About the author

Respected wine critic and vigneron James Halliday AM has a career that spans 47 years, but he is most widely known for his witty and informative writing about wine. As one of the founders of Brokenwood in the Hunter Valley and thereafter of Coldstream Hills in the Yarra Valley, James is an unmatched authority on every aspect of the wine industry, from the planting and pruning of vines through to the creation and marketing of the finished product. His winemaking has led him to sojourns in Bordeaux and Burgundy, and he had a long career as a wine judge in Australia and overseas. In 1995 he received the wine industry's ultimate accolade, the Maurice O'Shea Award. In 2010 James was made a Member of the Order of Australia for his services to the wine industry.

James has written or contributed to more than 70 books on wine since he began writing in 1970. His books have been translated into Japanese, French, German, Danish, Icelandic and Polish, and have been published in the United Kingdom and the United States, as well as in Australia. He is the author of *Varietal Wines*, *James Halliday's Wine Atlas of Australia*, *The Australian Wine Encyclopedia* and *A Life in Wine*.

The bestselling
and definitive guide
to Australian wine

ESTABLISHED 1986 — WINECOMPANION.COM.AU

Halliday

WINE COMPANION

2018

hardie grant books

Wine zones and regions of Australia

NEW SOUTH WALES

WINE ZONE		WINE REGION	
Big Rivers	(A)	Murray Darling	1
		Perricoota	2
		Riverina	3
		Swan Hill	4
Central Ranges	(B)	Cowra	5
		Mudgee	6
		Orange	7
Hunter Valley	(C)	Hunter	8
		Upper Hunter	9
Northern Rivers	(D)	Hastings River	10
Northern Slopes	(E)	New England	11
South Coast	(F)	Shoalhaven Coast	12
		Southern Highlands	13
Southern New South Wales	(G)	Canberra District	14
		Gundagai	15
		Hilltops	16
		Tumbarumba	17
Western Plains	(H)		

SOUTH AUSTRALIA

WINE ZONE		WINE REGION	
Adelaide Super Zone includes Mount Lofty Ranges, Fleurieu and Barossa wine regions			
Barossa		Barossa Valley	18
		Eden Valley	19
Fleurieu	(J)	Currency Creek	20
		Kangaroo Island	21
		Langhorne Creek	22
		McLaren Vale	23
		Southern Fleurieu	24
Mount Lofty Ranges		Adelaide Hills	25
		Adelaide Plains	26
		Clare Valley	27
Far North	(K)	Southern Flinders Ranges	28
Limestone Coast	(L)	Coonawarra	29
		Mount Benson	30
		Mount Gambier	31
		Padthaway	32
		Robe	33
		Wrattonbully	34
Lower Murray	(M)	Riverland	35
The Peninsulas	(N)	Southern Eyre Peninsula*	36

VICTORIA

WINE ZONE		WINE REGION	
Central Victoria	(P)	Bendigo	37
		Goulburn Valley	38
		Heathcote	39
		Strathbogie Ranges	40
Gippsland	(Q)	Upper Goulburn	41
		Alpine Valleys	42
Northeast Victoria	(R)	Beechworth	43
		Glenrowan	44
		King Valley	45
		Rutherglen	46
North West Victoria	(S)	Murray Darling	47
		Swan Hill	48
Port Phillip	(T)	Geelong	49
		Macedon Ranges	50
		Mornington Peninsula	51
		Sunbury	52
		Yarra Valley	53
Western Victoria	(U)	Ballarat*	54
		Grampians	55
		Henty	56
		Pyrenees	57

* For more information see page 50.

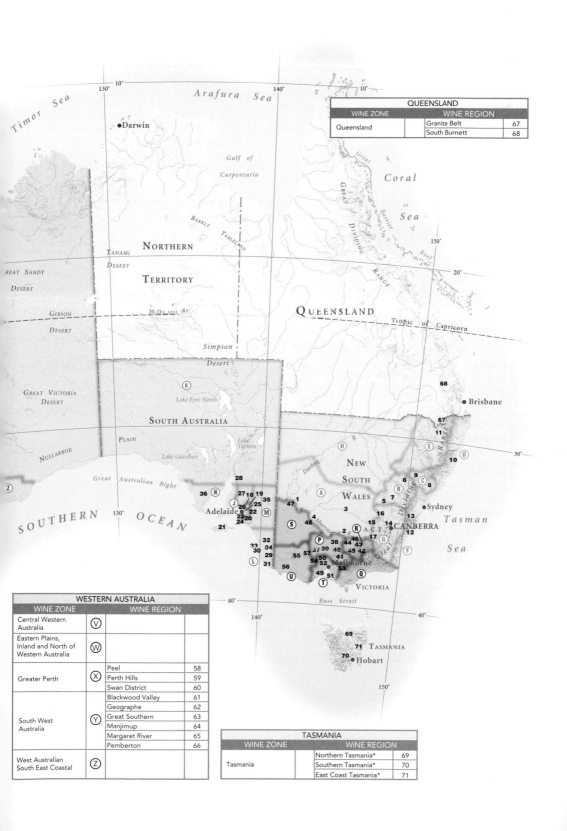

QUEENSLAND

WINE ZONE	WINE REGION	
Queensland	Granite Belt	67
	South Burnett	68

WESTERN AUSTRALIA

WINE ZONE		WINE REGION	
Central Western Australia	Ⓥ		
Eastern Plains, Inland and North of Western Australia	Ⓦ		
Greater Perth	Ⓧ	Peel	58
		Perth Hills	59
		Swan District	60
South West Australia	Ⓨ	Blackwood Valley	61
		Geographe	62
		Great Southern	63
		Manjimup	64
		Margaret River	65
		Pemberton	66
West Australian South East Coastal	Ⓩ		

TASMANIA

WINE ZONE	WINE REGION	
Tasmania	Northern Tasmania*	69
	Southern Tasmania*	70
	East Coast Tasmania*	71

Published in 2017 by Hardie Grant Books, an imprint of Hardie Grant Publishing

Hardie Grant Books (Melbourne)
Building 1, 658 Church Street
Richmond, Victoria 3121

Hardie Grant Books (London)
5th and 6th Floors
52–54 Southwark Street
London SE1 1UN

hardiegrantbooks.com

The *Australian Wine Companion* is a joint venture between James Halliday and Explore Australia Pty Ltd.

The map in this publication incorporates data copyright © Commonwealth of Australia (Geoscience Australia) 2004. Geoscience Australia has not evaluated the data as altered and incorporated within this publication and therefore gives no warranty regarding accuracy, completeness, currency or suitability for any particular purpose.

Australian wine zones and wine regions data copyright © Australian Wine and Brandy Corporation, April 2005

ISBN 978 1 74379 293 3

Typeset by Megan Ellis
Cover design by Murray Batten
Author photograph by Julian Kingma
Printed by McPherson's Printing Group, Maryborough, Victoria

Contents

Introduction	8
How to use this book	9
Winery of the year	14
Winemaker of the year	15
Wine of the year	16
Best value winery	17
Best new winery	18
Ten of the best new wineries	20
Ten of the best value wineries	22
Ten dark horses	24
Best of the best by variety	26
Best wineries of the regions	34
Regional production 2015–16	42
Varietal production 2015–16	44
Varietal wine styles and regions	46
Australia's geographical indications	50
Wine and food or food and wine?	54
Australian vintage charts	56
Australian vintage 2017: a snapshot	58
Acknowledgements	63
Australian wineries and wines	65
Index	756

Introduction

Australian wine is in a good place right now. The green shoots of a few years ago are now leaves, flowers and grapes. Thirty million glasses of Australian wines are enjoyed worldwide every day. For the FY16 domestic sales were up 6.9% to $2.97 billion, and export sales were up 11.4% to $2.11 billion.

Exports are the drivers of the rapidly changing environment, which has some similarities to the previous boom years between 2000 and '07 (when it peaked at $2.99 billion). Then the boom burst and the low point came as recently as '14, with sales of $1.808 billion. The upward trajectory is driven almost entirely by China and Hong Kong.

	Australian wine exports					
	Total		PR China		Hong Kong	
	Volume (litres)	Value AUD	Volume (litres)	Value AUD	Volume (litres)	Value AUD
	million	billion	million	million	million	million
2000	284	$1.34	0.3	$1.2	2	$13
2005	661	$2.75	4	$13	4	$23
2010	777	$2.16	55	$164	6	$44
2015	724	$1.89	68	$370	10	$132
MAT Dec '16	750	$2.22	99	$520	8	$110
MAT Mar '17	769	$2.29	108	$568	9	$119

Turning the coin over, France has 44% by value of the China market, Australia 25%, Chile 9.6%, Spain 6.5%, Italy 5.3%, and the US 2.3%. And just to keep New Zealand's success in the US market in focus, it has slightly less than 1% of the China market.

The biggest question is to what extent are there opportunities to increase exports to China beyond the existing routes to market? The most obvious answer is increasing white wine sales, which for moving annual total (MAT) March '17 amounted to $A20 million compared with $A500 million for red wine (in each case the figures are for bottled wine). The type of cuisine and time of year will have different demand outcomes, but this enormous disparity between white and red will change markedly over the next five years. Buying wine online has emerged as the most important single sales medium in China, and it results in a direct connection between the wine producer and the consumer. It also reaches beyond the largest existing markets in the Tier 1 and Tier 2 cities. The ever growing and mobile Chinese middle class will continue to drive consumption and create the world's largest single market.

There is also shopping by buyers purchasing premium wine on the Australian domestic market and shipping it to China for on-selling. Finally, compared with other forms of alcohol, most notably spirits, wine has both social and health benefits that will become increasingly understood as the market matures.

How to use this book

Wineries

Mount Mary ★★★★★

Coldstream West Road, Lilydale, Vic 3140 **Region** Yarra Valley
T (03) 9739 1761 **www**.mountmary.com.au **Open** Not
Winemaker Sam Middleton **Est.** 1971 **Dozens** 4000 **Vyds** 12ha
Mount Mary was one of the foremost pioneers of the rebirth of the Yarra Valley after 50 years without viticultural activity, and right from the outset produced wines of rare finesse and purity. Today its star shines brighter than that of any of the 174 wineries in the Yarra Valley. The late founder, Dr John Middleton, practised near-obsessive attention to detail long before that phrase slid into oenological vernacular. He relentlessly strove for perfection, and all four of the wines in the original Mount Mary portfolio achieved just that (within the context of each vintage). Charming grandson Sam Middleton is equally dedicated. An all-encompassing recent tasting of every vintage of these four wines left me in no doubt he is making even better wines since assuming the winemaker mantle in June 2011. Moreover, after protracted trials, two Rhône Valley inspired wines have been released, looking to the future yet also honouring John's late wife, Marli Russell. Winery of the Year 2018.

Winery name Mount Mary

The name of the producer, as it appears on the front label, is used throughout the book.

Winery rating ★★★★★

I look at the ratings for this year and the previous two years. If the wines tasted this year achieved a higher rating than last year, that higher rating has been given. If this year's wines were of lesser quality, I take into account the track record over the past two years (or longer where the winery is well known) and make a judgement call on whether it should retain its ranking or be given a lesser one. In what I call the mercy rating, in most instances a demotion is no more than half a star. Where no wines were submitted by a previously well rated winery with track record of providing samples, I may use my discretion to roll over last year's rating.

While there are (only) 1233 wineries profiled in this edition there are more than 2800 wineries to be found on www.winecompanion.com.au.

The percentage at the end of each rating summary on page 10 refers to the number of wineries achieving that rating within the total number of wineries in the *Wine Companion* database at the time of going to print. Two caveats: first, I retain a discretionary right to depart from the normal criteria; second, the basis of the ratings are best understood on the website, where all wine ratings appear.

Some may think my ratings are too generous, but less than half (43.7%) of the wineries in our database that are believed or known to be active are given ratings in this book, spread across the categories shown on page 10. Moreover, if I were to reduce the number of wineries in each category by (say) 50% the relative ranking would not change, other than a massive increase in the NR category, providing no useful guidance for the reader.

★★★★★   Outstanding winery regularly producing wines of exemplary quality and typicity. Will have at least two wines at 95 points or above, and have achieved a five-star rating for the previous two years. 239 wineries, 8.3%

Where the winery name itself is printed in red, that winery is generally acknowledged to have had a long track record of excellence in the context of its region – truly the best of the best. 101 wineries, 3.5%

★★★★★   Outstanding winery capable of producing wines of very high quality, and did so this year. Also will usually have at least two wines at 95 points or above. 229 wineries, 8%

★★★★☆   Excellent winery able to produce wines of high to very high quality, knocking on the door of a 5-star rating. Will normally have one wine at 95 points or above, and two (or more) at 90 or above, others 87–89. 239 wineries, 8.3%

★★★★   Very good producer of wines with class and character. Will have two (or more) wines at 90 points and above (or possibly one at 95 or above). 343 wineries, 11.9%

★★★☆   A solid, usually reliable, maker of good, sometimes very good, wines. Will have one wine at 90 points or above, others 86–89. 82 wineries, 2.8%

★★★   A typically good winery, but often has a few lesser wines. Will have wines at 86–89 points. 26 wineries, 0.9%

NR   The NR rating mainly appears on www.winecompanion.com.au. The rating is given in a range of circumstances: where there have been no tastings in the 12-month period; where there have been tastings, but with no wines scoring more than 88 points; or where the tastings have, for one reason or another, proved not to fairly reflect the reputation of a winery with a track record of success. NR wineries in the book are generally new wineries with no wine entries. 7 wineries.

Contact Details Coldstream West Road, Lilydale, Vic 3140 **T** (03) 9739 1761

The details are usually those of the winery and cellar door, but in a few instances may simply be a postal address; this occurs when the wine is made at another winery or wineries, and is sold only through the website and/or retail outlets.

Region Yarra Valley

A full list of zones, regions and subregions appears on pages 50 to 53. Occasionally you will see 'Various' as the region. This means the wine is made from grapes purchased from a number of regions; often by a winery without a vineyard of its own.

www.mountmary.com.au

An important reference point, normally containing material not found (for space reasons) in this book.

Open Not

Although a winery might be listed as not open or only open on weekends, many may in fact be prepared to open by appointment. A telephone call will establish whether it is possible or not. For space reasons we have simplified the open hours listing; where the hours vary each day, or for holidays, etcetera, we refer the reader to the website.

Winemaker Sam Middleton

In all but the smallest producers, the winemaker is simply the head of a team; there may be many executive winemakers actually responsible for specific wines in the medium to large companies (80 000 dozen and upwards). Once again, space constraints mean usually only two winemakers are named, even if they are part of a larger team.

Est. 1971

Keep in mind that some makers consider the year in which they purchased the land to be the year of establishment, others the year in which they first planted grapes, others the year they first made wine, and so on. There may also be minor complications where there has been a change of ownership or break in production.

Dozens 4000

This figure (representing the number of 9-litre (12-bottle) cases produced each year) is merely an indication of the size of the operation. Some winery entries do not feature a production figure: this is because the winery (principally, but not exclusively, the large companies) regards this information as confidential.

Vyds 12ha

Shows the hectares of vineyard(s) owned by the winery.

Summary Superbly refined, elegant and intense cabernets and usually outstanding and long-lived pinot noirs fully justify Mount Mary's exalted reputation. The Triolet blend is very good; more recent vintages of chardonnay are even better.

Surely self-explanatory, except that I have tried to vary the subjects I discuss in this part of the winery entry.

New wineries

 The vine leaf symbol indicates the 77 wineries that are new entries in this year's *Wine Companion*.

Tasting notes

There has been a progressive adoption of the 100-point system in wine shows and in reviews by other commentators. The majority follow the system outlined below, and which I used in precisely this form in the *Wine Companion* 2017. Space constraints mean that only 3859 notes are printed in full in this book, with points, drink-to dates and prices included for a further 2979 wines. Tasting notes for all wines receiving 84 points or above appear on www.winecompanion.com.au. See also page 26.

Ratings

97–99	GOLD	♟♟♟♟♟	**Exceptional.** Wines that have won a major trophy/ trophies in important wine shows, or are of that standard.
95–96		♟♟♟♟♟	**Outstanding.** Wines of gold medal standard, usually with a great pedigree.
94	SILVER	♟♟♟♟♟	Wines on the cusp of gold medal status, virtually indistinguishable from those wines receiving 95 points.
90–93		♟♟♟♟♟	**Highly Recommended.** Wines of silver medal standard, wines of great quality, style and character, and worthy of a place in any cellar.
89	BRONZE	♟♟♟♟	**Recommended.** Wines on the cusp of silver medal standard, the difference purely a judgement call.
86–88		♟♟♟♟	Wines of bronze medal standard; well produced, flavoursome wines, usually not requiring cellaring.
		✪	**Special Value.** Wines considered to offer special value for money within the context of their glass symbol status.
84–85		♟♟♟	**Acceptable.** Wines of good commercial quality, free from significant fault.
80–83		♟♟♟	**Over to You.** Everyday wines without much character and/or somewhat faulty.
75–79		♟♟♟	**Not Recommended.** Wines with one or more significant winemaking faults.

♟♟♟♟♟ **Yarra Valley Pinot Noir 2015** Bright, clear crimson–purple; everything about this wine exudes supreme class: the bouquet has a rose garden of perfume and spice, the palate a concerto for strings and clarinets, as predominantly red berry fruits glide around the finest quality tannins of the cello. The length and balance are awesome, and the wine will be singing soprano 20 years on from vintage. Cork. 13.5% alc. **Rating** 99 **To** 2028 $95

The tasting note opens with the vintage of the wine tasted. This tasting note will have been written within the 12 months prior to publication. Even that is a long time, and during the life of this book the wine will almost certainly change. More than this, remember that tasting is a highly subjective and imperfect art. The price of the wine is listed where information is available. Tasting notes for wines 95 points and above are printed in red.

The initials SC, JF, NG, CM, PR or TS, sometimes appearing at the end of a tasting note, signify that Steven Creber, Jane Faulkner, Ned Goodwin, Campbell Mattinson, Philip Rich or Tyson Stelzer tasted the wine and provided the tasting note and rating.

Cork

This is the closure used for this particular wine. The closures in use for the wines tasted are (in descending order): screwcap 90% (last year 88.4%), one-piece natural cork 5.3% (last year 5.8%), Diam 3.1% (last year 4.5%). The remaining 1.6% (in approximate order of importance) are ProCork, Twin Top, Crown Seal, Zork and Vino Lok. I believe the percentage of screwcap-closed wines will continue to rise for red wines; 98.3% of white wines tasted are screwcapped, leaving little room for any further increase.

13.5% alc.

As with closures, I have endeavoured to always include this information, which is in one sense self-explanatory. What is less obvious is the increasing concern of many Australian winemakers about the rise in alcohol levels, and much research and practical experimentation (picking earlier, higher fermentation temperatures in open fermenters, etcetera) is occurring. Reverse osmosis and yeast selection are two of the options available to decrease higher than desirable alcohol levels. Recent changes to domestic and export labelling mean the stated alcohol will be within a maximum of 0.5% difference to that obtained by analysis.

To 2028

Rather than give a span of drinking years, I have simply provided a (conservative) 'drink-to' date. Modern winemaking is such that, even if a wine has 10 or 20 years' future during which it will gain greater complexity, it can be enjoyed at any time over the intervening months and years.

$95

I use the price provided by the winery. It should be regarded as a guide, particularly if purchased retail.

Winery of the year

Mount Mary

In the second half of the 1960s, doctors in the Hunter Valley, Yarra Valley and Margaret River tentatively embarked on journeys into the unknown: small-scale winemaking with financial aims of minimal importance, but there nonetheless. All were familiar with the great wines of the world (notably from France) and established benchmarks for their wines accordingly; Bordeaux was a common denominator, Burgundy next in line.

Max Lake was the first to move to bottle wine for sale with Lake's Folly (1966) in the Hunter Valley; Tom Cullity (1967) and Kevin Cullen (1971) followed in Margaret River; then came Peter McMahon (1970) and John Middleton (1971) in the Yarra Valley.

All their legacies glitter brightly among the greatest Australian wineries today, but none more so than John Middleton's Mount Mary. It is still family-owned and run, with John's grandson, Sam Middleton, in calm, measured control of the winery, and with Sam's father, David, content that it should be so.

It is axiomatic to say that no two vintages are the same, and that the aim of a good (or great) winemaker is to make a better wine for a given set of growing season and vintage conditions than previously achieved. Or, to put it another way, there should always be an element of Socratean dissatisfaction. Such is Sam's approach to winemaking.

The 2015 vintage in the Yarra Valley was, quite simply, great, and Sam took full advantage of it, making exquisite wines. Just around the corner is the cool, dry 2017 vintage, promising to be as great as 1988 and '92, picture perfect across the Valley.

But there's more to the story. For some years there have been rumours of other varieties being planted at Mount Mary on an experimental basis, and wines made. Two of these have now been released under the label Marli Russell by Mount Mary, honouring John Middleton's wife by using her maiden name.

Here the compass takes in the Rhône Valley, with a Marsanne Roussanne white wine and a Grenache Mourvedre Shiraz red wine – the latter including Australia's foremost variety, Shiraz, a variety John had precious little time for. RIP John, it's just Socrates at work, and casts no aspersions on the glorious wines you made, nor gainsays your supreme vision in buying and planting Mount Mary in the first place.

Which brings me to the four master works, the foundations for which were created by John Middleton in 1971 and became legendary within a decade. A single word cannot possibly do justice to Mount Mary's Quintet, Pinot Noir, Chardonnay and Triolet. But they are joined at the hip by elegance. By all means add balance, purity and length, and as a codicil add longevity demonstrated by an all-consuming tasting in 2016 of every vintage released of the four wines.

Previous 'Winery of the Year' recipients were Paringa Estate (2007), Balnaves of Coonawarra (2008), Brookland Valley (2009), Tyrrell's (2010), Larry Cherubino Wines (2011), Port Phillip Estate/Kooyong (2012), Kilikanoon (2013), Penfolds (2014), Hentley Farm Wines (2015), Tahbilk (2016) and Mount Pleasant (2017).

Winemaker of the year

Paul Hotker

In the 2016 wine show calendar Bleasdale's chief winemaker, Paul Hotker, won five trophies for his 2015 Bleasdale Wellington Road Grenache Shiraz. It's not uncommon for a single wine to win multiple trophies. A haul of two or three trophies will greatly please the recipient and won't (usually) cause rumbles of discontent from those wines that were in the running, yet not awarded. It's just what happens.

But winning a trophy from five wine shows over the year in question is another thing, particularly when the fifth and final award came from the National Wine Show of Australia for Best Blended Dry Red. But the Wellington Road wasn't alone; the 2014 Second Innings Malbec won trophies from the Sydney Royal Wine Show and Winewise Championship. The next Second Innings vintage (2015) took another brace of trophies from the Perth Royal Wine Show and Royal Hobart Wine Show. Just to round things off, in 2016 the 2014 The Pioneer 1960 Malbec was awarded the trophy for Best Other Single Varietal Red at the Royal Queensland Wine Show.

This was no flash in the pan; in the 2015 show year Bleasdale Vineyards was awarded eight trophies from five shows, taking out a remarkable double at the Sydney Royal Wine Show for Best Cabernet-dominant Blend and Best Shiraz-dominant Blend.

Such extraordinary achievements could give the impression that Paul is a master blender following eerily closely in the footsteps of Wolfgang Blass 42 years ago. Wolfgang also dominated wine shows from Adelaide to Timbuktu with his red wine blends from Langhorne Creek.

This edition of *Wine Companion* features seven of Paul's wines: three shirazs and three malbecs received 95 points or above; a cabernet sauvignon (with gold from the National (Canberra) Wine Show) also joined the party. And at the other extreme Paul also makes a first class Adelaide Hills pinot gris year in, year out.

So how is it that Paul has developed such an uncanny touch in making Langhorne Creek red wines? In the early years there were some indications of his bourgeoning talent. In 1991–2 he was a vineyard/nursery hand at Olive Farm Wines and Vinitech Nurseries in the Swan Valley. Between '93 and '97 (his self-styled gap years) he was an international traveller, farm labourer, vineyard hand, bicycle courier, landscape gardener and builder's labourer. Between '98 and '02 he held various casual positions in vineyards and wineries straddling the Adelaide Hills, McLaren Vale, Robe, Yarra Valley, Margaret River, Geographe and Swan Valley. He also obtained a certificate in viticulture from Margaret River TAFE, then enrolled in the Bachelor of Science (Oenology) Degree course at the University of Adelaide, graduating in 2002.

He then jumped the ditch from 2003 to '06, working as viticulturist and assistant winemaker for Nautilus Estate in Marlborough. Between '07 and '13 he became a viticultural consultant; his major client was Shaw + Smith. So it's almost an anticlimax to record that since '07 he has been senior winemaker at Bleasdale Vineyards.

Previous 'Winemaker of the Year' recipients were Robert Diletti (2015), Peter Fraser (2016) and Sarah Crowe (2017).

Wine of the year

Henschke Hill of Grace 2012

In an article written for the *Weekend Australian* at the time of the launch of the 2012 Hill of Grace, I suggested that there were similarities between Burgundy's Domaine de la Romanée-Conti and Australia's Henschke. Both are family-owned and run, both are estate-based, both are priceless, and both have a central jewel in a dazzling, bejeweled crown. For Domaine the jewel is the 1.8ha Romanée-Conti vineyard; for Henschke it is the 4ha Hill of Grace. Each is owned exclusively, thus sending the brand goodwill into the stratosphere. Each winery also has other quality wines in their stables; DRC has seven, Henschke has 30.

The small size of a varietal vineyard magnifies the impact of growing season weather. In difficult vintages there is nowhere to turn other than to not release the wine or to significantly reduce the already limited quantity. Thus Hill of Grace was not made in 1960, 1974, 2000 and 2011.

At the other extreme are the great vintages, such as 2012 for Hill of Grace. Its release is as eagerly anticipated as any wine I can remember.

This is a magnificent, flawless wine. Balance, length, line and purity all receive emphatic ticks. But there's more still – it has a profound sense of place. Wherever else in Australia or the world can you find a medium-bodied shiraz that so calmly reflects the patchwork of vines largely between 50 and 150 years old?

Prue Henschke has developed a system for planting native grasses as a sward in the vineyard rows, and has established native plants around the vineyard to enhance the ecosystem services of beneficial insects. The better known organic composting and straw mulch helps maintain soil health. Biodynamic practices are interleaved with these strategies.

The bunches are hand-sorted in the vineyard, and again in the winery, by the full-time vineyard staff who are employed for picking, pruning and maintenance all year round, and who know the vines by their first names. Seventy per cent is crushed and destemmed, with 30% destemmed for whole berry ferment. It is matured in predominantly French hogsheads (65% new) for 18 months, and held for a further two to three years aging in bottle prior to release.

The wine is sold under Vino-Lok through the cellar door, website and all export markets; under screwcap for retailers and restaurants domestically.

Previous 'Wine of the Year' recipients were Bass Phillip Reserve Pinot Noir 2010 (2014), Xanadu Stevens Road Cabernet Sauvignon 2011 (2015), Serrat Shiraz Viognier 2014 (2016) and Best's Thomson Family Shiraz 2014 (2017).

Best value winery

Grosset

I am far from convinced that I chose the right name for this award. It could have connotations of cheapness (measured by low price), whereas its primary reference point is quality. Then I get caught in an unending series of qualifications, probably needing a very clever algorithm to cut through and make the very complex seem simple. Since I have no idea how an algorithm is constructed or works, I'm not going there.

I taste and score each wine without regard to price, after which the computer steps in and assesses whether the wine's score is within or above a predetermined price bar. If it is, it is given a red rosette, signifying it offers special value for money.

Simple? Too simple? Useful? Misleading? All of these, and more. For many years I considered each wine at the time of tasting in the context of its seeming value, and either gave or withheld the value rosette using my increasingly fallible memory.

For all its faults, it had the potential to bring into play the historic record of success for each wine, the overall quality of the vintage and the degree of difficulty (in diving parlance) of making the wine. Some of those factors are within the control of the winemaker, others are not. On its face, style (and style preference) dwell on the fringe.

Taking real life examples, how do you compare tank-fermented riesling or semillon on the one hand with barrel fermented chardonnay, or open fermented pinot noir or shiraz on the other hand? Or choose between classic and alternative varieties? Well, there are two answers.

First is the mathematical correlation between points and price on a grid system. This is done by computer, with no intervention by me. I only know the answer once the tasting notes plus points and prices go into the database.

Secondly, I either knowingly or subconsciously take into account some or all of the variables (but not the price) at the time I decide on the points. Thus, it's highly improbable that a winery with only one or two varietal strings to its bow would win this award.

Jeffrey Grosset is unchallenged as Australia's greatest maker of riesling, but he also makes sublime chardonnay and pinot noir from the Adelaide Hills, semillon sauvignon blanc from the Adelaide Hills and Clare Valley, and Gaia – his Bordeaux blend – from a high altitude vineyard in the Clare Valley. Nereus and Apiana, his vinous grandchildren, are unique blends, forging into unmapped territory.

Overall, Grosset is one of the top ten wineries in Australia, and there is no chance of it losing that status. And on a world scale, his wines are significantly underpriced.

Previous 'Best Value Winery of the Year' recipients were Hoddles Creek Estate (2015), West Cape Howe (2016) and Larry Cherubino Wines (2017).

Best new winery

Dappled Wine

One privilege of tasting, researching and writing about the 6000 or so wines selected for this year's *Wine Companion* (out of well over 9500 submitted) is discovering a hitherto unknown winemaker, winery and/or wine that blows your mind. I've never consciously thought through the implications of the combination of all three attributes but, by definition, it has to spring from the Best New Winery group.

Now I mean no disrespect to wineries previously selected, nor do I want to paint myself into a corner in the years to come. But people such as owner–winemaker Shaun Crinion of Dappled Wines come around once in the metaphorical blue moon.

It started in 1999 when he was working with his uncle at Laetitia Winery in California's Central Coast. A US citizen, Shaun intended to remain in the US, but the GFC made that too difficult for an unskilled 19-year-old.

And so he set off on a magic carpet tour of the world of wine, starting with Devil's Lair in Margaret River in 2000; followed in '01 by Corbett Canyon Vineyard, California (US); '02 Houghton, Swan Valley; '03 De Bortoli, Hunter Valley; '04–06 Pipers Brook, Northern Tasmania; '06 Bay of Fires, Northern Tasmania; '06–07 Williams Selyem, California (US); '08 Domaine Chandon, Yarra Valley; and '10 Domaine de Montille, Burgundy (Fr). With a wine pedigree like that he could gain employment wherever he wished without even mentioning that he is also an oenology graduate from Charles Sturt University ('01–05).

But in 2009 the magic carpet settled in the Yarra Valley, where Shaun created Dappled Wines (while also working part-time for Rob Dolan, 2009–16).

His longer term ambition is to buy or establish his own vineyard. It was easier, he says, when he had no domestic ties. Now 36, he and partner Catherine have two daughters aged two and four. Shaun, as a part-time house-husband and part-time winemaker, has been able to spend more time with his daughters than most fathers.

When I berated him for not previously submitting wines (after almost 10 years in the Yarra Valley) he responded, 'I've been brought up in wineries with great wines, wines that I've wanted to drink, and I wasn't sure my wines would appeal to you. I'm not a natural winemaker, but I did include some whole bunches in my '16 Straws Lane Gewurztraminer.' Well, I am in awe of that particular wine. Then there are the utterly beautiful labels from a graphic designer in Tasmania, with Catherine's active involvement.

An obvious question is how difficult is it to buy grapes for Dappled, and build continuing support. Shaun was able to buy 10.4 tonnes for this (2017) vintage, the grapes coming from three vineyards. He says he's greatly indebted to Simon Peirce of Steels Creek Estate, where he made the last two vintages, and who sells him up to three tonnes per year. Each of the three wineries supplied chardonnay, more than 50% of his total intake. He's quick to add he is also indebted to Rob Dolan (Best New Winery 2014) for what he has learnt.

Previous 'Best New Winery of the Year' recipients were Rob Dolan Wines (2014), Flowstone (2015), Bicknell fc (2016) and Bondar Wines (2017).

Ten of the best new wineries

Each one of these wineries making its debut in the *Wine Companion* has earned a five-star rating. They are thus the leaders of the 77 new wineries in this edition, although a number of other first-up wineries also achieved five stars. The ultimate selection criteria included the number of wines earning 95 points or above, and also value for money.

BEST NEW WINERY
Dappled Wine Yarra Valley / PAGE 212
The story of Dappled appears on page 18; further details appear in its winery entry on page 212.

Attwoods Wines Geelong / PAGE 87
Australian-born and -educated winemaker and owner Troy Walsh worked as a sommelier in London for 12 years, giving him the contacts needed when he returned to Australia and began the Flying Winemaker path of vintages in Australia and France. He focused on pinot noir and chardonnay in Burgundy and Geelong, becoming very familiar with the use of whole bunch fermentation. In 2010 he purchased an 18ha property 20km south of Ballarat, moving there with his family and close-planting 1.5ha of pinot noir and 0.5ha of chardonnay.

Dr Edge Tasmania / PAGE 237
Having worked as a winemaker for Petaluma, Peter Dredge moved to Tasmania in 2009, spending the next 7 years with Bay of Fires, becoming chief winemaker. In '15 he left Bay of Fires to set up a consultancy practice and become a self-employed winemaker for Dr Edge. Within a year he had formed a partnership to relaunch Meadowbank for the Ellis family, giving him access to 1.5ha of southern Tasmanian pinot noir, and buying other lots from the north and east coasts of Tasmania.

Elbourne Wines Hunter Valley / PAGE 247
In 2009 Adam and Alexys Elbourne fulfilled their dream of moving from Sydney to the Hunter Valley, purchasing a 22ha property on Marrowbone Road, with a 4ha chardonnay and shiraz vineyard (needing TLC) and enough land for their boutique racehorse stud and a Noah's Ark of animals including Wessex Saddleback pigs. The vineyard has been brought back to life, with Nick Paterson as contract winemaker.

Elderslie Adelaide Hills / PAGE 247
This winery brings together two families whose skills interlock at the hip – one winemaker, the other wine marketer. The winemaker is Adam Wadewitz, the wine marketer Nicole Roberts. Better still, they each have their partners (Nikki Wadewitz and Mark Roberts) on board, and they also have complementary intersecting real life jobs. Blue blood flows as freely as the wine in their veins.

"Heroes" Vineyard Geelong / **PAGE 338**

James Thomas was 16 when his parents planted a vineyard in the UK in 1996. He came to Australia in 2004, achieving a degree in oenology from La Trobe. Four years as assistant winemaker at Bannockburn Vineyards was followed by three years as head winemaker in England making sparkling wine. Returning to Australia in '14, he found and purchased an established 3.4ha vineyard. Sophisticated wine and a sophisticated label.

One Block Yarra Valley / **PAGE 505**

Jayden Ong has had a dazzling career in fine wine and fine food, starting with the Melbourne Wine Room (2000–06), and vintages at Curly Flat and Moorooduc Estate and Allies/Garagiste. He then gained a CSU degree in oenology, opened Cumulus Inc. restaurant with superstar chef Andrew McConnell and worked at Flying Winemaking in 2006–14. Small lot winemaking in the Yarra Valley was also threaded through the years. In '15 he and partner Morgan Ong purchased a small property and home at Mt Toolebewong, 700m above sea level in the Yarra Valley, now planted with an organic vineyard.

Shining Rock Vineyard Adelaide Hills / **PAGE 614**

Agronomist Darren Arney and psychologist wife Natalie Worth acquired the Shining Rock Vineyard from Lion Nathan in 2012. Planted by Petaluma in '00, the grapes sold until '15. The first vintage that year was made by Peter Leske (Revenir), then in '16 by Con Moshos (Tapanappa) in conjunction with Darren, the éminence grise of Brian Croser ever present.

Small Island Wines Southern Tasmania / **PAGE 626**

Tasmanian-born James Broinowski graduated in oenology from the University of Adelaide in 2013. He faced the same problem as other hopefuls with drive and ambition but no working capital. He turned to crowdfunding in '16, which enabled him to purchase pinot noir from Glengarry Vineyard in Northern Tasmania; he made a gold medal–winning Pinot Noir at the Hobart Wine Show 2016, plus 200 bottles of Rose. Further purchases of pinot noir in '16 and '17 will provide continuing payback to his supporters.

Woodvale Clare Valley / **PAGE 736**

This is the personal venture of Kevin Mitchell and wife Kathleen Bourne, and is not an offshoot of Kilikanoon. The raison d'être of the business is the making of small batches of Clare Valley's most esteemed varieties, riesling and shiraz, but also bringing grenache and cabernet sauvignon onboard to provide further choice. Four rieslings and shirazs from 2014 and '15 are very good indeed. The wines are available online.

Ten of the best value wineries

This year's ten wineries had single award recipients from each of the Clare Valley, Yarra Valley, Margaret River, Mornington Peninsula and the Great Southern, two from McLaren Vale and three from the Barossa Valley. If any or all of the wines made by these wineries were blind-tasted against similarly priced wines from France, elsewhere in Europe and the US, the Australian wines would win hands down. Grosset is Best Value Winery of the Year, and accordingly heads the list; the remainder are in alphabetical order.

BEST VALUE WINERY
Grosset Clare Valley / **PAGE 304**
The story of Grosset appears on page 17; further details appear in its winery entry on page 304.

Deep Woods Estate Margaret River / **PAGE 217**
This is one of the wineries to come in with a perfect score for its 12 wines. At the top end are the Yallingup Cabernet (98 points) and Reserve Chardonnay (97 points). The last four wines scored between 90 and 94 points, and offer exceptional value. The master puppeteer is the infinitely skilled winemaker Julian Langworthy (supported by Emma Gillespie).

Hardys McLaren Vale / **PAGE 314**
This is a reminder that just because the wines come from a large company with vineyard sources from every state, it is still totally reliant on the skill and commitment of their winemakers, here led by the brilliance of chief winemaker Paul Lapsley. Hardys had more (nine) wines scoring 97 and above than any other winery in this year's *Wine Companion*; only one (a left-field fortified muscadelle) did not receive a value rosette.

Landhaus Estate Barossa Valley / **PAGE 402**
Landhaus has clung on to its 5-star rating by its fingertips in recent years, receiving the benefit of the doubt in 2014 and '16. However, its performance this year has been exemplary: nine of its 10 wines scored 95 points or above, receiving the value rosette. Jane Faulkner provided the notes and points.

Montalto Mornington Peninsula / **PAGE 461**
Montalto brings together a large vineyard (by Mornington standards), part dating back to 1986, and the winemaking wizardry of the irrepressible Simon Black. Its forte is pinot noir and chardonnay, with shiraz, sauvignon blanc and pinot grigio sneaking in the back door. Ten of its 14 wines scored 94 points and above, relying on a mix of conventional and thoroughly left-field vinification practises.

Oakridge Wines Yarra Valley / **PAGE 499**

Winemaker David Bicknell is a fervent believer in single site wines, performing the very difficult task of using differing approaches to the vinification to express the character of the terroir, rather than obscure it. Thus the top range wines are not simply single vineyard, but single block wines. Chardonnay and pinot noir defined by their elegance are closest to his heart. Twelve of the 16 wines scoring 94 points and above received the value rosette.

Singlefile Wines Great Southern / **PAGE 621**

If there were to be a runner up in this category, Singlefile Wines would have been the recipient. While headquartered at its beautiful cellar door and restaurant in Denmark, it reaches out to the Frankland River, Mount Barker and Pemberton, as well as its own planting of chardonnay below and around the cellar door. Fifteen of its 17 wines scored 94 points and above, and received a value rosette.

Spinifex Barossa Valley / **PAGE 632**

While all the wines from Barossa vineyards are unusually complex, Spinifex's touch is always gentle. All but one of their wines scored 94 points and above, and received the value rosette. Two wines led the way with 97 points, the remainder achieved 95 or 96, with the single exception of one at 94 points ($24).

Teusner Barossa Valley / **PAGE 667**

Kym Teusner achieved a perfect score for his table wines this year. Two of the three top wines received 98 points, the third 97 points, then four wines scored 95 and 96, all against a background of very low prices given the quality and utterly beguiling complexity of the wines; five of the wines scored 94 (two) or 95 (three) and retail at $24 or less.

Yangarra Estate Vineyard McLaren Vale / **PAGE 743**

In the 2016 *Wine Companion* winemaker Peter Fraser was awarded the coveted Winemaker of the Year recognition, so it's no surprise that every one of his 11 wines this year should receive the value rosette: two from the highest category (receiving 97 points), the remainder bar one scoring 95 or 96 points. For the record, all of the wines were tasted and rated by Jane Faulkner.

Ten dark horses

To qualify for this award, each winery has to have received a 5-star rating for the first time, and have a history of lesser ratings. Boat O'Craigo is Dark Horse of the Year, and accordingly heads the list; the remaining wineries are in alphabetical order.

DARK HORSE OF THE YEAR
Boat O'Craigo Yarra Valley / **PAGE 126**
When Margaret and Steve Graham purchased a property at Kangaroo Ground, they correctly chose to plant shiraz and cabernet sauvignon on the warm site with its black volcanic basalt soil. In 2003, with son Travers joining the business, a vineyard in the foothills of the Black Spur Ranges was purchased, with gewurztraminer, sauvignon blanc, chardonnay and pinot noir vines already planted. The third stage was the 2011 acquisition of a substantial winery in Warranwood, equidistant between the vineyards.

Baillieu Vineyard Mornington Peninsula / **PAGE 94**
Charlie and Samantha Baillieu have re-established the former Foxwood Vineyard on the gentle slopes of Merricks North, growing chardonnay, viognier, pinot gris, pinot noir and shiraz. The north-facing vineyard is part of the 64ha Bulldog Run property owned by the Baillieus, and is immaculately maintained. Winemaker Geraldine McFaul took full advantage of the glorious 2015 vintage. The Baillieus' refurbished Merricks General Wine Store is a combined bistro/providore/cellar door.

Ballycroft Vineyard & Cellars Barossa Valley / **PAGE 95**
This micro-business is owned by Joe and Sue Evans. Joe's life on the land started in 1984 with a diploma of horticulture, then (in '87) a viticulture degree from Roseworthy/Adelaide University. Between 1992 and '99 he had various responsibilities at Rockford Wines. Since that time he has been at Greenock Creek Wines. Joe and Sue are a two-person band so visitors to the cellar door would be wise to make an appointment for a personal tasting with either one of them.

Cupitt's Winery Shoalhaven Coast / **PAGE 204**
Cupitt's Winery has been knocking on the door of a 5-star rating for a number of years, and blew it wide open for this edition of the *Wine Companion*. The tourist mecca of the southern NSW coast around Ulladulla is both blessing and bane. It's not a natural region for high quality grapes, nor a magnet for wine tourists. The Cupitt family, led by winemaker Rosie, has walked around the problem by buying grapes from regions as far as the Yarra Valley. The result is that the quality of the wines and the modesty of the prices is as commendable as it is unusual.

Firetail Margaret River / **PAGE 264**
Jessica Worrall and Rob Glass are fugitives from the oil and gas industry. In 2002 they purchased a 5.3ha vineyard in Margaret River that had been planted between 1979 and '81 to sauvignon blanc, semillon and cabernet sauvignon. The wines are made by Bruce Dukes and Peter Stanlake. Looking at the firepower of the contract

winemakers for Firetail, and the maturity of the vineyard in Margaret River, it is strange Firetall hasn't merited five stars before now. The wine quality is exemplary, and the prices are almost old-fashioned.

Iron Cloud Wines Geographe / **PAGE 361**
Owners Warwick Lavis and Geoff and Karyn Cross came together in 2003 to purchase what was then known as the Pepperilly Estate, which had been planted in '99 on red gravelly loam soil. West Australian peppermint trees line Henty Brook, the vineyard's natural water source. Michael Ng, chief winemaker for Rockcliffe came onboard in 2017, after Coby Ladwig (who made the '15 and '16 vintage wines) left to focus on his own brand (Rosenthal Wines) and become full-time winemaker for Singlefile Wines.

La Curio McLaren Vale / **PAGE 396**
Winemaker and owner Adam Hooper enrolled in the Bachelor of Oenology at Roseworthy College at 17, and got off to a flying start working as a winemaker with some of the best-known wineries in McLaren Vale (Geoff Merrill etc), interspersed with Flying Winemaker trips to Italy and France. Twenty years on and Adam is still enjoying the fruits of McLaren Vale, especially those of his labours at La Curio, which he started 10 years ago. The wines have always had a certain frisson, largely as a result of extreme cold soak prior to the fermentation of uncrushed whole berries.

Schulz Vignerons Barossa Valley / **PAGE 597**
Marcus and Roslyn Schulz are the fifth generation of one of the best-known (extended) wine families in the Barossa Valley, but in 2002 they went down a new path by initiating 'biological farming' of the 50-plus year-old vines. They moved away from irrigation and extensive spraying, and now the vines are virtually dry grown using natural nitrogen created by the active soil biology, with minimal chemical input. The 58.5ha vineyard is planted to 12 varieties and, as might be imagined, the lion's share of the grapes is sold to other makers in the Barossa.

Talisman Wines Geographe / **PAGE 654**
The untold story behind the establishment of Talisman Wines is that the property (situated high in the hills of the Ferguson Valley), which is surrounded by Wellington National Park, was initially purchased for its extreme beauty as a weekend escape for Kim and Jenny Robinson. It was not until years later (in 2000) that vineyard manager and local identity, Victor Bertola, encouraged them to plant the vineyard. They now have 9ha of cabernet, shiraz, malbec, zinfandel, chardonnay, riesling and sauvignon blanc, and have enjoyed much success at the Geographe Wine Show.

Vinden Estate Hunter Valley / **PAGE 706**
Vinden Estate provided an array of four semillons (from the 2014, '15 and '16 vintages) and two shirazs (from '10 and '14, the great Hunter vintage) for Ned Goodwin to taste, and he was duly impressed. Sandra and Guy Vinden have a beautiful home and cellar door, landscaped gardens and a vineyard that includes shiraz (2.5ha), merlot and alicante bouschet (2ha each), with the Broken Back Range in the distance. The wines are made onsite using estate-grown red grapes; semillon and chardonnay grapes are purchased from other growers.

Best of the best by variety

As usual, the number of wines in each group is limited. The varietal categories are the same as in previous years, as is the link of each wine with its region, so only the best are listed in full. That said, the cut-off point does reflect the strength of the particular category. Where the list would be unacceptably long, the wines printed in black are grouped by region and their names shortened while still enabling the exact wine to be identified in the tasting notes for the winery in question. In looking at the points, remember these are the best of the 9769 wines tasted for this edition.

Riesling

The Eden Valley empire strikes back with nine wines compared with six from Western Australia. One change in representation doesn't surprise, with three rieslings from Tasmania and one from Henty, the latter a climatic twin with Tasmania.

RATING	WINE	REGION
98	2016 Sons of Eden Cirrus Single Vineyard	Eden Valley
98	2016 Duke's Vineyard Magpie Hill Reserve	Porongurup
97	2016 Grosset Polish Hill	Clare Valley
97	2010 Jeanneret Doozie	Clare Valley
97	2016 Pikes The Merle Clare Valley	Clare Valley
97	2010 Twofold Aged Release	Clare Valley
97	2016 Harewood Estate	Denmark
97	2016 Glen Eldon Reserve	Eden Valley
97	2016 Kellermeister The Wombat General	Eden Valley
97	2012 Peter Lehmann Wigan	Eden Valley
97	2016 Poonawatta The Eden	Eden Valley
97	2015 Robert Oatley	Great Southern
97	2016 Seppelt Drumborg Vineyard	Henty
97	2016 Forest Hill Vineyard Block 1	Mount Barker
97	2015 Singlefile Single Vineyard	Mount Barker
97	2008 Abbey Creek Vineyard Museum Release	Porongurup
97	2016 Castle Rock Estate A&W Reserve	Porongurup
97	2016 Devil's Corner	Tasmania
97	2016 Pooley	Tasmania
97	2016 Stargazer Coal River Valley	Tasmania

Chardonnay

The field of 44 chardonnays was led by Margaret River (11), Yarra Valley (7), Adelaide Hills (5) and Mornington Peninsula (4). There was a greater spread thereafter, reflecting the great quality of Australian chardonnay; Beechworth, Geelong, Gippsland and Tasmania all provided three wines, Denmark two, Pemberton one. Space precluded listing all of these in full, but they are grouped by region, and wines with abbreviated names are found in full in the winery entry. This approach is used throughout this section where needed.

RATING	WINE	REGION
98	2015 Shaw + Smith Lenswood	Adelaide Hills
98	2015 Giaconda Estate Vineyard	Beechworth
98	2015 Hardys Eileen Hardy	Blend
98	2014 Singlefile The Vivienne	Denmark
98	2015 Flying Fish Cove Prize Catch	Margaret River
98	2014 Leeuwin Estate Art Series	Margaret River
98	2015 Pooley Cooinda Vale Single Vineyard	Tasmania
98	2015 Rochford Dans les Bois	Yarra Valley

97 **Adelaide Hills** 2016 Grosset Piccadilly, 2015 Ochota Barrels The Slint Vineyard, 2015 Penfolds Reserve Bin A, 2015 Shaw + Smith M3 **Beechworth** 2014 Giaconda Estate Vineyard, 2015 Giaconda Nantua Les Deux **Blend** 2014 Penfolds Bin 144 Yattarna **Denmark** 2015 Singlefile Family Reserve **Geelong** 2015 Austins & Co. Custom Collection Ellyse, 2011 Bannockburn Extended Lees, 2015 by Farr Three Oaks **Gippsland** 2015 Lightfoot & Sons Home Block, 2014 Narkoojee Reserve, 2015 Tambo Reserve **Margaret River** 2015 Credaro 1000 Crowns, 2015 Cullen Kevin John, 2015 Deep Woods Reserve, 2013 Devil's Lair 9th Chamber, 2015 Flying Fish Cove Wildberry, 2015 Mandoon Reserve, 2012 Robert Oatley The Pennant, 2015 Vasse Felix Heytesbury, 2014 Windows Petit Lot **Mornington Peninsula** 2015 Garagiste Merricks, 2015 Main Ridge, 2015 Ten Minutes by Tractor Judd, 2015 Ten Minutes by Tractor Wallis **Pemberton** 2016 Larry Cherubino 'Cherubino' **Tasmania** 2015 Dawson & James, 2015 Sinapius Home Vineyard **Yarra Valley** 2015 Dappled Appellation, 2015 Giant Steps Tarraford, 2016 Little Yarra, 2015 Mount Mary, 2014 Oakridge 864 Funder & Diamond, 2015 Oakridge 864 Funder & Diamond.

Semillon

The usual walk-over for the Hunter Valley, with all but two in the top group between five and eight years old, and another six on 96 points in the same age group.

RATING	WINE	REGION
97	2011 Brokenwood ILR Reserve	Hunter Valley
97	2012 David Hook Aged Release Old Vines Pothana Vineyard Belford	Hunter Valley
97	2011 Mount Pleasant Lovedale	Hunter Valley
97	2016 Silkman Reserve	Hunter Valley
97	2016 Tempus Two Uno	Hunter Valley
97	2005 Tyrrell's Museum Release Vat 1	Hunter Valley
97	2009 Coolangatta Aged Release Wollstonecraft	Shoalhaven Coast

96 **Adelaide Hills** 2016 Charlotte Dalton Love You Love Me, **Eden Valley** 2012 Henschke Hill of Peace, 2015 Henschke Louis **Hunter Valley** 2014 Chateau Francois, 2012 Eagles Rest Dam Block, 2016 First Creek Single Vineyard Murphys, 2016 Gundog Hunter's, 2014 Gundog Somerset, 2016 Gundog The Chase, 2010 Keith Tulloch, 2009 McLeish, 2006 Mistletoe Reserve, 2013 Silkman, 2015 Silkman, 2013 Tamburlaine Reserve, 2016 Thomas Braemore, 2011 Thomas Cellar Reserve Braemore, 2009 Two Rivers Stones Throw, 2012 Tyrrell's Belford.

Sauvignon Blanc

An interesting spread of regions, with the top group of five each from a different region. Adelaide Hills (6) fended off Margaret River for bragging rights. A high percentage of these wines have structure and complexity from some barrel fermentation.

RATING	WINE	REGION
96	2016 Michael Hall Piccadilly	Adelaide Hills
96	2016 Oakdene Jessica Single Vineyard	Geelong
96	2016 Stella Bella	Margaret River
96	2015 Moorilla Estate Muse St Matthias Vineyard	Tasmania
96	2016 Out of Step Willowlake Vineyard	Yarra Valley
95	**Adelaide Hills** 2015 Geoff Weaver Ferus, 2015 Geoff Weaver, 2016 Karrawatta Anna's, 2016 Shaw + Smith, 2016 Sidewood Estate **Frankland River** 2016 Alkoomi Black Label **Geelong** 2016 Bannockburn, 2016 "Heroes" Vineyard Otway **Geographe** 2015 Whicher Ridge **Gippsland** 2016 Tambo **Macedon Ranges** 2016 Hanging Rock Jim Jim **Margaret River** 2016 Deep Woods, 2016 Firetail, 2015 Flowstone, 2016 Robert Oatley, 2016 Watershed Senses **Mornington Peninsula** 2016 Port Phillip Estate **Orange** 2016 Logan **Pemberton** 2016 Castelli Empirica Fume, 2016 Larry Cherubino 'Cherubino' **Pyrenees** 2016 Taltarni Fume **Tasmania** 2013 Domaine A Lady A, 2016 Stefano Lubiana **Yarra Valley** 2016 Medhurst Estate Vineyard, 2016 Out of Step Lusatia Park D Block.	

Semillon Sauvignon Blends

Why does anyone outside of Margaret River bother? Not only does it monopolise the field on points, the wines have typically mouthwatering prices.

RATING	WINE	REGION
97	2016 Xanadu DJL River Sauvignon Blanc Semillon	Margaret River
97	2016 Larry Cherubino Cherubino Beautiful South White Blend	Porongurup
96	2015 Cape Mentelle Wallcliffe	Margaret River
96	2015 Cullen Vineyard Sauvignon Blanc Semillon	Margaret River
96	2015 Domaine Naturaliste Sauvage Sauvignon Blanc Semillon	Margaret River
96	2014 Stella Bella Suckfizzle Sauvignon Blanc Semillon	Margaret River

Other White Wines and Blends

Eleven wines, with the usual spread of regions.

RATING	WINE	REGION
97	2016 Hahndorf Hill GRU Gruner Veltliner	Adelaide Hills
97	2016 D'Sas Pinot Gris	Henty
97	2011 Tahbilk 1927 Vines Marsanne	Nagambie Lakes
97	2014 Mount Mary Triolet	Yarra Valley
96	2016 Hahndorf Hill White Mischief Gruner Veltliner	Adelaide Hills
96	2015 Dappled Straws Lane Gewurztraminer	Macedon Ranges
96	2015 Yangarra Estate Vineyard Roux Beaute Roussanne	McLaren Vale
96	2010 Tahbilk 1927 Vines Marsanne	Nagambie Lakes
96	2015 Mount Mary Triolet	Yarra Valley
96	2015 One Block Merricks Pinot Gris	Yarra Valley
96	2015 Yarra Yering Carrodus Viognier	Yarra Valley

Sparkling

All of these have been available (and tasted by Tyson Stelzer or myself) at some point over the past 12 months. I am aware that some practitioners, and some critics, are less convinced than I am about the quality of the Arras, but I am unrepentant.

White and Rose

RATING	WINE	REGION
97	2007 House of Arras Grand Vintage	Tasmania
96	2015 Clover Hill Cuvee Prestige Late Disgorged Blanc de Blancs	Tasmania
96	2006 House of Arras Blanc de Blancs	Tasmania
96	2003 House of Arras EJ Carr Late Disgorged	Tasmania

Sparkling Red

A tiny group of wines unique to Australia, eagerly sought by those who understand the peculiarities of the style and who, better still, are prepared to cellar them – the longer the better.

RATING	WINE	REGION
97	2007 Seppelt Show Sparkling Limited Release Shiraz	Grampians
96	2009 Ashton Hills Sparkling Shiraz	Clare Valley
96	NV Primo Estate Joseph Sparkling Red	McLaren Vale

Sweet

Suffice it to say *caveat emptor*, and read the tasting notes of the rieslings (off dry to luscious and intense) that monopolise the category this year.

RATING	WINE	REGION
96	2016 Bellarmine Riesling Select	Pemberton
96	2016 Pressing Matters R69 Riesling	Tasmania
95	2010 Petaluma Essence Botrytis	Coonawarra
95	2016 "Heroes" Vineyard Otway Hinterland Riesling	Geelong
95	2014 Brown Brothers Patricia Noble Riesling	King Valley
95	2015 Granite Hills Late Harvest	Macedon Ranges
95	2016 Mr Riggs Generation Series Sticky End Viognier	McLaren Vale
95	2014 De Bortoli Noble One Botrytis Semillon	Riverina
95	2012 Nugan Cookoothama Darlington Point Botrytis Semillon	Riverina
95	2016 Gala Late Harvest Riesling	Tasmania
95	2014 Riversdale Botrytis Riesling	Tasmania
95	2016 Oakridge Hazeldene Vineyard Botrytis Gris	Yarra Valley

Rose

Roses are the ultimate all-purpose wines, to be enjoyed when people meet for a drink, with any Asian cuisine, with seafood, with entrees of almost every kind and yet more. These are of world class, all full of vibrant fruits (mainly red), but dry.

RATING	WINE	REGION
96	2016 Hahndorf Hill	Adelaide Hills
96	2016 Deep Woods Harmony	Margaret River

96	2016 Deep Woods	Margaret River
96	2016 Eddie McDougall McDougall & Langworthy	Margaret River
96	2016 Victory Point	Margaret River
96	2016 Montalto Pennon Hill	Mornington Peninsula
95	**Adelaide Hills** 2015 Adelina Nebbiolo Rosato, 2016 Terre à Terre Piccadilly Valley Chardonnay **Barossa Valley** 2015 Landhaus Siren Grenache Mourvedre, 2016 Teusner Salsa, 2016 Turkey Flat **Bendigo** 2016 Sutton Grange Fairbank **Geelong** 2016 Farr Rising Saignee **McLaren Vale** 2016 Ochota Surfer Rosa **King Valley** 2016 D'Sas Rosato **Margaret River** 2016 Amelia Park, 2016 Flametree Pinot, 2016 Marq Serious, 2016 Preveli Wild Thing, 2016 Streicker Bridgeland Block, 2014 tripe.Iscariot Aspic **Mornington Peninsula** 2016 Garagiste Le Stagiaire **Mudgee/Orange** 2016 Simon Gilbert Saignee **Northeast Victoria** 2016 Eldorado Road Luminoso **Porongurup** 2016 Duke's **Pyrenees** 2016 Mitchell Harris **Tasmania** 2015 Delamere Hurlo's, 2016 Small Island Patsie's Blush **Yarra Valley** 2016 Chandon, 2016 Dominique Portet Fontaine, 2016 Handpicked Regional Selections, 2016 Medhurst Estate, 2016 Oakridge Baton Rouge.	

Pinot Noir

Put these alongside burgundies at twice the price, and they won't yield any ground. Yet the journey still has a long way to go, with new clones slotting in alongside MV6, an old clone unique to Australia. The average age of vines is also rising – the oldest are now more than 40 years old. A titanic struggle between Tasmania (10 wines), Yarra Valley (9) and Mornington Peninsula (8).

RATING	WINE	REGION
99	2015 Mount Mary	Yarra Valley
98	2015 Ashton Hills Reserve	Adelaide Hills
98	2014 Farrside by Farr	Geelong
98	2015 Dawson & James	Tasmania
98	2014 Delamere	Tasmania
98	2015 Home Hill Kelly's Reserve	Tasmania
98	2015 Toolangi Block E	Yarra Valley
97	**Adelaide Hills** 2015 Ashton Hills, 2015 Grosset, 2016 Grosset **Geelong** 2016 Clyde Park Single Block D, 2015 Sangreal by Farr, 2014 Tout Pres by Farr **Macedon Ranges** 2014 Curly Flat **Mornington Peninsula** 2016 Dexter Black Label, 2015 Eldridge Clonal Blend, 2015 Garagiste Terre de Feu, 2015 Montalto Main Ridge Block, 2015 Moorooduc Robinson, 2015 Moorooduc The Moorooduc McIntyre, 2015 Paradigm Hill Les Cinq, 2015 Ten Minutes by Tractor McCutcheon **Tasmania** 2016 Dr Edge, 2015 Freycinet, 2015 Gala Estate, 2015 Home Hill, 2015 Sailor Seeks Horse, 2015 Sinapius The Enclave, 2015 Tolpuddle **Yarra Valley** 2015 Hoddles Creek 1er, 2014 Mac Forbes Black Label Woori Yallock, 2015 Oakridge 864 A4 Block Willowlake, 2015 Oakridge Lusatia Park, 2015 Punch Lance's Vineyard, 2015 Yarra Yering, 2015 Yering Station Scarlett.	

Shiraz

These are truly the crème de la crème of Australian shiraz, coming from all points of the compass, reflecting the unequalled adaptability of shiraz to every type of climate. and its undisputed first place in hectares planted and tonnes produced.

RATING	WINE	REGION
99	2012 Penfolds Bin 95 Grange	Blend
99	2012 Henschke Hill Of Grace	Eden Valley
98	2014 Teusner Albert	Barossa Valley

98	2014 Giaconda Estate Vineyard Shiraz	Beechworth
98	2015 Clonakilla Murrumbateman Syrah	Canberra District
98	2010 Henschke Hill of Roses	Eden Valley
98	2015 Best's Thomson Family Great Western Shiraz	Grampians
98	2015 Mount Langi Ghiran Langi Shiraz	Grampians
98	2013 Moppity Escalier Shiraz	Hilltops
98	2014 De Iuliis Limited Release Shiraz	Hunter Valley
98	2015 Bekkers Syrah	McLaren Vale
98	2015 Hardys Eileen Hardy Shiraz	McLaren Vale
98	2013 Paxton Elizabeth Jean 100 Year Shiraz	McLaren Vale
98	2015 Yarra Yering Carrodus Shiraz	Yarra Valley

97 **Adelaide Hills** 2015 Bird in Hand, 2014 Shaw + Smith Balhannah, 2015 Shaw + Smith, 2015 Shaw + Smith Balhannah **Barossa Valley** 2015 Sons of Eden Zephyrus, 2014 St Hallett Old Block, 2014 Calabria Family Grand Reserve, 2014 Charles Melton Grains of Paradise, 2014 Charles Melton Voices of Angels, 2014 Elderton Command, 2015 Eperosa Magnolia 1896, 2012 Hentley Farm The Beauty, 2012 Hentley Farm The Creation, 2015 Hentley Farm Clos Otto, 2014 John Duval Wines Eligo, 2014 Kaesler Wines Alte Reben, 2014 Kalleske Johann Georg Old Vine, 2015 Kellermeister Black Sash, 2013 Landhaus Estate Rare, 2014 Maverick Ahrens' Creek, 2014 Penfolds Bin 798 RWT, 2013 Schubert Estate The Gander Reserve, 2015 Spinifex Moppa, 2015 Torzi Matthews 1903 Domenico Martino, 2015 Two Hands Wazza's Block, 2012 Peter Lehmann Stonewell, 2015 Spinifex La Maline **Canberra District** 2015 Gundog Estate Marksman's, 2015 McWilliam's 1877 **Clare Valley** 2013 Kilikanoon Attunga 1865, 2012 Kilikanoon Revelation, 2014 Wendouree **Coonawarra** 2014 Wynns Michael **Eden Valley** 2014 Henschke Mount Edelstone, 2014 Smidge Magic Dirt Shiraz, 2014 Sons of Eden Remus, 2015 Two Hands Yacca Block, 2015 Woods Crampton Frances & Nicole **Frankland River** 2014 Kerrigan + Berry **Geelong** 2015 Paradise IV J.H. Dardel **Geographe** 2013 Della Fay Reserve **Grampians** 2014 A.T. Richardson Chockstone, 2014 Best's Sparky's Block, 2013 Best's Wines Bin No. 0, 2015 Mount Langi Ghiran Mast **Hilltops** 2015 Moppity Reserve **Hunter Valley** 2015 Brokenwood Tallawanta, 2014 Gundog Estate The 48 Block, 2007 Meerea Park Alexander Munro, 2007 Mistletoe Grand Reserve, 2014 Pepper Tree Reserve Tallawanta, 2014 Scarborough The Obsessive **Langhorne Creek** 2015 Bleasdale Powder Monkey **Margaret River** 2015 Domaine Naturaliste Rachis **McLaren Vale** 2015 Brokenwood Rayner, 2015 Chalk Hill Alpha Crucis, 2013 Clarendon Hills Onkaparinga, 2014 DOWIE DOOLE Reserve, 2013 Hardys Upper Tintara, 2015 Hardys Tintara Blewitt Springs, 2014 Kay Brothers Block 6, 2015 Patritti Wines JPB, 2015 Reynella Basket Pressed, 2015 Richard Hamilton Centurion, 2014 Serafino Terremoto, 2015 Two Hands Dave's Block, 2014 Wines by Geoff Hardy The Yeoman, 2014 Wirra Wirra Whaite, 2015 Wirra Wirra Patritti, 2014 Woodstock The Stocks, 2014 Yangarra Ironheart **Mornington Peninsula** 2015 Foxeys Hangout **Nagambie Lakes** 2013 Tahbilk 1860 Vines **Porongurup** 2015 Duke's Magpie Hill Reserve **Yarra Valley** 2015 Boat O'Craigo Reserve, 2015 Giant Steps Tarraford, 2016 Pimba Wines, 2015 Punt Road Napoleone, 2014 Seville Estate Dr McMahon, 2015 Toolangi Estate.

Shiraz Viognier

Five wines; two challenge my belief that shiraz viognier fares best in cool regions.

RATING	WINE	REGION
97	2014 Murray Street Vineyards Reserve	Barossa Valley
97	2016 Serrat	Yarra Valley
97	2015 Yering Station Reserve	Yarra Valley
96	2013 Torbreck RunRig	Barossa Valley
96	2015 McKellar Ridge	Canberra District

Cabernet Sauvignon

The affinity of cabernet sauvignon with a maritime climate is put beyond doubt by its home in Bordeaux's Medoc region. So it comes as no surprise to find that most (but not all) of Australia's top quality cabernets come from regions with climates similar to Bordeaux. The dominance of Margaret River is likely to continue; not only is the climate ideally suited, but it is far more consistent than that of any other Australian region.

RATING	WINE	REGION
98	2014 Deep Woods Yallingup	Margaret River
98	2014 Domaine Naturaliste Morus	Margaret River
98	2012 The Evans & Tate	Margaret River
98	2010 Watershed Premium Awakening	Margaret River
98	2011 West Cape Howe King Billy	Mount Barker
97	**Barossa Valley** 2012 Hentley Farm von Kasper, 2014 Two Hands Aphrodite **Blend** 2015 Hardys HRB **Clare Valley** 2014 Wendouree **Coonawarra** 2013 Leconfield The Sydney Reserve, 2014 Wynns Johnsons **Frankland River** 2015 Larry Cherubino 'Cherubino', 2014 Singlefile The Philip Adrian, 2014 Singlefile, 2015 Singlefile The Philip Adrian **Margaret River** 2014 Amelia Park Reserve, 2014 Brokenwood Wildwood Road, 2014 Howard Park Leston, 2014 Moss Wood Wilyabrup, 2014 Stella Bella Serie Luminosa, 2014 Windows Basket Pressed **McLaren Vale** 2013 Clarendon Hills Hickinbotham, 2014 Hardys Thomas Hardy **Swan Valley** 2014 Houghton Jack Mann **Yarra Valley** 2015 Coldstream Hills Reserve, 2015 Yarra Yering Carrodus.	

Cabernet and Family

A thoroughly diverse range of Bordeaux blends and varieties on the one (larger) hand courtesy of Margaret River, and the classic Australian blend of cabernet and shiraz on the other.

RATING	WINE	REGION
99	2015 Yarra Yering Dry Red No. 1	Yarra Valley
98	2012 Yalumba The Caley Cabernet Shiraz	Coonawarra/Barossa
98	2015 Cullen Diana Madeline	Margaret River
98	2013 Vasse Felix Tom Cullity Cabernet Sauvignon Malbec	Margaret River
98	2015 Yarra Yering Agincourt Cabernet Malbec	Yarra Valley
97	Margaret River 2013 Pierro Reserve Cabernet Sauvignon Merlot, 2015 Woodlands Reserve de la Cave Cabernet Franc, 2015 Woodlands Reserve de la Cave Malbec **McLaren Vale** 2015 Hickinbotham Clarendon Vineyard The Peake Cabernet Shiraz **Yarra Valley** 2015 Mount Mary Quintet.	

Shiraz and Family

A South Australian stronghold, indeed stranglehold, mostly with some or all of shiraz, grenache and mourvedre.

RATING	WINE	REGION
98	2012 Hentley Farm Museum Release H-Block Shiraz Cabernet	Barossa Valley
98	2015 Head Ancestor Vine Springton Grenache	Eden Valley
98	2015 Bleasdale Wellington Road GSM	Langhorne Creek
98	2015 Bekkers Grenache	McLaren Vale
97	2015 Head Old Vine Greenock Grenache	Barossa Valley

97	2015 Hentley Farm H Block Shiraz Cabernet	Barossa Valley
97	2015 Hentley Farm The Quintessential Shiraz Cabernet	Barossa Valley
97	2015 Massena The Moonlight Run	Barossa Valley
97	2014 Murray Street Reserve Shiraz Cabernet	Barossa Valley
97	2014 Murray Street Reserve Shiraz Mataro	Barossa Valley
97	2015 Soul Growers 106 Vines Mourvedre	Barossa Valley
97	2015 Woods Crampton Old Vine Mataro	Barossa Valley
97	2014 Grosset Nereus	Clare Valley
97	2014 Wendouree Shiraz Mataro	Clare Valley
97	2013 Kellermeister Ancestor Vine Stonegarden Vineyard Grenache	Eden Valley
97	2015 BK Springs Hill Series Blewitt Springs Sparks Grenache	McLaren Vale
97	2013 Clarendon Hills Romas Grenache	McLaren Vale
97	2013 The Old Faithful Northern Exposure Grenache	McLaren Vale
97	2014 Yangarra High Sands Grenache	McLaren Vale

The Italians and Friends

Four wines, four varieties, four regions! Very Italian.

RATING	WINE	REGION
96	2015 Mount Langi Ghiran Spinoff Barbera	Grampians
96	2015 Rochford Valle del Re Nebbiolo	King Valley
96	2013 Beach Road Aglianico	Langhorne Creek/ McLaren Vale
96	2015 Coriole Sangiovese	McLaren Vale

Fortified

The points speak for themselves. These are unique to Australia in terms of their age, their complexity, their intensity, and their varietal make up. They arguably represent the best value of all Australian wines given the cost of production, notably in the amount of working capital tied up for decades.

RATING	WINE	REGION
100	1917 Seppeltsfield 100 Year Old Para Liqueur	Barossa Valley
99	NV All Saints Museum Muscadelle	Rutherglen
99	NV Chambers Rosewood Rare Muscadelle	Rutherglen
99	NV Chambers Rosewood Rare Muscat	Rutherglen
99	NV Morris Old Premium Rare Liqueur Topaque	Rutherglen

Best wineries of the regions

The nomination of the best wineries of the regions has evolved into a three-level classification (further explained on page 9). At the very top are the wineries with their names and stars printed in red; these have been generally recognised for having a long track record of excellence – truly the best of the best. Next are wineries with their stars (but not their names) printed in red, which have had a consistent record of excellence for at least the past three years. Those wineries with black stars have achieved excellence this year (and sometimes longer).

ADELAIDE HILLS
Ashton Hills ★★★★★
Barratt ★★★★★
Bird in Hand ★★★★★
BK Wines ★★★★★
Casa Freschi ★★★★★
Chain of Ponds ★★★★★
Charlotte Dalton Wines ★★★★★
Coates Wines ★★★★★
Coulter Wines ★★★★★
CRFT Wines ★★★★★
Elderslie ★★★★★
Geoff Weaver ★★★★★
Hahndorf Hill Winery ★★★★★
Jericho Wines ★★★★★
Karrawatta ★★★★★
Mike Press Wines ★★★★★
Mt Lofty Ranges Vineyard ★★★★★
Murdoch Hill ★★★★★
Ochota Barrels ★★★★★
Petaluma ★★★★★
Pike & Joyce ★★★★★
Riposte ★★★★★
Romney Park Wines ★★★★★
Scott ★★★★★
Shaw + Smith ★★★★★
Shining Rock Vineyard ★★★★★
Sidewood Estate ★★★★★
Tapanappa ★★★★★
The Lane Vineyard ★★★★★
Tomich Wines ★★★★★
Wicks Estate Wines ★★★★★

ADELAIDE
Heirloom Vineyards ★★★★★
Hewitson ★★★★★

Patritti Wines ★★★★★
Penfolds Magill Estate ★★★★★

ALPINE VALLEYS
Mayford Wines ★★★★★

BALLARAT
Tomboy Hill ★★★★★

BAROSSA VALLEY
1847 | Yaldara Wines ★★★★★
Ballycroft Vineyard & Cellars
    ★★★★★
Bethany Wines ★★★★★
Brothers at War ★★★★★
Caillard Wine ★★★★★
Charles Melton ★★★★★
Chateau Tanunda ★★★★★
Dorrien Estate ★★★★★
Dutschke Wines ★★★★★
Elderton ★★★★★
Eperosa ★★★★★
First Drop Wines ★★★★★
Gibson ★★★★★
Glaetzer Wines ★★★★★
Glen Eldon Wines ★★★★★
Grant Burge ★★★★★
Hayes Family Wines ★★★★★
Head Wines ★★★★★
Hemera Estate ★★★★★
Hentley Farm Wines ★★★★★
Jacob's Creek ★★★★★
John Duval Wines ★★★★★
Kaesler Wines ★★★★★
Kalleske ★★★★★
Kellermeister ★★★★★

Landhaus Estate ★★★★★
Langmeil Winery ★★★★★
Lanz Vineyards ★★★★★
Laughing Jack ★★★★★
Massena Vineyards ★★★★★
Maverick Wines ★★★★★
Murray Street Vineyards ★★★★★
Penfolds ★★★★★
Peter Lehmann ★★★★★
Purple Hands Wines ★★★★★
Rockford ★★★★★
St Hallett ★★★★★
St John's Road ★★★★★
Saltram ★★★★★
Schubert Estate ★★★★★
Schulz Vignerons ★★★★★
Schwarz Wine Company ★★★★★
Seppeltsfield ★★★★★
Sons of Eden ★★★★★
Soul Growers ★★★★★
Spinifex ★★★★★
Teusner ★★★★★
Thorn-Clarke Wines ★★★★★
Tim Smith Wines ★★★★★
Torbreck Vintners ★★★★★
Turkey Flat ★★★★★
Two Hands Wines ★★★★★
Westlake Vineyards ★★★★★
Wolf Blass ★★★★★
Woods Crampton ★★★★★
Yelland & Papps ★★★★★
Z Wine ★★★★★

BEECHWORTH
A. Rodda Wines ★★★★★
Fighting Gully Road ★★★★★
Giaconda ★★★★★
Golden Ball ★★★★★
Piano Piano ★★★★★

BENDIGO
Balgownie Estate ★★★★★
Bress ★★★★★
Pondalowie Vineyards ★★★★★
Turner's Crossing Vineyard ★★★★★

BLACKWOOD VALLEY
Dickinson Estate ★★★★★

CANBERRA DISTRICT
Capital Wines ★★★★★
Clonakilla ★★★★★
Collector Wines ★★★★★
Eden Road Wines ★★★★★
Four Winds Vineyard ★★★★★
Helm ★★★★★
McKellar Ridge Wines ★★★★★
Mount Majura Vineyard ★★★★★
Nick O'Leary Wines ★★★★★
Ravensworth ★★★★★

CENTRAL VICTORIA
Mount Terrible ★★★★★

CLARE VALLEY
Adelina Wines ★★★★★
Atlas Wines ★★★★★
Gaelic Cemetery Wines ★★★★★
Grosset ★★★★★
Jeanneret Wines ★★★★★
Jim Barry Wines ★★★★★
Kilikanoon Wines ★★★★★
Knappstein ★★★★★
Mitchell ★★★★★
Mount Horrocks ★★★★★
O'Leary Walker Wines ★★★★★
Paulett Wines ★★★★★
Pikes ★★★★★
Rhythm Stick Wines ★★★★★
Rieslingfreak ★★★★★
Sevenhill Cellars ★★★★★
Steve Wiblin's Erin Eyes ★★★★★
Taylors ★★★★★
Wendouree ★★★★★
Wilson Vineyard ★★★★★
Woodvale ★★★★★
Vickery Wines ★★★★★

COONAWARRA
Balnaves of Coonawarra ★★★★★
Brand's Laira Coonawarra ★★★★★
Katnook Coonawarra ★★★★★
Leconfield ★★★★★
Lindeman's (Coonawarra) ★★★★★
Majella ★★★★★
Parker Coonawarra Estate ★★★★★
Patrick of Coonawarra ★★★★★
Penley Estate ★★★★★
Redman ★★★★★

Wynns Coonawarra Estate ★★★★★
Zema Estate ★★★★★

CURRENCY CREEK
Shaw Family Vintners ★★★★★

DENMARK
Harewood Estate ★★★★★
Moombaki Wines ★★★★★
Rockcliffe ★★★★★
The Lake House Denmark ★★★★★

EDEN VALLEY
Brockenchack ★★★★★
Flaxman Wines ★★★★★
Forbes & Forbes ★★★★★
Heathvale ★★★★★
Henschke ★★★★★
Leo Buring ★★★★★
Mountadam ★★★★★
Pewsey Vale ★★★★★
Poonawatta ★★★★★
Robert Johnson Vineyards ★★★★★
Stage Door Wine Co ★★★★★
Yalumba ★★★★★

FRANKLAND RIVER
Alkoomi ★★★★★
Frankland Estate ★★★★★

GEELONG
Attwoods Wines ★★★★★
Austins & Co. ★★★★★
Banks Road ★★★★★
Bannockburn Vineyards ★★★★★
Brown Magpie Wines ★★★★★
Clyde Park Vineyard ★★★★★
Farr | Farr Rising ★★★★★
"Heroes" Vineyard ★★★★★
Lethbridge Wines ★★★★★
McGlashan's Wallington Estate
  ★★★★★
Oakdene ★★★★★
Paradise IV ★★★★★
Provenance Wines ★★★★★
Robin Brockett Wines ★★★★★
Scotchmans Hill ★★★★★
Shadowfax ★★★★★
Spence ★★★★★
Yes said the Seal ★★★★★

GEOGRAPHE
Capel Vale ★★★★★
Iron Cloud Wines ★★★★★
Talisman Wines ★★★★★
Whicher Ridge ★★★★★
Willow Bridge Estate ★★★★★

GIPPSLAND
Bass Phillip ★★★★★
Lightfoot & Sons ★★★★★
Narkoojee ★★★★★
Tambo Estate ★★★★★

GLENROWAN
Baileys of Glenrowan ★★★★★

GRAMPIANS
Best's Wines ★★★★★
Grampians Estate ★★★★★
Halls Gap Estate ★★★★★
Montara ★★★★★
Mount Langi Ghiran Vineyards
  ★★★★★
Seppelt ★★★★★
The Story Wines ★★★★★

GRANITE BELT
Boireann ★★★★★
Golden Grove Estate ★★★★★
Heritage Estate ★★★★★

GREAT SOUTHERN
Byron & Harold ★★★★★
Castelli Estate ★★★★★
Forest Hill Vineyard ★★★★★
Marchand & Burch ★★★★★
Paul Nelson Wines ★★★★★
Singlefile Wines ★★★★★
Staniford Wine Co ★★★★★
Trevelen Farm ★★★★★
Willoughby Park ★★★★★

GREAT WESTERN
A.T. Richardson Wines ★★★★★

HEATHCOTE
Flynns Wines ★★★★★
Heathcote Estate ★★★★★
Heathcote II ★★★★★
Jasper Hill ★★★★★

La Pleiade ★★★★★
Paul Osicka ★★★★★
Redesdale Estate Wines ★★★★★
Sanguine Estate ★★★★★
Vinea Marson ★★★★★

HENTY
Crawford River Wines ★★★★★
Henty Estate ★★★★★
Hentyfarm Wines ★★★★★

HILLTOPS
Moppity Vineyards ★★★★★

HUNTER VALLEY
Audrey Wilkinson ★★★★★
Bimbadgen ★★★★★
Briar Ridge Vineyard ★★★★★
Brokenwood ★★★★★
Chateau Francois ★★★★★
Chateau Pâto ★★★★★
De Iuliis ★★★★★
Drayton's Family Wines ★★★★★
Eagles Rest Wines ★★★★★
Elbourne Wines ★★★★★
First Creek Wines ★★★★★
Glenguin Estate ★★★★★
Gundog Estate ★★★★★
Hart & Hunter ★★★★★
Hungerford Hill ★★★★★
Keith Tulloch Wine ★★★★★
Lake's Folly ★★★★★
Leogate Estate Wines ★★★★★
McLeish Estate ★★★★★
Margan Family ★★★★★
Meerea Park ★★★★★
Mistletoe Wines ★★★★★
Mount Pleasant ★★★★★
Mount View Estate ★★★★★
Pepper Tree Wines ★★★★★
Pokolbin Estate ★★★★★
Silkman Wines ★★★★★
Sweetwater Wines ★★★★★
Tallavera Grove | Carillion ★★★★★
Tempus Two Wines ★★★★★
Thomas Wines ★★★★★
Tinklers Vineyard ★★★★★
Tulloch ★★★★★
Two Rivers ★★★★★

Tyrrell's Wines ★★★★★
Vinden Estate ★★★★★
Whispering Brook ★★★★★

KANGAROO ISLAND
The Islander Estate Vineyards
★★★★★

KING VALLEY
Brown Brothers ★★★★★
Wood Park ★★★★★

LANGHORNE CREEK
Angas Plains Estate ★★★★★
Bleasdale Vineyards ★★★★★
Bremerton Wines ★★★★★
John's Blend ★★★★★
Lake Breeze Wines ★★★★★

MACEDON RANGES
Bindi Wine Growers ★★★★★
Curly Flat ★★★★★
Granite Hills ★★★★★
Hanging Rock Winery ★★★★★
Lane's End Vineyard ★★★★★
Passing Clouds ★★★★★

MCLAREN VALE
Aramis Vineyards ★★★★★
Beach Road ★★★★★
Bekkers ★★★★★
Beresford Wines ★★★★★
Bondar Wines ★★★★★
Chalk Hill ★★★★★
Chapel Hill ★★★★★
Clarendon Hills ★★★★★
Coriole ★★★★★
d'Arenberg ★★★★★
Dandelion Vineyards ★★★★★
Dodgy Brothers ★★★★★
DOWIE DOOLE ★★★★★
Ekhidna ★★★★★
Fox Creek Wines ★★★★★
Gemtree Wines ★★★★★
Geoff Merrill Wines ★★★★★
Hardys ★★★★★
Haselgrove Wines ★★★★★
Hickinbotham Clarendon Vineyard
★★★★★
Hugh Hamilton Wines ★★★★★

Kangarilla Road Vineyard ★★★★★
Kay Brothers Amery Vineyards
  ★★★★★
La Curio ★★★★★
Maxwell Wines ★★★★★
Mitolo Wines ★★★★★
Mr Riggs Wine Company ★★★★★
Olivers Taranga Vineyards ★★★★★
Paxton ★★★★★
Penny's Hill ★★★★★
Pirramimma ★★★★★
Primo Estate ★★★★★
Reynella ★★★★★
Richard Hamilton ★★★★★
Rosemount Estate ★★★★★
Rudderless ★★★★★
SC Pannell ★★★★★
Serafino Wines ★★★★★
Shingleback ★★★★★
The Old Faithful Estate ★★★★★
Ulithorne ★★★★★
Way Wood Wines ★★★★★
Wirra Wirra ★★★★★
Yangarra Estate Vineyard ★★★★★
  ★★★★★
Zonte's Footstep ★★★★★

MANJIMUP
Peos Estate ★★★★★

MARGARET RIVER
Amelia Park Wines ★★★★★
Aravina Estate ★★★★★
Arlewood Estate ★★★★★
Ashbrook Estate ★★★★★
Brookland Valley ★★★★★
Burch Family Wines ★★★★★
Cape Grace Wines ★★★★★
Cape Mentelle ★★★★★
Chapman Grove Wines ★★★★★
Clairault | Streicker Wines ★★★★★
Cloudburst ★★★★★
Credaro Family Estate ★★★★★
Cullen Wines ★★★★★
Deep Woods Estate ★★★★★
Della Fay Wines ★★★★★
Devil's Lair ★★★★★
Domaine Naturaliste ★★★★★
Driftwood Estate ★★★★★

Evans & Tate ★★★★★
Evoi Wines ★★★★★
Fermoy Estate ★★★★★
Firetail ★★★★★
Flametree ★★★★★
Flowstone Wines ★★★★★
Flying Fish Cove ★★★★★
Forester Estate ★★★★★
Fraser Gallop Estate ★★★★★
Grace Farm ★★★★★
Happs ★★★★★
Hay Shed Hill Wines ★★★★★
Heydon Estate ★★★★★
Higher Plane ★★★★★
House of Cards ★★★★★
Ibizan Wines ★★★★★
Juniper Estate ★★★★★
Knee Deep Wines ★★★★★
Leeuwin Estate ★★★★★
Lenton Brae Wines ★★★★★
Marq Wines ★★★★★
McHenry Hohnen Vintners ★★★★★
Moss Wood ★★★★★
Palmer Wines ★★★★★
Passel Estate ★★★★★
Peccavi Wines ★★★★★
Pierro ★★★★★
Redgate ★★★★★
Sandalford ★★★★★
Stella Bella Wines ★★★★★
Thompson Estate ★★★★★
tripe.Iscariot ★★★★★
Umamu Estate ★★★★★
Vasse Felix ★★★★★
Victory Point Wines ★★★★★
Voyager Estate ★★★★★
Watershed Premium Wines ★★★★★
Wills Domain ★★★★★
Windows Estate ★★★★★
Wise Wine ★★★★★
Woodlands ★★★★★
Woody Nook ★★★★★
Xanadu Wines ★★★★★

MORNINGTON PENINSULA
Allies Wines ★★★★★
Baillieu Vineyard ★★★★★
Circe Wines ★★★★★
Crittenden Estate ★★★★★

Dexter Wines ★★★★★
Eldridge Estate of Red Hill ★★★★★
Elgee Park ★★★★★
Foxeys Hangout ★★★★★
Garagiste ★★★★★
Hurley Vineyard ★★★★★
Kooyong ★★★★★
Lindenderry at Red Hill ★★★★★
Main Ridge Estate ★★★★★
Montalto ★★★★★
Moorooduc Estate ★★★★★
Onannon ★★★★★
Paradigm Hill ★★★★★
Paringa Estate ★★★★★
Port Phillip Estate ★★★★★
Portsea Estate ★★★★★
Scorpo Wines ★★★★★
Stonier Wines ★★★★★
Ten Minutes by Tractor ★★★★★
Tuck's Ridge ★★★★★
Willow Creek Vineyard ★★★★★
Yabby Lake Vineyard ★★★★★

MOUNT BARKER
Plantagenet ★★★★★
Poacher's Ridge Vineyard ★★★★★
3 Drops ★★★★★
West Cape Howe Wines ★★★★★
Xabregas ★★★★★

MOUNT BENSON
Cape Jaffa Wines ★★★★★

MOUNT LOFTY RANGES
Michael Hall Wines ★★★★★

MUDGEE
Logan Wines ★★★★★
Robert Oatley Vineyards ★★★★★
Robert Stein Vineyard ★★★★★

NAGAMBIE LAKES
Tahbilk ★★★★★

NORTHEAST VICTORIA
Eldorado Road ★★★★★

ORANGE
Bloodwood ★★★★★
Colmar Estate ★★★★★

Cooks Lot ★★★★★
Philip Shaw Wines ★★★★★
Ross Hill Wines ★★★★★

PEMBERTON
Bellarmine Wines ★★★★★

PERTH HILLS
Millbrook Winery ★★★★★

PORONGURUP
Abbey Creek Vineyard ★★★★★
Castle Rock Estate ★★★★★
Duke's Vineyard ★★★★★

PYRENEES
Blue Pyrenees Estate ★★★★★
Dalwhinnie ★★★★★
DogRock Winery ★★★★★
Glenlofty Wines ★★★★★
Mitchell Harris Wines ★★★★★
Mount Avoca ★★★★★
Summerfield ★★★★★
Taltarni ★★★★★

QUEENSLAND
Witches Falls Winery ★★★★★

RIVERINA
De Bortoli ★★★★★
McWilliam's ★★★★★

RUTHERGLEN
All Saints Estate ★★★★★
Buller Wines ★★★★★
Campbells ★★★★★
Chambers Rosewood ★★★★★
Morris ★★★★★
Pfeiffer Wines ★★★★★
Stanton & Killeen Wines ★★★★★

SHOALHAVEN COAST
Coolangatta Estate ★★★★★
Cupitt's Winery ★★★★★

SOUTH AUSTRALIA
Angove Family Winemakers ★★★★★
Wines by Geoff Hardy ★★★★★

SOUTH WEST AUSTRALIA
Kerrigan + Berry ★★★★★
Snake + Herring ★★★★★

SOUTHERN FLEURIEU
Salomon Estate ★★★★★

SOUTHERN HIGHLANDS
Centennial Vineyards ★★★★★

SOUTHERN NEW SOUTH WALES
Hatherleigh Vineyard ★★★★★

STRATHBOGIE RANGES
Fowles Wine ★★★★★
Maygars Hill Winery ★★★★★

SUNBURY
Craiglee ★★★★★
Galli Estate ★★★★★

SWAN DISTRICT
Mandoon Estate ★★★★★

SWAN VALLEY
Houghton ★★★★★
John Kosovich Wines ★★★★★
Lamont's Winery ★★★★★
Sittella Wines ★★★★★

TASMANIA
Bay of Fires ★★★★★
Clover Hill ★★★★★
Dalrymple ★★★★★
Dawson & James ★★★★★
Delamere Vineyard ★★★★★
Devil's Corner ★★★★★
Domaine A ★★★★★
Dr Edge ★★★★★
Freycinet ★★★★★
Frogmore Creek ★★★★★
Gala Estate ★★★★★
Ghost Rock Vineyard ★★★★★
Heemskerk ★★★★★
Holm Oak ★★★★★
Home Hill ★★★★★
House of Arras ★★★★★
Jansz Tasmania ★★★★★
Josef Chromy Wines ★★★★★
Meadowbank Wines ★★★★★
Milton Vineyard ★★★★★

Moorilla Estate ★★★★★
Pipers Brook Vineyard ★★★★★
Pooley Wines ★★★★★
Pressing Matters ★★★★★
Riversdale Estate ★★★★★
Sinapius Vineyard ★★★★★
Small Island Wines ★★★★★
Stargazer Wine ★★★★★
Stefano Lubiana ★★★★★
Stoney Rise ★★★★★
Tamar Ridge | Pirie ★★★★★
Tolpuddle Vineyard ★★★★★

TUMBARUMBA
Coppabella of Tumbarumba ★★★★★

UPPER GOULBURN
Delatite ★★★★★

VARIOUS
Ben Haines Wine ★★★★★
Handpicked Wines ★★★★★
Ministry of Clouds ★★★★★
Smidge Wines ★★★★★
Twofold ★★★★★
Vinaceous Wines ★★★★★

VICTORIA
Di Sciascio Family Wines ★★★★★
Sentio Wines ★★★★★

WESTERN AUSTRALIA
Larry Cherubino Wines ★★★★★

WESTERN VICTORIA ZONE
Norton Estate ★★★★★

WRATTONBULLY
Ruckus Estate ★★★★★
Terre à Terre ★★★★★

YARRA VALLEY
Bicknell fc ★★★★★
Bird on a Wire Wines ★★★★★
Boat O'Craigo ★★★★★
Chandon Australia ★★★★★
Coldstream Hills ★★★★★
Dappled Wine ★★★★★
De Bortoli (Victoria) ★★★★★
Denton Viewhill Vineyard ★★★★★
Dominique Portet ★★★★★

Elmswood Estate ★★★★★
Gembrook Hill ★★★★★
Giant Steps ★★★★★
Helen's Hill Estate ★★★★★
Hillcrest Vineyard ★★★★★
Hoddles Creek Estate ★★★★★
Innocent Bystander ★★★★★
Journey Wines ★★★★★
Little Yarra Wines ★★★★★
Mac Forbes ★★★★★
Mandala ★★★★★
Mayer ★★★★★
Medhurst ★★★★★
Mount Mary ★★★★★
Nillumbik Estate ★★★★★
916 ★★★★★
Oakridge Wines ★★★★★
One Block ★★★★★
Out of Step ★★★★★
Pimba Wines ★★★★★
Pimpernel Vineyards ★★★★★
Punch ★★★★★
Punt Road ★★★★★

Rochford Wines ★★★★★
Rouleur ★★★★★
St Huberts ★★★★★
Santolin Wines ★★★★★
Serrat ★★★★★
Seville Estate ★★★★★
Soumah ★★★★★
Squitchy Lane Vineyard ★★★★★
Stefani Estate ★★★★★
Sutherland Estate ★★★★★
Tarrahill. ★★★★★
TarraWarra Estate ★★★★★
The Wanderer ★★★★★
Thick as Thieves Wines ★★★★★
Tokar Estate ★★★★★
Toolangi Vineyards ★★★★★
Trapeze ★★★★★
Wantirna Estate ★★★★★
Warramate ★★★★★
Warramunda Estate ★★★★★
Yarra Yering ★★★★★
Yering Station ★★★★★
Yeringberg ★★★★★

Regional production 2015–16

I have no option this year but to take a different approach to the statistics that are the bone of the wine industry: firstly, where are the varieties grown; and second, what are the varieties, and how do they rank in order of importance?

The table opposite provides a broad picture of the regional contributions, grouped by state and the three most significant regions in each state (except for South Australia, which has four). Murray Darling–Swan Hill takes in vineyards either side of the Murray River, marking (at various points) the border between New South Wales and Victoria, and encompasses regions on either side of the Murray.

For the purposes of the survey, the Murray Darling is treated as if it were a GI zone, and the crush for New South Wales and Victoria excludes the tonnes attributed to this hybrid zone.

The headline (or baseline, if you prefer) is a total crush of almost 1.81 million tonnes, substantially higher than the five-year average (2011–15) of 1.70 million tonnes. Go back to 2008 and you find the high point of 1.84 million tonnes from 166 000ha of vines. The prospects for 2017 are beset by qualifications, with 25 000ha removed from, and a November '16 hailstorm cutting a swathe through, parts of the Riverland and Murray Darling regions.

The expectation is for a similar crush; if there is a rise, it is likely to come from the dry land areas by virtue of the overall vintage, but it is probable there will be a modest rise in the price per tonne of dry-land red grapes rising across all price points.

The lead times must be measured in years; turning the total plantings around from the steady depletion of over 24 000ha since 2008 is not going to happen overnight, however thirsty the Chinese dragon may become. Moreover, the giddy rise in prices from 1997 to 2007 was followed by a dramatic fall as the value of grape prices and the volume and value of exports plummeted to their low point of MAT December 2010. Despite four years of growth in the value per litre, that of MAT March 2017 was $2.98 per litre, compared with $4.80 per litre in '07.

At the risk of over-emphasising the present and future demands of Asia, led by China, the figures for South Australia's 2016 crush are surely a combination of the dominance of Australia's largest producers in the Chinese market, of the demand for red wines – led by shiraz, cabernet sauvignon its lieutenant – and, of course, the excellence of the growing season weather.

Outside of South Australia (and the warm inland regions), Margaret River produced twice as much as the Yarra Valley and Tasmania, so its reputation for high quality from microscopic volumes of wine might have to be recalibrated.

The other aspect of the damned lies of statistics is that, based on knowledge of the response rate in both previous and current (2016) years, only 88% of the crush was captured by the information supplied. So the figures you see have been uniformly scaled up to 100%.

STATE/REGIONS	2016 TONNES	2015 TONNES	% CHANGE 2015–16	% OF CRUSH 2016
SOUTH AUSTRALIA	926,430	798,097	16%	51%
Langhorne Creek	68,090	43,348	57%	4%
Barossa Valley	61,580	49,790	24%	3%
McLaren Vale	46,433	31,668	47%	3%
Riverland	517,577	505,863	2%	29%
MURRAY DARLING–SWAN HILL	416,966	425,150	−2%	23%
NEW SOUTH WALES	348,441	367,271	−5%	19%
Hunter Valley	3,034	5,593	−46%	0%
Mudgee	1,997	3,215	−38%	0%
Riverina	311,639	324,550	−4%	17%
VICTORIA	63,933	70,011	−9%	4%
Mornigton Peninsula	3,198	2,097	53%	0%
Rutherglen	1,907	2,357	−19%	0%
Yarra Valley	9,378	11,652	−20%	1%
WESTERN AUSTRALIA	39,055	33,549	16%	2%
Greath Southern	7,615	5,459	39%	0%
Margaret River	20,639	18,925	9%	1%
Pemberton	2,805	2,062	36%	0%
TASMANIA	10,214	8,016	27%	1%
QUEENSLAND	2,168	694	212%	0%
AUSTRALIAN CAPITAL TERRITORY	0	24	−100%	0%
WARM INLAND REGIONS	1,259,180	1,266,499	−0.6%	70%
COOL/TEMPERATE REGIONS	548,027	436,312	26%	30%
TOTAL TONNES	1,807,207	1,702,812	6%	100%

Varietal production 2015–16

The table opposite shows some unexpected statistics. But to keep some perspective, I have arbitrarily divided the varieties into two groups, with a dividing line of 11 000 tonnes (verdelho) for major varieties, under 11 000 tonnes for minor.

The big red dog is shiraz, which is close to its all-time high production of 441 950 tonnes in 2008. While it has hit head winds in the US, it is in much demand in China. And it's hard to deny the special place Penfolds Grange has as Australia's most famous wine; it's relentlessly marketed, its quality (almost) always protected from CFOs by the winemaking team – almost, because I don't believe the 2011 should have been released. As a further postscript, in the great 1996 vintage Australia crushed a mere 81,674 tonnes.

Pinot noir and shiraz were cited by Wine Australia as being the main drivers of red wine growth in the domestic market, understandable given that pinot noir enjoyed the highest weighted average price per tonne in both 2015 and '16. The strange thing is that its plantings have remained virtually unchanged since '08, although its tonnage has increased by circa 8% (new plantings should have washed through the system long since).

Riesling's renaissance has long been talked about, its position with the third highest price in 2016, second highest in '15, seeming inexplicable: its '16 production is the lowest on record, its plantings having collapsed from 3893ha in '12 to 3157ha in '15.

Winemakers (outside the Barossa Valley) are anecdotally said to drink riesling, pinot noir and grenache. While they aren't doing much for the commercial health of the first two, they (or their surrogates) seem to be drinking enough to drag grenache back from the brink of oblivion. Less romantically, it's no longer in demand for fortified wines, but is for lovely medium-bodied table wines. As recently as 2002, 26 260 tonnes were crushed, falling to 11 335 tonnes in '10. Its 23% rise in price per tonne from '15 to '16 sees it as the most highly valued of the major varieties.

Which leaves me scant room to write about the alternative/lesser varieties in the bottom half of the table. Here tempranillo has doubled its area between 2007 and '15, leading the price per tonne for all varieties in the latter year (except the anomalies of the tiny production of arneis, fiano and – surprisingly – muscadelle).

Sangiovese had the second highest price after tempranillo, yet its plantings in 2015 were the smallest since '07.

One variety not mentioned is fiano, which consistently has a special texture seemingly independent of the vinification. There are two clones, with Jeffrey Grosset the font of knowledge. In my book *Varietal Wines* I recorded that Australia had 88ha planted, producing 340 tonnes, but since then it has enjoyed significant growth, with circa 2200 tonnes crushed in 2016, up from circa 1360 tonnes in '15.

	2016 TONNES	2016 WEIGHTED AVERAGE PURCHASE VALUE	2015 WEIGHTED AVERAGE PURCHASE VALUE	% CHANGE IN PRICE
SHIRAZ	430,185	684	600	14%
CHARDONNAY	406,028	382	316	21%
CABERNET SAUVIGNON	255,074	652	559	17%
MERLOT	111,959	433	415	4%
SAUVIGNON BLANC	100,769	553	514	8%
PINOT GRIS	73,372	619	597	1%
SEMILLON	64,066	345	310	11%
PINOT NOIR	47,860	891	856	4%
RIESLING	28,224	768	768	0%
PETIT VERDOT	20,299	350	344	2%
GEWURZTRAMINER	14,219	365	368	−1%
GRENACHE	13,235	887	719	23%
VERDELHO	11,005	400	397	1%
TEMPRANILLO	6,582	914	846	1%
DURIF	5,758	478	469	2%
SANGIOVESE	5,210	836	707	18%
MARSANNE	1,621	418	410	2%
NERO D'AVOLA	864	626	593	6%
MUSCADELLE	382	1,160	696	67%
ARNEIS	141	1,136	1,247	−9%

Varietal wine styles and regions

For better or worse, there simply has to be concerted action to highlight the link between regions, varieties and wine styles. It's not a question of creating the links: they are already there, and have been in existence for periods as short as 20 years or as long as 150 years. So here you will find abbreviated summaries of those regional styles (in turn reflected in the Best of the Best lists commencing on page 26).

Riesling

Riesling's link with the **Eden Valley** dates back at least to when Joseph Gilbert planted his Pewsey Vale vineyard, and the grape quickly made its way to the nearby **Clare Valley**. These two regions stood above all others for well over 100 years, producing wines that shared many flavour and texture characteristics: lime (a little more obvious in the Eden Valley), apple, talc and mineral, lightly browned toasty notes emerging with five–10 years bottle age. Within the last 20 or so years, the subregions of the **Great Southern** of Western Australia have established a deserved reputation for finely structured, elegant rieslings with wonderful length, sometimes shy when young, bursting into song after five years. The subregions are (in alphabetical order) **Albany**, **Denmark**, **Frankland River**, **Mount Barker** and **Porongurup**. **Canberra** is up with the best and **Tasmania**, too, produces high-class rieslings, notable for their purity and intensity courtesy of their high natural acidity. Finally, there is the small and very cool region of **Henty** (once referred to as Drumborg), its exceptional rieslings sharing many things in common with those of Tasmania.

Semillon

There is a Siamese-twin relationship between semillon and the **Hunter Valley**, which has been producing a wine style like no other in the world for well over 100 years. The humid and very warm climate (best coupled with sandy soils not common in the region) results in wines that have a median alcohol level of 10.5% and no residual sugar, are cold-fermented in stainless steel and bottled within three months of vintage. They are devoid of colour and have only the barest hints of grass, herb and mineral wrapped around a core of acidity. Over the next five to 10 years they develop a glowing green–gold colour, a suite of grass and citrus fruit surrounded by buttered toast and honey notes. As with rieslings, screwcaps have added decades to their cellaring life. The **Adelaide Hills** and **Margaret River** produce entirely different semillon, more structured and weighty, its alcohol 13–14%, and as often as not blended with sauvignon blanc, barrel fermentation of part or all common. Finally, there is a cuckoo in the nest: Peter Lehmann in the **Barossa/Eden Valley** has adapted Hunter Valley practices, picking early, fermenting in steel, bottling early, and holding the top wine for five years before release – and succeeding brilliantly.

Chardonnay

This infinitely flexible grape is grown and vinified in all 63 regions, and accounts for half of Australia's white wine grapes and wine. Incredibly, before 1970 it was all but unknown, hiding its promise here and there (**Mudgee** was one such place) under a cloak of anonymity. It was there and in the **Hunter Valley** that the first wines labelled chardonnay were made in 1971 (by Craigmoor and Tyrrell's). Its bold yellow colour, peaches and cream flavour and vanilla oak was unlike anything that had gone before and was accepted by domestic and export markets with equal enthusiasm. When exports took off into the stratosphere between 1985 and '95, one half of Brand Australia was cheerful and cheap oak-chipped chardonnay grown in the **Riverina** and **Riverland**. By coincidence, over the same period chardonnay from the emerging cool climate regions was starting to appear in limited quantities, its flavour and structure radically different to the warm-grown, high-cropped wine. Another 10 years on, and by 2005–06 the wine surplus was starting to build rapidly, with demand for chardonnay much less than its production. As attention swung from chardonnay to sauvignon blanc, the situation became dire. Lost in the heat of battle were supremely elegant wines from most cool regions, **Margaret River** and **Yarra Valley** the leaders of the large band. Constant refinement of the style, and the adoption of the screwcap, puts these wines at the forefront of the gradually succeeding battle to re-engage consumers here and abroad with what are world-class wines.

Sauvignon Blanc

Two regions, the **Adelaide Hills** and **Margaret River**, stood in front of all others until recently joined by **Orange**; these three produce Australia's best sauvignon blanc, wines with real structure and authority. It is a matter of record that Marlborough sauvignon blanc accounts for one-third of Australia's white wine sales; all one can say (accurately) is that the basic Marlborough style is very different, and look back at what happened with Australian chardonnay. Margaret River also offers complex blends of sauvignon blanc and semillon in widely varying proportions, and with varying degrees of oak fermentation.

Shiraz

Shiraz, like chardonnay, is by far the most important red variety and, again like chardonnay, is tremendously flexible in its ability to adapt to virtually any combination of climate and soil/terroir. Unlike chardonnay, a recent arrival, shiraz was the most important red variety throughout the 19th and 20th centuries. Its ancestral homes were the **Barossa Valley**, the **Clare Valley**, **McLaren Vale** and the **Hunter Valley**, and it still leads in those regions. With the exception of the Hunter Valley, it was as important in making fortified wine as table wine over the period 1850 to 1950, aided and abetted by grenache and mourvedre (mataro). In New South Wales the **Hilltops** and **Canberra District** are producing elegant, cool grown wines that usually conceal their power (especially when co-fermented with viognier) but not their silky length. Further north, but at a higher altitude, **Orange** is also producing fine, fragrant and spicy wines. All the other New South Wales regions are capable of producing good shiraz of seriously good character and quality; shiraz ripens comfortably, but quite late in the season. Polished, sophisticated wines are the result. Victoria has a cornucopia of regions at the cooler end of the spectrum; the coolest (though not too cool for comfort) are the **Yarra Valley**, **Mornington Peninsula**, **Sunbury** and **Geelong**, all producing fragrant, spicy medium-bodied wines. **Bendigo**, **Heathcote**, **Grampians** and **Pyrenees**, more or less running east–west across the centre of Victoria, are producing some of the most exciting medium-bodied shirazs in Australia, each with its own terroir stamp, but all combining generosity and elegance. In Western Australia, **Great Southern** and three of its five subregions, **Frankland River**, **Mount Barker** and **Porongurup**, are making magical shirazs, fragrant and spicy, fleshy yet strongly structured. **Margaret River** has been a relatively late mover, but it, too, is producing wines with exemplary varietal definition and finesse.

Cabernet Sauvignon

The tough-skinned cabernet sauvignon can be, and is, grown in all regions, but it struggles in the coolest (notably **Tasmania**) and loses desirable varietal definition in the warmer regions, especially in warmer vintages. Shiraz can cope with alcohol levels in excess of 14.5%, cabernet can't. In South Australia, **Coonawarra** stands supreme, its climate (though not its soil) strikingly similar to that of Bordeaux, the main difference lower rainfall. Perfectly detailed cabernets are the result, with no need of shiraz or merlot to fill in the mid-palate, although some excellent blends are made. **Langhorne Creek** (a little warmer) and **McLaren Vale** (warmer still) have similar maritime climates, doubtless the reason why McLaren Vale manages to deal with the warmth of its summer/autumn weather. The **Eden Valley** is the most reliable of the inner regions, the other principal regions dependent on a cool summer. From South Australia to Western Australia, where **Margaret River**, with its extreme maritime climate shaped by the warm Indian Ocean, stands tall. It is also Australia's foremost producer of cabernet merlot et al in the Bordeaux mix. The texture and structure of both the straight varietal and the blend is regal, often to the point of austerity when the wines are young, but the sheer power of this underlying fruit provides the balance and guarantees the future development of the wines over a conservative 20 years, especially if screwcapped. The **Great Southern** subregions of **Frankland River** and **Mount Barker** share a continental climate that is somewhat cooler than Margaret River's, and has a greater diurnal temperature range. Here cabernet has an incisive, dark-berry character and firm but usually fine tannins – not demanding merlot, though a touch of it and/or malbec can be beneficial. It is grown successfully through the centre and south of Victoria, but is often overshadowed by shiraz. In the past 20 years it has ceased to be a problem child and become a favourite son of the **Yarra Valley**; the forward move of vintage dates has been the key to the change.

Pinot Noir

The promiscuity of shiraz (particularly) and cabernet sauvignon is in sharp contrast to the puritanical rectitude of pinot noir. One sin of omission or commission, and the door slams shut, leaving the bewildered winemaker on the outside. **Tasmania** is the El Dorado for the variety, and the best is still to come with better clones, older vines and greater exploration of the multitude of mesoclimates that Tasmania has to offer. While it is north of Central Otago (New Zealand), its vineyards are all air conditioned by the Southern Ocean and Tasman Sea, and it stands toe-to-toe with Central Otago in its ability to make deeply-coloured, profound pinot with all the length one could ask for. Once on the mainland, Victoria's Port Phillip Zone, encompassing the **Geelong**, **Macedon Ranges**, **Sunbury**, **Mornington Peninsula** and **Yarra Valley** is the epicentre of Australian pinot noir, **Henty** a small outpost. The sheer number of high quality, elegant wines produced by dozens of makers in those regions put the **Adelaide Hills** and **Porongurup** (also capable of producing quality pinot) into the shade.

Other Red Varieties

There are many other red varieties in the *Wine Companion* database, and there is little rhyme or reason for the distribution of the plantings.

Sparkling Wines

The patter is eerily similar to that of pinot noir, **Tasmania** now and in the future the keeper of the Holy Grail, the **Port Phillip** Zone the centre of activity on the mainland.

Fortified Wines

Rutherglen and **Glenrowan** are the two (and only) regions that produce immensely complex, long-barrel-aged muscat and muscadelle, the latter called tokay for over a century, now renamed topaque. These wines have no equal in the world, Spain's Malaga nearest in terms of lusciousness, but nowhere near as complex. The other producer of a wine without parallel is Seppeltsfield in the **Barossa Valley**, which each year releases an explosively rich and intense tawny liqueur style that is 100% 100 years old.

Australia's geographical indications

The process of formally mapping Australia's wine regions is all but complete, though it will never come to an outright halt – for one thing, climate change is lurking in the wings.

The division into States, Zones, Regions and Subregions follows; those Regions or Subregions marked with an asterisk are not yet registered, and may never be, but are in common usage. The bizarre Hunter Valley GI map now has Hunter Valley as a Zone, Hunter as the Region and the sprawling Upper Hunter as a Subregion along with Pokolbin (small and disputed by some locals). Another recent official change has been the registration of Mount Gambier as a Region in the Limestone Coast Zone. I am still in front of the game with Tasmania, dividing it into Northern, Southern and East Coast. In a similar vein, I have included Ballarat (with 15 wineries) and the Southern Eyre Peninsula (three wineries).

State/Zone	Region	Subregion
AUSTRALIA		
Australia Australian South Eastern Australia★	★ The South Eastern Australia Zone incorporates the whole of the states of NSW, Vic and Tas, and only part of Qld and SA.	
NEW SOUTH WALES		
Big Rivers	Murray Darling Perricoota Riverina Swan Hill	
Central Ranges	Cowra Mudgee Orange	
Hunter Valley	Hunter	Broke Fordwich Pokolbin Upper Hunter Valley

State/Zone	Region	Subregion
Northern Rivers	Hastings River	
Northern Slopes	New England Australia	
South Coast	Shoalhaven Coast Southern Highlands	
Southern New South Wales	Canberra District Gundagai Hilltops Tumbarumba	
Western Plains		

SOUTH AUSTRALIA

State/Zone	Region	Subregion
Adelaide (Super Zone, includes Mount Lofty Ranges, Fleurieu and Barossa)		
Barossa	Barossa Valley Eden Valley	High Eden
Far North	Southern Flinders Ranges	
Fleurieu	Currency Creek Kangaroo Island Langhorne Creek McLaren Vale Southern Fleurieu	
Limestone Coast	Coonawarra Mount Benson Mount Gambier Padthaway Robe Wrattonbully	
Lower Murray	Riverland	
Mount Lofty Ranges	Adelaide Hills	Lenswood Piccadilly Valley
	Adelaide Plains Clare Valley	Polish Hill River★ Watervale★
The Peninsulas	Southern Eyre Peninsula★	

State/Zone	Region	Subregion
VICTORIA		
Central Victoria	Bendigo Goulburn Valley Heathcote Strathbogie Ranges Upper Goulburn	Nagambie Lakes
Gippsland		
Northeast Victoria	Alpine Valleys Beechworth Glenrowan King Valley Rutherglen	
North West Victoria	Murray Darling Swan Hill	
Port Phillip	Geelong Macedon Ranges Mornington Peninsula Sunbury Yarra Valley	
Western Victoria	Ballarat★ Grampians Henty Pyrenees	Great Western
WESTERN AUSTRALIA		
Central Western Australia		
Eastern Plains, Inland and North of Western Australia		
Greater Perth	Peel Perth Hills Swan District	Swan Valley

State/Zone	Region	Subregion
South West Australia	Blackwood Valley	
	Geographe	
	Great Southern	Albany
		Denmark
		Frankland River
		Mount Barker
		Porongurup
	Manjimup	
	Margaret River	
	Pemberton	
West Australian		
South East Coastal		

QUEENSLAND

Queensland	Granite Belt	
	South Burnett	

TASMANIA

Tasmania	Northern Tasmania★	
	Southern Tasmania★	
	East Coast Tasmania★	

AUSTRALIAN CAPITAL TERRITORY

NORTHERN TERRITORY

Wine and food or food and wine?

It all depends on your starting point: there are conventional matches for overseas classics, such as caviar (Champagne), fresh foie gras (Sauternes, riesling or rose) and new season Italian white truffles (any medium-bodied red). Here the food flavour is all important, the wine merely incidental.

At the other extreme come 50-year-old classic red wines: Grange, or Grand Cru Burgundy, or First Growth Bordeaux, or a Maurice O'Shea Mount Pleasant Shiraz. Here the food is, or should be, merely a low-key foil, but at the same time must be of high quality.

In the Australian context I believe not enough attention is paid to the time of year, which – particularly in the southern states – is or should be a major determinant in the choice of both food and wine. And so I shall present my suggestions in this way, always bearing in mind how many ways there are to skin a cat (but not serve it).

Spring

Sparkling
Oysters, cold crustacea, tapas, any cold hors d'oeuvres

Young riesling
Cold salads, sashimi

Gewurztraminer
Asian cuisine

Young semillon
Antipasto, vegetable terrine

Pinot gris
Crab cakes, whitebait

Verdelho, chenin blanc
Cold smoked chicken, gravlax

Mature chardonnay
Grilled chicken, chicken pasta, turkey, pheasant

Rose
Caesar salad, trout mousse

Young pinot noir
Seared kangaroo fillet, grilled quail

Merlot
Pastrami, warm smoked chicken

Cool climate medium-bodied cabernet sauvignon
Rack of baby lamb

Light to medium-bodied cool-climate shiraz
Rare eye fillet of beef

Young botrytised wines
Fresh fruits, cake

Summer

Chilled fino
Cold consommé

2–3-year-old semillon
Gazpacho

2–3-year-old riesling
Seared tuna

Young barrel-fermented semillon sauvignon blanc
Seafood or vegetable tempura

Young off-dry riesling
Prosciutto & melon/pear

Cool-climate chardonnay
Abalone, lobster, Chinese-style prawns

10–year-old semillon or riesling
Braised pork neck

Mature chardonnay (5+ years)
Braised rabbit

Off-dry rose
Chilled fresh fruit

Young light-bodied pinot noir
Grilled salmon

Aged pinot noir (5+ years)
Coq au vin, wild duck

Young grenache/sangiovese
Osso bucco

Hunter Valley shiraz (5–10 years)
Beef spare ribs

Sangiovese
Saltimbocca, roast poussin

Medium-bodied cabernet sauvignon (5 years)
Barbecued butterfly leg of lamb

Mature chardonnay
Smoked eel, smoked roe

All wines
Parmagiana

Autumn

Amontillado
Warm consommé

Barrel-fermented mature whites
Smoked roe, bouillabaisse

Complex mature chardonnay
Sweetbreads, brains

Aged (10-year-old) marsanne or semillon
Seafood risotto, Lebanese

Grenache
Grilled calf's liver, roast kid, lamb or pig's kidneys

Mature Margaret River cabernet merlot
Lamb fillet, roast leg of lamb with garlic and herbs

Cool climate merlot
Lamb loin chops

Fully aged riesling
Chargrilled eggplant, stuffed capsicum

Mature grenache/rhône blends
Moroccan lamb

Rich, full-bodied Heathcote shiraz
Beef casserole

Southern Victorian pinot noir
Peking duck

Young muscat
Plum pudding

Winter

Dry oloroso sherry
Full-flavoured hors d'oeuvres

Sparkling Burgundy
Borscht, wild mushroom risotto

Viognier
Pea and ham soup

Aged (10+ years) semillon
Vichysoisse (hot)

Sauvignon blanc
Coquilles St Jacques (pan-fried scallops)

Chardonnay (10+ years)
Cassoulet

2–4-year-old semillon sauvignon blanc
Seafood pasta

Tasmanian pinot noir
Squab, duck breast

Mature pinot noir
Mushroom ragout, ravioli

Mature cool-grown shiraz viognier
Pot au feu

10-year-old Grampians shiraz
Chargrilled rump steak

15–20-year-old full-bodied Barossa shiraz
Venison, kangaroo fillet

Coonawarra cabernet sauvignon
Braised lamb shanks/shoulder

Muscat (rare)
Chocolate-based desserts

Topaque (rare)
Creme brûlée

Vintage fortified shiraz
Dried fruits, salty cheese

Australian vintage charts

Each number represents a mark out of 10 for the quality of vintages in each region.

red wine   white wine   fortified

| 2013 | 2014 | 2015 | 2016 | | 2013 | 2014 | 2015 | 2016 | | 2013 | 2014 | 2015 | 2016 |

NSW

Hunter Valley
| 8 | 10 | 5 | 6 |
| 8 | 7 | 6 | 7 |

Mudgee
| 7 | 7 | 9 | 8 |
| 8 | 9 | 8 | 9 |

Orange
| 9 | 5 | 9 | 8 |
| 9 | 7 | 9 | 7 |

Canberra District
| 9 | 7 | 10 | 9 |
| 9 | 8 | 10 | 9 |

Hilltops
| 9 | 9 | 8 | 9 |
| 9 | 9 | 8 | 8 |

Southern Highlands
| 7 | 7 | 6 | 8 |
| 8 | 7 | 8 | 8 |

Tumbarumba
| 8 | 9 | 7 | 8 |
| 9 | 8 | 9 | 9 |

Riverina/Griffith
| 7 | 7 | 8 | 7 |
| 8 | 8 | 8 | 7 |

Shoalhaven
| 8 | 9 | 7 | 8 |
| 8 | 9 | 8 | 8 |

VIC

Yarra Valley
| 9 | 7 | 10 | 7 |
| 8 | 8 | 9 | 7 |

Mornington Peninsula
| 9 | 9 | 10 | 8 |
| 8 | 9 | 9 | 7 |

Geelong
| 9 | 8 | 10 | 7 |
| 8 | 7 | 9 | 8 |

Macedon Ranges
| 9 | 8 | 9 | 8 |
| 9 | 8 | 8 | 9 |

Sunbury
| 9 | 9 | 8 | 7 |
| 9 | 8 | 7 | 7 |

Gippsland
| 8 | 5 | 9 | 8 |
| 8 | 9 | 9 | 8 |

Bendigo
| 8 | 9 | 8 | 8 |
| 7 | 7 | 8 | 8 |

Heathcote
| 9 | 8 | 8 | 9 |
| 6 | 7 | 7 | 8 |

Grampians
| 9 | 9 | 8 | 6 |
| 8 | 9 | 8 | 7 |

Pyrenees
| 8 | 8 | 7 | 7 |
| 8 | 9 | 8 | 7 |

Henty
| 10 | 9 | 10 | 10 |
| 8 | 10 | 9 | 10 |

Beechworth
| 8 | 8 | 8 | 8 |
| 9 | 8 | 9 | 8 |

Nagambie Lakes
| 9 | 8 | 8 | 8 |
| 7 | 8 | 9 | 9 |

Upper Goulburn
| 9 | 9 | 9 | 8 |
| 9 | 9 | 7 | 9 |

Strathbogie Ranges
| 9 | 6 | 8 | 7 |
| 7 | 7 | 8 | 7 |

King Valley
| 8 | 7 | 9 | 7 |
| 8 | 9 | 8 | 8 |

Alpine Valleys
| 9 | 7 | 10 | 6 |
| 7 | 8 | 9 | 6 |

Glenrowan
| 9 | 9 | 8 | 8 |
| 7 | 7 | 7 | 9 |

Rutherglen
| 10 | 7 | 9 | 7 |
| - | - | 9 | 9 |

Murray Darling
| 8 | 8 | 9 | 7 |
| 7 | 8 | 7 | 8 |

SA

Barossa Valley

2013	2014	2015	2016
8	7	9	8
7	7	8	7

Eden Valley

2013	2014	2015	2016
8	8	9	8
8	8	10	9

Clare Valley

2013	2014	2015	2016
7	8	9	8
8	8	9	9

Adelaide Hills

2013	2014	2015	2016
9	8	9	8
8	8	10	7

McLaren Vale

2013	2014	2015	2016
9	7	8	8
8	8	8	7

Southern Fleurieu

2013	2014	2015	2016
6	8	7	8
5	8	6	8

Langhorne Creek

2013	2014	2015	2016
9	9	9	9
8	8	7	7

Kangaroo Island

2013	2014	2015	2016
8	8	8	9
8	9	8	9

Adelaide Plains

2013	2014	2015	2016
7	7	8	9
6	7	8	8

Coonawarra

2013	2014	2015	2016
9	8	9	9
8	8	8	8

Wrattonbully

2013	2014	2015	2016
9	9	9	10
8	8	9	10

Padthaway

2013	2014	2015	2016
8	8	9	x
8	9	9	x

Mount Benson & Robe

2013	2014	2015	2016
7	9	10	8
8	9	9	9

Riverland

2013	2014	2015	2016
8	8	9	8
8	8	8	7

WA

Margaret River

2013	2014	2015	2016
9	8	8	9
9	9	9	9

Great Southern

2013	2014	2015	2016
7	8	8	8
8	8	8	9

Manjimup

2013	2014	2015	2016
8	9	8	6
9	8	7	7

Pemberton

2013	2014	2015	2016
8	9	6	8
9	9	8	9

Geographe

2013	2014	2015	2016
6	9	7	8
7	8	7	8

Peel

2013	2014	2015	2016
9	8	x	8
9	8	x	7

Perth Hills

2013	2014	2015	2016
8	8	9	9
10	10	9	8

Swan Valley

2013	2014	2015	2016
9	8	7	6
8	8	8	7

QLD

Granite Belt

2013	2014	2015	2016
8	9	8	8
8	8	8	7

South Burnett

2013	2014	2015	2016
8	8	8	x
9	7	8	x

TAS

Northern Tasmania

2013	2014	2015	2016
7	8	8	8
8	9	8	8

Southern Tasmania

2013	2014	2015	2016
8	9	9	8
7	9	9	8

Australian vintage 2017: a snapshot

Accepting that exceptions will prove the rule, 2017 was a cool, late vintage of considerable quality. Heavy falls of winter and spring rain replenished ground water and filled soil to full capacity. Thus dormancy was extended, budburst occurring two to six weeks later than 2016, causing winemakers to use '02 or even the 1990s as measuring sticks. While bunch numbers were high, spring rain and wind interrupted flowering in some regions, leading to lower bunch weights and yield. While the official figures for the total crush won't be available until after this book goes to print, the guess is that the crush will be around 1.8 million tonnes for the third year in a row.

A feature of vintage was its leisurely pace after the mad scramble of 2016. There were textbook breaks between the early and late ripening varieties, but the arrival of warm, dry weather from the end of February through March and April meant healthy canopies through and after harvest.

The exceptions? First, the need for shoot and bunch thinning in the many regions with good fruit set. Next, the Granite Belt had a vintage it would rather forget. Also the Hunter Valley had a fiercely hot and largely dry harvest, yet the high quality of shiraz dares to be compared with the magnificent 2014 vintage. Finally, the Swan Valley had to deal with full-on flooding of its lower floodplains, with large crop losses.

SOUTH AUSTRALIA

The **Barossa** (including **Eden Valley**) experienced life-giving winter and spring rains, and vintage was a month later than 2016 ('02 is often cited as a reference point: '02 and '17 were very cool and late vintages, while '16 was hot and early). High yields had to be controlled; the reward was outstanding riesling and high quality shiraz, followed by the opposite extremes of cabernet sauvignon and Grenache. One response did suggest dilution of flavour could take the edge off some or all of the varieties. The **Clare Valley** started vintage two weeks later than 2016. The canopies were in better condition than those of many years past. Riesling and shiraz were the standouts for most, elegant cabernet sauvignon for others. The **Adelaide Hills** had a very wet winter, then average rainfall throughout the growing season coupled with low temperatures (similar to 2002 and '04) resulted in harvest four to six weeks later than '16. Control of yields (fruit and shoot thinning) was essential. This year has the potential to be one of the truly great vintages, with chardonnay and shiraz leading the way. The **Adelaide Plains** experienced the same cool, wet (until January) and late vintage. Yields were 30% above normal, with shiraz and cabernet sauvignon the best (no surprise there). In **McLaren Vale** the higher ground, coupled with cabernet sauvignon and grenache, produced wines of the highest quality for 2017. On the looser soils, vigilance was essential to combat fungal disease head on. Overall, elegance and balance characterise the '17 vintage. **Langhorne Creek** had above-average rains in winter, spring and summer, and a three-week delay in harvest. The snake in the Garden of Eden was an inundation of the floodplain, resulting in the loss of, or damage to, shiraz. **Southern Fleurieu** had temperatures 4°C below long-term average throughout a prolonged spring. A mild summer with no heat spikes to upset the apple cart means that a great vintage is expected. **Kangaroo Island** experienced the wettest winter ever recorded, with 1100mm, followed by a wet spring with rain every 10 days resulting in a very low yield (poor set at flowering). The white varieties, however, benefitted from the very late (four weeks) vintage. **Coonawarra** also cited 2002 and '04 as particular references for '17. Cabernet is a standout, with excellent colour, concentration and tannins. **Mount Benson** and **Robe** went hand-in-glove, although Robe showed the highest rainfall since records commenced in 1861. Much warmer conditions in March and April ensured high quality shiraz and cabernet sauvignon for those who kept crop levels low. **Wrattonbully** followed the Limestone Coast pattern, as did **Padthaway**. The **Riverland** had heavy (100mm) bursts of rain throughout spring and as late as Boxing Day; coupled with the low temperatures, harvest delays of four weeks were common. The yields were only slightly above average, but the temperature and rainfall created a wildcard situation, with little or no consistency from one vineyard to the next. Tough skinned cabernet sauvignon is the standout.

VICTORIA

The **Yarra Valley** arguably had the best vintage since 1992, and before that '88. It was marked by good rainfall and cool to mild temperatures that continued into summer. Rain and wind at flowering meant the Lower Yarra's yields were down somewhat. The Upper Yarra had good, but not excessive, yields, and the warm summer that finally arrived had no major heat spikes. All varieties came in later than any vintage since 2002, and at an unhurried pace. Chardonnay and pinot noir have just about every vigneron rubbing their hands with glee. The **Mornington Peninsula** was a carbon copy of the Yarra Valley, with good bunch numbers, but hen and chicken berries reduced yield. Flowering, and ultimately vintage, was two to three weeks later than 2016. The cool weather meant excellent retention of natural acidity, leading some to rate chardonnay and pinot gris as the best ever, while pinot noir has revealed great balance and elegance. **Geelong** had excellent winter and spring rains, resulting in a late but vigorous start to the season. Yields were variable depending on nutrient status. Pinot noir and shiraz yields in particular had to be carefully managed. **Sunbury** and the **Macedon Ranges** winemakers are ecstatic. One respondent rated the ripening conditions as the best this century, another went back further to the 1990s. Overall, low to moderate yields will be very high quality. **Bendigo** had a similar tale, with excellent late winter and spring rains filling the dams and subsoil alike. Benign, albeit cool, weather conditions saw very good fruit set. Lovely, strongly varietal but elegant cabernet sauvignon and merlot are the stars. Shiraz and cabernet are also doing well. **Heathcote** had average winter rain and a drier than normal spring until 80mm of rain in January set the vineyards up beautifully. Harvest commenced two to three weeks later than 2016, with generally moderate yields. Shiraz is the standout. The **Grampians** had the best vintage for at least a decade, with perfect weather from start to finish; summer was particularly mild and dry, with very few heat spikes. Riesling is outstanding. Shiraz is also textbook stuff, with spice and elegance in abundance. **Henty** (naturally) had a wet start, September's 145mm smashing the all-time record. The weather remained cool. The rain stopped in November, resulting in excellent fruit set. Come the start of harvest the canopies were utterly perfect, with riesling the first to benefit. The heavy winter rainfall in the **Pyrenees** was celebrated by all. The weather through the growing season was cooler than normal, resulting in a drawn out harvest with much longer hang time than encountered for many, many years. High quality shiraz and cabernet sauvignon are expected by almost all. **Beechworth** followed the Victorian rain and temperature pattern, with one major exception: picking wasn't late. Giaconda says that all varieties are of high to very high quality, but chardonnay is an absolute standout (watch for its release). **Nagambie Lakes** had average winter rainfall (for the first time in many years), then spring arrived with seemingly endless showers of rain. Summer opened warm and wet, with visions of a repeat of 2011, but the rain stopped in mid-February, and March was a joy with three balmy weeks of low 30°C temperatures and warm nights accelerating ripening. The result: distinct varietal flavours in the white wines, and reds with bright fruit and elegance. The **Strathbogie Ranges** had a year described succinctly as 'odd': a wet winter and spring; then a cool opening to summer with a mild, dry February; then three weeks in March with days around 30°C. This played hell with canopies. Overall, quality is average, high yield another factor. The **Upper Goulburn** had drier than average winter and spring, but mid- to late-summer rains were perfect. Summer and autumn brought cool to warm conditions with no heat spikes – the complete opposite of 2015 and '16. It was a very good year for white wines, but average for reds. The **Alpine Valleys** and **King Valley** had ample spring rainfall, and benign weather during flowering, creating above-average yields and the latest start to vintage for many years. Acid retention was excellent, and flavour development was ahead of baumes. Outstanding wines were produced from chardonnay, friulano, tempranillo, shiraz, sangiovese, prosecco and pinot grigio. **Glenrowan** ran its own race, with an early start to vintage and a compressed intake across the region, bringing back memories of 2016. Nonetheless, quality is high. The standout varieties are muscadelle, shiraz and durif. **Rutherglen**'s yields were moderate to high, producing good quality shiraz, cabernet sauvignon and chardonnay. The **Murray Darling**'s winter and growing season climate was virtually identical to the rest of Victoria, with no heat spikes and similar to vintages of 10–15 years ago. Whereas 2016 produced big flavoursome robust wines, the '17 wines have clear varietal aromas and refined palates.

NEW SOUTH WALES

The **Hunter Valley** has a history of hot dry years following a previous wet vintage and dry winter. Hot and dry certainly describes 2017 with temperatures over 35°C for 32 days, and peaks over 40°C between December and February, culminating in a three-day run of 44°C/47°C/46°C on February 10–12. Climate change fundamentalists will be shocked to learn that this was a great vintage; the red wines that were picked before the February heat blast nuzzling up close to the '14 vintage quality. Yields were average, with some semillon blocks carrying above-average crops to full ripeness. The **Upper Hunter** had regular rainfall through to December, minimising the need for irrigation. As the temperatures soared after Christmas, the good canopies of the vines carried the crop through to harvest. Overall it was a trouble-free vintage, starring semillon, chardonnay and shiraz. **Mudgee**'s very hot season posed challenges with low acids and slow flavour ripening, but canopies in good order well past harvest bodes well for the '18 vintage with a storehouse of carbohydrates in the vines. **Orange** had a topsy-turvy vintage. Winter and spring were awash with record rainfall from July through to November. Early February brought scorching heat, followed by a deluge in March, then heat again accompanied by powdery mildew. Good to high yield resulted in a late harvest notwithstanding the warmth of summer. Generalisations are dangerous but, depending on altitude, all of the varieties found favour here and there, the only exceptions being shiraz and riesling. The **Canberra District** started with soil that was filled with moisture after record winter rains. Spring was cool, with continued bursts of rain until Christmas. January and February brought record hot temperatures, followed by a normal, dry and cool autumn. The result: white wines, especially riesling, with great flavour at modest baumes; red wines with deep colour and perfect balance overall. **Hilltops** had the same wet winter and spring, rainfall easing in late November 2016. January and February were dry and sunny with mild temperatures. In mid-March 40mm of rain fell, which caused more nuisance than damage. The best varieties are chardonnay, riesling, sauvignon blanc and cabernet sauvignon, with red varieties picked between 12.5 and 13.5 baume. The **Tumbarumba** weather followed the general pattern, although the vintage was only a little later than that of the past eight to 10 years. All varieties performed well. Chardonnay led the bunch, although all the white varieties had great vibrancy and freshness coupled with excellent acid balance. Pinot noir may also be a show-stopper. **Southern Highlands** had a vintage it would rather forget. A cold and wet winter and spring was followed by heatwaves in January and ceaseless rain in February and March (rainfall in the latter month breaking the all-time record). Yields were very low, with much fruit left on the vine. The **Shoalhaven Coast** very often has different ripening patterns to other NSW regions; the one thing it shared this year was very high rainfall in March forcing the picking of everything still on the vine. This followed an up-and-down dry and very warm January, and a mild February interspersed with rain. In the end, yields were moderate. Sauvignon blanc proved the standout variety for some, while it was semillon for others. **Riverina** never had it so good. Vintage didn't get going in earnest until February after a long, wet winter, the red harvest was the latest in nearly 20 years, and not finished until the end of April. Sauvignon blanc, pinot gris and chardonnay are the best white wines; shiraz (as ever) leads the red pack.

WESTERN AUSTRALIA

Margaret River had above-average rainfall in winter, then intermittent rain in January, followed by a dry February, a wet March, and cool nights and dry days in April. This required constant vigilance in the vineyards to forestall disease. The reward was outstanding chardonnay and cabernet sauvignon, which Margaret River's big guns picked two weeks later than normal. Although the **Great Southern** is a vast region, it experienced the same cool, late vintage. One subregion set a record with budburst six weeks later than normal. The very wet winter and spring, followed by cool and basically dry weather, resulted in large crops being set; this in turn meant that fruit-thinning was essential. One report described five fruit-thinning passes through the vineyard as the growing season progressed. On average cool, dry conditions started and finished the growing season a month behind 2016. However, all bar one agree that riesling and pinot noir will be exceptional, with perfumed shiraz not far behind. Only one report was less enthusiastic, describing overall quality as above average, but not exceptional. **Manjimup** and **Pemberton** had a topsy-turvy growing season following a wet winter and spring, with rainfall continuing through to December. January was unremarkable, February cooler than average. High humidity and above-average rainfall continued through to March with vintage three to four weeks later than normal. It is hardly surprising that quite a lot of fruit was left unpicked. Chardonnay and pinot noir were the best. **Geographe** was basically more of the same: abundant spring rainfall stopped for perfect flowering conditions; followed by a cool summer with grapes maintaining a pure line of acidity; and a much later than usual start to harvest. A totally dry and long Indian summer through April made everyone smile. The **Swan Valley** made national news with a cyclone dumping 50–75mm of rain on two occasions, causing the Swan River to flood. The vineyards along the floodplain were submerged for a number of days, resulting in the total loss of the crop. The quality ranges from poor to above average. Crisp verdelho, perfumed grenache and shiraz are the picks. The **Perth Hills** had the same winter and spring rain as the rest of the state, resulting in a late growing season with a challenging spring. Yields were high and needed thinning. Merlot was the best performing variety. **Peel** had the hottest start for at least 10 years, but then settled down to the mildest season for that period. Yields were good to very good. All the reds ripened well, and some botrytis with chenin blanc needing hand-picking.

TASMANIA

Tasmania has much to sing about in 2017 with all three major districts telling a roughly similar tale. **Northern Tasmania** set the pattern, with higher than average rainfall in winter and spring prompting faster than usual growth, although temperatures remained a bit below average. As summer arrived the rain disappeared, but temperatures were still cooler than average. Late March weather was the warmest of the year – ideal for ripening. Yields are a little down with poor weather during flowering. The standout varieties are pinot noir, chardonnay and riesling. The overall quality is good to excellent. **East Coast Tasmania** had near-identical weather, with only two days above 30°C. The cool conditions delayed harvest by 10–12 days. The cooler weather, however, has led to remarkable flavour intensity in chardonnay, riesling and sauvignon blanc, while pinot noir has noticeably more colour intensity than the 2016 wines – the flavour is excellent. **Southern Tasmania** reported more of the same, although a very dry period from summer through to mid-autumn required vigilance in managing irrigation. Yields were moderate overall, but all the indications promise high quality across the board.

QUEENSLAND

The **Granite Belt** climate can be perfect, and it can be very dispiriting. Unfortunately, this year fell into the latter category, even though winter and spring were perfect, setting the stage for a top-flight vintage of moderate to good yields. Then a heatwave in late January through to early February caused acids to drop dramatically in a short time. When the heat subsided the rain came, with botrytis and downy mildew endemic. The best makers have found a few gems, with lower baume/alcohol than normal.

Acknowledgements

As I said last year, one of the inescapable outcomes of age is that for most of us, myself very definitely included, things take longer to do. Those years when you didn't even realise you were hard wired to instantly recall memories of all kinds recede into the distance. It didn't seem remarkable, it was just what one did, said or wrote. Now the insidious change means groping for a name or a word; you can learn tricks to prompt recall, but the cumulative loss of time is now inescapable. Thus I'm not doing any more than I used to, but I have to work longer hours to achieve the same result.

This led to the recruitment of Ned Goodwin MW and Jane Faulkner, who write in very different voices to each other (and to myself); Steven Creber also contributes, and Tyson Stelzer supplied the sparkling wine tasting notes. I'm overjoyed that Campbell Mattinson has agreed to rejoin the tasting team for the next edition and into the future.

It's lucky I have two helpers in the office (downstairs in my house) and another upstairs. They are my faithful servants Paula Grey, with over a quarter of a century of priceless time on the job, and Beth Anthony, with 17 years. They put up with my skill in constantly losing emails, printouts – anything physical – in the Bermuda Triangle of my desk, and print another copy, and another …

Beth was central in keeping track of all 9800 wines, sent this year to five different places, and ensuring the wines were correctly entered in the database. Her sister, Jake, sacrificed her Saturdays to steward for me for two months, as I had to taste six days per week. My wife Suzanne is most certainly not my servant, but that doesn't stop her looking after all I could possibly need.

Then there are the tribes at Hardie Grant who look after both the pre- and post-natal welfare of the *Wine Companion* in all its forms. All are important: some more important than others. From my selfish point of view, Sandy Grant is the *sine qua non* – he had the faith to form a joint venture, which I treasure dearly in all its forms.

Julie Pinkham and Simon McKeown are in the decision-making frontline, and I have never had a cross word – not even a niggle of annoyance – with or from either of them.

Then there is the one and only Annie Clemenger, who had the preposterous idea of having a book launch for the *Wine Companion* 2014. I am still bewildered by the runaway success of the *Wine Companion* awards event, and sincerely thank the winemakers and wineries that so willingly support it.

Editor Loran McDougall is the ultimate key to the book, rising to the challenge of herding cats as the last weeks and days pass in a whirl before the book goes off to the printer. The magic wand of Megan Ellis in typesetting the *Wine Companion* in the blink of an eye continues to amaze me, as does the eagle eye of Sarah Shrubb in proofreading the entire text.

Finally, my thanks to Tracy and Alan at the Coldstream Post Office, who receive the tsunami of wine boxes every year.

Australian wineries and wines

A note on alphabetical order
Wineries beginning with 'The' are listed under 'T'; for example,
'The Lane Vineyard'. Winery names that include a numeral are treated
as if the numeral is spelt out; for example, '2 Mates'
is listed under 'T'.

A. Retief ★★★★

PO Box 2503, Strawberry Hills, NSW 2012 **Region** Southern New South Wales
T 0400 650 530 www.aretief.com.au **Open** Not
Winemaker Alex Retief **Est.** 2008 **Dozens** 5000

Owner and winemaker Alex Retief's wine career was prompted by his parents planting a vineyard near Ladysmith, in Gundagai, in 1997. He enrolled in the wine science course at CSU, and in 2001 was accepted as the trainee winemaker at the university's winery. In mid '02 he went to California's Sonoma Valley, working at Fetzer Vineyards, returning to the Hunter Valley for the '03 vintage with Andrew Margan. He was winemaker there for two and a half years, punctuated by a harvest in Languedoc in '04, before heading back to France in '05 for a two-year appointment as winemaker at Chateau de Lagarde in Bordeaux. The A. Retief wines are made from contract-grown grapes in the Tumbarumba/Canberra District/Hilltops/Gundagai regions. He has his own boutique wine distribution company.

♥♥♥♥♀ **Tumbarumba Sauvignon Blanc 2014** From an established vineyard at 730m, fermented and matured for 12 months in French barriques. Quartz-green hue, the bouquet is, as expected, complex. What wasn't expected was the freshness the wine has retained, with no sign of break-up. Screwcap. 13% alc. **Rating** 91 **To** 2019 $28
The Alias Hilltops Mataro 2013 An attractive medium-bodied wine with bright fruits on the bouquet and a fresh palate of red cherries held in a fine cobweb of light, savoury/spicy tannins. Screwcap. 14% alc. **Rating** 90 **To** 2023 $40

♥♥♥♥ **Winbirra Vineyard Gundagai Shiraz 2015** **Rating** 89 **To** 2020 $28
Field Blend 2015 **Rating** 89 **To** 2025 $28

A. Rodda Wines ★★★★★

PO Box 589, Beechworth, Vic 3747 **Region** Beechworth
T 0400 350 135 www.aroddawines.com.au **Open** Not
Winemaker Adrian Rodda **Est.** 2010 **Dozens** 800 **Vyds** 2ha

Adrian Rodda has been winemaking since 1998, almost entirely working with David Bicknell at Oakridge. He was involved in the development of the superb Oakridge 864 Chardonnay, his final contribution to 864 coming in 2009. At the start of 2010 he and wife Christie, a doctor, decided to move to Beechworth, and it was no coincidence that he was a long-term friend of viticulturist Mark Walpole. Coincidences came with the Smith Vineyard and winery being available for lease; he now shares it with Mark, who makes his Beechworth wines there. Even more propitious was the availability of Smith Vineyard chardonnay, planted in 1974.

♥♥♥♥♥ **Smiths Vineyard Beechworth Chardonnay 2016** The grapes were pressed directly to French puncheons for wild fermentation and 10 months maturation on lees. The complexity, intensity and depth of this wine strikes like an arrow the moment it enters the mouth. It is Beechworth with a twist, more elegant than many from the region. New oak was kept to 30%, even the slightly funky solids aromas likewise under control. Screwcap. 13% alc. **Rating** 96 **To** 2026 $42 ✪
Willow Lake Vineyard Yarra Valley Chardonnay 2016 Made in exactly the same manner as the Smiths Vineyard, the intention for 'each wine to be an expression of the site and region'. The Upper Yarra, even more than the Lower Yarra, is all about finesse and length; grapefruit is the anchor of the fruit flavour, accompanied by white peach. 30% new oak has largely been swallowed by the intensity of the fruit. Screwcap. 13% alc. **Rating** 96 **To** 2026 $42 ✪
Aquila Audax Vineyard Beechworth Tempranillo 2015 Hand-picked, destemmed, 3 days cold soak, a 15% whole-bunch parcel fermented separately, 14 days post-ferment maceration, matured in French hogsheads (33% new) for 16 months. 'During fermentation the timing and combination of pumpovers, rack and returns, pigeage and plunging was to preserve aromatics and perfume' is at odds with the post-ferment maceration, but Adrian Rodda has managed to have his tempranillo and eat it. The bright colour is promising start, and the cascade of cherry all-sorts of the palate does the job there, and the oak decisions were precisely correct. Screwcap. 13.5% alc. **Rating** 95 **To** 2029 $36

Cuvee de Chez 2015 Sourced mainly from the great Smiths Vineyard, cabernet sauvignon leads both the statistics and the flavours, minty cassis to the fore. There is an overall piquancy to the palate: not unpleasant, but suggesting marginal ripeness of one or other component. Screwcap. 13.5% alc. **Rating** 94 **To** 2030 $38

ΨΨΨΨΨ **Aquila Audax Vineyard Tempranillo 2014 Rating** 93 **To** 2024 $36

A.T. Richardson Wines   ★★★★★

103 Hard Hill Road, Armstrong, Vic 3377 **Region** Great Western
T 0438 066 477 **www**.atrichardsonwines.com **Open** Not
Winemaker Adam Richardson **Est.** 2005 **Dozens** 2000 **Vyds** 7ha
Perth-born Adam Richardson began his winemaking career in 1995, along the way working for Normans, d'Arenberg and Oakridge Estate. Since that time he has held senior winemaking roles, ultimately with TWE America before moving back to Australia with wife Eva and children in late 2015. In 2005 he had put down roots in the Grampians region, establishing a vineyard with shiraz from old clones from the 19th century, and riesling. In '12 he extended the vineyard plantings with tannat and nebbiolo. The wines are exceptionally good, and given his experience and the quality of the vineyard, that should not come as a surprise. He has also set up a wine consultancy business, drawing on experience that is matched by few consultants based in Australia. Exports to Europe.

ΨΨΨΨΨ **Chockstone Grampians Shiraz 2014** This is Grampians shiraz at its autocratic best, taking some of the raw power of young, high quality cabernet sauvignon. The colour is superb, the bouquet extremely complex, built around the surging black fruits, earth and licorice of the full-bodied palate, which gains yet more depth from the ripe, but persistent tannins. Screwcap. 14% alc. **Rating** 97 **To** 2050 $25 ⊙

ΨΨΨΨΨ **Chockstone Grampians Shiraz 2015** 10yo vines, 2-3 days cold soak, open-fermented in small batches, 1-12 days post-ferment maceration, matured in 10% new American and used French and American oak for 9 months. Full, deep crimson-purple; exudes class from start to finish with burnished black cherry/berry fruits, spice, pepper and licorice. It is at once elegant, but persistent, and very long in the mouth. French oak and tannins make a snappy salute to the fruit. Great value. Screwcap. 14.5% alc. **Rating** 96 **To** 2040 $25 ⊙

Hard Hill Road Great Western Durif 2015 Machine-harvested, 4 days cold soak, open-fermented in small batches with cultured yeast, matured in American oak (50% new) for 12 months. Dense crimson-purple; a strange place for durif to bob up in, except for Adam Richardson's experience with the variety in the US (there called petit syrah). This is as good as durif comes in disciplined form, the extract controlled. Black fruits have a distinct spicy savoury edge, and the tannins are fine, oak unimportant. Screwcap. 14.5% alc. **Rating** 95 **To** 2025 $50

Chockstone Grampians Riesling 2016 Classic Grampians riesling, starting quietly on the bouquet, progressively building intensity and depth as the length of the palate reveals itself. While the boundaries are firmly marked by lime and Meyer lemon fruit, there's complexity to burn on the playing field. Give it a few years and shake your head at the price. Screwcap. 12% alc. **Rating** 94 **To** 2031 $18 ⊙

Chockstone Grampians Chardonnay 2016 Machine-harvested, whole berries fermented in French oak with cultured yeast, matured for 8 months. The picking decision was exactly right, the flavours pitched midway between white peach and pink grapefruit, acidity probably all natural, and significantly extending the length of the palate. Barrel-fermented, of course, but new oak has been appropriately restrained. Screwcap. 12.5% alc. **Rating** 94 **To** 2023 $25 ⊙

Chockstone Grampians Rose 2016 An equal blend of nebbiolo, shiraz, durif and tannat, the tannat and nebbiolo made as per white wines, the shiraz and durif not destemmed or crushed, the juice bled off. Bright, light crimson-pink; fragrant rose petal and strawberry aromas lead into a fresh, lively, crisp palate with a refreshingly dry finish. Screwcap. 13.5% alc. **Rating** 94 **To** 2018 $20 ⊙

Hard Hill Road Pyrenees Nebbiolo 2015 12yo vines, 5 days cold soak, open-fermented in small batches with cultured yeast, 30 days post-ferment maceration, matured in used oak for 12 months. Clear crimson; the perfumed bouquet is already on song with rose petals and cherry blossom, the palate pure nebbiolo, at this stage with its tannin muscles rippling through the cherry fruits. Just be patient. Screwcap. 14.5% alc. **Rating** 94 **To** 2030 $50

AAA Aaron Aardvark   NR

PO Box 626, North Melbourne, Vic 3051 **Region** Various Victoria
T 0432 438 325 **www**.theaardvark.com.au **Open** Not
Winemaker Vincubator **Est.** 2016 **Dozens** 1500
This is the joint venture of grapegrower John Brollo, a Yarra Valley vigneron growing sauvignon blanc; Dave and Jane Lawson, growing shiraz located beside the Loddon River near Bridgewater; and Mark Matthews, who is the contract winemaker, self-styled as 'Vincubator'.

Abbey Creek Vineyard   ★★★★★

2388 Porongurup Road, Porongurup, WA 6324 **Region** Porongurup
T (08) 9853 1044 **Open** By appt
Winemaker Castle Rock Estate (Robert Diletti) **Est.** 1990 **Dozens** 800 **Vyds** 1.6ha
This is the family business of Mike and Mary Dilworth, the name coming from a winter creek that runs alongside the vineyard and a view of The Abbey in the Stirling Range. The vineyard is split between pinot noir, riesling and sauvignon blanc. The Rieslings have had significant show success for a number of years.

♥♥♥♥♥ Museum Release Porongurup Riesling 2008 Scintillating. Has franked its early promise in full. Lime, orange rind, honeysuckle and beeswax. Gets it skates on, builds a power of flavour, then flies out through the finish. Screwcap. 12.5% alc. **Rating** 97 **To** 2023 $30 CM ✪

♥♥♥♥♥ Porongurup Riesling 2016 Quartz-white; fragrant crushed lime leaf aromas take no prisoners with their bracing freshness, and flint and mineral stare you down on the long, even palate. Has a long future ahead and could well spring a surprise as it ages. Screwcap. 11.8% alc. **Rating** 94 **To** 2026 $25✪

Across the Lake   ★★★★

White Dam Road, Lake Grace, WA 6353 **Region** Great Southern
T 0409 685 373 **Open** By appt
Winemaker Rockcliffe (Coby Ladwig) **Est.** 1999 **Dozens** 500 **Vyds** 2ha
The Taylor family has been farming (wheat and sheep) for over 40 years at Lake Grace; a small diversification into grapegrowing started as a hobby, but developed into more than that with 2ha of shiraz. They were motivated to support their friend Bill (WJ) Walker, who had started growing shiraz three years previously, and produced a gold medal-winning wine. Derek and Kristie Stanton have purchased the business.

♥♥♥♥♡ Shiraz 2014 Estate-grown, hand-picked, 20 days on skins, matured in oak (30% new) for 12 months. An old friend returns to the *Wine Companion*, the wine contract-made by Coby Ladwig. Savoury, spicy purple and black fruits grafted onto the medium-bodied palate, which is long and well balanced. A steal at the price. Screwcap. 14.5% alc. **Rating** 90 **To** 2034 $15✪

Adelina Wines   ★★★★★

PO Box 75, Sevenhill, SA 5453 **Region** Clare Valley
T (08) 8842 1549 **www**.adelina.com.au **Open** Not
Winemaker Colin McBryde, Jennie Gardner **Est.** 2002 **Dozens** 400

Established by Jennie Gardner and Col McBryde, both having prior experience in Australia (and elsewhere). The winery and vineyard are set in the Springfarm Valley, just south of the Clare township. The old vineyard, part dating back to 1910, is divided into three small blocks, with 1ha each of shiraz and grenache, and just under 0.5ha of cabernet sauvignon. The winery is a simple shed with the basic requisites to process the grapes and make wine. Most is estate-grown, along with grapes from a few sites in the Adelaide Hills.

ŸŸŸŸŸ **Clare Valley Shiraz Mataro 2015** A 50/50% blend, the estate shiraz circa 100yo, the mataro from the 80yo Ashton Vineyard, the components spending between 30 and 60 days on skins, matured in used oak or concrete for 12 months. Its best features are its texture and structure, but dark berry flavours are also compelling. A fascinating wine of high quality. Screwcap. 14.5% alc. **Rating** 96 **To** 2035 $29 ○
Adelaide Hills Nebbiolo Rosato 2015 Beautiful rose. Autumnal but well fruited. Candied citrus, raspberry, earth and dried herb characters. Rose petals too. Delightful, delicious and dry. Screwcap. 13.5% alc. **Rating** 95 **To** 2017 $29 CM ○
Polish Hill River Clare Valley Riesling 2016 The Polish Hill River produces riesling with a particular stamp, finer and more slatey than that from the main part of the Clare Valley. Here citrus flavours extend into grapefruit from the more common lime and lemon. Will come into its own over the next 5 years, and go much further thereafter. Screwcap. 11.1% alc. **Rating** 94 **To** 2036 $25 ○
Clare Valley Mataro 2015 From 80yo vines, fermented with cultured yeast, 97 days on skins, matured in used oak for 12 months. The time the wine spent on skins was well spent: this is a lovely cherry-infused wine with a perfect level of extract; the overall balance and length can't be faulted. Screwcap. 14.5% alc. **Rating** 94 **To** 2030 $40

ŸŸŸŸŸ **Eternal Return Adelaide Hills Arneis 2015** Rating 93 To 2018 $25 CM ○
Adelaide Hills Nebbiolo 2013 Rating 93 To 2026 $45 CM
Eternal Return Adelaide Hills Nebbiolo 2014 Rating 90 To 2021 $25 CM

After Hours Wine   ★★★★☆

455 North Jindong Road, Carbunup, WA 6285 **Region** Margaret River
T 0438 737 587 **www.afterhourswine.com.au Open** Fri–Mon 10–4
Winemaker Phil Potter **Est.** 2006 **Dozens** 3000 **Vyds** 8.6ha
In 2005 Warwick and Cherylyn Mathews acquired the long-established Hopelands Vineyard, planted to cabernet sauvignon (2.6ha), shiraz (1.6ha), merlot, semillon, sauvignon blanc and chardonnay (1.1ha each). The first wine was made in '06, after which they decided to completely rework the vineyard, which required many hours of physical labour. The vines were retrained, with a consequent reduction in yield and rise in wine quality and value.

ŸŸŸŸŸ **Oliver Margaret River Shiraz 2015** Medium crimson-purple hue; warm spices and earth nuances to the bouquet flow evenly into the medium-bodied palate. Here everything is precisely as and where it should be, blackberry and plum fruit leading the way, gently ripe tannins ex fruit and oak completing the picture of a wine with gold medals from Perth, Small Winemakers and Winewise Small Vignerons Awards, all '16. Screwcap. 14.5% alc. **Rating** 95 **To** 2030 $28 ○
Margaret River Chardonnay 2015 Machine-harvested, 8 hours skin contact prior to crushing, destemming and pressing, fermented in French oak (40% new) with cultured yeast, matured for 11 months. Bright straw-green, but not developing too quickly, the skin contact a courageous decision in this day and age. It has succeeded in creating the power and depth of the white peach stone fruit on the palate. A luscious wine. Gold medals Cool Climate and Small Winemakers wine shows '16. Screwcap. 13% alc. **Rating** 94 **To** 2020 $30 ○

ŸŸŸŸŸ **Margaret River Sauvignon Blanc Semillon 2016** Rating 90 To 2020 $19 ○

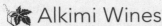 # Alkimi Wines

5/13A Elamo Road, Healesville, Vic 3777 (postal) **Region** Yarra Valley
T 0410 234 688 **www.**alkimiwines.com **Open** Not
Winemaker Stuart Dudine **Est.** 2014 **Dozens** 450

The name is taken from the phoenetic spelling of alchemy, the medieval concept of transmuting base metals into gold and similar works of magic. It's somehow appropriate for owner/winemaker Stuart Dudine, because there are unexplained gaps in his wine journey. We do know that he worked in Europe with Emmerich Knoll (a particularly gifted winemaker) in Austria, and with Stephane Ogier and Chateau Mont-Redon in France. His love of the Rhône Valley sprang from his time at Henschke, working with syrah, grenache and mourvedre. Since 2012 he has been based in the Yarra Valley, working (inter alia) for Yarra Yering, Oakridge and Mac Forbes. His overall raison d'etre is to find vineyard parcels that perform exceptionally well in their patch of soil, year in and year out, no matter the season.

ŸŸŸŸŸ **Intrépide Yarra Valley Marsanne 2016** From the Wattle Glen Vineyard at Mt Evelyn, hand-picked, whole-bunch pressed to used French oak for fermentation and 9 months maturation on lees (no mlf). The pale straw-green wine already has complex texture and structure, with a mix of vibrant grapefruit notes criss-crossed by flinty acidity and roasted almonds. Its bloodlines guarantee its capacity to develop over the next 10 years. Screwcap. 13% alc. **Rating** 95 **To** 2026 $26 ✪

Yarra Valley Syrah 2015 From the Warramunda Vineyard, 75% destemmed for an 18-day fermentation, 25% whole bunches, matured in oak (17% new Hungarian) for the remainder of the year before blending and bottling. 300 dozen made. Spice, pepper, lavender and clove aromas lead into a textured medium-bodied palate with black and blue fruits to the fore, fine tannins bringing up the rear. Sophisticated winemaking. Screwcap. 13.5% alc. **Rating** 94 **To** 2030 $30 ✪

ŸŸŸŸŸ **Heathcote Grenache Rose 2016 Rating** 92 **To** 2018 $25 ✪
Nagambie Roussanne 2015 Rating 90 **To** 2025 $25

Alkoomi ★★★★★

Wingebellup Road, Frankland River, WA 6396 **Region** Frankland River
T (08) 9855 2229 **www.**alkoomiwines.com.au **Open** 7 days 10–5
Winemaker Andrew Cherry **Est.** 1971 **Dozens** 52 000 **Vyds** 106.16ha

Established in 1971 by Merv and Judy Lange, Alkoomi has grown from a single hectare to be one of Western Australia's largest family-owned and operated wineries, with a vineyard of over 100ha. Now owned by Merv and Judy's daughter, Sandy Hallett, and her husband Rod, Alkoomi is continuing the tradition of producing high quality wines which showcase the Frankland River region. Alkoomi is actively reducing its environmental footprint; future plans will see the introduction of new varietals. Alkoomi operates cellar doors in Albany and at the winery (which also has a function centre). Exports to all major markets.

ŸŸŸŸŸ **Black Label Frankland River Sauvignon Blanc 2016** Rich and complex, the percentage of barrel ferment has worked to perfection, adding texture to the display of tropical fruits on the bouquet and palate. Right up with Margaret River. Screwcap. 12.5% alc. **Rating** 95 **To** 2018 $24 ✪

Black Label Frankland River Riesling 2016 An irresistible force of flavour. Lime leaf, fennel, apple and lemon/lime juice rush down the palate before partying on through the finish. Watch this develop; it should be some show. Screwcap. 12.5% alc. **Rating** 94 **To** 2030 $24 CM ✪

Melaleuca Frankland River Riesling 2016 Vines planted in '71, with the first harvest in '76. 100% free-run juice with some time on lees to enhance mid-palate texture. Still very much like a tightly coiled spring. Lime juice, lemon zest, citrus blossom and minerals in the bouquet. Taut and tense on the palate; the fruit is just a little overwhelmed at this stage by the penetrating acidity. An exciting work in progress. Screwcap. 12.5% alc. **Rating** 94 **To** 2030 $34 SC

Black Label Frankland River Chardonnay 2016 Estate-grown, fermented in new and 1-2yo French oak, a barrel selection made after 8 months. Classic cool-grown grapefruit and white peach aromas and flavours, backed by toasty oak and crisp acidity. Screwcap. 12.9% alc. Rating 94 To 2026 $24 ❂

ⓉⓉⓉⓉⓉ **White Label Frankland River SSB 2016** Rating 91 To 2020 $15 CM ❂
White Label Frankland River Riesling 2016 Rating 90 To 2022 $15 ❂

All Saints Estate ★★★★★

All Saints Road, Wahgunyah, Vic 3687 **Region** Rutherglen
T 1800 021 621 **www**.allsaintswine.com.au **Open** Mon–Sat 9–5.30, Sun 10–5.30
Winemaker Nick Brown, Chloe Earl **Est.** 1864 **Dozens** 25 000 **Vyds** 33.46ha
The winery rating reflects the fortified wines and table wines alike. The one-hat Terrace restaurant makes this a must see stop for any visitor to northeast Victoria. The towering castle façade is classified by the Historic Buildings Council. All Saints and St Leonards are owned and managed by fourth-generation Brown family members Eliza, Angela and Nick. Eliza is an energetic and highly intelligent leader, wise beyond her years, and highly regarded by the wine industry. The Brown family celebrated the winery's 150th anniversary in 2014. Exports to the UK, the US, Canada, Singapore and China.

ⓉⓉⓉⓉⓉ **Museum Rutherglen Muscadelle NV** This has Formula One acceleration from zero to 100km in the blink of the eye. The concentration and texture are such that you want to (and do) physically bite on the wine in the mouth. Amid the fireworks and white light display there is a certain calm for the so-fine spirit, the flavours equally amazing. It is based on 80yo components (compared to 20+ years for the Rare), and sits outside the normal Rutherglen classification. It is only bottled on order. 375ml. Vino-Lok. 18% alc. Rating 99 $1000
Rare Rutherglen Muscadelle NV Amber grading to near olive on the rim; a heady perfume of tea leaf, toffee and spice do justice to the intensity and drive of the palate, where malt and shortbread join the choir of the bouquet; the finish is (almost) never ending, but miraculously dries while its flavours are still with you, as much on your brain as in your mouth. 375ml. Vino-Lok. 18% alc. Rating 98 $120 ❂
Rutherglen Museum Muscat NV The ultimate in complexity and concentration; from a solera started in 1920, with only 250 litres released in 500 bottles of 500ml each year, the presentation doing full justice. It is a deep olive-brown, and pours reluctantly from the bottle, so viscous is it. This is at once concentrated, complex and labyrinthine, yet is amazingly light on its feet, with no spirit burn whatsoever. Its ultimate quality and rarity is the extraordinary length, which sets it apart. Vino-Lok. 18% alc. Rating 98 $1000
Rare Rutherglen Muscat NV Darker colour than the Muscadelle; liqueured raisins lead the Christmas pudding and heady spice aromas of the perfumed bouquet, morphing seamlessly into treacle, raisin and Christmas pudding with hard sauce. 375ml. Vino-Lok. 18% alc. Rating 97 $120 ❂

ⓉⓉⓉⓉⓉ **Grand Rutherglen Muscadelle NV** The faint hint of red colour at the heart of the Classic has gone, with dark walnut grading to lighter olive-brown on the rim. Less luscious, more intense and penetrating, tea leaf and burnt toffee to the fore; a little more complex than the Grand Muscat. 375ml. Vino-Lok. 18% alc. Rating 96 $72 ❂
Grand Rutherglen Muscat NV Is a neat match with the Grand Muscadelle; here it is richly fruity, with raisins, caramelised ginger and grilled nuts on the mid-palate, changing to an elegant back-palate with a pantry full of spices of Arabia; the overall balance is exceptional. 375ml. Vino-Lok. 18% alc. Rating 96 $72 ❂
Classic Rutherglen Muscadelle NV Golden brown, the clear rim showing age; exceptional complexity and depth for this level, the bouquet showing the range of flavours to come; terrific viscosity, rolling with Christmas cake and Callard & Bowser toffee wreathed in rancio drying the finish. A massive step up from the entry point (Rutherglen) wine. 375ml. Vino-Lok. 18% alc. Rating 95 $35 ❂

Shiraz 2015 Destemmed and crushed, open-fermented with plunging 2-3 times a day, gentle pressing via a hand-cranked wooden basket press made in 1883, matured in new and used puncheons and barriques for 16 months. Has more tannin structure than the vinification suggests, but the dark berry and spiced plum fruits stand staunchly in their way, protecting the overall balance of a medium to full-bodied shiraz. Screwcap. 14.4% alc. **Rating** 94 **To** 2035 $30 ✪

Rutherglen Muscadelle NV Pale golden brown; the scented bouquet of butterscotch and honey leads into a beautifully balanced and silky palate building on the flavours of the bouquet, before a gloriously fresh finish. While some may have been aged in oak for up to 5 years, this is all about freshness and nascent, youthful, varietal character. 375ml. Vino-Lok. 17% alc. **Rating** 94 $25 ✪

Classic Rutherglen Muscat NV The voluminous bouquet of essence of raisins leaps out of the glass; this has a wonderful mix of exuberant juicy muscat fruit on the one hand, and an elegantly cleansing finish demanding the next taste. 375ml. Vino-Lok. 18% alc. **Rating** 94 $35

ŸŸŸŸŸ **Family Cellar Marsanne 2015** Rating 93 To 2025 $35
Durif 2015 Rating 93 To 2025 $30
Rosa 2016 Rating 92 To 2019 $32
Alias II 2015 Rating 92 To 2030 $38
Sangiovese Cabernet 2016 Rating 92 To 2030 $26
Rutherglen Muscat NV Rating 92 $25 ✪
Alias I 2015 Rating 90 To 2023 $38
Cabernet Merlot 2015 Rating 90 To 2023 $40
Family Cellar Durif 2013 Rating 90 To 2022 $62

Allegiance Wines   ★★★★

Scenic Court, Alstonville, NSW 2477 **Region** Various
T 0434 561 718 **www**.allegiancewines.com.au **Open** Not
Winemaker Contract **Est.** 2009 **Dozens** 40 000
When Tim Cox established Allegiance Wines in 2009 he had the decided advantage of having worked in the Australian wine industry across many facets for almost 30 years. He worked on both the sales and marketing side, and also on the supplier side with Southcorp. He started Cox Wine Merchants to act as distributor for Moppity Vineyards, and successfully partnered with Moppity for over 5 years. This is a virtual wine business, owning neither vineyards nor winery, either having wines made for the business or purchased as cleanskins or as bulk wine.

ŸŸŸŸŸ **Alumni Aged Release Clare Valley Riesling 2012** Motoring along nicely, but with further to travel before it reaches its destiny. Soft, but not flabby, lime and apple juice flavours are backed by soft acidity, the wine in good balance. Screwcap. 12% alc. **Rating** 92 **To** 2022 $30

The Artisan McLaren Vale Grenache 2012 Full-bodied, from a great vintage. Like its Local Legend sibling, with generous fruit, but with better shape. Oak, too, seems to have played a part. Screwcap. 15% alc. **Rating** 90 **To** 2020 $40

The Artisan Grenache Shiraz Mataro 2015 Bright colour; this medium to full-bodied complex regional (grenache from the Barossa Valley and McLaren Vale, shiraz from Langhorne Creek and mataro from the Clare Valley) and varietal blend works well, the flavours ranging through a full spectrum from cherry to plum to blackberry. If the oak had been of higher quality this would have been a cracker. Screwcap. 14.5% alc. **Rating** 90 **To** 2028 $40

ŸŸŸŸ **The Artisan McLaren Vale Shiraz 2015** Rating 89 To 2028 $40
The Artisan Rutherglen Shiraz 2013 Rating 89 To 2028 $40
Local Legend McLaren Vale Grenache 2012 Rating 89 To 2020 $25

Allies Wines

15 Hume Road, Somers, Vic 3927 (postal) **Region** Mornington Peninsula
T 0412 111 587 **www.**allies.com.au **Open** Not
Winemaker David Chapman **Est.** 2003 **Dozens** 1000 **Vyds** 3.1ha
A former chef and sommelier, David Chapman began Allies in 2003 while working at
Moorooduc Estate. He makes Pinot Noir, emphasising the diversity of the Mornington
Peninsula by making a number of wines sourced from different districts. David spends much
of his time in the vineyard, working to ensure well exposed and positioned bunches, to achieve
ripe, pure flavours and supple tannins. His winemaking focuses on simple techniques that
retain concentration and character: no added yeasts, and no fining or filtration, are standard
practices. Production of Allies wines is small and will probably remain that way, given that any
expansion will limit the number of vines David can personally tend. Exports to Hong Kong.

Merricks Mornington Peninsula Pinot Noir 2016 The Merricks vineyard sits
high on an east-west ridge, at 33yo one of the earliest plantings on the Peninsula;
the largest crop since '11, but still a modest 1.6t/a. Slightly lighter colour than its
siblings; cherry and rhubarb aromas are taken into a vibrantly fresh and lingering
palate, with fine-grained tannins providing context and structure for the fruit to
drape itself on. Diam. 13.6% alc. **Rating** 95 **To** 2027 $45

Balnarring Mornington Peninsula Pinot Noir 2016 From a north-facing
vineyard at Balnarring, the warmer, drier site yielding smaller bunches than at
Merricks. The perfumed bouquet of red and dark cherries flows into a very well
structured palate happy to follow the old dictum: if you have a problem, flaunt it.
The problem is the firm tannins, but they are one of the strongest points of a wine
with considerable character. Diam. 13.2% alc. **Rating** 95 **To** 2028 $45

Tuerong Mornington Peninsula Pinot Noir 2016 From the most northerly
and least elevated of the vineyards. Has a very different face and personality
from its siblings, plum taking the lead on the bouquet and holding on to that
primacy through the palate and into the aftertaste. Tannins provide complexity
throughout the palate of a particularly attractive pinot. Diam. 13.1% alc. **Rating** 94
To 2026 $45

Assemblage Mornington Peninsula Pinot Noir 2016 50% Tuerong,
40% Balnarring and 10% Merricks, matured in a 3000l barrel with very thick
staves. Plum and cherries, red and black, provide the backbone for a generous
palate that scores with its vitality and freshness in a very warm vintage. The
picking date was spot on. Screwcap. 13.2% alc. **Rating** 94 **To** 2026 $30 ⬡

Alta Vineyards ★★★☆

99 Maud Street, Unley, SA 5061 **Region** Adelaide Hills
T (08) 8124 9020 **www.**altavineyards.com.au **Open** 7 days 11–5
Winemaker Sarah Fletcher **Est.** 2003 **Dozens** 4000 **Vyds** 23ha
Sarah Fletcher came to Alta after seven years working for Orlando Wyndham. There she came
face to face with grapes from all over Australia, and developed a particular regard for those
coming from the Adelaide Hills. So she joined Alta, which had already established a reputation
for its Sauvignon Blanc. The portfolio has been progressively extended with varieties suited to
the cool climate of the Adelaide Hills.

Adelaide Hills Sauvignon Blanc 2016 Selected from different sites to
accentuate different varietal characters. Gentle, cool, minimal intervention
winemaking employed, the goal being integrity and freshness of fruit character.
Passionfruit and nectarine is the first aromatic hit, lemongrass and snowpea
following. Well poised, the flavours juicy, but gathered in the arms of tight, almost
chalky acidity. Nicely done. Screwcap. 12.5% alc. **Rating** 91 **To** 2019 $23 SC ⬡

For Elsie Pinot Noir Rose 2016 Rating 89 **To** 2019 $23 SC

Amato Vino   ★★★★

PO Box 475, Margaret River, WA 6285 **Region** Margaret River
T 0409 572 957 **www**.amatovino.com.au **Open** Not
Winemaker Brad Wehr, Contract **Est.** 2003 **Dozens** 5000
Brad Wehr has long walked on the wild side with his wines and his labels. The three
brands within his portfolio are wine by brad, Mantra and Amato Vino (the last based on
SA's Riverland). It's not altogether surprising that he has become the Australian importer
for California's Bonny Doon Vineyard; some of the quirky humour of Bonny Doon is
exemplified by the wine by brad label. Exports to Ireland, Canada, South Korea and Singapore.

🍷🍷🍷🍷🍷 **Teroldego 2015** This northern Italian variety is a glossy purple-black. Very good
dark fruit and blueberries and fragrant to the core, enriched by Alpine herbs and
spice. A lively wine with the tannins and acidity working in tandem along the
glossy medium-bodied palate. Screwcap. 14.2% alc. **Rating** 93 **To** 2022 $40 JF
Mantra Barrel-Aged Margaret River Sauvignon Blanc 2016 Wild ferment
in used French oak, on lees 6 months, unfined/unfiltered. Smells of a lime daiquiri,
spicy, too, but this is all about texture and there's lots of it working alongside the
racy acidity. Savoury, moreish, salty, with a softness along the palate. Whiff of ethyl
acetate. Drink now. Screwcap. 12.5% alc. **Rating** 92 **To** 2020 $35 JF
Bela 2016 The second instalment made from the Balkan variety slankamenka
bela. Wild ferment in stainless steel, on lees 3 months, so it's ever-so-slightly
cloudy. It's salty, tastes of preserved lemon and daikon. It has texture, neat phenolics
and is mouth-wateringly fresh. Screwcap. 12.8% alc. **Rating** 92 **To** 2020 $25 JF ✪
Amato Vino Trousseau 2016 Wild ferment in a clay vessel, some whole
bunches, pressed to French oak hogsheads for 3 months, unfined/unfiltered. Pale
ruby with an orange tinge, wonderful perfume, smells of Campari served neat,
fresh herbs and licorice root. Very juicy, with tangy acidity and an undertone of
fruit sweetness. Super refreshing. Alas, only 30 dozen made. Screwcap. 13.9% alc.
Rating 92 **To** 2020 $40 JF
Amato Vino Riverland Bianco 2016 The label is cool and Bianco is actually a
blend of two whites – fiano and slankamenka. This brings out the best of both. A
touch reductive, lots of texture, some stone fruit and honey from fiano, and grip,
tang and saltiness from slankamenka. Screwcap. 13.6% alc. **Rating** 91 **To** 2021
$22 JF ✪
Montepulciano 2016 A robust wine with a neat interplay of savouriness to the
fruit flavours, so a mix of blackberries, cherries and pips, licorice, double espresso
and blackberry essence. Tannins have some grip; crunchy acidity on the finish.
Screwcap. 14.2% alc. **Rating** 90 **To** 2022 $25 JF

🍷🍷🍷🍷 **Wine by Brad Cabernet Merlot 2014 Rating** 89 **To** 2023 $19 JF ✪

Amberley   ★★★☆

10460 Vasse Highway, Nannup, WA 6275 **Region** South West Australia
T 1800 088 711 **www**.amberleyestate.com.au **Open** Not
Winemaker Lance Parkin **Est.** 1985 **Dozens** NFP
Initial growth was based on its ultra-commercial, fairly sweet Chenin Blanc. Became part of
Accolade, but is now simply a brand, without vineyards or winery. Exports to the UK, Canada
and the Pacific Islands.

🍷🍷🍷🍷🍷 **Secret Lane Margaret River Semillon Sauvignon Blanc 2016** A 70/30%
blend cool-fermented in tank using both wild and cultured yeast, and early
bottled. A slam dunk for Margaret River (and Amberley, of course), mercilessly
exposing the lack of intensity and length of the fused citrus, gooseberry and
lemongrass of this wine. Screwcap. 12.5% alc. **Rating** 91 **To** 2021 $20 ✪

🍷🍷🍷🍷 **Merlot 2015 Rating** 89 **To** 2018 $15 ✪

Amelia Park Wines

3857 Caves Road, Wilyabrup, WA 6280 **Region** Margaret River
T (08) 9755 6747 **www**.ameliaparkwines.com.au **Open** 7 days 10–5
Winemaker Jeremy Gordon **Est.** 2009 **Dozens** 20 000 **Vyds** 9.6ha
Jeremy Gordon had a winemaking career starting with Evans & Tate and thereafter Houghton,
before moving to the eastern states to broaden his experience. He returned to Margaret River,
and after several years he and wife Daniela founded Amelia Park Wines with business partner
Peter Walsh. Amelia Park initially relied on contract-grown grapes, but in 2013 purchased the
Moss Brothers site in Wilyabrup, allowing the construction of a new winery and cellar door.
Exports to the UK, the US, Singapore and China.

Reserve Margaret River Cabernet Sauvignon 2014 Ex a single vineyard
in Wilyabrup, night-harvested, crushed and destemmed, cool-fermented in static
fermenters with minimal pumpovers, 1 month on skins, matured in French
oak (33% new) for 18 months. Takes a millisecond of the first sip to establish its
glorious quality. It is silky smooth, as pure as the driven snow (well, you get what
I mean), exceptionally long, effortlessly communicating its cassis fruit coupled with
graphite, oak and perfect tannins. Screwcap. 14% alc. **Rating** 97 **To** 2040 $55 ✪

Reserve Frankland River Shiraz 2014 Frankland River is more noted for its
intensity and depth than for its elegance, but Jeremy Gordon has partially tamed
it with 18 months in French oak, and a controlled hand on the press. But don't
think this wine lacks tannins, they're there. A striking wine built to last. Screwcap.
14.5% alc. **Rating** 96 **To** 2040 $55 ✪

Margaret River Chardonnay 2016 Gin Gin, Davis and Dijon clones from
the home vineyard in Wilyabrup, whole-bunch pressed, settled overnight, cloudy
juice wild-fermented in French oak, matured on lees for 9 months with minimal
stirring. Vibrant, zesty and fresh, with white peach and grapefruit dividing the
spoils of the overall flavour set. It is terrifyingly good at its price. Screwcap.
13% alc. **Rating** 95 **To** 2025 $29 ✪

Reserve Margaret River Chardonnay 2015 The bouquet immediately
announces the reason why this is labelled Reserve: it's more complex and intense
than that of its varietal sibling. There is grapefruit as well as stone fruit, and the
palate is longer and more focused. It's based upon the best fruit from the best
blocks, the winemaking more a question of protecting the fruit than of trying to
increase its impact. Screwcap. 13% alc. **Rating** 95 **To** 2023 $50

Margaret River Rose 2016 30+yo estate grenache, hand-picked, crushed
and destemmed, 6 hours skin contact, wild-fermented and matured on lees for
2 months in used hogsheads. Pale salmon-pink; the bouquet is highly fragrant,
with a palate that more than matches the bouquet, bouncing hither and thither
with spicy red berries, bright acidity and a savoury finish. Wonderful rose.
Screwcap. 13% alc. **Rating** 95 **To** 2019 $25 ✪

Margaret River Cabernet Merlot 2015 Bright crimson-purple. Matured
in French oak, which contributes to both structure and flavour – which are
considerable. Cassis ticks one box, bay leaf another, the fine but persistent tannins
another, the length yet another, the price the final tick on the final box. Screwcap.
14.5% alc. **Rating** 95 **To** 2030 $29 ✪

Margaret River Semillon Sauvignon Blanc 2016 A small percentage of
the wine was wild-fermented in stainless steel barrels, a technique used more in
Margaret River than most other regions, but even there not widespread. This is a
delectably juicy wine with passionfruit, nectarine and a flash of minerality, the last
conceivably from the barrel-ferment component. Whatever, it all works very well.
Screwcap. 12.5% alc. **Rating** 94 **To** 2020 $22 ✪

Margaret River Chardonnay 2015 Rating 93 **To** 2021 $29
Trellis Margaret River SBS 2015 Rating 90 **To** 2017 $15 ✪

Amherst Winery

285 Talbot–Avoca Road, Amherst, Vic 3371 **Region** Pyrenees
T 0400 380 382 **www.**amherstwinery.com **Open** W'ends & public hols 11–5
Winemaker Luke Jones, Andrew Koerner **Est.** 1989 **Dozens** 1500 **Vyds** 5ha
In 1989 Norman and Elizabeth Jones planted vines on a property with an extraordinarily rich history, commemorated by the name Dunn's Paddock. Samuel Knowles was a convict who arrived in Van Diemen's Land in 1838. He endured continuous punishment until he fled to SA in 1846. He changed his name to Dunn and in 1851 married 18-year-old Mary Taaffe. They walked to Amherst, pushing a wheelbarrow carrying their belongings. The original lease title is in his name. Amherst Winery is sited on land once owned by Samuel Dunn. In Jan '13 son Luke and wife Rachel Jones acquired the Amherst Winery business; Luke has a wine marketing diploma and a diploma in Wine Technology. Exports to China.

ŸŸŸŸŸ **Daisy Creek Pyrenees Shiraz 2015** Estate-grown, matured for 15 months in French oak. The bouquet is expressive and attractive, the medium-bodied palate straddling black cherry, spice, pepper and earthy/foresty notes. The overall balance is very good indeed. Screwcap. 14% alc. **Rating** 92 **To** 2024 $20 **○**
Pyrenees Pinot Noir 2015 Hand-picked, wild-fermented, 8 days on skins, basket-pressed, matured in French oak for 8 months. More varietal expression than expected, for this is a marginal terroir for pinot. A problem is the build-up of tannins and fruit extract on the back-palate. Screwcap. 14% alc. **Rating** 90 **To** 2023 $25

ŸŸŸŸ **Rachel's Pyrenees Rose 2016 Rating** 89 **To** 2018 $20

Ampel

PO Box 243, Leichhardt, NSW 2040 **Region** Northern Tasmania
T 0418 544 001 **www.**vinous.com.au **Open** Not
Winemaker Jeremy Dineen **Est.** 2010 **Dozens** 1000
Tim Stock's distribution company, Vinous, was the distributor of Josef Chromy's wines until 2010, when the arrangement ended (amicably). Prior to this, Tim had become great friends with Jeremy Dineen, winemaker and general manager of the Chromy business. Jeremy was able to source grapes from a variety of vineyards for the Tasmanian wines that Tim needed for his customers on the mainland. The grapes are sourced from Helen and Gerald Phillips' vineyard in Yorktown in the north-west corner of the Tamar Valley. The vineyard was planted on land covered by virgin scrub, reflecting the impoverished quartz gravel soil. With virtually no organic matter present, it took six years for the first small crop to appear, but the vines have now built deep, substantial root systems. The Phillips' farming method is sustainable, with minimal treatments, a benefit of the free-draining soil. The plantings are two-thirds pinot noir and one-third pinot gris, the pinot noir inspiration coming from the Côte Chalonaise (light, fresh and fruity) in Burgundy and that of the pinot gris from Alsace (generous and broadly structured, yet aromatic).

ŸŸŸŸŸ **Pinot Gris 2016** Hand-picked, whole-bunch pressed, fermented with cultured yeast. Has that extra level of intensity and grip fostered by the Tasmanian climate; nashi pear, citrus and minerally acidity drive the bouquet and long palate, making light of the higher than usual alcohol. Screwcap. 14% alc. **Rating** 91 **To** 2020 $26

Anderson ★★★★☆

1619 Chiltern Road, Rutherglen, Vic 3685 **Region** Rutherglen
T (02) 6032 8111 **www.**andersonwinery.com.au **Open** 7 days 10–5
Winemaker Howard and Christobelle Anderson **Est.** 1992 **Dozens** 2000 **Vyds** 8.8ha
Having notched up a winemaking career spanning 28 years, including a stint at Seppelt (Great Western), Howard Anderson and family started their own winery, initially with a particular focus on sparkling wine but now extending across all table wine styles. Daughter Christobelle graduated from Adelaide University in 2003 with first class honours, and has worked in Alsace, Champagne and Burgundy either side of joining her father full-time in '05. The original estate

plantings of shiraz, durif and petit verdot (6ha) have been expanded with tempranillo, saperavi, brown muscat, chenin blanc and viognier.

ŶŶŶŶŶ Cellar Block Durif 2010 Dark and impenetrable colour, the first indication of its dry-grown pedigree. The bouquet has brooding licorice, sweet spice and blood plum aromas wrapped in a layer of quality oak. Softly but deeply textured on the palate, the black fruit flavours are seamlessly wound around a persistent spine of tannin. Screwcap. 14.2% alc. **Rating** 95 **To** 2035 $40 SC

Verrier Basket Press Durif Shiraz 2010 A multi trophy winner at Rutherglen Wine Show '12, aged for 12 months in French oak. A luscious bouquet, with aromas of Christmas cake, brandy-soaked fruit and sweet oak. Fleshy and richly flavoured, it keeps its shape and balance, the firm but well managed and integrated tannin an important feature. Screwcap. 14% alc. **Rating** 94 **To** 2030 $32 SC

Storyteller Durif 2013 Trophy for Best Other Variety at the Victorian Wines Show '14 leads an array of two gold and 11 silver medals awarded between '14 and '16. This is a riotously rich durif, bursting with red and black dried and fresh glace fruits that fill the mouth. Because the alcohol was controlled, the tannins likewise, this is a very good red meat wine. Screwcap. 14.1% alc. **Rating** 94 **To** 2023 $30 ○

ŶŶŶŶŶ Tempranillo 2014 Rating 90 **To** 2021 $21 ○
Methode Traditionnelle Sparkling Durif 2006 Rating 90 **To** 2017 $39 TS

Andrew Peace Wines ★★★★

Murray Valley Highway, Piangil, Vic 3597 **Region** Swan Hill
T (03) 5030 5291 **www**.apwines.com **Open** Mon–Fri 8–5, Sat 12–4
Winemaker Andrew Peace, David King **Est.** 1995 **Dozens** 180 000 **Vyds** 270ha
The Peace family has been a major Swan Hill grapegrower since 1980, moving into winemaking with the opening of a $3 million winery in '96. Varieties planted include chardonnay, colombard, grenache, malbec, mataro, merlot, pinot gris, riesling, sangiovese, sauvignon blanc, semillon, tempranillo and viognier. The planting of sagrantino is the largest of only a few such plantings in Australia. Exports to all major markets.

ŶŶŶŶŶ Australia Felix Premium Barrel Reserve Langhorne Creek Wrattonbully Cabernet Shiraz 2014 A best parcels, best barrel selection following 12 months maturation in French oak. It is medium to full-bodied, with cassis, fine tannins and cedary oak playing tag on the bouquet and palate alike. Both these regions can produce high-flavoured wines that retain plushness, as is the case here. Screwcap. 14.5% alc. **Rating** 94 **To** 2024 $28 ○

ŶŶŶŶŶ Australia Felix Premium Barrel Reserve Wrattonbully Cabernet Shiraz 2015 Rating 92 **To** 2030 $28

Angas Plains Estate ★★★★★

317 Angas Plains Road, Langhorne Creek, SA 5255 **Region** Langhorne Creek
T (08) 8537 3159 **www**.angasplainswines.com.au **Open** 7 days 11–5
Winemaker Peter Douglas **Est.** 1994 **Dozens** 3000 **Vyds** 15.2ha
In 1994 Phillip and Judy Cross began the Angas Plains Estate plantings, first with cabernet sauvignon, second shiraz and third a small block of chardonnay predominantly used as a sparkling base. The location, on ancient Angas River floodplains, together with cooling evening breezes from the local Lake Alexandrina, proved ideally suited to the red varieties. Skilled contract winemaking has resulted in some excellent wines from the estate-grown shiraz and cabernet sauvignon. Exports to Singapore, Hong Kong and China.

ŶŶŶŶŶ Special Reserve Langhorne Creek Shiraz 2013 A single 9t batch open-fermented for 8 days with twice daily pumpovers, matured in 20% new American oak and 80% used French hogsheads for 15 months, then a barrel selection. It is full-bodied like winemaker Peter Douglas, a gentle giant, and is made in his image. Diam. 14% alc. **Rating** 95 **To** 2038 $40

Special Reserve Langhorne Creek Cabernet Sauvignon 2014 Matured for 15 months in French hogsheads (80% new). Excellent crimson–purple hue introduces a disciplined cabernet that makes its varietal point clearly and firmly with blackcurrant, bay leaf and black olive nuances. No fireworks, just cabernet grown in a perfect spot. Screwcap. 14% alc. **Rating** 95 **To** 2039 $40
PJs Langhorne Creek Shiraz 2014 16yo vines, matured in 50/50% new and used French hogsheads for 12 months. The softness of the Langhorne Creek fruit hasn't been compromised, and the wine has elegance and intensity, not a common outcome. A lovely wine. Screwcap. 14.5% alc. **Rating** 94 **To** 2030 $25 ✪

🍷🍷🍷🍷🍷 PJs Langhorne Cabernet Sauvignon 2014 **Rating** 93 **To** 2034 $25 ✪

Angelicus   ★★★★
Lot 9 Catalano Road, Burekup, WA 6227 **Region** Geographe
T 0429 481 425 **www**.angelicus.com.au **Open** Not
Winemaker John Ward, Sue Ward **Est.** 1997 **Dozens** 800 **Vyds** 1.65ha
Dr John and Sue Ward moved from Sydney to WA with the aim of establishing a vineyard and winery. They moved to the Geographe region, where they purchased a 51ha block of granite-strewn rocky hillside facing north and west, looking towards the Indian Ocean. They began planting vines in 2009, the lion's share to grenache (bushvines, managed biodynamically), five clones of tempranillo, and verdelho.

🍷🍷🍷🍷🍷 **Geographe Garnacha 2016** Coming off bushvines, there's fruit intensity and ripeness, and it's convincing. Sweet raspberry and spiced red plums lead onto a medium-bodied palate with gritty tannins and refreshing acidity; just a little alcohol heat on the finish. Screwcap. 15% alc. **Rating** 93 **To** 2022 $25 JF ✪
Tempranillo 2016 It packs a lot of flavour and takes a savoury route with exotic spices, tobacco, black olives, crushed coriander seeds and pomegranate. Yet the palate is key – medium-bodied with stealth-like chalky tannins and cleansing acidity. Screwcap. 14.5% alc. **Rating** 92 **To** 2023 $25 JF ✪
Tempranillo 2015 Shows attractive, savoury varietal aromas without any obvious appearance of the 'cherry-cola' tempranillo character often seen in Australian examples. Medium-bodied, the flavours are in the red fruit spectrum with a suggestion of oak in play; fine-grained, dusty tannins lengthen the finish. Increasing vine age will add depth and complexity to future releases. Screwcap. 14% alc. **Rating** 91 **To** 2022 $25 SC
Verdejo 2016 The intriguing bouquet combines citrus, green herbs, pear and some skins or solids characters to great effect. Very fresh and bright through the palate, the fruit lively and the texture enhancing the flavours and mouthfeel. Chalky acidity runs its course and lingers on the finish. Good drinking. Screwcap. 12.5% alc. **Rating** 90 **To** 2020 $25 SC

Angove Family Winemakers   ★★★★★
Bookmark Avenue, Renmark, SA 5341 **Region** South Australia
T (08) 8580 3100 **www**.angove.com.au **Open** Mon–Sat 10–4, Sun & pub hols 10–3
Winemaker Tony Ingle, Paul Kernich, Ben Horley **Est.** 1886 **Dozens** 1 million
Vyds 480ha
Exemplifies the economies of scale achievable in the Riverland without compromising quality. Good technology provides wines that are never poor and sometimes exceed their theoretical station in life. The vast Nanya Vineyard has been redeveloped with changes in the varietal mix, row orientation and a partial move to organic growing. Angove's expansion into Padthaway (chardonnay), Watervale (riesling) and Coonawarra (cabernet sauvignon) via long-term contracts, and the purchase of the Warboys Vineyard in McLaren Vale in 2008, have resulted in outstanding premium wines. A large cellar door and cafe on the Warboys Vineyard at the corner of Chalk Hill Rd/Olivers Rd, McLaren Vale, is open 10–5 daily. Exports to all major markets.

 𝟗𝟗𝟗𝟗𝟗 **Single Vineyard Limited Release Sellicks Foothills McLaren Vale Shiraz 2015** This is a compelling wine offering a textural kaleidoscope of whole-bunch briar spice and finely tuned French oak cedars, slatey tannins and a crunchy mineral-clad core. This is heavy on deli smoked meum, iodine and ferrous notes, yet light and effortless. There is more chew and substance here than in the other Single Vineyard wines, yet not for a moment does it turn to jam juice. The most complete of the site-specific pack. Screwcap. 14% alc. **Rating 96 To 2035 $44** NG ✪

AMV-X McLaren Vale Shiraz 2016 This is a stellar expression of whole cluster–infused shiraz, with the 40% opted for as a reflection of the vineyard platformed across livewire slate and granitic terroir. This has abundant pulpy black and blue fruits, but they are compact and laced across a beam of anise and cardamom spice, melded to palate-spanking tannins. Screwcap. 14.2% alc. **Rating 95 To 2024 $30** NG ✪

Warboys Vineyard McLaren Vale Shiraz 2015 Strong crimson-purple hue; the vineyard is planted to old vine shiraz and grenache, and the elegance of the wine half-suggests a small percentage of grenache or partial whole bunch fermentation before maturation in French hogsheads. Red and black fruits, licorice, dark chocolate and built-in tannins provide an each-way bet for short (say 3 years) or long-term cellaring. Screwcap. 14.5% alc. **Rating 95 To 2035 $42**

Alternatus McLaren Vale Rose 2016 78% grenache, 18% tempranillo, 4.6% graciano and 2.4% carignan; grenache, tempranillo and graciano were pressed after 8 hours skin contact, the tempranillo and graciano co-fermented. A serious rose, and finishes long, crisp and bone dry; spicy red fruits ride in the saddle. Screwcap. 13% alc. **Rating 94 To 2017 $23** ✪

Single Vineyard Limited Release Blewitt Springs McLaren Vale Shiraz 2015 This medium-bodied shiraz is as sumptuous as it is svelte, floral and complex. There is a brilliant sheen to the vermilion hue; a lilac floral aroma, layered with blue and boysenberry fruits, and a peppery scamper across the mouth, given further lilt and energy by long, sinuous, iodine-soaked tannins. This wine is rich, yes; but expressive, full of crunch and highly aromatic. Screwcap. 14.5% alc. **Rating 94 To 2035 $44** NG

Alternatus McLaren Vale Grenache 2016 While it is ready to drink, don't underestimate the ability of the wine to provide pleasure in the future, for the purity of the varietal expression, with its array of raspberry, blueberry and red cherry fruit, is exemplary. In summer, should be slightly chilled to allow its fresh mouthfeel free rein. Great value. Screwcap. 14% alc. **Rating 94 To 2021 $23** ✪

Family Crest McLaren Vale Grenache Shiraz Mourvedre 2015 A blend of 60% Blewitt Springs grenache, 21% Sellicks Hills shiraz and 19% mourvedre; hand-picked, hand-sorted, each parcel separately fermented, matured in used French oak for 9 months. A worthy follow-on to the multi-trophy winning '14, it offers a perfectly balanced and structured mouthfeel to the spiced plum and red berry fruits without even a skerrick of confection or jam. Skilled winemaking, unbeatable value. Screwcap. 14.5% alc. **Rating 94 To 2020 $22** ✪

𝟗𝟗𝟗𝟗𝟗 **Wild Olive Organic McLaren Vale Shiraz 2015** Rating 93 To 2030 $20 ✪
Single Vineyard Ltd Release Willunga Shiraz 2015 Rating 93 $44 NG
Warboys Vineyard Grenache 2015 Rating 93 To 2023 $44 NG
AMV-X Tempranillo Mataro Grenache Graciano 2016 Rating 93 To 2022 $30 NG
Alternatus Fiano 2016 Rating 92 To 2021 $23 ✪
Nine Vines Grenache Shiraz Rose 2016 Rating 92 To 2017 $18 ✪
The Medhyk Shiraz 2015 Rating 92 To 2030 $65 NG
Warboys Vineyard Shiraz Grenache 2015 Rating 92 To 2022 $44 NG
Family Crest Shiraz 2015 Rating 91 To 2035 $25
Family Crest Cabernet Sauvignon 2015 Rating 91 To 2029 $22 ✪
Organic Merlot 2016 Rating 90 To 2021 $16 NG ✪
Alternatus McLaren Vale Tempranillo 2016 Rating 90 To 2018 $23

Angullong Wines

Victoria Street, Millthorpe, NSW 2798 **Region** Orange
T (02) 6366 4300 **www**.angullong.com.au **Open** 7 days 11–5
Winemaker Jon Reynolds, Liz Jackson **Est.** 1998 **Dozens** 17000 **Vyds** 216.7ha
The Crossing family (Bill and Hatty, and third generation James and Ben) has owned a 2000ha
sheep and cattle station for over half a century. Located 40km south of Orange, overlooking
the Belubula Valley, more than 200ha of vines have been planted. In all, there are 15 varieties,
with shiraz, cabernet sauvignon and merlot leading the way. Most of the production is sold.
Exports to Germany and China.

🍷🍷🍷🍷🍷 **Orange Sauvignon Blanc 2016** The fragrant, tropical fruit–accented bouquet
shows why Angullong was one of the first wineries to put Orange sauvignon
blanc on the front page. The palate lives up to the promise, intense tropical fruits
underwritten by citrussy acidity, leaving the mouth fresh and asking for more.
Great value. Screwcap. 13.5% alc. **Rating** 94 **To** 2018 $20 ✪
Fossil Hill Orange Shiraz Viognier 2014 The vintage was a challenging
one, but not for Angullong and this wine. A small amount of viognier was
co-fermented, aiding the bright colour, the fragrant bouquet and the supple
medium-bodied palate. The finish is well balanced and long. Screwcap. 14.5% alc.
Rating 94 **To** 2029 $26 ✪

🍷🍷🍷🍷🍷 **Crossing Reserve Shiraz 2015 Rating** 91 **To** 2030 $48
Fossil Hill Central Ranges Tempranillo 2015 Rating 91 **To** 2022 $26
Fossil Hill Orange Riesling 2016 Rating 90 **To** 2026 $24
Orange Chardonnay 2016 Rating 90 **To** 2020 $20 ✪
Crossing Reserve Cabernet Sauvignon 2015 Rating 90 **To** 2030 $48

Angus the Bull

PO Box 611, Manly, NSW 1655 **Region** Central Victoria
T (02) 8966 9020 **www**.angusthebull.com **Open** Not
Winemaker Hamish MacGowan **Est.** 2002 **Dozens** 20000
Hamish MacGowan took the virtual winery idea to its ultimate conclusion, with a single wine
(Cabernet Sauvignon) designed to be drunk with a perfectly cooked steak. Parcels of grapes
are selected from regions across Victoria and SA each year, the multi-regional blend approach
designed to minimise vintage variation. In 2012 a second wine, Wee Angus Cabernet Merlot,
was added. Exports to the UK, Canada, Ireland, the Philippines, Singapore, Thailand, Hong
Kong and NZ.

🍷🍷🍷🍷 **Wee Angus Cabernet Merlot 2014** Fruit sourced from Central Victoria.
Firmly in the mould that this brand has established: juicy, obvious, easy-drinking.
Plenty of fruit on the bouquet, with generous ripe plum and blackcurrant.
Merlot seems to have influence on the palate, the softness and red-berry flavours
consistent with that variety. Tannin is well managed to do the job required of it.
Screwcap. 13.5% alc. **Rating** 90 **To** 2019 $18 SC ✪

🍷🍷🍷🍷 **Cabernet Sauvignon 2014 Rating** 89 **To** 2020 $22 SC

Annie's Lane

Quelltaler Road, Watervale, SA 5452 **Region** Clare Valley
T (08) 8843 2320 **www**.annieslane.com.au **Open** 7 days 10–4
Winemaker Alex MacKenzie **Est.** 1851 **Dozens** NFP
The Clare Valley brand of TWE, the name coming from Annie Wayman, a turn-of-the-
century local identity. The brand consistently offers wines that over-deliver against their price
points. Copper Trail is the flagship release, and there are some very worthy cellar door and
on-premise wines.

🍷🍷🍷🍷🍷 **Quelltaler Clare Valley Riesling 2016** On song with its line of superfine
acidity striking at the heart of this wine, highlighting its Meyer lemon, zest, florals
and ginger spice along the way. Screwcap. 11% alc. **Rating** 95 **To** 2030 $27 JF ✪

Quelltaler Clare Valley Shiraz Cabernet 2014 Enticing dark crimson-purple.
There's a vibrant lift to this with florals, dark chocolate and gum leaves, the two
varieties balanced, the medium-bodied palate taking the oak and supple ripe
tannins in its stride. Screwcap. 14.5% alc, Rating 94 To 2024 $27 JF ◯

🍷🍷🍷🍷🍷 Copper Trail Clare Valley Shiraz 2014 Rating 93 To 2028 $80 JF
The Locals Cabernet Sauvignon 2014 Rating 92 To 2025 $23 JF ◯
The Locals Cabernet Sauvignon 2013 Rating 90 To 2023 $23

Anvers   ★★★★☆

633 Razorback Road, Kangarilla, SA 5157 **Region** Adelaide Hills
T (08) 8374 1787 **www**.anvers.com.au **Open** Not
Winemaker Kym Milne MW **Est.** 1998 **Dozens** 10 000 **Vyds** 24.5ha
Myriam and Wayne Keoghan's principal vineyard is in the Adelaide Hills at Kangarilla (16ha of
cabernet sauvignon, shiraz, chardonnay, sauvignon blanc and viognier), the second (97-year-
old) vineyard is at McLaren Vale (shiraz, grenache and cabernet sauvignon). Winemaker Kym
Milne has experience gained across many of the wine-producing countries in both northern
and southern hemispheres. Exports to the UK and other major markets.

🍷🍷🍷🍷🍷 WMK Adelaide Hills Shiraz 2014 From the estate Razorback Road Vineyard.
It's definitely full-bodied, but not heavy, with a swathe of dark plums, oak spice,
star anise and pomander-like aromas. Ripe, powerful tannins, yet there's a vivacity,
a brightness here, and if the cork lasts, so will this. 14.5% alc. Rating 95 To 2030
$48 JF

Aphelion Wine   ★★★★

18 St Andrews Terrace, Willunga, SA 5172 **Region** McLaren Vale
T 0404 390 840 **www**.aphelionwine.com.au **Open** Not
Winemaker Rob Mack **Est.** 2014 **Dozens** 200
Aphelion Wine is akin to a miniature painting done with single-hair paintbrushes. But when
you consider the credentials of winemaker Rob Mack, supported by co-founder wife Louise
Rhodes Mack, great oaks come to mind. Since 2007, Rob has accumulated two degrees (first
Accounting and Management in '07, then Bachelor of Wine Science from CSU in '16). He
has scaled the heights of direct marketing as wine buyer and planner (June '10-Jan '13) for
Laithwaites Wine People, and spent the next 18 months as production manager for Direct
Wines in McLaren Vale. Woven through this has been significant employment with five
wineries, four in McLaren Vale, which he obviously knows well. And I quote: 'In the interest
of continuing professional development, Rob will undertake a Northern Hemisphere vintage
position in Barolo, Piedmont, Italy this Sep–Nov ['17].' Aphelion has two wine projects: the
Grenache Project (four different wines) and the Sagrantino Project (one wine).

🍷🍷🍷🍷🍷 Grenache 2016 All the Aphelion grenache variations come from a single
80yo vineyard in Blewitt Springs, all hand-picked, all fermented to dryness, all
basket-pressed, none fined or filtered. A blend of berry, bunch and pressings, the
proportions not specified. It's not significantly richer or more complex, but has
some added power to the finish. Screwcap. 14.5% alc. Rating 91 To 2020 $29
Grenache Berry 2016 Whole berries, matured for 9 months in used French
barriques. Light, bright crimson; all red berry/cherry fruit with a savoury finish.
Screwcap. 14.5% alc. Rating 90 To 2020 $29
Grenache Bunch 2016 Half destemmed, half whole bunches. Has some weight
and juicy complexity, spicy notes joining the fray, then a savoury/stemmy finish.
Screwcap. 14.5% alc. Rating 90 To 2020 $29
Grenache Pressings 2016 The background information is far from clear – the
most likely scenario is that this is made up with the pressings from the Bunch
and Berry ferments. There is a saline character, and more tannins, although the
impact of the latter is limited by the use of basket pressing. Screwcap. 14.5% alc.
Rating 90 To 2020 $29

Apricus Hill

550 McLeod Road, Denmark, WA 6333 **Region** Denmark
T 0427 409 078 **www**.apricushill.com.au **Open** Fri–Mon 11–5, 7 days school hols
Winemaker James Kellie **Est.** 1995 **Dozens** 1000 **Vyds** 8ha
When the then owners of Somerset Hill Vineyard, Graham and Lee Upson, placed the vineyard on the market, James and Careena Kellie (of Harewood Estate) purchased it with two purposes: first, to secure a critical fruit source for Harewood, and second, to make and market a small range of single-vineyard, single-varietal wines for sale exclusively through the spectacular cellar door, with its sweeping vista. Thus Somerset Hill is now Apricus Hill.

🍷🍷🍷🍷🍷 **Single Vineyard Denmark Sauvignon Blanc 2016** Fermented and matured in French puncheons for 6 months (some solids). The barrel fermentation comes through on the bouquet, the palate focusing on the predominantly citrus and cut grass flavours that rapidly build intensity on the finish and aftertaste, tropical fruits dispatched to field on the boundary. Screwcap. 13% alc. **Rating** 94 To 2021 $27 ✪

🍷🍷🍷🍷🍷 **Single Vineyard Denmark Semillon 2016 Rating** 92 To 2026 $27
Single Vineyard Denmark Chardonnay 2016 Rating 92 To 2024 $27
Single Vineyard Denmark Pinot Noir 2016 Rating 91 To 2019 $27

Arakoon

7/229 Main Road, McLaren Vale, SA 5171 **Region** McLaren Vale
T (08) 8323 7339 **www**.arakoonwines.com.au **Open** By appt
Winemaker Raymond Jones **Est.** 1999 **Dozens** 3500 **Vyds** 3.5ha
Ray and Patrik Jones' first venture into wine came to nothing: a 1990 proposal for a film about the Australian wine industry with myself as anchorman. In 1999 they took the plunge into making their own wine and exporting it, along with the wines of others. As the quality of the wines has improved, so has the originally zany labelling been replaced with simple, but elegant, labels. Exports to Sweden, Denmark, Germany, Singapore, Malaysia and China.

🍷🍷🍷🍷🍷 **Doyen McLaren Vale Shiraz 2015** In the same ripe spectrum as its other reds but with bit more stuffing, as in the dark molten chocolate, the tar, the warm terracotta, the macerated fruit, the cedary oak and expansive tannins. All in abundance yet the palate smooths out with a peep of raspberry freshness. Screwcap. 15% alc. **Rating** 91 To 2024 $40 JF
Clarendon Shiraz 2015 It's bold, brassy, and a little too ripe, but fans of the style won't complain. The texture is smooth, with dark fruit infused with chocolate mint, lashings of oak and a wall of ripe, plump tannins. Screwcap. 15% alc. **Rating** 90 To 2024 $32 JF

Aramis Vineyards

411 Henley Beach Road, Brooklyn Park, SA 5032 **Region** McLaren Vale
T (08) 8352 2900 **www**.aramisvineyards.com **Open** By appt
Winemaker Renae Hirsch, Peter Leske **Est.** 1998 **Dozens** 12 000 **Vyds** 26ha
Aramis Vineyards was founded in 1998 by Lee Flourentzou. Located barely 2km from the Gulf of St Vincent, it is one of the coolest sites in McLaren Vale, planted to shiraz (18ha) and cabernet sauvignon (8ha), the two varieties best suited to the site. This philosophy leads Aramis to source grapes from other regions that best represent each variety, including sauvignon blanc and chardonnay from Adelaide Hills and riesling from Eden Valley. The city-based cellar door also features wines from other boutique producers. Exports to the US, Canada, Singapore, Malaysia, Thailand, Vietnam, Japan, Hong Kong and NZ.

🍷🍷🍷🍷🍷 **Black Label Adelaide Hills Gruner Veltliner 2015** My my, does this have varietal expression and intensity. Its impact is lightning fast and no less durable; citrus and green apple skin and zest join hands for maximum effect. Terrific now, and won't fall over anytime soon. Screwcap. 12.5% alc. **Rating** 95 To 2025 $25 ✪

Single Vineyard McLaren Vale Shiraz 2014 Interesting that Aramis crafts separate cuvees utilising the names 'shiraz' and 'syrah'. Both are exemplary examples of tannin management and freshness, with no structural pillar overdone through extraction, oak or other manipulation. This, the softer of the two, as the name 'shiraz' usually implies, is a billowing pillow of dark plum, cherry, anise and mace, ever so gently massaging the cheeks and roof of the mouth. The supports are such that the wine will age well. Screwcap. 14.5% alc. **Rating** 95 **To** 2025 $28 NG ✪

The Heir McLaren Vale Syrah 2012 Excellent retention of deep crimson hue; the complex bouquet runs through the gamut of regional fruit, the goal posts spice, dark chocolate and Christmas cake, the finish notably fresh and vibrant. Diam. 14.5% alc. **Rating** 95 **To** 2027 $55

White Label McLaren Vale Shiraz 2014 A juicy and rich wine that is paradoxically effortless, elegant and damn easy to drink. The usual violet and dark fruit equation is present in spades, yet it is the finely grained palpable grape tannins, the gentle milk-chocolate oak and the juicy lilt of acidity that makes this so enjoyable, especially at the price. Moreover, the wine is a welcome contrast to the fleets of freight trains coming out of these parts, acid overdriven and tannins on high beam. Screwcap. 14.5% alc. **Rating** 94 **To** 2022 $20 NG ✪

The Heir McLaren Vale Syrah 2013 Aged for 24 months in subtle French oak, 40% new and of a larger format than that used for the Shiraz, this is densely furled and altogether more carnal in its aromatic florals, cinnamon spice and smoked meat aromas, singed with a hint of reduction, than its softer brethren. Boysenberry and other blue fruits drift across the rich palate. Grippy and in need of time. Diam. 14.5% alc. **Rating** 94 **To** 2028 $55 NG

🍷🍷🍷🍷🍷 **Black Label Adelaide Hills Gruner Veltliner 2016** Rating 92 To 2022 $25 NG ✪

Black Label Adelaide Hills Chardonnay 2016 Rating 91 To 2019 $25 NG

Single Vineyard Shiraz 2013 Rating 91 To 2028 $28

Single Vineyard Cabernet Sauvignon 2015 Rating 90 To 2023 $28 NG

Single Vineyard Cabernet Sauvignon 2013 Rating 90 To 2033 $28

Aravina Estate ★★★★★

61 Thornton Road, Yallingup, WA 6282 **Region** Margaret River
T (08) 9750 1111 www.aravinaestate.com **Open** 7 days 10.30–4
Winemaker Ryan Aggiss **Est.** 2010 **Dozens** 10000 **Vyds** 28ha
In 2010 Steve Tobin and family acquired the winery and vineyard of Amberley Estate from Accolade, but not the Amberley brand. Steve has turned the property into a multifaceted business with a host of attractions: a restaurant, sports car collection, wedding venue and so forth. Exports to Indonesia, Malaysia, Hong Kong and China.

🍷🍷🍷🍷🍷 **Wildwood Ridge Reserve Margaret River Chardonnay 2015** Hand-picked, whole-bunch pressed, wild fermented in French barriques (35% new), matured on lees for 9 months. A very attractive, high class chardonnay with an effortless display of fruit on both the bouquet and palate, oak the messenger, but not the message per se. Pink grapefruit, white peach and a hint of cashew decorously fill the mouth; great line and length. Screwcap. 13% alc. **Rating** 96 **To** 2026 $60 ✪

Wildwood Ridge Reserve Margaret River Cabernet Sauvignon 2014 Includes 8% merlot, crushed to upright static fermenters with cultured yeast, one-third left on skins for extended maceration after mlf, matured for 18 months in French oak (50% new). Fragrant, with high-toned cassis aromas that replay on the palate, cassis again to the fore before French oak adds to the complexity and appeal of the wine. High quality cabernet tannins stand on the centre stage of the finish and aftertaste. Screwcap. 14.5% alc. **Rating** 95 **To** 2034 $60

Wildwood Ridge Reserve Margaret River Cabernet Sauvignon 2013 The beautiful flavours of Margaret River cabernet set sail here. Blackcurrant, gravel, bay leaves and dark chocolate. It's medium to full-bodied, but the kicker is the finish, which extends deliciously but firmly. A grand future awaits. A serious quality contender. Screwcap. 14% alc. **Rating** 95 **To** 2035 $50 CM

Margaret River Shiraz 2014 Both slippery smooth and peppery with black cherry, asphalt and clove notes combining to put on quite a show. Creamy oak adds velvet to the parade of savoury flavours. Tannin is beautifully massaged and the length is excellent. Screwcap. 14% alc. **Rating** 94 **To** 2030 $36 CM

????? Margaret River Vermentino 2015 Rating 93 To 2017 $32 CM
Block 4 Margaret River Chenin Blanc 2015 Rating 91 To 2022 $34 CM

Arlewood Estate   ★★★★★

Cnr Bussell Highway/Calgardup Road, Forest Grove, WA 6286 **Region** Margaret River
T (08) 9757 6676 **www.**arlewood.com.au **Open** Thurs–Mon 11–5
Winemaker Stuart Pym **Est.** 1988 **Dozens** 3500 **Vyds** 6.2ha
The antecedents of today's Arlewood shifted several times; they might interest a PhD researcher, but – with one exception – have no relevance to today's business. That exception was the 1999 planting of the vineyard by the (then) Xanadu winemaker Jurg Muggli. Garry Gossatti purchased the run-down, close-planted vineyard in 2008, and lived in the onsite house from 2008–12, driving to Perth one day per week for his extensive hospitality/hotel business (which paid Arlewood's bills). His involvement in the resurrection of the vineyard was hands-on, and the cool site in the south of Margaret River was, and remains, his obsession. He now drives down every weekend from Perth to talk to viticulturist Russell Oates and contract winemaker Stuart Pym, clearly believing that the owner's footsteps make the best fertiliser. Exports to the UK, Switzerland, Singapore, Malaysia, Hong Kong and China.

????? Margaret River Chardonnay 2015 From Happs Vineyard in Karridale, matured for 10 months in new and used oak. The intensity of the fruit hits the mouth in the proverbial flash, and doesn't diminish thereafter. It hits the sweet spot between citrus/grapefruit on the one hand, stone fruit/white peach on the other. This is all about the cool southern end of Margaret River. A wine needing no elaboration. Screwcap. 12.5% alc. **Rating** 96 **To** 2030 $30 **O**
Margaret River Cabernet Sauvignon 2014 A lengthy sojourn in French barriques (50% new) has left an indelible mark on the wine, but the fruit has ultimately carried the day with its intensity and length, the tannins humbled by the long time in barrel. Screwcap. 14% alc. **Rating** 95 **To** 2029 $30 **O**
La Bratta Bianco 2014 Sauvignon blanc, semillon and chardonnay from Happs Vineyard at Karridale. The sauvignon blanc and semillon were part barrel-fermented, the chardonnay barrel-fermented, the components kept separate until blending and bottling. Bright, gleaming green-straw; a complex wine with good texture, structure and length to its mix of citrus/stone fruit flavours. Explains the challenging price for a classic dry white. Screwcap. 13.5% alc. **Rating** 94 **To** 2023 $40

????? La Bratta Rosso 2014 Rating 92 To 2024 $50
La Bratta Rosso 2009 Rating 92 To 2024 $50
Margaret River Sauvignon Blanc Semillon 2016 Rating 91 To 2018 $20 **O**
Touriga 2014 Rating 90 To 2021 $20 **O**

 # Artis Wines   ★★★★☆

7 Flora Street, Stepney, SA 5069 **Region** Clare Valley/Adelaide Hills
T 0418 802 495 **www.**artiswines.com.au **Open** Not
Winemaker Andrew Miller **Est.** 2016 **Dozens** 450
What do you do after decades working for one of the largest wine groups in Australia (Orlando/Pernod-Ricard)? You start your own very small wine business making 450 dozen bottles of Clare Valley Riesling and Adelaide Hills Shiraz. And in doing so, you call upon your experience gained over the years working in France, Spain, the US, NZ, Argentina and Portugal, coupled with travel to many more wine regions.

????? Single Vineyard Clare Valley Riesling 2016 Berry-sorted in the vineyard. Free-run juice was split into two parcels, the first cool-fermented in stainless steel, the second fermented in used French barriques without refrigeration, the two parcels blended and returned to oak for a few weeks on light lees. This complex vinification has invested the wine with an extra level of texture, but left lime-accented varietal expression untouched in a riesling bursting with flavour, savoury/briny nuances adding complexity. Screwcap. 11.9% alc. **Rating** 96 **To** 2026 $37 ✪

Artwine ★★★★

72 Bird in Hand Road, Woodside, SA 5244 **Region** Adelaide Hills/Clare Valley
T (08) 8389 9399 **www**.artwine.com.au **Open** 7 days 11–5
Winemaker Joanne Irvine, Mike Sykes **Est.** 1997 **Dozens** 6500 **Vyds** 28ha
Artwine is the venture of Judy and Glen Kelly. It has three vineyards, two in Clare Valley: one on Springfarm Rd, Clare, the other on Sawmill Rd, Sevenhill (the latter also has two B&B cottages). The third vineyard is in the Adelaide Hills at Woodside, which houses their cellar door. Artwine currently has 15 varieties planted. The Clare Valley vineyards have tempranillo, shiraz, riesling, pinot gris, cabernet sauvignon, fiano, graciano, grenache, montepulciano, viognier and cabernet franc. The Adelaide Hills vineyard has prosecco, pinot noir, merlot and albarino. Exports to Singapore.

ɣɣɣɣɣ **Glass Half Full Riesling 2016** An impressive Clare Valley riesling simply made. The kaffir lime and lemon flavours are focused by the crunchy dry finish. Screwcap. 11.5% alc. **Rating** 94 **To** 2026 $22 ✪
Wicked Stepmother Fiano 2016 Estate-grown, machine-harvested; after short skin contact, the pressings and free-run juice are combined before cold settling, then cool-fermented in stainless steel. Does end up with that mineral texture of fiano, coupled with lemon zest. Screwcap. 12.5% alc. **Rating** 92 **To** 2021 $25 ✪
Leave Your Hat On Montepulciano 2015 Estate-grown, matured in used French oak for 14 months. Deeply, densely coloured, and no less densely flavoured. It is far removed from normal montepulciano, filling the mouth with its Magimix blend of dark berries and plums in a mocha landscape. This interrogates all who come across its path. Screwcap. 14.5% alc. **Rating** 91 **To** 2030 $45
In the Groove Gruner Veltliner 2016 From the Adelaide Hills. Cool-fermented in stainless steel. White pepper aromas on the bouquet, the flavours then shifting backwards and forwards between savoury/skinsy citrus and stone fruit. Gruner veltliner is here to stay. Screwcap. 12.5% alc. **Rating** 90 **To** 2022 $25
Prosecco NV A crunchy and varietal prosecco of nashi pear and lemon fruit with hints of fennel. Cool Adelaide Hills acidity defines a fresh and primary style, completed with well integrated, nicely balanced dosage. It finishes short and simple, but meets the easy-drinking prosecco brief confidently. Crown seal. 11% alc. **Rating** 90 **To** 2017 $25 TS

Arundel Farm Estate ★★★★

321 Arundel Road, Keilor, Vic 3036 **Region** Sunbury
T (03) 9338 9987 **www**.arundelfarmestate.com.au **Open** W'ends 10–5
Winemaker Mark Matthews, Claude Ceccomancini **Est.** 1984 **Dozens** 2000 **Vyds** 7ha
The first stage of the vineyard in 1984 was 0.8ha of shiraz and cabernet sauvignon. Rick Kinzbrunner of Giaconda made the first vintage in 1988 and for some years thereafter, but the enterprise lapsed until it was revived with new plantings in '96 and 2000. Today it is planted solely to shiraz and viognier. In October '11 Claude and Sandra Ceccomancini acquired the business and appointed Mark Matthews as winemaker.

ɣɣɣɣɣ **Sunbury Shiraz 2015** Hand-picked, 10% whole bunches and 1% viognier included, open-fermented, 20% completing fermentation in used French oak, 40% pressed off at the end of the ferment, 40% given 2 weeks post-ferment maceration, matured for 20 months. A surprisingly full-bodied shiraz, loaded with black fruits, licorice, spice and earth, ripe tannins a major contributor. Has the balance to justify the long-term cellaring needed for the wine to show its best. Screwcap. 14.5% alc. **Rating** 94 **To** 2040 $25 ✪

ɣɣɣɣɣ **Sunbury Viognier 2015 Rating** 91 **To** 2018 $25

Ashbrook Estate

379 Tom Cullity Drive, Wilyabrup, WA 6280 **Region** Margaret River
T (08) 9755 6262 **www**.ashbrookwines.com.au **Open** 7 days 10–5
Winemaker Catherine Edwards, Brian Devitt **Est.** 1975 **Dozens** 12500 **Vyds** 17.4ha
This fastidious producer of consistently excellent estate-grown table wines shuns publicity
and is less well known than is deserved, selling much of its wine through the cellar door and
to a loyal mailing list clientele. It is very much a family affair: Brian Devitt is at the helm,
winemaking is by his daughter Catherine, and viticulture by son Richard (also a qualified
winemaker). Exports to the US, Canada, Germany, Indonesia, Japan, Singapore, Hong Kong
and China.

♀♀♀♀♀ **Reserve Margaret River Chardonnay 2014** Hand-picked over 6 days.
Racked into new French barriques of various toast levels, rested on undisturbed
lees for 8 months, no mlf. Takes the elements of the standard chardonnay up to the
next level of complexity and power. No denying the supercharged oak influence,
but the depth and breadth of fruit matches it. Imposing. Needs time. Screwcap.
14% alc. **Rating** 96 **To** 2025 $65 SC ○
Margaret River Chardonnay 2015 The richly flavoured Mendoza clone makes
its presence felt, as does the spicy oak, but unequivocal varietal character is at the
heart of it. No mlf or battonage plays a part in enhancing that. Grapefruit, white-
fleshed stone fruit and green melon aromas and flavours are the drivers, the texture
and palate-extending acidity providing the ideal structure. Screwcap. 13.6% alc.
Rating 95 **To** 2022 $32 SC ○
Margaret River Cabernet Sauvignon Merlot 2013 2 years maturation in
premium French oak barriques. A real fragrance here, perhaps the petit verdot
(7%) and cabernet franc (6%) having their way. Underlying that is unmistakably
cedary, bay leaf–infused regional cabernet (77%) character and ripe red-berry
merlot (10%), all held within an elegant, finely framed oak and grape tannin
structure. Screwcap. 14.5% alc. **Rating** 94 **To** 2027 $30 SC ○

♀♀♀♀♀ **Margaret River Shiraz 2013 Rating** 93 **To** 2025 $30 SC
Reserve Cabernet Sauvignon 2013 Rating 93 **To** 2029 $65 SC
Margaret River Semillon 2016 Rating 92 **To** 2025 $25 SC ○
Margaret River Sauvignon Blanc 2016 Rating 91 **To** 2017 $25 SC

Ashton Hills

Tregarthen Road, Ashton, SA 5137 **Region** Adelaide Hills
T (08) 8390 1243 **www**.ashtonhills.com.au **Open** Sat–Mon 11–5
Winemaker Stephen George, Paul Smith **Est.** 1982 **Dozens** 1500 **Vyds** 3ha
Stephen George made Ashton Hills one of the great producers of Pinot Noir in Australia, and
by some distance the best in the Adelaide Hills. With no family succession in place, he sold the
business to Wirra Wirra in April 2015. It had been rumoured for some time that he (Stephen)
was considering such a move, so when it was announced, there was a sigh of relief that it
should pass to a business such as Wirra Wirra, with undoubted commitment to retaining the
extraordinary quality of the wines. Stephen will continue to live in the house on the property,
and provide ongoing consulting advice. Exports to the US, Hong Kong and China.

♀♀♀♀♀ **Reserve Pinot Noir 2015** 50% from the oldest (33yo) estate vines with three of
the five preferred clones (D5V12, Martini and 777) contributing, 33% matured in
new French oak. Has great colour, and the bouquet fills the senses with the first
whiff, spices leading the way, then the full cavalcade following on the palate: earth,
forest, plum, dark cherry, oak and fine but persistent tannins, all in play. Screwcap.
14.5% alc. **Rating** 98 **To** 2035 $70 ○
Piccadilly Valley Pinot Noir 2015 From the estate and adjacent Cemetery
Vineyard, matured in used French barriques. Good colour, both hue and depth;
may be the earliest harvest on record, but it certainly hasn't diminished the typicity
and/or quality of this distinguished producer. Dark cherry, plum, spices of all kinds

and savoury forest notes all slide sinuously through and around each other. This was a great vintage for Ashton Hills. Screwcap. 14% alc. **Rating** 97 **To** 2035 $35 ○

ⵚⵚⵚⵚⵚ Riesling 2016 Stephen George's reluctance to remove his riesling and replace it with pinot noir is easy to understand when you taste each release of the Riesling. Fully mature vines, and the site, produce a wine that, within its class, has the complexity, length, balance and varietal purity at the same level as his exalted Pinot Noirs. This is a great wine. Screwcap. 13% alc. **Rating** 96 **To** 2036 $30 ○
Clare Valley Sparkling Shiraz 2009 The old vines of Wendouree, half planted in 1919, bring an integrity, a finely mineral tannin structure and a savoury fruit presence that define one of Australia's greatest sparkling reds. Black plum, black cherry and even strawberry fruit of medium-bodied restraint are underlined by magnificently toned and effortlessly harmonious structure that speaks of the calm confidence of these grand old vines. Magnificent. Crown seal. 13.5% alc. **Rating** 96 **To** 2024 $45 TS ○
Estate Pinot Noir 2015 Matured in French oak. The two Martini clones of the five estate clones contributed almost 50% of the wine. The garnet-red hue introduces a wine with the distinctive complexity of the Adelaide Hills, with savoury/earthy/spicy overtones to the plummy fruit. The question is whether it is more advanced than it should be. Screwcap. 14% alc. **Rating** 94 **To** 2026 $45

Atlas Wines   ★★★★★

PO Box 458, Clare, SA 5453 **Region** Clare Valley
T 0419 847 491 **www**.atlaswines.com.au **Open** Not
Winemaker Adam Barton **Est.** 2008 **Dozens** 3000 **Vyds** 8ha
Owner and winemaker Adam Barton had an extensive winemaking career before establishing Atlas Wines: in McLaren Vale, the Barossa Valley, Coonawarra, the iconic Bonny Doon Vineyard in California and, most recently, at Reillys Wines in the Clare Valley. He has 6ha of shiraz and 2ha of cabernet sauvignon grown on a stony ridge on the eastern slopes of the region, and sources small batches from other distinguished sites in the Clare and Barossa valleys. The quality of the wines is extraordinarily good and extraordinarily consistent. Exports to Canada, Singapore, Hong Kong and China.

ⵚⵚⵚⵚⵚ 172° Watervale Riesling 2016 Fine and tightly structured with citrus blossom aromas, lime, lemon and Granny Smith apple, lengthened by crisp, minerally acidity. Precision engineering. Screwcap. 11.5% alc. **Rating** 95 **To** 2029 $30 ○
429° Clare Valley Shiraz 2015 Hand-picked, single vineyard, single batches from the White Hut district, then a barrel selection. Unreservedly full-bodied, with the blackest of black fruits, licorice, tar and earthy palisades protecting the power against all comers for years to come. Screwcap. 14.5% alc. **Rating** 94 **To** 2035 $43

ⵚⵚⵚⵚⵚ Clare Valley Shiraz 2015 Rating 92 **To** 2030 $27
The Spaniard 2015 Rating 90 **To** 2023 $27

Attwoods Wines   ★★★★★

45 Attwoods Road, Scotsburn, Vic 3352 **Region** Geelong
T 0407 906 849 **www**.attwoodswines.com.au **Open** Not
Winemaker Troy Walsh **Est.** 2010 **Dozens** 650 **Vyds** 2ha
Australian-born and educated winemaker and owner Troy Walsh began his journey into wine as a sommelier in London for 12 years (1990–2002), working his way up to some of the most exalted restaurants. In 2010 he followed the Flying Winemaker path of vintages in Australia and France each year. He also quickly ran his colours up the mast by focusing on pinot noir and chardonnay in Burgundy and Geelong. The wineries he worked with here and in France all used whole bunch fermentation as a significant part of the vinification process, and he uses the practice to a greater or lesser degree in most of his wines. Initially all of the grapes were contract-grown, and Troy continues to purchase grapes from two vineyards near Bannockburn. In 2010 Troy and wife Jane purchased an 18ha property 20km south of Ballarat, and moved the family from Melbourne, establishing a 1.5ha ultra-high density (1m × 1.2m spacing)

planting of pinot noir (MV6, 777 and Pommard) and 0.5ha of chardonnay. Attwoods also leases a 20yo vineyard at Garibaldi planted to 0.5ha each of pinot noir and chardonnay.

ŸŸŸŸŸ **Old Hog Geelong Chardonnay 2015** Pale, bright green-gold; there is a pattern of generosity and supple mouthfeel across all the Attwoods wines: where it comes from, with a starting gun of 12.8% alcohol, I don't know, but I certainly applaud it. Within the viscous white peach and nectarine exterior there's a laser beam of pink grapefruit, oak thereabouts. Cork. 12.8% alc. **Rating** 96 **To** 2025 $45 ✪
Le Sanglier Geelong Shiraz 2013 Slightly turbid colour, but the hue is good; a complex, but complete, medium-bodied shiraz with a spicy/peppery web behind the black cherry fruit, the loop ultimately closed by the generous use of high quality oak, integration the key. You might think this is all too much, but the finish is so mouthwatering and fresh. The answer lies in the alcohol of 13.2%. Diam. **Rating** 96 **To** 2030 $54 ✪

ŸŸŸŸŸ **Old Hog Geelong Pinot Noir 2015 Rating** 93 **To** 2018 $54

Atze's Corner Wines   ★★★★☆

Box 81, Nuriootpa, SA 5355 **Region** Barossa Valley
T 0407 621 989 **www**.atzescornerwines.com.au **Open** By appt
Winemaker Contract, Andrew Kalleske **Est.** 2005 **Dozens** 2000 **Vyds** 30ha
The seemingly numerous members of the Kalleske family have widespread involvement in grapegrowing and winemaking in the Barossa Valley. This venture is that of Andrew Kalleske, son of John and Barb Kalleske. In 1975 they purchased the Atze Vineyard, which included a small block of shiraz planted in '12, but with additional plantings along the way, including more shiraz in '51. Andrew purchases some grapes from the family vineyard. It has 20ha of shiraz, with small amounts of mataro, petit verdot, grenache, cabernet, tempranillo, viognier, petite sirah, graciano, montepulciano, vermentino and aglianico. The wines are all estate-grown and made in the onsite winery. Exports to the US.

ŸŸŸŸŸ **Eddies Old Vine Barossa Valley Shiraz 2015** Sourced from three vineyards planted in 1912, '51 and '75, each parcel popped into 25% new French and American oak, the remainder into hogsheads for 21 months. Everything integrated, but by no means a wallflower. Impenetrable black-red; dense, expansive tannins with ripe sweet fruit almost too sweet; hints of menthol, red licorice and chocolate. Cork. 15% alc. **Rating** 94 **To** 2031 $60 JF

ŸŸŸŸŸ **The Mob Barossa Valley Montepulciano 2015 Rating** 92 **To** 2021 $30 JF
The Bachelor Barossa Valley Shiraz 2015 Rating 91 **To** 2028 $30 JF
A Label Barossa Valley Vermentino 2016 Rating 90 **To** 2018 $25 JF

Audrey Wilkinson   ★★★★★

750 De Beyers Road, Pokolbin, NSW 2320 **Region** Hunter Valley
T (02) 4998 1866 **www**.audreywilkinson.com.au **Open** 7 days 10–5
Winemaker Jeff Byrne, Xanthe Hatcher **Est.** 1866 **Dozens** 30 000 **Vyds** 35.33ha
One of the most historic properties in the Hunter Valley, set in a particularly beautiful location and with a very attractive cellar door, has been owned by Brian Agnew and family since 2004. The wines are made from estate-grown grapes, the lion's share shiraz, the remainder (in descending order) semillon, malbec, verdelho, tempranillo, merlot, cabernet sauvignon, muscat and traminer; the vines were planted from the 1970s to the '90s. Also has a 3.45ha McLaren Vale vineyard of merlot and shiraz. Exports to the UK, Canada and China.

ŸŸŸŸŸ **Winemakers Selection Hunter Valley Semillon 2016** The palest straw hue with subtle aromatics of citrus blossom, lemon-lime zest, freshly cut herbs and grass, even a wet-pebble fragrance. Chalky texture with superfine acidity straight down the middle gives rise to a thirst-quenching quality of lemon barley water. Screwcap. 11.5% alc. **Rating** 95 **To** 2035 $30 JF ✪

The Ridge Hunter Valley Semillon 2016 There's racy lemony acidity, of course, with lots of flavour: lime drops, fennel, fresh goat's curd, bath salts and talc. It has the power booster on for a racy finish. Looking rather smart now and for a few more years. Screwcap. 12% alc. **Rating** 95 To 2028 $45 JF

ŸŸŸŸŸ **Winemakers Selection Orange Arneis 2016** Rating 93 To 2020 $30 JF
Winemakers Selection Canberra Shiraz 2015 Rating 92 To 2025 $40 JF
Hunter Valley Semillon 2016 Rating 91 To 2025 $25 JF
The Oakdale Hunter Chardonnay 2016 Rating 91 To 2022 $45 JF
Winemakers Selection Orange Chardonnay 2016 Rating 90 To 2022 $35 JF
Winemakers Selection Hunter Chardonnay 2016 Rating 90 To 2022 $40 JF
Hunter Valley Shiraz 2015 Rating 90 To 2025 $25 JF
Winemakers Selection Hunter Malbec 2016 Rating 90 To 2025 $65 JF
Winemakers Selection Blanc de Blanc 2013 Rating 90 To 2017 $40 TS

Austins & Co.

870 Steiglitz Road, Sutherlands Creek, Vic 3331 **Region** Geelong
T (03) 5281 1799 **www**.austinsandco.com.au **Open** By appt
Winemaker John Durham **Est.** 1982 **Dozens** 20 000 **Vyds** 61.5ha
Pamela and Richard Austin have quietly built their business from a tiny base, and it has flourished. The vineyard has been progressively extended to over 60ha. Son Scott (with a varied but successful career outside the wine industry) took over management and ownership in 2008. The quality of the wines is admirable. Exports to the UK, Canada, Hong Kong, Japan and China.

ŸŸŸŸŸ **Custom Collection Ellyse Chardonnay 2015** Named after the first grandchild of Pam and Richard Austin, Ellyse is made only in the best vintages. Fermented in French oak, a barrel selection made after 9 months. This is an exceptionally good chardonnay with clarity of expression, and even greater intensity and drive to its fusion of white peach, nectarine and pink grapefruit. Given its balance and wealth of fruit, it has no need for active French oak support, but of course it was barrel-fermented. Screwcap. 13% alc. **Rating** 97 To 2029 $60 ✪

ŸŸŸŸŸ **Greenbanks Geelong Pinot Noir 2015** The grapes are destemmed but not crushed, a warm ferment initiated with wild yeast, finishing with cultured yeast, matured in old puncheons for 9 months. Complex and compelling with more savoury whole-bunch characters than the vinification would suggest, characters that make the wine so satisfying, for there is a wealth of juicy red fruits that run right through to the finish. Screwcap. 13.5% alc. **Rating** 96 To 2028 $35 ✪
Custom Collection Spencer Geelong Shiraz 2015 The highest quality fruit selected, hand-picked and further sorted in the winery, wild-fermented in a 3t open fermenter, matured for 15 months in a thick-staved 500ml puncheon and an 800l concrete egg. The deep crimson-purple hue stands out; a full-bodied wine of complexity, intensity and balance; blackberry, cracked black pepper, spices and licorice soar across the bouquet and palate. The puncheon has contributed an identifiable addition of cedar, the egg working with texture, not flavour. Screwcap. 14.5% alc. **Rating** 96 To 2040 $60 ✪
Geelong Chardonnay 2015 19yo vines, hand-picked, whole-bunch pressed, wild-fermented in French oak (30% new), matured on lees for 10 months. A complex, rich, multilayered chardonnay with a full suite of stone fruit flavours balanced by citrussy acidity on its long and satisfying palate. Screwcap. 13% alc. **Rating** 95 To 2023 $35 ✪
Geelong Pinot Noir 2015 Has the X-factor that 6Ft6 lacks. The clear, bright colour introduces a bouquet with notes of spice and forest floor woven through the lively and long palate with plum, red cherry and sour cherry fruits liberally doused with spices. Screwcap. 13.5% alc. **Rating** 95 To 2025 $35 ✪

Custom Collection Ruby May Geelong Pinot Noir 2014 Hand-picked, chilled overnight, mostly destemmed, not crushed, 33% whole bunches, 4 days cold soak, open-fermented, plunged thrice daily, matured in French oak (33% new) for 12 months. Unexpectedly, the whole-bunch component provided the fleshy red fruits needed to provide balance and mid-palate vinosity. Complexity is a given, as is the length of the palate. Screwcap. 12.5% alc. **Rating** 95 **To** 2025 $60

Geelong Shiraz 2015 Hand-picked, destemmed, open-fermented, 15% whole bunches, matured in mostly used French oak for 12 months. Has the extreme power of its 6Ft6 sibling, but polishes the raw edges with the help of the whole-bunch inclusion and the quality of the fruit selection. If you are looking for the balance to provide a full-bodied shiraz that can be drunk now, the spicy elements and fractionally softer tannins of this wine should do the trick. Screwcap. 14.5% alc. **Rating** 95 **To** 2040 $35 ✪

6Ft6 Geelong Shiraz 2014 A rich, intensely flavoured full-bodied wine that takes cool climate shiraz into another dimension. Wonderfully spicy, its black-berried fruit flavours link with licorice and cracked pepper, the end result an unexpected freshness and elegance. Warm-grown shiraz can be wonderful, but will always be different from cool-grown. Screwcap. 14.5% alc. **Rating** 95 **To** 2034 $25 ✪

🍷🍷🍷🍷½ **6Ft6 Geelong Pinot Noir Rose 2016** **Rating** 92 **To** 2018 $25 ✪
6Ft6 Geelong Pinot Noir 2014 **Rating** 92 **To** 2022 $25 SC ✪
6Ft6 Geelong Shiraz 2015 **Rating** 92 **To** 2030 $25 ✪
6Ft6 Geelong Pinot Noir 2015 **Rating** 91 **To** 2023 $25
Greenbanks Geelong Pinot Noir 2014 **Rating** 91 **To** 2023 $35
Geelong Riesling 2016 **Rating** 90 **To** 2021 $25
6Ft6 Geelong Sauvignon Blanc 2015 **Rating** 90 **To** 2018 $25
6Ft6 King Valley Geelong Pinot Gris 2016 **Rating** 90 **To** 2018 $25
Geelong Pinot Noir 2014 **Rating** 90 **To** 2022 $35
Custom Collection Geelong Pinot Noir 2014 **Rating** 90 **To** 2023 $60

Auswan Creek ★★★★

218 Murray Street, Tanunda, SA 5352 **Region** Barossa Valley
T (02) 8203 2239 **www**.auswancreek.com.au **Open** Wed–Sun 10–5
Winemaker Ben Riggs **Est.** 2008 **Dozens** 30 000 **Vyds** 12ha

The Swan Wine Group was formed through the merger of Inspire Vintage and Australia Swan Vintage. The jewel in the business is a 10ha vineyard in Angaston, with 1.7ha of shiraz planted in 1908, 0.86ha planted in the '60s, 5.43ha of younger shiraz, topped up with 1.76ha of cabernet sauvignon and 1.26ha of grenache. The 2ha cellar door and winery vineyard in Tanunda provide the home base. The major part of the production comes from grapes purchased from growers across SA. The focus is exports to Singapore, Thailand and China.

🍷🍷🍷🍷½ **Peacock Reserve McLaren Vale Shiraz 2014** As saturated and inky as any table wine can be – no light pierces the colour; the extract is as formidable as the colour suggests, taking the wine to unknown territory: Clarendon Hills, Torbreck, Two Hands, Warrabilla – all kneel. Bitter chocolate, licorice, sticks and stones. Ready to drink 30+ years from vintage. Cork. **Rating** 92 **To** 2044 $80

🍷🍷🍷🍷 **Governor Selection Barossa Valley Cabernet Shiraz 2014** **Rating** 89 **To** 2024 $69

Avani ★★★★

98 Stanleys Road, Red Hill South, Vic 3937 **Region** Mornington Peninsula
T (03) 5989 2646 **www**.avanisyrah.com.au **Open** By appt
Winemaker Shashi Singh **Est.** 1987 **Dozens** 400 **Vyds** 4ha

Avani is the venture of Shashi and Devendra Singh, who have owned and operated restaurants on the Mornington Peninsula for over 25 years. This inevitably led to an interest in wine, but there was nothing inevitable about taking the plunge in 1998 and purchasing an established vineyard, Wildcroft Estate. Shashi enrolled in viticulture at CSU, but moved across to the wine science degree course. Phillip Jones began making the Avani wines in 2000, and in '04 Shashi began working at Bass Phillip, her role in the winery steadily increasing. Changes to the vineyard increased the planting density to 4000 vines per hectare, and reduced the cropping level to a little over 1 tonne per acre. There was a move to organic in '05, and thereafter to biodynamic practices in the vineyard. Even more radical was the decision to convert the existing plantings of five varieties to 100% shiraz. Shashi took total control of making the Avani wines at Phillip's Leongatha winery in '09, and in '12 they established their small onsite winery.

🍷🍷🍷🍷🍷 **Amrit Pinot Gris 2016** No sign of the oxidation that destroyed its Chardonnay sibling, and is indeed a very attractive pinot gris, whole-bunch pressed, barrel-fermented and matured on lees for 7 months. It is gloriously juicy, with the flavours extending from pear to stone fruits. Exceptional given its low alcohol. Diam. 12.3% alc. **Rating** 94 **To** 2020 $35

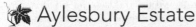 ## Aylesbury Estate

RMB 240, Ferguson, WA 6236 **Region** Geographe
T (08) 9728 3020 **www.**aylesburyestate.com.au **Open** Not
Winemaker Luke Eckersley, Coby Ladwig **Est.** 2015 **Dozens** 3500 **Vyds** 8.7ha
Ryan and Narelle Gibbs (and family) are the sixth generation of the pioneering Gibbs family in the Ferguson Valley. When the family first arrived in 1883, they named the farm Aylesbury, after the town in England whence they came. For generations the family ran cattle on the 200ha property, but in 1998 it was decided to plant 4.2ha of cabernet sauvignon as a diversification of the business. 2.5ha of merlot followed in '01, and 1.6ha of sauvignon blanc in '04. In '08 Ryan and Narelle took over ownership and management of the business from his father, selling the grapes until '15, when the first Aylesbury Estate wines were made.

🍷🍷🍷🍷🍷 **Waterfall Gully Ferguson Valley Sauvignon Blanc 2016** No frills – machine-harvested, cool-fermented with cultured yeast. So it's all from the vineyard, and there's plenty of flavour and mouthfeel as it ventures from tropical fruits into stone fruit territory. A touch more acidity might have transformed the wine. Screwcap. 12.5% alc. **Rating** 90 **To** 2018 $25

🍷🍷🍷🍷 **Waterfall Gully Cabernet Merlot 2015** **Rating** 89 **To** 2025 $25

BackVintage Wines

2/177 Sailors Bay Road, Northbridge, NSW 2063 **Region** Various
T (02) 9967 9880 **www.**backvintage.com.au **Open** Mon–Fri 9–5
Winemaker Julian Todd, Nick Bulleid MW, Mike Farmilo **Est.** 2003 **Dozens** 10 000
BackVintage Wines is a virtual winery in the fullest sense; not only does it not own vineyards, nor a winery, but also it sells only through its website or by phone. The winemaking team sources parcels of bulk or bottled wines it considers excellent quality and value for money, and is then responsible for the final steps before the wine goes to bottle. The value for money offered by these wines is self-evident, and quite remarkable.

🍷🍷🍷🍷🍷 **Tumbarumba Chardonnay 2015** A sophisticated chardonnay for the price with melon, sapid stone fruit flavours and and a bolt of citrus, all woven around a core of creamy cashew. Light weight in all and driven fairly long by Tumbarumba's altitudinal acidity. Screwcap. 12.7% alc. **Rating** 91 **To** 2022 $17 NG ✪
Adelaide Hills Pinot Gris 2016 Gris' baked apple, nashi pear and bitter almond are set alight by a perky dollop of riesling (8%), providing considerably more riesling friskiness than one would think: a nervy backbone supporting a core of lime. A successful style. Screwcap. 12.5% alc. **Rating** 90 **To** 2020 $13 NG ✪
Langhorne Creek Shiraz 2013 Straightforward warm climate shiraz blazing on all cylinders. Expect a cascade of dark fruits before a lick of reductive camphor and a wee tannic jolt from the addition of 6% cabernet sauvignon. 4% grenache rounds out the package. Screwcap. 14.4% alc. **Rating** 90 **To** 2028 $13 NG ✪

🍷🍷🍷🍷 **Block 8 McLaren Vale Shiraz 2014** **Rating** 89 **To** 2019 $13 NG ✪

Badger's Brook

874 Maroondah Highway, Coldstream, Vic 3770 **Region** Yarra Valley
T (03) 5962 4130 **www.**badgersbrook.com.au **Open** Wed–Sun 11–5
Winemaker Michael Warren, Gary Baldwin (Consultant) **Est.** 1993 **Dozens** 2500
Vyds 4.8ha
Situated next door to the well known Rochford, the vineyard is planted to chardonnay,
sauvignon blanc, pinot noir, shiraz (1ha each), cabernet sauvignon (0.35ha), merlot, viognier
(0.2ha each), with a few rows each of roussanne, marsanne and tempranillo. The Badger's
Brook wines, made onsite since 2012, are 100% estate-grown; the second Storm Ridge label
uses only Yarra Valley grapes. Also houses the Tramonto Kitchen & Bar. Exports to Asia.

ŶŶŶŶŶ **Yarra Valley Shiraz 2015** 15 months in French oak, 25% new. Things to like
about this wine: blood plum, licorice and woody, peppery spice (if such a thing
exists) on the bouquet, supple and juicy on the palate. The black and red fruit
flavours have energy and life, although it's essentially elegant and just medium-
weight, oak and tannin in balance. Screwcap. 13.5% alc. **Rating** 92 **To** 2025
$25 SC ✪
Yarra Valley Viognier Roussanne Marsanne 2015 An 85/7.5/7.5% estate-
grown blend. The flavours and structure are very similar to those of the '16; once
again, the viognier varietal character is plain to see, with apricot and tropical
nuances balanced and lengthened by the roussanne and marsanne, the latter
possibly the contributor of a brief spark of honeysuckle. Developing slowly and
surely. Screwcap. 13% alc. **Rating** 91 **To** 2019 $22 ✪
Yarra Valley Viognier Roussanne Marsanne 2016 A 90/5/5% blend.
Interesting: the back label says the wine is medium dry, but the residual sugar is
far from obvious. What is obvious is the apricot/stone fruit varietal flavours of
viognier, the roussanne and marsanne serving to provide a crisp, not oily, finish.
Screwcap. 13% alc. **Rating** 90 **To** 2018 $22
Yarra Valley Pinot Noir 2015 Estate-grown, mixed clones, hand-picked. Shows
a good array of varietal aromas, with sour cherry, cranberry and smoky spice in
the mix; a hint of vanilla is an oak influence. Lacks a little light and shade on the
palate, although there's sufficient depth and length of flavour for an easy pass mark.
Sappy tannins give the wine an appropriate, lightly astringent finish. Screwcap.
13% alc. **Rating** 90 **To** 2022 $28 SC
Yarra Valley Tempranillo 2015 Estate-grown, hand-picked, lots of whole
bunches included in the ferment, matured in French oak. A well made wine with
no issues from the use of so much whole bunches. It is medium-bodied, with
red and black cherry to the fore, and an airbrush of fine tannins on the finish.
Screwcap. 13.5% alc. **Rating** 90 **To** 2025 $28

ŶŶŶŶ **Yarra Valley Chardonnay 2016 Rating** 89 **To** 2020 $25 SC
Storm Ridge Yarra Valley Pinot Noir 2015 Rating 89 **To** 2022 $20
Yarra Valley Cabernet Sauvignon 2014 Rating 89 **To** 2029 $25

Baie Wines

120 McDermott Road, Curlewis, Vic 3222 **Region** Geelong
T 0400 220 436 **www.**baiewines.com.au **Open** By appt
Winemaker Robin Brockett **Est.** 2000 **Dozens** 2000 **Vyds** 6ha
Takes its name from the farming property Baie Park, owned by the Kuc family (headed by
Anne and Peter) for decades. In 2000 they established 2ha each of sauvignon blanc, pinot gris
and shiraz, the first vintage following in '06. The vineyard is planted on north-facing slopes
running down to the shore of Port Phillip Bay; the maritime influence is profound. Patriarch
Peter is a GP, used to working long hours and with attention to detail, and he and agriculturist
son Simon are responsible for the viticulture. Anne greets visitors at the waterfront estate, and
Simon's wife Nadine is the marketing force behind the business.

ŶŶŶŶŶ **Bellarine Peninsula Shiraz 2015** Harnesses a cool climate disposition of violet
florals, blueberry, tapenade, pepper grind, smoked meat and a ferrous iodine note
to a lustrous, smooth sheen. The acidity is bright, running from head to tail; the

tannins tightly massaged and gently tactile. The overall impression is of polish and class. Screwcap. 14% alc. **Rating** 95 **To** 2022 $30 NG ✪

🍷🍷🍷🍷 **Bellarine Peninsula Pinot Gris 2016** Rating 92 To 2019 $25 NG ✪
Bellarine Peninsula Rose 2016 Rating 90 To 2018 $25 NG

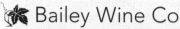

Bailey Wine Co ★★★★

PO Box 368, Penola, SA 5277 **Region** Coonawarra
T 0417 818 539 **www**.baileywineco.com **Open** Not
Winemaker Tim Bailey **Est.** 2015 **Dozens** 400
After 20 years living and working in Coonawarra, Tim (and Lucille) Bailey decided to take a busman's holiday by establishing their own small wine business. Tim's day job is winemaker at Leconfield, but he has also worked in the Sonoma Valley of California, and travelled through the Napa Valley as well as France. Tim and Lucille say they have a simple philosophy: 'Find great growers in the regions we love and let the vineyard shine through in the bottle.' Thus they sourced Clare Valley riesling and Grampians shiraz in 2016, and Adelaide Hills chardonnay and Coonawarra cabernet sauvignon for '17.

🍷🍷🍷🍷 **Bryksy Vineyard Watervale Riesling 2016** The floral bouquet is followed by citrus and apple blossom aromas, the palate tighter and crisper than the bouquet would suggest, its acidity accentuated by livewire acidity. This is a work in progress, guaranteed to burst into song by '21, and live much longer than that. Screwcap. 11% alc. **Rating** 93 **To** 2031 $25 ✪

Baileys of Glenrowan ★★★★★

779 Taminick Gap Road, Glenrowan, Vic 3675 **Region** Glenrowan
T (03) 5766 1600 **www**.baileysofglenrowan.com.au **Open** 7 days 10–5
Winemaker Paul Dahlenburg **Est.** 1870 **Dozens** 15 000 **Vyds** 143ha
Just when it seemed that Baileys would remain one of the forgotten outposts of the TWE group, the reverse has occurred. Since 1998 the utterly committed Paul Dahlenburg has been in charge of Baileys and has overseen an expansion in the vineyard and the construction of a 2000-tonne capacity winery. The cellar door has a heritage museum, winery viewing deck, contemporary art gallery and landscaped grounds, preserving much of the heritage value. Baileys has also picked up the pace with its Muscat and Tokay, reintroducing the Winemaker's Selection at the top of the tree, while continuing the larger-volume Founder series.

🍷🍷🍷🍷 **Winemakers Selection Rare Old Muscat NV** Dark mahogany; essence of raisins and a whisper of orange blossom; it has flavour and texture intensity and complexity even beyond that of the Rare Topaque; all the spices in Arabia, Christmas pudding, and cognac-soaked plums. Despite all this, has the essential freshness to cleanse the gloriously long finish and vibrating aftertaste. 375ml. Cork. 17.5% alc. **Rating** 98 $75 ✪
Winemakers Selection Rare Old Topaque NV The extreme age is obvious from the colour, with its olive rim; the bouquet is voluminous and intensely complex, the palate incredibly luscious and complex, with multi-spice, mandarin zest, tea leaf, and Callard & Bowser butterscotch flavours; the palate is like velvet, the rancio and spirit there but not excessive. A micro-sip avoided the obscenity of spitting it out when making this note. 375ml. Cork. 17.5% alc. **Rating** 97 $75 ✪

🍷🍷🍷🍷 **Organic Shiraz 2015** Small wonder this wine caused my tastebuds to suggest there was something special (and unusual) about it. The answer came by reading the back label, which specified 25% whole bunches, 2% muscadelle and maturation in French hogsheads and one large vat. It is elegant, positively sprightly, with a melody of purple and black fruits, the tannins superfine and the finish very long. Screwcap. 14% alc. **Rating** 96 **To** 2030 $28 ✪
Founder Series Classic Topaque NV Amber with a slight grading to light olive on the rim proclaiming its age; abundant flavour, with Christmas cake, singed toffee and abundant spice; the long finish is well balanced, although the sweetness

continues to the mid-palate, until rancio helps dry the finish. Great care at Baileys is being taken to maintain the quality and style of this wine, and this is as great a bargain as any wine on the market today. Vino-Lok. 17% alc. **Rating** 95 $30 ✪
Founder Series Classic Muscat NV The colour has developed past any hint of red (darker and deeper than the Topaque); a good example of the more elegant style that Paul Dahlenburg is seeking to make, with a perfumed rose petal and spice bouquet; the palate is positively elegant, without sacrificing fruit intensity or the lusciously sweet, raisined flavour; the spirit is part of the answer, also blending decisions. Great value. Three gold medals and Winestate Magazine Trophy for Best Fortified Wine of the Year '15. Vino-Lok. 17% alc. **Rating** 95 $30 ✪

♀♀♀♀♀ **Durif 2015 Rating** 92 **To** 2028 $28 SC
Shiraz 2015 Rating 91 **To** 2030 $28 SC
Petite Sirah 2015 Rating 90 **To** 2030 $28 SC

Baillieu Vineyard ★★★★★

32 Tubbarubba Road, Merricks North, Vic 3926 **Region** Mornington Peninsula
T (03) 5989 7622 www.baillieuvineyard.com.au **Open** At Merricks General Wine Store
Winemaker Geraldine McFaul **Est.** 1999 **Dozens** 2500 **Vyds** 9.2ha
Charlie and Samantha Baillieu have re-established the former Foxwood Vineyard, growing chardonnay, viognier, pinot gris, pinot noir and shiraz. The north-facing vineyard is part of the 64ha Bulldog Run property owned by the Baillieus, and is immaculately maintained. The refurbished Merricks General Wine Store is a combined bistro/providore/cellar door.

♀♀♀♀♀ **Mornington Peninsula Viognier 2016** It's not often you taste a viognier with clearer fruit expression than this. It fills the mouth with apricot/apricot kernel flavours yet doesn't cloy or finish very short. Unexpected though it is, there are no doubts about its exceptional quality. Screwcap. 13.5% alc. **Rating** 95 **To** 2018 $25 ✪
Mornington Peninsula Pinot Noir 2015 Light crimson; the perfumed bouquet promises – and delivers – delicious red fruits of all kinds. A great vintage, and the wine has uncommon drive and length. Always pretty, this takes the step up to the top echelon, promising further rewards to those who don't consume all their bottles in a hurry. Screwcap. 13% alc. **Rating** 95 **To** 2023 $35 ✪
Mornington Peninsula Shiraz 2015 Its deep, vibrant colour semaphores a shiraz that reflects the cool site, the exceptional '15 vintage, and skilled winemaking. It has a surfeit of spicy dark cherry and plum fruit, all the tannins one could wish for, and a long, well balanced finish. Still in its youth, of course, and with a rosy future. Screwcap. 13% alc. **Rating** 95 **To** 2035 $35 ✪
Mornington Peninsula Rose 2016 Estate-grown pinot noir and pinot meunier. This salmon-pink rose is a seriously good dry style filled with strawberry, spice and red cherry fruit. The flavours persist through to the aftertaste, augmented by light, citrussy acidity. Screwcap. 13.5% alc. **Rating** 94 **To** 2018 $25 ✪

♀♀♀♀♀ **Mornington Peninsula Chardonnay 2015 Rating** 93 **To** 2023 $35
Mornington Peninsula Pinot Gris 2016 Rating 92 **To** 2020 $30

Balgownie Estate ★★★★★

Hermitage Road, Maiden Gully, Vic 3551 **Region** Bendigo
T (03) 5449 6222 www.balgownieestatewines.com.au **Open** 7 days 11–5
Winemaker Tony Winspear **Est.** 1969 **Dozens** 15 000 **Vyds** 35.28ha
Balgownie Estate is the senior citizen of Bendigo, having celebrated its 40th vintage in 2012. A $3 million winery upgrade coincided with a doubling of the size of the vineyard. Balgownie Estate also has a cellar door in the Yarra Valley (Yarra Glen). The Yarra Valley operation fits in neatly with the Bendigo wines. Balgownie has the largest vineyard-based resort in the Yarra Valley, with over 65 rooms and a limited number of spa suites. In April '16 Chinese Interactive China Cultural Technology Investments purchased the Balgownie Bendigo and Yarra Valley operations for $29 million. Exports to the UK, the US, Canada, Fiji, Hong Kong, Singapore, China and NZ.

ΨΨΨΨΨ **Centre Block Bendigo Shiraz 2015** This is a looser knit single-site Bendigo shiraz than its brethren. The result is a choir of violet, iodine and blue fruits, lifted by a skein of white pepper melded to transparent acidity and moderate tannins. Slightly reduced, echoes the northern Rhône in its pointed, floral aromatics. Will age beautifully. Screwcap. 14.5% alc. **Rating** 96 **To** 2033 $55 NG **◐**

Old Vine Bendigo Shiraz 2014 A wine crafted from the best 12 rows of the original '69 plantings, aged for a longer period in oak. Graphite and licorella tension combine to give a pumice bite to the full-throttle notes of dark fruits and anise. The coffee-grind tannins are firmly embedded. Only time will tell, but this is a sumptuous show of force meeting regional style, rather than the compelling textural and aromatic study of the single block wines. Screwcap. 14.5% alc. **Rating** 95 **To** 2038 $120 NG

Yarra Valley Chardonnay 2015 Here awaits the soprano in the cooler Yarra dirt! Taut and tensile, the stone fruit melody strays more towards nectarine, juicy and tangy, as it punches its way across a palate decorated with high quality French oak and a leesy tension. Screwcap. 13.6% alc. **Rating** 94 **To** 2025 $45 NG

Railway Block Bendigo Shiraz 2015 The most concentrated of the single block Shiraz pillars, this leaves the lifted, floral aromatics behind in a journey to shiraz's world of spice: clove, anise, turmeric and black pepper. There are generous fruit flavours from the blue to black spectrum, yet the overall experience is one of energy, herb and power. Screwcap. 14.8% alc. **Rating** 94 **To** 2033 $55 NG

Rock Block Bendigo Shiraz 2015 This site is a tough position in which the vines struggle to embed their root system. The wine is a highly savoury blend of black olive and anise, impeccably balanced and sinuous, spiralling across the mouth as it tries to shed its firm carapace of moreish tannins and marked acidity. Screwcap. 14.5% alc. **Rating** 94 **To** 2035 $55 NG

ΨΨΨΨΨ **Bendigo Shiraz 2014** Rating 93 To 2034 $45 NG
Centre Block Bendigo Shiraz 2014 Rating 93 To 2032 $55 NG
Bendigo Chardonnay 2015 Rating 92 To 2022 $45 NG
Black Label Bendigo Cabernet Merlot 2014 Rating 91 To 2025 $25 NG
Bendigo Cabernet Sauvignon 2014 Rating 91 To 2028 $45 NG
Black Label Yarra Valley Chardonnay 2015 Rating 90 To 2021 $25 NG
Black Label Bendigo Shiraz 2015 Rating 90 To 2023 $25 NG

Ballandean Estate Wines ★★★★☆

Sundown Road, Ballandean, Qld 4382 **Region** Granite Belt
T (07) 4684 1226 **www**.ballandeanestate.com **Open** 7 days 9–5
Winemaker Dylan Rhymer, Angelo Puglisi **Est.** 1970 **Dozens** 12 000 **Vyds** 34.2ha
A rock of ages in the Granite Belt, owned by the ever-cheerful and charming Angelo Puglisi and wife Mary. Mary has introduced a gourmet food gallery at the cellar door, featuring foods produced by local food artisans as well as Greedy Me gourmet products made by Mary herself. 2012 was a stellar vintage for an energised Ballandean Estate, with smart new labels on a portfolio of excellent wines. Exports to Singapore, Taiwan and China.

ΨΨΨΨΨ **Limited Release Generation 3 2014** Except that this is the heaviest bottle, and that this is a blend of cabernet and shiraz, I know little about it, but believe it's a recognition of the three generations of the Puglisi family. It's a very good wine from a good Granite Belt vintage, the colour deep and clear, the blackcurrant/blackberry fruit duo working together very well, with no sign of jealousy. ProCork. **Rating** 95 **To** 2034 $69

ΨΨΨΨΨ **Opera Block Granite Belt Chardonnay 2015** Rating 91 To 2021 $30
Messing About Granite Belt Fiano 2016 Rating 90 To 2023 $30

Ballycroft Vineyard & Cellars ★★★★★

1 Adelaide Road, Greenock, SA 5360 **Region** Barossa Valley
T 0488 638 488 **www**.ballycroft.com **Open** 7 days 11–5
Winemaker Joseph Evans **Est.** 2005 **Dozens** 250 **Vyds** 3.5ha

This micro-business is owned by Joe and Sue Evans. Joe's life on the land started in 1984 and he later obtained a viticulture degree from Roseworthy. Between '92 and '99 he worked in various capacities at Rockford Wines, and since then at Greenock Creek Wines. Joe and Sue are a two-person band so would-be visitors to the cellar door would be wise to make an appointment for a personal tasting with one of them. Groups of up to eight people are welcome.

ŸŸŸŸŸ **Small Berry Barossa Valley Shiraz 2014** This is a ballsy wine that eschews the contemporary finesse card, yet is neither jammy nor hot. The alcohol is elevated and yet the confluence of molten dark fruit flavours, American oak and grape tannins is seamless. Miraculously poised and vinous, this has Greenock's turf stamped all over it. Reminiscent of Australian wine's Parker period in the late '90's? Some would say yes, for the worse. I say for the better. Screwcap. 14.7% alc. **Rating** 96 **To** 2035 $45 NG ✪

Small Berry Langhorne Creek Cabernet Sauvignon 2014 Despite the wine's corpulence and upfront high alcohol, cabernet's plume of tight-knit tannins, streak of spearmint and tobacco leaf, together with tangy cassis fruit, is in full regalia. Rather than an assault, the wine is a hedonistic free-flow across the palate, never straying into jam juice. The overall impression is one of unbridled richness. Screwcap. 15.6% alc. **Rating** 95 **To** 2038 $33 NG ✪

Small Berry New French Oak Langhorne Creek Cabernet Sauvignon 2014 The wine gushes with aromas of currant, spearmint and the cedar, vanilla and cinnamon spice of high quality, new French oak. After all, the wine has spent a whopping 28 months in the stuff, following an ambitious extraction regime of four pumpovers a day, for 10 days. While the immediate impression is one of … err … oak, the wine opens nicely over a day, suggesting that time in the cellar will reward those who like abundant fruit. A bit of a yeoman, yet amazingly balanced for the alcohol level. Cork. 15.6% alc. **Rating** 94 **To** 2038 $98 NG

Balnaves of Coonawarra   ★★★★★

15517 Riddoch Highway, Coonawarra, SA 5263 **Region** Coonawarra
T (08) 8737 2946 **www.**balnaves.com.au **Open** Mon–Fri 9–5, w'ends 12–5
Winemaker Pete Bissell **Est.** 1975 **Dozens** 9000 **Vyds** 74.33ha
Grapegrower, viticultural consultant and vigneron, Doug Balnaves has over 70ha of high quality estate vineyards. The wines are invariably excellent, often outstanding, notable for their supple mouthfeel, varietal integrity, balance and length; the tannins are always fine and ripe, the oak subtle and perfectly integrated. Coonawarra at its best. Exports to the UK, the US, Canada, Japan, Hong Kong and China.

ŸŸŸŸŸ **Chardonnay 2015** Pete Bissell gets chardonnay to a level unequalled by any other winemaker in the region. Hand-picked, whole-bunch pressed direct to Louis Latour barriques (20% new) for 45% wild and 55% cultured yeast fermentation, matured for 11 months on lees. Bissell nailed the harvest date of 20 Feb, posing the fruit between citrus and stone fruit, nougat, honey and creamy notes to come in the future. Screwcap. 13% alc. **Rating** 96 **To** 2025 $30 ✪

Cabernet Sauvignon 2015 Includes 2.7% petit verdot, matured for 18 months in French oak. This is classic Coonawarra cabernet with cassis, mulberry, mint and dried bay leaf coming together with fine, but firm, tannins to present an intense, earthy wine that doesn't even flick the needle of dead fruit/high alcohol. It thus has a certain austerity, of the kind you once found in classed growth Bordeaux from good vintages such as '70. Screwcap. 14.5% alc. **Rating** 96 **To** 2035 $40 ✪

The Tally Reserve Cabernet Sauvignon 2015 Hand-picked, a long maceration on skins, matured for 18 months in 66% new Chateau barriques. The highly expressive bouquet of cassis, mulberry and herbs married with oak feeds into a powerful palate where savoury tannins brook no argument about their purpose in life. They need petting and soothing for a minimum of 5 years before this comes back into the Balnaves family orbit. ProCork. 14% alc. **Rating** 96 **To** 2045 $90

Shiraz 2015 From the 41yo Paulownia Vineyard, matured for 18 months in French oak (35% new), immaculately made from quality estate grapes. The mix of plum, dark cherry and blackberry is only medium-bodied, but it has swallowed the oak with the ease that you will have in swallowing this wine. One of the style lighthouses in Coonawarra. Screwcap. 14% alc. **Rating** 95 **To** 2035 **$28** ✪
Cabernet Merlot 2015 A 90/10% blend from part of the oldest plantings ('76), matured for 15 months in French oak. Bright, crimson-purple; fruit flavours and tannin structure stake their respective claims from the outset, neither admitting defeat. Blackcurrant, mulberry and black olive flavours are in the red corner, ripe tannins from fruit and oak in the blue corner. This isn't a once-only prize fight; it will continue for many years. Screwcap. 14% alc. **Rating** 95 **To** 2035 **$28** ✪
The Blend 2015 60% merlot, 33% cabernet sauvignon, 5% cabernet franc, 2% petit verdot. The cabernet sauvignon component comes from new Entav clones 338 and 412, which have the same potential as the new merlot clones. The components were separately vinified, and blended before 14 months maturation in fine French oak. Balnaves has made this Bordeaux blend its own, defiantly thumbing its nose at Margaret River. It's on the light side of medium-bodied, but ticks all fruit boxes from blue and black, moving on to its supple mouthfeel ex fine tannins and oak. Screwcap. 14% alc. **Rating** 94 **To** 2027 **$19** ✪
Entav Clone Cabernet Petit Verdot 2016 An 85/15% blend open-fermented together with cultured yeast, matured in French oak and tank for 5 months. Good crimson-purple hue; the bouquet is fragrant, with bright purple and blue fruit aromas and controlled French oak. The structure of the medium to full-bodied palate is very good, especially given its short sojourn in oak. Powdery tannins are entirely appropriate, and the price is enticing. It will be fascinating to see how it develops. Screwcap. 14% alc. **Rating** 94 **To** 2026 **$28** ✪

Bangor Estate ★★★★☆

20 Blackman Bay Road, Dunalley, Tas 7177 **Region** Southern Tasmania
T 0418 594 362 **www**.bangorshed.com.au **Open** 7 days 10–5
Winemaker Winemaking Tasmania **Est.** 2010 **Dozens** 900 **Vyds** 4ha

Bangor Estate's story starts in 1830, when John Dunbabin, convicted of horse stealing, was transported to Van Diemen's Land. Through sheer hard work he earned his freedom and bought his own land, paving the way for five generations of farming at Bangor. Today it is a 6200ha property on the Forestier Peninsula in one of the most southerly parts of Tasmania, with 5100ha of native forest, grasslands and wetlands, and 35km of coastline. Both Matt and Vanessa Dunbabin have PhDs in plant ecology and plant nutrition, putting beyond question their ability to protect this wonderful property – until 2000ha were burnt in the 2013 bushfires that devastated their local town of Dunalley and surrounding areas. Time will heal this, but in the meantime they have decided to establish a cellar door in partnership with Tom and Alice Gray from Fulham Acquaculture, also badly affected by the fires. Hence the Bangor Farm 7 Oyster Shed was born. The vineyard is planted to 1.5ha each of pinot noir and pinot gris, and 1ha of chardonnay.

🍷🍷🍷🍷🍷 **Jimmy's Hill Reserve Tasmania Pinot Gris 2016** This pushes gris' aromatic envelope to an apotheosis of ripe stone fruit, apple, quince marmalade, almond paste and honeysuckle. The wine was barrel-fermented with wild yeast as an expression of gris' riper, broader and, dare I say, more interesting style. The only caveat is the heat on the finish. Screwcap. 14.5% alc. **Rating** 95 **To** 2024 **$36** NG

🍷🍷🍷🍷 **Tasmania Pinot Gris 2016** **Rating** 93 **To** 2025 **$35** NG
Abel Tasman Pinot Noir 2014 **Rating** 91 **To** 2023 **$43** NG
Tasmania Riesling 2016 **Rating** 90 **To** 2025 **$35** NG
Methode Traditionelle Vintage 2011 **Rating** 90 **To** 2018 **$45** TS

Banks Road

600 Banks Road, Marcus Hill, Vic 3222 **Region** Geelong
T (03) 5258 3777 **www**.banksroad.com.au **Open** Fri–Sun 11–5
Winemaker William Derham **Est.** 2001 **Dozens** 2000 **Vyds** 6ha
Banks Road is a small family-owned and -operated winery on the Bellarine Peninsula. The
estate vineyard is adopting biodynamic principles, eliminating the use of insecticides and
moving to eliminate the use of all chemicals on the land. The winery not only processes the
Banks Road grapes, but also makes wine for other small producers in the area.

ΨΨΨΨΨ **Soho Road Vineyard Bellarine Peninsula Chardonnay 2015** This is an
elegantly intense chardonnay, with pink grapefruit and white peach driving the
flavour, which has a particularly good edge (acid-derived) to lengthen and freshen
the finish and aftertaste. Screwcap. 12.2% alc. **Rating** 95 **To** 2024 $36
Yarram Creek Bellarine Pinot Noir 2015 Sourced from local vineyards and
small batch open-fermented with a small amount of whole bunches in some
ferments. Some wild-yeast ferments and some extended time on skins, matured
in French hogsheads (20% new). The hue is bright and clear crimson, and the
wine has great drive, length and focus. Whereas Soho Road is all about depth and
complexity, this has superbly focused linear drive, fruit and whole-bunch characters
tightly bound together. Great value. Screwcap. 13.2% alc. **Rating** 95 **To** 2023
$24 ✪
Soho Road Vineyard Bellarine Peninsula Pinot Noir 2015 The vineyard
overlooks Swan Bay and Port Phillip Heads, and is believed to be the oldest on
the Peninsula. The low-yielding vines (less than 1kg per vine) have produced a
complex and intense wine with attractive foresty/savoury overtones to the well
of dark cherry and plum fruit. Acidity lengthens and refreshes the generosity of a
high class pinot. Screwcap. 13.9% alc. **Rating** 95 **To** 2025 $36
Bellarine Pinot Grigio 2016 An exceptionally fragrant and pure expression of
the variety if nashi pear is the key aroma – which it is, according to most records.
If you wish, you can divide the aroma and flavour into pear skin and pear drops.
Full of interest. Screwcap. 12% alc. **Rating** 94 **To** 2020 $24 ✪
Geelong Pinot Noir 2014 Powerful and complex, the normally low yield
reduced further by poor fruit set in spring. It is layered and long, with savoury
black cherry and plum fruit in a web of earthy tannins that are, however, in overall
balance. May go the distance. Screwcap. 12.8% alc. **Rating** 94 **To** 2026 $30 ✪
Heathcote Sangiovese 2015 The same back label eulogy of the Bellarine
vineyard is used with this wine. Not a good look. However, there's no issue with
the wine, with savoury cherry fruit on the fresh, light to medium-bodied palate.
I don't think it will ever be more enjoyable than it is now, with its satin mouthfeel.
Screwcap. 13% alc. **Rating** 94 **To** 2023 $30 ✪

ΨΨΨΨΨ **Bellarine Pinot Gris 2015** Rating 92 To 2017 $30
Yarram Creek Bellarine Geelong Chardonnay 2015 Rating 91 To 2021 $24
Geelong Sauvignon Blanc 2015 Rating 90 To 2017 $24

Bannockburn Vineyards

Midland Highway, Bannockburn, Vic 3331 (postal) **Region** Geelong
T (03) 5281 1363 **www**.bannockburnvineyards.com **Open** By appt
Winemaker Matthew Holmes **Est.** 1974 **Dozens** 7000 **Vyds** 24ha
The late Stuart Hooper had a deep love for the wines of Burgundy, and was able to drink
the best. When he established Bannockburn, it was inevitable that pinot noir and chardonnay
would form the major part of the plantings, with lesser amounts of riesling, sauvignon blanc,
cabernet sauvignon, shiraz and merlot. Bannockburn is still owned by members of the Hooper
family, who continue to respect Stuart's strong belief in making wines that reflect the flavours
of the vineyard. Exports to Canada, China, Singapore and Hong Kong.

ΨΨΨΨΨ **Extended Lees Geelong Chardonnay 2011** Via a mix of stainless steel,
puncheons and barriques, it spent 4 years on lees. The result is beguiling.

Complexity on another level, and while there's so much flavour – the spiced lemons, buttered toasted brioche, chicken stock, hint of figs and stone fruit – it's also finely tuned with laser precision thanks to the gossamer thread of natural acidity. Screwcap. 13.5% alc. Rating 97 To 2022 $65 JF ☉

ɪɪɪɪɪ **S.R.H. 2013** From 12 rows of the oldest chardonnay vines, planted in '76. Wild-yeast fermented and aged in French oak for 3 years. There's a fair amount of colour yet the wine is still bright, youthful and richly flavoured. Oak spice, creamy nuances, leesy, the flavours are long and precise. Screwcap. 13.5% alc. **Rating** 96 To 2022 $75 JF ☉

Geelong Sauvignon Blanc 2016 A 100% varietal with compelling aromas: cold tea, white flowers and acacia blossom, complex and earthy. The palate is glorious – at once taut with fine acidity and flavoursome with creamed honey and pine needles; bursting with life. Screwcap. 13% alc. **Rating** 95 To 2026 $35 JF ☉

Geelong Chardonnay 2014 Whole-bunch pressed, wild-yeast fermented in French oak puncheons (20% new), mlf and on lees for 18 months. A full-bodied, complex wine with preserved ginger, lemon rind, curd and wood spice. There's texture. It's deep and powerful, yet the tight acidity reins this right in. It lingers. It demands time. Screwcap. 12.5% alc. **Rating** 95 To 2025 $60 JF

ɪɪɪɪɪ **Douglas 2013** Rating 91 To 2021 $30 JF
Geelong Pinot Noir 2015 Rating 90 To 2023 $60 JF

Barfold Estate ★★★★

57 School Road, Barfold, Vic 3444 **Region** Heathcote
T (03) 5423 4225 www.barfoldestate.com.au **Open** 7 days 10–5
Winemaker Craig and Sandra Aitken **Est.** 1998 **Dozens** 350 **Vyds** 4.2ha
Craig and Sandra Aitken's farm property is at Barfold in the southwestern corner of the Heathcote wine region, a cooler portion of the region producing spicy characters in shiraz. So far they have planted 3.8ha of shiraz and 0.4ha of cabernet sauvignon.

ɪɪɪɪɪ **Heathcote Sparkling Shiraz NV** The personality of Heathcote is encapsulated in medium-bodied dark plum fruit, white pepper and a note of paprika spice. Carefully handled, finely structured tannins define a long and seamless finish, precise and enticing. Diam. 13.4% alc. **Rating** 93 To 2019 $32 TS

 # Barnyard1978 ★★★★

12 Canal Rocks Road, Yallingup, WA 6282 **Region** Margaret River
T (08) 9755 2548 www.barnyard1978.com.au **Open** 7 days 10.30–5
Winemaker Todd Payne **Est.** 1978 **Dozens** 1250 **Vyds** 4ha
1978 was the year the first plantings were made by the then Sienna Estate, but under the new ownership of Raminta and Edidijus Rusilas a five-year restoration program of the somewhat neglected vineyard, plus new plantings, has paid dividends. So, too, has the opening of a restaurant with two separate tasting decks for different times of day; winner of a WA Builders Association award for its low environmental impact construction.

ɪɪɪɪɪ **Margaret River Chardonnay 2016** Gin Gin clone, hand-picked, destemmed and crushed, fermented with wild and cultured yeast, matured in French oak (30% new) for 7 months, lees-stirred for 3 months. White peach and pear fruit is gently held by tendrils ex oak, both length and balance immaculate. Screwcap. 13% alc. **Rating** 94 To 2026 $30 ☉

ɪɪɪɪɪ **Cabernet Sauvignon Cabernet Franc 2014** Rating 92 To 2024 $30

Barratt ★★★★★

Uley Vineyard, Cornish Road, Summertown, SA 5141 **Region** Adelaide Hills
T (08) 8390 1788 www.barrattwines.com.au **Open** W'ends 11.30–5
Winemaker Lindsay Barratt **Est.** 1993 **Dozens** 500 **Vyds** 5.6ha

This is the venture of former physician Lindsay Barratt. Lindsay has always been responsible for viticulture and, following his retirement in 2001, has taken full, hands-on responsibility for winemaking (receiving a graduate diploma in oenology from the University of Adelaide in '02). The quality of the wines is excellent. Exports to Singapore and Taiwan.

ㅜㅜㅜㅜㅜ **Uley Vineyard Piccadilly Valley Pinot Noir 2015** 32yo vines, destemmed, 35% whole bunches, open-fermented, cultured yeast after 5 days cold soak, 12 days on skins, matured in French barriques (22% new) for 10 months. The highly fragrant and flowery bouquet is a Siamese twin with the lively, juicy palate, complexity and length from the whole-bunch component. A seductive wine that grew and grew on retasting. Screwcap. 13.5% alc. **Rating** 96 **To** 2027 $37 ✪
Uley Vineyard Piccadilly Valley Chardonnay 2015 Clone I10V1, hand-picked, wild-yeast fermented in French oak (33% new), matured for 11 months. Quietly ticks all the boxes, the balance and length impressive, the flavour spectrum impeccable, the finish fresh. Screwcap. 13.5% alc. **Rating** 95 **To** 2024 $32 ✪
Piccadilly Valley Sauvignon Blanc 2016 Hand-picked, crushed, fermented with cultured yeast. Aromas of snow pea and herb open proceedings, but are quickly submerged by the intensity of the tropical and stone fruit on the long palate. Lots to offer. Screwcap. 13.5% alc. **Rating** 94 **To** 2018 $23 ✪

Barrgowan Vineyard   ★★★★★

30 Pax Parade, Curlewis, Vic 3222 **Region** Geelong
T (03) 5250 3861 **www**.barrgowanvineyard.com.au **Open** By appt
Winemaker Dick Simonsen **Est.** 1998 **Dozens** 150
Dick and Dib (Elizabeth) Simonsen began planting their shiraz (with five clones) in 1994, intending to make wine for their own consumption. With all five clones in full production, the Simonsens have a maximum production of 200 dozen and accordingly release small quantities of Shiraz, which sell out quickly. The vines are hand-pruned, the grapes hand-picked, the must basket-pressed, and all wine movements are by gravity. The quality is exemplary.

Barringwood   ★★★★

60 Gillams Road, Lower Barrington, Tas 7306 **Region** Northern Tasmania
T (03) 6287 6933 **www**.barringwood.com.au **Open** Thurs–Mon 10–5
Winemaker Josef Chromy Wines (Jeremy Dineen) **Est.** 1993 **Dozens** 3000 **Vyds** 5ha
Judy and Ian Robinson operated a sawmill at Lower Barrington, on the main tourist trail to Cradle Mountain, and when they planted 500 vines in 1993 the aim was to do a bit of home winemaking. The urge to expand the vineyard and make wine on a commercial scale soon occurred, and they embarked on a six-year plan, planting 1ha per year in the first four years and building the cellar and tasting rooms during the following two years. The recent sale of Barringwood to Neville and Vanessa Bagot hasn't seen any significant changes to the business.

ㅜㅜㅜㅜㅜ **Classic Cuvee 2013** A cuvee of poise and integrity, seamlessly uniting the strawberry and red cherry fruits of pinot with the citrus cut of chardonnay and the vibrancy of Tasmanian acidity (one-third mlf). 3 years on lees has built softness, creamy texture and hints of almond milk without disrupting the flow and freshness of vibrant Tasmanian fruit. It lingers with length, line and enticing appeal. Diam. 11.5% alc. **Rating** 94 **To** 2021 $45 TS

ㅜㅜㅜㅜㅜ **Pinot Gris 2016 Rating** 90 **To** 2021 $34 JF
Tasmanian Methode Traditionnelle Cuvee NV Rating 90 **To** 2017 $32 TS

Barristers Block   ★★★★

141 Onkaparinga Valley Road, Woodside, SA 5244 **Region** Adelaide Hills
T (08) 8389 7706 **www**.barristersblock.com.au **Open** 7 days 10.30–5
Winemaker Anthony Pearce, Peter Leske **Est.** 2004 **Dozens** 7000 **Vyds** 18.5ha

Owner Jan Siemelink-Allen has over 20 years in the industry, first as a grapegrower of 10ha of cabernet sauvignon and shiraz in Wrattonbully, then as a wine producer from that region. In 2006 she and her family purchased an 8ha vineyard planted to sauvignon blanc and pinot noir near Woodside in the Adelaide Hills. Exports to the UK, Germany, Vietnam, Malaysia, South Korea, Hong Kong, Singapore and China.

⟡⟡⟡⟡⟡ **The JP Wrattonbully Cabernet Sauvignon 2012** Has retained good colour and a cabernet-typical backbone of savoury tannins to the ample cassis fruit. Close to its plateau of peak drinking. Screwcap. 14.5% alc. **Rating** 91 **To** 2022 $69

Barton Estate ★★★★

2307 Barton Highway, Murrumbateman, NSW 2582 **Region** Canberra District
T (02) 6230 9553 **www.**bartonestate.com.au **Open** W'ends & public hols 10–5
Winemaker Capital Wines, Gallagher Wines **Est.** 1997 **Dozens** 500 **Vyds** 7.7ha
Bob Furbank and wife Julie Chitty are both CSIRO plant biologists: he is a biochemist (physiologist) and she is a specialist in plant tissue culture. In 1997 they acquired the 120ha property forming part of historic Jeir Station, and have since planted 15 grape varieties. The most significant plantings are to cabernet sauvignon, shiraz, merlot, riesling and chardonnay, the Joseph's coat completed with micro quantities of other varieties.

⟡⟡⟡⟡⟡ **Riley's Canberra Riesling 2016** A delightful bouquet, like the scent of an orchard in full blossom, perfumed and aromatic with the promise of the fruit to come. Softly textured on the palate, the light flavours of sweet red apple and orange citrus are framed by gentle acidity which doesn't intrude, but provides some verve to the mouthfeel and extends the finish. It's a wine of poise rather than power. Screwcap. 11.9% alc. **Rating** 94 **To** 2023 $25 SC ✪

⟡⟡⟡⟡⟡ **Canberra Blue Rose 2016 Rating** 90 **To** 2019 $20 SC ✪
Georgia Canberra Shiraz 2015 Rating 90 **To** 2025 $30 SC

Barton Jones Wines ★★★★

39 Upper Capel Road, Donnybrook, WA 6239 **Region** Geographe
T (08) 9731 2233 **www.**bartonjoneswines.com.au **Open** Thurs–Mon 10.30–4.30
Winemaker Contract **Est.** 1978 **Dozens** 2000 **Vyds** 3ha
The 22ha property on which Blackboy Ridge Estate is established was partly cleared and planted to 2.5ha of semillon, chenin blanc, shiraz and cabernet sauvignon in 1978. When current owners Adrian Jones and Jackie Barton purchased the property in 2000 the vines were already some of the oldest in the region. The vineyard and cellar door are on gentle north-facing slopes, with extensive views over the Donnybrook area. Exports to the UK.

⟡⟡⟡⟡⟡ **The Box Seat Geographe Semillon 2015** This spends 18 months in French oak for extra depth, yet the acidity is so crisp you can hear the crunch. Subtle leesy characters bolster the lemongrass and lemon juice flavours, and there's a smattering of dried herbs for good measure. Screwcap. 13.5% alc. **Rating** 94 **To** 2021 $25 JF ✪
The Bigwig Margaret River Shiraz 2015 While the fruit was sourced from over the border, as in Margaret River, gee it's a seductive wine. Exuberant mid-crimson with dark-red fruits spiced with cinnamon and star anise, and silky tannins to close. Screwcap. 14% alc. **Rating** 94 **To** 2024 $29 JF ✪

⟡⟡⟡⟡⟡ **The Top Drawer Cabernet Sauvignon 2015 Rating** 92 **To** 2021 $29 JF

Barwang ★★★★☆

Barwang Road, Young, NSW 2594 (postal) **Region** Hilltops
T (02) 9722 1200 **www.**mcwilliams.com.au **Open** Not
Winemaker Russell Cody, Andrew Higgins **Est.** 1969 **Dozens** NFP **Vyds** 100ha

Peter Robertson pioneered viticulture in the Young area when he planted vines in 1969 as part of a diversification program for his 400ha grazing property. When McWilliam's acquired Barwang in '89, the vineyard amounted to 13ha; today the plantings are 100ha. The label also takes in 100% Tumbarumba wines, as well as Hilltops/Tumbarumba blends. Exports to Asia.

ŸŸŸŸŸ **Hilltops Shiraz 2014** A seriously good and well priced cool climate shiraz. Medium-bodied and energetic, this has red and black fruits and some savoury notes. The palate is elegant, persistent and balanced, with gently grippy tannins providing the backbone to suggest that a few years in the cellar will reap rewards. Screwcap. 13.5% alc. **Rating** 93 **To** 2025 $23 PR ✪

ŸŸŸŸ **Tumbarumba Pinot Gris 2016 Rating** 89 **To** 2018 $23

Barwon Ridge Wines ★★★☆

50 McMullans Road, Barrabool, Vic 3221 **Region** Geelong
T 0418 324 632 **www.**barwonridge.com.au **Open** 1st w'end of month, public hols
Winemaker Leura Park (Nyall Condon) **Est.** 1999 **Dozens** 400 **Vyds** 3.6ha
In 1999 Geoff Anson, Joan Anson and Ken King (of Kings of Kangaroo Ground) planted Barwon Ridge. The vineyard nestles in the Barrabool Hills just to the west of Geelong. Geoff and Joan now operate the vineyard and they are focusing on producing premium fruit, with the wines now made at Leura Park. The vineyard is part of the re-emergence of winemaking in the Barrabool Hills, after the area's first boom through the 1840s to the 1880s. Barwon Ridge is planted to pinot noir, shiraz, cabernet sauvignon, marsanne and chardonnay.

ŸŸŸŸŸ **Geelong Cabernet Sauvignon 2015** Dark garnet-purple with intriguing, pleasant aromas of rosemary and black olives, lavender and cassis, cedary oak and wood spices. The palate has a pitch of ripe fruit, savoury as well, the tannins ripe with a slight astringency to the acidity. Screwcap. 13.4% alc. **Rating** 92 **To** 2027 $40 JF

ŸŸŸŸ **Geelong Shiraz 2015 Rating** 89 **To** 2025 $40 JF

Basalt Wines ★★★☆

1131 Princes Highway, Killarney, Vic 3283 **Region** Henty
T 0429 682 251 **www.**basaltwines.com **Open** 7 days 10–5
Winemaker Scott Ireland (contract) **Est.** 2002 **Dozens** 800 **Vyds** 2.8ha
Shane and Ali Clancey are part of the Great Ocean Road's community of Irish descendants spread around Port Fairy, and have turned a former potato paddock into a small, but very successful, wine business. In 2002 Shane began planting a multi-clone pinot noir vineyard, plus a small planting of tempranillo. Basalt Wines' grape intake is supplemented by a Drumborg vineyard, including 0.4ha of 26yo MV6 pinot noir and, even more importantly, riesling of the highest quality. Shane is viticulturist, assistant winemaker, wholesaler, and runs the cellar door, with Ali involved in various parts of the business, including the small flock of babydoll sheep which graze next to the winery.

ŸŸŸŸŸ **Great Ocean Road Riesling 2016** The Henty GI explains its minerally acidity, which is normally lacking in riesling in a maritime climate. Its mouthwatering lime zest flavours go hand in hand with the acidity. Very good now, great in 5+ years. Screwcap. 11.8% alc. **Rating** 94 **To** 2036 $29 ✪

ŸŸŸŸ **Great Ocean Road Pinot Noir 2015 Rating** 89 **To** 2022 $35

Basedow Wines ★★★☆

161–165 Murray Street, Tanunda, SA 5352 **Region** Barossa Valley
T 0418 847 400 **www.**basedow.com.au **Open** 7 days 10–5
Winemaker Richard Basedow, Rob Gibson **Est.** 1896 **Dozens** 5000 **Vyds** 214ha
Peter, Michael and Richard Basedow are the three Brothers Basedow (B3, as they call themselves), fifth-generation Barossans with distinguished forefathers. Grandfather Oscar

Basedow established the Basedow winery in 1896, while Martin Basedow established Roseworthy Agricultural College. As well as retaining consultant winemaker Rob Gibson, the brothers constructed a winery in the old Vine Vale Primary School property in 2008, using the schoolrooms as a cellar door. In '14 B3 Wines purchased the Basedow brand from James Estate, restoring continuity of ownership, and in November '15 the wheel turned full circle when they purchased the old family winery. Exports to the UK, Canada, Denmark, South Korea, Thailand, Singapore and China.

ᴛᴛᴛᴛᴛ **Eden Valley Riesling 2016** A distinctive Eden Valley fruit profile with Meyer lemon leading the way, emphasised here with relatively soft acidity that still leaves the wine in balance. One of those now or later rieslings. Screwcap. 11% alc. **Rating** 91 **To** 2025 $20 ✪

Bass Phillip   ★★★★★

Tosch's Road, Leongatha South, Vic 3953 **Region** Gippsland
T (03) 5664 3341 **www.**bassphillip.com **Open** By appt
Winemaker Phillip Jones **Est.** 1979 **Dozens** 1500
Phillip Jones handcrafts tiny quantities of superlative Pinot Noir which, at its best, has no equal in Australia. Painstaking site selection, ultra-close vine spacing and the very, very cool climate of South Gippsland are the keys to the magic of Bass Phillip and its eerily Burgundian Pinots. One of Australia's greatest small producers.

ᴛᴛᴛᴛᴛ **Premium Chardonnay 2015** Tightly coiled, superfine and elegant with its citrus bent, especially grapefruit and lemony freshness plus some white nectarines; this is not at all lean. Flavours build just the right amount of oak spice, with creamed-honey lees character reined in by a spider's silk thread of acidity. This is magical. ProCork. 12.5% alc. **Rating** 96 **To** 2025 JF
Reserve Pinot Noir 2015 It's like waiting in the starting blocks for a sprint race when the starter pistol hasn't gone off. As with the Premium, this needs time to amalgamate. The palate is somewhat denser, richer, with detailed tannins, cedary oak too, but beginning to melt into the body of the wine. There's power and complexity and more to come. ProCork. 13.3% alc. **Rating** 96 **To** 2030 JF
Estate Chardonnay 2015 A swathe of white stone fruit, grapefruit and zesty flavours wrap themselves around subtle, creamy lees notes and oak spice. This has depth and energy, and a long, satisfying finish. 12.6% alc. **Rating** 95 **To** 2025 JF
Gamay 2015 It is entirely fitting that someone so fanatical about pinot noir doesn't neglect gamay, for it is no poor cousin. It's striking how it has a strong beetroot character yet is full of fruit, namely rhubarb and cherries. Tannins are in the background, as the high acidity loads up the palate with freshness and drive. ProCork. 12.7% alc. **Rating** 95 **To** 2022 JF
Issan Vineyard Pinot Noir 2015 Attractive, bright mid-crimson; a touch reductive and meaty, but unfurls with a core of very good fruit, all dark sweet cherries and pips. Lovely texture; supple tannins with some pull on the finish. This is holding its own and more. The most complete of the pinots from this vintage. ProCork. 12.7% alc. **Rating** 95 **To** 2025 JF
Premium Pinot Noir 2015 This is a sleeper and doesn't want to budge. What it has now: a lovely fragrance of spiced cherries, pips, warm earth, wood spice, raspberry; slightly astringent acidity, fine tannins and a long finish. Still coming together. Be patient. ProCork. 13.2% alc. **Rating** 95 **To** 2030 JF

ᴛᴛᴛᴛᴛ **Pinot Rose 2016 Rating** 92 **To** 2020 $23 JF
Old Cellar Pinot 2015 Rating 92 **To** 2022 $36 JF
Estate Pinot Noir 2015 Rating 92 **To** 2022 JF
Crown Prince Pinot Noir 2015 Rating 91 **To** 2022 JF

Bass River Winery ★★★★

1835 Dalyston Glen Forbes Road, Glen Forbes, Vic 3990 **Region** Gippsland
T (03) 5678 8252 **www**.bassriverwinery.com **Open** Thurs–Tues 9–5
Winemaker Pasquale and Frank Butera **Est.** 1999 **Dozens** 1500 **Vyds** 4ha
The Butera family has established 1ha each of pinot noir and chardonnay and 2ha split equally to riesling, sauvignon blanc, pinot gris and merlot, with both the winemaking and viticulture handled by the father and son team of Pasquale and Frank. The small production is principally sold through the cellar door, with some retailers and restaurants in the South Gippsland area. Exports to Singapore.

🍷🍷🍷🍷🍷 **Single Vineyard Gippsland Riesling 2016** This is strongly reminiscent of an Alsatian expression of riesling rather than the cooler, more precise Germanic mould. Quince, pear, raw ginger, lime and mottled citrus fruits are splayed across a mid-weighted palate of astringency and bright acidity. Screwcap. 12% alc. **Rating** 93 **To** 2024 $25 NG ✪
1835 Chardonnay 2015 Despite striving for acid retention by blocking malolactic conversion, this is a generously aromatic and texturally embellished chardonnay by way of its wild yeast barrel fermentation and extended handling on lees across 30% new oak. Screwcap. 13% alc. **Rating** 91 **To** 2023 $40 NG
Single Vineyard Pinot Gris 2016 Whole-bunch pressed and partially barrel-fermented, this gris plays the freshness card with a full deck of textural interplay. Quince, green pear, marzipan and baked apple tones are given some tangy, leesy detail by the barrel-fermented quotient; zip and drive by that handled in tank. A good, snappy drink. Screwcap. 12% alc. **Rating** 91 **To** 2020 $25 NG
1835 Iced Riesling 2015 Truffled quince, very ripe pear and baked brown apple define the distinctly European nose, the palate with texture and an autumnal fruit basket. This is high on personality. Screwcap. 10% alc. **Rating** 91 **To** 2023 $30 NG
Vintage Brut Chardonnay Pinot Noir 2012 Endearing restraint and poise allow the subtle red apple fruit of pinot noir to meet the lemon of chardonnay, set against a backdrop of subtle, biscuity, bottle age complexity. It's a steely style of low dosage and grainy lees texture. A cuvee for sparkling fanatics, not big crowds. Diam. 12.5% alc. **Rating** 90 **To** 2022 $40 TS

🍷🍷🍷🍷 **Single Vineyard Gippsland Sauvignon Blanc 2016 Rating** 89 **To** 2019 $25 NG

Battle of Bosworth ★★★★☆

92 Gaffney Road, Willunga, SA 5172 **Region** McLaren Vale
T (08) 8556 2441 **www**.battleofbosworth.com.au **Open** 7 days 11–5
Winemaker Joch Bosworth **Est.** 1996 **Dozens** 15 000 **Vyds** 80ha
Owned and run by Joch Bosworth (viticulture and winemaking) and partner Louise Hemsley-Smith (sales and marketing), this winery takes its name from the battle which ended the War of the Roses, fought on Bosworth Field in 1485. The vineyards were established in the early 1970s in the foothills of the Mt Lofty Ranges. The vines are fully certified A-grade organic by ACO. The label depicts the yellow soursob (*Oxalis pes-caprae*), whose growth habits make it an ideal weapon for battling weeds in organic viticulture. Shiraz, cabernet sauvignon and chardonnay account for 75% of the plantings. The Spring Seeds wines are made from estate vineyards. Exports to the UK, the US, Canada, Sweden, Norway, Belgium, Hong Kong and Japan.

🍷🍷🍷🍷🍷 **Best of Vintage 2014** The continuing dearth of cabernet shiraz (or shiraz cabernet) is puzzling, if only because of the synergy that comes of the union. This brightly coloured, medium-bodied blend is at once juicy and textured, with blackberry and dark cherry fruit both contributing; long, with balanced oak and ripe tannins. Great stuff. Screwcap. 14.5% alc. **Rating** 95 **To** 2034 $50
Chanticleer McLaren Vale Shiraz 2014 Matured in used French oak that has both accentuated the regional signature of dark chocolate and given complexity to the mouthfeel. Altogether satisfying and convincing, plum and licorice adding interest. Certified organic. Screwcap. 14% alc. **Rating** 94 **To** 2025 $45

ΨΨΨΨΨ McLaren Vale Cabernet Sauvignon 2015 Rating 91 To 2030 $28
Puritan McLaren Vale Shiraz 2016 Rating 90 To 2021 $22
Spring Seed Wine Co. Scarlet Runner Shiraz 2015 Rating 90 To 2021 $22
Ding's McLaren Vale Shiraz 2014 Rating 90 To 2022 $15
McLaren Vale Shiraz 2014 Rating 90 To 2034 $28

Bay of Fires ★★★★★

40 Baxters Road, Pipers River, Tas 7252 **Region** Northern Tasmania
T (03) 6382 7622 **www.bayoffireswines.com.au Open** Mon–Fri 11–4, w'ends 10–4
Winemaker Penny Jones **Est.** 2001 **Dozens** NFP
Hardys purchased its first grapes from Tasmania in 1994, with the aim of further developing
and refining its sparkling wines, a process that quickly gave birth to House of Arras (see
separate entry). The next stage was the inclusion of various parcels of chardonnay from
Tasmania in the 1998 Eileen Hardy, then the development in 2001 of the Bay of Fires brand.
Bay of Fires has had outstanding success with its table wines: Pinot Noir was obvious, the
other wines typically of gold medal standard. Exports to the US, Asia and NZ.

ΨΨΨΨΨ **Eddystone Point Riesling 2015** Hand-picked, crushed, chilled, pressed,
fermented in stainless steel, matured for 4 months on yeast lees. The blossom-
filled bouquet announces a beautiful riesling that has taken the first step towards
maturity, sometimes a difficult transition, but not here. Delicate intensity is
inextricably linked on the palate, where citrus and Granny Smith apple join forces
to subjugate any attack from Tasmanian acidity – perfect balance the result. Top
gold Tasmanian Wine Show '17. Screwcap. 12.5% alc. **Rating** 96 **To** 2029 $25 **✪**
Pinot Noir 2015 From the Derwent River and Coal River valleys of southern
Tasmania. The vivid, deep crimson-purple hue is typical of Bay of Fires, and sets
the antennae waving furiously. The transition from the bouquet to the palate is
seamless and utterly coherent, with black cherry fruit peppered with spicy nuances,
French oak doing its duty. Screwcap. 13.5% alc. **Rating** 96 **To** 2026 $48 **✪**
Pinot Gris 2016 Hand-picked, whole-bunch pressed, 20% warm-fermented
in used French oak, the remainder in stainless steel, all matured for 4 months on
lees. Takes the approach used with Eddystone one step further; the fruit has great
intensity and, in particular, length. Screwcap. 13.5% alc. **Rating** 95 **To** 2021 $35 **✪**
Riesling 2016 Hand-picked, crushed, chilled and pressed, fermented in stainless
steel, matured for 4 months on yeast lees. A very good wine with pure varietal
fruit expression courtesy of lime and Meyer lemon flavours, but doesn't have the
crisp minerally acid drive expected on the finish. Could easily be just a pause
before it starts developing. Screwcap. 12.5% alc. **Rating** 94 **To** 2026 $35
Chardonnay 2015 From the Coal River Valley, East Coast and Derwent Valley,
whole-bunch pressed, fermented in French oak from five different coopers. Has
picked up positive green-gold colour earlier than might be expected. Is a user-
friendly, high quality chardonnay, ready now, with stone fruit and creamy/nutty
notes ex oak and possible mlf. Screwcap. 13.5% alc. **Rating** 94 **To** 2022 $45
Eddystone Point Pinot Noir 2015 Hand-picked from the Derwent Valley, East
Coast and Coal River Valley, fermented in temperature-controlled open stainless
steel fermenters, basket-pressed, matured in French oak (25% new). An elegant,
perfectly balanced pinot with pure red fruits, silky tannins and integrated oak, the
length impeccable. Screwcap. 13.5% alc. **Rating** 94 **To** 2025 $30 **✪**
Tasmanian Cuvee Pinot Noir Chardonnay Brut NV Nine years on tirage
is extraordinary. Krug-like in its lengthy elevage, giving the wine the depth and
complexity expected from first class champagne. Has bready/yeasty/nutty aromas
and flavours on the one hand, but on the other, the wine holds its citrus and green
apple fruit line very well. Cork. 12.5% alc. **Rating** 94 **To** 2018 $35

ΨΨΨΨΨ **Eddystone Point Pinot Gris 2016** Rating 92 To 2020 $25 **✪**
Tasmanian Pinot Noir Chardonnay Rose NV Rating 91 To 2017 $32 TS
Trial by Fires Piggy Skins Pinot Gris 2016 Rating 90 To 2019 $45

Beach Road

309 Seaview Road, McLaren Vale, SA 5171 **Region** Langhorne Creek/McLaren Vale
T (08) 8323 7344 **www.**beachroadwines.com.au **Open** Thurs–Mon 11–4
Winemaker Briony Hoare **Est.** 2007 **Dozens** 3000 **Vyds** 0.2ha

Briony (winemaker) and Tony (viticulturist) Hoare began their life partnership after meeting while studying wine science at the Roseworthy campus of Adelaide University. Their involvement in the industry dates back to the early 1990s, Briony working around Australia with many of the flagship wines of (then) Southcorp, Tony gaining extensive experience in Mildura, the Hunter Valley and McLaren Vale (where he spent five years as viticulturist for Wirra Wirra). In 2005 the pair decided to go it alone, setting up a wine consultancy, and in '07 launching Beach Road. The focus on Italian varieties stems from Briony's vintage in Piedmont, where she worked with barbera, nebbiolo, cortese and moscato. Along the way, however, they both had a lot of exposure to grenache, shiraz and mourvedre.

♟♟♟♟♟ **Aglianico 2013** The dry structural focus of aglianico, manifest in a ferruginous core of tannin, looms over warm, savoury aromas of tobacco leaf, dried Mediterranean herbs, black plum and smoked meat. The tannins splay across the long finish, taming the wine's warmth. Moreish and strong, auguring well for a long future. Screwcap. 12.5% alc. **Rating** 96 **To** 2025 $45 NG ✪
Fiano 2015 Fiano's capacity for a generous viscosity, plying the gums with textural intrigue, along with natural acid retention, is on full display. White flowers and a potpourri of herbs, plus a whiff of pungent fennel, drive the aromatic spectrum. Bitter almond and apricot ensue. A jangle of solid mineral melded to juicy acidity keep the wine purring. Screwcap. 13.5% alc. **Rating** 95 **To** 2018 $25 NG ✪
Nero d'Avola 2015 Firm, detailed and dutifully extracted tannins define and frame this fully flavoured wine. They are like pumice and dust, taming the avalanche of fruit: dark cherry, satsuma plum and orange rind flavours give an appetising bitterness reminiscent of amaro. Screwcap. 14.5% alc. **Rating** 95 **To** 2021 $45 NG

♟♟♟♟♟ **Shiraz NV Rating** 92 **To** 2023 $25 NG✪
Fiano 2014 Rating 91 **To** 2017 $25 NG

Beelgara | Cumulus ★★★★☆

892 Davys Plains Road, Cudal, NSW 2864 **Region** Riverina
T (02) 6966 0200 **www.**beelgarawines.com.au **Open** Not
Winemaker Rod Hooper **Est.** 1930 **Dozens** 600 000

Beelgara Estate was formed in 2001 after the purchase of the 60-year-old Rossetto family winery by a group of shareholders. The emphasis has changed significantly, with a concerted effort to go to the right region for each variety, while still maintaining good value for money. In '15 Beelgara (which also owns the Moss Bros, Riddoch Run and The Habitat brands) merged with Cumulus. The Cumulus wines are released under three brands: Rolling, from the Central Ranges zone; Climbing, solely from Orange fruit; and Cumulus, super-premium from the best of the estate vineyard blocks. Exports to most major markets.

♟♟♟♟♟ **Cumulus Orange Chardonnay 2015** Hand-picked, whole-bunch pressed, wild-fermented in French oak (30% new), remaining on lees until Nov, bottled Jan. While the wine shares many things with its Climbing sibling, the flavours and mouthfeel here are riper and rounder respectively. They don't take a step too far, the gentle complexity saying and doing all the right things to welcome you to the table. Screwcap. 12.5% alc. **Rating** 95 **To** 2022 $35 ✪
Cumulus Orange Chardonnay 2016 A small hand-picked parcel from one block, whole-bunch pressed and barrel-fermented in French oak, with various combinations of age and size of vessel employed. Unforced and effortless in feel, this is a wine with harmony. Fruit characters range from citrus to just-ripe stone fruit, and the oak provides nutty, creamy notes without intruding. Acidity is perfectly integrated. Screwcap. 12% alc. **Rating** 94 **To** 2020 $35 SC

ՇՇՇՇՉ Cumulus Climbing Orange Chardonnay 2015 Rating 90 To 2023 $24
Beelgara JT, The Patriarch Chardonnay 2015 Rating 90 To 2018 $30
Cumulus Climbing Orange Merlot 2014 Rating 90 To 2021 $24 SC

Bekkers ★★★★★

212 Seaview Road, McLaren Vale, SA 5171 **Region** McLaren Vale
T 0408 807 568 **www**.bekkerswine.com **Open** Thurs–Sat 10–4
Winemaker Emmanuelle and Toby Bekkers **Est.** 2010 **Dozens** 700 **Vyds** 5.5ha
This brings together two high-performance, highly experienced and highly credentialled business and life partners. Husband Toby Bekkers graduated with an honours degree in applied science in agriculture from the University of Adelaide, and over the ensuing years has had broad-ranging responsibilities as general manager of Paxton Wines in McLaren Vale, and as a leading exponent of organic and biodynamic viticulture. Wife Emmanuelle was born in Bandol in the south of France, and gained two university degrees, in biochemistry and oenology, before working for the Hardys in the south of France, which led her to Australia and a wide-ranging career, including Chalk Hill. Exports to the UK, Canada, France and China.

ՇՇՇՇՇ **McLaren Vale Syrah 2015** 64% Hickinbotham Clarendon Vineyard, 36% Gateway Vineyard, hand-picked, 18% whole bunches, 82% destemmed and sorted, 5 days cold soak, 12 days wild yeast ferment, matured 20 months in French puncheons (40% new). This makes the marriage of intensity and elegance seem simple, purity and power likewise. It is suspended in time and place with glorious fruit (no chocolate), gently savoury/spicy fine tannins and oak hiding in the panoply of fruit flavours. Screwcap. 14.5% alc. **Rating** 98 To 2045 $110 ✪
McLaren Vale Grenache 2015 Hand-picked from three vineyards on 17 Feb, 6 and 25 Mar, the parcels open-fermented with 20% whole bunches, 5-6 days cold soak before wild yeast fermentation, matured on fine lees in used French puncheons. As close to perfection as you are likely to come with McLaren Vale grenache. The perfumed bouquet sets the scene for the silky, supple red-fruited palate, superfine tannins always present, oak flavour absent. Has many of the characteristics of a great pinot noir. Screwcap. 15% alc. **Rating** 98 To 2030 $80 ✪

ՇՇՇՇՇ **McLaren Vale Syrah Grenache 2015** 70/30% blend; Blewitt Springs grenache, open-fermented and matured separately, 15-20% whole bunches, the remainder destemmed, aged on fine lees in used French oak. The wine repays the complex time-consuming vinification. The bouquet is fragrant with delicate red fruits and haunting spices, followed by an enchanting mouthfeel as red fruits flow serenely across the mouth, the deeper tones of plum and blackberry ex the shiraz adding complexity, but not impinging on the main message. Screwcap. 14.5% alc. **Rating** 95 To 2028 $80

Belford Block Eight ★★★★

65 Squire Close, Belford, NSW 2335 **Region** Hunter Valley
T 0410 346 300 **www**.blockeight.com.au **Open** Not
Winemaker Daniel Binet **Est.** 2012 **Dozens** 1000 **Vyds** 6ha
The existing 2ha each of semillon, shiraz and chardonnay were planted in 2000. The vineyard had been left to its own devices for two years before Jeff Ross and Todd Alexander purchased it in 2012. With the help of local consultant Jenny Bright, the vineyard was nursed back to health just in time for the celebrated '14 vintage. With a bit more TLC, and Daniel Binet continuing to make the wines, the future should be bright. Vines, olives, ducks, chickens, perch, yabbies and vegetables are all grown and harvested from the 40ha property.

ՇՇՇՇՉ **Reserve Hunter Valley Semillon 2016** There is considerably more intensity, crunch, sap and line of flavour to this wine than its less expensive sibling. The choir of lemon oil and the spectrum of other citrus fruit is reeled out as the fidelitous voice of the Hunter. It also boasts riper hints of quince and apricot. Screwcap. 11% alc. **Rating** 93 To 2030 $39 NG

Estate Hunter Valley Semillon 2016 Exactitude of flavour and length of finish are this wine's calling cards. Lemon drop and grapefruit rind notes ricochet across the mouth, and the saline acidity pulls them into a long finish without the meddling of oak or any artifice. Screwcap. 11% alc. **Rating** 91 **To** 2027 $29 NG

Bellarine Estate ★★★★

2270 Portarlington Road, Bellarine, Vic 3222 **Region** Geelong
T (03) 5259 3310 **www**.bellarineestate.com.au **Open** 7 days 11–4
Winemaker Robin Brockett **Est.** 1995 **Dozens** 1050 **Vyds** 10.5ha
This business runs parallel with the Bellarine Brewing Company, also situated in the winery, and the extended operating hours of Julian's Restaurant. It is a popular meeting place. The vineyard is planted to chardonnay, pinot noir, shiraz, merlot, viognier and sauvignon blanc. Exports to the US.

🍷🍷🍷🍷🍷 **Two Wives Geelong Shiraz 2015** There's a lot to relish – the glossy crimson-dark-purple hue, and while there's a lot of sweet, spicy oak, the ripe, plump and bright fruit still shines through. There's a plushness to the tannins, some grip on the finish yet everything is handled well. Screwcap. 14.5% alc. **Rating** 93 **To** 2026 $38 JF
OMK Geelong Viognier 2015 It's increasingly hard to find viognier that ticks the varietal box without being too big and blowzy. Here's one: acacia and lemon blossom with apricots and kernels, yet with zesty acidity too and a palate that is quite buoyant. Screwcap. 13% alc. **Rating** 92 **To** 2021 $32 JF
Phil's Fetish Geelong Pinot Noir 2015 Fragrant florals and forest undergrowth, with wood spices, all add savoury pitch to the nose, yet on the palate there's a ball of sweet ripe fruit, all macerated cherries and compote. Supple, pliable tannins; a lovely drink. Screwcap. 13.5% alc. **Rating** 92 **To** 2021 $38 JF
Julian's Geelong Merlot 2015 What's appealing about this merlot is that it has the right balance of fruit – red plums and blackberries meet the savoury aspect of spice, coffee grounds, wood and fresh herbs. Screwcap. 14% alc. **Rating** 92 **To** 2021 $38 JF

Bellarmine Wines ★★★★★

1 Balyan Retreat, Pemberton, WA 6260 **Region** Pemberton
T (08) 9842 8413 **www**.bellarmine.com.au **Open** By appt
Winemaker Dr Diane Miller **Est.** 2000 **Dozens** 5000 **Vyds** 20.2ha
This vineyard is owned by German residents Dr Willi and Gudrun Schumacher. Long-term wine lovers, the Schumachers decided to establish a vineyard and winery of their own, using Australia partly because of its stable political climate. The vineyard is planted to merlot, pinot noir, chardonnay, shiraz, riesling, sauvignon blanc and petit verdot. Exports to the UK, the US, Germany and China.

🍷🍷🍷🍷🍷 **Pemberton Riesling Select 2016** The label chart shows around 65g/l residual sugar. Once again, the sugar is partially masked by the fruit and acidity. It is seductive now, but has unlimited development potential. Lime and apple fruit are on the money. Screwcap. 7.5% alc. **Rating** 96 **To** 2036 $26 ✪
Pemberton Riesling Dry 2016 Right in the slot of the Bellarmine Riesling style. The floral bouquet of lemon, lime and apple blossom leads into a fresh, crisp palate with minerally acidity woven through the fruit and providing both length and drive. The wine needs 4–5 years to fully flower, but is already enticing. Screwcap. 12% alc. **Rating** 95 **To** 2027 $26 ✪
Pemberton Riesling Half-dry 2016 Very attractive style, although seems off-dry rather than half-dry, but there is in fact around 30g/l of residual sugar, perfectly balanced by the acidity. Screwcap. 9.5% alc. **Rating** 95 **To** 2031 $26 ✪

🍷🍷🍷🍷🍷 **Pemberton Sauvignon Blanc 2016 Rating** 90 **To** 2018 $20 NG ✪

Bellbrae Estate

520 Great Ocean Road, Bellbrae, Vic 3228 **Region** Geelong
T (03) 5264 8480 **www**.bellbraeestate.com.au **Open** 7 days 11–5
Winemaker David Crawford **Est.** 1999 **Dozens** 4000 **Vyds** 7ha

The Surf Coast area of Geelong enjoys a slightly milder climate overall than other areas of the Geelong viticultural region. Being so close to Bass Strait, Bellbrae Estate experiences a maritime influence that reduces the risk of frost in spring and provides more even temperature ranges during the summer – ideal growing conditions for producing elegant wines that retain their natural acidity. An additional 2ha of pinot noir and 1ha of chardonnay were planted in the spring of 2015, taking the estate to 8ha. Wines are released under the Bellbrae Estate and Longboard labels.

ƒƒƒƒƒ **Longboard Geelong Sauvignon Blanc 2016** No-frills stainless steel–fermented and early bottled. Has a handsome array of citrus and tropical fruits, and a clean, fresh finish. Screwcap. 12.5% alc. **Rating** 90 **To** 2018 $22
Bird Rock Geelong Pinot Noir 2015 Relatively light colour, albeit with a crimson hue; overall, light-bodied (even by pinot standards) with gentle red fruits and superfine tannins. All attractive as far as it goes, but needs more fruit weight. Screwcap. 13.5% alc. **Rating** 90 **To** 2020 $39

ƒƒƒƒ **Longboard Geelong Rose 2016 Rating** 89 **To** 2017 $25
Longboard Geelong Pinot Noir 2015 Rating 89 **To** 2018 $24
Longboard Geelong Shiraz 2015 Rating 89 **To** 2022 $24
Heathcote Shiraz 2015 Rating 89 **To** 2025 $36

Bellvale Wine

95 Forresters Lane, Berrys Creek, Vic 3953 **Region** Gippsland
T 0412 541 098 **www**.bellvalewine.com.au **Open** By appt
Winemaker John Ellis **Est.** 1998 **Dozens** 3500 **Vyds** 22ha

John Ellis is the third under this name to be actively involved in the wine industry. His background as a 747 pilot, and the knowledge he gained of Burgundy over many visits, sets him apart from the others. He has established pinot noir (14ha), chardonnay (6ha) and pinot gris (2ha) on the red soils of a north-facing slope. He chose a density of 7150 vines per hectare, following as far as possible the precepts of Burgundy. Exports to the UK, the US, Denmark, Germany, Singapore and Japan.

ƒƒƒƒƒ **Quercus Vineyard Gippsland Pinot Noir 2015** From a dry-grown vineyard, the wine spends 1 year in French oak, 15% new. A touch forward in colour and taste, yet sweet fruit and exotic spices flood the medium-bodied palate. There's rhubarb, sweet-sour cherries, menthol, a lemony astringency and sinewy tannins. Screwcap. 13.3% alc. **Rating** 92 **To** 2020 $35 JF
Gippsland Pinot Grigio 2016 Three clones, cool fermented at 18°C, aged for 4 months on stirred lees, some in used barriques. A wine with freshness its raison d'être, the oak an input to texture, not flavour. Nashi pear and apple fill the palate nicely before acidity trims the finish. Screwcap. 12.5% alc. **Rating** 90 **To** 2018 $25

ƒƒƒƒ **Gippsland Pinot Noir 2016 Rating** 89 **To** 2021 $23 JF

Belvoir Park Estate

39 Belvoir Park Road, Big Hill, Vic 3453 **Region** Bendigo
T (03) 5435 3075 **www**.belvoirparkestate.com.au **Open** W'ends 12.30–5
Winemaker Greg McClure **Est.** 1996 **Dozens** 1000 **Vyds** 3ha

When Greg and Mell McClure purchased Belvoir Park Estate in November 2010 from founders Ian and Julie Hall, it was in excellent condition. The house, guarded by 200-year-old red gums, overlooks the vineyard (riesling, merlot, shiraz and cabernet sauvignon). It was very much a lifestyle change for the McClures. Greg's involvement in the marketing side of many businesses is evident in the renovation and extension of the cellar door, which now includes a gallery. A new jetty has been built on the vineyard dam, and an annual wine festival is held in November.

🍷🍷🍷🍷🍷 **Symphony Bendigo Shiraz Cabernet Merlot 2015** Looks and tastes exactly as it should: full crimson-purple, medium-bodied+ and full of juicy blackberry and blackcurrant fruit with the special minty nuance of the region. A seriously nice wine. Screwcap. 13.9% alc. **Rating** 94 **To** 2035 **$28** ✪

Ben Haines Wine ★★★★★

5 Parker Street, Lake Wendouree, Vic 3350 (postal) **Region** Various
T 0417 083 645 **www**.benhaineswine.com **Open** Not
Winemaker Ben Haines **Est.** 2010 **Dozens** 1800

Ben Haines graduated from the University of Adelaide in 1999 with a degree in viticulture, waiting a couple of years (immersing himself in music) before focusing on his wine career. An early interest in terroir led to a deliberate choice of diverse regions, including the Yarra Valley, McLaren Vale, Adelaide Hills, Langhorne Creek, Tasmania and Central Victoria, as well as time in the US and France. His services as a contract winemaker are in high demand, and his name bobs up all over the place. Exports to the US.

🍷🍷🍷🍷🍷 **B Minor Yarra Valley Chardonnay 2015** Hand-picked, whole-bunch pressed, wild-yeast fermented with high solids in puncheons, matured for 14 months. Ben Haines at his best, the music sensitively played from start to finish. The most remarkable thing is his ability to conjure up so much varietal fruit with only 12.1% alcohol. So, forgetting numbers, the flavour set of white peach and grapefruit, intermixed with cashew, is totally commanding. Screwcap. **Rating** 96 **To** 2025 **$28** ✪

B Minor Yarra Valley Pinot Noir 2015 Hand-picked from a hillside site in Coldstream and a valley floor vineyard at Yering, a portion of each fermented with whole bunches, the remainder whole berries and left on skins for 28 days, matured for 18 months. Extreme attention to detail goes hand in glove with great grapes, hence great wine. Its song has siren allure, the opening bars on the bouquet with notes of spice and fruit forest floor threaded through predominantly red fruits. The palate picks up the theme without missing a beat, at once silky yet firm, and with great length. Screwcap. 13.2% alc. **Rating** 96 **To** 2029 **$28** ✪

Warramunda Volta Marsanne 2015 From the Warramunda Vineyard in Coldstream. Whole-bunch pressed, a cool wild yeast fermentation in puncheons for 6 months, partial mlf, matured on lees for 9 months. Exceptional mouthfeel and flavour, more citrus than honeysuckle or pear, the oak evident more as texture than flavour. Screwcap. 12.4% alc. **Rating** 95 **To** 2025 **$35** ✪

B Minor Upper Goulburn Shiraz Marsanne 2015 Fermented in two batches: 100% whole bunches (with 'a few whole bunches' of marsanne) wild yeast–open fermented, the other whole berries with a small percentage of crushed fruit and some marsanne skins, both batches matured on '14 marsanne lees for 14 months in used oak. The wine is vibrantly fresh, with red and black fruits rippling through the medium-bodied palate, fine tannins providing the ever-so-logical conclusion. Screwcap. 13.9% alc. **Rating** 95 **To** 2030 **$28** ✪

Return to the Vale Syrah 2015 Hand-picked, two separate open ferments: 100% whole berries given 4 weeks post-ferment maceration, the other 100% whole bunches, matured for 16 months in French puncheons, the final blend 90% whole bunch, 10% whole berry. Good colour and clarity; full-bodied, but with panache; blackberry, plum and dark chocolate weave through each other framed by fine, but persistent tannins. Diam. 14.3% alc. **Rating** 94 **To** 2035 **$55**

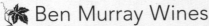

Ben Murray Wines ★★★★

PO Box 781, Tanunda, SA 5352 **Region** Barossa Valley
T 0438 824 493 **Open** Not
Winemaker Dan Eggleton **Est.** 2016 **Dozens** 500 **Vyds** 1ha

Ben Murray doesn't exist, but owners Dan Eggleton and Craig Thompson do. Each has had years of experience in various facets of the wine business, Dan with 20 years working for businesses ranging from major corporates to boutique enterprises. Craig brings a 1ha old vine grenache vineyard at Lyndoch into the venture, plus experience as a wine importer. The one thing they specifically have in common is a love of drinking wine.

ŸŸŸŸ♀ **Marananga Barossa Valley Grenache 2015** 60yo bushvines, hand-picked, destemmed, wild yeast–open fermented, hand-plunged, extended skin contact, matured in French oak (30% new). Bright, light crimson-purple; a lively, juicy, fresh wine, radically different from its Anima Reserve sibling, looking as if it's well under 14.5% alcohol. The red berry fruits have crisp acidity and no sign of confection. Screwcap. **Rating** 92 **To** 2021 $19 ✪
Cellar Release High Eden Riesling 2011 Machine-harvested, sorted, pressed directly to tank, wild-yeast fermented. It has the intensity, fuelled by acidity, of the cool, wet growing season. Just where it will head from here is a difficult question, one to which I don't have an answer. Screwcap. 12% alc. **Rating** 91 **To** 2020 $20 ✪
Marananga Barossa Valley Shiraz 2015 Hand-picked, wild yeast–open fermented, 10–16 days on skins, mainly matured in French oak (40% new) for 16 months. A full-bodied shiraz, deep in colour and black fruits, strong tannins and positive oak. At the moment still in separate boxes, needing several years to settle down and get on with life. Screwcap. 14.5% alc. **Rating** 90 **To** 2030 $70

ŸŸŸŸ **Anima Reserve Barossa Valley Grenache 2014** **Rating** 89 **To** 2018 $50

Bent Creek ★★★★

13 Blewitt Springs Road, McLaren Flat, SA 5171 **Region** McLaren Vale
T (08) 8383 0414 **www.**bentcreekvineyards.com.au **Open** W'ends 12–4
Winemaker Tim Geddes, Sam Rugari, David Garrick **Est.** 1999 **Dozens** 5000
Established in 1999, today Bent Creek is a joint partnership between Sam Rugari and David Garrick, collectively with over 40 years' experience in the wine industry. They source premium fruit from vineyards in McLaren Vale (with 70–100-year-old vines) to Piccadilly Valley in the Adelaide Hills, working closely with the growers. There is an overall focus on small parcels of high quality fruit that reflect the variety, vintage and unique terroir each has to offer. Exports to Indonesia, Hong Kong and China.

ŸŸŸŸ♀ **Black Dog McLaren Vale Shiraz 2015** Matured for 14 months in new and used American and French oak. A luscious, velvety regional shiraz oozing black fruits, both fresh and jammy (in a good way), with ripe tannins and oak. It doesn't require patience, but has so much left in the tank that it will go smoothly through the next 10 years. Screwcap. 14.5% alc. **Rating** 92 **To** 2029 $25 ✪
McLaren Vale Gamay Rosina Rose 2016 A fragrant bouquet with rose petal and strawberry aromas, the palate with red fruits to the fore, a touch of citrussy acidity bringing up the rear. Screwcap. 12.5% alc. **Rating** 91 **To** 2018 $20 ✪

ŸŸŸŸ **The Nude Old Vine Shiraz 2014** **Rating** 89 **To** 2030 $90

Beresford Wines ★★★★★

252 Blewitt Springs Road, McLaren Flat, SA 5171 **Region** McLaren Vale
T (08) 8383 0362 **www.**beresfordwines.com.au **Open** 7 days 10–5
Winemaker Chris Dix **Est.** 1985 **Dozens** 25 000 **Vyds** 28ha
This is a sister company to Step Rd Wines in Langhorne Creek, owned and run by VOK Beverages. The estate plantings are of cabernet sauvignon and shiraz (10ha each), chardonnay (5.5ha) and grenache (2.5ha), but they account for only a part of the substantial production. Some of the wines offer excellent value. Exports to the UK, the US, Germany, Denmark, Poland, Singapore, Hong Kong and China.

ŸŸŸŸŸ **Classic McLaren Vale Shiraz 2015** The savoury drive and buoyancy of the Classic really appeals. That's not to say it doesn't have dark plums, blackberries and currants, chocolate, soy sauce and spice, plus the richness and sweetness of the tannins, because those elements are all here. Packaged well and ready now. Screwcap. 14.5% alc. **Rating** 95 **To** 2027 $29 JF ✪

Grand Reserve McLaren Vale Shiraz 2015 A powerhouse of macerated black plums soaked in brandy, layers of savouriness, extract and the oak integrated. Chris Dix says the fruit is amazingly consistent, a pleasure to nurture into wine to create the ultimate expression of McLaren Vale shiraz: luxury in a glass. It will have its fans, but at a price. Screwcap. 14.1% alc. **Rating** 95 **To** 2045 $180 JF

Limited Release McLaren Vale Shiraz 2015 Deep purple-inky; a blockbuster with savoury umami flavours of black olives, dark chocolate, licorice, burnt caramel and oodles of oak, and yet integrated. The palate is a tidal wave of tannin and concentration, still coming together. Cork. 14.1% alc. **Rating** 94 **To** 2040 $80 JF

🍷🍷🍷🍷🍷 **Estate McLaren Vale Shiraz 2015 Rating** 93 **To** 2032 $50 JF
Classic McLaren Vale GSM 2015 Rating 93 **To** 2024 $29 JF
Estate McLaren Vale Grenache 2015 Rating 92 **To** 2023 $50 JF
McLaren Vale Sparkling Shiraz 2013 Rating 90 **To** 2017 $30 TS

Berton Vineyard ★★★★

55 Mirrool Avenue, Yenda, NSW 2681 **Region** Riverina
T (02) 6968 1600 **www**.bertonvineyards.com.au **Open** Mon–Fri 10–4, Sat 11–4
Winemaker James Ceccato, Bill Gumbleton **Est.** 2001 **Dozens** 1 million **Vyds** 32.14ha
The Berton Vineyard partners – Bob and Cherie Berton, James Ceccato and Jamie Bennett – have almost 100 years' combined experience in winemaking, viticulture, finance, production and marketing. 1996 saw the acquisition of a 30ha property in the Eden Valley and the planting of the first vines. Wines are released under the Berton Vineyard, Outback Jack and Head Over Heels labels. Exports to the UK, the US, Sweden, Norway, Russia, Japan and China.

🍷🍷🍷🍷🍷 **High Eden The Bonsai 2013** Shiraz and cabernet. Shiraz calls the tune in terms of varietal expression, with peppery, spicy, plummy aromas upfront supported by a chocolate/mocha back note which may include some oak influence. Rich in flavour (and alcohol, at 15%+) it maintains a feeling of elegance and suppleness, the tannins firm but fine enough to not intrude. Screwcap. 15% alc. **Rating** 93 **To** 2030 $40 SC

Reserve Barossa Shiraz 2014 Open-fermented on French oak chips and matured in French (30% new) and American (10% new) oak for 14 months. Small wonder that the French oak is as obvious as it is; there are enough good quality black fruits to capture attention and wallets – this is good value. Screwcap. 14.5% alc. **Rating** 90 **To** 2029 $17✪

Best's Wines ★★★★★

111 Best's Road, Great Western, Vic 3377 **Region** Grampians
T (03) 5356 2250 **www**.bestswines.com **Open** Mon–Sat 10–5, Sun 11–4
Winemaker Justin Purser **Est.** 1866 **Dozens** 20 000 **Vyds** 34ha
Best's winery and vineyards are among Australia's best-kept secrets. Indeed the vineyards, with vines dating back to 1866, have secrets that may never be revealed: for example, one of the vines planted in the Nursery Block has defied identification and is thought to exist nowhere else in the world. Part of the cellars, too, go back to the same era, constructed by butcher-turned-winemaker Henry Best and his family. The Thomson family has owned the property since 1920, with Ben, the fifth generation, having taken over management from father Viv. Best's consistently produces elegant, supple wines; the Bin No. 0 is a classic, the Thomson Family Shiraz (largely from vines planted in 1867) magnificent. In the *Wine Companion 2017* it was awarded the mantle of Wine of the Year from a field of almost 9000 wines. Very occasionally a pinot meunier (with 15% pinot noir) is made solely from 1868 plantings of those two varieties; there is no other Pinot Meunier of this vine age made anywhere else in the world. Justin Purser brings with him a remarkable CV, with extensive experience in Australia, NZ and Burgundy. Exports to the UK, the US, Canada, Sweden, Switzerland, Singapore, Hong Kong and China.

????? **Old Vine Great Western Pinot Meunier 2016** Made from the vines planted by Henry Best in 1868. Light, transparent crimson hue; the scented, flower-filled bouquet leads into what has to be the most deceptive palate of any Australian red wine. As you repeatedly taste the wine (and sneakily swallow a little) you pierce the veil in front of a rainbow of red fruit, spice and earthy notes, the fruit foremost. Here the history of wines made over recent decades proves a 25-year future. Screwcap. 12% alc. **Rating** 98 **To** 2046 $85

Thomson Family Great Western Shiraz 2015 Takes the keynote of intensity onto another level. Attention to detail in the vineyard throughout the growing season, and in the winery from the first juice to flow from the berries to the end of the bottling line are all reflected here. There is a total fusion of complex fruits, of licorice, spice and pepper sidelights, of fine, yet ripe, tannins that come from very old vines, and French oak, the texture running lengthways and sideways, but never breaking line. Screwcap. 14% alc **Rating** 98 **To** 2055 $200

Sparky's Block 1970 Vines Great Western Shiraz 2014 The best selection from the block planted in '70, Sparky the nickname of Marcus Thomson, born in '70. A great shiraz, the pity being only 50 dozen bottles produced. Its deep colour, and highly aromatic bouquet, spanning a rainbow of spices, lay the path for the very complex medium-bodied palate, with luscious dark fruits and superb tannins. Cork. 13.5% alc. **Rating** 97 **To** 2054 $150 ◐

Bin No. 0 Great Western Shiraz 2013 A quite beautiful medium-bodied wine with glorious red and black cherry fruit, superfine tannins and classy oak all in total harmony – so much so you can forget just where you are on the journey through to the finish. Screwcap. 14% alc. **Rating** 97 **To** 2043 $85

????? **House Block Great Western Riesling 2016** The wine immediately captures the palate with the intensity and depth of its Bickford's lime juice flavours; the acidity is part and parcel of the very long palate, and while there is abundant flavour to sustain immediate enjoyment, its best years are yet to come, its future unlimited. Screwcap. 10% alc. **Rating** 96 **To** 2036 $35 ◐

Great Western Pinot Meunier Pinot Noir 2016 Crafted from old (1868) and young (planted a century later) vines, plus a small amount of old-clone pinot noir. A vibrant, intense and perfectly balanced wine that always challenges perceptions of a delicate wine best suited to sparkling wine. The colour is fabulous, the red fruit flavours vibrant and lingering. Screwcap. 12.5% alc. **Rating** 96 **To** 2036 $45 ◐

White Gravels Hill Great Western Shiraz 2015 An explosion of spices, oriental and savoury, open proceedings for a lively free-spirited wine with some whole bunches in the ferment adding a dimension different from its stable mates. Red fruits have a greater say here, but remain totally within the house style. Screwcap. 13% alc. **Rating** 96 **To** 2030 $45 ◐

Great Western Riesling 2016 The floral bouquet is attractive, but doesn't prepare you for the waves of Meyer lemon and lime of the richly juicy fruit that floods the palate. History shows how long Grampians rieslings live and flourish, but it would be no sin to drink this tonight as long as you have a few bottles stashed away Screwcap. 11.5% alc. **Rating** 95 **To** 2029 $25 ◐

Foudre Ferment Concongella Vineyards Great Western Riesling 2016 Winemaker Justin Purser's worldwide wine knowledge gave him the courage to give the juice extended skin contact, and wild yeast ferment it in a large oak foudre. The complexity of the funky bouquet is striking, and the flavours are mouthfilling. It is fermented dry at only 11%, yet has intense Meyer lemon and lime fruit, and cool climate acidity, giving the fresh finish and aftertaste. Screwcap. 11% alc. **Rating** 95 **To** 2029 $35

Great Western Pinot Noir 2016 You might think that given the light colour and the low alcohol this wine was made for early consumption. And so it can be, but you'll be deprived of its long future. Its damson plum and cherry fruit is given complexity by savoury forest floor nuances coupled with full, but persistent, tannins. Screwcap. 12% alc. **Rating** 95 **To** 2029 $25 ◐

Bin No. 1 Great Western Shiraz 2015 Bright crimson-purple; fragrant spice, fruit and oak nuances are all on parade from the first whiff. The elegant, medium-bodied palate throws additional light on the complex array of cherry, plum, licorice and oak flavours; supple texture and silky tannins tie the bow on a lovely, dirt cheap shiraz. Screwcap. 14% alc. **Rating** 95 **To** 2030 $25 ✪

Bin No. 0 Great Western Shiraz 2015 Deep colour; the bouquet immediately wrests attention to its profound black fruits that follow in the full-bodied palate. Has remarkable power and intensity to its array of black fruits, licorice, spice and pepper flavours, all bound together by French oak. Intensity is the keyword. Screwcap. 14% alc. **Rating** 95 **To** 2035 $85

F.H.T. Great Western Shiraz 1999 From plantings in 1868, 1966, '70 and '92; includes 3% cabernet sauvignon; fermented for 7 days, mlf in tank, matured in American puncheons (22% new) for 16 months. F.H.T. stands for Fredrick Hamill Thomson, Viv Thomson's father, who passed away in '98. The overall yield of 20% of normal meant only one red wine was made at Best's in '99. Still substantial, on an upwards path; there is a wealth of black fruits, spice and licorice on the bouquet and palate, coupled with tannins that will keep the structure intact for years to come. My only reservation is the choice of American oak. Cork. 14.5% alc. **Rating** 95 **To** 2029 $150

Great Western Cabernet Sauvignon 2015 This is all about showing how elegance and intensity can be woven together to create the perfect medium-bodied palate. Blackcurrant, a waft of leaf, a glimmer of eucalypt and cedary oak/tannin nuances all join hands to support each other on the long, fresh palate. Don't be deceived: this will stand proud for 30+ years thanks to its immaculate balance. Screwcap. 14% alc. **Rating** 95 **To** 2045 $25 ✪

Great Western Sparkling Shiraz 2013 A grand expression of the mineral texture, depth of old vine black plum skin and blackberry fruit and savoury allure that defines the fame of this magnificent old estate. Superfine tannins, a creamy bead and perfectly gauged dosage unite on an enduring finish accented by dark chocolate and coffee. Crown seal. 14% alc. **Rating** 95 **To** 2025 $35 TS

Great Western Chardonnay 2016 Very much in the modern style of chardonnay, early picked to retain fresh fruit flavours and natural acidity not requiring adjustment – the risk is picking a few days too soon, leaving the wine skeletal. This (just) avoids that, and I like the buzzing energy on the long palate and the lingering citrussy acidity. Screwcap. 12.5% alc. **Rating** 94 **To** 2026 $25 ✪

LSV Great Western Shiraz Viognier 2015 Contract-grown shiraz from some of the most elevated vineyards in the region were co-fermented with 4% viognier. The co-fermentation has worked very well, lifting the fruit profile on the fragrant bouquet and supple palate alike, with a blend of juicy red and black fruits supported by tannins and oak. Screwcap. 14% alc. **Rating** 94 **To** 2030 $35

🍷🍷🍷🍷🍷 **Great Western Shiraz Nouveau 2016 Rating** 92 **To** 2021 $25 ✪

Bethany Wines ★★★★★

378 Bethany Road, Tanunda, SA 5352 **Region** Barossa
T (08) 8563 2086 **www**.bethany.com.au **Open** Mon–Sat 10–5, Sun 1–5
Winemaker Alex MacClelland **Est.** 1981 **Dozens** 25 000 **Vyds** 38ha

The Schrapel family has been growing grapes in the Barossa Valley for 140 years, and has had the winery since 1981. In their winery nestled high on a hillside on the site of an old bluestone quarry, Geoff and Rob Schrapel produce a range of consistently well made and attractively packaged wines. Bethany has vineyards in the Barossa and Eden valleys. Exports to the UK, Europe and Asia.

🍷🍷🍷🍷🍷 **Reserve Eden Valley Riesling 2016** Ultra-restraint with a waft of florals, lemony bath salts and chalky-citrussy acidity; refreshing on the palate. Tightly coiled, dry to the core. Finishes long. Screwcap. 11.5% alc. **Rating** 93 **To** 2027 $32 JF

Barossa Shiraz 2014 Produced from 80–100yo vines along the eastern edge of the Barossa Ranges. Open-fermented, and matured for 22 months in new and used French oak. A fine example of Barossa shiraz in medium-bodied, unencumbered form. Ripe red and black fruits on display; it has an easy generosity and just so tannins to match. Screwcap. 13.9% alc. Rating 91 To 2026 $30 SC

Between the Vines ★★★★

452 Longwood Road, Longwood, SA 5153 **Region** Adelaide Hills
T 0403 933 767 **www**.betweenthevines.com.au **Open** W'ends & public hols 12–5
Winemaker Matt Jackman, Simon Greenleaf **Est.** 2013 **Dozens** 400 **Vyds** 2.1ha
The estate vineyard (2.1ha of chardonnay) was planted in 1995, and purchased by Stewart and Laura Moodie in 2006. The vineyard is fully managed by Stewart and Laura, who do all the spraying/netting/wire lifting, pruning, fruit and shoot thinning, Laura having undertaken a year-long viticulture course. They employ backpackers for labour where needed, and only bring in professional teams for the harvest. In '13, the Moodies created the Between the Vines brand, grafting 0.2ha of tempranillo (on chardonnay rootstock). Output has increased, and small quantities of Pinot Noir and Tempranillo are bottled under their label. Matt Jackman makes the wine in consultation with the Moodies (Simon Greenleaf makes the sparkling wines).

🍷🍷🍷🍷 Single Vineyard Adelaide Hills Tempranillo 2013 This is a no nonsense, sock it to 'em tempranillo laden with red and black cherry fruit, plus firm acidity and controlled tannins. Retasting pulls it back from the initially threatening pose, and cellaring will aid the cause further. Screwcap. 14.5% alc. Rating 90 To 2023 $22

Bicknell fc ★★★★★

41 St Margarets Road, Healesville, Vic 3777 **Region** Yarra Valley
T 0488 678 427 **www**.bicknellfc.com **Open** Not
Winemaker David Bicknell **Est.** 2011 **Dozens** 300 **Vyds** 2.5ha
This is the busman's holiday for Oakridge chief winemaker David Bicknell and (former) viticulturist (present) partner Nicky Harris. It is focused purely on chardonnay and pinot noir, with no present intention of broadening the range; nor, indeed, the volume of production. As from '14 all the grapes have come from Val Stewart's close-planted vineyard at Gladysdale, planted in 1988. The partners have leased this vineyard, which will become the total focus of their business. From 2015 the wines will be labelled Applecross, the name of the highest mountain pass in Scotland, a place that David Bicknell's father was very fond of.

🍷🍷🍷🍷🍷 Applecross Yarra Valley Chardonnay 2015 Whole-bunch pressed, fermented in used French puncheons, no mlf, matured for 10 months on lees. Good things come in small parcels, here in no uncertain fashion. While it has all the finesse of the Upper Yarra, it has a shining purity to its intensity, and to the way the flavours build as the wine reaches the end of its journey in the mouth. White peach, nectarine, citrus — you name it. Screwcap. 13.3% alc. Rating 96 To 2027 $45
Yarra Valley Chardonnay 2014 0.7t/ha after dreadful conditions during flowering, whole-bunch pressed, fermented in a single used puncheon, no mlf, matured on lees for 11 months, 45 dozen made. '14 may have been a go along to get along vintage for pinot noir, but it produced excellent chardonnays in the Yarra Valley. This one has depth and power, and is strongly reminiscent of top White Burgundy. Screwcap. 13.7% alc. Rating 95 To 2027 $39
Applecross Yarra Valley Pinot Noir 2015 The life of a vigneron can be a most unhappy one, as it was for this vintage, starting with yield-reducing pruning, dropping the fruiting wire from 800–600mm, then losing 4 tonnes of grapes in 3 days to birds just prior to picking. The net result a yield of 0.6t/ha and only 75 dozen made, the last cut an OTT SO_2 addition, which will give the wine longevity, its future assured. Screwcap. 12.7% alc. Rating 94 To 2025 $45

Billy Button Wines

11 Camp Street, Bright, Vic 3741 **Region** Alpine Valleys
T 0418 559 344 **www.**billybuttonwines.com.au **Open** Thurs–Sun 12–6
Winemaker Jo Marsh **Est.** 2014 **Dozens** 3500

Jo Marsh speaks quietly, if not diffidently, making light of the numerous awards she won during her studies for her Degree in Agricultural Science (Oenology) at the University of Adelaide. She continued that habit when she won a contested position in Southcorp's (now Treasury Wine Estates) Graduate Recruitment Program; she was appointed assistant winemaker at Seppelt Great Western in 2003. By '08 she had been promoted to acting senior winemaker, responsible for all wines made onsite. After resigning from Seppelt, she became winemaker at Feathertop, and after two happy years decided to step out on her own in '14 to create Billy Button Wines. She has set up a grower network in the Alpine Valleys and makes a string of excellent wines.

ΨΨΨΨΨ **The Versatile Alpine Valleys Vermentino 2016** Hand-picked, whole-bunch pressed, wild-yeast fermented in stainless steel, matured on lees for 3 months with occasional stirring. Vermentino is definitely here to stay. It has a resolute character that comes through in almost all climates. The aftertaste welds together the citrus, spice and ginger notes of the bouquet and palate thanks to intense, refreshing acidity. Screwcap. 12.5% alc. **Rating** 95 **To** 2021 $25 ✪
The Affable Alpine Valleys Barbera 2015 It feels and tastes like the result of a strong vintage. It's both robust and frisky, with red and forest berry fruits chattering 'affably' away. Herb-like notes add a certain presence to the finish but fruit characters never relinquish the stage. Terrific drinking. Screwcap. 13.5% alc. **Rating** 94 **To** 2021 $30 CM ✪
The Alluring Alpine Valleys Tempranillo 2015 A thoroughly gorgeous wine. Perfumed and fruit-driven, and so pretty in that way, but with plenty of grunty, earthen, cola-infused tannin and more than a little attitude throughout. Berried fruit bursts though the palate and extends out through the finish. A flush of acid applies some kind of rein. More than anything, it carves the word 'exuberance' on your tongue. Screwcap. 13.5% alc. **Rating** 94 **To** 2023 $30 CM ✪
The Squid Alpine Valleys Saperavi 2015 Vinified in two parcels: the first destemmed and wild yeast–open fermented, matured in used barriques for 15 months; the second parcel wild-yeast fermented in a terracotta amphora and left on skins for 6 months, then transferred to a used puncheon for a further 9 months before blending. Deep, dense purple-crimson; extremely concentrated and powerful; the complex vinification has worked very well indeed – natural winemaking in reverse. The profile is interesting, with no more tannins on the finish than on the first sip. Screwcap. 14.5% alc. **Rating** 94 **To** 2025 $30 ✪

ΨΨΨΨΨ The Classic Alpine Valleys Chardonnay 2015 Rating 93 To 2020 $30
The Honest Alpine Valleys Fiano 2016 Rating 93 To 2021 $25 ✪
2 by 2 Shiraz Tempranillo 2015 Rating 93 To 2025 $25 ✪
The Torment King Valley Riesling 2016 Rating 92 To 2023 $25 ✪
Happy Alpine Valleys Gewurztraminer 2016 Rating 92 To 2022 $25 ✪
The Beloved Alpine Valleys Shiraz 2015 Rating 92 To 2029 $30
2 by 2 Sangiovese Cabernet 2015 Rating 92 To 2019 $25 ✪
The Rustic Alpine Valleys Sangiovese 2015 Rating 92 To 2022 $30 CM
2 by 2 Nebbiolo Barbera Rose 2015 Rating 91 To 2017 $25
Renegade Alpine Valleys Refosco 2015 Rating 91 To 2020 $30 CM
The Clandestine Schioppettino 2015 Rating 90 To 2020 $30 CM

Bimbadgen

★★★★★

790 McDonalds Road, Pokolbin, NSW 2320 **Region** Hunter Valley
T (02) 4998 4600 **www.**bimbadgen.com.au **Open** Fri–Sat 10–7, Sun–Thurs 10–5
Winemaker Rauri Donkin, Mike De Garis **Est.** 1968 **Dozens** 35000 **Vyds** 23.12ha

Bimbadgen's Palmers Lane vineyard was planted in 1968 and the McDonalds Road vineyard shortly thereafter, both sites providing a source of old vine semillon, shiraz and chardonnay. Since assuming ownership in '97, the Lee family has applied the same level of care and attention to cultivating Bimbadgen as they have to other properties in their portfolio. The small but impressive production is consumed largely by the owner's luxury hotel assets, with limited quantities available in the Sydney market. Exports to the UK, Switzerland, Germany, The Netherlands, Japan, Taiwan and China.

ŸŸŸŸŸ Family Collection Little Maverick Hunter Valley Shiraz 2014 A complex fragrance offers a plume of spiced plums, warm earth and dark fruit, menthol and charcoal, with the oak well stitched into place. The medium-weight palate takes everything in its stride, with ripe fine tannins, refreshing acidity and great length. Screwcap. 14% alc. **Rating** 95 **To** 2038 $100 JF
Estate Hunter Valley Semillon 2011 Very pale green; a fragrant, aromatic bouquet, then a well balanced palate with a juicy mix of lemon, lemongrass, and grass (three quite distinct flavours). Screwcap. 10% alc. **Rating** 94 **To** 2021 $20 ✪
Riverina Botrytis Semillon 2015 A glowing mid-gold colour; saffron-infused honey, apricots and lemon-cumquat marmalade entice on the nose while the neatly played lemony acidity balances out the sweetness. Screwcap. 12% alc. **Rating** 94 **To** 2019 $25 JF ✪

ŸŸŸŸŸ Signature Hunter Valley Semillon 2016 Rating 93 **To** 2026 $50 JF
MCA Range Orange Barbera 2015 Rating 93 **To** 2020 $29 JF
MCA Range Hunter Valley Fiano 2016 Rating 92 **To** 2021 $29 JF
Reserve Hunter Valley Shiraz 2015 Rating 92 **To** 2032 $65 JF
Hunter Valley Fortified Verdelho NV Rating 92 $29 JF
Signature Hunter Valley Semillon 2013 Rating 91 **To** 2025 $50 JF
Estate Hunter Valley Chardonnay 2013 Rating 90 **To** 2019 $50 JF
Hunter Valley Vermentino 2016 Rating 90 **To** 2019 $29 JF

Bindi Wine Growers   ★★★★★

343 Melton Road, Gisborne, Vic 3437 (postal) **Region** Macedon Ranges
T (03) 5428 2564 **www**.bindiwines.com.au **Open** Not
Winemaker Michael Dhillon, Stuart Anderson **Est.** 1988 **Dozens** 2000 **Vyds** 6ha
One of the icons of Macedon. The Chardonnay is top-shelf, the Pinot Noir as remarkable (albeit in a very different idiom) as Bass Phillip, Giaconda or any of the other tiny-production, icon wines. The addition of Heathcote-sourced shiraz under the Pyrette label confirms Bindi as one of the greatest small producers in Australia. Exports to the UK and the US.

ŸŸŸŸŸ Original Vineyard Pinot Noir 2015 27yo MV6 clone, hand-picked, 95% whole berries, 5% whole bunches, 16 days on skins, matured for 15 months in French barriques (30% new). The brilliantly clear colour signals a super-fragrant wine, spicy/savoury nuances attesting to the very cool climate of the Macedon Ranges, its balance and length impeccable. Screwcap. 14% alc. **Rating** 96 **To** 2030 $85

Bird in Hand   ★★★★★

Bird in Hand Road, Woodside, SA 5244 **Region** Adelaide Hills
T (08) 8389 9488 **www**.birdinhand.com.au **Open** Mon–Fri 10–5, w'ends 11–5
Winemaker Kym Milne MW, Peter Ruchs **Est.** 1997 **Dozens** 75 000 **Vyds** 29ha
This very successful business takes its name from a 19th-century gold mine. It is the venture of the Nugent family, headed by Dr Michael Nugent; son Andrew is a Roseworthy graduate. The family also has a vineyard in the Clare Valley, the latter providing riesling and shiraz. The estate plantings (merlot, pinot noir, cabernet sauvignon, sauvignon blanc, riesling, shiraz) provide only part of the annual crush, the remainder coming from contract growers. In 2010, a Bird in Hand cellar door was opened in Dalian, in China's northeastern Liaoning province, with a second following in Yingkou. Exports to all major markets.

🍷🍷🍷🍷🍷 **Adelaide Hills Shiraz 2015** Matured in French oak. Good colour; the Adelaide Hills wastes no time in imprinting its signature on what is an exceptionally good wine. The symphony of fruit, tannins and oak flavours plays without interruption as you navigate the complex palate, with luscious red and black cherry fruits dipped momentarily in dark chocolate. This is high quality fruit beautifully handled in the winery. Screwcap. 14.5% alc. **Rating** 97 **To** 2045 $42 ✪

🍷🍷🍷🍷🍷 **Nest Egg Mt Lofty Ranges Shiraz 2013** It's not exactly a cool climate style, but it does show traces of pepper and dried spice. Mostly it's beefy, rich and substantial, with thick, long chains of tannin and rivers of dark, berried, inky fruit and cedary, smoky, malty oak. Time is required, but its future is supremely bright. Screwcap. 14.5% alc. **Rating** 96 **To** 2035 $99 CM

M.A.C. Mt Lofty Ranges Shiraz 2013 A best barrels selection, matured for 24 months in tight-grained French oak, 2200 numbered bottles released. Remarkably youthful colour; a very classy wine, intense and long, with juicy red and black cherry and blackberry fruits supported (but not challenged) by cedary French oak and firm, dusty tannins. Screwcap. 14.5% alc. **Rating** 96 **To** 2043 $350

Marie Elizabeth Adelaide Hills Cabernet Sauvignon 2013 Has all the hallmarks of top class cabernet sauvignon, blackcurrant to the fore, plus nuances of black olive and sage; typical cabernet tannins run through the palate, their role to support, not challenge, the fruit. The balance between the French oak resulting from 24 months maturation and the opulent fruit is nigh on perfect. Screwcap. 14.5% alc. **Rating** 96 **To** 2043 $350

Adelaide Hills Chardonnay 2016 It's hard to imagine a chardonnay that so immediately establishes its harmony, elegance and inner peace. All the citrus and stone fruit flavours are there, the French oak important yet totally integrated, acidity there if the question is asked. Screwcap. 13.5% alc. **Rating** 95 **To** 2024 $42

Nest Egg Adelaide Hills Chardonnay 2015 Well made, with a web of fig, nectarine and peach (part white, part yellow) fruit complemented by well handled oak. Impossible to fault, but it lacks the X-factor of the very best Aus chardonnays. Screwcap. 13.5% alc. **Rating** 95 **To** 2023 $79

Adelaide Hills Chardonnay 2015 Wild-yeast fermented, mlf and lees stirring in a mix of new and used French barriques. The harmony and elegance of this wine are not in doubt. White peach, apple and apricot align themselves with the subtle oak and supple finish. Screwcap. 13.5% alc. **Rating** 95 **To** 2022 $35 ✪

M.A.C. Mt Lofty Ranges Shiraz 2012 A barrel selection following 24 months maturation in French oak. Good depth and hue; there is only one issue about what is clearly a very good wine: the amount of French oak. The answer to that question may well vary from taster to taster, but I take a (heavily qualified) position, and say it is too much. Screwcap. 14.5% alc. **Rating** 95 **To** 2032 $350

Nest Egg Adelaide Hills Merlot 2013 Open-fermented, 21 days on skins, pressed to French oak for 18 months. As long as you are content that there is no reason why merlot shouldn't be full-bodied, this ticks all the boxes. It has cassis, black olive and bay leaf supported by ripe tannins and obvious (but not excessive) French oak. Screwcap. 14% alc. **Rating** 95 **To** 2028 $99

🍷🍷🍷🍷🍷 **Adelaide Hills Pinot Rose 2016 Rating** 93 **To** 2017 $20 JF ✪
Nest Egg Cabernet Sauvignon 2013 Rating 93 **To** 2030 $99 CM
Adelaide Hills Montepulciano 2015 Rating 93 **To** 2029 $45
Clare Valley Riesling 2016 Rating 92 **To** 2030 $25 SC ✪
Honeysuckle Clare Valley Riesling 2016 Rating 91 **To** 2020 $25 JF
Adelaide Hills Pinot Gris 2016 Rating 90 **To** 2019 $25 JF

Bird on a Wire Wines   ★★★★★

51 Symons Street, Healesville, Vic 3777 (postal) **Region** Yarra Valley
T 0439 045 000 **www.**birdonawirewines.com.au **Open** By appt
Winemaker Caroline Mooney **Est.** 2008 **Dozens** 500

This is now the full-time business of winemaker Caroline Mooney, who grew up in the Yarra Valley and who has had (other full-time) winemaking jobs in the valley for over 10 years. The focus is on small, single vineyard sites owned by growers committed to producing outstanding grapes. Exports to the UK.

ŸŸŸŸŸ Yarra Valley Chardonnay 2014 A finely structured wine reflecting the particularly good chardonnay vintage in the Yarra Valley. Nothing has been overplayed, and the wine will grow and grow over the next 5 years, but not lose its shape. Screwcap. 13% alc. **Rating** 95 **To** 2029 $45

Yarra Valley Syrah 2014 Reflects the low-yielding vintage with its fuller than usual body. Spice, leather, licorice and blackberry all take a bow at the first and subsequent curtain calls – and subsequent there are, for the wine progressively reveals more and more, drawing you back to its juicy essence notes and tannins. Screwcap. 14.5% alc. **Rating** 95 **To** 2029 $45

ŸŸŸŸŸ Yarra Valley Nebbiolo 2015 Rating 90 **To** 2025 $47

Birthday Villa Vineyard

101 Mollison Street, Malmsbury, Vic 3446 **Region** Macedon Ranges
T (03) 5423 2789 **www.**birthdayvilla.com.au **Open** W'ends 11–5
Winemaker Cameron Leith (Passing Clouds) **Est.** 1976 **Dozens** 300 **Vyds** 2ha
The Birthday Villa name comes from the 19th-century Birthday Mine at nearby Drummond discovered on Queen Victoria's birthday. Gewurztraminer (1.5ha) was planted in 1962; cabernet sauvignon (0.5ha) followed later. The quality of the Gewurztraminer comes as no surprise, as the very cool climate is suited to the variety. On the other hand, the Cabernet Sauvignon comes as a major surprise, although cool vintages provide a challenge.

ŸŸŸŸŸ Malmsbury Gewurztraminer 2016 Hand-picked, whole-bunch pressed, fermented in tank with cultured yeast. The scented, floral musk bouquet is handsomely varietal, and the textured palate adds to the appeal. It's entirely the result of first class fruit coming from the vineyard in a vintage that suited the very cool Malmsbury site. Screwcap. 12.8% alc. **Rating** 91 **To** 2022 $28

Malmsbury Gewurztraminer 2015 Less overtly varietal than the '16, but makes up for that with its length, balance and firm, lingering finish. Screwcap. 12% alc. **Rating** 90 **To** 2021 $28

Bittern Estate

8 Bittern-Dromana Road, Bittern, Vic 3918 **Region** Mornington Peninsula
T 0417 556 529 **www.**bitternestate.com.au **Open** By appt
Winemaker Alex White, Carl Tiesdell-Smith **Est.** 2013 **Dozens** 4500 **Vyds** 7ha
The Zerbe family has been involved in horticulture for many generations since arriving from Prussia in 1854, planting fruit trees in what is now suburban Melbourne. Generations later, in 1959, the family planted an apple and pear orchard called Tathravale. In '96, Gary and Karen Zerbe began planting the Bittern Vineyard on this property, the extended family providing the third generation of grapegrowers. In that year the family produced its first full array of wine styles under the Bittern Estate label. There was an involvement with Box Stallion, but following land sales by third parties, that venture has terminated. Continuity is provided by the winemaking team of Alex White and Carl Tiesdell-Smith. Exports to China.

ŸŸŸŸŸ Mornington Peninsula Chardonnay 2015 Destemmed and crushed before 6 hours skin contact prior to pressing; clear juice was barrel-fermented to age on lees, then transferred to French oak for completion of mlf. Bright pale straw-green; has a racy grapefruit stream at its heart, oak phenolics framing that fruit on both bouquet and palate. Screwcap. 13.4% alc. **Rating** 90 **To** 2020 $25

Mornington Peninsula Arneis 2013 Crushed and destemmed, then skin-contacted for 8 hours before cold settling for cool fermentation of clear juice. Has the complex raft of citrus pith, zest and lemongrass arneis can provide on both the bouquet and palate. Screwcap. 13.6% alc. **Rating** 90 **To** 2020 $20 ✪

BK Wines ★★★★★

Burdetts Road, Basket Range, SA 5138 **Region** Adelaide Hills
T 0410 124 674 **www**.bkwines.com.au **Open** By appt
Winemaker Brendon Keys **Est.** 2007 **Dozens** 3500

BK Wines is owned by NZ-born Brendon Keys and wife Kirsty. Brendon has packed a great deal of high and low living into the past decade, managing a chalet in the French Alps for eight months. Bouncing between Australia and NZ before working in California with the well known Paul Hobbs, he then helped Paul set up a winery in Argentina. Brendon's tag-line is 'wines made with love, not money', and he has not hesitated to confound the normal rules of engagement in winemaking. If he isn't remembered for this, the labels for his wines should do the trick. Exports to the UK, the US, Canada, Singapore, Hong Kong and Japan.

ŸŸŸŸŸ **Springs Hill Series Blewitt Springs Sparks McLaren Vale Grenache 2015**
100% whole bunches, wild-yeast fermented, 1 month on skins, matured in used French puncheons. Blewitt Springs does it again, and again, and again ... It gives the wine a freshness, a purity, a focus and a sublime balance to its red cherry, raspberry and redcurrant rainbow of flavours. I rarely swallow when I'm tasting, but did here. Screwcap. 13.5% alc. **Rating** 97 **To** 2025 $44 **✪**

ŸŸŸŸŸ **Springs Hill Series Blewitt Springs Red Blend 2015** An (unspecified percentage) blend of mourvedre, shiraz and grenache from Blewitt Springs, 100% whole bunches, wild-yeast fermented, 1 month on skins, matured in French puncheons (10% new). It has remarkable colour, deep and bright, setting the scene for a wine of perfect balance and flavours of every manner of red, purple, blue and black fruits. There is so much going on it is perhaps inevitable that it should back off infinitesimally on the finish. Screwcap. 13% alc. **Rating** 96 **To** 2030 $44 **✪**

Swaby Single Vineyard Piccadilly Valley Chardonnay 2015 Hand-picked clone I10V1, whole-bunch pressed, wild-yeast fermented in French oak (30% new), matured for 9 months. Has layered complexity, with minerally acidity and French oak woven through the folds of green apple and white peach fruit. Still on an upwards curve of development. Screwcap. 12.5% alc. **Rating** 95 **To** 2024 $55

One Ball Single Vineyard Kenton Valley Adelaide Hills Chardonnay 2015 The vinification has worked well, all with a gentle touch that keeps the focus on the generous white peach/grapefruit/fig fruit. A very attractive wine. Screwcap. 12.8% alc. **Rating** 95 **To** 2021 $32 **✪**

Archer Beau Single Barrel Piccadilly Valley Adelaide Hills Chardonnay 2015 A single best (new) barrique selection, matured for 11 months in barrel, then a further year in bottle, 20 dozen made. The flavours are strongly citrus (grapefruit), but have the intensity to stare down suggestions of wannabe sauvignon blanc. Vino-Lok. 12.5% alc. **Rating** 95 **To** 2021 $85

Remy Single Barrel Lenswood Adelaide Hills Pinot Noir 2015 A best barrel selection from the Gower Pinot Noir, named after the the Keys' youngest son, wild-yeast fermented, matured in 100% new French oak for 9 months. Star-bright crimson-purple hue; has a fragrant spicy/earthy bouquet and a very tight and as yet unevolved palate where stem, fruit and oak tannins provide formidable opposition to wild strawberry fruit, often noted for its acidity. I'm not sure I really like the wine, but I am impressed by it. Vino-Lok. 12% alc. **Rating** 95 **To** 2023 $85

Mazi Whole Bunch Blewitt Springs McLaren Vale Syrah 2014 From the dry-grown Springs Hill Vineyard, 100% whole bunches, matured in a new French puncheon for 12 months, plus a further 18 months in bottle, 50 dozen made. It's oh so hard to finesse a single barrel wine, its destiny written the moment it is pumped into the barrel. If you accept the consequences of this approach, the wine can't be faulted. Screwcap. 13.5% alc. **Rating** 95 **To** 2034 $85

Skin n' Bones Single Vineyard Lenswood Adelaide Hills Pinot Noir 2016 No skin and bones about the colour or, for that matter, aromas and flavours; a ripe, dark compote of plums and spices belie its modest alcohol – which plays an important role in letting the light in. Screwcap. 12.8% alc. **Rating** 94 **To** 2026 $32

Springs Hill Series Blewitt Springs Sparks McLaren Vale Grenache 2016
Good colour; grenache is as grenache does – in McLaren Vale, that is. Rich cherry and plum fruits with a stack of spices, and no confection notes; long and juicily rounded in the mouth. Screwcap. 13.5% alc. **Rating** 94 **To** 2028 $44

ŢŢŢŢŢ **Skin n' Bones Skin Contact White 2015 Rating** 92 **To** 2020 $32
Saignee of Pinot Noir Lenswood Rose 2016 Rating 92 **To** 2019 $25 **✪**
One Ball Kenton Valley Chardonnay 2016 Rating 91 **To** 2022 $32
Inox Lenswood Adelaide Hills Pinot Grigio 2016 Rating 90 **To** 2017 $25
Skin n' Bones Lenswood Pinot Noir 2015 Rating 90 **To** 2022 $32

Black Bishop Wines ★★★★

1 Valdemar Court, Magill, SA 5072 (postal) **Region** Adelaide Hills
T 0422 791 775 www.blackbishopwines.com.au **Open** Not
Winemaker Damon Koerner **Est.** 2012 **Dozens** 2000
Black Bishop was established by three mates from school, Jack Horsnell, Damon Koerner and Chris Bishop, each 27 years old. Chris has an ongoing love for Barossa Shiraz, and thought that it made sense to make his own wine rather than purchasing it from others; Damon grew up in the Watervale district of the Clare Valley, and studied oenology and viticulture at Adelaide University, working vintages across Australia and abroad since graduation; and Jack grew up living and working in Adelaide Hills hotels, often drinking ('way') too much local wine.

ŢŢŢŢŢ **Single Vineyard Adelaide Hills Sauvignon Blanc 2015** A subtle, thoughtfully made wine. Aromas are clearly sauvignon blanc, in the citrus, passionfruit, faintly grassy rather than tropical fruit spectrum. The flavours and mouthfeel build quietly layer by layer, finishing with good length and well concealed acidity. A food wine in the best sense. Screwcap. 12.8% alc. **Rating** 90 **To** 2018 $20 SC **✪**

Black Range Estate ★★★★

638 Limestone Road, Yea, Vic 3717 **Region** Upper Goulburn
T (03) 5797 2882 **Open** Not
Winemaker Paul Evans **Est.** 2001 **Dozens** 400 **Vyds** 24ha
Rogan Lumsden and Jessica Ng were based in Hong Kong, he as a pilot for Dragonair, she inflight manager for Cathay Pacific, but each was thinking of life after airlines. In 2000 they purchased the property where they now live, and planted the first vines (7ha of shiraz and 2.4ha of merlot), following up with 4.5ha of pinot noir and 10.1ha of pinot gris in '03. The first vintage of Merlot and Shiraz was made that year. Plan A was to sell the grapes, with what they term 'wild ideas of adding accommodation and a restaurant following our retirement years later'. The vagaries of the industry made them graft 4.5ha of merlot to pinot noir in '14, even though in '13 (following inspiration from running the Medoc Marathon three times after learning it came complete with wine tasting tables as it wound its way through the vineyards) they had asked Paul Evans to make a merlot – the first time they had taken the final step of having wine made for them.

ŢŢŢŢŢ **Rogan Yea Valley Merlot 2014** The challenge was a big one: make a merlot in the style of St Emilion. The wine does have some elegance, and a slightly savoury edge to its cassis and plum fruit. The fine tannins are another plus. Screwcap. 13% alc. **Rating** 92 **To** 2023 $22 **✪**

Black Stump Wines ★★★☆

Riverton Railway Station, Riverton, SA 5412 **Region** Various
T 0415 971 113 www.blackstumpwines.com **Open** By appt
Winemaker Tim Mortimer **Est.** 1988 **Dozens** 400
Tim Mortimer went down a number of blind alleys trying to find the best way to gain an economic foothold in the wine industry. After seven years of experimentation, he decided to focus on riesling from the Great Southern and elsewhere in South West Australia, infilling with red wines from SA headed by Nebbiolo and Shiraz. One unique wine for his virtual

winery (which owns neither vineyards nor a winery) is Nebbiolo Moscato – a thoroughly lateral idea.

🍷🍷🍷🍷♀ **Frankland River Riesling 2016** A well made riesling, true to its variety and its Frankland River birthplace. Lime, lemon and minerally acidity are bonded on the long, even palate. Screwcap. 12.5% alc. **Rating** 90 **To** 2021 $18 ○

BlackJack Vineyards ★★★★

Cnr Blackjack Road/Calder Highway, Harcourt, Vic 3453 **Region** Bendigo
T (03) 5474 2355 **www.**blackjackwines.com.au **Open** W'ends & most public hols 11–5
Winemaker Ian McKenzie, Ken Pollock **Est.** 1987 **Dozens** 4000 **Vyds** 6ha
Established by the McKenzie and Pollock families on the site of an old apple and pear orchard in the Harcourt Valley, BlackJack is best known for some very good Shirazs. Despite some tough vintage conditions, BlackJack has managed to produce supremely honest, full-flavoured and powerful wines, all with a redeeming edge of elegance. Exports to Canada and China.

🍷🍷🍷🍷♀ **Bendigo Shiraz 2014** A rock solid red with layers of flavour from lavender, pepper, menthol and bitumen to dark fruits, all black plums and currants. Oak still obvious but will amalgamate; full-bodied fleshy tannins and a refreshing twang of acidity. Screwcap. 13.5% alc. **Rating** 93 **To** 2025 $38 JF
Block 6 Bendigo Shiraz 2014 Bright crimson; a mix of dark plums, cherry pips, and that alluring Aussie bush fragrance plus black pepper and loads of new oak spice. Sleek texture and a sweet-sour note that's kept in check by the full-bodied palate and robust flavours. Screwcap. 13.5% alc. **Rating** 92 **To** 2024 $38 JF
Chortle's Edge Shiraz 2014 Chortle's Edge over-delivers on its commitment to make a good, uncomplicated drink. Pale to mid ruby and just shy of medium-bodied, yet there's plenty of juicy succulent fruit, cinnamon, wood spices. Soft acidity and giving tannins. Screwcap. 13.5% alc. **Rating** 90 **To** 2019 $20 JF ○
The Major's Line Bendigo Shiraz 2014 Exudes its regional origins, with dark plums, currants, gum leaves, menthol and black pepper that follow through on the almost full-bodied palate. The oak is well handled, the acidity bright and the ripe tannins flow through with ease. Screwcap. 13.5% alc. **Rating** 90 **To** 2022 $28 JF

Bleasdale Vineyards ★★★★★

1640 Langhorne Creek Road, Langhorne Creek, SA 5255 **Region** Langhorne Creek
T (08) 8537 4000 **www.**bleasdale.com.au **Open** Mon–Sun 10–5
Winemaker Paul Hotker, Matt Laube **Est.** 1850 **Dozens** 100000 **Vyds** 49ha
This is one of the most historic wineries in Australia, in 2015 celebrating 165 years of continuous winemaking by the direct descendants of the founding Potts family. Not so long before the start of the 21st century, its vineyards were flooded every winter by diversion of the Bremer River, which provided moisture throughout the dry, cool, growing season. In the new millennium, every drop of water was counted. The vineyards have been significantly upgraded and refocused, with shiraz accounting for 45% of plantings, supported by seven other proven varieties. Bleasdale has completely revamped its labels and packaging, and has headed to the Adelaide Hills for sauvignon blanc, pinot gris and chardonnay under the direction of gifted winemaker (and viticulturist) Paul Hotker. Exports to all major markets.

🍷🍷🍷🍷🍷 **Wellington Road Langhorne Creek GSM 2015** 49% grenache, 45% shiraz, 6% mataro, the grenache and shiraz destemmed together and open-fermented, 12 days on skins, matured in used French puncheons for 6 months. Five trophies: Cowra, Qld, Melbourne, Sydney and National wine shows '16. Bright crimson; the magical manipulation of fruit, tannins and oak provides a wine that transcends the normal stature of the best GSMs. This is a wine to stand alongside the greatest examples from the Rhône Valley. Moreover, its balance is such that it will be as great in 20 years as it is now. Screwcap. 14% alc. **Rating** 98 **To** 2040 $35 ○
The Powder Monkey Single Vineyard Langhorne Creek Shiraz 2015
Destemmed, 15% whole berries, 9–12 days on skins, matured in French oak (27% new) for 12 months, gold medal Melbourne Wine Awards '16. It is very

concentrated and powerful, but there's no sign of a midriff bulge. The fruits are all black, both berry and cherry, the oak and tannins built into the very fabric of the wine. Screwcap. 14% alc. **Rating** 97 **To** 2035 $65 ✪

999999 **Generations Langhorne Creek Shiraz 2015** Destemmed, open-fermented, 9–12 days on skins, matured for 12 months in French oak (22% new), gold medal Adelaide Wine Show '16. A thoroughly inviting bouquet of mixed spices, purple and black fruits and cedary oak; the palate is likewise labrador-friendly, awash with plum and black cherry fruit, but retaining its shape and focus. An ever-reliable wine that fully justifies its price. Screwcap. 14% alc. **Rating** 95 **To** 2030 $35 ✪

Bremerview Langhorne Creek Shiraz 2015 Destemmed, 15% whole berries, open-fermented, 12 days on skins, matured in French oak (15% new) for 12 months. Gold medals at Melbourne and National wine shows '16. A masterful play between luscious Langhorne Creek fruit and a spicy, savoury finish. A medium-bodied shiraz that holds interest from the first sip to the finish and aftertaste of the last sip. It's a needle stuck in the groove to comment on the dizzying value for money. Screwcap. 14% alc. **Rating** 95 **To** 2030 $20 ✪

The Broad-Side Langhorne Creek Shiraz Cabernet Sauvignon Malbec 2015 A 63/26/13% blend, destemmed and crushed, open-fermented with pumpovers, 7–11 days on skins, matured for 9 months in American and French oak (10% new). Top gold Adelaide and top gold Rutherglen wine shows '16, the value verging on the absurd. With black fruits in the ascendant, impressive tannin structure and flavour complexity. Licorice and bramble also appear on the finish and aftertaste. Screwcap. 14% alc. **Rating** 95 **To** 2030 $16 ✪

Wellington Road Langhorne Creek Shiraz Cabernet Sauvignon 2015 60% shiraz 26% cabernet sauvignon, 9% malbec, the shiraz and malbec destemmed, the cabernet destemmed and crushed, open-fermented, 11–15 days on skins, matured in French oak (25% new) for 12 months. The two important wine shows (Melbourne and National) that gave the wine gold medals in '16 got it right, the two that gave it 'only' silver got it wrong. This is positively mouthwatering and lipsmacking stuff, deserving serious attention, but more likely to be greedily gulped. Screwcap. 14% alc. **Rating** 95 **To** 2030 $29 ✪

Mulberry Tree Langhorne Creek Cabernet Sauvignon 2015 Destemmed and crushed, open-fermented, 11–15 days on skins, matured for 12 months in French oak (15% new), gold medal National Wine Show '16. Vibrant colour; pure cassis fruit leads the way on the bouquet and medium-bodied palate, but when you look behind the stats and find harvest baumes from 13.2 to 14.1 and cap management in the fermenters, you realise the nature and extent of Paul Hotker's magical touch. Screwcap. 14% alc. **Rating** 95 **To** 2030 $20 ✪

Frank Potts 2015 64% cabernet sauvignon, 14% merlot, 13% malbec, 9% petit verdot, destemmed and crushed (the malbec destemmed only), open-fermented, 9–14 days on skins, matured in French oak (28% new) for 12 months. Bright crimson; Langhorne Creek is a very special place, as Wolf Blass realised decades before others. This wine exemplifies the freshness and softness of the bright fruit expression of all the red varieties grown there. This is so seductive it pains me to spit it out, but that I must do. Screwcap. 14% alc. **Rating** 95 **To** 2035 $35 ✪

Generations Langhorne Creek Malbec 2015 Destemmed, 20% whole berries, open-fermented, matured in French puncheons (12% new) for 12 months. Malbec has flourished in Langhorne Creek for over 100 years, and outpointed Argentinean malbec at the Sydney International Wine Competition. This is a powerful wine with layered plum and blackberry fruits, the tannins firmer than is normal for Langhorne Creek. Screwcap. 14% alc. **Rating** 95 **To** 2035 $35 ✪

Second Innings Langhorne Creek Malbec 2015 Picked from 7 Mar to 15 Apr, destemmed, 15% whole berries, 2–3 days cold soak, open-fermented, 9–12 days on skins, matured for 12 months in French oak (10% new), trophy Hobart, golds National Wine Show, Melbourne and Rutherglen '16. Deep crimson-purple; a lavish, full-bodied, dark plum–laden wine. Langhorne Creek is malbec's home away from home. Screwcap. 14% alc. **Rating** 95 **To** 2025 $20 ✪

Double Take Langhorne Creek Malbec 2014 From local grower Rick Eckert's vineyard, destemmed, open-fermented, 11 days on skins, matured for 11 months in used French puncheons, trophy Australian National Single Vineyard Show, gold Langhorne Creek Wine Show '16. Deeply coloured; a limited quantity made, only in the best vintages. Significantly fuller-bodied than Second Innings, promising much for those who wait. Screwcap. 14.5% alc. **Rating** 95 **To** 2034 $65

Adelaide Hills Pinot Gris 2016 Hand-picked, whole-bunch pressed, part fermented in tank, part in used French oak. As in previous years, a superior pinot gris, with a wealth of flavours spanning pear all the way to citrus, thus providing above-average length. Screwcap. 13% alc. **Rating** 94 **To** 2019 $19 ✪

16 Year Old Rare Langhorne Creek Verdelho NV More orange to the colour than the tawnies, not surprising. For long a famous wine in Langhorne Creek (and Madeira). Has lovely spicy, Callard & Bowser butterscotch and Easter cake flavours. 500ml. Cork. 18.5% alc. **Rating** 94 $69

🍷🍷🍷🍷 **Adelaide Hills Chardonnay 2016** **Rating** 91 **To** 2021 $25
18 Year Old Rare Tawny NV **Rating** 91 $69
Grand Langhorne Creek Tawny NV **Rating** 90 $39

Bloodwood ★★★★★

231 Griffin Road, Orange, NSW 2800 **Region** Orange
T (02) 6362 5631 **www**.bloodwood.biz **Open** By appt
Winemaker Stephen Doyle **Est.** 1983 **Dozens** 4000 **Vyds** 8.43ha

Rhonda and Stephen Doyle are two of the pioneers of the Orange district, 2013 marking Bloodwood's 30th anniversary. The estate vineyards (chardonnay, riesling, merlot, cabernet sauvignon, shiraz, cabernet franc and malbec) are planted at an elevation of 810–860m, which provides a reliably cool climate. The wines are sold mainly through the cellar door and by an energetic, humorous and informatively run mailing list. Has an impressive track record across the full gamut of wine styles, especially Riesling; all of the wines have a particular elegance and grace. Very much part of the high quality reputation of Orange. Exports to Malaysia.

🍷🍷🍷🍷🍷 **Riesling 2016** Lime, lemon zest, riper quince and a sherbety Pez-like quality are de rigueur, yet what sets this Riesling apart is a volcanic pulse that meshes flavour, mineral and juicy, free-flowing acidity into a delectable whole. Extended lees handling proves rewarding. Indeed, there is nothing hard about this. A beauty now, or over the next decade plus. Screwcap. 12.4% alc. **Rating** 95 **To** 2028 $25 NG ✪

Schubert 2015 Creamily reticent, with calm, soothing aromatics lilting towards white peach, topped with the curd of vanillan oak, sitting ever so subtly atop the package. The fruit is just ripe enough, the acidity linear and juicy, while the lees work handily, imbuing a mealy core of mineral punch and nougat. The wine finishes with a whiplash of nectarine acidity. Screwcap. 13% alc. **Rating** 95 **To** 2028 $30 NG ✪

Shiraz 2014 A nourishing shiraz as much for its cool calmness as for its savoury dusting of firm leather-polished tannins, impeccably managed oak and dutiful acidity. This is quintessentially Australian. Dark fruit tones pay gentle homage to the Rhône with a melody of pepper and charcuterie notes à go-go, while the resounding generosity of flavour across the wine's mid-weighted bow brings it all back home. Screwcap. 14% alc. **Rating** 95 **To** 2025 $28 NG ✪

🍷🍷🍷🍷 **Chardonnay 2016** **Rating** 93 **To** 2023 $28 NG
Silk Purse 2016 **Rating** 93 **To** 2026 $28 NG
Big Men in Tights 2016 **Rating** 92 **To** 2020 $18 NG ✪

Blue Pyrenees Estate ★★★★★

Vinoca Road, Avoca, Vic 3467 **Region** Pyrenees
T (03) 5465 1111 **www**.bluepyrenees.com.au **Open** Mon–Fri 10–4.30, w'ends 10–5
Winemaker Andrew Koerner, Chris Smales **Est.** 1963 **Dozens** 60 000 **Vyds** 149ha

Forty years after Remy Cointreau established Blue Pyrenees Estate (then known as Chateau Remy), the business was sold to a small group of Sydney businessmen. Former Rosemount senior winemaker Andrew Koerner heads the winery team. The core of the business is the very large estate plantings, most decades old, but with newer arrivals, including viognier. Blue Pyrenees has a number of programs designed to protect the environment and reduce its carbon footprint. Exports to Asia, primarily China.

ΨΨΨΨΨ **Section One Shiraz 2014** Includes 1% viognier. From the oldest shiraz vines on the property, planted in the 1970s. 24 months in French and American oak barriques. Real depth on the bouquet and palate, with dense blackberry and blueberry characters, chocolate and spice, and a distinctive Pyrenees feel. Plenty to come as well. Screwcap. 14.5% alc. **Rating** 95 **To** 2034 $42 SC
Estate Red 2013 73% cabernet sauvignon, 19% merlot, with shiraz and malbec both at 4% makes a harmonious blend. Bursting with dark red plums, cherries and wood spices, there's mint/menthol but not too much. The oak is integrated and adds to the sleek full-bodied palate; sits comfortably in its savoury profile. Screwcap. 14.5% alc. **Rating** 95 **To** 2030 $42 JF

ΨΨΨΨΩ **Cabernet Sauvignon 2014 Rating** 93 **To** 2029 $24 SC **○**
Bone Dry Rose Pinot Noir 2016 Rating 92 **To** 2017 $22 **○**
Shiraz 2014 Rating 92 **To** 2026 $24 SC **○**
Champ Blend Blanc 2015 Rating 90 **To** 2020 $32 SC
Dry Grown Shiraz 2013 Rating 90 **To** 2020 $28 SC
Midnight Cuvee 2011 Rating 90 **To** 2026 $90 TS
Sparkling Shiraz NV Rating 90 **To** 2020 $28 TS

Blue Rock Wines ★★★★☆

PO Box 692, Williamstown, SA 5351 **Region** Eden Valley
T 0419 817 017 **www.**bluerockwines.com.au **Open** Not
Winemaker Zissis Zachopoulos **Est.** 2005 **Dozens** 4000 **Vyds** 15ha
This is the venture of the brothers Zachopoulos: Nicholas, Michael and Zissis, the last with a double degree – viticulture and wine science – from CSU. Michael and Nicholas manage the 104ha property, situated in the Eden Valley at an elevation of 475m. Most blocks are north-facing, the slopes providing frost protection with their natural air drainage, the soils likewise rich and free-draining. The vineyards have been planted so far to mainstream varieties, with an ongoing planting program extending to 8ha of tempranillo, pinot gris, pinot noir, grenache and mataro. Most of the 450–500-tonne production is the subject of a sales agreement with Grant Burge. 75 tonnes are retained each year to make the Blue Rock wines.

ΨΨΨΨΨ **Limited Release Family Reserve Series Pantelis Barossa Cabernet Sauvignon 2012** Machine-harvested, crushed and destemmed, open-fermented with cultured yeast, matured in French and Hungarian oak for 30 months. Reflects the exceptional vintage. The wine has unexpected elegance to go with its highly expressive cassis/blackcurrant fruit, the tannins superfine, the oak evident but integrated. All up, a very impressive Barossa cabernet, its balance perfect. Screwcap. 14.5% alc. **Rating** 96 **To** 2042 $30 **○**
Limited Release Family Reserve Series Black Velvet Barossa Shiraz 2013 Includes 3% viognier, co-fermented in 1500l open fermenters with cultured yeast, 14 days post-ferment maceration, matured in 50% new French and 50/50% new and used American oak for 2 years. A lot of time and money have been invested in the wine, which is not reflected in the price. Shortly put, it's a bargain. It is only medium-bodied, the tannins fine, the long palate with cool-grown black cherry, blackberry and spice. Screwcap. 14% alc. **Rating** 94 **To** 2017 $25 **○**

ΨΨΨΨΩ **Eden Valley Vineyard Series Riesling 2016 Rating** 93 **To** 2024 $15 **○**
Eden Valley Vineyard Series Cabernet 2014 Rating 91 **To** 2029 $18 **○**

Boat O'Craigo

458 Maroondah Highway, Healesville, Vic 3777 **Region** Yarra Valley
T (03) 5962 6899 **www.**boatocraigo.com.au **Open** Fri–Sun 10.30–5.30
Winemaker Rob Dolan (Contract) **Est.** 1998 **Dozens** 3000 **Vyds** 21.63ha
When Margaret and Steve Graham purchased a property at Kangaroo Ground, naming it in honour of their Scottish ancestors, they correctly chose to plant shiraz and cabernet sauvignon on the warm site with its black volcanic basalt soil. In '03 the maiden vintage followed and, with son Travers joining the business, they purchased a vineyard in the foothills of the Black Spur Ranges, with gewurztraminer, sauvignon blanc, chardonnay and pinot noir. The third stage was the '11 acquisition of a substantial winery in Warranwood, equidistant between the vineyards.

ΥΥΥΥΥ **Reserve Yarra Valley Shiraz 2015** From a single block on the Kangaroo Ground vineyard, hand-picked and sorted, whole berry open-fermented, matured in French oak (50% new) for 18 months, then a barrel selection. Yes, there's more new oak, but there is much more depth to the predominantly black fruits of the medium to full-bodied palate; licorice, bramble and black pepper all dwell in the halls of the fruit. Diam. 14% alc. **Rating** 97 **To** 2040 $55 ✪

ΥΥΥΥΥ **Braveheart Yarra Valley Cabernet Sauvignon 2015** Yarra Valley cabernet at its elegant best. It effortlessly communicates its varietal message, with blackcurrant fruit at the sweet spot of ripeness, bay leaf and dried herb also part of the fruit flavour spectrum. The tannins are precisely balanced, oak likewise. Screwcap. 13.8% alc. **Rating** 96 **To** 2030 $30 ✪
Black Spur Yarra Valley Pinot Noir 2016 MV6 clone from the estate Healesville vineyard, hand-picked, 20% whole bunches, 80% whole berries, wild-yeast fermented, plunged twice daily, matured in French oak (30% new) for 9 months. Bright, full crimson; very well made, its multifaceted red fruits with focus, length and balance, the whole-bunch contribution adding to the savoury element that takes this wine out of the ruck without tarnishing the purity of the whole berry fruits. Screwcap. 13.5% alc. **Rating** 95 **To** 2026 $30 ✪
Black Cameron Yarra Valley Shiraz 2015 From the estate Kangaroo Ground vineyard. '15 was almost as great for shiraz as for pinot noir. Red, purple and black fruits are anchored by fine-grained tannins and French oak, the mouthfeel complex, but very inviting. Screwcap. 14% alc. **Rating** 95 **To** 2030 $30 ✪

ΥΥΥΥΥ **Braveheart Yarra Valley Cabernet Sauvignon 2014** Rating 93 To 2029 $30
Yarra Valley Methode Traditionnelle 2012 Rating 93 To 2022 $36 TS
Black Spur Sauvignon Blanc 2015 Rating 92 To 2017 $22 CM ✪
Black Spur Sauvignon Blanc 2016 Rating 91 To 2018 $22 ✪
Reserve Yarra Valley Chardonnay 2016 Rating 91 To 2026 $45
Black Spur Yarra Valley Gewurztraminer 2016 Rating 90 To 2019 $22

Boireann   ★★★★★

26 Donnellys Castle Road, The Summit, Qld 4377 **Region** Granite Belt
T (07) 4683 2194 **www.**boireannwinery.com.au **Open** Fri–Sun 10–4
Winemaker Peter Stark **Est.** 1998 **Dozens** 1200 **Vyds** 1.6ha
Peter and Therese Stark have a 10ha property set among the great granite boulders and trees that are so much a part of the Granite Belt. They have planted no fewer than 11 varieties, including four that go to make the Lurnea, a Bordeaux blend; shiraz and viognier; grenache and mourvedre providing a Rhône blend; and a straight merlot. Tannat, pinot noir (French) and sangiovese, barbera and nebbiolo (Italian) make up the viticultural League of Nations. Peter is a winemaker of exceptional talent, producing cameo amounts of quite beautifully made red wines that are of a quality equal to Australia's best. Peter says he has decided to think about retiring, and the property was sold in May 2017.

ΥΥΥΥΥ **Granite Belt Shiraz S2 2015** S2 is the second shiraz of the vintage, picked 6 Apr, open-fermented, 7 days on skins, matured in French barriques (25% new) for 11 months. Deep crimson-purple; the very expressive bouquet is followed by an even more intense and powerful palate; spice, pepper and licorice jam and black cherry on the medium to full-bodied palate. Fruit and oak tannins give the wine a stature that S1 doesn't have. Screwcap. 13.5% alc. **Rating** 95 **To** 2035 $35 **۞**

Granite Belt Shiraz Viognier 2015 From the oldest shiraz block planted on its own roots, 5% viognier co-fermented, hand-plunged for 7 days, matured in French barriques (30% new). The impact of the viognier is evident in the bright colour and the elevated perfume of the bouquet. Red and black fruits each have their share of the action all the way through to the finish and aftertaste of the medium-bodied palate. Screwcap. 13.5% alc. **Rating** 95 **To** 2029 $35 **۞**

La Cima Granite Belt Sangiovese 2015 Destemmed, open-fermented for 6 days, matured in French barriques for 11 months. One can only wonder at Peter Starks' instinctive feel for getting the best out of Italian varieties that can cause so much pain for winemakers and consumers alike. Here it is light pressing and finishing the fermentation in barrel that gives a sangiovese that has retained varietal expression without hard extract. Screwcap. 13% alc. **Rating** 95 **To** 2025 $30 **۞**

La Cima Granite Belt Barbera Superiore 2015 From a lower-cropping block than its La Cima varietal sibling, 'with more depth and ripeness', destemmed and crushed, open-fermented, hand-plunged for 8 days, matured for 11 months in French oak. Deeper colour than that of its sibling, and a distinctly deeper palate, albeit with similar flavours. The main difference is in the texture and structure; its longevity is assured. Screwcap. 14% alc. **Rating** 95 **To** 2030 $35 **۞**

The Lurnea 2015 A full Bordeaux blend of 42% cabernet sauvignon, 23% petit verdot, 21% merlot and 14% cabernet franc, matured in French barriques (50% new). The crimson-purple colour is a reassuring start; the wine has the Full Monty of cassis and redcurrant fruits tempered by dried herb notes, only just allowing a suggestion that a part of the blend didn't achieve full phenolic ripeness. Screwcap. 13% alc. **Rating** 94 **To** 2029 $30 **۞**

La Cima Rosso 2015 60% nebbiolo and 40% barbera, the barbera component 'to soften the firm tannins of the nebbiolo and retain the Italian spicy flavours', matured for 11 months in French barriques. A lovely, fragrant, juicy red berry bouquet and, more importantly, palate with no tannin fireworks, for they are fine and soft. No need to wait. Screwcap. 13.5% alc. **Rating** 94 **To** 2021 $28 **۞**

Granite Belt Mourvedre 2015 A tiny production from only 200 vines, open-fermented for 6 days, basket-pressed, matured in used French barriques for 11 months. Very good colour, particularly given the micro-make; the smoky, sultry black fruit aromas and flavours of this late ripening variety are backed up by persistent, albeit fine, tannins on the full-bodied palate. This wine has a magical quality all of its own. Screwcap. 13.5% alc. **Rating** 94 **To** 2030 $35

♙♙♙♙♙ La Cima Granite Belt Barbera 2015 Rating 92 To 2020 $28
Granite Belt Shiraz S1 2015 Rating 91 To 2025 $20 **۞**
La Cima Granite Belt Nebbiolo 2015 Rating 91 To 2022 $35
Granite Belt Tannat 2015 Rating 91 To 2030 $35

Bondar Wines   ★★★★★

Rayner Vineyard, 24 Twentyeight Road, McLaren Vale, SA 5171 **Region** McLaren Vale
T 0419 888 303 **www.**bondarwines.com.au **Open** By appt
Winemaker Andre Bondar **Est.** 2013 **Dozens** 500 **Vyds** 11ha
Husband and wife Selina Kelly and Andre Bondar began a deliberately unhurried journey in 2009, which culminated in the purchase of the celebrated Rayner Vineyard post-vintage '13. Andre had been a winemaker at Nepenthe wines for 7 years, and Selina had recently completed a law degree, but was already somewhat disillusioned about the legal landscape. They changed focus, and began to look for a vineyard capable of producing great shiraz. The Rayner Vineyard had all the answers, a ridge bisecting the land, Blewitt Springs sand on the eastern side, and the Seaview, heavier clay loam soils over limestone on the western side. They are continuing to close-plant counoise, and mataro, carignan and cinsaut will follow. An Adelaide Hills Syrah is in their sights. Exports to the UK.

TTTTT **Violet Hour McLaren Vale Shiraz 2015** There must be a bit of magic behind Bondar. All the wines have a certain ethereal quality and none more so than this shiraz. Excellent dark purple-red hue, highly fragrant with dark fruits, savoury spices and remains on a medium-bodied frame – it has plenty of depth. Succulent, velvety tannins, a long finish; seductive, and leaves you wanting more. Screwcap. 14% alc. **Rating** 95 To 2028 $28 JF ✪

Rayner Vineyard Grenache 2016 Old vines, hand-picked, 75% left on skins for 35 days gentle extraction for texture, the remainder 9 days on skins, cool ferment for aromatics, old hogsheads for 6 months. This has all the prettiness the variety can muster – the florals, raspberry and musk, and Middle Eastern spices – but the medium-bodied palate is the real charmer. Fine sandpaper tannins, savoury too, supple and with purity. Screwcap. 14% alc. **Rating** 95 To 2028 $38 JF

Junto McLaren Vale GSM 2016 Grenache 80%, shiraz 15%, mataro 5%. There's more to that blend than meets the eye: grenache 43yo, half left on skins for 35 days; shiraz up to 65yo; some whole bunches (the mataro 100%); aged 8 months in old oak. Beautifully fragrant, savoury too, with supple, fine tannins, a real succulence and juiciness. Screwcap. 13.5% alc. **Rating** 95 To 2024 $28 JF ✪

Junto McLaren Vale GSM 2015 75/21/4% blend. All old oak. 130 dozen. You can't help but admire the combination of mid-palate oomph and overall freshness/ vigour/life. Redcurrant and cranberry meet leather, woodspice and earth. A subtle musk-like sweetness provides extra spark. A lovely wine to drink. Screwcap. 14% alc. **Rating** 94 To 2024 $25 CM ✪

TTTTY **Adelaide Hills Chardonnay 2016 Rating** 93 To 2024 $35 JF
McLaren Vale Grenache Rose 2016 Rating 93 To 2018 $25 CM ✪

Bonking Frog ★★★★

7 Dardanup West Road, North Boyanup, WA 6237 **Region** Geographe
T 0408 930 332 **www**.bonkingfrog.com.au **Open** Fri–Sun 12–5
Winemaker Naturaliste Vintners (Bruce Dukes) **Est.** 1996 **Dozens** 1200 **Vyds** 3ha
Julie and Phil Hutton put their money where their hearts are, electing to plant a merlot-only vineyard in 1996. Presumably knowing the unpredictable habits of merlot when planted on its own roots, they began by planting 3500 Swartzman rootstock vines, and then 12 months later field-grafted the merlot scion material. Small wonder their backs are still aching. I don't doubt for a millisecond the sincerity of their enthusiasm for the variety when they say, 'Fruity, plummy, smooth and velvety. Hints of chocolate too. If you're new to wine and all things merlot, this is a wonderful variety to explore.' And the frogs? Well they bonk – loudly.

TTTTT **Summer Geographe Merlot Rose 2016** Bright, light crimson; has lots of small red fruits/berries on the bouquet and palate which won it a gold medal at the Perth Wine Show '16. But it can't quite make up its mind whether it is dry or off-dry – or perhaps it's my mind. Screwcap. 12% alc. **Rating** 94 To 2018 $22 ✪

Born & Raised ★★★☆

33 Bangaroo Street, North Balgowlah, NSW 2093 (postal) **Region** Various Vic
T 0413 860 369 **www**.bornandraisedwines.com.au **Open** Not
Winemaker David Messum **Est.** 2012 **Dozens** 1000
David and Helen Messum have covered a fair bit of ground in relatively quick time since starting specialised wine and hospitality marketing agency Just a Drop in 2009. Interaction with David's clients led him to the conclusion that he should be making wine as well as finding ways for others to market their wines. Part of the realisation came from working with hipster winery Pyramid Valley and major quality-oriented producer Craggy Range in NZ. David likes to dabble in wild-yeast ferments, odd varietal couplings, sometimes staying in the realm of conventionally made wine (wild yeast is no big deal these days) and at times going way out, as he did with his 2014 Sauvignon Blanc, which spent 104 days on skins.

TTTT **The Chance Field Blend 2016** Not a true field blend – riesling 46%, moscato giallo 42%, gewurztraminer 12% – and the nose is a bit cheesy, but the super-dry palate is much better. Flavours of musk, ginger spice, lemon and lime with chalky acidity. Screwcap. 11.6% alc. **Rating** 89 **To** 2019 $24 JF

Botobolar

89 Botobolar Road, Mudgee, NSW 2850 **Region** Mudgee
T (02) 6373 3840 **www**.botobolar.com **Open** Thurs–Tues 11–4
Winemaker Kevin Karstrom **Est.** 1971 **Dozens** 4000 **Vyds** 19.4ha
One of the first organic vineyards in Australia, with present owner Kevin Karstrom continuing the practices established by founder (the late) Gil Wahlquist. Preservative-free reds and low-preservative dry whites extend the organic practice of the vineyard to the winery. Shiraz produces the best wines to appear under the Botobolar label, with gold medal success at the Mudgee Wine Show. A solar generator has been installed on the hill behind the winery in its first step towards lowering its carbon footprint. Botobolar also has a cellar door in the centre of Mudgee: The Shop by Botobolar at 28 Church Street, open 7 days.

�♥ **Preservative Free Mudgee Shiraz 2016** It's a fair bet this wine went from fermenter to bottle asap, resulting in the deep, dense crimson–purple colour and depth of black fruits, possibly helped by organically grown grapes. Given the screwcap and the density of the wine, it may cellar as well as its McLaren Vale opposite, Battle of Bosworth. Screwcap. 13% alc. **Rating** 90 **To** 2021 $20❂

Bourke & Travers ★★★★

PO Box 457, Clare, SA 5453 **Region** Clare Valley
T 0400 745 057 **www**.bourkeandtravers.com **Open** Not
Winemaker David Travers, Michael Corbett **Est.** 1998 **Dozens** 200 **Vyds** 6ha
Owner David Travers' family has been continuously farming in Aus for 157 years, chiefly raising sheep, and broadacre cereals and legumes. In the 1870s David's great-grandfather, Nicholas Travers, established a vineyard south of Leasingham, between what is now Kilikanoon and O'Leary Walker. However, his son Paul left this property to establish a large sheep and grazing property near Port Lincoln, and son Gerald (David's father) retains these properties today, David remaining heavily involved in their operation. He (David) established Bourke & Travers on Armagh Creek in 1996, and planted the first grapes (shiraz) in '98. The Bourke in the brand comes from David's mother, Kathleen Bourke (her maiden name).

♥♥♥♥♥ **Single Vineyard Clare Valley Shiraz 2010** Matured in new French oak for 20 months. A pocket rocket, with earthy/briary undertones to the uniformly black fruits. Ripe tannins join the oak to frame a wine of real presence. Where has this wine been hiding for 7 years? Screwcap. 14.5% alc. **Rating** 93 **To** 2030 $40
Single Vineyard Clare Valley Shiraz 2012 Matured in new (12%) and used French oak for 14 months. 5 years on and the vintage is still holding centre stage with its power, length and balance. It now has a military ribbon – not quite the Victoria Cross, but serious – as some of the nuanced complexities of age are starting to move into focus. Screwcap. 14% alc. **Rating** 92 **To** 2027 $40
Single Vineyard Clare Valley Shiraz 2013 A small parcel kept separate and matured in new and used French oak for 14 months. A full-bodied shiraz that tastes of highish alcohol, or +14.5%. It has good colour, positive black fruits in Clare Valley style, the tannins potent, but not dry. Screwcap. **Rating** 90 **To** 2023 $40

Bowen Estate ★★★★

15459 Riddoch Highway, Coonawarra, SA 5263 **Region** Coonawarra
T (08) 8737 2229 **www**.bowenestate.com.au **Open** 7 days 10–5
Winemaker Emma Bowen **Est.** 1972 **Dozens** 12000 **Vyds** 33ha
Regional veteran Doug Bowen presides over one of Coonawarra's landmarks, but he has handed over full winemaking responsibility to daughter Emma, 'retiring' to the position of viticulturist. In May 2015 Bowen Estate celebrated its 40th vintage with a tasting of 24 wines (Shiraz and Cabernet Sauvignon) from 1975 to 2014. Exports to the Maldives, Singapore, China, Japan and NZ.

🍷🍷🍷🍷♀ Coonawarra Cabernet Sauvignon 2015 This has slipped into a very ripe frame with blackberries in syrup, menthol, bay leaves and cedary oak. Full-bodied; while there's a plushness to the palate, there's a lot of fruit/oak sweetness. Savoury tannins provide power and grip. Screwcap. 15.5% alc. **Rating** 90 **To** 2023 $34 JF

🍷🍷🍷🍷 Coonawarra Shiraz 2015 Rating 89 To 2021 $34 JF

Box Grove Vineyard ★★★★☆

955 Avenel-Nagambie Road, Tabilk, Vic 3607 **Region** Nagambie Lakes
T 0409 210 015 **www**.boxgrovevineyard.com.au **Open** By appt
Winemaker Sarah Gough **Est.** 1995 **Dozens** 2500 **Vyds** 27ha
This is the venture of the Gough family, with industry veteran (and daughter) Sarah Gough managing the vineyard, winemaking and marketing. Having started with 10ha each of shiraz and cabernet sauvignon under contract to Brown Brothers, Sarah decided to switch the focus of the business to what could loosely be called 'Mediterranean varieties'. These days prosecco, vermentino, primitivo and roussanne are the main varieties, plus shiraz and cabernet sauvignon from the original plantings. Osteria (an Italian word meaning a place that serves wine and food) holds tastings and meals prepared by visiting Melbourne chefs by appointment. Exports to Singapore and China.

🍷🍷🍷🍷♀ Primitivo 2014 The time and effort taken to make this wine are not reflected in the price. The snake in the Garden of Eden is the alcohol: while it is in line with Italian Amarone, the fruit here struggles to hide the fiery heat of the alcohol. Food is the obvious antidote. Screwcap. 15.6% alc. **Rating** 90 **To** 2018 $28

Brand's Laira Coonawarra ★★★★★

14860 Riddoch Highway, Coonawarra, SA 5263 **Region** Coonawarra
T (08) 8736 3260 **www**.brandslaira.com.au **Open** Mon–Fri 9–4.30, w'ends 11–4
Winemaker Peter Weinberg, Amy Blackburn **Est.** 1966 **Dozens** NFP **Vyds** 278ha
Three days before Christmas 2015, Casella Family Brands received an early present when it purchased Brand's Laira from McWilliam's. Over the years McWilliam's had moved from 50% to 100% ownership of Brand's and thereafter it purchased an additional 100ha of vineyards (taking Brand's to its present 278ha) and had expanded both the size of and the quality of the winery. Exports to select markets.

🍷🍷🍷🍷🍷 Blockers Cabernet Sauvignon 2014 25+yo vines, machine-harvested, a mix of open and roto-fermenters with cultured yeast, 7 days on skins, 85% post-ferment maceration for 5 weeks, matured for 19 months in 85% French and 15% American oak (35% new). The structure and texture reflect the steps in the vinification, with fine-grained tannins in a support role for the blackcurrant fruit, which was picked at the right time. Screwcap. 14% alc. **Rating** 94 **To** 2030 $24

🍷🍷🍷🍷♀ Foundation Shiraz 2013 Rating 92 To 2028 $23 ❂
Old Station Cabernet Shiraz 2013 Rating 92 To 2025 $25 JF ❂
Old Station Rose 2016 Rating 90 To 2018 $20 JF ❂

Brangayne of Orange ★★★★☆

837 Pinnacle Road, Orange, NSW 2800 **Region** Orange
T (02) 6365 3229 **www**.brangayne.com **Open** Mon–Fri 11–4, Sat 11–5, Sun 11–4
Winemaker Simon Gilbert **Est.** 1994 **Dozens** 3000 **Vyds** 25.7ha
The Hoskins family (formerly orchardists) moved into grapegrowing in 1994 and have progressively established high quality vineyards. Brangayne produces good wines across all mainstream varieties, ranging, remarkably, from Pinot Noir to Cabernet Sauvignon. It sells a substantial part of its crop to other winemakers. Exports to China.

🍷🍷🍷🍷♀ Chardonnay 2016 With its cool, citrus and stone fruit aromas and well handled oak (it only spent 4 months in older French barrels) this well crafted, cool climate and racy chardonnay is linear, but not lean, and should fill out nicely over the next 2–3 years. Screwcap. 13.5% alc. **Rating** 91 **To** 2022 $20 PR ✪

Cabernet Sauvignon 2014 Bright, medium crimson in colour, this elegant and finely boned cabernet has some gently leafy aromas to go with the red berry fruit and touch of tobacco leaf. The palate is medium-bodied and nicely balanced, and there's enough in the way of fine-grained tannins for this to age in the medium term. Screwcap. 13.5% alc. **Rating** 90 **To** 2024 $32 PR

🍷🍷🍷🍷 **Pinot Grigio 2016 Rating** 89 **To** 2021 $20 PR

Brash Higgins   ★★★★☆

California Road, McLaren Vale, SA 5171 **Region** McLaren Vale
T (08) 8556 4237 **www**.brashhiggins.com **Open** By appt
Winemaker Brad Hickey **Est.** 2010 **Dozens** 1000 **Vyds** 7ha
Move over TWE's 'vintrepreneurs', for Brad Hickey has come up with 'creator' and 'vinitor' to cover his role (and that of partner Nicole Thorpe) in establishing Brash Higgins. His varied background, including 10 years as head sommelier at some of the best New York restaurants, then a further 10 years of baking, brewing and travelling to the best-known wine regions of the world, may provide some clue. More tangibly, he planted 4ha of shiraz, 2ha of cabernet sauvignon, and recently grafted 1ha of shiraz to nero d'Avola on his Omensetter Vineyard looking over the Willunga Escarpment. Exports to the US and Canada.

🍷🍷🍷🍷🍷 **GR/M Co-Ferment McLaren Vale Grenache Mataro 2015** Something of a carbon copy of the excellent '14. It's light but insistent, fleshy but structured. Spice, garden herbs, raspberried fruits, roasted nuts. It's many good things rolled into one delicious whole, and yet it remains light on its feet at all times. Screwcap. 14.5% alc. **Rating** 94 **To** 2022 $37 CM

🍷🍷🍷🍷🍷 **NDV Amphora Project Nero d'Avola 2015 Rating** 92 **To** 2025 $42 CM

Brash Vineyard   ★★★★

PO Box 455, Yallingup, WA 6282 **Region** Margaret River
T 0427 042 767 **www**.brashvineyard.com.au **Open** Not
Winemaker Bruce Dukes (Contract) **Est.** 2000 **Dozens** 1000 **Vyds** 18.35ha
Brash Vineyard was established in 1998 as Woodside Valley Estate. While most of the grapes were sold to other Margaret River producers, Cabernet Sauvignon, Shiraz, Chardonnay and Merlot were made, and in '09 the Cabernet Sauvignon and the Shiraz earned the winery a 5-star rating. It is now owned by Chris and Anne Carter (managing partners, who live and work there), Brian and Anne McGuinness, and Rik and Jenny Nitert. The vineyard is now mature, and is producing high quality fruit.

🍷🍷🍷🍷🍷 **Single Vineyard Cabernet Sauvignon 2015** This leads with its juicy blackberries and mulberries, choc-mint and violets. Powerful tannins and slightly raspy acidity are having a tussle, all pointing to a smooth finish eventually. Screwcap. 14.1% alc. **Rating** 93 **To** 2028 $40 JF

Single Vineyard Sauvignon Blanc 2016 This vintage is more punchy and fruity, with star fruit, passionfruit pith and dried pears, but it's also zesty, with lemongrass, lemony acidity and pine-needle freshness. A hint of riper fruit/ sweetness rounds it out on the finish. Screwcap. 13.5% alc. **Rating** 92 **To** 2020 $23 JF ✪

Chardonnay 2015 Steely expression of the variety, particularly in a regional context, with crisp apple and nashi pear shooting through juicy nectarine. Nutty oak lends a modest hand; you'd expect another year or so in bottle to do this wine wonders. Screwcap. 13.2% alc. **Rating** 92 **To** 2022 $35 CM

Single Vineyard Shiraz 2015 Flashing a fair bit of oak, all cedary and charry; hopefully it will subside with bottle age. In the meantime, plenty of plums and pepper on the full-bodied palate, with decent structure to the tannins. Has an appeal. Screwcap. 14.3% alc. **Rating** 91 **To** 2025 $35 JF

Brave Goose Vineyard ★★★★

PO Box 852, Seymour, Vic 3660 **Region** Central Victoria
T 0417 553 225 **www**.bravegoosevineyard.com.au **Open** By appt
Winemaker Nina Stocker **Est.** 1988 **Dozens** 200 **Vyds** 6.5ha
The Brave Goose Vineyard was planted in 1988 by former chairman of the Grape & Wine Research and Development Corporation, Dr John Stocker, and wife Joanne. In '87 they found a property on the inside of the Great Dividing Range, near Tallarook, with north-facing slopes and shallow, weathered ironstone soils. They established 2.5ha each of shiraz and cabernet sauvignon, and 0.5ha each of merlot, viognier and gamay, but made only small amounts under the Brave Goose label. The brave goose in question was the sole survivor of a flock put into the vineyard to repel cockatoos and foxes. Two decades on, Jo and John handed the reins of the operation to their winemaker daughter Nina and son-in-law John Day.

ŸŸŸŸŸ Central Victoria Cabernet Merlot 2015 This is a full-bodied wine of a 85% cabernet sauvignon, 10% merlot and 5% malbec constitution. Ripe currant, black plum and red cherry flavours, all corseted by streamlined ripe grape tannins and a smudge of creamy French vanillan oak (10% new) splay across the mouth. Anise, mint and bitter chocolate echo along the finish, guided long by a beam of juicy acid. Forceful structural attributes and impeccable fruit ripeness augur well for a long future. Screwcap. 14% alc. **Rating** 93 **To** 2035 $25 NG ○
Central Victoria Shiraz 2015 An assemblage of dusty red and dark fruits are tucked within a carapace of vanilla pod oak and moderate, gritty tannins. The oak is still unresolved, yet far from excessive. It simply needs time to find its place amid emerging notes of briar, clove, pepper and barbecued meat. This wine seems more elementally Central Victorian than it does varietal. Screwcap. 13.5% alc. **Rating** 91 **To** 2027 $25 NG

Bream Creek

Marion Bay Road, Bream Creek, Tas 7175 **Region** Southern Tasmania
T (03) 6231 4646 **www**.breamcreekvineyard.com.au **Open** At Dunalley Waterfront Cafe
Winemaker Greer Carnal, Glenn James **Est.** 1974 **Dozens** 6000 **Vyds** 7.6ha
Until 1990 the Bream Creek fruit was sold to Moorilla Estate, but since then the winery has been independently owned and managed by Fred Peacock, legendary for the care he bestows on the vines under his direction. Fred's skills have seen an increase in production and outstanding wine quality across the range, headed by the Pinot Noir. The list of trophies and gold, silver and bronze medals won is extensive. Fred's expertise as a consultant is in constant demand. Exports to China.

ŸŸŸŸŸ Vintage Cuvee Traditionnelle 2010 Fred Peacock praises the '10 season for its natural acidity, and blended a higher proportion of chardonnay to create a tighter style. More than 5 years on lees has created a creamy bead and nougat and meringue notes to its crunchy grapefruit, strawberry and white peach character. It concludes even and harmonious. Cork. 12.8% alc. **Rating** 91 **To** 2018 $42 TS

Bremerton Wines

Strathalbyn Road, Langhorne Creek, SA 5255 **Region** Langhorne Creek
T (08) 8537 3093 **www**.bremerton.com.au **Open** 7 days 10–5
Winemaker Rebecca Willson **Est.** 1988 **Dozens** 30000 **Vyds** 120ha
Bremerton has been producing wines since 1988. Rebecca Willson (Chief Winemaker) and Lucy Willson (Marketing Manager) are the first sisters in Australia to manage and run a winery. With 120ha of premium vineyards (80% of which goes into their own labels), they grow cabernet sauvignon, shiraz, verdelho, chardonnay, sauvignon blanc, malbec, merlot, fiano, graciano and petit verdot. Exports to most major markets.

ŸŸŸŸŸ Old Adam Langhorne Creek Shiraz 2014 Classic Langhorne Creek flavours of sweet black plums, chocolate and coffee grounds, and there's more. It's richly flavoured and full-bodied but not heavy, with cedary oak and plush tannins. Balanced. Complex. Hedonistic. Cork. 15% alc. **Rating** 95 **To** 2028 $56 JF

Old Adam Langhorne Creek Shiraz 2013 A strict fruit selection from the best blocks on the estate vineyard is used for this wine. It has remarkable intensity and power to its dark berry fruits, chocolate, spice, licorice and ripe tannins. Its alcohol is responsible for that intensity, but doesn't heat up the finish. The cork has been perfectly inserted. 15% alc. **Rating** 95 **To** 2034 $56

Batonnage Langhorne Creek Shiraz Malbec 2015 Seamless, the palate long and detailed, the tannins supple and ripe. It's complex, full-bodied yet fine. There's texture, a grit with bright acidity keeping this buoyant. It needs more time in bottle and will reward the patient. Screwcap. 14.5% alc. **Rating** 95 **To** 2032 $32 JF ✪

Batonnage Langhorne Creek Shiraz Malbec 2014 Often a standout in the Bremerton range for its polish and completeness. Ready now with an abundance of Middle Eastern spices, licorice, lavender, mulberries and plums; the palate is full-bodied and seamless, the oak integrated, the tannins plush and the finish long. Screwcap. 14.5% alc. **Rating** 95 **To** 2031 $32 JF ✪

B.O.V. 2013 50/50% cabernet sauvignon and shiraz, with the blend well knitted and precise. There's density and suppleness, dark plums and blackberries. Really spicy, with a sprinkling of dark cocoa; ripe tannins and the oak in its place. And ready now. Cork. 15% alc. **Rating** 95 **To** 2025 $85 JF

ƳƳƳƳƳ Selkirk Shiraz 2015 Rating 93 To 2023 $22 JF ✪
Coulthard Cabernet Sauvignon 2015 Rating 93 To 2022 $22 JF ✪
Walter's Reserve Cabernet 2013 Rating 93 To 2023 $56 JF
Special Release Graciano 2015 Rating 93 To 2022 $24 JF ✪
CHW Traditional Method Sparkling Shiraz 2014 Rating 93 To 2019 $25 TS
Special Release Fiano 2015 Rating 92 To 2022 $24 ✪
Special Release Mourvedre 2015 Rating 92 To 2020 $24 JF ✪
Special Release Malbec 2015 Rating 92 To 2025 $24 JF ✪
Special Release Vermentino 2015 Rating 91 To 2018 $24
Special Release Mourvedre 2014 Rating 91 To 2021 $24 JF
Betty & Lu Langhorne Creek Sauvignon Blanc 2016 Rating 90 To 2017 $17 ✪
Special Release Langhorne Creek Vermentino 2016 Rating 90 To 2018 $24 JF
Langhorne Creek Racy Rose 2016 Rating 90 To 2018 $17 JF ✪
Coulthard Cabernet Sauvignon 2014 Rating 90 To 2022 $22 JF
Walter's Reserve Cabernet 2012 Rating 90 To 2022 $56
Tamblyn Cabernet Shiraz Malbec Merlot 2015 Rating 90 To 2022 $18 JF ✪
Special Release Tempranillo Graciano 2015 Rating 90 To 2022 $24 JF
Wiggy Sparkling Chardonnay 2011 Rating 90 To 2017 $32 TS
Mistelle Barrel Aged Fortified Chardonnay NV Rating 90 $20 JF ✪

Bress   ★★★★★

3894 Harmony Way, Harcourt, Vic 3453 **Region** Bendigo
T (03) 5474 2262 **www**.bress.com.au **Open** W'ends & public hols 11–5 or by chance
Winemaker Adam Marks **Est.** 2001 **Dozens** 5000 **Vyds** 17ha
Adam Marks has made wine in all parts of the world since 1991, and made the brave decision (during his honeymoon in 2000) to start his own business. Having initially scoured various regions of Australia for the varieties best suited to those regions, the focus has switched to three Central Victorian vineyards: Bendigo, Macedon Ranges and Heathcote. The Harcourt vineyard in Bendigo is planted to riesling (2ha), shiraz (1ha) and 3ha of cabernet sauvignon and cabernet franc; the Macedon vineyard to chardonnay (6ha) and pinot noir (3ha); and the Heathcote vineyard to shiraz (2ha). Exports to the Philippines, Singapore and Hong Kong.

ƳƳƳƳƳ Gold Macedon Pinot Noir 2015 Made with minimal additions and messing about in the cellar: natural yeast and malolactic bacteria are encouraged, rather than inoculated. Filtering and fining are eschewed unless absolutely necessary. The tang of sour cherry cascades into darker fruit tones, all jittering along on a skein of

controlled volatility and bright, cool climate acidity. A welcome change of textures comes, too, with each glass. Screwcap. 13% alc. **Rating** 96 **To** 2022 **$45** NG ✪
Gold Chook Heathcote Shiraz 2015 This cuvee is capable of evoking the highly strung nervousness and soaring aromatics of fine syrah. However, it is first and foremost a shiraz. This means a weightier context and a wine bursting with blue and black fruits tucked within plush seams of detailed tannins. A trickle of iodine, tar, anise and acidity keep it careening onward. Finishes ever so sweet, with a welcome rasp of savoury spice. Screwcap. 14% alc. **Rating** 95 **To** 2032 **$45** NG

🍷🍷🍷🍷🍷 **Silver Chook Harcourt Cabernet Franc 2016** **Rating** 91 **To** 2021 **$24** NG

Briar Ridge Vineyard ★★★★★

Mount View Road, Mount View, NSW 2325 **Region** Hunter Valley
T (02) 4990 3670 **www**.briarridge.com.au **Open** 7 days 10–5
Winemaker Gwyneth Olsen **Est.** 1972 **Dozens** 9500 **Vyds** 39ha
Semillon and shiraz have been the most consistent performers, underlying the suitability of these varieties to the Hunter Valley. Briar Ridge has been a model of stability, and has the comfort of substantial estate vineyards from which it is able to select the best grapes. It also has not hesitated to venture into other regions, notably Orange. In 2013 Gwyneth (Gwyn) Olsen was appointed winemaker after an impressive career in Australia and NZ. In '12 she added the distinction of graduating as Dux of the AWRI Advanced Wine Assessment course to her CV. Exports to the UK, Europe and Canada.

🍷🍷🍷🍷🍷 **Dairy Hill Single Vineyard Hunter Valley Semillon 2016** Like its Stockhausen sibling, is pure and refined, but with a greater degree of elegance on a palate that flows serenely from start to finish. All the fruit and acid components are here already and in great balance. Honey will join the lime in the years to come, acidity the foundation for that future. Screwcap. 11.5% alc. **Rating** 94 **To** 2026 **$35**
Fume Semillon Sauvignon Blanc 2016 The impact of the barrel ferment is evident, but not assertive, but the sum of the parts is greater than the individual components – two varieties, two regions, and the imprint of the highly skilled winemaker. This is a wine with attitude and flavour to burn, perfect for dinner table conversation now or later. Screwcap. 12% alc. **Rating** 94 **To** 2020 **$23** ✪
Big Bully Limited Release Wrattonbully Cabernet Sauvignon 2014 Machine-harvested, crushed and destemmed, open-fermented, matured for 18 months in French and American oak (35% new). I rather like the name, but it's not entirely true of this boisterous, warm-hearted wine, with rich blackcurrant fruit. Drink as the mood takes you. Screwcap. 13.5% alc. **Rating** 94 **To** 2034 **$35**

🍷🍷🍷🍷🍷 **Stockhausen Hunter Valley Semillon 2016** **Rating** 93 **To** 2023 **$28**
Tempranillo Shiraz 2016 **Rating** 93 **To** 2020 **$25** ✪
Briar Hill Single Vineyard Chardonnay 2016 **Rating** 90 **To** 2019 **$35**
Limited Release Tempranillo 2016 **Rating** 90 **To** 2023 **$35**

Brick Kiln ★★★★

21 Greer St, Hyde Park, SA 5061 **Region** McLaren Vale
T (08) 8357 2561 **www**.brickiln.com.au **Open** At Red Poles Restaurant
Winemaker Linda Domas, Phil Christiansen **Est.** 2001 **Dozens** 1500 **Vyds** 8ha
This is the venture of Malcolm and Alison Mackinnon. They purchased the Nine Gums Vineyard in 2001. It had been planted to shiraz in 1995–96. The majority of the grapes are sold, with a lesser portion contract-made for the partners under the Brick Kiln label, which takes its name from the Brick Kiln Bridge adjacent to the vineyard. Exports to the UK, Canada, China, Hong Kong and Singapore.

🍷🍷🍷🍷🍷 **Single Vineyard McLaren Vale Shiraz 2015** Dark crimson, this is an opulent wine with a kinetic power nicely tucked beneath seams of vanillan oak supports and well meshed grape tannins. Aromas of black fruits all billow across a core of blueberry and molten kirsch. This note grows more intense with air, sapid and intensely drawn across a trickle of peppery acidity. Screwcap. 14.8% alc. **Rating** 93 To 2033 $35 NG

Brindabella Hills

156 Woodgrove Close, Wallaroo, ACT 2618 **Region** Canberra District
T (02) 6230 2583 **www.**brindabellahills.com.au **Open** W'ends, public hols 10–5
Winemaker Dr Roger Harris, Brian Sinclair **Est.** 1986 **Dozens** 1500 **Vyds** 5ha
Distinguished research scientist Dr Roger Harris presides over Brindabella Hills, which increasingly relies on estate-produced grapes, with small plantings of riesling, shiraz, chardonnay, sauvignon blanc, merlot, sangiovese, cabernet sauvignon, cabernet franc and viognier. Wine quality has been consistently good. Roger has decided to retire, with no family prepared to continue the business, so this will be the last entry for the *Wine Companion*. He hopes a new owner may appear, but isn't able to wait indefinitely.

ΨΨΨΨΨ Canberra District Riesling 2016 This showcases the Canberra region's thrilling idiom of riesling which, while exhibiting the Full Monty of citrus flavours tweaked with some candied rind, never leans into the Rose's lime territory of the Eden and Clare. Hints of stone fruits, too, are etched by a fine-boned, mineral-clad palate of a giddy daintiness, but razor-sharp precision and thrilling intensity. Screwcap. 12% alc. **Rating** 95 To 2029 $25 NG ✪

ΨΨΨΨΨ Canberra District Shiraz 2015 Rating 93 To 2023 $28 NG
Brio Canberra District Sangiovese 2013 Rating 90 To 2020 $20✪

Brini Estate Wines

698 Blewitt Springs Road, McLaren Vale, SA 5171 **Region** McLaren Vale
T (08) 8383 0080 **www.**briniwines.com.au **Open** By appt
Winemaker Adam Hooper (Contract) **Est.** 2000 **Dozens** 4500 **Vyds** 16.4ha
The Brini family has been growing grapes in the Blewitt Springs area of McLaren Vale since 1953. In 2000 John and Marcello Brini established Brini Estate Wines to vinify a portion of the grape production; up to that time it had been sold to companies such as Penfolds, Rosemount Estate and d'Arenberg. The flagship Limited Release Shiraz is produced from dry-grown vines planted in 1947, the other wines from dry-grown vines planted in '64. Exports to Vietnam and China.

ΨΨΨΨΨ Christian Single Vineyard McLaren Vale Shiraz 2012 Matured for 18 months in new and 1yo French and American oak. The colour is very good for a 5yo shiraz, and the aromas and flavours reflect a great vintage slowly moving to maturity and the long plateau that will follow. No shy, retiring flower, but it does have the finesse lacking in the other Brini reds. Screwcap. 14.5% alc. **Rating** 95 To 2032 $45
Limited Release Single Vineyard Sebastian Shiraz 2013 Made from the best grapes from the '47 plantings, oak maturation similar to most Brini Shirazs. The extra quality is obvious, supple mouthfeel a feature, the edge of bitter chocolate likewise. Screwcap. 14.5% alc. **Rating** 94 To 2033 $60

ΨΨΨΨΨ Sebastian Single Vineyard Shiraz 2013 Rating 93 To 2029 $34
Blewitt Springs Single Vineyard Shiraz 2014 Rating 92 To 2029 $24✪
McLaren Vale Rose 2016 Rating 91 To 2018 $22✪
Single Vineyard McLaren Vale Merlot 2014 Rating 91 To 2021 $22✪

Brockenchack

13/102 Burnett Street, Buderim, Qld 4556 **Region** Eden Valley
T (07) 5458 7700 **www.**brockenchack.com.au **Open** By appt
Winemaker Shawn Kalleske, Joanne Irvine **Est.** 2007 **Dozens** 4500 **Vyds** 16ha

Trevor (and wife Marilyn) Harch have long been involved in liquor distribution in Qld, owning one of Australia's leading independent liquor wholesalers. Over the years, Trevor became a regular visitor to the Barossa/Eden Valley, and in 1999 purchased the Tanunda Cellars Wine Store. In 2007, Trevor and Marilyn purchased a vineyard in the Eden Valley and retained Shawn Kalleske as winemaker. The vineyard has 8ha of shiraz, 2ha each of riesling and cabernet sauvignon, and 1.3ha each of pinot noir, pinot gris and chardonnay. The majority of wines released are labelled in honour of one or other member of the Harch family. Brockenchack comes from the first names of the four grandchildren: Bronte, Mackenzie, Charli and Jack. Exports to Germany, Japan, China and NZ.

ŸŸŸŸŸ **William Frederick Eden Valley Shiraz 2013** Impenetrable black-purple hue with plums of the same colour – not overripe but essency and doused in kirsch, licorice and menthol. Aged for 2 years in 100% new French oak, which accentuates the massive tannins and cedary, charry characters. Screwcap. 15.5% alc. **Rating** 93 **To** 2030 $150 JF
Zip Line Eden Valley Shiraz 2015 While it's full-bodied and richly flavoured with dark plums, mocha, menthol and woodsy spices, the brightness of the fruit shines through. Rather silky texture, and ripe tannins. Plenty of pleasure to be had. Screwcap. 14.5% alc. **Rating** 92 **To** 2027 $24 JF ✪
Mackenzie William 1896 Eden Valley Riesling 2016 Hints of wild flowers, pepper and all manner of citrus flavours flowing onto a linear palate, with a steely line of lemony acidity and a smidge of sweetness to tuck in the corners. Screwcap. 12% alc. **Rating** 91 **To** 2028 $20 JF ✪
Jack Harrison Eden Valley Shiraz 2013 Very much in the riper spectrum, from the dark crimson-black hue to the density of fruit. It also features currants, chocolate, licorice and a sweet sensation to the cedary, charry oak and mouth-filling tannins. Screwcap. 15.2% alc. **Rating** 90 **To** 2032 $58 JF

Brokenwood   ★★★★★

401–427 McDonalds Road, Pokolbin, NSW 2321 **Region** Hunter Valley
T (02) 4998 7559 www.brokenwood.com.au **Open** Mon–Sat 9.30–5, Sun 10–5
Winemaker Iain Riggs, Stuart Hordern **Est.** 1970 **Dozens** 100 000 **Vyds** 64ha
A deservedly fashionable winery producing consistently excellent wines. Its big-selling Hunter Semillon provides the volume to balance the limited quantities of the flagships ILR Semillon and Graveyard Shiraz. Next there is a range of wines coming from regions including Beechworth (a major resource is the associated Indigo Vineyard), Orange, Central Ranges, McLaren Vale, Cowra and elsewhere. In 2017 Iain Riggs celebrated his 35th vintage at the helm of Brokenwood, offering a unique mix of winemaking skills, management of a diverse business, and an unerring ability to keep Brokenwood's high profile fresh and newsworthy. He has also contributed a great deal to various wine industry organisations. Exports to all major markets.

ŸŸŸŸŸ **ILR Reserve Hunter Valley Semillon 2011** When I first tasted this wine in Oct '15 I made this note: 'It has a lovely combination of lemongrass freshness with perfect first stage development of sweet fruit and incipient honey (which will take years to fully evolve). In the meantime, citrus rules the roost, allied with mouthwatering acidity.' Fifteen months down the track, nothing more needs to be said. Screwcap. 11% alc. **Rating** 97 **To** 2031 $75
Tallawanta Hunter Valley Shiraz 2015 The 9ha Tallawanta Vineyard was planted in 1920 by the Elliott family. Hand-picked, 3 days cold soak, fermented with cultured yeast, matured in a large format 3yo French cask for 15 months. The decision to use no new oak is as intriguing as it is successful. The vintage wasn't great, but this medium-bodied wine has soared above the challenges, its earthy/savoury/leathery flavours pure Hunter terroir. Screwcap. 13% alc. **Rating** 97 **To** 2045 $140 ✪
Rayner Vineyard McLaren Vale Shiraz 2015 Crushed and chilled, and transported to the Hunter Valley, open-fermented, plunged, matured in 100% French oak. Finishing the primary fermentation in oak, the way

Brokenwood made its shiraz in the 1970s and early '80s, has provided maximum rewards with this lovely shiraz. Coupled with its 14% alcohol, it has given the wine carpet slippers that muffle its approach and catch you by surprise. Screwcap. **Rating** 97 **To** 2040 $100 ◎

Wildwood Road Margaret River Cabernet Sauvignon 2014 Matured in French oak (30% new) for 18 months. Bright crimson-purple; Brokenwood didn't pussyfoot around looking for budget cabernet: this is the real deal, with superb structure and balance to its display of cassis, black olive, spice and bay leaf. Tannins are a vital part of great cabernet. Screwcap. 14.5% alc. **Rating** 97 **To** 2034 $80 ◎

♀♀♀♀♀ **Supa Indigo Vineyard Chardonnay 2016** Whole-bunch pressed, wild-yeast fermented in French oak (30% new), matured for 10 months. This is made from the Bernard clone 76, and has an intensity and crisp acidity to its fruit not achieved by older clones. It creates a purity of varietal expression – or clonal, if you prefer circuitous logic. Green apple, grapefruit and white peach are on duty here, with a zesty, fresh aftertaste. Screwcap. 12.5% alc. **Rating** 96 **To** 2027 $75 ◎

Indigo Vineyard Beechworth Chardonnay 2015 Features the very good Dijon clones, hand-picked, whole-bunch pressed, fermented and matured in French oak (33% new). While this shares the white peach and grapefruit flavour of its Orange sibling, there is an added thrust and drive to the palate, the long finish reflecting that drive. Screwcap. 12.5% alc. **Rating** 96 **To** 2025 $55 ◎

Four Winds Vineyard Canberra District Riesling 2016 Whole-bunch pressed, free-run wild-yeast fermented in stainless steel. The riesling class at the Canberra Regional Wine Show is very strong, and very competitive, making its gold medal significant, but not the least surprising. Full of lime juice flavours coupled with all-important acidity. In drinkability, riesling of this quality runs rings around 1yo Hunter semillon. Screwcap. 11.5% alc. **Rating** 95 **To** 2031 $35 ◎

Hunter Valley Semillon 2016 Right in the heart of Brokenwood style: has all the flavours of citrus and lemongrass needed for immediate enjoyment, the acidity fresh and cleansing. Its balance and mouthfeel assure the future of the wine, which in 5 years will have added a leg, if not two. Dodged all the bullets of the '16 vintage. Screwcap. 10.5% alc. **Rating** 95 **To** 2026 $25 ◎

Indigo Vineyard Beechworth Chardonnay 2016 Whole-bunch pressed, wild-yeast fermented in French oak (30% new), matured for 10 months. Beechworth produces chardonnay that has fruit complexity largely unrelated to fermentation-created funk/complexity. There is also a drive that gathers pace as the wine moves along the palate to the long, lingering finish. Screwcap. 12.5% alc. **Rating** 95 **To** 2027 $55

Forest Edge Vineyard Orange Chardonnay 2015 Whole-bunch pressed and wild yeast fermentation in French oak play their part in this first class chardonnay. Grapefruit and white peach aromas and flavours are joined by toasty oak and cashew nuances on the long finish and aftertaste. Screwcap. 13% alc. **Rating** 95 **To** 2022 $55

Forest Edge Vineyard Orange Pinot Noir 2016 MV6 clone, cold-soaked, 10% whole bunches, matured in mostly used French barriques for 10 months. Very good colour and clarity; the fragrant red cherry and spice bouquet has an instant replay when the wine is tasted, but given another dimension by the briar, bramble, foresty tannins. A very smart medium-bodied pinot with good length and balance – and future. Screwcap. 14% alc. **Rating** 95 **To** 2030 $55

Indigo Vineyard Beechworth Shiraz 2015 3–4 days cold soak, 4–5 days ferment with plunging, matured for 12 months in a new 2800l French cask. Top gear stuff, exulting in its shiny black fruits and spices of all kinds. The mouthfeel is supple and smooth, the weight medium to full-bodied, French oak playing its role in tune with the other components. Screwcap. 13.5% alc. **Rating** 95 **To** 2035 $65

Quail McLaren Vale Hunter Valley Shiraz 2015 From the Graveyard Vineyard (4 days cold soak, 5 days ferment, mlf in new French oak), and the Wade Block 2 Vineyard in McLaren Vale (6 days + mlf in a roto fermenter), matured in new American oak for 15 months. Very complex; the heavy lifting is done by the

McLaren Vale Wade Vineyard, with fine, but mouthcoating, tannins. It won't be fully approachable for a decade. Screwcap. 13% alc. **Rating** 95 **To** 2045 **$**180

Wade Block 2 Vineyard McLaren Vale Shiraz 2014 Transported in a chilled tanker to the Hunter Valley, Vinomatic fermentation, matured in new and used French (80%) and American (20%) oak. Bright, clear, moderately deep crimson-purple; a full-bodied wine from this very special vineyard, black fruits, oak and tannin all waving their flags, demanding attention. 5 years should bring calm, and the wine will sail on thereafter. Screwcap. 14% alc. **Rating** 95 **To** 2039 **$**65

Beechworth Sangiovese 2016 3–4 days cold soak, 4–5 days ferment with plunging, matured in used French puncheons. Bright, clear scarlet; Brokenwood has waltzed past the tannin trap without a care in the world. Delicious red fruits of cherry and wild strawberry, the mouthfeel pure silk, the oak and tannins not even on stage. Screwcap. 13.5% alc. **Rating** 95 **To** 2030 **$**35 ✪

Forest Edge Vineyard Orange Chardonnay 2016 Whole-bunch pressed, wild-yeast fermented in French oak (35% new), matured for 10 months. The extreme reduction of years gone by (earning the soubriquet Mr Stinky) is no more: just finely gauged complexity and a trace of funk, the palate of grapefruit and white peach elegant, the French oak doing all that was asked of it. Screwcap. 12.5% alc. **Rating** 94 **To** 2026 **$**55

Maxwell Vineyard Hunter Valley Chardonnay 2015 Hand-picked, whole-bunch pressed, wild yeast fermentation in French oak, mainly used, but which comes through clearly on the bouquet; the wine has a powerful V8 engine throbbing away, remarkable given its modest alcohol. The Brokenwood winemaking team knows how to handle the unpredictable Hunter Valley summer months better than most. Screwcap. 12.5% alc. **Rating** 94 **To** 2021 **$**55

Four Winds Vineyard Canberra District Shiraz 2015 The grapes were transported to Brokenwood, destemmed, 20% whole bunches, 3 days cold soak, open-fermented, matured in a 1yo French 2800l cask. Full, bright crimson-purple; a full-bodied wine with its future already laid out as the tannins soften and all the spicy/peppery red and black cherry fruit escape the bonds that presently prevent communication are released. Screwcap. 13.5% alc. **Rating** 94 **To** 2040 **$**75

Shiraz 2014 Hand-picked, open and roto fermenters, matured in 80% French oak (30% new) and 20% used American oak for 15 months. Good colour; a fresh, elegant, medium-bodied shiraz that ticks all the boxes. It's already welcoming visitors and will continue doing so in the coming years, the fruits predominantly red, the tannins ripe and fine, the French oak exactly measured. Screwcap. 13.5% alc. **Rating** 94 **To** 2030 **$**35

Beechworth Tempranillo 2016 The second vintage of this wine, hand-picked, a short cold soak, 4 days fermentation with hand plunging, matured in French puncheons (10% new) for 6 months. Deeper coloured, and larger in every dimension than the Sangiovese. Brokenwood played its cards like a world champion in all the steps of the vinification. This is a very good Tempranillo, but doesn't have the wonderful charm of the Sangiovese, its fruit template darker and more savoury. Screwcap. 13.5% alc. **Rating** 94 **To** 2026 **$**35

🍷🍷🍷🍷🍷 **Hunter Valley Shiraz 2015** **Rating** 92 **To** 2035 **$**50
Beechworth Sangiovese 2015 **Rating** 92 **To** 2020 **$**35 JF
Beechworth Tempranillo 2015 **Rating** 92 **To** 2023 **$**35
Poppy's Block Hunter Valley Semillon 2015 **Rating** 91 **To** 2028 **$**45 JF
Indigo Vineyard Beechworth Pinot Noir 2015 **Rating** 90 **To** 2022 **$**55
Beechworth Pinot Noir 2015 **Rating** 90 **To** 2025 **$**35

Bromley Wines ★★★★

PO Box 571, Drysdale, Vic 3222 **Region** Geelong
T 0487 505 367 **www**.bromleywines.com.au **Open** Not
Winemaker Darren Burke **Est.** 2010 **Dozens** 300

In his previous life, Darren Burke worked as an intensive care nurse in Australia and the UK, but at the age of 30 he fell to the allure of wine and enrolled in the Bachelor of Applied

Science (Oenology) at Adelaide University. Thereafter he became graduate winemaker at Orlando, then at Alkoomi Wines, fitting in a vintage in Chianti. With successful vintages in 2005 and '06 completed, and the impending birth of wife Tammy's first child, the couple decided to move back to the east coast. There Darren worked at several wineries on the Bellarine Peninsula before taking up his winemaking post at Leura Park Estate. Says Darren, 'The essence of Bromley is family. All our wines carry names drawn from our family history. Family is about flesh and blood, sweat and tears, love and laughter.' Exports to Singapore.

ΤΤΤΤΩ **Eclipse 2016** This is an ultra-refreshing nebbiolo rose with body, yet is devilishly dry on the finish; racy acidity, cherry pip, watermelon rind, woodsy spices and Campari-esque flavours. Screwcap. 13% alc. **Rating** 93 **To** 2019 $24 JF ✪
Mosaic 2016 For a pinot grigio, this could pass for rosé with its pale salmon hue, the result of 12 hours skin contact before being pressed to 50% French hogsheads, the remainder to stainless steel. I like the wine, as there's texture, chew from neatly handled phenolics, florals and spiced pears then a twist of refreshing acidity to seal the deal. Screwcap. 12% alc. **Rating** 92 **To** 2019 $24 JF ✪
Heathcote Shiraz 2015 Reductive and meaty, giving it austerity, but it's appealing as it moves into the core of ripe black plums doused in star anise, morello cherries and smoky, menthol oak. Succulent palate with fleshy tannins and good acidity to close. Screwcap. 13.8% alc. **Rating** 92 **To** 2024 $32 JF

Brookland Valley ★★★★★

Caves Road, Wilyabrup, WA 6280 **Region** Margaret River
T (08) 9755 6042 **www.**brooklandvalley.com.au **Open** 7 days 11–5
Winemaker Courtney Treacher **Est.** 1984 **Dozens** NFP
Brookland Valley has an idyllic setting, plus its cafe and Gallery of Wine Arts, which houses an eclectic collection of wine, food-related art and wine accessories. After acquiring a 50% share of Brookland Valley in 1997, Hardys moved to full ownership in 2004; it is now part of Accolade Wines. The quality, value for money and consistency, of the wines are exemplary.

ΤΤΤΤΤ **Estate Margaret River Chardonnay 2015** Fermented in French oak, matured for 9 months on lees. Pale quartz-green; high quality in every respect, intense, very long, the pink grapefruit and white peach driving the agenda, oak merely a conveyance. Screwcap. 13.5% alc. **Rating** 96 **To** 2023 $48 ✪
Estate Margaret River Chardonnay 2016 Whole-bunch pressed, wild yeast fermentation in French barriques, including mlf, matured on lees for 8 months with stirring. The vinification was sure-footed from start to finish. The result is a delicate wine with delicious stone fruit and pear flavours, the oak playing a pure support role, having been used as a means to an end. Screwcap. 13.5% alc. **Rating** 95 **To** 2026 $48
Reserve Margaret River Chardonnay 2015 Whole-bunch pressed, barrel-fermented, and given extended lees contact. A rich, complex and luscious chardonnay speaking loud and clear of its Margaret River origin, but looking back wistfully over its shoulder to see where it came from style-wise. Gold medal Sydney Wine Show '16. Screwcap. 13.5% alc. **Rating** 95 **To** 2025 $75
Estate Margaret River Cabernet Merlot 2014 Hand-picked, open-fermented, matured in French oak for 14 months. Oak makes its presence felt on the bouquet, but takes second place on the palate. Here cassis/blackcurrant fruits, bay leaf and black olive are decorously joined by fine, ripe tannin. Gold medal Sydney Wine Show '16. Screwcap. 13.5% alc. **Rating** 95 **To** 2034 $57

ΤΤΤΤΩ **Verse 1 Margaret River Chardonnay 2016 Rating** 90 **To** 2020 $15 ✪
Verse 1 Margaret River Shiraz 2014 Rating 90 **To** 2022 $15 ✪

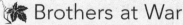 # Brothers at War ★★★★★

16 Gramp Avenue, Angaston, SA 5353 **Region** Barossa
T 0405 631 889 **www.**brothersatwar.com.au **Open** Not
Winemaker Angus Wardlaw **Est.** 2014 **Dozens** 600

David Wardlaw was one of the bastions of the Barossa Valley in the second half of the 20th century, working alongside greats such as Peter Lehmann, John Vickery, Jim Irvine and Wolf Blass. For son Angus Wardlaw, a life in wine was inevitable, working first (in 2009) at Dorrien Estate and after four years starting at Kirrihill Wines in the Clare Valley. He has a love for all things Eden Valley. His brother Sam Wardlaw, with a love of all things Barossa, started in the production side of the business when he worked for Premium Wine Bottlers until '09, when he was employed by Andrew Seppelt at Murray Street Vineyards, spending the next six years there. Matt Carter's role is mysterious; while he started as a cellarhand at Colonial Wine for a couple of vintages, he has since moved into civil construction, currently running large infrastructure projects but returning from time-to-time to drink plenty of the Brothers at War wines.

ŸŸŸŸŸ **Fist Fight Barossa Shiraz 2015** 50% 60+yo Eden Valley vines, 50% 30+yo Barossa Valley vines, 100% whole berries, crushed and destemmed, 5 days cold soak, cultured yeast, open-fermented, 15 days on skins, 20% new French puncheons and 80% used French hogsheads for 12 months. The fight is a very good one, the problem being the micro-make of only 990 bottles. This lovely young wine has Eden Valley DNA from top to toe. Screwcap. 14% alc. **Rating** 95 **To** 2035 $30 **◐**

I'm Always Right Eden Valley Cabernet Sauvignon 2015 40+yo vines, 20% whole berries, 5 days cold soak, open-fermented with cultured yeast, 15 days on skins, matured for 12 months in French hogsheads (20% new). The wine has intense cassis and black olive fruit, with the barest glimpse of mint. It is medium to full-bodied as befits cabernet, but the tannins are supple, the oak keeping the boat in trim. Great bargain. Screwcap. 14.5% alc. **Rating** 95 **To** 2030 $30 **◐**

Nothing in Common Eden Valley Riesling 2016 From 70yo vines. Tangy, zesty lime and lemon flavours combine with crunchy acidity and refuse to leave the palate for a seeming eternity – as long as it took me to (hand) write this tasting note. Great stuff. Screwcap. 11.8% alc. **Rating** 94 **To** 2026 $25 **◐**

ŸŸŸŸŸ **Mum's Love Eden Valley Rose 2016 Rating** 90 **To** 2019 $20 **◐**

Brothers in Arms   ★★★★☆

Lake Plains Road, Langhorne Creek, SA 5255 **Region** Langhorne Creek
T (08) 8537 3182 **www**.brothersinarms.com.au **Open** By appt
Winemaker Jim Urlwin **Est.** 1998 **Dozens** 25 000 **Vyds** 85ha
The Adams family has been growing grapes at Langhorne Creek since 1891, when the vines at the famed Metala vineyards were planted. Guy Adams is the fifth generation to own and work the vineyard, and over the past 20 years has both improved the viticulture and expanded the plantings. In 1998 they decided to hold back a small proportion of the production for the Brothers in Arms label, and now they dedicate 85ha to Brothers in Arms (40ha each of shiraz and cabernet sauvignon and 2.5ha each of malbec and petit verdot). Exports to the UK, the US, Canada, Sweden, Denmark, South Korea, Malaysia, Singapore, Hong Kong and China.

ŸŸŸŸŸ **Langhorne Creek Cabernet Sauvignon 2014** Picked later than Side by Side (1–4 Apr), matured for 18 months in French puncheons, and a fine example of medium-bodied Langhorne Creek cabernet, with supple fruit in a cassis spectrum, plus the bay leaf/black olive nuance needed for fruit complexity. Needless to say, the tannins are soft. Screwcap. 14.5% alc. **Rating** 95 **To** 2029 $50

No. 6 Langhorne Creek Shiraz Cabernet 2014 76% shiraz, 23% cabernet sauvignon and 1% petit verdot, matured in French barriques (10% new). A lively medium-bodied blend with a supple palate typical of Langhorne Creek, its complex suite of earthy/fruity flavours rolling serenely across the mouth, coming back again and again as the wine is revisited, the fruit fist in the velvet glove having the last word. Great value. Screwcap. 14.5% alc. **Rating** 94 **To** 2034 $22 **◐**

ŸŸŸŸ **Side by Side Cabernet Sauvignon 2014 Rating** 89 **To** 2024 $27

Brown Brothers

Milawa–Bobinawarrah Road, Milawa, Vic 3678 **Region** King Valley
T (03) 5720 5500 **www.**brownbrothers.com.au **Open** 7 days 9–5
Winemaker Joel Tilbrook, Cate Looney **Est.** 1885 **Dozens** 1 million+ **Vyds** 570ha
Draws upon a considerable number of vineyards spread throughout a range of site climates,
ranging from very warm to very cool. An expansion into Heathcote added significantly to its
armoury. In 2010 Brown Brothers took a momentous step, acquiring Tasmania's Tamar Ridge
for $32.5 million. In May '16 it acquired Innocent Bystander and stock from Giant Steps,
and with it a physical presence in the Yarra Valley. The premium quality varietal wines to
one side, Brown Brothers has gained two substantial labels, Innocent Bystander Moscato and
Innocent Bystander Prosecco. It is known for the diversity of varieties with which it works,
and the wines represent good value for money. Deservedly one of the most successful family
wineries – its cellar door receives the greatest number of visitors in Australia. A founding
member of Australia's First Families of Wine. Exports to all major markets.

ΨΨΨΨΨ **Patricia Chardonnay 2014** With Brown Brothers' foray into Tasmania, no
surprise 55% of the fruit for Patricia comes off the Kayena Vineyard, the rest from
White Hills. This is a sterling wine, at once linear, minerally, tight; a thoroughbred.
Excellent fruit definition with creamed honey and leesy notes, spine-tinglingly
long and pure. Screwcap. 12.5% alc. **Rating** 95 **To** 2024 $45 JF
Patricia Shiraz 2013 A powerhouse of colour and flavour, with its black fruit
profile, licorice, dried herbs and a spice rack of aromas yet surprisingly supple
tannins; just shy of full-bodied. Good to feel the restraint with chalky raspberry
sorbet–like acidity. Very fresh. Screwcap. 14.5% alc. **Rating** 95 **To** 2026 $65 JF
Patricia Pinot Noir Chardonnay 2010 From Brown Brothers' high altitude
Whitlands Vineyard (since sold to Domaine Chandon). It spent 5 years on tirage,
developing its complex bouquet of lemon and brioche, the elegant and very long
palate with flavours of nougat, lemon curd and almond. A wine of exceptional
balance. Cork. 12.5% alc. **Rating** 95 **To** 2018 $47
Patricia Noble Riesling 2014 Now isn't this a beauty. Mid-amber hue with the
promise of honey-drenched apricots, saffron-infused cumquat marmalade, and the
aroma of toffee as it's about to set. While those are the richer elements at play, this
also shines with citrus lemony freshness, the sweetness perfectly controlled by fine
bright acidity. Screwcap. 9.5% alc. **Rating** 95 **To** 2022 $35 JF ✪
Ten Acres Heathcote Shiraz 2013 Estate-grown, matured for 12 months
in French and American oak. A classy wine that manages to combine elegance
and intensity; sparkling bright red fruits on entry to the mouth turn darker on
the finish, and hold the whip hand over the tannins and oak on the long palate.
Screwcap. 14.5% alc. **Rating** 94 **To** 2028 $29 ✪

ΨΨΨΨΨ **Patricia Pinot Noir Chardonnay 2011** Rating 93 To 2018 $48 TS
18 Eighty Nine Dry Rose 2016 Rating 92 To 2017 $19 ✪
Vintage Release Heathcote Durif 2014 Rating 92 To 2024 $21 ✪
Ten Acres Shiraz Cabernet 2014 Rating 91 To 2029 $29
Vintage Release Tempranillo & Graciano 2015 Rating 91 To 2023 $21 ✪
Vintage Release Heathcote Durif 2015 Rating 91 To 2024 $21 JF ✪
Pinot Chardonnay Meunier NV Rating 91 To 2018 $27 TS
18 Eighty Nine Pinot Grigio 2016 Rating 90 To 2018 $19 ✪
Vintage Release Banksdale Gamay 2015 Rating 90 To 2020 $21 ✪
Vintage Release Banksdale Gamay 2014 Rating 90 To 2019 $21 ✪
Patricia Cabernet Sauvignon 2012 Rating 90 To 2022 $65 JF
Single Vineyard Prosecco 2016 Rating 90 To 2017 $21 TS ✪
Cuvee Premium Sparkling Brut Chardonnay Pinot Noir NV Rating 90
To 2017 $19 TS ✪

Brown Hill Estate

Cnr Rosa Brook Road/Barrett Road, Rosa Brook, WA 6285 **Region** Margaret River
T (08) 9757 4003 **www.**brownhillestate.com.au **Open** 7 days 10–5
Winemaker Nathan Bailey, Haydn Millard **Est.** 1995 **Dozens** 3000 **Vyds** 22ha
The Bailey family is involved in all stages of wine production, with minimum outside help.
Their stated aim is to produce top-quality wines at affordable prices, via uncompromising
viticultural practices emphasising low yields. They have shiraz and cabernet sauvignon (8ha
each), semillon, sauvignon blanc and merlot (2ha each). The quality of the best wines in the
portfolio is very good.

🍷🍷🍷🍷🍷 **Perseverance Margaret River Cabernet Merlot 2014** A 70/30% blend with
abundant currant, cedar, mulch and tobacco leaf notes from attack to finish. But
it is the impeccably polished and tightly knit milk chocolate tannins that serve
as the wine's raison d'être. A mellifluous synergy of fruit and judiciously handled
structural components. Screwcap. 14% alc. **Rating** 95 To 2030 $50 NG

🍷🍷🍷🍷🍷 **Golden Horseshoe Margaret River Chardonnay 2016** Rating 93 To 2022
$35 NG
Fimiston Reserve Margaret River Shiraz 2015 Rating 93 To 2032 $35 NG
Hannans Cabernet Sauvignon 2015 Rating 93 To 2025 $22 NG ✪
Charlotte Sauvignon Blanc 2016 Rating 92 To 2018 $21 NG ✪
Ivanhoe Cabernet Sauvignon 2015 Rating 92 To 2030 $35 NG
Bill Bailey Shiraz Cabernet Sauvignon 2014 Rating 91 To 2030 $60 NG
Jubilee Margaret River Semillon 2016 Rating 90 To 2022 $25 NG
Great Boulder Margaret River Cabernet Shiraz Merlot Malbec 2014
Rating 90 To 2028 $40 NG

Brown Magpie Wines

125 Larcombes Road, Modewarre, Vic 3240 **Region** Geelong
T (03) 5266 2147 **www.**brownmagpiewines.com **Open** 7 days 11–4 Jan
Winemaker Loretta and Shane Breheny **Est.** 2000 **Dozens** 5000 **Vyds** 9ha
Shane and Loretta Breheny's 20ha property is situated predominantly on a gentle, north-facing
slope, with cypress trees on the western and southern borders providing protection against the
wind. Vines were planted over 2001–02, with pinot noir (4ha) taking the lion's share, followed
by pinot gris and shiraz (2.4ha each) and 0.1ha each of chardonnay and sauvignon blanc.
Viticulture is Loretta's love; winemaking (and wine) is Shane's.

🍷🍷🍷🍷🍷 **Single Vineyard Geelong Shiraz 2015** Open-fermented with 20% whole
bunches and a high proportion of whole berries, plunged 3–4 times daily,
extended post-ferment maceration, matured in barrel for 15 months. The whole
bunches helped balance the extract from post-ferment maceration, leaving great
flavour, texture, intensity and complexity. Its length and balance are also of a high
order. Red and black cherry, spice, licorice and espresso coffee join with the
tannins and oak of a great wine. Screwcap. 13.9% alc. **Rating** 96 To 2040 $38 ✪
Modewarre Mud Reserve Single Vineyard Geelong Shiraz 2014 Open-
fermented with 5% whole bunches, the balance destemmed, four ferments
selected, matured in oak for 12 months, a further selection resulting in two
hogsheads matured for a further 12 months. Given the vintage and the vinification,
it is no surprise that the wine should be as intense, long and tightly focused as it is,
dripping with red and black fruits, spices and licorice. Verges on mouthwatering.
Screwcap. 13.6% alc. **Rating** 96 To 2039 $60 ✪

🍷🍷🍷🍷🍷 **Single Vineyard Geelong Pinot Noir 2015** Rating 92 To 2030 $38
Loretta Blanc de Noir 2013 Rating 90 To 2017 $38 TS

Brygon Reserve

529 Osmington Road, Margaret River, WA 6280 **Region** Margaret River
T 1800 754 517 **www.**brygonreservewines.com.au **Open** 7 days 11–5
Winemaker Okigh McManus **Est.** 2009 **Dozens** NFP

Since its establishment in 2009 by Robert and Laurie Fraser-Scott, this business has grown very rapidly, although details of its production are not available. Having originally relied on contract winemaking, it opened a winery and cellar door in February '15. The winery has its own bottling plant and bulk wine storage facilities, with at least some of the wine produced under contract elsewhere in Margaret River. The plethora of wines are under six major brands: Hummingbird, The Bruce, Brygon Reserve, Flying High, Third Wheel and Lions Lair. Unless otherwise stated, all come from Margaret River. There are some ancillary brands used in export or special markets, and thus not sold through retail outlets in Australia. Exports to the US, Vietnam, Macau, Taiwan, Thailand, Hong Kong, Singapore and China.

ỸỸỸỸỢ **Brygon Reserve Small Batch Oak Aged Chardonnay 2012** Has discovered the fountain of youth, white peach the fruit flavour driver, and offering much enjoyment now. Difficult to guess where it will head, and how much character it will develop at its peak. Screwcap. 13% alc. **Rating** 92 **To** 2021 $75
Brygon Reserve Flying High Semillon Sauvignon Blanc 2016 While simply cool-fermented in stainless steel, and largely driven by the semillon, has considerable focus and intensity, the finish long, crisp and clean. Will calmly travel through several more years. Screwcap. 12.7% alc. **Rating** 90 **To** 2020 $25
Brygon Reserve Humming Bird Series Semillon Sauvignon Blanc 2016 Still semillon-dominant, this has more softening by a tropical fruit influence than its Flying High sibling. Nice wine, simply made and needing no elaboration. Screwcap. 12.7% alc. **Rating** 90 **To** 2018 $25
Brygon Reserve Gold Label Vintage Reserve Chardonnay 2012 Bright green-gold; while now at its peak, has held its varietal fruit well, likewise its balance between French and barrel ferment oak. Don't delay past the end of the decade. Screwcap. 12.5% alc. **Rating** 90 **To** 2019 $50
Brygon Reserve Small Batch Oak Aged Shiraz 2012 Six different typefaces, most with meaningless information such as 'selected (by a scrawled name)'. Lighter colour than its siblings and the fruit is fresher, even though haunted by its oak. Screwcap. 13.5% alc. **Rating** 90 **To** 2022 $75
Brygon Reserve Gold Label Vintage Reserve Cabernet Sauvignon 2012 Has held its hue remarkably well; a savoury medium-bodied cabernet with varietal dried herb, earth and black olive notes buzzing around the core of blackcurrant fruit, French oak part of the mix, the tannins very much alive. Screwcap. 13.5% alc. **Rating** 90 **To** 2022 $50

ỸỸỸỸ **Brygon Reserve Flying High Sauvignon Blanc 2016 Rating** 89 **To** 2017 $25
Brygon Reserve Private Bin Block 3 Chardonnay 2012 Rating 89 **To** 2017 $60
Brygon Reserve Flying High Shiraz 2015 Rating 89 **To** 2023 $25
Brygon Reserve Small Batch Oak Aged Margaret River Cabernet Sauvignon 2012 Rating 89 **To** 2022 $75

Buckshot Vineyard

PO Box 119, Coldstream, Vic 3770 **Region** Heathcote
T 0417 349 785 **www.**buckshotvineyard.com.au **Open** Not
Winemaker Rob Peebles **Est.** 1999 **Dozens** 700 **Vyds** 2ha

This is the venture of Meegan and Rob Peebles, and comes on the back of Rob's 20+ year involvement in the wine industry, including six vintages in Rutherglen, starting in 1993, followed by 10 years at Domaine Chandon, and squeezing in weekend work at Coldstream Hills' cellar door in '93. It is the soils of Heathcote, and a long-time friendship with John and Jenny Davies, that sees the flagship Shiraz, and a smaller amount of Zinfandel (with some shiraz) coming from a small block, part of a 40ha vineyard owned by the Davies southwest of Colbinabbin. Rob makes the wines at Domaine Chandon. Exports to the US.

ɣɣɣɣɣ Reserve de la Cave Margaret River Malbec 2015 Only 300 bottles were produced of what is, unquestionably, one of the world's great cabernet francs. A gorgeous deep ruby red, this fragrant wine has a core of dark cherry/mulberry fruit while the 100% new oak sits very discreetly in the background. With its superb depth of fruit, silky palate and ripe, fine and very persistent tannins, there is little doubt that this will provide enormous pleasure now and over the next 10–20 years. Screwcap. 13.5% alc. **Rating** 97 **To** 2030 $90 PR

ɣɣɣɣ The Square Peg Zinfandel 2015 A convincing example of a variety that doesn't always hit the heights in Australia. Deeply coloured, this ripe but not overripe wine has aromas of dark cherry and plum fruit, together with a little blackstrap licorice that follows onto the very flavoursome and nicely balanced palate. Gently grippy tannins round out a wine that should provide pleasure for at least the next 3–4 years. Screwcap. 14.5% alc. **Rating** 89 **To** 2020 $26 PR

Bull Lane Wine Company ★★★★

PO Box 77, Heathcote, Vic 3523 **Region** Heathcote
T 0427 970 041 **www.**bulllane.com.au **Open** Not
Winemaker Simon Osicka **Est.** 2013 **Dozens** 400
After a successful career as a winemaker with what is now TWE, Simon Osicka, together with viticulturist partner Alison Phillips, returned to the eponymous family winery just within the eastern boundary of the Heathcote region in 2010. Spurred on by a decade of drought impacting on the 60-year-old dry-grown vineyard, and a desire to create another style of shiraz, Simon and Alison spent considerable time visiting Heathcote vineyards with access to water in the lead-up to the '10 vintage. After the weather gods gave up their tricks of '11, Bull Lane was in business. Exports to Denmark.

ɣɣɣɣɣ Via del Toro Pyrenees Nebbiolo 2015 From the Malakoff Vineyard, the grapes were hand-sorted, with whole berries open-fermented in small pots, then 3 weeks on skins before maturation in used French oak for 16 months. Good colour for nebbiolo; savoury tannins are an integral part of the character of any good nebbiolo, but so are the small red fruits in the heart of the wine. An unqualified success. Screwcap. 14.5% alc. **Rating** 94 **To** 2025 $32

ɣɣɣɣɣ Heathcote Shiraz 2015 Rating 93 **To** 2029 $28

Buller Wines ★★★★★

2804 Federation Way, Rutherglen, Vic 3685 **Region** Rutherglen
T (02) 6032 9660 **www.**bullerwines.com.au **Open** Mon–Sat 9–5, Sun 10–5
Winemaker Dave Whyte **Est.** 1921 **Dozens** 10 000 **Vyds** 32ha
In 2013, after 92 years of ownership and management by the Buller family, the business was purchased by Gerald and Mary Judd, a well known local couple and family with extensive roots in the northeast. They are hands-on in the business, and have overseen investment in the cellar, storage, operations and, importantly, vineyards. Exports to all major markets.

ɣɣɣɣɣ Calliope Rare Tokay NV A wonderfully complex array of cold black tea, honey and butterscotch achieve the unexpected, but precious, near-dry finish, luring you back again and again. Pure magic. Screwcap. 18% alc. **Rating** 97 $120

Calliope Rare Rutherglen Muscat NV Deep amber, shading towards olive on the sides of the glass when swirled. Extremely complex and intense, so no doubt about its extreme age; the desiccated raisin base at the start of each component up to 70 years ago is the setting for all the other rancio and spice components. A bargain given its rarity and age. Screwcap. 18% alc. **Rating** 97 $120

ɣɣɣɣɣ Calliope Grand Rutherglen Tokay NV The amber-mahogany hue has a faint touch of olive-green on the rim; the bouquet is complex, with rancio evident, plus an indefinable note; an unctuous palate with a wanton display of desiccated/caramelised/crystallised fruits and tea leaf. Screwcap. 18% alc. **Rating** 95 $65

Calliope Grand Rutherglen Muscat NV Very complex; a surprising touch of topaque-like fruit flavour in the middle of the luscious sea of grapey/raisin fruit and a wealth of Christmas pudding and toffee. Screwcap. 18% alc. **Rating** 95 **$65**

🍷🍷🍷🍷🍷 Balladeer Rutherglen Cabernet Sauvignon 2015 Rating 90 To 2029 $28

Bundalong Coonawarra ★★★★☆

109 Paul Road, Comaum, SA 5277 (postal) **Region** Coonawarra
T 0419 815 925 **www**.bundalongcoonawarra.com.au **Open** Not
Winemaker Andrew Hardy, Peter Bissell **Est.** 1990 **Dozens** 650 **Vyds** 65ha
James Porter has owned the Bundalong property for many years. In the second half of the 1980s, encouraged by an old shallow limestone quarry on the property, he sought opinions about the suitability of the soil for grapegrowing. In '89 the first plantings of cabernet sauvignon were made, followed by shiraz. The primary purpose of the 65ha vineyard was to supply grapes to major companies. Trial vintages were made in '94 and '96, followed by the first serious vintage in 2008. The strategy has been only to make wine in the very best vintages in Coonawarra, with the '08, '12, '14 and '15 the only vintages so far accredited.

🍷🍷🍷🍷🍷 **Single Vineyard Cabernet Sauvignon 2015** Matured for 18 months in French oak. Classic Coonawarra cabernet, one foot in the style of yesteryear, the other firmly planted today. The bouquet is fragrant, with blackcurrant and an airbrush of Coonawarra mint, fine-grained tannins first out of the block on the long, medium-bodied palate. It's those tannins, not oak, that shape the overall impact of a very good wine. Screwcap. 13.8% alc. **Rating** 95 **To** 2035 **$27** ○

🍷🍷🍷🍷🍷 Single Vineyard Shiraz 2015 Rating 93 To 2035 $27 ○

Burch Family Wines ★★★★★

Miamup Road, Cowaramup, WA 6284 **Region** Margaret River
T (08) 9756 5200 **www**.burchfamilywines.com.au **Open** 7 days 10–5
Winemaker Janice McDonald, Mark Bailey **Est.** 1986 **Dozens** NFP **Vyds** 183ha
Burch Family Wines acts as an umbrella name for the Howard Park and MadFish brands. Over the last 30 years the Burch family has slowly acquired vineyards in Margaret River and Great Southern. The Margaret River vineyards range from Leston in Wilyabrup, to Allingham in southern Karridale; Great Southern includes Mount Barrow and Abercrombie (the latter acquired in 2014), with Houghton cabernet clones, planted in 1975, all in Mount Barker. At the top of the portfolio are the Abercrombie Cabernet Sauvignon and the Allingham Chardonnay, followed by the Rieslings, Chardonnay and Sauvignon Blanc; next come pairs of Shiraz and Cabernet Sauvignon under the Leston and Scotsdale labels. The Miamup and the Flint Rock regional ranges were established in '12. MadFish is the second label producing the full range of varietal wines, Gold Turtle the second tier of MadFish. The feng shui–designed cellar door is a must see. A founding member of Australian First Families of Wines. Exports to all major markets.

🍷🍷🍷🍷🍷 **Howard Park Leston Margaret River Cabernet Sauvignon 2014**
Fermented in stainless steel, select parcels remaining on skins post fermentation, others pressed at dryness, each batch matured separately in French barriques (40% new) for 18 months. Vibrant and pure, cassis fruit to the fore, French oak synergistic, tannins and echoes of bay leaf/olive simply reaffirming the nigh-on perfect varietal expression. Screwcap. 14.5% alc. **Rating** 97 **To** 2039 **$46** ○

🍷🍷🍷🍷🍷 **Howard Park Scotsdale Great Southern Cabernet Sauvignon 2014** This is in superb form, its curranty flavour and combination of earthen/tobacco-like notes pulled inexorably through to a taut-but-lengthy finish. It's a champion for medium-weight cabernet; quality without stress, length without overreach, flavour without borders. Screwcap. 14.5% alc. **Rating** 96 **To** 2040 **$46** CM ○
Howard Park Porongurup Riesling 2016 Bone dry, this superb single vineyard wine from the remote Porongurup subregion of the Great Southern is restrained, with precise nashi, grapefruit and gentle floral aromas. On the admirably persistent

palate there is a fine vein of laser-like acidity and you just know this will reward at least another 5–10 years cellaring. Screwcap. 11.5% alc. **Rating** 95 **To** 2026 $34 PR ✪

Howard Park Porongurup Riesling 2015 From the former Gibraltar Rock Vineyard, one of the two oldest in Porongurup, acquired by Burch Family in '10. The wine has changed (for the better) since Sept '15, its flowery blossom bouquet introducing a palate that comes thundering home on the finish, with all banners flying well into the aftertaste. Screwcap. 12.4% alc. **Rating** 95 **To** 2025 $34 ✪

Howard Park Museum Release Great Southern Riesling 2012 A still very bright green-gold and with aromas of lime, quince and toast, this is travelling beautifully under screwcap. And while approachable now with its flavoursome, gently textured and very long palate, there is a fine vein of acidity running through the wine, meaning that this will still be looking pristine 5 years from now. 12% alc. **Rating** 95 **To** 2022 $41 PR

Howard Park Miamup Margaret River Sauvignon Blanc Semillon 2016 A blend of 87% sauvignon blanc and 13% semillon that was fermented in a combination of both stainless steel and oak, this has some ripe fresh tropical fruit notes that are balanced by a fine thread of acidity that runs through a wine that is simultaneously vibrant, fresh, textured and long. Screwcap. 13% alc. **Rating** 95 **To** 2021 $28 PR

Howard Park Allingham Margaret River Chardonnay 2015 From the cool Karridale district. White peach, nectarine and pink grapefruit are the drivers, not the French oak. It has great length and an intense aftertaste, the flavours drawing saliva from the mouth. Irresistible. Screwcap. 13% alc. **Rating** 95 **To** 2023 $89

Howard Park Flint Rock Great Southern Shiraz 2014 Frankland River and Mount Barker, open-fermented in small vats, matured for 15 months in new and used French oak. A serious, powerful full-bodied wine that might be confused with cabernet in a blind tasting thanks to savoury tannins that provide a platform for the blackberry, black cherry and plum fruits, with a dusting of spice and pepper; oak also contributes. Screwcap. 14.5% alc. **Rating** 95 **To** 2034 $28 ✪

Howard Park Sauvignon Blanc 2016 Part fermentation with cultured yeast in stainless steel, part wild-yeast fermented in used French oak results in a wine that has the best of both worlds, neither of which has any resemblance to Marlborough sauvignon blanc. Its balance of tropical fruits, tempered by savoury notes that provide texture as much as citrussy notes, is excellent. Screwcap. 13% alc. **Rating** 94 **To** 2020 $31

Howard Park Miamup Margaret River Chardonnay 2016 From southern Margaret River, the parcels vinified separately, each hand-picked, cooled overnight, sorted, whole-bunch pressed, fermented in new and used French oak, matured for 7 months with regular lees stirring and mlf. The fragrant and fresh bouquet heralds a fresh and inviting zesty palate, the flavours ranging through citrus and stone fruits of all kinds, oak playing a pure support role. A wine with time on its side. Screwcap. 13% alc. **Rating** 94 **To** 2023 $28 ✪

♟♟♟♟♟ MadFish Gold Turtle Chardonnay 2016 **Rating** 92 **To** 2020 $20 ✪
Howard Park Flint Rock Pinot Noir 2016 **Rating** 92 **To** 2026 $28
Howard Park Leston Margaret River Shiraz 2015 **Rating** 91 **To** 2035 $46 PR
Howard Park Margaret River Merlot 2014 **Rating** 91 **To** 2024 $35
Howard Park Miamup Cabernet Sauvignon 2014 **Rating** 91 **To** 2029 $28
Howard Park Scotsdale Frankland Shiraz 2015 **Rating** 90 **To** 2025 $46 PR

Burge Family Winemakers   ★★★★☆

1312 Barossa Way, Lyndoch, SA 5351 **Region** Barossa Valley
T (08) 8524 4644 **www**.burgefamily.com.au **Open** Fri, Sat, Mon 10–5
Winemaker Rick Burge **Est.** 1928 **Dozens** 3500 **Vyds** 10ha
Burge Family Winemakers, with Rick Burge at the helm (not to be confused with Grant Burge, although the families are related), has established itself as an icon producer

of exceptionally rich, lush and concentrated Barossa red wines. 2013 marked 85 years of continuous winemaking by three generations of the family. Exports to Canada, Germany, Belgium, The Netherlands, Hong Kong, Singapore and Japan.

ŸŸŸŸŸ **Garnacha Dry Grown Barossa Valley Grenache 2014** Red berries, cloves, assorted spices, a flash of licorice and the allure of fresh florals. It's not a heavy wine but it trips deliciously through the mouth, balance and texture both key features. There's warmth to the finish, to a minor degree, but it could be argued that it comes with the territory. Screwcap. 15.5% alc. **Rating** 91 **To** 2024 $25 CM
The Hipster Barossa Valley Garnacha Monastrell Tempranillo 2013
Mid-weight red with as much earth and spice notes as red-berried fruit. An old school 'earth wine' served with a fresh, low-oak face. Highly drinkable and enjoyable. Screwcap. 14.5% alc. **Rating** 91 **To** 2021 $25 CM

Burke & Wills Winery

3155 Burke & Wills Track, Mia Mia, Vic 3444 **Region** Heathcote
T (03) 5425 5400 **www**.wineandmusic.net **Open** By appt
Winemaker Andrew Pattison, Robert Ellis **Est.** 2003 **Dozens** 1500 **Vyds** 3.4ha
After 18 years at Lancefield Winery in the Macedon Ranges, Andrew Pattison moved his operation a few kilometres north in 2004 to set up Burke & Wills Winery in Heathcote, continuing to produce wines from both regions. With vineyards at Mia Mia and Redesdale, he now has 2ha of shiraz, 1ha of cabernet sauvignon and Bordeaux varieties and 0.4ha of gewurztraminer. He still sources a small amount of Macedon Ranges fruit from his former Malmsbury vineyard; additional grapes are contract-grown in Heathcote. Exports to Malaysia.

ŸŸŸŸŸ **Vat 1 French Oak Heathcote Shiraz 2015** An impressive deep crimson. Matured in a combination of new, 1 and 4yo French barriques, this beautifully put together and balanced Heathcote shiraz has dark fruits, black pepper, and other spice rack spices. The medium-bodied, concentrated yet stylish palate is equally good. Screwcap. 14% alc. **Rating** 92 **To** 2025 $36 PR
Pattison Family Reserve Macedon Ranges Chardonnay 2015 This impressive and well priced chardonnay has some complex and attractive gun flint aromas to go with some nice reduction. Good melon and fig fruit. The oak has been nicely handled and is already well integrated, the palate balanced and long. Screwcap. 13% alc. **Rating** 90 **To** 2020 $25 PR

Bush Track Wines ★★★★

219 Sutton Lane, Whorouly South, Vic 3735 **Region** Alpine Valleys
T 0409 572 712 **www**.bushtrackwines.com.au **Open** By appt
Winemaker Jo Marsh, Eleana Anderson **Est.** 1987 **Dozens** 350 **Vyds** 9.65ha
Bob and Helen McNamara established the vineyard in 1987, the 5.53ha of shiraz with 11 different clones, the other plantings 2ha of chardonnay, 1.72ha of cabernet sauvignon and 0.4ha of sangiovese. They have made small volumes of wines since 2006. Improvement in vineyard practices, and the services of Jo Marsh (Billy Button Wines) and Eleana Anderson (Mayford Wines), should secure the future of Bush Track Wines.

ŸŸŸŸŸ **Ovens Valley Alpine Valleys Shiraz 2015** All class from its glorious dark purple hue to the glossy feel as it glides across the tongue. Full-bodied with supple tannins, integrated oak, and a whisper of eucalypt, pepper and juniper berries. A core of succulent fruit. Screwcap. 14% alc. **Rating** 95 **To** 2024 $25 JF ✪

ŸŸŸŸŸ **Alpine Valleys Cabernet Sauvignon 2015 Rating** 92 **To** 2021 $25 JF ✪

Buttermans Track

PO Box 82, St Andrews, Vic 3761 **Region** Yarra Valley
T 0425 737 839 **www**.buttermanstrack.com.au **Open** Not
Winemaker James Lance, Gary Trist **Est.** 1991 **Dozens** 600 **Vyds** 2.13ha

I became intimately acquainted with Buttermans Track in the latter part of the 1980s when Coldstream Hills, at that stage owned by my wife Suzanne and myself, purchased grapes from the Roberts family's Rising Vineyard. I had to coax a 3-tonne truck with almost no brakes and almost no engine to tackle the hills and valleys of the unsealed Buttermans Track. Louise and Gary Trist began planting a small vineyard in '91 on a small side road just off the Buttermans Track. Between then and 2003 they established 0.86ha of pinot noir, 0.74ha of shiraz and 0.53ha of sangiovese. The Trist family sold the grapes to Yarra Valley wineries until '08. From that year onwards a small parcel of sangiovese was retained for the Buttermans Track label, which has now extended to include the other two varieties.

ΨΨΨΨΨ **Yarra Valley Sangiovese Rose 2016** This is a punchy, light and delicately copper-toned rose, its tangerine, cumquat and sour strawberry notes running along a tensile rail of acidity. Given a smudge of skin contact, fermented with wild yeast and matured in older French oak, this lip-smacking rose was bottled unfined and unfiltered with plenty of energy from fore to aft. Screwcap. 13% alc. **Rating** 93 **To** 2019 $26 NG

Yarra Valley Sangiovese 2015 This is a deep crimson–coated, mid to fully packed sangiovese with bright acidity, and the variety's hallmark edgy tannins. Full of fruit and spread with the textural detail attesting to plenty of love and care across sustainable viticulture. This is in the here and now, although it will age very well. Screwcap. 13.7% alc. **Rating** 93 **To** 2027 $32 NG

Yarra Valley Pinot Noir 2016 Very light and edgy, with a sappy skein of early-harvest fruit in the ferment; a smidgeon (5%) of whole bunch. Sour cherry, sweet strawberry, orange rind and a fountain of tangy red fruit define the aroma, reverberating across the pumice-inflected midriff, given further grip by well applied French oak (30% new). Light, aromatic and easy to drink, if not particularly complex. Screwcap. 13.2% alc. **Rating** 92 **To** 2023 $40 NG

Byrne Vineyards   ★★★★

PO Box 15, Kent Town BC, SA 5071 **Region** South Australia
T (08) 8132 0022 **www.**byrnevineyards.com.au **Open** Not
Winemaker Peter Gajewski, Phil Reedman **Est.** 1963 **Dozens** 35 000 **Vyds** 384ha
The Byrne family has been involved in the SA wine industry for three generations, with vineyards spanning Clare Valley, Eden Valley, Adelaide Plains and Riverland. The vines vary from 20 to over 50 years of age. Exports to the UK, Canada, France, Germany, Denmark, Sweden, Norway, Thailand, the Philippines, Singapore, Japan and China.

ΨΨΨΨΨ **Flavabom Field White 2016** A field blend of muscadelle, chenin blanc, colombard and semillon, co-fermented, resulting in a textural, savoury drink. Peachy, musk, spicy and succulent, grippy from neat phenolics and so satisfying. Screwcap. 14% alc. **Rating** 92 **To** 2020 $25 JF ✪

Limited Release Clare Valley Grenache 2013 80yo bushvines produce this dense, richly flavoured red in a riper, extracted style with oak influencing the nose and mouthfeel. Stewed plums, sarsaparilla, grainy ripe tannins, full-bodied and warm on the finish. Screwcap. 15.5% alc. **Rating** 91 **To** 2023 $59 JF

ΨΨΨΨ **Antiquarian Clare Valley Sangiovese 2013 Rating** 88 **To** 2022 $59 JF
Thomson Estate Clare Valley Sangiovese 2013 Rating 87 **To** 2021 $28 JF

Byron & Harold   ★★★★★

351 Herdigan Road, Wandering, WA 6308 **Region** Great Southern
T 0402 010 352 **www.**byronandharold.com.au **Open** Not
Winemaker Luke Eckersley **Est.** 2011 **Dozens** 35 000 **Vyds** 18ha
The owners of Byron & Harold make a formidable partnership, covering every aspect of winemaking, sales and marketing, and business management and administration. Paul Byron and Ralph (Harold) Dunning together have more than 65 years of experience in the Australian wine trade, working at top levels for some of the most admired wineries and wine distribution companies. Andrew Lane worked for 20 years in the tourism industry, including

in a senior role with Tourism Australia, leading to the formation of the Wine Tourism Export Council. More recently he developed the family vineyard (Wandering Lane). Exports to the UK, Canada, China and NZ.

🍷🍷🍷🍷🍷 **The Partners Great Southern Riesling 2016** Mandarin, citrus blossom, sour stone fruits and green apple are glazed with ginger and given flight across the precise, linear palate by mineral chalkiness. This is long, vibrant and piercingly intense of flavour and force. Screwcap. 12.6% alc. **Rating** 96 **To** 2036 $28 NG ✪
First Mark Mount Barker Riesling 2015 Comes at you like an express train, pulsating with lemon blossom and lemon zest on the bouquet, then an intense lime and Granny Smith apple palate bolstered by crunchy acidity. Great now, better still in 10 years. Screwcap. 12.5% alc. **Rating** 95 **To** 2027 $28 ✪
The Partners Great Southern Cabernet Sauvignon 2014 Cassis, bay leaf and cedar are all upfront on the bouquet, the secondary aromas of lanolin and mocha-like oak providing a counterpoint. Full-bodied but essentially elegant, the dark red and black fruit flavours run smoothly through the length of the palate with dusty tannins chiming in to control the finish. Screwcap. 14.5% alc. **Rating** 95 **To** 2035 $40 SC
Wandering Lane Great Southern Riesling 2016 A riesling that bounces with a stone-fruited mineral goodness on the nose, before a sluice of slate and flow of transparent acidity takes the light, dry palate for a long ride across a bed of talc and citrus zest. Screwcap. 12% alc. **Rating** 94 **To** 2028 $22 NG ✪

🍷🍷🍷🍷🍷 **Chapter & Verse Riesling 2015** Rating 92 To 2030 $24 NG ✪
Margaret's Muse Chardonnay 2015 Rating 91 To 2022 $28
Chapter and Verse Great Southern Shiraz 2013 Rating 91 To 2028 $35
Rose & Thorns Mount Barker Riesling 2015 Rating 90 To 2023 $24 NG
Chapter & Verse Great Southern Cabernet Shiraz 2014 Rating 90 To 2022 $24 NG

Caillard Wine ★★★★★
5 Annesley Street, Leichhardt, NSW 2040 (postal) **Region** Barossa Valley
T 0433 272 912 **www.**caillardwine.com **Open** Not
Winemaker Dr Chris Taylor, Andrew Caillard MW **Est.** 2008 **Dozens** 700
Andrew Caillard MW has had a long and varied career in wine, including vintages at Brokenwood and elsewhere, but has also taken the final step of making his own wine, with the support of wife Bobby. Andrew says the inspiration to make Mataro (and now Shiraz) came while writing the background for Penfolds' The Rewards of Patience tastings. He learnt that both Max Schubert and John Davoren had experimented with mataro, and that the original releases of Penfolds St Henri comprised a fair percentage of the variety. For good measure, Andrew's great (times four) grandfather, John Reynell, planted one of Australia's first vineyards at Reynella, around 1838. Exports to Hong Kong and China.

🍷🍷🍷🍷🍷 **Shiraz 2015** Off to a flying start, for it tastes and feels as if the alcohol is closer to 13.5% than 14.2% (the latter far from unacceptable). Likewise, the French oak maturation (part new, part used) has left the black cherry, plum and blackberry fruits in total command. It is supple, medium-bodied and perfectly balanced, the tannins whisper-smooth. Screwcap. **Rating** 96 **To** 2035 $55 ✪
Shiraz 2014 Open-fermented with some whole bunches, matured in French barriques (10% new) for 15 months. Bright crimson-purple; classic (in the best sense) Barossa shiraz, the bouquet leading inexorably into the medium to full-bodied palate where black fruits dominate, underpinned by nuances of plum, mulberry, licorice and firm savoury tannins. Put your house on the wine flourishing in 20+ years. Screwcap. 14.1% alc. **Rating** 95 **To** 2034 $55
Mataro 2014 Fermented and matured in new and used French oak. Andrew Caillard's team has made an art of mataro as well as of the labels on the Caillard releases. This is a wine as much about texture as it is about flavour, each acting in synergistic support of the other, wild herbs linking with sour cherry and spice. Screwcap. 14.2% alc. **Rating** 94 **To** 2029 $55

Calabria Family Wines   ★★★★☆

1283 Brayne Road, Griffith, NSW 2680 **Region** Riverina/Barossa Valley
T (02) 6969 0800 **www.**calabriawines.com.au **Open** Mon–Fri 8.30–5, w'ends 10–4
Winemaker Bill Calabria, Emma Norbiato **Est.** 1945 **Dozens** NFP **Vyds** 55ha
Along with a number of Riverina producers, Calabria Family Wines (until 2014 known as
Westend Estate) has successfully lifted both the quality and the packaging of its wines. Its
3 Bridges range is anchored on estate vineyards. Calabria Family Wines is moving with the
times, increasing its plantings of durif, and introducing aglianico, nero d'Avola, and St Macaire
(on the verge of extinction, and once grown in Bordeaux, this 2ha is the largest planting
in the world). Equally importantly, it is casting its net over the Barossa Valley, Canberra
District, Hilltops and King Valley premium regions, taking this one step further by acquiring
a 12ha vineyard in the Barossa Valley. Exports to the UK, the US and other major markets,
including China.

🍷🍷🍷🍷🍷 **The Iconic Grand Reserve Barossa Valley Shiraz 2014** The vintage
represents a milestone as centenarian vines are at its heart. And it beats strongly.
It's hard not to be mesmerised as the flood of ripe fruit flows onto the structured,
full-bodied palate, bringing with it spice, cedary oak, menthol and plush tannins.
Yet it is not unwieldy. There's composure and depth; it's comfortable with its
shape because it's balanced, it's glossy and convincing. Well played. Cork. 15% alc.
Rating 97 **To** 2045 $175 JF

🍷🍷🍷🍷🍷 **3 Bridges Reserve Botrytis Semillon 2010** Burnished amber, a luscious
palate and very fresh, with poached apricots doused in cinnamon and saffron, lime
marmalade with some burnt toffee. The acidity perfectly balances the sweetness
while more exotic flavours dance across the tongue. 375ml. Screwcap. 10% alc.
Rating 94 **To** 2020 $45 JF

🍷🍷🍷🍷🍷 **3 Bridges Barossa Valley Shiraz 2015** Rating 93 **To** 2028 $25 JF⚬
Golden Mist Botrytis Semillon 2008 Rating 93 **To** 2020 $65 JF
Francesco Show Reserve Grand Liqueur Muscat NV Rating 92 $45 JF
3 Bridges Tumbarumba Chardonnay 2016 Rating 91 **To** 2021 $25 JF
3 Bridges Barossa Valley Cabernet 2015 Rating 91 **To** 2025 $25 JF
3 Bridges Riverina Durif 2015 Rating 91 **To** 2027 $25 JF
3 Bridges Riverina Botrytis Semillon 2015 Rating 91 **To** 2021 $25 JF
Francesco Show Reserve Grand Tawny NV Rating 91 $45 JF
Tumbarumba Pinot Noir 2016 Rating 90 **To** 2020 $15 JF⚬
Richland Anniversary Shiraz 2015 Rating 90 **To** 2027 $16 JF⚬
Calabria Private Bin Nero d'Avola 2016 Rating 90 **To** 2021 $15 JF⚬

Caledonia Australis | Mount Macleod   ★★★★

PO Box 626, North Melbourne, Vic 3051 **Region** Gippsland
T (03) 9329 5372 **www.**southgippslandwinecompany.com **Open** Not
Winemaker Mark Matthews **Est.** 1995 **Dozens** 4500 **Vyds** 16.18ha
Mark and Marianna Matthews acquired Caledonia Australis in 2009. Mark is a winemaker
with vintages in numerous wine regions around the world. He works as a winemaking
teacher, and also runs a contract winemaking business. Marianna has experience with major
fast-moving consumer goods brands globally. The Matthews have converted the main
chardonnay block to certified organic, and are rehabilitating around 8ha of wetlands with the
local catchment authority. Exports to Canada and Japan.

🍷🍷🍷🍷🍷 **Caledonia Australis Pinot Noir 2015** All fruit sorted, 5–10% whole-bunch
inclusion in 1-tonne fermenters, wild-yeast fermented, matured in French oak
(10% new) for 18 months. Has the depth of fruit expected from east Gippsland
and a distinctive plummy/strawberry taste; good length and balance. Assured
winemaking. Screwcap. 14% alc. **Rating** 94 **To** 2023 $30⚬

🍷🍷🍷🍷🍷 **Caledonia Australis Chardonnay 2014** Rating 91 **To** 2021 $30

Calneggia Family Vineyards Wines   ★★★★

1142 Kaloorup Road, Kaloorup, WA 6280 **Region** Margaret River
T (08) 9368 4555 **www**.cfvwine.com.au **Open** Not
Winemaker Brian Fletcher **Est.** 2010 **Dozens** 1500 **Vyds** 34ha
The Calneggia family has owned vineyards and been involved in wine in the Margaret River region for over 25 years. The family owns several premium vineyards across the region and produces the Rosabrook, Bunkers, Bramble Lane, Brian Fletcher Signature Wines and now their first Calneggia Family Vineyards Estate wines, in conjunction with long-term winemaker Brian Fletcher.

ŸŸŸŸŸ **Margaret River Cabernet Merlot 2014** This drinks like a medium–bodied claret on the lighter side, with currants of both hues, a potpourri of herb, bell pepper and a hint of mint sashaying along a scale of tight tannins, a lick of oak and a stream of acidity. Screwcap. 14.3% alc. **Rating** 91 **To** 2025 $25 NG
Margaret River Sauvignon Blanc Semillon 2016 The sauvignon blanc was intentionally harvested early for zest and raciness, while the semillon's lanolin and lemon drop viscosity fill the wine out and provide a few layers to mull over. Screwcap. 13.1% alc. **Rating** 90 **To** 2017 $25 NG

ŸŸŸŸ **Margaret River Rose 2016 Rating** 89 **To** 2017 $25 NG

 # Camfield Family Wines   ★★★★

247 Moonambel Highway/Warrenmang Road, Moonambel, Vic 3478 **Region** Pyrenees
T (03) 9830 1414 **www**.camfieldfamilywines.com **Open** Not
Winemaker Dominic Bosch **Est.** 2003 **Dozens** 2000 **Vyds** 21ha
The Camfield family first settled in the Pyrenees in the mid 1880s on the periphery of the Gold Rush. In 1910 the family moved to Moonambel and sheep farming. Since that time various branches of the family have moved to other places and other occupations, but when Ross Camfield purchased the land for the Camfield Family Vineyard, it was directly across the road from the property owned by the family in 1910. In 2003 they planted 21ha of vineyard (10ha shiraz, 6ha sangiovese, 5ha pinot gris). Right from the time the first wine was made, the focus was on exports. To assist their Chinese distribution partners, the business has Chinese-speaking relationship managers. Exports to the US, Vietnam and China.

ŸŸŸŸŸ **Family Selection Pyrenees Pinot Gris 2015** Bright copper-pink; the bouquet is complex, with spices, dried fruits and marzipan, the palate very rich indeed. Strawberry, honeysuckle and more marzipan flavours are saved from cloying by unusual savoury acidity. Screwcap. 13.5% alc. **Rating** 92 **To** 2018 $25 ✪
Family Selection Pyrenees Shiraz 2013 Plum and blackberry fruit is framed by obvious oak, but the texture is good, as is the length. Screwcap. 14.5% alc. **Rating** 90 **To** 2023 $35

ŸŸŸŸ **Family Selection Pyrenees Sangiovese 2013 Rating** 89 **To** 2019 $35

Campbells   ★★★★★

Murray Valley Highway, Rutherglen, Vic 3685 **Region** Rutherglen
T (02) 6033 6000 **www**.campbellswines.com.au **Open** Mon–Sat 9–5, Sun 10–5
Winemaker Colin Campbell, Julie Campbell **Est.** 1870 **Dozens** 36000 **Vyds** 72ha
Campbells has a long and rich history, with five generations of the family making wine for over 150 years. There were difficult times: phylloxera's arrival in the Bobbie Burns Vineyard in 1898; the Depression of the 1930s; and premature deaths. But the Scottish blood of founder John Campbell has ensured that the business has not only survived, but quietly flourished. Indeed, there have been spectacular successes in unexpected quarters (white table wines, especially Riesling) and expected success with Muscat and Topaque. 99-point scores from Robert Parker and a 100-point score from *The Wine Spectator* put Campbells in a special position. It is fair to say that the nigh-on half-century fourth-generation stewardship of Malcolm and Colin Campbell has been the most important so far, but the five members of the fifth generation all working in the business are well equipped to move up the ladder

when Colin and/or Malcolm retire. A founding member of Australia's First Families of Wine. Exports to the UK, the US and China.

ŸŸŸŸŸ **Isabella Rare Topaque NV** The dark mahogany and olive rim precedes a mind-blowingly powerful rich and complex wine at the top of the topaque tree. I'm sure this has become even more intense, and more compellingly textured, than previous tastings, yet it isn't the slightest bit stale. I suppose it's just the sheer bliss of tasting these wines that causes me to write as if I have not previously encountered them. Screwcap. 18% alc. **Rating** 97 $120 **☉**

ŸŸŸŸŸ **Merchant Prince Rare Muscat NV** Wines of this intensity can be a life-changing experience. If it were any thicker or denser it would be impossible to pour. It has might but it also has glory: it packs bags of tarry, toffeed, burnt fruits and honeyed flavours, but it still manages to skip through the palate at a speed more youthful wines often cannot manage. Few wines, the world over, come as guaranteed to impress as this does. Screwcap. 18% alc. **Rating** 96 $120 CM
Grand Rutherglen Topaque NV Deep olive-brown; a wonderful example of muscadelle/topaque, with all the cold tea, butterscotch, Christmas cake and burnt toffee expected of the variety at its zenith. I have to admit to a special love of topaque, while recognising the greatness of the muscat Rutherglen makes. Screwcap. 17.5% alc. **Rating** 95 $65
Grand Rutherglen Muscat NV Much deeper colour than the Classic, mahogany rimmed with olive. This is for veteran tasters − if you are a P-plate driver you don't get behind the wheel of a Ferrari. Here a sword of rancio brings burnt and sweet flavours of every description into play: Christmas pudding and the works. Screwcap. 17.5% alc. **Rating** 95 $65
Classic Rutherglen Topaque NV Butterscotch, cold tea and honey all roll around the mouth in a glistening, almost velvety, fashion. It is very sweet, but the rancio cleanses the finish and aftertaste. Screwcap. 17.5% alc. **Rating** 94 $38
Rutherglen Topaque NV There's an argument that the youngest tier of topaque is the most enjoyable, it's so immediately compelling (and dangerous). There are shortbread biscuits, spices galore and honey all to be had. Screwcap. 17.5% alc. **Rating** 94 $19 **☉**
Classic Rutherglen Muscat NV This is the magic hall of Rutherglen muscat, the flavours coming unbidden by you at such a rate it's hard to record them in any orderly fashion. Singed butterscotch, malt, dried and crystallised fruits, then the vinous masochism of the rancio. Screwcap. 17.5% alc. **Rating** 94 $38

ŸŸŸŸŸ **Rutherglen Sparkling Shiraz NV** Rating 93 To 2020 $30 TS
Limited Release Rutherglen Roussanne 2016 Rating 92 To 2021 $25 **☉**
Rutherglen Muscat NV Rating 92 $19 **☉**
Limited Release Rutherglen Marsanne Viognier 2016 Rating 91 To 2021 $28

Cannibal Creek Vineyard ★★★★

260 Tynong North Road, Tynong North, Vic 3813 **Region** Gippsland
T (03) 5942 8380 **www.**cannibalcreek.com.au **Open** 7 days 11–5
Winemaker Patrick Hardiker **Est.** 1997 **Dozens** 3000 **Vyds** 5ha
Patrick and Kirsten Hardiker moved to Tynong North in 1988, initially grazing beef cattle, but aware of the viticultural potential of the sandy clay loam and bleached subsurface soils weathered from the granite foothills of the Black Snake Ranges. Plantings began in '97, using organically based cultivation methods; varieties include pinot noir, chardonnay, sauvignon blanc, merlot and cabernet sauvignon. The family established the winery in an old farm barn built in the early 1900s by the Weatherhead family, with timber from Weatherhead Hill (visible from the vineyard); it also houses the new cellar door and restaurant. In 2016 a new cellar door and restaurant, designed by Enarchitects and hand built by Patrick, was opened.

ŸŸŸŸŸ **Reserve Sauvignon Blanc 2016** The Reserve bottling differentiates itself from the regular cuvee by way of barrel fermentation. This has imbued the wine with a creamy textural weave, a leesy smokiness and impressive breadth across the mouth. Herb, a faint whiff of passionfruit, galangal and verdant foliage all linger within. Despite the wine's ethereal grace, the finish bursts with intensity of flavour and tenacious length. Screwcap. 12% alc. **Rating** 94 **To** 2021 $35 NG

Chardonnay 2015 Reticent at first, this picks up the pace as notes of melon, green fig and apricot wind across a tensile beam of mineral crunch and cool climate, unadulterated acidity. The oak is seamlessly integrated, providing further structural support and some cinnamon spice on the sapid finish. This will age well over the medium term. Screwcap. 13% alc. **Rating** 94 **To** 2023 $35 NG

♀♀♀♀♀ **Cabernet Merlot 2015 Rating** 93 **To** 2025 $38 NG
Vin de Liqueur 2015 Rating 93 $38 NG
Sauvignon Blanc 2016 Rating 92 **To** 2020 $32 NG
Pinot Noir 2015 Rating 91 **To** 2023 $38 NG
Merlot 2015 Rating 91 **To** 2021 $38 NG
Blanc de Blancs 2013 Rating 90 **To** 2018 $32 TS

🍷 Cantina Abbatiello ★★★★

90 Rundle Street, Kent Town, SA 5067 (postal) **Region** Adelaide
T 0421 200 414 **Open** Not
Winemaker Contract **Est.** 2015 **Dozens** NFP
Luca Abbatiello was born and raised in a small village in the south of Italy 'Vagabondo' means nomad, and as he grew up the wanderlust took hold, wine and food remaining important wherever he went. And while he worked for Michelin-starred restaurants in England (where he first headed) he says he still missed the homemade food of Italy. This led him and his partner to move to Australia in 2014, gravitating to Adelaide. Here he found the family food that he had missed, and a work environment full of opportunities. The most recent of those has been the creation of his virtual winery Cantina Abbatiello.

♀♀♀♀♀ **Vagabondo McLaren Vale Shiraz 2012** Harvested with a berry sorting platform incorporated in the machine, crushed and destemmed, wild-yeast fermented, matured for 2 years in used oak. The medium-bodied palate has dark/black fruits, good length and good balance. It retains the freshness of the great vintage, its value self-evident. Screwcap. 13% alc. **Rating** 91 **To** 2027 $20 ✪
Vagabondo Adelaide Hills Sauvignon Blanc 2016 Cool-fermented in tank with sauvignon blanc yeast QL23, 5 months on light lees. Crisp, positive mouthfeel and flavour, citrus more than tropical fruit, but overall good varietal expression. Adelaide Hills does it again. Screwcap. 12.5% alc. **Rating** 90 **To** 2017 $18 ✪

Cape Barren Wines ★★★★

PO Box 738, North Adelaide, SA 5006 **Region** McLaren Vale
T (08) 8267 3292 **www**.capebarrenwines.com **Open** By appt
Winemaker Rob Dundon **Est.** 1999 **Dozens** 12 100 **Vyds** 16.5ha
Cape Barren was founded in 1999 by Peter Matthews, who sold the business in late 2009 to Rob Dundon and Tom Adams, who together have amassed in excess of 50 years' experience in winemaking, viticulture and international sales. The wines are sourced from dry-grown vines between 70 and 125 years old. With changes in vineyard blocks, the '15 vintage red wines are from 70yo shiraz and 79yo grenache. Chardonnay, sauvignon blanc and gruner veltliner are sourced from the Adelaide Hills. Exports to the US, Canada, China and other markets across Asia.

♀♀♀♀♀ **Native Goose McLaren Vale Shiraz 2015** A vivid, deep purple hue bodes positively for the crushed blueberry, anise, clove and black olive notes that cascade like waves across a velvety, fully packed palate. The oak caresses rather than bludgeons, feeling more like a structural adjunct, helping to tame the wine's compelling richness. Screwcap. 14.7% alc. **Rating** 93 **To** 2030 $23 NG ✪
Old Vine Reserve Release McLaren Vale Shiraz 2014 The deep sands and limestone energy of the elevated Blewitt Springs vineyard mark this wine; vines

ranging from 55–125yo fuel this elixir. The wine pushes the envelope of excess, but manages to squeeze its bulging, black-fruited muscles into an attire with a semblance of taste. Cork. 15% alc. **Rating** 93 **To** 2034 $40 NG

Native Goose Chardonnay 2016 Peach, baked apple and nectarine notes are iced with new oak. A cool climate riff of juicy acidity gives thrust to the parry of a creamy nougat core. Screwcap. 13% alc. **Rating** 90 **To** 2020 $23 NG

McLaren Vale Cabernet Sauvignon Merlot Cabernet Franc 2015 Sourced from Blewitt Springs, this is greater than the sum of its varietal personalities. A forceful palate with a dark-fruited sheen is etched by fine-boned tannins and a lash of oak. Screwcap. 14.5% alc. **Rating** 90 **To** 2024 $18 NG ✪

♟♟♟♟ **Funky Goose Gruner Veltliner 2016** Rating 89 To 2021 $21 NG

Cape Bernier Vineyard ★★★★☆

230 Bream Creek Road, Bream Creek, Tas 7175 **Region** Southern Tasmania
T (03) 6253 5443 **www**.capebernier.com.au **Open** By appt
Winemaker Frogmore Creek (Alain Rousseau) **Est.** 1999 **Dozens** 1800 **Vyds** 4ha
Andrew and Jenny Sinclair took over from founder Alastair Christie in 2014. The vineyard plantings consist of 2ha of pinot noir (including three Dijon clones), 1.4ha of chardonnay and 0.6ha of pinot gris on a north-facing slope with spectacular views of Marion Bay. The property is one of several in the region that are changing from dairy and beef cattle to wine production and tourism. Exports to Singapore.

♟♟♟♟♟ **Pinot Noir 2015** Late rains are said by Cape Bernier to provide a lighter mouthfeel than previous vintages, but all things are relative: this is no wimp, with complexity riding high and bramble and forest fruits running through the long palate and lingering aftertaste. Both interesting and challenging (in the best possible way). Screwcap. 13.3% alc. **Rating** 95 **To** 2030 $42

Unwooded Chardonnay 2016 Sets the pace for unwooded chardonnay with its intensity, purity and drive; neither the Yarra Valley or Margaret River could afford to impose the limit on expression of chardonnay of this potential. Grapefruit, peach and melon are all on show, plus Tasmanian acidity. Screwcap. 12.7% alc. **Rating** 94 **To** 2026 $26 ✪

♟♟♟♟♟ **Pinot Gris 2016** Rating 91 To 2019 $29

Cape Grace Wines ★★★★★

281 Fifty One Road, Cowaramup, WA 6284 **Region** Margaret River
T (08) 9755 5669 **www**.capegracewines.com.au **Open** 7 days 10–5
Winemaker Dylan Arvidson, Mark Messenger **Est.** 1996 **Dozens** 2000 **Vyds** 6ha
Cape Grace can trace its history back to 1875, when timber baron MC Davies settled at Karridale, building the Leeuwin lighthouse and founding the township of Margaret River; 120 years later, Robert and Karen Karri-Davies planted their vineyard to chardonnay, shiraz and cabernet sauvignon, with smaller amounts of cabernet franc, malbec and chenin blanc. Robert is a self-taught viticulturist; Karen has over 15 years of international sales and marketing experience in the hospitality industry. Winemaking is carried out on the property; consultant Mark Messenger is a veteran of the Margaret River region. Exports to Singapore and China.

♟♟♟♟♟ **Reserve Margaret River Cabernet Sauvignon 2013** Two barrels made the cut for the Reserve. Both new French barriques with the wine aged for 16 months, creating an intensely flavoured, full-bodied and sweet-fruited cabernet of exceptional length. Screwcap. 14.5% alc. **Rating** 96 **To** 2032 $85 JF

Margaret River Cabernet Sauvignon 2014 A neat interplay of concentrated fruit and savouriness with blackberries and currants balancing out the cedary oak, warm earth and new leather characters. It's full-bodied, with refreshing acidity and supple tannins. Screwcap. 13.9% alc. **Rating** 95 **To** 2033 $55 JF

♟♟♟♟♟ **Margaret River Shiraz 2014** Rating 91 To 2023 $35 JF

Cape Jaffa Wines ★★★★★

459 Limestone Coast Road, Mount Benson via Robe, SA 5276 **Region** Mount Benson
T (08) 8768 5053 www.capejaffawines.com.au **Open** 7 days 10–5
Winemaker Anna and Derek Hooper **Est.** 1993 **Dozens** 10000 **Vyds** 22.86ha
Cape Jaffa was the first of the Mount Benson wineries, its winery made from local rock
(between 800 and 1000 tonnes are crushed each year). Cape Jaffa's fully certified biodynamic
vineyard provides 50% of production, with additional fruit sourced from a certified
biodynamic grower in Wrattonbully. Having received the Advantage SA Regional Award
in '09, '10 and '11 for its sustainable initiatives in the Limestone Coast, Cape Jaffa is now a
Hall of Fame inductee. Exports to the UK, Canada, Thailand, the Philippines, Hong Kong,
Singapore and China.

ŸŸŸŸŸ **Epic Drop Limestone Coast Shiraz 2015** A barrel selection of the wines
made from the best batches of the vintage. This is unflinchingly full-bodied, with
black fruits, dark chocolate, plentiful tannins and positive oak. Needs many years to
fully open up. Screwcap. 14.5% alc. **Rating** 95 **To** 2035 $29 ✪
La Lune Mt Benson Shiraz 2014 From Cape Jaffa's favourite estate block
6, open-fermented, hand-plunged, matured in tight-grained French oak. Great
colour; the intensity of this biodynamic certified wine is insidious, building
another level in a carefully orchestrated wine each time you go back to it.
Screwcap. 14.5% alc. **Rating** 95 **To** 2034 $60
Limestone Coast Shiraz 2015 A gold medal at the competitive Limestone
Coast Wine Show in '16 reflects the balance and drinkability of the wine, exactly as
intended by Cape Jaffa. Also impressive is its excellent colour, fresher and brighter
than Epic Drop. Fantastic value. Screwcap. 14.5% alc. **Rating** 94 **To** 2025 $20 ✪
Epic Drop Limestone Coast Shiraz 2014 A barrel selection of the wines
made from the best batches of the Limestone Coast vintage. A striking wine in
every respect; the mouthfeel of the red and black cherry fruits is smooth and
supple, the wine light to medium-bodied despite its alcohol. Oak and tannins have
walk on, walk off parts. Screwcap. 15% alc. **Rating** 94 **To** 2024 $29 ✪
Upwelling Limestone Coast Cabernet Sauvignon 2015 85% from
Wrattonbully, 15% Mount Benson, matured for 12 months in French oak
(15% new). Very good depth to the crimson-purple hue, a clue to the depth
and controlled richness of the cassis, blackberry and bay leaf on the bouquet and
palate alike. The texture and structure are admirable, too, the only question the
(surprising) amount of oak. Screwcap. 14% alc. **Rating** 94 **To** 2029 $29 ✪

ŸŸŸŸŸ **La Lune Mount Benson Field Blend 2015** **Rating** 93 **To** 2022 $42 JF
En Soleil Wrattonbully Pinot Gris 2016 **Rating** 91 **To** 2018 $27
Limestone Coast Sauvignon Blanc 2016 **Rating** 90 **To** 2018 $20 JF ✪

Cape Mentelle ★★★★★

331 Wallcliffe Road, Margaret River, WA 6285 **Region** Margaret River
T (08) 9757 0888 www.capementelle.com.au **Open** 7 days 10–4.30
Winemaker Frederique Perrin Parker, Antoine Robert, Coralie Lewis **Est.** 1970
Dozens 80000 **Vyds** 150ha
Part of the LVMH (Louis Vuitton Möet Hennessy) group. Cape Mentelle is firing on all
cylinders, with the winemaking team fully capitalising on the extensive and largely mature
vineyards, which obviate the need for contract-grown fruit. It is hard to say which of the wines
is best; the ranking, such as it is, varies from year to year. That said, Sauvignon Blanc Semillon,
Chardonnay, Shiraz and Cabernet Sauvignon lead the portfolio, and Cape Mentelle is one of
those knocking on the door of the Winery of the Year Award. Exports to all major markets.

ŸŸŸŸŸ **Wallcliffe 2015** The best parcels of sauvignon blanc and semillon are the soul
of Wallcliffe. This is one of the finest from Margaret River for its complexity and
deliciousness. Super restraint, taking its high notes off the citrus scale with lemon-
lime zest and pith plus lemongrass, then wraps that all up in a savoury parcel, with
length to match. Screwcap. 13.5% alc. **Rating** 96 **To** 2025 $49 JF ✪

Margaret River Cabernet Sauvignon 2014 Includes 15% merlot. An excellent wine with neatly compact flavours and definition. Beautiful tannin structure, silky and refined, the cassis, the oak, the spices all dutifully playing their part. Screwcap. 14% alc. **Rating** 96 **To** 2035 $98 JF

Wallcliffe 2014 Offers intense fresh herbs, cut grass, lime zest/oil and Chinese gooseberries with its bouquet and palate and barrel-ferment complexity. Lively acidity is the backbone of its length and structure. Screwcap. 13% alc. **Rating** 95 **To** 2023 $49 JF

Margaret River Chardonnay 2015 Careful with this wine: it is so well composed that before you know it, your glass will be empty. A succulent palate with stone fruit, ginger cream and leesy notes, the integrated oak adding flavour and depth, plus struck match. Screwcap. 13.5% alc. **Rating** 95 **To** 2027 $45 JF

Wallcliffe Cabernet Sauvignon Cabernet Franc 2014 A complex bouquet of cassis and cranberries mingles with an array of spices with bitter chocolate and black tea. Silky and generous palate, yet medium-bodied, with the tannins and oak all in line. Screwcap. 14% alc. **Rating** 95 **To** 2030 $49 JF

ΨΨΨΨΨ Margaret River Shiraz 2014 Rating 93 To 2027 $41 JF
       Margaret River Zinfandel 2015 Rating 93 To 2025 $65 JF
       Margaret River Zinfandel 2014 Rating 93 To 2021 $56
       Margaret River Sauvignon Blanc Semillon 2016 Rating 92 To 2020 $26 JF
       Margaret River Shiraz 2015 Rating 92 To 2030 $41 JF

Cape Naturaliste Vineyard   ★★★★☆

1 Coley Road (off Caves Road), Yallingup, WA 6282 **Region** Margaret River
T (08) 9755 2538 **www.**capenaturalistevineyard.com.au **Open** 7 days 10.30–5
Winemaker Bruce Dukes **Est.** 1997 **Dozens** 5000 **Vyds** 10.7ha
Cape Naturaliste Vineyard has a long and varied history going back 150 years, when it was a coach inn for travellers journeying between Perth and Margaret River. Later it became a dairy farm, and in 1970 a mining company purchased it, intending to extract nearby mineral sands. The government stepped in and declared the area a national park, whereafter (in '80) Craig Brent-White purchased the property. The vineyard is planted to cabernet sauvignon, shiraz, merlot, semillon and sauvignon blanc, and is run on an organic/biodynamic basis.

ΨΨΨΨΨ **Torpedo Rocks Reserve Margaret River Shiraz Cabernet Merlot 2013**
       American oak (10%) used with the shiraz and it works, furrowing the fruity brow
       of the wine with some tannic austerity and creamy, vanilla mocha. Blue and black
       fruit allusions are prominent, as is anise in the background. The patina of tannins
       is finely tuned, harnessing the intensity of the fruit into a wine of power and
       thrust. The alcohol, too, is well absorbed. Screwcap. 14.7% alc. **Rating** 95 **To** 2026
       $60 NG
       Torpedo Rocks Reserve Margaret River Cabernet Sauvignon 2013 The
       Reserve bottling differentiates itself from the regular Torpedo Rocks with the
       use of superior oak. This cuvee is more lifted, with a skein of spearmint toning
       down the volume of black fruits cascading across the palate. The oak, too, is more
       effective in conferring a savoury authority while imparting welcome tannins.
       A more balanced wine. Screwcap. 14.6% alc. **Rating** 94 **To** 2030 $60 NG

ΨΨΨΨΨ Reserve Margaret River Merlot 2013 Rating 93 To 2025 $50 NG
       Margaret River Cabernet Sauvignon 2013 Rating 93 To 2025 $40 NG
       Torpedo Rocks Semillon 2015 Rating 92 To 2022 $27 NG
       Margaret River Sauvignon Blanc 2016 Rating 92 To 2019 $20 NG❂
       Margaret River Cabernet Sauvignon 2015 Rating 92 To 2025 $25 NG❂
       Torpedo Rocks Margaret River Shiraz 2013 Rating 91 To 2023 $40 NG
       Margaret River SSB 2016 Rating 90 To 2019 $20 NG❂

Capel Vale

118 Mallokup Road, Capel, WA 6271 **Region** Geographe
T (08) 9727 1986 **www**.capelvale.com **Open** 7 days 10–4
Winemaker Daniel Hetherington **Est.** 1974 **Dozens** 50000 **Vyds** 90ha
Established by Perth-based medical practitioner Dr Peter Pratten and wife Elizabeth in 1974.
The first vineyard adjacent to the winery was planted on the banks of the quiet waters of
Capel River. The viticultural empire has since been expanded, spreading across Geographe
(15ha), Mount Barker (15ha), Pemberton (28ha) and Margaret River (32ha). There are four
tiers in the Capel Vale portfolio: Debut (varietals), Regional Series, Black Label Margaret
River Chardonnay and Cabernet Sauvignon, and at the top the Single Vineyard Wines.
Exports to all major markets.

Regional Series Pemberton Semillon 2016 100% fermented in French oak,
this beautifully made wine has aromas of cut grass, greengage and lemon zest.
Subtle and restrained, there is lovely mid-palate intensity for what is a compelling
example of the style. Screwcap. 11% alc. **Rating** 92 **To** 2022 $25 PR ●
Regional Series Margaret River Chardonnay 2015 A portion of this wine
went through mlf together with some battonage during maturation in older
French wood to give the wine texture and immediate drinkability. It's worked,
and the result is a delicious, good value, persistent and fruit-driven drink-now
chardonnay. Screwcap. 13.5% alc. **Rating** 92 **To** 2020 $25 PR ●
Regional Series Mount Barker Riesling 2016 Clear varietal expression in a
wine that is generous in every way; lime juice/apple, balanced acidity and good
length. Needs more urgency. Screwcap. 12% alc. **Rating** 91 **To** 2023 $25
Black Label Margaret River Chardonnay 2015 The oak influence won't be
ignored here. Nutty, biscuity, spicy aromas to the fore, varietal citrus and peach
character present, but less obvious. Richly textured, but held tight by acidity, the
fruit flavour is a little hard to find within the structure. The oak is back again
on the finish. It's a serious style, but perhaps needs time to really come together.
Screwcap. 13% alc. **Rating** 91 **To** 2025 $35 SC

Debut Sauvignon Blanc Semillon 2016 Rating 89 **To** 2018 $18 PR ●

Capercaillie Wines

4 Londons Road, Lovedale, NSW 2325 **Region** Hunter Valley
T (02) 4990 2904 **www**.capercailliewines.com.au **Open** 7 days 10–4.30
Winemaker Peter Lane **Est.** 1995 **Dozens** 10000 **Vyds** 8ha
A successful winery in terms of the quality of its wines, as well as their reach outwards from
the Hunter Valley. The Capercaillie wines have generous flavour. Its fruit sources are spread
across South Eastern Australia, although the portfolio includes wines that are 100% Hunter
Valley. Exports to Dubai and China.

The Creel 2016 From low-yielding 70yo vines in Pokolbin, hand-picked, free-
run juice cold-settled overnight, cool-fermented with neutral yeast. A festival
of lemon juice, lemongrass and lemon sherbet flavours balanced on a tightrope
walker's strand of mouthwatering acidity. Screwcap. 10.1% alc. **Rating** 94
To 2036 $35

Hunter Valley Chardonnay 2014 Rating 90 **To** 2017 $32

Capital Wines

13 Gladstone Street, Hall, ACT 2618 **Region** Canberra District
T (02) 6230 2022 **www**.capitalwines.com.au **Open** Thurs–Sun 10–5
Winemaker Andrew McEwin, Phil Scott **Est.** 1986 **Dozens** 3500 **Vyds** 5ha
Capital Wines started as Kyeema Wines, established by Andrew and Marion McEwin in 1986.
They purchased a 4ha vineyard 4km south of Murrumbateman in 2000, planted in 1984 to
shiraz, cabernet sauvignon and chardonnay (Kyeema had sourced fruit from this vineyard

since its first vintage), extending the plantings with merlot, shiraz and tempranillo in '02, and removing the cabernet in '07. Kyeema became Capital Wines in '08, with a much expanded range of wines. Exports to Thailand.

ŢŢŢŢŢ **The Whip Canberra District Riesling 2016** It's easy to sit back, relax and just enjoy this for what it is – a gorgeous, very approachable riesling. It will go some distance thanks to the line of very fine lemony acidity. Meyer lemon and lime juice freshness and blossom add to its appeal. Screwcap. 10.7% alc. **Rating** 95 To 2028 $21 JF ◐

Gundaroo Vineyard Canberra District Riesling 2016 Crafted with precision. Crystalline acidity drives right through the middle, holding everything firmly in place. A posy of wild flowers and blossom aromas, plus ricotta cheese with lemon juice, forms part of the complex bouquet and palate. A keeper. Screwcap. 10.7% alc. **Rating** 95 To 2033 $29 JF ◐

Kyeema Vineyard Canberra District Shiraz 2015 Mid-ruby-black; reductive, slightly feral at first with cured meat aromas, then wham! They dissipate and a flurry of spicy red fruit and florals takes over. Some creaminess on the mid-weighted palate, and a beautiful tannin structure. Ultimately, a deliciously savoury wine. Screwcap. 13.8% alc. **Rating** 95 To 2028 $52 JF

Kyeema Vineyard Canberra District Shiraz Viognier 2015 Plenty of dark garnet colour; reductive, but unfurls with a savoury outlook. Supple palate with plump tannins, the oak completely absorbed into the wine – merely a whiff of char and spice (18 months French oak, 93% new). Yes there's lovely sweet plum fruit in this with some apricot kernel, but it's the palate that really entices. Screwcap. 13.8% alc. **Rating** 95 To 2026 $52 JF

The Ambassador Tempranillo 2015 Is it the juicy, tangy and bright cherries and raspberries? Or the zesty snappy acidity? Whatever it is, this is such a good drink. The palate balances all the exuberance of the variety with its raw silk tannins and considerable depth. Screwcap. 14% alc. **Rating** 94 To 2022 $27 JF ◐

ŢŢŢŢŢ **The Swinger Canberra Sauvignon Blanc 2016** Rating 93 To 2021 $21 JF ◐
Kyeema Vineyard Canberra Merlot 2015 Rating 93 To 2026 $46 JF
Kyeema Vineyard Tempranillo Shiraz 2015 Rating 93 To 2021 $36 JF
The Frontbencher Shiraz 2015 Rating 91 To 2020 $27 JF
Kyeema Vineyard Chardonnay Viognier 2016 Rating 90 To 2020 $36 JF
The Backbencher Merlot 2015 Rating 90 To 2021 $27 JF

Cargo Road Wines   ★★★★☆

Cargo Road, Orange, NSW 2800 **Region** Orange
T (02) 6365 6100 **www.**cargoroadwines.com.au **Open** W'ends & public hols 11–5
Winemaker James Sweetapple **Est.** 1983 **Dozens** 3000 **Vyds** 14.65ha
Originally called The Midas Tree, the vineyard was planted in 1983 by Roseworthy graduate John Swanson, who established a 2.5ha vineyard that included zinfandel – 15 years ahead of his time. The property was acquired in '97 by Charles Lane, James Sweetapple and Brian Walters. They have rejuvenated the original vineyard and planted more zinfandel, sauvignon blanc, cabernet and riesling. Exports to the UK and Singapore.

ŢŢŢŢŢ **Orange Riesling 2016** The citrus and apple blossom bouquet soars from the glass immediately it is swirled, telling of the luscious lime and grapefruit flavours of the palate. Its purity and length guarantee its future development if you can summon up the willpower not to drink it in a big hurry. Screwcap. 10.5% alc. **Rating** 95 To 2026 $28

Carlei Estate | Carlei Green Vineyards ★★★★☆

1 Alber Road, Upper Beaconsfield, Vic 3808 **Region** Yarra Valley/Heathcote
T (03) 5944 4599 **www.**carlei.com.au **Open** W'ends 11–6
Winemaker Sergio Carlei **Est.** 1994 **Dozens** 10 000 **Vyds** 2.25ha

Sergio Carlei has come a long way, graduating from home winemaking in a suburban garage to his own (commercial) winery in Upper Beaconsfield. Carlei Estate falls just within the boundaries of the Yarra Valley. Along the way Carlei acquired a Bachelor of Wine Science from CSU, and established a vineyard with organic and biodynamic accreditation adjacent to the Upper Beaconsfield winery, plus 7ha in Heathcote. Contract winemaking services are now a major part of the business. Exports to the US, Singapore and China.

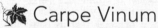 **Estate Heathcote Viognier 2016** A tangy viognier, ticking all the boxes of aromatic exuberance: apricot, orange blossom and honeysuckle. The palate is mid-weighted, streamlined and surprisingly vibrant rather than toned by the variety's usual viscosity. Some smart barrel work serves as a useful restraining order, reeling it all in to a crunchy whole. Screwcap. 14.5% alc. **Rating** 93 **To** 2020 $49 NG
Carlei Estate Botrytis Semillon 2010 Crunchy, tangy and brimming with tropical fruits, ironbark honey, candied citrus rind, ginger spice and orange blossom, this is a joy to drink. The intense flavours are drawn across a live-wire thread of bright, juicy acidity, spinning across the palate. Screwcap. 14% alc.
Rating 93 **To** 2020 $49 NG
Estate Director's Cut Central Victoria Shiraz 2009 This flaxen, dense wine smoulders with an oaky char following 24 months of barrel age in the most 'hedonistic barrels', according to the back label. The wine has flow, skirting across the mouth with an arsenal of dark fruit flavours, hoisin sauce and lacquered duck. The tannins are lathered in coffee and bitter chocolate. The finish, as the alcohol level suggests, is throat tickling. Cork. 14.9% alc. **Rating** 90 **To** 2025 $99 NG

 Green Vineyards Sauvignon Blanc 2015 Rating 89 **To** 2020 $29 NG

🍂 Carpe Vinum   NR
PO Box 333, Penola, SA 5277 **Region** Limestone Coast
T 0452 408 488 **www**.carpevinum.com.au **Open** Not
Winemaker Tom Carson, Sue Bell **Est.** 2011 **Dozens** 750 **Vyds** 4ha
Carpe Vinum is the venture of Malcolm and Henry Skene. In 2011 Malcolm returned from many years overseas of postgraduate studies and then work in Europe (and the UK), while Henry had been building his legal practice in Melbourne. Both had a keen interest in wine, and one night over dinner they decided to seize the day and set about making their own Cabernet Sauvignon, the variety they loved best of all. Not quite by chance, the Skene family had owned the Krongart property near Penola since 1869, and in the mid-1990s their uncle/father planted 4ha of cabernet sauvignon. Its isolation and other distractions meant that it had gone untended for years until they were able to persuade viticulturist Fred Boot to leave Yabby Lake (he had spent the previous 14.5 years at the Strathbogie Ranges vineyards) and begin the resuscitation of the vineyard. It's still a work in progress, with Tom Carson making the '14 and '15 vintages at Yabby Lake, and Sue Bell making the '16 vintage. The '14 wine said more about the state of the vineyard than the skills of winemaker Tom Carson.

Casa Freschi   ★★★★★
159 Ridge Road, Ashton, SA 5137 **Region** Adelaide Hills/Langhorne Creek
T 0409 364 569 **www**.casafreschi.com.au **Open** By appt
Winemaker David Freschi **Est.** 1998 **Dozens** 2000 **Vyds** 7.55ha
David Freschi graduated with a degree in oenology from Roseworthy College in 1991 and spent most of the decade working in California, Italy and NZ. In '98 he and his wife decided to trade in the corporate world for a small family-owned winemaking business, with 2.4ha of vines established by his parents in '72; an additional 1.85ha of nebbiolo is now planted adjacent to the original vineyard. Says David, 'The names of the wines were chosen to best express the personality of the wines grown in our vineyard, as well as to express our heritage.' A second 3.2ha vineyard has been established in the Adelaide Hills, planted to chardonnay, pinot gris, riesling and gewurztraminer. Exports to the UK, Singapore, the Philippines and Japan.

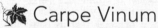 **Ragazzi Adelaide Hills Pinot Grigio 2016** Hand-picked from a dry-grown vineyard at 580m, eight parcels whole-bunch pressed and separately fermented in

French oak, aged on lees for 8 months, 10% undergoing mlf. Wines such as this are game changers: I have to concede that pinot gris is a high quality variety when given respect. Its power is explosive, the palate long and intense, citrus and pear entwined with sparkling acidity. Screwcap. 13% alc. **Rating** 95 **To** 2021 $28 ❂

La Signora 2014 70% nebbiolo, 15% each of shiraz and malbec, 22 individual parcels separately open-fermented with wild yeast, macerated for 3–4 weeks, matured for 18 months in used French oak. The bouquet is fragrant, spicy cherry/ sour cherry expanding in the best way on the long medium-bodied palate. It's interesting how nebbiolo dominates flavours, the other two varieties contributing more to weight and structure. Cork. 13.5% alc. **Rating** 95 **To** 2030 $45

Langhorne Creek Nebbiolo 2014 21 plantings (10 clones) are destemmed and separately open-fermented with wild yeast, hand-plunged and macerated for 2–3 weeks, matured in used French puncheons for 18 months. Reflects the long experience of Casa Freschi with nebbiolo. Clear, light scarlet, it is super refined, with dusky red cherry/berry on the bouquet and finely structured palate alike. The balance, line and length are all good. Cork. 13.5% alc. **Rating** 94 **To** 2029 $55

ΨΨΨΨ♀ **Adelaide Hills Chardonnay 2015** Rating 92 To 2021 $50
Ragazzi Langhorne Creek Nebbiolo 2015 Rating 91 To 2021 $28

Casella Family Brands ★★★★

Wakely Road, Yenda, NSW 2681 **Region** Riverina
T (02) 6961 3000 **www**.casellafamilybrands.com **Open** Not
Winemaker Alan Kennett, Peter Mallamace **Est.** 1969 **Dozens** 12.5 million **Vyds** 2891ha
The fairytale success story for Casella, gifted the opportunity to establish yellow tail as a world brand overnight by, Southcorp withdrawing the distribution of (inter alia) its best-selling Lindemans Bin 65 Chardonnay in the US, is now almost ancient history. yellow tail will remain the engine room for Casella well into the future, but it has now moved decisively to build a portfolio of premium and ultra-premium wines through its acquisition of Peter Lehmann in 2014, and then Brand's Laira winery, cellar door and the use of the brand name from McWilliam's in '15. McWilliam's no doubt had its reasons for the sale, but it had invested much time and money in expanding both the vineyards and the winery; the Peter Lehmann and Brand's Laira brands will transform the future shape of Casella's business. The fact that Casella now has 2891ha of vineyards spread across Australia is a case of putting its money where its mouth is. It is second only to Treasury Wine Estates in export sales (by value), followed by Pernod-Ricard and Accolade. Exports to all major markets.

ΨΨΨΨ♀ **Limited Release Cabernet Sauvignon 2013** Blackberries and plums laced with lavender and wood spice. Cedary oak adds to the full-bodied palate; a rich chocolate flavour, a hint of fennel and ripe tannins the size of a night-club bouncer. Wrattonbully. Screwcap. 14% alc. **Rating** 93 **To** 2025 $45 JF

1919 Shiraz 2010 The charry oak has been ramped up and dries the finish, which is a shame as the fruit in this is very good, mixed with soy sauce and salted chocolate. Reasonably fresh on the finish. McLaren Vale. Cork. 14.5% alc. **Rating** 92 **To** 2022 $100 JF

Limited Release Shiraz 2013 Full-bodied, with a wave of tannin slightly drying on the finish. A structured, smooth palate, just won't quite budge at the moment. Limestone Coast. Screwcap. 14% alc. **Rating** 90 **To** 2025 $45 JF

1919 Shiraz 2012 The wine stain is halfway through the cork and that's a worry, because this should be fresher. As it stands, a core of deep dark fruit, chocolate and spice, lashings of sweet coconut-cedary oak, tannins drying. McLaren Vale. Cork. 14.5% alc. **Rating** 90 **To** 2021 $100 JF

Limited Release Shiraz 2012 Pushes the envelope with its ripeness and sweetness, with cedary oak, all chocolate and ripe tannins. Just shy of full-bodied. McLaren Vale. Cork. 14% alc. **Rating** 90 **To** 2022 $45 JF

Winemaker's Series No: 1 Young Brute The Pride of Wrattonbully 2015 Shiraz 80%, cabernet sauvignon 20% with the label stating 'a big, robust, juicy red blend'. Yep, sums up the wine rather well. Brimming with bright sweet Wrattonbully fruit, decent amount of tannin and spice, and at a good price. Screwcap. 14% alc. **Rating** 90 **To** 2024 $25 JF

1919 Cabernet Sauvignon 2010 Impenetrable red-black. A powerful, dense wine, with blackberry and chocolate flavours. There's still life here but it's almost snuffed out by the considerable oak tannins and flavour. Cork. 14.5% alc. **Rating** 90 **To** 2022 $100 JF

♥♥♥♥ Limited Release Cabernet Sauvignon 2012 **Rating** 89 **To** 2022 $45 JF

Cassegrain Wines

764 Fernbank Creek Road, Port Macquarie, NSW 2444 **Region** Hastings River
T (02) 6582 8377 **www.**cassegrainwines.com.au **Open** 7 days 10–5
Winemaker John Cassegrain, Alex Cassegrain **Est.** 1980 **Dozens** 50000 **Vyds** 34.9ha
Cassegrain has continued to evolve and develop. It still draws on the original Hastings River vineyard of 4.9ha, the most important varieties being semillon, verdelho and chambourcin, with pinot noir and cabernet sauvignon making up the numbers. However, Cassegrain also part-owns and manages Richfield Vineyard in the New England region, with 30ha of chardonnay, verdelho, semillon, shiraz, merlot, cabernet sauvignon and ruby cabernet. Grapes are also purchased from Tumbarumba, Orange and the Hunter Valley. Exports to Japan, China and other major markets.

♥♥♥♥♥ **Seasons Winter Cabernet Sauvignon 2015** Dusty and tannic but the core of currant fruit provides plenty to wrap your tongue around. Oak is subtle, but adds just enough to both the texture and flavour to help keep you coming back for more. Screwcap. 14% alc. **Rating** 90 **To** 2024 $22 CM

♥♥♥♥ Edition Noir Semillon 2016 **Rating** 89 **To** 2020 $28 CM
Edition Noir New England Durif 2015 **Rating** 89 **To** 2021 $28 CM

Castelli Estate ★★★★★

380 Mount Shadforth Road, Denmark, WA 6333 **Region** Great Southern
T (08) 9364 0400 **www.**castelliestate.com.au **Open** 7 days 10–5
Winemaker Mike Garland **Est.** 2007 **Dozens** 10000
Castelli Estate will cause many small winery owners to go green with envy. When Sam Castelli purchased the property in late 2004, he was intending simply to use it as a family holiday destination. But because there was a partly constructed winery he decided to complete the building work and simply lock the doors. However, wine was in his blood, courtesy of his father, who owned a small vineyard in Italy's south. The temptation was too much, and in '07 the winery was commissioned. Fruit is sourced from some of the best vineyards in WA, in Frankland River, Mount Barker, Pemberton and Porongurup. Exports to Singapore and China.

♥♥♥♥♥ **Il Liris Chardonnay 2015** Has all the power and glory of the '14, conjured up from the same (theoretical) slender base of 13.1% alcohol. Indeed, it's almost shocking compared to most top chardonnays from Margaret River – not necessarily better, but bigger and richer. Vino-Lok. **Rating** 96 **To** 2023 $70 ✪

Great Southern Shiraz 2015 A lovely cool-grown shiraz, jumping out of its skin with a starburst of juicy red fruits on the bouquet, promptly followed up by the medium-bodied palate. In the wake of heat in early Mar, hand-picking and sorting was rewarded by the quality of the fruit. Screwcap. 14.3% alc. **Rating** 96 **To** 2030 $36 ✪

Great Southern Riesling 2016 Quartz-white; the bouquet is pungently floral, with wild flower aromas joining citrus and apple blossom. The palate moves decisively to lime juice within the framework of talcy acidity, the aftertaste little short of spectacular. Screwcap. 12% alc. **Rating** 95 **To** 2030 $26 ✪

Empirica Pemberton Fume Blanc 2016 Extended skin contact of sauvignon blanc via cold soak of crushed grapes, partial wild yeast–barrel fermentation.

The funky bouquet comes as no surprise, but the intense palate's lack of ugly phenolics is a (very pleasant) surprise, its length impressive. A walk on the wild side that hasn't lost its way. Screwcap. 12.4% alc. **Rating** 95 **To** 2026 $28 **✪**

Empirica Pinot Gris 2016 A distinguished pinot gris, stacked with flavour of ripe nashi pear and poached pear with spice lurking in the background. There is some residual sugar, but it's woven into the texture of the wine. Screwcap. 13.5% alc. **Rating** 95 **To** 2020 $28 **✪**

Cabernet Merlot 2014 A generous wine with plumes of cassis and redcurrant fruit balanced by integrated French oak and ripe tannins. Looked better and better each time it was retasted. Screwcap. 14.2% alc. **Rating** 95 **To** 2039 $20

Frankland River Cabernet Sauvignon 2014 A cabernet all about elegance, length and finesse rather than austere power, it comes to meet you halfway, but doesn't settle for second place. It is a celebration of cassis, bay leaf and fine, persistent, faintly earthy, tannins, French oak in the background. Screwcap. 14.8% alc. **Rating** 95 **To** 2029 $32 **✪**

Il Liris Rouge 2014 57% cabernet sauvignon, 35% shiraz, 8% malbec. The bouquet and palate alike reflect the (positive) inputs of the three varieties, with the cassis of the cabernet, spicy black fruits of shiraz and the plum of malbec. It has great intensity and length, with firm tannins needing to soften, which they will do over the next 2–3 years. Vino-Lok. 14.7% alc. **Rating** 95 **To** 2034 $75

Empirica Geographe Tempranillo 2015 'Renowned vineyard' (I didn't know there was one), small batch making, cold soak, hand-plunged, minimal oak. A particularly compelling tempranillo full of supple cherry fruit through to the long finish; very good aftertaste. Screwcap. 14.8% alc. **Rating** 95 **To** 2025 $32 **✪**

🍷🍷🍷🍷🍷 **Pemberton Sauvignon Blanc Semillon 2015** Rating 93 To 2017 $22 **✪**
Pemberton Chardonnay 2016 Rating 93 To 2026 $36
Shiraz Malbec 2014 Rating 93 To 2020 $22 **✪**
Frankland River Cabernet Sauvignon 2015 Rating 93 To 2030 $38
The Sum Riesling 2016 Rating 90 To 2023 $18 **✪**
Empirica Gewurztraminer 2016 Rating 90 To 2021 $28

Castle Rock Estate   ★★★★★

2660 Porongurup Road, Porongurup, WA 6324 **Region** Porongurup
T (08) 9853 1035 **www.**castlerockestate.com.au **Open** 7 days 10–5
Winemaker Robert Diletti **Est.** 1983 **Dozens** 4500 **Vyds** 11.2ha

An exceptionally beautifully sited vineyard (riesling, pinot noir, chardonnay, sauvignon blanc, cabernet sauvignon and merlot), winery and cellar door on a 55ha property with sweeping vistas of the Porongurup Range, operated by the Diletti family. The standard of viticulture is very high, and the vineyard itself is ideally situated. The two-level winery, set on a natural slope, maximises gravity flow. The Rieslings have always been elegant and have handsomely repaid time in bottle; the Pinot Noir is the most consistent performer in the region; the Shiraz is a great cool climate example; and Chardonnay has joined a thoroughly impressive quartet, elegance the common link. Rob Diletti's excellent palate and sensitive winemaking mark Castle Rock as one of the superstars of WA. Exports to China.

🍷🍷🍷🍷🍷 **A&W Reserve Porongurup Riesling 2016** A wine of crystal clarity in every way, and marries elegance with power as it unfolds. Lime and slatey acidity are intertwined on the exceptionally long and pure palate. Few '16 rieslings from anywhere in Aus could point to the future as convincingly as this wine. Screwcap. 11.5% alc. **Rating** 97 **To** 2036 $35 **✪**

🍷🍷🍷🍷🍷 **Diletti Chardonnay 2015** Barrel-fermented (25% new), matured on lees for 10 months. Up-scales its Great Southern sibling: a bit more fruit weight (and hence alcohol), more new oak and more time in bottle. None of this impairs the finesse or balance of the wine. Screwcap. 12.5% alc. **Rating** 96 **To** 2030 $30 **✪**

Porongurup Riesling 2016 A 10+-year track record leaves no doubt about its longevity, nor the way it will burst into song with 5+ years of bottle age, and continue that song for another 5+ years; length and balance are the cornerstones of this beautiful wine. Screwcap. 11.5% alc. **Rating** 95 **To** 2030 $25 ●

Great Southern Chardonnay 2016 Fermented in used oak, 2 months on lees in barrel with stirring. Tangy, zesty and full of life, the sort of wine luring those of the ABC (Anything But Chardonnay) club back to the variety. It's not the least oaky, but is very, very mouthwatering. Screwcap. 12% alc. **Rating** 94 **To** 2022 $20 ●

Great Southern Pinot Noir 2015 The bouquet has two distinct strains: cherry and raspberry, and more savoury/bramble and faintly spicy. The palate plays out in the same fashion due to very clever control of oak. Spice will build with more age in bottle. Screwcap. 13.8% alc. **Rating** 94 **To** 2023 $38

Great Southern Cabernet Sauvignon 2014 The first straight cabernet release from Castle Rock since '94. Matured for 15 months in French oak (25% new). Picked at precisely the right time. The wine has savoury dried herb nuances giving complexity (but no green notes) to the blackcurrant fruit, cabernet tannins and cedary oak of a complete wine. Screwcap. 13.5% alc. **Rating** 94 **To** 2029 $24 ●

♟♟♟♟♟ Skywalk Great Southern Riesling 2016 Rating 92 To 2026 $20 ●
Porongurup Sauvignon Blanc 2016 Rating 92 To 2018 $20 ●

Centennial Vineyards ★★★★★

'Woodside', 252 Centennial Road, Bowral, NSW 2576 **Region** Southern Highlands
T (02) 4861 8722 **www**.centennial.net.au **Open** 7 days 10–5
Winemaker Tony Cosgriff **Est.** 2002 **Dozens** 10000 **Vyds** 28.65ha
Centennial Vineyards, a substantial development jointly owned by wine professional John Large and investor Mark Dowling, covers 133ha of beautiful grazing land, with the vineyard planted to pinot noir (6.21ha), chardonnay (7.14ha), sauvignon blanc (4.05ha), tempranillo (3.38ha), pinot gris (2.61ha) and smaller amounts of savagnin, riesling, arneis, gewurztraminer and pinot meunier. Production from the estate vineyards is supplemented by purchases of grapes from Orange to meet the challenge of Southern Highlands' capricious weather. Exports to the US, Denmark, Singapore, China and South Korea.

♟♟♟♟♟ **Reserve Single Vineyard Shiraz Viognier 2015** 4% viognier and 6% shiraz included as whole bunches, the balance destemmed/crushed on top, 4 weeks on skins, matured in French oak (19% new), selected barrels blended at 12 months. The fragrant bouquet is a true reflection of the supple, medium-bodied palate and its display of spiced cherry fruit flavours. Savoury/foresty fine-grained tannins give the wine authority on the finish. Diam. 14.8% alc. **Rating** 95 **To** 2030 $33 ●

Winery Block Tempranillo 2015 Hand-picked, crushed and destemmed, open-fermented, a barrel selection made after 9 months maturation. Tony Cosgriff is delighted with the wine, correctly noting that tempranillo is best suited to a cool climate because of its early ripening nature. Gloriously juicy, with red cherry fruits, yet only light to medium-bodied. Sensitive, albeit complex, winemaking. Screwcap. 12.9% alc. **Rating** 95 **To** 2027 $25 ●

Reserve Single Vineyard Riesling 925 2016 5% was cane-cut a week before the main picking, whole-bunch pressed, clear juice fermented with cultured yeast, the ferment stopped early, 925 meaning 9% alcohol at 25g/l residual sugar. Typical skilled (and thoughtful) winemaking; super fresh and crisp, perfect balance, hence perfect length. Screwcap. 9% alc. **Rating** 95 **To** 2026 $26 ●

Reserve Selection Riesling 115 2016 From Orange and the Southern Highlands. This has a snap, crackle, pop palate with a complex array of juicy citrus fruits of all kinds riddled with jolts of electric acidity. The bin number 115 means 11% alcohol and 5g/l of residual sugar, and it's the tension between the residual sugar and titratable acidity that make this wine so interesting (and good). Screwcap. 11.4% alc. **Rating** 94 **To** 2026 $26 ●

Reserve Selection Pinot Gris 2015 From a vineyard in Orange at 850m, hand-picked, 50% wild-yeast fermented in barrel, 50% in tank with cultured yeast; matured for 9 months in used French oak. If you want complexity in your pinot gris, this is a very good way to go about it. The bouquet is a little too complex viewed on its own, but the palate puts matters right with its length and intensity, bringing varietal fruit and crunchy acidity into play. Screwcap. 13.4% alc. Rating 94 To 2018 $26 ✪

Road Block Savagnin 2015 Hand-picked, whole-bunch pressed, fermented in French oak (5% new), 60% mlf; matured for 9 months. As enjoyable as it is interesting. The savagnin (from young vines, I assume) has relished the barrel fermentation and maturation, with gloriously juicy fruit flavours of Meyer lemon and apple to the fore. Screwcap. 13% alc. **Rating** 94 **To** 2020 $20 ✪

Reserve Single Vineyard Barbera 2015 10% of the fruit was dried, the remainder crushed and destemmed on top, warm-fermented in tank with cultured yeast, 3 weeks on skins, matured in French oak (12% new), selected barrels blended at 12 months. The left field vinification was well conceived and executed, adding both weight and texture. There is a savoury sweet (not sweet and sour) basket of flavours and Italian spices, the tannins soft, but present. Screwcap. 14.8% alc. Rating 94 To 2027 $30 ✪

Finale Late Autumn Chardonnay 2013 Has excellent balance and freshness: so much so it could be enjoyed on its own, particularly if served ice cold. Screwcap. 10.2% alc. **Rating** 94 **To** 2021 $23 ✪

ŢŢŢŢŢ **Reserve Rose 2016** Rating 93 To 2018 $26 ✪
Reserve Pinot Noir 2015 Rating 93 To 2025 $33
Road Block Riesling 2016 Rating 92 To 2026 $22 ✪
Reserve Chardonnay 2015 Rating 92 To 2023 $33
Finale Autumn Sauvignon Blanc 2016 Rating 92 To 2020 $23 ✪
Winery Block Pinot Grigio 2016 Rating 91 To 2017 $24
Reserve Merlot 2015 Rating 91 To 2030 $28
Orange Sauvignon Blanc 2016 Rating 90 To 2017 $22
Old Block Chardonnay 2014 Rating 90 To 2024 $20 ✪
Reserve Selection Arneis 2015 Rating 90 To 2018 $26
Orange Shiraz 2015 Rating 90 To 2025 $25
Reserve Shiraz 2015 Rating 90 To 2030 $30
Reserve Cabernet Merlot 2015 Rating 90 To 2030 $30
Bong Bong Quattro Rosso 2015 Rating 90 To 2018 $19 ✪

Ceravolo Estate ★★★★

Suite 5, 143 Glynburn Road, Firle, SA 5070 (postal) **Region** Adelaide Plains/Hills
T (08) 8336 4522 **www.**ceravolo.com.au **Open** Not
Winemaker Joe Ceravolo, Michael Sykes **Est.** 1985 **Dozens** 15 000 **Vyds** 23.5ha
Dentist turned vigneron and winemaker Joe Ceravolo, and wife Heather, have been producing single vineyard wines from their 16ha estate on the Adelaide Plains since 1999, enjoying wine show success with Shiraz, Petit Verdot, Merlot and Sangiovese. Their son Antony, and his wife Fiona, have joined to take their family business into the next generation. The Ceravolos have also established vineyards (7.5ha) around their home in the Adelaide Hills, focusing on Italian varieties such as primitivo, picolit, pinot grigio, dolcetto, barbera and cortese. Wines are released under Ceravolo and St Andrews Estate labels. Exports to Denmark, Germany, Dubai, South Korea, Japan, Taiwan and China.

ŢŢŢŢŢ **Adelaide Hills Cortese 2016** It's crisp and fresh. It's lemony and textural. It's a variety that hails from Italy's Piedmont region. Never the most complicated, but a good drink for its zesty appeal and acidity. Screwcap. 11.5% alc. **Rating** 92 To 2019 $25 JF ✪

Adelaide Hills Dolcetto Rose 2016 Thanks to dolcetto's high acidity and pretty aromatics, it produces good rose. Proof here. Savoury with raspberry and strawberry nuances, there's texture and a lemony twang on the dry finish. Screwcap. 12.5% alc. **Rating** 91 **To** 2018 $20 JF ✪

Adelaide Plains Petit Verdot 2014 The colour is an impenetrable red-noir and it's richly flavoured with super-ripe fruit compote, lots of woodsy spices and sweet

oak, all leading onto a full-bodied dense palate with robust tannins. It's a mouthful but comes together well. Cork. 15% alc. **Rating** 91 **To** 2024 $25 JF
Adelaide Hills Pinot Grigio 2016 A racy, leaner style, refreshing, with hints of white blossom fleshed out with pears and stone fruit. Finishes dry. Screwcap. 13% alc. **Rating** 90 **To** 2018 $20 JF ♦

ΥΥΥΥ   **Adelaide Plains Petit Verdot 2013 Rating** 89 **To** 2021 $25 JF

Ceres Bridge Estate ★★★★

84 Merrawarp Road, Stonehaven, Vic 3221 **Region** Geelong
T (03) 5271 1212 **www**.ceresbridge.com.au **Open** By appt
Winemaker Challon Murdock **Est.** 1996 **Dozens** 400 **Vyds** 7.4ha
Challon and Patricia Murdock began the long, slow and very frustrating process of establishing their vineyard in 1996. They planted 1.8ha of chardonnay in that year, but 50% of the vines died. Instead of deciding it was all too difficult, they persevered by planting 1.1ha of pinot noir in 2000, and replanting in '01. In '05 they signified their intention to become serious by planting shiraz, nebbiolo, sauvignon blanc, viognier, tempranillo and pinot grigio. Those vines are now mature, with the nebbiolo, in particular, proving its worth.

ΥΥΥΥΥ   **Nebbiolo 2015** This nebbiolo boasts sapid red to dark berry fruits, black cherry, sandalwood and wood smoke flaring across a taut acid spice. Nebbiolo's spindly tannins comply with the wine's Italianate dry, structural focus. Screwcap. 12.5% alc. **Rating** 92 **To** 2022 $25 NG ♦
Pinot Noir 2015 A mid-weighted pinot noir furled around a weave of bright acidity and finely grained French oak supports. Black cherry, camphor, tomato skin and briar are given voltage by a cheeky volatile zing, all in keeping with this wine's livewire composure. Screwcap. 13.5% alc. **Rating** 90 **To** 2021 $22 NG

Chaffey Bros Wine Co ★★★★☆

26 Campbell Road, Parkside, SA 5063 (postal) **Region** Barossa Valley
T 0417 565 511 **www**.chaffeybros.com **Open** Not
Winemaker Daniel Chaffey Hartwig, Theo Engela **Est.** 2008 **Dozens** 7000
Chaffey Bros was co-founded by Daniel Chaffey Hartwig, whose great-uncle Bill Chaffey founded Seaview Wines in McLaren Vale, and who was himself a descendant of the Chaffey brothers who came to Australia to create the Riverina and Riverland regions by designing and implementing the original irrigation schemes. Daniel, born and raised in the Barossa Valley, picked grapes during school holidays, and later on worked at Penfolds' cellar door. After eight years of selling and helping other people create wine labels, he became a bulk wine merchant dealing in both Australian and overseas wines and wineries and also developing a range of branded wines. Exports to Canada, Denmark, The Netherlands, Singapore, Macau, Hong Kong and China.

ΥΥΥΥΥ   **This Is Not Your Grandma's Eden Valley Riesling 2012** Has fulfilled the promise it showed when first tasted 3 years ago, although I'm tempted to say this is exactly your grandmother's wine, so perfectly does it capture all things Eden Valley, with juicy lime fruit complexed by a touch of green apple skin, and structured on its foundation of crisp acidity. Still on a rise to even better things around the corner. Screwcap. 12.3% alc. **Rating** 95 **To** 2026 $22 ♦

ΥΥΥΥΥ   **Synonymous Barossa = Shiraz 2015 Rating** 93 **To** 2022 $28 SC
Pax Aeterna Old Vine Grenache 2016 Rating 93 **To** 2021 $30 JF
Not Your Grandma's Rose 2016 Rating 92 **To** 2018 $22 JF ♦
Tripelpunkt Eden Valley Riesling 2016 Rating 91 **To** 2023 $25 JF
Not Your Grandma's Riesling 2016 Rating 91 **To** 2026 $22 JF ♦
Kontrapunkt Eden Valley Kerner 2016 Rating 91 **To** 2021 $33 JF
Dufte Punkt Eden Valley Gewürztraminer Riesling Weißer Herold 2016
Rating 91 **To** 2020 $25 JF
Battle for Barossa La Resistance Grenache Shiraz Mourvedre 2015
Rating 90 **To** 2020 $25 CM

Chain of Ponds ★★★★★

c/- 83 Pioneer Road, Angas Plains, SA 5255 (postal) **Region** Adelaide Hills
T (08) 8389 1415 **www.chainofponds.com.au Open** Not
Winemaker Greg Clack **Est.** 1993 **Dozens** 25 000

It is years since the Chain of Ponds brand was separated from its then 200ha of estate vineyards, which were among the largest in the Adelaide Hills. It does, however, have long-term contracts with its major growers and, prior to the 2015 vintage, Greg Clack came onboard as full-time chief winemaker. In May '16 Chain of Ponds closed its cellar door and moved to Project Wine's small batch processing facility at Langhorne Creek, completing its withdrawal from the Adelaide Hills, other than its grape purchasing contracts. Exports to the UK, the US, Canada, Singapore, Hong Kong, the Philippines and China.

🍷🍷🍷🍷🍷 **Ledge Single Vineyard Adelaide Hills Shiraz 2015** Destemmed and crushed into small open fermenters, 2 days cold soak, 10 days on skins, matured in French hogsheads for 20 months. A high quality wine with juicy black fruits backed by fine but persistent tannins. Screwcap. 14.5% alc. **Rating** 95 **To** 2034 $38
Amadeus Single Vineyard Adelaide Hills Cabernet Sauvignon 2015 Destemmed, 2 days cold soak, open-fermented, matured for 20 months in French oak (30% new). A very elegant and pure cabernet utterly belying its alcohol, the full-bodied palate ending with pure-bred cabernet tannins. Screwcap. 15% alc. **Rating** 95 **To** 2040 $38
Stopover Single Vineyard Adelaide Hills Barbera 2015 Hand-picked, 3 days cold soak, open-fermented, completing fermentation in French oak (30% new); matured for 12 months. It's not often an Australia barbera has the bright, vibrant, juicy fruit that overflows in this wine, 5% shiraz completing the structure. Screwcap. 14% alc. **Rating** 95 **To** 2030 $38
Grave's Gate Adelaide Hills Shiraz 2015 Includes 12% cabernet, 8 days on skins, pressed to 1–3yo French and American oak to finish primary ferment and mature for 18 months. Designed to focus on the black cherry and blackberry fruit, and succeeds in so doing, the only blemish the level of oak, which will cure itself with a few more years in bottle. Screwcap. 14.5% alc. **Rating** 94 **To** 2029 $20 ✪

🍷🍷🍷🍷🍷 **Amelia's Letter Adelaide Hills Pinot Grigio 2016 Rating** 92 **To** 2018 $20 ✪
Black Thursday Adelaide Hills Sauvignon Blanc 2016 Rating 90 **To** 2017 $20 ✪
Section 400 Adelaide Hills Pinot Noir 2016 Rating 90 **To** 2021 $20 ✪
Morning Star Adelaide Hills Pinot Noir 2015 Rating 90 **To** 2022 $38

Chalice Bridge Estate ★★★★☆

796 Rosa Glen Road, Margaret River, WA 6285 **Region** Margaret River
T (08) 9319 8200 **www.chalicebridge.com.au Open** By appt
Winemaker Jason Brown **Est.** 1998 **Dozens** 3000 **Vyds** 122ha

Planting of the vineyard began in 1998; there are now 29ha of chardonnay, over 28ha each of cabernet sauvignon and shiraz, 12.5ha of semillon, 18ha of sauvignon blanc, 7.5ha of merlot and a small amount of savagnin; it is the second largest single vineyard in Margaret River. Sensible pricing helps, cross-subsidised by the sale of the major part of the annual crop. Exports to the UK, Macau, Hong Kong and China.

🍷🍷🍷🍷🍷 **The Estate Margaret River Semillon Sauvignon Blanc 2015** Bright straw-green; despite semillon being the major partner, lively tropical fruits – passionfruit, lychee and guava – make the first impression, with only a hint of grass/snow pea in the background. Screwcap. 12.5% alc. **Rating** 91 **To** 2017 $25
The Estate Margaret River Sauvignon Blanc 2016 Night-harvested, crushed, pressed, cool-fermented in stainless steel. Crisp, clean and fresh; citrus joins hands with stone fruit joins hands with tropical fruits. Neatly covers the field with no-frills winemaking. Screwcap. 12.5% alc. **Rating** 90 **To** 2018 $25

The Quest Margaret River Cabernet Sauvignon 2015 The colour is there or thereabouts, the light to medium-bodied palate with enough blackcurrant/cassis to join with – not be dominated by – brambly/savoury tannins and light French oak. Screwcap. 14% alc. **Rating** 90 **To** 2023 $35

ŸŸŸŸ **The Estate Margaret River Sauvignon Blanc 2015** Rating 89 To 2017 $25
The Quest Margaret River Chardonnay 2016 Rating 89 To 2019 $34
The Estate Margaret River Chardonnay 2016 Rating 89 To 2020 $25
The Estate Margaret River Cabernet Merlot 2014 Rating 89 To 2024 $25
The Estate Margaret River Cabernet Merlot 2013 Rating 89 To 2025 $25

Chalk Hill   ★★★★★

58 Field Street, McLaren Vale, SA 5171 **Region** McLaren Vale
T (08) 8323 6400 **www.chalkhill.com.au Open** Not
Winemaker Emmanuelle Bekkers **Est.** 1973 **Dozens** 20000 **Vyds** 89ha
The growth of Chalk Hill has accelerated after passing from parents John and Diana Harvey to grapegrowing sons Jock and Tom. Both are heavily involved in wine industry affairs in varying capacities. Further acquisitions mean the vineyards now span each district of McLaren Vale, planted to both the exotic (savagnin, barbera and sangiovese) and mainstream (shiraz, cabernet sauvignon, grenache, chardonnay and cabernet franc) varieties. The Alpha Crucis series is especially praiseworthy. Exports to most markets; exports to the US under the Alpha Crucis label, to Canada under the Wits End label.

ŸŸŸŸŸ **Alpha Crucis McLaren Vale Shiraz 2015** It's McLaren Vale but not as you know it. There's perfume and power and such vibrancy to the fruit, a certain detail not seen before with this series. The restraint dial is on. Excellent crimson colour, wafts of red and black fruit, red licorice, with light Middle Eastern spices, especially sumac. Full-bodied with velvety tannins and a long, persistent finish. Screwcap. 14.5% alc. **Rating** 97 **To** 2040 $85 JF ○

ŸŸŸŸŸ **ACWS Renae Hirsch McLaren Vale Shiraz 2015** Fascinating concept to have one site (Chalk Hill's Heritage Block) and six winemakers taking select parcels of fruit, putting their winemaking stamp onto the subsequent wine. This shines for the purity of fruit – 25% whole bunches in the ferment and aged in used French oak puncheons. Florals, red fruited, startling fine and long tannins with raspberry sorbet–like acidity. Screwcap. 14.5% alc. **Rating** 96 **To** 2038 $60 JF ○
ACWS Bec Willson McLaren Vale Shiraz 2015 Open-top fermenter, on skins 10 days, pressed to mostly used French oak, 8 months on lees, racked off lees back into barrel for another 8 months. Such a glossy colour and equally glossy palate, with bright, tangy, sweet dark fruits, dark chocolate with menthol, dried herbs too. Full-bodied, with some oak spice and lively acidity to finish. Screwcap. 14.5% alc. **Rating** 96 **To** 2038 $60 JF ○
ACWS Corrina Wright McLaren Vale Shiraz 2015 Fruit crushed, natural open ferment, pressed to French oak (20% new). The plushest and richest wine of the series. A core of dark plums and currants, choc-coated licorice bullets and espresso coffee with everything beautifully contained. The tannins are rich and pliable, the acidity refreshing. Screwcap. 15% alc. **Rating** 96 **To** 2038 $60 JF ○
ACWS Kerri Thompson McLaren Vale Shiraz 2015 Hand-picked, 40% whole bunches, wild-yeast fermented on top of some riesling skins, pressed to French oak (30% new). Unfined and unfiltered. Excellent colour – dark crimson. Intensely fruited and rich but by no means heavy; full-bodied, luscious palate, succulent with plush tannins and a bit more oomph. Screwcap. 15% alc. **Rating** 96 **To** 2038 $60 JF ○
ACWS Peter Schell McLaren Vale Shiraz 2015 25% whole bunches, rest destemmed but not crushed, open fermenters, natural yeast, aged in French oak (65% new). The oak makes its presence felt, adding char and spice. A touch drying, and the most savoury of all the wines. Has its fair share of dark fruit, chocolate, licorice, while earthy flavours abound and the firm tannins drive on the full-bodied palate. Screwcap. 14.5% alc. **Rating** 96 **To** 2039 $60 JF ○

ACWS Tim Knappstein McLaren Vale Shiraz 2015 Inoculated, 25% whole bunches, 36% whole berries and 39% destemmed and crushed and aged in French barriques (35% new). Intriguing perfume to this – floral with Mediterranean herbs and rosemary infusing the dark fruit. Fleshy, ripe tannins, there's power to this, but tamed. Screwcap. 14.5% alc. **Rating** 96 **To** 2035 $60 JF ✪

Clarendon McLaren Vale Syrah 2015 A new edition to the Chalk Hill stable, with the back label giving credit to winemaker Renae Hirsch and the vineyard, Hickinbotham Block 126, fruit off rows 8 to 16, 275 dozen made. This is classy stuff. The dark fruit is succulent, and there's the right amount of spice and flavour. It's savoury, full-bodied, with velvety tannins. The wine spends 15 months in French puncheons; the superbly integrated oak adds another layer to this already complex, compelling wine. Screwcap. 14.5% alc. **Rating** 96 **To** 2035 $50 JF ✪

McLaren Vale Shiraz 2015 Perfect example of how on song Chalk Hill is with its wines, and none better than the '15 vintage. A core of perfectly ripe fruit – dark plums, black and red berries, flecked with anise, Mediterranean herbs, milk chocolate and woodsy spices. Incredibly fresh on the palate, with juicy raspberry acidity and neatly pitched tannins. Screwcap. 14.5% alc. **Rating** 95 **To** 2026 $25 JF ✪

Luna McLaren Vale Shiraz 2015 A wine that offers great value on the one hand and exceptional quality on the other deserves to be rewarded, without forgetting the all-important drinkability factor. Excellent dark purple-black, brimming with bright fruit – dark plums and blackberries interspersed with licorice, dark chocolate, dried herbs and florals. Tannins are supple, acidity refreshing and bright. It's a ripper and a bargain. Screwcap. 14.5% alc. **Rating** 95 **To** 2026 $19 JF ✪

McLaren Vale Grenache Tempranillo 2016 One the most joyous wines the way it hums along with its Spanish tune – a blend of 50% grenache, 36% tempranillo and for good Iberian measure 14% graciano. A heady mix of florals, raspberries, sarsaparilla and juicy acidity. There's some depth, as the flavours are layered, the tannins supple and buoyant. Screwcap. 14% alc. **Rating** 95 **To** 2026 $25 JF ✪

Chalkers Crossing ★★★★☆

285 Grenfell Road, Young, NSW 2594 **Region** Hilltops
T (02) 6382 6900 **www**.chalkerscrossing.com.au **Open** Mon–Fri 9–5
Winemaker Celine Rousseau **Est.** 2000 **Dozens** 14 000 **Vyds** 27ha

Chalkers Crossing's Rockleigh Vineyard was planted in 1996–97, and is supplemented by purchased grapes from Tumbarumba. Winemaker Celine Rousseau was born in France's Loire Valley, trained in Bordeaux and has worked in Bordeaux, Champagne, Languedoc, Margaret River and the Perth Hills. This Flying Winemaker (now an Australian citizen) has exceptional skills and dedication. In 2012 she was appointed general manager as well as winemaker. In '16 her '14 Shiraz won multiple trophies at a number of shows. Exports to the UK, Canada, Denmark, Sweden, Thailand, Hong Kong and China.

🍷🍷🍷🍷🍷 **Hilltops Riesling 2016** A powerful riesling that is nevertheless light on its feet, with an aromatic spectrum that strays into white peach and apricot, straddling a carapace of lemon- and lime-tinged acidity. The finish has compelling length, suggesting a long future. Screwcap. 13% alc. **Rating** 93 **To** 2031 $18 NG ✪

Hilltops Cabernet Sauvignon 2015 Currant, bitter chocolate, spearmint, tea leaf and cedar notes are hinged to a mid-weighted palate of varietal strictness: firm, stiff upper-lipped tannins and marked acidity. Screwcap. 13.5% alc. **Rating** 92 **To** 2031 $30 NG

Tumbarumba Chardonnay 2015 Far from the madding crowd of tensile, skinny chardonnays, this is all peaches and cream. Yet despite the wine's intensity of flavour and overall breadth, the eschewing of mlf and vineyards at an altitude of 720m imbue a mineral edge and tension to the package. Screwcap. 12.5% alc. **Rating** 91 **To** 2025 $25 NG

Hilltops Semillon 2016 A barrel-fermented semillon of weight and textural force. The oak remains the dominant sensory component. Notes of lemon oil, quince and pear are waiting in the wings if time allows them to shine. Screwcap. 12.5% alc. **Rating** 90 **To** 2022 $18 NG ✪

Hilltops Shiraz 2013 A wine with a herbal riff of spearmint and sage, spiced with anise and cardamom. Blue fruits provide the bass and cracked white pepper the seismic rhythm of cool climate shiraz. Finishes abrasive and a tad too short to merit a higher score. Screwcap. 14% alc. **Rating** 90 **To** 2022 $30 NG

🍷🍷🍷🍷 CC2 **Hilltops Chardonnay 2016 Rating** 89 **To** 2022 $18 NG ✪

Chalmers ★★★★☆

11 Third Street, Merbein, Vic 3505 **Region** Heathcote
T 0400 261 932 **www** chalmerswine.com.au **Open** Not
Winemaker Bart van Olphen, Tennille Chalmers **Est.** 1989 **Dozens** 7000 **Vyds** 27ha
Following the 2008 sale of their very large vineyard and vine nursery propagation business, the Chalmers family has refocused its wine businesses. All fruit comes from the 80ha property on Mt Camel Range in Heathcote, which provides the grapes for the individual variety, single vineyard Chalmers range (Vermentino, Fiano, Greco, Lambrusco, Rosato, Nero d'Avola, Sagrantino and Aglianico). The entry-level Montevecchio label is based around blends and more approachable styles. A second vineyard at Merbein is a contract grapegrower, but also has a small nursery block housing the Chalmers' clonal selections. In '13 a program of micro-vinification of the rarer, and hitherto unutilised, varieties from the Nursery Block was introduced. In '17 a new winery was commissioned in time for most of that year's vintage, and from '18 all winemaking will be carried out at Merbein. Exports to the UK.

🍷🍷🍷🍷🍷 **Heathcote Nero d'Avola 2016** The absence of oak hasn't deprived the wine of anything it might have gained or, to put it another way, its multi-cherry flavours wouldn't be clearly etched. They cover the field from morello to sour, to red to … And the mouthfeel has no reductive characters whatsoever. Screwcap. 13.5% alc. **Rating** 91 **To** 2020 $27
Montevecchio Bianco 2016 40% vermentino, 32% garganega, 26% malvasia, 2% moscato giallo. This simply has to be a great example of synergy from a high field blend, for there is interesting grip and length and a field of flavours. Best enjoyed sooner than later. Screwcap. 12.5% alc. **Rating** 90 **To** 2019 $24
Heathcote Rosato 2016 A 70/30% blend of sagrantino and aglianico. Salmon-pink with a very expressive, strong, spicy, savoury bouquet. The palate is equally flavour-filled, but I only wish it was totally dry. Screwcap. 13% alc. **Rating** 90 **To** 2018 $27
Montevecchio Rosso 2015 The light but fresh colour is entirely appropriate for a light but fresh blend, with spicy red fruits at the fore. A drop-dead fun wine for a BYO Italian restaurant. Don't even think of cellaring it. Screwcap. 13.5% alc. **Rating** 90 **To** 2020 $24
Heathcote Aglianico 2013 I can do business with this wine. It has no sharp edges to worry about; it is light to medium-bodied, with spicy/juicy red and sour cherry fruits and a clean finish. Screwcap. 13% alc. **Rating** 90 **To** 2021 $42

🍷🍷🍷🍷 **Heathcote Vermentino 2016 Rating** 89 **To** 2018 $27
Heathcote Sagrantino 2014 Rating 89 **To** 2024 $43

Chambers Rosewood ★★★★★

Barkly Street, Rutherglen, Vic 3685 **Region** Rutherglen
T (02) 6032 8641 **www**.chambersrosewood.com.au **Open** Mon–Sat 9–5, Sun 10–5
Winemaker Stephen Chambers **Est.** 1858 **Dozens** 10 000 **Vyds** 50ha
Chambers' Rare Muscat and Rare Muscadelle (or Topaque or Tokay, what's in a name?) are the greatest of all in the Rutherglen firmament, the other wines in the hierarchy also magnificent. Stephen Chambers comes into the role as winemaker, the sixth generation of the

Chambers family, but father Bill, with his startling light blue eyes, is seldom far away. Exports to the UK, the US, Canada, Belgium, Denmark, South Korea, Singapore, China and NZ.

ΨΨΨΨΨ **Rare Rutherglen Muscadelle NV** Dark mahogany. The impact of the wine in the mouth is as extraordinary as that of the Rare Muscat; a micro-sip floods the senses as they go into overdrive trying to capture the myriad interlocking flavours. The everlasting finish and aftertaste is the key to understanding this wine: it is not just the 5% or so of the oldest component (say 90 years), but the 5% of the most youthful (say 5–6 years) which, by skill worthy of Michelangelo, has given the wine the vibrant freshness drawing you back again and again, without diminishing its complexity. 375ml. Screwcap. 18% alc. **Rating** 99 To 2017 $250

Rare Rutherglen Muscat NV Dense mahogany. With incredibly concentrated and complex, startling viscosity as it enters the mouth: yet it has a quicksilver lightness on the back-palate. The layers of flavour are almost countless, with sour cherry/morello cherry, Turkish coffee and the finest black chocolate (Swiss or Belgian). This wine is truly something that all wine lovers must experience at least once; one sip was taken for this entire note and the flavour is still building. 375ml. Screwcap. 18% alc. **Rating** 99 To 2017 $250

Grand Rutherglen Muscadelle NV It's the end of a day's tasting and there's no way I'm going to spit out wines of this world class – indeed world beating – quality. Malt, mocha, wild honey, caramel and every exotic spice you can think of – all these and more flavours blaze the mouth until you have swallowed it. The aftertaste is wondrously fresh. 375ml. Screwcap. 18% alc. **Rating** 98 To 2017 $100

Grand Rutherglen Muscat NV The olive rim to the walnut-brown heart of the colour sets the scene; the heady essence of raisin bouquet pushes any discussions of the fortifying spirit to the back row; in its place there is an Arabian bazaar of spices, with a nod to Turkish baklava, then a rolling wave of Christmas pudding with a garnish of dark chocolate and caramelised rose nuts. The ultimate magic of the Chambers wines lies in the freshness of the finish. 375ml. Screwcap. 18.5% alc. **Rating** 97 To 2017 $55

Chandon Australia   ★★★★★

727 Maroondah Highway, Coldstream, Vic 3770 **Region** Yarra Valley
T (03) 9738 9200 **www.**chandon.com.au **Open** 7 days 10.30–4.30
Winemaker Dan Buckle, Glenn Thompson, Adam Keath **Est.** 1986 **Dozens** NFP
Vyds 170ha
Established by Möet & Chandon, this is one of the two most important wine facilities in the Yarra Valley; the tasting room has a national and international reputation, having won a number of major tourism awards in recent years. The sparkling wine product range has evolved, and there has been increasing emphasis placed on the table wines, now released under the Chandon label. An energetic winemaking team under the leadership of Dan Buckle has maintained the high quality standards. Exports to all major markets.

ΨΨΨΨΨ **Pinot Noir Rose 2016** Pale pink; a delicious rose with perfumed red fruit aromas and flavours, strawberry and red cherry to the fore; enticing long and dry finish. Screwcap. 12.5% alc. **Rating** 95 To 2019 $32 ❂

Barrel Selection Yarra Valley Shiraz 2015 Bright crimson-purple; a Yarra Valley shiraz that ticks every box: the bouquet is fragrant, the supple, smooth medium-bodied palate full of black cherry fruit sprinkled with pepper and spice, the finish and aftertaste fresh. Screwcap. 13.5% alc. **Rating** 95 To 2030 $46

ΨΨΨΨΨ **Methode Traditionelle Pinot Noir Shiraz NV Rating** 93 To 2017 $32 TS
Yarra Valley Chardonnay 2015 Rating 92 To 2021 $32 JF
Altius Methode Traditionelle Upper Yarra 2012 Rating 92 To 2018 $59 TS
Barrel Selection Pinot Meunier 2016 Rating 91 To 2023 $46 PR

Chapel Hill

1 Chapel Hill Road, McLaren Vale, SA 5171 **Region** McLaren Vale
T (08) 8323 8429 **www**.chapelhillwine.com.au **Open** 7 days 11–5
Winemaker Michael Fragos, Bryn Richards **Est.** 1973 **Dozens** 50000 **Vyds** 44ha
A leading medium-sized winery in the region. Owned since 2000 by the Swiss Thomas Schmidheiny group, which owns the respected Cuvaison winery in California and vineyards in Switzerland and Argentina. Wine quality is unfailingly excellent. The production comes from estate plantings of shiraz, cabernet sauvignon, chardonnay, verdelho, savagnin, sangiovese and merlot, plus contract-grown grapes. The red wines are not filtered or fined, and there are no tannin or enzyme additions, just SO_2 – natural red wines. Exports to all other major markets.

House Block McLaren Vale Shiraz 2015 Hand-picked, crushed and destemmed into small 2-tonne open fermenters, neutral yeast, 10 days on skins, matured for 20 months in French hogsheads (16% new). Deep crimson-purple; this is a powerful full-bodied shiraz, swaggering with black fruits, licorice and earth met face-on by ripe tannins, oak a means, not an end. Part of the Scarce Earth series. Screwcap. 14.5% alc. **Rating** 96 **To** 2040 $65 ✪

Road Block McLaren Vale Shiraz 2015 Hand-picked, bunch-sorted, crushed and destemmed, open-fermented, matured 20 months in French hogsheads (17% new). Saturnine black fruits, grumbling with concentration and power, burbles of licorice and bitter chocolate, swirls of ripe tannins. No L or P plate drivers allowed. Scarce Earth. Screwcap. 14.5% alc. **Rating** 96 **To** 2040 $65 ✪

McLaren Vale Grenache Shiraz Mourvedre 2015 A 56/33/11% blend separately vinified, matured in used French oak for 17 months. Despite its undoubted richness and complexity, it has a freshness and verve that eludes other regions. Its ability to age is unquestioned, but there's a powerful argument for early consumption of at least some of the dozen bottles you should buy. Screwcap. 14.5% alc. **Rating** 96 **To** 2030 $25 ✪

Gorge Block McLaren Vale Cabernet Sauvignon 2015 Picked by a selective harvester, open-fermented, 20 days on skins, matured 20 months in French hogsheads (18% new). An expressive and complex bouquet and full-bodied palate, each singing of black fruits, earth, licorice and dark chocolate. The tannins are an important part of the package, oak (appropriately) less so. Screwcap. 14.5% alc. **Rating** 96 **To** 2045 $65 ✪

The Vicar McLaren Vale Shiraz 2015 Crushed and destemmed, open-fermented 12 days on skins, matured in French hogsheads (22% new) for 22 months. Full-bodied, crammed full of black fruits, tar, earth, licorice, dark chocolate, and cabernet-like tannins. No velvet slipper here, instead vinous flagellation – stop, stop, I love it. Screwcap 14.5% alc. **Rating** 95 **To** 2040 $75

McLaren Vale Shiraz 2014 Absolutely achieves expressing 'a profound sense of place'; unctuous black fruits swathed in dark chocolate drive the bouquet and medium to full-bodied palate with relentless precision, yet keep balance and length. Oak and tannins are part of the package, but you sense them, rather than feel their impact. Screwcap. 14.5% alc. **Rating** 95 **To** 2034 $30 ✪

McLaren Vale Cabernet Sauvignon 2015 Open-fermented, 12 days on skins, matured in French hogsheads (20% new) for 21 months. A good example of the varietal character that McLaren Vale can generate, not the least reliant on expensive oak or elevated alcohol. This is old money, with blackcurrant striding out confidently in the lead, bay leaf and dried herbs scurrying after it. Will develop along the path it has already set. Screwcap. 14.5% alc. **Rating** 95 **To** 2030 $30 ✪

Gorge Block McLaren Vale Chardonnay 2015 Hand-picked and sorted, free-run juice fermented in French oak, matured for 11 months. A notably complex chardonnay, with more texture and more varietal fruit than most McLaren Vale examples. The picking decision was spot on, hitting the sweet spot for a stylish, harmonious wine. Screwcap. 13% alc. **Rating** 94 **To** 2023 $25 ✪

McLaren Vale Shiraz 2015 14–35yo vines, hand-picked, open-fermented, 10 days on skins, matured 21 months in French hogsheads (21% new). An expressive bouquet, blackberry, licorice, bitter chocolate and oak all on display, flowing onto the palate in the same formation until bold tannins attack. This has balance, and will flourish with 10 years in bottle. Screwcap. 14.5% alc. **Rating** 94 To 2035 $30 ✪

McLaren Vale Cabernet Sauvignon 2014 A sense of place indeed, communicated by the first whiff of the bouquet, cigar box and dark chocolate close behind cassis fruit; the medium to full-bodied palate brings the expected tannins into play, oak of textural, as much as flavour, importance in a notably well balanced wine. Screwcap. 14.5% alc. **Rating** 94 To 2029 $30 ✪

ŶŶŶŶŶ **The Parson Cabernet Sauvignon 2015** Rating 93 To 2030 $18 ✪
McLaren Vale Sangiovese Rose 2016 Rating 92 To 2018 $18 JF ✪
The Parson McLaren Vale Shiraz 2015 Rating 92 To 2022 $18 CM ✪
The Vinedresser McLaren Vale Shiraz 2015 Rating 92 To 2025 $26
McLaren Vale Shiraz Mourvedre 2015 Rating 92 To 2030 $25 ✪
The Parson McLaren Vale GSM 2015 Rating 91 To 2020 $18 ✪
McLaren Vale Sangiovese 2013 Rating 91 To 2021 $25 CM

Chapman Grove Wines   ★★★★★

37 Mount View Terrace, Mount Pleasant, WA 6153 **Region** Margaret River
T (08) 9364 3885 **www**.chapmangrove.com.au **Open** Not
Winemaker Richard Rowe (Consultant) **Est.** 2005 **Dozens** 7000 **Vyds** 32ha
A very successful venture under the control of CEO Ron Fraser. The wines come from the estate vineyards planted to chardonnay, semillon, sauvignon blanc, shiraz, cabernet sauvignon and merlot. The wines have three price levels: at the bottom end, the standard Chapman Grove range; then the Reserve Range; and, at the top, ultra-premium wines under the Atticus label. Exports to Canada, Hong Kong, Singapore, the Philippines, Taiwan and China.

ŶŶŶŶŶ **Atticus Grand Reserve Chardonnay 2016** Hand-picked, matured in French oak (50% new) for 10 months. As ever, a distinguished wine, with a particular texture engendered by its citrussy acidity; the heavy lifting is provided by the immaculate white peach and pink grapefruit of a palate that is intense yet delicate, delicacy stemming from the way the wine flows through the mouthfeel and long finish. Cork. 12.8% alc. **Rating** 96 To 2026 $90

Reserve Margaret River Semillon 2016 85% cool-fermented in tank, 15% in French oak. A relative rarity as a single variety in Margaret River, usually coupled with sauvignon blanc. It has nettle, cut grass, snow pea and citrus aromas and flavours, and will absolutely burst into song when 5yo, adding dimensions of flavour and structure. Screwcap. 13% alc. **Rating** 94 To 2026 $27 ✪

Margaret River Sauvignon Blanc 2016 Conveys complexity without compromising its core of varietal flavour, flavour that nods to the Loire Valley. Fresh herbal/snow pea nuances dance with a mix of citrus fruit verging on stone fruit as much as tropical, its length and balance unimpeachable. Screwcap. 12.8% alc. **Rating** 94 To 2017 $22

ŶŶŶŶŶ **Reserve Margaret River Semillon Sauvignon Blanc 2016** Rating 93 To 2021 $27 ✪
Reserve Margaret River Sauvignon Blanc 2016 Rating 92 To 2021 $27

Charles Cimicky   ★★★★

Hermann Thumm Drive, Lyndoch, SA 5351 **Region** Barossa Valley
T (08) 8524 4025 **www**.charlescimickywines.com.au **Open** Tues–Fri 10.30–3.30
Winemaker Charles Cimicky **Est.** 1972 **Dozens** 20 000 **Vyds** 25ha
These wines are of good quality, thanks to the sophisticated use of good oak in tandem with high quality grapes. Historically, Cimicky has an ultra-low profile, but he has relented

sufficiently to send some wines. Exports to the US, Canada, Switzerland, Germany, Malaysia and Hong Kong.

🍷🍷🍷🍷🍷 **Trumps Barossa Valley Shiraz 2015** A complex wine with black fruits, a twig of dried herbs and a long, medium to full bodied palate. The tannins are plentiful, but under control. Screwcap. 14.5% alc. **Rating** 92 **To** 2035

Reserve Barossa Valley Shiraz 2014 Has the Cimicky style stamp written large across its back-palate, a savoury/black olive/herb wash adding complexity to the wines, especially via the tannins. Extreme patience is needed, but there won't be a long window of opportunity. This has the added cross of the '14 vintage to bear. Screwcap. 15% alc. **Rating** 92 **To** 2029

The Autograph Barossa Valley Shiraz 2015 A powerful full-bodied wine with a truckload of black fruits and – here's the pity – even more dry tannins. In a weird way, it's balanced, and may come out one day long into the future. Screwcap. **Rating** 90 **To** 2035

Charles Melton

Krondorf Road, Tanunda, SA 5352 **Region** Barossa Valley
T (08) 8563 3606 **www**.charlesmeltonwines.com.au **Open** 7 days 11–5
Winemaker Charlie Melton, Krys Smith **Est.** 1984 **Dozens** 15 000 **Vyds** 32.6ha
Charlie Melton, one of the Barossa Valley's great characters, with wife Virginia by his side, makes some of the most eagerly sought à la mode wines in Australia. There are 7ha of estate vineyards at Lyndoch, 9ha at Krondorf and 1.6ha at Light Pass, the lion's share shiraz and grenache, and a small planting of cabernet sauvignon. An additional 30ha property was purchased in High Eden, with 10ha of shiraz planted in 2009, and a 5ha field of grenache, shiraz, mataro, carignan, cinsaut, picpoul and bourboulenc was planted in '10. The expanded volume has had no adverse effect on the quality of the rich, supple and harmonious wines. Exports to all major markets.

🍷🍷🍷🍷🍷 **Grains of Paradise Shiraz 2014** Aged on lees for 24 months in 60/40% American and French barriques. The bouquet is exceptionally complex and fragrant, with spiced plum and oak translating to the equally complex medium-bodied palate. Its fundamental elegance is captured by the long palate and aftertaste. A wine with unlimited exploration opportunities. Screwcap. 14.5% alc. **Rating** 97 **To** 2044 $66

Voices of Angels Shiraz 2014 Fermented with 10-15% whole bunches and 3% riesling, aged on lees in new French oak for 28 months. Grains of Paradise is all about comforting elegance, but this wine throws down the gauntlet with its more edgy, clearly articulated complexity. It has elements of cool climate style, due to the whole bunch inclusion and riesling. Different as chalk and cheese from Grains of Paradise. Screwcap. 14.5% alc. **Rating** 97 **To** 2044 $66

🍷🍷🍷🍷🍷 **Nine Popes 2014** Grenache, shiraz, mourvedre, variously wild and cultured yeast-fermented, some batches including whole bunches, some co-fermented, matured on lees in French barriques for 24 months. Charlie Melton was an early mover with this blend, and has vast accumulated experience and knowledge. He nailed the wine this vintage, its storehouse of red, purple and black fruits coursing fluidly along the palate – so much so that deconstruction is at best of little worth. It's just a lovely wine. Screwcap. 14.5% alc. **Rating** 96 **To** 2034 $70

Rose of Virginia 2016 Brief skin contact after crushing, then a 6-week cold fermentation, has given the wine far more colour than most Aus roses. Red cherries ride high on the bouquet and palate, the long, dry finish and aftertaste continuing the theme through to the end. As always, a wine of high quality. Screwcap. 12.5% alc. **Rating** 94 **To** 2020 $25 ✪

The Kirche 2014 67% cabernet sauvignon, 33% shiraz, separately fermented and matured in French oak (30% new) for 26 months before blending. An impressive example of this traditional blend dating back to the early '60s when cabernet plantings began to proliferate across SA. It's a powerful number, needing time to relax its grip. Screwcap. 14.5% alc. **Rating** 94 **To** 2034 $37

Richelieu 2014 'Only made in the best grenache years' from blocks with an average vine age of 115 years, cool-fermented with 10% whole bunches, 7–10 days on skins, matured on lees in mostly used oak for 24–30 months. A tapestry of rich flavours augmented by substantial French oak inputs, and a balanced share of tannins. Built to last. Screwcap. 14.5% alc. **Rating** 94 **To** 2024 $66

Charlotte Dalton Wines ★★★★★

PO Box 125, Verdun, SA 5245 **Region** Adelaide Hills
T 0466 541 361 **www.**charlottedaltonwines.com **Open** Not
Winemaker Charlotte Hardy **Est.** 2015 **Dozens** 700

Charlotte Hardy has been making wines for 15 years, with a star-studded career at Craggy Range (NZ), Chateau Giscours (Bordeaux) and David Abreu (California), but has called SA home since 2007. Her winery is part of her Basket Range house, which has been through many incarnations since starting life as a pig farm in 1858. Much later it housed the Basket Range store, and at different times in the past two decades it has been the winery to Basket Range Wines, The Deanery Wines and now Charlotte Dalton Wines.

🍷🍷🍷🍷🍷 **Love You Love Me Adelaide Hills Semillon 2016** Barrel-fermented and lees-stirred. The (apparent) choice of used oak was spot on, leaving the architecture of the semillon to effortlessly carry the palate on its long journey. This is a table wine equivalent to Spanish manzanilla drawn fresh from the barrel on a crisp morning. Screwcap. 12.6% alc. **Rating** 96 **To** 2031 $39 ◐

Eliza The Broderick Vineyard Basket Range Pinot Noir 2016 50/50% 777 and MV6 clones, hand-picked, whole bunches into a fermenter, the extra weight gradually crushing the berries, no plunging or pumpovers, Charlotte adding dry ice, gentle foot stomping the day before basket pressing to new French oak. This has resulted in a very good pinot, extra spicy and foresty, with ample red fruits to provide balance. Screwcap. 12.8% alc. **Rating** 95 **To** 2026 $39

Love Me Love You Adelaide Hills Shiraz 2016 From the oldest plantings of shiraz in the Adelaide Hills, the clone ex Wendouree, hand-picked, 30% whole bunches, matured in French oak (20% new), 'seemed complete' in mid Aug, so racked to tank, settled for 1 month (no filtration) and bottled. This has elegance and poise, its plum/black cherry fruits framed by fine, persistent tannins and integrated oak. Screwcap. 13.5% alc. **Rating** 95 **To** 2031 $42

Beyond the Horizon Adelaide Hills Shiraz 2015 From the same small vineyard as the Love You Love Me Shiraz, and matured for 18 months in French oak (75% new). Its dominant message is light-bodied freshness and elegance with juicy poached blackcurrant fruits to the fore. It's a lovely wine, although may prove to be a work in progress. Screwcap. 12.6% alc. **Rating** 95 **To** 2025 $47

Chateau Francois ★★★★★

1744 Broke Road, Pokolbin, NSW 2321 **Region** Hunter Valley
T (02) 4998 7548 **Open** W'ends 9–5
Winemaker Don Francois **Est.** 1969 **Dozens** 200

I have known former NSW Director of Fisheries Dr Don Francois for almost as long as I have been involved with wine, which is a very long time indeed. I remember his early fermentations of sundry substances other than grapes (none of which, I hasten to add, was the least bit illegal) in the copper bowl of an antiquated washing machine in his suburban laundry. He established Chateau Francois one year before Brokenwood, and our winemaking and fishing paths have crossed many times since. Some years ago Don suffered a mild stroke, and no longer speaks or writes with any fluency, but this has not stopped him from producing a range of absolutely beautiful Semillons that flourish marvellously with age. I should add that he is even prouder of the distinguished career of his daughter, Rachel Francois, at the NSW bar. The semillon vines are now 48 years old, producing exceptional wine that is sold for the proverbial song year after year. Five-star value.

ΨΨΨΨΨ **Pokolbin Semillon 2014** '14 is celebrated for its red wines, but the semillons are very good as well, picked when the fruit was perfect rather than threading the needle of impending rain. This has a gold-plated 15-year life ahead, but the lemon juice and lemon curd flavours are already evident, acidity providing both balance and length. It is enjoyable now, but it will steadily become more complex. Screwcap. 11% alc. **Rating** 96 **To** 2029 $20 **C**
Pokolbin Semillon 2015 This wasn't an easy vintage, but the 46yo vines and the sloping hillside vineyard give it a start over many others. This is a fine, delicious wine now, but will bloom over the next 10 years, and live long thereafter. Screwcap. 11% alc. **Rating** 95 **To** 2030 $20 **C**
Pokolbin Semillon 2016 The Hunter Valley's often tempestuous climate makes generalisations hazardous, but this small single vineyard with its vines approaching 50yo rarely misses a beat. Its display is pure Hunter semillon, with lemon zest/lemongrass, lemon curd and unsweetened juice all corralled by crisp, minerally acidity. Screwcap. 11% alc. **Rating** 94 **To** 2029 $20 **C**

ΨΨΨΨΨ **Pokolbin Shiraz 2015 Rating** 92 **To** 2025 $18 **C**

Chateau Pâto

67 Thompsons Road, Pokolbin, NSW 2321 **Region** Hunter Valley
T (02) 4998 7634 **Open** By appt
Winemaker Nicholas Paterson **Est.** 1980 **Dozens** 500 **Vyds** 2.5ha
Nicholas Paterson's day job is at Mistletoe and elsewhere, but his heart is here. The lion's share of plantings is shiraz (the first plantings), with smaller blocks of chardonnay, marsanne, roussanne, viognier and mourvedre; most of the grapes are sold, with a tiny quantity of shiraz being made into a marvellous wine. Father David's legacy is being handsomely guarded.

ΨΨΨΨΨ **DJP Hunter Valley Shiraz 2014** It's partly the shape and feel of the tannins, the savouriness, the new leather and freeze-dried raspberry powder aromas that affirm Hunter Valley shiraz. There's a depth and savoury intensity, and while aged in French puncheons for 16 months, the finish is a bit taxing and not ready to have its day. Come back in a few years. Screwcap. 14.9% alc. **Rating** 95 **To** 2032 $50 JF
Hunter Wine Country Old Pokolbin Vineyard Shiraz 2014 Sourced from three vineyards with plantings going back to the '60s. Dark crimson colour, florals and brightness to the dark plums, Cherry Ripe, new leather and oak spice build on the palate. At once structured, richly flavoured and with shapely tannins – some grit and a lot of give. Screwcap. 14.1% alc. **Rating** 95 **To** 2038 $40 JF

Chateau Tanunda

9 Basedow Road, Tanunda, SA 5352 **Region** Barossa Valley
T (08) 8563 3888 **www.**chateautanunda.com **Open** 7 days 10–5
Winemaker Neville Rowe **Est.** 1890 **Dozens** 130 000 **Vyds** 100ha
This is one of the most historically significant winery buildings in the Barossa Valley, built from bluestone quarried at nearby Bethany in the late 1880s. It has been restored by John Geber and family, and a new small batch basket press has been installed. Chateau Tanunda owns almost 100ha of vineyards in Bethany, Eden Valley, Tanunda and Vine Vale, with additional fruit sourced from a group of 30 growers covering the panoply of Barossa districts. The wines are made from hand-picked grapes, basket-pressed, and are neither fined nor filtered. There is an emphasis on single vineyard and single district wines under the Terroirs of the Barossa label. The grand building houses the cellar door and the Barossa Small Winemakers Centre, offering wines from boutique winemakers. Exports to all major markets have been a major reason for the increase in production from 50 000 to 130 000 dozen, success due to the unrelenting, market-oriented approach of John Geber.

ΨΨΨΨΨ **Terroirs of the Barossa Greenock Shiraz 2015** Saturated, molten black fruit flavours melded to lavish oak-grip and spice. The alcohol, while pushing envelopes, somehow refrains from singing the throats and nostril hairs. The tannin management is impeccable, the grape and oak manifests orchestrated effortlessly to serve as a colander for the thick fruit extract. Cork. 15% alc. **Rating** 95 **To** 2038 $49 NG

50 Year Old Vines Barossa Shiraz 2014 A limited release drawn from old, low-yielding vines. A thrust of dark fruit flavours and Christmas cake spice is contrasted with generous oak and granular, bitter chocolate tannins. A shade of light in the form of tangy red fruits lingers on a pulsating finish. Cork. 14.5% alc. **Rating** 95 **To** 2035 $75 NG

The Chateau Bethanian Barossa Valley Shiraz 2015 A wine of both compelling intensity of flavour and concentration, yet one of considerable refinement, too. With new and seasoned French and American oak, this is typical of the regional approach. The boysenberry fruit envelops the palate as the wine opens, auguring for a long future. Cork. 14% alc. **Rating** 94 **To** 2038 $35 NG

Grand Barossa Shiraz 2015 Boasts a satin velour of impeccably massaged tannins and gentle acidity, coating the mouth as a creamy duo. Swishing the wine about the gums reveals ample boysenberry fruit, hints of anise and an echo of pepper and mace on the finish. Cork. 14.5% alc. **Rating** 94 **To** 2025 $25 NG ✪

Grand Barossa Shiraz 2014 Northern Rhône scent: ground pepper, blue fruits and charcuterie; a skein of hi-fi acidity embedded in the mid-weighted frame. Typical of the region on some levels, although blue fruit billows across the palate as the wine opens. Screwcap. 14.5% alc. **Rating** 94 **To** 2024 $25 NG ✪

🍷🍷🍷🍷🍷 **The Chateau Single Vineyard Shiraz 2014** Rating 93 To 2028 $35 NG
Newcastle Cinsault Carignan 2015 Rating 93 To 2022 $22 NG ✪
Chorus Barossa 2014 Rating 93 To 2022 $17 NG ✪
50 Year Old Vines Cabernet Sauvignon 2013 Rating 93 To 2028 $75 NG
Grand Barossa Cabernet Sauvignon 2015 Rating 92 To 2028 $25 NG ✪
Chorus Tempranillo Garnacha Graciano 2014 Rating 91 To 2022 $17 NG ✪
Barossa Tower Shiraz 2015 Rating 90 To 2022 $19 NG ✪
Dahlitz Single Vineyard Merlot 2014 Rating 90 To 2025 $20 NG ✪

Cherry Tree Hill ★★★★

Hume Highway, Sutton Forest, NSW 2577 **Region** Southern Highlands
T (02) 8217 1409 **www.**cherrytreehill.com.au **Open** 7 days 9–5
Winemaker Anton Balog (Contract) **Est.** 2000 **Dozens** 4000 **Vyds** 14ha
The Lorentz family, then headed by Gabi Lorentz, began the establishment of the Cherry Tree Hill vineyard in 2000 with the planting of 3ha each of cabernet sauvignon and riesling; 3ha each of merlot and sauvignon blanc followed in '01; and, finally, 2ha of chardonnay in '02. The inspiration was childhood trips on a horse and cart through his grandfather's vineyard in Hungary, and Gabi's son (and current owner) David completes the three-generation involvement as manager of the business.

🍷🍷🍷🍷🍷 **Riesling 2016** Slate and lime, as to be expected, kick things off. But the palate kicks into a riot of quince marmalade, barley sugar, ginger and candied citrus rind, doused in a judicious dollop of sweetness as a homage to a Kabinett riesling. The acidity is soft, lilting and natural. Screwcap. 13.2% alc. **Rating** 94 **To** 2025 $35 NG

🍷🍷🍷🍷🍷 **Chardonnay 2015** Rating 93 To 2023 $25 NG ✪
Diana Reserve Chardonnay 2015 Rating 93 To 2023 $40 NG
Sauvignon Blanc 2016 Rating 90 To 2019 $20 NG ✪

Chrismont ★★★★

251 Upper King River Road, Cheshunt, Vic 3678 **Region** King Valley
T (03) 5729 8220 **www.**chrismont.com.au **Open** 7 days 10–5
Winemaker Warren Proft **Est.** 1980 **Dozens** 25 000 **Vyds** 100ha
Arnie and Jo Pizzini's substantial vineyards in the Cheshunt and Whitfield areas of the upper King Valley have been planted to riesling, sauvignon blanc, chardonnay, pinot gris, cabernet sauvignon, merlot, shiraz, barbera, sagrantino, marzemino and arneis. The La Zona range ties

in the Italian heritage of the Pizzinis and is part of the intense interest in all things Italian. It also produces a Prosecco, contract-grown in the King Valley. In January '16 the Chrismont Cellar Door, Restaurant and Larder was opened. As well as a 7-day cellar door, the new development can seat up to 300 guests, and is designed to host weddings, corporate events business conferences and group celebrations. A feature is the 'floating' deck over the vineyard, which can seat up to 150 people and has floor-to-ceiling glass looking out over the Black Ranges and King Valley landscape. Exports to the Philippines, Malaysia and Singapore.

ᵀᵀᵀᵀᵀ **La Zona King Valley Pinot Grigio 2016** Very good concentration and varietal expression. Nashi pear, Granny Smith apple and Meyer lemon announce themselves on the bouquet, and follow suit on the long palate. The finish and aftertaste do nothing to upset the apple cart. Screwcap. 11.5% alc. **Rating** 94 To 2020 $22 ○

La Zona King Valley Fiano 2016 Fiano doesn't know when to give up. Grow it anywhere, make it anyhow, and it will still come up with a textured palate of ever-changing fruit expression reflecting the outcomes of terroir, here with citrus, almond and touches of stone fruit. Screwcap. 13% alc. **Rating** 94 To 2023 $26 ○

ᵀᵀᵀᵀᵀ **King Valley Pinot Gris 2015** Rating 93 To 2020 $26 ○
La Zona King Valley Sangiovese 2015 Rating 93 To 2025 $26 ○
La Zona King Valley Barbera 2015 Rating 93 To 2022 $26 ○
La Zona King Valley Sagrantino 2015 Rating 93 To 2027 $30
La Zona King Valley Rosato 2016 Rating 90 To 2018 $18 ○

Churchview Estate ★★★★☆

8 Gale Road, Metricup, WA 6280 **Region** Margaret River
T (08) 9755 7200 **www**.churchview.com.au **Open** Mon–Sat 10–5
Winemaker Greg Garnish **Est.** 1998 **Dozens** 45 000 **Vyds** 65ha
The Fokkema family, headed by Spike Fokkema, immigrated from The Netherlands in the 1950s. Business success in the following decades led to the acquisition of the 100ha Churchview Estate property in '97, and to the progressive establishment of substantial vineyards (65ha planted to 16 varieties), managed organically. Exports to all major markets.

ᵀᵀᵀᵀᵀ **The Bartondale Margaret River Chardonnay 2015** Hand-picked, whole-bunch pressed to a combination of oak formats and barrel-fermented under the aegis of ambient yeasts, this is a chardonnay big on personality and flavour: cashew, cinnamon spice, nougat and an abundance of stone fruit blended with Asian pear. While made in the contemporary streamlined Australian fashion, matchstick flintiness is exchanged for concentration of fruit and an intensity of flavour. Screwcap. 13.5% alc. **Rating** 95 To 2023 $55 NG

ᵀᵀᵀᵀᵀ **The Bartondale Cabernet Sauvignon 2015** Rating 93 To 2033 $55 NG
St Johns Margaret River Marsanne 2016 Rating 92 To 2022 $35 NG
St Johns Margaret River Cabernet Sauvignon Malbec Merlot Petit Verdot 2015 Rating 92 To 2035 $35 NG
The Bartondale Laine Brut Zero 2010 Rating 92 To 2022 $55 TS
Estate Range SBS 2016 Rating 91 To 2017 $20 NG ○
Estate Range Chardonnay 2015 Rating 91 To 2020 $20 NG ○
The Bartondale Margaret River Shiraz 2015 Rating 90 To 2025 $55 NG
St Johns Limited Release Vintage Brut 2013 Rating 90 To 2017 $35 TS

Ciavarella Oxley Estate ★★★★

17 Evans Lane, Oxley, Vic 3678 **Region** King Valley
T (03) 5727 3384 **www**.oxleyestate.com.au **Open** Mon–Sat 9–5, Sun 10–5
Winemaker Tony Ciavarella **Est.** 1978 **Dozens** 3000 **Vyds** 1.6ha
Cyril and Jan Ciavarella's vineyard was begun in 1978, with plantings being extended over the years. One variety, aucerot, was first produced by Maurice O'Shea of McWilliam's Mount Pleasant 60 or so years ago; the Ciavarella vines have been grown from cuttings collected

from an old Glenrowan vineyard before the parent plants were removed in the mid-'80s. Tony Ciavarella left a career in agricultural research in mid-2003 to join his parents at Ciavarella. Cyril and Jan retired in '14, Tony and wife Merryn taking over management of the winery.

🍷🍷🍷🍷🍷 **Sangiovese 2015** Ticks the boxes, complexity in particular. Ciavarella says cherry and pomegranate, which I reckon is on the money, but watermelon? The tannins are balanced and ripe. Screwcap. 13.8% alc. **Rating** 94 **To** 2023

🍷🍷🍷🍷🍷 **Zinfandel 2015 Rating** 91 **To** 2020

Cirami Estate   ★★★★

78 Nixon Road, Monash, SA 5342 **Region** Riverland
T (08) 8583 5366 **www**.rvic.org.au **Open** Mon–Fri 9–4
Winemaker Eric Semmler **Est.** 2008 **Dozens** 1000 **Vyds** 46.4ha
Cirami Estate is owned by the Riverland Vine Improvement Committee Inc., a sizeable non-profit organisation. It is named after Richard Cirami, who was a pioneer in clonal selection and variety assessment, and was on the RVIC committee for over 20 years. The vineyard includes 40 varieties at 0.3ha or greater, and another 2ha planted to over 60 varieties, the latter Cirami Estate's collection of nursery plantings.

🍷🍷🍷🍷🍷 **Montepulciano 2014** Montepulciano packs a lot of flavour into a neat ball with acidity and supple tannins supporting, yet remains medium-bodied. The upfront plump red fruits are fragrant and juicy, and there's woodsy spice and plenty of personality. Screwcap. 14.5% alc. **Rating** 93 **To** 2020 $18 JF
Verdejo 2016 It's refreshing. It's zesty. It has personality wrapped around the juicy palate, all lemon-lime juice with neat acidity and green coolness in a basil spectrum, and a bright finish. Screwcap. 12.5% alc. **Rating** 91 **To** 2018 $15 JF ❂
Albarino 2016 A variety that offers enticing aromas – think white blossom and lemon/lime zest and texture. Some creamy notes, snappy acidity and a crisp finish seal the deal. Screwcap. 12.5% alc. **Rating** 90 **To** 2020 $15 JF ❂

Circe Wines   ★★★★★

PO Box 22, Red Hill, Vic 3937 **Region** Mornington Peninsula
T 0417 328 142 **www**.circewines.com.au **Open** Not
Winemaker Dan Buckle **Est.** 2010 **Dozens** 800 **Vyds** 2.9ha
Circe was a seductress and minor goddess of intoxicants in Homer's Odyssey. Circe Wines is the partnership of winemaker Dan Buckle and marketer Aaron Drummond, very much a weekend and holiday venture, inspired by their mutual love of pinot noir. They have a long-term lease of a vineyard in Hillcrest Road, not far from Paringa Estate. 'Indeed,' says Dan, 'it is not far from the Lieu-dit "Buckle" Vineyard my dad planted in the 1980s.' Circe has 1.2ha of vines, half chardonnay and half MV6 pinot noir. They have also planted 1.7ha of pinot noir (MV6, Abel, 777, D2V5 and Bests' Old Clone) at a vineyard in William Road, Red Hill. Dan Buckle's real job is chief winemaker at Chandon Australia. Exports to the UK.

🍷🍷🍷🍷🍷 **Utopies Grampians Shiraz 2015** As the bouquet promises, a powerful wine, but delivers that power smoothly and fluently, black cherry and blackberry both in play, as are spices and a hint of black pepper. Overall length and balance can't be faulted. Screwcap. 13.5% alc. **Rating** 96 **To** 2035 $50 ❂

 ## Clackers Wine Co.   ★★★★☆

13 Wicks Road, Kuitpo, SA 5172 **Region** Adelaide Hills
T 0402 120 680 **www**.clackerswineco.com.au **Open** Not
Winemaker Greg Clack **Est.** 2015 **Dozens** 299
Greg Clack has been in the wine industry for 14 years, the first 11 in McLaren Vale with Haselgrove Wines. In 2014 he took himself to the Adelaide Hills as chief winemaker at Chain of Ponds – this remains his day job, nights and days here and there devoted to Clackers Wine

Co. Its raison d'être is the discovery of small, high quality batches of single vineyard McLaren Vale grenache. The first vintage of 2015 was an unqualified success.

♥♥♥♥♥ **McLaren Vale Grenache 2015** A near-perfect evocation of McLaren Vale grenache, near because of a stubborn refusal on my part to accept 15.3% alcohol as the norm. It has beautiful varietal expression with all the red fruits you are ever likely to come across (but no confection), and the wine flows effortlessly across and along the palate. Screwcap. **Rating** 96 **To** 2030 $32 ✪

Clairault | Streicker Wines ★★★★★

3277 Caves Road, Wilyabrup, WA 6280 **Region** Margaret River
T (08) 9755 6225 **www**.clairaultstreicker.com.au **Open** 7 days 10–5
Winemaker Bruce Dukes **Est.** 1976 **Dozens** 19000 **Vyds** 113ha
This multifaceted business is owned by New York resident John Streicker. It began in 2002 when he purchased the Yallingup Protea Farm and Vineyards. This was followed by the purchase of the Ironstone Vineyard in '03, and finally the Bridgeland Vineyard, which has one of the largest dams in the region: 1km long and covering 18ha. The Ironstone Vineyard is one of the oldest vineyards in Wilyabrup. In April 2012 Streicker acquired Clairault, bringing a further 40ha of estate vines, including 12ha now over 40 years old. The two brands are effectively run as one venture. A large part of the grape production is sold to winemakers in the region. Exports to the US, Canada, Dubai, Malaysia, Singapore, Hong Kong and China.

♥♥♥♥♥ **Clairault Estate Margaret River Chardonnay 2015** Hand-picked and whole-bunch pressed, fermented in French barriques (40% new), no mlf, matured for 9 months. They don't come more seductive than this. There is a perfect union of fruit, oak and acidity: white peach, nectarine and a creamy kiss of oak are tethered by citrussy acidity. Screwcap. 13% alc. **Rating** 96 **To** 2028 $38 ✪
Streicker Ironstone Block Margaret River Cabernet Sauvignon 2013
Hand-picked, destemmed and the berries just split, pressed to French barriques (45% new) for 18 months. This has more density than the Clairault Cabernet, and also more texture. Blackcurrant allows some earthy, but ripe, tannins into the game. Despite its full-bodied expression, the balance is exceptional, and will underwrite its future development. Screwcap. 14.1% alc. **Rating** 96 **To** 2038 $45 ✪
Clairault Margaret River Sauvignon Blanc Semillon 2016 A 79/21% blend, 80% cool-fermented in stainless steel, 20% fermented in French barriques. A compelling exercise in wine power politics, playing the sauvignon blanc v semillon game and stainless steel v barrel fermentation split. All this adds up to flamboyant flavours and texture, white stone fruit with a crosscut of acidity on the long palate. Screwcap. 13% alc. **Rating** 95 **To** 2021 $22 ✪
Streicker Bridgeland Block Margaret River Sauvignon Semillon 2015
Hand-picked, cold-pressed, fermented in French oak (33% new) on light solids; matured for 9 months with lees stirring. The net result is a wine with a distinctive funky/smoky bouquet, then a palate of exceptional intensity and drive. The flavours are largely in a grassy/green pea spectrum, with just enough room for passionfruit and gooseberry to jump onboard, but are grasped by the rocky acidity and lemon zest of the finish. Screwcap. 12.5% alc. **Rating** 95 **To** 2022 $30 ✪
Clairault Margaret River Chardonnay 2015 Crushed, some whole bunches included, fermented in French oak (40% new), part undergoing mlf; matured for 9 months. The mlf hasn't deprived the wine of freshness, and it has much of the same synergy as its Estate sibling. The bouquet is complex, faintly (positively) reductive, the stone fruit flavours foremost, the oak subtle. Screwcap. 13% alc.
Rating 95 **To** 2026 $27 ✪
Streicker Ironstone Block Old Vine Margaret River Chardonnay 2014
The colour is still an amazingly youthful straw-green, the bouquet and palate likewise youthful. Estate-grown, whole-bunch pressed, fermented in French barriques, this wine has remarkable grapefruit/apple flavours of exceptional intensity and longevity from the Gin Gin clone. Screwcap. 13.5% alc. **Rating** 95
To 2029 $41

Streicker Bridgeland Block Margaret River Rose 2016 Vivid pink; very
expressive, scented red berry/strawberry bouquet, the palate vibrantly juicy,
with crisp acidity on the long finish. Skilled winemaking of estate-grown fruit;
exceptional quality. Screwcap. 13% alc. **Rating** 95 **To** 2020 $28 **۞**
Streicker Bridgeland Block Margaret River Syrah 2014 50% hand-picked,
destemmed, the berries left uncrushed, 33% stalks added back, 4 days later the
remainder picked and destemmed, pressed to French oak (33% new) to finish
fermentation and maturation for 14 months. The juicy red and black cherry
fruit are vibrant and fresh. If there is an issue, it is the low level of tannin-based
structure, but I'll forgive it that. Screwcap. 14% alc. **Rating** 95 **To** 2030 $43
Clairault Estate Margaret River Cabernet Sauvignon 2013 From the '76
plantings, matured in French barriques for 18 months. The colour is excellent, as are
the balance and depth of the fruit which, while predominantly cassis/blackcurrant,
does have the occasional glint of red fruits before ripe, but savoury, tannins move in
to end the conversation. Screwcap. 14% alc. **Rating** 95 **To** 2033 $43

♟♟♟♟♀ Clairault Cabernet Sauvignon 2015 Rating 92 To 2029 $27
Clairault Cabernet Sauvignon Merlot 2015 Rating 90 To 2023 $22
Streicker Blanc de Blancs 2013 Rating 90 To 2021 $45 TS

Clare Wine Co ★★★★

PO Box 852, Nuriootpa, SA 5355 **Region** Clare Valley
T (08) 8562 4488 **www**.clarewineco.com.au **Open** Not
Winemaker Reid Bosward, Stephen Dew **Est.** 2008 **Dozens** 5000 **Vyds** 36ha
An affiliate of Kaesler Wines, its primary focus is on exports. Its vines are predominantly
given over to shiraz and cabernet sauvignon. It also has riesling and semillon, but no
chardonnay, which is presumably purchased from other Clare Valley growers. Exports to
Malaysia, Singapore, Hong Kong and China.

♟♟♟♟♟ Watervale Riesling 2016 Literally crawling with crystal clear varietal fruit
expression, lime juice, crushed lime leaf and zest resting on a bed of balanced
acidity. All this, and a retro label, making it a monte for wine bar/cafe dining.
Screwcap. 11.5% alc. **Rating** 94 **To** 2026 $20 **۞**

♟♟♟♟♀ Cabernet Sauvignon 2013 Rating 90 To 2023 $20 **۞**

Clarendon Hills ★★★★★

Brookmans Road, Blewitt Springs, SA 5171 **Region** McLaren Vale
T (08) 8363 6111 **www**.clarendonhills.com.au **Open** By appt
Winemaker Roman Bratasiuk **Est.** 1990 **Dozens** 15000 **Vyds** 63ha
Age and experience, it would seem, have mellowed Roman Bratasiuk – and the style of his
wines. Once formidable and often rustic, they are now far more sculpted and smooth, at times
bordering on downright elegance. Roman took another major step by purchasing an 160ha
property high in the hill country of Clarendon at an altitude close to that of the Adelaide Hills.
Here he has established a vineyard with single-stake trellising similar to that used on the steep
slopes of Germany and Austria; it produces the Domaine Clarendon Syrah. He makes up to
20 different wines each year, all consistently very good, a tribute to the old vines. Exports to
the US and other major markets.

♟♟♟♟♟ Onkaparinga Syrah 2013 Deeply coloured; this is a wine I can do business
with; yes, of course it's definitely full-bodied, but its muscles ripple smoothly, with
layers oozing blackberry, licorice and dark chocolate. The tannins oil the passage
of the fruits rather than impeding them, making this dangerously drinkable. Cork.
14.5% alc. **Rating** 97 **To** 2043 $100 **۞**
Romas Grenache 2013 Keeps the colour flag flying high, and kicks on from
there. It is grenache built for the ages, and has exceptional balance that will
guarantee its future. It is supple to the point of being silky, and ablaze with red
fruits and spice. Cork. 14.5% alc. **Rating** 97 **To** 2035 $100 **۞**

Hickinbotham Cabernet Sauvignon 2013 This brings memories of Roman Bratasiuk's first release of his wines, comparing them to First Growth Bordeaux, but not reaping dividends. Had this been one of the wines in the comparison, it would have done so. For any cabernet lover looking for a cabernet with a 30–40 year life, this stands alongside the best Australia has to offer. All of that said, be aware of the unbridled power of the wine. Cork. 14.5% alc. **Rating** 97 To 2053 $100 ○

ΨΨΨΨΨ **Hickinbotham Syrah 2013** Deep crimson-purple; spice, tar, licorice and sombre black fruits on the bouquet lead into an intense, full-bodied palate that catches you by surprise with its (relative) lightness of foot. Savoury tannins are there in abundance, as is French oak, but with sufficient protein on hand, you could enjoy a glass (possibly even two) of this wine. Cork. 14.5% alc. **Rating** 96 To 2048 $100
Clarendon Grenache 2013 Deep, bright colour, rare for grenache of any age unless it be Clarendon Hills; the palate is full, supple and round, with red fruits in the ascendant, floral notes slipping in behind. Has all the structure and ripeness one could wish for. Cork. 14.5% alc. **Rating** 95 To 2028 $55
Onkaparinga Grenache 2013 Strong colour; the alcohol doesn't register as heat, but does in the way the flavours refuse to leave the mouth after the wine has been spat out (or swallowed); the bouquet, too, is fragrant, not heavy. This is high quality wine, even if its style won't please all. Cork. 15.2% alc. **Rating** 95 To 2033 $100
Brookman Cabernet Sauvignon 2013 This is unequivocally full-bodied, its well of blackcurrant and blackberry fruit in a basket of tannins and oak; the tannins tip the scales at the moment, but there is enough fruit depth to see them off in the years to come. Cork. 14.5% alc. **Rating** 95 To 2033 $75
Domaine Clarendon Syrah 2013 Exceptional youthful crimson-purple; the estate-grown grapes provide a full-bodied wine with a realm of spicy black fruits and licorice, the tannins muted but present, ditto oak. Will quite possibly pull out the proverbial rabbit with more time. Cork. 14.7% alc. **Rating** 94 To 2028 $35

ΨΨΨΨΨ **Moritz Syrah 2013 Rating** 93 To 2028 $75

Clarnette & Ludvigsen Wines ★★★★

Westgate Road, Armstrong, Vic 3377 **Region** Grampians
T 0409 083 833 **www.**clarnette-ludvigsen.com.au **Open** By appt
Winemaker Leigh Clarnette **Est.** 2003 **Dozens** 400 **Vyds** 15.5ha
Winemaker Leigh Clarnette and viticulturist Kym Ludvigsen's career paths crossed in late 1993 when both were working for Seppelt, Kym with a 14ha vineyard in the heart of the Grampians, all but 1ha of chardonnay, 0.5ha of viognier and 0.25ha of riesling planted to rare clones of shiraz, sourced from old plantings in the Great Western area. They met again in 2005 when both were employed by Taltarni. The premature death of Kym in '13 was widely reported, in no small measure due to his (unpaid) service on wine industry bodies. With next generations on both sides, the plans are to continue the business. Exports to China.

ΨΨΨΨΨ **Grampians Shiraz 2015** 30% new and 1yo French hogsheads for 15 months. Beguiling cool climate shiraz aromas emerge from the glass as you smell this wine; pepper, Middle Eastern spice, and dark, plummy fruit. The oak chimes in as a subplot. No more than medium-bodied, it flows easily across the palate with ripe flavours, soft in texture but underpinned by sneaky acidity. Screwcap. 14.8% alc. **Rating** 94 To 2022 $35 SC

ΨΨΨΨΨ **Reserve Grampians Shiraz 2014 Rating** 93 To 2029 $50 SC

Claymore Wines ★★★★☆

7145 Horrocks Way, Leasingham, SA 5452 **Region** Clare Valley
T (08) 8843 0200 **www.**claymorewines.com.au **Open** 7 days 10–5
Winemaker Marnie Roberts **Est.** 1998 **Dozens** 25 000 **Vyds** 27ha

Claymore Wines is the venture of Anura Nitchingham, a medical professional who imagined that it would lead the way to early retirement (which, of course, it did not). The starting date depends on which event you take: the first 4ha vineyard at Leasingham purchased in 1991 (with 70-year-old grenache, riesling and shiraz); '96, when a 16ha block at Penwortham was purchased and planted to shiraz, merlot and grenache; '97, when the first wines were made; or '98, when the first releases came onto the market. The labels are inspired by U2, Pink Floyd, Prince and Lou Reed. Exports to the UK, Canada, Denmark, Malaysia, Singapore, Taiwan, Hong Kong and China.

ŶŶŶŶŶ **Dark Side of the Moon Clare Valley Shiraz 2014** Rich, soft and well balanced is usually a good composition. Lashings of dark, ripe fruit on the bouquet, bolstered by aromas of licorice and deftly handled oak. Mouthfilling and generous, the seamless texture lets it glide along the palate easily, satisfying as it goes. The tannin is just firm enough to temper the fullness of flavour. Screwcap. 14.5% alc. **Rating** 94 **To** 2026 $25 SC **✪**
Signature Series Ian Rush Shiraz 2013 Named for Liverpool FC's prolific goal scorer of the '80s. Only three barrels (1000 bottles) produced. An imposing bouquet of heady oak and rich, almost raisiny aromas. Densely flavoured with deep, dark fruit and sweet spice, the tannin is implacable but strikes the right balance for a long future. Screwcap. 16% alc. **Rating** 94 **To** 2033 $95 SC

ŶŶŶŶŶ **God is a DJ Clare Valley Riesling 2016** Rating 93 To 2024 $25 JF **✪**
Dark Side of the Moon Clare Shiraz 2015 Rating 93 To 2028 $25 JF **✪**
Black Magic Woman Reserve Cabernet Sauvignon 2013 Rating 93 To 2025 $45 JF
Joshua Tree Watervale Riesling 2016 Rating 91 To 2022 $20 JF **✪**
Voodoo Child Chardonnay 2015 Rating 90 To 2020 $22 SC
Whole Lotta Love Clare Valley Rose 2015 Rating 90 To 2018 $20 SC **✪**

Clockwork Wines   ★★★★

8990 West Swan Road, West Swan, WA 6056 (postal) **Region** Swan Valley
T 0401 033 840 **Open** Not
Winemaker Rob Marshall **Est.** 2008 **Dozens** 7000 **Vyds** 5ha
This is a separate business from that of Oakover Wines, although both are owned by the Yukich family. Grapes are sourced from around WA, with the majority coming from Margaret River, and from Geographe, Frankland River and the Clockwork Vineyard in the Swan Valley. The 2007 Clockwork Cabernet Merlot, somewhat luckily, perhaps, found itself in the line-up for the Jimmy Watson Trophy at its first show entry, part of a dominant contingent from Margaret River thanks to its great vintage.

ŶŶŶŶŶ **Shiraz 2015** A bit of a tease, this shiraz, as at first it highlights upfront fruit, then morphs into more detail. Plums, spice, cedary oak; it's juicy, with a backbone of crunchy acidity and ripe, grainy tannins. A bargain to boot and will garner more complexity in time. Screwcap. 14.5% alc. **Rating** 92 **To** 2025 $20 JF **✪**

Clonakilla   ★★★★★

Crisps Lane, Murrumbateman, NSW 2582 **Region** Canberra District
T (02) 6227 5877 **www**.clonakilla.com.au **Open** 7 days 10–5
Winemaker Tim Kirk, Bryan Martin **Est.** 1971 **Dozens** 17 000 **Vyds** 13.5ha
The indefatigable Tim Kirk, with an inexhaustible thirst for knowledge, is the winemaker and manager of this family winery founded by his father, scientist Dr John Kirk. It is not at all surprising that the quality of the wines is exceptional, especially the Shiraz Viognier, which has paved the way for numerous others, but remains the icon. Demand for the wines outstrips supply, even with the 1998 acquisition of an adjoining 20ha property by Tim and wife Lara Kirk, planted to shiraz and viognier; the first Hilltops Shiraz being made in 2000, from the best vineyards; the 2007 purchase by the Kirk family of another adjoining property, and the planting of another 1.8ha of shiraz, plus 0.4ha of grenache, mourvedre and cinsaut; and in the same year, the first vintage of O'Riada Shiraz. Exports to all major markets.

ŸŸŸŸŸ **Murrumbateman Syrah 2015** From the T&L Block, 100% whole berries, wild-yeast fermented, 1 month on skins, matured for 22 months in French puncheons. This has everything a medium-bodied shiraz grown in the right climate should have under the baton of a master winemaker. Black cherry is the dominant flavour, but is flanked on either side by red cherry and blackberry. The palate is silky and supple on the journey until the end, when decorous tannins and French oak add their voices. Screwcap. 14% alc. **Rating** 98 **To** 2040 $96 ✪

ŸŸŸŸŸ **Canberra District Riesling 2016** Pale straw-green; accelerates continuously from the first floral whiff through to the aftertaste; the mid-palate progressively builds ripe lime flavours as the wine is retasted, but is matched by the flinty acidity of the finish and lingering aftertaste. Sustained by that acidity, it has an outstanding future. Screwcap. 12% alc. **Rating** 96 **To** 2031 $36 ✪

Ballinderry 2015 38% merlot, 35% cabernet franc, 27% cabernet sauvignon from vines planted between '71 and '87, 3 weeks on skins; matured for 22 months in French oak (30% new). There is an utterly symbiotic and synergistic union between the deliciously ripe and sweet red and black fruits of the long, medium-bodied palate. High quality French oak does the job, but doesn't seek the limelight any more than the tannins. Screwcap. 14.5% alc. **Rating** 96 **To** 2035 $45 ✪

Canberra District Viognier 2016 Estate-grown 17yo (Yarra Yering clone planted in '99) and 30yo (the original plantings) vines, two-thirds whole-bunch pressed, the remainder 24 hours skin contact, wild-yeast fermented in 600l demi-muids, matured for 11 months in oak. The vinification is a triumph. It not only avoids oily phenolics; it gives the wine real texture and structure, yet doesn't obliterate varietal character. Screwcap. 13.5% alc. **Rating** 95 **To** 2021 $45

Ceoltoiri 2016 A Chateau Neuf du Pape-inspired blend, this year with mourvedre (46%) the dominant component (usually grenache), with grenache, shiraz, cinsaut, counoise and roussanne, 100% whole berry ferments, matured in used French oak for 11 months. A light-bodied wine with a complex web of flavours, spiced red and purple fruits to the fore. The alcohol is a positive contributor to a palate that keeps on building with new cadences not previously sensed. Whatever else can be said, the length is seriously good. Screwcap. 14% alc. **Rating** 95 **To** 2026 $36

Hilltops Shiraz 2016 From five vineyards, 2–3 days cold soak, mostly open-fermented with pigeage, some whole bunches included, 8 days post-ferment maceration, matured in French oak (17% new) for 11 months. The usual Clonakilla signature of perfectly balanced fruit, tannins and oak, always complex yet always with great mouthfeel, black fruits to the fore, with a gentle sprinkle of spice and pepper. Screwcap. 14% alc. **Rating** 94 **To** 2031 $28 ✪

ŸŸŸŸŸ **Viognier Nouveau 2016** **Rating** 91 **To** 2018 $25 CM

Cloudbreak Wines   ★★★★

5A/1 Adelaide Lobethal Road, Lobethal, SA 5241 **Region** Adelaide Hills
T 0431 245 668 **www**.cloudbreakwines.com.au **Open** Not
Winemaker Simon Greenleaf, Randal Tomich **Est.** 1998 **Dozens** 22 000 **Vyds** 80ha
Cloudbreak Wines is a joint venture between Randal Tomich and Simon Greenleaf, who share a friendship of over 20 years. Cloudbreak specialises in cool climate wines grown on the Tomich family's Woodside Vineyard. Randal has extensive experience in winemaking, specialising in vineyard development. The vineyards upon which Cloudbreak Wines is based comprise chardonnay (22ha), sauvignon blanc (18ha), pinot noir (15ha), gruner veltliner (6ha), and riesling, gewurztraminer and shiraz (5ha each). Exports to Singapore and China.

ŸŸŸŸŸ **Winemakers Reserve Adelaide Hills Sauvignon Blanc 2016** No-frills winemaking. It should be called Viticulturists Reserve, for it wears a tri-corner hat with excellent varietal fruit spanning grass, citrus and tropical aromas and flavours, striding out on the finish. Screwcap. 13% alc. **Rating** 93 **To** 2019 $30

Single Vineyard Adelaide Hills Pinot Noir 2015 Estate-grown Dijon clones 114 and 115 plus MV6, hand-picked at dawn, cold-soaked, fermented and matured in French oak. Excellent colour; a complex wine with signs of whole-bunch inclusion in the form of savoury, green tannins. Screwcap. 13.5% alc. **Rating** 90 **To** 2020 $30

Cloudburst ★★★★★

PO Box 1294, Margaret River, WA 6285 **Region** Margaret River
T (08) 6323 2333 **www**.cloudburstwine.com **Open** Not
Winemaker Will Berliner **Est.** 2005 **Dozens** 450 **Vyds** 5ha

An extremely interesting young winery. Will Berliner and wife Alison Jobson spent several years in Australia searching for a place that resonated with them, and on their first visit to Margaret River were immediately smitten, drawn by its biodiversity, beaches, farms, vineyards, community and lifestyle. When they purchased their land in 2004 they hadn't the slightest connection with wine and no intention of ever getting involved. Within 12 months Will's perspective had entirely changed, and in '05 he began planting the vineyard and applying biodynamic preparations, seeking to build microbial life in the soil. They planted the vineyard as if it were a garden, with short rows, and initially planted 0.2ha of each of cabernet sauvignon and chardonnay, and 0.1ha of malbec. By 2018 the vineyard will have doubled in size, but without changing the varieties or their proportions. The packaging is truly striking and imaginative. The unseen hand is that of the Watson family, the wines being made at Woodlands by Will under the watchful eye of Stuart Watson. Exports to the US.

🍷🍷🍷🍷🍷 **Chardonnay 2015** Distinctive flavour profile. It leans heavily on elegance as a quality marker but lines of smoked bran, wheat, nectarine and sweet pear-like flavour bring both savouriness and fruitiness to the table. Everything here feels fresh-faced and limpid. Screwcap. 13.3% alc. **Rating** 95 **To** 2022 CM

Cabernet Sauvignon 2014 Silken, superfine cabernet with black olive, blackcurrant and bay leaf notes doing most of the bidding. Cedary oak plays a clear role too but it's all seamless, it all slips along smoothly. Screwcap. 13.4% alc. **Rating** 95 **To** 2034 $275 CM

Malbec 2014 A pure display of blue- and black-berried fruit comes gently wrapped in smoky oak. It's presented in pristine condition; notes of liquid violets come floating forward as the wine breathes, emphasising its quality (and seductive charms) further. Screwcap. 13.9% alc. **Rating** 94 **To** 2028 $225 CM

Clover Hill ★★★★★

60 Clover Hill Road, Lebrina, Tas 7254 **Region** Northern Tasmania
T (03) 5459 7900 **www**.cloverhillwines.com.au **Open** By appt
Winemaker Robert Heywood, Peter Warr **Est.** 1986 **Dozens** 12 000 **Vyds** 23.9ha

Clover Hill was established by Taltarni in 1986 with the sole purpose of making a premium sparkling wine. It has 23.9ha of vineyards (chardonnay, pinot noir and pinot meunier) and its sparkling wine quality is excellent, combining finesse with power and length. The American owner and founder of Clos du Val (Napa Valley), Taltarni and Clover Hill has brought these businesses and Domaine de Nizas (Languedoc) under the one management roof, the group known as Goelet Wine Estates. Exports to the UK, the US and other major markets.

🍷🍷🍷🍷🍷 **Cuvee Prestige Late Disgorged Blanc de Blancs 2015** There is brightness to a medium straw hue, and a silky and seamless accord between primary and secondary character. Ripe fruit succulence of grilled pineapple and juicy white peach are cut with fresh citrus definition and the energy of partial malic acidity. More than a decade on lees has blessed it with glorious layers of silky, creamy texture and captivating nuances of butter, glace pear and vanilla nougat. At its glorious peak now. Diam. 12.3% alc. **Rating** 96 **To** 2019 $150 TS

Cuvee Exceptionnelle Blanc de Blancs 2010 Chardonnay was where it all began for Clover Hill, and there is a tension and definition to this grape that defines the estate's longest-lived wines to this day. There's intensity of grapefruit, lemon butter and even the exuberance of star fruit amid the toast and burnt butter of bottle age. In creamy texture, mouthfilling intensity and undeviating line and length, this is a grand release for Clover Hill, with plenty of energy still coiled into its folds. Diam. 12.6% alc. **Rating** 95 **To** 2022 $65 TS

Tasmanian Cuvee Methode Traditionnelle Rose NV 54% chardonnay, 43% pinot noir, 3% pinot meunier. A delicious rose, with vibrant rose petal, watermelon and spice aromas, it spends 2 years on tirage, and the base wine is taken through partial mlf. Its freshness and drive, coupled with a seemingly low dosage, gives a pleasingly dry, lingering aftertaste. Cork. 12.5% alc. **Rating** 94 **To** 2018 $35

ŢŢŢŢŢ **Brut Rose 2013** Rating 92 To 2017 $65 TS
Tasmania Cuvee Rose NV Rating 91 To 2017 $34 TS
Clover Hill 2012 Rating 90 To 2018 $50 TS
Tasmanian Cuvee NV Rating 90 To 2018 $35 TS

Clyde Park Vineyard ★★★★★

2490 Midland Highway, Bannockburn, Vic 3331 **Region** Geelong
T (03) 5281 7274 **www**.clydepark.com.au **Open** 7 days 11–5
Winemaker Ben Mullen, Terry Jongebloed **Est.** 1979 **Dozens** 6000 **Vyds** 10.1ha
Clyde Park Vineyard, established by Gary Farr but sold by him many years ago, has passed through several changes of ownership. Now owned by Terry Jongebloed and Sue Jongebloed-Dixon, it has significant mature plantings of pinot noir (3.4ha), chardonnay (3.1ha), sauvignon blanc (1.5ha), shiraz (1.2ha) and pinot gris (0.9ha), and the quality of its wines is consistently exemplary. Exports to the UK and Hong Kong.

ŢŢŢŢŢ **Single Block D Bannockburn Pinot Noir 2016** MV6 clone planted in '88, 60% whole bunches, wild-yeast fermented, 35 days on skins, matured for 11 months in French oak (33% new), 165 dozen made. The bouquet is complex, spicy and inviting; the palate has the power and drive of a tip-top Premier Cru from Vosne-Romanée, and a superior outlook for cellaring, its inherent quality protected for decades by the screwcap. 12.8% alc. **Rating** 97 **To** 2041 $75 ❂

ŢŢŢŢŢ **Single Block B3 Bannockburn Chardonnay 2016** Clone P58 planted 32 years ago, hand-picked, whole-bunch pressed, matured in French oak (33% new), 120 dozen made. More complex, but also more elegant, than its varietal sibling, with a seamless flow of stone fruit, oak and gently citrussy acidity streaming across the palate. Screwcap. 13% alc. **Rating** 96 **To** 2025 $75 ❂

Single Block F College Bannockburn Pinot Noir 2016 MV6 planted in '89, hand-picked, 60% whole bunches, wild-yeast fermented, 21 days on skins, matured in French oak (33% new). The bouquet tells you this is very different from Block B2, even though they abut each other. The palate is rounder, with sweet red fruits on a bed of spice and forest floor. Screwcap. 13% alc. **Rating** 96 **To** 2030 $75 ❂

Single Block B2 Bannockburn Pinot Noir 2016 MV6, 60% whole bunches, wild-yeast fermented/macerated 21 days on skins, 11 months in French oak (33% new). A highly expressive red and purple-fruited bouquet segues into a well built palate in the power-laden Clyde Park style. It is so well balanced it will cruise through what will be a long life. Screwcap. 12.5% alc. **Rating** 95 **To** 2031 $75

Geelong Shiraz 2016 Dense colour with just a glimpse of crimson; an ultra-powerful shiraz, showing little sign of its 11 months in oak; black fruits, pepper, spice, licorice and tar all keep each other in a rugby scrum, as much savoury as fruity. That all this came from 13.5% alcohol is breathtaking, and redoubles the case for very, very long cellaring. Screwcap. **Rating** 95 **To** 2051 $40

Geelong Pinot Noir 2016 This is all about compressed power demanding to be left alone until its dark fruits soften and allow exploration of the latent flavours. It's also about the difference between the '15 and '16 vintages in pinot's dress circle around Melbourne. Screwcap. 13% alc. **Rating** 94 **To** 2031 $40

Locale Geelong Pinot Noir 2016 Made from purchased grapes grown across the region. This is a powerhouse in its price class – in Burgundy it would be labelled Bourgogne. It can certainly be drunk now, but will equally certainly see

its deep-seated cherry, spice and tannin flavour and structure come into full flower. Screwcap. 13% alc. **Rating** 94 **To** 2029 $25 ✪
Locale Geelong Shiraz 2015 From the parcels left over after blending of the '15 Shiraz, not bottled until Jan '17. It's vigorous and complex, with notes of stem and spice, licorice and pepper smoothly connected to give the wine an irresistible appeal. Screwcap. 13.5% alc. **Rating** 94 **To** 2029 $25 ✪

♟♟♟♟♟ Geelong Chardonnay 2016 **Rating** 93 **To** 2023 $40

Coal Valley Vineyard ★★★★☆

257 Richmond Road, Cambridge, Tas 7170 **Region** Southern Tasmania
T (03) 6248 5367 **www.**coalvalley.com.au **Open** 7 days 11–5 (closed Jul)
Winemaker Alain Rousseau, Todd Goebel **Est.** 1991 **Dozens** 1500 **Vyds** 4.5ha
Since acquiring Coal Valley Vineyard in 1999, Gill Christian and Todd Goebel have increased the original 1ha hobby vineyard to 4.5ha of pinot noir, riesling, cabernet sauvignon, merlot, chardonnay and tempranillo. More remarkable were Gill and Todd's concurrent lives: one in India, the other in Tasmania (flying over six times a year), and digging 4000 holes for the new vine plantings. Todd makes the Pinot Noir and Tempranillo onsite, and dreams of making all the wines. Exports to Canada.

♟♟♟♟♟ Riesling 2016 The flowery, blossom-filled bouquet doesn't bear false witness: the palate is filled with lime, lemon and Granny Smith apple flavours, zesty acidity perfectly balanced and lengthening the palate even further. All of this said, it's best years are in front of it. Screwcap. 12.9% alc. **Rating** 95 **To** 2026 $30 ✪
Chardonnay 2015 Hand-picked, pressed to French oak (25% new) and fermented with cultured yeast, no mlf, matured for 8 months with some lees stirring. Has all the focus, intensity and drive one could wish for; the fruit/oak balance is spot on, the varietal and regional expression likewise. Screwcap. 12.5% alc. **Rating** 94 **To** 2026 $34
Pinot Noir 2015 Hand-picked, destemmed and crushed, fermented in tank with cultured yeast, matured in French oak (33% new) for 10 months. Very good colour; the highly expressive bouquet is riddled with spices and forest fruits, characters that drive the long, savoury palate which is bursting with potential. Its crisp acidity needs to yield to the flavours that will develop over the next 5 years. Screwcap. 13.5% alc. **Rating** 94 **To** 2030 $39

Coates Wines ★★★★★

185 Tynan Road, Kuitpo, SA 5172 **Region** Adelaide Hills
T 0417 882 557 **www.**coates-wines.com **Open** W'ends & public hols 11–5
Winemaker Duane Coates **Est.** 2003 **Dozens** 2500
Duane Coates has a Bachelor of Science, a Master of Business Administration and a Master of Oenology from Adelaide University; for good measure he completed the theory component of the Masters of Wine degree in 2005. Having made wine in various parts of the world, and in SA, he is more than qualified to make and market Coates wines. Nonetheless, his original intention was to simply make a single barrel of wine employing various philosophies and practices outside the mainstream; there was no plan to move to commercial production. The key is organically grown grapes. Exports to the UK and the US.

♟♟♟♟♟ McLaren Vale Grenache Shiraz Mourvedre 2015 This has drinkability written all over its core of black olive tapenade and molten black fruits. Strongly reminiscent of a southern Rhône red: forceful in personality, albeit with a grippy tannic platform, real acidity and not a lick of jamminess. Among the finest, most suave and savoury GSMs tasted. Screwcap. 14% alc. **Rating** 96 **To** 2023 $30 NG ✪
Adelaide Hills The Chardonnay 2016 Whole-bunch pressed to 20% new French oak, fermented wild and stirred twice while remaining on gross lees for almost a year. Melon and stone fruits mingle on the nose, but the soul of the wine is surely the kernel of nougatine, cashew and roasted hazelnut that defines the wine's midriff. This is a more generous chardonnay than the status quo, but far from fat. Screwcap. 13% alc. **Rating** 95 **To** 2025 $30 NG ✪

The Garden of Perfume & Spice Syrah 2015 From the Adelaide Hills, Robe and Langhorne Creek, each parcel wild-yeast fermented for 3 weeks, 12 months in French barriques (30% new); 300 dozen made. An elegant wine singing the same song from the first whiff of the bouquet through to the finish, blackberry and blueberry faithfully replayed on the immaculately balanced palate, likewise oak and gently savoury/foresty tannins. Screwcap. 14% alc. **Rating** 95 **To** 2028 $30 **◐**

McLaren Vale Langhorne Creek The GSM 2015 A 48/33/19% blend co-fermented over 22 days, 35% whole bunches, the balance crushed and destemmed, 11 months in French oak. The logistics of picking the three components at the same time for co-fermentation must have been daunting for a one-man operation, but the result has been very rewarding. The bouquet is super-fragrant, and the red fruits of the palate come home at a rate of knots. Really lovely, early drinking wine. Screwcap. 14.5% alc. **Rating** 95 **To** 2025 $25 **◐**

McLaren Vale and Langhorne Creek The Cabernet Shiraz 2014 Has absorbed 32 months in French oak well; black cherry and satsuma plum, a herbal potpourri of bay leaf and dried sage. Syrah's blue-fruited florals and their confluence with the sterner, herbal visage of cabernet is showcased with aplomb. The tannins are finely wrought, firm and detailed; the acidity bright, the finish long. Screwcap. 14.5% alc. **Rating** 95 **To** 2035 $30 NG **◐**

Adelaide Hills The Chardonnay 2015 Wild yeast fermentation in French barriques (30% new), then aged on lees with mlf. The straw-green colour shows some early development, as does the precocious bouquet with its tropical element neatly balanced on the palate by grapefruit and white peach in classic cool-grown style. Screwcap. 13.5% alc. **Rating** 94 **To** 2022 $25 **◐**

McLaren Vale Syrah 2015 20 months oak maturation, partially in new French oak. This syrah has a real spring in its step, thanks to 80yo Blewitt Springs' fruit conferring an energetic crunch. Smoked meat, tar and blue and black fruits of all descriptions are given a prosaic lift by alluring florals. The palate is defined by slinky tannins, assuaging acidity and maritime salinity, all giving shape to the flavours. Screwcap. 14.5% alc. **Rating** 94 **To** 2030 $25 NG **◐**

McLaren Vale The Mourvedre 2015 80% crushed and destemmed, 20% whole bunches, 22 days on skins, matured in a new French hogshead and French barriques (70% used) for 11 months. Not the easiest variety to make as a 100% varietal, but Coates succeeds here, with plush purple fruits and spices running through the medium-bodied, well balanced palate. Screwcap. 14.5% alc. **Rating** 94 **To** 2023 $30 **◐**

ＹＹＹＹＹ **The Gimp McLaren Vale Shiraz 2015 Rating** 93 **To** 2035 $30 NG
Langhorne Creek The Cabernet Sauvignon 2015 Rating 93 **To** 2038 $30 NG
Robe Vineyard The Malbec 2015 Rating 93 **To** 2027 $25 NG **◐**
The Reserve Adelaide Hills Chardonnay 2015 Rating 91 **To** 2022 $40
Langhorne Creek Adelaide Hills La Petite Rouge 2015 Rating 91 **To** 2023 $18 **◐**

Cockfighter's Ghost ★★★★☆

576 De Beyers Road, Pokolbin, NSW 2320 **Region** Hunter Valley
T (02) 4993 3688 **www.**cockfightersghost.com.au **Open** 7 days 10–5
Winemaker Jeff Byrne, Xanthe Hatcher **Est.** 1988 **Dozens** 30 000 **Vyds** 38ha
This winery's name comes from the legend of one of the early explorers: his horse, Cockfighter, drowned one night while crossing a creek near their vineyard, but its ghost is said to live on. Cockfighter's Ghost and Poole's Rock were founded in 1988 by the late David Clarke OAM. Upon his passing, the brands, vineyards and winery in Pokolbin were acquired by the Agnew family, who also own the neighbouring Audrey Wilkinson. All brands under the Agnew Wines umbrella have kept separate identities. There has also been significant investment in winery upgrades. Grapes are sourced from estate vineyards in McLaren Vale, Pokolbin and the Upper Hunter Valley, and also from key regions including the Adelaide Hills, Langhorne Creek, Orange and Tasmania.

ŢŢŢŢŢ **Cockfighter's Ghost Reserve Hunter Valley Semillon 2016** Back in racy
territory with its backbone of sprightly acidity, tight on the palate with tangy and
tart freshly squeezed Granny Smith apple juice, lime juice too. Enjoy it now with
seafood. Screwcap. 11.5% alc. **Rating** 95 **To** 2032 $30 JF ✪

ŢŢŢŢ♀ **Poole's Rock McLaren Vale Shiraz 2016** Rating 93 To 2026 $45 JF
Cockfighter's Reserve Coonawarra Cabernet 2015 Rating 93 To 2030
$40 JF
Poole's Rock Tasmania Pinot Noir 2016 Rating 92 To 2024 $65 JF
Cockfighter's Ghost Hunter Semillon 2016 Rating 91 To 2024 $25 JF
Cockfighter's Ghost McLaren Vale Shiraz 2015 Rating 90 To 2024 $25 JF
Cockfighter's Langhorne Creek Cabernet 2015 Rating 90 To 2024 $25 JF

Cofield Wines   ★★★★

Distillery Road, Wahgunyah, Vic 3687 **Region** Rutherglen
T (02) 6033 3798 **www.**cofieldwines.com.au **Open** Mon–Sat 9–5, Sun 10–5
Winemaker Damien Cofield, Brendan Heath **Est.** 1990 **Dozens** 13 000 **Vyds** 15.4ha
Sons Damien (winery) and Andrew (vineyard) have taken over responsibility for the business
from parents Max and Karen Cofield. Collectively, they have developed an impressively broad-
based product range with a strong cellar door sales base. The Pickled Sisters Cafe is open for
lunch Wed–Mon, (02) 6033 2377). A 20ha property at Rutherglen, purchased in 2007, is
planted to shiraz, durif and sangiovese.

ŢŢŢŢŢ **Provincial Parcel Alpine Valleys Beechworth Chardonnay 2015** Hand-
picked, wild-yeast fermented in French barriques, then 15 months in barrel on
lees. Shows many of the good qualities associated with top chardonnay from the
region (particularly Beechworth). Complex bouquet, with stone fruit and citrus
enhanced by the nutty, creamy oak characters. Perfect weight; flavoursome but still
elegant and textural. Screwcap. 13% alc. **Rating** 94 **To** 2022 $36 SC
Reserve Release Pinot Noir Chardonnay 2006 The full straw hue retains
brightness after more than a decade, a sure prelude to the integrity that this cuvee
has maintained. Fresh butter, roast almonds, ginger, wild honey, creme brulee
and all manner of spice are the blessings of almost 9 years on lees, supporting
dried peach fruit. It's very long, seamless and silky, with beautifully defined and
mouthfilling texture. 11.6% alc. **Rating** 94 **To** 2018 $45 TS

ŢŢŢŢ♀ **Minimal Footprint Quartz Vein Petit Verdot 2013** Rating 93 To 2025
$32 SC
Rutherglen Muscat NV Rating 93 $25 SC ✪
Rutherglen Shiraz 2014 Rating 92 To 2024 $26 SC
Rutherglen Shiraz Durif 2015 Rating 92 To 2035 $24 SC ✪
Rutherglen Topaque NV Rating 92 $25 ✪
Rutherglen Sangiovese 2015 Rating 90 To 2023 $22 SC
Rutherglen Durif 2014 Rating 90 To 2035 $26 SC
Minimal Footprint Quartz Vein Durif 2013 Rating 90 To 2021 $35 SC
Prosecco NV Rating 90 To 2017 $20 TS ✪

Coldstream Hills   ★★★★★

31 Maddens Lane, Coldstream, Vic 3770 **Region** Yarra Valley
T (03) 5960 7000 **www.**coldstreamhills.com.au **Open** 7 days 10–5
Winemaker Andrew Fleming, Greg Jarratt, James Halliday (Consultant) **Est.** 1985
Dozens 25 000 **Vyds** 100ha
Founded by the author, James Halliday, Coldstream Hills is now a small part of Treasury Wine
Estates, with 100ha of owned estate vineyards as its base, three in the Lower Yarra Valley and
two in the Upper Yarra Valley. Chardonnay and Pinot Noir continue to be the principal focus;
Merlot and Cabernet Sauvignon came on-stream in 1997, Sauvignon Blanc around the same
time, Reserve Shiraz later still. Vintage conditions permitting, Chardonnay and Pinot Noir are
made in Reserve, Single Vineyard and varietal forms. In addition, Amphitheatre Pinot Noir

was made in tiny quantities in 2006 and '13. In '10 a multimillion-dollar winery was erected around the original winery buildings and facilities; it has a capacity of 1500 tonnes. There is a plaque in the fermentation area commemorating the official opening on 12 October '10 and naming the facility the 'James Halliday Cellar'. Exports to the UK, the US and Singapore

ŸŸŸŸŸ **Reserve Yarra Valley Cabernet Sauvignon 2015** A simply great Yarra Valley cabernet that is different from but every bit the equal of anything from Margaret River. Deep purple in colour, this has a core of dark cherry and blackcurrant fruit, a little cigar box and cedar from 15 months in new and older French oak. Powerful yet supremely refined and elegant, persistent and fine-grained tannins round out a wine destined to provide many years of drinking pleasure. Screwcap. 14% alc. **Rating** 97 **To** 2022 $60 PR ◐

ŸŸŸŸŸ **Reserve Yarra Valley Chardonnay 2016** This is the latest in a long line of superb chardonnays from one of the Yarra Valley's finest exponents. Brightly coloured, aromas of grapefruit, stone fruit and a little struck match lead onto the palate with is powerful, seamless and long. Still tightly wound; a long life seems assured. Screwcap. 13% alc. **Rating** 95 **To** 2022 $60 PR

Deer Farm Vineyard Pinot Noir 2016 From the vines planted in the Upper Yarra Valley in '94, this very bright and beautifully detailed wine has a touch of spice to go with the red cherry fruit aromas while the palate is pure, layered and long. Ripe persistent tannins run throughout a wine that has excellent depth while remaining light on its feet. Screwcap. 14% alc. **Rating** 95 **To** 2024 $50 PR

Reserve Yarra Valley Shiraz 2015 From the dark crimson hue and heady aromas to the fine-grained tannins, this is seductive, yet demands to be noticed. Succulent red and black-berried fruit, florals with cedary oak spice following through onto the fuller bodied, smooth palate. The oak is supportive, the acidity ultra-refreshing. Finishes on a high note: the epitome of cool climate shiraz. Screwcap. 14% alc. **Rating** 95 **To** 2030 $45 JF

Yarra Valley Chardonnay 2016 Sourced across hillside plots in both the Upper and Lower Yarra Valley, this is a judicious meld of tension and impeccably ripe melon and stone fruit flavours, nudged with cashew. The wine leaves an indelible impression of coolness; of place; so sensitive, inconspicuous and well judged are the handling of oak and mineral thread. There is nothing forceful about this. Rather, it is an exercise in restraint and yet, also of flavour line and lingering length. A lovely drink. Screwcap. 13.5% alc. **Rating** 94 **To** 2025 $35 NG

Blanc de Blancs 2011 Both Coldstream Hills' sparklings are sourced from the heights of the Deer Farm Vineyard in the cool Upper Yarra, and the cold and wet '11 season has made for a particularly bright, pale and enduring style. Primary apple and lemon fruit remain the themes, with lees age building complexity of lemon meringue, nougat and vanilla, blessing it with a finely textured mouthfeel and dainty bead. It lingers with great confidence and energy, yet is calm and composed. Cork. 11.5% alc. **Rating** 94 **To** 2021 $45 TS

ŸŸŸŸŸ **Rising Vineyard Chardonnay 2016** Rating 93 **To** 2025 $45 PR
Yarra Valley Merlot 2015 Rating 93 **To** 2023 $35 JF
Yarra Valley Pinot Noir 2016 Rating 92 **To** 2023 $35 JF
Pinot Noir Chardonnay 2013 Rating 92 **To** 2017 $35 TS
The Dr's Block Pinot Noir 2016 Rating 90 **To** 2026 $50 PR

Coliban Valley Wines   ★★★☆

313 Metcalfe-Redesdale Road, Metcalfe, Vic 3448 **Region** Heathcote
T 0417 312 098 **www**.colibanvalleywines.com.au **Open** W'ends 10–5
Winemaker Helen Miles **Est.** 1997 **Dozens** 300 **Vyds** 4.4ha
Helen Miles, who has a degree in science, and partner Greg Miles have planted 2.8ha of shiraz, 1.2ha of cabernet and 0.4ha of merlot near Metcalfe, in the cooler southwest corner of Heathcote. The granitic soils and warm climate allow organic principles to be used successfully. The shiraz is dry-grown, while the cabernet sauvignon and merlot receive minimal irrigation.

ŢŢŢŢŢ **Heathcote Riesling 2016** No-frills fermentation through to dryness, and the wine is a pleasing surprise for a region not noted for its rieslings. It has not only good lemon and lime fruit, but excellent natural crisp acidity that energises the mouthfeel and aftertaste. Screwcap. 12.5% alc. **Rating** 92 **To** 2026 $20 ✪

Collector Wines ★★★★★

12 Bourke Street, Collector, NSW 2581 (postal) **Region** Canberra District
T (02) 6116 8722 **www**.collectorwines.com.au **Open** Not
Winemaker Alex McKay **Est.** 2007 **Dozens** 3000
Owner and winemaker Alex McKay makes exquisitely detailed wines, bending to the dictates of inclement weather on his doorstep, heading elsewhere if need be. He was part of a talented team at Hardys' Kamberra Winery, and when it was closed down by Hardys' new owner CHAMP, decided to stay in the district. He is not known to speak much, and when he does, his voice is very quiet. So you have to remain alert to appreciate his unparalleled sense of humour. No such attention is needed for his wines, which are consistently excellent, their elegance appropriate for their maker. Exports to The Netherlands and Japan.

ŢŢŢŢŢ **Lamp Lit Canberra District Marsanne 2016** This assemblage of Mediterranean varieties (7% roussanne and 6% viognier, along with the marsanne) tastes fully ripe. An achievement of assiduous viticulture, transformed into a waxy, textural wine of considerable detail by skilful winemaking. Each parcel underwent full mlf following fermentation in a combination of steel tank and oak. Viognier's apricot, exotica and honeysuckle leaps over the pack aromatically, while the rest find a flinty confluence with this sort of blend's natural proclivity for richness. Screwcap. 12.9% alc. **Rating** 95 **To** 2024 $33 NG ✪
Reserve Canberra District Shiraz 2015 Optimally ripe and threaded with a fine needle of the pepper and ground spice that mark fine, cool climate Australian shiraz. Star anise and clove waft across a wave of dark cherry and blue-fruit allusion. Aromatic, with 2% of viognier in the blend, the wine is medium-bodied, uncoiling its multitude of layers with time in the glass. The finish is granitic, crunchy, firm, long and soothing, with the tannins and spice sheathing and guiding the fruit, but never drying it out. Screwcap. 13% alc. **Rating** 95 **To** 2030 $59 NG

ŢŢŢŢŢ **City West Riesling 2016 Rating** 93 **To** 2028 $36 NG
Marked Tree Red Canberra Shiraz 2015 Rating 92 **To** 2023 $28 NG
Shoreline Canberra Sangiovese 2016 Rating 92 **To** 2018 $25 NG ✪
Rose Red City Canberra Sangiovese 2015 Rating 92 **To** 2018 $33 NG

Colmar Estate ★★★★★

790 Pinnacle Road, Orange, NSW 2800 **Region** Orange
T 0419 977 270 **www**.colmarestate.com.au **Open** W'ends & public hols 10.30–5
Winemaker Chris Derrez, Lucy Maddox **Est.** 2013 **Dozens** 2000 **Vyds** 5.9ha
The inspiration behind the name is clear when you find that owners Bill Shrapnel and his wife Jane have long loved the wines of Alsace: Colmar is the main town in that region. The Shrapnels realised a long-held ambition when they purchased an established, high-altitude (980m) vineyard in May 2013. Everything they have done has turned to gold, notably grafting cabernet sauvignon to pinot noir, merlot to chardonnay, and shiraz to pinot gris. The plantings are now 1.51ha of pinot noir (clones 777, 115 and MV6), 1.25ha of chardonnay (clones 95, 96 and P58), 1.24ha of riesling and lesser quantities of sauvignon blanc, pinot gris and traminer.

ŢŢŢŢŢ **Block 1 Orange Chardonnay 2015** Hand-picked from just eight rows of P58 clone planted in '91, matured in French puncheons (50% new) with lees stirring. This is a very elegant and graceful chardonnay, picked at precisely the right time, and made with sensitivity, in particular the amount of new oak. It all comes together perfectly, white peach and nectarine to the fore, citrussy acidity brining the long finish to a conclusion. Screwcap. 13% alc. **Rating** 96 **To** 2023 $38 ✪

Orange Riesling 2016 From an excellent riesling site, the depth in this wine shows what can be achieved at 11.5% alc. A charming bouquet with green apple, subtle citrus and floral aromas in play. Tight and fine-boned on the palate, the length of flavour is a feature. Screwcap. **Rating** 95 **To** 2024 $28 SC ○

Orange Chardonnay 2015 Three trophies at the Orange Wine Show '16, including Best Wine of Show. Early picking has not resulted in a preponderance of grapefruit – if anything, the reverse. Nor has the small amount of new oak (if any) held the wine back. Screwcap. 12.5% alc. **Rating** 95 **To** 2023 $32 ○

Block 6 Orange Riesling 2016 Hand-picked, destemmed and crushed, cool-fermented with cultured yeast on light solids, matured in stainless steel. Cleverly made, the light solids giving texture offset by barely perceptible residual sugar. Floral citrus blossom aromas are followed by flavours of lime and green apple tied together by balanced acidity. Screwcap. 12% alc. **Rating** 94 **To** 2026 $32

Orange Gewurztraminer 2016 Trophy Best Other White Orange Wine Show '16. Unequivocally varietal bouquet, with lychee, musk stick and Turkish Delight all putting their hands up. The palate is often more problematic with gewurztraminer, but this is well done, with delicate but persistent flavour and fine acidity. No overt sweetness, no hardness. Screwcap. 13% alc. **Rating** 94 **To** 2018 $28 SC ○

Block 3 Orange Pinot Noir 2015 Clones 115, 777 and MV6, hand-picked, destemmed, various batches crushed or left as whole berries, 3 days cold soak, warm-fermented, 9–14 days on skins, matured in French puncheons (33% new) for 11 months. With another 3 years in bottle this wine will have a 10+-year drinking window. Intense red, black and morello cherry fruit with an opposing force of tannin and acidity. Balance is key. Screwcap. 13.5% alc. **Rating** 94 **To** 2028 $45

♥♥♥♥♡ **Orange Pinot Rose 2016 Rating** 92 **To** 2018 $26 SC

Colvin Wines ★★★★

19 Boyle Street, Mosman, NSW 2088 (postal) **Region** Hunter Valley
T (02) 9908 7886 **www.**colvinwines.com.au **Open** Not
Winemaker Andrew Spinaze, Mark Richardson **Est.** 1999 **Dozens** 500 **Vyds** 5.2ha
In 1990 Sydney lawyer John Colvin and wife Robyn purchased the De Beyers Vineyard, which has a history going back to the second half of the 19th century. By 1967, when a syndicate bought 35ha of the original vineyard site, no vines remained. The syndicate planted semillon on the alluvial soil of the creek flats and shiraz on the red clay hillsides. Up to 1998 all the grapes were sold to Tyrrell's, but since '99 quantities have been made for the Colvin Wines label. These include Sangiovese, from a little over 1ha of vines planted by John in '96.

♥♥♥♥♥ **De Beyers Vineyard Hunter Valley Chardonnay 2016** Only 25 dozen bottles made, and there is a marked oak input from the single barrel. That said, there is good varietal fruit, more stone fruit than citrus, and it has refused to be bowed by the oak. Screwcap. 12% alc. **Rating** 94 **To** 2023 $65

♥♥♥♥♡ **De Beyers Vineyard Hunter Valley Semillon 2015 Rating** 93 **To** 2025 $35
Museum Release De Beyers Sangiovese 2007 Rating 90 **To** 2022 $45

Condie Estate ★★★★☆

480 Heathcote-Redesdale Road, Heathcote, Vic 3523 **Region** Heathcote
T 0404 480 422 **www.**condie.com.au **Open** W'ends & public hols 11–5
Winemaker Richie Condie **Est.** 2001 **Dozens** 1500 **Vyds** 6.8ha
Richie Condie worked as a corporate risk manager for a multinational company off the back of a Bachelor of Commerce degree, but after establishing Condie Estate, completed several viticulture and winemaking courses, including a diploma of winemaking at Dookie. Having first established 2.4ha of shiraz, Richie and wife Rosanne followed with 2ha of sangiovese and 0.8ha of viognier. In 2010 they purchased a 1.6ha vineyard that had been planted in 1990, where they have established a winery and cellar door. Richie says to anyone thinking

of going into wine production: 'Go and work in a small vineyard and winery for at least one year before you start out for yourself. You need to understand how much hard physical work is involved in planting a vineyard, looking after it, making the wine, and then selling it.'

ŶŶŶŶŶ **The Max Shiraz 2015** Vibrant purple-crimson; this top wine is a barrel selection – all up 30% new French oak barriques. The spicy, charry characters are still settling into the wine. Florals, pepper and dark fruits tussle for a lead role yet combine harmoniously. The palate soars, with suppleness of the fruit and tannins, and citrussy acidity. Screwcap. 14.6% alc. **Rating** 95 **To** 2032 $50 JF

ŶŶŶŶŶ **The Gwen Shiraz 2015 Rating** 93 **To** 2028 $28 JF
Giarracca Sangiovese 2016 Rating 92 **To** 2027 $30 JF

Conte Estate Wines ★★★★

270 Sand Road, McLaren Flat, SA 5171 **Region** McLaren Vale
T (08) 8383 0183 **www.**conteestatewines.com.au **Open** By appt
Winemaker Danial Conte **Est.** 2003 **Dozens** 5000 **Vyds** 77ha
The Conte family has a large vineyard, predominantly established since 1960 but with 2.5ha of shiraz planted 100 years earlier. The vineyard includes shiraz, grenache, cabernet sauvignon, sauvignon blanc and chardonnay. While continuing to sell a large proportion of the production, winemaking has become a larger part of the business. Exports to the US, Canada and China.

ŶŶŶŶŶ **La Vita Nuda McLaren Vale Vermentino 2014** Crushed and pressed in an airbag press, the unclarified juice cool-fermented in stainless steel, 9 months on lees. The bouquet is (unexpectedly) very aromatic, with pine tree/pine nuts and citrus zest providing plenty of interest; the palate takes some of those characters and adds pear and apple. Screwcap. 12.5% alc. **Rating** 90 **To** 2020 $20 ✪
Nuovo Cammino McLaren Vale Aglianico 2014 There's reason to stop and take note of this southern Italian variety, with its maraschino cherry fruit tamed by spicy/earthy/wild herb notes on the aftertaste. It has sultry Italian maiden charm that keeps your eyes on it. Screwcap. 13.5% alc. **Rating** 90 **To** 2022 $25
Sticky Gecko Noble Rot McLaren Vale Gewurztraminer 2010 Bronze-gold in colour, it challenges the d'Arenberg super-stickies with its harvest at 23° baume; extremely luscious, with spiced mandarin and cumquat flavours, it has the all-important acidity to provide balance, but does demand a rich dessert to be anointed with this wine. 500ml. Screwcap. 10.5% alc. **Rating** 90 **To** 2020 $25

ŶŶŶŶ **Primrose Lane McLaren Vale Chardonnay 2016 Rating** 89 **To** 2020 $25

Cooks Lot ★★★★★

Ferment, 87 Hill Street, Orange, NSW 2800 **Region** Orange
T (02) 9550 3228 **www.**cookslot.com.au **Open** Tues–Sat 11–5
Winemaker Duncan Cook **Est.** 2002 **Dozens** 4000
Duncan Cook began making wines for his eponymous brand in 2002, while undertaking his oenology degree at CSU. He completed his degree in '10, and now works with a number of small growers from Orange wishing to be part of the production of wines with distinctive regional character. In '12 Duncan transferred his business from Mudgee to Orange, the current releases focusing on grapes grown in Orange. Exports to China.

ŶŶŶŶŶ **Allotment No. 333 Orange Riesling 2016** This is a very smart riesling with exceptional focus, length and purity, the key its chalky acidity permeating bitter lemon fruit, leaving the mouth asking for more asap. The National Cool Climate Wine Show isn't a major show (three trophies), and the Highland Wine Show (gold medal) even less so, but the success of the wine was fully deserved. Screwcap. 11.5% alc. **Rating** 95 **To** 2036 $22 ✪
Allotment No. 1010 Orange Shiraz 2015 Attractive wine: the colour is good, the bouquet expressive and aromatic with spice-infused black cherry fruit, the medium-bodied palate lining up in support. Here, too, black cherry leads the way,

the supple texture driven by fine, ripe tannins and well handled oak. Cooks Lot has found its kitchen. Screwcap. 13.5% alc. **Rating** 95 **To** 2030 $22 ✪

Allotment No. 8 Handpicked Orange Shiraz 2014 Hand-picked, open wild-yeast fermented, plunged four times daily, free-run juice and pressings matured separately in French oak for 12 months. Bright, clear crimson; while only just medium-bodied in extract, this has intense red berry/cherry aromas and flavours complexed by notes of bramble and spice, the length impressive. Trophy Best Shiraz Orange Wine Show. Screwcap. 13.5% alc. **Rating** 95 **To** 2029 $46

Allotment No. 666 Orange Pinot Gris 2016 Most cool-fermented with some untoasted oak in stainless steel, a small portion separately fermented in barrel. Absolutely entitled to use gris, its mouth-coating fruit bordering on outright fleshy; pear and nougat are fenced in by tight acidity. Trophy Best Pinot Gris Orange Wine Show. Screwcap. 13% alc. **Rating** 94 **To** 2020 $22 ✪

Allotment No. 9 Handpicked Orange Pinot Noir 2015 Wild-yeast fermented, some whole bunches, plunged four times daily, free-run juice and pressings matured separately in French puncheons for 12 months. Has much attitude, if not downright aggression (in pinot terms); fragrant dark cherry/berry fruit plus some whole bunch/forest floor nuances. The rich palate takes off from an earthy/foresty bed, and earned it three trophies (including Best Wine of Show) at the Australian Highland Wine Show. Screwcap. 13.5% alc. **Rating** 94 **To** 2027 $35

ＹＹＹＹＹ **Allotment No. 168 Chardonnay 2015** Rating 92 To 2023 $22 ✪
Allotment No. 1111 Pinot Noir 2015 Rating 92 To 2023 $22 ✪
Allotment No. 8989 Cabernet Merlot 2015 Rating 92 To 2025 $22 ✪
Allotment No. 689 Sauvignon Blanc 2016 Rating 90 To 2017 $22
Allotment No. 365 Rose 2016 Rating 90 To 2017 $22

Coolangatta Estate   ★★★★★

1335 Bolong Road, Shoalhaven Heads, NSW 2535 **Region** Shoalhaven Coast
T (02) 4448 7131 **www**.coolangattaestate.com.au **Open** 7 days 10–5
Winemaker Tyrrell's **Est.** 1988 **Dozens** 5000 **Vyds** 10.5ha
Coolangatta Estate is part of an 150ha resort with accommodation, restaurants, golf course, etc; some of the oldest buildings were convict-built in 1822. The standard of viticulture is exceptionally high (immaculate Scott Henry trellising), and the contract winemaking is wholly professional. Coolangatta has a habit of bobbing up with medals at Sydney and Canberra wine shows, including gold medals for its mature Semillons. In its own backyard, Coolangatta won the trophy for Best Wine of Show at the South Coast Wine Show for 14 consecutive years.

ＹＹＹＹＹ **Aged Release Individual Vineyard Wollstonecraft Semillon 2009** The vivid quartz-green colour is a sure sign of a wine that has seven trophies and nine gold medals to its credit. It has entered what will be a long plateau of perfection; lemongrass, lemon curd and Meyer lemon juice fruit flavours stream across a perfectly balanced and long palate. Screwcap. 11% alc. **Rating** 97 **To** 2029 $40 ✪

ＹＹＹＹＹ **Individual Vineyard Wollstonecraft Semillon 2016** From a single estate block planted in '96, whole-bunch presssed, cool-fermented in stainless steel. Slightly more weight on the mid-palate than the Estate, but it's odd that there are two estate wines made by Tyrrell's using the same vinification methods that sell at the same price. Screwcap. 12% alc. **Rating** 95 **To** 2021 $25 ✪

Estate Grown Semillon 2016 From estate vines planted in '03 and '06, whole-bunch pressed, cool-fermented in stainless steel. There is little more to the palate but it follows the same path as the Wollstonecraft. Bright and juicy, with citrus/Meyer lemon fruit, finishing with crisp acidity. Gold medals Perth and Cowra wine shows '16. Screwcap. 11.6% alc. **Rating** 95 **To** 2026 $25 ✪

ＹＹＹＹ **Alexander Berry Chardonnay 2016** Rating 89 To 2021 $25

Coombe Farm

673–675 Maroondah Highway, Coldstream, Vic 3770 **Region** Yarra Valley
T (03) 9739 0173 **www**.coombeyarravalley.com.au **Open** 7 days 10–5 (Wed–Sun Jun–Aug)
Winemaker Nicole Esdaile **Est.** 1999 **Dozens** 7000 **Vyds** 60ha

Once the Australian home of world-famous opera singer Dame Nellie Melba, The Melba Estate is now also the home of Coombe Farm. The renovated motor house and stable block of the estate now house the cellar door as well as a providore, gallery and restaurant which overlooks the gardens. Tours of the gardens are also available. The quality of the estate-grown wines has been consistently good. Exports to the UK and Japan.

Tribute Series Evelyn Yarra Valley Chardonnay 2015 This is more powerful, more fruity, more complex and distinctly longer than its varietal sibling, yet retains the elegance of that wine. Even in this wine, the amount of new oak and the time in oak is abstemious, leading to the question where is the X-factor, and will it appear with more time in bottle? Screwcap. 13% alc. **Rating** 94 **To** 2023 $50

Yarra Valley Pinot Gris 2016 Rating 93 To 2018 $25 ✪
Yarra Valley Chardonnay 2015 Rating 92 To 2022 $37
Yarra Valley Pinot Noir 2016 Rating 90 To 2031 $37
Tribute Series Fullerton Pinot Noir 2014 Rating 90 To 2019 $50

Cooper Burns

494 Research Road, Nuriootpa, SA 5355 **Region** Barossa Valley
T (08) 7513 7606 **www**.cooperburns.com.au **Open** By appt
Winemaker Russell Burns **Est.** 2004 **Dozens** 3000

Cooper Burns is the winemaking partnership of Mark Cooper and Russell Burns. It is a virtual winery focusing on small batch, handmade wine from the Eden Valley and the northern end of the Barossa Valley. Production has been increased to add a Riesling and Grenache to the Shirazs. Exports to the US and Hong Kong.

The Bloody Valentine Barossa Valley Shiraz 2013 Almost a drag queen dancing in inky mascara, vermilion to opaque; giddy with a heady perfume of violet, boysenberry, mulberry and dark cherry. Before skidding across the floor, the high heels are replaced by platform boots. Some smoked meat, tar, anise, vanilla and finely massaged tannins are interwoven across the plush veneer, turning the parade in the direction of savouriness. Impeccably made. Smooth, seamless and polished. Diam. 14.5% alc. **Rating** 95 **To** 2028 $100 NG

Eden Valley Riesling 2015 Rating 93 To 2026 $22 NG ✪

Cooter & Cooter

82 Almond Grove Road, Whites Valley, SA 5172 **Region** McLaren Vale
T 0438 766 178 **www**.cooter.com.au **Open** Not
Winemaker James Cooter **Est.** 2012 **Dozens** 1800 **Vyds** 23ha

James and Kimberley Cooter have taken the slow road to establishing their business; the cursive script on the wine labels has been that of various Cooter businesses in SA since 1847. James came from a family with a modern history of more than 20 years in the wine industry. Kimberley is also a hands-on winemaker, having spent her early years with father Walter Clappis, a veteran McLaren Vale winemaker. Now, with over 20 vintages between them, she and James have established their own vineyard on the southern slopes of Whites Valley. It has 18ha of shiraz and 3ha of cabernet sauvignon planted in 1996, and 2ha of old vine grenache planted in the '50s. They also buy Clare Valley grapes to make Riesling.

Watervale Riesling 2016 From two small vineyards, kept separate until final blending, both conventionally fermented (other than both kept on lees). Dyed in the wool Watervale riesling: bracingly fresh and crisp with unsweetened lemon and lime, with pith and zest notes also on duty. Good length, too. Screwcap. 12% alc. **Rating** 93 **To** 2026 $22 ✪

McLaren Vale Shiraz 2015 Includes 5% grenache, separately vinified and matured, open-fermented for 14 days, matured in used French oak for 15 months. Wears its region on its sleeve, opening and finishing with savoury dark chocolate, but providing lots of mid-palate blackberry fruit with a starlet of red ex the grenache. Has broad appeal. Screwcap. 14% alc. **Rating** 91 **To** 2030 $22 **○**

Adelaide Hills Pinot Noir 2016 Two vineyards and two clones: 114 at Piccadilly, MV6 at Kuitpo, picked two weeks apart, kept separate until blending, 25% whole bunches, 7 days on skins. A relatively light-bodied pinot, with purity rather than power or complexity the essence of the wine. Largely red-fruited, it soothes the mouth, and leaves no doubt about its varietal expression. Screwcap. 13% alc. **Rating** 90 **To** 2021 $30

Coppabella of Tumbarumba ★★★★★

424 Tumbarumba Road, Tumbarumba, NSW 2653 (postal) **Region** Tumbarumba
T (02) 6382 7997 **Open** Not
Winemaker Jason Brown **Est.** 2011 **Dozens** 4000 **Vyds** 71.9ha
Coppabella is owned by Jason and Alecia Brown, owners of the highly successful Moppity Vineyards in Hilltops. They became aware of the quality of Tumbarumba chardonnay and pinot noir, in particular the quality of the grapes from the 71ha Coppabella vineyard, when purchasing grapes for the Moppity Vineyards business. This was the second vineyard established (in 1993) by the region's founder, Ian Cowell, but frost and other problems led him to lease the vineyard to Southcorp, an arrangement that continued until 2007. The reversion of the management of the vineyard coincided with several failed vintages, and this precipitated a decision by the owner to close the vineyard and remove the vines. In October '11, at the last moment, the Browns purchased the vineyard, and have since invested heavily in it, rehabilitating the vines and grafting a number of blocks to the earlier-ripening Dijon clones of pinot noir and chardonnay. Coppabella is run as an entirely separate venture from Moppity.

🍷🍷🍷🍷🍷 **The Crest Single Vineyard Chardonnay 2016** Hand-picked, part whole-bunch pressed and wild-yeast fermented in barriques and puncheons (30% new), part fermented in stainless steel and kept on lees for 6 months. The bouquet is complex and attractive, but it's the power, focus, drive, length and purity of the palate that takes you prisoner from the first sip. It scales the heights of white peach, green apple and pink grapefruit, the 30% new oak swallowed by the fruit, acidity a given. Terrific value. Screwcap. 13.5% alc. **Rating** 96 **To** 2026 $35 **○**

Sirius Single Vineyard Chardonnay 2016 From Block 20, hand-picked, whole-bunch pressed direct to French hogsheads for fermentation and 9 months maturation. Intense cool climate style, grapefruit pith, zest and juice dominating the lesser white peach/pear contributions. The oak was/is an important contributor to a good wine. Screwcap. 12.5% alc. **Rating** 95 **To** 2023 $60

Single Vineyard Chardonnay 2015 It must be a very, very difficult task keeping track of the Moppity, Lock & Key and Coppabella Chardonnays, all variously plundering Tumbarumba and/or the Hilltops at prices often close to each other. This has a degree more ripeness than the '16 Lock & Key, and is positively silky in the mouth. Yes, it's a different vintage, but there's only a dollar difference in the price. Screwcap. 13% alc. **Rating** 95 **To** 2022 $26 **○**

Procella I Hilltops Shiraz 2015 Medium to full-bodied, but with flavour and structured complexity; there are spicy/cedary notes woven through the cherry and blackberry fruits on the bouquet and palate, harmonious and juicy. Very nice wine, balance its key asset. Screwcap. 14% alc. **Rating** 95 **To** 2035 $45

Procella III Hilltops Cabernet Sauvignon 2015 Deep, healthy colour; a very powerful full-bodied cabernet that has repaid the investment in the vineyard and winery. Blackcurrant/cassis, bay leaf, dried herbs and cedary oak come through the vigour and purity on the finish. Give it a decade and you'll have a great wine, then double up for another decade. Screwcap. 14% alc. **Rating** 95 **To** 2040 $45

The Crest Single Vineyard Pinot Noir 2015 777, MV6 and D5V12 clones from varying elevations in the vineyard, hand-picked, wild-yeast fermented, 30% whole bunches; matured for 12 months in French barriques. Excellent colour; you will find, if you didn't already know, that Jason Brown pinpoints the Coppabella (and Moppity) brands with deadly precision, over-delivering on quality while leaving the money in the till. This has abundant dark cherry fruits and the texture and structure fit well. Screwcap. 13.5% alc. **Rating** 94 **To** 2029 $35

♥♥♥♥♡ Single Vineyard Sauvignon Blanc 2016 Rating 92 To 2018 $26
Single Vineyard Pinot Noir 2016 Rating 91 To 2021 $26

Corduroy   ★★★★

15 Bridge Terrace, Victor Harbor, SA 5211 (postal) **Region** Adelaide Hills
T 0405 123 272 **www**.corduroywines.com.au **Open** Not
Winemaker Phillip LeMessurier **Est.** 2009 **Dozens** 320
Phillip and Eliza Le Messurier have moved to the Adelaide Hills, but are continuing the model they originally created in the Hunter under the tutelage of Andrew Thomas at Thomas Wines. In the new environment, they are matching place and variety to good effect.

♥♥♥♥♥ Pedro's Paddock Adelaide Hills Pinot Noir 2016 Very different from its Single Vineyard sibling, with a greater volume of fruit on the bouquet and palate, ditto complexity. It is all MV6 clone, and has been wild-yeast fermented. Is there some whole bunch here? Spicy, savoury forest floor notes dot the landscape of the wine from the first whiff through to the satisfying finish and aftertaste. Screwcap. 12.2% alc. **Rating** 95 **To** 2026 $42

♥♥♥♥♡ Single Vineyard Adelaide Hills Shiraz 2015 Rating 93 To 2035 $34
Single Vineyard Clare Valley Riesling 2016 Rating 91 To 2026 $22 **✪**
Mansfield Rathmine Vineyard Chardonnay 2016 Rating 91 To 2026 $42
Single Vineyard Adelaide Hills Pinot Noir 2016 Rating 91 To 2023 $28
Single Vineyard Adelaide Hills Chardonnay 2016 Rating 90 To 2019 $28

Coriole   ★★★★★

Chaffeys Road, McLaren Vale, SA 5171 **Region** McLaren Vale
T (08) 8323 8305 **www**.coriole.com **Open** Mon–Fri 10–5, w'ends & public hols 11–5
Winemaker Alex Sherrah **Est.** 1967 **Dozens** 32 000 **Vyds** 48.5ha
While Coriole was not established until 1967, the cellar door and gardens date back to 1860, when the original farm houses that now constitute the cellar door were built. The oldest shiraz forming part of the estate plantings dates back to 1917, and since '85, Coriole has been an Australian pioneer of sangiovese and the Italian white variety fiano. Shiraz has 65% of the plantings, and it is for this variety that Coriole is best known. Exports to all major markets.

♥♥♥♥♥ The Soloist McLaren Vale Shiraz 2014 From a single estate block planted in '69, matured in French oak. This sings a different song from its Estate sibling, with more intensity, cut and length to the expressive and complex palate. This is McLaren Vale at its best, and carries its alcohol with consummate ease. Screwcap. 14.7% alc. **Rating** 96 **To** 2034 $45 **✪**
Lloyd McLaren Vale Shiraz 2014 It's easy to be seduced by the beautiful deep purple colour but it's the flavours, the palate, that really matter. They star in this complex wine. Savoury toned, full-bodied, ripe and concentrated, and yet there's this line of definition and detail. The oak, sitting at 30% new French hogsheads, is seamlessly integrated. Screwcap. 14.5% alc. **Rating** 96 **To** 2036 $100 JF
McLaren Vale Sangiovese 2015 Coriole was the first to plant sangiovese in Australia ('85), this wine being its 29th consecutive release. Its colour is bright and clear crimson, the bouquet and palate riding high on a cornucopia of cherries of every description, the tannins ripe and interwoven with the fruit. A seriously good sangio. Screwcap. 14.5% alc. **Rating** 96 **To** 2030 $27 **✪**
McLaren Vale Fiano 2016 Tip-top fiano with its heady aromas of mandarin, lemon rind and honeysuckle, then it teases out a raft of flavours onto a palate full of texture – Mediterranean herbs, creamed honey. Flintiness and chalk-like acidity are the final touch. Boom. Screwcap. 13% alc. **Rating** 95 **To** 2020 $27 JF **✪**

The Soloist McLaren Vale Shiraz 2015 It glides and swirls; this wine takes you on a journey and the ride is so smooth. It starts with a single vineyard, the glorious fruit shining strongly through the 80% new French oak hogsheads (aged 2 years). This has power and presence. The palate is enveloped with ripe glossy tannins, long and persistent on the finish. Screwcap. 14.7% alc. **Rating** 95 **To** 2030 $45 JF

McLaren Vale Nero 2016 Coriole has long championed Italian grape varieties, with nero d'Avola turning into one of its stars. This is a beauty, with a core of juicy red fruits, especially raspberry, and a whisper of Mediterranean dried herbs, supple tannins, a lighter frame and a neat acid line keeping it so damn lively. Three trophies, including Wine of Show at the Australian Alternative Varieties Wine Show '16. Screwcap. 14% alc. **Rating** 95 **To** 2020 $25 JF ○

Estate McLaren Vale Shiraz 2014 Estate-grown vines approximately 40yo. A delicious medium to full-bodied, generously endowed shiraz. It is supple and velvety, black fruits encased in black chocolate, the tannins fine and soft, the length faultless. Screwcap. 14.5% alc. **Rating** 94 **To** 2029 $30 ○

Estate McLaren Vale Cabernet Sauvignon 2014 Matured for 18 months in French oak. A complex amalgam of black fruits, rosemary and thyme married with bitter chocolate and fine tannins. The tannins and oak are positive contributions to texture and structure. Screwcap. 14.5% alc. **Rating** 94 **To** 2034 $30 ○

♥♥♥♥♡ **McLaren Vale Picpoul 2016** Rating 93 To 2020 $25 JF ○
Estate McLaren Vale Shiraz 2015 Rating 93 To 2026 $30 JF
Redstone McLaren Vale Shiraz 2015 Rating 93 To 2021 $20 JF ○
Scarce Earth Galaxidia Shiraz 2015 Rating 93 To 2032 $60 JF
Dancing Fig Mourvedre Grenache Shiraz 2015 Rating 93 To 2025 $25 JF ○
Mary Kathleen Cabernet Merlot 2014 Rating 90 To 2029 $65 JF
Estate McLaren Vale Cabernet Sauvignon 2015 Rating 90 To 2024 $30 JF
McLaren Vale Sangiovese Shiraz 2015 Rating 90 To 2020 $20 JF ○
Vita McLaren Vale Sangiovese 2014 Rating 90 To 2019 $65 JF

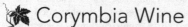

🍂 Corymbia Wine ★★★★

30 Nolan Avenue, Upper Swan, WA 6069 **Region** Swan Valley
T 0439 973 195 **www**.corymbiawine.com.au **Open** Not
Winemaker Genevieve Mann **Est.** 2013 **Dozens** 200 **Vyds** 0.72ha
This is a Flying Winemaker exercise in reverse. Rob Mann was chief winemaker at Cape Mentelle in the Margaret River, where he and wife Genevieve lived, but Rob's father had established a family vineyard in the Swan Valley more than 25 years ago, Rob and his father working together in Rob's early years as a winemaker. The Mann team settled on 0.4ha of tempranillo, 0.2ha of malbec and 0.12ha of cabernet sauvignon for the Corymbia wine production, but just to make the story more complex, it is Genevieve, not Rob, who makes the wines. They now live in the Napa Valley in California, where Rob is chief winemaker for the illustrious Newton Winery, coming back for what is obviously a pretty short vintage.

♥♥♥♥♥ **Corymbia 2014** A blend of tempranillo and cabernet sauvignon. Very good colour; a particularly impressive wine given the constraints of the heat of the region; spicy/savoury components add both freshness and complexity to the black cherry fruits. Screwcap. 13.5% alc. **Rating** 94 **To** 2024 $35

♥♥♥♥♡ **Corymbia 2016** Rating 92 To 2026 $35

Costanzo & Sons ★★★★

602 Tames Road, Strathbogie, Vic 3666 **Region** Strathbogie Ranges
T 0447 740 055 **www**.costanzo.com.au **Open** By appt
Winemaker Ray Nadeson (Contract) **Est.** 2011 **Dozens** 500 **Vyds** 6ha
This is the venture of Joe Costanzo and Cindy Heath, Joe having grapegrowing in his DNA. He was raised on his parents' 20ha vineyard in NSW on the Murray River, the family business selling grapes to Brown Brothers, Seppelt, Bullers and Miranda Wines. By the age of 17 he had

decided to follow in their footsteps, working full-time in vineyards, and studying viticulture for five years. He and Cindy searched for the perfect vineyard, and in 2011 finally acquired one that had been planted between 1993 and '94 to 1.5ha each of sauvignon blanc and chardonnay, and 3ha of pinot noir.

ŸŸŸŸŸ Single Vineyard Reserve Strathbogie Ranges Sauvignon Blanc 2015
Wild yeast ferment in French oak puncheons and 10 months in barrel. Loire Valley inspired and well executed. Classic gunflint aromas with varietal and oak characters playing a part, and a textured, almost unctuous mouthfeel; the subtle, savoury sauvignon flavours persist through the palate and long finish. A lovely wine. Screwcap. 14.5% alc. **Rating** 94 **To** 2022 $40 SC

ŸŸŸŸŸ Methode Traditionelle Blanc de Noir 2014 Rating 90 **To** 2019 $40 TS

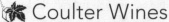 ## Coulter Wines   ★★★★★

6 Third Avenue, Tanunda, SA 5352 (postal) **Region** Adelaide Hills
T 0448 741 773 **www**.coulterwines.com **Open** Not
Winemaker Chris Coulter **Est.** 2015 **Dozens** 250
Chris Coulter had a 22-year previous life as a chef, but fell in love with wine in the early 1990s, and managed to fit in a vintage at Coldstream Hills as a cellar rat. In 2007 he undertook a winemaking degree, and secured work with Australian Vintage Limited, gaining large volume winemaking experience first in Mildura and then at the then Chateau Yaldara in the Barossa Valley, remaining there through 2014 under Australian Vintage Limited, and thereafter as part of the 1847 winemaking team after its acquisition of the Yaldara site. Coulter Wines was born in the 2015 vintage as a side project, making wines from another universe – adding nothing other than SO_2, movements are by gravity, and the wine is unfiltered where practicable. He purchases and hand-picks grapes from premium vineyards in the Adelaide Hills (chardonnay, sangiovese and barbera). A Mataro is planned for 2017.

ŸŸŸŸŸ C1 Adelaide Hills Chardonnay 2016 Single vineyard, whole-bunch pressed, full solids juice wild-yeast fermented in reshaved Hungarian oak, lees stirred, not fined or filtered. Delicious wine, perfectly ripened grapes with evenly poised white stone fruit (white peach, nectarine) and citrus (grapefruit) gives energy and velocity to the palate, oak merely a vehicle. Screwcap. 13% alc. **Rating** 95 **To** 2026 $30 ✪
C2 Adelaide Hills Sangiovese 2016 Hand-picked from a single vineyard, 30% whole bunches, 2-day carbonic maceration, basket-pressed, matured in used French hogsheads for 5 months, unfined. Bright, clear crimson; totally delicious, silky and slippery, the tannins totally domesticated (remarkable without fining), the balance impeccable. Screwcap. 14% alc. **Rating** 95 **To** 2022 $28 ✪

ŸŸŸŸŸ C5 Adelaide Hills Barbera 2016 Rating 91 **To** 2021 $28

Cowaramup Wines   ★★★★☆

19 Tassel Road, Cowaramup, WA 6284 **Region** Margaret River
T (08) 9755 5195 **www**.cowaramupwines.com.au **Open** By appt
Winemaker Naturaliste Vintners (Bruce Dukes) **Est.** 1995 **Dozens** 4000 **Vyds** 17ha
Russell and Marilyn Reynolds run a biodynamic vineyard with the aid of sons Cameron (viticulturist) and Anthony (assistant winemaker). Plantings began in 1996 and include merlot, cabernet sauvignon, shiraz, semillon, chardonnay and sauvignon blanc. Notwithstanding low yields and the discipline that biodynamic grapegrowing entails, wine prices are modest. Wines are released under the Cowaramup, Clown Fish and New School labels.

ŸŸŸŸŸ Reserve Limited Edition Ellensbrook Margaret River Chardonnay 2015
Fermented and matured for 12 months in new French oak. That oak has an impact on the wine, but not at the cost of the powerful fruit; white peach, apple and grapefruit are all in play on the long palate. Screwcap. 12.5% alc. **Rating** 96 **To** 2025 $30 ✪

ⓉⓉⓉⓉⓉ Clown Fish Sauvignon Blanc Semillon 2016 Rating 93 To 2020 $20 ○
Clown Fish Cabernet Merlot 2015 Rating 92 To 2029 $20 ○

Coward & Black Vineyards ★★★★

448 Tom Cullity Drive, Wilyabrup, WA 6280 **Region** Margaret River
T (08) 9755 6355 **www.**cowardandblack.com.au **Open** 7 days 9–5
Winemaker Clive Otto (Contract) **Est.** 1998 **Dozens** 1500 **Vyds** 9.5ha
Patrick Coward and Martin Black have been friends since they were five years old. They acquired a property directly opposite Ashbrook and on the same road as Vasse Felix, and began the slow establishment of a dry-grown vineyard; a second block followed five years later. In all there are 2.5ha each of cabernet sauvignon and shiraz, and 1.5ha each of chardonnay, semillon and sauvignon blanc. The cellar door is integrated with another of their businesses, The Margaret River Providore, which sells produce from their organic garden and olive grove.

ⓉⓉⓉⓉⓉ Margaret River Semillon Sauvignon Blanc 2016 The punchy, mouth-watering tropical fruit flavours of the sauvignon blanc are at play while the semillon holds its own with lemon balm/verbena aromatics and superfine acidity. A balanced whole. Screwcap. 12.5% alc. **Rating** 92 To 2019 $21 JF ○
Margaret River Chardonnay 2016 Oscillates. That's what this wine does. At first it seems unforgiving, lean with slightly unripe fruit and bracing acidity. Then it swings, offering some gingery spice and balanced oak nuances amid the citrus spectrum. Hedge your bets. Screwcap. 12.3% alc. **Rating** 92 To 2022 $28 JF
Margaret River Show Shiraz 2015 Apart from the mid-crimson hue, the red plums sprinkled with pepper and juniper, it's the fine and soft tannins that stand out. It's medium-bodied, savoury, and with a lick of cedary oak. Screwcap. 13.6% alc. **Rating** 92 To 2022 $27 JF
Winston Margaret River Cabernet Shiraz 2015 Equal percentages of the varieties and each aged separately in one-third new French oak for 18 months. The strength of cabernet shows aromatically with blackberry and mulberries, bay leaf and woodsy spices; some gritty shiraz tannins are a little drying and sinewy on the finish. Screwcap. 13.6% alc. **Rating** 91 To 2024 $27 JF

ⓉⓉⓉⓉ Margaret River Semillon Sauvignon Blanc 2015 Rating 89 To 2019 $21 JF

Crabtree Watervale Wines ★★★★

North Terrace, Watervale SA 5452 **Region** Clare Valley
T (08) 8843 0069 **www.**crabtreewines.com.au **Open** 7 days 10.30–4.30
Winemaker Kerri Thompson **Est.** 1979 **Dozens** 6000 **Vyds** 13.2ha
Crabtree is situated in the heart of the historic and iconic Watervale district, the tasting room and courtyard (set in the produce cellar of the original 1850s homestead) looking out over the estate vineyard. The winery was founded in 1984 by Robert Crabtree, who built a considerable reputation for medal-winning Riesling, Shiraz and Cabernet Sauvignon. In 2007 it was purchased by an independent group of wine enthusiasts; the winery firmly continues in the established tradition of estate-grown premium wines (Robert remains a shareholder).

ⓉⓉⓉⓉⓉ Riesling 2016 100% from the estate vineyard, hand-picked and sorted. The bouquet is floral, with citrus, apple and a hint of herb, the palate fleshy (in riesling terms) with ripe citrus fruits and comforting acidity on the finish and aftertaste. Screwcap. 12.5% alc. **Rating** 94 To 2026 $26 ○

ⓉⓉⓉⓉⓉ Bay of Biscay Grenache Rose 2016 Rating 90 To 2018 $22

cradle of hills ★★★★☆

76 Rogers Road, Sellicks Hill, SA 5174 **Region** McLaren Vale
T (08) 8557 4023 **www.**cradle-of-hills.com.au **Open** By appt
Winemaker Paul Smith **Est.** 2009 **Dozens** 800 **Vyds** 6.88ha
Paul Smith's introduction to wine was an unlikely one: the Royal Australian Navy, and in particular the wardroom cellar at the tender age of 19. A career change took Paul to the world

of high-performance sports, and he met his horticulturist wife Tracy. From 2005 they travelled the world with their two children, spending a couple of years in Europe, working in and learning about the great wine regions, and how fine wine is made. Paul secured a winemaking diploma, and they now have almost 7ha of cabernet sauvignon and shiraz (roughly 50% each), supplementing this with purchased grenache and mourvedre.

ŸŸŸŸŸ **Darkside McLaren Vale Shiraz Mourvedre 2013** 70% shiraz, 25% mourvedre, 5% grenache, open-fermented, hand-plunged, up to 2 weeks post-ferment maceration, basket-pressed, matured in French hogsheads (30% new) for 2 years. The fragrant, gently spicy bouquet leads into a medium-bodied palate with very good mouthfeel, length and balance, the flavours ranging through plum, red and black cherry fruit, dark chocolate coupled with silky tannins providing a savoury touch on the finish. Screwcap. 14.5% alc. **Rating** 95 **To** 2028 $29 ❂
Maritime McLaren Vale Cabernet Shiraz 2013 A 60/40% blend, open-fermented in 1.5t vats, hand-plunged, up to 2 weeks post-ferment maceration, basket-pressed, matured in French hogsheads (30% new) for 2 years. Very different from its Row 5 Cabernet Sauvignon sibling, here with the fruit foremost, bringing blackcurrant and blackberry fruit to the table, regional dark chocolate more important than cedary oak. Screwcap. 14.5% alc. **Rating** 94 **To** 2028 $29 ❂

ŸŸŸŸŸ **Old Rogue Sellicks Hill McLaren Vale Shiraz 2015** Rating 91 To 2030 $24

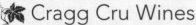

Cragg Cru Wines   ★★★★

Unit 4, 2 Whinnerah Avenue, Aldinga Beach, SA 5173 (postal) **Region** McLaren Vale
T 0432 734 574 **www**.craggcruwines.com.au **Open** Not
Winemaker Robert Cragg **Est.** 2015 **Dozens** 225
Robert Cragg was first involved in the periphery of the wine industry in 2005, when he had the task of pruning and grafting grape vines on his family property, making his first wine from those vines. He moved on to be a cellarhand at Southern Highlands Wines in Moss Vale, was appointed assistant winemaker, but almost immediately moved to the Hunter Valley in '12, where he became familiar with organic winemaking techniques. After two years he was offered a job in McLaren Vale, where he works full-time, but in spare hours and days established his business together with partner Jessica Ward. Exports to the UK, the US, Canada, Belgium, The Netherlands, Hong Kong and China.

ŸŸŸŸŸ **Single Vineyard Fiano 2016** Has that cool precision of fiano, and its textural subtext, most likely just its acidity, but it's a particular form of acidity. The fact that fiano has this standoffish nature simply encourages you to come back for more. Screwcap. 12.5% alc. **Rating** 91 **To** 2020 $22 ❂
Grenache Touriga 2016 The touriga has given the wine more colour and more flavour, not the usual role for touriga (we don't know the blend percentages). Indeed, I like this wine for its freshness and happy-go-lucky drinkability. Screwcap. 14.5% alc. **Rating** 90 **To** 2021 $25

ŸŸŸŸ **Single Vineyard Grenache 2016** Rating 89 To 2020 $25

Craiglee   ★★★★★

Sunbury Road, Sunbury, Vic 3429 **Region** Sunbury
T (03) 9744 4489 **www**.craiglee.com.au **Open** Sun & public hols 10–5
Winemaker Patrick Carmody **Est.** 1976 **Dozens** 2500 **Vyds** 9.5ha
A winery with a proud 19th-century record, Craiglee recommenced winemaking in 1976 after a prolonged hiatus. Produces one of the finest cool climate Shirazs in Australia, redolent of cherry, licorice and spice in the better (warmer) vintages, lighter-bodied in the cooler ones. Mature vines and improved viticulture have made the wines more consistent (except 2011) over the past 10 years or so. Exports to the UK, the US, Italy, Hong Kong and China.

Craigow ★★★★☆

528 Richmond Road, Cambridge, Tas 7170 **Region** Southern Tasmania
T (03) 6248 5379 **www**.craigow.com.au **Open** 7 days Christmas to Easter
Winemaker Frogmore Creek (Alain Rousseau) **Est.** 1989 **Dozens** 800 **Vyds** 8.75ha
Hobart surgeon Barry Edwards and wife Cathy have moved from being grapegrowers with
only one wine to a portfolio of impressive wines, with long-lived Riesling of particular quality,
closely attended by Pinot Noir, while continuing to sell most of their grapes.

🍷🍷🍷🍷🍷 **Pinot Noir 2015** Destemmed, wild-yeast fermented in an open 1-tonne
fermenter, pressed to French oak (20% new) for 8 months maturation. Tasmania
meets Central Otago with exceptional depth of crimson-purple colour and the
power and concentration of black cherry, spices and liqueured plum flavours. Just
when you think there is too much of a good thing, dusty/savoury tannins point
the ship in the right direction for a long voyage. Screwcap. 14% alc. **Rating** 95
To 2030 $45
Riesling 2016 Ripe stone fruit, orange blossom, quince and ginger crystal tones,
a rich, explosive riesling glimpsing the Pfalz, with a compelling thrust and parry of
powerful fruit flavours and fresh mineral tension, all careening along lime-doused
acidity. A phenolic pucker imparts further texture while punctuating the long
finish. Screwcap. 13% alc. **Rating** 94 To 2026 $32 NG

🍷🍷🍷🍷♀ **Dessert Riesling 2008** Rating 93 To 2025 $29 NG
Unwooded Chardonnay 2016 Rating 91 To 2022 $34 NG

Crawford River Wines ★★★★★

741 Hotspur Upper Road, Condah, Vic 3303 **Region** Henty
T (03) 5578 2267 **www**.crawfordriverwines.com **Open** By appt
Winemaker John and Belinda Thomson **Est.** 1975 **Dozens** 3000 **Vyds** 10.5ha
Time flies, and it seems incredible that Crawford River celebrated its 40th birthday in 2015.
Once a tiny outpost in a little-known wine region, Crawford River is a foremost producer
of Riesling (and other excellent wines) thanks to the unremitting attention to detail and skill
of its founder and winemaker, John Thomson (and moral support from wife Catherine). His
talented elder daughter Blinder has returned part-time after completing her winemaking
degree and working along the way in Marlborough (NZ), Bordeaux, Rivera del Duress
(Spain), Bolgheri and Tuscany, and the Nahe (Germany), with Crawford River filling in the
gaps. She continues working in Spain, effectively doing two vintages each year. Younger
daughter Fiona is in charge of sales and marketing. Exports to the UK.

🍷🍷🍷🍷🍷 **Riesling 2016** A wine that stops you in your tracks for it has intensity of flavour
yet feels effortless. The silk thread of acidity down the middle keeps the fine palate
in place right through to a finish that is luxuriously long. Screwcap. 13.5% alc.
Rating 96 To 2030 $45 JF ✪
Young Vines Riesling 2016 It's ready now yet will age, as these wines do. It has
plenty of flavour from fresh lemon and limes, their rind and glace too, plus a touch
of mandarin and stone fruit. The acidity is softish, chalky; there's texture and it's
pristine. Screwcap. 13.5% alc. **Rating** 95 To 2024 $32 JF ✪

🍷🍷🍷🍷♀ **Beta Sauvignon Blanc Semillon 2014** Rating 93 To 2024 $32 JF
Cabernet Merlot 2014 Rating 92 To 2022 $35 JF
Semillon Sauvignon Blanc 2013 Rating 91 To 2020 $25 JF
Rose 2016 Rating 91 To 2019 $27 JF

Credaro Family Estate ★★★★★

2175 Caves Road, Yallingup, WA 6282 **Region** Margaret River
T (08) 9756 6520 **www**.credarowines.com.au **Open** 7 days 10–5
Winemaker Dave Johnson **Est.** 1993 **Dozens** 10000 **Vyds** 150ha
The Credaro family first settled in Margaret River in 1922, migrating from northern Italy.
Initially a few small plots of vines were planted to provide the family with wine in the

European tradition. However, things began to change significantly in the '80s and '90s, and changes have continued through to 2015. The most recent has been the acquisition of a 40ha property, with 18ha of vineyard, in Wilyabrup (now called the Summus Vineyard) and the expansion of winery capacity to 1200 tonnes with 300 000 litres of additional tank space. Credaro now has seven separate vineyards (150ha in production), spread throughout the Margaret River: Credaro either owns or leases each property and grows/manages the vines with its own viticulture team. Exports to Thailand, Singapore and China.

ΨΨΨΨΨ **1000 Crowns Margaret River Chardonnay 2015** This and the '15 Kinship Chardonnay have identical estate origins: part from Credaro's most southern vineyard near Witchcliffe, part from its Metricup Vineyard. Both whole-bunch pressed, wild-yeast fermented, and fermented and matured in French oak (30% new). Absolutely stunning purity and length, and a gold-plated future. Gold medals Margaret River Wine Show '16 and Sydney International Wine Competition '16. Screwcap. 12.5% alc. **Rating** 97 **To** 2030 $65 ✪

ΨΨΨΨΨ **1000 Crowns Margaret River Shiraz 2015** Five gold medals in prestigious Aus (4) and UK (1) wine shows. Part estate-grown (Witchcliffe), part contract (Wilyabrup), whole-berry fermentation, 14+ days on skins, matured for 10 months in French oak (20% new). This is a standout shiraz, marrying elegance with intensity and length on the medium-bodied palate, with flavours of dark cherry, plum and a whisk of oak. Screwcap. 14% alc. **Rating** 96 **To** 2035 $85

Kinship Margaret River Chardonnay 2015 This is a very good chardonnay, sharing all the resources used with and for its 1000 Crowns sibling. It also won a gold medal at the Margaret River Wine Show '16, doubling up with a gold medal from Perth. Richer and fuller than 1000 Crowns, it will develop more quickly against the yardstick of its sibling. Presumably it was a case of best barrel selection for 1000 Crowns. Screwcap. 12.5% alc. **Rating** 95 **To** 2022 $32 ✪

Kinship Margaret River Cabernet Sauvignon 2015 Two estate vineyards produced two very different parcels, Altus given 16 days on skins, Summus 30 days on skins post-ferment. Cabernet franc, malbec and petit verdot were included in the blend, which spent 18 months in French oak (30% new). Full-bodied and dramatically different from its stablemates, with blackcurrant fruit wreathed in firm tannins. It needs time, but has the balance to assure the outcome. Gold medal National Cool Climate Wine Show. Screwcap. 14% alc. **Rating** 95 **To** 2035 $32 ✪

Kinship Margaret River Shiraz 2015 25yo vines; whole berries fermented in static fermenters with cultured yeast, 14 days on skins, matured in French oak (20% new) for 10 months. Has awesome drive and intensity, with savoury/spicy black cherry and plum fruit, tannins adding their not inconsiderable weight; the oak integration is also perfect. Screwcap. 14% alc. **Rating** 94 **To** 2035 $32

ΨΨΨΨΨ **Five Tales Shiraz 2015 Rating** 93 **To** 2026 $21 ✪
Five Tales Cabernet Merlot 2015 Rating 93 **To** 2024 $21 ✪

CRFT Wines   ★★★★★

PO Box 197, Aldgate, SA 5154 **Region** Adelaide Hills
T 0413 475 485 **www**.crftwines.com.au **Open** Not
Winemaker Candice Helbig, Frewin Ries **Est.** 2012 **Dozens** 1200
Life and business partners NZ-born Frewin Ries and Barossa-born Candice Helbig crammed multiple wine lives into a relatively short period before giving up secure jobs and establishing CRFT in time for their inaugural 2013 vintage. Frewin started with four years at Cloudy Bay before heading to St Emilion, then to the iconic pinot noir maker in Sonoma, Williams Selyem, then four years with Kingston Estate, and subsequent time as a contract winemaker. Candice is a sixth-generation Barossan, trained as a laboratory technician. She spent eight years with Hardys, gaining her degree in oenology and viticulture from CSU, then moved to Boar's Rock and Mollydooker in '11. They say growth will come from additional single vineyards rather than by increasing the size of the make of any particular wine. They share the Lenswood winery (the original Nepenthe winery) with other kindred spirits. A shed-cum-cellar door

is in the planning stage, as is the possibility of planting some gruner veltliner. Exports to the UK and Singapore.

ŸŸŸŸŸ **Fechner Vineyard Moculta Eden Valley Shiraz 2015** Sourced from an east-facing vineyard near Moculta in the northern end of the Eden Valley. Medium-bodied with spicy fresh raspberry fruit and well handled oak, this restrained and persistent wine should provide considerable pleasure now and over the next 5 or so years. Screwcap. 14% alc. **Rating** 93 **To** 2027 $49 PR

Crittenden Estate   ★★★★★

25 Harrisons Road, Dromana, Vic 3936 **Region** Mornington Peninsula
T (03) 5981 8322 **www**.crittendenwines.com.au **Open** 7 days 10.30–4.30
Winemaker Rollo Crittenden **Est.** 1984 **Dozens** 8000 **Vyds** 4.4ha
Garry Crittenden was one of the pioneers on the Mornington Peninsula, establishing the family vineyard over 30 years ago, and introducing a number of avant garde pruning and canopy management techniques. In the manner of things, much has changed – and continues to change – in cool climate vineyard management. While pinot noir and chardonnay remain the principal focus, Garry's constant desire to push envelopes saw the establishment of a range of Italian varietals (Pinocchio) and Iberian Peninsula varieties (Los Hermanos). In 2015 winemaking returned to the family vineyard on the Mornington Peninsula in a newly built facility, with son Rollo Crittenden very much in charge. Exports to the UK and the US.

ŸŸŸŸŸ **Kangerong Mornington Peninsula Chardonnay 2015** Fermented wild, with 30% mlf following whole bunch pressing to an array of French oak, the wine stirred regularly. Expanding across a beam of mineral crunch, curdy leesy detail, vanillan oak supports and a core of toasted hazelnut and truffle notes, this is reminiscent of a solid Meursault. This is impressive in a very different way from the chiselled 'Peninsula' bottling. Screwcap. 13% alc. **Rating** 96 **To** 2025 $45 NG ✪
Peninsula Chardonnay 2015 This boasts a superb thrust of thirst-slaking wet stone notes with fruit flavours a distant echo, a testament to a wine marked with cool climate, maritime genetics. A parry of chalky, pumice-like mineral and crunchy acidity follow. Hints of apricot, candied citrus rind and quince. The intensity of flavour, despite the absence of obvious fruit, is compelling. A combined ferment of inoculated and wild yeast, before partial mlf (20%) and regular batonnage in assorted French oak has made this a benchmark 'entry' wine to the range. Screwcap. 13.2% alc. **Rating** 95 **To** 2025 $34 NG ✪
The Zumma Mornington Peninsula Pinot Noir 2015 An enticingly bright, perfumed pinot of pure, crunchy, almost brazen red cherry flavours, pouring across seams of vibrant, cool climate acidity. There is some lightly toasted cedar oak in support, but as an adjunct rather than a shout. This is very good, each fresh glass providing a different shade of texture and flavour. Screwcap. 13.4% alc. **Rating** 95 **To** 2023 $55 NG

ŸŸŸŸŸ **The Zumma Chardonnay 2015** **Rating** 93 **To** 2023 $55 NG
Peninsula Pinot Gris 2015 **Rating** 93 **To** 2020 $34 NG
Cri de Coeur Pinot Noir 2015 **Rating** 93 **To** 2025 $80 NG
Kangerong Pinot Noir 2015 **Rating** 93 **To** 2020 $45 NG
Peninsula Pinot Noir 2015 **Rating** 92 **To** 2021 $34 NG

Cullen Wines   ★★★★★

4323 Caves Road, Wilyabrup, WA 6280 **Region** Margaret River
T (08) 9755 5277 **www**.cullenwines.com.au **Open** 7 days 10–4.30
Winemaker Vanya Cullen, Trevor Kent **Est.** 1971 **Dozens** 20 000 **Vyds** 49ha
One of the pioneers of Margaret River, and has always produced long-lived wines of highly individual style from the mature estate vineyards. The vineyard has progressed beyond organic to biodynamic certification and, subsequently, has become the first vineyard and winery in Australia to be certified carbon neutral. This requires the calculation of all the carbon used

and CO_2 emitted in the winery; the carbon is then offset by the planting of new trees. Winemaking is in the hands of Vanya Cullen, daughter of the founders; she is possessed of an extraordinarily good palate and generosity to the cause of fine wine. It is impossible to single out any particular wine from the top echelon. Exports to all major markets.

 TTTTT **Diana Madeline 2015** 87% cabernet sauvignon, 11% merlot, 1% each of malbec and cabernet franc, from the Cullen Vineyard; matured for 17 months in French barriques (66% new). It is inappropriate to use the word 'elegant' in describing the wine, simply because it is on another, higher level, making the word hackneyed in this instance. The fragrant bouquet, the silky palate and perfectly shaped tannins of the finish are unique to this wine. Screwcap. 13% alc. **Rating** 98 **To** 2040 $125 ❂
Kevin John 2015 Picked on fruit and flower days, wild-yeast fermented in French barriques for 5 months (75% new) and allowed to go through mlf. Asserts its blue blood ancestry with vital freshness and citrussy acidity retained despite the mlf. The layers of white flowers, white flesh stone fruit and grapefruit will become progressively richer and more complex, but it's so well balanced and full of life there is every reason to enjoy this chardonnay young. Screwcap. 13% alc. **Rating** 97 **To** 2025 $115 ❂

TTTTT **Cullen Vineyard Margaret River Sauvignon Blanc Semillon 2015** A 74/26% blend fermented and matured in new French oak for 5 months. The complex bouquet brings toasty oak, cut grass and hints of stone fruit into play, the palate pulling out all the stops with its mix of tropical fruits and citrussy acidity. Screwcap. 13% alc. **Rating** 96 **To** 2025 $35 ❂
Mangan Vineyard Margaret River Merlot Malbec Petit Verdot 2016 A 78/15/7% blend, matured in French oak (34% new) for 7 months. Bright crimson-purple hue; a super-fragrant bouquet, followed by an immaculately balanced and structured palate full of juicy red fruits. Terrific value, drink anytime over the next 20 years. Screwcap. 13% alc. **Rating** 96 **To** 2036 $35 ❂
Mangan East Block 2015 80% malbec, 20% petit verdot, wild-yeast fermented, basket-pressed; matured for 7 months in new and used French oak. Strikingly deep crimson-purple; utterly different from Diana Madeline, with powerful fruit and tannins ex the 1.1t/ha yield of the petit verdot. One to put away for the favourite grandchild. Screwcap. 13.5% alc. **Rating** 96 **To** 2040 $45 ❂
Mangan Vineyard Margaret River Sauvignon Blanc Semillon 2016 57% sauvignon blanc, 38% semillon, 5% verdelho, 12% fermented and matured in oak (45% new). As ever, fresh, lively and highly expressive, fruit doing all the talking; all sorts of gooseberry citrus on the bouquet and palate, with lemongrass, and precisely judged acidity. Screwcap. 13% alc. **Rating** 95 **To** 2021 $29 ❂
Legacy Series Kevin John Flower Day Margaret River Chardonnay 2013 Wild-yeast fermented and matured in new biodynamic French oak barrels for 9 months before bottling. There's no doubting the quality of the fruit, but the mere fact that it was fermented and matured in 100% new oak has inevitably left its mark on the wine. It's about as far as Vanya Cullen can go with biodynamics, and defies conventional judging. Screwcap. 14% alc. **Rating** 95 **To** 2023 $250

Cupitt's Winery   ★★★★★

58 Washburton Road, Ulladulla, NSW 2539 **Region** Shoalhaven Coast
T (02) 4455 7888 **www.**cupittwines.com.au **Open** Wed–Sun 10–5
Winemaker Rosie, Wally and Tom Cupitt **Est.** 2007 **Dozens** 4000 **Vyds** 3ha
Griff and Rosie Cupitt run a combined winery and restaurant complex, taking full advantage of the location on the south coast of NSW. Rosie studied oenology at CSU and has more than a decade of vintage experience, taking in France and Italy; she also happens to be the Shoalhaven representative for Slow Food International. The Cupitts have 3ha of vines centred on sauvignon blanc and semillon, and also buy viognier and shiraz from Tumbarumba, shiraz, chardonnay and sauvignon blanc from the Southern Highlands, and verdelho from Canowindra (Cowra). Rosie has been joined in the winery by sons Wally and Tom.

ŸŸŸŸŸ **Hilltops Riesling 2016** The continental climate of the region is clearly suited to riesling, but relatively little is planted. This has freshness and drive, with Meyer lemon and Granny Smith apple flavours, the acidity a mix of citrus and mineral-inflected nuances. Screwcap. 11.5% alc. **Rating** 95 **To** 2026 $28 ✪

Alphonse Sauvignon 2016 Whole-bunch pressed, part fermented and matured in French hogsheads with extended lees contact. A surprising wine with many of the mouthfeel and flavour characteristics of semillon. CO_2 lifts the lemongrass/mineral duo that races along the palate, culminating in a mouthwatering finish. Points for the degree of difficulty. Screwcap. 12.5% alc. **Rating** 95 **To** 2021 $32 ✪

Alphonse Sauvignon 2015 Hand-picked, whole-bunch pressed, part fermented and matured in French barriques. A well made and sophisticated wine, with texture foremost and a nod to France. Citrus fruit and acidity play lead roles in a wine having nothing in common with Marlborough. Screwcap. 12% alc. **Rating** 95 **To** 2022 $32 ✪

Hilltops Shiraz 2015 The wine instantaneously hits its sweet spot as it enters the mouth for the first time, and doesn't miss a beat thereafter. It is at the lighter end of the medium-bodied scale, but it racks up the intensity and purity of the red and black cherry fruits. Tannins (in particular) and oak both contribute to the length of the palate. A snip at the price. Screwcap. 14% alc. **Rating** 95 **To** 2030 $28 ✪

Hilltops Nebbiolo 2015 Wild yeast fermentation with a long maceration on skins and maturation in French hogsheads for 18 months has worked very well. There are cherry allsorts fruit flavours with warm spices and totally domesticated tannins. Elegant Aus nebbiolos are rare. Screwcap. 14% alc. **Rating** 95 **To** 2025 $36

Yarra Valley Chardonnay 2015 Part fermented in French oak, part in tank, matured on lees for 12 months. Has the length that is the recognised hallmark of good Yarra Valley chardonnay. The grapes were picked at the right time, allowing optimal development of white peach/grapefruit flavours, oak not spoiling the party in any way. Screwcap. 12.8% alc. **Rating** 94 **To** 2024 $32

ŸŸŸŸŸ **Hilltops Merlot 2015** **Rating** 93 **To** 2025 $35
Mia Bella Yarra Valley Arneis 2016 **Rating** 92 **To** 2020 $28
The Pointer Tumbarumba Pinot Noir 2016 **Rating** 92 **To** 2025 $30
Hilltops Carolyn's Cabernet 2015 **Rating** 91 **To** 2025 $40
Hilltops Viognier 2016 **Rating** 90 **To** 2020 $28
Dusty Dog Hilltops Shiraz 2014 **Rating** 90 **To** 2020 $52

Curator Wine Company ★★★★☆

28 Jenke Road, Marananga, SA 5355 **Region** Barossa Valley
T 0411 861 604 **www.**curatorwineco.com.au **Open** By appt
Winemaker Tom White **Est.** 2015 **Dozens** 600 **Vyds** 8ha

This business is owned by Tom and Bridget White, who have made a number of changes in direction over previous years, and have now decided to focus on Shiraz and Cabernet Sauvignon from the Barossa Valley, a decision that has been rewarded. The vineyard at Marananga is planted on ancient red soils rich in ironstone and quartzite, and the wines are naturally fermented.

ŸŸŸŸŸ **Barossa Valley Shiraz 2014** It's not until you have taken several breaths after tasting the wine that the alcohol makes its presence felt, but there's a power of black fruits, licorice and new French oak to do battle with the alcohol. It's a strangely compelling wine – while I don't want to drink table wine with such alcohol, the quality is undeniable. Diam. 15.5% alc. **Rating** 95 **To** 2044 $55

Barossa Valley Shiraz 2013 The move to 40% used French oak from the '15 vintage could well see a new star in the firmament, '14 marking a step to reduce the amount of new oak. There is shiraz of the highest quality held in oak bondage for the foreseeable future in this wine, but its quality can't be denied. Diam. 15.5% alc. **Rating** 94 **To** 2033 $55

Curlewis Winery

55 Navarre Road, Curlewis, Vic 3222 **Region** Geelong
T (03) 5250 4567 **www**.curlewiswinery.com.au **Open** By appt
Winemaker Rainer Breit, Stefano Marasco **Est.** 1998 **Dozens** 1300 **Vyds** 2.8ha
Rainer Breit and partner Wendy Oliver purchased their property in 1996 with 1.6ha of
then 11yo pinot noir vines. Rainer, a self-taught winemaker, uses the full bag of pinot noir
winemaking tricks: cold soaking, hot fermentation, post-ferment maceration, part inoculated
and part wild yeast use, prolonged lees contact, and bottling the wine neither fined nor
filtered. While self-confessed 'pinotphiles', they planted some chardonnay, supplemented by
a little locally grown shiraz and chardonnay. Rainer and Wendy sold the business in 2011 to
Leesa Freyer and Stefano Marasco. Leesa and Stefano also own and operate the Yarra Lounge
in Yarraville, Melbourne. Exports to Canada, Sweden, the Maldives, Malaysia, Singapore and
Hong Kong.

ŢŢŢŢŢ **Special Home Block Reserve Pinot Noir 2014** Very good garnet hue; an
array of cherries, damson plums with cedary oak fragrance and woodsy spices
follow through onto the medium-bodied palate, where the tannins have a firm
grip. A slight astringency leads to a close with perky acidity. Extra time in bottle
advisable. Screwcap. 13.5% alc. **Rating** 94 **To** 2026 $70 JF

ŢŢŢŢŢ **Bel Sel Chardonnay 2016 Rating** 93 **To** 2021 $30 JF
Reserve Pinot Noir 2014 Rating 90 **To** 2022 $65 JF
Bel Sel Pinot Noir 2014 Rating 90 **To** 2021 $30 JF

Curly Flat ★★★★★

263 Collivers Road, Lancefield, Vic 3435 **Region** Macedon Ranges
T (03) 5429 1956 **www**.curlyflat.com **Open** W'ends 12–5
Winemaker Phillip Moraghan, Matt Regan **Est.** 1991 **Dozens** 6000 **Vyds** 13ha
Phillip Moraghan and Jenifer Kolkka began developing Curly Flat in 1991, drawing in part on
Phillip's working experience in Switzerland in the late '80s, and with a passing nod to Michael
Leunig. With ceaseless help and guidance from the late Laurie Williams (and others), they have
painstakingly established 8.5ha of pinot noir, 3.5ha of chardonnay and 1ha of pinot gris, and a
multi-level, gravity-flow winery. Exports to the UK, Japan and Hong Kong.

ŢŢŢŢŢ **Pinot Noir 2014** A pinot noir lit by a satin sheen of red berry fruits spread across
the mouth by juicy acidity and impeccably wrought tannins. Growing darker of
fruit and broader of midriff as it opens, a lick of briar, wood smoke and truffle
imbue a carnal edge to a shimmering, mellifluous finish. Delicious out of the gates.
Screwcap. 13.6% alc. **Rating** 97 **To** 2026 $58 NG ✪

ŢŢŢŢŢ **Chardonnay 2015** 50% mlf has conferred complexity, stability and poise on
one hand, and retained natural acidity on the other. This strikes a creamy chord
that parlays well with the wine's sheer extract, stone fruit and vanilla pod notes.
The finish is long and emphatic, careening across a high-pitched scale of mineral
crunch and layered complexity. Screwcap. 13.2% alc. **Rating** 95 **To** 2028 $54 NG

ŢŢŢŢŢ **Pinot Gris 2016 Rating** 93 **To** 2020 $36 NG
Williams Crossing Pinot Noir 2015 Rating 92 **To** 2021 $34 NG
Macedon NV Rating 92 **To** 2017 $45 TS
Williams Crossing Chardonnay 2015 Rating 91 **To** 2021 $28 NG

Curtis Family Vineyards

514 Victor Harbor Road, McLaren Vale, SA 5171 **Region** McLaren Vale
T 0439 800 484 **www**.curtisfamilyvineyards.com **Open** Not
Winemaker Mark and Claudio Curtis **Est.** 1973 **Dozens** 10 000
The Curtis family traces its history back to 1499 when Paolo Curtis was appointed by
Cardinal de Medici to administer Papal lands in the area around Cervaro. (The name Curtis is
believed to derive from Curtius, a noble and wealthy Roman Empire family.) The family has

been growing grapes and making wine in McLaren Vale since 1973, having come to Australia some years previously. Exports to the US, Canada, Thailand and China.

ŸŸŸŸŸ **Limited Series McLaren Vale Grenache 2015** From 100yo vines, open-fermented, matured for 18 months in French hogsheads. Very good, bright, clear crimson colour; has managed to keep the oak subservient to the plum and red cherry fruit, fine-grained tannins providing texture and structure. Impressive stuff, good now or much later. Screwcap. 14% alc. **Rating** 95 **To** 2030 $100

Cavaliere McLaren Vale Shiraz 2016 Hand-picked 60yo vines, crushed and destemmed, open-fermented with cultured yeast, 14 days on skins, matured in new French hogsheads for 10 months. The deep, vivid colour signals a newborn full-bodied wine that needs many years to open its door for business. It is balanced, and its impenetrable black forest of fruit, French oak and powerful, but supple, tannins will all play a role. Diam. 14% alc. **Rating** 94 **To** 2041 $70

Limited Series McLaren Vale Shiraz 2015 60yo vines, crushed and destemmed, 14 days on skins, basket-pressed direct to new French hogsheads for 18 months maturation. Interesting use of a screwcap for this wine, and Diam for its siblings. The estate vineyard, the alcohol and the vinification are the same for all three, the major difference being the three vintages and length of time in new oak. Full-bodied by normal standards, but has sufficiently good balance to justify the use of the word 'elegant'. 14% alc. **Rating** 94 **To** 2040 $100

Pasha Limited Series McLaren Vale Shiraz 2014 Deeply coloured, little or no change; this is beyond the conventional meaning of the term 'full-bodied', so full is the extract of thickly painted fruit that sits in the mouth with flavours of licorice, chocolate, stewed plums, blackberry jam and bramble. The hope is that it will lose weight as it slowly ages. Diam. 14% alc. **Rating** 94 **To** 2044 $150

Cavaliere McLaren Vale Cabernet Sauvignon 2015 Full-bodied with considerable complexity and depth, fruit and oak locked in unarmed combat, blackberry to the fore, but the oak not yielding. The tannins are balanced and integrated, as is the hint of dark chocolate. Classy packaging. Diam. 14% alc. **Rating** 94 **To** 2035 $70

ŸŸŸŸŸ **Cavaliere McLaren Vale Shiraz 2014** Rating 93 **To** 2034 $70
Gold Label McLaren Vale Shiraz 2014 Rating 92 **To** 2029 $70
Cavaliere McLaren Vale Shiraz 2015 Rating 91 **To** 2035 $70
Neverland Merlot 2015 Rating 90 **To** 2021 $18 ✪
The Nut House Wine Co Merlot 2015 Rating 90 **To** 2021 $18 ✪

d'Arenberg ★★★★★

Osborn Road, McLaren Vale, SA 5171 **Region** McLaren Vale
T (08) 8329 4888 **www.darenberg.com.au** **Open** 7 days 10–5
Winemaker Chester Osborn, Jack Walton **Est.** 1912 **Dozens** 270 000 **Vyds** 197.2ha
Nothing, they say, succeeds like success. Few operations in Australia fit this dictum better than d'Arenberg, which has kept its 100-year-old heritage while moving into the 21st century with flair and élan. At last count the d'Arenberg vineyards, at various locations, have 24 varieties planted, as well as 120 growers in McLaren Vale. There is no question that its past, present and future revolve around its considerable portfolio of richly robed red wines, Shiraz, Cabernet Sauvignon and Grenache being the cornerstones. The quality of the wines is unimpeachable, the prices logical and fair. It has a profile in both the UK and the US that far larger companies would love to have. d'Arenberg celebrated 100 years of family grapegrowing in '12 on the property that houses the winery, cellar door and restaurant. A founding member of Australia's First Families of Wine. Exports to all major markets.

ŸŸŸŸŸ **The Fruit Bat Single Vineyard McLaren Vale Shiraz 2013** More towards medium-bodied, and more accessible as a young wine than its brethren. Ripe, juice-dripping damson plum aromas lead the way, but the bouquet also offers up floral notes of rose perfume and Asian spice. The flavours show some regional earthiness, but there's a lightness of touch which carries it easily along to the lingering, sweet-fruited finish. Screwcap. 14.8% alc. **Rating** 96 **To** 2035 $99 SC

The Apotropaic Triskaidekaphobia Single Vineyard Shiraz 2013 This takes the ever-idiosyncratic d'Arenberg wine names altogether too far. The vinification is as usual, with 20 months maturation in used French oak. It is full-bodied, with a wealth of black fruits of every size and description on the mid-palate; the back-palate and finish add a dimension of earthy/savoury, tannin-linked, notes. Screwcap. 14.6% alc. **Rating** 96 **To** 2043 $99

The Piceous Lodestar Single Vineyard McLaren Vale Shiraz 2013 All the usual deep colour and ripe fruit aromas and flavours, but in addition polished tannins frame the fruit in an unexpected way. There are bright nuances, even elegance, that the other d'Arenberg wines don't have. It's probably the particular vineyard speaking. Screwcap. 14.8% alc. **Rating** 96 **To** 2043 $99

The Old Bloke & The Three Young Blondes Shiraz Roussanne Viognier Marsanne 2012 The usual d'Arenberg vinification with 20 months maturation in used French barriques. The cepage (shiraz, roussanne, viognier and marsanne) is very unusual, and the '12 vintage overall is on the way to recognition as the best between '00 and '16 for the Barossa Valley and McLaren Vale reds. The wine has the structure needed to sail through the next 30+ years (a marriage of rich black fruits and complex tannin). Screwcap. 14.7% alc. **Rating** 96 **To** 2052 $200

The Bamboo Scrub Single Vineyard McLaren Vale Shiraz 2014 From vines planted in '84, machine-harvested, open-fermented and foot-trodden with 14 days on skins, then matured for 16 months in oak. Blewitt Springs' cooler climate always leaves its mark; fine red and black fruits at the core of a wine made to go the distance and then some; texture and structure underscore the fruit, tannins to the fore. Screwcap. 13.9% alc. **Rating** 95 **To** 2039 $99

Shipsters' Rapture Single Vineyard McLaren Vale Shiraz 2014 Vines planted in '69, open-fermented and foot-trodden, 14 days on skins, then 16 months in oak. An archetypal full-bodied regional shiraz with an abundance of interwoven strands of black fruits, dark chocolate and fine-grained, but persistent, tannins. A supple high quality wine. Screwcap. 14.6% alc. **Rating** 95 **To** 2034 $99

The Dead Arm McLaren Vale Shiraz 2014 Part hand, part machine-harvested, crushed and destemmed, 2–3 weeks on skins in open (headed down) fermenter, matured for 20 months in French oak (8% new) and a dab of American oak. Deep crimson-purple; ultra full-bodied and densely packed with the darkest black fruits, licorice, 70% cacao dark chocolate and ripe tannins. Will live forever. Screwcap. 14.4% alc. **Rating** 95 **To** 2049 $65

Scarce Earth The Eight Iron Single Vineyard McLaren Vale Shiraz 2013 Very much McLaren Vale in personality, although of course the vineyard applies its own stamp as well. The first impression is of baked earth, with the term 'ironstone' coming to mind, although that may be geologically flawed. Notes of anise, caraway and lavender are sprinkled through the ripe red fruit, the palate buoyant and long in flavour. Screwcap. 14.5% alc. **Rating** 95 **To** 2038 $99 SC

The Swinging Malaysian Single Vineyard McLaren Vale Shiraz 2013 Seems to be a more approachable example of this label. Red and black fruits dominate the bouquet, with blood plum and juicy, almost jubey raspberry aromas. All those elements carry through to the palate, which then offers another dimension, with flavours of clove and other sweet spices seasoning the brew. A very good release. Screwcap. 14.6% alc. **Rating** 95 **To** 2035 $99 SC

Tyche's Mustard Single Vineyard McLaren Vale Shiraz 2013 Ultra-powerful, with a lava-like molten flow of black fruits, spices, chocolate and licorice sweeping all before it until the last gasp, when ripe tannins come to the rescue. All of these d'Arenberg wines are heroic. Screwcap. 14.8% alc. **Rating** 95 **To** 2043 $99

The Amaranthine Single Vineyard McLaren Vale Shiraz 2013 Standard vinification, matured for 20 months in used French oak. Deep, dense crimson-purple colour, excellent for its age; a concentrated, boldly full-bodied shiraz with a deep well of black fruits, licorice and bitter chocolate; the tannins are still resolving themselves, but are in balance and will underwrite the future of the wine. Screwcap. 14% alc. **Rating** 95 **To** 2033 $99

The High Trellis McLaren Vale Cabernet Sauvignon 2014 Crushed and destemmed, open-fermented with headed down boards, 2–3 weeks on skins, matured for 22 months in French oak (10% new). A prime example of the affinity between McLaren Vale and cabernet, even if the flavours are slightly left field and it does best in cooler vintages. Medium to full-bodied, and the cassis and black olive fruit does have dark chocolate notes, and persistent tannins. Gold medal Adelaide Wine Show '16. Screwcap. 14.4% alc. **Rating** 95 **To** 2034 $18 ❂

The Amaranthine Single Vineyard McLaren Vale Shiraz 2014 From vines planted in '68, machine-harvested, open-fermented and foot-trodden with 12 days on skins, then oak-matured for 16 months. Shares the excellent full crimson-purple hue of the '14 Single Vineyard series; a strikingly spicy/savoury medium to full-bodied wine, its juicy core surrounded by foresty bitter chocolate notes, its tannins rounding off the finish. Screwcap. 14.6% alc. **Rating** 94 **To** 2034 $99

The Pickwickian Brobdingnagian Single Vineyard Shiraz 2013 Density and warmth seem to be the recurring themes through this wine. The aromas and flavours conjure up blackberry, but it's more reminiscent of something cooked, perhaps conserve, than freshly picked fruit. A bitumen-like character in the bouquet and on the palate adds a dark, impenetrable quality. Needs a good spell in the cellar to show its worth. Screwcap. 14.4% alc. **Rating** 94 **To** 2030 $99 SC

Shipsters' Rapture Single Vineyard McLaren Vale Shiraz 2013 Always a deep, dark sort of wine, and no different with this vintage. On the bouquet and palate, 'tarry' is the most characteristic descriptor, with licorice not far behind and a touch of alcohol warmth poking through. A pine/mint-like aroma, black fruit and bitter chocolate flavours are typical of the vineyard. This will take much time to fully evolve. Screwcap. 14.7% alc. **Rating** 94 **To** 2040 $99 SC

The Bamboo Scrub Single Vineyard McLaren Vale Shiraz 2013 You can doubtless get lost in the bamboo scrub as easily as you can get lost in the sea of black/dark chocolate fruits of these d'Arenberg wines. The problem is not one of quality, but of fearful symmetry, the point of difference here the lift on the aftertaste. A glass half full job – it's there, but is it a positive or a negative? Difference is not of itself to be admired willy-nilly. Screwcap. 15% alc. **Rating** 94 **To** 2043 $99

The Derelict Vineyard McLaren Vale Grenache 2014 True to form for The Derelict, it's grenache with some serious substance. The distinctive varietal aroma is there, with the sweet fruit elements apparent, but there's also a dark vinosity that will need age to completely reveal itself. Likewise on the palate, there's a latent depth of flavour which is still a little buried in the drying, persistent tannin. Patience required. Screwcap. 14.3% alc. **Rating** 94 **To** 2033 $29 SC ❂

The Bonsai Vine McLaren Vale Grenache Shiraz Mourvedre 2014 Matured for 12 months in 50/50% used French and American barriques. Deeply coloured, it's a particularly luscious and enjoyable GSM. The medium to full-bodied palate is stacked with red and black fruits and perfectly weighted tannins, and has an earthy/savoury twist on the finish. Great value. Screwcap. 14.3% alc. **Rating** 94 **To** 2034 $29 ❂

The Coppermine Road McLaren Vale Cabernet Sauvignon 2014 Crushed and destemmed, open-fermented with headed down boards, 2–3 weeks on skins, matured for 18 months in French oak (7% new). A powerful cabernet with pronounced tannins woven throughout the black fruits of the full-bodied palate; has depth and length, and the balance to benefit from extended cellaring. Screwcap. 14.1% alc. **Rating** 94 **To** 2039 $65

Dal Zotto Wines   ★★★★☆

Main Road, Whitfield, Vic 3733 **Region** King Valley
T (03) 5729 8321 **www**.dalzotto.com.au **Open** 7 days 10–5
Winemaker Michael Dal Zotto **Est.** 1987 **Dozens** 30 000 **Vyds** 48ha
The Dal Zotto family is a King Valley institution; ex-tobacco growers, then contract grapegrowers, they are now primarily focused on their Dal Zotto wine range. Led by Otto

and Elena, and with sons Michael and Christian handling winemaking and sales/marketing respectively, the family is producing increasing amounts of wine of consistent quality from its substantial estate vineyard. The cellar door is in the centre of Whitfield, and is also home to their Trattoria (open weekends). Exports to the UAE, the Philippines and China appear to be flying, production up from 15 000 dozen.

 🍷🍷🍷🍷🍷 **Museum Release King Valley Riesling 2006** Underlines the quality that will reward the patience of those who cellar Dal Zotto's current vintage, subject always to the quality of the current year. This Museum Release is superb, towering over the other Dal Zotto Rieslings. Screwcap. 13% alc. **Rating** 95 **To** 2022 $70

🍷🍷🍷🍷🍷 **Museum Release King Valley Riesling 2005** **Rating** 93 **To** 2021 $65
King Valley Arneis 2016 **Rating** 92 **To** 2019 $27 SC
Pucino King Valley Prosecco 2016 **Rating** 91 **To** 2017 $23 TS
King Valley Riesling 2015 **Rating** 90 **To** 2023 $18 ✪
Pucino King Valley Prosecco NV **Rating** 90 **To** 2017 $20 TS
Pucino Col Fondo 2014 **Rating** 90 **To** 2017 $27 TS

Dalfarras   ★★★★☆

PO Box 123, Nagambie, Vic 3608 **Region** Nagambie Lakes
T (03) 5794 2637 **www.**tahbilk.com.au **Open** At Tahbilk
Winemaker Alister Purbrick, Alan George **Est.** 1991 **Dozens** 8750 **Vyds** 20.97ha
The project of Alister Purbrick and artist wife Rosa (née Dalfarra), whose paintings adorn the labels of the wines. Alister is best known as winemaker at Tahbilk (see separate entry), the family winery and home, but this range of wines is intended to (in Alister's words) 'allow me to expand my winemaking horizons and mould wines in styles different from Tahbilk'.

🍷🍷🍷🍷🍷 **Pinot Grigio 2016** A striking wine with strawberry, pear and stone fruits all on display, in some ways more like a gris, the ultimate compliment. Top gold Melbourne Wine Awards '16. Screwcap. 13% alc. **Rating** 95 **To** 2017 $18 ✪

🍷🍷🍷🍷🍷 **Sangiovese 2015** **Rating** 91 **To** 2025 $19 ✪

Dalrymple   ★★★★★

1337 Pipers Brook Road, Pipers Brook, Tas 7254 **Region** Northern Tasmania
T (03) 6382 7229 **www.**dalrymplevineyards.com.au **Open** Not
Winemaker Peter Caldwell **Est.** 1987 **Dozens** 4000 **Vyds** 17ha
Dalrymple was established many years ago by the Mitchell and Sundstrup families; the vineyard and brand were acquired by Hill-Smith Family Vineyards in late 2007. Plantings are split between pinot noir and sauvignon blanc, and the wines are made at Jansz Tasmania. In '10 Peter Caldwell was appointed, responsible for the vineyard, viticulture and winemaking. He brought with him 10 years' experience at Te Kairanga Wines (NZ), and two years with Josef Chromy Wines. His knowledge of pinot noir and chardonnay is comprehensive. In Dec '12 Hill-Smith Family Vineyards acquired the 120ha property on which the original Frogmore Creek Vineyard was established; 10ha of that property is pinot noir specifically for Dalrymple.

🍷🍷🍷🍷🍷 **Pipers River Pinot Noir 2015** Deep crimson-purple; the rich plum and black cherry bouquet is followed by a full-bodied palate with a galaxy of dark forest berry and complex spicy/savoury fruit flavours. The texture and structure guarantee a very long life. Screwcap. 14% alc. **Rating** 95 **To** 2030 $34 ✪
Single Site Ouse Pinot Noir 2014 Fruit intensity is in abundance here, heightened by the whole bunches (up to 40%) in the ferment, aged in French oak barriques (40% new). A mélange of cranberry juice, stewed rhubarb and damson plums, fleshy and juicy on the palate; wood spice, fennel and wood smoke add to the complexity, with the fine natural acidity keeping the plump tannins in place. Screwcap. 13% alc. **Rating** 95 **To** 2027 $61 JF

Dalwhinnie

448 Taltarni Road, Moonambel, Vic 3478 **Region** Pyrenees
T (03) 5467 2388 **www.**dalwhinnie.com.au **Open** 7 days 10–5
Winemaker David Jones **Est.** 1976 **Dozens** 3500 **Vyds** 25ha
David and Jenny Jones are making wines with tremendous depth of flavour, reflecting the
relatively low-yielding but well maintained vineyards. The vineyards are dry-grown and
managed organically, hence the low yield, but the quality more than compensates. A 50-tonne
high-tech winery allows the wines to be made onsite. Exports to the UK, the US and China.

Moonambel Shiraz 2015 Dalwhinnie seldom misses the target, and certainly
didn't in '15. Black fruits of all descriptions have a (fruit) sweet edge that is quite
delicious, the mouthfeel supple, the palate of effortless length, French oak just a
cog in the engine. Screwcap. 14.5% alc. **Rating** 96 **To** 2040 $65 ◐
Moonambel Cabernet 2015 Clear, deep crimson-purple; just as you would
expect from the region, fully mature vines, the winemaker and the judicious use of
French oak. The flavours are deep and deceptively powerful, tannins plentiful, but
submerged in the fruit, the overall balance and length faultless. Screwcap. 14% alc.
Rating 96 **To** 2040 $55 ◐

Moonambel Chardonnay 2016 **Rating** 90 **To** 2022 $45

Dandelion Vineyards

PO Box 138, McLaren Vale, SA 5171 **Region** McLaren Vale
T (08) 8556 6099 **www.**dandelionvineyards.com.au **Open** Not
Winemaker Elena Brooks **Est.** 2007 **Dozens** NFP **Vyds** 124.2ha
This is a highly impressive partnership between Peggy and Carl Lindner (40%), Elena and
Zar Brooks (40%), and Fiona and Brad Rey (20%). It brings together vineyards spread across
the Adelaide Hills, Eden Valley, Langhorne Creek, McLaren Vale, Barossa Valley and Fleurieu
Peninsula. Elena is not only the wife of industry dilettante Zar, but also a gifted winemaker.
Exports to all major markets.

Wonderland of the Eden Valley Riesling 2016 From Colin Kroehn's
vineyard planted in 1912, hand-picked and small batch fermented. Its very high
acidity of 8.8g/l and pH of 2.91 put it fairly and squarely into (normally) German
territory, and it has been fermented to dryness. The wine will live for decades,
and counter to my usual practice, the points are for 2020+, not today. Screwcap.
10.5% alc. **Rating** 95 **To** 2046 $60
Menagerie of the Barossa Grenache Shiraz Mataro 2015 An 80/15/5%
field blend; open-fermented with wild yeast for 14 days, matured for 12 months in
used French barriques. An altogether superior Barossa blend with very good colour
and a concerto of supple red and black fruits on the finely balanced, medium-
bodied palate. Great value. Screwcap. 14.5% alc. **Rating** 95 **To** 2030 $27 ◐
Fairytale of the Barossa Rose 2015 90yo grenache bushvines, free-run juice
fermented and matured in used French oak, matured on yeast lees for 20 weeks.
A very well made, complex rose; the spicy/savoury structure is infilled with bright
bramble/cherry pip flavours, and the length is impressive. Screwcap. 13% alc.
Rating 94 **To** 2017 $27 ◐
Lionheart of the Barossa Shiraz 2015 Hand-picked, open-fermented, wild
yeast, 8 days on skins, basket-pressed to French barriques (some new), matured
for 18 months. Deep crimson-purple; a full-bodied shiraz in classic Barossa Valley
mode; blackberry, plum, licorice, warm spice and soft, plum tannins all add up to a
totally hedonistic play. Screwcap. 14.5% alc. **Rating** 94 **To** 2030 $27 ◐
Pride of the Fleurieu Cabernet Sauvignon 2015 Destemmed and crushed,
open fermented for 14 days, matured in used French barriques for 18 months.
Full-bodied, its varietal expression is shaped by the Mediterranean climate,
resulting in a rich, robust wine with blackcurrant and a hint of dark chocolate,
balance achieved without fuss. Screwcap. 14.5% alc. **Rating** 94 **To** 2035 $27 ◐

⚑⚑⚑⚑⚑ Fairytale of the Barossa Rose 2016 Rating 93 To 2019 $27 ◐
Pride of the Fleurieu Cabernet Sauvignon 2014 Rating 92 To 2024 $27
Lion's Tooth of McLaren Vale Shiraz Riesling 2014 Rating 90 To 2024 $27
Damsel of the Barossa Merlot 2015 Rating 90 To 2023 $27

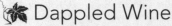

Dappled Wine ★★★★★

1 Sewell Road, Steels Creek, Vic 3775 **Region** Yarra Valley
T 0407 675 994 **www**.dappledwines.com.au **Open** By appt
Winemaker Shaun Crinion **Est.** 2009 **Dozens** 800
Owner and winemaker Shaun Crinion was introduced to wine in 1999, working for his winemaker uncle at Laetitia Winery & Vineyards on the central coast of California. His career since then has been so impressive I can't cut it short, so here (with minor abbreviations) it is in full: 2000 Devil's Lair, Margaret River; Corbett Canyon Vineyard, California; '02 Houghton, Middle Swan; '03 De Bortoli, Hunter Valley; '04–06 Pipers Brook, Tasmania; '06 Bay of Fires, Tasmania; '06–07 Williams Selyem, California; '08 Domaine Chandon, Yarra Valley; '10 Domaine de Montille, Burgundy; '09–16 Dappled Wines (plus part-time for Rob Dolan). His longer-term ambition is to buy or establish his own vineyard.

⚑⚑⚑⚑⚑ Appellation Yarra Valley Chardonnay 2015 An exquisitely sculpted wine, its magic lying as much in what it doesn't say as in what it does – a perfect union of stone and citrus fruit, acidity and oak. Screwcap. 13% alc. **Rating** 97 To 2025 $27 ◐

⚑⚑⚑⚑⚑ Straws Lane Macedon Ranges Gewurztraminer 2015 Has more pristine varietal character on the bouquet and palate alike than I've encountered for a very long time. The musk, lychee and warm spice bouquet illuminates and intensifies the palate to the degree found in Alsace every day of the week, and oh so rarely in Australia. Screwcap. 13% alc. **Rating** 96 To 2023 $27 ◐
Swallowfield Upper Yarra Valley Chardonnay 2015 This has a very complex bouquet, and an equally complex palate; new French oak and a fearless early picking approach have a hologram-like impact, ever shifting around a spear of pink grapefruit. Unexpectedly, it came second on a recount to the Appellation Yarra Valley Chardonnay. Screwcap. 12.5% alc. **Rating** 96 To 2023 $38 ◐
Appellation Upper Yarra Valley Pinot Noir 2015 Deep pinot colour; an exotic and expressive bouquet has spice, dark berry and charcuterie aromas; the supple palate, with damson plum and black cherry, is utterly delicious. If more is needed, the tannins are akin to a spider web at dawn in the vineyard with shiny droplets of water on its interstices. Screwcap. 13% alc. **Rating** 96 To 2028 $27 ◐
La Petanque Mornington Peninsula Chardonnay 2015 If I were a Mornington Peninsula chardonnay winemaker, I would be shying away from this challenge to my raison d'être. This uncompromising purity (no mlf) is apt to take no prisoners. Screwcap. 13.5% alc. **Rating** 95 To 2023 $38
Swallowfield Upper Yarra Valley Pinot Noir 2015 Bright, clear colour; lifts the bar with its greater use of new French oak matched by deeper fruits; although the alcohol is the same as the Appellation Upper Yarra Valley Pinot, the power of this wine demands patience. In 10 years it will have shown a clean pair of heels to its sibling. Quite beautiful labels. Screwcap. 13% alc. **Rating** 95 To 2030 $38
Fin de la Terre Yarra Valley Syrah 2015 Deep crimson-purple; radiates its sense of place with aromas of black cherry, licorice and cracked pepper, savoury tannins joining the party on the complex, well balanced palate. Still settling in, but is a winner in the medium term. Screwcap. 14% alc. **Rating** 94 To 2030 $38

David Hook Wines ★★★★☆

Cnr Broke Road/Ekerts Road, Pokolbin, NSW 2320 **Region** Hunter Valley
T (02) 4998 7121 **www**.davidhookwines.com.au **Open** 7 days 10–4.30
Winemaker David Hook **Est.** 1984 **Dozens** 10 000 **Vyds** 8ha

David Hook has over 25 years' experience as a winemaker for Tyrrell's and Lake's Folly, also doing the full Flying Winemaker bit with jobs in Bordeaux, the Rhône Valley, Spain, the US and Georgia. The Pothana Vineyard has been in production for over 30 years, and the wines made from it are given the 'Old Vines' banner. This vineyard is planted on the Belford Dome, an ancient geological formation that provides red clay soils over limestone on the slopes, and sandy loams along the creek flats; the former for red wines, the latter for white.

ŸŸŸŸŸ **Aged Release Old Vines Pothana Vineyard Belford Semillon 2012** When first tasted in Jan '13, I wrote 'will develop with sure-footedness' and gave it 94 points, its price $25. Well, I wasn't wrong: this is now a gloriously elegant and pure Hunter Valley semillon, the lemon zest and minerally acidity still in full voice, plus a splash of lime. It's still only a baby, with a casual decade in front of it to grow to maturity. Screwcap. 10.5% alc. **Rating** 97 **To** 2027 $50 ○

ŸŸŸŸŸ **Hilltops Nebbiolo 2015** Warm open fermentation, lightly pressed and matured in new and used French oak for 12 months. Nebbiolo is utterly unpredictable: sometimes tempestuous, sometimes coquettish, happily in the latter mood here. Red rose and cherry blossom aromas, then a vibrant palate with red fruits caressing the tongue, tannins in remission. Screwcap. 13.5% alc. **Rating** 94 **To** 2024 $38

ŸŸŸŸŸ **Orange Vermentino 2016** Rating 92 To 2019 $35
Orange Sangiovese 2015 Rating 92 To 2020 $30
Old Vines Pothana Vineyard Belford Semillon 2016 Rating 90 To 2019 $25
Orange Hilltops De Novo Rosso 2015 Rating 90 To 2020 $30
Orange Riesling 2016 Rating 90 To 2026 $35

Dawson & James   ★★★★★
1240B Brookman Road, Dingabledinga, SA 5172 **Region** Southern Tasmania
T 0419 816 335 **www.**dawsonjames.com.au **Open** Not
Winemaker Peter Dawson, Tim James **Est.** 2010 **Dozens** 1200 **Vyds** 3.3ha
Peter Dawson and Tim James had long and highly successful careers as senior winemakers for Hardys/Accolade wines. Tim jumped ship first, becoming managing director of Wirra Wirra for seven years until 2007, while Peter stayed longer. Now both have multiple consulting roles. They have both long had a desire to grow and make wine in Tasmania, a desire which came to fruition in '10. Exports to the UK and Singapore.

ŸŸŸŸŸ **Pinot Noir 2015** A sumptuous and svelte pinot noir, reminiscent of Chambolle-Musigny. A lustrous ruby hue parlays with wood smoke, bonbons and a hint of undergrowth. Layers of flavour play out across an expansive palate, finishing with a lick of briar. Screwcap. 12.9% alc. **Rating** 98 **To** 2023 $68 NG ○
Chardonnay 2015 Superlative chiselled chardonnay, unwinding on the palate in mineral-clad notches of stone fruits, toasted nuts and oatmeal, every detail embedded and driven long by sensitively handled reductive tension and juicy, cool climate acidity. Despite the lowish alcohol, nothing about this is anorexic. Screwcap. 12.2% alc. **Rating** 97 **To** 2026 $58 NG ○

DCB Wine   ★★★★
505 Gembrook Road, Hoddles Creek, Vic 3139 **Region** Yarra Valley
T 0419 545 544 **www.**dcbwine.com.au **Open** Not
Winemaker Chris Bendle **Est.** 2013 **Dozens** NFP
DCB is a busman's holiday for Chris Bendle, currently a winemaker at Hoddles Creek Estate, where he has been since 2010. He has previously made wine in Tasmania, NZ and Oregon, so he is the right person to provide wines that are elegant, affordable, and reward the pleasure of drinking (Chris's aim). It should be said that the wines offer excellent value.

ŸŸŸŸŸ **Yarra Valley Chardonnay 2016** Given the quality, this is a bargain. No shortage of flavour, with a compilation of white stone fruit, freshly grated Granny Smith apple, ginger powder. Softish acidity. A gentle wine, long on the finish. Lots to like. Screwcap. 13.1% alc. **Rating** 93 **To** 2023 $20 JF ○

Yarra Valley Pinot Noir 2016 You're out with friends, you want to drink well but also go home with money in your wallet. This fits the bill, as it were. Supple juicy fruit, tangy cherries and pips, a whiff of oak spice, soft tannins and drinkability by the bucket load. Screwcap. 13.4% alc. **Rating** 92 **To** 2022 $20 JF ✪

De Beaurepaire Wines ★★★★

182 Cudgegong Road, Rylstone, NSW 2849 **Region** Mudgee
T (02) 6379 1473 **www**.debeaurepairewines.com **Open** W'ends by appt
Winemaker Jacob Stein (Contract) **Est.** 1998 **Dozens** 1000 **Vyds** 52.3ha
The large De Beaurepaire vineyard was planted by Janet and Richard de Beaurepaire in 1998, and is situated on one of the oldest properties west of the Blue Mountains, at an altitude of 570–600m. The altitude, coupled with limestone soils, and frontage to the Cudgegong River, provides grapes (and hence wines) very different from the normal Mudgee wines. The vineyard is planted to merlot, shiraz, cabernet sauvignon, pinot noir, petit verdot, viognier, chardonnay, semillon, verdelho and pinot gris; most of the grapes are sold.

♀♀♀♀♀ **La Comtesse Rylstone Chardonnay 2015** Clone I10V5, part barrel- and part tank-fermented, matured for 5 months in French oak (20% new). Bell-clear varietal character in a grapefruit juice, zest and pith spectrum, the finish long and satisfying. Screwcap. 14% alc. **Rating** 92 **To** 2021 $25 ✪

De Bortoli ★★★★★

De Bortoli Road, Bilbul, NSW 2680 **Region** Riverina
T (02) 6966 0100 **www**.debortoli.com.au **Open** Mon–Sat 9–5, Sun 9–4
Winemaker Darren De Bortoli, Julie Mortlock **Est.** 1928 **Dozens** NFP **Vyds** 311.5ha
Famous among the cognoscenti for its superb Noble One, which in fact accounts for only a minute part of its total production, this winery turns out low-priced varietal and generic wines that are invariably competently made. They come in part from estate vineyards, but also from contract-grown grapes. In June 2012 De Bortoli received a $4.8 million grant from the Federal Government's Clean Technology Food and Foundries Investment Program. This grant supported an additional investment of $11 million by the De Bortoli family in their project called 'Re-engineering Our Future for a Carbon Economy'. De Bortoli is a founding member of Australia's First Families of Wine. Exports to all major markets.

♀♀♀♀♀ **Noble One Botrytis Semillon 2014** Full golden-bronze; long experience has taught De Bortoli how to maximise the sweetness and richness without cloying the mouth. Indeed, the finish to the honey, creme brulee and cumquat marmalade flavours is seemingly almost dry – which it isn't, of course. 375ml. Screwcap. 10% alc. **Rating** 95 **To** 2024 $33 ✪

De Bortoli (Victoria) ★★★★★

Pinnacle Lane, Dixons Creek, Vic 3775 **Region** Yarra Valley
T (03) 5965 2271 **www**.debortoli.com.au **Open** 7 days 10–5
Winemaker Stephen Webber, Sarah Fagan **Est.** 1987 **Dozens** 350 000 **Vyds** 430ha
Arguably the most successful of all Yarra Valley wineries, not only in terms of the sheer volume of production, but also taking into account the quality of its wines. It is run by the husband and wife team of Leanne De Bortoli and Steve Webber, but owned by the De Bortoli family. The wines are released in three quality and price groups: at the top Single Vineyard, then Estate Grown, and in third place, Villages. Small volume labels also increase the offer with Riorret Single Vineyard Pinot Noir, Melba, La Bohème, an aromatic range of Yarra Valley wines, and Vinoque, enabling trials (at the commercial level) of new varieties and interesting blends in the Yarra. The BellaRiva Italian varietal wines are sourced from the King Valley, and Windy Peak from Vic regions, including the Yarra, King Valley and Heathcote. Finally, in mid-2016, De Bortoli purchased one of the most distinguished Upper Yarra vineyards, Lusatia Park. Exports to all major markets.

ŶŶŶŶŶ **Riorret Lusatia Park Yarra Valley Pinot Noir 2015** The Lusatia Park Vineyard will provide many outstanding wines in the years to come. This wine is all about purity and finesse, with a strict hands-off approach to the whole-berry fermentation. There are already hints of forest, of violets and of fraises du bois. Diam. 13.5% alc. **Rating** 96 **To** 2023 $45 ✪

Melba Reserve Yarra Valley Cabernet Sauvignon 2014 From the A2, B3 and D2 estate blocks, 28 days maceration, matured for 12 months in French oak (35% new), four aerative rackings. Where the Estate is peaceful, this is incisive and bright, cassis to the fore, riding high on a bedrock of ripe, clear tannins (and French oak), and driving through to the finish and aftertaste without a moment's hesitation. Screwcap. 13.5% alc. **Rating** 96 **To** 2039 $45 ✪

Riorret Lusatia Park Yarra Valley Chardonnay 2016 From Block A on the Lusatia Park Vineyard, whole-bunch pressed, wild-yeast fermented with full mlf, matured for 9 months in used barriques. Lusatia Park is in the Upper Yarra, and this – coupled with the modest alcohol – led to the decision to take the wine through mlf. It certainly hasn't stripped the elegance or fresh, juicy/limey acidity of this lovely chardonnay. The Yarra Valley length of flavour is on full display, oak (obviously) simply a means to an end. Diam. 12.8% alc. **Rating** 95 **To** 2026 $45

Riorret Balnarring Mornington Pinot Noir 2016 Hand-picked and sorted, 25% whole bunches, 14 days on skins, matured for 9 months in oak (30% new). Minimal working of the whole-berry ferment is a keystone of the De Bortoli vinification, especially with the terroir series. Deep crimson-purple, it certainly shows no suggestion of under-extraction. In pinot terms it borders on full-bodied with its black cherry engine, and insists on 3–4 years to allow the development of what will be a first class pinot. Diam. 13.2% alc. **Rating** 95 **To** 2026 $50

Section A5 Yarra Valley Chardonnay 2016 Wild-yeast fermented including full mlf, matured in used barriques for 9 months. This is a polished wine with good balance and length, but tasted shortly after bottling seemed a little hesitant to speak. No worries about its future. Screwcap. 12.8% alc. **Rating** 94 **To** 2024 $50

La Bohème Act Two Yarra Valley Dry Pinot Noir Rose 2016 Pale salmon; it looks and tastes as if partly fermented on skins/whole fruit, not just juice run-off for fermentation after it has gained colour from maceration. Some barrel-ferment notes also at work. Screwcap. 12.7% alc. **Rating** 94 **To** 2017 $22 ✪

Riorret Lusatia Park Yarra Valley Pinot Noir 2016 Block B of the Lusatia Park Vineyard, hand-picked and sorted, 15% whole bunches, 15 days on skins, matured for 9 months in oak (30% new). The crimson-purple hue is good, and the bouquet has wafts of spice woven through the dominant cherry and plum fruit. Like many '16 Yarra pinots, will benefit from cellaring to soften the undercurrent of toughness. Diam. 13.5% alc. **Rating** 94 **To** 2021 $50

Estate Grown Yarra Valley Shiraz 2014 Open-fermented, 25% whole bunches, matured for 10 months in a 23hl foudre and 500l barrels. An elegant, medium-bodied shiraz offering cool climate fragrance, red fruits and spices, the tannins fine, the oak integrated. The whole-bunch inclusion adds to the spicy, savoury parts of the wine. Screwcap. 13.5% alc. **Rating** 94 **To** 2024 $30 ✪

Estate Grown Yarra Valley Cabernet Sauvignon 2014 From four estate vineyards, made in the same way as the Melba Reserve. Attention to detail from start to finish is the cornerstone of the De Bortoli winemaking ethos. The cabernet fruit gives a varietal earthy/dusty edge to the blackcurrant fruit, coupled with fine, supple tannins. The balance and length of the palate are excellent. Screwcap. 13.5% alc. **Rating** 94 **To** 2029 $30 ✪

ŶŶŶŶŶ **La Bohème Act Four Syrah Gamay 2016 Rating** 93 **To** 2020 $20 ✪
Vinoque Yarra Valley Nebbiolo Rose 2016 Rating 92 **To** 2018 $25 ✪
BellaRiva King Valley Pinot Grigio 2016 Rating 90 **To** 2019 $17 ✪
Vinoque The Oval Vineyard Yarra Valley Pinot Blanc 2016 Rating 90 **To** 2018 $25
Vinoque Chalmers Vineyard Heathcote Greco 2016 Rating 90 **To** 2023 $25

La Bohème Act Three Pinot Gris & Friends 2016 Rating 90 To 2021 $22
Villages Yarra Valley Pinot Noir 2016 Rating 90 To 2021 $22
La Bohème The Missing Act Cabernet and Friend 2015 Rating 90
To 2023 $22
Prosecco NV Rating 90 To 2017 $18 TS
La Bohème Cuvee Blanc NV Rating 90 To 2017 $24 TS

De Iuliis ★★★★★

1616 Broke Road, Pokolbin, NSW 2320 **Region** Hunter Valley
T (02) 4993 8000 **www.**dewine.com.au **Open** 7 days 10–5
Winemaker Michael De Iuliis **Est.** 1990 **Dozens** 10 000 **Vyds** 30ha
Three generations of the De Iuliis family have been involved in the establishment of their
vineyard. The family acquired a property at Lovedale in 1986 and planted 18ha of vines in '90,
selling the grapes from the first few vintages to Tyrrell's but retaining increasing amounts for
release under the De Iuliis label. In '99 the land on Broke Road was purchased, and a winery
and cellar door were built prior to the 2000 vintage. In '11 the business purchased 12ha of
the long-established Steven Vineyard in Pokolbin. Winemaker Michael De Iuliis completed
postgraduate studies in oenology at the Roseworthy campus of Adelaide University and was
a Len Evans Tutorial scholar. He has lifted the quality of the wines into the highest echelon.

🍷🍷🍷🍷🍷 **Limited Release Hunter Valley Shiraz 2014** This ripper is produced by
blending the best barrels from a number of sites. It is positively unctuous, painting
the mouth with a mesmerising array of red, purple, blue and black fruits, the
flavours lingering long in the mouth after the wine is swallowed, yet it is no more
than medium-bodied. Screwcap. 14.6% alc. **Rating** 98 To 2054 $80 ❂

🍷🍷🍷🍷🍷 **Hunter Valley Semillon 2016** Top gold in the semillon class at the Sydney
Wine Show '16. The crossover with 1yo riesling can confuse, but the acidity is
more pronounced, the lemongrass notes are peculiar to semillon and, as they
age, the wines will adopt different personalities, honeyed nuances developing
at 10+ years, the crackling acidity unchanged. Screwcap. 10.9% alc. **Rating** 95
To 2031 $20 ❂
Steven Vineyard Hunter Valley Shiraz 2015 Light, bright crimson-purple;
the celebrated Steven Vineyard is approaching its 50th birthday, and has enabled
Mike De Iuliis to produce this elegant, medium-bodied shiraz that is a celebration
of its terroir, Hunter earth and leather woven through the tapestry of red and
purple fruits. Screwcap. 13% alc. **Rating** 94 To 2030 $40

🍷🍷🍷🍷🍷 **Aged Release Hunter Semillon 2011** Rating 93 To 2022 $30 JF
Limited Release Hunter Chardonnay 2014 Rating 93 To 2022 $35 JF
Single Vineyard Hunter Semillon 2016 Rating 92 To 2028 $25 JF ❂
LDR Vineyard Hunter Shiraz Touriga 2015 Rating 92 To 2025 $40 JF
Hunter Valley Chardonnay 2016 Rating 90 To 2021 $20 JF ❂

De Salis Wines ★★★★

Lofty Vineyard, 125 Mount Lofty Road, Nashdale, NSW 2800 **Region** Orange
T 0403 956 295 **www.**desaliswines.com.au **Open** 7 days 11–5
Winemaker Charles Svenson, Mitchell Svenson **Est.** 1999 **Dozens** 4000 **Vyds** 8.76ha
This is the venture of research scientist Charles (Charlie) Svenson and wife Loretta. Charlie
became interested in winemaking when, aged 32, he returned to study microbiology and
biochemistry at UNSW. In 2009, after a prolonged search, Charlie and Loretta purchased
a vineyard first planted in 1993, then known as Wattleview and now as Lofty Vineyard. At
1050m, it is the highest vineyard in the Orange GI, with pinot noir (6 clones), chardonnay,
merlot, pinot meunier and sauvignon blanc. In 2015 they purchased the Forest Edge Vineyard
with pinot noir (2ha, including three clones), sauvignon blanc (2.5ha) and chardonnay (1.5ha).
The majority of the fruit from this vineyard is sold to Brokenwood.

$\mathbb{Y}\mathbb{Y}\mathbb{Y}\mathbb{Y}\mathbb{Y}$ **Lofty Chardonnay 2015** By far the best balanced of the De Salis '15 Chardonnays, picked twice (12.1 and 12.3° baume), the acidity reduced by full mlf to 8.75g/l. The problem lies in balanced ripening of the grapes; the vineyard must be very cool indeed. Screwcap. 12.7% alc. **Rating** 90 **To** 2022 $05

Dead Man Walking ★★★★☆

11a Bizana Street, West Footscray, Vic 3012 **Region** Adelaide Hills/Clare Valley
T 0400 118 020 www.deadmanwalkingwine.com **Open** Not
Winemaker Thomas Kies **Est.** 2015 **Dozens** 380
Thomas Kies explains the slightly ghoulish name he has chosen for his business thus: 'Don't put it off, don't procrastinate, don't leave it until it's too late. That's why [I] created the label after spending years working in the wine industry, with time spent at wineries in Tasmania, Victoria and overseas, and later as a wine distributor in Melbourne.' He works with growers in the Adelaide Hills and Clare Valley to select small parcels of grapes to be made with small batch techniques, hopefully showcasing the quality and purity of their fruit.

$\mathbb{Y}\mathbb{Y}\mathbb{Y}\mathbb{Y}\mathbb{Y}$ **Clare Valley Riesling 2016** Picked early to preserve natural acidity of 7.2g/l and a pH of 2.87, the result a classic Clare riesling of lime, lemon and Granny Smith apple fruit with an exhilarating line of acidity that leaves the mouth fresh and begging for more. Screwcap. 11.5% alc. **Rating** 95 **To** 2026 $25 **○**

$\mathbb{Y}\mathbb{Y}\mathbb{Y}\mathbb{Y}\mathbb{Y}$ Adelaide Hills Pinot Gris 2016 Rating 91 To 2022 $25

Deakin Estate ★★★☆

Kulkyne Way, via Red Cliffs, Vic 3496 **Region** Murray Darling
T (03) 5018 5555 www.deakinestate.com.au **Open** Not
Winemaker Frank Newman **Est.** 1980 **Dozens** 205 000 **Vyds** 350ha
Deakin Estate is owned by Freixenet of Spain, as is Katnook Estate. For over 10 years, Dr Phil Spillman steered the development of Deakin Estate, his rather large shoes filled by Frank Newman. Frank has had a long and varied career, starting at Penfolds working alongside Max Schubert, then Angove (for more than a decade) and BRL Hardy at Renmano. The very large production, with an enlarged range of brands, is only part of the story: with other labels produced at the estate, the annual crush of 2500 tonnes for Deakin is doubled, as is the production of bottled wines under those other labels. Exports to all major markets.

$\mathbb{Y}\mathbb{Y}\mathbb{Y}\mathbb{Y}\mathbb{Y}$ **La La Land Tempranillo 2015** Has retained excellent crimson-purple hue, the flavours equally surprisingly fresh and juicy, with a seductive lift to the red fruits on the finish. A great success. Screwcap. 13.5% alc. **Rating** 92 **To** 2020 $18 **○**

$\mathbb{Y}\mathbb{Y}\mathbb{Y}\mathbb{Y}$ Shiraz 2016 Rating 89 To 2019 $10 JF **○**

Deep Woods Estate ★★★★★

889 Commonage Road, Yallingup, WA 6282 **Region** Margaret River
T (08) 9756 6066 www.deepwoods.com.au **Open** Wed–Sun 11–5, 7 days during hols
Winemaker Julian Langworthy, Emma Gillespie **Est.** 1987 **Dozens** 30 000 **Vyds** 14ha
Owned by Perth businessman Peter Fogarty and family, who also own Lake's Folly in the Hunter Valley, and Millbrook in the Perth Hills. The 32ha property has 14ha of cabernet sauvignon, shiraz, merlot, cabernet franc, chardonnay, sauvignon blanc, semillon and verdelho. Named Winery of the Year by Ray Jordan in his *The West Australian Wine Guide 2017*, Julian Langworthy distinguishing himself as one of the foremost talents in Australia, the 2014 Reserve Cabernet Sauvignon named as both Wine of the Year and Red Wine of the Year in the Jordan book. Exports to Germany, Malaysia, Singapore, Japan and China.

$\mathbb{Y}\mathbb{Y}\mathbb{Y}\mathbb{Y}\mathbb{Y}$ **Yallingup 2014** Made from 31yo vines, this is a selection of the five best barriques (three new) from the larger make of Reserve Cabernet. The colour is still a bright crimson-purple hue, the bouquet complex, the palate shocking in the quite extraordinary power and complexity of its blackcurrant, bramble and glittering tannins. How it manages to end up fresh on the finish is beyond my imagination or comprehension. Screwcap. 14.5% alc. **Rating** 98 **To** 2044 $130 ✪

Reserve Margaret River Chardonnay 2015 Hand-picked, chilled overnight, whole-bunch pressed, wild-yeast fermented in new and used French oak, limited lees contact. Glinting straw-green; the palate is almost aching in its intensity and length, arcing through white peach, nectarine, grapefruit zest and mouthwatering acidity. The finish and aftertaste give a high fidelity replay of all that has gone before. Screwcap. 13% alc. **Rating** 97 **To** 2035 $45 ✪

ŸŸŸŸŸ **Harmony Margaret River Rose 2016** 70% shiraz, 22% tempranillo, 8% grenache crushed separately, promptly removed from the skins, fermented in tank with aromatic yeast. An ultra-fragrant bouquet with delicately spicy small red fruits, the lissom palate of wild strawberries with an unusual blend of delicacy, yet arresting flavours and finish. Trophy Best Rose Margaret River Wine Show '16, gold medal Melbourne Wine Awards. Screwcap. 13% alc. **Rating** 96 **To** 2018 $15 ✪

Margaret River Rose 2016 68% tempranillo, 27% shiraz, 5% vermentino, the vermentino barrel-fermented, the tempranillo and shiraz oxidatively handled pre-fermentation. The bouquet leaps out of the glass with a mix of talc, sour cherry and citrus zest, the bone dry, savoury palate all about texture, with spice and red fruits in second place. Screwcap. 12.5% alc. **Rating** 96 **To** 2018 $30 ✪

Reserve Block 7 Margaret River Shiraz 2015 Partly from the first planting at Deep Woods in '87, partly from an adjacent, mature vineyard. Whole bunches, cold soak and partial barrel fermentation, then a selection of the best French barriques that have matured the wine for 14 months. Deeply coloured, it is full-bodied, yet dazzlingly light on its feet on the finish and aftertaste, fruit, tannins and oak all on the same page. Screwcap. 14.5% alc. **Rating** 96 **To** 2035 $45 ✪

Reserve Margaret River Cabernet Sauvignon 2015 From the oldest estate vines, plus grapes from a nearby grower, crushed and destemmed, 16 months maturation in new and used French barriques. A perfumed, brambly bouquet leads into a medium-bodied palate that caresses the mouth with blackcurrant, redcurrant and herbs. Screwcap. 14% alc. **Rating** 96 **To** 2030 $65 ✪

Margaret River Sauvignon Blanc 2016 Incorporates a small percentage of barrel ferment and lees stirring. This is an exceptionally vigorous and complex wine with a banner headline to both the bouquet and palate of passionfruit and citrus. The superabundant flavours deal with the extremely high natural acidity of 9g/l. This is irresistible. Screwcap. 12.5% alc. **Rating** 95 **To** 2018 $20 ✪

Margaret River Cabernet Sauvignon Merlot 2015 78% cabernet sauvignon, 18% merlot, 4% petit verdot; matured for 18 months in French oak (30% new). An immaculately bred and raised wine, transparently displaying its cassis and bay leaf fruit, its quality French oak and its superfine tannins on its medium-bodied palate. Balanced and can be enjoyed now. Screwcap. 14% alc. **Rating** 95 **To** 2025 $35 ✪

Margaret River Shiraz et al 2015 85% shiraz, 10% malbec, 5% grenache, part matured in large French barrels for 12–15 months. Full, bright crimson-purple hue; while it overflows with the aromas and flavours of succulent plums, blackberries and spicy red fruits, its soft, velvety tannin mouthfeel makes it a classic now or later drinking proposition. Screwcap. 14.5% alc. **Rating** 94 **To** 2021 $20 ✪

ŸŸŸŸŸ **Ivory Semillon Sauvignon Blanc 2016 Rating** 92 **To** 2018 $15 ✪
Margaret River Chardonnay 2016 Rating 92 **To** 2019 $20 ✪
Ebony Cabernet Shiraz 2015 Rating 90 **To** 2020 $15 ✪

DEGEN   ★★★★☆

365 Deasys Road, Pokolbin, NSW 2320 **Region** Hunter Valley
T 0427 078 737 **www**.degenwines.com.au **Open** W'ends 10–5
Winemaker Various contract **Est.** 2001 **Dozens** 1880 **Vyds** 4.5ha
In June 1997 marine engineer Tom Degen, together with IT project manager wife Jean, took a weekend drive to the Hunter Valley with no particular plan in mind, but as a consequence of that drive, became the owners of an 11ha wild, heavily wooded bush block, dotted with

boulders, with no fencing or water. The weekend drive became an every weekend drive to mount their John Deere tractor and slowly but surely clear tonnes of timber, remove the boulders, build a dam and work the soil. In Sept 2001 they planted 1.8ha of shiraz, 1.7ha chardonnay and 1ha semillon, and by '13 opened the cellar door and Wine Stay (accommodating 4 guests).

ȲȲȲȲȲ **Single Vineyard Hunter Valley Chardonnay 2014** Made by the incredibly talented Liz Jackson. It is still at the start of its life. Perfectly balanced, and the marvellously fresh white peach, melon and grapefruit flavours barely show the French oak. Lovely wine. Screwcap. 13.1% alc. **Rating** 95 **To** 2023 $30 ✪
Single Vineyard Hunter Valley Shiraz 2014 Made by Andrew Leembruggen. Medium to full red-purple; the power and intensity of the '14 vintage ignites this medium to full-bodied shiraz, augmented by French and American oak and ripe tannins. Born to age. Screwcap. 13% alc. **Rating** 94 **To** 2034 $35

Delamere Vineyard

Bridport Road, Pipers Brook, Tas 7254 **Region** Northern Tasmania
T (03) 6382 7190 **www.**delamerevineyards.com.au **Open** 7 days 10–5
Winemaker Shane Holloway, Fran Austin **Est.** 1983 **Dozens** 5000 **Vyds** 13.5ha
Delamere was one of the first vineyards planted in the Pipers Brook area. It was purchased by Shane Holloway and wife Fran Austin and their families in 2007. Shane and Fran are in charge of viticulture and winemaking. The vineyard has been expanded with 4ha of pinot noir and chardonnay. Exports to China.

ȲȲȲȲȲ **Pinot Noir 2014** Seriously good, marrying finesse with complexity and intensity, capable of causing havoc in a blind tasting with its overtones of Vosne-Romanée in Burgundy. There is a framework of foresty notes, but the focus is on the painting in the frame, gently spicy plum and black cherry fruit in perfect harmony with the oak and tannins. Screwcap. 13.8% alc. **Rating** 98 **To** 2030 $45 ✪

ȲȲȲȲȲ **Block 3 Chardonnay 2014** From the oldest estate vines, whole-bunch pressed, wild-yeast fermented (including mlf) and matured for 12 months in new oak with lees stirring, aged a further year in bottle. Powerful, complex and intense, with layer upon layer of flavours orbiting around grapefruit, unfazed by the new oak, which is simply woven into the fruit. Diam. 13.7% alc. **Rating** 96 **To** 2029 $110
Pinot Noir 2015 30+yo estate vines, open-fermented with wild yeast, 20% whole bunches, matured in French oak. The bouquet is highly expressive, with savoury earthy notes jostling for space with red cherry fruits and new French oak. The palate has the exceptional intensity that is the hallmark of Delamere, the vines and meticulous viticulture providing the springboard for a pinot of real style and individuality. Screwcap. 13.9% alc. **Rating** 96 **To** 2030 $50 ✪
Hurlo's Rose 2015 Named in honour of family friend John Hurlstone, a connoisseur of fine wine. From the oldest estate pinot noir vines, destemmed, pressed, fermented in French oak (50% new), matured for 10 months on lees. Except for the difference in the sequence of pressing, made exactly as a pinot noir table wine might be made, and given a price to match. The gentle savoury complexity of the bouquet changes gears in no uncertain fashion on the intense and long palate of fraises du bois. Screwcap. 13.6% alc. **Rating** 95 **To** 2020 $80
Block 8 Pinot Noir 2014 From the oldest estate vines, destemmed, 30% whole bunches, 5 days cold soak, open-fermented, hand-plunged twice daily, pressed to French oak (50% new) after 14 days, matured for 10 months. Exceptionally complex, with dark cherry fruit and savoury forest floor characters enjoying star billing, but with a host of lesser parts playing support roles, the whole-bunch inclusion the most notable. Diam. 13.9% alc. **Rating** 95 **To** 2024 $110
Naissante Pinot Noir 2015 From growers in the Tamar Valley. Hand-picked, wild-yeast fermented with 30-40% whole bunches, matured in French barriques. The light colour gives no clue about the intensity of the wine in the mouth, a substantial part from the whole bunch fermentation, introducing foresty/herbal

notes that sit well with the red cherry and strawberry fruit flavours; the tannins, too, make a positive contribution. Screwcap. 13.9% alc. **Rating** 94 To 2027 $27 **○**

🍷🍷🍷🍷🍷 Chardonnay 2015 Rating 93 To 2025 $50
Naissante Riesling 2014 Rating 92 To 2024 $27
Chardonnay 2014 Rating 92 To 2024 $45
Rose NV Rating 92 To 2017 $30 TS
Cuvee 2013 Rating 91 To 2017 $50 TS
Naissante Fume Blanc 2015 Rating 90 To 2020 $27
Blanc de Blanc 2011 Rating 90 To 2019 $65 TS
Blanc de Blanc 2010 Rating 90 To 2017 $65 TS

Delatite ★★★★★

26 High Street, Mansfield, Vic 3722 **Region** Upper Goulburn
T (03) 5775 2922 **www.**delatitewinery.com.au **Open** 7 days 11–5
Winemaker Andy Browning **Est.** 1982 **Dozens** 5000 **Vyds** 26ha
With its sweeping views across to the snow-clad Alps, this is uncompromising cool climate viticulture. Increasing vine age (many of the plantings are well over 30 years old), and the adoption of organic (and partial biodynamic) viticulture, seem also to have played a role in providing the red wines with more depth and texture; the white wines are as good as ever; all are wild-yeast fermented. In 2011 Vestey Holdings Limited, the international pastoral giant, acquired a majority holding in Delatite, and has said it represents one of 'what we hope will be a number of agricultural businesses here'. Exports to Denmark, China, Japan and Malaysia.

🍷🍷🍷🍷🍷 Vivienne's Block Reserve Riesling 2016 48yo estate vines, whole-bunch pressed, wild-yeast fermented. High quality, intense and very long, with lime juice and zest filling the palate. Screwcap. 13% alc. **Rating** 95 To 2030 $39
Deadman's Hill Gewurztraminer 2016 Vines with an average age of 25 years, whole-bunch pressed, mostly wild-yeast fermented in stainless steel, a small portion (9%) in used puncheons. Delatite has always had a high reputation for its Gewurztraminer. It has spicy/lychee/rose petal aromas and flavours as the starting point, but it also has a very complex texture and structure underpinning its length. Screwcap. 14.5% alc. **Rating** 95 To 2023 $27 **○**

🍷🍷🍷🍷🍷 Tempranillo 2015 Rating 93 To 2027 $35
Riesling 2016 Rating 91 To 2024 $27
Pinot Gris 2016 Rating 91 To 2018 $27
High Ground Sauvignon Blanc 2016 Rating 90 To 2017 $20 **○**
High Ground Pinot Noir 2016 Rating 90 To 2023 $20 **○**
Devil's River Cabernet Merlot 2012 Rating 90 To 2022 $35

Delinquente Wine Co ★★★★

36 Brooker Terrace, Richmond, SA 5033 **Region** Riverland
T 0437 876 407 **www.**delinquentewineco.com **Open** Not
Winemaker Various **Est.** 2013 **Dozens** 3500
A Hollywood actress was famous for saying, 'I don't care what they say about me as long as they spell my name right.' Con-Greg Grigoriou might say, 'I don't care how bad people think my wine labels are as long as they remember them.' Con-Greg grew up on a vineyard in the Riverland, and spent a lot of time in wineries, with his father and grandfather, and has decided to concentrate on southern Italian grape varieties. It's a virtual winery operation, buying fruit from growers who share his vision and having the wine made wherever he is able to find a facility prepared to assist in the making of micro-quantities. Delinquente is getting a lot of airplay from the smart set, and it's no surprise to see production jump from 600 to 3500 dozen. Exports to the UK, the US, Singapore and Japan.

🍷🍷🍷🍷🍷 The Bullet Dodger Riverland Montepulciano 2016 Deep vermilion hue verging on opaque. The wine is explosive with dark fruit flavours without being sweet, heavy, or in any way jammy, due to dry, arched and savoury tannins. They splay themselves across the mouth, restraining the fruit while forcing flavour into every corner of the mouth and imbuing a sense of energy. Dusty and delicious. Screwcap. 14.5% alc. **Rating** 92 **To** 2020 $22 NG ○

Pretty Boy Riverland Nero d'Avola Rosato 2016 Musky palate, firmly glimpsing ripe red and dark fruit flavours glazed with orange zest, without foraging in the territory of excess. A bead of unresolved CO_2 combines nicely with the gentle ebb and flow of tangy acidity and phenolics, conferring a sense of savouriness. Screwcap. 12% alc. **Rating** 90 **To** 2018 $22 NG

Roxanne the Razor Riverland Nero d'Avola Montepulciano 2016 An 80/20% blend, this is a juicy wine redolent of dark cherries, violet and plum. The finish is dusted with Asian five-spice. A juicy core of carbonic pulp is hewn to well etched tannins, conferring focus and length. Screwcap. 14% alc. **Rating** 90 **To** 2020 $22 NG

ΨΨΨΨ   **Screaming Betty Riverland Vermentino 2016** Rating 89 To 2019 $22 NG

Dell'uva Wines   ★★★★★

194 Richards Road, Freeling, SA 5372 **Region** Barossa Valley
T (08) 8525 2245 **www**.delluvawines.com **Open** By appt
Winemaker Wayne Farquhar **Est.** 2014 **Dozens** 500

Owner and winemaker Wayne Farquhar moved from horticulture to viticulture, acquiring his first vineyard in 1979. His viticultural career was low-key for a number of years, but having tasted wines from all over the world over a decade of business travel, he decided to establish Dell'uva Wines off the back of his existing (conventional) vineyard on the western ridge of the Barossa Valley. In short order he established small plots of an A–Z of varieties: aglianico, albarino, ansonica, arinto, barbera, cabernet sauvignon, canaiolo nero, carmenere, carnelian, chardonnay, dolcetto, durif, fiano, freisca, garnacha, graciano, grillo, lagrein, merlot, marsanne, mencia, montepulciano, moscato bianco, mourvedre, negroamaro, nero d'Avola, pinot blanc, pinot grigio, pinot noir, primitivo, roussanne, sagrantino, sangiovese, saperavi, shiraz, tannat, tempranillo, touriga nacional, verdelho, vermentino, verdicchio, viognier. With only 20ha available, the production of each wine is necessarily limited, the vinification as unconventional as the vineyard mix, utilising barrels, ceramic eggs, demijohns and tanks. The winemaking techniques have been chosen to throw maximum attention onto the inherent quality of the varieties, and this story has a long way to run.

Della Fay Wines   ★★★★★

3276 Caves Road, Yallingup, WA 6284 **Region** Margaret River
T (08) 9755 2747 **www**.kellysvineyard.com.au **Open** By appt
Winemaker Michael Kelly **Est.** 1999 **Dozens** 3000 **Vyds** 8ha

This is the venture of the Kelly family, headed by district veteran Michael Kelly, who gained his degree in wine science from CSU before working at Seville Estate and Mount Mary in the Yarra Valley and Domaine Louis Chapuis in Burgundy, then coming back to WA working for Leeuwin Estate and Sandalford. From there he became the long-term winemaker at Fermoy Estate, but he and his family laid the groundwork for their own brand, buying prime viticultural land in Caves Road, Yallingup, in 1999. They planted 2ha each of cabernet sauvignon, nebbiolo and sauvignon blanc, and 1ha each of chardonnay and vermentino. Shiraz from the Geographe region is also included. 'Della Fay' honours the eponymous Kelly family matriarch. Exports to The Netherlands, South Korea, Singapore and China.

ΨΨΨΨΨ   **Reserve Geographe Shiraz 2013** From the Barreca family vineyard in
Geographe, that Michael Kelly believes is the best region in WA. The deep purple-crimson hue is an impressive start, and while the initial impression is of a surfeit of new oak, retasting puts the vibrant and intense fruit far in front. Screwcap. 14.5% alc. **Rating** 97 **To** 2038 $25 ○

ΨΨΨΨΨ   **Margaret River Cabernet Sauvignon 2014** An uncompromisingly full-bodied
cabernet with a Bordeaux-like austerity to it despite its overcoat of new French oak. It's built for the long haul, with a rock solid foundation of tannins. Screwcap. 14% alc. **Rating** 95 **To** 2044 $30 ○

Denton Viewhill Vineyard

160 Old Healesville Road, Yarra Glen, Vic 3775 **Region** Yarra Valley
T (03) 9012 3600 **www**.dentonwine.com **Open** By appt
Winemaker Luke Lambert **Est.** 1996 **Dozens** 2000 **Vyds** 31.3ha

Leading Melbourne architect John Denton and son Simon began the establishment of the vineyard with a first stage planting in 1997, completing the plantings in 2004. The name Viewhill derives from the fact that a granite plug 'was created 370 million years ago, sitting above the surrounding softer sandstones and silt of the valley'. This granite base is most unusual in the Yarra Valley, and, together with the natural amphitheatre that the plug created, has consistently produced exceptional grapes. The principal varieties planted are pinot noir, chardonnay and shiraz, with lesser quantities of nebbiolo, cabernet sauvignon, merlot, cabernet franc and petit verdot.

ΨΨΨΨΨ **DM Chardonnay 2015** Take a core of pristine fruit, add layers of considered winemaking – the right oak and its spices, the lees, the creamy-nuttiness – and a picture starts to emerge of a complex wine. This also has a depth to it, with super tangy acidity injected through the flavours: like a whirling dervish, it might leave you dizzy. Screwcap. 13.5% alc. **Rating** 96 **To** 2025 $43 JF ❂
DM Pinot Noir 2015 While it lays its drinkability card firmly on the table, it's a neatly composed wine with tangy cherries and cranberries, all spiced up with ginger, freeze-dried raspberry powder and woodsy spices, some twigs too. Medium-bodied, with chewy tannins and zesty acidity ensuring that this is an ultra-refreshing drink. Diam. 13.5% alc. **Rating** 95 **To** 2023 $43 JF

ΨΨΨΨΨ **Denton Shed Pinot Noir 2016** Rating 93 **To** 2019 $30 JF
Denton Shed Chardonnay 2016 Rating 91 **To** 2021 $30 JF
DM Nebbiolo 2014 Rating 91 **To** 2025 $50 JF

Deonte Wines

Lot 111 Research Road, Tanunda, SA 5352 **Region** Barossa Valley
T (03) 9819 4890 **www**.deontewines.com.au **Open** By appt
Winemaker Benjamin Edwards **Est.** 2012 **Dozens** 15 000 **Vyds** 10.29ha

This is the venture of Zhijun (George) Hu, who has started a virtual winery with the primary purpose of exporting to China. The initial focus has been on the Yarra Valley, Coonawarra and the Barossa Valley, shiraz figuring prominently, either as a single variety, or as part of a blend with cabernet sauvignon. Having neither a vineyard nor a winery affords George maximum flexibility in purchasing grapes and/or bulk wine, and he does have ongoing exclusive grape supply contracts from 10.29ha in the Barossa Valley. Exports to China.

ΨΨΨΨΨ **Exceptional Barrels Seppeltsfield Barossa Valley Shiraz 2014** Deep, crimson-purple; the bouquet signals what is to come, with a deep well of spiced plum and oak aromas. In full-bodied Deonte style, the mid-palate upstaged by the crescendo of extract on the finish. Screwcap. 14.3% alc. **Rating** 90 **To** 2025 $52

ΨΨΨΨ **Exceptional Barrels Nuriootpa Barossa Valley Shiraz 2014** Rating 89 **To** 2024 $59

Deviation Road

207 Scott Creek Road, Longwood, SA 5153 **Region** Adelaide Hills
T (08) 8339 2633 **www**.deviationroad.com **Open** 7 days 10–5
Winemaker Kate and Hamish Laurie **Est.** 1999 **Dozens** 6000 **Vyds** 11.05ha

Deviation Road was created in 1998 by Hamish Laurie, great-great-grandson of Mary Laurie, SA's first female winemaker. He initially joined with father Dr Chris Laurie in '92 to help build the Hillstowe Wines business; the brand was sold in 2001, but the Laurie family retained the vineyard, which now supplies Deviation Road with its grapes. Wife Kate joined the business in '01, having studied winemaking and viticulture in Champagne, then spent four years at her family's Stone Bridge winery in Manjimup. It also has 3ha of pinot noir and shiraz at Longwood, where its cellar door is situated. Exports to the UK, the US and Hong Kong.

ŸŸŸŸŸ **Pinot Gris 2016** The quality of this pinot gris derives from the vineyard (no surprise), and from the winery (20% fermented in French oak). It loses no time in establishing its complexity and intensity, and for good measure, its future. The bouquet is good, but the palate is the prize-winner with its mix of gooseberry, stone fruits and citrussy acidity. Screwcap. 12.5% alc. **Rating** 95 **To** 2020 $30 **✪**
Chardonnay 2015 Fermented and matured in French barriques. Juicy, fresh and vibrant, white peach and pink grapefruit sustained and lengthened by crisp acidity. Screwcap. 12% alc. **Rating** 94 **To** 2023 $45
Altair Brut Rose NV A gorgeously elegant cuvee that articulates the character of Adelaide Hills pinot noir and chardonnay with the utmost grace and finesse. Subtle strawberry hull, red cherry, pink grapefruit and lemon define a primary and pristine style, impeccably supported by vibrant Adelaide Hills acidity and invisible dosage. Cork. 12% alc. **Rating** 94 **To** 2017 $30 TS **✪**

ŸŸŸŸŸ **Loftia Adelaide Hills Vintage Brut 2014** **Rating** 93 **To** 2024 $45 TS

Devil's Cave Vineyard ★★★★

250 Forest Drive, Heathcote, Vic 3523 **Region** Heathcote
T 0438 110 183 **www**.devilscavevineyard.com **Open** By appt
Winemaker Luke Lomax, Steve Johnson **Est.** 2012 **Dozens** 550 **Vyds** 0.4ha
This is an acorn and oak story. After retiring from 40+ years of business in Heathcote, Steve and Gay Johnson purchased the property to enjoy their retirement. In 2010 they planted 0.4ha of shiraz, the name coming from an adjacent cave locally known as 'the Devil's Cave'. In 2012 Steve asked Luke Lomax (his niece's husband) to help with the first vintage of 33 dozen bottles. Luke was assistant winemaker for Yabby Lake, with particular responsibility for Heathcote Estate wines. The cameraderie was such that the Johnsons formed a partnership with Luke and Jade Lomax, and it's been onwards and upwards since then, with an impressive collection of gold and silver medals for the '13, '14 and '15 Shirazs. The plantings continue, the partnership also sourcing shiraz and cabernet sauvignon from Coliban Glen Vineyard.

ŸŸŸŸŸ **Heathcote Shiraz 2015** Hand-picked, destemmed, open-fermented, hand-plunged, basket-pressed, matured in French oak. This doesn't push the richness envelope too far. It is a neatly cadenced wine, with purple and black fruits resting on a gently savoury/earthy bed. Screwcap. 14% alc. **Rating** 91 **To** 2029 $33
Heathcote Grenache Rose 2016 Very pale pink, no more than blush; a fragrant rose petal/rosehip bouquet leads into a delicate, dry palate with flavours taking in a touch of citrus alongside red fruits. Well made, the modest alcohol a feature. Screwcap. 13% alc. **Rating** 90 **To** 2017 $25

Devil's Corner ★★★★★

The Hazards Vineyard, Sherbourne Road, Apslawn, Tas 7190 **Region** East Coast Tasmania
T (03) 6257 8881 **www**.devilscorner.com.au **Open** 7 days 10–5 (Nov–Apr)
Winemaker Tom Wallace **Est.** 1999 **Dozens** 70 000 **Vyds** 175ha
This is one of the separately managed operations of Brown Brothers' Tasmanian interests, taking The Hazards Vineyard on the east coast as its chief source: it is planted to pinot noir, chardonnay, sauvignon blanc, pinot gris, riesling, gewurztraminer and savagnin. The avant-garde labels mark a decided change from the past, and also distinguish Devil's Corner from the other Tasmanian activities of Brown Brothers. Exports to all major markets.

ŸŸŸŸŸ **Riesling 2016** Won three trophies at the Tasmanian Wine Show '17 thanks to its mix of extreme purity, intensity and length. Its balance and its aftertaste of lime, Granny Smith apple and lemon follows with the inevitability of day into night. It has limitless longevity, but I'll settle for 30 years. Screwcap. 12% alc. **Rating** 97 **To** 2046 $20 **✪**

🍷🍷🍷🍷🍷 **Mt Amos Pinot Noir 2015** Partial whole bunches, cold-soaked, open-fermented, matured in French oak (35% new). The aromatic bouquet has both cherry and plum fruit to spare, the palate veering to the savoury/spicy side, bringing texture and structure into the game. It's very well balanced, with a classically long palate and aftertaste. Screwcap. 13% alc. **Rating** 95 **To** 2028 $65
Resolution Pinot Noir 2015 Has all the striking intensity and length of very cool-grown pinot. The bouquet is alluring, with cherry, red berry and spice tumbling over each other, the supple, long palate picking up those flavours, then finishing with a savoury flourish. Very good now, great later. Screwcap. 13% alc. **Rating** 94 **To** 2025 $30 ○

🍷🍷🍷🍷🍷 **Resolution Chardonnay 2013 Rating** 93 **To** 2021 $30
Pinot Noir 2016 Rating 92 **To** 2025 $23 ○
Pinot Noir 2015 Rating 91 **To** 2023 $20 ○
Sauvignon Blanc 2015 Rating 90 **To** 2017 $20 ○
Sparkling NV Rating 90 **To** 2017 $23 TS

Devil's Lair   ★★★★★

Rocky Road, Forest Grove via Margaret River, WA 6285 **Region** Margaret River
T 1300 651 650 **www**.devils-lair.com **Open** Not
Winemaker Luke Skeer **Est.** 1981 **Dozens** NFP
Having rapidly carved out a high reputation for itself through a combination of clever packaging and impressive wine quality, Devil's Lair was acquired by Southcorp in 1996. The estate vineyards have been substantially increased since, now with sauvignon blanc, semillon, chardonnay, cabernet sauvignon, merlot, shiraz, cabernet franc and petit verdot, supplemented by grapes purchased from contract growers. Production has increased from 40000 dozen to many times greater, largely due to its Fifth Leg and Dance With the Devil wines. Exports to the UK, the US and other major markets.

🍷🍷🍷🍷🍷 **9th Chamber Margaret River Chardonnay 2013** A powerful chardonnay with energy, drive and flavour to match, yet remains quite airy. Creamy, nutty, flinty, struck match, lots of moreish sulphides and leesy characters, actually plenty of flavour but not too much. It's balanced, fresh, the oak, the spice and fruit all neatly played, the palate long, pure and goes at its own pace. 250 dozen. Screwcap. 13% alc. **Rating** 97 **To** 2023 $100 JF ○

🍷🍷🍷🍷🍷 **Margaret River Chardonnay 2015** A pristine wine with great length and detail. The fruit, as always, points the way with its mix of grapefruit and white stone fruit, a liberal dose of ginger spice and fennel, and leads to a superfine palate with matching acidity. Screwcap. 12.5% alc. **Rating** 95 **To** 2025 $50 JF
Margaret River Cabernet Sauvignon 2014 The heady aromas set the scene with ribbons of black and red currants, cassis and leafy freshness playing with cedary spice from the integrated oak, and chiselled tannins morphing into the silky medium-bodied palate. Screwcap. 14.5% alc. **Rating** 95 **To** 2034 $50 JF
The Hidden Cave Margaret River Cabernet Shiraz 2014 Not a common blend in the Margaret River, but works well here, driven with precision by the cabernet's extremely attractive display of cassis, tempered by the softer fruit of the shiraz. The tannins are balanced and integrated, the oak likewise, all making for a very smart wine. Screwcap. 14.5% alc. **Rating** 94 **To** 2029 $24 ○

🍷🍷🍷🍷🍷 **Fifth Leg Treasure Hunter Reserve Margaret River Sauvignon Blanc 2015 Rating** 92 **To** 2017
Fifth Leg Treasure Hunter Reserve Margaret River Cabernet Merlot 2014 Rating 92 **To** 2029
Dance with the Devil Chardonnay 2016 Rating 91 **To** 2020 $25 JF
The Hidden Cave Sauvignon Blanc Semillon 2016 Rating 90 **To** 2019 $25 JF
Fifth Leg Sauvignon Blanc Semillon 2015 Rating 90 **To** 2018 $18 SC ○
The Hidden Cave Chardonnay 2016 Rating 90 **To** 2020 $24
Fifth Leg Shiraz 2014 Rating 90 **To** 2021 $18 SC ○

Dexter Wines

210 Foxeys Road, Tuerong, Vic 3915 (postal) **Region** Mornington Peninsula
T (03) 5989 7007 **www**.dexterwines.com.au **Open** Not
Winemaker Tod Dexter **Est.** 2006 **Dozens** 2000 **Vyds** 7.1ha
Tod Dexter arrived in the US with the intention of enjoying some skiing; having done that, he became an apprentice winemaker at Cakebread Cellars, a well known Napa Valley winery. After seven years he returned to Australia and the Mornington Peninsula, and began the establishment of the vineyard in 1987, planted to pinot noir (4ha) and chardonnay (3.1ha). To keep the wolves from the door he became winemaker at Stonier, and leased his vineyard to Stonier. Having left Stonier to become Yabby Lake winemaker, and spurred on by turning 50 in 2006 (and at the urging of friends), he and wife Debbie established the Dexter label. Exports to the UK, the US, Denmark, Norway and the UAE.

ŸŸŸŸŸ Black Label Mornington Peninsula Pinot Noir 2016 This is a rare as hen's teeth cuvee from this estate, released seldom and only in top vintages. The pinot's nose makes immediate connection with the earth's mulch and wood smoke. These flavours reverberate across a fulsome palate, drawn across a bow of whole-bunch spike, cool climate acidity and nicely meshed tannins. Red and black cherry appear. Screwcap. 13.5% alc. **Rating** 97 **To** 2028 $75 NG ✪

Di Sciascio Family Wines

2 Pincott Street, Newtown, Vic 3220 **Region** Various Vic
T 0417 384 272 **www**.disciasciofamilywines.com.au **Open** Not
Winemaker Matthew Di Sciascio, Andrew Santarossa **Est.** 2012 **Dozens** 1000
Matthew Di Sciascio's journey through wine has been an odyssey of Homeric proportions. His working life began as an apprentice boilermaker in his father's business. In 1991 he accompanied his father on a trip to Italy, where a shared bottle of wine in the kitchen of his uncle sowed the seed that flowered back in Australia, helping with garage winemaking by his father and friends. In '97, the vinous pace increased, with vineyard work in the Yarra Valley and enrolment in Dookie Agricultural College's viticultural course. It accelerated further with the establishment of Bellbrae Estate in Geelong, and enrolling (in 2002) in the new Deakin University Wine and Science degree, graduating in '05 as co-dux. In Dec '10 the responsibility for seriously ill parents and a young daughter led to the decision to sell his share of Bellbrae to his financial partners, and (in '12) to start this venture.

ŸŸŸŸŸ D'Sas Henty Pinot Gris 2016 This is at the peak of pinot gris quality in this country. A great wine by any standards, filling the mouth with a rainbow of flavours, yet skipping lightly while it does so. It must be said that the frigid climate of Henty also helps the cause. Screwcap. 14% alc. **Rating** 97 **To** 2023 $36 ✪

ŸŸŸŸŸ D'Sas King Valley Rosato 2016 Light, vibrant puce; rose petal and wild strawberry aromas are followed by a bone-dry and gloriously long palate. Here there's an interplay between crisp acidity and a persistent veil of fruits, the latter contributing more to the mouthfeel than the former. Brilliant sangiovese rose. Screwcap. 12.5% alc. **Rating** 95 **To** 2020 $32 ✪
D'Sas Heathcote Sangiovese 2015 A complex bouquet of wattle seed, Turkish Delight, red cherries and watermelon comes together seamlessly on the palate. Here red berries take control, supported by sangio tannins. Make no mistake – this is a very smart wine. Screwcap. 13.5% alc. **Rating** 95 **To** 2028 $40
D'Sas King Valley Pinot Grigio 2016 Quartz-green; this is a delicious pinot grigio, full of nashi pear, citrus and green apple aromas and flavours, so full that they are layered, yet don't lose their freshness and drive. The finish is as fresh as a spring day. Screwcap. 12% alc. **Rating** 94 **To** 2020 $32
D'Sas Henty Field Blend 2015 A blend of viognier, savagnin, pinot gris, riesling, fiano and gewurztraminer all grown in the nursery block of Jack and Lois Doevens' Drumborg vineyard. The cool climate has imposed steel handcuffs to hold all the fruit flavours together, the finish prodigiously long given the character of some of the varieties. Screwcap. 13.5% alc. **Rating** 94 **To** 2021 $32

Reserve Heathcote Shiraz 2015 Bright crimson; the freshness of this wine suggests less alcohol than that of the standard wine, not (as is the case) higher. The elegant, intense medium-bodied palate is full of red fruits, leaving only a little space for black fruits to make their presence felt; the oak is in tune, albeit at a higher level. Screwcap. 14.5% alc. **Rating** 94 **To** 2030 $60

ΨΨΨΨΨ Heathcote Shiraz 2015 **Rating** 90 **To** 2030 $40

 # Dickinson Estate
2414 Cranbrook Road, Boyup Brook, WA 6244 **Region** Blackwood Valley
T (08) 9769 1080 **www**.dickinsonestate.com.au **Open** Not
Winemaker Coby Ladwig, Luke Eckersley **Est.** 1994 **Dozens** 6500 **Vyds** 13.5ha
Trevor and Mary Dickinson went from a 20-year life at sea with the Australian Navy to farmers at Boyup Brook in 1987. They learned on the job, initially cropping and breeding sheep for wool, then cattle and fat lambs. In '94 they diversified further, planting 13.5ha of shiraz, chardonnay, sauvignon blanc and cabernet sauvignon, and appointing the highly experienced team of Coby Ladwig and Luke Eckersley to make the wines. Exports to China.

ΨΨΨΨΨ Blackwood Valley Shiraz 2015 It has a complex bouquet with black fruits, spices and French oak to the fore, the medium-bodied palate closely tracking the bouquet and adding soft, ripe tannins to the package. A flying start, auguring well for the future. Screwcap. 14.5% alc. **Rating** 95 **To** 2030 $23 ✪
Blackwood Valley Cabernet Sauvignon 2015 Well made. There is a consistent style to the Dickinson Estate red wines involving soft, textured tannins, positive use of French oak (possibly some barrel fermentation and maturation) and fruit picked earlier rather than later. The blackcurrant/bay leaf/black olive of this medium-bodied wine is right in the slot. Screwcap. 13.5% alc. **Rating** 95 **To** 2030 $23 ✪

ΨΨΨΨΨ Blackwood Valley Sauvignon Blanc 2016 **Rating** 91 **To** 2018 $23 ✪
Blackwood Valley Chardonnay 2016 **Rating** 91 **To** 2023 $23 ✪

DiGiorgio Family Wines
Riddoch Highway, Coonawarra, SA 5263 **Region** Coonawarra
T (08) 8736 3222 **www**.digiorgio.com.au **Open** 7 days 10–5
Winemaker Peter Douglas **Est.** 1998 **Dozens** 25 000 **Vyds** 353.53ha
Stefano DiGiorgio emigrated from Abruzzo, Italy, in 1952. Over the years, he and his family gradually expanded their holdings at Lucindale to 126ha. In '89 he began planting cabernet sauvignon, chardonnay, merlot, shiraz and pinot noir. In 2002 the family purchased the historic Rouge Homme winery and its surrounding 13.5ha of vines from Southcorp. The plantings have since been increased to almost 230ha, the lion's share to cabernet sauvignon. The enterprise offers full winemaking services to vignerons in the Limestone Coast zone. Exports to all major markets.

ΨΨΨΨΨ Coonawarra Cabernet Sauvignon 2014 Speaks equally loudly of its place and variety, the two having formed a special bond over the past 50+ years. Blackcurrant, earth, briar and black olive weave an intricate, continuously moving pattern on the long palate. Screwcap. 13.5% alc. **Rating** 92 **To** 2030 $23 ✪
Emporio Coonawarra Merlot Cabernet Sauvignon Cabernet Franc 2014 An estate-grown 60/36/4% blend, matured in predominantly new oak for an extended period, bottled Jan '16. A full-bodied wine with a complex blend of red and black currant, plum and black olive fruit flavours backed by sturdy tannins and oak. Screwcap. 13.9% alc. **Rating** 91 **To** 2029 $23 ✪

Dinny Goonan

880 Winchelsea-Deans Marsh Road, Bambra, Vic 3241 **Region** Geelong
T 0438 408 420 **www**.dinnygoonan.com.au **Open** 7 days Jan, w'ends & public hols
Winemaker Dinny and Angus Goonan **Est.** 1990 **Dozens** 1500 **Vyds** 5.5ha
The establishment of Dinny Goonan dates back to 1988, when Dinny bought a 20ha
property near Bambra, in the hinterland of the Otway Coast. Dinny had recently completed
a viticulture diploma at CSU, and initially a wide range of varieties was planted in what is
now known as the Nursery Block, to establish those best suited to the area. As these came
into production Dinny headed back to CSU, where he completed a wine science degree.
Production is focused on shiraz and riesling, with more extensive plantings of these varieties.

Single Vineyard Riesling 2016 A particularly intense young riesling with the
Full Monty of lime juice, zest and pith, and a few apple skins thrown in for good
measure. Just head for your nearest or best Chinese restaurant and congratulate
yourself. Screwcap. 12% alc. **Rating** 95 **To** 2036 $25 ✪

Cabernets 2015 Rating 93 **To** 2025 $27 ✪
Botrytis Semillon 2015 Rating 92 **To** 2021 $30
Single Vineyard Shiraz 2015 Rating 90 **To** 2023 $30

Dirty Three Wines

64 Cashin Street, Inverloch, Vic 3996 **Region** Gippsland
T 0413 547 932 **www**.dirtythreewines.com.au **Open** Thurs–Sun 11–5.30
Winemaker Marcus Satchell **Est.** 2012 **Dozens** 1500 **Vyds** 4ha
The name originates from the three friends (and families) who decided to pool their talents
in making and marketing wine. Marcus Satchell, Cameron McKenzie and Stuart Gregor are
all well known in the nether world of small volume, high quality winemaking on the fringes
of their real jobs. Stuart and Cam also had the distraction of Four Pillars Gin in Healesville, a
fairytale story of success in its own right. There's been a minor change in the name (adding
'Wines') and an ownership change to Marcus and partner Lisa Sartori.

Dirt 3 South Gippsland Pinot Noir 2016 Dirt 3 is the estate vineyard –
Holgates Road – with 25% whole bunches used. This is ready to drink. The
tannins are firm but giving, with refreshing perky acidity among the dark fruits,
juniper berries, star anise and wood spices, plus some damp undergrowth and
orange peel. Screwcap. 13.4% alc. **Rating** 94 **To** 2025 $55 JF

South Gippsland Pinot Noir 2016 Rating 93 **To** 2024 $35 JF
Dirt 2 South Gippsland Pinot Noir 2016 Rating 93 **To** 2024 $55 JF
Holgates Road Pinot Noir 2015 Rating 93 **To** 2025 $48 JF
South Gippsland Riesling 2016 Rating 92 **To** 2023 $30 JF
Dirt 1 South Gippsland Pinot Noir 2016 Rating 92 **To** 2024 $55 JF
Three Gippsland Pinot Noir 2015 Rating 92 **To** 2023 $33 JF

Doc Adams

2/41 High Street, Willunga, SA 5172 **Region** McLaren Vale
T (08) 8556 2111 **www**.docadamswines.com.au **Open** By appt
Winemaker Adam Jacobs **Est.** 2005 **Dozens** 5000 **Vyds** 27ha
Doc Adams is a partnership between viticulturist Adam Jacobs and orthopaedic surgeon Dr
Darren Waters (and their wives). Adam graduated from CSU with a degree in viticulture and
has had over 20 years' experience as a consultant viticulturist. Darren has grown low-yielding
shiraz vines in McLaren Vale since 1998. Exports to China.

1838 First Vines McLaren Vale Shiraz 2015 50% from 103yo vines (not
1838), 50% from 75yo vines. Deep crimson-purple; a full-bodied shiraz with black
fruits, tar, licorice and a breath of regional dark/bitter chocolate; tannins and oak
are necessarily present, but are obscured by the voluminous folds of the dark fruit.
Screwcap. 14.9% alc. **Rating** 94 **To** 2045 $48

Dodgy Brothers

PO Box 655, McLaren Vale, SA 5171 **Region** McLaren Vale
T 0450 000 373 **www**.dodgybrotherswines.com **Open** Not
Winemaker Wes Pearson **Est.** 2010 **Dozens** 2000

This is a partnership between Canadian-born Flying Winemaker Wes Pearson, viticulturist Peter Bolte and grapegrower Peter Sommerville. Wes graduated from the University of British Columbia's biochemistry program in 2008, along the way working at wineries including Chateau Leoville Las Cases in Bordeaux. In '08 he and his family moved to McLaren Vale, and after working at several wineries, he joined the Australian Wine Research Institute as a sensory analyst. Peter Bolte has over 35 vintages in McLaren Vale under his belt, and was the original Dodgy Brother. Peter Sommerville's vineyard provides cabernet sauvignon, cabernet franc and petit verdot for the Dodgy Brothers Bordeaux blend. Exports to Canada.

ᵀᵀᵀᵀᵀ **Archetype McLaren Vale Shiraz 2014** 1.3 tonnes from a special vineyard, crushed, destemmed, open-fermented, matured in French oak (75% new) for 10 months; 90 dozen made. The complex bouquet ranges through black fruits, polished leather and licorice; the medium-bodied palate is seductively juicy and supple, with a long, lingering fruit-filled finish and aftertaste. A classy example of McLaren Vale shiraz, the handling of cedary French oak spot on. Screwcap. 14.6% alc. **Rating** 96 **To** 2030 $40 ⦿
Juxtaposed Push Old Vine McLaren Vale Grenache 2015 An exotic grenache with scents of Turkish Delight, violet and kirsch, hailing from 90yo vines in Clarendon. This is sumptuous. The tannins are sandy, detailed and svelte; the acidity is gentle, but there. Ethereal. Screwcap. 14.4% alc. **Rating** 96 **To** 2028 $35 NG ⦿
Sellicks Foothills McLaren Vale Shiraz 2015 From three vineyards, one a cooler site boasting vines in excess of 70yo. This is a warm meets cool climate type of expression. Dark fruits and violet florals saturate the nose and provide a smooth carpet, reverberating across the palate. Yet things shift gears. The acidity flows and the tannins are impeccably managed, giving a savoury pucker to the ride. Screwcap. 14.5% alc. **Rating** 94 **To** 2033 $26 NG ⦿

ᵀᵀᵀᵀᵀ **Sellicks Foothills McLaren Vale Shiraz 2014** Rating 91 To 2029 $24
Archetype McLaren Vale Grenache 2014 Rating 90 To 2022 $35

DogRidge Wine Company

129 Bagshaws Road, McLaren Flat, SA 5171 **Region** McLaren Vale
T (08) 8383 0140 **www**.dogridge.com.au **Open** 7 days 11–5
Winemaker Fred Howard **Est.** 1991 **Dozens** 10 000 **Vyds** 56ha

Dave and Jen Wright had a combined background of dentistry, art and a CSU viticultural degree when they moved from Adelaide to McLaren Flat to become vignerons. They inherited vines planted in the early 1940s as a source for Chateau Reynella fortified wines, and their vineyards now range from 2001 plantings to some of the oldest vines in the immediate district. At the McLaren Flat vineyards, DogRidge has 70+-year-old shiraz and grenache. Quality at one end, value-packed at the other end. Exports to the UK, the US and other major markets.

ᵀᵀᵀᵀᵀ **Most Valuable Player McLaren Vale Cabernet Sauvignon 2012** This is a beautiful wine from a truly great vintage. The note of Jan '14 is absolutely true of the wine of today. 'Very good colour; cassis is the fruit driver, accompanied by nuances of plum, cedar, oak and earth, the tannins exactly what is needed to provide long-term structure.' Screwcap. 14.5% alc. **Rating** 96 **To** 2032 $65 ⦿

ᵀᵀᵀᵀᵀ **Square Cut McLaren Vale Cabernet 2014** Rating 93 To 2029 $25 ⦿
Shirtfront McLaren Vale Shiraz 2015 Rating 92 To 2035 $25 ⦿
Running Free Grenache Rose 2015 Rating 91 To 2017 $22 ⦿
Noble Rot Sticky White Frontignac 2016 Rating 91 To 2019 $25

DogRock Winery

114 Degraves Road, Crowlands, Vic 3377 **Region** Pyrenees
T 0409 280 317 **www.**dogrock.com.au **Open** By appt
Winemaker Allen Hart **Est.** 1999 **Dozens** 500 **Vyds** 6.2ha
This is the micro-venture of Allen (now full-time winemaker) and Andrea (viticulturist) Hart.
Having purchased the property in 1998, planting of shiraz, riesling, tempranillo, grenache,
chardonnay and marsanne began in 2000. Given Allen's former post as research scientist/
winemaker with Foster's, the attitude taken to winemaking is unexpected. The estate-grown
wines are made in a low-tech fashion, without gas cover or filtration, the Harts saying,
'All wine will be sealed with a screwcap and no DogRock wine will ever be released under
natural cork bark'. DogRock installed the first solar-powered irrigation system in Australia,
capable of supplying water 365 days a year, even at night or in cloudy conditions.

🍷🍷🍷🍷🍷 **Degraves Road Pyrenees Shiraz 2015** Crushed, wild yeast–open fermented,
hand-plunged, pressed after 9 days, matured for 16 months in French oak
(60% new). It has a fragrant bouquet and beautifully structured and balanced
medium-bodied palate; cherry and plum fruit is first and foremost, the tannins
silky, the oak evident but integrated. Gold medal Victorian Wine Show '16.
Screwcap. 14% alc. **Rating** 96 **To** 2035 $35 ✪
Degraves Road Pyrenees Riesling 2016 While logistic limitations have
resulted in the use of a chardonnay-style bottle, it distracts only momentarily
before the sheer power and intensity of the very long palate, and even longer
aftertaste, take your breath away. Lemon zest, pith and unsweetened flavours do the
heavy lifting in this striking wine. Screwcap. 11.5% alc. **Rating** 95 **To** 2026 $25 ✪
Pyrenees Shiraz 2015 Crushed, wild yeast–open fermented, pressed after 7 days,
14 months in French (60% new) and American (10% new) oak. Marries generous
ladles of predominantly purple and black fruits with a savoury, oaky undertow
reflecting texture as much as flavour. Its medium to full-bodied frame assures a
long future ahead. Screwcap. 14% alc. **Rating** 94 **To** 2033 $25 ✪
Degraves Road Pyrenees Grenache 2015 Wild-yeast fermented for 9 days,
and briefly matured in French oak. This is a pure expression of concentrated and
powerful grenache that will flourish in bottle in the same way as the best examples
from the southern Rhône Valley. Screwcap. 14.5% alc. **Rating** 94 **To** 2023 $35
Pyrenees Grenache 2015 A junior brother to Degraves Road, simply built on
a lighter frame, but with delicious red fruits and an appealing twist of savoury spice
on the finish. Screwcap. 14.5% alc. **Rating** 94 **To** 2023 $25 ✪

🍷🍷🍷🍷🍷 **Grampians Tempranillo 2015** Rating 93 To 2023 $25 ✪
Grampians Cabernet Sauvignon 2015 Rating 92 To 2027 $25 ✪
Degraves Road Pyrenees Chardonnay 2016 Rating 90 To 2021 $25

Dolan Family Wines

PO Box 500, Angaston, SA 5353 **Region** Barossa Valley
T 0438 816 034 **www.**dolanfamilywines.com.au **Open** Not
Winemaker Nigel and Timothy Dolan **Est.** 2007 **Dozens** 1000
Nigel is a fifth-generation member of the Dolan family, son Tim the sixth: truly, wine is in
their blood. Nigel's father Bryan enrolled in the first oenology course offered by Roseworthy,
graduating in 1949. There was no nepotism involved when Nigel was appointed chief
winemaker of Saltram in 1992, winning major accolades during his 15 years in that role. He
is a consultant and has responsibility for Dolan Family Wines. Nigel's son Tim is a graduate
of the Adelaide University oenology course, and has worked internationally as well as in
Australia. This is a virtual winery business, with neither vineyards nor winery – just lots of
experience. Exports to Hong Kong.

🍷🍷🍷🍷🍷 **x22 Langhorne Creek Shiraz 2014** Nigel Dolan has made wine from the
Metala Vineyard of Guy and Liz Adams for 22 vintages, hence the name of the
wine. Open-fermented, 12 days on skins, matured for 18 months in French
hogsheads (15% new). Its origin provides its luscious and supple cascade of red and

black fruits, giving great mouthfeel and a long finish. Invites the second glass in no uncertain fashion. Screwcap. 14.5% alc. **Rating** 94 **To** 2034 $48

▼▼▼▼♀ **Rifleman's Clare Valley Riesling 2016 Rating** 93 **To** 2026 $20 ◐
Stonewell District Barossa Shiraz 2014 Rating 92 **To** 2029 $48

Domain Barossa ★★★☆

25 Murray Street, Tanunda, SA 5352 **Region** Barossa Valley
T (08) 8304 8879 **www**.domainbarossa.com **Open** By appt
Winemaker Chris Polymiadis **Est.** 2002 **Dozens** 20000
Domain Barossa is now under the ownership of Ron Collins, who can trace his viticultural roots back through five generations. Grapes are predominantly sourced from the winery's 30 year-old vines on the outskirts of Angaston, with a focus on traditional local favourites, such as shiraz and grenache shiraz mataro.

▼▼▼▼♀ **Toddler GSM 2015** An unpretentious rendition of three varieties that excel in the Barossa, and in this blend it's all upfront fruit with a touch of spice and easygoing tannins. Screwcap. 14.5% alc. **Rating** 90 **To** 2020 $20 JF ◐

Domaine A ★★★★★

105 Tea Tree Road, Campania, Tas 7026 **Region** Southern Tasmania
T (03) 6260 4174 **www**.domaine-a.com.au **Open** Mon–Fri 10–4
Winemaker Peter Althaus **Est.** 1973 **Dozens** 5000 **Vyds** 11ha
The striking black label of the premium Domaine A wine, dominated by the single multicoloured 'A', signified the change of ownership from George Park to Peter Althaus many years ago. The wines are made without compromise, and reflect the low yields from the immaculately tended vineyards. They represent aspects of both Old World and New World philosophies, techniques and styles. Exports to the UK, Canada, Denmark, Switzerland, Taiwan, Hong Kong, Singapore, Japan and China.

▼▼▼▼▼ **Lady A Sauvignon Blanc 2013** Fermented and matured in 100% new French oak. Still bright straw-green, it is as complex as its long-term history would suggest. The fruit rises above the oak, bolstered by good natural acidity. The comparison with the wines of the late Didier Dageneau (Loire Valley) is inevitable, and Lady A doesn't fail the test. Cork. 13.5% alc. **Rating** 95 **To** 2022 $60
Pinot Noir 2011 20–25yo vines, seven clones, hand-picked, sorted, crushed, open-fermented with cultured yeast, 12 days on skins, matured in used French oak for 18 months. Typical deep colour of Domaine A: southern Tasmania wasn't affected by the rain that soaked Vic and SA. This is still in rude health at 6yo, with black cherry and plum framed by ripe tannins and quality oak. Cork. 12.5% alc. **Rating** 95 **To** 2031 $90
Merlot 2011 25yo vines, hand-picked, destemmed and crushed, open-fermented with cultured yeast, 12 days on skins, 24 months in French oak (50% new). It has a generous helping of dried bay leaf/herbs, olives and bramble influences, but is not green, and certainly not bitter. It's pre-Parker Bordeaux-like, its texture, structure and length admirable. Cork. 14% alc. **Rating** 95 **To** 2031 $85
Petit a 2011 66% cabernet sauvignon, 32% merlot, 2% petit verdot from 20–25yo vines, destemmed/crushed, open-fermented with cultured yeast, 12 days on skins, used French oak for 24 months. The Domain A red wines from this vintage are right up with the best of previous vintages. This has a healthy serve of bramble and earth alongside its dark plum and blackberry fruits, texture and structure its strengths. Diam. 13% alc. **Rating** 94 **To** 2031 $45

Domaine Asmara ★★★★☆

Gibb Road, Toolleen, Vic 3551 **Region** Heathcote
T (03) 5433 6133 **www**.domaineasmara.com **Open** 7 days 9–6.30
Winemaker Sanguine Estate **Est.** 2008 **Dozens** 2000 **Vyds** 12ha

Chemical engineer Andreas Greiving had a lifelong dream to own and operate a vineyard, and the opportunity came along with the global financial crisis. He was able to purchase a vineyard planted to shiraz, cabernet sauvignon, cabernet franc, durif and viognier, and have the wines contract made. The venture is co-managed by dentist wife Hennijati. The red wines are made from controlled yields of 1–1.5 tonnes per acre, hence their concentration. Exports to the UK, Malaysia, Vietnam, Hong Kong and China.

ỸỸỸỸỸ Infinity Heathcote Shiraz 2015 67% completed fermentation in French oak, the balance open-fermented in stainless steel, matured for 15 months in French oak (67% new). Deep, dense crimson-purple; the bouquet is very complex, with French oak thumping the drum, the inky, full-bodied palate answering with oceans of black fruits, licorice and a reprise of the oak. A wine to polarise opinions – not my style at all, but deserves respect. Cork. 15% alc. **Rating** 95 **To** 2035 $75
Reserve Heathcote Cabernet Sauvignon 2015 25% barrel-fermented, the balance in open stainless steel, matured for 10 months in French oak (30% new). A tangy, juicy cabernet with a savoury flavour profile not tracking the alcohol (seemingly lower, which is a plus). Cork. 14.7% alc. **Rating** 94 **To** 2030 $45
Private Reserve Heathcote Durif 2015 Matured for 10 months in 25% new French oak, 25% new American oak and 50% used American oak for 10 months. Dense, inky colour; a full-bodied wine that has contemptuously swept away the new oak by its massive extract of both fruit and tannins, the proverbial ox and open fire needed. Cork. 14.5% alc. **Rating** 94 **To** 2045 $45

ỸỸỸỸỿ Private Collection Heathcote Shiraz 2015 Rating 91 To 2030 $35
Reserve Heathcote Shiraz 2014 Rating 90 To 2024 $45

Domaine Carlei G2 ★★★★

1 Alber Road, Upper Beaconsfield, Vic 3808 **Region** Various Vic
T (03) 5944 4599 **Open** By appt
Winemaker David Carlei **Est.** 2010 **Dozens** 2000
This is the venture of David Carlei, son of Sergio Carlei; the two have worked together for some years, David having studied wine marketing at CSU. His focus is on using organic and/or biodynamic grapes; maceration of white wines on skins for up to 90 days, followed by prolonged lees contact with minimal fining. The reds see a similar process: whole clusters, wild yeast fermentation and prolonged maceration periods with ageing on lees. They are, in short, natural wines, the red wines with more intrinsic quality than most of their peers. Exports to the US, the UK and China.

ỸỸỸỸỸ Yarra Valley Syrah 2012 This is very good and would receive a higher score if it were a little more youthful and vibrant. However, it brims with a crunchy, effusive energy. This is Crozes-Hermitage Australien: violet, nori dried seaweed, blueberry and boysenberry and the sapid waft of bbq. Pepper-doused tannins and a litany of spice careen across the slinky, pulsating finish. Kapow! Diam. **Rating** 94 **To** 2020 $39 NG

Domaine Dawnelle ★★★★

PO Box 89, Claremont, Tas 7011 **Region** Southern Tasmania
T 0447 484 181 **www**.domainedawnelle.com **Open** Not
Winemaker Michael O'Brien **Est.** 2013 **Dozens** 430 **Vyds** 1.2ha
Domaine Dawnelle is a partnership between Michael O'Brien and Kylie Harrison. The name of the venture honours Michael's great-grandmother (and farm) in rural NSW. He studied at CSU, and is a qualified viticulturist and winemaker with 20 years' experience in mainland Australia, abroad and, more recently, Tasmania. As well as planting 1.2ha of vineyard overlooking the Derwent River, he manages the Tinderbox Vineyard, providing the partnership with grapes until the estate vineyard comes into full bearing.

ŢŢŢŢŢ **Chardonnay 2016** The fruit comes off two disparate sites but is picked on the same day, whole-bunch pressed to stainless steel and left on lees for 8 months with no mlf. Little wonder this is tightly coiled with a razor-sharp palate; appealing nonetheless. Lemon/grapefruit juice and pith, a hint of grilled nuts and an ultra-refreshing style. Screwcap. 13.2% alc. **Rating** 93 **To** 2024 $36 JF

Tinderbox Vineyard Pinot Noir 2014 There's a core of sweet cherries and plums overlaid with earthy, dusty tones plus more unusual aromas of lavender and menthol/pine needles. Full-bodied, with a plushness to the tannins and a slight ripe-unripe fruit character, but neatly put together and immediately drinkable. Cork. 13.8% alc. **Rating** 93 **To** 2021 $56 JF

ŢŢŢŢ **Riesling 2016 Rating** 89 **To** 2027 $36 JF

Domaine Naturaliste   ★★★★★

Cnr Hairpin Road/Bussell Highway, Carbunup, WA 6280 **Region** Margaret River
T (08) 9755 1188 **www**.domainenaturaliste.com.au **Open** Not
Winemaker Bruce Dukes **Est.** 2012 **Dozens** 4000
Bruce Dukes' career dates back over 25 years, its foundations built around a degree in agronomy from the University of WA, followed by a master's degree in viticulture and agronomy from the University of California, Davis, thence to a four-year stint at Francis Ford Coppola's iconic Niebaum-Coppola winery in the Napa Valley. Back in WA he worked with a consultancy and contract winemaking business in Margaret River in 2000. The winery was set up to handle small and large amounts of fruit, but it was not until '12 that he made his own wine under the Domaine Naturaliste label. The quality of all the wines he makes is excellent. Exports to the UK, the US, Canada and China.

ŢŢŢŢŢ **Morus Margaret River Cabernet Sauvignon 2014** 3 weeks on skins, matured in French (Troncais) oak (52% new) for 14 months. An opulent and wonderfully rich cabernet that doesn't lose its shape or integrity as it fills your senses. When John Wade was in his winemaking prime in the '80s he discovered that Burgundian-coopered Troncais oak, normally associated with pinot noir, worked magically with cabernet, and it's part of the richness of this wine. Cassis and mulberry go hand in hand (as they can do in Coonawarra), aided and abetted by the tannins softened in the maceration period. ProCork. 14% alc. **Rating** 98 **To** 2044 $85 ✪

Rachis Margaret River Syrah 2015 From vines planted in '78, cool-fermented, one-third whole bunches included, matured for 12 months on lees in French puncheons (33% new). An immaculately crafted syrah, it is elegant, perfectly balanced, fragrant, very long, absurdly cheap and effortlessly complex. Spice and some pepper join the red and black cherry fruits of the palate, fine and ripe tannins, and quality French oak. Screwcap. 13.8% alc. **Rating** 97 **To** 2035 $30 ✪

ŢŢŢŢŢ **Sauvage Margaret River Sauvignon Blanc Semillon 2015** A 75/25% blend matured on lees for 10 months in French puncheons (33% new). A hauntingly complex bouquet has passionfruit, lemongrass and French oak aromas, the palate with unusual depth and classic length. Multi trophy winner. Screwcap. 13% alc. **Rating** 96 **To** 2021 $30 ✪

Artus Margaret River Chardonnay 2015 Bruce Dukes at his best, conjuring up the complexity of a top French white burgundy with a base of natural acidity. The barrel ferment has led to complex, funky nuances, and the texture of the wine builds progressively until it moves through towards the exceptionally long finish and aftertaste. Screwcap. 13% alc. **Rating** 96 **To** 2025 $45 ✪

Rebus Margaret River Cabernet Sauvignon 2015 Separate parcels fermented and matured in French barriques (40% new) for 12 months, thereafter a barrel selection. Puppet master Bruce Dukes has assembled the components on a string, with blackcurrant fruit, French oak and rippling tannins all dancing to his tune. Screwcap. 13.8% alc. **Rating** 96 **To** 2030 $35 ✪

Discovery Margaret River Sauvignon Blanc Semillon 2016 Has the Bruce Dukes stamp on it, providing a wine that has purity and finesse, yet also haunting complexity to its flavours. I'll happily buy into Dukes' keywords – gooseberry and guava – but there's also a tracer bullet of zesty/pithy citrus on the long, emphatic finish. Screwcap. 13% alc. **Rating** 95 **To** 2017 $24 ✪

Floris Margaret River Chardonnay 2015 Barrel ferment characters are evident, but it is the grapefruit and white peach that drives the extreme length of the palate and its aftertaste. This will develop slowly and surely. Screwcap. 13% alc. **Rating** 95 **To** 2023 $30 ✪

Discovery Margaret River Syrah 2014 95% syrah, 3% viognier and 2% malbec, whole berries cool-fermented to create partial carbonic maceration. It has that intangible savoury freshness that can only be achieved with grapes picked around 13° baume, not 15°. This has it in spades, with a starlight scatter of spices, fruit flavours, neither predominantly black nor red, tannins positively adding to the result. Screwcap. 13.5% alc. **Rating** 95 **To** 2039 $24 ✪

Discovery Chardonnay 2015 The model for a budget-priced chardonnay, graceful and fluid, with equally balanced stone fruits and citrus, the overall effect one of freshness and elegance. Screwcap. 13% alc. **Rating** 94 **To** 2021 $24 ✪

🍷🍷🍷🍷🍷 **Discovery Cabernet Sauvignon 2014** Rating 92 To 2024 $24 ✪
Margaret River Syrah 2013 Rating 91 To 2020 $24

Domaines & Vineyards ★★★★☆

PO Box 875, West Perth, WA 6872 **Region** Western Australia
T 0400 880 935 **www**.dandv.com.au **Open** Not
Winemaker Robert Bowen **Est.** 2009 **Dozens** 10 000

One of the best-known winemakers in WA is Rob Bowen, with over 35 years' experience with several of WA's leading wineries, most recently Houghton. In 2009 he joined forces with a team of viticulturists (led by David Radomilijac) who collectively furnish the project with an extensive range of knowledge and expertise. The theme is to produce premium wines with a strong sense of place, all grapes hand-picked from the best available vineyards in the Margaret River and Pemberton regions. Two ranges of wines are produced: Robert Bowen (from Margaret River and Pemberton) and Pemberley (from the Pemberley Farms Vineyard owned by David). Exports to the UK, Singapore and China.

🍷🍷🍷🍷🍷 **Robert Bowen Margaret River Chardonnay 2015** A neatly composed and balanced wine: linear and tight, yet has a depth of flavour too. Starts with a flush of nectarines and other white stone fruit and leesy nutty nuances, with the oak seamlessly integrated. Screwcap. 13.2% alc. **Rating** 95 **To** 2022 $50 JF

Robert Bowen Pemberton Chardonnay 2015 Whole-bunch pressed, wild-yeast ferment, 50% new French oak for 11 months with most through mlf. In the richer spectrum, and yet it works. Stone fruit, melon with clotted cream, butterscotch, nutty leesy notes all encompass its full body with tangy acidity. Screwcap. 13.2% alc. **Rating** 94 **To** 2021 $50 JF

🍷🍷🍷🍷🍷 **Pemberley Pemberton Chardonnay 2015** Rating 93 To 2023 $25 JF ✪
Robert Bowen Pemberton Pinot Noir 2015 Rating 92 To 2022 $40 JF
Robert Bowen Mount Barker Cabernet 2014 Rating 92 To 2028 $40 JF

Domaines Tatiarra ★★★★

2 Corrong Court, Eltham, Vic 3095 (postal) **Region** Heathcote
T 0428 628 420 **www**.tatiarra.com **Open** Not
Winemaker Ben Riggs **Est.** 1991 **Dozens** 5000 **Vyds** 13.4ha

This shiraz-only producer is owned by a group of investors and their core asset is a 60ha property of Cambrian earth identified and developed by Bill Hepburn. The majority of the wine comes from the Tatiarra (an Aboriginal word meaning 'beautiful country') property. The wines are made at Scotchmans Hill winery in Geelong, with Ben Riggs commuting from McLaren Vale. Exports to the UK, the US, Canada, Denmark, Switzerland, Singapore and China.

ŦŦŦŦŢ **Culled Barrel Heathcote Shiraz 2014** From barrels culled from the final selection for the regular Shiraz, this has a certain lift, bounce and astringency that the more expensive cuvee does not. While less expensive, the fruit intensity and bitter chocolate flavours that fans of this sort of wine expect do not fall short. Screwcap. 15% alc. **Rating** 92 **To** 2028 $22 NG ✪

Cambrian Heathcote Shiraz 2014 You know what to expect when the wine hits the glass. An inky crimson verging on opaque, with few punches pulled. Saturated dark fruit flavours, plus bitter chocolate and coffee grind, before a gauntlet of tannin and alcohol is laid across this molten wine's stern. Screwcap. 15% alc. **Rating** 90 **To** 2030 $30 NG

ŦŦŦŦ **Caravan of Dreams Shiraz Pressings 2014** **Rating** 89 **To** 2030 $60 NG

Dominique Portet   ★★★★★

870–872 Maroondah Highway, Coldstream, Vic 3770 **Region** Yarra Valley
T (03) 5962 5760 **www.**dominiqueportet.com **Open** 7 days 10–5
Winemaker Ben Portet **Est.** 2000 **Dozens** 15 000 **Vyds** 4.3ha
Dominique Portet was bred in the purple. He spent his early years at Chateau Lafite (where his father was régisseur) and was one of the first Flying Winemakers, commuting to Clos du Val in the Napa Valley, where his brother was winemaker. He then spent over 20 years as managing director of Taltarni and Clover Hill. After retiring from Taltarni, he moved to the Yarra Valley, a region he had been closely observing since the mid-1980s. In 2001 he found the site he had long looked for and built his winery and cellar door, planting a quixotic mix of viognier, sauvignon blanc and merlot next to the winery. Son Ben is now executive winemaker, leaving Dominique with a roving role as de facto consultant and brand marketer. Ben (35) has a winemaking CV of awesome scope, covering all parts of France, South Africa, California and four vintages at Petaluma. Exports to the UK, Canada, Denmark, India, Dubai, Hong Kong, Singapore, Malaysia, China and Japan.

ŦŦŦŦŦ **Origine Yarra Valley Chardonnay 2015** From mature vines in the Upper Yarra Valley. Grapefruit flavours ride shotgun, coupled with natural acidity. While the wine was fermented and matured for 9 months in French barriques, only 25% were new, minimising the flavour of oak, but not its textural effect. Screwcap. 13% alc. **Rating** 96 **To** 2035 $45 ✪

Fontaine Yarra Valley Rose 2016 50% merlot, 40% shiraz, 10% cabernet sauvignon, hand-picked, fermented in stainless steel with lees stirring. Pale salmon-pink; the super-fragrant bouquet paves the way for a posy of red fruits that covers all the bases. The palate is juicy and long, the acidity perfect, the finish dry. A beauty. Screwcap. 13.5% alc. **Rating** 95 **To** 2017 $22 ✪

Heathcote Shiraz 2014 Destemmed, 10% whole bunches, matured in French oak (20% new) for 14 months. The power and the depth of the fruit are remarkable. It has tiers of purple and black fruits, plus spice/pepper and licorice in abundance, ripe tannins and French oak completing the picture. Cork. 14% alc. **Rating** 95 **To** 2039 $48

Fontaine Yarra Valley Cabernet Sauvignon 2015 There is a purity to the wine, evident right from the bouquet through the palate and on to the aftertaste; flavour, texture and structure are indivisible, but insistent. Small wonder it won a gold medal at the Yarra Valley Wine Show '16. Exceptional bargain. Screwcap. 14% alc. **Rating** 95 **To** 2030 $22 ✪

Yarra Valley Cabernet Sauvignon 2014 From 20+yo vines at Coldstream and Steels Creek, hand-picked and sorted, crushed, 25 days on skins, matured in French oak (40% new) for 14 months. There is a hard to place and unexpected spicy character to the bouquet that largely disappears on the complex, medium to full-bodied palate. Here black fruits, led by blackcurrant, set the tone, but do allow space for a swish of black olive, cedar and cabernet tannins. Cork. 14% alc. **Rating** 95 **To** 2039 $55

ŦŦŦŦŢ **Yarra Valley Brut Rose LD NV** **Rating** 93 **To** 2020 $30

Dorrien Estate

Cnr Barossa Valley Way/Siegersdorf Road, Tanunda, SA 5352 **Region** Barossa Valley
T (08) 8561 2200 **www**.cellarmasters.com.au **Open** Not
Winemaker Corey Ryan (Chief) **Est.** 1982 **Dozens** 1 million

Dorrien Estate is the physical base of the vast Cellarmasters network – the largest direct-sale outlet in Australia. It also makes wine for many producers across Australia at its modern winery, which has a capacity of 14.5 million litres in tank and barrel; however, a typical make of each wine will be little more than 1000 dozen. Most of the wines made for others are exclusively distributed by Cellarmasters. Acquired by Woolworths in May 2011.

Mockingbird Lane Single Vineyard Hayshed Block Clare Valley Riesling 2016 The high prices paid across Australia for riesling suggest its long-discussed renaissance is now a fact, and the price of this wine is further evidence. From a small single block, its calling card is the perfumed bouquet and delicate, but long, palate with lacy acidity. Screwcap. 11.5% alc. **Rating** 96 **To** 2031 $50 ✪

Mockingbird Hill Slate Lane Polish Hill River Riesling 2015 This comes from the slatey soils of the Polish Hill River district, and does them proud. Freshly squeezed lime juice is held in a close embrace by minerally acidity, the line, length and balance all exactly measured and managed. Screwcap. 12.5% alc. **Rating** 95 **To** 2030 $32 ✪

Dorrien Estate Bin 1A Chardonnay 2015 75% Mount Benson, 25% Yarra Valley. The components were separately vinified, and (seemingly) barrel-fermented. White peach and nectarine are a (very good) conventional start, but the complex nutty/tangy finish takes the wine into gold medal territory. Screwcap. 13.5% alc. **Rating** 95 **To** 2022 $31 ✪

Redemption Tumbarumba Chardonnay 2015 Whole-bunch pressed, fermented in French oak, matured for 9 months. A very good wine with drive, verve and pure, cool-grown chardonnay precision. Pink grapefruit leads the charge, but has stone fruit backup, oak a major influence on texture and structure. Screwcap. 13% alc. **Rating** 95 **To** 2027 $42

Black Wattle Vineyards Mount Benson Shiraz 2013 The Black Wattle vineyards are mature, and the combination of the cool climate of Mount Benson and the good vintage has given the winemaking team a dream start – gratefully accepted. Blackberry, plum, anise and spice are framed by supple tannins and a well judged touch of oak. Screwcap. 14% alc. **Rating** 95 **To** 2025 $33 ✪

Black Wattle Vineyards Mount Benson Cabernet Sauvignon 2013 Exceptional, deep crimson-purple; a high quality example of a wine with a distinguished lineage, to this day lying outside the norm for Mount Benson with the depth and intensity of its cassis/black olive fruit and firm, but integrated, tannins. Screwcap. 14% alc. **Rating** 95 **To** 2035 $33 ✪

Mockingbird Hill Slate Lane Polish Hill River Riesling 2016 No-frills winemaking: a cool, long ferment in stainless steel. The dial ratchets up with the price, but the quality is in step. Polish Hill River is known for its slate soils, and they come through clearly here, accompanied by lime (dominant) and lemon fruit. Screwcap. 11.5% alc. **Rating** 94 **To** 2026 $30 ✪

Avon Brae High Eden & Flaxman Valley Chardonnay 2015 In total, 97% Eden Valley (75% High Eden, 22% Flaxman Valley), crushed and pressed, fermented in new and used French oak. An impressive chardonnay, full of white peach, nectarine and grapefruit flavours, oak restrained. Screwcap. 13% alc. **Rating** 94 **To** 2021 $30 ✪

Tolley Elite Adelaide Hills Chardonnay 2015 90% tank-fermented, 10% in barrel. The quality of the fruit is beyond question – it is very good – and the airbrush of oak doesn't leave a gap in the mouthfeel or flavour, which bonds stone fruit, grapefruit and melon into a single stream of flavour. Screwcap. 12.5% alc. **Rating** 94 **To** 2020 $38

Cormack & Co Margaret River SBS 2015 **Rating** 92 **To** 2019 $24 ✪
Tolley Elite Adelaide Hills Chardonnay 2014 **Rating** 92 **To** 2021 $38

John Glaetzer Stonyfell Black Shiraz 2014 Rating 92 To 2029 $28
Mockingbird Hill Slate Lane Shiraz 2014 Rating 92 To 2034 $27
Mockingbird Hill Clare Valley Shiraz 2014 Rating 92 To 2029 $23 ❂
Krondorf Growers Bowen & Bowen Barossa Grenache Rose 2016
Rating 91 To 2017 $24
Krondorf The Growers Rohrlach & Bowen Barossa Grenache Rose 2015
Rating 91 To 2017 $24
Cormack & Co Margaret River Chardonnay 2016 Rating 90 To 2021 $24
Krondorf Symmetry Chardonnay 2014 Rating 90 To 2019 $31
Redemption Hilltops Shiraz 2015 Rating 90 To 2025 $28
Wordsmith Heathcote Shiraz 2014 Rating 90 To 2029 $30
Archway Fleurieu Peninsula Malbec 2014 Rating 90 To 2021 $25
Dorrien Estate Light Pass Road Barossa Zinfandel 2015 Rating 90
To 2022 $26

DOWIE DOOLE ★★★★★

598 Bayliss Road, McLaren Vale, SA 5171 **Region** McLaren Vale
T (08) 7325 6280 **www**.dowiedoole.com **Open** 7 days 10–5
Winemaker Chris Thomas **Est.** 1995 **Dozens** 25 000 **Vyds** 53ha
DOWIE DOOLE was founded in 1995 by Drew Dowie and Norm Doole. They had been
connected to the McLaren Vale community for many years as grapegrowers in the region.
Vineyard management is now led by champions of sustainable viticulture practices Dave
Gartelmann and Drew Dowie. In May '16, with winemaker and managing director Chris
Thomas leading a group of like-minded investors, DOWIE DOOLE acquired 35ha of vines
of the 53ha Conte Tatachilla Vineyard, book-ended by 50 year-old bushvine grenache and
recently grafted (in '12) vermentino, aglianico and lagrein. Exports to all major markets.

🍷🍷🍷🍷🍷 **Reserve McLaren Vale Shiraz 2014** From a block replanted in '74; the
vinification is essentially the same as for Cali Road, with one major exception:
the oak used is French. An object lesson on the benefits of French oak. This is a
wine with precision and brilliance, an edgy character that simply illuminates the
fruit, and leaves the mouth thirsting for more. Grace and power. Diam. 14.5% alc.
Rating 97 To 2044 $80 ❂

🍷🍷🍷🍷🍷 **The Banker McLaren Vale Cabernet Sauvignon 2013** Excellent colour,
still young and vibrant; varietal and regional expressions are evenly matched,
both contributing to the density and fabric of a richly plumed cabernet, its heart
of cassis wrapped in a veneer of high quality dark chocolate, ripe tannins and
integrated oak. Diam. 14.5% alc. **Rating** 96 To 2038 $66 ❂
**The Fruit of the Vine The Sculptor McLaren Vale Cabernet Sauvignon
2012** A special batch of 50 dozen made from the estate Tintookie Vineyard in
Blewitt Springs. This is a high quality cabernet that ticks every box. The colour
is still deep crimson-purple, the bouquet and palate flush with blackcurrant fruit,
the tannins fine but persistent (as they should be), the finish long, the future as far
distant as you wish it to be. Diam. 14.5% alc. **Rating** 96 To 2042 $80
Cali Road McLaren Vale Shiraz 2014 From an east-facing slope planted in '00,
crushed, 13 days on skins, pressed direct to American hogsheads (50% new) for
2 years maturation. An exceptionally powerful and intense wine, yet no more than
full-bodied; dark berries, dark chocolate, mocha and savoury tannins make up a tag
team of boundless energy. Diam. 14.5% alc. **Rating** 95 To 2034 $50
Cali Road McLaren Vale Shiraz 2013 A very generous, ultra-typical McLaren
Vale style that is not the least extractive; supple black fruits have a cross-grain
of dark chocolate and vanilla, all seamlessly joined. Diam. 14.5% alc. **Rating** 95
To 2033 $50
Mr G's C.S.M. 2013 A 40/27/22/11% blend of cabernet sauvignon, shiraz,
merlot and mourvedre, separately fermented, matured in used oak for 2 years.
A more elegant take on McLaren Vale red blends than usual, and works very well

indeed. The fragrant bouquet signalling the fresh and lively array of red fruits on the palate suggests only one thing: have another glass. Screwcap. 14.5% alc. **Rating** 95 **To** 2028 $35 ○

Estate McLaren Vale Chenin Blanc 2016 Start with 83yo vines from Blewitt Springs, hand-pick at low baume and high natural acidity, cool ferment in stainless steel for 2–3 weeks and you end up with a wine of startling freshness, acidity and vibrant citrus and apple flavours. DOWIE DOOLE gives the wine a 20+-year cellaring future, and I'll run with that. Screwcap. 12.2% alc. **Rating** 94 **To** 2035 $20 ○

Estate McLaren Vale Shiraz 2015 From three blocks, each vinified separately until final barrel selection and blending, matured in 50/50% American and French hogsheads (25% new). Has excellent balance, texture and velvety mouthfeel to its luscious black fruits, discreetly supported by savoury notes ex tannins and oak. Good wine at a good price. Screwcap. 14.5% alc. **Rating** 94 **To** 2029 $25 ○

C.T. McLaren Vale Shiraz 2014 From blocks in Blewitt Springs and Tatachilla, open-fermented separately for 10 days, pressed direct to used French (70%) and American barrels for 24 months. A rich yet supple and smooth shiraz that stays well within the line in the sand for alcohol issues; the flavours of plum and black berry fruits sit well together, and the overall balance of fruit and oak is impeccable. A prosperous future awaits. Screwcap. 14.2% alc. **Rating** 94 **To** 2034 $35

McLaren Vale Cabernet Sauvignon 2014 A no-frills, yet nigh-on perfect example of McLaren Vale cabernet, which gives equal time to the expression of place and of variety in a generous medium-bodied frame. Blackcurrant, dark chocolate, black olive, a splash of oak and supple tannins all contribute. Screwcap. 14% alc. **Rating** 94 **To** 2029 $25 ○

ⓎⓎⓎⓎⓎ **Estate McLaren Vale Chenin Blanc 2015** **Rating** 93 **To** 2020 $25 ○
Adelaide Hills Sauvignon Blanc 2015 **Rating** 91 **To** 2017 $25
B.F.G. McLaren Vale Grenache 2015 **Rating** 91 **To** 2022 $35
Estate McLaren Vale Merlot 2013 **Rating** 91 **To** 2023 $25

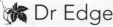 Dr Edge   ★★★★★

5 Cato Avenue, West Hobart, Tas 7000 (postal) **Region** Southern Tasmania
T 0439 448 151 **www.**dr-edge.com **Open** Not
Winemaker Peter Dredge **Est.** 2015 **Dozens** 500
After having worked as a winemaker for Petaluma, Peter Dredge moved to Tasmania in 2009, spending 7 years within the Accolade group, becoming chief winemaker at Bay of Fires. He moved proactively to become a consultant and self-employed winemaker to shortcircuit the uncertainty then existing around Accolade and its future. In '15 he sourced a small amount of pinot noir from Joe Holyman of Stoney Rise and Gerald Ellis of Meadowbank to start his own label. He made the wine at Moorilla as a contract client with sole control of the winemaking process. In '15, during vintage, the Ellis family, owners of Meadowbank, approached Pete to form a partnership to relaunch Meadowbank. As part of the deal, Meadowbank gave Pete a sole lease arrangement to 1.5ha of pinot noir from the '16 vintage and onwards.

ⓎⓎⓎⓎⓎ **Pinot Noir 2016** A blend of roughly 50% Derwent Valley, 30% East Coast and 20% Tamar Valley wines, plus clones 777 and 115 with various techniques including whole bunch, cold soak and maceration carbonique, all parcels pressed at the tail end of fermentation to French oak (15% new). This is the most fragrant and complex of the Pinots, with red cherry, dark cherry and damson plum. It has the tannin structure of Burgundy, which lengthens the finish and aftertaste. Utterly gorgeous. Screwcap. 12.5% alc. **Rating** 97 **To** 2030 $50 ○

ⓎⓎⓎⓎⓎ **South Tasmania Pinot Noir 2016** MV6. A highly expressive bouquet with scents of cherry blossom and rose petals, the palate painted by juicy red fruits, inducing repeated visits to the glass. The palette has a mesmerising intensity of red and purple fruits without sacrificing elegance or purity. A truly beautiful pinot. 50 dozen made. Screwcap. 12.5% alc. **Rating** 96 **To** 2025 $50 ○

East Tasmania Pinot Noir 2016 The most fragrant/scented of the four '16 Dr Edge pinots; the palate is pure, intensely red-fruited, with remarkable freshness and length. It caresses the mouth and fills the senses with its magical bouquet. 50 dozen made. Screwcap. 12.5% alc. **Rating** 96 **To** 2030 $50 ✪

North Tasmania Pinot Noir 2016 The colour is marginally deeper, with a little more purple in the hue; the bouquet and palate introduce notes of darker fruits, headed by plums of various types. The palate has the most structure, verging on robust. Typical of the Tamar Valley, which is as it should be. 50 dozen made. Screwcap. 12.5% alc. **Rating** 94 **To** 2026 $50

Drake ★★★★

PO Box 417, Hamilton, NSW 2303 **Region** Yarra Valley
T 0417 670 655 **www**.drakesamson.com.au **Open** Not
Winemaker Mac Forbes, Matt Dunne **Est.** 2012 **Dozens** 2500
Drake is a handshake business of Nicholas Crampton, winemaker Matt Dunne, and a friend of Nicholas, Andrew Dunn. Mac Forbes is the executive winemaker for Drake wines made in the Yarra Valley, it being the intention to focus future activities on the Yarra. Quality is uniformly high. Exports to NZ.

♀♀♀♀♀ **Heathcote Shiraz 2015** 30yo vines, hand-picked, destemmed, open-fermented and matured in French oak. Generosity is its watchword, with blackberry, plum and a splash of licorice filling the mouth. Will live as long as your patience and then some. Terrific value. Screwcap. 13.5% alc. **Rating** 92 **To** 2030 $20 ✪

Off the Books Heathcote Shiraz 2015 Delivers a ball of juicy dark fruit, laced with spice, plus gloss and sheen to the palate, firm tannins and chalky, lemony acidity. Incredibly bright and lively. Screwcap. 13.5% alc. **Rating** 91 **To** 2021 $22 JF✪

Samson Yarra Valley Pinot Noir 2015 The latest rendition from winemakers Mac Forbes and Matt Dunne, sourcing fruit from Hoddles Creek, Coldstream and Yarra Junction. Highly aromatic with wild strawberries, cherries and blood orange, plus some herbaceous tones. The palate is lean, tangy and tart, with acidity doing the talking – it's refreshing and needs bbq red meat as per the food matching on the back label. Screwcap. 12% alc. **Rating** 90 **To** 2021 $35 JF

♀♀♀♀ **Yarra Valley Chardonnay 2016 Rating** 89 **To** 2020 $20 JF

Drayton's Family Wines ★★★★★

555 Oakey Creek Road, Cessnock, NSW 2321 **Region** Hunter Valley
T (02) 4998 7513 **www**.draytonswines.com.au **Open** details on website
Winemaker Edgar Vales, Max and John Drayton **Est.** 1853 **Dozens** 45 000 **Vyds** 72ha
This substantial Hunter Valley producer has suffered more than its share of misfortune over the years, but has risen to the challenges. Edgar Vales is the chief winemaker after previous experience as assistant winemaker with David Hook and First Creek Wines. His arrival coincided with the release of a range of high quality wines. Exports to Ireland, Bulgaria, Turkey, Vietnam, Malaysia, Indonesia, Singapore, Taiwan and China.

♀♀♀♀♀ **Heritage Vines Chardonnay 2013** From the oldest chardonnay vines, planted by Max Drayton in '64. Hand-picked, free-run juice fermented in French oak (30% new), 40% wild yeast fermentation, 60% with cultured yeast, matured for 6 months. It has drive and intensity courtesy of the almost 50yo vines and faultless winemaking. White peach with a dressing of citrus, the oak balanced and integrated. Screwcap. 13.5% alc. **Rating** 95 **To** 2023 $60

Heritage Vines Shiraz 2013 The vines are over 100yo. The Hunter hit the jackpot with the very good '11 and '13 vintages, followed by the fabled '14. This is a delicious medium-bodied wine, with region and variety in synergistic harmony, aided by balanced and integrated French oak. The flavours are of cherry and berry, red and dark, the tannins supple. Screwcap. 14% alc. **Rating** 95 **To** 2033 $60

Heritage Vines Semillon 2013 From 120yo estate plantings, hand-picked, free-run juice, fermented with cultured yeast. Still quartz-white, with no sign whatsoever of development; the bouquet and palate do show some signs of an extra level of fruit, but it still remains in primary youth, and needs another 5 1 years. Screwcap. 11.5% alc. **Rating** 94 **To** 2028 $60

Vineyard Reserve Pokolbin Semillon 2012 From the oldest vines on The Flat block, hand-picked, fermented in stainless steel with cultured yeast, 3 months on lees. Bright straw-green; an intense and vibrant semillon, lemon/lime fruit still on what will be a leisurely journey to maximum flavour and texture as hints of lime and toast develop – around '20. Screwcap. 11% alc. **Rating** 94 **To** 2027 $30 ✪

♟♟♟♟♟ **Bin 5555 Hunter Valley Shiraz 2014 Rating** 93 **To** 2044 $20 ✪
Vineyard Reserve Pokolbin Shiraz 2014 Rating 92 **To** 2029 $30
Hunter Valley Semillon 2016 Rating 91 **To** 2026 $20 ✪

Driftwood Estate ★★★★★

3314 Caves Road, Wilyabrup, WA 6282 **Region** Margaret River
T (08) 9755 6323 **www.driftwoodwines.com.au Open** 7 days 10–5
Winemaker Eloise Jarvis, Paul Callaghan **Est.** 1989 **Dozens** 15000
Driftwood Estate is a well established landmark on the Margaret River scene. Quite apart from offering a brasserie restaurant capable of seating 200 people (open 7 days for lunch and dinner) and a mock Greek open-air theatre, its wines feature striking and stylish packaging and opulent flavours. Wines are released in three ranges: The Collection, Artefacts and Oceania. Exports to the UK, Canada, Singapore and China.

♟♟♟♟♟ **Artifacts Margaret River Sauvignon Blanc Semillon 2016** The sauvignon blanc component is wild yeast–barrel fermented, which adds complexity to both the bouquet and palate, the semillon providing crisp, lemony acidity that balances the finish and aftertaste. Having unpicked the parcel, the overall impression is one of complete harmony. Screwcap. 13.1% alc. **Rating** 95 **To** 2020 $25 ✪

Single Site Margaret River Chardonnay 2016 Whole-bunch pressed, wild-yeast fermented in French oak (37% new), matured for 10 months with lees stirring, four barrels selected and blended. This is no shrinking violet; its intensity and drive are admirable, but there is no heat. A juicy quality that runs through the length of the palate, the solids fermentation working to perfection, as does the acid balance. Screwcap. 13.4% alc. **Rating** 95 **To** 2024 $45

Artifacts Margaret River Cabernet Sauvignon 2015 88.4% cabernet sauvignon, 5.4% petit verdot, 3.1% cabernet franc, 2.9% shiraz and 0.2% merlot, co-fermented with cultured yeast, 35 days on skins, matured for 15–18 months in used French oak. Brilliantly coloured; an unusually fresh and elegant wine in the context of the baseline style of Margaret River. The expressive and fragrant bouquet exudes cassis and redcurrant, and the supple, medium-bodied palate has a perfect blend of fruits (blueberry and blackcurrant), harmonious French oak and fine-grained, persistent tannins. Screwcap. 14.5% alc. **Rating** 95 **To** 2030 $30 ✪

♟♟♟♟♟ **The Collection Classic White Margaret River 2016 Rating** 93 **To** 2022 $20 ✪
Artifacts Margaret River Cabernet 2014 Rating 93 **To** 2026 $32 SC
Artifacts Margaret River Meritage 2015 Rating 93 **To** 2028 $30
Artifacts Margaret River Meritage 2014 Rating 92 **To** 2029 $30
Artifacts Margaret River Shiraz 2014 Rating 91 **To** 2022 $26 SC

Dromana Estate ★★★★

555 Old Moorooduc Road, Tuerong, Vic 3933 **Region** Mornington Peninsula
T (03) 5974 4400 **www.dromanaestate.com.au Open** Wed–Sun 11–5
Winemaker Peter Bauer **Est.** 1982 **Dozens** 7000 **Vyds** 53.9ha
Since it was established over 30 years ago, Dromana Estate has undergone many changes, most notably the severance of involvement with the Crittenden family. After several changes of

ownership, it is now owned by Weeping Elm Wines Pty Ltd, trading as Dromana Estate. Mornington Estate is its second label.

ƚƚƚƚƚ **Mornington Peninsula Pinot Noir 2016** Bold flavours hold the fort: those typical of pinot noir from the lower, warmer area of Mornington Peninsula, such as dark and maraschino cherries with the savoury salami. There's a sweet spot alongside fleshy ripe tannins. Full-bodied and loads of immediate appeal. Screwcap. 13.5% alc. **Rating** 93 **To** 2026 $39 JF

Mornington Estate Shiraz 2015 A rather smart shiraz with plenty of dark fruit, yet retains its savoury outlook with pepper, licorice and cloves. Oak in check and adding to the savoury tannins tempered by refreshing acidity. No more than medium-bodied and ready to pour. Screwcap. 14.5% alc. **Rating** 93 **To** 2024 $25 JF ✪

Mornington Peninsula White #1 2016 This is bright and breezy, lively with mouthwatering lemony acidity, and as floral and spicy as anything. For the record, it's a blend of 67% gewurztraminer, the rest pinot gris. Screwcap. 12.5% alc. **Rating** 90 **To** 2019 $25 JF

ƚƚƚƚ **Mornington Estate Pinot Noir 2016** **Rating** 89 **To** 2021 $25 JF

Dudley Wines ★★★★

1153 Willoughby Road, Penneshaw, Kangaroo Island 5222 **Region** Kangaroo Island
T (08) 8553 1333 **www.**dudleywines.com.au **Open** 7 days 10–5
Winemaker Brodie Howard **Est.** 1994 **Dozens** 3500 **Vyds** 14ha
This is one of the most successful wineries on Kangaroo Island, owned by Jeff and Val Howard, with son Brodie as winemaker at the onsite winery. It has three vineyards on Dudley Peninsula: Porky Flat Vineyard, Hog Bay River and Sawyers. Two daughters and a daughter-in-law manage the cellar door sales, marketing and bookkeeping. Most of the wines are sold through licensed outlets on the Island.

ƚƚƚƚƚ **Porky Flat Kangaroo Island Shiraz 2014** Dark crimson and vibrant; heady aromas of dark plums dunked in cinnamon and smells of a 19th century Victorian cedar chest of drawers. Supple, silky medium-bodied palate with ripe tannins and the oak a neat interplay. Screwcap. 14.5% alc. **Rating** 91 **To** 2026 $38 JF

ƚƚƚƚ **Pink Bay Kangaroo Island Rose 2016** **Rating** 89 **To** 2019 $20 JF

Duke's Vineyard ★★★★★

Porongurup Road, Porongurup, WA 6324 **Region** Porongurup
T (08) 9853 1107 **www.**dukesvineyard.com **Open** 7 days 10–4.30
Winemaker Robert Diletti **Est.** 1998 **Dozens** 3500 **Vyds** 10ha
When Hilde and Ian (Duke) Ranson sold their clothing manufacturing business in 1998, they were able to fulfil a long-held dream of establishing a vineyard in the Porongurup subregion of Great Southern with the acquisition of a 65ha farm at the foot of the Porongurup Range. They planted shiraz and cabernet sauvignon (3ha each) and riesling (4ha). Hilde, a successful artist, designed the beautiful, scalloped, glass-walled cellar door sales area, with its mountain blue cladding. Great wines at great prices.

ƚƚƚƚƚ **Magpie Hill Reserve Riesling 2016** The sheer power and concentration of this wine are startling, especially in the context of the normally reserved Porongurup style. Citrus and a touch of Granny Smith apple help build the layers of fruit which rest on the mainframe of crunchy/minerally acidity. Despite this precocious display of flavour, the wine has perfect balance and prodigious length. Screwcap. 12.5% alc. **Rating** 98 **To** 2036 $30 ✪

Magpie Hill Reserve Shiraz 2015 6 days on skins, matured for 18 months in French oak (35% new). Deep crimson; doubles the intensity and layered richness of the Single Vineyard Shiraz, the length prodigious. On the way through, blackberry, black cherry, licorice and spice all compete for attention, tannins significant, but balanced. Screwcap. 13.5% alc. **Rating** 97 **To** 2040 $35 ✪

🍷🍷🍷🍷🍷 **Invitation Winemaker Tony Davis Riesling 2016** 15-day cold ferment, 5 weeks on lees. Quartz-white; the perfumed bouquet, full of lime and lemon blossom, sets the scene, and the palate takes the stage without hesitation. It is as long as it is intense, its future assured. Screwcap. 12% alc. **Rating** 96 **To** 2030 **$30** ●
Magpie Hill Reserve Cabernet Sauvignon 2015 A more autocratic wine than the Single Vineyard, which befits its status. The colour is superb, the fruit carrying an earthy edge right from the outset, yet the flavours are unequivocally ripe, blackcurrant cassis to the fore. Bordeaux would be happy with this. Screwcap. 13.6% alc. **Rating** 96 **To** 2035 **$35** ✪
Single Vineyard Riesling 2016 Lemon/lime and apple blossom aromas; while it has the texture and structure of a young high class Porongurup riesling, it is already showing hints of the lime and (ultimately) honey characters that will develop over the next 5 years in the first stage of its development, before settling down to the next 10+ years as it reaches full maturity. Screwcap. 12.5% alc. **Rating** 95 **To** 2031 **$25** ✪
Single Vineyard Rose 2016 85% cabernet sauvignon, 15% shiraz drawn off from Estate reds (saignee) and cool-fermented. Pale salmon-pink; a supremely aromatic/scented bouquet; the palate is intense and long, with strawberry fruit and a juicy, but dry, finish. Screwcap. 12.5% alc. **Rating** 95 **To** 2017 **$20** ✪
Single Vineyard Shiraz 2015 Matured in French barriques (20% new) for 15 months. An ever reliable standout bargain of high quality cool-grown shiraz. The fragrant bouquet speaks of black cherry and spices of all kinds threaded through the fruit. See how long the aftertaste lingers in the mouth. Screwcap. 13.5% alc. **Rating** 95 **To** 2030 **$26** ✪
Single Vineyard Cabernet Sauvignon 2015 A delicious wine bringing all the components of cassis/blackcurrant fruit, quality French oak and ripe tannins to the table. There is just enough bay leaf/black olive/earth to ensure complexity is part of the deal. Screwcap. 13.6% alc. **Rating** 95 **To** 2030 **$26** ✪
Single Vineyard Off Dry Riesling 2016 Distinguished wine from a great vineyard, and a great contract winemaker, but at the moment it's in no man's land. The small amount of residual sugar will only come into the game when the wine is 5yo, and for 10 years thereafter. Screwcap. 12.3% alc. **Rating** 94 **To** 2031 **$25** ✪

Dutschke Wines ★★★★★

Lot 1 Gods Hill Road, Lyndoch, SA 5351 **Region** Barossa Valley
T (08) 8524 5485 **www**.dutschkewines.com **Open** By appt
Winemaker Wayne Dutschke **Est.** 1998 **Dozens** 6000 **Vyds** 15ha

Winemaker and owner Wayne Dutschke set up business with uncle (and grapegrower) Ken Semmler in 1990 to produce their first wine. Since then, Dutschke Wines has built its own small winery around the corner from Ken's vineyard, and the portfolio has increased. While Wayne has now been making small batch wines for over 25 years, his use of whole-berry ferments, open fermenters, basket presses and a quality oak regime have all remained the same. He was crowned Barossa Winemaker of the Year in 2010, inducted into the Barons of Barossa in '13, and is the author of a children's book about growing up in a winery called *My Dad has Purple Hands*. Exports to the US, Canada, Denmark, Germany, The Netherlands and Taiwan.

🍷🍷🍷🍷🍷 **Oscar Semmler St Jakobi Vineyard Barossa Valley Shiraz 2014** Open-fermented, 12 days on skins, matured for 19 months in French hogsheads (75% new). Deep crimson-purple; absolutely from the big end of town, yet has grace, Rolls Royce style. The balance is impeccable, the mouthfeel totally harmonious, the black fruits, licorice and spice supported by fine-grained tannins, the new oak integrated but positive. Screwcap. 14.5% alc. **Rating** 96 **To** 2044 **$70** ✪
St Jakobi Single Vineyard Lyndoch Barossa Valley Shiraz 2015 From Ken Semmler's vineyard, planted in '78, matured in French hogsheads (33% new) for 18 months. Deep crimson-purple; a full-bodied Barossa Valley shiraz straddling traditional and newer winemaking practices (the latter French oak). Its depth and balance will see this wine transform itself over the next 10 years and flourish for 20+ years thereafter. Screwcap. 14.5% alc. **Rating** 95 **To** 2045 **$45**

SAMI St Jakobi Vineyard Lyndoch Barossa Valley Cabernet Sauvignon
2015 Machine-harvested, open-fermented, 10 days on skins, matured in
French hogsheads (33% new) for 18 months. The Barossa struggles to achieve
the X-factor with cabernet, but this goes oh so close. Its colour and bouquet are
impressive, as are the juicy cassis fruit and fine tannins, quality French oak adding
further to the wine, the length admirable. Screwcap. 14.5% alc. **Rating** 95 **To** 2030
$35 ●

GHR Neighbours Barossa Valley Shiraz 2015 Open-fermented, 7–24 days
on skins, pressed, 18 months in French and American oak (35% new). Full-bodied
and notably complex, but supple throughout the palate. Blackberry and blood
plum fruit is framed by oak and well judged tannins. A great future. Screwcap.
14.5% alc. **Rating** 94 **To** 2039 $32

♈♈♈♈♈ Uncle St Jakobi Vineyard 2015 Rating 91 To 2025 $27

Eagles Rest Wines

Lot 1, 534 Oakey Creek Road, Pokolbin, NSW 2320 **Region** Hunter Valley
T (02) 4998 6714 **www**.eaglesrestwines.com.au **Open** 7 days 10–5
Winemaker Jeff Byrne **Est.** 2007 **Dozens** 5000 **Vyds** 20ha
Eagles Rest has flown under the radar since its establishment in 2007, and still does. The estate
is planted to 11ha of chardonnay, 10ha shiraz, 6ha semillon and 2ha verdelho.

♈♈♈♈♈ Dam Block Hunter Valley Semillon 2012 This is freakish, still with the colour
of a 1yo semillon, not a 5yo. What is more, the palate lives up to the promise of
the colour: fine, long and pure, with lemon, lime and grapefruit citrus flavours
locked together by tightly wound acidity. Screwcap. 10.9% alc. **Rating** 96 **To** 2026
$25 ●

Maluna Hunter Valley Chardonnay 2012 This is one of the new generation
Hunter Valley chardonnays that belie the climate. It is intense, vibrant and lively,
with lemon, grapefruit and lemongrass flavours riding high, wide and handsome,
the finish long and clean. Yes, there's oak present as a result of barrel fermentation,
but it's more to do with structure than flavour. Screwcap. 12% alc. **Rating** 95
To 2022 $45 ●

Maluna Hunter Valley Chardonnay 2014 A vibrant à la mode chardonnay
that the Hunter Valley can do so well, making wines that appear cool climate in
style. The accent is on grapefruit/white peach flavours underpinned by bright
acidity and integrated French oak. Screwcap. **Rating** 94 **To** 2022

Maluna Hunter Valley Shiraz 2014 From the great '14 vintage, only
500 dozen made. As is typical, it is medium-bodied, with an earthy/savoury
background to the plum and blackberry fruits, accentuated here by the impact
of French oak. The tannins are typical, and provide the structure for long-term
ageing. Screwcap. 14.2% alc. **Rating** 94 **To** 2044

♈♈♈♈♈ Hunter Valley Chardonnay 2011 Rating 93 To 2020 $29

Echelon

68 Anzac Street, Chullora, NSW 2190 **Region** Various
T (02) 9722 1200 **www**.echelonwine.com.au **Open** Not
Winemaker Various **Est.** 2009 **Dozens** NFP
Echelon is the brainchild of Nicholas Crampton, a wine marketer who understands wine
(by no means a common occurrence). He persuaded McWilliam's (Echelon's owner) to give
free rein to his insights, and enlisted the aid of winemaker Corey Ryan. Brands under the
Echelon umbrella are Last Horizon (single vineyard wines from Tasmania, made by Adrian
Sparks), Partisan (from McLaren Vale), Armchair Critic and Under & Over (from established
vineyards in the best regions) and Zeppelin (made by Corey Ryan and Kym Teusner, sourced
from Barossa vineyards owned by Teusner or Sons of Eden, and often up to 80 years old).

♈♈♈♈♈ **Last Horizon Tamar Valley Riesling 2016** Whole-bunch pressed and cool fermented. A very good riesling with excellent depth, structure and length to a complex array of lime, lemon and apple fruit within a frame of minerally acidity, the length faultless. Screwcap. 12% alc. **Rating** 95 To 2026 $32 ♦

♈♈♈♈♈ **Last Horizon Tamar Valley Pinot Noir 2016** Rating 93 To 2022 $33

Eclectic Wines

687 Hermitage Road, Pokolbin, NSW 2320 **Region** Hunter Valley
T 0410 587 207 **www**.eclecticwines.com.au **Open** Fri–Mon
Winemaker First Creek Wines, David Hook, Paul Stuart **Est.** 2001 **Dozens** 3000
This is the venture of Paul and Kate Stuart, nominally based in the Hunter Valley, where they live and have a vineyard planted to shiraz and mourvedre; 'nominally', because Paul's 30+ years in the wine industry have given him the marketing knowledge to sustain the purchase of grapes from various regions, including Canberra. He balances the production of his own wines under the Eclectic label while also acting as an independent marketing and sales consultant to other producers, selling his clients' wine in different markets from those in which he sells his own. Exports to The Netherlands, Taiwan and China.

♈♈♈♈♈ **Hunter Valley Semillon 2016** This boasts the honeydew, lemon drop, hay and lanolin X-factors that make Hunter semillon such a thrilling ride of livewire acidity, unadulterated fruit and Brylcreem soapiness. Long and chiselled. Screwcap. 12% alc. **Rating** 95 To 2029 $28 NG ♦
Pewter Label Reserve Hunter Valley Shiraz 2014 A modern expression of Hunter shiraz, minus the shoe polish tannins, instead with a beam of violet, wakame and juicy blue fruits, firmly glimpsing the Rhône in its aromatic, mid-weighted guise. Screwcap. 14% alc. **Rating** 94 To 2026 $38 NG

♈♈♈♈♈ **Hunter Valley Chardonnay 2016** Rating 93 To 2023 $28 NG
Hunter Valley Semillon 2015 Rating 91 To 2028 $28 NG
Hunter Central Ranges Pinot Grigio 2016 Rating 91 To 2019 $25 NG
Hunter Valley Verdelho 2015 Rating 90 To 2018 $25 NG

Eddie McDougall Wines

PO Box 2012, Hawthorn, Vic 3122 **Region** King Valley
T 0413 960 102 **www**.eddiemcdougall.com **Open** Not
Winemaker Eddie McDougall **Est.** 2007 **Dozens** 5000
Eddie McDougall's wine education began with part-time work in restaurants and bars while obtaining a Bachelor of International Business degree. The next step was a vineyard job at Shadowfax, then a postgraduate degree in wine technology and viticulture at the University of Melbourne. Next came Giant Steps, Clyde Park, O'Leary Walker and Wood Park. The top Barolo producer, Vietti, and the legendary Mas de Daumas Gassac in Languedoc took his winemaking CV onto the world platform. He has given an entirely new (and different) meaning to the term 'Flying Winemaker': as well as the wines he makes in Australia, he makes wine at the Eighth Estate Winery in Hong Kong using grapes flown from France. In 2013 he was one of the 12 elite wine professionals selected for the annual Len Evans Tutorial, regarded as the world's most esteemed wine judging program. Exports to Singapore, Hong Kong, Macau, Taiwan and China.

♈♈♈♈♈ **McDougall & Langworthy Margaret River Rose 2016** An eclectic blend of tempranillo, shiraz, grenache and vermentino; given that only 250 dozen were made, this must have been a labour of love. Pale pink; the bouquet is exceptionally fragrant, with red fruits and exotic spices galore; like a great pinot, the bouquet is mesmeric. The palate, too, vibrates with energy, with wild strawberries filling the mouth. Screwcap. 12.5% alc. **Rating** 96 To 2018 $38 ♦

Eden Hall   ★★★★☆

6 Washington Street, Angaston, SA 5353 **Region** Eden Valley
T 0400 991 968 **www.**edenhall.com.au **Open** 7 days 11–5
Winemaker Kym Teusner, Christa Deans **Est.** 2002 **Dozens** 4000 **Vyds** 32.3ha
David and Mardi Hall purchased the historic Avon Brae Estate in 1996. The 120ha property
has been planted to cabernet sauvignon (the lion's share, with 13ha), riesling (9.25ha), shiraz
(6ha) and smaller amounts of merlot, cabernet franc and viognier. The majority of the
production is contracted to Yalumba, St Hallett and McGuigan Simeon, with 10% of the best
grapes held back for the Eden Hall label. Exports to Canada and China.

🍷🍷🍷🍷🍷 **Reserve Riesling 2016** Picks up where its standard sibling leaves off. Riper
fruit and the use of free-run juice gives rise to a wine with multiple layers to its
tapestry of Meyer lemon and Rose's lime juice flavours. The house style has soft
acid as its benchmark, inviting earlier rather than later consumption. Screwcap.
12.3% alc. **Rating** 95 **To** 2026 $35 ✪
Block 4 Shiraz 2015 Hand-picked from specific rows of Block 4, matured for
18 months in French oak (40% new). While on the heavy side of medium-bodied,
has very good focus, length and line. Blackberry, plum and black cherry fruit drive
the agenda, savoury tannins help placing the vines' lineage in the Eden Valley.
Distinguished stuff. Screwcap. 14.5% alc. **Rating** 94 **To** 2035 $40
Block 3 Cabernet Sauvignon 2015 Matured for 17 months in French oak
(40% new). Eden Valley's more temperate climate (than the Barossa Valley) is more
suited for cabernet sauvignon. This is a deep-seated full-bodied cabernet, full
of contrasting cassis and blackcurrant and black olive/bay leaf fruit, tannins à la
cabernet, augmented by French oak. Screwcap. 14.5% alc. **Rating** 94 **To** 2040 $40

🍷🍷🍷🍷🍷 **Riesling 2016 Rating** 93 **To** 2025 $22 ✪
Springton Barossa Shiraz 2015 Rating 92 **To** 2030 $25 ✪
Gruner Veltliner 2016 Rating 91 **To** 2025 $35

Eden Road Wines   ★★★★★

3182 Barton Highway, Murrumbateman, NSW 2582 **Region** Canberra District
T (02) 6226 8800 **www.**edenroadwines.com.au **Open** Wed–Sun 11–4
Winemaker Celine Rousseau, Brigitte Rodda **Est.** 2006 **Dozens** 9500 **Vyds** 3ha
The name of this business, now entirely based in the Canberra District, reflects an earlier
stage of its development, when it also had a property in the Eden Valley. That has now been
separated, and since 2008 Eden Road's operations have centred on Hilltops, Canberra District
and Tumbarumba. Eden Road has purchased the former Doonkuna winery and mature
vineyard, and its marketing has been greatly assisted by winning the Jimmy Watson Trophy in
'09. Exports to the UK, the US, the Maldives and Hong Kong.

🍷🍷🍷🍷🍷 **Maragle Single Vineyard Chardonnay 2015** What's quite breathtaking about
Maragle is its abundance of flavour, reined in to a linear frame. Not such an easy
balance to strike, here done so with laser precision. Flinty, with leesy notes, citrus
and stone fruit, ginger spice, smoky and wood spices, superfine acidity and great
length. Screwcap. 12.6% alc. **Rating** 96 **To** 2025 $40 JF
Tumbarumba Chardonnay 2014 A blend of fruit off the Maragle and
Courabyra vineyards – best of both, perhaps. This is all class, with the richness
and ginger-creamed-honey flavour of the Courabyra offset by the linearity of the
other. It's certainly harmonious – long, savoury, detailed, and with superb balance.
Complete. Screwcap. 13.1% alc. **Rating** 96 **To** 2025 JF
Courabyra Single Vineyard Chardonnay 2015 It's pale and bright, but what
jumps out is this amazing flavour – probably lees-derived, because it's like clotted
cream infused with ginger and honey. There's also stone fruit, Meyer lemon and
more spice. The palate is another thing altogether: super tight, linear and the
epitome of restraint. Screwcap. 12% alc. **Rating** 95 **To** 2025 JF
Gundagai Syrah 2015 This certainly needs more time in bottle before it'll
unfurl to reveal its potential. In the meantime, it offers a deep purple–crimson hue,

wood spices, blue fruits, roasted hazelnuts, gravel and overall vibrancy. Firm tannins yet a detailed, medium-bodied palate. Scewcap. 13.5% alc. **Rating** 95 **To** 2030 JF

ΨΨΨΨΨ **The Long Road Chardonnay 2015 Rating** 92 **To** 2022 $28 JF
Skinny Flat White 2016 Rating 92 **To** 2020 $30 JF
Murrumbateman Canberra District Syrah 2015 Rating 92 **To** 2025 JF
Canberra Riesling 2016 Rating 91 **To** 2022 $28 JF
The Long Road Pinot Gris 2016 Rating 91 **To** 2020 $28 JF
Pinot Noir 2016 Rating 90 **To** 2024 JF

Edenmae Estate Wines   ★★★★

7 Miller Street, Springton, SA 5235 **Region** Eden Valley
T 0409 493 407 **www**.edenmae.com.au **Open** Fri–Sun 10–6
Winemaker Michelle Barr **Est.** 2007 **Dozens** 1800 **Vyds** 12ha
Owner/winemaker Michelle Barr runs Edenmae on a minimal intervention/organic viticulture basis. The vineyard is planted to riesling and shiraz (4ha each), pinot noir and cabernet sauvignon (2ha each), most around 40yo, some younger. Its cellar door offers their full portfolio for tasting and local platters.

ΨΨΨΨΨ **Maluka Single Vineyard Eden Valley Shiraz 2013** From 43yo estate dry-grown vines, matured in French oak for 2 years. The very good crimson-purple colour reflects the intensity and controlled power of the palate, with its multiple layers of French oak; black cherry fruit, licorice and a touch of black pepper join the party on the finish. Screwcap. 14% alc. **Rating** 94 **To** 2033 $38

ΨΨΨΨ **Belle Single Vineyard Cabernet Sauvignon 2013 Rating** 93 **To** 2033 $32

Eight at the Gate   ★★★★

42A Grant Avenue, Rose Park, SA 5067 (postal) **Region** Wrattonbully
T 0400 873 126 **www**.eightatthegate.com.au **Open** Not
Winemaker Peter Douglas (Contract) **Est.** 2002 **Dozens** 800 **Vyds** 60ha
Sisters Jane Richards and Claire Davies are part of a southeast SA farming family. Each of the sisters had four children, hence (slightly indirectly) the name of their enterprise. They came to it by diverse pathways: Jane left the land, successfully weaving her way up the corporate ladder in the technology world, on a journey that took her to New York and San Francisco. Claire set down her roots in the land, graduating from Roseworthy, working as an assistant winemaker, thereafter as a viticultural consultant in the Di Davidson Consulting group, one of Australia's best. The sisters came together in 2002, buying Lanacoona Estate, with an established vineyard planted in 1995, now significantly expanded to the present 60ha under the expert eagle eye of Claire. Most of the grapes are sold, but since 2005 they have made small amounts of wine for family consumption. With Peter Douglas onboard as contract winemaker, production has inched upwards, and in 2016 they finally labelled Eight at the Gate wines.

ΨΨΨΨΨ **Single Vineyard Wrattonbully Chardonnay 2016** It seems little or no oak was involved, but the wine did win a gold medal at the Australian Small Winemakers Show '16. It's been well made, from the harvest date choice through to the wine in the bottle, with fresh stone fruit flavours to the fore, and just sufficient acidity. Very good value. Screwcap. 12.7% alc. **Rating** 90 **To** 2020 $20
Cabernet Shiraz 2013 Bright crimson-purple; the wine has abundant texture and structure underwriting the blend of blackcurrant, plum and blackberry fruits. The tannins are rounded, and the oak soft, but they are still in the process of integrating with the fruit. Screwcap. 14% alc. **Rating** 90 **To** 2025 $26

1847 | Yaldara Wines   ★★★★★

Chateau Yaldara, Hermann Thumm Drive, Lyndoch, SA 5351 **Region** Barossa Valley
T (08) 8524 5328 **www**.1847wines.com **Open** 7 days 9.30–5
Winemaker Alex Peel, Chris Coulter **Est.** 1996 **Dozens** 50 000 **Vyds** 53.9ha

1847 Wines is wholly owned by Treasure Valley Wines Pty Ltd, which is Chinese-owned. The year is that when Barossa pioneer Johann Gramp planted his first vines in the region. There is in fact no other connection between Gramp and the business he established and 1847 Wines. It (1847 Wines) has 80ha of estate vineyards in the general vicinity of the original plantings by Gramp. A 1000-tonne winery was built for the '14 vintage, handling the core production, together with new varieties and blends. This is underpinned by the acquisition of Chateau Yaldara in '14, providing a major retail outlet and massively enhanced production facilities. Exports to China.

🍷🍷🍷🍷🍷 **1847 Limited Release 40 Year Old Rare Tawny NV** The olive-mahogany colour attests to its age. This is a very good tawny, concentrated and complex, with burnt toffee, Christmas cake, spice, cumquat and more, the fortifying spirit clean and rancio at the right level. Above all else, is not stale. The price is ambitious, of course. Cork. 20% alc. **Rating** 96 $420

1847 Limited Release 30 Year Old Rare Tawny NV There is no doubt that this Limited Release quartet of 10 to 40 Year Old (as an average in each case) tawnies are true to label. Do not think for one moment that further development will take place in the bottle – it won't. The prices may seem high, but don't reflect the much higher cost of production. Cork. 20% alc. **Rating** 96 $230

1847 20 Year Old Aged Tawny NV Lighter colour than the 10 Year Old, grading towards a tawny hue on the rim; spicy Christmas cake complexity is neatly balanced by rancio. Cork. 20% alc. **Rating** 95 $100

1847 10 Year Old Aged Tawny NV Red-brown hue; juicy, rich, already showing some rancio development; good balance. A complex wine, fresh and fruity before an essentially dry finish. Cork. 18% alc. **Rating** 94 $40

🍷🍷🍷🍷🍷 **1847 Old Vine Barossa Valley Grenache 2015** Rating 93 To 2029 $120
1847 Grand Pappy's Adelaide Hills Chardonnay 2015 Rating 90 To 2019 $50
1847 Old Vine Barossa Valley Grenache 2014 Rating 90 To 2025 $120
1847 Barossa Valley Sparkling Petit Verdot 2013 Rating 90 To 2019 $35 TS

Ekhidna   ★★★★★

67 Branson Road, McLaren Vale, SA 5171 **Region** McLaren Vale
T (08) 8323 8496 **www**.ekhidnawines.com.au **Open** 7 days 11–5
Winemaker Matthew Rechner **Est.** 2001 **Dozens** 8000

Matt Rechner entered the wine industry in 1988, spending most of the years since at Tatachilla in McLaren Vale, starting as laboratory technician and finishing as operations manager. Frustrated by the constraints of large winery practice, he decided to strike out on his own in 2001. The quality of the wines has been such that he has been able to build a winery and cellar door, the winery facilitating the use of various cutting-edge techniques. Exports to the UK, Singapore and China

🍷🍷🍷🍷🍷 **Matt's LP McLaren Vale Shiraz 2014** From vineyards 20–100+yo, all parcels handled separately, crushed, 5–7 days cold soak, open-fermented with cultured yeast, matured in mainly French oak (2% new). Full to the brim with supple juicy black fruits, mocha oak and tantalising spicy tannins; it is full-bodied, yet effortlessly carries its weight, beckoning you back for another sip, and another. Screwcap. 14.5% alc. **Rating** 95 To 2034 $30 ✪

McLaren Vale Cabernet Shiraz 2013 Cabernet calls the shots from start to finish, not necessarily what one might expect from McLaren Vale. More surprising is the quality of the wine given its ludicrously low price tag – it is medium-bodied, tightly focused, and its savoury, dark berry fruits have excellent tannin backup. A steal. Screwcap. 14.5% alc. **Rating** 94 To 2028 $20 ✪

🍷🍷🍷🍷🍷 **McLaren Vale GSM 2015** Rating 91 To 2022 $20 ✪
McLaren Vale Mourvedre 2014 Rating 90 To 2029 $20 ✪

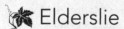 # Elbourne Wines

236 Marrowbone Road, Pokolbin, NSW 2320 **Region** Hunter Valley
T 0416 190 878 **www**.elbournewines.com.au **Open** By appt
Winemaker Nick Paterson **Est.** 2009 **Dozens** 500 **Vyds** 4ha

Adam and Alexys Elbourne have done what many thousands of young families have dreamt of doing: selling their house in Sydney and moving to the unpolluted environment of the Hunter Valley to bring up their family. Their house sold in two weeks, making the search for property more urgent than most. But you make your own luck, and they had already made many trips to the Hunter, simply to enjoy the wine and food scene – and Alexys was raised on an 80ha property on the banks of the Patterson River. So it seemed inevitable that they would find and buy the 22ha Marrowbone Road property, with 2ha each of rundown chardonnay and shiraz and enough land to have a boutique racehorse stud and a Noah's Ark of animals including rare Wessex Saddleback pigs. The last pieces of the puzzle were the two-year restoration of the vineyard under the direction of one of the great viticulturists of the Hunter Valley, Neil Stevens, who continues to manage the vineyard, and the appointment of Nick Paterson as contract winemaker.

ɤɤɤɤɤ **Single Vineyard Hunter Valley Shiraz 2014** You are not likely to forget the striking label with a very large E in its centre. A problem for Elbourne is that it will most likely be a long time before a red vintage as great as this will come along again. But Elbourne has made hay, with an intense and very long shiraz given high quality French oak to frame its red and black fruits, the tannins willowy. Screwcap. 14.5% alc. **Rating** 96 **To** 2044 $33 ❂

Hunter Valley Shiraz 2011 Small wonder this wine won a gold medal at the Hunter Valley Wine Show '14. It has made the best use of a very good vintage to produce a classic Hunter shiraz that has flourished in bottle, and will continue to do so for a decade or two. It is fuller and richer than the '14 despite its lower alcohol, skilled used of French oak common to both wines. Screwcap. 13% alc. **Rating** 96 **To** 2041 $38 ❂

Hunter Valley Chardonnay 2012 Early picking has conferred great freshness, elegance and length on the wine, reflected in its trophies and gold medals. Obviously, the judges at these shows had no questions about the fruit depth (or lack thereof). Screwcap. 12% alc. **Rating** 95 **To** 2020 $35 ❂

ɤɤɤɤɤ **Hunter Valley Chardonnay 2013** Rating 93 To 2020 $28
Single Vineyard Hunter Valley Chardonnay 2014 Rating 92 To 2021 $28
Single Vineyard Hunter Valley Chardonnay 2015 Rating 90 To 2021 $28

Elderslie

PO Box 93, Charleston, SA 5244 **Region** Adelaide Hills
T 0404 943 743 **www**.eldersliewines.com.au **Open** Not
Winemaker Adam Wadewitz **Est.** 2015 **Dozens** 600 **Vyds** 8ha

This may be a new kid off the block, but it brings together two families with blue blood wine in their veins. In their respective roles as winemaker (Adam Wadewitz) and wine marketer (Nicole Roberts) they bring a wealth of experience gained in many parts of the wine world. They each have their partners (Nikki Wadewitz and Mark Roberts) onboard, and also have their real-life jobs. In 2016 Nicole accepted the position of executive officer of the Adelaide Hills Wine Region, having had brand development roles with three of the Hills' leading winemakers, Shaw + Smith, Grosset and The Lane Vineyard. Over the past 20 years Adam has carved out a career at the highest imaginable level, aided by becoming joint dux of the Len Evans Tutorial in 2009. He was senior winemaker at Best's, where he made the 2012 Jimmy Watson winner; became the youngest judge to serve as a panel chair at the National Wine Show; and is now senior winemaker for Shaw + Smith and their associated Tolpuddle Vineyard in Tasmania.

ɤɤɤɤɤ **Hills Blend #1 Adelaide Hills Pinot Blanc 2016** A single wine, like the first swallow of spring, cannot change my views about the worth of pinot blanc. While the fruit aromas and flavours are unremarkable, the texture and structure of this wine are exceptional. Grainy, minerally, fantastically long and complex, this haunts the mouth for an impossibly long time after it is tasted. Screwcap. 13% alc. **Rating** 95 **To** 2026

Hills Blend #2 Adelaide Hills Pinot Meunier Pinot Noir 2016 A highly fragrant bouquet with a full suite of red fruits that translates directly into the palate, which adds fine, but firm, tannins to the equation. Plenty of attitude, and likewise potential development. Screwcap. 13.5% alc. **Rating** 95 **To** 2026

Elderton   ★★★★★

3–5 Tanunda Road, Nuriootpa, SA 5355 **Region** Barossa Valley
T (08) 8568 7878 **www**.eldertonwines.com.au **Open** Mon–Fri 10–5, w'ends, hols 11–4
Winemaker Richard Langford **Est.** 1982 **Dozens** 45 000 **Vyds** 65ha

The founding Ashmead family, with mother Lorraine supported by sons Allister and Cameron, continues to impress with their wines. The original source was 30ha of fully mature shiraz, cabernet sauvignon and merlot on the Barossa floor; subsequently 16ha of Eden Valley vineyards (shiraz, cabernet sauvignon, chardonnay, zinfandel, merlot and roussanne) were incorporated into the business. Energetic promotion and marketing in Australia and overseas are paying dividends. Elegance and balance are the keys to these wines. Exports to all major markets.

ⓎⓎⓎⓎⓎ **Command Barossa Shiraz 2014** This is power corseted by a filmy, gossamer texture and sheer, strident vinosity. Dark fruit, anise, tar, camphor and a Cadbury milk chocolate creaminess coat the palate. There is a barrel-ferment smokiness, too. The extraction levels are exact, the use of French and American oak sensitive. All is in a harmony and perfectly suited to the style. Screwcap. 14.5% alc. **Rating** 97 **To** 2040 $130 NG ✪

ⓎⓎⓎⓎⓎ **Western Ridge Barossa Valley Grenache Carignan 2015** A seldom seen blend in this country, carignan's bracing rasp of acidity and tannin offers a mitigating spike to grenache's red cherry, kirsch and amaro. This wine showcases the synergy between the two varieties beautifully, Screwcap. 14.5% alc. **Rating** 96 **To** 2028 $60 NG ✪

Ashmead Barossa Cabernet Sauvignon 2015 Brims with cabernet's varietal stash of attributes: currant and a swag of dark plum, dried sage, bouquet garni and a gentle lilt of grassiness. At first gentle and massaged by the sheer density of flavour, the tannins grow in stature as the wine opens, with acidity serving as an echo chamber, drawing the flavours back across the senses. Screwcap. 14.5% alc. **Rating** 96 **To** 2035 $120 NG

Ode to Lorraine Barossa Cabernet Sauvignon Shiraz Merlot 2014 A wine defined by the thrust of Barossan density and the tenacious vinosity of older vines, finely tuned to the parry of chalky tannins, and tangy acidity. Plums of all types, pastille, a potpourri of herbs and the pull of mint all play a part in a wine that leaves a resounding impression of elegance. Screwcap. 14% alc. **Rating** 95 **To** 2032 $60 NG

Neil Ashmead Grand Tourer Barossa Valley Shiraz 2015 A blend of ancient estate-grown shiraz vines and sensitive winemaking, the overall impression is one of strapping power melded to an avuncular aromatic profile, all corseted by tannins and oak buried in the mass of dark fruit, and a savoury interplay. The finish is an endless melody of vinosity and force of personality. Screwcap. 14.6% alc. **Rating** 94 **To** 2034 $60 NG

Barossa Valley Golden Semillon 2016 Made by cutting the cordon and thus concentrating the sugars in the bunches sans botrytis influence, the wine is a brilliant hue of yellow tinged with iridescent green at the edges. Mango, papaya, quince marmalade and a tang of ginger spice that plays long across the mouth are bound to an energetic skein of zesty acidity that tows the wine long. Screwcap. 10.5% alc. **Rating** 94 **To** 2026 $30 NG ✪

🍷🍷🍷🍷🍷 Eden Valley Riesling 2016 Rating 92 To 2030 $30 NG
　　　 Eden Valley Chardonnay 2016 Rating 92 To 2030 $30 NG
　　　 E Series Shiraz Cabernet 2015 Rating 91 To 2022 $19 NG ○
　　　 Barossa GSM 2014 Rating 91 To 2024 $34 NG

Eldorado Road ★★★★★

46–48 Ford Street, Beechworth, Vic 3747 **Region** Northeast Victoria
T (03) 5725 1698 **www.**eldoradoroad.com.au **Open** Fri–Sun 11–5
Winemaker Paul and Ben Dahlenburg, Laurie Schulz **Est.** 2010 **Dozens** 1500 **Vyds** 4ha
Paul Dahlenburg (nicknamed Bear), Lauretta Schulz (Laurie) and their children have leased a 2ha block of shiraz planted in the 1890s with rootlings supplied from France (doubtless grafted) in the wake of phylloxera's devastation of the Glenrowan and Rutherglen plantings. Bear and Laurie knew about the origins of the vineyard, which was in a state of serious decline after years of neglect. The owners of the vineyard were aware of its historic importance and were more than happy to lease it. Four years of tireless work reconstructing the old vines has resulted in tiny amounts of exceptionally good shiraz; they have also planted a small area of nero d'Avola and durif.

🍷🍷🍷🍷🍷 **Luminoso Rose 2016** Nero d'Avola matured in used French puncheons for 6 months on full lees. Salmon-pink; textured and savoury, its crisp acidity simultaneously lengthens and dries out the finish. Great food style. Screwcap. 13.7% alc. **Rating** 95 **To** 2020 $23 ○
Onyx Durif 2015 Estate-grown on weathered red granite soils, open-fermented, extended fermentation and maceration in skins, matured in Burgundian oak. Durif is the toughest assignment in the book to capture perfume in the bouquet and light and life penetrating the fruit and tannin components. Paul Dahlenburg has achieved the near-impossible. Screwcap. 14.4% alc. **Rating** 95 **To** 2040 $35 ○
Quasimodo Shiraz Durif Nero d'Avola 2014 Notwithstanding the region and blend suggesting a full-bodied wine, this is an elegant, medium-bodied style with a complex web of spicy blue, purple and black fruits, the tannins fine, the oak subtle. Controlled alcohol is the key to its success, making it ready whenever you are. Screwcap. 13.3% alc. **Rating** 94 **To** 2023 $28 ○

🍷🍷🍷🍷🍷 Beechworth Chardonnay 2015 Rating 93 To 2020 $35
　　　 IV Nations Vintage Fortified 2015 Rating 93 $25 ○
　　　 Comrade Nero d'Avola 2015 Rating 90 To 2022 $35

Eldredge ★★★★

659 Spring Gully Road, Clare, SA 5453 **Region** Clare Valley
T (08) 8842 3086 **www.**eldredge.com.au **Open** 7 days 11–5
Winemaker Leigh Eldredge **Est.** 1993 **Dozens** 8000 **Vyds** 20.9ha
Leigh and Karen Eldredge have established their winery and cellar door in the Sevenhill Ranges at an altitude of 500m above Watervale. The mature estate vineyard is planted to shiraz, cabernet sauvignon, merlot, riesling, sangiovese and malbec. Exports to the UK, the US, Canada, Singapore and China.

🍷🍷🍷🍷🍷 **Blue Chip Clare Valley Shiraz 2015** Another release in the style that has characterised this label over many years. A heady and forceful bouquet, exuding aromas of very ripe blackberry, principally, along with vanillan oak, and the warm, sweet scent that comes with brandied plum pudding. Full and richly flavoured, the black fruit rolls along the palate in a glycerine-textured wave escorted by imposing tannins. Screwcap. 14.8% alc. **Rating** 94 **To** 2030 $35 SC
Reserve Clare Valley Malbec 2014 Aged for 18 months in new French oak, and its influence is obvious, particularly on the bouquet. Whether it's too much or not is a matter of opinion. What's not in contention is the succulent, abundant fruit on offer. Ripe, soft red berries – raspberry, mulberry, boysenberry – fill the bouquet and spill onto the palate, flooding it with flavour. Delicious now or later. Screwcap. 14.8% alc. **Rating** 94 **To** 2030 $38 SC

ŦŦŦŦ♀ **Clare Valley Riesling 2016** Rating 93 To 2030 $22 SC **O**
RL Clare Valley Cabernet Malbec 2014 Rating 93 To 2035 $30 SC
JD Clare Valley Sangiovese 2015 Rating 92 To 2027 $20 SC **O**
Mollie 2016 Rating 90 To 2020 $20 SC **O**

Eldridge Estate of Red Hill   ★★★★★

120 Arthurs Seat Road, Red Hill, Vic 3937 **Region** Mornington Peninsula
T 0414 758 960 **www**.eldridge-estate.com.au **Open** Mon–Fri 12–4, w'ends & hols 11–5
Winemaker David Lloyd **Est.** 1985 **Dozens** 1000 **Vyds** 2.8ha
The Eldridge Estate vineyard was purchased by David and (the late) Wendy Lloyd in 1995.
Major retrellising work has been undertaken, changing to Scott Henry, and all the wines are
estate-grown and made. David has also planted several Dijon-selected pinot noir clones (114,
115 and 777), which have been contributing since 2004; likewise the Dijon chardonnay clone
96. Attention to detail permeates all he does in vineyard and winery. Exports to the US.

ŦŦŦŦŦ **Clonal Blend Pinot Noir 2015** Clones with 25% 777, the remainder equal
quantities of MV6, 115, Pommard, G5V15 and Clone 1. A beautiful pinot, half
made in the vineyard, half in the winery. Its power takes a few seconds to start,
but thereafter takes no prisoners. It has the fabulous red fruit flavours and intensity
of the great vintage. Looked better each time it was retasted. Screwcap. 13.5% alc.
Rating 97 To 2030 $75 **O**

ŦŦŦŦŦ **Single Clone Pinot Noir 2015** All the Eldridge Estate Pinots have star-bright
colour, an instantaneous come-on, and all have exceptional fragrance. This is
100% MV6, and the wine shows why this clone is the go-to clone in Aus, its fruit
and savoury flavours welding to the roof and crevices of the mouth, retaining their
grip long after the wine is swallowed. A meaty touch to the bouquet also makes a
contribution. Screwcap. 13.5% alc. **Rating** 96 To 2030 $68 **O**
Eldridge Clone 1 Pinot Noir 2015 This clone was selected in Burgundy
for David Lloyd and brought back to Australia, where it underwent the lengthy
quarantine period. Has power that out-muscles all but MV6, but in the politest
possible way. The fruits are a little darker, with some plum joining the fray, its
grip increasing as it travels through to the finish. Screwcap. 13.5% alc. **Rating** 96
To 2029 $68 **O**
Wendy Chardonnay 2015 Honours the memory of David Lloyd's wife
Wendy ('54-2014), made from Dijon clones 95 and 96, whole-bunch pressed
and fermented in quality French oak. While elegance and attention to detail are
its watchwords, it has greater intensity and length than its sibling, but still has the
feeling of a miniature painting. Screwcap. 13% alc. **Rating** 95 To 2025 $55
Pinot Noir 2015 This is the flag bearer of Eldridge Estate, with the largest
make in the portfolio (all things being relative in the context of the total annual
production of 1000 dozen), an equal blend of the clones used in the Clonal Blend.
The fragrance, balance and length are all in perfect alignment, red fruits of just
about every kind in an ethereal smoothie, a dip of spice and forest floor on the
side. Screwcap. 13.5% alc. **Rating** 95 To 2027 $60
Fume Blanc 2016 Bright straw-green; takes all the problems that can dog
sauvignon blanc in its stride; the barrel ferment comes through with influences
of a smoky bouquet rendered unimportant by the sheer power of the lemongrass,
ripe citrus and passionfruit of the palate, the finish shining brightly. Screwcap.
13.5% alc. **Rating** 94 To 2020 $30 **O**
Chardonnay 2015 Five clones, including Dijon selections, are whole-bunch
pressed and fermented in French oak. Has freshness and brightness, modulated
chardonnay fruit in control from start to finish. Screwcap. 13% alc. **Rating** 94
To 2025 $45
North Patch Chardonnay 2015 From a small patch near the cellar door; the
five-clonal blend and standard whole-bunch press vinification process of Eldridge
Estate. All these wines have fruit picked at the precise moment, with grapefruit,
melon and white stone fruits. Screwcap. 13% alc. **Rating** 94 To 2022 $40

Gamay 2015 I expected this wine to be very different from the Pinots, but the benison of the '15 vintage and David Lloyd's light hand on the tiller narrows the gap somewhat. It has wondrous texture and structure (gamay is often one-dimensional), with black cherries to the fore. Screwcap. 13% alc. Rating 94 To 2025 $40

Elgee Park ★★★★★

24 Junction Road, Merricks North, Vic 3926 **Region** Mornington Peninsula
T (03) 5989 7338 **www**.elgeeparkwines.com.au **Open** At Merricks General Wine Store
Winemaker Geraldine McFaul (Contract) **Est.** 1972 **Dozens** 1600 **Vyds** 4.4ha
The pioneer of the Mornington Peninsula in its 20th-century rebirth, owned by Baillieu Myer and family. The vineyard is planted to riesling, chardonnay, viognier (some of the oldest vines in Australia), pinot gris, pinot noir, merlot and cabernet sauvignon. The vineyard is set in a picturesque natural amphitheatre with a northerly aspect, looking out across Port Phillip Bay towards the Melbourne skyline.

🍷🍷🍷🍷🍷 **Family Reserve Mornington Peninsula Pinot Gris 2016** The fact that this pinot gris was fermented in used oak followed by lees stirring is very obvious, the wine with greater complexity and weight than the majority. The pear and apple fruit is sotto voce, making the wine food friendly. Screwcap. 13% alc. **Rating** 94 **To** 2020 $35

🍷🍷🍷🍷🍷 **Family Reserve Viognier 2016 Rating** 92 To 2018 $30
Family Reserve Riesling 2016 Rating 90 **To** 2018 $30
Family Reserve Viognier 2015 Rating 90 **To** 2018 $30

Ellis Wines ★★★★☆

3025 Heathcote-Rochester Road, Colbinabbin, Vic 3559 (postal) **Region** Heathcote
T 0401 290 315 **www**.elliswines.com.au **Open** Not
Winemaker Guy Rathjen **Est.** 1998 **Dozens** 700 **Vyds** 54.6ha
Bryan and Joy Ellis own this family business, daughter Raylene Flanagan is the sales manager, and seven of the vineyard blocks are named after family members. For the first 10 years the Ellises were content to sell the grapes to a range of distinguished producers. However, since then a growing portion of the crop has been vinified.

🍷🍷🍷🍷🍷 **Premium Heathcote Shiraz 2014** Open-fermented for 14+ days, plunged, pressed to tank, then racked to French oak (60% new) for 14 months. Good colour; an intense bouquet with licorice and spice spun through black cherry and berry fruits, given further complexity by the French oak and tannins. The most surprising feature is the ease with which it has absorbed the oak. Screwcap. 14.7% alc. **Rating** 95 **To** 2034 $42

🍷🍷🍷🍷🍷 **Signature Label Heathcote Shiraz 2014 Rating** 90 **To** 2024 $34

Elmswood Estate ★★★★★

75 Monbulk-Seville Road, Seville, Vic 3139 **Region** Yarra Valley
T (03) 5964 3015 **www**.elmswoodestate.com.au **Open** W'ends 12–5
Winemaker Han Tao Lau **Est.** 1981 **Dozens** 2000 **Vyds** 6.9ha
Planted to cabernet sauvignon, chardonnay, merlot, sauvignon blanc, pinot noir, shiraz and riesling on the red volcanic soils of the far southern side of the Yarra Valley. The cellar door operates from 'The Pavilion', a fully enclosed glass room situated on a ridge above the vineyard, with 180 degree views of the Upper Yarra Valley. It seats up to 110 guests, and is a popular wedding venue. Exports to Hong Kong and China.

🍷🍷🍷🍷🍷 **Yarra Valley Chardonnay 2016** 35yo P58 clone, hand-picked over 3 days, chilled overnight, hand-sorted on a vibrating table, whole-bunch pressed, fermented in French oak (19% new) and matured for 9 months on lees. It is flinty, in full pursuit of Chablis, its 9.4g/l titratable acidity challenging some. The lipsmacking finish is fine by me. Screwcap. 13.1% alc. **Rating** 95 **To** 2026 $35 ✪

Yarra Valley Merlot 2015 Hand-picked, chilled overnight, mainly destemmed whole berries, some crushed, open-fermented, 2–4 weeks on skins, matured for 15 months in French oak (40% new). Bright, clear crimson-purple; the medium-bodied palate has fresh, elegant red fruits on the one hand, fine-grained persistent tannins on the other. Diam. 13.9% alc. **Rating** 95 **To** 2030 $35 ✪

Yarra Valley Syrah 2015 Chilled overnight, small open fermenters with 10% whole bunches, 2–4 weeks on skins, matured for 10 months in French oak (33% new), 200 dozen made. Good hue; juicy dark cherry and plum fruit is backed by spice on the bouquet on the way in, and cedar and fine tannins on the way out. Very good overall balance. Screwcap. 14% alc. **Rating** 94 **To** 2029 $35

Yarra Valley Cabernet Sauvignon 2015 From the deep red loamy basaltic soils of the Upper Yarra Valley, always challenging cabernet's ability to achieve full ripeness. The answer here is early pruning, increasing trellis height and leaf removal around the fruiting zone. Standard Elmswood vinification (of a high order) produces a deeply coloured, potent cabernet with a strong savoury dried herb and bay leaf subtext. Diam. 14.3% alc. **Rating** 94 **To** 2034 $35

♟♟♟♟♟ **Yarra Valley Pinot Noir 2015** **Rating** 90 **To** 2022 $38

Eperosa   ★★★★★

24 Maria Street, Tanunda, SA 5352 **Region** Barossa Valley
T 0428 111 121 **www.**eperosa.com.au **Open** By appt
Winemaker Brett Grocke **Est.** 2005 **Dozens** 1600 **Vyds** 7.83ha
Eperosa owner Brett Grocke qualified as a viticulturist in 2001, and, through Grocke Viticulture, consults and provides technical services to over 200ha of vineyards spread across the Barossa Valley, Eden Valley, Adelaide Hills, Riverland, Langhorne Creek and Hindmarsh Valley. He is ideally placed to secure small parcels of organically managed grapes, hand-picked, whole-bunch fermented and foot-stomped, and neither filtered nor fined. The wines are of impeccable quality – the use of high quality, perfectly inserted, corks will allow the wines to reach their full maturity decades hence. Exports to the UK.

♟♟♟♟♟ **Magnolia 1896 Barossa Valley Shiraz 2015** From the 1896 planting, wild-yeast fermented, matured in used French puncheons. The sheer power and intensity of this full-bodied wine neutralises any downside from the high alcohol, the overall flavour and mouthfeel on the savoury side, not jammy. Flows across the mouth adding touches of licorice and jet black fruits. Cork. 15.5% alc. **Rating** 97 **To** 2045 $100 ✪

♟♟♟♟♟ **Elevation Barossa Valley Shiraz 2015** Single dry-grown vineyard at 325m, '65 and '96 plantings. Deep crimson; a sumptuously rich and velvety wine with flavours ranging from spicy/briary to liqueur plums, the tannins ripe and plump. A hedonistic wine from start to finish. Cork. 15.3% alc. **Rating** 96 **To** 2035 $45 ✪

L.R.C. Greenock Barossa Valley Shiraz 2015 From a single row of the '67 planting. The fragrant bouquet has unexpected meaty nuances among numerous others, the palate rich, with spicy savoury notes running through the multifaceted black berry fruits, the tannins ripe and balanced. Reaches the back-palate and finishes with grace. Cork. 14.8% alc. **Rating** 96 **To** 2040 $50 ✪

Stonegarden Eden Valley Shiraz 2015 1858 and 1950s plantings. Like all the Eperosa Shirazs, superb colour, legs of wine slowly trickling down the sides of the glass; the bouquet has aromas of wild game and earth, the palate is profound and rich. Here the alcohol does make its presence felt, although its impact is diminished by the power of the fruit. Cork. 15.7% alc. **Rating** 95 **To** 2045 $100

Stonegarden 1858 Eden Valley Grenache 2015 A vineyard such as this is (or should be) a national living treasure. The wine is deeply coloured, and has fruit to match before the rocket fuel ignites as the first taste nears the end of its journey through the mouth. Brett Grocke knows infinitely more about viticulture generally than I do, and if you could double infinity, I'd do so for this vineyard. Cork. 15.8% alc. **Rating** 94 **To** 2029 $75

Y Y Y Y Y Synthesis Barossa Grenache Mataro 2015 Rating 93 To 2029 $32
Blanc Barossa Semillon 2015 Rating 92 To 2025 $36
Totality Barossa Mataro Shiraz Grenache 2015 Rating 92 To 2025 $36

Epsilon   ★★★★☆

43 Hempel Road, Daveyston, SA 5355 **Region** Barossa Valley
T 0417 871 951 **www.**epsilonwines.com.au **Open** By appt
Winemaker Aaron Southern **Est.** 2004 **Dozens** 2500 **Vyds** 7ha
Epsilon, the fifth star of the Southern Cross constellation, is a great example of how a
background star can come to the fore. Established in 1994 with fruit that contributed to an
intra-regional blend, fifth-generation Barossa grapegrowers Aaron and Julie Southern were
inspired to make a wine that would reflect their shiraz vineyard on the western slopes of the
Barossa Valley. Exports to the UK, the US, Canada and South-East Asia.

Y Y Y Y Y **Barossa Valley Shiraz 2015** Tiptoes an elegant aromatic line of lilac, violet,
iodine and sapid blueberry notes, laced with star anise and clove. Fine-grained,
slinky tannins and saline acidity serve as a confluence of the free-flowing fruit and
expanding, more savoury, tones of smoked meats, black olive and licorice root.
Northern Rhône? A wine of a deft hand, and fresh fruit picked at the optimal
window of opportunity. This is complex wine, offering superb value. Screwcap.
14.8% alc. **Rating** 96 To 2025 $20 NG **○**
Nineteen Ninety Four Greenock Barossa Valley Shiraz 2013 Blueberry,
iodine and sarsaparilla notes are reeled in by a a ferruginous core of grape and oak
tannins. Vinous and concentrated, attesting to the older vine heritage of the fruit,
this shiraz is compelling as much for its corpulence as for its poise and drinkability,
both transcending and belying its alcohol. Lacks the aromatic appeal of its younger
vine sibling. Screwcap. 15% alc. **Rating** 94 To 2025 $45 NG

Ernest Hill Wines   ★★★★☆

307 Wine Country Drive, Nulkaba, NSW 2325 **Region** Hunter Valley
T (02) 4991 4418 **www.**ernesthillwines.com.au **Open** 7 days 10–5
Winemaker Mark Woods **Est.** 1999 **Dozens** 6000 **Vyds** 12ha
This is part of a vineyard originally planted in the early 1970s by Harry Tulloch for Seppelt
Wines; it was later renamed Pokolbin Creek Vineyard, and later still (in '99) the Wilson family
purchased the upper (hill) part of the vineyard, and renamed it Ernest Hill. It is now planted to
semillon, shiraz, chardonnay, verdelho, traminer, merlot, tempranillo and chambourcin. Exports
to the US and China.

Y Y Y Y Y **Cyril Premium Hunter Semillon 2015** The bouquet and fore-palate suggest it
is in an early stage of transition as it closes for business, but the finish tells another
story altogether with its minerally drive. This may fuel the wine's ability to attract
whenever tasted. Screwcap. 11% alc. **Rating** 94 To 2025 $25 **○**
William Henry Premium Hunter Shiraz 2011 Excellent retention of crimson
colour; has prospered since it was first tasted by me 4 years ago, with a happy
combination of terroir and varietal fruit. Plum and blackberry are still in the lead,
leather and earth moving back into the fabric of the wine, the use of French oak
perfect. Diam. 13.7% alc. **Rating** 94 To 2026 $70

Y Y Y Y Y **Alexander Reserve Hunter Chardonnay 2015** Rating 92 To 2021 $35

Ernest Schuetz Estate Wines   ★★★★

778 Castlereagh Highway, Mudgee, NSW 2850 **Region** Mudgee
T 0402 326 612 **www.**ernestschuetzestate.com.au **Open** W'ends 10.30–4.30
Winemaker Jacob Stein, Robert Black **Est.** 2003 **Dozens** 7200 **Vyds** 4.1ha
Ernest Schuetz's involvement in the wine industry started in 1988 at the age of 21. Working
in various liquor outlets and as a sales representative for Miranda Wines, McGuigan Simeon
and, later, Watershed Wines gave him an in-depth understanding of all aspects of the wine

market. In 2003 he and wife Joanna purchased the Arronvale Vineyard (first planted in '91), at an altitude of 530m. When the Schuetzs acquired the vineyard it was planted to merlot, shiraz and cabernet sauvignon, and they have since grafted 1ha to riesling, pinot blanc, pinot gris, zinfandel and nebbiolo. Exports to Vietnam and China.

ΨΨΨΨΨ **St Isabel Barrel Fermented Mudgee Pinot Blanc Pinot Gris Riesling 2015** 42% pinot blanc, 38% pinot gris and 20% riesling, 20% picked early and air-dried on racks for 19 days, whole-bunch pressed, wild-yeast fermented (including mlf) in three French hogsheads, on lees for 12 months, stirred for the first two. A richly textured tapestry, and has given pinot gris and pinot blanc a presence they normally lack. What seems to be a low level of residual sugar has worked well. Truly interesting. Screwcap. 13.5% alc. **Rating** 94 **To** 2030 $40
Family Reserve Mudgee Black Syrah 2014 Wild yeast–open fermented, 30% whole bunches, matured in 66% American and 33% Hungarian oak, one-third new, for 24 months. Lavishly flavoured with plum and blackberry fruit, a crown of new oak ex the conclusion of fermentation in it, and ripe tannins. The accelerator has been flat to the floor from start to finish, leaving you (metaphorically) gasping for air. Screwcap. 14.5% alc. **Rating** 94 **To** 2044 $30 ✪
Epica Amarone Method Mudgee Cabernet Shiraz 2014 50% cabernet sauvignon, 40% shiraz, 10% merlot, hand-picked, air-dried on racks for 4 weeks, 50% destemmed, 50% whole bunches, hand-plunged and foot-stomped for 10 days on skins, matured in new French hogsheads for 24 months. Jacob Stein must have aged a lifetime in making this wine – and even though we have details of every aspect of the wine, you either enjoy it and its courage, or you walk on by. The price is a steal vis à vis the cost of production. Screwcap. 16% alc. **Rating** 94 **To** 2044 $70
St Martin de Porres Unfiltered Mudgee Zinfandel Nebbiolo 2014 A 'field blend' of mainly zinfandel, the 20% nebbiolo and 10% cabernet component air-dried for 7 days, 60% destemmed, 40% whole bunches wild yeast–open fermented, matured in two hogsheads. This is almost docile compared to Epica, and is easy to enjoy. Zinfandel comes through with its varietal colours flying high, redcurrant to the fore. Screwcap. 14.5% alc. **Rating** 94 **To** 2029 $45

ΨΨΨΨΨ **Museum Release Family Reserve Mudgee Shiraz 2009 Rating** 93 **To** 2020 $50

Espier Estate   ★★★★
Room 1208, 401 Docklands Drive, Docklands, Vic 3008 **Region** South Eastern Australia **T** (03) 9670 4317 **www**.jnrwine.com **Open** Mon–Fri 9–5
Winemaker Sam Brewer **Est.** 2007 **Dozens** 25 000
This is the venture of Robert Luo and Jacky Lin. Sam Brewer has worked for Southcorp and De Bortoli, and in the US and China, and has been closely linked with the business since its establishment. The principal focus of the business is export to Asian countries, with China and Hong Kong the main areas. Much of the volume is linked to contract-made wines under the Espier Estate label, with prices ranging from entry level to premium styles. Exports to Asia.

ΨΨΨΨΨ **Feel Reserve Heathcote Shiraz 2015** Medium to full-bodied density in the mouth, belied by well aligned and detailed milk chocolate tannins and mellifluous acidity, making it feel far lighter and setting it in flight. Plum, currant and black cherry flavours glide from nose to throat. A very well balanced wine brimming with drinkability factor. Cork. 14.5% alc. **Rating** 92 **To** 2022 $30 NG
Estate Range 1916 Cabernet Sauvignon 2015 Menthol and blackcurrant smother the aroma. Reverberating on the full palate, they are squeegeed into form by well meaning oak, dried sage herbal cut and stiff upper lip cabernet tannins. Very bright acidity rushes along the back straight. All part of the regional course. Cork. 14.5% alc. **Rating** 90 **To** 2022 $20 NG ✪

ΨΨΨΨ **Dream Shiraz 2015 Rating** 89 **To** 2022 $20 NG

Estate 807

807 Scotsdale Road, Denmark, WA 6333 **Region** Denmark
T (08) 9840 9027 **www**.estate807.com.au **Open** Thurs–Sun 10–4
Winemaker James Kellie, Mike Garland **Est.** 1998 **Dozens** 1500 **Vyds** 4.2ha
Dr Stephen Junk and Ola Tylestam purchased Estate 807 in 2009. Stephen was a respected embryologist working in IVF, while Ola came from a financial background. They chose the property due to its range of pinot noir and chardonnay clones (there are also plantings of cabernet and sauvignon blanc). Farm animals are used in the vineyard: chickens and ducks eat the pests and sheep and alpacas provide manure and keep the vineyard neat and tidy.

ꭹꭹꭹꭹꭹ **Great Southern Riesling 2014** From a single vineyard in Porongurup. Opens with a polite chirp, but then accelerates across the palate with a gale of minerally acidity blowing from behind. The latent citrus fruit will grow over time. Screwcap. 12% alc. **Rating** 92 **To** 2029 $23 ✪
Reserve Chardonnay 2016 Dijon clone 77 hand-picked from a single estate vineyard. Can only be described as pretty, so perfectly balanced are the delicate varietal fruit flavours, the shimmer of barrel ferment oak, the heart of pink grapefruit beating quietly but regularly. Screwcap. 12% alc. **Rating** 91 **To** 2021 $29

Esto Wines

PO Box 1172, Balhannah, SA 5242 **Region** Adelaide Hills
T 0109 069 320 **www**.estowines.com.au **Open** Not
Winemaker Charlotte Hardy, Phil Christiansen **Est.** 1994 **Dozens** 200 **Vyds** 23.5ha
The Dean family have been grapegrowers in the Adelaide Hills since 1994, and have progressively established three vineyards: the largest is 13ha planted in '94 at Balhannah, with a clonal mix of shiraz, semillon, chardonnay, sauvignon blanc and pinot noir, from which Charlotte Hardy makes Semillon and Sauvignon Blanc for the Esto label. Shiraz, made by Phil Christiansen, is also made from this block. The next block (mostly pinot noir and chardonnay, with a postage stamp-sized planting of sangiovese) nestles in the Piccadilly Valley in the afternoon shadow of Mt Lofty. All of the grapes from this vineyard are purchased by a distinguished group of Adelaide Hills winemakers. The third block, of 6.5ha – The Farside – is mostly sauvignon blanc and pinot gris, the bulk of which is purchased by Petaluma.

ꭹꭹꭹꭹꭹ **Semillon 2016** Machine-harvested, and wild-yeast fermented. It takes a second for the drive on the finish to make its mark, with cut grass and left field lemon juice embraced by a cloak of acidity. Screwcap. 12.5% alc. **Rating** 90 **To** 2021 $29

ꭹꭹꭹꭹ **Sauvignon Blanc 2016** **Rating** 89 **To** 2018 $22

Evans & Tate

★★★★★

Cnr Metricup Road/Caves Road, Wilyabrup, WA 6280 **Region** Margaret River
T (08) 9755 6244 **www**.evansandtate.com.au **Open** 7 days 10.30–5
Winemaker Matthew Byrne, Lachlan McDonald **Est.** 1970 **Dozens** NFP **Vyds** 12.3ha
The 47-year history of Evans & Tate has been one of constant change and, for decades, expansion, acquiring large wineries in SA and NSW. For a series of reasons, nothing to do with the excellent quality of its Margaret River wines, the empire fell apart in 2005; McWilliam's finalised its acquisition of the Evans & Tate brand, cellar door and vineyards (and since a part share in the winery) in December '07. Exports to all major markets.

ꭹꭹꭹꭹꭹ **The Evans & Tate Margaret River Cabernet Sauvignon 2012** Astonishing colour, still bright crimson; the bouquet and palate are full of juicy cassis fruit, yet the overall extract – especially the gossamer tannins – is delicate. A truly beautiful medium-bodied cabernet of exceptional purity and length. Trophies include Best Red Wine Margaret River Wine Show '15, and Best Cabernet Sauvignon Sydney Wine Show '16. Screwcap. 14% alc. **Rating** 98 **To** 2032 $100 ✪

ꭹꭹꭹꭹꭹ **Metricup Road Cabernet Merlot 2014** **Rating** 93 **To** 2025 $24 JF ✪
Butterball Margaret River Chardonnay 2016 **Rating** 92 **To** 2021 $20 ✪

Metricup Road Margaret River Shiraz 2014 Rating 92 To 2024 $24 ◐
Breathing Space Margaret River Rose 2016 Rating 90 To 2017 $19 CM ◐
Breathing Space Margaret River Cabernet Sauvignon 2014 Rating 90
To 2024 $14 ◐

Evoi Wines　　★★★★★

92 Dunsborough Lakes Drive, Dunsborough, WA 6281 **Region** Margaret River
T 0407 131 080 **www**.evoiwines.com **Open** By appt
Winemaker Nigel Ludlow **Est.** 2006 **Dozens** 12000
NZ-born Nigel Ludlow has a Bachelor of Science in human nutrition, but after a short career as a professional triathlete, he turned his attention to grapegrowing and winemaking, with a graduate diploma in oenology and viticulture from Lincoln University, NZ. Time at Selaks Drylands winery was a stepping stone to Flying Winemaking stints in Hungary, Spain and South Africa, before a return as senior winemaker at Nobilo. He thereafter moved to Vic, and finally to Margaret River. It took time for Evoi to take shape, the first vintage of chardonnay being made in the lounge room of his house. By 2010 the barrels had been evicted to more conventional storage, and since '14 the wines have been made in leased space at a commercial winery. Quality has been exceptional. Exports to the UK, Norway and Hong Kong.

🍷🍷🍷🍷🍷 **The Satyr Reserve 2014** Statuesque, with a furl of tight, alluvial tannins running the main seam; bright maritime acidity and an impeccably woven tapestry of oak sew down the edges. The fruit runs the gamut of currant, blue and black fruits. Dried sage, anise and a litany of herbal notes pummel all into a compact, savoury ball of great potential. A very fine cabernet, aided by 18% petit verdot and 9% malbec. Screwcap. 14.5% alc. **Rating** 96 To 2039 $55 NG ◐
Reserve Margaret River Chardonnay 2015 Whole-bunch pressed to assorted French barriques before partial wild yeast fermentation and mlf. Almost skeletal of composure, etched with vanilla bean oak and the smoky crunch of mineral-inducing lees. The acidity, maritime and saline too, propels the wine along. It finishes with a flourish of nectarine, oatmeal and nougat. Screwcap. 14% alc. **Rating** 95 To 2025 $55 NG
Margaret River Cabernet Sauvignon 2015 A spread of cassis, cocoa, bay leaf, bouquet garni and an array of dried herbs mark this release as a cooler expression of Evoi cabernet. Dollops of petit verdot and malbec add to the tapestry. The wine is highly savoury and mid-weighted, with an emphasis on herb over fruit. The tannins are palate-whetting and gravelly, forming the structural supports with a well rendered cedar oak frame. Screwcap. 14.5% alc. **Rating** 94 To 2035 $32 NG

🍷🍷🍷🍷🍸 **Margaret River SBS 2016** Rating 93 To 2019 $24 NG ◐
Margaret River Chardonnay 2015 Rating 93 To 2025 $28 NG
art by Evoi Cabernet Sauvignon 2015 Rating 92 To 2030 $20 ◐
Bakenal SBS 2015 Rating 91 To 2018 $15 NG ◐

Faber Vineyard　　★★★★☆

233 Haddrill Road, Baskerville, WA 6056 **Region** Swan Valley
T (08) 9296 0209 **www**.fabervineyard.com.au **Open** Fri–Sun 11–4
Winemaker John Griffiths **Est.** 1997 **Dozens** 2500 **Vyds** 4.5ha
John Griffiths, former Houghton winemaker, teamed with wife Jane Micallef to found Faber Vineyard. They have established shiraz, verdelho (1.5ha each), brown muscat, chardonnay and petit verdot (0.5ha each). Says John, 'It may be somewhat quixotic, but I'm a great fan of traditional warm-area Australian wine styles, wines made in a relatively simple manner that reflect the concentrated ripe flavours one expects in these regions. And when one searches, some of these gems can be found from the Swan Valley.' Exports to Hong Kong and China.

🍷🍷🍷🍷🍷 **Reserve Swan Valley Shiraz 2014** Open-fermented, 2 days cold soak, 10 days on skins, matured for 22 months in French oak. Deep crimson-purple; full-bodied, with great depth to the sombre black fruits; the tannins are also front and centre, but balanced by the fruit, and are rounded, not abrasive. Utterly true to the philosophy of its maker, and its terroir. Cork. **Rating** 95 To 2030 $71

Millard Vineyard Swan Valley Shiraz 2013 Open-fermented, matured for 22 months in French oak. Seriously full-bodied, and very powerful through the mid-palate before releasing part of its grip on the finish, allowing a faint dimple of red fruit to shine in the blackness. Cork. Rating 94 To 2030 $18

Frankland River Cabernet Sauvignon 2014 Has retained very good colour; a delicious medium-bodied cabernet with juicy cassis/blackcurrant fruit, bay leaf/black olive and fine-grained tannins. Well handled oak frames a pretty picture with a very good future. Cork. **Rating** 94 **To** 2030 $55

Swan Valley Liqueur Muscat NV When first tasted 4 years ago I wrote 'The very essence of toffee, grilled nuts, raisins and pain grillee; a lovely rich and unctuous example, with a baked fruit character that is all Swan Valley in character.' Still the same, unctuously sweet and rich, needing a little more rancio cut to lift it into the top rank. 500ml. Cork. 18% alc. **Rating** 94 $60

TTTTT **Ferguson Valley Malbec 2015** Rating 92 $33 PR
Riche Swan Valley Shiraz 2015 Rating 91 To 2030 $27
Millard Vineyard Swan Valley Shiraz 2014 Rating 91 To 2028 $48

Farmer and The Scientist

Jeffreys Road, Corop, Vic 3559 **Region** Heathcote
T 0400 141 985 **www.**farmerandthescientist.com **Open** Not
Winemaker Brian and Jess Dwyer, Ron Snep **Est.** 2013 **Dozens** 1200 **Vyds** 8ha
The Farmer is Bryan Dwyer, the Scientist wife Jess. Bryan is a viticulturist who learnt his craft with Southcorp, Jess has a degree in science amplified by teaching. She in fact became doubly qualified by working in wineries and vineyards from a young age. Ron Snep plays an important and successful role in the winery.

TTTTT **Heathcote Grenache Shiraz Mourvedre 2015** A 55/30/15% blend matured in American and French oak. The moderately deep, bright crimson-purple hue doesn't deceive: this is a very smart blend, with red fruits doing all the talking on the bouquet and medium-bodied palate. The tannins have good structure, and there is no alcohol-induced heat. Screwcap. 14.9% alc. **Rating** 93 **To** 2030 $25 **☉**
Heathcote Rose 2016 Estate grenache from a small block on the Mt Camel range. Has an exotic bouquet of fairy floss and raspberry, repeated with precision on the fresh, fruit-filled palate. Few would pick up the 'hint of residual sweetness' mentioned on the back label, perhaps thanks to brisk lemony acidity. A very well made wine offering great value. Screwcap. 12.4% alc. **Rating** 92 **To** 2017 $18 **☉**

TTTT **Heathcote Shiraz 2015** Rating 89 To 2025 $25
Heathcote Tempranillo 2015 Rating 89 To 2019 $25

Farmer's Leap Wines

41 Hodgson Road, Padthaway, SA 5271 **Region** Padthaway
T (08) 8765 5155 **www.**farmersleap.com **Open** Not
Winemaker Renae Hirsch **Est.** 2004 **Dozens** 10 000 **Vyds** 295.4ha
Scott Longbottom and Cheryl Merrett are third-generation farmers in Padthaway. They commenced planting the vineyard in 1995 on the family property, and now there are shiraz, cabernet sauvignon, chardonnay and merlot. Initially the majority of the grapes were sold, but increasing quantities held for the Farmer's Leap label have seen production rise from 2500 dozen. Exports to Canada, Singapore, South Korea, Japan, Taiwan, Hong Kong and China.

TTTTT **The Brave Padthaway Shiraz 2012** Plum, cherry and blueberry lay siege to the aroma, while a sluice of anise seizes the day for the savoury camp. Smoked meat and five-spice reverberate from nose to palate. Vanillan oak laces the fruit flavours, supine and powerful. Oak supports keep it all from slipping into a Bacchanalian melée. Cork. 15% alc. **Rating** 93 **To** 2023 $42 NG

TTTT **The Brave Padthaway Shiraz 2013** Rating 89 To 2029 $42 NG
Padthaway Cabernet Sauvignon 2014 Rating 89 To 2022 $25 NG

Farr | Farr Rising   ★★★★★

27 Maddens Road, Bannockburn, Vic 3331 **Region** Geelong
T (03) 5281 1733 **www**.byfarr.com.au **Open** Not
Winemaker Nick Farr **Est.** 1994 **Dozens** 5500 **Vyds** 13.8ha
By Farr and Farr Rising continue to be separate brands from separate vineyards, the one major change being that Nick Farr has assumed total responsibility for both labels, leaving father Gary free to pursue the finer things in life without interruption. This has in no way resulted in any diminution in the quality of the Pinot Noir, Chardonnay, Shiraz and Viognier made. The vineyards are based on ancient river deposits in the Moorabool Valley. There are six different soils spread across the Farr property, with the two main types being rich, friable red and black volcanic loam, and limestone, which dominates the loam in some areas. The other soils are quartz gravel through a red volcanic soil, ironstone (called buckshot) in grey sandy loam with a heavy clay base, sandstone base and volcanic lava. The soil's good drainage and low fertility are crucial in ensuring small yields of intensely flavoured fruit. Exports to the UK, Canada, Denmark, Sweden, Hong Kong, Singapore, Taiwan, the Maldives, China and Japan.

ΨΨΨΨΨ **Farrside by Farr Geelong Pinot Noir 2014** Clones 114, 115, 667 and MV6, 60–70% destemmed, 4 days cold soak, wild-yeast fermented, pigeaged 2–3 times daily, matured for 18 months in French oak (50–60% new). The compex bouquet is the calm before the storm of the palate, which strikes the second the wine enters the mouth, and doesn't abate until long after the wine has gone from the glass. Great fusion of plum/black cherry fruit with a savoury carpet of spices and sweet earth. Cork. 13.5% alc. **Rating** 98 **To** 2029 $83 ✪

Three Oaks Vineyard by Farr Chardonnay 2015 Bright, gleaming straw-green; impeccably groomed, shirt tucked in, not a hair out of place, intensity, balance and length of a high order. Trying to pinpoint the flavours is akin to chasing a rainbow. Diam. 13% alc. **Rating** 97 **To** 2029 $80 ✪

Sangreal by Farr Geelong Pinot Noir 2015 Clones 114 and 115 planted in '94, believed to have mutated into a single 'Sangreal' clone, 66% whole bunches, 4 days cold soak, wild yeast–open fermented for 8 days, matured in new French oak for 18 months. Deeply coloured, depth and savoury complexity: the cornerstones of great pinots. Spices from an Arabian bazaar intermingle sinuously with vibrant berry fruits, a skein of refreshing acidity adding another dimension to a wine that continuously draws saliva from the mouth. Cork. **Rating** 97 **To** 2035 $80 ✪

Tout Pres by Farr Pinot Noir 2014 Six clones mutated into a single Tout Pres clone planted at 7300 vines per ha, the densest planting on the estate, hence Tout Pres translating to 'very cosy', 100% whole bunches open-fermented, matured in new French oak. Dramatic in its opening stanza, with a highly fragrant bouquet of mixed red and purple spices, the palate sleek and extraordinarily long. Every time you go back to it more is revealed, all of it very good. If you think Burgundy, it has to be Vosne-Romanée. Cork. 13% alc. **Rating** 97 **To** 2029 $110 ✪

ΨΨΨΨΨ **By Farr Shiraz 2015** Open-fermented with 2–4% viognier, 20% whole bunches; matured for 18 months in French oak (20% new). The aromas are particularly complex and fragrant, charcuterie and allspice decorating the concourse of black cherry and satsuma plum of the bouquet and medium to full-bodied palate. The management of the viognier addition, the tannins and the oak made perfect by long practice. Cork. 13.5% alc. **Rating** 96 **To** 2035 $65 ✪

Farr Rising Geelong Saignee 2016 Multiple pinot noir clones, hand-picked, pressed, wild-yeast fermented in used French oak, matured for 10 months. Salmon-pink; has the mouthfeel of pinot noir table wine – it's more than a rose. Rose petal, cherry blossom and spice aromas lead into a supple, long palate raising the bar on its complex web of spices. The magic is saignee: run off from a vat of high quality pinot table wine (to be). Diam. 13.5% alc. **Rating** 95 **To** 2020 $29 ✪

Farr Rising Geelong Shiraz 2015 85–95% destemmed, 19 days wild yeast fermentation in tank, matured for 18 months in French oak (10% new). For a split second you think this could be the odd man out in the Farr empire, but elegance isn't the mission here – just sustained intensity to the panoply of dark fruits soaring on the almost juicy finish and aftertaste. The quality of the grapes and the skill of Nick Farr make a deadly duo. Diam. 14% alc. **Rating** 95 **To** 2035 $48

Feathertop Wines   ★★★★

Great Alpine Road, Porepunkah, Vic 3741 **Region** Alpine Valleys
T (03) 5756 2356 **www**.feathertopwinery.com.au **Open** 7 days 10–5
Winemaker Kel Boynton, Nick Toy **Est.** 1987 **Dozens** 9000 **Vyds** 16ha
Kel Boynton has a beautiful vineyard, framed by Mt Feathertop rising above it. The initial American oak input has been softened in more recent vintages to give a better fruit-oak balance. Kel has planted a spectacular array of 22 varieties, headed by savagnin, pinot gris, vermentino, sauvignon blanc, fiano, verdelho, riesling, friulano, pinot noir, tempranillo, sangiovese, merlot, shiraz, montepulciano and nebbiolo, with smaller plantings of prosecco, pinot meunier, dornfelder, durif, malbec, cabernet sauvignon and petit verdot. Exports to Austria.

♥♥♥♥♥ Fiano 2016 Feathertop's first foray with fiano and it's a promising start. Luscious palate with honeysuckle and ginger cream, dried herbs; quite spicy, with lemon acidity. Screwcap. 13% alc. **Rating** 92 **To** 2020 $25 JF ✪
King Valley Riesling 2015 This gets into shape quickly with a tisane of lemons and limes, basil and mint then the talc-like acidity and lemon pith spread across the palate to a fresh finish. Screwcap. 11.5% alc. **Rating** 91 **To** 2021 $25 JF
Blanc de Blanc 2012 The cool climes of the Alpine Valleys infuse tension and stamina into chardonnay, heightened by low dosage, making for a style of high-tensile acidity. 3.5 years of lees age have built fine texture and subtle almond meal character, but the focus remains resolutely on bright lemon and apple fruit that belies its age. Patience. Crown seal. 12% alc. **Rating** 91 **To** 2027 $40 TS
Alpine Valleys Pinot Gris 2016 Layers of dried and poached pears flecked with star anise and powdered ginger. The palate has plenty of the weight and richness typical of the gris style in Australia. Screwcap. 13.5% alc. **Rating** 90 **To** 2020 $25 JF
Limited Release Alpine Valleys Cabernet Sauvignon 2014 Spending 2 years in French oak (25% new), this smells of black jubes, with currants, a neat layer of spice, cedar, pepper and juniper berries leading onto a lighter-framed palate. Screwcap. 13.5% alc. **Rating** 90 **To** 2023 $30 JF
Alpine Valleys Tempranillo 2015 Super crunchy and lively tempranillo with a jet of raspberry and cherry cola, tobacco fragrance, and a neat tension between its acidity and tannins. Screwcap. 14% alc. **Rating** 90 **To** 2021 $30 JF

♥♥♥♥ Alpine Valleys Vermentino 2015 Rating 88 **To** 2020 $25 JF
Alpine Valleys Pinots 2015 Rating 88 **To** 2020 $30 JF
Alpine Valleys Friulano 2015 Rating 87 **To** 2018 $25 JF

Fergusson   ★★★★

82 Wills Road, Yarra Glen, Vic 3775 **Region** Yarra Valley
T (03) 5965 2237 **www**.fergussonwinery.com.au **Open** 7 days 11–5
Winemaker Rob Dolan **Est.** 1968 **Dozens** 2000 **Vyds** 6ha
One of the very first Yarra wineries to announce the rebirth of the Valley, now best known as a favoured destination for tourist coaches, offering hearty fare in comfortable surroundings and wines of both Yarra and non-Yarra Valley origin. For this reason the limited quantities of its estate wines are often ignored, but they should not be.

♥♥♥♥♥ Benjamyn Reserve Yarra Valley Cabernet Sauvignon 2015 Crushed and destemmed, open-fermented, 2 days cold soak, pressed when dry to French oak (30% new), matured for 16 months. Classic cabernet: autocratic from the outset, with tight, firm tannins sewn through the earthy black fruits and black olives on the full-bodied palate. Screwcap. 13.7% alc. **Rating** 94 **To** 2035 $40

♥♥♥♥♥ Jeremy Yarra Valley Shiraz 2015 Rating 90 **To** 2025 $30

Fermoy Estate

838 Metricup Road, Wilyabrup, WA 6280 **Region** Margaret River
T (08) 9755 6285 **www**.fermoy.com.au **Open** 7 days 10–5
Winemaker Jeremy Hodgson **Est.** 1985 **Dozens** 16 000 **Vyds** 47ha
A long-established winery with 17ha of semillon, sauvignon blanc, chardonnay, cabernet sauvignon and merlot. The Young family acquired Fermoy Estate in 2010, and built a larger cellar door which opened in '13, signalling the drive to increase domestic sales. It is happy to keep a relatively low profile, however difficult that may be given the quality of the wines. Jeremy Hodgson brings with him a first class honours degree in oenology and viticulture, and a CV encompassing winemaking roles with Wise Wines, Cherubino Consultancy and, earlier, Plantagenet, Houghton and Goundrey Wines. Exports to Europe, Asia and China.

ⵊⵊⵊⵊⵊ **Reserve Margaret River Cabernet Sauvignon 2014** From 30yo estate vines, a final barrel selection resulting in a blend of 75% new oak and 25% 1yo. There is more depth on the palate, and the tannins are firmer here, wrapped around a core of juicy cassis fruit. The way the fruit has absorbed the new oak without batting an eyelid speaks volumes about its quality. Screwcap. 14.5% alc. **Rating** 95 To 2034 $85
Margaret River Cabernet Sauvignon 2014 Includes 8% shiraz; matured for 18 months in new and used French oak. Good colour; rich cassis and bay leaf/black olive notes fill the bouquet and medium-bodied palate alike; the tannins are plentiful, but relatively soft. Screwcap. 14% alc. **Rating** 94 To 2029 $40

ⵊⵊⵊⵊⵣ **Reserve Margaret River Chardonnay 2016** Rating 93 To 2025 $60 JF
Margaret River Rose 2016 Rating 93 To 2019 $30 JF
Reserve Margaret River Shiraz 2015 Rating 93 To 2035 $65
Margaret River Merlot 2014 Rating 93 To 2029 $30
Margaret River Sauvignon Blanc 2016 Rating 91 To 2022 $25 JF
Margaret River Semillon Sauvignon Blanc 2016 Rating 91 To 2019 $22 JF ✪
Margaret River Chardonnay 2016 Rating 91 To 2023 $30 JF
Margaret River Merlot 2015 Rating 90 To 2022 $30 JF

Fernfield Wines ★★★★

112 Rushlea Road, Eden Valley, SA 5235 **Region** Eden Valley
T 0402 788 526 **www**.fernfieldwines.com.au **Open** Fri–Mon 11–4
Winemaker Rebecca and Scott Barr **Est.** 2002 **Dozens** 1500 **Vyds** 0.7ha
The establishment date of 2002 might, with a little poetic licence, be shown as 1864. Bryce Lillecrapp is the fifth generation of the Lillecrapp family; his great-great-great-grandfather bought land in the Eden Valley in 1864, subdividing it in 1866, establishing the township of Eden Valley and building the first house, Rushlea Homestead. Bryce restored this building and opened it in 1998 as a bicentennial project; it now serves as Fernfield Wines' cellar door. Ownership has now passed to daughter Rebecca Barr and husband Scott.

ⵊⵊⵊⵊⵣ **Gold Leaf Reserve Single Vineyard Eden Valley Shiraz Viognier 2013** 50% of the viognier was fermented in a French barrique and aged on lees, 50% in stainless steel, the shiraz open-fermented and matured in used oak for 22 months, a single barrel selected and matured for a further 12 months, 32 dozen made. The mouthfeel is very good, the flavours likewise. The only question is the amount of American oak the wine has to carry. Screwcap. 14.3% alc. **Rating** 93 To 2028 $47
Old River Red Eden Valley Merlot 2014 Open-fermented, 5 days on skins, 6-hourly plunging, aged in French hogsheads for 24 months. The trials and tribulations of merlot outside of Margaret River are well chronicled, with new clones offering hope for the future. That said, this wine has good texture, structure and redcurrant/plum fruit. Screwcap. 14.5% alc. **Rating** 90 To 2029 $35

Ferngrove

276 Ferngrove Road, Frankland River, WA 6396 **Region** Frankland River
T (08) 9363 1300 **www.ferngrove.com.au Open** Mon–Sat 10–4
Winemaker Marco Pinares, Marelize Russouw **Est.** 1998 **Dozens** NFP **Vyds** 340ha
Known for producing consistent examples of cool climate wines across multiple price
brackets, the Ferngrove stable includes the Stirlings, Orchid, Frankland River and Symbols
ranges. Ferngrove Vineyards Pty Ltd enjoys the benefits of majority international ownership,
but remains Australian-run. Exports to all major markets.

ŸŸŸŸŸ **Malbec Cabernet Rose 2016** A 70/30% blend with an exceptionally fragrant
bouquet full of red fruits, the palate likewise ranging through red cherry, raspberry
and touches of spice. Raises the question whether it's possible to have too much
of a good thing; the answer is blowing in the wind. Screwcap. 14% alc. **Rating** 93
To 2020 $20 ✪

Shiraz 2014 Matured for 18 months in new and used French oak. Classic
Frankland River shiraz, medium-bodied and lively, with red and black cherry fruit
liberally sprinkled with spice and pepper, long in the mouth and aftertaste. Utterly
exceptional value. Screwcap. 13.5% alc. **Rating** 93 To 2029 $20 ✪

Cossack Riesling 2016 18yo estate vines, cool-fermented and left on lees
until bottling. A generous, layered, ripe palate offers plenty of flavour for earlyish
enjoyment. Very different from the Cossack wine of yesteryear, and fairly priced.
Screwcap. 13% alc. **Rating** 90 To 2023 $23

 # Fetherston Vintners

1/99a Maroondah Highway, Healesville, Vic 3777 **Region** Yarra Valley
T (03) 5962 6354 **www.fetherstonwine.com.au Open** Not
Winemaker Chris Lawrence **Est.** 2015 **Dozens** 750
The establishment of Fetherston Vintners in 2015 by Chris Lawrence and Camille Koll was,
in hindsight, the logical consequence of their respective careers in wine, food and hospitality.
Chris began his career in the kitchen in establishments all over Australia. In '09 he enrolled
in the science (oenology) degree with the University of Southern Queensland, graduating in
'14 as valedictorian, receiving the Faculty Medal for Science. During his time at Yering Station
('10–'14) he worked his way up from junior cellar hand to assistant winemaker. A vintage at
Domaine Serene in Oregon's Willamette Valley in '12 gave him further insight into the study
of great chardonnay and pinot noir. In '14 he took on the role of winemaker at Sunshine
Creek in the Yarra Valley. Camille is Yarra born and bred, growing up at Hoddles Creek. After
finishing school, she began a 7-year stint at Domaine Chandon, giving her invaluable insight
into professional branding, marketing and customer service. She is now working in hospitality
management in her day job. Chris's late grandfather was Tony Fetherston.

ŸŸŸŸŸ **Yarra Valley Chardonnay 2015** Mendoza clone, whole-bunch pressed,
fermented with wild and 'innovative' yeast in new and used French barriques.
Good quality fruit, good vintage, good winemaking and the Yarra Valley all go to
make a delicious chardonnay of great length and finesse, with a decade in front
of it if you wish to go down that path. Screwcap. 13.5% alc. **Rating** 95 To 2026
$25 ✪

Yarra Valley Shiraz 2015 30% whole bunches, 70% whole berries, 14 days post-
ferment maceration, matured in French barriques (30% new) for 12 months, 80
dozen made. Deep crimson-purple; this is a voluptuous wine, all the elements in
high relief on the bouquet, black cherry and plum on the palate, spice, licorice and
pepper on the finish ex soft tannins. Screwcap. 14% alc. **Rating** 94 To 2030 $25 ✪

ŸŸŸŸŸ **Yarra Valley Pinot Noir 2015 Rating** 90 To 2021 $28

Fighting Gully Road

Kurrajong Way, Mayday Hill, Beechworth, Vic 3747 **Region** Beechworth
T (03) 5727 1434 **www**.fightinggully.com.au **Open** By appt
Winemaker Mark Walpole, Adrian Rodda **Est.** 1997 **Dozens** 3000 **Vyds** 8.3ha
Mark Walpole (who began his viticultural career with Brown Brothers in the late 1980s) and partner Carolyn De Poi found their elevated north-facing site to the south of Beechworth in 1995. They commenced planting the Aquila Audax Vineyard in 1997 with cabernet sauvignon and pinot noir, subsequently expanding with significant areas of sangiovese, tempranillo, shiraz, petit manseng and chardonnay. In 2009 they were fortunate to lease the oldest vineyard in the region, planted by the Smith family in 1978 to chardonnay and cabernet sauvignon – in fact Mark shares the Smith Family vineyard lease with long-term friend Adrian Rodda (see separate entry). Says Mark, 'We are now making wine in a building in the old and historic Mayday Hills Lunatic Asylum – a place that should be full of winemakers!'

ŢŢŢŢŢ **Beechworth Chardonnay 2015** Bright straw-green; the bouquet has à la mode struck match complexity, but it's the powerful, intense and very long palate that shows once again the synergy between Beechworth and chardonnay. Grapefruit and white peach are the chief protagonists on the palate, highly strung acidity adding its voice. First class wine. Screwcap. 13% alc. **Rating** 96 **To** 2027 $38 ✪
Beechworth Pinot Noir 2015 Dijon clone 114, part whole-bunch fermented. Pinot often struggles to provide clear varietal character in the climate of Beechworth, but this succeeded – another example of a top pinot vintage. Complex, with the whole bunch introducing spicy/savoury notes to the purple fruits of the long, well balanced finish. Screwcap. 13.5% alc. **Rating** 95 **To** 2023 $28 ✪
Moelleux Beechworth Petit Manseng 2016 Exudes mandarin, cumquat, apricot, assorted candied citrus rind, jasmine and honey blossom aromas, strung tautly across a beam of effusive, saliva-generating acidity. Unbeknownst to many, these sprightly wines are seldom hewn of botrytised berries, but fermented slowly with dried, late harvest grapes. There is 70g/l residual sugar tucked into this, but the acidity is such a whirlwind that it is palpably swept away with not a cloying note. 375ml. Screwcap. 12% alc. **Rating** 94 **To** 2022 $28 NG ✪

ŢŢŢŢŢ **Beechworth Sangiovese Rose 2016 Rating** 93 **To** 2019 $25 NG ✪
Aglianico 2014 Rating 93 **To** 2021 $45

Fikkers Wine

1 Grandview Crescent, Healesville, Vic 3777 (postal) **Region** Yarra Valley
T 0437 142 078 **www**.fikkerswine.com.au **Open** Not
Winemaker Anthony Fikkers **Est.** 2010 **Dozens** 1400
Proprietor/winemaker Anthony Fikkers started his winemaking career in the Hunter Valley before moving to settle permanently in the Yarra Valley. His modus operandi is to seek out small parcels of wine in similar fashion to Mac Forbes, with whom he worked as assistant winemaker. He certainly believes that variety is the spice of life, making the Two Bricks range, the larger-volume wines either unoaked or lightly oaked and a range of Single Vineyard varietals, the vineyard sources changing from year to year reflecting availability.

ŢŢŢŢŢ **Two Bricks Yarra Valley Sangiovese 2016** From Killara Estate, whole berries wild-yeast fermented for 25 days before pressing, matured in French oak (15% new) for 8 months. Superb colour; 1yo sangiovese with depth and attitude from fruit rather than tannins? Rare, but here's one, indeed with RPJ (Robert Parker Jr) gobfuls of red fruits. Lovely stuff. Screwcap. 14% alc. **Rating** 95 **To** 2026 $28 ✪
Single Vineyard Yarra Valley Sauvignon Blanc 2016 Unsurprisingly, a very complex bouquet and palate; the intensity of the fruit is typical Yarra Valley, very long and fresh in the mouth, with citrussy acidity in control, tropical flavours cast to the four winds. Screwcap. 13.5% alc. **Rating** 94 **To** 2020 $30 ✪

Two Bricks Yarra Valley Pinot Noir 2016 A very fragrant bouquet with spicy red fruits; the savoury whole-bunch flavours are obvious (even though only 30%), but there is sufficient fruit to provide sweetness and overall balance. Screwcap. 13.5% alc. Rating 94 To 2029 $30 🔒

🍷🍷🍷🍷 Two Bricks Yarra Valley Pinot Gris 2016 Rating 92 To 2022 $28
Two Bricks Yarra Valley Shiraz 2016 Rating 91 To 2023 $28

Final Cut Wines ★★★★

1a Little Queen Street, Chippendale, NSW 2008 (postal) **Region** Barossa Valley
T (02) 9403 1524 **www.**finalcutwines.com **Open** Not
Winemaker David Roe **Est.** 2004 **Dozens** 4000
The names of the wines point to the involvement of owners David Roe and Les Lithgow (of the film industry). Theirs is a virtual winery, the wines made from high quality, contract-grown grapes. David becomes involved in vintage, but it is otherwise long-distance winemaking from the directors' studio in Sydney. Exports to the US, Canada and the Far East.

🍷🍷🍷🍷🍷 Take Two Barossa Valley Shiraz 2015 Fermented on a small percentage of viognier skins plus some whole bunches, matured for 12 months in French hogsheads (50% new). Thoroughly atypical Barossa Valley shiraz, with a strong spicy/savoury make-up to both bouquet and palate. In addition, the wine is no more than medium-bodied. Interesting to say the least, and tasted over a 24-hour period. Screwcap. 14.5% alc. Rating 94 To 2025 $49

 Finniss River Wines ★★★☆

15 Beach Road, Christies Beach, SA 5165 **Region** Currency Creek
T (08) 8326 9894 **www.**finnissvineyard.com.au **Open** 7 days 10–6
Winemaker Adam Parkinson **Est.** 1999 **Dozens** 3000 **Vyds** 146ha
The Hickinbotham family established several great vineyards, the last of these being that of Finniss River in 1999. The planting mix was good, dominated by 31.3ha of shiraz and 20.9ha of cabernet sauvignon. Between then and February 2015, when Adam and Lauren Parkinson purchased the vineyard, all the grapes were sold, which brought Adam, during his time as general manager of a winery in McLaren Vale, as well as general manager of one of Australia's largest vineyard management companies, into contact with the family and its grapes. Grape sales still remain, and will remain for the foreseeable future, but the cellar door is the outlet for local sales, and exports to China, the US and Singapore have already been established.

🍷🍷🍷🍷 Shiraz 2015 Crushed and destemmed, 8 days on skins, matured in new French oak for 8 months. Deep crimson-purple; this is an interesting shiraz, but why use 100% new French oak? There is no doubt about the quality of the fruit, and you are left to wonder how good the wine might have been if new and used oak had had a 50/50% split. Screwcap. 14.9% alc. Rating 90 To 2030 $22

🍷🍷🍷🍷 Cabernet Sauvignon 2015 Rating 89 To 2030 $22

Fire Gully ★★★★

Metricup Road, Wilyabrup, WA 6280 **Region** Margaret River
T (08) 9755 6220 **www.**firegully.com.au **Open** By appt
Winemaker Dr Michael Peterkin **Est.** 1988 **Dozens** 5000 **Vyds** 13.4ha
A 6ha lake created in a gully ravaged by bushfires gave the name. In 1998 Mike Peterkin of Pierro purchased it. He manages the vineyard in conjunction with former owners Ellis and Margaret Butcher. He regards the Fire Gully wines as entirely separate from those of Pierro: the plantings are cabernet sauvignon, merlot, shiraz, semillon, sauvignon blanc, chardonnay, viognier and chenin blanc. Exports to all major markets.

🍷🍷🍷🍷🍷 Margaret River Chardonnay 2015 Whole-bunch pressed to tank, partial wild yeast fermentation and 70% of the material undergoing mlf in barrel before 9 months maturation in French oak (30% new). Peach, apricot and melon flavours are framed with a dusting of vanilla pod oak, yet the overall impression is one of chiselled precision. Screwcap. 14% alc. **Rating** 94 **To** 2023 $32 NG

🍷🍷🍷🍷🍷 **Margaret River Rose 2016** Rating 93 To 2018 $32 NG
Margaret River Shiraz 2014 Rating 90 To 2022 $32 NG

Fireblock   ★★★★☆

28 Kiewa Place, Coomba Park, NSW 2428 (postal) **Region** Clare Valley
T (02) 6554 2193 **Open** Not
Winemaker O'Leary Walker **Est.** 1926 **Dozens** 3000 **Vyds** 6ha
Fireblock (formerly Old Station Vineyard) is owned by Bill and Noel Ireland, who purchased the almost-70-year-old Watervale vineyard in 1995. The vines planted in 1926 (3ha of shiraz and 2ha of grenache) are dry-grown; the riesling (1ha) was replanted to the Geisenheim clone in 2008 when town water became available. The wines are skilfully contract-made, winning trophies and gold medals at capital city wine shows. Exports to Sweden and Malaysia.

🍷🍷🍷🍷🍷 **Watervale Riesling 2015** Little or no colour change; a lovely riesling now, starting to develop lime/lemon fruit to push acidity into its all-important support role, leaving spring day freshness in the aftertaste. Another 3 years of cellaring will see this in full song. Screwcap. 12% alc. **Rating** 95 **To** 2025 $17 ❂

🍷🍷🍷🍷🍷 **Watervale Riesling 2016** Rating 93 To 2026 $17 ❂
1926 Old Bush Vine GSM 2014 Rating 93 To 2024 $18 ❂
Old Vine Clare Valley Shiraz 2013 Rating 92 To 2033 $20 ❂
Old Vine Clare Valley Shiraz 2014 Rating 91 To 2024 $20 ❂
Old Vine Clare Valley Grenache 2014 Rating 90 To 2022 $17 ❂

Firetail   ★★★★★

21 Bessell Road, Rosa Glen, WA 6285 **Region** Margaret River
T (08) 9757 5156 **www**.firetail.com.au **Open** 7 days 11–5
Winemaker Bruce Dukes, Peter Stanlake **Est.** 2002 **Dozens** 1200 **Vyds** 5.3ha
Jessica Worrall and Rob Glass are fugitives from the oil and gas industry. In '02 they purchased a 5.3ha vineyard in Margaret River that had been planted between '79 and '81 to sauvignon blanc, semillon and cabernet sauvignon. The wines are made by Bruce Dukes and Peter Stanlake. Looking at the firepower of the contract winemakers for Firetail, and the maturity of the vineyard in Margaret River, it is strange Firetail hasn't merited five stars before now. The wine quality is exemplary and the prices are almost old-fashioned.

🍷🍷🍷🍷🍷 **Margaret River Sauvignon Blanc 2016** A complex and textured sauvignon blanc, with the full range of flavour boxes: cut grass and green pea, citrus and apple, and gooseberry and tropical, topped and tailed by lemony acidity. Gold medal Margaret River Wine Show '16. Screwcap. 12.7% alc. **Rating** 95 **To** 2022 $19 ❂
Margaret River Cabernet Sauvignon 2014 Bright crimson-purple hue; an elegant, medium-bodied cabernet with bright cassis fruit and a lively mouthfeel derived from the moderate alcohol. Gold medal WA Wine Show '15 and ranked equal eighth in the UK *Decanter* magazine's best 80 Margaret River cabernets Jan '17. Cork. 13.7% alc. **Rating** 95 **To** 2029 $27 ❂

🍷🍷🍷🍷🍷 **Margaret River Cabernet Sauvignon 2012** Rating 92 $27

First Creek Wines   ★★★★★

600 McDonalds Road, Pokolbin, NSW 2320 **Region** Hunter Valley
T (02) 4998 7293 **www**.firstcreekwines.com.au **Open** 7 days 10–5
Winemaker Liz and Greg Silkman **Est.** 1984 **Dozens** 35 000
First Creek Wines is the brand of First Creek Winemaking Services, a major contract winemaker. Liz Silkman (née Jackson) had an exceptional year in 2011: she was a finalist in the *Gourmet Traveller* Winemaker of the Year awards, winner of the Hunter Valley Winemaker of the Year, and won Best Red Wine of Show at the NSW Wine Awards for the Winemakers Reserve Shiraz 2010. Exports to the UK, Sweden and China.

🍷🍷🍷🍷🍷 **Single Vineyard Murphys Semillon 2016** The bouquet suggests there's more happening here than simple best practice, but the power and varietal intensity of the palate sweeps such thoughts away. Very interesting how Hunter Valley semillon producers are now charging high prices ($60–$100) for semillons that tick both present and future boxes. Screwcap. **Rating** 96 **To** 2030 $60 ✪

Winemaker's Reserve Hunter Valley Chardonnay 2011 The gleaming green-tinged colour heralds a beautifully developed and proportioned chardonnay. White peach, almond and grapefruit sing together with precision; gentle but sufficient acidity on the finish carrying the song through to its natural conclusion. No need to rush it, but it's hard to imagine there is much room left for improvement. Screwcap. 13.5% alc. **Rating** 96 **To** 2021 $60 ✪

Winemaker's Reserve Hunter Valley Semillon 2016 Has more depth and incipient texture than many of its vintage siblings across the Hunter. Curiously, the acidity is less brusque than is normal. A high quality wine that drinks as well today as it will in a decade. Screwcap. 11% alc. **Rating** 95 **To** 2029 $45

Single Vineyard Black Cluster Semillon 2014 Exhibits all the attributes of an outstanding young Hunter semillon. The bouquet has vitality, showing the expected elements of lemongrass, freshly cut hay and scented soap. Those characters are reprised on the palate, which is perfectly poised; fresh and textured and long. Cellaring recommended, but a pleasure to drink now. Screwcap. **Rating** 95 **To** 2026 $50 SC

Winemaker's Reserve Hunter Valley Semillon 2011 This wine's generosity as a 1yo has now fully flowered, with a blossom-filled bouquet, and a palate with some of the citrus notes you would expect from a youngish riesling, but adding honeysuckle and a hint of partially dried fruit. Acidity is, and will remain, the staff of life for the wine. Screwcap. 10% alc. **Rating** 95 **To** 2023 $50

Winemaker's Reserve Hunter Valley Semillon 2009 This is a wild child: the bouquet heads off on a tangent all of its own, but the ravishing palate flicks the bouquet out of the picture with its almost painful intensity. A remarkable semillon with complexity its raison d'être. Screwcap. 11% alc. **Rating** 95 **To** 2021 $50

Winemaker's Reserve Hunter Valley Chardonnay 2016 A typical high quality modern Hunter Valley style, the fruit flavours balanced between stone and citrus fruits, honeydew melon the bridge to connect the points, the oak balanced and integrated. Screwcap. **Rating** 95 **To** 2026 $60

Winemaker's Reserve Hunter Valley Shiraz 2011 Still in its first phase of development, although you can sense the luminous, gently earthy and fragrant fruit characters that await with another 5+ years of maturation. Right now, it is intense and long, with spice, black fruits and a waft of new oak all contributing to its flavour. Screwcap. 13% alc. **Rating** 95 **To** 2031 $60

Winemaker's Reserve Hunter Valley Chardonnay 2010 Has reached the end of its development phase, but will hold its present form for some years yet. It is very complex, with juicy white peach and grapefruit engaged in a courtly dance on a long and intricately detailed palate. Screwcap. 12.5% alc. **Rating** 94 **To** 2020 $60

🍷🍷🍷🍷🍷 **Hunter Valley Shiraz 2014 Rating** 92 **To** 2030 $35 SC

First Drop Wines   ★★★★★

Beckwith Park, Barossa Valley Way, Nuriootpa, SA 5355 **Region** Barossa Valley
T (08) 8562 3324 **www**.firstdropwines.com **Open** Wed–Sat 10–4
Winemaker Matt Gant **Est.** 2005 **Dozens** 10 000

The First Drop Wines of today has been transformed since its establishment in 2005. It now has a real winery, part of the old Penfolds winery at Nuriootpa, shared with Tim Smith Wines. The group of buildings is now called Beckwith Park, in honour of the man who did so much groundbreaking work for Penfolds: Ray Beckwith OAM, who died in 2012, but not before his 100th birthday; his other recognition came in the form of the Maurice O'Shea Award. Exports to the UK, the US, Canada, Denmark, Japan, Hong Kong and NZ.

🍷🍷🍷🍷🍷 **Does Your Dog Bite? Single Vineyard Wilton Eden Valley Syrah 2014**
Of the three Does Your Dog Bite? wines, this has the edge, and is the only one
with almost one-third whole bunches in the ferment and much less oak – 33%
new French hogsheads. In a savoury spectrum, wafts of spice and red fruits with
briary characters, full-bodied (just); very fine silky tannins, superbly balanced and
long on the finish. Peter Sellers fans will chuckle about the name; as for the label,
that's another story. Screwcap. 13% alc. **Rating** 96 **To** 2033 $50 JF ⊘

Two Percent Barossa Shiraz 2015 The 2% is moscatel; perhaps that adds to
the lift of the aromatics, or not. Regardless, this is big and bodacious yet perfectly
contained. Full-bodied, slippery texture with a suppleness to the ripe and almost
sweet tannins and oak in check. Screwcap. 15% alc. **Rating** 95 **To** 2030 $38 JF

Does Your Dog Bite? Single Vineyard Moculta Eden Valley Syrah 2014
The Moculta and Craneford Does Your Dog Bite? wines are made identically:
16 months in 100% new French oak puncheons. Both are appealing, for different
reasons: this is more savoury and spicy, with a core of dark plums and cherries
covered in licorice root, richly fruited but not overripe. Full-bodied, plush tannins,
a persistent finish, integrated oak. Screwcap. 14.5% alc. **Rating** 95 **To** 2034 $50 JF

Minchia Adelaide Hills Montepulciano 2013 A powerful, sturdy rendition of
the variety, and while the 50% new French oak puncheons make their presence
felt, everything is balanced. It's awash with satsuma and dark plums, licorice, soy
sauce and ferrous notes that move onto a full-bodied palate, with giving tannins
and plenty of grip on the finish. Screwcap. 14% alc. **Rating** 95 **To** 2024 $38 JF

Mother's Milk Barossa Shiraz 2015 Dark-garnet-black à la Barossa, and while
there's an abundance of concentrated flavour, there's a vibrancy, too. Black plums in
kirsch, licorice; slurpy but not a jam-packed wine, and there's an ease to the finish
with supple tannins. Screwcap. 14.5% alc. **Rating** 94 **To** 2025 $25 JF ⊘

McLaren Vale Touriga Nacional 2015 Plenty of flavour and aromatics with
this variety – florals, spice, densely packed red-black fruits. There's a plushness with
pliable tannins, and it's rich and thick and oh so enjoyable. Screwcap. 14% alc.
Rating 94 **To** 2023 $25 JF ⊘

🍷🍷🍷🍷🍷 **Mere et Fils Adelaide Hills Chardonnay 2015 Rating** 93 **To** 2022 $25 JF ⊘
Vivo Adelaide Hills Arneis 2016 Rating 93 **To** 2019 $25 JF ⊘
Does Your Dog Bite Craneford Syrah 2014 Rating 93 **To** 2030 $50 JF
Mother's Ruin McLaren Vale Cabernet Sauvignon 2015 Rating 93
To 2023 $25 JF ⊘
The Matador Barossa Garnacha 2015 Rating 91 **To** 2021 $25 JF
Forza Adelaide Hills Nebbiolo 2011 Rating 91 **To** 2020 $50 JF

 First Foot Forward ★★★★☆

6 Maddens Lane, Coldstream, Vic 3770 **Region** Yarra Valley
T 0402 575 818 **www**.firstfootforward.com.au **Open** By appt
Winemaker Martin Siebert **Est.** 2013 **Dozens** 400
Owner and winemaker Martin Siebert's daytime job is at Tokar Estate, where he has been
chief winemaker for a number of years. In 2013 he had the opportunity to purchase pinot
noir and chardonnay from a mature vineyard in The Patch, high in the Dandenong Ranges on
the southern edge of the Yarra Valley. It is cooler and wetter than the floor of the Yarra Valley,
so much so that the fruit is consistently picked after Tokar's cabernet sauvignon, reducing the
stress that might otherwise have occurred. He says that so long as the fruit is available, he will
be purchasing it, adding a Sauvignon Blanc from Steels Creek to slightly broaden the offer to
quality-focused restaurants and specialty wine stores around Melbourne.

🍷🍷🍷🍷🍷 **Yarra Valley Pinot Noir 2015** This shows the '15 Yarra Valley pinot noir vintage
to best advantage: while red berry fruits remain its core, there is a remarkable drive
and intensity to the palate as it picks up savoury forest floor nuances and classy
tannins. Screwcap. 13.5% alc. **Rating** 95 **To** 2025 $25 ⊘

Gruyere Vineyard Yarra Valley Viognier 2016 First Foot Forward has
mastered balancing on the viognier razor's edge, achieving full varietal flavour,

and avoiding oily phenolics. A very snappy wine. Screwcap. 13.5% alc. **Rating** 94
To 2020 $25 **○**

� The Patch Vineyard Chardonnay 2013 Rating 93 To 2022 $25 **○**
The Patch Vineyard Pinot Noir 2016 Rating 92 To 2021 $25 **○**
The Patch Vineyard Chardonnay 2015 Rating 91 To 2021 $25
The Patch Vineyard Pinot Noir Rose 2016 Rating 91 To 2019 $25

First Ridge ★★★★

Cnr Castlereagh Highway/Burrundulla Road, Mudgee, NSW **Region** Mudgee
T 0407 701 014 **www**.firstridge.com.au **Open** 7 days 10–4
Winemaker James Manners **Est.** 1998 **Dozens** 5000 **Vyds** 20ha
Eighteen years ago Sydney architect John Nicholas and wife Helen began the establishment
of what is now a 20ha vineyard on undulating hillsides above the open valley below. The
soils vary from shallow topsoils of basalt and quartz on the highest ridges to deeper loams
over neutral clays. Barbera and sangiovese and vermentino are planted on the ridges, fiano,
pinot grigio, tempranillo, shiraz and merlot on the deeper soils. The vineyard manager, Colin
Millot, began work in McLaren Vale 30 years ago, moving to Mudgee in 1995 to manage
the Rosemount Hill of Gold and Mountain Blue Vineyards. James Manners (son of famed
chef Ned Manners) plays his part in realising the desire of the Nicholases to 'enjoy tables of
abundant food, friends and fiery conversation, not unlike a vibrant Italian table'.

♥♥♥♥♀ Mudgee Barbera 2015 Light crimson-purple; an altogether attractive wine
with supple plum fruits, fine tannins and a hint of oak. Balance is its greatest asset.
Screwcap. 14.5% alc. **Rating** 91 To 2028 $30
Mudgee Rose 2016 A sangiovese rose, with a slight salmon tinge to the hue.
Has a complex texture, suggesting barrel fermentation (partial or total). Well made.
Screwcap. 12.8% alc. **Rating** 90 To 2017 $20

♥♥♥♥ Mudgee Vermentino 2016 Rating 89 To 2020 $25

Five Geese ★★★★☆

389 Chapel Hill Road, Blewitt Springs, SA 5171 (postal) **Region** McLaren Vale
T (08) 8383 0576 **www**.fivegeese.com.au **Open** Not
Winemaker Mike Farmilo **Est.** 1999 **Dozens** 5000 **Vyds** 28ha
Sue Trott is devoted to her Five Geese wines, which come from vines planted in 1927 and
'65 (shiraz, cabernet sauvignon, grenache and mataro), nero d'Avola a more recent arrival. She
sold the grapes for many years, but in '99 decided to create her own label and make a strictly
limited amount of wine from the pick of the vineyards, which are run on organic principles.
Exports to the UK, South Korea and Singapore.

♥♥♥♥♀ McLaren Vale Shiraz 2014 The Blewitt Springs district is second to none in
McLaren Vale, and the maturation in appropriate oak has been put to good use in
this estate-grown wine, its colour an early warning of its quality. True blue Aussie
value, over-delivering with panache. Screwcap. 14.5% alc. **Rating** 92 To 2029
$20 **○**
The Pippali Old Vine McLaren Vale Shiraz 2014 From 30yo vines in
McLaren Flat, matured for 18 months in new and second-fill French barriques.
Good hue, although not especially deep; it's remarkable how the fruit has held its
own against the oak, for on the whole it is on the light side of medium-bodied.
Hugely drinkable. Cork. 14.5% alc. **Rating** 92 To 2029 $28
McLaren Vale Cabernet Sauvignon 2014 From 30yo vines in McLaren Flat
on deep alluvial iron-rich soil, matured for 18 months in new and used French
barriques. A richly plumed cassis-accented bouquet and palate, the latter with
a coat of dark chocolate and ripe tannins. Will develop serenely over the years.
Screwcap. 14.5% alc. **Rating** 92 To 2029 $24 **○**

♥♥♥♥ Volpacchiotto McLaren Vale Rose 2016 Rating 89 To 2018 $20

Five Oaks Vineyard

60 Aitken Road, Seville, Vic 3139 **Region** Yarra Valley
T (03) 5964 3704 **www.fiveoaks.com.au Open** W'ends & public hols 11–5
Winemaker Wally Zuk **Est.** 1995 **Dozens** 1000 **Vyds** 3ha

Wally Zuk and wife Judy run all aspects of Five Oaks – far removed from Wally's background in nuclear physics. He has, however, completed the wine science degree at CSU, and is thus more than qualified to make the Five Oaks wines. The lion's share of the vineyard is planted to cabernet sauvignon (2.6ha), with 0.2ha each of riesling and merlot. Exports to Canada, Macau, Hong Kong and China.

SGS Yarra Valley Cabernet Sauvignon 2015 From a very low-yielding vintage (1t/acre), crushed, 36 hours cold soak, fermented in stainless steel with cultured yeast, matured in French oak (55% new) for 18 months. It's only light to medium-bodied, but it's remarkable how so much French oak has been absorbed by the cassis/choc-mint fruit. It's elegant, offering now or later consumption. Screwcap. 14% alc. **Rating** 91 **To** 2025 $55

Flametree

Cnr Caves Road/Chain Avenue, Dunsborough, WA 6281 **Region** Margaret River
T (08) 9756 8577 **www.flametreewines.com Open** 7 days 10–5
Winemaker Cliff Royle, Julian Scott **Est.** 2007 **Dozens** 20 000

Flametree, owned by the Towner family (John, Liz, Rob and Annie), has had extraordinary success since its first vintage in 2007. The usual practice of planting a vineyard and then finding someone to make the wine was turned on its head: a state-of-the-art winery was built, and grape purchase agreements signed with growers in the region. Show success was topped by the winning of the Jimmy Watson Trophy with its 2007 Cabernet Merlot. If all this were not enough, Flametree secured the services of winemaker Cliff Royle. Exports to the UK, Canada, Indonesia, Malaysia, Singapore and Hong Kong.

Margaret River Shiraz 2015 Wild-yeast fermented in batches in open and static fermenters, plunged and/or pumped over twice daily, select parcels with whole bunches, matured for 10 months in French oak. A complex, full-bodied shiraz with black cherry, plum, licorice and spices all well and truly in play. The texture and structure of the wine are built around ripe, fine tannins. A long life ahead. Screwcap. 14% alc. **Rating** 96 **To** 2035 $27 ○

S.R.S. Wallcliffe Margaret River Chardonnay 2016 Flametree's flagship white highlights great fruit from the (unofficial) subregion of Wallcliffe coupled with thoughtful winemaking. The result is a flinty, complex and savoury wine with plenty of flavour; moreish leesy characters plus grapefruit and pith, and tangy as anything. Screwcap. 13% alc. **Rating** 95 **To** 2024 $65 JF

Margaret River Pinot Rose 2016 Chilled overnight to around 8°C, whole bunches loaded into the press, rotated a few times and after 3 hours 500l/t pressed to tank, the remaining 120l/t to used French puncheons. Very few roses on the market would have as much winemaking effort as that invested in this wine. It is complex and savoury, with flashes of spice, and has a long, dry finish. Screwcap. 13% alc. **Rating** 95 **To** 2017 $25 ○

S.R.S. Wilyabrup Margaret River Cabernet Sauvignon 2014 Sourced from Wilyabrup, long regarded as the regional benchmark for cabernet. Blackcurrant, dark chocolate and juicy red berry aromas and flavours are enhanced by cedary oak and framed by sublime tannin. The concentration, elegance and structure are exemplary. Screwcap. 14% alc. **Rating** 95 **To** 2034 $65 SC

Margaret River Cabernet Sauvignon Merlot 2014 A beautiful purity runs through the wine, beginning with a bouquet of varietal cassis, redcurrant and floral notes, and the regional influence of bay leaf, tobacco and herb. Smoothly textured and supple, the flavours mirror the aromas, framed by superfine, melting tannin. Delicious. Screwcap. 14% alc. **Rating** 94 **To** 2028 $30 SC ○

ŸŸŸŸŸ Embers Cabernet Sauvignon 2014 Rating 93 To 2024 $20 CM ❂
Margaret River Chardonnay 2015 Rating 92 To 2022 $27 CM
Embers Cabernet Sauvignon 2015 Rating 92 To 2023 $22 JF ❂
Embers Sauvignon Blanc 2015 Rating 91 To 2017 $20 CM ❂
Margaret River Chardonnay 2016 Rating 91 To 2022 $27 JF
Embers Sauvignon Blanc 2016 Rating 90 To 2018 $22 JF
Margaret River SBS 2016 Rating 90 To 2018 $24 JF

Flaxman Wines   ★★★★★

662 Flaxmans Valley Road, Flaxmans Valley, SA 5253 **Region** Eden Valley
T 0411 668 949 **www**.flaxmanwines.com.au **Open** Thurs–Sun 11–5
Winemaker Colin Sheppard **Est.** 2005 **Dozens** 1500 **Vyds** 2ha
After visiting the Barossa Valley for over a decade, Melbourne residents Colin Sheppard
and wife Fi decided on a seachange, and in 2004 found a small, old vineyard overlooking
Flaxmans Valley. It consists of 1ha of 60+ and 90-year-old riesling, 1ha of 65+ and 90-year-
old shiraz and a 0.8ha of 60+ year-old semillon. The vines are dry-grown, hand-pruned and
hand-picked, and treated – say the Sheppards – as their garden. Yields are restricted to under
4t/ha, and exceptional parcels of locally grown grapes are also purchased. Colin has worked at
various Barossa wineries for many years, and his attention to detail (and understanding of the
process) is reflected in the consistently high quality of the wines.

ŸŸŸŸŸ Eden Valley Riesling 2016 This has the indelible imprint of Eden Valley from
attack to pulsating finish: lime gelato all the way. Most impressive is the wine's
juxtaposition of intensity and concentration of flavour through its midriff, and the
energising natural acidity, rapier-like and yet beguiling and gentle in the context of
the region. Screwcap. 12% alc. **Rating** 96 To 2032 $27 NG ❂
Shhh Eden Valley Cabernet 2014 Beautifully handled, with crushed clove,
tobacco, cassis, star anise and dried sage mellifluously flowing across a mid to fully
loaded palate, architected to drinkable perfection by chiselled tannins and succulent
acidity. The oak is buried. Screwcap. 14% alc. **Rating** 95 To 2028 $45 NG

ŸŸŸŸŸ Reserve Chardonnay 2015 Rating 93 To 2022 $50 NG
Estate Eden Valley Shiraz 2014 Rating 93 To 2025 $60 NG
The Stranger Shiraz Cabernet 2014 Rating 92 To 2029 $37 NG
Eden Valley Chardonnay 2015 Rating 90 To 2022 $27 NG

Flowstone Wines   ★★★★★

11298 Bussell Highway, Forest Grove, WA 6286 **Region** Margaret River
T 0487 010 275 **www**.flowstonewines.com **Open** By appt
Winemaker Stuart Pym **Est.** 2013 **Dozens** 1000 **Vyds** 2.25ha
Flowstone is the venture of Stuart Pym and Phil Giglia. Stuart's involvement with wine
commenced in 1983, when he moved to Margaret River to help his parents establish their
vineyard and winery in Wilyabrup (since sold). Lengthy winemaking careers at Voyager
Estate (1991–2000), Devil's Lair ('00–'08) and Stella Bella ('08–'13) were rounded out with
concurrent vintage work overseas. Phil is a self-confessed wine tragic, his fascination starting
at the University of WA's Wine Club. The two met at a Margaret River Great Estates lunch
in the late '90s, and hatched the idea of starting a small business, which took shape in '03
when the property was purchased. 0.5ha of chardonnay was planted the following year, the
remainder in '09. Estate grapes are augmented by contract-grown grapes. The attention to
detail of the venture is typified by the appeal of the label design, the labels themselves made
from 81% limestone, the remainder bonding resin (there is no wood fibre or pulp).

ŸŸŸŸŸ Queen of the Earth Margaret River Chardonnay 2014 This walks a fine
line between moreish complexity or way too much funk. Personally, it sneaks
in with the former as there's plenty of stuffing: 18 months in French barriques
(50% new) and the fruit has absorbed it, offering complex match-strike and flinty
notes, bacon and lemon, grapefruit and pith, lots of texture. The key is the fresh,
tight acidity. Screwcap. 13.3% alc. **Rating** 96 To 2024 $55 JF ❂

Queen of the Earth Margaret River Cabernet Sauvignon 2013 From a dry-grown vineyard in Wilyabrup planted in the late '70s. Hand-picked, open-fermented for 17 days then to French oak barriques for 3 years, and once bottled allowed to relax for 15 months. What a wine. Complex yet refined, with florals, cassis and warm earth, full-bodied but long and pure with svelte tannins. Only 92 dozen made. Screwcap. 14.2% alc. **Rating** 96 **To** 2030 $74 JF ✪

Margaret River Sauvignon Blanc 2015 Single vineyard, the whole berries pressed to old barriques and a (600l) demi-muid for 11 months with lees stirring. A wine that is palate-focused and free of the nervy pressures of immediacy, says winemaker Stuart Pym. This is intensely flavoured, high-toned and complex: imagine crushed gravel, Chinese tea-smoke, and lemon verbena with crackling acidity yet texture galore. Screwcap. 13% alc. **Rating** 95 **To** 2024 $32 JF ✪

Margaret River Chardonnay 2014 Many layers: creamed honey, lemon curd, ginger fluff cake, all manner of stone fruit and their skins plus a refined texture. There's almost an overload of flavour but then the sparky acidity tucks everything in neatly. Screwcap. 12.5% alc. **Rating** 95 **To** 2024 $36 JF

Margaret River Shiraz Grenache 2015 50% shiraz, 48% grenache and 2% mourvedre, the shiraz crushed and destemmed for open fermentation, the grenache and the mourvedre 100% whole-bunch open-fermented and foot-stomped; the shiraz was pressed at 6° baume to finish fermentation in used oak; matured for 7 months in used barriques and puncheons, 230 dozen made. Vivid crimson-purple; the energy of the blaze of red fruits on the palate is utterly compelling, and creates the long finish and aftertaste, underlined by superfine tannins. Screwcap. 14% alc. **Rating** 95 **To** 2023 $25 ✪

Margaret River Cabernet Sauvignon Touriga 2013 The cabernet is from a single vineyard in Wilyabrup, 70% in the blend, the touriga from Yallingup, planted in the late '70s. Each made in a similar fashion, but kept separate, aged 2 years in French oak barriques (20% new). Harmonious in its composition, there's an ease, a suppleness to the tannins – plenty of grip, though – and the fruit is neatly compiled into the more savoury aspects of the wine. Screwcap. 14.1% alc. **Rating** 95 **To** 2027 $36 JF

🍷🍷🍷🍷🍷 **Margaret River Gewurztraminer 2015 Rating** 93 **To** 2023 $32 JF
Moonmilk 2016 Rating 92 **To** 2020 $19 JF ✪

Flying Fish Cove   ★★★★★

Caves Road, Wilyabrup, WA 6284   **Region** Margaret River
T (08) 9755 6600 **www.**flyingfishcove.com **Open** 7 days 11–5
Winemaker Simon Ding **Est.** 2000 **Dozens** 21 000 **Vyds** 25ha
Flying Fish Cove has two strings to its bow: contract winemaking for others, and the development of its own brand, partly based on 25ha of estate plantings. Long-serving winemaker Simon Ding had a circuitous journey before falling prey to the lure of wine. He finished an apprenticeship in metalwork in 1993. On returning to Australia in '96 he obtained a Bachelor of Science degree and joined the Flying Fish Cove team in 2000. Exports to the US and Malaysia.

🍷🍷🍷🍷🍷 **Prize Catch Margaret River Chardonnay 2015** Chilled for 12 hours, 200l/t pressed to new French oak for wild yeast fermentation, matured for 8 months with 2 months lees stirring. Dazzling purity and intensity has been its own reward; while oak frames the picture, you would never guess it was 100% new. Exceptional length. Screwcap. 13% alc. **Rating** 98 **To** 2027 $95 ✪

The Wildberry Reserve Margaret River Chardonnay 2015 Hand-picked, whole-bunch pressed, with the first 500l/t wild-yeast fermented in French oak (50% new), lees-stirred for 10 months. White peach, pink grapefruit, and just a touch of cashew ex the oak race along the palate, staying on song for a long time in the aftertaste. Screwcap. 13% alc. **Rating** 97 **To** 2026 $45 ✪

ŶŶŶŶŶ **The Wildberry Reserve Margaret River Cabernet Sauvignon 2015**
Crushed and destemmed, cultured yeast, 14 days on skins, matured in French oak
(50% new), 350 dozen made. Bright crimson; a super-elegant, light to medium-
bodied cabernet riding high on its juicy cassis and redcurrant fruit. It has managed
to absorb the oak with apparent ease, and even more striking, not in mainstream
Margaret River style. Screwcap. 14.3% alc. **Rating** 95 **To** 2030 $45

ŶŶŶŶŶ **Margaret River Chardonnay 2016 Rating** 93 **To** 2026 $22 ⊘
The Italian Job Vermentino 2014 Rating 93 **To** 2021 $25 ⊘
Margaret River Cabernet Merlot 2014 Rating 91 **To** 2023 $22 CM ⊘

Flynns Wines ★★★★★
29 Lewis Road, Heathcote, Vic 3523 **Region** Heathcote
T (03) 5433 6297 **www.**flynnswines.com **Open** W'ends 11.30–5
Winemaker Greg and Natala Flynn **Est.** 1999 **Dozens** 2000 **Vyds** 4.12ha
Greg and Natala Flynn spent 18 months searching for their property, which is 13km north of
Heathcote on red Cambrian soil. They have established shiraz, sangiovese, verdelho, cabernet
sauvignon and merlot. Greg is a Roseworthy marketing graduate, and has had over 25 years
working at the coal face of retail and wholesale businesses, interweaving 10 years of vineyard
and winemaking experience, supplemented by the two-year Bendigo TAFE winemaking
course. Just for good measure, Natala has joined in the vineyard and winery, and likewise
completed the TAFE course.

ŶŶŶŶŶ **MC Heathcote Shiraz 2014** Dark purple-black, a great colour and there's a lot
going on in this full-bodied, richly flavoured wine – and a lot to enjoy. Dark fruit
and blueberries with menthol, licorice and wood spices, plus beautifully supple yet
powerful tannins. Yes there's oak, but it's integrated; then a long and vibrant finish.
Screwcap. 14.8% alc. **Rating** 95 **To** 2032 $35 JF ⊘
James Flynn Heathcote Shiraz 2013 Awash with black plums, licorice and
oak, with wafts of coconut rough and new leather. A style many will relish; glossy,
structured and velvety plush tannins, yet everything amalgamated. It makes a
statement: look at me. Screwcap. 15% alc. **Rating** 95 **To** 2033 $70 JF

Forbes & Forbes ★★★★★
30 Williamstown Road, Springton, SA 5235 **Region** Eden Valley
T (08) 8568 2709 **www.**forbeswine.com.au **Open** At Taste Eden Valley, Angaston
Winemaker Colin Forbes **Est.** 2008 **Dozens** 400 **Vyds** 5ha
This venture is owned by Colin and Robert Forbes, and their respective partners. Colin says,
'I have been in the industry for a "frightening" length of time', beginning with Thomas Hardy
& Sons in 1974. While Colin is particularly attached to riesling, the property owned by the
partners in Eden Valley has 2ha each of riesling and merlot, and 1ha of cabernet sauvignon.

ŶŶŶŶŶ **Single Vineyard Eden Valley Riesling 2016** Quintessential Eden Valley
riesling with Meyer lemon and Rose's lime juice joined together by livewire
acidity. Totally delicious, and as the '08 shows, has a 20+-year life for those who
want to have their cake and eat it. Screwcap. 11.4% alc. **Rating** 95 **To** 2036 $21 ⊘
Cellar Matured Eden Valley Riesling 2008 Is developing as surely (and
slowly) as expected/hoped for in its two previous tastings, the first in '08, the
next in '14, which can't be improved on: 'Still exceptionally pale colour, and
no less youthful on the palate; here lime, lemon and apple all intersect with
bracing acidity; this acidity is part of its tenacity, but will not prevent the ongoing
development of flavour to and past '20.' Fantastic value. Screwcap. 12.6% alc.
Rating 95 **To** 2028 $28 ⊘

ŶŶŶŶŶ **Red Letter Day Sparkling Red NV Rating** 90 **To** 2020 $30 TS

Forest Hill Vineyard ★★★★★

Cnr South Coast Highway/Myers Road, Denmark, WA 6333 **Region** Great Southern
T (08) 9848 2399 **www**.foresthillwines.com.au **Open** Thurs–Sun 10.30–4.30
Winemaker Liam Carmody, Guy Lyons **Est.** 1965 **Dozens** 12000 **Vyds** 65ha
This family-owned business is one of the oldest 'new' winemaking operations in WA, and was
the site of the first grape plantings in Great Southern in 1965. The Forest Hill brand became
well known, aided by the fact that a '75 Riesling made by Sandalford from Forest Hill grapes
won nine trophies. The quality of the wines made from the oldest vines (dry-grown) on the
property is awesome (released under the numbered vineyard block labels). Exports to Taiwan,
Hong Kong, Singapore and China.

ŸŸŸŸŸ **Block 1 Mount Barker Riesling 2016** Whole-bunch pressed, the free-run
juice kept separate for this wine; a long, cool ferment with a Champagne yeast
followed. A subdued bouquet, making you unprepared for the explosive intensity
and length of the brilliantly detailed palate, with all its future flavours shimmering
translucently in the background. Screwcap. 13% alc. **Rating** 97 **To** 2036 $38 ❂

ŸŸŸŸŸ **Block 8 Mount Barker Chardonnay 2014** Whole bunches chilled overnight
before sorting and pressing to new and used French barriques for cool
fermentation, 8.4g/l of acidity making partial mlf essential for balance. Entirely
about purity, finesse and varietal fruit expression, the acidity the glue holding the
parts together. Screwcap. 13.5% alc. **Rating** 96 **To** 2029 $45 ❂

Block 9 Mount Barker Shiraz 2014 Destemmed into open fermenters,
pumped over twice daily, matured for 18 months in French oak. Savoury bitter
chocolate and licorice notes intersect with the black fruits of the bouquet and
palate alike. All about nuanced complexity, tannins and oak the canvas on which
the primary flavours are painted. Screwcap. 14% alc. **Rating** 96 **To** 2044 $60 ❂

Block 5 Mount Barker Cabernet Sauvignon 2014 Made from the best
fruit from the oldest ('75) plantings, destemmed to closed fermenters, with twice
daily aerative pumpovers, then matured in new and used French barriques for
18 months. As expected, a high quality cabernet in every way; only medium-
bodied, but beautifully nuanced and poised, blackcurrant fruit, bay leaf, oak and
fine – almost silky – tannins. Screwcap. 14% alc. **Rating** 96 **To** 2039 $65 ❂

Estate Mount Barker Chardonnay 2016 From four blocks in the Forest
Hill and Highfields Vineyards, crushed, cooled, pressed direct to French barriques
(30% new) for wild yeast fermentation and subsequent maturation with partial mlf.
Has very good mouthfeel and length, primarily zesty pink grapefruit flavours with
some cashew notes. Screwcap. 13.5% alc. **Rating** 95 **To** 2020 $30 ❂

Estate Mount Barker Shiraz 2015 Crushed and destemmed, to French
barriques, matured for 15 months before blending and egg white fining. While
only medium-bodied, this is a classic Mount Barker cool-grown shiraz, supple and
perfectly balanced, its black cherry/berry fruits studded with ripe, but fine, tannins
and integrated oak. Screwcap. 14.5% alc. **Rating** 95 **To** 2030 $30 ❂

Estate Mount Barker Cabernet Sauvignon 2015 Simple vinification similar
to its Cabernet Merlot sibling, here 20 days on skins and 16 months maturation
in French barriques. The poor fruit set and low yields of '15 have resulted in an
intense, very savoury cabernet with dried herb and earthy notes running through
blackcurrant fruit. Needs time. Screwcap. 14% alc. **Rating** 94 **To** 2030 $32

ŸŸŸŸŸ **Estate Mount Barker Riesling 2016 Rating** 93 **To** 2026 $26 SC ❂
Highbury Fields Cabernet Merlot 2014 Rating 93 **To** 2029 $22 ❂
Estate Gewurztraminer 2016 Rating 92 **To** 2026 $26
Highbury Fields Chardonnay 2016 Rating 91 **To** 2021 $22 ❂
Highbury Fields Great Southern Shiraz 2015 Rating 90 **To** 2022 $22

Forester Estate   ★★★★★

1064 Wildwood Road, Yallingup, WA 6282 **Region** Margaret River
T (08) 9755 2788 **www.foresterestate.com.au Open** By appt
Winemaker Kevin McKay, Todd Payne **Est.** 2001 **Dozens** 25 000 **Vyds** 33.5ha
Forester Estate is owned by Kevin and Jenny McKay, with a 500-tonne winery, half devoted
to contract winemaking, the other half for the Forester label. Winemaker Todd Payne has
had a distinguished career, starting in the Great Southern, thereafter the Napa Valley, back to
Plantagenet, then Esk Valley in Hawke's Bay, plus two vintages in the Northern Rhône Valley,
one with esteemed producer Yves Cuilleron in 2008. His move back to WA completed the
circle. The estate vineyards are planted to sauvignon blanc, semillon, chardonnay, cabernet
sauvignon, shiraz, merlot, petit verdot, malbec and alicante bouschet. Exports to Japan.

⦙⦙⦙⦙⦙ **Margaret River Chardonnay 2015** Hand-picked, chilled overnight, crushed
and pressed, some to barrel, most to tank for the start of fermentation, thence
to French barriques (36% new) for the balance of fermentation and 9 months
maturation. Classic Margaret River chardonnay, half and half white peach and
grapefruit, with abundant depth. Screwcap. 13% alc. **Rating** 95 **To** 2025 $38
Margaret River Cabernet Merlot 2014 43% cabernet sauvignon, 42% merlot,
5% each petit verdot, malbec and cabernet franc, matured in French barriques
(15% new). Has the Margaret River vibrancy of predominantly cassis fruit
decorated with splashes of bay leaf, black olive and cedary oak. Isn't great, but is
very good, and great value. Screwcap. 14% alc. **Rating** 95 **To** 2029 $24 **○**
Margaret River Cabernet Sauvignon 2014 There's no need to embellish
Margaret River cabernet with lots of French oak or other varieties if you are
seeking purity of varietal expression, as this wine handsomely demonstrates. Cassis
is the cornerstone, a touch of black olive and ripe tannins doing the rest. It will
age as long as patience remains. Screwcap. 14% alc. **Rating** 95 **To** 2029 $38
Yelverton Reserve Margaret River Cabernet 2011 93% cabernet sauvignon,
4% cabernet franc, 2% petit verdot and 1% merlot, open-fermented, 30 days on
skins, matured in French barriques (50% new) for 20 months, gold medal Margaret
River Wine Show '16. Gets the show on the right road, promptly sustained
by delicious cassis fruit running from go to whoa. Forester Estate has done the
cellaring work for you, and whether you drink it now or later is a personal choice.
Screwcap. 13.5% alc. **Rating** 95 **To** 2026 $62
Margaret River Sauvignon Blanc 2016 The bouquet fully reflects the partial
barrel fermentation of the wine, the complexity sitting well within the parameters
of the luscious passionfruit, gooseberry and cut grass palate. No Marlborough here.
Screwcap. 13% alc. **Rating** 94 **To** 2019 $27 **○**
Margaret River Semillon Sauvignon Blanc 2016 Has crystal clear Margaret
River SSB varietal expression, with snow pea and grassy notes cohabiting with
tropical guava and passionfruit flavours. Thus there is ample fruit complexity to
make barrel fermentation unnecessary, and the future will add further interest.
Screwcap. 13% alc. **Rating** 94 **To** 2020 $24 **○**
Jack out the Box Margaret River Fer 2014 The only commercial planting
I know of fer (from the southwest of France) in Australia, grafted onto rootstock
by Forester. Matured for 20 months in used oak. Deeply coloured; it has a fragrant
spicy/pepper bouquet and a powerful, dark-fruited, full-bodied palate with robust
tannins. Screwcap. 13.5% alc. **Rating** 94 **To** 2029 $40

⦙⦙⦙⦙⦙ **Margaret River Alicante 2011 Rating** 90 **To** 2020 $40

Foster e Rocco   ★★★★☆

PO Box 438, Heathcote, Vic 3523 **Region** Heathcote
T 0407 057 471 **www.fostererocco.com.au Open** Not
Winemaker Adam Foster, Lincoln Riley **Est.** 2008 **Dozens** 2500
Long-term sommeliers and friends Adam Foster and Lincoln Riley have established a business
that has a very clear vision: food-friendly wine based on the versatility of sangiovese. They

make their wine at Syrahmi, building it from the ground up, with fermentation in both stainless steel and a mixture of used French oak. Exports to the US, Japan and China.

ΨΨΨΨΨ **Heathcote Sangiovese 2013** Hand-sorted in the vineyard, 100% destemmed, wild yeast–open fermented, 5 days cold soak, 21 days fermentation and maceration, 14 months in used oak. Very good colour, and, as in the case of the unoaked Nuovo, all about delicious, spiced red and sour cherry fruit, docile tannins a great finish. Screwcap. 14% alc. **Rating** 95 **To** 2023 $34
Nuovo Heathcote Sangiovese 2016 Machine-harvested, destemmed, wild yeast–open fermented, 20 days on skins. You would swear there's sweet spicy oak involved, so it's the sangio tannins, so often savage, that are providing the texture and bewitching the wine. Screwcap. 13.5% alc. **Rating** 94 **To** 2026 $25

ΨΨΨΨΨ **Heathcote Rose 2016** **Rating** 91 **To** 2020 $25

Four Sisters ★★★★

199 O'Dwyers Road, Tahbilk, Vic 3608 **Region** Central Victoria
T (03) 5736 2400 **www**.foursisters.com.au **Open** Not
Winemaker Alan George, Jo Nash, Alister Purbrick **Est.** 1995 **Dozens** 45 000
The four sisters who inspired this venture were the daughters of the late Trevor Mast, a great winemaker who died before his time. The business is owned by the Purbrick family (the owner of Tahbilk). It orchestrates the purchase of the grapes for the brand, and also facilitates the winemaking. The production is wholly export-focused, with limited sales in Australia. It exports to 15 countries, including China, and that number may well diminish if Chinese distribution fulfils all its potential.

ΨΨΨΨΨ **Pinot Grigio 2016** Distinct light pink; faint touches of wild strawberry hide in the skirts of the dominant pear and citrus flavours. Has good length to the crisp, dry palate. Excellent value. Screwcap. 14% alc. **Rating** 90 **To** 2018 $16 ✪
Central Victoria Shiraz 2015 This wine was tasted after full-bodied shirazs of up to $70, and suggested the prices of this and the others should be swapped. It's a delicious drink-now style, its medium-bodied palate full of red and purple fruits, oak and tannins bit players. Exceptional value. Screwcap. 14.5% alc. **Rating** 90 **To** 2021 $16 ✪
Central Victoria Merlot 2015 Pretty much hits the sweet spot for what is expected of merlot at this price. Ripe, bright fruit on the bouquet with a lick of sweet oak, and a generous, supple palate, the red-berry flavours buoyant and fresh. Screwcap. 14.5% alc. **Rating** 90 **To** 2019 $16 SC ✪

ΨΨΨΨ **Central Victoria Cabernet Sauvignon 2015** **Rating** 89 **To** 2020 $16 SC ✪

Four Winds Vineyard ★★★★★

9 Patemans Lane, Murrumbateman, NSW 2582 **Region** Canberra District
T (02) 6227 0189 **www**.fourwindsvineyard.com.au **Open** W'ends 10–4
Winemaker Jaime and Bill Crowe **Est.** 1998 **Dozens** 2500 **Vyds** 11.9ha
Graeme and Suzanne Lunney conceived the idea for Four Winds in 1997, planting the first vines in '98, moving to the property full-time in '99, and making the first vintage in 2000. Daughter Sarah looks after promotions, and youngest daughter Jaime, complete with a degree in forensic biology, has joined husband Bill in the winery. She brings with her several years' experience with the former Kambera winery, and three vintages in the Napa Valley.

ΨΨΨΨΨ **Canberra District Riesling 2016** Almost Germanic in style in terms of varietal character and structure. A charming bouquet, showing delicate lemon and lime aromas with a floral, blossomy feel. Pure riesling flavours run along the palate, the fruit sweetness in harmony with the fine, lightly etched acidity. The length is a feature, with all elements gently persisting through the finish and aftertaste. Screwcap. 11.5% alc. **Rating** 95 **To** 2025 $25 SC ✪

Tom's Block Shiraz 2015 Sarah Crowe says the family is excited about this wine, having made 20 dozen in '14 and none in '16, putting the 220 dozen of this wine into focus. Matured for 12 months in French oak, plus a further 12 months in bottle before release. The perfumed bouquet and bright crimson purple colour segue to the light to medium-bodied palate that dances in the mouth like a firetail finch, the flavours all things red, the tannins pure silk. Screwcap. 14.2% alc. **Rating** 95 **To** 2025 $75

Canberra District Shiraz 2015 Rating 92 **To** 2026 $30 CM
Canberra District Sangiovese 2015 Rating 92 **To** 2021 $30 CM
Canberra District Shiraz Rose 2016 Rating 91 **To** 2018 $22 SC ❂

Fowles Wine

Cnr Hume Freeway/Lambing Gully Road, Avenel, Vic 3664 **Region** Strathbogie Ranges
T (03) 5796 2150 **www**.fowleswine.com **Open** 7 days 9–5
Winemaker Victor Nash, Lindsay Brown **Est.** 1968 **Dozens** 70 000 **Vyds** 120ha
This family-owned winery is led by Matt Fowles, with chief winemaker Victor Nash heading the winemaking team. The large vineyard is primarily focused on riesling, chardonnay, shiraz and cabernet sauvignon, but also includes arneis, vermentino, pinot gris, sauvignon blanc, pinot noir, mourvedre, sangiovese and merlot. Marketing is energetic, with the well known Ladies Who Shoot Their Lunch label available as large posters, the wines also available presented in a 6-bottle gun case. Exports to the UK, the US, Canada and China.

Ladies Who Shoot Their Lunch Riesling 2016 One of the gems in this series: a luscious riesling with texture and layers of flavour without being heavy. Part stainless steel ferment, part large oak cask help with that, as does a splash of pinot gris, with exacting acidity ensuring this remains vibrant and age-worthy. Screwcap. 13% alc. **Rating** 94 **To** 2027 $35 JF

Ladies Who Shoot Their Lunch Chardonnay 2015 Rating 93 **To** 2023 $35 JF
Stone Dwellers Rose 2016 Rating 93 **To** 2019 $22 JF ❂
Ladies Who Shoot Their Lunch Shiraz 2015 Rating 93 **To** 2025 $35 JF
Ladies Who Shoot Their Lunch Wild Ferment Chardonnay 2016 Rating 92 **To** 2024 $35 JF
Stone Dwellers Shiraz 2015 Rating 92 **To** 2025 $25 JF ❂
Stone Dwellers Riesling 2016 Rating 91 **To** 2023 $22 JF ❂
Ladies Who Shoot Their Lunch Shiraz 2014 Rating 91 **To** 2022 $35 JF
The Rule Strathbogie Ranges Shiraz 2015 Rating 90 **To** 2025 $50 JF

Fox Creek Wines

140 Malpas Road, McLaren Vale, SA 5171 **Region** McLaren Vale
T (08) 8557 0000 **www**.foxcreekwines.com **Open** 7 days 10–5
Winemaker Scott Zrna, Ben Tanzer **Est.** 1995 **Dozens** 35 000 **Vyds** 21ha
Fox Creek is the venture of the extended Watts family, headed by Jim (a retired surgeon). Although Fox Creek is not certified organic, it uses sustainable vineyard practices, avoiding all systemic chemicals. In June 2015 Fox Creek announced a $500 000 winery expansion, developed in close collaboration with the winemaking team. Exports to all major markets.

Three Blocks McLaren Vale Cabernet Sauvignon 2014 The synergy between McLaren Vale and cabernet sauvignon has long been noted, but this is a particularly good example. It is as pure as it is elegant, the cassis fruit perfectly ripened and equally perfectly handled in the winery with its hint of French oak. Totally, absolutely delicious. Screwcap. 14% alc. **Rating** 96 **To** 2029 $35 ❂
Reserve McLaren Vale Shiraz 2015 A phalanx of dark fruits and cherry bonbon notes, all soaked in creamy vanilla chocolate, serve as the attack. Sinuous grape tannins and a prism of sexy French oak frame the fruit flavours. Screwcap. 14.5% alc. **Rating** 95 **To** 2035 $80 NG

Old Vine McLaren Vale Shiraz 2015 Deep vermilion verging on opaque, this oozes dark and blue fruits and florals. A hint of anise gives further accent. Encased in slick milk-chocolate oak and massaged by pulpy grape tannins, the wine never strays into excess. Screwcap. 14.5% alc. **Rating** 94 **To** 2032 $60 NG

McLaren Vale Merlot 2015 Dark berries pop across a streamlined palate of bright acidity, svelte tannins and a dusting of well handled oak. A sweet core of kirsch segues to damson plum, licking the finish. In all, a fine merlot exuding energy and drinkability. Screwcap. 14.5% alc. **Rating** 94 **To** 2024 $20 NG ✪

♥♥♥♥♀ **McLaren Vale Vermentino 2016** **Rating** 93 **To** 2018 $23 NG ✪
Short Row McLaren Vale Shiraz 2015 **Rating** 93 **To** 2028 $35 NG
Jim's Script McLaren Vale Cabernet Sauvignon Merlot Cabernet Franc Petit Verdot 2014 **Rating** 92 **To** 2026 $27
McLaren Vale Cabernet Sauvignon 2015 **Rating** 91 **To** 2024 $20 NG ✪
Red Baron McLaren Vale Shiraz 2015 **Rating** 90 **To** 2022 $17 NG ✪
JSM McLaren Vale Shiraz Cabernet Sauvignon Cabernet Franc 2014 **Rating** 90 **To** 2029 $27
Limited Release McLaren Vale Nero d'Avola 2015 **Rating** 90 **To** 2020 $35 NG
Vixen NV **Rating** 90 **To** 2018 $27 TS

Fox Gordon   ★★★★

44 King William Road, Goodwood, SA 5034 **Region** Barossa Valley/Adelaide Hills
T (08) 8377 7707 **www**.foxgordon.com.au **Open** Not
Winemaker Natasha Mooney **Est.** 2000 **Dozens** 10 000
This is the venture of Sam and Rachel Atkins (née Fox) and winemaker Natasha (Tash) Mooney. Tash has had first class experience in the Barossa Valley, particularly during her time as chief winemaker at Barossa Valley Estate. The partners initially produced only small quantities of high quality wine, allowing them time to look after their children; the venture was planned in the shade of the wisteria tree in Tash's back garden. The grapes come from dry-grown vineyards farmed under biodiversity principles. Classy packaging adds the final touch. Exports to the UK, Canada, Germany, India, Singapore, Hong Kong and China.

♥♥♥♥♀ **Abby Adelaide Hills Viognier 2015** Fox Gordon has established a reputation for making enjoyable viognier, and this assemblage of yellow peach, apricot and citrus shows why. Screwcap. 13% alc. **Rating** 91 **To** 2018 $23 ✪

Princess Adelaide Hills Fiano 2016 The texture and self-generated drive of fiano is very obvious, as are the savoury overtones to the mix of citrus and herbal flavours. Quite where the notes of sage come from in the cool environment is a question to ponder. **Rating** 91 **To** 2020 $23 ✪

Eight Uncles Barossa Shiraz 2015 Good depth to the crimson-purple hue; matured in French oak, this is utterly authentic Barossa shiraz. Medium+-bodied, black fruits doing the hard lifting, French oak per se not obvious – and, indeed, why should it impact on the flavour of the wine? It does provide texture. Great value. Screwcap. 13.9% alc. **Rating** 91 **To** 2030 $20 ✪

The Dark Prince Adelaide Hills Nero d'Avola 2015 The flavour descriptors of dark cherry, blackberry and so forth – even the name of the wine – suggest a brooding full-bodied wine, when it's nothing like that. It's light to medium-bodied with easy fruit and tannins, and lots of fresh enjoyable fruits. Screwcap. 14.5% alc. **Rating** 91 **To** 2023 $25

Sassy Adelaide Hills Sauvignon Blanc 2016 While no tricks have been used during the winemaking, the wine has real presence and attitude by the time it reaches all the corners of the mouth. Crisp acidity and citrus carry the tropical nuances of lychee and guava. Screwcap. 13.9% alc. **Rating** 90 **To** 2018 $19 ✪

Charlotte's Web Adelaide Hills Pinot Grigio 2016 A distinct tinge of pink heralds an expressive pinot grigio with its mix of nashi pear and Granny Smith apple. A bit more depth to the same flavour set would be a very good wine. Screwcap. 14% alc. **Rating** 90 **To** 2018 $20 ✪

Foxeys Hangout

/95 Wiiiii Hill Road, Red Hill, Vic 3937 **Region** Mornington Peninsula
T (03) 5989 2022 **www.**foxeys-hangout.com.au **Open** W'ends & public hols 11–5
Winemaker Tony and Michael Lee **Est.** 1998 **Dozens** 5000 **Vyds** 3.4ha
This is the venture of Tony Lee and journalist wife Cathy Gowdie. Cathy explains where it
all began:'We were not obvious candidates for a seachange. When we talked of moving to the
country, friends pointed out that Tony and I were hardly back-to-nature types."Do you own a
single pair of shoes without heels?" asked a friend. At the end of a bleak winter, we bought an
old farmhouse on 10 daffodil-dotted acres at Red Hill and planted a vineyard.' They planted
pinot noir, chardonnay, pinot gris and shiraz on the north-facing slopes of the old farm.

ΨΨΨΨΨ **Mornington Peninsula Shiraz 2015** Bright, full crimson-purple; positively
vibrates with its intense, highly focused black pepper, black cherry and spice
aromas and flavours. Dances in the mouth with an ever-changing display of fruits,
texture and structure. Great cool climate shiraz. Screwcap. 13.5% alc. **Rating** 97
To 2035 $45 ✪

ΨΨΨΨΨ **Red Fox Mornington Peninsula Pinot Noir 2015** Good colour, bright and
full; the bouquet has excellent varietal expression, with plum and black cherry
to the fore, and the palate adds significant power and precision courtesy of a
backdrop of savoury/stemmy tannins. A high quality pinot at a mouthwatering
price. Screwcap. 13.5% alc. **Rating** 96 To 2027 $28 ✪
Mornington Peninsula Chardonnay 2015 Mostly whole-bunch pressed,
with 'some rougher handling to extract more solids', two barrels whole-bunch
fermented to add a textural component, matured in French oak (25% new). White
peach, cashew and grapefruit all coalesce on a palate that has more freshness and
cut than many of its Mornington Peninsula peers. Crisp acidity on the finish is
another plus. Screwcap. 13% alc. **Rating** 95 To 2023 $38
Mornington Peninsula Pinot Noir 2015 Part whole-bunch wild yeast
fermentation, matured in French oak (25% new). The light, but bright and
clear, hue gives no hint of the power of the savoury, complex palate. Everything
about the wine follows the page line by line, and does so without obvious effort.
Burgundians would doff their caps to this. Screwcap. 13.5% alc. **Rating** 95
To 2025 $38
Mornington Peninsula Rose 2016 Made from shiraz and pinot noir, with
extended pre-fermentation skin contact. Vivid, clear crimson-puce; the striking
highly scented/perfumed bouquet leads into a palate that is full of cherry fruit and
a garland of savoury spices. Has attitude+. Screwcap. 13% alc. **Rating** 94 To 2018
$28 ✪

Frankland Estate

Frankland Road, Frankland, WA 6396 **Region** Frankland River
T (08) 9855 1544 **www.**franklandestate.com.au **Open** details on the website
Winemaker Hunter Smith, Brian Kent **Est.** 1988 **Dozens** 15 000 **Vyds** 34.5ha
A significant operation, situated on a large sheep property owned by Barrie Smith and Judi
Cullam. The vineyard has been established progressively since 1988; the introduction of an
array of single vineyard Rieslings has been a highlight, driven by Judi's conviction that terroir
is of utmost importance, and the soils are indeed different. The Isolation Ridge Vineyard is
now organically grown. Frankland Estate has held important International Riesling tastings
and seminars for more than a decade. Exports to all major markets.

ΨΨΨΨΨ **Poison Hill Vineyard Riesling 2016** Captivating and powerful from the word
go, starting with its lime and grapefruit flavours, then wet rocks before a mineral
sensation with chalky acidity. Everything balanced with laser accuracy; a joy to
behold. Screwcap. 11.3% alc. **Rating** 96 To 2029 $40 JF ✪
Isolation Ridge Vineyard Riesling 2016 All the hallmarks of this site are at
play: camomile and blossom, the lightness of touch on the palate with its citrus

notes, the steely freshness and acidity so pure it creates an ultra-fine and long finish. Screwcap. 12.5% alc. **Rating** 96 **To** 2029 $40 JF ✪

Cabernet Sauvignon 2014 Very good colour; this lines up hand in hand with the '14 Shiraz, like an exercise in varietal purity and attention to detail in both vineyard and winery. Blackcurrant fruit with notes of dried herbs and a hint of earth is supported by first class cabernet tannins and a measured touch of French oak. Exceptional value. Screwcap. 13.5% alc. **Rating** 96 **To** 2039 $28 ✪

Olmo's Reward 2014 The finest, most complete Olmo's Reward to date, comprising cabernet franc (58%), cabernet sauvignon (26%), malbec (11%), petit verdot (5%). Red fruits, earth and spice sashay across the medium-bodied frame meeting finely crafted tannins. Pure and long on the finish and seems effortless. Certainly effortless to drink. Screwcap. 14.2% alc. **Rating** 96 **To** 2030 $85 JF

Shiraz 2015 The variety and the terroir both seek to impose their stamp over the other: both fail in their attempt, the perfect win-win outcome. Blackberry fruit, spice and black pepper lead the way on the bouquet and medium-bodied palate alike, French oak (subtle) and tannins (ripe, but fine) completing a great portrait of cool-grown shiraz. Screwcap. 14% alc. **Rating** 95 **To** 2035 $28 ✪

Isolation Ridge Vineyard Shiraz 2015 This will morph into something rather special. It has the hallmarks of a finely tuned expressive Frankland River shiraz, with heady aromatics of florals, dark fruit, licorice, pepper, wood spices, chiselled tannins and clearly defined oak. Some creaminess on the palate adds another layer of complexity. Screwcap. 14% alc. **Rating** 95 **To** 2030 $40 JF

Riesling 2016 Quartz-white; the bouquet has floral blossom and hints of bath powder, the palate is powerful and grippy (in a good sense) with rocky minerality and a very long aftertaste. Demands 5+ years, and will repay 10+ handsomely. Screwcap. 12.5% alc. **Rating** 94 **To** 2026 $28 ✪

Chardonnay 2015 Frankland Estate has been working diligently in the vineyard and it's starting to show. Lemon barley water, citrus zest with some ginger spice and daikon radish crunch to the mouthwatering acidity; linear and very refined. Screwcap. 13% alc. **Rating** 94 **To** 2025 $28 JF ✪

Chardonnay 2014 A sleek feline chardonnay that has that slight understatement of all the Frankland Estate self-grown wines. Here the fruit is in the tangy citrus arc, but so well poised that no one aroma or flavour takes hold. Developing with quiet confidence. Screwcap. 13% alc. **Rating** 94 **To** 2023 $28 ✪

🍷🍷🍷🍷🍷 Rocky Gully Shiraz 2015 **Rating** 93 **To** 2027 $20 JF ✪
Rocky Gully Riesling 2015 **Rating** 92 **To** 2030 $20 ✪
Isolation Ridge Vineyard Chardonnay 2014 **Rating** 91 **To** 2021 $28
Rocky Gully Riesling 2016 **Rating** 90 **To** 2023 $20 ✪

Franklin Tate Estates   ★★★☆

Gale Road, Kaloorup, WA 6280 **Region** Margaret River
T (08) 9267 8555 **www**.franklintateestates.com.au **Open** Not
Winemaker Rory Clifton-Parks, Gary Stokes **Est.** 2010 **Dozens** 32 000 **Vyds** 101ha
This is the second winery established by Franklin and Heather Tate in 2010. In '07 they created Miles from Nowhere (see separate entry), but this is a quite separate venture. Franklin is a second-generation vigneron in Margaret River, with his parents, John and Toni Tate, pioneers in founding Evans & Tate in '74. Franklin was of course part of the establishment during the rapid growth of the winery from the 1990s until 2005. The lion's share of the plantings on their two vineyards (planted many years ago) are sauvignon blanc, semillon, chardonnay, shiraz and cabernet sauvignon, with minor plantings of verdelho, petit verdot and viognier. There are two tiers in the wine range: the Estate series and the Alexander's Vineyard Reserve range. Exports to the US, Canada, Malaysia, Singapore and Thailand.

🍷🍷🍷🍷🍷 Tate Alexander's Vineyard Margaret River Cabernet Sauvignon 2014
A savoury wine defined by cabernet's verdant baritone of bay leaf, dried sage, tobacco and green bean. The mid-palate lacks some concentration and currant

flecks the wine's edges, rather than flowing through its centre, as a result. The oak is well handled, farming the fruit rather than overwhelming it. Screwcap. 14.4% alc. Rating 90 To 2022 $24 NG

TTTT Tate Margaret River SBS 2016 Rating 89 To 2018 $16 NG ○

Fraser Gallop Estate ★★★★★

493 Metricup Road, Wilyabrup, WA 6280 **Region** Margaret River
T (08) 9755 7553 **www**.frasergallopestate.com.au **Open** 7 days 11–4
Winemaker Clive Otto, Kate Morgan **Est.** 1999 **Dozens** 11 000 **Vyds** 20ha
Nigel Gallop began the development of the vineyard in 1999, planting cabernet sauvignon, semillon, petit verdot, cabernet franc, malbec, merlot, sauvignon blanc and multi-clone chardonnay. The dry-grown vines have modest yields, followed by kid glove treatment in the winery. With Clive Otto (formerly of Vasse Felix) onboard, a 300-tonne winery was built, with highly qualified assistant winemaker Kate Morgan part of the team. The wines have had richly deserved success in wine shows and journalists' reviews. Exports to the UK, Canada, Sweden, Indonesia and Singapore.

TTTTT Margaret River Semillon Sauvignon Blanc 2016 Partial barrel fermentation embroiders the already powerful and deep flavours with an extra degree of texture and complexity; the flavours are predominantly on the green bean/grass/snow pea side, augmented by the coiled spring of acidity. Screwcap. 12.5% alc. Rating 95 To 2023 $24 ○
Parterre Margaret River Semillon Sauvignon Blanc 2015 A 50/50% blend that spent 10 months in French oak and stainless steel. Its complexity extends from the first whiff through to the finish and aftertaste, deriving in part from the spread of fruit flavours (citrus, tropical and white peach) and the carefully managed oak. The suggestion of white Bordeaux whispers in the wings. Screwcap. 12% alc. Rating 95 To 2018 $35 ○
Margaret River Chardonnay 2016 One of the more elegant and restrained Margaret River chardonnays, the accent on the very high quality fruit grown on the immaculate estate vineyards, not on winemaker Clive Otto's thumbprints. The flavours are more in the white peach/nectarine spectrum than citrus until the parting shot of citrussy acidity. Screwcap. 13% alc. Rating 95 To 2023 $26 ○
Parterre Margaret River Chardonnay 2016 With its grapefruit, nectarine, nutty and gentle vanilla aromas (from 10 months in 30% new French oak), there is a lot to like about this wine. The palate is equally good, and despite the initial richness, there is a nice line of acidity that runs through the wine, keeping it perfectly balanced. Screwcap. 13.5% alc. Rating 95 To 2022 $39 PR
Parterre Margaret River Semillon Sauvignon Blanc 2016 A blend of 73% semillon and 27% sauvignon blanc that spent 10 months in a mix of French oak and 265l stainless steel barrels, this a lovely example of the style. With its gentle stone fruit and freshly cut grass aromas, it manages to be simultaneously textured, racy, restrained and long. Screwcap. 12.5% alc. Rating 94 To 2022 $35 PR

TTTTY Misceo 2015 Rating 93 To 2025 $30
Palladian Cabernet Sauvignon 2015 Rating 91 To 2028 $88 PR

Freeman Vineyards ★★★★☆

101 Prunevale Road, Prunevale, NSW 2587 **Region** Hilltops
T (02) 6384 4299 **www**.freemanvineyards.com.au **Open** By appt
Winemaker Dr Brian Freeman, Xanthe Freeman **Est.** 2000 **Dozens** 5000 **Vyds** 173ha
Dr Brian Freeman spent much of his life in research and education, in the latter role as head of CSU's viticulture and oenology campus. In 2004 he purchased the 30-year-old Demondrille vineyard. He has also established a vineyard next door, and in all has 22 varieties that range from staples such as shiraz, cabernet sauvignon, semillon and riesling through to more exotic, trendy varieties such as tempranillo, and on to corvina, rondinella and harslevelu.

ΨΨΨΨΨ **Robusta Corvina 2012** This is a beguiling wine, with plenty of dried extract in the vein of Amarone, the forceful dried grape wine from Italy's Veneto region. Dried fig, orange rind, black fruits of every description and a resounding echo of thyme on the finish are chiselled by firm dusty tannins and bright, slaking acidity. Long, tactile and ageworthy. Screwcap. 19.5% alc. **Rating** 95 $55 NG
Secco Rondinella Corvina 2012 Harvested late Apr–early May; part dried slowly for 10 days, the desiccated grapes added to the remaining hand-picked grapes; matured post-ferment in used oak prior to bottling in '14, then cellared for 2 years prior to release. It has a fragrant bouquet and a vibrant palate, its acidity more obvious than its alcohol, and notes of morello cherry rather than (for example) plums. **Rating** 94 **To** 2025 $40

ΨΨΨΨΨ **Rondo Rondinella Rose 2016 Rating** 93 **To** 2018 $20 **✪**
Sangiovese 2015 Rating 93 **To** 2023 $30 NG
Tempranillo 2013 Rating 93 **To** 2021 $25 NG **✪**
Corona Corvina Rondinella 2015 Rating 91 **To** 2020 $20 **✪**
Dolcino 2015 Rating 91 **To** 2019 $25 CM

Freycinet   ★★★★★

15919 Tasman Highway via Bicheno, Tas 7215 **Region** East Coast Tasmania
T (03) 6257 8574 **www**.freycinetvineyard.com.au **Open** details on the website
Winemaker Claudio Radenti, Lindy Bull **Est.** 1969 **Dozens** 9000 **Vyds** 15.9ha
The Freycinet vineyards are situated on the sloping hillsides of a small valley. The soils are brown dermosol on top of Jurassic dolerite, and the combination of aspect, slope, soil and heat summation produces red grapes with unusual depth of colour and ripe flavours. One of the foremost producers of pinot noir, with an enviable track record of consistency – rare in such a temperamental variety. The Radenti (sparkling), Riesling and Chardonnay are also wines of the highest quality. In 2012 Freycinet acquired part of the neighbouring Coombend property from Brown Brothers. The 42ha property extends to the Tasman Highway, and includes a 5.75ha mature vineyard and a 4.2ha olive grove. Exports to the UK and Singapore.

ΨΨΨΨΨ **Pinot Noir 2015** From the original plantings, hand-picked, 5% whole bunches, the remainder crushed and destemmed; roto-fermented for 8 days, then matured in French oak (27% new) for 12 months. The colour and bouquet are good, the palate another thing again, soaring with its energy and drive, its length prodigious. Complex, earthy dark fruits are tied together by savoury pinot tannins of the highest quality. Screwcap. 14.5% alc. **Rating** 97 **To** 2026 $70 **✪**

ΨΨΨΨΨ **Riesling 2016** A fine example of Tasmanian riesling, the variety that robustly challenges chardonnay's claim to be the leading white variety of the island. The acidity is a given, but there is totally delicious lime juice flavour in abundance, and even a hint of passionfruit. Screwcap. 13% alc. **Rating** 96 **To** 2031 $30 **✪**
Louis Pinot Noir 2015 From blocks planted in '95 adjacent to the original plantings, roto-fermented, matured for 10 months in French oak. Excellent clarity of colour; dark cherry, savoury, earthy, bramble characters are framed by French oak. This is still resolutely primary, albeit very long, and will open up over the next 5 years, kicking on thereafter. Screwcap. 14.5% alc. **Rating** 95 **To** 2030 $37
Chardonnay 2015 Fermented in French oak, lees-stirred. A very intense bouquet and palate with pink grapefruit to the fore and figgy/creamy/nutty notes to the rear. Interesting wine, probably best over the next few years. Screwcap. 13.5% alc. **Rating** 94 **To** 2021 $42

ΨΨΨΨΨ **Wineglass Bay Sauvignon Blanc 2016 Rating** 93 **To** 2018 $29
Cabernet Merlot 2013 Rating 93 **To** 2028 $36
Radenti Chardonnay Pinot Noir 2011 Rating 92 **To** 2019 $65 TS

Frogmore Creek

699 Richmond Road, Cambridge, Tas 7170 **Region** Southern Tasmania
T (03) 6248 4484 **www**.frogmorecreek.com.au **Open** 7 days 10–5
Winemaker Alain Rousseau, John Bown **Est.** 1997 **Dozens** 40 000 **Vyds** 55ha
Frogmore Creek is a Pacific Rim joint venture, the owners being Tony Scherer of Tasmania and Jack Kidwiler of California. The business has grown very substantially, first establishing its own organically managed vineyard, and thereafter by a series of acquisitions. First was the purchase of the Hood/Wellington Wines business; next was the purchase of the large Roslyn Vineyard near Campania; and finally (in Oct 2010) the acquisition of Meadowbank Estate, where the cellar door is now located. In Dec '12 the original Frogmore Creek vineyard was sold to Hill-Smith Family Vineyards. Exports to the US, NZ, Japan and China.

♟♟♟♟♟ **Methode Traditionelle Cuvee 2010** Pinot noir (88%) declares its grand presence in a full straw-yellow hue and dramatic brushstrokes of deep red cherry and mirabelle plum fruit. 7 years of age have built captivating layers of butterscotch, brioche, vanilla and glace fig. Yet for all its complexity and succulent richness, it pulls seamlessly into a vibrant and honed tail of bright southern Tasmanian acidity, perfectly balanced by intimately integrated dosage. It exudes persistence, stamina and sheer jubilation. Diam. 12.2% alc. **Rating** 95 **To** 2020 TS

♟♟♟♟♟ **Winemaker's Reserve Late Disgorged Cuvee 2004 Rating** 93 **To** 2018 TS
42°S Pinot Grigio 2016 Rating 91 **To** 2018 $26 PR
Meadowbank Blanc de Blancs 2011 Rating 90 **To** 2018 $45 TS
Meadowbank Chardonnay Pinot Noir NV Rating 90 **To** 2017 $32 TS

Gaelic Cemetery Wines

PO Box 54, Sevenhill, SA 5453 **Region** Clare Valley
T (08) 8843 4370 **www**.gaelic-cemeterywines.com **Open** Not
Winemaker Neil Pike, Steve Baraglia **Est.** 2005 **Dozens** 1500 **Vyds** 6.5ha
This is a joint venture between winemaker Neil Pike, viticulturist Andrew Pike and Adelaide retailers Mario and Ben Barletta. It hinges on a single vineyard owned by Grant Arnold, planted in 1996, adjacent to the historic cemetery of the region's Scottish pioneers. Situated in a secluded valley of the Clare hills, the low-cropping vineyard, say the partners, 'is always one of the earliest ripening shiraz vineyards in the region and mystifyingly produces fruit with both natural pH and acid analyses that can only be described as beautiful numbers'. The result is hands-off winemaking. Exports to all major markets.

♟♟♟♟♟ **Premium Clare Valley Riesling 2016** Fermented with wild and cultured yeast. The difference between this and Celtic Farm is striking: while there is an abundance of fruit, this has greater structure and texture, its minerally acidity bolder. Has all the ingredients to develop into a great riesling with a minimum of 5 years in bottle. Screwcap. 11% alc. **Rating** 96 **To** 2036 $36 ✪
Celtic Farm Clare Valley Riesling 2016 Made as an approachable wine for early consumption, but notched up gold medals at the Clare Valley Wine Show and the Canberra International Riesling Competition. The bouquet and palate exude lime and Meyer lemon fruit, but there is also good acidity. Screwcap. 11% alc. **Rating** 95 **To** 2026 $23 ✪
Premium Clare Valley Shiraz 2013 A powerful and rich wine that has found some chocolate buried in the soil, bringing a complex suite of flavours and extra length to the palate. A very well composed wine with an unexpected lightness of foot on the palate. Cork. 14.5% alc. **Rating** 95 **To** 2038 $45

♟♟♟♟ **Celtic Farm Clare Valley Shiraz Cabernet 2014 Rating** 89 **To** 2021 $23

Gala Estate

14891 Tasman Highway, Cranbrook, Tas 7190 **Region** East Coast Tasmania
T 0408 681 014 **www**.galaestate.com.au **Open** 7 days 10–4 (closed winter)
Winemaker Greer Carland, Glen James **Est.** 2009 **Dozens** 3500 **Vyds** 11ha
This vineyard is situated on a 4000ha sheep station, with the sixth, seventh and eighth generations, headed by Robert and Patricia (Amos) Greenhill, custodians of the land granted to Adam Amos in 1821; it is recognised as the second-oldest family business in Tasmania. The 11ha vineyard is heavily skewed to pinot noir (7ha), the remainder planted (in descending order of area) to chardonnay, pinot gris, riesling, shiraz and sauvignon blanc. The main risk is spring frost, and overhead spray irrigation serves two purposes: it provides adequate moisture for early season growth, and frost protection at the end of the growing season.

ΨΨΨΨΨ Estate Pinot Noir 2015 Deep colour; bring it on: this has more pinot fruit per square inch than almost any other wine in its class. Essence of black cherry and plum is magically lightened by the spray of spices and fine, foresty/savoury tannins that run through the majestically long palate and aftertaste. French oak? Yes, that too. Screwcap. 13.4% alc. **Rating** 97 **To** 2025 $45 **☉**

ΨΨΨΨΨ Riesling 2016 A riveting riesling, its perfumed bouquet full of citrus blossom, coming into full flower on the lime-driven palate, finishing with perfectly balanced, but incisive, acidity. The aftertaste lingers long, making another mouthful mandatory. Screwcap. 11.5% alc. **Rating** 96 **To** 2031 $30 **☉**
Estate Pinot Noir 2014 Deep colour typical of Gala; complex, brooding, rich and sensual, clearly grown on a special vineyard. Satsuma plum, kirsch, spices and fine tannins are all on uninhibited display. A long future ahead. Screwcap. 14% alc. **Rating** 95 **To** 2030 $45
Late Harvest Riesling 2016 Natural Tasmanian acidity means this style can be produced almost at will, the essential flavour of riesling raised onto another level of intensity and length while retaining balance and length. Rose's lime juice in a screwcapped bottle that just happens to have a gentle amount of alcohol. 8.9% alc. **Rating** 95 **To** 2026 $35 **☉**
Pinot Gris 2016 Tasmania may be reticent about its sauvignon blancs, but it has long been one of the best regions for pinot gris. Here the flavours take in white flesh stone fruit and citrus as well as pear, natural acidity providing all the structure needed. Screwcap. 13.2% alc. **Rating** 94 **To** 2020 $30 **☉**

ΨΨΨΨ Sauvignon Blanc 2016 Rating 89 **To** 2017 $30

Galafrey

Quangellup Road, Mount Barker, WA 6324 **Region** Mount Barker
T (08) 9851 2022 **www**.galafreywines.com.au **Open** 7 days 10–5
Winemaker Kim Tyrer **Est.** 1977 **Dozens** 3500 **Vyds** 13.1ha
The Galafrey story began when Ian and Linda Tyrer gave up high-profile jobs in the emerging computer industry and arrived in Mount Barker to start growing grapes and making wine, the vine-change partially prompted by their desire to bring up their children-to-be in a country environment. The dry-grown vineyard they planted continues to be the turning point, the first winery established in an ex-whaling building (long since replaced by a purpose-built winery). The premature death of Ian at a time when the industry was buckling at the knees increased the already considerable difficulties the family had to deal with, but deal with it they did. Daughter Kim Tyrer is now CEO of the business, with Linda still very much involved in the day-to-day management of Galafrey. Exports to China.

ΨΨΨΨΨ Dry Grown Vineyard Mount Barker Riesling 2016 Super dry with a dash of lemon–lime juice, it's also slatey and steely, racy and lean with its bracingly fresh chalky acidity ensuring great length. Plus it'll be oh so age-worthy. Screwcap. 12% alc. **Rating** 95 **To** 2027 $25 JF **☉**

🍷🍷🍷🍷🍷 Dry Grown Vineyard Mount Barker Shiraz 2014 Rating 91 To 2022 $30 JF
Dry Grown Vineyard Mount Barker Cabernet Sauvignon 2014 Rating 91
To 2021 $30 JF

Galli Estate ★★★★★

1507 Melton Highway, Plumpton, Vic 3335 **Region** Sunbury
T (03) 9747 1444 **www**.galliestate.com.au **Open** 7 days 11–5
Winemaker Ben Ranken **Est.** 1997 **Dozens** 10 000 **Vyds** 160ha
Galli Estate has two vineyards: Heathcote, which produces the red wines (Shiraz, Sangiovese, Nebbiolo, Tempranillo, Grenache and Montepulciano), and the cooler climate vineyard at Plumpton, producing the whites (Chardonnay, Pinot Grigio, Sauvignon Blanc and Fiano). All wines are biodynamically estate-grown and made, with wine movements on the new moon. Exports to Canada, Singapore, China and Hong Kong.

🍷🍷🍷🍷🍷 **Pamela 2016** The four Burgundy chardonnay clones, 76, 95, 96 and 227, whole-bunch pressed direct to French oak (33% new). The wine has the concentration, power and length expected of its clonal and cool-grown regional make-up. It is surprising that it has achieved so much character at its low alcohol level. Screwcap. 12% alc. **Rating** 95 **To** 2023 $55
Adele Nebbiolo 2013 Hand-picked, 100% whole berries, 5 days cold soak, wild-yeast fermented, 70 days on skins, matured for 18 months in used French oak. Light, but bright hue; a remarkable nebbiolo, for it has good varietal character and, thanks to its 10-week maceration, its tannins are fine. Having achieved all this, will live on, and on. Screwcap. 14.8% alc. **Rating** 95 **To** 2033 $38

🍷🍷🍷🍷🍷 **Adele Chardonnay 2015** Rating 93 To 2022 $38
Adele Syrah 2015 Rating 93 To 2030 $38
Camelback Heathcote Sangiovese 2015 Rating 92 To 2025 $20 ✪
Artigiano Block Two Heathcote Shiraz 2015 Rating 91 To 2025 $30
Camelback Sunbury Cabernet Sauvignon Merlot 2015 Rating 91
To 2023 $20 ✪
Adele Sangiovese 2015 Rating 91 To 2023 $38
Adele Fiano 2015 Rating 90 To 2020 $38

Gallows Wine Co ★★★★

Lennox Road, Carbunup River, WA 6280 **Region** Margaret River
T (08) 9755 1060 **www**.gallows.com.au **Open** 7 days 10–5
Winemaker Charlie Maiolo, Neil Doddridge **Est.** 2008 **Dozens** 11 000 **Vyds** 27ha
This is the venture of the Maiolo family, headed by winemaker Charlie. The macabre name is that of one of the most famous surf breaks on the Margaret River coast. The vineyard is planted to semillon, sauvignon blanc, chardonnay, pinot noir, shiraz, merlot and cabernet sauvignon. The site climate is strongly influenced by Geographe Bay, 5km to the north, and facilitates the production of wines with a large spectrum of flavours and characteristics.

🍷🍷🍷🍷🍷 **The Bommy Margaret River Shiraz 2014** Offers fresh, juicy blackberry aromas on the bouquet, aligned with the typically gamey/savoury twang that is so often seen in Margaret River shiraz. Shows real energy on the palate, with red and black fruit flavours bounding along, buoyant and lively, reined in by a measure of tarry tannin. It has plenty of drink-now appeal, so cellaring is an option more than a necessity. Screwcap. 13.5% alc. **Rating** 93 **To** 2024 $31 SC
The Bommy Margaret River Shiraz 2013 The bright colour sends the message of the juicy, bright red and black cherry fruit plus a wisp of blackberry juice. A wine that makes only one request: drink over the next 3–4 years while all that freshness is in full flower. Screwcap. 13.5% alc. **Rating** 93 **To** 2023 $31
The Bommy Margaret River Cabernet Sauvignon 2014 Matured for 18 months in French and American oak. The fragrant red-fruited bouquet pays respect to the perfect alcohol and medium-bodied palate. This in no way

diminishes the texture of the wine in the mouth, which is very good thanks to soft tannins and French oak. Screwcap. 13.5% alc. **Rating** 93 **To** 2030 $31

The Bommy Margaret River Chardonnay 2015 Fermented in French oak (35% new), matured for 9 months. Nectarine and peach come onto the first wave, grapefruit acidity onto the second (larger) break. The new oak component isn't obvious, but that isn't a bad thing. Screwcap. 14% alc. **Rating** 92 **To** 2023 $28

The Bommy Margaret River Semillon Sauvignon Blanc 2016 A 55/45% blend, fermented in tank. The semillon component seems even more influential than its 55%; cut grass, green pea and lemony acidity are more obvious than the lychee/gooseberry notes of the sauvignon blanc. Either way, it's a bracingly fresh and crisp wine. Screwcap. 12.5% alc. **Rating** 91 **To** 2020 $26

The Gallows Margaret River Cabernet Sauvignon Merlot 2014 The hue is good, although light; as that might suggest, the wine is only just into medium-bodied, but it does have length and intensity to its bright cassis flavours trimmed by just a touch of dried herbs. Screwcap. 14% alc. **Rating** 90 **To** 2025 $23

♥♥♥♥ Carpark Margaret River Shiraz Merlot 2014 Rating 89 To 2020 $23

Gapsted ★★★★

3897 Great Alpine Road, Gapsted, Vic 3737 **Region** Alpine Valleys
T (03) 5751 1383 **www**.gapstedwines.com.au **Open** 7 days 10–5
Winemaker Michael Cope-Williams, Toni Pla Bou, Matt Fawcett **Est.** 1997
Dozens 200 000 **Vyds** 256.1ha

Gapsted is the major brand of the Victorian Alps Winery, which started life (and continues) as a large-scale contract winemaking facility. However, the quality of the wines made for its own brand has led to the expansion of production not only under that label, but also under a raft of cheaper, subsidiary labels. As well as the substantial estate plantings, Gapsted sources traditional and alternative grape varieties from the King and Alpine Valleys. Exports to the UK, Sweden, Norway, the UAE, Thailand, Hong Kong, Singapore, China and Japan.

♥♥♥♥♡ **Valley Selection King Valley Pinot Gris 2016** 10% barrel-fermented. A more than usually intense palate, intensity translating into length, making the price grand larceny. Another arrow in the quiver of mature pinot gris vines grown in appropriate climates. Screwcap. 13.5% alc. **Rating** 92 **To** 2019 $18 ❂

Limited Release King Valley Fiano 2016 Fiano strikes once again, 10% petit manseng making the wine a unique blend, but not having the textural drive of fiano, which has deliciously edgy/savoury/sour lemon zest noes that positively sing. Screwcap. 13.5% alc. **Rating** 92 **To** 2021 $25 ❂

Limited Release Alpine Valleys Saperavi 2014 89% saperavi, 11% shiraz, fermented separately with cultured yeast, 7 days on skins, matured in used American oak for 23 months. The colour not quite as dense as might be expected: perhaps the shiraz and 23 months in oak are part of the picture. The wine itself is attractive, with medium to full-bodied black fruits that have a raw, juicy appeal. A killer for wine options games. Screwcap. 14.5% alc. **Rating** 91 **To** 2029 $31

Ballerina Canopy Cabernet Sauvignon 2013 From the Barossa Valley, Wrattonbully and the King Valley, matured in French and American oak for 17 months. The wine has clear medium-bodied varietal expression, clever use of oak and soft tannins all adding up to easygoing drinkability. Screwcap. 14.5% alc. **Rating** 90 **To** 2023 $31

Garagiste ★★★★★

4 Lawrey Street, Frankston, Vic 3199 (postal) **Region** Mornington Peninsula
T 0439 370 530 **www**.garagiste.com.au **Open** Not
Winemaker Barnaby Flanders **Est.** 2006 **Dozens** 2500 **Vyds** 3ha

Barnaby Flanders was a co-founder of Allies Wines (see separate entry) in 2003, with some of the wines made under the Garagiste label. Allies has now gone its own way, and Barnaby has a controlling interest in the Garagiste brand. The focus is on the Mornington Peninsula. The grapes are hand-sorted in the vineyard and again in the winery. Chardonnay is whole-bunch pressed, barrel-fermented with wild yeast in new and used French oak, mlf variably used, 8–9 months on lees. Seldom fined or filtered. Exports to Singapore, Hong Kong and China.

ȲȲȲȲȲ **Merricks Mornington Peninsula Chardonnay 2015** Like the crescendo of Nessun Dorma, sung by Pavarotti, this soars and the length goes on and on. To get there, there's a balance of grapefruit, pith and white stone fruit, flinty, gingery and peppery. The oak adds another layer of complexity, as does the lees character. You won't want to come down. Screwcap. 13% alc. **Rating** 97 **To** 2025 $45 JF ✪
Terre de Feu Mornington Peninsula Pinot Noir 2015 This is a stunning wine. Fruit off the Merricks Grove vineyard, 100% whole bunches, wild yeast ferment, aged 10 months in French hogsheads (50% new). Utterly compelling and highly delicious. Earthy rhubarb and beetroot fragrance with star anise, cinnamon quills and Tuscan prosciutto lead to black cherries and pips with blood orange. On the full-bodied palate the tannins hold sway – ripe, smoky and powerful, with refreshing acidity to close. Screwcap. 13.5% alc. **Rating** 97 **To** 2030 $75 JF ✪

ȲȲȲȲȲ **Le Stagiaire Mornington Peninsula Chardonnay 2016** Sets the pulse racing with its linearity, crisp acidity and extraordinary length. But there's a wealth of flavour too – the white stone fruit, citrus zest and juice, the kick of spice and just the right amount of lees-creamy influence to add another layer of complexity but not weight. Oh, and a bargain. Screwcap. 13% alc. **Rating** 96 **To** 2026 $30 JF ✪
Merricks Mornington Peninsula Pinot Noir 2015 Small open fermenters, wild yeast, 22 days on skins, French oak hogsheads (25% new), for 10 months. It's sapid and tastes as if there are whole bunches in it. It's a savoury, meaty wine, and earthy-toned, yet has a core of dark cherries and plums, with some power and grit. Screwcap. 13.5% alc. **Rating** 96 **To** 2026 $45 JF ✪
Le Stagiaire Mornington Peninsula Rose 2016 Well, look at this. A proper rose with flavour depth and super dry. A pale morello-cherry-salmon-pink, and crisp, yet there's texture, a hint of watermelon and rind, zesty lemony mouthwatering acidity. Screwcap. 13% alc. **Rating** 95 **To** 2020 $29 JF ✪
Le Stagiaire Mornington Peninsula Pinot Gris 2016 A mid-straw-copper-pink hue and packed with flavour – not too much. The right amount of spiced pears drizzled with honey, creamy lees and grilled nuts. And a neat line of acidity keeping the wine dancing along to a persistent finish. Screwcap. 13.5% alc. **Rating** 94 **To** 2021 $29 JF ✪
Le Stagiaire Mornington Peninsula Pinot Noir 2016 It's wrong, in a way, to call this the entry-level wine, but as point of comparison it will have to do. A selection of fruit from the four sites, destemmed with a small portion of whole bunches, wild yeast and aged in French oak hogsheads 10% new for 10 months. It ticks all the boxes – flavour, balance, neatly etched tannins with some grip on the finish, lightly spiced, just shy of full-bodied and ready to rock 'n roll. Screwcap. 13.5% alc. **Rating** 94 **To** 2025 $30 JF ✪
Balnarring Mornington Peninsula Pinot Noir 2015 Almost identical winemaking with the Merricks wine, so this turns out to be a contrast in the vineyards. A plusher, riper fruit profile here and a different feel to the acidity and tannin structure – grip and power. The dark fruit is studded with cloves and licorice, with wafts of cured meats and dried herbs. Screwcap. 13.5% alc. **Rating** 94 **To** 2025 $45 JF

Garners Heritage Wines   ★★★★

54 Longwood/Mansfield Road, Longwood East, Vic 3666 **Region** Strathbogie Ranges
T (03) 5798 5513 **www.**garnerswine.com.au **Open** W'ends 11–4, 0410 649 030
Winemaker Lindsay Brown **Est.** 2005 **Dozens** 500 **Vyds** 1.8ha
Leon and Rosie Garner established Garners Heritage Wine in 2005, celebrating their tenth anniversary in '15. The 1.8ha boutique vineyard may be small, and the newest in the Strathbogie Ranges, but it has produced high class Shirazs. Although the region is classified as

cool climate, the property is at the base of the mountain range, where the warm summers are ideal for growing shiraz. A very small amount is exported to Hong Kong.

🍷🍷🍷🍷🍷 **Leon's Strathbogie Ranges Shiraz 2015** This wine was deliberately made from very ripe grapes, reflecting the late Leon Garner's wish to make a bigger wine, spending 17 months in French puncheons (40% new) and used French and American oak. Right now, the wine isn't open for business, and it may be some years before it is. Screwcap. 15.5% alc. **Rating** 90 **To** 2035

Gartelmann Wines

701 Lovedale Road, Lovedale, NSW 2321 **Region** Hunter Valley
T (02) 4930 7113 **www**.gartelmann.com.au **Open** Mon–Sat 10–5, Sun 10–4
Winemaker Jorg Gartelmann, Liz Silkman **Est.** 1970 **Dozens** 7000
In 1996 Jan and Jorg Gartelmann purchased what was previously the George Hunter Estate – 16ha of mature vineyards, most established by Oliver Shaul in '70. In a change of emphasis, the vineyard was sold, and Gartelmann now sources its grapes from the Hunter Valley and other NSW regions, including the cool Rylstone area in Mudgee. Exports to the US, Germany, Singapore and China.

🍷🍷🍷🍷🍷 **Diedrich Orange Shiraz 2015** This soars with pretty aromas of florals, red-berried fruits, a dusting of spice and is equally rewarding on the palate. An elegant wine, medium-weighted, with supple, sleek tannins, crisp, lemony acidity and plenty of joy in between. Really hard to put down. Screwcap. 14.6% alc. **Rating** 95 **To** 2030 $50 JF

🍷🍷🍷🍷🍷 **Phillip Alexander Mudgee Cabernet 2015** **Rating** 93 **To** 2022 $28 JF
Jonathan Mudgee Cabernet Sauvignon 2015 **Rating** 93 **To** 2028 $35 JF
Rylstone Petit Verdot 2015 **Rating** 93 **To** 2026 $35 JF
Benjamin Hunter Valley Semillon 2014 **Rating** 91 **To** 2025 $35 JF
Stephanie Orange Pinot Gris 2016 **Rating** 91 **To** 2017 $25 JF
Diedrich Hunter Clare Valley Shiraz 2011 **Rating** 90 **To** 2028 $50 JF

Gatt Wines

417 Boehms Springs Road, Flaxman Valley, SA 5235 **Region** Eden Valley
T (08) 8564 1166 **www**.gattwines.com **Open** Not
Winemaker David Norman **Est.** 1972 **Dozens** 8000 **Vyds** 53.35ha
When you read the hyperbole that sometimes accompanies the acquisition of an existing wine business, about transforming it into a world-class operation, it is easy to sigh and move on. When Ray Gatt acquired Eden Springs, he proceeded to translate words into deeds. As well as the 19.82ha Eden Springs Vineyard, he also acquired the historic Siegersdorf Vineyard (19.43ha) on the Barossa floor, and the neighbouring Graue Vineyard (11.4ha). The change of name from Eden Springs to Gatt Wines in 2011 was sensible. Exports to Denmark, Germany, South Korea, Japan, Macau, Hong Kong and China.

🍷🍷🍷🍷🍷 **Eden Springs High Eden Shiraz 2010** The gently aromatic bouquet and medium-bodied palate have red cherry, raspberry, spice and pepper that gain intensity as the wine travels through to the long, lingering finish and aftertaste. A gold medal at Monaco Women and Wines of the World is a needless (and dubious) distinction for a lovely wine. Cork. 13.5% alc. **Rating** 95 **To** 2030 $40
Eden Springs High Eden Riesling 2015 Estate-grown wine from a vineyard with an altitude of 46–513m. The flavour register is in a super-generous lime citrus spectrum, enhanced by crisp, minerally acidity. Screwcap. 12% alc. **Rating** 94 **To** 2027 $30 ✪

Gembrook Hill

Launching Place Road, Gembrook, Vic 3783 **Region** Yarra Valley
T (03) 5968 1622 **www**.gembrookhill.com.au **Open** By appt
Winemaker Timo Mayer, Andrew Marks **Est.** 1983 **Dozens** 1500 **Vyds** 5ha
Ian and June Marks established Gembrook Hill, one of the oldest vineyards in the coolest part
of the Upper Yarra Valley. Son Andrew assists Timo Mayer on the winemaking front, each also
having his own label (see separate entries for The Wanderer and Mayer). The northeast-facing
vineyard is in a natural amphitheatre; the low-yielding sauvignon blanc, chardonnay and pinot
noir are not irrigated. The minimal approach to winemaking produces wines of a consistent
style with finesse and elegance. Exports to the UK, the US, Denmark, Japan and Malaysia.

🍷🍷🍷🍷🍷 **Yarra Valley Chardonnay 2016** Estate-grown and barrel-fermented. Shows the
intensity and extreme length of Upper Yarra fruit, pink grapefruit and white peach
sharing the limelight with its current of highwire acidity, oak simply a conveyance.
Diam. 13.5% alc. **Rating** 95 **To** 2025 $40
Yarra Valley Pinot Noir 2015 From 33yo dry-grown estate vines. It takes its
time getting into its stride, the bouquet clean but reticent in showing its gently
spiced red fruits, the palate upping the ante into satsuma plum and red cherry
fruits. Even here it has its skirts wrapped around its ankles, but the future is assured.
Diam. 13.5% alc. **Rating** 94 **To** 2030 $55

🍷🍷🍷🍷🍷 **Yarra Valley Sauvignon Blanc 2015** **Rating** 92 **To** 2017 $33
Yarra Valley Pinot Noir 2014 **Rating** 91 **To** 2020 $55
Blanc de Blancs 2011 **Rating** 91 **To** 2026 $55 TS
Yarra Valley Sauvignon Blanc 2016 **Rating** 90 **To** 2018 $34

Gemtree Wines

167 Elliot Road, McLaren Flat, SA 5171 **Region** McLaren Vale
T (08) 8323 8199 **www**.gemtreewines.com **Open** 7 days 10–5
Winemaker Mike Brown, Joshua Waechter **Est.** 1998 **Dozens** 90 000 **Vyds** 138.47ha
Gemtree is a family-owned winery dedicated to growing better wine – naturally. Paul and Jill
Buttery established the Gemtree vineyards in McLaren Vale in 1980. Now their son Andrew
runs the business, their daughter Melissa Brown is the viticulturist and her husband Mike
is the chief winemaker. The vineyards are certified organic and farmed biodynamically, and
the wine portfolio is of high quality. Exports to the UK, the US, Canada, Sweden, Denmark,
Norway, Finland, Hong Kong, China and NZ.

🍷🍷🍷🍷🍷 **McLaren Vale Grenache 2016** This is a radically alternative paradigm to
many of this estate's wines. Succulent and expansive across the palate with red
currant, pomegranate, strawberry and flavours of cherry soused in spirit, this
medium-bodied, delicately textured grenache is given a rasp of briar, an inflection
of reduction and a lick of cardamom and exotic clove on the finish. From both
organic and fully fledged biodynamically farmed vineyards, this is very good and
brimming with drinkability. Cork. 14.5% alc. **Rating** 95 **To** 2024 $50 NG
Amatrine McLaren Vale Savagnin Chardonnay 2015 A quirky blend that
hits all the right notes on the drinkability scale. A saline perk of oyster shell gives
lift to a whiff of apricot and chamomile, reminiscent somehow of a quaffing
Chablis. At 60% savagnin, the blend is pierced by a skein of chalky acidity, leaving
an overall impression of a tactile, savoury dryness. A versatile wine at the table.
Screwcap. 13.2% alc. **Rating** 95 **To** 2022 $7 NG ✪

🍷🍷🍷🍷🍷 **The Phantom Red 2014** **Rating** 93 **To** 2028 $42 SC
Cinnabar McLaren Vale GSM 2016 **Rating** 92 **To** 2024 $25 NG ✪
Dragon's Blood Cabernet Sauvignon 2016 **Rating** 92 **To** 2029 $16 NG ✪
The Phantom Red 2015 **Rating** 92 **To** 2025 $45 NG
Uncut McLaren Vale Shiraz 2015 **Rating** 91 **To** 2020 $30 NG
Dragon's Blood McLaren Vale Shiraz 2015 **Rating** 91 **To** 2023 $16 NG ✪
Moonstone McLaren Vale Savagnin 2016 **Rating** 90 **To** 2020 $20 NG ✪

Luna de Fresa Tempranillo Rose 2016 **Rating** 90 **To** 2018 $20 NG ✪
Luna Roja McLaren Vale Tempranillo 2015 **Rating** 90 **To** 2022 $28 SC
Aprils Dance Sparkling NV **Rating** 90 **To** 2017 $30 TS

Geoff Merrill Wines ★★★★★

291 Pimpala Road, Woodcroft, SA 5162 **Region** McLaren Vale
T (08) 8381 6877 **www**.geoffmerrillwines.com.au **Open** Mon–Fri 10–4.30, Sat 12–4.30
Winemaker Geoff Merrill, Scott Heidrich **Est.** 1980 **Dozens** 55 000 **Vyds** 45ha

If Geoff Merrill ever loses his impish sense of humour or his zest for life, high and not-so-high, we shall all be the poorer. The product range consists of three tiers: premium (varietal); Reserve, being the older wines, reflecting the desire for elegance and subtlety of this otherwise exuberant winemaker; and, at the top, Henley Shiraz. Exports to all major markets.

🍷🍷🍷🍷🍷 Henley McLaren Vale Shiraz 2008 One of the first to adopt a big, heavy bottle with silk screen printing. Matured for 35 months in French oak, bottled Aug '11, released Jun '17, 230 dozen made. All the components have come together in a savoury, earthy wine well into its secondary phase of development, but with unlimited ability to age gracefully. Cork. 14.5% alc. **Rating** 95 **To** 2033 $170

Jacko's McLaren Vale Shiraz 2012 Matured for 24 months in American oak (20% new). A deliciously fresh and vibrant wine underlining just how great the '12 vintage was. Multifaceted red and black berry fruits are juicy, yet have ample texture and structure. This will continue to cruise along for another decade at least. Screwcap. 14.5% alc. **Rating** 95 **To** 2027 $28 ✪

Bush Vine McLaren Vale Grenache Rose 2016 From 60–90yo vines, hand-picked, 18 hours on skins (less time on skins than previous roses), cool-fermented with cultured yeast. Given. Light magenta; red cherry/strawberry/raspberry fruits drive the bouquet and the marvellously juicy and supple palate that has exceptional length and aftertaste. Screwcap. 13.5% alc. **Rating** 94 **To** 2017 $21 ✪

🍷🍷🍷🍷 Reserve Cabernet Sauvignon 2011 **Rating** 91 **To** 2027 $45
Reserve Chardonnay 2015 **Rating** 90 **To** 2021 $35

Geoff Weaver ★★★★★

2 Gilpin Lane, Mitcham, SA 5062 (postal) **Region** Adelaide Hills
T (08) 8272 2105 **www**.geoffweaver.com.au **Open** Not
Winemaker Geoff Weaver **Est.** 1982 **Dozens** 3000 **Vyds** 12.3ha

This is the business of one-time Hardys chief winemaker Geoff Weaver. The Lenswood vineyard was established between 1982 and '88, and invariably produces immaculate Riesling and Sauvignon Blanc, and long-lived Chardonnays. The beauty of the labels ranks supreme. Exports to the UK, Hong Kong and Singapore.

🍷🍷🍷🍷🍷 Lenswood Chardonnay 2013 Hand-picked, chilled, whole-bunch pressed to French barriques (50% new) for wild yeast fermentation and lees contact, partial mlf, 12 months maturation. This is the cat's pyjamas, with its pyrotechnic display of grapefruit-driven fruit flavours, bright acidity and long finish. Is ambling surely along its development path. Screwcap. 13% alc. **Rating** 96 **To** 2023 $40 ✪

Lenswood Sauvignon Blanc 2015 Hand-picked, but otherwise conventional cold fermentation in stainless steel. A picture-perfect display of all the tropical fruits (except durian) you've ever tasted; even a Dutch master couldn't display them on a single canvas. Despite this embarrassment of riches, the palate finishes fresh and crisp. Screwcap. 13.5% alc. **Rating** 95 **To** 2017 $25 ✪

Ferus Lenswood Sauvignon Blanc 2015 Wild-yeast fermented in French barriques followed by 12 months maturation on lees in those barrels. The impact on the mouthfeel is, as intended, substantial, filling the mouth with complex, smoky overtones to the luscious sauvignon blanc fruits of the palate. In the same school as Cloudy Bay. Screwcap. 13.5% alc. **Rating** 95 **To** 2018 $42

Lenswood Riesling 2015 Hand-picked and cold-fermented in stainless steel. It's a lady in waiting: the acidity of the vintage will prove its knight in shining armour as it approaches maturity, and all its perfume and high-toned citrus fruit will appear. Screwcap. 12.5% alc. **Rating** 94 **To** 2030 $25 ♥

Lenswood Pinot Noir 2012 Has matured as expected when first tasted 3 years ago. The colour is still healthy, the red fruit flavours, a mix of juicy and savoury characters, still energise the light-bodied palate. While the drink to date remains '19, best enjoyed now. Screwcap. 12% alc. **Rating** 94 **To** 2019 $40

George Wyndham ★★★★☆

700 Dalwood Road, Dalwood, NSW 2335 **Region** Hunter Valley
T (02) 4938 3444 **www**.wyndhamestate.com **Open** Not
Winemaker Steve Meyer **Est.** 1828 **Dozens** 800 000 **Vyds** 87ha
This historic property is now merely a shopfront for the Wyndham wines. The Bin wines often surprise with their quality, representing excellent value; the Show Reserve wines, likewise, can be very good. The wines come from various parts of South Eastern Australia, sometimes specified, sometimes not. Exports to Canada, Europe and Asia.

🍷🍷🍷🍷♀ **Black Cluster Single Vineyard Hunter Valley Shiraz 2013** Brilliant purple-dark-crimson; concentrated flavours with spiced plum compote, bitumen, licorice and charry oak – lots of new oak characters of bacon and wood spice. Full-bodied, deep with tannins so dense you could carve them, but just the right amount of refreshing acidity to keep the pulse. Screwcap. 13.6% alc. **Rating** 93 **To** 2030 $70 JF

🍷🍷🍷🍷 **Founder's Reserve Langhorne Creek Shiraz 2014** Rating 89 To 2020 $22

 # Georges Wines ★★★★

32 Halifax Street, Adelaide, SA 5000 **Region** Clare Valley
T (08) 8410 9111 **www**.georges-exile.com **Open** Not
Winemaker O'Leary Walker **Est.** 2004 **Dozens** 3500 **Vyds** 10ha
This venture began with Nick George's acquisition of the Springwood Vineyard in the Armagh Valley district of the Clare Valley. The 10ha vineyard was planted between 1996 and 2000, shiraz by some distance the most important of the varieties. Nick understood the proud history of the vineyard, which for a number of years supplied Leasingham with all of its grapes. He appointed O'Leary Walker as contract winemaker, an astute move.

🍷🍷🍷🍷♀ **The Exile Clare Valley Shiraz 2013** This is a step up of intensity of fruit, forcefully reflective of the finest parcels across the estate's holdings. This bottling boasts a more velvety, plush velour than its entry-level sibling, along with palpable creamy vanillan oak pillars following 24 months in a combination of new and used French oak. There is gravitas and flow, flecked with licorice and a hint of mint. The ripe tannins are soaked in coffee liqueur. Screwcap. 14.5% alc. **Rating** 93 **To** 2028 $29 NG

Georges Exile Clare Valley Shiraz 2013 This is a plummy, full-bodied shiraz. Matured in French oak for 18 months, the freshness of this wine is admirable, especially for the bargain price. There is little in the way of after-dinner mints, which to this taster is often the bane of the Clare. Strident, plush and enjoyable. Screwcap. 15% alc. **Rating** 92 **To** 2023 $19 NG ✪

🍷🍷🍷🍷 **Georges Exile Watervale Riesling 2015** Rating 89 To 2023 $19 NG ✪

Ghost Rock Vineyard ★★★★★

1055 Port Sorrell Road, Northdown, Tas 7307 **Region** Northern Tasmania
T (03) 6428 4005 **www**.ghostrock.com.au **Open** 7 days 11–5
Winemaker Justin Arnold **Est.** 2001 **Dozens** 10 400 **Vyds** 23ha

Cate and Colin Arnold purchased the former Patrick Creek Vineyard (planted exclusively to pinot noir in 1989) in 2001. The vineyards, situated among the patchwork fields of Sassafras to the south, and the white sands of the Port Sorell Peninsula to the north, now total 23ha: pinot noir (14 clones) remains the bedrock of the plantings, with other varieties including chardonnay, pinot gris, riesling and sauvignon blanc. Son Justin has assumed winemaking responsibilities in the new 100-tonne winery, having previously plied his trade in the Yarra Valley (Coldstream Hills), Margaret River (Devil's Lair) and Napa Valley (Etude), and his wife Alicia runs the cooking school and cellar door.

ΨΨΨΨΨ **Riesling 2016** Hand-picked, cool-fermented, 5½ months on lees with stirring, a small portion matured in two 'neutral' barrels for 5 weeks. Quite apart from the painstaking vinification, it is the balance between residual sugar of 7.8g/l and titratable acidity of 9.79g/l that makes this riesling so Germanic in its personality. The wine has great length to its flinty/minerally aspect, tied to ripe lime and green apple flavours. Screwcap. 13% alc. **Rating** 96 **To** 2029 $29 ✪

Two Blocks Pinot Noir 2015 8% retained for whole-bunch inclusion in the ferments, 10 day cold soak before 50/50% wild/cultured yeast fermentation, pressed to barrel at 3° baume, matured for 11 months. The bouquet is particularly fragrant and spicy, the long palate guarded by sentinels of foresty/savoury tannins. I greatly like the style, but I suspect not all will agree with me. Screwcap. 13.5% alc. **Rating** 95 **To** 2025 $38

Small Batch Chardonnay 2016 Employs the finest grapes from the vineyard, barrel-fermented with specific cultured yeast. Picked riper than its sibling, no mlf used, but the acidity is less dominant; natural balance is achieved. Excellent length and integration of oak. Screwcap. 13.4% alc. **Rating** 94 **To** 2023 $44

The Pinots 2016 50/50% pinot meunier and pinot gris, crushed, 72 hours cold soak, wild-yeast fermented in tank. Post fermentation, one very old barrel was filled and back-blended. Pale crimson heralds a wine with a surprising level of red berry fruit flavours, the creamy texture no less surprising. Despite its fruit, it is bone dry and won't quail at the thought of more time in bottle. Screwcap. 13.6% alc. **Rating** 94 **To** 2020 $29 ✪

ΨΨΨΨΨ **Sauvignon Blanc 2016** **Rating** 93 **To** 2021 $29
Chardonnay 2016 **Rating** 93 **To** 2021 $34
Pinot Gris 2016 **Rating** 93 **To** 2019 $29

Giaconda   ★★★★★

30 McClay Road, Beechworth, Vic 3747 **Region** Beechworth
T (03) 5727 0246 **www**.giaconda.com.au **Open** By appt
Winemaker Rick Kinzbrunner **Est.** 1985 **Dozens** 3000 **Vyds** 5.5ha

These wines have a super-cult status and, given the small production, are extremely difficult to find; they are sold chiefly through restaurants and via their website. All have a cosmopolitan edge befitting Rick Kinzbrunner's international winemaking experience. The Chardonnay is one of Australia's greatest, and is made and matured in the underground wine cellar hewn out of granite. This permits gravity flow, and a year-round temperature range of 14–15°C, promising even more for the future. Exports to the UK and the US.

ΨΨΨΨΨ **Estate Vineyard Chardonnay 2015** Hand-picked, whole-bunch crushed and pressed, fermented in French oak (30% new), 100% mlf, matured for 22 months. The bouquet is very complex, yet subtle, due to ephemeral husky/creamy nuances. The sheer power of the palate is of a category unique to Giaconda (and perhaps Leeuwin Estate), for it is on you before you realise it, the acidity bright and fresh. Screwcap. 14% alc. **Rating** 98 **To** 2027 $129 ✪

Estate Vineyard Shiraz 2014 Destemmed and crushed, with some whole bunches, wild-yeast fermented on skins for an extended period, basket-pressed and transferred to French oak (40% new) for 2 years maturation. This challenges Giaconda's Chardonnay (don't get into a lather, it doesn't quite succeed) for top ranking in the stable; it has an utterly seductive mouthfeel with two strands of flavour welded together: the first black cherry and blackberry, the second

peppery/savoury/spicy notes. It is at the ultimate peak of elegance. Cork.
13.8% alc. **Rating** 98 **To** 2039 $79 ○

Nantua Les Deux Chardonnay 2015 Gleaming light green-gold; has
the hallmark complexity of all Kinzbrunner's Chardonnays. The bouquet has
reduction/struck match easily accommodated by the depth of the stone fruit,
grilled cashew and creamy flavours, in turn balanced by citrus-tinged acidity.
Screwcap. 13.8% alc. **Rating** 97 **To** 2025 $48 ○

Estate Vineyard Chardonnay 2014 Hand-picked, lightly crushed and basket-
pressed to French oak (30% new) for fermentation and ageing, up to 2 years
in barrel. Has all the opulent complexity this wine is famous for, yet has a fine
stainless steel backbone that will ensure its development over 10 years. The flavours
run through grapefruit juice and zest, grilled almond, nutty oak and minerally
acidity. Screwcap. 13.8% alc. **Rating** 97 **To** 2025 $115 ○

ΨΨΨΨΨ **Estate Vineyard Pinot Noir 2015** Crushed and whole berries and whole
bunches are open-fermented, 28 days on skins, matured for 14 months in French
oak (30% new). There is a tussle between crabapple and red cherry fruits on the
one hand, and firm, savoury tannins on the other. Rick is a realist, knowing he
can't make a pinot as good as this every year. As it is, a little more fruit sweetness
wouldn't go astray. Screwcap. 13.5% alc. **Rating** 94 **To** 2025 $89

Giant Steps   ★★★★★

336 Maroondah Highway, Healesville, Vic 3777 **Region** Yarra Valley
T (03) 5962 6111 **www.**giantstepswine.com.au **Open** Mon–Fri 11–late, w'ends 9–late
Winemaker Phil Sexton, Steve Flamsteed **Est.** 1997 **Dozens** 12 500 **Vyds** 45ha
In May 2016 the sale by Giant Steps of the Innocent Bystander brand and stock was completed.
The former Innocent Bystander restaurant and shop has been substantially remodelled to put
the focus on the high quality, single vineyard, single varietal wines in what is demonstrably a
very distinguished portfolio. Its vineyard resources comprise the Sexton Vineyard (32ha) in the
Lower Yarra and Applejack Vineyard (13ha) in the Upper Yarra, the Primavera Vineyard (8ha
in the Upper Yarra, under long-term supervised contract) and Tarraford Vineyard (8.5ha in the
Lower Yarra, under long-term lease). Exports to the UK and the US.

ΨΨΨΨΨ **Tarraford Vineyard Yarra Valley Chardonnay 2015** The fragrance of the
bouquet has the allure of great Burgundy, making you loath to leave the aromas
and move on to the palate. When you do, you won't be disappointed, for a silken
wave of luscious (all things are relative) and multifaceted stone and citrus fruits
awaits your arrival. Screwcap. 13.5% alc. **Rating** 97 **To** 2027 $45 ○

Tarraford Vineyard Yarra Valley Syrah 2015 95% whole bunch fermentation
in a single 4000l open French oak vat, matured in French puncheons (new and
used) for 18 months. This joins a distinguished band of Yarra Valley shirazs of the
highest quality from vines planted in the '70s and '80s. It is full-bodied in the best
sense, simply thanks to the intensity of the black fruit, spice, pepper and licorice
symphony of flavours. I will have been gone for generations before this wine calls
time. Screwcap. 13.8% alc. **Rating** 97 **To** 2055 $50 ○

ΨΨΨΨΨ **Lusatia Park Vineyard Yarra Valley Chardonnay 2016** Each of the '16 Giant
Steps Chardonnays was vinified in exactly the same way (wild-yeast fermented
in French puncheons, 20% new, no battonage, matured for 10 months), and each
was bottled 23 Jan '17. The Upper Yarra Valley gives the wine a finely honed
elegance, casting a spell on the mouth. It's very long, and very fine. Tasted 1 week
after bottling: hard on the wine, hard on the taster. Screwcap. 13.5% alc. **Rating** 96
To 2028 $45 ○

Applejack Vineyard Yarra Valley Pinot Noir 2016 MV6 and 114 clones,
wild-yeast fermented in open stainless steel and oak vats, 50% whole bunches,
delestage by gravity, matured in French oak (25% new) for 11 months. A highly
fragrant bouquet of red flowers and fruits leads a silky, elegant and relatively light-
bodied palate, but don't be deceived: this has the greatest symmetry and length of
the '16 Giant Steps Pinots. Screwcap. 13.8% alc. **Rating** 96 **To** 2030 $50 ○

Primavera Vineyard Yarra Valley Pinot Noir 2016 MV6 clone, wild yeast–open fermented in a stainless steel vat, 75% whole bunches, matured in French oak (25% new) for 11 months. The bouquet is very fragrant and enticing, promising and delivering a palate with satin smooth red fruits and spices. The most juicy of the Upper Yarra pair (Applejack Vineyard is also Upper Yarra). Screwcap. 13.5% alc. Rating 96 To 2033 $50 ✪

Tarraford Vineyard Yarra Valley Chardonnay 2016 Lower Yarra Valley, with a layered texture on the palate that reflects the inherent power from its low yield. At this stage, has the greatest drive of the '16 Chardonnays, but whether it will retain that advantage is in the lap of the gods. Screwcap. 13.5% alc. Rating 95 To 2030 $45

Sexton Vineyard Yarra Valley Chardonnay 2016 This is typical of the Lower Yarra Valley; it has a particular flavour and texture on the back-palate and finish, with a faint honeysuckle/cashew note; on retasting (several times), grapefruit also struck a blow. Screwcap. 13.5% alc. Rating 95 To 2027 $45

Sexton Vineyard Yarra Valley Pinot Noir 2016 230m, MV6 clone, wild-yeast fermented in a 4000l oak vat, 20% whole bunches, matured in French oak (25% new) for 11 months. Deep colour; the bouquet breathes black cherries, dark spices, the palate the fullest, and more plummy than either Primavera or (at the other extreme) Applejack. Overall, the most powerful, but most closed/reductive of the trio. Screwcap. 13.8% alc. Rating 95 To 2035 $50

Yarra Valley Syrah 2015 Gloriously complex, starting with its dark garnet-purple hue; heady perfume of black plums, cherry pips, rosehips, florals, menthol, earth and stems. There's exuberant fruit on the structured yet very finely tuned palate – tannins gritty, ripe and textural, the acidity cleansing and the finish long and precise. Screwcap. 14% alc. Rating 95 To 2030 $35 JF ✪

🍷🍷🍷🍷🍷 Yarra Valley Pinot Noir 2016 Rating 93 To 2023 $35 NG
Yarra Valley Merlot 2015 Rating 92 To 2025 $35 NG
Yarra Valley Chardonnay 2016 Rating 91 To 2024 $35 NG

Gibson   ★★★★★

190 Willows Road, Light Pass, SA 5355 **Region** Barossa Valley
T (08) 8562 3193 **www.**gibsonwines.com.au **Open** 7 days 11–5
Winemaker Rob Gibson **Est.** 1996 **Dozens** 10000 **Vyds** 14.2ha
Rob Gibson spent much of his working life as a senior viticulturist for Penfolds, involved in research tracing the characters that particular parcels of grapes give to a wine, which left him with a passion for identifying and protecting what is left of the original vineyard plantings in Australia. He has a vineyard in the Barossa Valley at Light Pass (merlot), and one in the Eden Valley (shiraz and riesling), and also purchases grapes from McLaren Vale and the Adelaide Hills. Exports to Germany, Thailand, Hong Kong and China.

🍷🍷🍷🍷🍷 **Eden Valley Riesling 2016** The estate Burkes Hill Vineyard is extraordinarily rocky and, more importantly for riesling, east-facing. This is classic and beautiful, with exceptional balance and length riding on its magic carpet of lime and lemon fruit, rimmed with crisp acidity. Screwcap. 10.5% alc. Rating 96 To 2031 $23

The Dirtman Barossa Shiraz 2015 The back label implies that this is a blend of Barossa Valley and Eden Valley fruit. It has deep, but vibrant colour, and is full-bodied, yet magically has elegance and finesse to its mid-palate, and black cherry fruit before the firm, intense, but not dry, tannin pickup on the finish. Screwcap. 14.8% alc. Rating 96 To 2040 $33

Reserve Shiraz 2014 Includes 10% cabernet sauvignon. Open ferment, then 18 months in barrel, 67% French, 33% American. An earthy feel on the bouquet, with aromas of tar and baked soil conjuring up a sense of its warm Barossa origins. The underlying fruit has a deep, dense quality like the blackest of plums. Although supple, it has a restrained intensity which argues for a long cellar life. Screwcap. 14.5% alc. Rating 94 To 2034 $51 SC

ƯƯƯƯỢ Wilfreda Barossa Mataro Shiraz Grenache 2015 Rating 93 To 2027
$29 SC
Reserve Merlot 2013 Rating 93 To 2025 $47 SC
Discovery Road Fiano 2016 Rating 92 SC

Gilbert Family Wines ★★★★

PO Box 773, Mudgee, NSW 2850 **Region** Orange/Mudgee
T (02) 6373 1454 **www**.thegilbertsarecoming.com.au **Open** Not
Winemaker Simon and Will Gilbert **Est.** 2010 **Dozens** 3500 **Vyds** 25.81ha
For some time now Simon Gilbert has devoted himself to his consultancy and wine brokering business, Wineworks of Australia. As that business has grown, Simon has returned to the winery wearing his Wineworks of Australia hat, overseeing the winemaking of the estate-grown grapes, all exported. Separate from his consultancy business, he has established gilbert by Simon Gilbert, and makes the wines for this label at the same winery. Distribution is limited to specialist wine retailers and restaurants. Fifth and sixth generations Simon, Will and Mark Gilbert have drawn on the family history (Joseph Gilbert was among the first to plant grapes in the Eden Valley, in 1842) to produce Gilbert + Gilbert Wines (from the winery's previous name) sourced from the Eden Valley. Exports to Hong Kong and China.

ƯƯƯƯƯ Mudgee Orange Saignee Rose 2016 A sangiovese/shiraz/barbera blend
grown at 645m. Pale pink; a perfumed dried and fresh rose petal bouquet, and a
palate to match. This is quite something, with spicy/juicy fruit flavours running
through the palate like a rivulet in spring. Screwcap. 12.5% alc. **Rating** 95
To 2018 $24 ✪

ƯƯƯƯỢ Orange Shiraz 2015 Rating 93 To 2029 $36
Orange Pinot Grigio 2016 Rating 90 To 2018 $26
Barrel Select Orange Pinot Noir 2015 Rating 90 To 2022 $42
Orange Riesling RS28 2015 Rating 90 To 2020 $36

Gilberts ★★★★☆

30138 Albany Highway, Kendenup via Mount Barker, WA 6323 **Region** Mount Barker
T (08) 9851 4028 **www**.gilbertwines.com.au **Open** Fri–Mon 10–5
Winemaker West Cape Howe **Est.** 1985 **Dozens** 3000 **Vyds** 9ha
Once a part-time occupation for sheep and beef farmers Jim and Beverly Gilbert, but now a full-time and very successful one. The mature vineyard (shiraz, chardonnay, riesling and cabernet sauvignon), coupled with contract winemaking at West Cape Howe, has long produced high class riesling. The 3 Devils Shiraz is named in honour of their sons. Exports to Singapore.

ƯƯƯƯƯ Reserve Mount Barker Shiraz 2013 Gee this is good. It's fresh, not
overworked and showcases the estate's 30+yo vines with a bouquet of red fruits,
joss sticks, dark chocolate, spices and some charry oak. Medium-weighted with
savoury, fine tannins. Screwcap. 13% alc. **Rating** 95 To 2024 $30 JF ✪
Mount Barker Riesling 2016 Genteel and gentle with its delicate blend of
white and wild flowers, and Meyer lemon zest and juice with chalky acidity.
There's texture and an abundance of appeal. Approachable now, but no question it
will go some distance. Screwcap. 12% alc. **Rating** 94 To 2028 $24 JF ✪

ƯƯƯƯỢ 3 Devils Shiraz 2014 Rating 93 To 2022 $18 JF ✪
Hand Picked Chardonnay 2015 Rating 90 To 2022 $25 JF
3 Lads Cabernet Sauvignon 2014 Rating 90 To 2023 $25 JF

Gioiello Estate ★★★★☆

350 Molesworth-Dropmore Road, Molesworth, Vic 3718 **Region** Upper Goulburn
T 0437 240 502 **www**.gioiello.com.au **Open** Not
Winemaker Scott McCarthy (Contract) **Est.** 1987 **Dozens** 3500 **Vyds** 8.97ha

The Gioiello Estate vineyard was established by a Japanese company and originally known as Daiwa Nar Darak. Planted between 1987 and '96, it accounts for just under 9ha on a 400ha property of rolling hills, pastures, bushland, river flats, natural water springs and billabongs. Now owned by the Schiavello family, the vineyard continues to produce high quality wines.

ŸŸŸŸŸ **Old House Upper Goulburn Merlot 2014** Hand-picked, crushed, open-fermented, matured in French barriques for 18 months. Fragrant cherry and plum aromas lead into a palate with vibrant spicy, savoury nuances threaded through the fruits promised by the bouquet. This is merlot à la Bordeaux, with good length and balance. Screwcap. 13.5% alc. **Rating** 95 **To** 2029 $45

Old Hill Upper Goulburn Chardonnay 2015 Wild-yeast fermented in French barriques, matured for 12 months. A well made, elegant wine with good balance, length and varietal expression. Not a hair out of place, but no X-factor either. Screwcap. 13.2% alc. **Rating** 94 **To** 2023 $40

ŸŸŸŸŸ **Mt Concord Upper Goulburn Syrah 2014 Rating** 93 **To** 2029 $45

Gipsie Jack Wine Co ★★★★

1509 Langhorne Creek Road, Langhorne Creek, SA 5255 **Region** Langhorne Creek
T (08) 8537 3029 **www.**gipsiejack.com.au **Open** 7 days 10–5
Winemaker John Glaetzer, Ben Potts **Est.** 2004 **Dozens** 7000
The partners of Gipsie Jack are John Glaetzer and Ben Potts, who made a little over 500 dozen from two growers in their inaugural vintage in 2004. Glaetzer and Potts say, 'We want to make this label fun, like in the "old days". No pretentiousness, no arrogance, not even a back label. A great wine at a great price, with no discounting.' Exports to Switzerland and Singapore.

ŸŸŸŸŸ **Langhorne Creek Shiraz 2014** Full-bodied, with lots of flavour and fruit from stewed plums and currants to cedary oak, licorice and mint chocolate. There's succulence alongside the ripe, powerful tannins. Screwcap. 14% alc. **Rating** 90 **To** 2021 $18 JF ✪

Gisborne Peak ★★★☆

69 Short Road, Gisborne South, Vic 3437 **Region** Macedon Ranges
T (03) 5428 2228 **www.**gisbornepeakwines.com.au **Open** 7 days 11–5
Winemaker John Ellis **Est.** 1978 **Dozens** 2000 **Vyds** 5.5ha
Bob Nixon began the development of Gisborne Peak way back in 1978, planting his dream vineyard row by row. The tasting room has wide shaded verandahs, plenty of windows and sweeping views. The vineyard is planted to pinot noir, chardonnay, semillon, riesling and lagrein.

ŸŸŸŸŸ **Macedon Ranges Pinot Rose 2015** Looks good in the glass; salmon-pink with a faintly orange tinge. Strawberries mainly on the bouquet, less-ripe red fruits providing a contrast. Essentially dry on the palate, although the fruit sweetness softens the edges and adds mouthfeel. Flavours are subtle, but lingering, the finish defined with light astringency. Screwcap. 12.5% alc. **Rating** 90 **To** 2018 $28 SC

ŸŸŸŸ **Macedon Ranges Semillon 2014 Rating** 89 **To** 2020 $25 SC

Glaetzer Wines ★★★★★

PO Box 824, Tanunda, SA 5352 **Region** Barossa Valley
T (08) 8563 0947 **www.**glaetzer.com **Open** Not
Winemaker Ben Glaetzer **Est.** 1996 **Dozens** 15 000 **Vyds** 20ha
With a family history in the Barossa Valley dating back to 1888, Glaetzer Wines was established by Colin Glaetzer after 30 years of winemaking experience. Son Ben worked in the Hunter Valley and as a Flying Winemaker in many of the world's wine regions before returning to Glaetzer Wines and assuming the winemaking role. The wines are made with great skill and abundant personality. Exports to all major markets.

🍷🍷🍷🍷🍷 **Anaperenna 2015** 82% shiraz, 18% cabernet sauvignon from 30–100yo vines from Ebenezer, open-fermented, plunged, matured for 16 months in new French (92%) and American (8%) hogsheads. A very good example of full-bodied Barossa Valley shiraz, the cabernet simply riding shotgun; the palate has exceptional depth to its layers of black fruits, licorice, earth, oak and tannins, but emerges with perfect balance. Cork. 15% alc. **Rating** 96 **To** 2035 $52 ✪

Bishop Barossa Valley Shiraz 2015 Classic Glaetzer, full-bodied and taking no prisoners. Black fruits, licorice, dark chocolate, ripe tannins and oak are woven together so tightly it's hard to tell where one starts and/or another finishes. It's hard to deny the quality. Screwcap. 15% alc. **Rating** 95 **To** 2030 $33 ✪

Amon-Ra Unfiltered Barossa Valley Shiraz 2015 From vines 50–130yo, open-fermented, plunged, matured 16 months in new French (95%) hogsheads for 16 months. It's hard to say which of the fruit, alcohol, tannins or oak makes the biggest impact in this blockbuster wine, beyond the normal parameters of full-bodied shiraz. In the context of its style, it is difficult to criticise. Cork. 15.5% alc. **Rating** 95 **To** 2045 $100

🍷🍷🍷🍷🍷 **Wallace Barossa Valley Shiraz Grenache 2015** Rating 90 To 2021 $23

Glen Eldon Wines   ★★★★★

143 Nitschke Road, Krondorf, SA 5352 **Region** Barossa Valley
T (08) 8568 2644 **www**.gleneldonwines.com.au **Open** By appt
Winemaker Richard Sheedy **Est.** 1997 **Dozens** 6000 **Vyds** 50ha

Owners Richard and Mary Sheedy (and their four children) have established the Glen Eldon property in the Eden Valley. The shiraz and cabernet sauvignon come from their vineyards in the Barossa Valley; viognier and merlot are contract-grown; the riesling is from the Eden Valley. Exports to the US, Canada and China.

🍷🍷🍷🍷🍷 **Reserve Eden Valley Riesling 2016** Purely free-run juice and bottled early; it is tried and true, and delivers the quality of the fruit on a 24 carat plate. The intensity of lime, lemon and grapefruit flavours bowls you over, the length of the finish and aftertaste quite special. Screwcap. 11.5% alc. **Rating** 97 **To** 2036 $50

🍷🍷🍷🍷🍷 **Eight Barrels Single Vineyard Eden Valley Shiraz 2013** From a single block on the Glen Eldon homestead, and described on the back label as having chocolate, plum, spice, white pepper and silky, fine tannins. I'd add that its juicy freshness makes it taste like 13.5%, not 14.5% alcohol. ProCork. **Rating** 96 **To** 2038 $50

Eden Valley Riesling 2016 Classic lemon and lime fruit flavours establish themselves immediately the wine is tasted for the first time, and don't let go, the natural acidity holding the line exactly as it should. Screwcap. 11.5% alc. **Rating** 95 **To** 2031 $20

Baby Black Barossa Heathcote Shiraz 2014 It is fair to assume this is a 50/50% blend of a best barrel selection between Richard Sheedy and Adrian Munari. It has been matured in a mix of American and French oak for 2 years, yet the black cherry and blackberry fruit comes out on top, with ripe tannins going about their business. Screwcap. 14% alc. **Rating** 95 **To** 2034 $60

Dry Bore Barossa Shiraz 2014 A single-site selection from the Glen Eldon Vineyard. It spent 18–24 months in French and American oak, and packs a lethal punch despite its moderate alcohol. I'm happy to believe it has the balance to repay cellaring by softening its phenolics and tannins over time. Screwcap. 14% alc. **Rating** 94 **To** 2034 $30

🍷🍷🍷🍷🍷 **Barossa Cabernet Sauvignon 2013** Rating 90 To 2028 $30

Glenguin Estate   ★★★★★

Milbrodale Road, Broke, NSW 2330 **Region** Hunter Valley
T (02) 6579 1009 **www**.glenguinestate.com.au **Open** Thurs–Mon 10–5
Winemaker Robin Tedder MW, Rhys Eather **Est.** 1993 **Dozens** 2000 **Vyds** 6ha

Glenguin Estate was established by the Tedder family, headed by Robin Tedder MW, close to Broke and adjacent to Wollombi Brook. The backbone of the production comes from 24-year-old plantings of Busby clone semillon and shiraz. Tannat (1ha) and a new planting of grafted semillon, with cuttings from Braemore/HVD, complete the picture. Vineyard manager Andrew Tedder, who has considerable experience with organics and biodynamics, is overseeing the ongoing development of Glenguin's organic program.

TTTTT **Aged Release Glenguin Vineyard Semillon 2013** Just 4 years' bottle development, lifting the intensity of all the constituents, citrus to the fore. A vinous example of having one's cake and eating it, because youthful and mature flavours live happily together. Screwcap. 11% alc. **Rating** 95 **To** 2028 $35 ✪
Aged Release The Old Broke Block Semillon 2003 Here the process of development has invested the wine with flavours of honey and toast, yet the citrussy acidity provides balance. In pre-screwcap days, this wine would be (at least) tired, more likely completely stuffed. Screwcap. 11% alc. **Rating** 95 **To** 2023 $40
Aged Release Aristea Hunter Valley Shiraz 2009 Estate-grown on the Schoolhouse Block, matured in large format French oak (50% new) for 12 months. Excellent colour; settling comfortably into a leather armchair to watch the passing parade of years go by without a ripple. Purple and black fruits, bramble, earth, soft tannins and oak all contribute. Screwcap. 13.5% alc. **Rating** 95 **To** 2039 $80

TTTT **Glenguin Vineyard Semillon 2015 Rating** 89 **To** 2021 $27

Glenlofty Wines   ★★★★★
123 Warrenmang-Glenlofty Road, Glenlofty, Vic 3469 (postal) **Region** Pyrenees
T (03) 5354 8228 **www**.glenloftywines.com.au **Open** Not
Winemaker Blue Pyrenees **Est.** 1995 **Dozens** 12 000 **Vyds** 137ha
The vineyard was established by Southcorp after exhaustive soil and climate research. In August 2010 Treasury Wine Estates sold the vineyard to Canadian-based Roger Richmond-Smith and winemaking moved to Blue Pyrenees Estate. Glenlofty Wines also purchased the nearby 30ha Decameron Station, bringing the total vineyard holdings to almost 140ha.

TTTTT **The Sawmill Vineyard Pyrenees Shiraz 2015** The Sawmill Vineyard is from a single block within Glenlofty's 32 blocks – this is the first single vineyard release. It is full-bodied, with lashings of black fruits/berries supported by a swarm of tannins that are balanced by the lavish fruit. Screwcap. 14.5% alc. **Rating** 95 **To** 2035 $45
Pyrenees Shiraz 2014 Includes 5% cabernet sauvignon and 2% viognier. Vibrant crimson-purple, it has a fragrant, fruit-filled bouquet leading into an intensely flavoured, red and black-fruited medium-bodied palate. Complexity grows each time you come back to the wine. Screwcap. 14.7% alc. **Rating** 95 **To** 2034 $28 ✪
Single Vineyard Pyrenees Cabernet Sauvignon 2013 Richly varietal bouquet; cassis leading the way, with an assortment of dark fruit and a touch of bracken-like foliage in the background. Juicy mouthfeel; the red and black fruit flavours and sweet/savoury oak characters are absorbed within the texture, which is framed by insistent, fine-grained tannin. A fine example of Pyrenees cabernet in the making. Screwcap. 15% alc. **Rating** 94 **To** 2035 $24 SC ✪

TTTTT **Single Vineyard Cabernet Sauvignon 2012 Rating** 93 **To** 2030 $24 SC ✪
Single Vineyard Pyrenees Chardonnay 2015 Rating 92 **To** 2022 $24 SC ✪
Pyrenees Marsanne Roussanne 2014 Rating 92 **To** 2022 $22 SC ✪
Pyrenees Marsanne Roussanne 2015 Rating 91 **To** 2025 $28
Pyrenees Marsanne Roussanne 2013 Rating 91 **To** 2021 $22 SC ✪
Single Vineyard Pyrenees Shiraz 2013 Rating 90 **To** 2025 $22 SC
Single Vineyard Pyrenees Shiraz Viognier 2013 Rating 90 **To** 2022 $24 SC
Pyrenees Merlot 2015 Rating 90 **To** 2028 $28
Pyrenees Merlot 2012 Rating 90 **To** 2024 $22 SC

Glenwillow Wines

Bendigo Pottery, 146 Midland Highway, Epsom, Vic 3551 **Region** Bendigo
T 0428 461 076 **www**.glenwillow.com.au **Open** W'ends 11–5
Winemaker Greg Dedman, Adam Marks **Est.** 1999 **Dozens** 750 **Vyds** 2.8ha
Peter and Cherryl Fyffe began their vineyard at Yandoit Creek, 10km south of Newstead, in 1999, planting 1.8ha of shiraz and 0.3ha of cabernet sauvignon, later branching out with 0.6ha of nebbiolo and 0.1ha of barbera. The vineyard, planted on a mixture of rich volcanic and clay loam interspersed with quartz and buckshot gravel, has an elevated north-facing aspect, which minimises the risk of frost.

🍷🍷🍷🍷🍷 **Reserve Bendigo Shiraz 2014** Made by Adam Marks (The Wanderer) from the best 6 rows of the estate vineyard; hand-picked and foot-crushed in open fermenters, retaining some whole bunches in the ferment, and pressed to French oak. The colour isn't deep, but is bright, setting the scene for a medium-bodied wine that has a complex, expressive bouquet and a decidedly complex palate full of savoury and spicy characters running through the long finish and lingering aftertaste. Screwcap. 14.4% alc. **Rating** 95 **To** 2029 $60

🍷🍷🍷🍷🍷 **Sparkling Shiraz 2014** Rating 93 To 2024 $35 TS
Bendigo Nebbiolo d'Yandoit 2015 Rating 92 To 2023 $32

Goaty Hill Wines

530 Auburn Road, Kayena, Tas 7270 **Region** Northern Tasmania
T 1300 819 997 **www**.goatyhill.com **Open** 7 days 11–5
Winemaker Jeremy Dineen (Contract) **Est.** 1998 **Dozens** 5000 **Vyds** 19.5ha
Kristine Grant, Markus Maislinger and Natasha and Tony Nieuwhof are close friends from two families who moved from Victoria to make wine in the pristine climate of the Tamar Valley. Most of the estate-grown grapes are now made into the Goaty Hill brand, although they still sell some of their premium fruit to Jansz Tasmania. There aren't any goats on the property, but there is, according to the owners, a friendly collection of children and dogs.

🍷🍷🍷🍷🍷 **Sauvignon Blanc 2016** A gold medal at the Tasmanian Wine Show '17, rewarded for its harmonious fruit flavours and freshness. The winemaking was of the no-frills persuasion, but the balance is spot on. Screwcap. 13% alc. **Rating** 94 **To** 2019 $30 ✪

🍷🍷🍷🍷🍷 **Pinot Noir 2013** Rating 92 To 2023 $38
Maia 2012 Rating 91 To 2018 $42 TS
Botrytis Riesling 2016 Rating 91 $30
Pinot Gris 2016 Rating 90 To 2019 $30

Golden Ball

1175 Beechworth Wangaratta Road, Beechworth, Vic 3747 **Region** Beechworth
T (03) 5727 0284 **www**.goldenball.com.au **Open** By appt
Winemaker James McLaurin **Est.** 1996 **Dozens** 850 **Vyds** 3.2ha
There are now two vineyards, the first named Original, planted in 1996 to 1.8ha, and the Lineage vineyard of 1.4ha close-planted in 2005. The Original is planted to chardonnay, cabernet sauvignon, merlot and malbec, while in '06 Lineage was planted to shiraz, savagnin, cabernet sauvignon, petit verdot and sagrantino, with only the shiraz and savignon in commercial production, but by '18 or '19 one would expect Lineage to be moving into commercial production. Exports to Singapore.

🍷🍷🍷🍷🍷 **Saxon Beechworth Shiraz 2014** From the Lineage Vineyard, hand-picked, wild yeast–open fermented, 3–4 weeks on skins, matured in French oak (35% new) for 20 months. Combines richness and depth with elegance and balance; spicy plum cake aromas are repeated by the palate on entry, then cleansing acidity and brighter red fruits arrive on the finish and aftertaste. Diam. 14.2% alc. **Rating** 95 **To** 2034 $55

Gallice Beechworth Cabernet Merlot Malbec 2013 The wine abounds with attitude, the fruit flavours bright and fresh, redcurrant, blackcurrant and sundry spices all featuring. Dusty tannins come into the spotlight on the finish, the oak nipping at their heels. Diam. 13.8% alc. **Rating** 95 **To** 2028 $55

là-bas Beechworth Chardonnay 2015 Hand-picked Mendoza and 95 clones (50/50%), whole-bunch pressed, a cool wild yeast fermentation in French oak (35% new), matured for 18 months. Well made, but it's not the Smith Vineyard fruit any more, so it's harder to tap into X-factor sources. It's got some deliberate funk, and has length and balance. Screwcap. 13.5% alc. **Rating** 94 **To** 2025 $65

ΨΨΨΨΨ **bona fide Beechworth Savagnin 2016 Rating** 90 **To** 2024 $30

Golden Grove Estate ★★★★★

Sundown Road, Ballandean, Qld 4382 **Region** Granite Belt
T (07) 4684 1291 **www**.goldengroveestate.com.au **Open** 7 days 9–4
Winemaker Raymond Costanzo **Est.** 1993 **Dozens** 4000 **Vyds** 12.4ha
Golden Grove Estate was established by Mario and Sebastian Costanzo in 1946, producing stone fruits and table grapes. The first wine grapes (shiraz) were planted in '72, but it was not until '85, when ownership passed to (CSU graduate) son Sam and his wife Grace, that the use of the property began to change. In '93 chardonnay and merlot joined the shiraz, followed by cabernet sauvignon, sauvignon blanc and semillon. The baton has been passed down another generation to CSU graduate Ray Costanzo, who has lifted the quality of the wines remarkably, and has also planted tempranillo, durif, barbera, malbec, mourvedre, vermentino and nero d'Avola. Its consistent wine show success over recent years with alternative varieties is impressive.

ΨΨΨΨΨ **Granite Belt Vermentino 2016** 20% barrel-fermented in new oak, and a small amount of full-solids barrel-ferment semillon. The winemaking provides smoky, almost gunflint-like aromas followed by notes of green apple and pear. Excels on the palate, with lovely mouthfeel and zingy acidity carrying the fresh and vibrant flavours all the way. Screwcap. 12.5% alc. **Rating** 95 **To** 2019 $26 SC ❖

Joven Granite Belt Tempranillo 2016 This is exactly what young tempranillo should taste like: a core of juicy fruit laced with wood spice, sarsaparilla and red licorice leading onto a medium-bodied palate with neatly packed tannins and raspberry sorbet–like acidity. Fruit of the forest and exotic spices abound, along with a savoury undercurrent. Screwcap. 13.5% alc. **Rating** 95 **To** 2021 $26 JF ❖

Granite Belt Semillon 2010 Has classic semillon aromas, just beginning to show some waxy/toasty development, but still full of fresh citrus and lemongrass character. Similar theme on the palate, where brisk acidity takes a firm grip, the flavours of lemon and honeysuckle still to fully evolve. Needs yet more time. Screwcap. 11.5% alc. **Rating** 94 **To** 2025 $20 SC ❖

Granite Belt Chardonnay 2016 Crushed, held on skins overnight, wild-yeast fermented in stainless steel and new French oak. As well made as ever; the new oak is a little more obvious than expected on the bouquet, less so on the lively grapefruit/melon/white peach palate. Its intensity and length are on the money. Screwcap. 12.5% alc. **Rating** 94 **To** 2024 $26 ❖

ΨΨΨΨΨ **Granite Belt Semillon Sauvignon Blanc 2016 Rating** 93 **To** 2018 $20 SC ❖
Granite Belt Rose 2016 Rating 92 **To** 2018 $16 SC ❖
Granite Belt Mourvedre 2014 Rating 92 **To** 2024 $28 SC
Granite Belt Malbec 2014 Rating 92 **To** 2023 $28 JF
Heathcote Nero d'Avola 2015 Rating 92 **To** 2022 $28 SC
Members Only Granite Belt Sangiovese 2016 Rating 90 **To** 2020 $30

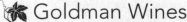 # Goldman Wines ★★★★☆

11 Ercildoune Street, Cessnock, NSW 2325 (postal) **Region** Hunter Valley
T 0467 808 316 **www**.goldmanwines.com.au **Open** Not
Winemaker Jo Marsh **Est.** 2014 **Dozens** 1500

Owner Callan Goldman grew up in the Hunter Valley, coming into contact with many of the people involved in growing grapes or making wine (or both) in the region. But his real job then and now is working as a civil engineer in northwest WA to fund his various wine production plans. Jo Marsh of Billy Button Wines made the majority of the impressive porfolio for the venture in 2015, '16 and '17. The '17 wines have been made by Jo at her new winery in the Ovens Valley.

🍷🍷🍷🍷🍷 **Hunter Valley Semillon 2014** Is in the early stages of transformation to fully fledged maturity, but is open for business (not the sometimes awkward transition), with lemon rind, juice and grass flavours on the powerful and focused palate. Quite how such quality comes from purchased grapes and contract winemaking is beyond me – this is a gift horse. Screwcap. 11.2% alc. **Rating** 94 **To** 2025 $21 ✪
Wrattonbully Cabernet Sauvignon 2012 From a perfect vintage and a quality vineyard, matured in new French oak, 70 dozen made. At the opulent end of the spectrum, particularly the impact of the oak; it's all high quality stuff (both fruit and oak), but the question is whether the oak will ever yield first place to the fruit. Screwcap. 14.5% alc. **Rating** 94 **To** 2032 $38

🍷🍷🍷🍷♀ **Beechworth Chardonnay 2013 Rating** 93 **To** 2021 $33
Hunter Valley Shiraz 2014 Rating 92 **To** 2024 $20 ✪
Hunter Valley Shiraz Viognier 2014 Rating 92 **To** 2024 $20 ✪
Hunter Valley Viognier 2014 Rating 90 **To** 2017 $17 ✪

Gomersal Wines ★★★★
203 Lyndoch Road, Gomersal, SA 5352 **Region** Barossa Valley
T (08) 8563 3611 **www**.gomersalwines.com.au **Open** 7 days 10–5
Winemaker Barry White, Peter Pollard **Est.** 1887 **Dozens** 9250 **Vyds** 20ha
The 1887 establishment date has a degree of poetic licence. In 1887 Friedrich W Fromm planted the Wonganella Vineyards, following that with a winery on the edge of the Gomersal Creek in '91; it remained in operation for 90 years, finally closing in 1983. In 2000 a group of friends 'with strong credentials in both the making and consumption ends of the wine industry' bought the winery and re-established the vineyard, planting 17ha of shiraz, 2ha of mourvedre and 1ha of grenache. Exports to The Netherlands, South Korea, Singapore and China.

🍷🍷🍷🍷♀ **Reserve Barossa Valley Shiraz 2013** Deep, dense, but bright crimson-purple; a very full-bodied shiraz of great character and good quality. You can't help but wonder how good it might have been with 14% alcohol and 2 years in French (not American) oak, but it leads nowhere. At this price you shouldn't quibble. Screwcap. 15% alc. **Rating** 93 **To** 2043 $25 ✪
Cellar Door Release Barossa Valley Mataro 2013 A super-generous, super-full-bodied and super-low-priced wine, 29 months in second-use hogsheads; a rigid barrel selection meant only 162 dozen were released. Its oak and tannin profile should encourage you to buy as much as possible and drink as little as possible before (say) '23. Screwcap. 15.5% alc. **Rating** 91 **To** 2043 $17 ✪

🍷🍷🍷🍷 **Barossa Valley Shiraz 2014 Rating** 89 **To** 2029 $17 ✪

Goodman Wines ★★★★☆
15 Symons Street, Healesville, Vic 3777 (postal) **Region** Yarra Valley
T 0447 030 011 **www**.goodmanwines.com.au **Open** Not
Winemaker Kate Goodman **Est.** 2012 **Dozens** 500
Kate Goodman started her winemaking career in McLaren Vale and the Clare Valley, thereafter spending seven years winemaking at Seppelt in the Grampians. In 2000 she became chief winemaker at Punt Road Wines and remained there until '14, when she left to set up Goodman Wines, leasing a winery together with fellow winemaker Caroline Mooney (of Bird on a Wire). Using some lead time planning, and with the knowledge and approval of Punt

Road's owners, she had made wines over the '12 and '13 vintages, all from mature Upper Yarra Valley vineyards. From '17 she is also winemaker for Penley Estate and Zonzo Estate.

ŢŢŢŢŢ **Yarra Valley Chardonnay 2015** From the Willowlake Vineyard, hand-picked, whole-bunch pressed, wild-yeast fermented and matured in French oak (20% new), no mlf. Layered and rich, ripe citrus – Meyer lemon and a whisk of grapefruit – white peach and creamy cashew flavours all coming to the party with the first stages of bottle development. Screwcap. 12.5% alc. **Rating** 95 **To** 2023 $40
Yarra Valley Pinot Noir 2015 Hand-picked, 25% whole bunches, the balance destemmed, open-fermented, 14 days on skins, matured in French oak (10% new). A very powerful wine in the context of the Upper Yarra, although Willowlake Vineyard is the oldest vineyard in the Upper Yarra. It rides high, wide and handsome on its pile of red and black fruits. Left field for its district and vintage, but will richly reward the patient. Screwcap. 13% alc. **Rating** 94 **To** 2030 $40

ŢŢŢŢŢ **Heathcote Vermentino 2016 Rating** 91 **To** 2023 $28

Gooree Park Wines   ★★★★

Gulgong Road, Mudgee, NSW 2850 **Region** Mudgee
T (02) 6378 1800 **www**.gooreepark.com.au **Open** Mon–Fri 10–5, w'ends 11–4
Winemaker Rueben Rodriguez **Est.** 2008 **Dozens** 3000 **Vyds** 546ha
Gooree Park Wines is part of a group of companies owned by Eduardo Cojuangco, other companies including a thoroughbred horse stud and a pastoral enterprise and vineyards based in Mudgee and Canowindra. Eduardo's interest in all forms of agriculture has resulted in the planting of over 500ha of vines, starting with the Tullamour Vineyard in Mudgee in 1996, Fords Creek in Mudgee in '97, and Mt Lewis Estate at Canowindra in '98.

ŢŢŢŢŢ **Don Eduardo Mudgee Shiraz Cabernet 2015** 60/40% with a 50/50 split between new American and French oak, aged for 1 year, with the final wine a barrel selection. Deep crimson and bright; full-bodied, dark fruit richly coated with dark chocolate, oak spices and tannin aplenty, dry on the finish. Screwcap. 14.5% alc. **Rating** 91 **To** 2025 $35 JF
Crowned Glory Mudgee Cabernet Sauvignon 2015 Richly flavoured with blackberries and currants coated in dark chocolate; wood spice and varnish fold into a full-bodied palate. Somewhat dry on the finish. Oak sitting atop but should integrate in time. Screwcap. 14.6% alc. **Rating** 91 **To** 2027 $32 JF

Gotham Wines   ★★★☆

8 The Parade West, Kent Town, SA 5067 **Region** South Australia
T (08) 7324 3031 **www**.gothamwines.com.au **Open** Not
Winemaker Peter Pollard **Est.** 2004 **Dozens** 65 000
In 2014 a group of wine enthusiasts, including former BRL Hardy CEO Stephen Millar, came together to purchase the Gotham Wines brands. The intention was (and is) to build on the existing domestic and export distribution of the wines, which include Wine Men of Gotham, Gotham, Stalking Horse and Step X Step brands, from Langhorne Creek, Clare Valley, Barossa Valley and McLaren Vale. Exports to most major markets.

ŢŢŢŢŢ **Clare Valley Riesling 2016** From the mix of lime and lemon blossom, zest and juice, and honeydew melon to the gentleness on the palate, there's plenty to savour here. Screwcap. 12% alc. **Rating** 92 **To** 2023 $15 JF ❂

ŢŢŢŢ **Langhorne Creek Shiraz 2015 Rating** 89 **To** 2023 $20 JF

Grace Farm   ★★★★★

741 Cowaramup Bay Road, Gracetown, WA 6285 **Region** Margaret River
T (08) 9384 4995 **www**.gracefarm.com.au **Open** By appt
Winemaker Jonathan Mettam **Est.** 2006 **Dozens** 3000 **Vyds** 8.17ha

Situated in the Wilyabrup district, Grace Farm is the small, family-owned vineyard of Elizabeth and John Mair, taking its name from the nearby coastal hamlet of Gracetown. Situated beside picturesque natural forest the vineyard is planted to cabernet sauvignon, chardonnay, sauvignon blanc and semillon. Viticulturist Tim Quinlan conducts tastings (by appointment), explaining Grace Farm's sustainable viticultural practices.

ΨΨΨΨ **Margaret River Cabernet Sauvignon 2015** Estate-grown, matured for 12 months in used French oak 'to throw the emphasis on the fruit'. Deeply coloured; a prime example of Margaret River cabernet, cassis and black olive fruit supported by ripe, grainy tannins. The balance is such that it can be enjoyed as much tonight as in 10 or 20 years. Screwcap. 14.5% alc. **Rating** 95 **To** 2035 $30 **☻**

ΨΨΨΨΨ **Margaret River Sauvignon Blanc Semillon 2016** Rating 91 To 2020 $21 **☻**
Margaret River Chardonnay 2015 Rating 90 To 2024 $30

Grampians Estate

1477 Western Highway, Great Western, Vic 3377 **Region** Grampians
T (03) 5354 6245 **www.**grampiansestate.com.au **Open** 7 days 10–5
Winemaker Andrew Davey, Don Rowe, Tom Guthrie **Est.** 1989 **Dozens** 2000 **Vyds** 8ha
Graziers Sarah and Tom Guthrie began their diversification into wine in 1989, but their core business continues to be fat lamb and wool production. Both activities were ravaged by the 2006 bushfires, but each has recovered. They have acquired the Garden Gully winery at Great Western, giving them a cellar door and a vineyard with 138-year-old shiraz and 80+-year-old riesling. Exports to Singapore and China.

ΨΨΨΨ **Mafeking Shiraz 2015** A neatly pitched core of very good fruit, yet definitely savoury. It's reined in on the medium-bodied palate with fine tannins and citrussy acidity. It's just damn pleasing. Screwcap. 13.5% alc. **Rating** 95 **To** 2028 $25 JF **☻**
Streeton Reserve Shiraz 2014 Mid-ruby-dark-purple with incredibly vibrant fruit; layers of savouriness, spice and florals all flow onto the medium-bodied palate. There's no shortage of complexity; it's all finely composed. Screwcap. 13.5% alc. **Rating** 95 **To** 2032 $75 JF
GST Grenache Shiraz Tempranillo 2015 A 60/30/10% blend creates a juicy wine with the fruit sweetness and spice of the grenache to the fore. It's immediately enjoyable, with wafts of red fruits, florals, and licorice allsorts and a hint of savouriness. A lighter-framed palate and grainy tannins with zesty acidity finish it off neatly. Screwcap. 13.8% alc. **Rating** 94 **To** 2020 $28 JF **☻**

Granite Hills

1481 Burke and Wills Track, Baynton, Vic 3444 **Region** Macedon Ranges
T (03) 5423 7273 **www.**granitehills.com.au **Open** 7 days 11–6
Winemaker Llew Knight, Ian Gunter **Est.** 1970 **Dozens** 5000 **Vyds** 12.5ha
Granite Hills is one of the enduring classics, pioneering the successful growing of riesling and shiraz in an uncompromisingly cool climate. It is based on riesling, chardonnay, shiraz, cabernet sauvignon, cabernet franc, merlot and pinot noir (the last also used in its sparkling wine). The Rieslings age superbly, and the Shiraz was the forerunner of the cool climate school in Australia. Exports to Japan and China.

ΨΨΨΨ **Macedon Ranges Late Harvest 2015** From a small hand-picked and selected parcel of partially botrytised riesling, the fermentation stopped with 80g/l of residual sugar, the result a totally delicious glass of lime, passionfruit and lychee flavours, then a cleansing finish. Screwcap. 8% alc. **Rating** 95 **To** 2025 $20 **☻**

ΨΨΨΨΨ **Macedon Ranges Riesling 2015** Rating 93 To 2025 $30 PR
Macedon Ranges Shiraz 2010 Rating 90 $35 PR

Grant Burge

279 Krondorf Road, Barossa Valley, SA 5352 **Region** Barossa Valley
T 1800 088 711 **www**.grantburgewines.com.au **Open** 7 days 10–5
Winemaker Craig Stansborough **Est.** 1988 **Dozens** 400000
Grant and Helen Burge established the eponymous Grant Burge business in 1988. It grew into one of the largest family-owned wine businesses in the valley. In February 2015, Accolade Wines announced it had acquired the Grant Burge brand, and the historic Krondorf Winery. The 356ha of vineyards remain in family ownership, and will continue to supply premium grapes to the Accolade-owned business. Exports to all major markets.

Filsell Old Vine Barossa Shiraz 2015 A mix of open and tank fermentation, matured for 21 months in 30% new oak (65% French, 36% American), the remainder used. The vines are nearing 100yo, and have produced a full-bodied shiraz that proclaims its DNA in full voice. Blackberry fruit, licorice and tarry nuances are decorated with substantial, but ripe, tannins. The saving grace is the alcohol of 14%, not 15%. Screwcap. **Rating** 95 **To** 2035 $43
Filsell Old Vine Barossa Shiraz 2014 The wine reflects the quality of the grapes, picked when ripe but not overripe. Blackberry and plum provide the heart of the wine, other inputs coming from chocolate and oak, neatly buttressed by ripe, but firm, tannins. Screwcap. 14.5% alc. **Rating** 95 **To** 2039 $37
Corryton Park Barossa Cabernet Sauvignon 2013 Matured in French oak for 20 months, it comes from the vineyard purchased by Grant Burge in '99, in one of the highest and coolest points of the Barossa Valley. It reflects its place, cassis intermingling with dried bay leaf and the barest hint of mint. Screwcap. 14% alc. **Rating** 95 **To** 2033 $37
The Vigneron Centenarian Barossa Semillon 2015 From the Zerk family 101yo block of semillon near Lyndoch and made to throw all the focus on the herb and lemongrass fruit, citrussy acidity prolonging the finish and aftertaste. Will do well with more time in bottle. Screwcap. 12% alc. **Rating** 94 **To** 2025 $30 ✪
Balthasar Eden Valley Shiraz 2014 Flavours of red and black berry fruits, spice, dark chocolate and cedary oak have been blended into a medium to full-bodied wine smoothie. Diam. 14% alc. **Rating** 94 **To** 2034 $37
Abednego Barossa Valley Shiraz Mourvedre Grenache 2014 37.5% shiraz, 35% mourvedre, 27.5% grenache, a mix of open and stainless steel fermentation, 65% matured in 2500l French vats, 35% in used French oak for 16 months. As long as you are prepared to be patient, this is a distinguished Barossa Valley blend, taking it right up to McLaren Vale. Spiced red and black fruits leap from the glass on the bouquet, following through onto the fore-palate. Diam. 13.5% alc. **Rating** 94 **To** 2034 $76
Cameron Vale Barossa Cabernet Sauvignon 2014 87.2% cabernet sauvignon, 10% merlot, 1.5% petit verdot and 1.3% shiraz; fermented with wild and cultured yeast, matured for 20 months in French oak (34% new). This is at the elegant end of the spectrum of Barossa Valley cabernet. It has blackcurrant fruit along with dried herb and bay leaf notes, the tannins fine but persistent, the finale almost juicy. Screwcap. 13.5% alc. **Rating** 94 **To** 2024 $27 ✪

Helene Tasmania Grande Cuvee 2006 Rating 93 To 2018 $50 TS
Miamba Barossa Shiraz 2015 Rating 91 To 2025 $27
Daly Road Barossa Shiraz Mourvedre 2014 Rating 91 To 2029 $27
5th Generation Barossa Shiraz 2015 Rating 90 To 2025 $18 ✪
Virtuoso Barossa GSM 2015 Rating 90 To 2019 $19 CM ✪
Virtuoso Barossa GSM 2015 Rating 90 To 2020 $19 ✪

Green Door Wines ★★★★☆

1112 Henty Road, Henty, WA 6236 **Region** Geographe
T 0439 511 652 **www**.greendoorwines.com.au **Open** Fri–Sun 11–4.30
Winemaker Ashley Keeffe, Jane Dunkley **Est.** 2007 **Dozens** 1000 **Vyds** 3.5ha

Ashley and Kathryn Keeffe purchased what was then a rundown vineyard in '06. With a combination of new and pre-existing vines, there are now 1ha of fiano and mourvedre, 0.75ha of grenache, 0.5ha of vardelho and tempranillo, and 0.25ha of shiraz. The wines are made in a small onsite winery (with the aid of consultant winemaker Jane Dunkley) using a range of winemaking methods, including the use of amphora pots.

🍷🍷🍷🍷🍷 **Amphora Geographe Tempranillo 2015** Geographe is turning into a hotbed of Iberian activity, with tempranillo the star. Check this out for its perfume of red licorice, florals and cherries and woodsy spices. The medium-bodied palate is supple and open, with a mineral thread to the acidity, then whoosh – the stealth-like tannins kick in. Screwcap. 13.5% alc. **Rating** 95 **To** 2022 $35 JF ○

🍷🍷🍷🍷🍷 **El Toro Geographe Tempranillo 2015** Rating 93 To 2022 $25 JF ○
Spanish Steps Geographe GSM 2015 Rating 91 To 2021 $20 JF ○
Flamenco Geographe Rose 2016 Rating 90 To 2018 $19 JF ○

Greenway Wines

350 Wollombi Road, Broke, NSW 2330 **Region** Hunter Valley
T 0418 164 382 **www**.greenwaywines.com.au **Open** W'ends 10–3 or by appt
Winemaker Michael McManus **Est.** 2009 **Dozens** 280 **Vyds** 2.4ha
This is the venture of John Marinovich and Anne Greenway, who purchased the vineyard in 2009 after many years of dreaming of becoming vignerons. They acquired a vineyard that had been first planted in 1999, with 2ha of merlot, the remainder shiraz and a little gewurztraminer. They say 'We were not prepared for how beautiful our little vineyard would be. It's bordered by the foothills of the Brokenback mountains on one side, and skirted by Wollombi Brook on the other.'

🍷🍷🍷🍷🍷 **The Architect Hunter Valley Shiraz 2014** 165 dozen made. Light but bright colour; a wonderfully juicy and expressive wine with its array of red and purple fruits presented in a web of silken tannins on the long, light to medium-bodied palate. Ready now or later. Screwcap. 13% alc. **Rating** 95 **To** 2029 $25 ○

🍷🍷🍷🍷🍷 **Grace Hunter Valley Gewurz Traminer 2014** Rating 92 To 2020 $16
Red Shed Hunter Valley Rose 2014 Rating 90 To 2018 $18

Grey Sands ★★★★

6 Kerrisons Road, Glengarry, Tas 7275 **Region** Northern Tasmania
T (03) 6396 1167 **www**.greysands.com.au **Open** Sat–Mon 12–5 (mid-Nov–mid-Apr)
Winemaker Peter Dredge, Bob Richter **Est.** 1989 **Dozens** 1000 **Vyds** 3.5ha
Bob and Rita Richter began the establishment of Grey Sands in 1989, slowly increasing the plantings to the present total. The ultra-high density of 8900 vines per hectare reflects the experience gained by the Richters during a three-year stay in England, when they visited many vineyards across Europe, as well as Bob's graduate diploma from Roseworthy College. Plantings include pinot noir, merlot, pinot gris and malbec. Exports to Singapore.

🍷🍷🍷🍷🍷 **Pinot Noir 2012** A bright, medium brick-red at 5yo, this pinot is in terrific nick. With its attractive autumnal/forest floor notes, there is more than enough red fruit and gently grippy tannins to ensure that this will keep on keeping for some time yet. Diam. 13.2% alc. **Rating** 92 **To** 2022 $50 PR

Grey-Smith Wines NR

PO Box 288, Coonawarra, SA 5263 **Region** Coonawarra
T 0429 499 355 **www**.grey-smith.com.au **Open** Not
Winemaker Ulrich Grey-Smith **Est.** 2012 **Dozens** 160
Ulrich Grey-Smith travelled wine roads near and far for decades before establishing his eponymous business. The original foundation for this career was the completion of the bachelor degree in oenology at Roseworthy Agricultural College (1987–90). His business goes well beyond the small amount of sparkling wine he makes, to all sides of making and

selling wine. He works as a consultant, as a freelance winemaker, and for many years was executive officer and secretary of the Limestone Coast Grape & Wine Council Inc (albeit on a part-time basis). He was also involved in the sharp end of helping run the annual Limestone Coast Wine Show, crossing over to the other side of the road as an associate judge and judge, as far afield as Mudgee, Cowra, Riverina, Riverland, Swan Hill and Macedon.

Groom   ★★★★☆

28 Langmeil Road, Tanunda, SA 5352 (postal) **Region** Barossa Valley
T (08) 8563 1101 www.groomwines.com **Open** Not
Winemaker Daryl Groom **Est.** 1997 **Dozens** 1940 **Vyds** 27.8ha
The full name of the business is Marschall Groom Cellars, a venture owned by David and Jeanette Marschall and their six children, and Daryl and Lisa Groom and their four children. Daryl was a highly regarded winemaker at Penfolds before he moved to Geyser Peak in California. Years of discussion between the families resulted in the purchase of a 35ha block of bare land adjacent to Penfolds' 130-year-old Kalimna Vineyard. Shiraz was planted in 1997, giving its first vintage in '99. The next acquisition was an 8ha vineyard at Lenswood in the Adelaide Hills, planted to sauvignon blanc. In 2000, 3.2ha of zinfandel was planted on the Kalimna Bush Block. Exports to the US, Canada, Hong Kong, Taiwan and China.

🍷🍷🍷🍷🍷 **Barossa Valley Shiraz 2014** A cascade of red and dark berries, black plum and cherry bound through the mouth, given flight by gentle extraction (a mere 6 days on skins) and a brushstroke of oak. The filmy tannins are finely wrought and serve to thread a structural weave, holding it all together. This is a plump, eminently approachable warm climate wine that wears a tattoo of drinkability with pride, especially amid its regional peers. Cork. 14% alc. **Rating** 95 **To** 2030 $50 NG

🍷🍷🍷🍷🍷 **Barossa Valley Shiraz 2015 Rating** 92 **To** 2030 $50 NG
Adelaide Hills Sauvignon Blanc 2016 Rating 91 **To** 2018 $24 NG
Bush Block Barossa Valley Zinfandel 2015 Rating 91 **To** 2023 $30 NG

Grosset   ★★★★★

King Street, Auburn, SA 5451 **Region** Clare Valley
T (08) 8849 2175 www.grosset.com.au **Open** 10–5 Wed–Sun (Spring)
Winemaker Jeffrey Grosset, Brent Treloar **Est.** 1981 **Dozens** 11 000 **Vyds** 22.2ha
Jeffrey Grosset wears the unchallenged mantle of Australia's foremost riesling maker. Grosset's pre-eminence is recognised both domestically and internationally; however, he merits equal recognition for the other wines in his portfolio: Semillon Sauvignon Blanc from Clare Valley/Adelaide Hills, Chardonnay and Pinot Noir from the Adelaide Hills and Gaia, a Bordeaux blend from the Clare Valley. These are all benchmarks. His quietly spoken manner conceals a steely will. Trial plantings (2ha) of fiano, aglianico, nero d'Avola and petit verdot suggest some new wines may be gestating. Exports to all major markets. Best value winery *Wine Companion* 2018.

🍷🍷🍷🍷🍷 **Polish Hill Clare Valley Riesling 2016** As always, made using free-run juice, and fermented with a neutral cultured yeast, placing all the focus on the expression of variety and place. The bouquet is gloriously floral with sweet lemon blossom aromas, the palate with diamond-cut purity and clarity. Natural acidity is part of the DNA of this classic wine, underlining its spring day freshness. Screwcap. 12.7% alc. **Rating** 97 **To** 2031 $54 ✪
Piccadilly Chardonnay 2016 Fermented in French barriques (40% new) with partial mlf and 10 months' maturation. The wine proclaims its provenance from the first whiff through to the finish. It is sublimely elegant and balanced, with white peach at the centre of its flavour spectrum, natural acidity providing an extra degree of length. This will grow another leg with 5 years' bottle development. Screwcap. 13.5% alc. **Rating** 97 **To** 2029 $65 ✪
Adelaide Hills Pinot Noir 2016 This is all about the opening of the peacock's tail on the finish and aftertaste. The star-bright crimson colour semaphores that there's a lot to come, yet the bouquet is holding its cards close to its chest. The

palate lets it all hang out as a swathe of small red fruits and savoury whole-bunch components contest bragging rights, ultimately having to sign a truce after the glorious finish and aftertaste. Screwcap. 13.5% alc. **Rating** 97 **To** 2024 $77 **☉**

Adelaide Hills Pinot Noir 2015 From 35yo estate vines part crushed, part whole bunches; open-fermented, 8 days on skins, matured on lees for 8 months in French oak (60% new). Clear crimson-purple; a savoury/spicy edge to red and purple fruits on the bouquet heralds a striking palate with a drive and fruit intensity that has some similarities to Ashton Hills. The ride along the palate through to the aftertaste grows inexorably yet harmoniously. Screwcap. 13.5% alc. **Rating** 97 **To** 2030 $77 **☉**

Nereus 2014 Part of the quest to determine what variety will be the best junior partner for his shiraz – nero d'Avola emerged in front of malbec and mataro this vintage, and looks as if it will continue to be the best. Grosset is seeking perfume, structure and drinkability, which this has in spades. It's simply bloody gorgeous. Screwcap. 13.7% alc. **Rating** 97 **To** 2030 $49 **☉**

ƔƔƔƔƔ **Springvale Clare Valley Riesling 2016** As good as any Grosset Springvale Riesling of the past decade, with beautifully balanced and very expressive lime juice fruit and crystalline acidity flowing through the gloriously long palate. Drink now or soonish if you value freshness, in 5–10 years if you value complexity. Screwcap. 12.7% alc. **Rating** 96 **To** 2029 $40 **☉**

Semillon Sauvignon Blanc 2016 Clare Valley semillon and Adelaide Hills sauvignon blanc. The initial impact is the minerally lemongrass flavours and acidity of the semillon before the back-palate, finish and aftertaste are driven by gently tropical/gooseberry fruits. Screwcap. 13.5% alc. **Rating** 95 **To** 2019 $35 **☉**

Apiana 2016 A 60/40% blend of semillon and fiano. The components are whole-bunch pressed and separately fermented in tank. The wine has wildflower nuances to the striking bouquet, and an incredible tactile grip on the mid-palate, countered by the fiano. Screwcap. 13% alc. **Rating** 95 **To** 2025 $40

Gaia 2014 The Bordeaux blend meticulously conceived and brought alive by Jeffrey Grosset. It is old money, seeing no reason to flaunt its character; the bouquet and palate bring an elegant parade of black and redcurrant, wild herbs and finely ground tannins to the table, oak chairs to complete the setting. Screwcap. 13.7% alc. **Rating** 95 **To** 2029 $82

Piccadilly Chardonnay 2015 A juicy supple wine with nectarine, white peach and creamy flavours gently filling the mouth, pear and apple also joining in on the back-palate and finish. The French oak influence has more to do with texture than flavour. Screwcap. 13.5% alc. **Rating** 95 **To** 2023 $65

Alea Clare Valley Riesling 2016 Only just off dry. Delicious – how could it not be – now, but will be a giant slayer with 5–10 years in bottle. Screwcap. 12% alc. **Rating** 94 **To** 2031 $36

Grove Estate Wines   ★★★★☆

4100 Murringo Road, Young, NSW 2594 **Region** Hilltops
T (02) 6382 6999 **www**.groveestate.com.au **Open** 7 days 10–5
Winemaker Brian Mullany **Est.** 1989 **Dozens** 4000 **Vyds** 46ha
The Grove Estate partners of the Mullany, Kirkwood and Flanders families purchased the then unplanted property situated on volcanic red soils at an elevation of 530m with the intention of producing premium cool climate wine grapes for sale to other winemakers. Over the ensuing years plantings included cabernet sauvignon, shiraz, merlot, zinfandel, barbera, sangiovese, petit verdot, chardonnay, semillon and nebbiolo. In 1997 a small amount of cabernet sauvignon was vinified under the Grove Estate label, and the winemaking gathered pace thereafter. Nebbiolo has been particularly successful, as has the shiraz viognier. Exports to China.

ƔƔƔƔƔ **Sommita Hilltops Nebbiolo 2015** Hand-picked, open-fermented with wild yeast, 50 days on skins, matured in used oak for 10 months. Excellent colour; unmistakably nebbiolo, sour and red cherry with an underlay of fine, savoury tannins on the long oak. Screwcap. 14% alc. **Rating** 95 **To** 2025 $45

ŸŸŸŸ♀ The Cellar Block Hilltops Shiraz Viognier 2015 Rating 92 To 2029 $35
The Italian Hilltops Nebbiolo Sangiovese Barbera 2015 Rating 90
To 2022 $25

Gundog Estate ★★★★★

101 McDonalds Road, Pokolbin, NSW 2320 **Region** Hunter Valley
T (02) 4998 6873 **www**.gundogestate.com.au **Open** 7 days 10–5
Winemaker Matthew Burton **Est.** 2006 **Dozens** 8000 **Vyds** 5ha
Matt Burton makes four different Hunter Semillons and Shiraz from the Hunter Valley,
Murrumbateman and Hilltops. He and wife Renee run the cellar door from the historic
Pokolbin school house, next to the old Rosemount/Hungerford Hill building on McDonalds
Road. The Burton McMahon wines are a collaboration between Matt Burton and Dylan
McMahon of Seville Estate. In 2016 Gundog opened a second cellar door at 42 Cork Street,
Gundaroo (Thurs–Sun 10–5). Exports to the UK.

ŸŸŸŸŸ **Marksman's Canberra District Shiraz 2015** Whole and crushed berries
soaked for 3 days, warm open ferment, matured for 14 months in barrel
(30% new), 240 dozen made. Deep crimson-purple; an elegant yet powerful and
long wine. Black forest fruits, bramble, licorice and spice dance on the soft cushion
of tannins and oak, reaching a climax on the finish and aftertaste. Screwcap.
14% alc. **Rating** 97 **To** 2040 $60 ❂
The 48 Block Hunter Valley Shiraz 2014 It's forcing the issue to compare
the quality of the superb '14 Gundog Shirazs, but the complexity and richness of
this wine puts it in first place, and it will keep its shape and fruit flavour a little bit
longer. This was part of the Lindemans Ben Ean Vineyard before bean counters
managed to give it away. Screwcap. 13.8% alc. **Rating** 97 **To** 2054 $80 ❂

ŸŸŸŸŸ **Hunter's Semillon 2016** From the most generous parcels of Gundog's semillon.
Its flavour and texture reflect its origin, with a tactile mouthfeel and intensity
reverberating into the finish and aftertaste. The flavours, too, range through
lemongrass, lemon curd and slippery acidity. Screwcap. 11% alc. **Rating** 96
To 2030 $25 ❂
The Chase Hunter Valley Semillon 2016 The Chase is of absolute purity
of varietal expression, the opposite of Gundog's Wild Semillon. Free-run juice is
cold-settled then fermented with a neutral yeast. Yet its bouquet surges out of the
glass with lemongrass/hay aromas, the palate then imprinting its suite of flavours
for a seeming eternity. Gold medal at the Hunter Valley Wine Show '16. Screwcap.
10.5% alc. **Rating** 96 **To** 2031 $30 ❂
Somerset Vineyard Hunter Valley Semillon 2014 For me, the standout of
the three Gundog '14 Semillons with its extraordinary intensity and drive, creating
a very rich palate. Screwcap. 11% alc. **Rating** 96 **To** 2029 $50 ❂
Hilltops Shiraz 2015 Sourced from the Freeman Vineyard; 12 months
maturation in French puncheons (25% new). An exercise in the intensity and
purity of cool-grown shiraz, with intense black fruits, licorice, spice and black
pepper all waving their hands demanding to be heard. The medium to full-bodied
palate is perfect. Screwcap. 14.5% alc. **Rating** 96 **To** 2035 $35 ❂
Somerset Vineyard Hunter Valley Shiraz 2014 The abiding class and virtue
of this wine is its extreme length, built on freshness and elegance. Its fragrance
is notable, as is the harmony of the fruit flavours. I spent an hour tasting (and
retasting) these wines. Screwcap. 13.8% alc. **Rating** 96 **To** 2049 $80
Old Road Hunter Valley Shiraz 2014 Good colour; the keywords are depth
and richness, the persistence of dark fruits matched by tannins. As with all three
Gundog Shirazs, teasing out the differences isn't easy because of their harmony, but
it can be done. Working backwards and forwards, the fragrance builds progressively.
Screwcap. 13.8% alc. **Rating** 96 **To** 2049 $80
Vernon Vineyard Hunter Valley Semillon 2014 Stands out for its multifaceted
complexity, opening with a clap of cymbals and finishing with another clap in
a different register. Its tropical fruit flavours surely come from its alcohol, which

is higher than any other Hunter semillon of significance. Screwcap. 12.5% alc. **Rating** 95 **To** 2026 $50

Sunshine Vineyard Hunter Valley Semillon 2014 This vineyard was the birthplace of the great Lindeman Semillons of the '50s and '60s until it fell prey to corporate vinocide and (in time) was used to launch balloons, but it has since been redeemed. Doesn't show its upper end alcohol; flavour harmony, balance, line and length all ticked. Screwcap. 12% alc. **Rating** 95 **To** 2029 $50

Canberra District Shiraz 2015 Fermented and held on skins for 10 days, matured in French puncheons (30% new) for 12 months. A complex bouquet and medium-bodied palate, savoury/spicy components travelling side by side with purple and black fruits; fine tannins, part fruit, part oak, provide further interest and length. Screwcap. 14.5% alc. **Rating** 95 **To** 2035 $40

Burton McMahon Gippsland Pinot Noir 2016 Sappy and long on introduction, the wine glides across a carpet of sour cherry, wild strawberry, musk, sandalwood and dank, wet leaves. This is mellifluous stuff with the 20% of whole cluster fruit beautifully absorbed. Screwcap. 13.2% alc. **Rating** 94 **To** 2025 $38 NG

Indomitus Rutilus Canberra District Shiraz 2015 This shiraz is produced with minimal messing about, from 30% whole bunches in the ferment and 12 months in seasoned French oak with viognier (4%) for good measure. The result is dense, aromatic and on the better side of vibrant, straddling a mid-weighted frame and a core of concentrated fruit. Screwcap. 14.5% alc. **Rating** 94 **To** 2025 $50 NG

ΨΨΨΨΨ **Wild Hunter Valley Semillon 2016** Rating 93 To 2023 $30
Burton McMahon D'Aloisio's Vineyard Yarra Valley Chardonnay 2016 Rating 93 To 2025 $34 NG
Burton McMahon Syme on Yarra Vineyard Yarra Valley Pinot Noir 2016 Rating 92 To 2025 $38 NG
Burton McMahon George's Vineyard Yarra Valley Chardonnay 2016 Rating 91 To 2025 $34 NG

Haan Wines ★★★★
148 Siegersdorf Road, Tanunda, SA 5352 **Region** Barossa Valley
T (08) 8562 4590 **www.**haanwines.com.au **Open** Not
Winemaker Sarah Siddons (Contract) **Est.** 1993 **Dozens** 3500 **Vyds** 16.3ha
Hans and Fransien Haan established their business in 1993 when they acquired a vineyard near Tanunda. The plantings are shiraz (5.3ha), merlot (3.4ha), cabernet sauvignon (3ha), viognier (2.4ha), cabernet franc (1ha) and malbec, petit verdot and semillon (0.4ha each). Oak undoubtedly plays a role in the shaping of the style of the Haan wines, but it is perfectly integrated, and the wines have the fruit weight to carry the oak. Exports to Switzerland, the Czech Republic, China and other markets.

ΨΨΨΨΨ **Barossa Valley Merlot Prestige 2013** A fleshier, riper style as the vintage dictated, but everything stitched well, from the ripe powerful tannins to the core of luscious dark plums, spice, black olives, the oak adding flavour and bolstering its framework. Warm on the finish. Diam. 15% alc. **Rating** 93 **To** 2020 $65 JF
Barossa Valley Viognier Ratafia NV A mid-amber pale, orange colour; laden with butter menthol, burnt toffee, freshly made cumquat–lime marmalade and apricot kernels. It's smooth on the palate, sweet but reined in by good acidity and the neutral spirit. Best with cheese. Screwcap. **Rating** 92 $20 JF ☻

Hahndorf Hill Winery ★★★★★
38 Pain Road, Hahndorf, SA 5245 **Region** Adelaide Hills
T (08) 8388 7512 **www.**hahndorfhillwinery.com.au **Open** 7 days 10–5
Winemaker Larry Jacobs **Est.** 2002 **Dozens** 6000 **Vyds** 6.5ha
Larry Jacobs and Marc Dobson, both originally from South Africa, purchased Hahndorf Hill Winery in 2002. Larry gave up a career in intensive care medicine in 1988 when he

bought an abandoned property in Stellenbosch, and established the near-iconic Mulderbosch Wines. When Mulderbosch was purchased at the end of '96, the pair migrated to Australia and eventually found their way to Hahndorf Hill. In '06, their investment in the winery and cellar door was rewarded by induction into the South Australian Great Tourism Hall of Fame. In '07 they began converting the vineyard to biodynamic status, and they were among the first movers in implementing a carbon offset program. They imported three clones of gruner veltliner from Austria, in '16 expanding the Austrian varieties further by planting St Laurent. In '16 it was Best Producer of Show <100 tonnes at the Adelaide Hills Wine Show, the White Mischief Gruner Veltliner winning the trophy for Best Gruner Veltliner, the Rose winning the trophy for Best Rose at the Winewise Small Vignerons Award (and a gold medal at the Melbourne Wine Awards). Exports to the UK, Singapore and China.

🍷🍷🍷🍷🍷 **GRU Adelaide Hills Gruner Veltliner 2016** Six clones, hand-picked at various baumes, each batch treated differently, some cool, some warm-fermented in stainless steel, 30% wild-yeast fermented in old barriques with extended lees contact. The exceptionally complex vinification puts most winemakers of chardonnay to shame. It has electric vibrancy and drive, capturing your senses without warning. Its combination of delicacy, attention to detail and intensity is amazing. Gold medal Adelaide Wine Show '16. Screwcap. 12% alc. **Rating** 97 **To** 2026 $28 **☉**

🍷🍷🍷🍷🍷 **White Mischief Adelaide Hills Gruner Veltliner 2016** The bouquet has clear touches of white pepper and spice, the palate with more generous fruit than most gruners, and more texture. The flavours have some white peach, some guava fruit and acidity to freshen the finish. Screwcap. 13% alc. **Rating** 96 **To** 2026 $23 **☉**
Adelaide Hills Rose 2016 39% trollinger, 36% pinot noir, 25% merlot, picked and crushed together. The perfumed and spicy rose petal bouquet has the keys to open the door of a palate with exceptional drive to its mouthwatering array of all things red. It is dry and delicate yet totally intriguing, and perfectly balanced. Gold medal and trophy Winewise '16, gold medal Melbourne Wine Awards '16. Screwcap. 13% alc. **Rating** 96 **To** 2020 $23 **☉**
Adelaide Hills Shiraz 2014 Hand-picked, largely destemmed and crushed, with some whole bunches, cold-soaked pre-fermentation, matured in French barriques for 11 months. Every single atom of this medium-bodied wine is in its due place, and in balance with every other atom; its sense of place, its varietal expression and its oak integration are all immaculate. Flavours? Spice, cherry and plum, reflecting harvesting at the right moment. Screwcap. 14% alc. **Rating** 95 **To** 2034 $35 **☉**
Adelaide Hills Sauvignon Blanc 2016 Chilled, destemmed and crushed, fermented with cultured yeast. If the Yarra Valley is a reluctant host for sauvignon blanc, the Adelaide Hills is a willing and winning host. This wine glories in the vibrancy of its tropical and stone fruits, with the palate long, the aftertaste lingering. Screwcap. 12.5% alc. **Rating** 94 **To** 2018 $23 **☉**
Adelaide Hills Pinot Grigio 2016 Chilled and crushed, the pressings separated, cool-fermented in stainless steel. The bouquet is highly fragrant with rose petal and powder puff aromas, the palate precisely reflecting the aim of Hahndorf Hill to produce a true grigio style. Screwcap. 12% alc. **Rating** 94 **To** 2020 $25 **☉**
Zsa Zsa Zweigelt Nouveau 2016 The only zweigelt currently produced in Australia; hand-picked, whole bunches undergoing carbonic maceration in stainless steel, matured in used French barriques for 14 weeks. A striking wine, with mouthfilling morello cherry fruit and absolutely no tannins, no residual sugar, just balanced acidity. Also, despite only 14 weeks in used French barriques, is a complete wine with no reduction. Screwcap. 11.5% alc. **Rating** 94 **To** 2026 $33

Haldon Estate Wines   ★★★★

59 Havelock Road, Beechworth, Vic 3747 **Region** Beechworth
T (03) 5728 2858 **www.**haldonestatewines.com.au **Open** W'ends & most hols 11–5
Winemaker Tracey Richards **Est.** 2010 **Dozens** 900 **Vyds** 2.2ha

Tracey Richards and her partner Ranald (Ran) Currie still have day jobs to pay the bills, but have already had remarkable success with the wines they have made and marketed. Tracey has had a long love affair with wine, and studied oenology at CSU from 2000–05, graduating dux of her class. With an introduction from Rick Kinzbrunner's nephew, Peter Graham, she started working vintages at Giaconda from '03, and continued to do so each vintage until '12. They have planted 2.2ha of estate vines, which include chardonnay, riesling, semillon, sauvignon blanc, pinot noir, nebbiolo and cabernet sauvignon. The house on the 3.8ha property is no ordinary abode, having been built in 1893. Tracey says they live in the house full-time 'and freeze most winters'. The vineyard established by the partners is in fact its third incarnation, the first dating back to the 1850s. Haldon has a little cellar door in a farm outbuilding built circa 1900–30, now (after it was gutted) restored.

ŶŶŶŶŶ **The Clarence John Beechworth Nebbiolo Cabernet Sauvignon 2015**
Nebbiolo and cabernet sauvignon are odd bedfellows; the latter dominates aromatically. A sinewy, austere style which is appealing, with raspy tannins, new leather and green peppercorns, black pepper too; nebbiolo's acidity enlivens the palate. Screwcap. 13.9% alc. **Rating** 91 **To** 2021 $39 JF
Beechworth Sauvignon Blanc Semillon 2016 The mid-gold colour aside, there's a savoury element that appeals here, with smoky nuances, lime curd, quite a tight palate with dried herbs, the oak adding spice and a sensation of sweetness even with the acidity. Screwcap. 13.9% alc. **Rating** 90 **To** 2020 $29 JF
Beechworth Shiraz 2015 Gets into gear with spiced plum compote and cedary-woodsy characters with aged balsamic. There's an underlying ripe/overripe fruit character leading onto a mid-weighted palate with tapering tannins. Screwcap. 13.9% alc. **Rating** 90 **To** 2022 $39 JF
The Cutting Shiraz Merlot Cabernet 2015 The shiraz and merlot come from the King Valley, the cabernet sauvignon from Beechworth, roughly equal portions and aged for 2 years. All brambleberries, currants and leafy freshness, medium-weighted with a fineness to the tannins, and a slight astringency on the finish. Easy-drinking appeal. Screwcap. 13.3% alc. **Rating** 90 **To** 2021 $29 JF

ŶŶŶŶ **The Piano Player Beechworth Rose 2015 Rating** 89 **To** 2019 $22 JF
Beechworth Chardonnay 2015 Rating 88 **To** 2019 $39 JF
The Edgar Wallace Beechworth Cabernet Sauvignon 2015 Rating 87 **To** 2019 $39 JF

Halls Gap Estate ★★★★★

4113 Ararat-Halls Gap Road, Halls Gap, Vic 3381 **Region** Grampians
T 0413 595 513 **www.**hallsgapestate.com.au **Open** Wed–Mon 10–5
Winemaker Duncan Buchanan **Est.** 1969 **Dozens** 2000 **Vyds** 10.5ha
I first visited this vineyard when it was known as Boroka Vineyard and marvelled at the location in the wild country of Halls Gap. It wasn't very successful: Mount Langi Ghiran acquired it in 1998 and it was a useful adjunct to Mount Langi Ghiran for a while, but by 2013 it had outlived its purpose. It was then that the opportunity arose for the Drummond family, led by Aaron, to purchase the somewhat rundown vineyard. They moved quickly; while the '13 vintage was made at Mount Langi Ghiran, thereafter it was controlled under contract by Circe Wines (Aaron Drummond's partnership business with Dan Buckle). At the start of '14 Dan and Aaron hired Duncan Buchanan (ex Dromana Estate viticulturist and winemaker), giving him the dual task of managing their Mornington Peninsula vineyard and spending all-important time at Halls Gap.

ŶŶŶŶŶ **Fallen Giants Vineyard Riesling 2016** Generous bouquet. Aromas of fresh (and even baked) apple, a touch of slightly tropical fruit and then lime leaf in the background. Entry on the palate has a minerally, quartz-like feel, softening through the middle with flavours of nashi pear and Meyer lemon. Slatey acidity picks up again through the finish and lingers in the aftertaste. Screwcap. 11.5% alc. **Rating** 95 **To** 2026 $25 SC ✪

Fallen Giants Vineyard Shiraz 2015 Initially, a savoury impression on the bouquet, with gamey, charcuterie-like aromas. Sitting in the glass, the dark fruit emerges, flanked by notes of white pepper and Middle Eastern spices. Supple and seamless on the palate, there's a sense of restrained power and of a long cellar life ahead. Screwcap. 14% alc. **Rating** 95 **To** 2035 $30 SC ✪

🍷🍷🍷🍷🍷 **Fallen Giants Vineyard Cabernet Sauvignon 2015 Rating** 93 **To** 2025 $30
Fallen Giants Vineyard Block 1 Riesling 2015 Rating 92 **To** 2023 $30 SC

Hamelin Bay   ★★★★☆

McDonald Road, Karridale, WA 6288 **Region** Margaret River
T (08) 9758 6779 **www**.hbwines.com.au **Open** 7 days 10–5
Winemaker Julian Scott **Est.** 1992 **Dozens** 10 000 **Vyds** 23.5ha
The Hamelin Bay vineyard was established by the Drake-Brockman family, pioneers of the region. Richard Drake-Brockman's great-grandmother, Grace Bussell, was famous for her courage when, in 1876, aged 16, she rescued survivors of a shipwreck not far from the mouth of the Margaret River. Richard's great-grandfather Frederick, known for his exploration of the Kimberley, read about the feat in Perth's press and rode 300km on horseback to meet her – they married in 1882. Hamelin Bay's vineyard and winery is located within a few kilometres of Karridale, at the intersection of the Brockman and Bussell Highways, which were named in honour of these pioneering families. Exports to the UK, Canada, Malaysia, Singapore and China.

🍷🍷🍷🍷🍷 **Five Ashes Reserve Margaret River Shiraz 2012** Hand-picked, destemmed, fermented with cultured yeast, matured for 16 months in French barriques (50% new). Has retained excellent colour; the bouquet and palate run on the same rail line, with a potent savoury mix of black fruits, licorice, tapenade, smoked meat, cedary oak and more. From the cool Karridale district, and shows it. Screwcap. 14% alc. **Rating** 95 **To** 2037 $49
Five Ashes Reserve Margaret River Cabernet Sauvignon 2012 A barrel selection matured in French oak for 16 months. Savoury, spicy black fruits on the medium to full-bodied palate join with cedary oak and tannins and a faint whisper of mint (not a negative). High quality wine. Screwcap. 14% alc. **Rating** 95 **To** 2032 $49
Five Ashes Vineyard Margaret River Semillon Sauvignon Blanc 2016 A 76/24% blend, 8 weeks on lees in tank, otherwise no-frills vinification. Has more complexity on the bouquet and significantly greater and richer fruit on the palate than its Sauvignon Blanc sibling. Here Meyer lemon marries with passionfruit in heterovinous union. Screwcap. 13% alc. **Rating** 94 **To** 2022 $25 ✪
Five Ashes Vineyard Margaret River Chardonnay 2015 Very crisp and fresh, grapefruit flavours lead the way, oak subtle but evident; acidity similar, and certainly cleans out the finish and aftertaste. Screwcap. 13% alc. **Rating** 94 **To** 2026 $30 ✪

🍷🍷🍷🍷🍷 **Five Ashes Vineyard Margaret River Shiraz 2013 Rating** 93 **To** 2033 $32
Five Ashes Vineyard Cabernet Merlot 2014 Rating 93 **To** 2029 $25 ✪
Five Ashes Vineyard Merlot 2015 Rating 92 **To** 2030 $25 ✪
Five Ashes Vineyard Cabernet Sauvignon 2012 Rating 92 **To** 2022 $32
Five Ashes Vineyard Sauvignon Blanc 2016 Rating 90 **To** 2018 $25

Hancock & Hancock   ★★★★

210 Chalk Hill Road, McLaren Vale, SA 5171 **Region** McLaren Vale
T 0417 291 708 **Open** Not
Winemaker Larry Cherubino, Mike Brown **Est.** 2007 **Dozens** NFP **Vyds** 8.09ha
This is the venture of industry doyen Chris Hancock and brother John, who returned to their family roots when they purchased the McLaren Vale vineyard La Colline in 2007. Chris graduated as dux of the oenology degree at Roseworthy Agricultural College in 1963, taking up immediate employment with the Penfold family. In '76 he joined Rosemount Estate,

and when it was acquired by Southcorp, stayed on with the business in the upper echelon of its management. When the late Bob Oatley re-entered the wine business, establishing what is now Robert Oatley Vineyards (ROV) Chris rejoined the family and is today Deputy Executive Chairman of ROV. Unsurprisingly the wines are distributed by Oatley Family Wine Merchants. Exports to the UK, Hong Kong and China.

ŸŸŸŸ♀ **Home Vineyard McLaren Vale Grenache Rose 2016** Pale pink; very much in the modern style, fragrant and red-fruited; it is light on its feet, yet taps out an insistent message. Clever winemaking, knowing when to leave the wine alone. Screwcap. 13% alc. **Rating** 92 **To** 2018 $23 **○**

Handpicked Wines ★★★★★

50 Kensington Street, Chippendale, NSW 2008 **Region** Various
T (02) 9475 7888 **www**.handpickedwines.com.au **Open** Mon–Fri 11–10, w'ends 10–10
Winemaker Gary Baldwin, Peter Dillon **Est.** 2001 **Dozens** 50 000 **Vyds** 63ha
Handpicked is part of DMG Fine Wines, a global wine business with its head office in Australia. Its roots go back over 50 years to China, and the vision of Ming Guang Dong, who built a successful broad-based business. His four children were educated in the UK, Australia or Singapore, and today they are all involved in the business, with William Dong at the helm. Having worked with what became Handpicked Wines, he bought the business with the aim of creating great wines from great regions under one label. Today it makes wines in Italy, Chile, France and Spain, but the main arm is Australia, where Handpicked has 33ha in the Yarra Valley, 18ha in the Mornington Peninsula and 12ha in the Barossa Valley. It secured the services of Gary Baldwin as executive chief winemaker, and constructed a winery at the company's flagship Capella Vineyard at Bittern, on the Mornington Peninsula, destined to become the hospitality base for the business. In November 2014, Peter Dillon was successfully headhunted to assist Gary Baldwin; Dillon has established his credentials as a winemaker of the highest quality over the past 13 years. Exports to Italy, the Philippines, South Korea, Myanmar, Cambodia, Vietnam, Japan, Hong Kong and China.

ŸŸŸŸŸ **Regional Selections Yarra Valley Rose 2016** A small amount of marsanne was included with pinot noir 'to give the wine extra body and texture'. Very pale pink, it has a distinctly spicy/savoury twist to the small red berry fruit at its core, evident both in the fragrant bouquet and the crisp palate. A cut above. Screwcap. 13.4% alc. **Rating** 95 **To** 2018 $28 **○**
Collection Tasmania Pinot Noir 2015 From the Tamar Valley and Pipers River. Unexpectedly, does not have the usual Tasmanian depth to the bright and clear hue; that said, it is a complex, savoury, foresty/stemmy pinot with drive and length that may divide opinion. I like it Screwcap. 13.7% alc. **Rating** 95 **To** 2025 $60
Collection Mornington Peninsula Pinot Noir 2015 Like its '15 siblings, has bright, clear and light colour; the gently spiced fresh bouquet leads into an elegant, carefully choreographed, red berry palate. It's a very nice pinot needing a little more drive/X-factor for top points. Screwcap. 13% alc. **Rating** 94 **To** 2023 $60

ŸŸŸŸ♀ **Capella Vineyard Mornington Peninsula Pinot Noir 2015** Rating 93 To 2025 $80

Hanging Rock Winery ★★★★★

88 Jim Road, Newham, Vic 3442 **Region** Macedon Ranges
T (03) 5427 0542 **www**.hangingrock.com.au **Open** 7 days 10–5
Winemaker Robert Ellis **Est.** 1983 **Dozens** 20 000 **Vyds** 14.5ha
The Macedon area has proved marginal in spots, and the Hanging Rock vineyards, with their lovely vista towards the Rock, are no exception. John Ellis thus elected to source additional grapes from various parts of Victoria to produce an interesting and diverse range of varietals at different price points. In 2011 John's children Ruth and Robert returned to the fold: Robert has an oenology degree from Adelaide University, since then working as a Flying Winemaker in Champagne, Burgundy, Oregon and Stellenbosch. Ruth has a degree in wine marketing from Adelaide University. Exports to the UK, the US and other major markets.

ΨΨΨΨΨ **Jim Jim Macedon Ranges Sauvignon Blanc 2016** Hand-picked over three dates, giving flavour complexity. 10% barrel fermentation adds more to a sauvignon blanc of considerable stature. The mouthfeel has very good texture, the flavours ranging from cut grass to passionfruit and ultimately a slash of citrus pith, zest and juice. Screwcap. 13.2% alc. **Rating** 95 **To** 2019 $30 ✪
Jim Jim Macedon Ranges Pinot Noir 2014 Bright, light crimson; clear varietal character from the opening whiff through to the finish; vibrant red and purple fruits rising to expand on the back-palate and aftertaste. Lovely pinot with years in front of it. Screwcap. **Rating** 95 **To** 2021 $50
Cambrian Rise Heathcote Shiraz 2014 Blended from several vineyards, and has luscious red and black berry fruits in abundance, the style achieved with three decades of experience. Ripe tannins and oak provide balance and texture to a hedonistic wine. Screwcap. 14.5% alc. **Rating** 94 **To** 2034 $30 ✪
Reserve Heathcote Shiraz 2006 Good colour for age; the complex bouquet has ribbons of black fruits, earth, spice and oak; the palate adds licorice and an element of lifted acidity, but otherwise follows the lead of the bouquet. Diam. **Rating** 94 **To** 2026 $105

ΨΨΨΨΨ **Heathcote Shiraz 2013** Rating 93 **To** 2033 $75
Cuvee Eight Macedon Late Disgorged NV Rating 93 **To** 2022 $115 TS
The Jim Jim Three Macedon Ranges Riesling Pinot Gris Gewurztraminer 2016 Rating 92 **To** 2026 $30
Macedon Ranges Pinot Noir 2015 Rating 90 **To** 2021 $35
Macedon Rose Brut NV Rating 90 **To** 2017 $35 TS

Hanging Tree Wines   ★★★☆

294 O'Connors Road, Pokolbin, NSW 2325 **Region** Hunter Valley
T (02) 4998 6601 **www.**hangingtreewines.com.au **Open** 7 days 10–5
Winemaker Andrew Thomas (Contract) **Est.** 2003 **Dozens** 2500 **Vyds** 2.8ha
Hanging Tree Wines (which started life as the Van De Scheur Estate) has been developed into a luxury resort. The homestead has two master suites and two deluxe rooms; the verandahs have accommodated wedding parties for up to 102 seated guests. The wines, from the estate plantings of semillon, chardonnay, shiraz and cabernet sauvignon, are made by leading contract-winemaker Andrew Thomas.

ΨΨΨΨΨ **Limited Release Hunter Valley Semillon 2011** While picked late, has nothing else in common with its '14 sibling. Here green herbs and lemon zest are coupled with bracing acidity on the long finish. Still has a long life ahead. Screwcap. 12.5% alc. **Rating** 92 **To** 2026 $27

ΨΨΨΨ **Limited Release Hunter Valley Semillon 2014** Rating 89 **To** 2019 $25

Hanrahan Estate   ★★★★☆

3 Hexham Road, Gruyere, Vic 3770 **Region** Yarra Valley
T 0421 340 810 **www.**hanrahan.net.au **Open** Fri–Mon 11–5
Winemaker Yering Station (Willy Lunn) **Est.** 1997 **Dozens** 1800 **Vyds** 9.11ha
Bev Cowley (Ansett Cabin Manager) and long-term partner Bill Hanrahan (Ansett Captain) began the establishment of their vineyard in 1997 on what was previously a cattle grazing property. The idea was to have a more relaxing lifestyle away from the Ansett international service that flew for several years throughout Asia. They planted 5ha of pinot noir, 3.3ha of shiraz and 0.8ha of chardonnay. The quality of the grapes led to a contract with Yering Station, and their label was launched in 2002. Following the tragic death of husband Bill in 2007, Bev threw herself into the development of the project, helped by family and friends, and in particular by Dave Willis, her vineyard manager. Bev has also worked with Yarra Ranges Tourism, and introduced a concept called Reverse BYO® – you bring your own food and Bev provides the wine and other beverages, resulting in many picnic spots around the estate.

🍷🍷🍷🍷🍷 **Single Vineyard Yarra Valley Chardonnay 2014** Pale straw-green, a very good start; it has the length, purity and focus of top class Yarra chardonnay. Grapefruit and white peach have juicy acidity that both fills and freshens the palate and its aftertaste. Screwcap. 13% alc. **Rating** 95 **To** 2024 $38

🍷🍷🍷🍷🍷 **Lockie Single Vineyard Yarra Valley Pinot Noir 2015** Rating 93 To 2022 $42
Single Vineyard Yarra Valley Shiraz 2014 Rating 92 To 2029 $38
Angus Single Vineyard Yarra Valley Shiraz 2015 Rating 90 To 2023 $38

Happs ★★★★★

575 Commonage Road, Dunsborough, WA 6281 **Region** Margaret River
T (08) 9755 3300 **www.**happs.com.au **Open** 7 days 10–5
Winemaker Erl Happ, Mark Warren **Est.** 1978 **Dozens** 14 000 **Vyds** 35.2ha
One-time schoolteacher, potter and winemaker Erl Happ is the patriarch of a three-generation family. More than anything, Erl has been a creator and experimenter, building the self-designed winery from mudbrick, concrete form and timber, and making the first crusher. In 1994 he began an entirely new 30ha vineyard at Karridale, planted to no less than 28 varieties, including some of the earliest plantings in Australia of tempranillo. The Three Hills label is made from varieties grown at this vineyard. Erl passed on to son Myles a love of pottery, and Happs Pottery now has four potters, including Myles. Exports to the US, Denmark, The Netherlands, Malaysia, Hong Kong, China and Japan.

🍷🍷🍷🍷🍷 **Three Hills Eva Marie 2015** This is a white Bordeaux-inspired blend of sauvignon blanc (61.5%), semillon (31%) and a dollop of muscadelle. Margaret River really struts its maritime salinity and alluvial energy across wines such as these. Mid-weighted and highly textural, with an immaculate sheen of cedary vanillan oak, finds an effortless confluence with bright acidity. Screwcap. 13% alc. **Rating** 95 **To** 2023 $30 NG ✪
Three Hills Charles Andreas 2015 A Bordeaux blend, with 50% cabernet, 17% merlot, 17% malbec and 16% petit verdot, this is a tightly knit, powerful expression defined by a thrust of fine-grained tannins lofting over a coterie of plum, blackcurrant, pastille, sage and bay leaf. There is serious gravitas about this and it will age exceptionally well. Screwcap. 14% alc. **Rating** 95 **To** 2030 $45 NG

🍷🍷🍷🍷🍷 **Three Hills Margaret River Chardonnay 2015** Rating 93 To 2024 $45 NG
Three Hills Margaret River Malbec 2015 Rating 93 To 2030 $38 NG
Margaret River SBS 2016 Rating 92 To 2024 $24 NG ✪
Margaret River Rose 2016 Rating 92 To 2018 $22 NG ✪
Margaret River Cabernet Merlot 2015 Rating 92 To 2025 $24 NG ✪
Margaret River Shiraz 2015 Rating 91 To 2023 $30 NG
Margaret River Chardonnay 2015 Rating 90 To 2024 $24 NG
Three Hills Margaret River Grenache Shiraz Mataro 2015 Rating 90 To 2023 $30 NG
Margaret River Merlot 2015 Rating 90 To 2023 $24 NG

Harbord Wines ★★★★

PO Box 41, Stockwell, SA 5355 **Region** Barossa Valley
T (08) 8562 2598 **www.**harbordwines.com.au **Open** Not
Winemaker Roger Harbord **Est.** 2003 **Dozens** 500
Roger Harbord is a well known and respected Barossa winemaker, with over 20 years' experience, the last 10 as chief winemaker for Cellarmasters Wines, Normans and Ewinexchange. He has set up his own virtual winery as a complementary activity; the grapes are contract-grown (sources include Vine Vale, Moppa, Greenock and Marananga), and he leases winery space and equipment to make and mature the wines. Exports to the UK, the US, Singapore and China.

🍷🍷🍷🍷🍷 **Tendril Barossa Valley Shiraz 2015** Made in small batches, matured in used French and American hogsheads for 14 months. It may not be exciting or electrifying, but it is built upon the foundations of some seriously good quality shiraz. On the full side of medium-bodied, it has a velvety mouthfeel, the flavours ranging through plum, blackberry and a touch of spice. Screwcap. 14.5% alc. Rating 94 To 2035 $25 ✪

Harcourt Valley Vineyards   ★★★★☆

3339 Calder Highway, Harcourt, Vic 3453 **Region** Bendigo
T (03) 5474 2223 **www.**harcourtvalley.com.au **Open** 7 days 11–5
Winemaker Quinn Livingstone **Est.** 1975 **Dozens** 2500 **Vyds** 4ha
Using 100% estate-grown fruit Quinn Livingstone (second-generation winemaker) is making a number of small batch wines from the property. Minimal fruit handling is used in the winemaking process. The tasting area overlooks the vines, with a large window that allows visitors to see the activity in the winery. Founder Barbara Broughton died in '12, aged 91, and Quinn's mother, Barbara Livingstone, has now retired. Exports to China.

♥♥♥♥♥ **Barbara's Bendigo Shiraz 2015** A first class evocation of all that is great with Bendigo shiraz: a deep and profound well of spiced black fruits provide a velvety mouthfeel and a long finish. The tannin and oak management is the icing on the cake. Screwcap. 14.5% alc. **Rating** 95 To 2030 $25 ✪

♥♥♥♥♡ **Mt Camel Range Heathcote Shiraz 2015 Rating** 93 To 2025 $25 ✪

Hardys   ★★★★★

202 Main Road, McLaren Vale, SA 5171 **Region** McLaren Vale
T (08) 8329 4124 **www.**hardyswine.com.au **Open** Mon–Fri 11–4, w'ends 10–4
Winemaker Paul Lapsley (Chief) **Est.** 1853 **Dozens** NFP
The 1992 merger of Thomas Hardy and the Berri Renmano group may have had some elements of a forced marriage, but the merged group prospered over the next 10 years. So successful was it that a further marriage followed in early 2003, with Constellation Wines of the US the groom, BRL Hardy the bride, creating the largest wine group in the world (the Australian arm was known as Constellation Wines Australia, or CWA); but it is now part of the Accolade Wines group. The Hardys wine brands are headed by Thomas Hardy Cabernet Sauvignon, Eileen Hardy Chardonnay, Pinot Noir and Shiraz; then the Sir James range of sparkling wines; next the HRB wines, the William Hardy quartet; then the expanded Oomoo range and the Nottage Hill wines. The 'Big Company' slur is ill deserved. These are some of Australia's greatest wines. Exports to all major markets.

♥♥♥♥♥ **Eileen Hardy Chardonnay 2015** From Tasmania, the Yarra Valley and Tumbarumba. Gleaming straw-green; manages to effortlessly combine power and intensity with elegance and glorious varietal fruit expression. White stone fruit is at the very heart of a palate that aspires to perfection. Quality French oak and minerally acidity play their parts, albeit largely forgotten in the wealth of fruit. Screwcap. 13.5% alc. **Rating** 98 To 2030 $95 ✪

Eileen Hardy Shiraz 2015 From 80yo vines in McLaren Vale, wild yeast–open fermented, basket-pressed, matured in French oak (70% new). Deep, dense crimson-purple; it instantaneously stamps its extreme quality in the same way as prior vintages. It fuses blackberry, plum, dark chocolate and oak into a single stream of superbly balanced flavour, making deconstruction a waste of time at best, sacrilege at worst. Screwcap. 14.5% alc. **Rating** 98 To 2045 $125 ✪

Barrel Selected Rare Liqueur Sauvignon Blanc NV Bottle no. 97. Pale golden amber; a totally unique style produced from Australia's oldest sauvignon blanc vines, grown in McLaren Vale. Needless to say, very intense and very complex rancio with spicy, caramelised citrus fruit, honeycomb, butterscotch and almost fresh citrus notes buried on the finish. Remarkable balance. 500ml. Vino-Lok. 18% alc. **Rating** 98 $100 ✪

Tintara Sub Regional Blewitt Springs McLaren Vale Shiraz 2015 This is a northern Rhône lookalike, with a spicy savoury background to its beautifully structured and textured palate, full of spice, purple and black fruits and fine tannins. Screwcap. 14.5% alc. **Rating** 97 To 2040 $80 ✪

Upper Tintara McLaren Vale Shiraz 2013 Vines over 100yo are on the site of the original Hardys Tintara winery; open-fermented, pneumatic-plunged. It is a beautifully weighted medium-bodied wine with a spray of red and black fruits, fine tannins and only a wisp of dark chocolate. A 50-year wine in the making despite its already evident elegance. Screwcap. 14% alc. **Rating** 97 **To** 2063 $70 ○

HRB Cabernet Sauvignon 2015 Bin D670. Hardys has been making regional blends since 1865, so this simply follows Thomas Hardy's prescription. Coonawarra and Frankland River, blended with McLaren Vale 150 years after the edict. The full-bodied palate has the black-fruited power of a weightlifter and the balance of a highwire walker. It is one of those wines with an 100-year life stamped on it. Screwcap. 14% alc. **Rating** 97 **To** 2055 $40 ○

Thomas Hardy Cabernet Sauvignon 2014 The bouquet tells you what is to follow on the full-bodied palate. towering blackcurrant fruit with bay leaf, black olive and earth all dripping from the fruit where they meet implacable tannins and a lick of French oak. Screwcap. 14% alc. **Rating** 97 **To** 2049 $130 ○

ΨΨΨΨΨ **HRB Pinot Noir 2015** Bin D667. Yarra Valley/Tasmania. This is a thoroughly modern version of a regional blend. Still in its infancy, the bouquet as yet reticent, the palate filled with dark cherry and plum fruit, and a complex texture and structure promising much with a few more years in bottle, the aftertaste already complex. Screwcap. 13.5% alc. **Rating** 95 **To** 2028 $30 ○

Tintara Yeenunga Single Vineyard McLaren Vale Shiraz 2015 From a vineyard high above the Onkaparinga Gorge, it is a rich, full-bodied shiraz full of black fruits, dark chocolate and firm tannins. Its quality, balance and length are plain to see, but it's not open for business yet. An outstanding candidate for the cellar. Screwcap. 14% alc. **Rating** 95 **To** 2040 $80

HRB Shiraz 2015 Bin D671. The individual vineyard components (from McLaren Vale and Clare Valley) are matured separately in French oak (25% new) for 16 months. Very skilled blending allows the dark chocolate and plum flavours of McLaren Vale to show in wine, with particularly good texture and structure ex the Clare Valley portion. The result is a wine that is no more than medium-bodied. Screwcap. 14% alc. **Rating** 95 **To** 2030 $40

HRB Shiraz 2014 Bin D662. McLaren Vale/Frankland River/Clare Valley. Only Hardys has the viticultural resources to make a synergistic blend such as this, the unexpected result a coherent medium-bodied wine that is light on its feet, skipping through the Full Monty of red and black berry fruits, the tannins adding to the overall picture of elegance. Screwcap. 14.5% alc. **Rating** 95 **To** 2040 $30 ○

HRB Riesling 2016 Bin D669. Why does Hardys blend Clare Valley and Tasmania riesling? Because it can, and was the first to do so. It's got heaps of depth and attitude, but just how brilliantly successful the ploy may be will only be known in 5–10 years. Until then, Tasmanian acidity keeps the Clare Valley fruit with its nose to the ground. Screwcap. 12.5% alc. **Rating** 94 **To** 2031 $40

HRB Chardonnay 2015 Bin D664. A blend of grapes from Tumbarumba, Yarra Valley, Margaret River, Adelaide Hills and Pemberton, all separately barrel-fermented and matured until the complicated blending trials took place with Paul Lapsley wielding the baton. It is intense and powerful, the flavours of perfectly ripened cool-grown chardonnay paying little or no attention to the oak. Screwcap. 13.5% alc. **Rating** 94 **To** 2028 $30 ○

Tintara McLaren Vale Shiraz 2015 Dense crimson-purple; the bouquet provides the path for the medium to full-bodied palate to follow, inky black fruits and dark chocolate the cornerstone, ripe tannins integrated from the outset. If all this isn't enough, licorice and dark cherry are also on display. Screwcap. 14.5% alc. **Rating** 94 **To** 2028 $28 ○

Barrel Selected Rare Tawny NV Grenache shiraz, bottle no. 788. Golden brown; an impressive blend of very old and young material with daunting alcohol and nutty rancio complexity. The alcohol will frighten the odd horse or two. 500ml. Vino-Lok. 20% alc. **Rating** 94 $100

ŶŶŶŶŶ Tintara McLaren Vale Sangiovese 2015 Rating 93 To 2021 $28
Tintara McLaren Vale Grenache Shiraz Mataro 2016 Rating 92
To 2025 $28
Tintara McLaren Vale Fiano 2016 Rating 90 To 2021 $28
Brave New World McLaren Vale Grenache Shiraz Mourvedre 2016
Rating 90 To 2021 $20 ✪
HRB Cabernet Sauvignon 2014 Rating 90 To 2024 $30

Hare's Chase   ★★★★☆

PO Box 46, Melrose Park, SA 5039 **Region** Barossa Valley
T (08) 8277 3506 **www**.hareschase.com **Open** Not
Winemaker Peter Taylor **Est.** 1998 **Dozens** 5000 **Vyds** 16.8ha
Hare's Chase is the creation of two families, headed respectively by Peter Taylor as winemaker,
with over 30 vintages' experience and Mike de la Haye as general manager; they own
an 100-year-old vineyard in the Marananga Valley area of the Barossa Valley. The simple,
functional winery sits at the top of a rocky hill in the centre of the vineyard, which has some
of the best red soil available for dry-grown viticulture. In 2016 Peter and Mike say 'After 15
years of developing Hare's Chase, we are starting to believe we may one day give up our day
jobs.' Exports to the US, Canada, Switzerland, Singapore, Hong Kong, Malaysia and China.

ŶŶŶŶŶ **Barossa Valley Shiraz 2013** This has been made with great skill, for while it
has the alcohol, fruit power and depth, tannins and American oak that mark it as
Barossa Valley and nothing else, it has an open weave, a lightness of touch rarely
encountered. Great value, its future guaranteed by its balance. Screwcap. 14.5% alc.
Rating 96 To 2033 $38 ✪

ŶŶŶŶŶ Ironscraper Barossa Shiraz 2015 Rating 93 To 2029 $35 JF

Harewood Estate   ★★★★★

Scotsdale Road, Denmark, WA 6333 **Region** Denmark
T (08) 9840 9078 **www**.harewood.com.au **Open** details on website
Winemaker James Kellie, Paul Nelson **Est.** 1988 **Dozens** 15 000 **Vyds** 19.2ha
In 2003 James Kellie, responsible for the contract making of Harewood's wines since
1998, purchased the estate with his father and sister as partners. A 300-tonne winery was
constructed, offering both contract winemaking services for the Great Southern region and
the ability to expand the Harewood range to include subregional wines. In January 2010
James, together with wife Careena, purchased his father's and sister's shares to become 100%
owners. Exports to the UK, the US, Denmark, Switzerland, Indonesia, Hong Kong, Malaysia,
Macau, Singapore, China and Japan.

ŶŶŶŶŶ **Denmark Riesling 2016** A notably elegant wine exhibiting white floras, apricot
and lemon zest. The acidity is juicy rather than hard: a palpably energetic bead,
yet never obtuse, serving to draw up the saliva and make one hanker for the next
glass and a South-East Asian salad. A beautiful, balletic riesling. Screwcap. 12% alc.
Rating 97 To 2028 $24 NG ✪

ŶŶŶŶŶ **Mount Barker Riesling 2016** A warmer expression of apricot, quince and ripe
apple, threaded with a spicy after-tang of ginger, this coats the mouth with an
uncanny Germanic richness despite its delicacy. Natural acidity reverberates across
the cheeks, with the flavours long and sinuous. Screwcap. 12.5% alc. Rating 96 To
2028 $24 NG ✪
Porongurup Riesling 2016 Made solely with free-run juice as is the wont of all
of Harewood's subregional-specific rieslings, this is grapefruit zest and lime cordial,
driven across a dry, pumice-like palate by zesty acidity and a Pez-like prickle of
unresolved CO_2 for zip and aromatic lift. Powerful in the context of the stable, the
wine is chiselled and strident across the palate, finishing with an emphatic phenolic
pucker. Screwcap. 12.5% alc. Rating 95 To 2028 $24 NG ✪

Reserve Denmark Semillon Sauvignon Blanc 2016 Lemon oil, lanolin, ripe apricot and durian aromas spring from the glass, before a bite and dusting of coconut sprinkles is conferred by high quality new French oak. The palate boasts considerable breadth and some leesy detail following partial barrel fermentation, while strutting across a riff of highwired, slatey acidity. Screwcap. 13% alc. Rating 94 To 2022 $27 NG ❂

ΤΤΤΤΩ Reserve Denmark Chardonnay 2015 Rating 93 To 2023 $34 NG
Frankland River Riesling 2016 Rating 92 To 2026 $24 NG ❂
Great Southern SBS 2016 Rating 92 To 2020 $21 NG ❂
Denmark Pinot Noir 2016 Rating 92 To 2021 $21 NG ❂
F Block Great Southern Pinot Noir 2016 Rating 92 To 2026 $27 NG
Denmark Chardonnay 2016 Rating 91 To 2023 $27 NG
Great Southern Cabernet Merlot 2015 Rating 91 To 2030 $21 NG ❂

Hart & Hunter ★★★★★

Gabriel's Paddock, 463 Deasys Road, Pokolbin, NSW 2325 Region Hunter Valley
T 0401 605 219 www.hartandhunter.com.au Open Thurs–Sun 10–4
Winemaker Damien Stevens, Jodie Belleville Est. 2009 Dozens 2500
This is the venture of winemaking couple Damien Stevens and Jodie Belleville, with partners Daniel and Elle Hart. The grapes are purchased from highly regarded growers within the Hunter, with the emphasis on single vineyard wines and small batch processing. Continuing success for the venture led to the opening of a cellar door in late 2015, offering not only the three best-known Hunter varieties, but also experimental wines and alternative varieties.

ΤΤΤΤΤ Single Vineyard Series The Hill Shiraz 2011 Excellent retention of red–purple hue; first tasted by Tyson Stelzer 4 years ago (95 points) with comments on its concentration and balance. Since then it has calmly fulfilled expectations, and it is absolutely certain it will flourish over the next 10 years and well beyond as a classic Hunter Valley shiraz with a magical mix of plummy and earthy flavours on a long, even finish. Screwcap. 13.5% alc. Rating 96 To 2036 $75 ❂
Single Vineyard Series Oakey Creek Semillon 2016 A great example of modern Hunter Valley semillon that disputes riesling's entitlement to citrus as its unique DNA. This is strikingly racy, with lemon juice, lemongrass and a dash of lime all coated by minerally acidity. Balance and length are spot on. Screwcap. 11% alc. Rating 95 To 2029 $30 ❂
Single Vineyard Series The Remparts Semillon 2016 The distinctly floral bouquet introduces a palate that has some of the richness which develops in older semillons, but has nothing to do with premature development. This doesn't confront you with its acidity, but it's built deep within the walls of the palate. Screwcap. 11% alc. Rating 95 To 2029 $30 ❂
Single Vineyard Series Oakey Creek Semillon 2013 Brilliant green-quartz; first tasted 3 years ago, and is fulfilling all the promise it then had, although it's still got a decade-long journey in front of it. The secret of Hunter Valley semillon is its purity and freshness, acidity a constant number that seems to soften as the wine ages, when in fact it's the growth of and change in the fruit flavours that mark its development. Screwcap. 10.5% alc. Rating 95 To 2027 $39
Single Vineyard Series Syrah 2014 The light, but bright and clear colour is unexpected in the context of '14, but it's explained by the modest alcohol, and validated by the purity and freshness of the red-berried palate. It has got some of the earmarks of pinot noir, and pleads to be enjoyed over the next 3–5 years. Screwcap. 13% alc. Rating 95 To 2024 $40
Dr B's Fiano 2016 Is there a new star in the Hunter sky? This fiano has freshness, purity and intensity, coming from the same forge as young, high quality semillon. It will be fascinating to watch the development of this (and subsequent vintages) over time. Screwcap. 11.5% alc. Rating 94 To 2023 $28 ❂

ΤΤΤΤΩ Twenty Six Rows Chardonnay 2015 Rating 93 To 2022 $40
Fox Force Five Shiraz 2015 Rating 90 To 2030 $47

Hart of the Barossa

Cnr Vine Vale Road/Light Pass Road, Tanunda, SA 5352 **Region** Barossa Valley
T 0412 586 006 **www.**hartofthebarossa.com.au **Open** By appt
Winemaker Michael and Alisa Hart, Troy Kalleske **Est.** 2007 **Dozens** 2200 **Vyds** 6.5ha
The ancestors of Michael and Alisa Hart arrived in SA in 1845, their first address (with seven children) a hollow tree on the banks of the North Para River. Michael and Alisa personally tend the vineyard, which is the oldest certified organic vineyard in the Barossa Valley, and includes a patch of 110-year-old shiraz. The quality of the wines coming from these vines is exceptional; unfortunately, there is only enough to fill two hogsheads a year (66 dozen bottles). The other wines made are also impressive, particularly given their prices. Exports to Germany, Hong Kong, Taiwan and China.

🍷🍷🍷🍷🍷 **Ye Faithful Limited Release Old Vine Shiraz 2014** Bless this wine, for it makes clear the argument that old vines, in this case 110 years, are distinctive and distinguished. The full-bodied palate is glossy and seamless, the tannins velvety and powerful, and the finish long. In between there's licorice, sweet oak and a core of exceptional fruit. Screwcap. 14.5% alc. **Rating** 95 **To** 2034 $79 JF

🍷🍷🍷🍷🍸 **The Blesing Limited Release Cabernet Sauvignon 2014** Rating 90 **To** 2025 $32 JF

Haselgrove Wines

187 Sand Road, McLaren Vale, SA 5171 **Region** McLaren Vale
T (08) 8323 8706 **www.**haselgrove.com.au **Open** By appt
Winemaker Andre Bondar **Est.** 1981 **Dozens** 40 000 **Vyds** 9.7ha
Italian-Australian industry veterans Don Totino, Don Luca, Tony Carrocci and Steve Maglieri decided to purchase Haselgrove 'over a game of cards and couple of hearty reds' in 2008. They have completely changed the product range, its price and its presentation: the Legend Series $75 to $150, the Origin Series at $35, and First Cut at $18. Then there is the very large custom crush facility which provides all-important cash flow. Exports to Canada, Malaysia, Hong Kong, China and NZ.

🍷🍷🍷🍷🍷 **Col Cross Single Vineyard McLaren Vale Shiraz 2015** From a single vineyard of old vines, age not specified, crushed into open fermenters, 8 days on skins, pressed to used French hogsheads for 18 months. Excellent colour with its full-bodied powerful structure, the dark ripe concentrated fruit adding a layer to its savoury profile with a mix of soy sauce, licorice, dark chocolate, dried herbs and Middle Eastern spices. Diam. 14.5% alc. **Rating** 96 **To** 2029 $90 JF
Catkin McLaren Vale Shiraz 2015 Fruit from four vineyards, fermented separately and each adding something special to the end result – a balanced wine. Nothing is out of place: the right amount of fruit, savouriness, textural tannins, full-bodied but not weighty and a lovely flourish in the finish. Screwcap. 14.5% alc. **Rating** 95 **To** 2025 $40 JF
The Lear McLaren Vale Shiraz 2015 This is really polished, with velvety rich tannins teased out of the powerful thrust of dark fruit, menthol and spice. It's structured and full-bodied yet seems effortless. Screwcap. 14.5% alc. **Rating** 95 **To** 2029 $90 JF
Protector McLaren Vale Cabernet Sauvignon 2015 No doubting the variety with its leafy freshness of currants, blackberries; it is supple, with equally pliable tannins, some grip and lemony acidity. A vivacious wine that hasn't succumbed to oak flavours. Nicely played. 14.5% alc. **Rating** 95 **To** 2025 $40 JF

🍷🍷🍷🍷🍸 **Scarce Earth The Ambassador Shiraz 2015** Rating 93 **To** 2024 $85 JF
Switch Grenache Shiraz Mourvedre 2015 Rating 93 **To** 2024 $40 JF
Staff Adelaide Hills Chardonnay 2016 Rating 91 **To** 2021 $30 JF

Hastwell & Lightfoot

301 Foggos Road, McLaren Vale, SA 5171 **Region** McLaren Vale
T (08) 8323 8692 **www**.hastwellandlightfoot.com.au **Open** Fri-Sun 11-5
Winemaker James Hastwell **Est.** 1988 **Dozens** 4500 **Vyds** 16ha
Established in 1988 by Mark and Wendy Hastwell and Martin and Jill Lightfoot. Having initially sold much of the production, they have made a significant commitment to the Hastwell & Lightfoot brand, producing wines from estate-grown varieties. The vines are grafted onto devigorating rootstocks that restrain the development of dead fruit characters in warmer seasons. James Hastwell, son of Mark and Wendy, has his winery just 2km from the vineyard. Exports to the UK, the US, Canada, Malaysia, Taiwan, Singapore and China.

McLaren Vale Vermentino 2016 Vermentino and McLaren Vale are firm friends. This has an attractive mix of citrus and gently tropical fruits, given structure and length by crisp, lingering acidity. Screwcap. 13% alc. **Rating** 90 **To** 2021 $21 ✪

McLaren Vale Shiraz 2013 Rating 89 **To** 2028 $25

Hatherleigh Vineyard

35 Redground Heights Road, Laggan, NSW 2583 **Region** Southern New South Wales
T 0418 688 794 **www**.nickbulleid.com/hatherleigh **Open** Not
Winemaker Nick Bulleid, Stuart Hordern **Est.** 1996 **Dozens** 250 **Vyds** 1ha
This is the venture of long-term Brokenwood partner and peripatetic wine consultant Nick Bulleid. It has been a slowly, slowly venture, with all sorts of obstacles along the way, with 1ha of pinot noir planted between 1996 and '99, but part thereafter grafted to a better clone, resulting in a clonal mix of MV6 (predominant) with two rows of clone 777 and a few vines of clone 115. The wines are made at Brokenwood under the joint direction of Stuart Hordern and Nick, and are available though the website.

Pinot Noir 2013 Winemaker/owner Nick Bulleid MW's small vineyard at Laggan (910m) is a quixotic busman's holiday. It's a seriously cool region (snow at budburst this vintage), and it took time for the pieces to come together – the vines have become mature and Nick's accumulated knowledge has grown. Made with 20% whole bunches and matured in new and used French barriques. It is light-bodied, but with classic secondary flavours, warm spices and foresty notes powering the palate. Ready now. Screwcap. 13% alc. **Rating** 95 **To** 2023

Hay Shed Hill Wines

511 Harmans Mill Road, Wilyabrup, WA 6280 **Region** Margaret River
T (08) 9755 6046 **www**.hayshedhill.com.au **Open** 7 days 10–5
Winemaker Michael Kerrigan **Est.** 1987 **Dozens** 24000 **Vyds** 18.55ha
Mike Kerrigan, former winemaker at Howard Park, acquired the business in late 2006 (with co-ownership by the West Cape Howe syndicate) and is now the full-time winemaker. He had every confidence that he could dramatically lift the quality of the wines, and has done precisely that. The five wines in the Vineyard, White Label and Block series are all made from estate-grown grapes. The Block series are the ultimate site-specific wines, made from separate blocks within the vineyard. They consist of Block 1 Semillon Sauvignon Blanc, Block 6 Chardonnay, Block 8 Cabernet Franc and Block 2 Cabernet Sauvignon. The Pitchfork wines are made from contract-grown grapes in the region. Exports to the UK, the US, Denmark, Singapore, Malaysia, Japan, Hong Kong and China.

Margaret River Sauvignon Blanc Semillon 2016 A perfect example of Margaret River SBS. All the work has been done in the vineyard, the winery a hands-off zone as varietal fruit, not oak, has shaped the wine. Some grassy/pea pod aromas quickly yield to the even flow of passionfruit, pineapple and guava on the supple palate. Screwcap. 12.5% alc. **Rating** 95 **To** 2018 $22 ✪
Block 1 Margaret River Semillon Sauvignon Blanc 2016 44yo dry-grown vines, the two components picked, pressed and co-fermented, the wine matured

in used French barriques. A fresh, positively juicy, mouthfeel to stone and tropical fruit flavours. Delicious. Screwcap. 12% alc. **Rating** 95 **To** 2021 $30 ✪

Margaret River Chardonnay 2015 Fermented in French barriques (30% new), matured for 10 months. Margaret River complexity and depth are intensified by the low yields and use of free-run juice, which have soaked up the oak. Grapefruit flavours settle comfortably on the mid-palate, and are sustained through the length of the wine. Screwcap. 13% alc. **Rating** 95 **To** 2025 $28 ✪

Block 2 Margaret River Cabernet Sauvignon 2013 Deep crimson-purple; a richly textured and structured wine still in the early phase of its life, primary, lush cassis at its heart. The oak is yet to fully integrate, but will do so given time. Screwcap. 14% alc. **Rating** 94 **To** 2030 $55

Morrison's Gift 2014 40% cabernet sauvignon, 20% each of merlot and petit verdot and 10% each of malbec and cabernet franc; the vines 35–48yo. Matured for 15 months in French barriques (20% new). A luscious cascade of red, blue and black fruits and berries, the oak somewhat more than expected. The tannins are soft, the overall balance good. Screwcap. 14% alc. **Rating** 94 **To** 2029 $25 ✪

Margaret River Malbec 2015 Hand-picked, cold-soaked, open-fermented with cultured yeast, 18 days on skins, matured in French barriques (20% new) for 12 months. Crimson-purple; a high quality medium to full-bodied malbec full of plum and black fruits, the texture complex and satisfying, the tannins perfectly balanced and integrated. Screwcap. 14% alc. **Rating** 94 **To** 2029 $30

🍷🍷🍷🍷🍷 **Margaret River Pinot Noir Rose 2016** Rating 92 To 2018 $22 ✪
Margaret River Shiraz Tempranillo 2015 Rating 92 To 2029 $22
Margaret River Tempranillo 2015 Rating 92 To 2030 $30
G40 Mount Barker Riesling 2016 Rating 92 To 2026 $25
Margaret River Grenache 2015 Rating 91 To 2030 $30
Pitchfork Cabernet Merlot 2014 Rating 91 To 2022 $17 SC ✪
Pitchfork Semillon Sauvignon Blanc 2016 Rating 90 To 2018 $17 ✪
Pitchfork Margaret River Chardonnay 2016 Rating 90 To 2020 $17 ✪
Pitchfork Margaret River Shiraz 2014 Rating 90 To 2019 $17 SC ✪
Margaret River Cabernet Merlot 2015 Rating 90 To 2024 $22
Pitchfork Cabernet Merlot 2015 Rating 90 To 2023 $17

🍂 Hayes Family Wines   ★★★★★

102 Mattiske Road, Stone Well, SA 5352 **Region** Barossa Valley
T 0419 706 552 **www.**hayesfamilywines.com **Open** By appt
Winemaker Andrew Seppelt **Est.** 2014 **Dozens** 200 **Vyds** 5ha
Brings together the Hayes, Seppelt and Schulz families, each bringing a contribution to the partnership. Andrew Seppelt has 20+ years of winemaking in the Barossa, Marcus Schulz has more than 50 years of grapegrowing in the northern Barossa, and Brett Hayes and family have 25+ years of agriculture and business experience. In late 2016 the business was expanded by the purchase of a 5ha old vineyard in the Stone Well district on the western ridge of the Barossa Valley. The business is off to a flying start with its '15 vintage wines.

🍷🍷🍷🍷🍷 **Barossa Valley Shiraz 2015** A deceptive medium-bodied shiraz that reveals more about itself each time it is retasted, in particular the intense juicy black fruits that are wrapped within folds of new French oak and supple tannins. Ostentatious? No. Classy? Yes. Screwcap. 14.3% alc. **Rating** 95 **To** 2030 $32 ✪

Barossa Valley Mataro Shiraz 2015 An 80/20% blend from the Ebenezer district. The colour is bright but light; a beautifully made wine that has ensured the quality of fruit by picking at exactly the right time, and then keeping the oak where it should be. The flavours are of purple (plum) and blue fruits, the tannins fine and perfectly weighted. If owners look like their dogs, this looks like its elegant labels (front and back). Screwcap. 14.1% alc. **Rating** 95 **To** 2025 $32 ✪

Barossa Valley Mataro 2015 Bottle no. 18 of 300. There's a laudable approach with all the Hayes Family wines of picking while there's fruit freshness and adequate acidity. This fragrant mataro has delicious red fruits and superfine tannins. Screwcap. 14% alc. **Rating** 94 **To** 2023 $26 ✪

Head Wines

Lot 1 Stonewell Road, Stonewell, SA 5352 **Region** Barossa Valley
T 0413 114 233 **www.**headwines.com.au **Open** By appt Feb–Apr
Winemaker Alex Head **Est.** 2006 **Dozens** 5000 **Vyds** 7.5ha
Head Wines is the venture of Alex Head, who came into the wine industry in 1997 with a degree in biochemistry from Sydney University. Experience in fine wine stores, importers and an auction house was followed by vintage work at wineries he admired: Tyrrell's, Torbreck, Laughing Jack and Cirillo Estate. The naming of the wines reflects his fascination with Côte-Rôtie in the Northern Rhône Valley. The two facing slopes in Côte-Rôtie are known as Côte Blonde and Côte Brune. Head's Blonde comes from an east-facing slope in the Stone Well area, while The Brunette comes from a very low-yielding vineyard in the Moppa area. In each case, open fermentation (with whole bunches) and basket pressing precedes maturation in French oak. Exports to Denmark, The Netherlands and Japan.

🍷🍷🍷🍷🍷 **Ancestor Vine Springton Eden Valley Grenache 2015** An assiduously detailed grenache boasting strident vinosity across a velour of raspberry, currant and plum, macerated in dark cherry liqueur and given lift and a mediating spike by 20% whole bunches. This can only come from ancient vines, here 156yo. Filigreed, sandy tannins and a bead of zesty acidity give form to the cascade of fruit. Screwcap. 14.5% alc. **Rating** 98 **To** 2035 $100 NG ✪

Rare Barossa Valley Tawny NV Old vine grenache aged in a shed and finished off for detail and composure in whisky barrels. It gives a thrilling ride of toasted walnut, treacle and ginger spice, spread across the palate with a peacock's flourish of compelling complexity, perfectly integrated spirit and searing length. Screwcap. 20% alc. **Rating** 98 $50 NG ✪

Old Vine Greenock Barossa Valley Grenache 2015 From a 101yo vineyard, chiselled of slate. Grenache's liquid kirsch qualities are on full display. These are restrained by a dollop of old vine mataro for ferruginous grip, 10% stems in the ferment and a gentle extraction regime, employing whole berries, wild yeast and 17 months' oak maturation. Pure, unadulterated pleasure. Screwcap. 14.5% alc. **Rating** 97 **To** 2026 $35 NG ✪

🍷🍷🍷🍷🍷 **The Brunette Moppa Barossa Valley Shiraz 2015** Barossan sweetness and a regional warmth are offset against an ethereal palate of polished tannins, a dark sheen of fruit and impeccably melded oak. A mid-weighted wine. Some smoked meat, tapenade, hoisin and pepper spice provide an echo and clear definition of the variety. Screwcap. 14.2% alc. **Rating** 96 **To** 2035 $55 NG ✪

Head Red Barossa Valley Shiraz 2015 The back label puts it succinctly: 'this is the best value blend of Barossa Valley shiraz I can make each year'. The bouquet is super-fragrant, the medium-bodied palate vibrant and fresh, the flavours circling red and black fruits, multi-spices and a touch of black licorice, the tannins judged to perfection. Screwcap. 14% alc. **Rating** 95 **To** 2025 $25 ✪

The Blonde Stone Well Barossa Valley Shiraz 2015 A classy wine of cascading sweet fruit flavours and myriad spices. 33% new French oak is impeccably integrated; the fine, papery tannins are polished and the acidity marked and racy, an imprint of the limestone substrata on which the vineyard is planted. Screwcap. 14.3% alc. **Rating** 95 **To** 2035 $45 NG

Stonegarden Eden Valley Riesling 2016 A highly Germanic expression of riesling that is not afraid of melding its tensile engine of acidity to a chassis of phenolic grunt. A warm palate, all autumnal fruits and quince compote, suggests a sunnier clime. This is Eden Valley meets the Pfalz, expanding ever onward across a long finish bristling with a citrus tang and ginger spice. Very fine. Screwcap. 12% alc. **Rating** 94 **To** 2031 $25 NG ✪

The Contrarian Krondorf Barossa Valley Shiraz 2015 An annual endeavour to express a single Barossan site in a contrarian fashion. One's first impression is of smoked meat, black cherry fruit, cinnamon oak and a ferruginous core of bramble, anise and spice melded to sinewy, gritty tannins, the legacy of judicious extraction across a wild yeast ferment and 20% stem retention, before ageing in large format French oak. Screwcap. 14.2% alc. **Rating** 94 **To** 2033 $35 NG

ŶŶŶŶ♀ **Barossa Valley Grenache Rose 2016 Rating** 93 **To** 2018 $25 NG ✪
Nouveau Barossa Valley Pinot Noir Touriga Nacional Montepulciano 2016 Rating 93 **To** 2019 $20 NG ✪
Head Red Barossa Valley GSM 2015 Rating 92 **To** 2021 $25 ✪

Heafod Glen Winery ★★★★

8691 West Swan Road, Henley Brook, WA 6055 **Region** Swan Valley
T (08) 9296 3444 **www**.heafodglenwine.com.au **Open** Wed–Sun 10–5
Winemaker Liam Clarke **Est.** 1999 **Dozens** 2500 **Vyds** 3ha
A combined vineyard and restaurant business, each set on outdoing the other, each with major accolades. Founder Neil Head taught himself winemaking, but in 2007 employed Liam Clarke (with a degree in viticulture and oenology), and a string of significant show successes for Verdelho, Viognier and Reserve Chardonnay has followed. Chesters Restaurant has received many awards over the years. Exports to Japan.

ŶŶŶŶŶ **HB2 Vineyard Swan Valley Semillon 2016** Whole-bunch pressed, multiple yeast strains for barrel fermentation in French oak. Tangy, lively and crisp, it looks as if its stay in oak wasn't long. It has a mix of lemongrass, lemon sherbet and Meyer lemon juice, finishing with crisp acidity. Already an interesting wine, but more will come to those who wait. Screwcap. 11.5% alc. **Rating** 94 **To** 2023 $27

Heartland Wines ★★★★

The Winehouse, Wellington Road, Langhorne Creek, SA 5255 **Region** Langhorne Creek
T (08) 8333 1363 **www**.heartlandwines.com.au **Open** 7 days 10–5
Winemaker Ben Glaetzer **Est.** 2001 **Dozens** 50 000 **Vyds** 200ha
A joint venture of industry veterans: winemakers Ben Glaetzer and Scott Collett, and wine industry management specialist Grant Tilbrook. Heartland focuses on cabernet sauvignon and shiraz from Langhorne Creek, John Glaetzer (head winemaker at Wolf Blass for over 30 years, and Ben's uncle) liaising with growers and vineyards he has known for over three decades, the wines made by Ben at Barossa Vintners. Exports to all major markets.

ŶŶŶŶ♀ **Langhorne Creek One 2014** Cabernet sauvignon and shiraz. Hugely oaky on the bouquet, but the richness of the fruit manages to find a way through, and it's a powerful combination. A flood of flavour, with ripe blackberries and sweet oakiness to the fore, somewhat larger than life, but satisfying withal. Screwcap. **Rating** 93 **To** 2028 $79 SC
First Release Langhorne Creek Malbec 2015 This is a catchy wine. The bouquet is a riot of berry fruit; raspberry, boysenberry, blueberry and more. Ultra-fresh and inviting. A background of scented oak fits in easily. The palate picks up the theme, juicy and long. Fun to drink. Screwcap. 14.5% alc. **Rating** 92 **To** 2026 $50 SC
Directors' Cut Langhorne Creek Shiraz 2014 The licorice aroma of Langhorne Creek shiraz is the introduction to the bouquet here, followed by toasty oak, Asian spice and black fruit, roughly in that order. Velvety in texture, sweet-fruited and generous in flavour, it's an attractive package. Screwcap. **Rating** 91 **To** 2032 $32 SC
Langhorne Creek Shiraz 2014 No surprises from this release, which will keep its followers happy. Rich, ripe blackberry fruit in spades and a generous dollop of oak are the order of the day, with some sweet spice and chocolate in tow. The tannin is just enough for good balance without attracting too much attention. Screwcap. 14.5% alc. **Rating** 90 **To** 2021 $18 SC ✪
Spice Trader Langhorne Creek Shiraz Cabernet Sauvignon 2014
Easygoing, undemanding, and ultimately quite satisfying. This is a wine that

does its job very well. It offers ripe berry aromas, a touch of spice, a hint of
chocolate and warm earthiness on the bouquet. The palate is soft, although quite
mouthfilling, with slightly sweet-toned fruit which has a definite regionality about
it. On the money. Screwcap. 14.5% alc. Rating 90 To 2020 $15 SC **◑**

Directors' Cut Langhorne Creek Cabernet Sauvignon 2014 No escaping
the fact that oak is playing a big part here, its mocha and coffee aromas much in
evidence. The cabernet character makes its move on the palate, with blackcurrant
and blackberry flavours leading the way, and some cooler, leafy notes providing
another dimension. Screwcap. 14.5% alc. **Rating** 90 **To** 2034 $32 SC

Sposa e Sposa 2014 A blend of lagrein and dolcetto which has been a staple
Heartland combination for a few years now. Quite Italianate on the bouquet,
the fruit having a savoury sort of vinosity, matched with a biscuity, nutty quality.
A supple palate, mid-weight wine, the flavours melding with light but grippy
tannin. Just a fraction hot on the finish. Screwcap. 14.5% alc. **Rating** 90 **To** 2021
$18 SC **◑**

♥♥♥♥   Old Magnificent Shiraz 2015 Rating 89 To 2030 $100 SC

Heathcote Estate   ★★★★★

98 High Street, Heathcote, Vic 3523 **Region** Heathcote
T (03) 5433 2488 **www.**yabbylake.com **Open** 7 days 10–5
Winemaker Tom Carson, Chris Forge **Est.** 1998 **Dozens** 5000 **Vyds** 34ha
Heathcote Estate and Yabby Lake Vineyards are owned by the Kirby family, of Village
Roadshow Ltd. They purchased a prime piece of Heathcote red Cambrian soil in 1999,
planting shiraz (30ha) and grenache (4ha), the latter an interesting variant on viognier. The
wines are matured exclusively in French oak. The arrival of the hugely talented Tom Carson
as Group Winemaker has added lustre to the winery and its wines. The cellar door, situated in
an old bakery in the Heathcote township, provides a relaxed dining area. Exports to the US,
the UK, Canada, Sweden, Singapore, Hong Kong and China.

♥♥♥♥♡   Single Vineyard Shiraz 2015 This brightly coloured and complex wine has red
and black fruits and a little fresh earth, and the oak (French 20% new) has been
beautifully handled. There is good depth of fruit on the tightly wound palate. Just
needs 6 months to open up a little and then another 7–10 years plus for it to really
hit its straps. Screwcap. 14% alc. **Rating** 93 **To** 2030 $45 PR

Heathcote II   ★★★★★

290 Cornella-Toolleen Road, Toolleen, Vic 3551 **Region** Heathcote
T (03) 5433 6292 **www.**heathcote2.com **Open** W'ends 11–5
Winemaker Peder Rosdal **Est.** 1995 **Dozens** 500 **Vyds** 6.5ha
This is the venture of Danish-born, French-trained, Flying Winemaker (California, Spain and
Chablis) Peder Rosdal and viticulturist Lionel Flutto. The establishment of the vineyard dates
back to 1995, with further plantings since of shiraz (with the lion's share of 2.7ha), cabernet
sauvignon, cabernet franc, merlot, tempranillo and grenache. The vines are dry-grown on the
famed red Cambrian soil, and the wines are made onsite using hand-plunging, basket pressing
and (since 2004) French oak maturation. Exports to Denmark, Japan and Singapore.

♥♥♥♥♥   HD Shiraz 2012 Hand-sorted into new open-top French puncheons, 3 days
cold soak, hand-plunged, basket-pressed, matured for 22 months in French oak
(75% new). Deep crimson-purple; everything about this ultra full-bodied wine is
dialled up to maximum power: jet black fruits, tannins and French oak. All it needs
is 20+ years to come into a plateau of perfection. Its saving graces now are its
modest alcohol (no heat) and balance. Cork. 13.5% alc. **Rating** 96 **To** 2032 $89

Myola 2012 35% each of cabernet franc and merlot, 30% cabernet sauvignon,
separately vinified, 3 days cold soak, then a Bordeaux yeast-initiated fermentation,
matured in French oak for 12 months, blended and returned to oak (30% new) for
a further 10 months. Wow, does this pack a punch. There's no heat, just profound

fruit and tannins matched to size. The cassis flavours of cabernet are foremost, but blueberry and mulberry also contribute. Cork. 14% alc. **Rating** 96 **To** 2032 $55
Shiraz 2012 3 days cold soak, open-fermented, plunged, 14 days on skins, matured for 22 months in French oak (35% new). A full-bodied, rich display of intense black fruits backed by fine, persistent tannins and integrated cedary French oak. This also has balance, modest alcohol and a high quality cork. 13.5% alc. **Rating** 95 **To** 2037 $39

Heathcote Winery ★★★★

183–185 High Street, Heathcote, Vic 3523 **Region** Heathcote
T (03) 5433 2595 **www**.heathcotewinery.com.au **Open** 7 days 10–5
Winemaker Brendan Pudney **Est.** 1978 **Dozens** 8000 **Vyds** 14ha
The cellar door of Heathcote Winery is situated in the main street of Heathcote, housed in a restored miner's cottage built by Thomas Craven in 1854 to cater for the huge influx of gold miners. The winery is immediately behind the cellar door, and processed the first vintage in 1983, following the planting of the vineyards in '78. Shiraz and Shiraz Viognier account for 90% of the production.

ŶŶŶŶŶ **Cravens Place Shiraz 2015** Matured in used American and French oak. Has energy and freshness to its tapestry of red and black fruits, tannins and oak relegated to observer status. Has more juicy/spicy fruit than many of its peers. Nice surprise ex modest alcohol. Screwcap. 14% alc. **Rating** 92 **To** 2025 $22
The Origin Single Vineyard Shiraz 2014 From a single block on the Newlans Lane Vineyard. Full-bodied, with black fruits wrapped in French oak. This has its line flowing through from start to finish without a single break or hesitation, but needs time in the cellar. Screwcap. 14.5% alc. **Rating** 91 **To** 2034 $55
Mail Coach Viognier 2016 Yarra Yering and Elgee Park have viognier dating back to the '60s and early '70s, making the back label assertion of first mover of this wine dubious. Regardless, it does have some energy and freshness to its varietal expression, without undue oily phenolics. Screwcap. 13% alc. **Rating** 90 **To** 2020 $28

ŶŶŶŶ **Slaughterhouse Paddock Single Vineyard Shiraz 2014** **Rating** 89 **To** 2029 $55

Heathvale ★★★★★

300 Saw Pit Gully Road, via Keyneton, SA 5353 **Region** Eden Valley
T (08) 8564 8248 **www**.heathvale.com **Open** At Taste Eden Valley, Angaston
Winemaker Trevor March, Chris Taylor **Est.** 1987 **Dozens** 1200 **Vyds** 10ha
The origins of Heathvale go back to 1865, when William Heath purchased the property, building the homestead and establishing the vineyard. The wine was initially made in the cellar of the house, which still stands on the property (now occupied by owners Trevor and Faye March). The vineyards were re-established in 1987, and consist of shiraz, cabernet sauvignon, riesling, sagrantino and tempranillo. Between 2011 and '12 fundamental changes for the better took place. Stylish new labels are but an outward sign of the far more important changes to wine style, with winemaking now under the control of consultant Chris Taylor (Quattro Mano) and the introduction of French oak. Exports to China.

ŶŶŶŶŶ **The Reward Eden Valley Barossa Shiraz 2015** The wine is highly fragrant and expressive, with red and black cherry fruit supported by persistent but fine tannins, cedary oak ex maturation in 50% new French oak. Packaging is another plus. Screwcap. 14.5% alc. **Rating** 95 **To** 2035 $50
The Belief Eden Valley Sagrantino 2015 Wines from the handful of other plantings of sagrantino in Aus have kicked like an enraged mule with bitter tannins that put nebbiolo to shame. This is radically different, and the March family must be very happy with this delicious wine with its savoury/spicy dark/morello cherry fruit flavours. Its length and balance seal the deal – President Trump could do no better. Screwcap. 14.5% alc. **Rating** 95 **To** 2023 $37

The Encounter Eden Valley Barossa Cabernet Sauvignon 2015 The Eden Valley is able to produce cabernet with unequivocal cool climate savoury characters, this wine a prime example. Maturation in French oak (30% new) has built on the fruit foundation, providing context and structure on the medium to full-bodied palate. Screwcap. 14.5% alc. **Rating** 94 **To** 2030 $42

ŶŶŶŶŶ The Witness Eden Valley Riesling 2016 Rating 90 To 2024 $27 SC

Heemskerk ★★★★★

660 Blessington Road, White Hills, Tas 7258 (postal) **Region** Southern Tasmania
T 1300 651 650 **www.**heemskerk.com.au **Open** Not
Winemaker Peter Munro **Est.** 1975 **Dozens** NFP
The Heemskerk brand established by Graham Wiltshire when he planted the first vines in 1965 (in the Pipers River region) is a very different business these days. It is part of TWE, and sources its grapes from vineyards including the Riversdale Vineyard in the Coal River Valley for riesling; the Lowestoft Vineyard in the Derwent Valley for pinot noir; and the Tolpuddle Vineyard in the Coal River Valley for chardonnay.

ŶŶŶŶŶ Abel's Tempest Chardonnay 2015 An immediately arresting chardonnay built on the framework of Tasmanian acidity. The flavours are of grapefruit, peach and nectarine, a mouthwatering, perfectly balanced trio. Some may baulk at the suggestion of balance, pointing to acidity, but it's like salt – some can't have too much, others can't hack it. Screwcap. 13.5% alc. **Rating** 95 **To** 2023 $25 ✪
Abel's Tempest Pinot Noir 2015 Good depth to the crimson hue; an aromatic bouquet with cherry and plum fruits coupled with spicy nuances, the medium-bodied palate flavours following on directly from the bouquet; excellent persistence of the fruit, and line, length and balance tick all the boxes. Tasmania is as Tasmania does. Screwcap. 13% alc. **Rating** 95 **To** 2023 $32 ✪
Abel's Tempest Pinot Gris 2016 Pale straw; an elegant wine in terms of its suite of apple and pear flavours, and its overall fruit purity, amplified by its acid balance. Screwcap. 13.5% alc. **Rating** 94 **To** 2019 $32

ŶŶŶŶŶ South Tasmania Chardonnay Pinot Noir 2011 Rating 93 To 2021 $60 TS
Georg Jensen Hallmark Cuvee NV Rating 93 To 2020 $40 TS
Abel's Tempest Chardonnay Pinot Noir NV Rating 91 To 2019 $32 TS

Heggies Vineyard ★★★★

Heggies Range Road, Eden Valley, SA 5235 **Region** Eden Valley
T (08) 8561 3200 **www.**heggiesvineyard.com **Open** By appt
Winemaker Peter Gambetta **Est.** 1971 **Dozens** 15 000 **Vyds** 62ha
Heggies was the second of the high-altitude (570m) vineyards established by the Hill-Smith family. Plantings on the 120ha former grazing property began in 1973; the principal varieties are riesling, chardonnay, viognier and merlot. There are then two special plantings: a 1.1ha reserve chardonnay block, and 27ha of various clonal trials. Exports to all major markets.

ŶŶŶŶŶ Eden Valley Chardonnay 2015 Brightly coloured, this attractive and well made Eden Valley chardonnay has aromas of rockmelon and stone fruits, and the gently spicy oak (all barriques and about 45% new) has been well handled. The palate is youthful, structured and long; I imagine this will need at least another 2 years to really hit its straps. Screwcap. **Rating** 90 **To** 2020 PR

Heirloom Vineyards ★★★★★

Salopian Inn, cnr Main Road/McMurtrie Road, McLaren Vale, SA 5171 **Region** Adelaide
T (08) 8556 6099 **www.**heirloomvineyards.com.au **Open** 7 days 10–5
Winemaker Elena Brooks **Est.** 2004 **Dozens** NFP
This is (yet another) venture for Zar Brooks and his wife Elena. They met during the 2000 vintage, and one thing led to another, as they say. Dandelion Vineyards and Zonte's Footstep came along first, and continue, but other partners are involved in those ventures (and are

co-owners of the Salopian Inn, with the cellar door in the restaurant). The lofty aims here are 'to preserve the best of tradition, the unique old vineyards of SA, and to champion the best clones of each variety, embracing organic and biodynamic farming'. I don't doubt the sincerity of the sentiments, but there's a fair degree of Brooksian marketing spin involved. Exports to all major markets.

ΨΨΨΨΨ **A'Lambra Eden Valley Shiraz 2014** Made in the 'most is best' fashion, with high quality Eden Valley shiraz in abundance, and lots of high quality oak. Such wines often pall on the second or third taste – this complex shiraz worms its way through the barricades as it bursts into operatic song on the spicy black cherry and licorice back-palate and finish. Screwcap. 14.5% alc. **Rating** 96 **To** 2040 $80
Eden Valley Riesling 2016 Aromas of lemon, grapefruit, honeysuckle and beeswax. Characteristically, it's still a little stern on the palate. It tastes of the place it's from. The citrus flavours are muted, but the underlying depth is evident, the slatey acidity guiding it along. Secure under screwcap, it feels as though in a cool cellar it could live forever. 10.5% alc. **Rating** 95 **To** 2036 $30 SC ✪
Barossa Shiraz 2015 Skilfully made, pushing the boundary of ripeness to a point where the richness of the Barossa (and shiraz) is expressed without becoming overdone. Blackberry, blueberry, sweet spice and almost (but not fully) dried fruit aromas fill the bouquet, and the palate is a flowing wave of juicy plummy flavour with a seasoning of French oak and supple, fine-grained tannin. Screwcap. 14.5% alc. **Rating** 95 **To** 2040 $40 SC
Adelaide Hills Sauvignon Blanc 2016 A serious take on this ubiquitous regional/varietal blend, and impressively executed. Sitting firmly at the savoury/ herbal end of the spectrum in terms of aromas and flavours; citrus, gooseberry and snow pea dominate, with minerally, almost reductive characters working in seamlessly. Length on the palate is a feature, as is the fine, linear, persistent acidity. Screwcap. 12.5% alc. **Rating** 94 **To** 2021 $30 SC ✪
Adelaide Hills Chardonnay 2015 Organic/biodynamic grapes, bunch-sorted, free-run juice wild-yeast fermented, 15% tank-pressed and matured, 85% matured in French barriques (30% new) for 12 months. This is a perfectly groomed chardonnay, not a hair out of place on the supple palate; the flavours halfway between white peach and grapefruit, oak a bridge between the two. Screwcap. 12.5% alc. **Rating** 94 **To** 2025 $30 ✪
McLaren Vale Shiraz 2014 Well, there is no doubting where this comes from, laden as it is with savoury bitter chocolate and a circle of black fruits, tannins and oak handled with complete confidence. Full-bodied yet balanced, with a long future in its DNA. Screwcap. 14.5% alc. **Rating** 94 **To** 2034 $40

ΨΨΨΨΨ **Adelaide Hills Pinot Grigio 2016** **Rating** 92 **To** 2020 $30 SC
The Velvet Fog Adelaide Hills Pinot Noir 2015 **Rating** 91 **To** 2020 $40
Adelaide Hills Pinot Grigio 2015 **Rating** 90 **To** 2017 $30

Helen & Joey Estate   ★★★★☆

12–14 Spring Lane, Gruyere, Vic 3770 **Region** Yarra Valley
T (03) 9728 1574 **www**.hjestate.com.au **Open** Mon & Fri 11–5, w'ends 11–5
Winemaker Stuart Dudine **Est.** 2011 **Dozens** 11000 **Vyds** 35ha
This is the venture of Helen Xu, who purchased the large Fernando Vineyard on Spring Lane (next to Yeringberg) in 2010. It is planted to pinot noir, cabernet sauvignon, merlot, chardonnay, pinot gris, shiraz and sauvignon blanc. Helen's background is quite varied. She has a Masters degree in analytical chemistry, and was a QA manager for Nestlé for several years. She now owns a business in Shanghai, working with textile ink development together with husband Joey, and they currently split their time between China and Australia. Exports to Singapore, Japan and China.

ΨΨΨΨΨ **Alena Yarra Valley Chardonnay 2015** Whole-bunch pressed before being fermented with natural yeasts in a mixture of new and older barriques and with zero mlf. The result is a tightly wound and flinty Yarra chardonnay that has good weight, texture and length. Screwcap. 13.2% alc. **Rating** 92 **To** 2020 $45 PR

Alena Yarra Valley Cabernet Sauvignon 2015 Deep crimson-purple in colour, this medium-bodied and elegant Yarra cabernet has some ripe blackcurrant fruit aromas together with a little cedar from being matured in 225l French barriques (30% new). The wine finishes with good depth of fruit, and fine, persistent tannins. Screwcap. 14.2% alc. **Rating** 90 **To** 2025 $45 PR

Helen's Hill Estate ★★★★★

16 Ingram Road, Lilydale, Vic 3140 **Region** Yarra Valley
T (03) 9739 1573 **www**.helenshill.com.au **Open** 7 days 10–5
Winemaker Scott McCarthy **Est.** 1984 **Dozens** 15 000 **Vyds** 53ha
Helen's Hill Estate is named after the previous owner of the property, Helen Fraser. Venture partners Andrew and Robyn McIntosh and Roma and Allan Nalder combined childhood farming experience with more recent careers in medicine and finance to establish and manage the day-to-day operations of the estate. It produces two labels: Helen's Hill Estate and Ingram Rd, both made onsite. Scott McCarthy started his career early by working vintages during school holidays before gaining diverse and extensive experience in the Barossa and Yarra valleys, Napa Valley, Languedoc, the Loire Valley and Marlborough. The winery, cellar door complex and elegant 140-seat restaurant command some of the best views in the valley. Exports to Hong Kong, the Maldives and China.

ŸŸŸŸŸ **Range View Reserve Pinot Noir 2014** The fragrant and expressive bouquet of red and black cherry fruits flows into a juicy, lively palate with a silken web of fine, ripe tannins and French oak, the orchestra playing in the pits below front stage. Screwcap. 12.8% alc. **Rating** 96 **To** 2030
Breachley Block Single Vineyard Yarra Valley Chardonnay 2016 Three clones, wild-fermented in French oak (28% new); 10-month maturation. A fragrant bouquet and perfectly poised palate, with grapefruit and minerally acidity the drivers of a long, lingering finish and fresh aftertaste. Screwcap. 12.8% alc. **Rating** 95 **To** 2028 $35
First Light Reserve Pinot Noir 2014 Single vineyard, single clone, hand-picked, matured in French barriques for 14 months. The clone is MV6, selected from Clos Vougeot in Dec 1831. It became – and remains – the most widely planted red across Australia, mostly on its own roots. Here the purple of plum joins black cherry rolling inexorably along to the finish and aftertaste. Screwcap. 12.8% alc. **Rating** 95 **To** 2029
Ingram Road Single Vineyard Yarra Valley Chardonnay 2016 Multi-clone, wild-yeast fermented in French oak (10% new); 10-month maturation. Generous and rich, with nectarine and white peach to the fore, neatly tightened on the finish by grapefruit/citrus acidity. Ready now. Screwcap. 13.4% alc. **Rating** 94 **To** 2022 $20

Helm ★★★★★

19 Butt's Road, Murrumbateman, NSW 2582 **Region** Canberra District
T (02) 6227 5953 **www**.helmwines.com.au **Open** Thurs–Mon 10–5
Winemaker Ken and Stephanie Helm **Est.** 1973 **Dozens** 5000 **Vyds** 17ha
Ken Helm celebrated his 40th vintage in 2016. Over the years he has achieved many things, through dogged persistence on the one hand, vision on the other. Riesling has been an all-consuming interest for him, ultimately rewarded with rieslings of consistently high quality. He has also given much to the broader wine community, extending from the narrow focus of the Canberra District to the broad canvas of the international world of riesling: in '00 he established the Canberra International Riesling Challenge, retiring as Chairman in '16, but keeping an active eye on the Challenge. In '14 his youngest child Stephanie (and husband Ben Osborne, Helm's vineyard manager) purchased Yass Valley Wines, rebranding it as 'The Vintner's Daughter', and he also persuaded Stephanie to join him as winemaker at Helm. Exports to Macau and Hong Kong.

ŸŸŸŸŸ **Premium Canberra District Riesling 2016** For the first time sourced for the estate vineyard planted in 2008. The most intense and penetrating of the four riesling releases in '16. Unsweetened lime juice/pith fruit nestles in a cradle of calm but firm acidity. Length is the inevitable consequence of the balance and intensity. Screwcap. 11.5% alc. **Rating** 96 **To** 2036 $52 **۞**

Premium Canberra District Cabernet Sauvignon 2013 Matured for 2 years in French oak (50% new). Bright crimson-purple; it has a cedary autocracy wrapped around a heart of cassis and bay leaf; the tannins are firm, but completely ripe, and the finish is long and detailed. Screwcap. 13.5% alc. **Rating** 95 **To** 2033 $52

Tumbarumba Riesling 2016 The fourth release from a vineyard at 630m with granitic sandy loam soils. The floral bouquet leads into a fine, elegant palate with intense lemon/lime fruit and a very, very long, penetrating and lingering finish. Screwcap. 11% alc. **Rating** 95 **To** 2033 $30 **۞**

Classic Dry Canberra District Riesling 2016 Hand-picked, and only free-run juice used. Elegance and finesse coupled with layered mouthfeel and depth to its citrus bowl of fruit; hints of apple blossom carry on into the palate, albeit playing second fiddle to the dominant citrus built on the structure of integrated and balanced acidity. Screwcap. 11.8% alc. **Rating** 95 **To** 2031 $38

Canberra District Cabernet Sauvignon 2015 The '15 vintage was the earliest in 40 years. From the Lustenberger Vineyard, matured until Jan '17 in new and used French oak. It is medium-bodied, with juicy berry fruits, supple tannins and integrated oak. It doesn't have a single green bone in its body. This is better (by a slim margin) than the '13. Screwcap. 13.5% alc. **Rating** 95 **To** 2035 $35 **۞**

Central Ranges Riesling 2016 The bouquet offers a compelling combination of lime juice, lime zest and minerally acidity; the acidity is presently throwing its weight around and cramping the fruit on the palate – given time, this will be a very good riesling. Screwcap. 11.5% alc. **Rating** 94 **To** 2021 $30 **۞**

Hemera Estate ★★★★★

1516 Barossa Valley Way, Lyndoch, SA 5351 **Region** Barossa Valley
T (08) 8524 4033 **www.**hemeraestate.com.au **Open** 7 days 10–5
Winemaker Jason Barrette **Est.** 1999 **Dozens** 15000 **Vyds** 44ha

Hemera Estate was originally founded by Darius and Pauline Ross in 1999 as Ross Estate Wines. The name change came about in 2012 after the business was sold to Winston Wine. This purchase also saw renewed investment in the winery, vineyard and tasting room, with a focus on consistently producing high quality wines. Running very much on an estate basis, the winery and tasting room are located on the 44ha vineyard in the southern Barossa Valley, planted to 11 varieties, with blocks of old vine grenache (105yo) and riesling (48yo). Exports to the UK, the US and China.

ᵠᵠᵠᵠᵠ **Limited Release Home Block Barossa Valley Shiraz 2015** Sourced mostly from home Blocks 3A and 6A, pressed to French and American oak barrels (75% new) for 18 months. It's dark and dense, richly flavoured and powered by tannin. The oak, while a powerful presence, has soaked into the wine with dark cherries, currants and plums shining through. Spice, coconut rough, soy sauce and licorice add to the flavour profile. Screwcap. 14.7% alc. **Rating** 93 **To** 2024 $85 JF

JDR Barossa Valley Shiraz 2013 Black-red hue; the fruit has dropped away, leaving sweet oak, charcuterie, Dutch licorice, eucalypt and leather notes dominating the nose. It's a big Barossa shiraz, full-bodied, with formidable tannin structure, and somewhat drying on the finish. Only for fans of the style. Screwcap. 14.6% alc. **Rating** 92 **To** 2025 $110 JF

Estate Barossa Cabernet Sauvignon 2015 A mix of cassis, currants and leafy freshness, cedary oak, soy sauce, eucalypt and bitter herbs. Vitality and freshness on the medium to full-bodied palate, with sandpaper tannins, which need more time to ameliorate, and crunchy acidity to close. Screwcap. 14.5% alc. **Rating** 92 **To** 2025 $40 JF

Estate Barossa Valley Shiraz 2015 Aged in French and American oak (30% new) for 18 months, then a barrel selection for the final blend. Incredibly approachable thanks to giving tannins and ripe fleshy fruit. Oak spice works

into the dark cherry and plum fruit characters. Screwcap. 14.5% alc. **Rating** 91
To 2028 $40 JF
Estate Barossa Valley GSM Grenache Shiraz Mataro 2015 51/32/17%.
A neat blend of succulent ripe fruit on a supple juicy palate, nicely shaped, too.
Lightly spiced, with plump tannins making it ready now. Screwcap. 14.5% alc.
Rating 91 To 2021 $35 JF

ŸŸŸŸ **Estate Barossa Valley Riesling 2016** Rating 89 To 2023 $25 JF
Old Vine Barossa Valley Grenache 2014 Rating 89 To 2020 $35 JF

Henry's Drive Vignerons ★★★★
41 Hodgson Road, Padthaway, SA 5271 **Region** Padthaway
T (08) 8132 1048 **www.henrysdrive.com Open** 7 days 10–4
Winemaker Andrew Miller **Est.** 1998 **Dozens** 65 000 **Vyds** 94.9ha
Named after the proprietor of the 19th-century mail coach service that once ran through
their property, Henry's Drive Vignerons is the wine operation established by Kim Longbottom
and her late husband Mark. Kim is continuing to build the family tradition of winemaking,
with brands such as Henry's Drive, Pillar Box, The Scarlet Letter and The Postmistress. Exports
to the UK, the US, Canada, Denmark, Singapore, Hong Kong, China and NZ.

ŸŸŸŸŸ **Magnus Padthaway Shiraz 2013** Picked late Mar, ferment finished in barrel,
then matured for 22–24 months in new French puncheons. Deep purple-crimson;
a war of worlds à la HG Wells, with layers of new French oak and equal layers of
black cherry and blackberry fruit confronting each other. It's classic more is better,
most is best stuff. The rewards will come when and if the stand-off ends. Screwcap.
14.5% alc. **Rating** 94 To 2033 $65
Padthaway Shiraz Cabernet 2013 A 68/32% blend from 25yo estate vines,
open-fermented in small pots, fermentation completed in 60% French and
40% American oak (new and used) for 15–18 months, then a barrel selection.
Deep colour; in flamboyant full-bodied style, but amid the sea of flavours there
is a point of near calm, suggesting that the required patience will be rewarded.
Screwcap. 14% alc. **Rating** 94 To 2033 $35

ŸŸŸŸŸ **H Padthaway Syrah 2015** Rating 92 To 2030 $25 ✪
Padthaway Shiraz 2013 Rating 92 To 2038 $35

Henschke ★★★★★
1428 Keyneton Road, Keyneton, SA 5353 **Region** Eden Valley
T (08) 8564 8223 **www.henschke.com.au Open** Mon–Fri 9–4.30, Sat 9–12
Winemaker Stephen Henschke **Est.** 1868 **Dozens** 30 000 **Vyds** 121.72ha
Regarded as the best medium-sized red wine producer in Australia, Henschke has gone from
strength to strength over the past three decades under the guidance of winemaker Stephen
and viticulturist Prue Henschke. The red wines fully capitalise on the very old, low-yielding,
high quality vines and are superbly made with sensitive but positive use of new small oak: Hill
of Grace is second only to Penfolds Grange as Australia's red wine icon. A founding member
of Australia's First Families of Wine. 2012 Hill of Grace is Wine of the Year in the 2018 *Wine
Companion*. Exports to all major markets.

ŸŸŸŸŸ **Hill of Grace 2012** One of the greaest Australian shirazs, hand-picked from
vines up to 152yo, hand-sorted, 70% crushed and destemmed, 30% destemmed
for whole berry open ferment, then matured in predominantly French hogheads
(65% new) for 18 months. It is a magnificent, flawless wine, with balance, length,
line and purity. It has perfect colour, fragrant dark cherry/berry aromas and
flavours, positive tannin and French oak support. As it ages over the next 45 years,
it will achieve a lustre, a silk and satin mouthfeel, flavours and spices ever-changing
and intermingling. Screwcap. 14.5% alc. **Rating** 99 To 2062 $825
Hill of Roses 2010 Is it worth the price? Yes, absolutely. Is entirely sourced from
the Hill and Grace Vineyard. You are buying history. You are buying part of the

most valuable vineyard land in Australia, as rare as Romanée-Conti in Burgundy, both in reality beyond price or value because they will never be for sale at any price. The use of 100% French oak gives the wine an additional point of difference from Hill of Grace, in which American oak still plays a minor role. This to one side, the wine has superb colour, a racy, superfine palate of exceptional length and the balance that is endowed by that balance (or vice versa, it doesn't matter). Vino-Lok. 14.5% alc. **Rating** 98 **To** 2040 $380

Mount Edelstone 2014 102yo single vineyard, matured in 92% French and 8% American hogsheads (28% new) for 18 months. Only a fraction of the normal crop, as was the case in many parts of SA and Vic. The colour is that of an 18-month-old (not 36 months) shiraz, the aromas of black fruits, licorice and black pepper, the tannins firm and enduring, yet in balance with the powerful fruit. I remain to be convinced this is suited to drinking while the '13 comes around: the best solution is to leave both to themselves for 5 or so years. Screwcap. 14.5% alc. **Rating** 97 **To** 2044 $225

ΤΤΤΤΤ **Louis 2015** A delectably juicy semillon, one of the brightest and freshest I can remember. Just what the 5% fermented and matured in used French oak contributed is irrelevant, because it's the dancing lemon-infused flavours that make this wine so attractive. There is every reason to agree with the 20+-year cellaring potential suggested by Henschke. Screwcap. 12% alc. **Rating** 96 **To** 2035 $33 ✪

Hill of Peace 2012 Entirely from the Hill of Grace Vineyard. 40% barrel-fermented and matured in used French oak, the remainder in stainless steel. This semillon has been a carefully guarded secret since '12, when the vintage promoted the idea that it's in no way intended as a pun to say the wine is graceful, for that is its cardinal virtue, having calmly moved through the 5 years since vintage. It has the depth of flavour that is unique to old vines, achieved without any phenolic weight whatsoever. Screwcap. 12% alc. **Rating** 96 **To** 2032 $50 ✪

Giles Adelaide Hills Pinot Noir 2015 From 25yo vines on the estate Lenswood vineyard, picked between 19 Feb and 13 Mar, an exceptionally long period for a single vineyard wine. Open-fermented in wax-lined vats, matured for 9 months in French barriques (19% new). It has a very fragrant and flowery bouquet setting the scene for red cherry and wild strawberry fruits on the palate, lengthened by fine tannins, oak lost in the crowd. Elegance and purity are its keywords. Screwcap. 13% alc. **Rating** 96 **To** 2029 $55 ✪

The Alan Lenswood Pinot Noir 2013 Hand-picked from 20 Feb to 1 Mar from the Lenswood vineyard, open-fermented in wax-lined vats, matured for 15 months in used French barriques. A powerful wine, plums joining red and black cherry fruits in a savoury overlay suggesting the incorporation of some whole bunches. Vino-Lok. 13.5% alc. **Rating** 96 **To** 2028 $93

Tappa Pass Vineyard Selection Barossa Shiraz 2014 This compelling and complex wine starts with a heady fragrance of cinnamon, licorice, asphalt and ripe red fruits with a floral lift plus cedary oak; full-bodied, with powerful, precise, velvety tannins, and a stunning palate – elegant with amazing length. Vino-Lok. 14.5% alc. **Rating** 96 **To** 2036 $100 JF

Cyril Henschke 2013 83% cabernet sauvignon, 7% cabernet franc, 5% merlot, matured in French hogsheads (42% new) for 18 months. Cabernet from the Eden Valley has its own cool personality – and absolute authority. It is blackcurrant rather than cassis, with tannins that are firm but not dry, and an elusive touch of mint. The franc and merlot have helped the cabernet show a bit of love, the French oak likewise. Screwcap. 14% alc. **Rating** 96 **To** 2038 $165

Julius Eden Valley Riesling 2016 A wine of ultimate coherence running from the bouquet through to the aftertaste, continuously reflecting the lime juice that is the essence and foundation of a riesling, giving immediate or long-term pleasure. It will never lose its bloodline. Screwcap. 11.5% alc. **Rating** 95 **To** 2031 $41

Green's Hill Adelaide Hills Riesling 2016 Beautifully pure aromatics, with hints of citrus blossom and white stone fruit. Finely poised on the palate, the flavours subtle and seamless, the acidity playing its part by insinuation more than blunt force. Still very much in an evolutionary phase; expect to see a long life ahead. Screwcap. **Rating** 95 **To** 2030 $35 SC ✪

Peggy's Hill Eden Valley Riesling 2016 You have to start with the aftertaste in describing the wine, because that's where 90% of the action is, as its intensity and length take you back to the flowery, talc bouquet and all that lies between. Henschke puts a 20+-year cellaring potential on it, and I'm not going to argue with that. Screwcap. 12% alc. **Rating** 95 **To** 2036 $25 ✪

Croft Adelaide Hills Chardonnay 2015 The mature vineyard, and the disciplined approach to picking the grapes using knowledge gained over 10+ years, give the wine more depth and mouthfeel than its Archer's Vineyard sibling. Grapefruit, white peach and apple are joined at the hip with touches of roasted cashew and gently toasty oak. Screwcap. 13.5% alc. **Rating** 95 **To** 2025 $47

Johann's Garden 2015 70% grenache, 25% mataro and 5% shiraz from various Barossa Valley vineyards. Aromas of red fruits and a hint of spice, the light-bodied palate bursting with fresh red fruits. A definite drink-soon style – while all the exuberant fruits are on full display. Vino-Lok. 14.5% alc. **Rating** 95 **To** 2022 $56

Abbotts Prayer Vineyard 2013 59% cabernet sauvignon, 41% merlot, matured in French hogsheads (41% new) for 18 months before blending. The key is the medium-bodied and supple palate, tannins nowhere to be seen. Whatever else one can say, the wine is so well balanced it is ready for consumption from the start, yet has a 20-year horizon thanks to its mix of cassis, plum and black olive flavours. Vino-Lok. 14% alc. **Rating** 95 **To** 2033 $100

Marble Angel Vineyard Cabernet Sauvignon 2013 100% cabernet sauvignon from 40+yo vines at Light Pass, matured in French hogsheads (41% new) for 18 months. Following the superb '12, Marble Angel was never going to be easy, but this does better than most Barossa cabernets. Its tannin structure is a feature, giving the wine length and emphatic mouthfeel, the heart of a very good cabernet. Vino-Lok. 14.5% alc. **Rating** 95 **To** 2033 $97

The Rose Grower Eden Valley Nebbiolo 2012 The Roseler family are long-term landholders, their name meaning 'rose grower' in Italian, the vineyard often wreathed in fog ('nebbiolo' is Italian for fog). The wine has the power and intensity of a top class pinot noir, with rose petal overtones and an exceptionally long finish, yet (amazingly) with silky, soft tannins. Vino-Lok. 13% alc. **Rating** 95 **To** 2027 $60

The Bootmaker Barossa Valley Mataro 2015 96% old vine mataro and 4% old vine grenache, the wine paying tribute to the wide skillset of the Silesian Lutheran settlement of the Barossa Valley. Mataro seldom makes a wine as supple as this, and I don't think this can be ascribed to the 4% grenache inclusion. There's a special quality to the tannins that counterintuitively lifts the aura of the red fruits on the palate. The balance is such that a 20+-year life is assured. Vino-Lok. 14.5% alc. **Rating** 95 **To** 2035 $75

Louis 2014 From 50yo estate semillon vines in the Eden Valley. The early stages of bottle development have invested the wine with mouthfeel and an extra degree of depth, with more to come over the next 5+ years. Screwcap. 12% alc. **Rating** 94 **To** 2024 $33

Five Shillings 2016 67% shiraz, 33% mataro from the Eden and Barossa Valleys matured in 72% Reserve and 28% American hogsheads (4% new) for 8 months prior to blending. It's not hard to see why the vintage should have prompted the release of this inaugural limited release wine. Quite simply, it ticks all the boxes: varietal typicity of the two components, length, balance and overall mouthfeel. All it needs is (say) 5 years in bottle. Screwcap. 14.5% alc. **Rating** 94 **To** 2036 $33

Henry's Seven 2014 Henry's Seven is the area, not the varieties of the vineyard planted by Henry Evans in 1853 at Keyneton. The wine has four varieties (shiraz, grenache, mataro and viognier), the colour no doubt assisted by the viognier, the bouquet likewise. It is fresh and spirited, yet also supple and balanced, with a full array of dark berry, purple and black fruits, the tannins perfectly integrated. Screwcap. 14% alc. **Rating** 94 **To** 2029 $37

Stone Jar Eden Valley Tempranillo 2015 91% tempranillo and 7% mataro co-fermented and blended with 2% graciano, matured in used French hogsheads for 10 months. Juicy cherry fruits in the ascendant, coupled with a lesser amount of plum. Medium-bodied, supple and smooth, the tannins and oak are polished to the point of becoming invisible. Trophy Best Other Varieties Barossa Wine Show '16. Screwcap. 14% alc. **Rating** 94 **To** 2030 $50

Johanne Ida Selma Lenswood Blanc de Noir MD NV A beautifully characterful, expressive and powerful blanc de noirs that masterfully captures the depth of pinot noir and the tension of the heights of Lenswood. Pinot noir speaks in a deep voice of satsuma plums, black cherries and mixed spice, riding a line of focused, finely poised acidity. 16 vintages and two decades of maturity unite to build layers of dark fruitcake, ginger nut biscuits and dark chocolate, culminating in a long and full yet impeccably tense finish. Crown seal. 12% alc. **Rating** 94 **To** 2020 $60 TS

Eden Valley Noble Rot Semillon 2016 18% aged on lees for 6 months in used French barriques, the remainder on lees in tank. Typical Henschke, coming up with X-factor in virtually all of its wines. This has excellent balance between fruit, acidity and high residual sugar, and texture to go with the flavours. Will stand up to any dessert. Screwcap. 10.5% alc. **Rating** 94 **To** 2022 $40

ŶŶŶŶŶ **Joseph Hill Gewurztraminer 2015** Rating 93 To 2025 $36
Tappa Pass Barossa Shiraz 2015 Rating 93 To 2030 $115
Adelaide Hills Noble Gewurztraminer 2016 Rating 93 To 2026 $33
Joseph Hill Gewurztraminer 2016 Rating 92 To 2030 $36
Eleanor's Cottage SBS 2015 Rating 92 To 2020 $25 ✪
Henry's Seven 2015 Rating 92 To 2028 $37 JF
The Rose Grower Eden Valley Nebbiolo 2013 Rating 92 To 2030 $60
Coralinga Adelaide Hills Sauvignon Blanc 2016 Rating 91 To 2018 $27
Archer's Vineyard Adelaide Hills Chardonnay 2015 Rating 91 To 2022 $35
Coralinga Adelaide Hills Sauvignon Blanc 2015 Rating 90 To 2018 $27
Innes Vineyard Littlehampton Adelaide Hills Pinot Gris 2016 Rating 90 To 2018 $37
Tilly's Vineyard 2015 Rating 90 To 2017 $20 ✪
Keyneton Euphonium 2014 Rating 90 To 2024 $60
Abbotts Prayer Vineyard 2012 Rating 90 To 2027 $97
Muscat of Tappa Pass 2015 Rating 90 To 2017 $35

Hentley Farm Wines   ★★★★★

Cnr Jenke Road/Gerald Roberts Road, Seppeltsfield, SA 5355 **Region** Barossa Valley
T (08) 8562 8427 **www**.hentleyfarm.com.au **Open** 7 days 11–5
Winemaker Andrew Quin **Est.** 1999 **Dozens** 20 000 **Vyds** 39.6ha
Keith and Alison Hentschke purchased Hentley Farm in 1997, as an old vineyard and mixed farming property. Keith has thoroughly impressive credentials, having studied agricultural science at Roseworthy, graduating with distinction, later adding an MBA. During the 1990s he had a senior production role with Orlando, before moving on to manage Fabal, one of Australia's largest vineyard management companies. Establishing Hentley Farm might seem all too easy, but it needed all his knowledge to create such a great vineyard. A total of 38.2ha were planted between 1999 and 2005. In '04 an adjoining 6.5ha vineyard, christened Clos Otto, was acquired. Shiraz dominates the plantings, with 32.5ha. Situated on the banks of Greenock Creek, the vineyard has red clay loam soils overlaying shattered limestone, lightly rocked slopes and little topsoil. Joining Keith in the vineyard and winery are Greg Mader as viticulturist and Andrew Quin as winemaker, both with very impressive CVs. *Wine Companion* 2015 Winery of the Year. Exports to the US and other major markets.

ŶŶŶŶŶ **Museum Release H-Block Shiraz Cabernet 2012** All the Museum Release wines were re-tasted for this edition, but none had changed in any material way. First tasted Mar '14: A 65/35% blend; the intense bouquet of black fruits leads into the luscious, velvety palate that achieves the impossible of being light on its feet, thanks in no small measure to the cassis fruit component; the velvety tannins and fully integrated oak help sweep the wine along the course of its very long palate. Cork. 14.8% alc. **Rating** 98 **To** 2052 $265

Clos Otto Barossa Valley Shiraz 2015 Individual estate parcels, destemmed and crushed, open-fermented with cultured yeast, 8 days on skins, matured in French oak (70% new) for 22 months, blended after 6 months in oak. An exotic bouquet with new shoe leather and a sprinkle of sultry spices, the full-bodied palate with supple blackberry fruits to the fore and an underlay of integrated French oak. There is a finesse to the overall texture, structure and flavour that is remarkable. Cork. 14.8% alc. **Rating** 97 **To** 2045 $180

Museum Release The Beauty Barossa Valley Shiraz 2012 All the Museum prices have increased by 50% since their initial release. First tasted Feb '14: Deep purple-crimson; the intensity, focus and power of this wine might seem an unlikely foundation for finesse, but it achieves this with its effortless black fruits, licorice and a wisp of bitter chocolate; this in turn creates the magical length and harmony of the back-palate and finish. Cork. 15% alc. **Rating** 97 **To** 2037 $85 ✪

Museum Release The Creation Barossa Valley Shiraz 2012 First tasted Mar '14: This is winemaker Andrew Quin's unique wine from the vintage. There is so much fruit concentration in the full-bodied palate that the alcohol is simply a number, the oak long since swallowed by the fruit; blackberry, black cherry and licorice aromas spear through the bouquet, the rich and supple palate feeding off a similar suite of fruit flavours, the ripe tannins perfectly balanced, and sustaining the long finish. Cork. 15% alc. **Rating** 97 **To** 2052 $265

The Quintessential Barossa Valley Shiraz Cabernet 2015 A 60/40% blend, destemmed and crushed, 70% with 35 days on skins, 30% with 8 days on skins, matured in French oak (30% new) for 12 months. The blackcurrant/cassis/herb notes of the cabernet unexpectedly come out on top of the blackberry and plum of the shiraz. This medium-bodied wine has been carefully handled, emerging with absolutely perfect balance. Screwcap. 14.5% alc. **Rating** 97 **To** 2035 $62 ✪

H Block Shiraz Cabernet 2015 A 67/33% blend, fermented separately, 9 days on skins, matured for 22 months in French oak (50% new), blended after 6 months in oak. A very complex wine, the complexity primarily coming from the duel between blackberry and blackcurrant fruit, oak a second for both parties. So yes, oak is obvious, but it is integrated, and impossible to dislike. The tannins are impeccable, in the usual Hentley Farm style. Cork. 15% alc. **Rating** 97 **To** 2040 $165

Museum Release von Kasper Barossa Valley Cabernet Sauvignon 2012 First tasted Mar '14: Acknowledges the foresight of Otto Kasper in choosing a site on the banks of Greenock Creek in '97, 21 months in French oak has barely touched the sides of what is a monumental cabernet, the depth of its flavour mosaic of cassis, black olive, sage and earth almost indescribable. The one thing the wine needs is to lie dormant for not less than 3 years, preferably 5, its life thereafter anyone's guess. Cork. 14.5% alc. **Rating** 97 **To** 2052 $120 ✪

ⵉⵉⵉⵉⵉ **The Beauty Barossa Valley Shiraz 2015** Includes 3% viognier, destemmed only, co-fermented, 9 days on skins, matured in French oak (35% new) for 16 months. Fruit, oak and tannins are in perfect alignment, all expressive; the juicy blackberry and satsuma plum fruit has clearly gained freshness from the viognier. A lovely Barossa Valley shiraz. Screwcap. 14.5% alc. **Rating** 96 **To** 2040 $62 ✪

The Beast Barossa Valley Shiraz 2015 This is power in liquid form. It is unequivocally full-bodied, and should be allowed to mature for a minimum of 5 years, preferably 10. Its black fruits are shot through with spice, licorice and savoury tannins that would do cabernet proud. Cork. 15.2% alc. **Rating** 96 **To** 2045 $89

The Creation Barossa Valley Shiraz 2015 Made in the same way as Clos Otto other than maturation in American oak (50% new). The American oak is much more assertive than French, its signal soaring on the first whiff, likewise the first sip. It works well here, tipping its hat to Grange, the flavours coating every corner of the mouth, yet doesn't overstay its welcome. Cork. 15% alc. **Rating** 96 To 2040 $165

Museum Release The Beast Barossa Valley Shiraz 2012 I can do no more than repeat what I wrote when first tasted in Mar '14: From a single block high on the hill, with shallow soils and even sunlight exposure resulting in very small berries. Deep, saturated crimson-purple paints the scene, with untold layers of black fruits, ripe tannins and integrated oak; bitter chocolate and poached plum flavours are in the mix too. Cork. 15% alc. **Rating** 96 **To** 2052 $120

The Marl Barossa Valley Grenache 2016 You see the attention to detail with this wine: 94% on skins for 6 days, 6% for 52 days. This is space age Barossa Valley grenache, showing that it is possible to make great wine at 13.5% alcohol without any confection/Turkish Delight characters, just a delicious flower vase collection of red fruits. Big-time bargain. Screwcap. **Rating** 96 **To** 2023 $21 ✪

The Old Legend Barossa Valley Grenache 2016 15% picked early with a large percentage of whole bunches in the ferment adding plush fruit and vibrancy; 60% spent 40 days on skins for earth, spice and tannins; 20% was picked late in the season, providing richness and colour. The result is a rich and powerful wine with texture and structure to burn. Closer to traditional style, but without confection. Will be long-lived. Screwcap. 14% alc. **Rating** 96 **To** 2031 $62 ✪

Barossa Valley Viognier 2016 Single vineyard, whole-bunch pressed directly to French oak (33% new) for wild, full solids, fermentation and 7 months maturation with 6 months battonage. Gleaming straw-green; a fascinating way to walk the fine line between bland viognier and OTT oily flavour. It has tightly furled energy and drive, stone fruit (apricot) and citrussy acidity, oak merely a shadow in the background. Screwcap. 12.5% alc. **Rating** 95 **To** 2022 $42

Poppy Barossa Field Blend 2016 Chardonnay, riesling, viognier, fiano, white fronti and pinot gris. This demonstrates Andrew Quin's skill as much as any of his towering reds. He has retained freshness and zest, complexity ex barrel fermentation adding another dimension. I cannot recall a bits and pieces, puppy dogs' tails white to even equal this. Screwcap. 12% alc. **Rating** 95 **To** 2022 $25 ✪

Barossa Valley Shiraz 2016 The colour is typical Hentley Farm, deep, but with a vivid crimson-purple rim; the expressive black fruits bouquet and the medium to full-bodied, richly textured palate follow the same path. The blackberry essence flavours are intense and luscious, bright and fresh. Screwcap. 14.5% alc. **Rating** 95 **To** 2046 $28 ✪

The Stray Mongrel 2016 59% grenache, 37% shiraz and 4% zinfandel, open and closed fermenters, half 7 days on skins, 45% 40 days on skins, the zinfandel 69 days. Vibrant blend, just tipping the medium-bodied scales, and inviting immediate/ early consumption. The logistics of managing so many ferments is awesomely difficult, but pays big dividends. Screwcap. 14% alc. **Rating** 95 **To** 2026 $28 ✪

von Kasper Barossa Valley Cabernet Sauvignon 2015 Parcels are separately fermented and taken to barrel for mlf and 6 months maturation before blending and returned to oak for a further 18 months in French oak (30% new). Deep, bright colour; an ultra-powerful, full-bodied cabernet sauvignon in bold Barossa Valley style. Given the fresh, easy-to-drink-now other wines from Hentley Farm, it shouldn't be hard to keep your hands off this for 5+ years. Cork. 14.5% alc. **Rating** 95 **To** 2045 $89

Eden Valley Riesling 2016 From three growers, the parcels cold-settled, fermented in stainless steel with cultured yeast. An elegant style with a notable lightness of foot. Airy acidity is omnipresent on the palate, but citrussy fruit has no trouble balancing it. Of course you can drink it now, but it will grow another leg over the next 5 years. Screwcap. 11.8% alc. **Rating** 94 **To** 2031 $24 ✪

Brass Monkey Vineyards Adelaide Hills Pinot Grigio 2016 This is a seriously good grigio – it has real character and attitude. There are layers of energetic flavours, with pear and apple bouncing against citrussy fruit and acidity. Could equally have been called gris. Screwcap. 12% alc. **Rating** 94 **To** 2018 $21 ✪

Barossa Valley Rose 2016 85% grenache, 15% shiraz, 24 hours skin contact, fermented in stainless steel with cultured yeast, no mlf. Vivid crimson-pink; the ultra-fragrant red berry bouquet introduces an equally vibrant and fruity palate with a long finish and balancing acidity. Lovely rose at a seductive price. Screwcap. 12% alc. **Rating** 94 **To** 2018 $21 ○

Museum Release Clos Otto Barossa Valley Shiraz 2011 One-third of the block was rack-dried for 3 weeks, matured for 22 months in French oak (70% new). My original tasting note from Mar '13 was written without knowledge of the rack drying, which answers my speculation. My points and drink-to date are unchanged. 'Full purple-crimson, excellent for the vintage; bottled Feb '13, after 22 months in barrel. It must have taken courage (and constant vineyard work) to achieve this alcohol, needed for the development of the plush, spiced plums and blackberry fruit, with a farewell savoury twist.' Cork. 14.8% alc. **Rating** 94 **To** 2026 $265

The Rogue Barossa Field Blend 2016 46% grenache, 13% malbec, 9% each of mataro and shiraz, 7% tempranillo, 3% nero d'Avola and 2% zinfandel. Not a field blend (ie from a single vineyard), but that's irrelevant: the wine has been unified by 9 months maturation in used oak. It has a really attractive juicy freshness to both the bouquet and palate, and is intended for early consumption, and endless discussion by loyal followers of Hentley Farm. Screwcap. 14.5% alc. **Rating** 94 **To** 2026 $24 ○

𝒴𝒴𝒴𝒴𝒴 **Black Beauty Sparkling Shiraz NV** Rating 93 To 2024 $62 TS
The Marl Barossa Shiraz 2016 Rating 90 To 2026 $21 ○
The Marl Barossa Cabernet Sauvignon 2016 Rating 90 To 2021 $21 ○
Barossa Valley Cabernet Sauvignon 2016 Rating 90 To 2030 $28

Henty Estate   ★★★★★

657 Hensley Park Road, Hamilton, Vic 3300 (postal) **Region** Henty
T (03) 5572 4446 **www.**henty-estate.com.au **Open** Not
Winemaker Peter Dixon **Est.** 1991 **Dozens** 1400 **Vyds** 7ha
Peter and Glenys Dixon have hastened slowly with Henty Estate. In 1991 they began the planting of 4.5ha of shiraz, 1ha each of cabernet sauvignon and chardonnay, and 0.5ha of riesling. In their words, 'we avoided the temptation to make wine until the vineyard was mature', establishing the winery in 2003. Encouraged by neighbour John Thomson, they have limited the yield to 3–4 tonnes per hectare on the VSP-trained, dry-grown vineyard.

𝒴𝒴𝒴𝒴𝒴 **Chardonnay 2014** Hand-picked, fermented in 100% new French oak, 16 months maturation with lees stirring. A very distinguished cool climate chardonnay that has absorbed the impact of oak, using it to magnify both texture and pristine grapefruit flavours. Will develop at a leisurely pace, gaining depth and even more complexity as it does so. Screwcap. 12.8% alc. **Rating** 95 **To** 2023

Shiraz 2015 Matured for 12 months across 75% French Vosge oak, 30% new, with the remainder Hungarian, this is a beautifully detailed shiraz. Lilac florals greet the drinker, before smoked meat aromas and blue and black fruit allusions segue to a peppery thread of acidity melded to well massaged, pulpy grape tannins. Again, there is a buoyant joy to this wine, making it very easy to drink. Dangerously so. Screwcap. 13.2% alc. **Rating** 95 **To** 2025 $26 NG ○

Wannon Run Shiraz 2014 Ultra-expressive medium-bodied cool climate shiraz at a bargain price. The bright, clear crimson colour sets the scene for the interplay of red (dominant) and black fruits, licorice, spice and pepper on the bouquet and palate. One sip leads to another, and another – suddenly you have ripped past the National Health and Medical Research Foundation's advisory limits. Don't worry, this feeds the soul as well as the body. Screwcap. 13.2% alc. **Rating** 95 **To** 2024 $20 ○

Wannon Run Shiraz 2013 Retains vivid crimson-purple hue; the '13 and '14 are as near to identical as two vintages of a given wine could ever be: red and black fruits, spice, cracked pepper and licorice all seamlessly contributing to the elegant medium-bodied palate. These wines will go the distance, however attractive they may be now. Screwcap. 13.2% alc. **Rating** 95 **To** 2028 $20 ○

ŸŸŸŸ⵿ **Wannon Run Shiraz 2015** Rating 93 To 2023 $20 NG ✪
Cabernet Sauvignon 2015 Rating 93 To 2026 $26 NG ✪
Rose 2015 Rating 90 To 2017 $20 ✪

Hentyfarm Wines ★★★★★

250 Wattletree Road, Holgate, NSW 2250 **Region** Henty
T 0423 029 200 **www.**hentyfarm.com.au **Open** Not
Winemaker Justin Purser **Est.** 2009 **Dozens** 1500
Dr John Gladstones names the Henty GI the coolest climate in Australia, cooler than Tasmania and the Macedon Ranges. This is both bane and blessing, for when it's cold, it's bitterly so. The other fact of life it has to contend with is its remoteness, lurking just inside the SA/Vic border. The rest is all good news, for this region is capable of producing riesling, chardonnay and pinot noir of the highest quality. Seppelt's Drumborg Vineyard focuses on riesling, pinot noir and chardonnay, Crawford River on riesling, both adding lustre to the region. In 2009 Jonathan (Jono) Mogg and partner Belinda Low made several weekend trips in the company of (then) Best's winemaker Adam Wadewitz and his partner Nikki. They were able to buy grapes from renowned Henty grower Alastair Taylor, and the first vintage of Chardonnay was made in '09. In '11 a Pinot Noir was added to the portfolio and Riesling and Pinot Meunier in '15. The pinot gris is grown by 'biological grape farmers' Jack and Lois Doevan. The wines are made under contract by Justin Purser at Best's Wines. Exports to China.

ŸŸŸŸŸ **Riesling 2016** The cool Henty region has a five-decade history of producing long-lived rieslings by Seppelt and Crawford River; this is a pristine example, the citrus verging on grapefruit, minerally acidity providing the spine. Altogether special. Screwcap. 11.6% alc. **Rating** 95 **To** 2036 $25 ✪
Chardonnay 2015 Penfolds clone P58, hand-picked, part slightly crushed berries, part whole bunches, 80% fermented in French oak with mixed yeasts, 20% in stainless steel, matured for 6 months. The low alcohol, low pH and high acidity describe a tight ring around the white peach and grapefruit flavours, which will grow as the wine ages. Screwcap. 12.4% alc. **Rating** 95 **To** 2027
Pinot Gris 2016 The gris name certainly reflects the power and depth of the wine. This pinot gris shows that the variety performs best in the coolest climates. It has so much intensity it might well be thought to be riesling in a blind tasting; far from the often anodyne nature of some pinot gris. Screwcap. 12.9% alc. **Rating** 95 **To** 2019 $25 ✪
Pinot Meunier 2015 There is ample depth (and clarity) to the colour, and exceptional energy to the palate with its plum and black cherry fruit. Savoury complexity builds through to the finish and lingering aftertaste. Worth pursuing. Screwcap. 13.6% alc. **Rating** 95 **To** 2025 $35 ✪
Pinot Noir 2015 28yo 114 and 115 clones, hand-picked, 75% whole berries, 25% whole bunches, open-fermented,14 days on skins plus post-ferment maceration, matured in French oak (5% new) for 9 months. The very light colour proves the old adage not to judge a pinot by its colour, for the spicy/savoury bouquet and (even more) the delicate, yet intense red fruits of the detailed palate are striking. For pinot lovers, to be sure, but the length and balance of the wine cannot be denied. Screwcap. 12.8% alc. **Rating** 95 **To** 2023
Gewurztraminer 2016 Fresh spice and lychee aromas are strongly varietal, and also drive the flavours on the palate. No-frills winemaking (I assume, in the absence of any info), the high quality coming from the interaction of the often low-flavoured grapes with the extremely cool Henty climate. Screwcap. 12.3% alc. **Rating** 94 **To** 2026 $25

Herbert Vineyard ★★★★☆

Bishop Road, Mount Gambier, SA 5290 **Region** Mount Gambier
T 0408 849 080 **www.**herbertvineyard.com.au **Open** By appt
Winemaker David Herbert **Est.** 1996 **Dozens** 450 **Vyds** 2.4ha

David and Trudy Herbert have planted 1.9ha of pinot noir, and a total of 0.5ha of cabernet sauvignon, merlot and pinot gris (the majority of the pinot noir is sold for sparkling wine). They have built a two-level (mini) winery overlooking a 1300-square metre maze, which is reflected in the label logo.

ŸŸŸŸŸ **Barrel Number 1 Mount Gambier Pinot Noir 2014** One of several pinots from Herbert over the past few years to prove the suitability of Mount Gambier for pinot noir. Excellent retention of hue; this really has gold-plated varietal character, with terrific drive to its finish and aftertaste, forest and red fruits in sync. Screwcap. 13% alc. **Rating** 95 **To** 2022 $37

The Maze Mount Gambier Shiraz Cabernets Merlot 2015 50% shiraz, 37% cabernet sauvignon, 3% cabernet franc and 10% merlot, the shiraz from Wrattonbully, meaning the regional claim on the front label can't be made – it should be Limestone Coast. This to one side, the wine is vibrant and juicy, all the grapes co-fermented, shiraz's ripeness balanced by the estate-grown Bordeaux varieties at much lower alcohol levels. The wine was matured in French oak, some new. Screwcap. 14.6% alc. **Rating** 94 **To** 2030 $25 ❂

ŸŸŸŸŸ **Wrattonbully Shiraz 2015 Rating** 90 **To** 2030 $22

Heritage Estate   ★★★★★

Granite Belt Drive, Cottonvale, Qld 4375 **Region** Granite Belt
T (07) 4685 2197 **www.**heritagewines.com.au **Open** 7 days 9–5
Winemaker John Handy **Est.** 1992 **Dozens** 5000 **Vyds** 10ha
Heritage Estate (owned by Bryce and Paddy Kassulke) has two estate vineyards in the Granite Belt, one at Cottonvale (north) at an altitude of 960m, where it grows white varieties, and the other at Ballandean, a slightly warmer site, where red varieties and marsanne are planted. Heritage Estate has been a prolific award-winner in various Qld wine shows and it has invested in a new bottling line, enabling it to use screwcaps. After a series of difficult vintages, with the Cottonvale vineyard hit by hail in 2013, Heritage Estate has bounced back impressively, taking full advantage of the excellent '14 vintage. A winery to watch.

ŸŸŸŸŸ **Granite Belt Pinot Gris 2016** The grapes were chilled, crushed and held on skins for 16 hours, the juice tested for phenolics and then fined. This wine has more flavour and texture than all but one or two gris treated without barrel ferment, and is right up there with the top barrel-fermented examples. The mouthwatering finish is exceptional, the flavours a fusion of strawberry and lemon zest. Virtuoso winemaking. Screwcap. 13% alc. **Rating** 95 **To** 2022 $25 ❂

Old Vine Reserve Granite Belt Shiraz 2016 From 60+yo vines at the estate vineyard at Ballandean, 2 weeks pre- and 1 week post-ferment maceration, matured in French puncheons (20% new), bottled Jan '17. The good colour and, as one would expect, good varietal character showcase the high quality vintage; excellent balance and length, with an interplay of cherry, plum and blackberry, backed up by ripe tannins and enough French oak to satisfy. Very well made. Screwcap. 13.8% alc. **Rating** 95 **To** 2036 $30 ❂

Reserve Granite Belt Chardonnay 2016 Whole-bunch pressed with free-run, wild-yeast fermented in French puncheons (25% new), the pressings (around 25% of the wine) fermented in used puncheons with cultured yeast, no mlf, matured for 8 months with monthly lees stirring. Screwcap. 13% alc. **Rating** 94 **To** 2025 $35

Wild Ferment Granite Belt Marsanne 2016 The vines are fruit-thinned 'in order to avoid a potentially bland wine'; crushed and pressed, fined, wild-yeast fermented with some solids, matured for 7 months on lees with stirring. A very interesting approach to marsanne in the vineyard and in the winery, the wine with considerable mouthfeel and drive, unlike many (Tahbilk an obvious and honourable exception). The crisp/crunchy texture and pungent acidity all work very well. Screwcap. 13.2% alc. **Rating** 94 **To** 2026 $30 ❂

Granite Belt Shiraz Mourvedre Grenache 2016 A 50/25/25 % blend matured in French oak, reflecting John Handy's aim to maximise fruit expression. Excellent bright crimson-purple; a totally delicious medium-bodied palate exemplifying the ability of the Granite Belt to make high quality wine if the vintage conditions are right. Screwcap. 14% alc. **Rating** 94 **To** 2029 $25 ✪

Granite Belt Verdelho 2015 Rating 93 **To** 2017 $20 ✪
Vintage Reserve Granite Belt Fiano 2016 Rating 93 **To** 2022 $28
Granite Belt Verdelho 2016 Rating 92 **To** 2019 $22 ✪
Sauvignon Blanc 2015 Rating 91 **To** 2017 $20 ✪

 "Heroes" Vineyard

14 Deal Avenue, Jan Juc, Vic 3228 (postal) **Region** Geelong
T 0490 345 149 **www**.heroesvineyard.com **Open** Not
Winemaker James Thomas **Est.** 2016 **Dozens** 950 **Vyds** 3.9ha
James Thomas was 16 when his parents planted a vineyard in the UK in 1996. He came to Australia in 2004. After achieving a postgraduate degree in oenology from La Trobe, he spent four years as assistant winemaker at Bannockburn Vineyards, followed by three years as head winemaker in England, making sparkling wine. Returning to Australia in 2014, his homing pigeon instinct led him to become head winemaker at Clyde Park for the 2014–16 vintages (inclusive). Wanting to establish his own winery, he looked at many possible sites in Geelong, but didn't imagine he would be able to find a 3.4ha vineyard planted to pinot noir, shiraz, riesling and sauvignon blanc. He is deeply wedded to organic vineyard practices, and is moving towards certification. He has also increased the plantings with 0.5ha chardonnay. I was much taken by the sophistication of the labels, even more by the quality of his wines.

Otway Hinterland Sauvignon Blanc 2016 Whole-bunch pressed, wild-yeast fermented in stainless steel and one new puncheon (just over 25% of the blend), 5 months on lees. The result is a perfectly executed style, managing to bring together clear varietal expression within a palate with texture, structure and, most importantly, balance. Screwcap. 12.9% alc. **Rating** 95 **To** 2022 $28 ✪
Otway Hinterland Shiraz 2016 Fermented in two batches, one 'carbo-crush' (10% whole bunches for carbonic maceration), the other destemmed (whole berries), 4 weeks on skins, blended, matured in French oak (20% new) for 10 months. Bright, full crimson-purple; a powerful and very complex shiraz that repays all the effort invested in the vineyard and winery. Black fruits, licorice and spice run through the full-bodied palate, tannins and oak standing either side of the main game. Screwcap. 13.7% alc. **Rating** 95 **To** 2036 $35 ✪
Otway Hinterland Riesling 2016 Whole-bunch pressed, wild yeast fermentation arrested at 69g/l residual sugar, titratable acidity of 8.4g/l and a pH of 2.9. A perfectly made Kabinett-style riesling, the acidity precisely balanced by the residual sugar, leaving the wine to revel in its lime juice flavour set. I'll drink this anywhere, anytime. Screwcap. 7.4% alc. **Rating** 95 **To** 2031 $32 ✪

 Hersey Vineyard   **NR**

1003 Main Street, Hahndorf, SA 5245 (postal) **Region** Adelaide Hills
T 0401 321 770 **Open** Not
Winemaker Damon Koerner **Est.** 2014 **Dozens** 2000 **Vyds** 10ha
The Hersey Vineyard was established by Ursula Pridham, Australia's first female qualified winemaker, and was run organically and biodynamically long before it became fashionable. However, years passed, and it was largely abandoned before the Hersey family (led by Jono Hersey) purchased the vineyard in early 2013 – but had to spend a year rescuscitating the vines. Even then the yields for 2015 and '16 were pathetically low, with only 1.2 tonnes from 3.5ha of chardonnay. The 10ha vineyard is separated into five parcels sprawled across 52ha of forest, scrub and paddocks, all with different aspects. Pinot gris, syrah and merlot are purchased from Adelaide Hills' vineyards, while soil preparation is underway, in order to plant gamay and syrah in the near future.

Hesketh Wine Company ★★★★

28 The Parade, Norwood, SA 5067 **Region** Various
T (08) 8362 8622 **www**.heskethwinecompany.com.au **Open** Nt
Winemaker Phil Lehmann, Charlie Ormsby, James Lienert **Est.** 2006 **Dozens** 40 000
Headed by Jonathon Hesketh, this is part of WD Wines Pty Ltd, which also owns Parker
Coonawarra Estate and St John's Road in the Barossa Valley. Jonathon spent 7 years as the
Global Sales & Marketing Manager of Wirra Wirra, and two and a half years as General
Manager of Distinguished Vineyards in NZ. He also happens to be the son of Robert
Hesketh, one of the key players in the development of many facets of the SA wine industry.
Jonathon says, 'After realising long ago that working for the man (Greg Trott) was never
going to feed two dogs, four children, two cats, four chickens and an ever-so-patient wife,
the family returned to Adelaide in early 2006 to establish Hesketh Wine Company.' Exports
to all major markets.

🍷🍷🍷🍷🍷 **Regional Selection Adelaide Hills Sauvignon Blanc 2016** Pretty much
all the descriptors you'd like to see are here; vibrant, snapping fresh aromas of
nectarine, nettle and passionfruit. Juicy flavour, just a hint of fruit sweetness, and
crisp acidity that does its job without imposing itself. Ticks the boxes. Screwcap.
13% alc. **Rating** 92 $18 To 2018 SC ✪
Small Parcels Barossa Valley Bonvedro 2015 Once thought to be carignan
in Australia is bonvedro — a rare variety from Spain. Regardless of the confusion,
this is a ripper red, bright and breezy. Florals, raspberries, spicy, medium-bodied
and super tangy refreshing acidity to finish. Just drink it. Screwcap. 14% alc.
Rating 90 To 2019 $25 JF
Small Parcels Barossa Valley Negroamaro 2015 The fruit comes off the
Kalleske family's Koonunga Hill vineyard and Hesketh turns it into a lively, juicy
wine. The medium–light palate hosts a fair amount of fruit flavours, black olives
and sarsaparilla tempered by crunchy acidity; tannins are not obvious. Screwcap.
14.5% alc. **Rating** 90 To 2019 $25 JF

🍷🍷🍷🍷 **Bright Young Things Sauvignon Blanc 2016 Rating** 89 To 2017 $14 SC ✪
Midday Somewhere Shiraz 2015 Rating 89 $12 PR ✪

Heslop Wines ★★★★

PO Box 93, Mudgee, NSW 2850 **Region** Mudgee
T (02) 6372 3903 **www**.heslopwines.com.au **Open** Not
Winemaker Robert Heslop **Est.** 2011 **Dozens** 300 **Vyds** 4ha
This is the venture of Bob and Julie Heslop, who returned to Mudgee (where Julie was born)
in 1984, purchasing a property across the road from Julie's father's vineyard; the vendor was
Ferdie Roth, a member of the famous Mudgee wine family, who had planted the muscat
hamburg vines still on the property. Bob's winemaking career began at Kay Bros in McLaren
Vale, while undertaking oenology studies at CSU. Using sustainable viticulture practices, they
have planted 4ha to a Joseph's Coat of 11 varieties.

🍷🍷🍷🍷🍷 **Mudgee Touriga Nacional 2014** 30yo vines, hand-picked, crushed, open-
fermented with cultured yeast, 5 days on skins, matured in used oak for
12 months, gold medal Mudgee Wine Show '16. Has a very savoury, spicy fruit-
driven bouquet and medium to full-bodied palate, tannins playing a role. The
bouquet yields more interest each time you return to it, and the tannins don't
cause gridlock. Cork. 13.5% alc. **Rating** 94 To 2029 $35

🍷🍷🍷🍷🍷 **Mudgee Shiraz Blend 2014 Rating** 91 To 2024 $30
Mudgee Late Harvest Sauvignon Blanc 2014 Rating 91 To 2020 $20 ✪

Hewitson ★★★★★

66 Seppeltsfield Road, Nuriootpa, SA 5355 **Region** Adelaide
T (08) 8212 6233 **www**.hewitson.com.au **Open** 7 days 9–5
Winemaker Dean Hewitson **Est.** 1996 **Dozens** 35 000 **Vyds** 4.5ha

Dean Hewitson was a winemaker at Petaluma for 10 years, during which time he managed to do three vintages in France and one in Oregon as well as undertaking his Masters at the University of California, Davis. It is hardly surprising that the wines are immaculately made from a technical viewpoint. Dean sources 30-year-old riesling from the Eden Valley and 70-year-old shiraz from McLaren Vale; he also makes a Barossa Valley Mourvedre from vines planted in 1853 at Rowland Flat, and Barossa Valley Shiraz and Grenache from 60-year-old vines at Tanunda. Exports to the UK, the US and other major markets.

ŢŢŢŢŢ **Private Cellar Falkenberg Vineyard Barossa Valley Shiraz 2013** 220 dozen made, matured in French barriques for 30 months. It is profoundly, luxuriantly, hedonistically juicy, the flavours midway between red and black, or – if you prefer – some of each. There's plenty of French oak too, and the only thing that might debar early enjoyment isn't present: tannins – they are in the mix, but perfectly integrated. Cork. 14% alc. **Rating** 96 **To** 2043 $88

Miss Harry Barossa Valley Harriet's Blend 2014 Grenache, shiraz, mourvedre, carignan and cinsaut. This is flush with gloriously juicy red, blue and purple fruits, the components picked with unerring accuracy. While there is prodigious flavour, there's no overripe fruit. It weaves in some of the magic of the Rhône Valley's iconic Chateau Rayas, the ultimate compliment. Screwcap. 14% alc. **Rating** 96 **To** 2024 $25 ✪

Private Cellar Falkenberg Vineyard Barossa Valley Shiraz 2014 A single vineyard, 90yo vines, and the wine aged in new French barriques for 2 years: this is the foundation for Hewitson's premier shiraz. There's an unmistakable Barossa stamp – it's richly flavoured with menthol, dark fruits, a velvety sensation to the ripe tannins – and it's long. There's detail here, yet it is still in the big, voluptuous category, and done well. Cork. 14% alc. **Rating** 95 **To** 2030 $88 JF

Gun Metal Eden Valley Riesling 2016 The very dry growing season produced small berries, hand-picked, whole-bunch pressed, free-run juice. As complex and concentrated as the growing conditions would suggest, and the magnums ($48) look particularly appealing. Lemon juice and lemon curd flavours are buttressed by talcy acidity. Screwcap. 12.5% alc. **Rating** 94 **To** 2031 $24 ✪

LuLu Adelaide Hills Sauvignon Blanc 2016 This has an extra level of interest and intensity to its fruit, although there have been no frills to the winemaking. The flavours have two paths side by side, one featuring citrus, the other tropical fruits, both tethered by bright acidity on the finish. The siren song calling for early enjoyment should not be resisted. Screwcap. 12% alc. **Rating** 94 **To** 2017 $23 ✪

Belle Ville Barossa Valley Rose 2016 80% grenache, 20% cinsaut from 90yo vines, bottled immediately after settling. Very pale pink; soft, spicy red and blue fruit is part of grenache's contribution to the blend; there is also an extra dimension to the mouthfeel. Screwcap. 12.5% alc. **Rating** 94 **To** 2019 $23 ✪

Ned & Henry's Barossa Valley Shiraz 2015 Excellent depth and hue; Dean Hewitson implants his own unique thumbprint on Barossa Valley shiraz with this wine, always comprehensively over-delivering on price, achieving its power from the black fruit tannins, not the alcohol. However, it does need a year or two to settle down. Screwcap. 14% alc. **Rating** 94 **To** 2030 $28 ✪

Minimal Intervention Barossa Sangiovese 2015 Generous flavours run in the red spectrum, notwithstanding the crosscut of savoury tannins. It has been grown and made without compromise, and will be utterly at home in any Italianate restaurant you introduce it to. Screwcap. 14% alc. **Rating** 94 **To** 2028 $25 ✪

Minimal Intervention Fleurieu Tempranillo 2015 This wine has a very good purple-crimson hue, the dark berry fruits of the bouquet translating onto a medium+-bodied palate with black cherry fruit neatly framed by a mix of spicy/savoury/licorice-accented tannins. Will age gracefully. Screwcap. 14% alc. **Rating** 94 **To** 2030 $25 ✪

Old Garden Vineyard Barossa Valley Mourvedre 2013 Old Garden is an understatement, as the vines were planted in 1853. All the elements that make this wine special are in abundance: licorice, tar, menthol and herbs. It's full-bodied, smooth, with abundant tannins, creamy vanillan oak and spicy fruitcake. A very good wine. Just holding it back is the charry oak from 100% new French barrels. Cork. 14% alc. **Rating** 94 **To** 2029 $88 JF

ΥΥΥΥΥ **Ned & Henry's Barossa Valley Shiraz 2016** Rating 93 To 2029 $28 JF
Baby Bush Barossa Valley Mourvedre 2014 Rating 92 To 2022 $28 JF

Heydon Estate ★★★★★

325 Tom Cullity Drive, Wilyabrup, WA 6280 **Region** Margaret River
T (08) 9755 6995 **www.**heydonestate.com.au **Open** 7 days 10–5
Winemaker Mark Messenger **Est.** 1988 **Dozens** 1800 **Vyds** 10ha
Margaret River dentist and cricket tragic George Heydon and wife Mary have been involved in the region's wine industry since 1995. They became 50% partners in Arlewood, and when that partnership was dissolved in 2004 they retained the property and the precious 2ha of cabernet sauvignon and 2.5ha of Gin Gin clone chardonnay planted in '88. Additional plantings from '95 include Dijon chardonnay clones, sauvignon blanc, semillon, shiraz and petit verdot. The estate is now biodynamic, near neighbour Vanya Cullen having inspired the decision. Exports to the UK, Singapore and Hong Kong.

ΥΥΥΥΥ **The Willow Single Vineyard Margaret River Chardonnay 2013** Ambient fermentation in just the right percentage of new French oak (40%) is a lesson in harnessing Margaret River's tendency towards ample peachy stone fruit, through the deft touch of winemaking expertise. A trail of oatmeal and mineral funk sluices across an impeccably balanced palate: tensile and generous all at once. Screwcap. 13.5% alc. **Rating** 96 **To** 2023 $60 NG ✪
W.G. Grace Single Vineyard Margaret River Cabernet Sauvignon 2011 The aromas are the expected mix of blackcurrant and dark fruits, sluiced with tobacco, mulch and a moreish beef bouillon. However, the wine comes across as forward and relatively soft. The tannins build in composure as the fruit expands across the cheeks. This is already approachable; perhaps the structural carapace is buried beneath the fruit density. Screwcap. 14% alc. **Rating** 95 **To** 2022 $75 NG

ΥΥΥΥΥ **W.G. Grace Cabernet Sauvignon 2012** Rating 93 To 2021 $75 NG
The Doc Petit Verdot 2014 Rating 93 To 2030 $45 NG
The Urn Botrytis Semillon 2014 Rating 93 To 2024 $25 NG ✪
The Sledge Shiraz 2014 Rating 92 To 2035 $40 NG

Hickinbotham Clarendon Vineyard ★★★★★

92 Brooks Road, Clarendon, SA 5157 **Region** McLaren Vale
T (08) 8383 7504 **www.**hickinbothamwines.com.au **Open** By appt
Winemaker Charlie Seppelt, Chris Carpenter **Est.** 2012 **Dozens** 3500 **Vyds** 87ha
Alan Hickinbotham established the vineyard bearing his name in 1971 when he planted dry-grown cabernet sauvignon and shiraz in contoured rows on the sloping site. He was a very successful builder, this his first venture into wine, but his father, Alan Robb Hickinbotham, had a long and distinguished career, co-founding the oenology diploma at Roseworthy in '36. In 2012 Clarendon, and the stately sandstone house on the property, was purchased by Jackson Family Wines; it is run as a separate business from Yangarra Estate Vineyard, with different winemaking teams and wines. Exports to all major markets.

ΥΥΥΥΥ **The Peake Cabernet Shiraz 2015** Take the best parcels of cabernet sauvignon from Trueman, same for Brookes Road shiraz, a 56/44% blend, and another selection at the final assemblage to ensure it's the best of the best. It's morphed into a harmonious entity. Complex, detailed on every level, with powdery tannins, cassis, dark plums, cured meats and spice; very refreshing, full-bodied, deep and superbly balanced. Screwcap. 14% alc. **Rating** 97 **To** 2035 $175 JF

ΥΥΥΥΥ **Brooks Road McLaren Vale Shiraz 2015** In a word, breathtaking. Yes it's powerful, richly flavoured and full-bodied, but the angel is in the detail. Black-crimson-purple fruit notes flecked with bay leaves, dark chocolate with cinnamon spice. The oak is neatly tucked in, the tannins plump and slightly grainy, with exceptional length. Screwcap. 14% alc. **Rating** 96 **To** 2033 $75 JF ✪

The Revivalist Merlot 2015 While this has structure, depth and power, it's also finely crafted and elegant. Excellent colour, savoury yet with a whisper of florals and dark fruit, cassis among the oak spice, dried herbs and black olives. Fuller-bodied and expansive tannins with an appealing amaro-like finish. Not quite tamed; only time can do that. Cork. 13.5% alc. **Rating** 95 **To** 2030 $75 JF

Trueman Cabernet Sauvignon 2015 While the aromatics are lively, the palate has clamped shut, no matter that the hallmarks of a superb wine are here. Fragrant cassis, tobacco, black olives, eucalypt and black plums dipped in chocolate with some fruit sweetness get through on the firm palate, but the tannins are intense and the oak (70% new) a little unforgiving. Come back to this in '25. Screwcap. 14% alc. **Rating** 95 **To** 2035 $75 JF

Higher Plane ★★★★★

98 Tom Cullity Drive, Cowaramup, WA 6284 **Region** Margaret River
T (08) 9755 9000 **www**.higherplanewines.com.au **Open** At Juniper Estate, 7 days 10–5
Winemaker Mark Messenger **Est.** 1996 **Dozens** 2500 **Vyds** 14.55ha

In 2006 Higher Plane was purchased by the late Roger Hill and Gillian Anderson (of Juniper Estate), but kept as a stand-alone brand, with different distributors, etc. The Higher Plane vineyards are planted to all the key varieties: chardonnay and sauvignon blanc are foremost, with cabernet sauvignon, merlot, tempranillo, fiano, semillon, cabernet franc, malbec and petit verdot making up the rest. Exports to Hong Kong.

🍷🍷🍷🍷🍷 **Reserve Margaret River Cabernet Sauvignon 2013** There's an ethereal quality to this: nothing forced, just perfectly ripe fruit shining through. Exquisitely perfumed, the oak seamlessly integrated, the tannins filigreed and the palate supple yet quite detailed and elegant. Sheer joy. Not unreasonable to start drinking it now. Screwcap. 14% alc. **Rating** 96 **To** 2025 $45 JF ✪

Margaret River The Messenger 2013 Winemaker Mark Messenger has a knack with cabernet sauvignon and its mates, as in malbec/cabernet franc/merlot/petit verdot, which are drawn into this. His namesake wine is a barrel selection, and while there's a certain power and depth, it's contained beautifully. Succulent fruit, earthy-savoury notes, finely chiselled tannins and a persistent finish. Screwcap. 14% alc. **Rating** 96 **To** 2027 $50 JF ✪

Reserve Margaret River Chardonnay 2015 Whole-bunch pressed to barrel and left on lees in French oak (40% new) for 10 months. The best barrels are selected for the Reserve, and while it's finely tuned, linear, and with gossamer-like acidity, there's a depth of flavour with a mix of grapefruit, oak spice and lees. Screwcap. 13% alc. **Rating** 95 **To** 2024 $37 JF

Margaret River Chardonnay 2014 Hand-picked, fermented in French oak and held on yeast lees for 10 months, then a best barrels selection. An intensely flavoured and tightly structured wine, driven by its fruit first and foremost. Grapefruit, green apple and white peach are braced by lemony acidity, oak held in restraint. Will be long-lived. Screwcap. 13% alc. **Rating** 95 **To** 2024 $37

Margaret River Cabernet Merlot 2014 Estate-grown, small batch fermentation, matured in French oak for 18 months. A generously built palate with luscious cassis to the fore, cleverly supported by cedary oak and ripe tannins on the finish. Screwcap. 14% alc. **Rating** 95 **To** 2029 $25 ✪

Margaret River Fiano 2016 Whole-bunch pressed, fermented in used oak. Wildflower blossom aromas explode into the bright, lively, textured palate that typifies the best of Australian fiano, lengthened significantly by crunchy acidity on the powerful, long finish. Screwcap. 12.5% alc. **Rating** 94 **To** 2020 $25 ✪

Margaret River Tempranillo 2015 Hand-picked, open-fermented, matured in used French oak. Excellent colour flags a tempranillo with real attitude from concentrated and focused dark cherry fruit on the bouquet and medium to full-bodied palate. Its balance saves it from becoming belligerent, but protein is needed. Screwcap. 13.5% alc. **Rating** 94 **To** 2030 $25 **☉**

ㅇㅇㅇㅇ **Margaret River SSB 2016** Rating 92 To 2019 $?? JF **☉**
Forest Grove Margaret River Chardonnay 2015 Rating 91 To 2022 $25

Highland Heritage Estate   ★★★★

4698 Mitchell Highway, Orange, NSW 2800 **Region** Orange
T (02) 6363 5602 **www**.daquinogroup.com.au **Open** 7 days 9–5
Winemaker John Hordern, Rex D'Aquino **Est.** 1984 **Dozens** 5000 **Vyds** 15ha
Owned and operated by the D'Aquino family, the vineyard, restaurant and cellar door are located on 125ha 3km east of the city of Orange. The vineyard is planted to 15ha of chardonnay, sauvignon blanc, riesling, pinot noir, merlot and shiraz. At an elevation of 900m, on deep alluvial and rich basalt soils, the cool to cold climate and long growing season produce elegant reds and crisp, clean whites. Exports to all major markets.

ㅇㅇㅇㅇㅇ **Fume Blanc 2015** This has been barrel-aged in new French oak, setting a creamy, pungent tone to the herbaceous greengage and gooseberry voice of sauvignon, while imbuing a core of creamy lanolin, lemon oil and a riper tone of quince and stone fruits. The palate is multilayered and very ripe for the idiom, but never slips into tropical sweetness. Screwcap. 13.5% alc. **Rating** 93 **To** 2023 $20 NG **☉**

Nikki D Riesling 2011 Grown on the riesling-suitable elevated basalts of Orange, this is a delicate wine infused with abundant citrus, quince, cumquat, mango and pineapple notes. The acidity is tangy, punchy and juicy; the wine grows in stature in the glass. The finish is long and penetrative. Screwcap. 8% alc. **Rating** 93 **To** 2022 $20 NG **☉**

Orange Riesling 2013 Fine developed aromas of quince, marzipan, beeswax, Rose's lime and orange blossom, all licked with a gentle waft of kerosene. The palate is light and beginning to tiptoe across the dainty, balletic precipice of precision and intensity of flavour. While the acid is natural, the finish peters out just short of the line. Screwcap. 11.5% alc. **Rating** 91 **To** 2020 $20 NG **☉**

Orange Sauvignon Blanc 2015 A nice counterpoint to the estate's Fume Blanc. This is a vibrant sauvignon, playing on the verdant carriage of piquant pepper, greengage, gooseberry and mint, carried long and tangy by high country acidity and optimal ripeness, despite the lowish alcohol. Screwcap. 11.5% alc. **Rating** 91 **To** 2019 $20 NG **☉**

Orange Pinot Noir 2015 A pallid cherry red, this mid-weighted pinot is nevertheless solid, building in the glass. Aromas of dark cherry, strawberry and hints of roasted beetroot, sarsaparilla and mulch play across the chunky mid-palate. Despite the alcohol, the overall impression is savoury, not hot. The wine pushes across the mouth based on strength of personality and flavour, rather than finesse. Screwcap. 14.5% alc. **Rating** 90 **To** 2025 $25 NG

ㅇㅇㅇㅇ **Orange Chardonnay 2015** Rating 89 To 2023 $20 NG

Hill-Smith Estate   ★★★★☆

Flaxmans Valley Road, Eden Valley, SA 5235 **Region** Eden Valley
T (08) 8561 3200 **www**.hillsmithestate.com **Open** By appt
Winemaker Teresa Heuzenroeder **Est.** 1979 **Dozens** 5000 **Vyds** 12ha
The Eden Valley vineyard sits at an altitude of 510m, providing a cool climate that extends the growing season; rocky, acidic soil, coupled with winter rainfall and dry summers, results in modest crops. The Parish Vineyard in the Coal River Valley was purchased from Frogmore Creek in 2012; other white wines otherwise lacking a home have been put under the Hill-Smith Estate umbrella.

ㅇㅇㅇㅇㅇ **Parish Vineyard Single Estate Coal River Valley Riesling 2016** The wine has a quiet dignity, calming you until the game seems over, and you find a wall of minerally, textured power on the aftertaste. Retasting (with the wisdom of hindsight), you can see the signs of the nature of the wine, but it does make you bend at the knee. Screwcap. 12.5% alc. **Rating** 94 **To** 2026

♥♥♥♥♡ **Adelaide Hills Chardonnay 2015 Rating** 93 **To** 2021 $30 JF
Eden Valley Chardonnay 2015 Rating 91 **To** 2021 $24 JF

Hillbrook Wines ★★★★

Cnr Hillbrook Road/Wheatley Coast Road, Quinninup, WA 6258 **Region** Pemberton
T (08) 9776 7202 **www.**hillbrookwines.com.au **Open** Fri–Sun & public hols 12–5
Winemaker Rob Diletti (Castle Rock Estate) **Est.** 1996 **Dozens** 1000 **Vyds** 8ha
When Brian Ede and partner Anne Walsh left Alice Springs in 1996 to move to Pemberton, they made (in their words) the ultimate tree change. As well as establishing sauvignon blanc (3.4ha), merlot (2ha), semillon (1.2ha), pinot noir (0.8ha) and a smattering of chardonnay, they have 600 olive trees. A substantial portion of the estate-produced grapes are sold, only part vinified for the Hillbrook label.

♥♥♥♥♡ **Pemberton Semillon Sauvignon Blanc 2016** A 60/40% blend, the semillon firmly in the driver's seat with its citrus/lemongrass flavours and crisp acidity on the long palate. Screwcap. 13% alc. **Rating** 90 **To** 2018 $18 ✪

Hillcrest Vineyard ★★★★★

31 Phillip Road, Woori Yallock, Vic 3139 **Region** Yarra Valley
T (03) 5964 6689 **www.**hillcrestvineyard.com.au **Open** By appt
Winemaker David and Tanya Bryant **Est.** 1970 **Dozens** 500 **Vyds** 8.1ha
The small, effectively dry-grown vineyard was established by Graeme and Joy Sweet, who ultimately sold it to David and Tanya Bryant. The pinot noir, chardonnay, merlot and cabernet sauvignon grown on the property were of the highest quality and, when Coldstream Hills was in its infancy, were particularly important resources for it. For some years the wines were made by Phillip Jones (Bass Phillip), but the winemaking is now carried out onsite by David and Tanya. Exports to Singapore.

♥♥♥♥♡ **Village Yarra Valley Chardonnay 2015** Influenced by mentor Phillip Jones (from Bass Phillip), this is at the opulent end of the Yarra Valley chardonnay spectrum. Bright gold with green tinges, with aromas of ripe stone fruit, fig and nougat; the medium-bodied palate is flavoursome and textured and with enough acidity to keep it balanced. Diam. 12.9% alc. **Rating** 90 **To** 2020 $30 PR

Hither & Yon ★★★★

17 High Street, Willunga, SA 5172 **Region** McLaren Vale
T (08) 8556 2082 **www.**hitherandyon.com.au **Open** 7 days 11–4
Winemaker Richard Leask **Est.** 2012 **Dozens** 5000 **Vyds** 90ha
Brothers Richard and Malcolm Leask arrived as youngsters in McLaren Vale in the 1970s, following a family move from the Hunter Valley. Since father Ian Leask established the first family vineyard in '80, a further six sites spread across McLaren Vale have been added. Currently 13 varieties are planted over 90ha, with more plantings planned. In 2011 Richard and Malcolm started the Hither & Yon label, focusing on small single vineyard parcels, which change each year depending on the vintage and site. Richard manages all the vineyards and makes the wines, Malcolm handles production, sales and the historic cellar door. The labels feature the brand's ampersand, created by a different artist for each wine.

♥♥♥♥♡ **McLaren Vale Cabernet Sauvignon 2015** A supremely honest McLaren Vale cabernet, with warm (but not hot) blackcurrant fruit and a cache of dark chocolate buried alongside the tannins that will emerge with age. Screwcap. 14% alc. **Rating** 93 **To** 2030 $25 ✪
McLaren Vale Tempranillo 2016 Made from two pickings, almost 3 weeks apart. Open-fermented, whole berries and bunches, and 6 months in well used

French oak all part of the recipe. Unequivocally varietal bouquet, with lifted aromas of fresh cherry, blueberry, and cola extract spliced with a more savoury element. Fresh, juicy and flavoursome, but moderated by the fine tannin. Delicious. Screwcap. 14% alc. **Rating** 93 **To** 2021 $25 SC ♥

Old Jarvie The Saviour McLaren Vale Tempranillo Garnacha Monastrell 2015 A take on a Spanish blend of the 'interesting but easy-drinking' genre. Individual traits from the three varieties are there, but it's the overall feel of the wine that carries the day. Dusty, spicy, generous of fruit but avoiding overt ripeness. You'll enjoy this without effort, which is probably just as it's intended to be. Screwcap. 14% alc. **Rating** 92 **To** 2021 $30 SC

Old Jarvie The Charitable McLaren Vale Nero d'Avola Aglianico Rose 2016 50% nero d'Avola, 50% aglianico. That's a blend you don't trip over every day tasting Australian rose. Unsurprisingly, it's a savoury style built for the table. The general impression is of red fruit, in the cranberry and sour cherry vein, with a sweet spice character running through the bouquet and palate. Screwcap. 12.9% alc. **Rating** 91 **To** 2019 $30 SC

McLaren Vale Grenache Mataro 2016 A solid citizen of the Vale, with spoonfuls of red cherry, raspberry and dark chocolate all attesting to its place in the wine world. Nice control of alcohol in a hot, compressed vintage. Screwcap. 14.5% alc. **Rating** 91 **To** 2023 $25

Old Jarvie The Even Hand McLaren Vale Grenache Shiraz Mataro 2015 57% grenache, 22% shiraz, 21% mataro. Initially lots of sweetness on the bouquet; aromas of candied orange peel and other Christmas pudding ingredients, but there are earthy, savoury notes in the background. The ripe fruit theme continues as you taste, but persistent tannin frames the palate and gives the wine a nicely firm edge. Screwcap. 14.5% alc. **Rating** 90 **To** 2025 $30 SC

Old Jarvie The Widowmaker McLaren Vale Tannat Petit Verdot Cabernet Sauvignon 2014 An unusual blend. The tannins are insidious, never seeking to take control, but never stepping back either. The red and black fruits are such that, contrary to all expectations, the wine ends up no more than medium-bodied. Screwcap. 14% alc. **Rating** 90 **To** 2029 $30

♥♥♥♥ McLaren Vale Aglianico 2014 **Rating** 89 **To** 2020 $30

Hobbs of Barossa Ranges   ★★★★☆

550 Flaxman's Valley Road, Angaston, SA 5353 **Region** Barossa Valley
T 0427 177 740 **www.**hobbsvintners.com.au **Open** At Artisans of Barossa
Winemaker Peter Schell, Chris Ringland **Est.** 1998 **Dozens** 1500 **Vyds** 6.22ha
Hobbs of Barossa Ranges is the high-profile, if somewhat challenging, venture of Greg and Allison Hobbs. The estate vineyards revolve around 1ha of shiraz planted in 1908, 1ha planted in '88, 1ha planted in '97 and 1.82ha planted in 2004. In '09 0.4ha of old white frontignac was removed, giving space for another small planting of shiraz. The viticultural portfolio is completed with 0.6ha of semillon planted in the 1960s, and an inspired 0.6ha of viognier ('88). All the wines, made by Peter Schell (at Spinifex), push the envelope. The only conventionally made wine is the Shiraz Viognier, with a production of 130 dozen. Gregor, an Amarone-style Shiraz in full-blooded table wine mode, and a quartet of dessert wines, are produced by cane cutting, followed by further desiccation on racks. The Grenache comes from a Barossa floor vineyard, the Semillon, Viognier and White Frontignac from estate-grown grapes. Exports to the US, Denmark, Singapore, Taiwan and China.

♥♥♥♥♥ **1905 Shiraz 2014** Hand-picked 110yo vines, crushed and destemmed, open-fermented with wild yeast, 10 days on skins, matured for 24 months in new French hogsheads. The single vineyard was planted in 1905, and has provided a wine that is a pure rendition of Barossa shiraz at its greatest, the problem being production of only 130 dozen bottles. Its primary flavours are deepest black, yet there is a fleeting lick of red berries as you take the wine into your mouth. Likewise the cedary French oak offers another (harmonious) take on the texture and flavour. Diam. 14.1% alc. **Rating** 96 **To** 2040 $120

Semillon 2011 Hand-picked from a single vineyard, crushed and destemmed, open-fermented on skins with wild yeast, 50% matured in used French oak for 6–8 months where it completed mlf, 50% matured in stainless steel, matured in bottle for 5 years before release. You would have no hope of guessing how the wine was made, nor how it old it was, if it were tasted blind. The colour is still pale green, the flavours built around lemon curd, lemongrass and lemon. It's so left field it's back to square one. Screwcap. 13.4% alc. **Rating** 94 **To** 2031 $30 ✪

Gregor Single Vineyard Shiraz 2014 40yo vines, hand-picked and air-dried Amarone style, crushed and destemmed, wild yeast–open fermented, 10 days on skins, matured in a new French oak 1350l vat and puncheons. In some years the Amarone effect is not as obvious; here it is dialled up to maximum impact, which I can't grow to love (others have no problem). With only 200 dozen produced, it sells out quickly. Diam. 15.2% alc. **Rating** 94 **To** 2034 $150

Hoddles Creek Estate   ★★★★★

505 Gembrook Road, Hoddles Creek, Vic 3139 **Region** Yarra Valley
T (03) 5967 4692 **www**.hoddlescreekestate.com.au **Open** By appt
Winemaker Franco D'Anna, Chris Bendle **Est.** 1997 **Dozens** 20 000 **Vyds** 33.3ha
The D'Anna family has established a vineyard on the property that has been in the family since 1960. The vineyards (chardonnay, pinot noir, sauvignon blanc, cabernet sauvignon, pinot gris, merlot and pinot blanc) are hand-pruned and hand-harvested, and a 300-tonne, split-level winery was built in 2003. Son Franco is the viticulturist and inspired winemaker; he started to work in the family liquor store at 13, graduating to chief wine buyer by the time he was 21, then completed a Bachelor of Commerce degree at Melbourne University before studying viticulture at CSU. A vintage at Coldstream Hills, then two years' vintage experience with Peter Dredge at Witchmount, and Mario Marson (ex Mount Mary) as mentor in the '03 vintage, has put an old head on young shoulders. The Wickhams Rd label uses grapes from an estate vineyard in Gippsland, and purchased grapes from the Yarra Valley and Mornington Peninsula. Best Value Winery *Wine Companion* Awards '15. Exports to The Netherlands, Dubai, Singapore, Japan and China.

♟♟♟♟♟ **1er Yarra Valley Chardonnay 2015** A fruit selection (hand-picked), fermented and matured for 12 months in French barriques (30% new). Bright straw-green; it has obvious complexity, and the extra length that the best Yarra Valley chardonnays have compared to those of other regions. Grapefruit juice, zest and pith are the anchor of the flavour, and also build the trajectory of the wine through to the finish. Screwcap. 13.2% alc. **Rating** 97 **To** 2025 $45 ✪

1er Yarra Valley Pinot Noir 2015 Estate-grown, 20% whole bunches, matured for 12 months in French oak (35% new), then 6 months in tank. The bouquet is gloriously fragrant and flowery, the red and blue fruits immediately picked up by the palate, which then moves on with its vibrant spicy whole-bunch notes adding more layers to its seemingly endless finish. Ultra-detailed grapegrowing and vinification. Screwcap. 13.2% alc. **Rating** 97 **To** 2030 $45 ✪

♟♟♟♟♟ **Yarra Valley Pinot Noir 2015** Six clones separately fermented, 25% whole bunches, 21 days on skins, matured for 10 months in French oak (25% new). Superb colour; the perfumed bouquet of red berries and plums sets the scene for the perfectly balanced and very long palate, with a contrast between its juicy fruits and fine-grained tannins. This is a ridiculous bargain, whether enjoyed tonight or in a decade. Screwcap. 13.2% alc. **Rating** 96 **To** 2025 $20 ✪

Wickhams Road Yarra Valley Chardonnay 2016 Hand-picked, fermented and matured in French oak (20% new) for 8 months. Quite obviously, the difference between this and its Gippsland sibling comes from the terroir. This is lighter on its feet, more elegant and longer on the palate; the flavour wheel has all of those from its sibling, adding nuances of pear and green apple. Screwcap. 12.5% alc. **Rating** 95 **To** 2030 $18 ✪

Yarra Valley Chardonnay 2015 Eight estate-grown clones, 80% crushed and destemmed, 20% whole bunches, mix of wild and cultured yeasts, 100% barrel-fermented in French oak (25% new), matured for 10 months.

Sits comfortably alongside its Pinot Noir sibling, with the same attention to detail and similar over-delivery against price expectations. White peach, melon grapefruit and French oak are spun so tightly together it's hard to weigh up their individual contributions, and not necessary to do so. Screwcap. 13.2% alc. Rating 95 To 2025 $20 ○

Yarra Valley Pinot Gris 2016 70% whole bunches foot-stomped and allowed to ferment naturally after 3 days, then pressed to used oak, the remaining 30% treated as a red wine: berry ferment for 7 days until dry, hand-plunged and then pressed to used oak. Mid-depth salmon-pink; the most unusual vinification has resulted in a rose with red wine texture, length, intensity and complexity. Screwcap. 12.5% alc. **Rating** 95 To 2019 $22 ○

Wickhams Road Gippsland Chardonnay 2016 This comes at you like a stealth bomber, its intensity, length, varietal fruit and lingering aftertaste utterly unexpected. Grapefruit and white stone fruit each claim bragging rights, neither prevailing, but flipping French oak out of the ring. Fantastic value, and awesome power. Screwcap. 12.5% alc. **Rating** 94 To 2029 $18 ○

Wickhams Road Yarra Valley Pinot Noir 2016 Clear crimson-purple; the fragrant bouquet opens with a wraith of spice, red flowers and red fruits; the lively, fresh and juicy palate picks up the theme without losing a beat. Great now or later – ridiculous price for a wine of this quality (and joy). Screwcap. 13.5% alc. **Rating** 94 To 2023 $18 ○

�♀ **Wickhams Road Gippsland Pinot Noir 2016** Rating 93 To 2026 $18 ○
Yarra Valley Pinot Blanc 2016 Rating 90 To 2017 $22

Hoggies Estate Wines ★★★☆

Stentiford Vineyard, Lot 95 Skinner Road, Coonawarra, SA 5263 **Region** Coonawarra
T (08) 8736 3268 **www**.hoggieswine.com **Open** By appt
Winemaker Gavin Hogg **Est.** 1996 **Dozens** 16 000 **Vyds** 27.5ha
A complicated story. Founded by Gavin Hogg and Mike Press in 1996 and based on an 80ha vineyard in the Wrattonbully region, the Kopparossa label was born in 2000. The vineyard (not the brand) was sold in '02, and Mike retired to build his eponymous winery and vineyard in the Adelaide Hills. Various twists and turns followed between then and '09, when Gavin purchased a 24ha vineyard on the Murray River, adjacent to his parents' vineyard; the majority of the fruit from the Hoggies Vineyard is used for the Hoggies Estate brand, and for various private labels. The Kopparossa wines come from the 3.5ha estate vineyard in Coonawarra. Exports to the UK, the US, Canada, Morocco, Vietnam, Japan, Hong Kong and China.

♀♀♀♀♀ **Olivia Coonawarra Cabernet Sauvignon 2013** Spent 2 years in new Troncais (French) oak, but hasn't bowed to the oak, although, obviously enough, it does intersect with cassis/blackcurrant fruit right from the outset. Because the tannins are fine (but persistent, as is proper), the wine just edges into medium-bodied territory: for drinking whenever the mood takes you. Gold medal Limestone Coast Wine Show '16. Screwcap. 14% alc. **Rating** 94 To 2028 $20 ○

♀♀♀♀ **Coonawarra Riesling 2014** Rating 89 To 2021 $15 ○

Hollick ★★★★

Riddoch Highway, Coonawarra, SA 5263 **Region** Coonawarra
T (08) 8737 2318 **www**.hollick.com **Open** Mon–Fri 9–5, w'ends & public hols 10–5
Winemaker Joe Cory **Est.** 1983 **Dozens** 40 000 **Vyds** 87ha
In April 2014 the Hollick family announced that a major investment had been made in their business by the large Chinese group Hong Kong Yingda Investment Co. Ltd. Involved in hospitality and tourism in China, part of its business involves vineyard and winery operations. The Hollick family continues to own a part of the business, and continues to manage it in the same way as usual. Major benefits to Hollick are working capital and access to the Chinese market; and Hong Kong Yingda Investment Co. Ltd will gain expertise from the Hollick family. Exports to most major markets.

ƳƳƳƳƳ **The Nectar 2016** This is very good: balletic, airy and strident across a palate of precise mineral crunch and tangy, botrytis acidity; a dainty, sweet riesling that finishes almost palpably dry as flavours of quince marmalade, lime splice and ginger seemingly evaporate across its spine. There is not a cloying note. Screwcap. 10.3% alc. **Rating** 94 **To** 2026 $25 NG ❂

ƳƳƳƳƳ **Wilgha Shiraz 2014 Rating** 93 **To** 2034 $54 NG
Ravenswood Cabernet Sauvignon 2014 Rating 93 **To** 2030 $77 NG
Neilson's Block Merlot 2014 Rating 91 **To** 2022 $54 NG
Bond Road Chardonnay 2015 Rating 90 **To** 2021 $25 NG

Hollydene Estate   ★★★★

3483 Golden Highway, Jerrys Plains, NSW 2330 **Region** Hunter Valley
T (02) 6576 4021 **www**.hollydeneestate.com **Open** 7 days 9–5
Winemaker Matt Burton **Est.** 1965 **Dozens** 2000 **Vyds** 40ha
Karen Williams has three vineyards and associated properties, all established in the 1960s. They are Hollydene Estate, Wybong Estate and Arrowfield, the latter one of the original vinous landmarks in the Upper Hunter. The three vineyards produce grapes for the Juul and Hollydene Estate labels. Also produces sparkling wines from the Mornington Peninsula. Exports to Indonesia and China.

ƳƳƳƳƳ **Blanc de Blancs 2008** A beautifully composed sparkling that sets a benchmark for the Mornington, contrasting dynamism, energy and calm. Tangy lemon, crunchy apple and white peach fruit are cut with an electric line of high-velocity acidity, yet never harsh or hard, well toned by the silky, buttery calm of long lees age. Marvellous. Diam. 12.5% alc. **Rating** 94 **To** 2020 $50 TS

ƳƳƳƳƳ **Blanc de Noirs 2008 Rating** 93 **To** 2019 $35 TS
Show Reserve Chardonnay 2014 Rating 90 **To** 2022 $35 SC

Holm Oak   ★★★★★

11 West Bay Road, Rowella, Tas 7270 **Region** Northern Tasmania
T (03) 6394 7577 **www**.holmoakvineyards.com.au **Open** 7 days 11–5
Winemaker Rebecca Duffy **Est.** 1983 **Dozens** 10 000 **Vyds** 11.62ha
Holm Oak takes its name from its grove of oak trees, planted around the beginning of the 20th century and originally intended for the making of tennis racquets. Winemaker Rebecca Duffy, daughter of owners Ian and Robyn Wilson, has extensive winemaking experience in Australia and California, and husband Tim, a viticultural agronomist, manages the vineyard (pinot noir, cabernet sauvignon, chardonnay, riesling, sauvignon blanc and pinot gris, with small amounts of merlot, cabernet franc and arneis). Exports to the US, Canada, Norway and Japan.

ƳƳƳƳƳ **The Wizard Chardonnay 2015** Whole-bunch pressed, wild-yeast fermented (including 100% mlf) and matured in French oak, a barrel selection made in Jan '16, and matured further in 100% new oak. Gleaming green-gold; the wine is described by Holm Oak as bigger, richer and more complex than the Estate wine. I would add a big asterisk and say it retains finesse and purity, the mlf needed to secure its balance. Screwcap. 13% alc. **Rating** 96 **To** 2025 $60 ❂
Pinot Noir 2015 Destemmed and wild-yeast fermented in small open fermenters, plunged, pressed to French oak (20% new) at dryness, matured for 10 months. A sumptuous pinot overflowing with red and purple fruit and a contrasting touch of forest to add to both flavour and texture. Tasmania challenges Central Otago with wines such as this. Screwcap. 13% alc. **Rating** 96 **To** 2028 $32 ❂
The Wizard Pinot Noir 2015 From 6 rows of one of the old pinot blocks, mainly D5V12, including some newer clones, open-fermented, 30% whole bunches, hand-plunged, matured in French oak, 12 barrels (60% new) selected for this wine and matured for a further 6 months. Much lighter colour than expected, but it is strikingly spicy/savoury with a stream of red fruits that overwhelms the

other claimants. This is a book that needs to be reread many times to understand its hidden meanings. Screwcap. 13.5% alc. **Rating** 96 **To** 2030 $60 ✪

Riesling 2016 The expressive bouquet has lime blossom, lime leaf and spice aromas, the palate filling the senses with the opposing influences of a titratable acidity of 7.5g/l and 8g/l of residual sugar. The flavours are akin to strobe lighting as they dash around the palate, lasting well into the aftertaste, and the finish is cleansing and pure. Screwcap. 12% alc. **Rating** 95 **To** 2029 $25 ✪

Chardonnay 2015 Whole-bunch pressed, wild-yeast fermented in French oak (30% new), 30% mlf, 9 months in oak. A very elegant, perfectly poised and highly expressive chardonnay with grainy acidity adding to the textural play behind the white peach and almond kernel flavours of the palate. Astute winemaking. Screwcap. 12.5% alc. **Rating** 95 **To** 2027 $30 ✪

Sauvignon Blanc 2016 Cool-fermented in stainless steel with the addition of a small amount of oak blocks, the bouquet shows little sign of it. When it comes to the palate, there is a massive change on the finish and aftertaste, where its spicy, herbal, zesty, lime notes take off like the proverbial scalded cat. Screwcap. 12% alc. **Rating** 94 **To** 2023 $25 ✪

ΨΨΨΨΨ **Pinot Gris 2016 Rating** 90 **To** 2020 $25
Arneis 2016 Rating 90 **To** 2020 $25

Home Hill ★★★★★

38 Nairn Street, Ranelagh, Tas 7109 **Region** Southern Tasmania
T (03) 6264 1200 **www.**homehillwines.com.au **Open** 7 days 10–5
Winemaker Gilli and Paul Lipscombe **Est.** 1994 **Dozens** 2000 **Vyds** 5ha
Terry and Rosemary Bennett planted their first 0.5ha of vines in 1994 on gentle slopes in the beautiful Huon Valley. Between '94 and '99 the plantings were increased to 3ha of pinot noir, 1.5ha of chardonnay and 0.5ha of sylvaner. Home Hill has had great success with its exemplary Pinot Noirs, consistent multi-trophy and gold medal winners in the ultra-competitive Tasmanian Wine Show. Impressive enough, but pales into insignificance in the wake of winning the Jimmy Watson Trophy at the Melbourne Wine Awards '15.

ΨΨΨΨΨ **Kelly's Reserve Pinot Noir 2015** This is a selection of the best barrels, with one small section of the vineyard always providing the core of the wine. It is a monumental pinot with a turbocharged V12 engine throbbing gently but insistently as it waits for the race to start. It captures every corner of the mouth with its brooding array of foresty red, purple and blue fruits, the powerful tannins fully justified and giving the wine a 20-year future. Keep your hands off it as long as you can. Screwcap. 13.9% alc. **Rating** 98 **To** 2035 $75 ✪

Estate Pinot Noir 2015 Manicured estate vineyards and the inclusion of a small amount of whole bunches are the starting line for a wine that is never less than great; the wine show records of this and the Kelly's Reserve are totally deserved. This remarkable wine is at once juicy yet lushly textured, its drive and length foregone conclusions, its red cherry/berry fruit core at peace with the tannins and oak. Screwcap. 13.6% alc. **Rating** 97 **To** 2028 $42 ✪

Horner Wines ★★★★

12 Shedden Street, Cessnock, NSW 2325 **Region** Hunter Valley
T 0427 201 391 **www.**nakedwines.com.au **Open** Not
Winemaker Ashley Horner **Est.** 2013 **Dozens** 6500 **Vyds** 12ha
Horner Wines is the family venture of Ashley and Lauren Horner. They have a certified organic vineyard planted to chardonnay, viognier and shiraz. Grapes are also sourced from organic vineyards in Orange and Cowra. Ashley had a 14-year career working at Rosemount Estate, Penfolds, Kamberra Estate, Saint Clair (NZ) and Mount Pleasant, ultimately becoming winemaker at Tamburlaine and completing a Diploma in Wine Technology at Dookie College. Lauren has a degree in hospitality/tourism, and is now involved in the

running of Horner Wines. The move from grapegrowing to winemaking was precipitated by the fall in demand for grapes, and they sell the wines through www.nakedwines.com.au.

🍷🍷🍷🍷🍷 **Little Jack Organic Riesling 2016** From Orange. Mandarin and crushed lime leaf aromas lead into a structured palate with good grip and freshness anchored by crisp acidity. The mid-palate needs to fill out, which it will with a few more years in bottle. Screwcap. 11.8% alc. **Rating** 90 **To** 2023 $17 **⊙**

Family Reserve Shiraz 2016 Estate-grown, hand-picked, 4 days cold soak, cool-fermented, matured for 9 months in French hogsheads (25% new). Very respectable colour; the oak profile is presently stronger than the blackberry and plum fruit on the medium-bodied palate, but could retract its claws over the next 5 years or so, and merit higher points. Screwcap. 14% alc. **Rating** 90 **To** 2026 $25

Houghton ★★★★★

148 Dale Road, Middle Swan, WA 6065 **Region** Swan Valley
T (08) 9274 9540 **www**.houghton-wines.com.au **Open** 7 days 10–5
Winemaker Ross Pamment **Est.** 1836 **Dozens** NFP
Houghton's reputation was once largely dependent on its (then) White Burgundy, equally good when young or 5 years old. In the last 20 years its portfolio has changed out of all recognition, with a kaleidoscopic range of high quality wines from the Margaret River, Frankland River, Great Southern and Pemberton regions to the fore. The Jack Mann and Gladstones red wines stand at the forefront, but to borrow a saying of the late Jack Mann, 'There are no bad wines here.' With a history of 180 years, its future now lies in the hands of Accolade Wines. Exports to the UK and Asia.

🍷🍷🍷🍷🍷 **Jack Mann Cabernet Sauvignon 2014** From the Justin Vineyard in Frankland River. Includes 5% merlot, destemmed, wild yeast–open fermented, matured for 16 months in Bordeaux-coopered French oak (50% new). This is a wine built for the ages on its rock of ages blend of deep-seated cassis fruit, high quality oak and full-on cabernet tannins. Screwcap. 14% alc. **Rating** 97 **To** 2054 $133 **⊙**

🍷🍷🍷🍷🍷 **The Bandit Frankland River Cabernet Sauvignon 2012** This reflects the vast experience Houghton has with Frankland River cabernet, having made it for decades. So it's no surprise to find cassis/blackcurrant/blackberry woven together with cedary oak and ripe, persistent tannins. What is surprising is the age and price of the wine. Screwcap. 13.5% alc. **Rating** 94 **To** 2027 $20 **⊙**

🍷🍷🍷🍷🍷 **Crofters Chardonnay 2016 Rating** 93 **To** 2022 $19 **⊙**

House of Arras ★★★★★

Bay of Fires, 40 Baxters Road, Pipers River, Tas 7252 **Region** Northern Tasmania
T (03) 6362 7622 **www**.houseofarras.com.au **Open** Mon–Fri 11–4, w'ends 10–4
Winemaker Ed Carr **Est.** 1995 **Dozens** NFP
The rise and rise of the fortunes of the House of Arras has been due to two things: first, the exceptional skills of winemaker Ed Carr, and second, its access to high quality Tasmanian chardonnay and pinot noir. While there have been distinguished sparkling wines made in Tasmania for many years, none has so consistently scaled the heights of Arras. The complexity, texture and structure of the wines are akin to that of Bollinger RD and Krug; the connection stems from the 7–15+ years the wines spend on lees prior to disgorgement.

🍷🍷🍷🍷🍷 **Grand Vintage 2007** 100% Tasmanian, 77% chardonnay, 23% pinot noir, gleaming straw-green hue, and very, very complex, in full-blown Arras style at its towering best, with layer upon layer of complexity ex brioche, toast, flint, white peach and apple. Although it spent over 8 years on tirage, the overall mouthfeel strongly suggests this exceptional wine has time to go. Cork. 12.5% alc. **Rating** 97 **To** 2018 $77 **⊙**

ΨΨΨΨΨ **Blanc de Blancs 2006** At a full decade of age, the delightfully toasty/nutty/ honey personality of mature chardonnay has emerged with clarity and jubilation, backed by impeccably focused and enduring acidity, perfectly balanced with low dosage of less than 6g/l. There is an effortless harmony here that testifies to Ed Carr's exacting craftsmanship, promising enduring potential. Cork. 12.5% alc. **Rating** 96 **To** 2021 $80 TS

EJ Carr Late Disgorged 2003 At a full 14yo (12 on lees) this is a showpiece for the grand endurance of Australian sparkling, still showing more energy, vitality and potential than most champagnes from the same vintage. Grapefruit, lemon and apple still abound in this chardonnay-charged style (more than 60%), while maturity has blessed it with delightfully silky structure and captivating layers of nougat, lemon meringue, dried peach, vanilla and mixed spice. A thrilling line of bright, enduring acidity promises the confidence to see out two decades. Marvellous. Cork. 12.5% alc. **Rating** 96 **To** 2023 $130 TS

Grand Vintage 2008 '08 is one of my favourite vintages in Tasmania, and this cuvee captures the tension of its mood in a pale, bright straw hue and focused lemon and apple fruit. An almost two-thirds chardonnay dominance is proclaimed in white fruit definition and layers of struck flint reduction. 7 years on lees has built more in texture than flavour, lending just subtle almond meal and charcuterie complexity. The tightly coiled acidity of this enduring season calls for time to unwind. Patience. Cork. 12.5% alc. **Rating** 95 **To** 2023 $70 TS

Blanc de Blancs 2007 At a full 10 years (8 on lees), the bright, pale-straw hue is a marvel. Age has blessed it with delightful layers of freshly churned butter, almond nougat, toast and the slightest wisp of wood smoke, yet the focus remains resolutely transfixed on impeccably vibrant lemon, grapefruit and crunchy apple fruit. The acidity draws out a long finish of refreshingly minuscule dosage of 3.5g/l and finely played bitter phenolic grip. Cork. 12.5% alc. **Rating** 94 **To** 2022 $80 TS

A by Arras Premium Cuvee NV 59% pinot noir, 33% chardonnay, 8% pinot meunier aged 3+ years on tirage and 6 months on cork. Has it all: balance, life, length and complexity, dancing the line between supple richness and minerality to perfection. Natural acidity helps to deliver the particularly good finish and aftertaste of this slimmed-down version of Arras. Cork. 12.5% alc. **Rating** 94 **To** 2018 $30 ✪

Rose 2006 A pretty, pale salmon-copper hue predicts nothing of the grand complexity and character that is packed into this impeccably crafted Tasmanian rose. 7 years on lees has built a toasty, creamy, spicy style, bolstering the personality and depth of Tasmanian pinot noir (two-thirds of the blend). It culminates in a finish of great persistence, enlivened by bright, enduring acidity and bitter yet fine, well placed phenolic grip. Cork. 12.5% alc. **Rating** 94 **To** 2018 $80 TS

ΨΨΨΨΨ **Brut Elite NV Rating** 91 **To** 2019 $40 TS

House of Cards   ★★★★★

3220 Caves Road, Yallingup, WA 6282 **Region** Margaret River
T (08) 9755 2583 **www.**houseofcardswine.com.au **Open** 7 days 10–5
Winemaker Travis Wray **Est.** 2011 **Dozens** 5000 **Vyds** 12ha

House of Cards is owned and operated by Elizabeth and Travis Wray, Travis managing the vineyard and making the wines, Elizabeth managing sales and marketing. The name of the winery is a reflection of the gamble that all viticulturists and winemakers face every vintage: 'You have to play the hand you are dealt by Mother Nature.' They only use estate-grown grapes, open-top fermentation, hand-plunging and manual basket pressing. It's certainly doing it the hard way, but it must seem all worthwhile when they produce wines of such quality.

ΨΨΨΨΨ **The Royals Single Vineyard Margaret River Chardonnay 2016** Gin Gin clone, whole-bunch pressed to French hogsheads (45% new), wild-yeast fermented, 10% mlf, matured for 11 months. The opulence of high quality Margaret River chardonnay comes through on the first whiff, and is equally quickly built up by the richly textured, complex palate. The handling and choice of oak is a feature, the 10% mlf there as a seasoning is on food; the length and finish flow unhesitatingly through to the aftertaste. Screwcap. 13% alc. **Rating** 95 To 2026 $36

The Royals Single Vineyard Margaret River Cabernet Sauvignon 2015
Open-fermented, 35 days extended skin contact, basket-pressed, matured in French oak (30% new) for 18 months. A totally convincing medium to full-bodied cabernet that repays all the vinification steps; cassis, bay leaf and dried herbs hit the bouquet and palate in precisely the same way; an all-up classic medium-bodied cabernet style. Screwcap. 14% alc. **Rating** 95 **To** 2035 $39

Single Vineyard The Ace 2015 50% cabernet sauvignon, 25% each of malbec and petit verdot, 20% drained off the cabernet portion, open-fermented, 35 days extended skin contact; 50% whole-bunch inclusion in the petit verdot ferment, 50% of the cabernet and malbec finish ferment on barrel, all matured for 18 months in French barriques (50% new). Juicy, vibrant and long. Release Nov '17. But even at Feb '17, shows its class and finesse on the long palate, finished with French oak and fine, savoury tannins. Cork. 14.2% alc. **Rating** 95 To 2035 $65

The Joker Margaret River Sauvignon Blanc 2016 Machine-harvested, pressed at low pressure so only free-run juice used, fermented with two cultured yeasts. Sophisticated winemaking has resulted in a very intense wine, power accumulating at a rate of knots on the very long palate, with texture as well as lemon zest/minerally acidity. Screwcap. 12.5% alc. **Rating** 94 **To** 2020 $21 ✪

The Joker Margaret River Shiraz 2015 Open-fermented, 20% whole-berry carbonic maceration, hand-plunged, basket-pressed, matured in used French oak for 12 months. This has exceptional drive and freshness, with spice and licorice to spare. It has quasi cool climate characters uncommon in the temperate climate of Margaret River. Compelling wine at a bargain price. Screwcap. 14% alc. **Rating** 94 To 2030 $24 ✪

♟♟♟♟♟ Lady Luck Single Vineyard Petit Verdot 2014 Rating 93 To 2035 $48
Black Jack Single Vineyard Malbec 2015 Rating 93 To 2040 $48

Howard Vineyard   ★★★★☆

53 Bald Hills Road, Nairne, SA 5252 **Region** Adelaide Hills
T (08) 8188 0203 www.howardvineyard.com **Open** Tues–Sun 10–5
Winemaker Tom Northcott **Est.** 2005 **Dozens** 6000 **Vyds** 60ha
Howard Vineyard is a family-owned Adelaide Hills winery set among towering gum trees and terraced lawns. Pinot noir, chardonnay, pinot gris and sauvignon blanc are sourced from the 470m altitude Schoenthal 'Beautiful Valley' Vineyard, near Lobethal, while Howard's Nairne Vineyard, in the warmer Mt Barker district, is home to shiraz, cabernet sauvignon and cabernet franc. All the wines are estate-grown. Exports to Hong Kong and China.

♟♟♟♟♟ Amos Adelaide Hills Chardonnay 2016 Bernard clones 76 and 95, hand-sorted, whole-bunch pressed, free-run juice to French oak (33% new), 20% wild yeast ferment and aged 9 months. Lots of white stone fruit and fuzz, a touch of ripe pear too, long on the palate with a fine line of natural acidity. Finishes just short, but still very good. Screwcap. 13.4% alc. **Rating** 93 To 2024 $40 JF

Clover Adelaide Hills Pinot Gris 2016 An unexpectedly complex and arresting powder-puff bouquet is reflected in the strongly varietal nashi pear palate, but one with a twist of orange peel and strongly structured acidity. There is no suggestion (by the winery) of left field vinification, which makes these characters even more interesting. Screwcap. 12.8% alc. **Rating** 94 To 2019 $24 ✪

Adelaide Hills Riesling 2016 This is quite full-bodied for a riesling. It is textural, with lemon peel, zest and pith and plenty of racy acidity cutting through. Lots to like. Screwcap. 12% alc. **Rating** 92 To 2024 JF

Clover Adelaide Hills Shiraz 2015 Matured in French oak for 12+ months. Bright crimson-purple; the plum and red/dark cherry fruits have a savoury edge of licorice and finely tuned tannins running through the well balanced, medium-bodied palate. Screwcap. 13% alc. **Rating** 92 **To** 2029 $24 **○**

Adelaide Hills Sauvignon Blanc 2016 Really restrained aromas working on a citrus theme with wafts of aniseed, some freshly cut grass and pine needles. Zesty palate, mouthwatering even, chalky acidity, some texture and a touch of sweetness on the finish. Screwcap. 13.2% alc. **Rating** 91 **To** 2020 JF

Clover Adelaide Hills Sauvignon Blanc 2016 Stainless steel–fermented with limited lees stirring. Mainstream Adelaide Hills style, with stone and tropical fruits surrounded by savoury snow pea and Granny Smith apple, punchy acidity cleansing the finish. Screwcap. 13.2% alc. **Rating** 90 **To** 2017 $24

Picnic Adelaide Hills Cabernet Franc Rose 2016 Chilled in the press for 8 hours. Pale pink; red cherry, strawberry and musk aromas and flavours; neat counterbalance between subliminal sweetness (5g/l) and acidity. Screwcap. 13% alc. **Rating** 90 **To** 2017 $18 **○**

Amos Adelaide Hills Shiraz 2015 Dark purple hue; plums and cherries, some sour cherries with fresh herbs, black olives and lots of wood spice, the oak not impinging. The palate's on the lean side, supple enough, just without the expected vibrancy. Screwcap. 13% alc. **Rating** 90 **To** 2024 $45 JF

Amos Adelaide Hills Cabernet Sauvignon 2015 The flagship wine, with 120 dozen made. The leafiness, the cassis, the florals, the freshly rolled tobacco and cedary spice kick all bode well – there's plenty to like in this more restrained style. The lean palate is less convincing; while refreshing, there's a slight green edge to the tannins. Screwcap. 13% alc. **Rating** 90 **To** 2026 $55 JF

Amos Adelaide Hills Cabernet Sauvignon Cabernet Franc 2014 75/25% blend. You'd expect to see more depth for a blend spending 2 years in 75% new French puncheons. There's no question about the elegance of this wine, and you can easily argue that the oak is an integral part of that elegance. Ultimately, it is a wine that declines to be convincingly classified – it's all a question of personal taste. 100 dozen made. Screwcap. 13.2% alc. **Rating** 90 **To** 2024 $50

Clover Adelaide Hills Cabernet Franc 2015 The notoriously difficult cabernet franc spent only 6 months in used French barriques, leaving the wine with a light, brilliant crimson colour, aromas of rose petals and violets, the light-bodied red cherry/strawberry fruits dancing on the tongue. 200 dozen made. Screwcap. 12% alc. **Rating** 90 **To** 2021 $24

Clover Adelaide Hills Pinot Noir Chardonnay 2016 With a pretty, pale salmon hue, this is a young and fresh cuvee that celebrates the rose petal, strawberry and cassis of Adelaide Hills pinot noir and cuts it with the lemon tension of chardonnay, culminating in a fresh and dry finish with some phenolic grip. Cork. 12.5% alc. **Rating** 90 **To** 2017 $24 TS

🍷🍷🍷🍷 **Picnic Adelaide Hills Cabernet Sauvignon Cabernet Franc Shiraz 2015** **Rating** 89 **To** 2020 $18 **○**

Hugh Hamilton Wines ★★★★★

94 McMurtrie Road, McLaren Vale, SA 5171 **Region** McLaren Vale
T (08) 8323 8689 **www.**hughhamiltonwines.com.au **Open** 7 days 11–5
Winemaker Nic Bourke **Est.** 1991 **Dozens** 20000 **Vyds** 21.4ha
In 2014, fifth-generation family member Hugh Hamilton handed over the reins to daughter Mary, the sixth generation of the family. It was she who developed the irreverent black sheep packaging. But it's more than simply marketing: the business will continue to embrace both mainstream and alternative varieties, its 85-year-old shiraz and 65-year-old cabernet sauvignon at its Blewitt Springs vineyard providing the ability to develop the Pure Black label. This reflects changes in the way the vines are trellised, picking and fermenting in small open fermenters, using gravity for wine movements, and maturation in high quality French oak. The cellar door is lined with the original jarrah from Vat 15 of the historic Hamilton's Ewell winery, the largest wooden vat ever built in the southern hemisphere. Exports to the UK, the US, Canada, Sweden, Finland, Malaysia and China.

ŸŸŸŸŸ **Black Blood III Black Sheep Vineyard McLaren Vale Shiraz 2015**
From the deep sands of Blewitt Springs. The bouquet signals the bright, lively
medium-bodied palate with its mix of red and black cherry, plum and spice fruit.
The tannins are superfine, adding length and class. The three Black Blood shirazs
are the most convincing trio, linking different vineyard soils to the wine in the
glass. Screwcap. 14.5% alc. **Rating** 96 **To** 2030 $79

Pure Black Shiraz 2013 The colour is seductive – black–dark purple with a
blood red tinge, and glossy; so is the wine. There's a swathe of black fruits, licorice,
dark chocolate, anise, menthol and oak that has been seamlessly integrated. Make
no mistake, this is structured to the max, but everything is balanced: the tannins are
voluptuous, the length powerful. Cork. 14.5% alc. **Rating** 96 **To** 2038 $180 JF

Black Blood II Church Vineyard McLaren Vale Shiraz 2015 Alluvial soils.
Very different from the Black Blood I: more open and fragrant, the medium
to full-bodied palate with a mix of red and black fruits, supple and rich, with
perfectly weighted tannins. Screwcap. 14.5% alc. **Rating** 95 **To** 2035 $79

Jekyll & Hyde McLaren Vale Shiraz Viognier 2015 A 93/7% blend, the
shiraz vines dating back to '47, the adjacent viognier of much newer origin. The
two varieties are picked together and co-fermented with a 3-day cold soak, 6-day
ferment and 5-day post-ferment maceration, matured for 17 months in French
oak (23% new) and new American oak (2%). This is full-bodied, but moves deftly
across the palate in a continuous stream of black fruits, dark chocolate and cedar,
the tannins ripe and synchronous. Screwcap. 15% alc. **Rating** 95 **To** 2035 $50

The Villain McLaren Vale Cabernet Sauvignon 2015 Open-fermented with
cultured yeast, 14 days on skins, matured for 20 months in French oak (20% new).
Potent blackcurrant and bay leaf aromas lead into a full-bodied palate, tannins a
positive feature adding a note to 'take me seriously'. I've come to agree I should
do so. Great value. Screwcap. 14.5% alc. **Rating** 95 **To** 2040 $29 ❍

Black Blood I Cellar Vineyard McLaren Vale Shiraz 2015 Black cracking
clays. Full-bodied, entirely in the black fruit and licorice spectrum, forbidding
but compelling. Strong tannins are made to measure, the oak largely irrelevant.
Screwcap. 14.5% alc. **Rating** 94 **To** 2040 $79

ŸŸŸŸŸ **Black Ops Shiraz Saperavi Nero d'Avola 2015 Rating** 93 **To** 2035 $32
Shearer's Cut McLaren Vale Shiraz 2015 Rating 90 **To** 2029 $24

Hugo
★★★★☆

246 Elliott Road, McLaren Flat, SA 5171 **Region** McLaren Vale
T (08) 8383 0098 **www.**hugowines.com.au **Open** Mon–Fri 10–5, Sat 12–5, Sun 10.30–5
Winemaker John Hugo **Est.** 1982 **Dozens** 7200 **Vyds** 25ha
Came from relative obscurity to prominence in the late 1980s with some lovely ripe, sweet
reds, which, while strongly American oak-influenced, were outstanding. It picked up the pace
again after a dull period in the mid-'90s, and has made the most of the recent run of good
vintages. The estate plantings include shiraz, cabernet sauvignon, chardonnay, grenache and
sauvignon blanc, with part of the grape production sold. Exports to the UK and Canada.

ŸŸŸŸŸ **McLaren Vale Shiraz 2014** Has held its hue very well; the heady bouquet
speaks loud and clear of McLaren Vale, the palate (curiously, but happily) backing
off the cheer squad into an elegant, medium-bodied shiraz that is intense, yet
light on its feet, with black fruits, integrated oak and fine-grained tannins. It is a
cool wine in the fullest sense. Gold medals Adelaide and Small Winemakers '16.
Screwcap. 14.5% alc. **Rating** 95 **To** 2034 $25 ❍

Reserve McLaren Vale Shiraz 2014 There is more of everything in this wine:
colour, fruit depth, new oak and ripe tannins. They're all in balance too. The
wine's greatest days are down the track, its gold medal at the Sydney International
Winemakers Show '17 a hint. Screwcap. 14.5% alc. **Rating** 94 **To** 2039 $55

McLaren Vale Grenache Shiraz 2015 80% bushvine grenache planted in '51,
20% estate shiraz planted in '88, crushed and fermented together, 6 days on skins,
matured in used French and American hogsheads for 15 months. The blend has

proved synergistic, particularly the co-fermentation, which is not always possible. Regardless, power and focus join forces on the medium to full-bodied palate with red, purple and black fruits all contributing. Screwcap. 14.5% alc. **Rating** 94 To 2025 $25 ◐

🍷🍷🍷🍷🍷 McLaren Vale Grenache Shiraz Rose 2016 Rating 93 To 2017 $20 ◯

Hungerford Hill ★★★★★

2450 Broke Road, Pokolbin, NSW 2320 **Region** Hunter Valley
T (02) 4998 0710 **www.**hungerfordhill.com.au **Open** Sun–Thurs 10–5, Fri–Sat 10–7
Winemaker Bryan Currie **Est.** 1967 **Dozens** 17 000 **Vyds** 28ha
Sam and Christie Arnaout purchased Hungerford Hill in December 2016 to refocus the 50-year-old label on its Hunter Valley origin, with significant new Lower Hunter vineyards at Sweetwater (see separate entry) and Dalwood (the oldest continuously operating vineyard in Australia). Hungerford Hill will use these vineyards to bolster is Hunter Valley wines while continuing its 20+ year association with the cool climate Tumbarumba and Hilltops regions.

🍷🍷🍷🍷🍷 Epic McLaren Vale Shiraz 2014 This is a well made wine that clearly reflects the terroir of McLaren Vale and its impact on shiraz. It is medium to full-bodied, and the fruit, oak and tannin triptych is of high calibre. Why turn your back on the vintage when creating an 'epic'? '14 was one of the greatest Hunter Valley vintages for shiraz since '65. Screwcap. 14.5% alc. **Rating** 96 To 2044 $120
Single Vineyard Tumbarumba Pinot Noir 2015 Brilliantly clear colour sets the scene for a similarly pure and bright palate full of crunchy red cherries and wild strawberries. It will likely be gulped rather than sipped, but should be given the respect it deserves. Screwcap. 14% alc. **Rating** 95 To 2030 $65
Liquid Metal 2016 Semillon, sauvignon blanc and muscadelle. This is crisp and lively, Hunter Valley contributing the semillon, Tumbarumba the other two varieties. The finish and aftertaste are very good indeed. Screwcap. 12.5% alc. Rating 94 To 2022 $40

🍷🍷🍷🍷🍷 Cardinal Sparkling Shiraz NV Rating 93 To 2020 $36 TS
Tumbarumba Pinot Gris 2016 Rating 91 To 2020 $27
Hunter Valley Shiraz 2015 Rating 91 To 2023 $45
Heavy Metal 2014 Rating 91 To 2034 $55
Hilltops Cabernet Sauvignon 2015 Rating 91 To 2025 $45
Hunter Valley Semillon 2016 Rating 90 To 2026 $27
Tumbarumba Pinot Noir 2016 Rating 90 To 2023 $40
Tumbarumba Tempranillo 2015 Rating 90 To 2022 $40

Hunter-Gatherer Vintners ★★★★

362 Pipers Creek-Pastoria Road, Pipers Creek, Vic 3444 **Region** Macedon Ranges
T 0407 821 049 **www.**hgwines.com.au **Open** W'ends 12–5
Winemaker Brian Martin **Est.** 2015 **Dozens** 1000 **Vyds** 5ha
In late 2015 winemaker Brian Martin purchased a vineyard which had passed through a number of ownerships since its establishment in 1999. It was first known as Loxley Vineyard, and later Harmony Row. It has a long-established cellar door, and offers Shiraz, Pinot Noir, Riesling and Chardonnay (and a couple of sparkling wines) under the Hunter-Gatherer label. Alternative varieties are marketed under the Marvio label.

🍷🍷🍷🍷🍷 Macedon Pinot Noir 2015 From the estate vineyard and a vineyard at Romsey, matured in French oak for 15 months. It is a pinot with considerable attitude, the colour full and bright, the bouquet and palate gifted with abundant red and black cherry fruits given texture and context by fine, ripe tannins. Screwcap. 13.5% alc. Rating 94 To 2027
Heathcote Shiraz 2010 Open-fermented, hand-plunged, matured for 20 months in French oak. Where has this wine been for 7 years? In suspended animation? The colour is still deep crimson-purple, the palate rich and opulent,

with stewed plum and blackberry fruit, the tannins ripe and totally integrated. Screwcap. 15% alc. **Rating** 94 **To** 2030 $25

Sparkling Shiraz 2013 An enticing expression of Heathcote shiraz, with deep black plum and black cherry fruit, juicy black pastilles, fine mineral tannins and the complexity of pepper and sage. It's impeccably underscored by dark chocolate and coffee oak, harmonising evenly on a long finish of creamy bead and well judged dosage. 14% alc. **Rating** 94 **To** 2021 $35 TS

Huntington Estate   ★★★★☆

Ulan Road, Mudgee, NSW 2850 **Region** Mudgee
T 1800 995 931 **www**.huntingtonestate.com.au **Open** Mon–Sat 10–5, Sun 10–4
Winemaker Tim Stevens **Est.** 1969 **Dozens** 13 000 **Vyds** 43.8ha
Since taking ownership of Huntington Estate from the founding Roberts family, Tim Stevens has sensibly refrained from making major changes. The policy of having older vintage wines available is continuing, making the cellar door a first port of call for visitors to Mudgee. On the other side, the Music Festival suffers only one problem: there are not enough tickets to satisfy the demand. It really has a well deserved life of its own, and will do so for years to come. Exports to China.

🍷🍷🍷🍷🍷 **Tim Stevens Signature Shiraz 2015** Fruit ex Block 1, spends 18 months in barrel – 60% new American oak. At this youthful exuberant stage, the oak is showing off, but in time it will settle. The fruit radiates all plums, raspberries and blackberries, with more complexing notes of coconut rough chocolate. Firm tannins and lemony acid add more freshness. Screwcap. 14.5% alc. **Rating** 95 **To** 2026 $70 JF

🍷🍷🍷🍷🍷 **Cabernet Sauvignon 2009 Rating** 93 **To** 2024 $26 **○**
Special Reserve Semillon 2015 Rating 92 **To** 2025 $30 JF
Shiraz 2014 Rating 91 **To** 2025 $28 JF
Special Reserve Shiraz 2014 Rating 91 **To** 2028 $35 JF
Gewurztraminer 2016 Rating 90 **To** 2020 $23 JF
Special Reserve Cabernet Sauvignon 2011 Rating 90 **To** 2024 JF
Late Harvest Semillon 2016 Rating 90 **To** 2019 $40 JF

Hurley Vineyard   ★★★★★

101 Balnarring Road, Balnarring, Vic 3926 **Region** Mornington Peninsula
T (03) 5931 3000 **www**.hurleyvineyard.com.au **Open** 1st w'end each month 11–5
Winemaker Kevin Bell **Est.** 1998 **Dozens** 1000 **Vyds** 3.5ha
It's never as easy as it seems. Despite leading busy city lives, Kevin Bell and wife Tricia Byrnes have done most of the hard work in establishing Hurley Vineyard themselves, with family and friends. Most conspicuously, Kevin has completed the Applied Science (Wine Science) degree at CSU, drawing on Nat White for consultancy advice, and occasionally from Phillip Jones of Bass Phillip and Domaine Fourrier in Gevrey Chambertin. He has not allowed a significant heart issue to prevent him continuing with his first love.

🍷🍷🍷🍷🍷 **Lodestone Mornington Peninsula Pinot Noir 2015** An assemblage of Dijon clones 114, 115, 777 and MV6, this is an incarnation of violet florals, creamy strawberry and the delights of dank autumn leaves with a seasoning of cinnamon oak and mace, the tannins chiffon and silk. Matured for 18 months in French oak, one-third new, this brims with salacious sex appeal ... as all good pinot noir should. Diam. 13.5% alc. **Rating** 96 **To** 2025 $70 NG **○**

Garamond Mornington Peninsula Pinot Noir 2015 A manifest of precision, intensity and concentration of flavour and persistence. Sapid flavours of dark cherry, kirsch and satsuma plum waft over a chassis of filigreed acidity and ambitious oak. There is a febrile energy to this; brooding, even. Far from a finessed pinot, this is charged. Diam. 13.5% alc. **Rating** 96 **To** 2030 $80 NG

Hommage Mornington Peninsula Pinot Noir 2015 A tightly furled wine initially, with a beam of cherries of both colours, damson plum and baking spice strung across expansive French oak, all cedar and bristling tannins. The wine expands in the glass, exhibiting a higher red-fruited pitch, slightly medicinal. Still clenched within a carapace of toasted oak, the wine's concentration of fruit augurs well for cellaring. Diam. 15.5% alc. Rating 94 To 2028 $70 NG

Estate Mornington Peninsula Pinot Noir 2015 Rating 93 To 2023 $45 NG

Ibizan Wines ★★★★★

15 Bridgelands Road, Rosa Glen, WA 6285 **Region** Margaret River
T (08) 9757 5021 **www.ibizanwines.com.au Open** By appt
Winemaker Naturaliste Vintners (Bruce Dukes) **Est.** 2000 **Dozens** 1000 **Vyds** 7.7ha
Brian and Michelle Lowrie found a vineyard in the beautiful but seldom visited Upper Chapman Valley district of Margaret River in 2000. It had 2.7ha of cabernet sauvignon believed to have been planted in 1976, and 5ha of semillon and sauvignon blanc planted in the early '80s. Until '10 the grapes were sold, but in that year the semillon and sauvignon blanc were vinified for Ibizan Wines, and had immediate and significant show success. The name, incidentally, comes from the two red cloud kelpies who have faithfully kept company with Brian and Michelle in the vineyard over the years. They resemble the Egyptian Ibizan hounds who looked after the pharoahs, hence the Egyptian eye on the striking labels.

Margaret River Semillon Sauvignon Blanc 2016 This sure dazzles with its fine mix of tropical fruits tempered by lemon and lime juice plus pine-needle freshness; almost thirst-quenching thanks to the zesty acidity. This is a charmer. Screwcap. 12.4% alc. **Rating** 95 **To** 2020 $22 JF ✪
Old Vine Margaret River Cabernet Sauvignon 2015 By Margaret River standards, the vines are old – planted in '78. This has regionality stamped all over it, from the blackberry, mulberry fruits, earthy tones of allspice to the fine tannin profile. Oak is balanced into the linear, slightly sinewy frame. There's nothing heavy or heavy-handed. Screwcap. 13.5% alc. **Rating** 95 **To** 2026 $27 JF ✪
Old Vine Margaret River Cabernet Sauvignon 2014 From the cool southern parts of Margaret River, matured for 14 months in French oak. This is all about elegance and purity of varietal expression, cabernet tannins hiding in the background, leaving the field open for cassis and red cherry fruit to take command. Screwcap. 13.5% alc. **Rating** 95 **To** 2029 $29

Margaret River Semillon Sauvignon Blanc 2015 Rating 92 To 2020 $22

Idavue Estate ★★★★

470 Northern Highway, Heathcote, Vic 3523 **Region** Heathcote
T 0429 617 287 **www.idavueestate.com Open** W'ends 10.30–5
Winemaker Andrew and Sandra Whytcross **Est.** 2000 **Dozens** 600 **Vyds** 5.7ha
Owners and winemakers Andrew and Sandra Whytcross both undertook a two-year winemaking course through the Bendigo TAFE; with assistance from son Marty, they also look after the vineyard, which is planted to shiraz (3ha), cabernet sauvignon (1.9ha), and semillon and chardonnay (0.4ha each). The red wines are made in typical small batch fashion with hand-picked fruit, hand-plunged fermenters and a basket press.

Blue Note Heathcote Shiraz 2015 Dense and tightly knit; Heathcote's tenacious rush of dark fruit flavours are neatly tucked within a bonnet of finely managed tannins, gentle acidity and the right amount of oak. Some cinnamon, pepper and violet are in there somewhere, too. Screwcap. 14% alc. **Rating** 93 **To** 2020 $45 NG
Heathcote Shiraz 2015 Everything to be expected from Heathcote in a glass: a vermilion robe, and dark, densely concentrated fruit flavours of all descriptions. Held together by pulpy, juicy, deftly extracted grape tannins, all intermingling with bitter chocolate and coffee grind oak that is a mere complement to the cascading, rich fruit flavours. Screwcap. 14% alc. **Rating** 91 **To** 2029 $35 NG

In Dreams

179 Glenview Road, Yarra Glen, Vic 3775 **Region** Yarra Valley
T (03) 8413 8379 **www**.indreams.com. **Open** Not
Winemaker Nina Stocker **Est.** 2013 **Dozens** 3000
In Dreams produces two wines: Chardonnay and Pinot Noir from fruit sourced predominantly from the Upper Yarra Valley. The cooler microclimate of the area matches with the traditional winemaking techniques, such as small batch fermentation and delicate use of French oak. Nina Stocker, past winemaker of Catalina Sounds and daughter of eminent wine scientist, Dr John Stocker, makes wines that allow the fruit to express itself.

In Dreams Chardonnay 2015 An impressive wine with energy and focus to its mix of pink grapefruit and white stone fruit, fresh acidity drawing out the length of the palate, oak a vehicle. Screwcap. 13.3% alc. **Rating** 95 $25 ☉

In Dreams Pinot Noir 2015 Matured in French barriques (20% new) for 11 months before blending. This is a very attractive pinot, made with exceptional attention to detail. If only it had (say) 13% alcohol, it would have been a world beater. Screwcap. 12.7% alc. **Rating** 94 **To** 2022 $30 ☉

Indigo Vineyard

1221 Beechworth–Wangaratta Road, Everton Upper, Vic 3678 **Region** Beechworth
T (03) 5727 0233 **www**.indigovineyard.com.au **Open** Wed–Sun 11–4
Winemaker Stuart Hordern, Marc Scalzo **Est.** 1999 **Dozens** 3300 **Vyds** 46.15ha
Indigo Vineyard has a little over 46ha of vineyards planted to 11 varieties, including the top French and Italian grapes. The business was and is primarily directed to growing grapes for sale to Brokenwood, but since 2004 increasing amounts have been vinified for the Indigo label. The somewhat incestuous nature of the whole business sees the Indigo wines being made at Brokenwood (Marc Scalzo makes the Pinot Grigio).

Beechworth Pinot Noir 2016 This is a delicious pinot noir, with Beechworth's darker fruit spectrum of damson plum and bing cherry delicately juxtaposed against ethereal powdery tannins, well managed oak and 25% of stems put into the potion for a whiff of autumnal mulch. This helps to stamp a savoury authority while mitigating any sense of sweetness. Screwcap. 13.3% alc. **Rating** 93 **To** 2023 $36 NG

Secret Village Beechworth Pinot Noir 2016 Strawberry, sour cherry and vanilla cream are braced by cardamom and clove. This is a dainty, fine-boned pinot noir with substantial energy and finesse. Screwcap. 13.3% alc. **Rating** 93 **To** 2022 $65 NG

Secret Village Beechworth Shiraz 2015 Bright vermilion, this is purple and blue fruits à go go. The whole is one of intense flavours and firm, tannic structure. Black olive, smoked meat, cardamom and anise tease one back for another glass, lingering on the long finish. Screwcap. 13.5% alc. **Rating** 93 **To** 2024 $55 NG

Alpine Valleys Beechworth Chardonnay 2016 55% Alpine Valley fruit, with the remainder from Beechworth; is tightly furled, saline and mineral-kissed. The wine did not undergo mlf, leaving the French oak, faint stone-fruit notes and leesy crunch to imbue personality. Screwcap. 13.1% alc. **Rating** 92 **To** 2024 $36 NG

Secret Village Beechworth Chardonnay 2016 Contemporary in its styling, with an engine of stone fruit, cashew, nougat and citrus flavours strung across a chassis of granitic mineral, nervy acidity and vanillan oak. This is edgy, sub-alpine chardonnay, verging on skeletal. Screwcap. 12.5% alc. **Rating** 92 **To** 2024 $50 NG

Beechworth Shiraz 2015 Beechworth's granitic energy spins a web of blueberry, violet and anise across a skein of vibrant, peppery acidity. There are new oak vanillas and cedar too, following 16 months in French oak, 30% of which was new. Screwcap. 13.5% alc. **Rating** 92 **To** 2023 $36 NG

Alpine Valleys Beechworth Pinot Grigio 2016 A pointed, yet textural example of grigio, crafted with roussanne solids (3%) added to older oak, following a cool tank fermentation for the grigio component. The idea was to build textural breadth and detail, and boy has it worked, the phenolic bite just enough for intrigue. Screwcap. 13.2% alc. **Rating** 91 **To** 2021 $25 NG

McNamara Alpine Valleys Chardonnay 2016 This chardonnay is in stark contrast to its Beechworth brethren. It is altogether riper, softer, and brimming with pear, apple and quince. The texture is gently sudsy, relying on assuaging phenolics for direction and poise, rather than acidity and mineral grunt. Screwcap. 13.3% alc. **Rating** 90 **To** 2022 $32 NG

Beechworth Rose 2016 Dutifully dry and thirst-slaking, with bright cherry notes curled around a phenolic pucker, a hint of twig and a lick of bitter amaro on the finish. Screwcap. 13.5% alc. **Rating** 90 **To** 2018 $25 NG

ŸŸŸŸ **Umpires Decision Cowra Chardonnay 2016** Rating 89 **To** 2021 $25 NG

Inkwell ★★★★

PO Box 33, Sellicks Beach, SA 5174 **Region** McLaren Vale
T 0430 050 115 **www.**inkwellwines.com **Open** By appt
Winemaker Dudley Brown **Est.** 2003 **Dozens** 800 **Vyds** 12ha
Inkwell was born in 2003 when Dudley Brown returned to Australia from California and bought a rundown vineyard on the serendipitously named California Road. He inherited 5ha of neglected shiraz, and planted an additional 7ha to viognier (2.5ha), zinfandel (2.5ha) and heritage shiraz clones (2ha). The five-year restoration of the old vines and establishment of the new reads like the ultimate handbook for aspiring vignerons, particularly those who are prepared to work non-stop. The reward has been rich. Dudley is adamant that the production will be capped at 1000 dozen; almost all the grapes are sold. Exports to the US and Canada.

ŸŸŸŸŸ **Deeper Well McLaren Vale Shiraz 2011** Matured in French oak (50% new) for 2 years and given 3 years in bottle prior to release. 744 bottles only. The bold fruit, the spread of tannin, the reach, the impact. From the toughest of seasons comes a wine with no holds barred. Asphalt, cakey blackberry, cleansing acidity and ribs of dry, coffeed tannin. It sits, remarkably, in the upper reaches of the ripeness spectrum and accordingly carries some alcohol warmth. Impressive it most certainly is. Screwcap. 14.7% alc. **Rating** 94 **To** 2034 $70 CM

ŸŸŸŸŸ **Road to Joy Shiraz Primitivo 2014** Rating 93 **To** 2026 $26 CM ✪

🍇 Inner City Winemakers ★★★★

28 Church Street, Wickham, NSW 2293 **Region** Hunter Valley
T (02) 4962 3545 **www.**innercitywinemakers.com.au **Open** Tues–Sun 10–5
Winemaker Rob Wilce **Est.** 2010 **Dozens** 900
Owner/winemaker Rob Wilce has over 20 years' experience in the business, mainly spent with wine companies in the Hunter Valley. While his job was in marketing and sales, he has worked many vintages with different winemakers in the valley, learning the basic winemaking skills. He realised he simply didn't have the capital to establish a vineyard and winery, and so came up with the idea of a virtual winery, purchasing a small warehouse at Wickham, on the edge of Newcastle's CBD and harbour. The small warehouse was too small right from the word go, and is now 'ridiculously small', but he spreads vintage intake by buying grapes from the Hunter Valley, Orange, Hilltops and New England, thus starting in January and finishing at the end of April. He says his winemaking can best be described as rustic, with Heath Robinson winemaking equipment, but it gets the job done. He has a wine club with just under 200 members, and they do the wine marketing for him and the two part-time employees who join him over vintage.

ŸŸŸŸŸ **Vintage Chardonnay 2015** From Orange; crushed, basket-pressed, 50% fermented in stainless steel, 50% in new and used French oak, blended and returned to oak for 6 months. The fermentation and maturation regime has worked well: the bouquet and palate are both expressive and complex, the palate with a touch of (good) reduction adding to the appeal of the white stone fruit and nutty oak. Screwcap. 13.8% alc. **Rating** 94 **To** 2025 $28 ✪

Hilltops Cabernet Sauvignon 2015 48 hours cold soak, open-fermented, plunged every 4 hours for 5 days, basket-pressed to a 1000l flexcube and a used French barrel, French and American oak staves added to the flexcube after mlf, the wine matured for 12 months. The quality of the grapes shines through, with layer upon layer of cassis/blackcurrant, bay leaf and black olive. Given its full-bodied profile, the way the tannins have been resolved is impressive, as is the subtle American oak. Screwcap. 14.5% alc. **Rating** 94 **To** 2035 $50

ŸŸŸŸŸ **Street Art Series Gewurztraminer 2015 Rating** 90 **To** 2018 $25

Innocent Bystander ★★★★★

314 Maroondah Highway, Healesville, Vic 3777 **Region** Yarra Valley
T (03) 5720 5500 **www**.innocentbystander.com.au **Open** By appt
Winemaker Joel Tilbrook, Cate Looney **Est.** 1997 **Dozens** 49 000 **Vyds** 45ha
On 5 April 2016 Brown Brothers and Giant Steps announced that the Innocent Bystander brand (including Mea Culpa) and stock had been sold to Brown Brothers. As part of the acquisition, Brown Brothers purchased the White Rabbit Brewery site adjacent to Giant Steps, and this has become the cellar door home of Innocent Bystander. Its business is in two completely different wine categories, both fitting neatly together. On the one hand is the big volume (confidential) of vintage moscato, the grapes coming from the King Valley, and non vintage prosecco, similarly sourced. The other side of the business is the premium, high quality Yarra Valley single varietal wines, with substantial brand value. Exports to the UK, the US and other major markets.

ŸŸŸŸŸ **Yarra Valley Syrah 2015** Serial winner, vintage by vintage, of show awards, this winning gold at the Yarra Valley Wine Show '16; matured in French oak. It gets your attention from the first whiff, the first sip. The black fruits have special texture and structure, demanding that you take the next mouthful before you have finished the first; the tannins also add to both flavour (spicy) and texture (fine, persistent). Great value. Screwcap. 13.8% alc. **Rating** 95 **To** 2030 $25 ✪

ŸŸŸŸŸ **Yarra Valley Pinot Noir 2016 Rating** 93 **To** 2023 $25 ✪
Yarra Valley Chardonnay 2016 Rating 90 **To** 2020 $25

Ipso Facto Wines ★★★★

PO Box 1886, Margaret River, WA 6285 **Region** Margaret River
T 0402 321 572 **Open** Not
Winemaker Kate Morgan **Est.** 2010 **Dozens** 300
This is the realisation of owner/winemaker Kate Morgan's dream of making her own wine with her own label. After graduating from Curtin University with a degree in viticulture and oenology she worked vintages in Australia and overseas before returning to WA. There she worked at Houghton, Stella Bella and for the last three years as assistant winemaker at Fraser Gallop Estate. The wines are made with minimal additions (only SO_2 added), and are wild-yeast fermented.

ŸŸŸŸŸ **Margaret River Cabernet Sauvignon 2015** Sourced from a vineyard in the cooler Wallcliffe subregion, this beautifully crafted wine is at the elegant end of the Margaret River cabernet spectrum. Perfumed with a touch of bell pepper to go with the mainly cherry fruit, the medium-bodied palate is persistent, nicely structured and long. Screwcap. 13% alc. **Rating** 93 **To** 2025 $35 PR
Margaret River Chenin 2012 Whole-bunch pressed into barrel, where it went through a natural yeast fermentation, this looks youthful in every respect. Aromatically, there are citrus notes plus some complexity from the well handled French oak; the medium-bodied, textured and dry palate has excellent purity and length. Screwcap. 12.5% alc. **Rating** 92 **To** 2020 $32 PR
Margaret River Cabernet Sauvignon 2014 Fermented with ambient yeasts in open-top fermenters before being bottled unfined and filtered after spending 10 months in barrel, this gentle Margaret River cabernet smells of red fruits, violets

and a little bell pepper; the medium-bodied palate has good depth, finishing with ripe, fine-grained tannins. Screwcap. 14% alc. **Rating** 91 **To** 2022 $35 PR

Iron Cloud Wines ★★★★★

Suite 16, 18 Stirling Highway, Nedlands, WA 6009 (postal) **Region** Geographe
T 0401 860 891 **www**.pepperilly.com **Open** Not
Winemaker Coby Ladwig **Est.** 1999 **Dozens** 2500 **Vyds** 11ha
In 2003 owners Warwick Lavis and Geoff and Karyn Cross purchased the then-named Pepperilly Estate, which had been planted in 1999 on red gravelly loam soils. Peppermint trees line the Henty Brook, the natural water source for the vineyard. In '17 Michael Ng, chief winemaker for Rockcliffe succeeded Coby Ladwig (who made the '15 and '16 vintage wines).

ŶŶŶŶŶ **The Alliance Ferguson Valley Chardonnay 2015** Takes the fruit flavours of its Rock of Solitude sibling by the scruff of its neck and engenders almost fierce drive, with crunchy acidity woven through grapefruit and apple skin. The finish is long, brilliantly clear and fresh. Screwcap. 13.5% alc. **Rating** 95 **To** 2027 $45
Rock of Solitude Purple Patch Single Vineyard Ferguson Valley GSM 2015 Juicy, spicy, peppery red fruits of a cool-grown GSM create a new field of opportunity, radically different from that of SA. The alcohol simply doesn't impact: it's a number without significance. This really hums with its energy, captivating your palate as it swoops by. Screwcap. 14.5% alc. **Rating** 95 **To** 2029 $32 ❂
Rock of Solitude Single Vineyard Ferguson Valley Chardonnay 2015 Unforced and fruit-driven, demonstrating the superior Burgundy clones 76, 95, 96 and 277 that work magic wherever they are grown: one of the 21st century advances in the grape – hence wine – quality. The fragrant citrus blossom bouquet opens the door for white peach and grapefruit to strut their stuff on the long palate. Oak? Yes, it's there, but don't worry about finding it. Screwcap. 13.5% alc. **Rating** 94 **To** 2023 $32

ŶŶŶŶŶ **Pepperilly Single Vineyard Ferguson Valley SBS 2016** Rating 90 **To** 2020 $25

Ironwood Estate ★★★★☆

2191 Porongurup Road, Porongurup, WA 6234 **Region** Porongurup
T (08) 9853 1126 **www**.ironwoodestatewines.com.au **Open** Wed–Mon 11–5
Winemaker Wignalls Wines (Michael Perkins) **Est.** 1996 **Dozens** 2500 **Vyds** 5ha
Ironwood Estate was established in 1996 under the ownership of Mary and Eugene Harma. An estate vineyard of riesling, sauvignon blanc, chardonnay, shiraz, merlot and cabernet sauvignon (in more or less equal amounts) was planted on a northern slope of the Porongurup Range. Exports to Japan and Singapore.

ŶŶŶŶŶ **Porongurup Shiraz 2014** An A-grade bargain. Balanced and long in the mouth, this medium-bodied shiraz has compelling complex fruits in a largely black spectrum, licorice and black pepper add-ons at no extra cost. Grows each time it is retasted. Screwcap. 13.8% alc. **Rating** 95 **To** 2034 $20 ❂

ŶŶŶŶŶ **Porongurup Rocky Rose 2016** Rating 90 **To** 2029 $18 ❂

Irvine ★★★★

PO Box 308, Angaston, SA 5353 **Region** Eden Valley
T (08) 8564 1046 **www**.irvinewines.com.au **Open** At Taste Eden Valley, Angaston
Winemaker Rebekah Richardson **Est.** 1983 **Dozens** 10 000 **Vyds** 80ha
When James (Jim) Irvine established his eponymous winery, he chose a singularly difficult focus for the business: the production of great merlot from the Eden Valley. Throughout the years of establishment, and indeed thereafter, he was a much-in-demand consultant, bobbing up in all sorts of places. Yet when he decided to sell the business in 2014, its potential was greatly increased with the dowry provided by the purchasing Wade and Miles families. In 1867 Henry Winter Miles planted 0.8ha of shiraz. Successive generations of the Miles family had added to the vineyard portfolio from 1967, both acquiring existing vineyards and planting

others (Ben's Block vineyard at Penrice is home to 120yo vines). Henry's great-grandson Peter Miles and partner John Wade collectively own 160ha spread through the Barossa and Eden Valleys although only 80ha fall within the new Irvine partnership. Exports to the UK, Switzerland, the UAE, Singapore, Malaysia, Japan, Taiwan, Hong Kong and China.

ΨΨΨΨΨ **James Irvine Eden Valley Grand Merlot 2012** Luxurious bouquet with aromas of truffle, framboise liqueur and the scent derived from many months in high quality French oak. Supple and silky, but the firmness of tannin is strict, and there's no mistaking that this is a serious wine. An extra degree of complexity is missing, given the asking price. Cork. 14.5% alc. **Rating** 94 **To** 2025 $130 SC

ΨΨΨΨΨ **Springhill Eden Valley Riesling 2016 Rating** 93 **To** 2029 $22 ✪
Single Vineyard Eden Valley Zinfandel 2013 Rating 93 **To** 2020 $50 SC
The Estate Eden Valley Merlot 2014 Rating 92 **To** 2022 $25 SC ✪
The Estate Eden Valley Shiraz 2015 Rating 91 **To** 2023 $25 SC
The Estate Eden Valley Cabernet Merlot Cabernet Franc 2015
Rating 91 **To** 2023 $25 SC

Ius Wines   ★★★★

Mary Street, Coonawarra, SA 5263 **Region** South Australia
T 0488 771 046 **www.iuswines.com.au Open** Not
Winemaker Sam Brand **Est.** 2012 **Dozens** 10000
Ius is a collaboration between Sam Brand and Tom Cosgrove. Grapes are sourced via ongoing agreements with the Brand family and local growers. The wines are made at several wineries in Coonawarra. Tom Cosgrove is a seventh-generation Australian with a 25-year track record in sales and distribution of fresh foods and wine. Future plans include a cellar door/ function facility.

ΨΨΨΨΨ **Hinterland Coonawarra Cabernet Sauvignon 2013** A deep, lustrous crimson. Highly attractive. Cassis, mint, dried sage, a whiff of the Australian scrub and attenuated tannins are pummelled by clear-cut acidity and plenty of medium toasted French oak. The regional voice is vivid and forceful. Screwcap. 14% alc. **Rating** 93 **To** 2028 $30 NG

J&J Wines   ★★★★☆

Lot 115 Rivers Lane, McLaren Vale, SA 5172 **Region** McLaren Vale
T (08) 8339 9330 **www.jjvineyards.com.au Open** Third Thurs each month 10.30–5.30
Winemaker Winescope (Scott Rawlinson) **Est.** 1998 **Dozens** 5000 **Vyds** 5.5ha
J&J is owned and operated by three generations of the Mason family. The estate vineyards are organically managed, but are significantly supplemented by contract-grown grapes. It has come a long way since 2004, the first year when some of the estate grapes were vinified to make wine for the private use of the family. Exports to Hong Kong.

ΨΨΨΨΨ **Eminence McLaren Vale Shiraz 2014** Open-fermented and matured in French oak. Flavour is never in question with the J&J reds; the distinguishing factor here is the level of finesse. It hits and holds and then turns intricate and fine. The palate is drenched in plum and smoky oak; the finish is both taut and elongated. Cork. 14% alc. **Rating** 95 **To** 2032 $55 CM
Rivers Lane Reserve McLaren Vale Shiraz 2014 Takes a while to get a handle on this shiraz because the tannins are so evenly spread along the palate. Initially it seems too tannic, but it's not. The medium-bodied palate has more black than red fruits, and those fruits slide fluidly and securely along the palate and into the finish and aftertaste. Screwcap. 14% alc. **Rating** 94 **To** 2034 $32

ΨΨΨΨΨ **McLaren Vale Shiraz 2013 Rating** 93 **To** 2026 $25 CM ✪
Rivers Lane Reserve McLaren Vale Shiraz 2013 Rating 92 **To** 2025 $32 CM
Rivers Lane Organic McLaren Vale Shiraz 2014 Rating 91 **To** 2023 $25 CM
Boots Hill McLaren Vale Shiraz 2014 Rating 91 **To** 2021 $22 CM ✪
Adelaide Hills Sauvignon Blanc 2015 Rating 90 **To** 2017 $19 CM ✪

Jack Estate

15025 Riddoch Highway, Coonawarra, SA 5263 **Region** Coonawarra
T (08) 8736 3130 **www**.jackestate.com **Open** By appt
Winemaker Shannon Sutherland, Conrad Slabber **Est.** 2011 **Dozens** 9000 **Vyds** 221ha
The Lees family has been involved in agriculture for over a century, but it was left to Adrian and Dennise Lees (and their son Matthew) to make the transition from general agriculture to viticulture. In 2011 the family was able to acquire the large Mildara Blass winery and barrel storage to accommodate the Limestone Coast-sourced wines, and the far larger amount from the Murray Darling region, where the family owns 220ha of vineyards (plus 1ha of cabernet sauvignon in Coonawarra). Rachel Lees is responsible for marketing, Matthew is the winery manager. Exports to Malaysia, the Philippines, Thailand, Singapore and China.

ＴＴＴＴＴ **Coonawarra Wrattonbully Shiraz 2014** This is a take-home-tonight red that ticks all the boxes from quality to a keen price. It's juicy and exuberant, with a core of ripe sweet red fruit, a sprinkling of woodsy spices and powdery, fine tannins. Complexity is not part of the equation, but drinkability is, and should be celebrated. Screwcap. 14.5% alc. **Rating** 94 **To** 2021 $22 JF ⊙
Mythology Coonawarra Cabernet Sauvignon 2013 All up, 40 months in French oak and the wine is sitting comfortably, all components neatly brought together into a harmonious whole. This is elegant. Perfectly ripe fruit, wafts of cassis, mint and dark chocolate all lead on to a full-bodied, yet smooth, palate with finely detailed tannins. Screwcap. 14.5% alc. **Rating** 94 **To** 2030 $55 JF

ＴＴＴＴＴ **Mythology Coonawarra Chardonnay 2015 Rating** 93 **To** 2022 $39 JF
Coonawarra Cabernet Sauvignon 2014 Rating 93 **To** 2023 $25 JF ⊙
Mythology Coonawarra Shiraz 2013 Rating 90 **To** 2028 $55 JF

Jack Rabbit Vineyard

85 McAdams Lane, Bellarine, Vic 3221 **Region** Geelong
T (03) 5251 2223 **www**.jackrabbitvineyard.com.au **Open** 7 days 10–5
Winemaker Nyall Condon **Est.** 1989 **Dozens** 8000 **Vyds** 2ha
Jack Rabbit vineyard is owned by David and Lyndsay Sharp of Leura Park Estate. Its 2ha of vineyards (planted equally to pinot noir and cabernet sauvignon) take second place to its Restaurant at Jack Rabbit (details on the website), plus the House of Jack Rabbit tasting room, cellar door and cafe. The estate vineyards are supplemented by contract-grown fruit.

ＴＴＴＴ **Geelong Pinot Grigio 2016** Pale straw hue with some dried pears, sweet and sour lemon drops, ginger spice and sprightly citrussy acidity. Uncomplicated, refreshing and convincing. Screwcap. 12.8% alc. **Rating** 89 **To** 2019 $30 JF
Bellarine Peninsula Pinot Noir 2015 Opens with puckering acidity; a sinewy and tight lean frame, but then the amaro note kicks in alongside morello cherries, charcuterie, stems and unusual herbal aromatics. Confit duck will help enormously. Screwcap. 12.5% alc. **Rating** 89 **To** 2022 $35 JF

Jackson Brooke ★★★★

126 Beaconsfield Parade, Northcote, Vic 3070 (postal) **Region** Henty
T 0466 652 485 **www**.jacksonbrookewine.com.au **Open** Not
Winemaker Jackson Brooke **Est.** 2013 **Dozens** 120
Jackson Brooke graduated from the University of Melbourne in 2004 with a science degree, and having spent a summer working at Tarrington Vineyards, went to study oenology at Lincoln University in NZ. A vintage at Wedgetail Estate in the Yarra Valley, followed by stints in Japan, Southern California and then three years as assistant winemaker to Ben Portet. Some reverse swing from creating his own wine label led to a full-time teaching career. He had already married and his first daughter Olivia was born in March 2014. With his accumulated knowledge of boutique winemaking he has abandoned any idea of building a winery for the foreseeable future, renting space in the little winery at Tarrington Vineyards. He has edged up

annual production from 1 tonne in '13 to 3 tonnes in '15, and 6 tonnes in '16 (15–20 tonnes is the ultimate plateau).

ΥΥΥΥΥ **Henty Chardonnay 2015** One-third fermented in new French oak, two-thirds in stainless steel, full mlf, matured for 7 months. If nothing else, it is easy to see why the wine was taken through full mlf, for it is crisp and fresh, grapefruit (not stone fruit) and apple its flavour profile. Typical Henty ultra-cool style, with a very long life ahead. Cork. 13.5% alc. **Rating** 94 **To** 2025 $25 **○**

ΥΥΥΥ **Henty Syrah 2015 Rating** 91 **To** 2022 $25

Jacob's Creek ★★★★★

2129 Barossa Valley Way, Rowland Flat, SA 5352 **Region** Barossa Valley
T (08) 8521 3000 **www**.jacobscreek.com **Open** 7 days 10–5
Winemaker Ben Bryant **Est.** 1973 **Dozens** NFP **Vyds** 1000ha
Jacob's Creek (owned by Pernod-Ricard) is one of the largest-selling brands in the world, and the global success of the base range has had the perverse effect of prejudicing many critics and wine writers who fail (so it seems) to objectively look behind the label and taste what is in fact in the glass. There is an ever-changing plethora of brands, such as Limited Edition, Private Collection, Reserve, Signature, most with a new label livery – but this shouldn't distract from the quality of the wines. Exports to the UK, the US, Canada and China, and other major markets.

ΥΥΥΥΥ **Limited Edition Shiraz Cabernet 2010** There has been no stinting in the making of this wine, made by Bernard Hickin to celebrate his long service at Jacob's Creek, bottled 4 years before his retirement. Made from 63% Barossa shiraz and 33% Coonawarra cabernet (plus 4% shiraz), fermented separately with cultured yeast, 2–3 weeks on skins, matured for 24 months in new oak (88% French, 12% American). The quality of the fruit and the vintage has allowed the 100% new oak to be absorbed by the intense, perfectly ripened collage of blackberry, blackcurrant and plum fruit, the tannins sufficient for the long haul. One of the very best Jacob's Creek reds. Cork. 14.5% alc. **Rating** 96 **To** 2035 $180

Lyndale Barossa Chardonnay 2016 Matured in French oak (60% new) for 9 months. This isn't a powerhouse, yet has soaked up the oak without batting an eyelid, white peach leading the way along the fruit path, escorted by grapefruit. It is so well balanced it is nigh-on certain that it will grow depth to accompany the length it now has. Screwcap. 12.7% alc. **Rating** 95 **To** 2024 $50

Biodynamic McLaren Vale Shiraz 2014 Sold exclusively from the Jacob's Creek Visitor Centre. Dense inky colour; it literally shouts its McLaren Vale birthplace from the rooftops with its full-bodied, yet supple, palate. You can be sure this black fruit dipped in chocolate wine is from a certified biodynamic producer, and that during its 24-month elevage, racking was carried out on a full or new moon. Cork. 14.5% alc. **Rating** 95 **To** 2034 $65

ΥΥΥΥ **Barossa Signature Chardonnay 2016 Rating** 92 **To** 2020 $20 **○**
Reserve Margaret River Chardonnay 2016 Rating 92 **To** 2021 $18 **○**
Reserve Adelaide Hills Chardonnay 2016 Rating 91 **To** 2021 $18 **○**
Centenary Hill Barossa Valley Shiraz 2012 Rating 91 **To** 2024 $82 PR
Le Petit Rose 2016 Rating 90 **To** 2017 $17 **○**
Organic McLaren Vale Shiraz 2014 Rating 90 $65 PR

James & Co Wines ★★★★

359 Cornishtown Road, Rutherglen, Vic 3685 **Region** Beechworth
T (02) 6032 7556 **www**.jamesandcowines.com.au **Open** Not
Winemaker Ricky James **Est.** 2011 **Dozens** 450
Ricky and Georgie James intended to buy land in Beechworth and establish a vineyard planted primarily to sangiovese. They say, 'Serendipity led us to Mark Walpole, and we were

given the chance to purchase fruit from his Fighting Gully Road Vineyard.' In the meantime, they had set up their home in Rutherglen, and intend to float between the two regions – in their words,'James & Co. is a winery with a vineyard of no fixed address.'

ŶŶŶŶŶ Beechworth Sangiovese Rose 2016 50% of the wine saignee, the remainder picked early and pressed specifically for this wine. Pale pink, with a very expressive spicy bouquet and (for rose) an intense red cherry/berry spicy palate. Screwcap. 14% alc. **Rating** 94 **To** 2021 $24 **☉**
Beechworth Cabernet Sauvignon 2015 Cold-soaked, fermented cool (20°C) and matured in new and used French oak. Normally blended with sangiovese, but this vintage made cabernet that was so good it was in part bottled separately. It is deeply savoury, with dried herbs, bay leaf and dark chocolate woven through blackcurrant fruit. Screwcap. 14% alc. **Rating** 94 **To** 2035 $40

ŶŶŶŶŶ Beechworth Sangiovese 2014 Rating 93 **To** 2024 $35
Beechworth Sangiovese Cabernet 2014 Rating 92 **To** 2022 $24 **☉**
Beechworth Sangiovese 2015 Rating 92 **To** 2023 $35
Beechworth Sangiovese Cabernet 2015 Rating 90 **To** 2033 $24

Jamieson Estate

PO Box 6598, Silverwater, NSW 2128 **Region** Mudgee
T (02) 9737 8377 **www**.jamiesonestate.com.au **Open** Not
Winemaker James Manners **Est.** 1998 **Dozens** 1000 **Vyds** 10ha
Generations of the Jamieson family have been graziers in the region for 150 years, and were able to select 100ha of the most suitable soil from their property on which to establish their vineyard. Beginning in 1998, they planted 89ha of vines, selling the grapes to leading wineries in the region. When the buyers did not renew their contracts, they removed 79ha of vines (leaving 10ha of shiraz), and are now producing small quantities of Semillon Sauvignon Blanc, Chardonnay, Shiraz and Cabernet Sauvignon. Exports to Taiwan and China.

ŶŶŶŶŶ Guntawang Mudgee Shiraz 2015 Has all the colour a rich shiraz can muster plus a cascade of black and red fruits, pepper and spice, a slick palate, juicy with ripe tannins and some grip on the finish. Screwcap. 14.5% alc. **Rating** 92 **To** 2023 $22 JF **☉**

Jane Brook Estate Wines

229 Toodyay Road, Middle Swan, WA 6056 **Region** Swan Valley
T (08) 9274 1432 **www**.janebrook.com.au **Open** 7 days 10–5
Winemaker Mark Baird **Est.** 1972 **Dozens** 20000 **Vyds** 18.2ha
Beverley and David Atkinson have worked tirelessly to build up the Jane Brook Estate wine business over the past 45 years. All wines are produced from the estate vineyards in Swan Valley (6.5ha) and Margaret River (Shovelgate Vineyard) (11.7ha). Exports to China.

ŶŶŶŶŶ Shovelgate Vineyard Margaret River Sauvignon Blanc Semillon 2016 This has mesmerising intensity, its flavours like Roman candles dancing in the mouth as they change back and forth, tropicals to the fore, but grassy, green pea and citrus all to be had. Oak? I didn't think about that, but if you've asked, no. Screwcap. 12.2% alc. **Rating** 95 **To** 2021 $23 **☉**

ŶŶŶŶŶ Shovelgate Vineyard Cabernet Sauvignon 2013 Rating 92 **To** 2027 $35
Back Block Shiraz 2014 Rating 91 **To** 2024 $28

Jansz Tasmania

1216b Pipers Brook Road, Pipers Brook, Tas 7254 **Region** Northern Tasmania
T (03) 6382 7066 **www**.jansztas.com **Open** 7 days 10–4.30
Winemaker Louisa Rose **Est.** 1985 **Dozens** 38000 **Vyds** 30ha
Jansz is part of Hill-Smith Family Vineyards, and was one of the early sparkling wine labels in Tasmania, stemming from a short-lived relationship between Heemskerk and Louis Roederer.

Its 15ha of chardonnay, 12ha of pinot noir and 3ha of pinot meunier correspond almost exactly to the blend composition of the Jansz wines. It is the only Tasmanian winery entirely devoted to the production of sparkling wine (although the small amount of Dalrymple Estate wines is also made here), and is of high quality. Part of the former Frogmore Creek Vineyard purchased by Hill-Smith Family Vineyards in Dec 2012 is dedicated to the needs of Jansz Tasmania. Exports to all major markets.

ΤΤΤΤΤ **Vintage Cuvee 2011** Jansz vintage is sourced exclusively from the Jansz vineyard in Piper's River in northeastern Tasmania, and the cool '11 vintage represents a surprisingly powerful release. It's more toasty and biscuity than ever, with the theatrics of barrel fermentation (50%) conspiring with 4.5 years lees age to produce layered complexity of ginger cake, biscuits, even notes of fruit mince spice, coffee and chocolate. The cool restraint of Tasmanian fruit triumphs on the finish. Cork. 12% alc. **Rating** 93 **To** 2018 $56 TS
Vintage Rose 2013 Sealed with Diam for the first time – yes! This is an intense vintage for Jansz, upholding its gorgeous, pale salmon hue and contrasting this with rumbling depth of fruit power and the complexity of oak fermentation and lees age. The 100% pinot noir from the Jansz vineyard is alive with wild strawberries and red cherries, at once fleshy yet focused and tense. Barrel fermentation and maturity build a creamy bead and dark chocolate, coffee and ginger nut biscuit complexity which linger long through the finish. 13% alc. **Rating** 93 **To** 2018 $53 TS
Premium Cuvee NV This is a cuvee of contrasts, juxtaposing crunchy citrus rind with the generous flesh of peach and mirabelle plums, the freshness of ripe fruit with the toasty, nutty, biscuity complexity of age, and the cut of cool Tasmanian acidity with the sweetness of dosage. A little bitter phenolic grip provides bite to the finish. Cork. 12% alc. **Rating** 91 **To** 2017 $31 TS
Premium Rose NV Under Diam for the first time ever (hoorah!), Jansz Rose retains its gorgeously subtle pale salmon hue. More toasty and biscuity and less perfumed than usual; there are notes of wild strawberries, watermelon and hints of tomato, concluding with cool Tasmanian acidity and gentle phenolic grip. A value-for-money rose, though it's lost the finesse it enjoyed when Nat Fryar was at the helm of Jansz. 12% alc. **Rating** 91 **To** 2017 $31 TS

Jasper Hill   ★★★★★
Drummonds Lane, Heathcote, Vic 3523 **Region** Heathcote
T (03) 5433 2528 www.jasperhill.com.au **Open** By appt
Winemaker Ron Laughton, Emily McNally **Est.** 1979 **Dozens** 2000 **Vyds** 26.5ha
The red wines of Jasper Hill are highly regarded and much sought after. As long as vintage conditions allow, these are wonderfully rich and full-flavoured wines. The vineyards are dry-grown and are managed organically. Exports to the UK, the US, Canada, France, Denmark, Hong Kong and Singapore.

ΤΤΤΤΤ **Emily's Paddock Shiraz Cabernet Franc 2015** The cabernet franc is only 3%, which strictly speaking should not appear on the front label (5% is the minimum). It has a fragrant savoury/spicy bouquet, characters that come through strongly on the palate. The tannins are not a force per se, the savoury bitter chocolate notes coming from the fruit. Cork. 15% alc. **Rating** 96 **To** 2035
Georgia's Paddock Heathcote Shiraz 2015 Matured for 12 months in French barriques (20% new). It is medium to full-bodied, with red and black fruits competing for space alongside spices and firm, but balanced, tannins. Carries its alcohol with aplomb on the long palate. Cork. 15% alc. **Rating** 95 **To** 2035 $78
Georgia's Paddock Heathcote Nebbiolo 2015 The light, but bright, cherry red colour announces a seriously good nebbiolo; it has a fragrant bouquet, and a very long palate driven by savoury red fruits, not by tannins, dry or otherwise. A great place to start for those seeking to get their heads around nebbiolo. Cork. 14% alc. **Rating** 95 **To** 2030 $66

ΤΤΤΤΤ **Georgia's Paddock Heathcote Riesling 2016** Rating 90 To 2021 $41

jb Wines ★★★★☆

PO Box 530, Tanunda, SA 5352 **Region** Barossa Valley
T 0408 794 389 **www.**jbwines.com **Open** By appt
Winemaker Joe Barritt **Est.** 2005 **Dozens** 700 **Vyds** 18ha
The Barritt family has been growing grapes in the Barossa since the 1850s, but this particular venture was established in 2005 by Lenore, Joe and Greg Barritt. It is based on shiraz, cabernet sauvignon and chardonnay (with tiny amounts of zinfandel, pinot blanc and clairette) planted between 1972 and '03. Greg runs the vineyard operations; Joe, with a Bachelor of Agricultural Science degree from Adelaide University, followed by 10 years of winemaking in Australia, France and the US, is now the winemaker. Exports to Hong Kong.

♥♥♥♥♀ **Oohlala Barossa Valley Pinot Meunier Rose 2014** It was news to me that pinot meunier is being grown in the Barossa Valley Pale salmon pink; a very interesting wine, the back label speaking of a touch of sweetness balanced by acidity. It's hard to taste that sweetness, which is a good thing in a light-bodied, fresh and crisp rose. Very good value. 500ml. Screwcap. 12.4% alc. **Rating** 90 **To** 2018 $15 JH

Jeanneret Wines ★★★★★

Jeanneret Road, Sevenhill, SA 5453 **Region** Clare Valley
T (08) 8843 4308 **www.**jeanneretwines.com **Open** Mon–Fri 9–5, w'ends 10–5
Winemaker Ben Jeanneret, Harry Dickinson **Est.** 1992 **Dozens** 18000 **Vyds** 6ha
Ben Jeanneret has progressively built the range and quantity of wines he makes at the onsite winery. In addition to the estate vineyards, Jeanneret has grape purchase contracts with owners of an additional 20ha of hand-pruned, hand-picked, dry-grown vines spread throughout the Clare Valley. The Rieslings are very good indeed, the red wines extractive and difficult to enjoy. Exports to Sweden, Malaysia and Japan.

♥♥♥♥♥ **Doozie 2010** The pale, but bright, straw-green colour of this riesling seems to have changed little over the past 7 years, but the wine has made its move into a long plateau of maturity, the rate of change slowing. It's making this change with certainty, the flavours of lime and lemon suggesting they have sweetened the wine (they haven't); the acidity has softened its attack. A truly lovely wine, ready now or in another 7 years. Screwcap. 12.9% alc. **Rating** 97 **To** 2029 $40

♥♥♥♥♥ **Single Vineyard Sevenhill Riesling 2016** Vibrantly live and pure riesling, crackling with unsweetened citrus juice and pith, doing so with an almost savoury precision. The '10 Museum release shows what will occur over the next 6–7 years, so cellar this. Screwcap. 12.5% alc. **Rating** 95 **To** 2029 $25 ❂
Single Vineyard Watervale Riesling 2016 Much deeper and juicier than its Sevenhill sibling, trading precision for generosity, with Meyer lemon and Bickford's lime juice. This is the wine to drink now, although it will develop well if you are only interested in mature riesling. Screwcap. 12% alc. **Rating** 95 **To** 2026 $25 ❂

♥♥♥♥♀ **25 Year Old Rabelos Clare Valley Tawny NV Rating** 90 $50

Jericho Wines ★★★★★

13 Seacombe Crescent, Seacombe Heights, SA 5047 (postal) **Region** Adelaide Hills/McLaren Vale
T 0499 013 554 **www.**jerichowines.com.au **Open** Not
Winemaker Neil and Andrew Jericho **Est.** 2012 **Dozens** 3000
Neil Jericho made wine for over 35 years in Victoria, mainly in the Rutherglen and King Valley regions. In this venture the whole family is in play, with wife Kaye, a 'vintage widow'; eldest daughter Sally, who worked for Wine Australia for 10 years then obtained marketing and accounting degrees from the University of Adelaide; and son Andrew, who obtained his Bachelor of Oenology from the University of Adelaide (in 2003), having worked for 10 years in McLaren Vale, but then moved outside the square for experience at the highly regarded Grace Vineyard in the Shanxi Province of China. Son Kim was torn between oenology and

hospitality courses and graphic design, and opted for the latter, providing help with label and design.

ŶŶŶŶŶ Selected Vineyard McLaren Vale GSM 2015 An 87/10/3% blend, the grenache from 40yo unirrigated bushvines. A luscious mouthful – and mouthfeel – achieved at relatively low alcohol; it overflows with its cornucopia of red fruits plus a few sprigs of purple and black also in play, giving that extra something to a very distinguished grenache. Screwcap. 14.2% alc. **Rating** 96 **To** 2030 $25 **☉**
Single Vineyard Adelaide Hills Syrah 2015 10% stalks retained, 35 days on skins, matured in used French barriques for 12 months, released with a further 12 months bottle age. The bouquet is full of fragrant red fruits and spices, the palate underlining the power of the fruit with its long, balanced finish and aftertaste. Diam. 12.9% alc. **Rating** 95 **To** 2035 $35 **☉**
Single Vineyard McLaren Vale Shiraz 2014 This is an elegant shiraz with vibrantly fresh fruits and positive acidity. There are notes of pepper, spice and licorice, normally appearing in cool climate shiraz, but not giving rise here to any suggestion of unripe fruit – is it Blewitt Springs, I wonder? Regardless, it deserves applause – and its points. Diam. 13.8% alc. **Rating** 95 **To** 2029 $35 **☉**
Selected Vineyard Adelaide Hills Fume Blanc 2016 Fermented in used French barrels, matured with lees stirring for 7 months. Has worked very well, giving texture and structure without diminishing the bright citrus, stone and tropical fruits. Screwcap. 13.3% alc. **Rating** 94 **To** 2019 $25 **☉**
Selected Vineyards Adelaide Hills Fiano 2016 Made strictly adhering to the KISS principle: crushed, pressed, cool-fermented in stainless steel, bottled. The haunting bouquet of field flowers and spices introduces a palate with a mix of lemon/lemon zest, pear and apple flavours within the carapace of textured power that is the mark of fiano. Screwcap. 13.5% alc. **Rating** 94 **To** 2020 $25 **☉**

Jim Barry Wines   ★★★★★

33 Craigs Hill Road, Clare, SA 5453 **Region** Clare Valley
T (08) 8842 2261 **www.**jimbarry.com **Open** Mon–Fri 9–5, w'ends, hols 9–4
Winemaker Peter Barry, Tom Barry **Est.** 1959 **Dozens** 80 000 **Vyds** 300ha
The patriarch of this highly successful wine business, Jim Barry, died in 2004, but the business continues under the active management of several of his many children, led by the irrepressible Peter Barry. The ultra-premium release is The Armagh Shiraz, with the McCrae Wood red wines not far behind. Jim Barry Wines is able to draw upon mature Clare Valley vineyards, plus a small holding in Coonawarra. After studying and travelling, third-generation winemaker Tom and commercial manager Sam Barry have joined the business, launching The Barry Bros label. In November 2016, Jim Barry Wines released the first commercial Assyrtiko grown and made in Australia. A founding member of Australia's First Families of Wine. Exports to all major markets.

ŶŶŶŶŶ The Armagh Shiraz 2014 This is superbly honed, brimming with power and depth, full-bodied yet with a certain refinement. Astonishing colour, all dark ruby with purple tinges, the tannins velvety and savoury, the finish long. Every detail taken care of and the end result complete. Surprisingly approachable, but built to last a considerable distance. Screwcap. 14% alc. **Rating** 96 **To** 2044 $295 JF
The Florita Clare Valley Riesling 2016 There's so much zest appeal in this, plus all the purity and class a riesling with this provenance can muster. Complex, with a heady aroma of white florals, aniseed and fenugreek, lemon barley water; pith-like texture and superfine acidity, so it's racy, long and oh so pure. Screwcap. 11.3% alc. **Rating** 95 **To** 2038 $50 JF
The Lodge Hill Riesling 2016 It has a floral prettiness and plenty of limey flavour, and a minerally, sherbet-like sizzle to the finish is the perfect icing to a delicious cake. Screwcap. 12% alc. **Rating** 94 **To** 2028 $22 CM **☉**
Watervale Riesling 2016 Jim Barry's Rieslings have low pH (as low as 2.86), and acidity as high are 7.3g/l. This is a vibrantly alive wine, with vivid lime and

mineral flavours on the long palate. Please yourself whether you drink it now or 10 years hence. Value++. Screwcap. 12% alc. **Rating** 94 **To** 2029 $19
The Forger Shiraz 2015 Quite assertive as it plays a bright tune with its raspberry, jubes and plums then unleashes a savoury chord brimming with woodsy spices, earth and new oak. Integrated neatly. There's a whisper of violets, the tannins raspy, the body structured, and the acidity fresh. Screwcap. 14.2% alc. **Rating** 94 **To** 2030 $35 JF
The McRae Wood Clare Valley Shiraz 2014 First made in '92 as a junior brother to the Armagh from an estate vineyard planted in '64. It sits well in the mouth, but its quality comes into high relief on the finish and aftertaste. Here dark berry fruits, spice, licorice and leather all dance a jig together. It's on the way to greatness. Screwcap. 14% alc. **Rating** 94 **To** 2034 $55

ŸŸŸŸŸ **Cellar Release The Florita Riesling 2011** Rating 93 To 2021 $55 JF
Clare Valley Assyrtiko 2016 Rating 93 To 2021 $35
Single Vineyard Shiraz 2015 Rating 93 To 2028 $35 JF
PB Shiraz Cabernet Sauvignon 2014 Rating 93 To 2029 $60 JF
Single Vineyard Riesling 2016 Rating 92 To 2026 $35 JF
Clare Valley Assyrtiko 2015 Rating 92 To 2020 $35
The Benbournie Cabernet Sauvignon 2013 Rating 92 To 2031 $70 JF
Barry and Son's Shiraz 2015 Rating 90 To 2021 $25 JF
The Barry Brothers Shiraz Cabernet 2015 Rating 90 To 2020 $20 JF
Single Vineyard Cabernet 2015 Rating 90 To 2027 $35 JF

Jim Brand Wines   ★★★☆

PO Box 18, Coonawarra, SA 5263 **Region** Coonawarra
T (08) 8736 3252 **www.**jimbrandwines.com.au **Open** Not
Winemaker Brand family, Bruce Gregory (consultant) **Est.** 2000 **Dozens** 3000 **Vyds** 9.5ha
The Brand family story starts with the arrival of Eric Brand in Coonawarra in 1950. He married Nancy Redman and purchased a 24ha block from the Redman family, relinquishing his job as a baker and becoming a grapegrower. It was not until '66 that the first Brand's Laira wine was made. The family sold 50% of the Brand's Laira winery in '94 to McWilliam's, Jim Brand staying on as chief winemaker until he died in 2005. Sam Brand is the fourth generation of this family, which has played a major role in Coonawarra for over 50 years. Exports to Fiji, Hong Kong and China.

ŸŸŸŸŸ **Silent Partner Coonawarra Cabernet Sauvignon 2014** Mid-ruby; this is merging into camphor, cigar box, cedar and a dried array of garden herb, chief among them Australian bush tomato and a spray of menthol–cum–eucalyptus. There is a core of dark chocolate and plum, clinging to its youth. Strongly regional. Screwcap. 14.5% alc. **Rating** 91 **To** 2025 $36 NG

ŸŸŸŸ **Jim's Vineyard Coonawarra Shiraz 2014** Rating 89 To 2023 $36 NG

Jinks Creek Winery   ★★★☆

Tonimbuk Road, Tonimbuk, Vic 3815 **Region** Gippsland
T (03) 5629 8502 **www.**jinkscreekwinery.com.au **Open** Sun 12–5
Winemaker Andrew Clarke **Est.** 1981 **Dozens** 2000 **Vyds** 3.52ha
Planting of the Jinks Creek vineyard antedated the building of the winery by 11 years, and the wines are made from estate-grown grapes. Perched above the vineyard with an uninterrupted view of the Bunyip State Forest and Black Snake Ranges, a refurbished 100-year-old wool shed has been renovated to house a restaurant, art gallery and cellar door. It is constructed entirely from recycled materials. Exports to the US.

ŸŸŸŸ **Pinot Gris 2014** I can do no more than quote verbatim the back label description: 'Floral, honey and spicy notes, oiliness on the palate, and a long balanced acid finish.' This is a totally accurate description, taking it into a rare space in the world of pinot gris. Screwcap. 12.5% alc. **Rating** 89 **To** 2017 $25

Yarra Valley Cabernet Franc 2013 Cabernet franc is a very difficult mistress for any winemaker to tackle, with its sweet/sour fruit and overtones of tobacco leaf. It's not easy to come to terms with the wine, even less to decide what points to give it. You could add or subtract five points from mine without any comeback from me. Screwcap. 13% alc. **Rating** 89 **To** 2017 $30

John Duval Wines

PO Box 622, Tanunda, SA 5352 **Region** Barossa Valley
T (08) 8562 2266 **www**.johnduvalwines.com **Open** At Artisans of Barossa
Winemaker John Duval **Est.** 2003 **Dozens** 7000
John Duval is an internationally recognised winemaker, having been the custodian of Penfolds Grange for almost 30 years as part of his role as chief red winemaker there. In 2003 he established his eponymous brand; he continues to provide consultancy services to clients all over the world. While his main focus is on old vine shiraz, he has extended his portfolio with other Rhône varieties. Exports to all major markets.

Eligo The Barossa Shiraz 2014 Matured for 20 months in French oak (75% new). The massive difference in most of the best Barossa Valley shirazs of today compared to the wines of 20 years ago has been the adoption of French oak. It freshens the flavour profile, allowing the varietal fruit freedom to communicate its message. That said, this wine needs a decade, if not several, to reach its peak. Cork. 14.5% alc. **Rating** 97 **To** 2040 $120 ❂

Entity Barossa Shiraz 2015 Matured for 17 months in French oak (35% new). Reflects John Duval's long career as the chief architect of Grange. This brings depth, texture and complexity to a palette (sic) of black fruits, ripe tannins and oak. It cries out for patience, and the greater your patience, the greater the reward. Screwcap. 14.5% alc. **Rating** 96 **To** 2045 $50 ❂

Plexus Barossa Marsanne Roussanne Viognier 2016 Matured for 6 months in French oak. I'd really love to taste this wine in 3–5 years. It's pleasant now, its balance and freshness admirable, but it's the potential for flavour and complexity development that is eye – or mouth – catching. It's specific to this wine: the blend is common enough, but often bland. Screwcap. 12.5% alc. **Rating** 94 **To** 2025 $30 ❂

Plexus Barossa Valley Shiraz Grenache Mourvedre 2015 Matured for 15 months in French oak (10% new). Richly robed in luscious fruits supported by gentle tannins and a dab of oak. It is well made (of course) and is strongly Barossan in temperament. What you make of this will depend on your personal preference. Screwcap. 14.5% alc. **Rating** 94 **To** 2029 $40

Plexus Marsanne Roussanne Viognier 2015 Rating 93 **To** 2021 $30 CM
Plexus Marsanne Roussanne Viognier 2014 Rating 92 **To** 2017 $30 CM
Annexus Grenache 2015 Rating 92 **To** 2025 $70

John Gehrig Wines

Oxley-Milawa Road, Oxley, Vic 3678 **Region** King Valley
T (03) 5727 3395 **www**.johngehrigwines.com.au **Open** 7 days 10–5
Winemaker Ross Gehrig **Est.** 1976 **Dozens** 5600 **Vyds** 85ha
The Gehrig family has been making wine for five generations in Rutherglen, but in August 2011 the shape and size of the business increased rapidly. The purchase of an 80ha vineyard from Rutherglen Winemakers saw estate plantings rise from 6ha to 85ha; the vineyard purchased by Gehrig has a rich history, with an 1870 building known as Snarts Winery operating until the 1940s. Heritage listed, it has been restored and now operates as the cellar door. Work to rehabilitate the vineyard continues; part is used for the significantly increased John Gehrig production, the remainder of the grapes are sold.

King Valley Riesling 2013 Is developing very well indeed, with marvellous length and balance. Bickford's lime juice is tightly linked with Meyer lemon.

Campbell Mattinson gave it 94 points 3 years ago – I'm confident he would match my rating on retasting. Screwcap. **Rating** 95 To 2028
RG King Valley Riesling 2009 Bright gleaming straw-green; is developing surely and slowly, last tasted in Apr '13, and building on the framework of minerally, savoury acidity. I think it's now on the plateau of development, with fruit and acid neatly sewn together. Screwcap. 12% alc. **Rating** 94 To 2022 $32

ŶŶŶŶŶ **Rutherglen Durif 2013** Rating 92 To 2028 $35
King Valley Riesling 2015 Rating 90 To 2025
King Valley Riesling 2014 Rating 90 To 2020 $22
King Valley Chenin Blanc 2013 Rating 90 To 2023 $22
Grand Tawny NV Rating 90 $32

John Kosovich Wines

Cnr Memorial Ave/Great Northern Hwy, Baskerville, WA 6056 **Region** Swan Valley
T (08) 9296 4356 **www.**johnkosovichwines.com.au **Open** 7 days 10–5.30
Winemaker Anthony Kosovich **Est.** 1922 **Dozens** 3000 **Vyds** 10.9ha
John Kosovich Wines operated as Westfield Wines until 2003, when it changed its name to honour John's 50th vintage. The name change did not signify any change in either philosophy or direction for this much-admired producer of gloriously complex Rare Muscats. The 7.4ha of old vines in the Swan Valley accompany 3.5ha established in Pemberton in 1989. Son Anthony joined his father in 1994, and has since taken primary responsibility for the wines.

ŶŶŶŶŶ **Muscat 1974** Extreme concentration through prolonged storage at warm temperatures (à la Madeira) has created a wine so viscous and dense that it stains the sides of the glass in the same way as the Seppelt 100 Year Old Para does. Raisined to the point of burnt toffee, amazingly dense, the acidity and rancio on the finish coming as a relief to balance that lusciousness. Very difficult to decide points for a wine so unique and rare. Diam. 19% alc. **Rating** 98 $155 **⊙**
Rare Muscat NV Base material from '50 is blended with vintages from '74–96. The intensity here has to be seen/tasted to be believed. It oozes up and down the glass as you sip at it, its flavours of burnt toffee and intense raisin licked at by notes of fresh, black, sweet coffee. Quite staggering, really. It's like stepping into a whole new world. 375ml. Diam. 19% alc. **Rating** 97 $95 CM **⊙**

ŶŶŶŶŶ **Reserve Chenin Blanc 2011** In the zone. Drinking beautifully. Apple, citrus, spice and assorted exotica. It feels textural and yet there's no oak involved. Drink now; drink well. Screwcap. 12.5% alc. **Rating** 95 To 2020 $35 CM **⊙**

ŶŶŶŶŶ **Reserve Pemberton Cabernet Malbec 2014** Rating 93 To 2025 $40 CM

John's Blend

18 Neil Avenue, Nuriootpa, SA 5355 (postal) **Region** Langhorne Creek
T (08) 8562 1820 **www.**johnsblend.com.au **Open** At The Winehouse, Langhorne Creek
Winemaker John Glaetzer **Est.** 1974 **Dozens** 2000 **Vyds** 23ha
John Glaetzer was Wolf Blass's right-hand man almost from the word go, the power behind the throne of the three Jimmy Watson trophies awarded to Wolf Blass wines ('74, '75, '76) and the small matter of 11 Montgomery trophies for the Best Red Wine at the Adelaide Wine Show. This has always been a personal venture on the side, as it were, of John and wife Margarete, officially sanctioned, of course, and needing little marketing effort. Exports to Canada, Switzerland, Indonesia, Singapore and Japan.

ŶŶŶŶŶ **Margarete's Langhorne Creek Shiraz 2014** From four vineyards, vinified separately, fermented and matured for 26 months in new French hogsheads. Practice makes perfect, and John Glaetzer has practised unrelentingly for 42 years. The vinification, oak usage and the reliable climate of Langhorne Creek mean that you know what you will get without taking the cork out of the bottle. 14.5% alc. **Rating** 95 To 2035 $35 **⊙**

Individual Selection Langhorne Creek Cabernet Sauvignon 2013 The 39th release. So far as I know, this has the longest elevage of any Australian red wine, although the detailed arithmetic tracking its movements ending with bottling in the winter of '16 seems very tight. All of which is of academic interest, for the end result is extremely good, as long as dietary restrictions don't prevent your drinking oak along with your wine. Cork. 14.5% alc. **Rating** 95 **To** 2033 $35 **○**

Jones Winery & Vineyard ★★★★☆

Jones Road, Rutherglen, Vic 3685 **Region** Rutherglen
T (02) 6032 8496 **www.**joneswinery.com **Open** Mon, Thurs, Fri 10–4, w'ends 10–5
Winemaker Mandy Jones **Est.** 1860 **Dozens** 2000 **Vyds** 9.8ha
Jones Winery & Vineyard was established in 1860 and stands as testament to a rich winemaking tradition. Since 1927, the winery has been owned and operated by the Jones family. Two blocks of old vines have been preserved (including 1.69ha of shiraz), supported by further blocks progressively planted between '75 and 2008. Today, Jones Winery & Vineyard is jointly operated by winemaker Mandy Jones, who brought years of experience working in Bordeaux, and her brother Arthur Jones. Together they produce a small range of boutique wines.

🍷🍷🍷🍷🍷 **Rare Rutherglen Muscat NV** Mid-mahogany; quite heady, with a gamut of spices from star anise and cinnamon to powdered ginger and smells of dark fruitcake, burnt toffee and raisins. Richly flavoured, luscious but not heavy, with a brandy note to the spirit, and the considerable sweetness balanced by the acidity and depth of flavour. A treasure. Vino-Lok. 18.5% alc. **Rating** 95 $160 JF
LJ 2015 It has all the richness and depth a full-bodied shiraz can muster yet there's nothing heavy-handed here as the fruit – from 110yo vines – is the real star, wound around savoury-earthy notes, licorice and star anise, with ripe tannins on the finish. Plenty to like. Screwcap. 14.9% alc. **Rating** 94 **To** 2038 $65 JF
Classic Rutherglen Muscat NV Mid-amber with a touch of orange; luscious palate, all fruitcake and spice, orange marmalade, raisins soaked in brandy, plus butterscotch and caramel. The spirit is clean, warming and neatly balanced. 500ml. Vino-Lok. 18.5% alc. **Rating** 94 $35 JF

🍷🍷🍷🍷🍷 **Rutherglen Malbec 2015 Rating** 93 **To** 2029 $38 JF
Rutherglen Shiraz 2015 Rating 92 **To** 2028 $35 JF
Rutherglen Durif 2015 Rating 92 **To** 2029 $38 JF
MO Rutherglen Marsanne 2016 Rating 91 **To** 2020 $24 JF
CORRELL Blanc Aperitif NV Rating 90 $38 JF

Josef Chromy Wines ★★★★★

370 Relbia Road, Relbia, Tas 7258 **Region** Northern Tasmania
T (03) 6335 8700 **www.**josefchromy.com.au **Open** 7 days 10–5
Winemaker Jeremy Dineen **Est.** 2004 **Dozens** 30 000 **Vyds** 60ha
After escaping from Czechoslovakia in 1950, establishing Blue Ribbon Meats, using the proceeds of that sale to buy Rochecombe and Heemskerk vineyards, then selling those and establishing Tamar Ridge before it, too, was sold, Joe is at it again: this time he's invested $40 million in a wine-based business. If this were not remarkable enough, Joe is in his 80s, and has recovered from a major stroke. The foundation of the new wine business is the Old Stornoway Vineyard, with 60ha of mature vines, the lion's share to pinot noir and chardonnay. Joe's grandson, Dean Cocker, is business manager of the restaurant, function and wine centre. The homestead is now a dedicated wine centre and cellar door, offering WSET (Wine & Spirit Education Trust) courses. Exports to all majot markets.

🍷🍷🍷🍷🍷 **ZDAR Chardonnay 2013** A full-bodied chardonnay, built on the foundation of substantial barrel (12 months) and bottle age (3 years), following fermentation in new (one-third) and used barriques. The creamy, detailed texture is accentuated by weekly lees stirring. Stone fruits, cashew, nougat, truffled lees and vanillan oak fill the olfactory senses. The wine is weighty and confident in its strapping richness. Screwcap. 13.5% alc. **Rating** 95 **To** 2025 $75 NG

Pinot Noir 2015 A calm and effortless example of the synergy between pinot noir and the broad sweep of Tasmania's climate. Every cherry/berry fruit you would expect in a very good pinot, with a harmonious and relaxed mouthfeel and balance, spices around the corner waiting to appear over the next few years. Screwcap. 14.5% alc. **Rating** 95 **To** 2025 $38

Riesling 2016 One of many Tasmanian rieslings that are of very high quality, their cornerstone the acidity the climate bestows, often balanced by some residual sugar. The intensity of this zesty, lime-etched wine draws on its minerally/slatey acidity, cleansing the mouth and inviting another glass, especially if served with fresh Tasmanian seafood. Screwcap. 12.5% alc. **Rating** 94 **To** 2026 $28 ✪

Chardonnay 2015 Bright straw-green; its varietal expression is not in question – grapefruit zest, white peach – nor is the subtle nutty oak contribution. There's just a curious absence of X-factor in many Tasmanian chardonnays, which you may regard as unjust in the context of this wine. Screwcap. 13.5% alc. **Rating** 94 **To** 2023 $38

Vintage 2011 The depth and power of Relbia estate pinot noir is bolstered by the richness of 5 years of lees age, producing a particularly intense and characterful Chromy Vintage. White peach, fig and mirabelle plum fruit of succulent ripeness and commanding presence linger very long and full, toned by the vibrant yet ripe acid flow of the cool '11 season. A creamy texture and grand layers of ginger nut biscuits, chocolate and coffee proclaim lees maturity. A great release for Chromy. Diam. 12.5% alc. **Rating** 94 **To** 2018 $45 TS

Botrytis Riesling 2016 A wine with a poised, balletic twist of residual sugar and acidity. A resinous golden hue edged with amber segues to a fruit bowl of pear, quince and apricot; some as compote, others ginger. A whiff of volatility serves the wine well, as does the beam of tangy acidity that whirls and twirls the sweetness, brushing it away like an electric toothbrush, to near-palpable dryness. As light as a feather. Screwcap. 9.5% alc. **Rating** 94 **To** 2030 $28 NG ✪

ⵖⵖⵖⵖ Sauvignon Blanc 2016 **Rating** 93 **To** 2020 $28 NG
Pinot Gris 2016 **Rating** 93 **To** 2020 $28
DELIKAT SGR Riesling 2016 **Rating** 93 **To** 2025 $28 NG
RS6 Tasmania Riesling 2016 **Rating** 93 **To** 2025 NG
ZDAR Pinot Noir 2013 **Rating** 91 **To** 2024 $75 NG
PEPIK Sparkling Rose NV **Rating** 91 **To** 2017 $32 TS
PEPIK Chardonnay 2016 **Rating** 90 **To** 2021 $25 NG
Tasmanian Cuvee Methode Traditionelle NV **Rating** 90 **To** 2017 $32 TS

Journey Wines ★★★★★

1a/29 Hunter Road, Healesville, Vic 3777 (postal) **Region** Yarra Valley
T 0427 298 098 **www**.journeywines.com.au **Open** Not
Winemaker Damian North **Est.** 2011 **Dozens** 2500
The name chosen by Damian North for his brand is particularly appropriate given the winding path he has taken before starting (with his wife and three youngish children) his own label. Originally a sommelier at Tetsuya's, he was inspired to enrol in the oenology course at CSU, gaining his first practical winemaking experience as assistant winemaker at Tarrawarra Estate. Then, with family in tow, he moved to Oregon's Benton-Lane Winery to make pinot noir, before returning to become winemaker at Leeuwin Estate for five years. The wheel has turned full circle as the family has returned to the Yarra Valley, securing 2ha of chardonnay, 2.5ha of pinot noir and 2ha of shiraz under contract arrangements, and making the wines at Medhurst. Exports to the UK, Singapore and Thailand.

ⵖⵖⵖⵖ Yarra Valley Chardonnay 2015 80% from Gruyere in the Lower Yarra Valley, and 20% from Gladysdale in the Upper Yarra, picked 2 weeks later, whole-bunch pressed, wild-yeast fermented, matured in French puncheons (25% new) with 10 months' maturation. A distinctly complex bouquet leads into a palate of intensity and great length. The flavours are classic Yarra Valley: white peach and grapefruit/citrus with a tingling, fresh finish. Screwcap. 13.5% alc. **Rating** 96 **To** 2028 $34 ✪

Yarra Valley Pinot Noir 2015 From the Lone Star Creek and Willowlake Vineyards in the Upper Yarra Valley, 80% destemmed, 20% whole bunches small-batch wild yeast–open fermented, hand-plunged, 15 days on skins, matured in French oak (25% new) for 9 months. Balances savoury/foresty characters with positive red cherry and plum fruit to very good effect; the tannins are positive yet silky, lengthening the palate and aftertaste. Screwcap. 13% alc. **Rating** 95 To 2027 $38

Journeys End Vineyards   ★★★★

Level 7, 420 King William Street, Adelaide, SA 5000 (postal) **Region** South Eastern Australia
T 0431 709 305 **www**.journeysendvineyards.com.au **Open** Not
Winemaker Ben Riggs (Contract) **Est.** 2001 **Dozens** 10 000
An interesting virtual winery, which, while focused on McLaren Vale shiraz, also has contracts for other varieties in the Adelaide Hills, Coonawarra and Langhorne Creek. The Shiraz uses five different clones to amplify the complexity that comes from having grapegrowers in many different parts of McLaren Vale. Exports to all major markets.

ŶŶŶŶŶ **Coonawarra Station Cabernet Sauvignon 2012** The label looks as if it was inspired by the Woodley Treasure Chest series, suggesting a great classic, not a $21 wine. This was made in a great vintage, so why the price? Repeated tasting comes up with the same answer: a wine with the rectitude typical of cool-grown cabernet, so don't look a gift horse in the mouth. Screwcap. 14.5% alc. **Rating** 92 To 2027 $21 ✪
Three Brothers Reunited Shiraz 2014 You get exceptional value with this shiraz, mainly McLaren Vale in origin. Made by Ben Riggs, and on the light side of medium-bodied, but does have cherry fruits with hints of spice and chocolate. Absolutely ready to go. Screwcap. 14.5% alc. **Rating** 90 To 2020 $13 ✪

Juniper Estate   ★★★★★

98 Tom Cullity Drive, Cowaramup, WA 6284 **Region** Margaret River
T (08) 9755 9000 **www**.juniperestate.com.au **Open** 7 days 10–5
Winemaker Mark Messenger **Est.** 1973 **Dozens** 12 000 **Vyds** 19.5ha
When Roger Hill and Gillian Anderson purchased the Wrights' vineyard in 1998, the 10ha vineyard was already 25 years old, but in need of retrellising and a certain amount of nursing to bring it back to health. All of that has happened, along with the planting of additional shiraz and cabernet sauvignon. The Juniper Crossing wines use a mix of estate-grown grapes and grapes from other Margaret River vineyards, while the Juniper Estate releases are made only from the estate plantings. Since Roger's death in '13, Gillian has continued running Juniper Estate and Higher Plane. Exports to the UK, the US, Ireland, Canada, Hong Kong, the Philippines, Singapore and NZ.

ŶŶŶŶŶ **Small Batch Margaret River Tempranillo 2015** Bright crimson-purple; it would be easy to let this slip by without much comment simply because it has been crafted (not a word I often use) with such care. The evocative bouquet has cherry blossom fragrance, the supple, slinky medium-bodied palate with juicy black cherry fruits crosscut by fine-grained, but persistent, savoury tannins. Elegance personified. Screwcap. 13.5% alc. **Rating** 95 To 2028 $25 ✪
Single Vineyard Margaret River Malbec 2014 Open-fermented, matured in French oak for 16 months. Normally blended, but so exceptional in this vintage that a small quantity was bottled. Excellent colour; it fills the mouth with plum, plum skin, spice and cinnamon flavours, and finishes with the pillowy tannins sometimes missing from malbec. Screwcap. 14% alc. **Rating** 95 To 2029 $37.50
Juniper Crossing Margaret River Semillon Sauvignon Blanc 2016 Notably lively, juicy and intense, with Meyer lemon, lemongrass and a whisper of passionfruit pervading both the bouquet and palate, the length amplified by crisp acidity. Great value. Screwcap. 13% alc. **Rating** 94 To 2019 $22 ✪

Juniper Crossing Margaret River Cabernet Merlot 2014 It asserts its class from the outset and at this price level, that's something of a rarity. It's mid-weight, feels authentic, is both dark and bright at once, and comes polished with an appropriate smear of smoky/chocolatey oak. Tannin management too is impeccable. It's a wine of a winery on song. Screwcap. 14% alc. **Rating** 94 To 2030 $22 CM ❍

❦❦❦❦❦ **Small Batch Margaret River Fiano 2016 Rating** 93 To 2020 $25 ❍
Juniper Crossing Chardonnay 2016 Rating 92 To 2023 $23 ❍
Juniper Crossing Shiraz 2015 Rating 92 To 2025 $23 ❍

Just Red Wines ★★★★

2370 Eukey Road, Ballandean, Qld 4382 **Region** Granite Belt
T (07) 4684 1322 **www.**justred.com.au **Open** Fri–Mon 10–5
Winemaker Michael Hassall **Est.** 1998 **Dozens** 1500 **Vyds** 2.8ha
Tony, Julia and Michael Hassall have planted shiraz and merlot (plus cabernet sauvignon, tannat and viognier not yet in production) at an altitude of just under 900m. They minimise the use of chemicals wherever possible, but do not hesitate to protect the grapes if weather conditions threaten an outbreak of mildew or botrytis.

❦❦❦❦❦ **Granite Belt Shiraz Viognier 2015** 8% viognier was co-fermented with the shiraz. An attractive, lively red cherry/berry bouquet and palate reflect the impact of the viognier, lifting the freshness and length of the palate. The only question is the slightly nippy finish. Screwcap. 13.5% alc. **Rating** 90 To 2021 $19 ❍

Kaesler Wines ★★★★★

Barossa Valley Way, Nuriootpa, SA 5355 **Region** Barossa Valley
T (08) 8562 4488 **www.**kaesler.com.au **Open** 7 days 11–5
Winemaker Reid Bosward **Est.** 1990 **Dozens** 20 000 **Vyds** 36ha
The first members of the Kaesler family settled in the Barossa Valley in 1845. The vineyards date back to 1893, but the Kaesler family ownership ended in 1968. After several changes, the present (much-expanded) Kaesler Wines was acquired by a small group of investment bankers (who have since acquired Yarra Yering), in conjunction with former Flying Winemaker Reid Bosward and wife Bindy. Reid's experience shows through in the wines, which now come from estate vineyards adjacent to the winery, and 10ha in the Marananga area. The latter includes shiraz planted in 1899, with both blocks seeing plantings in the 1930s, '60s, then each decade through to the present. Exports to all major markets.

❦❦❦❦❦ **Alte Reben Barossa Valley Shiraz 2014** From the estate vineyard planted in 1899 at Marananga, matured in French oak (30% new) for 18 months, not fined or filtered. Full-bodied, but very well balanced, and has a purity, a strong sense of place to its black/forest berry fruit; the French oak, too, plays a positive role. A great example of the genre. Cork. 14% alc. **Rating** 97 To 2044 $150 ❍

❦❦❦❦❦ **The Bogan 2014** From estate vineyards planted in 1899 and 1965, matured in French oak (25% new) for 13 months. A powerful, distinctly savoury shiraz with an abundance of earthy black fruits that don't deviate an inch during their passage along the palate. Will flourish for decades in the bottle. Cork. 15% alc. **Rating** 96 To 2034 $50 ❍
Old Bastard 2014 Hailing from plantings dating from 1893, this wine struts with a largesse and swagger of one comfortable in its skin. Opaque and foreboding at first sight, the wine is aromatically reticent. At least at the beginning. In time the monster bares dark fruits of every description, plus cardamom and barbecued meats. Oak kicks in as the guardian for a long future. Spice provides punctuation. One for the boardroom. Cork. 14.5% alc. **Rating** 95 To 2032 $220 NG
Old Vine Barossa Valley Semillon 2016 The estate vines were planted in '60 and produce grapes of high quality. The most important winemaking decision was

to pick earlier, resulting in freshness and deep-seated varietal flavour on the long, well balanced, citrus-based palate. Screwcap. 11.5% alc. **Rating** 94 **To** 2029 $20 **○**

🍷🍷🍷🍷🍷 Avignon Barossa Valley Grenache Mourvedre 2014 **Rating** 92 **To** 2021 $35
Stonehorse Grenache Shiraz Mourvedre 2014 **Rating** 92 **To** 2023 $25 **○**
Small Valley Vineyard Adelaide Hills Sauvignon Blanc 2016 **Rating** 90
To 2019 $28
Small Valley Vineyard Adelaide Hills Chardonnay 2016 **Rating** 90
To 2022 $32
Stonehorse Shiraz 2014 **Rating** 90 **To** 2029 $25
Uvaggio 2015 **Rating** 90 **To** 2020 $35 NG
Rizza Barossa Valley Riesling 2016 **Rating** 90 **To** 2026 $20 NG **○**

Kakaba Wines

PO Box 348, Hahndorf, SA 5245 **Region** Adelaide Hills
T 0438 987 010 **www.kakaba.com.au Open** Not
Winemaker Greg Clack **Est.** 2006 **Dozens** 5000
When I send an email to a new winery for the Companion, I ask what inspired the vigneron to entertain the folly of starting a new winery. Chris Milner, with wife Jill in tow, responded by saying, 'it has been an enjoyable journey and, incredible as it may seem, moderately profitable, which I attribute to having zero overheads (no vineyards and no winery), zero employees (Jill and I don't get paid) and zero bank debt (too much debt will kill you every time!)'. He had the great advantage of having worked in the wine business since the late 1990s, mainly in the finance and commercial operations of various businesses. In 2006 there was an opportunity to source premium wine from the Adelaide Hills, and sell it to other wineries as bulk either during vintage or shortly thereafter. This worked very well in '06 and '07, but then came the super-abundant vintage of '08, with supply exceeding demand. Because of his wisdom the business survived, and continued, finally moving to bottle some wine under its own labels.

🍷🍷🍷🍷🍷 Reserve Adelaide Hills Shiraz 2014 Completed its fermentation in used
French oak, then matured for 20 months. A very well made wine that reflects its
place of origin and the impact of the vintage, its medium to full-bodied palate
saturated with plum and blackberry fruit that sits comfortably on a bed of dark
spices and rounded tannins. Screwcap. 14.5% alc. **Rating** 94 **To** 2030 $39

🍷🍷🍷🍷🍷 Reserve Adelaide Hills Pinot Noir 2014 **Rating** 93 **To** 2021 $39
Reserve Adelaide Hills Cabernet Sauvignon 2014 **Rating** 93 **To** 2025 $39
Reserve Adelaide Hills Sauvignon Blanc 2016 **Rating** 91 **To** 2019 $24 PR

Kalleske

6 Murray Street, Greenock, SA 5360 **Region** Barossa Valley
T (08) 8563 4000 **www.kalleske.com Open** 7 days 10–5
Winemaker Troy Kalleske **Est.** 1999 **Dozens** 15 000 **Vyds** 48ha
The Kalleske family has been growing and selling grapes on a mixed farming property at Greenock for over 140 years. Sixth-generation Troy Kalleske, with brother Tony, established the winery and created the Kalleske label in 1999. The vineyard is planted to shiraz (27ha), grenache (6ha), mataro (2ha), chenin blanc, durif, viognier, zinfandel, petit verdot, semillon and tempranillo (1ha each). The vines vary in age, with the oldest dating back to 1875; the overall average age is around 50 years. All are grown biodynamically. Exports to all major markets.

🍷🍷🍷🍷🍷 Johann Georg Old Vine Single Vineyard Barossa Valley Shiraz 2014
From the oldest estate vineyard, planted in 1875. This has instantaneous appeal,
its mouthfeel gently velvety, the flavours of perfectly ripened blackberries, plums
and licorice, oak and tannins doing no more than provide respectful support. A
lovely old vine wine that rose above the tribulations of the '14 vintage. Screwcap.
14.5% alc. **Rating** 97 **To** 2044 $120 **○**

🍷🍷🍷🍷🍷 Greenock Single Vineyard Barossa Valley Shiraz 2015 Matured in new
and used American and French oak. Blackberry, plum and hints of spicy oak come

together well on the bouquet and palate alike. The tannins are only just evident, and the wine is no more than medium-bodied. Continues a line of attractive wines. Screwcap. 14.5% alc. **Rating** 95 **To** 2035 $40

Eduard Old Vine Barossa Valley Shiraz 2011 From three dry-grown estate blocks planted between 1905 and '60; destemmed and open-fermented on skins for 8–10 days with twice-daily pumpovers, pressed to new and used French and American hogsheads for fermentation and 2 years maturation. A powerful, concentrated and layered wine with some smoky/charcuterie nuances to the black fruits of the bouquet and palate, but the tannins are soft and in balance. Screwcap. 14.5% alc. **Rating** 94 **To** 2034 $85

ҮҮҮҮҮ **Moppa Barossa Valley Shiraz 2015** Rating 93 To 2025 $28
Pirathon by Kalleske Shiraz 2015 Rating 93 To 2025 $23 JF ✪
Old Vine Grenache 2015 Rating 93 To 2023 $45 JF
Merchant Cabernet Sauvignon 2015 Rating 93 To 2025 $28 JF
Dodger Single Vineyard Tempranillo 2015 Rating 93 To 2022 $25 JF ✪
Barossa Valley Rosina Rose 2015 Rating 91 To 2020 $20 ✪
Clarry's Barossa Valley GSM 2016 Rating 91 To 2021 $21 ✪
Buckboard Barossa Valley Durif 2015 Rating 91 To 2025 $25 JF
Barossa Valley Rosina Rose 2016 Rating 90 To 2017 $20 CM ✪
Zeitgeist Barossa Valley Shiraz 2016 Rating 90 To 2018 $26 CM
Fordson Zinfandel 2015 Rating 90 To 2022 $25 JF
Fordson Zinfandel 2014 Rating 90 To 2021 $24

Kangarilla Road Vineyard   ★★★★★

Kangarilla Road, McLaren Vale, SA 5171 **Region** McLaren Vale
T (08) 8383 0533 **www.**kangarillaroad.com.au **Open** Mon–Fri 9–5, w'ends 11–5
Winemaker Kevin O'Brien **Est.** 1997 **Dozens** 65 000 **Vyds** 14ha
In Jan 2013 Kangarilla Road founders Kevin O'Brien and wife Helen succeeded in breaking the mould for a winery sale, and crafted a remarkable win–win outcome. They sold their winery and surrounding vineyard to Gemtree Vineyards, which has had its wine made at Kangarilla Road since '01 under the watchful eye of Kevin. The O'Briens have retained their adjacent JOBS Vineyard and the Kangarilla Road wines continue to be made by Kevin at the winery. Luck of the Irish, perhaps. Exports to the UK, the US and other major markets.

ҮҮҮҮҮ **McLaren Vale Shiraz 2015** From several McLaren Vale vineyards, open-fermented with heading down boards, matured for 16 months in French and American hogsheads (25% new). This deeply coloured shiraz is a great example of McLaren Vale's synergistic union with the variety. Dark black fruits, licorice, spice and dark chocolate all add to the palate, along with powdery tannins from both fruit and oak. Screwcap. 14.5% alc. **Rating** 95 **To** 2030 $25 ✪

The Devil's Whiskers McLaren Vale Shiraz 2014 Dense crimson-purple; a full-bodied shiraz that keeps attention throughout the tasting journey. The fruits are in the black spectrum, licorice and dark chocolate travelling companions aided by ripe tannins and integrated oak, the finish almost juicy, adding even more attraction. Screwcap. 14.5% alc. **Rating** 95 **To** 2034 $40

The Devil's Whiskers McLaren Vale Shiraz 2013 From the opening whiff through to the finish and aftertaste, the wine rings the bell of McLaren Vale, its black fruits wrapped in Belgian chocolate; while filled with these flavours, high quality oak and supple tannins lend support and structure, and the aftertaste is savoury, not fruit-sweet. Screwcap. 14.5% alc. **Rating** 95 **To** 2033 $40

ҮҮҮҮҮ **The Monty Rose 2016** Rating 91 To 2018 $20 ✪
Brierly Vineyard Montepulciano 2014 Rating 91 To 2020 $30
Duetto 2015 Rating 90 To 2019 $25
Brierly Vineyard McLaren Vale Montepulciano 2015 Rating 90 $30 PR

Karatta Wines

232 Clay Wells Road, Robe, SA 5276 **Region** Robe
T (08) 8735 7255 **www**.karattawines.com.au **Open** details on website
Winemaker Chris Gray **Est.** 1994 **Dozens** 4000 **Vyds** 39.6ha
Owned by David and Peg Woods, Karatta Wines was named after Karatta House, one of Robe's well known heritage-listed icons, built in 1858 and restored by David and Peg. Peg's family was also involved with the 1880s Karatta steam freighter that plied the south coast from Adelaide to Kangroo Island to Port Lincoln. Vineyards include the 12 Mile Vineyard and Tenison Vineyard, both in the Robe region. In 2017 Karatta opened a tasting room/cellar door in the heart of Robe.

Brush Heath 12 Mile Vineyard Robe Cabernet Sauvignon 2015 Fresh, cool climate varietal aromas on display, with blackcurrant fruit cheek by jowl with grassy, herbal notes. A medium-weight palate, the flavours very pure, red and black berry-like, with a cedary (perhaps oak-derived) element adding a layer of complexity. The tannin is light, but in balance, and there's an easy, harmonious feeling to the wine in general. Screwcap. 14.2% alc. **Rating** 92 **To** 2025 $25 SC ●
Dune Thistle 12 Mile Vineyard Robe Shiraz 2015 Just-ripe blackberry and blood plum are in evidence on the bouquet, with sweet spice and licorice having a presence. An even flow along the palate, the flavours in the same fruit spectrum, and while there's not a lot of weight, there is enough depth and length to carry it through. It feels as if it could do with an extra gear, but it won't disappoint anybody. Screwcap. 14.2% alc. **Rating** 91 **To** 2022 $25 SC
Pincushion 12 Mile Vineyard Robe Malbec 2015 Interesting to see a straight malbec from this region. A deep, almost inky colour to begin. A little shy on the bouquet initially, but opens up to show typically raspberry varietal fruit with a minerally, iodine-like character in the background. Juicy, ripe flavour on the palate; a little one-dimensional perhaps, but it has an attractive freshness and vibrancy which appeals. Screwcap. 14.5% alc. **Rating** 90 **To** 2021 $35 SC

Karrawatta

818 Greenhills Road, Meadows, SA 5201 **Region** Adelaide Hills/Langhorne Creek
T (08) 8537 0511 **www**.karrawatta.com.au **Open** By appt
Winemaker Mark Gilbert **Est.** 1996 **Dozens** 990 **Vyds** 46.6ha
Mark Gilbert is the great-great-great-grandson of Joseph Gilbert, who established the Pewsey Vale vineyard (and winery) in 1847. What is not generally known is that Joseph Gilbert had named the property Karrawatta, a name already in use for another property. The right to use the name was decided on the toss of a coin in a local SA pub, forcing Gilbert (who lost) to relinquish the Karrawatta name and adopt Pewsey Vale instead. The Karrawatta of today is not in the Barossa Ranges, but the Adelaide Hills; there is a neat coincidence here, because in 1847 Pewsey Vale was the highest vineyard planting in SA, and Mark Gilbert's Karrawatta is one of the highest plantings in the Adelaide Hills. It is true that he only has 13.8ha of vines here, and 32.8ha in Langhorne Creek, but never let the facts get in the way of a good story.

Anna's Adelaide Hills Sauvignon Blanc 2016 Hand-picked, whole-bunch pressed, wild-yeast fermented in used French barriques with partial mlf. The vinification has worked to perfection, giving texture, structure and complexity to a very intense sauvignon. Its aromas and flavours dwell mainly in a cut grass/snow pea spectrum, but there are contrasting notes of sweet citrus and tropical fruits. Screwcap. 12.7% alc. **Rating** 95 **To** 2018 $26 ●
Sophie's Hill Adelaide Hills Pinot Grigio 2016 Hand-picked, whole-bunch pressed, fermented in used French barriques, some mlf. Karawatta suggests this is the leaner style of Italian grigio. I don't agree. It's in a high quality gris style with intense lime and nashi pear flavours and a cleansing finish. Screwcap. 13.4% alc. **Rating** 95 **To** 2019 $26 ●
Spartacus Langhorne Creek Cabernet Malbec Shiraz 2014 Like Spartacus, this is fearless with its bold, big flavours. Plenty of concentrated yet bright fruit,

chocolate, ferrous and salt-bush characters, and a slickness to the texture. Full-bodied and ripe tannins makes you sit up and take notice. One for the gladiator in your life. Diam. 14.6% alc. **Rating** 95 **To** 2038 $92 JF

Dairy Block Adelaide Hills Shiraz 2015 The back label says this is a small parcel from the estate, hand-picked, which I'll buy. But I won't buy the assertion that it was whole-bunch pressed, as the colour is deep crimson-purple, and this isn't a rose. Matured for 18 months in French barriques, it is an imposing cool-grown shiraz, its dark fruits intertwined with potpourri spices, the palate velvety and succulent. Screwcap. 15% alc. **Rating** 94 **To** 2035 $38

 Anth's Garden Adelaide Hills Chardonnay 2016 **Rating** 93 **To** 2025 $52 JF

KarriBindi ★★★★

111 Scott Road, Karridale, WA 6288 (postal) **Region** Margaret River
T (08) 9758 5570 **www**.karribindi.com.au **Open** Not
Winemaker Kris Wealand **Est.** 1997 **Dozens** 2000 **Vyds** 32.05ha
KarriBindi is owned by Kevin, Yvonne and Kris Wealand. The name is derived from Karridale and the surrounding karri forests, and from Bindi, the home town of one of the members of the Wealand family. In Nyoongar, 'karri' means strong, special, spiritual, tall tree and 'bindi' means butterfly. The Wealands have established sauvignon blanc (15ha), chardonnay (6.25ha), cabernet sauvignon (4ha), plus smaller plantings of semillon, shiraz and merlot. KarriBindi supplies a number of high-profile Margaret River wineries, reserving approximately 20% of its grapes for its own label. Exports to Singapore and China.

 Margaret River Semillon Sauvignon Blanc 2016 10% of the blend of 55% semillon to 45% sauvignon blanc was fermented in new French oak, before being transferred back to tank for settling. The result is a pungent, crisp, aromatic white that pulls few punches in the greengage and nettle stakes. The slaking acidity and fringe of oak combine nicely, pulling it all into a racy, energetic whole. Screwcap. 12.8% alc. **Rating** 92 **To** 2019 $20 NG ✪

Margaret River Shiraz 2012 A mid-weighted wine of gravelly tannins, lilting acidity and savoury notes of soy, five-spice and mace. Some mocha melds effortlessly with some barrel-ferment bacon back and the cavalry of blue and dark fruits that fill out the wine's fore and aft. A graceful shiraz showing some tertiary complexity and a savoury soul. Screwcap. 13.7% alc. **Rating** 91 **To** 2020 $25 NG

Margaret River Sauvignon Blanc 2016 A dollop of this was fermented in new French oak, serving to give a savoury bite and to take the edge off the gushing spearmint, nettle, gooseberry and quince flavours. A livewire, balanced tightrope act of precision and exuberance. Screwcap. 13% alc. **Rating** 90 **To** 2018 $20 NG ✪

Kate Hill Wines ★★★★☆

101 Glen Road, Huonville, Tas 7109 (postal) **Region** Southern Tasmania
T (03) 6223 5641 **www**.katehillwines.com.au **Open** Not
Winemaker Kate Hill **Est.** 2008 **Dozens** 1000 **Vyds** 3ha
When Kate Hill (and husband Charles) came to Tasmania in 2006, Kate had worked as a winemaker in Australia and overseas for 10 years. Kate's wines are made from grapes from a number of vineyards across southern Tasmania, the aim being to produce approachable, delicate wines. Exports to Singapore.

Riesling 2015 From Derwent River and the Coal River Valley, a 3-week cool ferment. 6 months maturation in tank on lees has added a dimension to the mid-palate; pure Bickford's lime juice flavours run along silver rails of minerally acidity. Calmly moving through the transition from youth to maturity without missing a beat. Screwcap. 12% alc. **Rating** 95 **To** 2025 $28 ✪

Pinot Noir 2013 **Rating** 90 **To** 2021 $36

Katnook Coonawarra

Riddoch Highway, Coonawarra, SA 5263 **Region** Coonawarra
T (08) 8737 0300 **www**.katnookestate.com.au **Open** Mon–Sat 10–5, Sun 11–5
Winemaker Wayne Stehbens **Est.** 1979 **Dozens** 90 000 **Vyds** 198ha
Second in size (in the region) to Wynns Coonawarra Estate, Katnook has made significant
strides since its acquisition by Freixenet, the Spanish Cava producer; at one time selling most
of its grapes, it now sells only 10%. The historic stone woolshed in which the second vintage
in Coonawarra (1896) was made, and which has served Katnook since 1980, has been restored.
Likewise, the former office of John Riddoch has been restored and is now the cellar door,
and the former stables now serve as a function area. Well over half the total estate plantings are
cabernet sauvignon and shiraz, with the Odyssey Cabernet Sauvignon and Prodigy Shiraz the
icon duo at the top of a multi-tiered production. Exports to all major markets.

ΨΨΨΨΨ Odyssey Cabernet Sauvignon 2013 Crushed and destemmed, fermented in
a mix of open and closed fermenters, 5–10 days on skins, matured for 36 months
in French (56% new) and used American oak. Obviously, oak leaves a footprint on
the wine, but there is a wealth of blackcurrant/cassis, bay leaf and spice to provide
balance to a warm-hearted, generous wine that can be enjoyed now or in 20+
years. Cork. 14.5% alc. **Rating** 96 **To** 2037 $100
Amara Vineyard Cabernet Sauvignon 2015 Fermented in both closed and
open fermenters for 5–10 days, matured for 11 months in barriques, 93% French
(45% new), 7% American. A distinguished Coonawarra cabernet with abundant
mulberry and cassis fruit that has absorbed the new French oak without a
murmur. The tannins are firm (as they should be) and the long-term future of the
wine is assured. Screwcap. 14% alc. **Rating** 95 **To** 2035 $50
The Caledonian Cabernet Shiraz 2015 55% cabernet sauvignon, 35% shiraz,
the remaining 10% tannat and petit verdot; matured for 14 months in French
oak (40% new). The oak is obvious on the bouquet, but less so on the complex,
full-bodied palate, with its array of blackberry, blackcurrant, plum and spicy oak
flavours, the tannins built to size. Screwcap. 14% alc. **Rating** 95 **To** 2030 $50

ΨΨΨΨΨ Estate Cabernet Sauvignon 2014 Rating 93 **To** 2029 $40
Squire's Blend Cabernet Merlot 2014 Rating 90 **To** 2024 $22

Kay Brothers Amery Vineyards

57 Kays Road, McLaren Vale, SA 5171 **Region** McLaren Vale
T (08) 8323 8211 **www**.kaybrothersamerywines.com **Open** details on website
Winemaker Colin Kay, Duncan Kennedy, Colin Kay (Consultant) **Est.** 1890
Dozens 10 500 **Vyds** 22ha
A traditional winery with a rich history and just over 20ha of priceless old vines; while the
white wines have been variable, the red and fortified wines can be very good. Of particular
interest is Block 6 Shiraz, made from 120+-year-old vines; both vines and wines are going
from strength to strength. Celebrated its 125th anniversary in 2015. Exports to the US, Canada,
Switzerland, Germany, Malaysia, Hong Kong, Singapore, South Korea, Thailand and China.

ΨΨΨΨΨ Block 6 McLaren Vale Shiraz 2014 The lavish depth of fruit and sheer
concentration and intensity of flavour bury the oak constructs that frame this wine.
A veneer of American and French oak, new and used, is melded precisely to ripe
grape tannins for focus and as guarantors of a long future. Hailing from a plot of
vines dating back 122 years, this offers unparalleled vinosity, sumptuous textural
layers and an exotic tang of hoisin and five-spice on the cascading finish. Screwcap.
14.5% alc. **Rating** 97 **To** 2036 $85 NG ✪

ΨΨΨΨΨ Hillside McLaren Vale Shiraz 2014 A wine of exuberant dark fruit, toned and
rippling across a muscular frame sculpted by creamy oak, American and French,
impeccably wrought grape tannins and just enough acidity for zest and poise. This
is the sort of generous wine that wears its heart on its sleeve, oozing a ripeness

seldom found elsewhere. It is all McLaren Vale! The oak, while heady, will be absorbed in time. Screwcap. 14% alc. **Rating** 95 **To** 2034 $45 NG

Griffon's Key Reserve McLaren Vale Grenache 2015 Ruby red, this is nose to palate drinking material bursting with personality: raspberry liqueur, bing cherry, anise and some briar reverberate across a juicy palate, given some fibrous texture with judicious oak and some whole cluster spike. Expansive, pulpy, generous and a testament to the confluence between McLaren Vale turf and lustrous grenache. Screwcap. 14.5% alc. **Rating** 95 **To** 2028 $45 NG

Ironmonger 2014 A blend of shiraz and cabernet, ex old vine material. Damson plum leads the phalanx of dark fruits, before a briar crown of tobacco, sage and mint add to the complexity. Smoked meat, too. True to form, a ferruginous core of tannins cleans up the finish and tows the wine long, tactile and juicy. Screwcap. 14.5% alc. **Rating** 94 **To** 2035 $35 NG

ŶŶŶŶŶ **Basket Pressed Grenache 2015** Rating 93 To 2023 $25 NG ❂
Basket Pressed McLaren Vale Merlot 2015 Rating 93 To 2023 $25 NG ❂
McLaren Vale Grenache Rose 2016 Rating 91 To 2019 $22 NG ❂
Basket Pressed McLaren Vale Shiraz 2015 Rating 91 To 2025 $28 NG
Basket Pressed McLaren Vale Mataro 2015 Rating 91 To 2028 $28 NG

Keith Tulloch Wine ★★★★★

Hermitage Road, Pokolbin, NSW 2320 **Region** Hunter Valley
T (02) 4998 7500 **www.**keithtullochwine.com.au **Open** 7 days 10–5
Winemaker Keith Tulloch, Brendon Kaczorowski **Est.** 1997 **Dozens** 12 000 **Vyds** 9.1ha
Keith Tulloch is, of course, a member of the Tulloch family, which has played a leading role in the Hunter Valley for over a century. Formerly a winemaker at Lindemans and Rothbury Estate, he developed his own label in 1997. There is the same almost obsessive attention to detail, the same almost ascetic intellectual approach, the same refusal to accept anything but the best as that of Jeffrey Grosset. Exports to the UK, the UAE, Indonesia and Japan.

ŶŶŶŶŶ **Museum Release Hunter Valley Semillon 2010** This was the basic release in '10, yet is anything but basic 7 years along the track. It still has the elegance of all Keith Tulloch's releases, the citrus flavours dialled towards, yet still not at, maximum intensity and complexity. Would I have any qualms about drinking my last bottle tonight? None. Screwcap. 11.5% alc. **Rating** 96 **To** 2025 $65 ❂

The Doctor Hunter Valley Shiraz 2014 Named to reflect the 50 years Keith Tulloch's father Dr Harry Tulloch has spent supporting viticulture in the Hunter Valley. Six blocks from the Mars and Kester Vineyards, made by father and son. This nails the vintage, with perfect balance of dark berry fruits supported by spicy/earthy tannins and oak. Screwcap. 13.5% alc. **Rating** 96 **To** 2044 $150

Field of Mars Block 1 Hunter Valley Shiraz 2013 A reminder that '13 was in itself one of the quartet ('07, '11, '13 and '14) of very good Hunter red vintages. This is a great expression of terroir, the back lights coming from the savoury/earthy/leathery characters lying behind and below the blackberry fruits. Adding the parts, you come up with great mouthfeel and superb length. Screwcap. 13.5% alc. **Rating** 96 **To** 2048 $100

Winemakers Selection Marsanne 2016 33 dozen made from 50yo estate vines, completed primary fermentation and mlf in the barrel. It's got a great deal going for it, good now (zesty, vibrant), or in 10 years (honeysuckle, honey), living on its acidity. Screwcap. 11.8% alc. **Rating** 95 **To** 2027 $75

Epogee Winemakers Selection Marsanne Viognier Roussanne 2016 Complex parcels were split into nine lots with equal proportions of tank, barrel and skin contact fermentation. This painstaking vinification has been its own reward, with complex intensity, and every reason to suppose this will blossom over the next 5 years. Screwcap. 13% alc. **Rating** 95 **To** 2022 $40

Field of Mars Block 2A Hunter Valley Semillon 2015 Hand-picked, only 120 dozen made. Delicious now, the fruit flavours snowballing as they run along the palate and gather pace and intensity on the finish. Not an easy vintage in the Hunter Valley. Screwcap. 11% alc. **Rating** 94 **To** 2035 $50

Field of Mars Block 6 Hunter Valley Chardonnay 2015 Well handled barrel-ferment inputs into stone fruit and citrus fruit seem to be it until another taste reveals previously hidden intensity on the finish. The only uncertainty is where the wine is headed. Screwcap. 13.5% alc. **Rating** 94 **To** 2022 $60

Tawarri Vineyard Hunter Valley Shiraz 2015 The vineyard is situated on the slopes of the Great Dividing Range at 460m, the wine matured in French oak for 15 months. It is deeply coloured, with black fruits and peppery notes quite different from most Hunter Valley shiraz. A wine full of questions that can't be answered for a decade. Screwcap. 14.4% alc. **Rating** 94 **To** 2035 $48

Museum Release The Kester Hunter Valley Shiraz 2009 A good example of the tenacity of Hunter Valley shiraz, for the colour is still a bright crimson, the palate lively and fresh, throwing you back to the fragrant bouquet. Overall, juicy and fresh, and not in a hurry to go anywhere. Screwcap. 13.8% alc. **Rating** 94 **To** 2029 $90

ΨΨΨΨΨ Hunter Valley Semillon 2016 Rating 93 To 2029 $30
Field of Mars Block 1 Hunter Valley Shiraz 2014 Rating 92 To 2034 $100
Hunter Valley Botrytis Semillon 2015 Rating 92 To 2019 $38

Kellermeister   ★★★★★

Barossa Valley Highway, Lyndoch, SA 5351 **Region** Barossa Valley
T (08) 8524 4303 **www**.kellermeister.com.au **Open** 7 days 9.30–5.30
Winemaker Mark Pearce **Est.** 1976 **Dozens** 30 000 **Vyds** 20ha

Since joining Kellermeister from Wirra Wirra in 2009, Mark Pearce has successfully worked through challenging times to ensure the survival of the winery and its brands; and upon the retirement of founders Ralph and Val Jones in late '12, the Pearce family acquired the business. Surrounded by a young, close-knit team, Mark is committed to continuing to build on the legacy that the founders began more than 40 years ago. His winemaking focus is on continuing to preserve Kellermeister's best wines, while introducing new wines, made with the intention of expressing the purity of the provenance of the Barossa. Exports to the US, Canada, Switzerland, Denmark, Israel, Taiwan, China and Japan.

ΨΨΨΨΨ **The Wombat General Hand Picked Eden Valley Riesling 2016** From the best riesling block on the Fechner Vineyard, hand-picked, whole-bunch pressed with free-run juice (450l/t). Beautiful wine, the palate with exceptional intensity and purity, the lemon/lime fruit with a jewelled crown of crunchy acidity. The longer you hold the wine in the mouth, the more impressive it becomes. A ridiculously low price. Screwcap. 12.5% alc. **Rating** 97 **To** 2036 $22 ❂

Black Sash Barossa Valley Shiraz 2015 100yo vines at Ebenezer, matured in French hogsheads (75% new). A striking crimson–purple, it takes the meaning of full-bodied shiraz to the extreme, its raison d'être sombre black fruits on the edge of bitterness, but not tripping the wire. The French oak is very evident, but I have no fears for the wine's future, which stretches out decades ahead. Screwcap. 14.5% alc. **Rating** 97 **To** 2045 $65 ❂

Ancestor Vine Stonegarden Vineyard Eden Valley Grenache 2013 The vineyard was planted circa 1868 with a grenache field blend. The wine has spent a very long time in large oak vats, and was only recently bottled with Amorim's top of the range cork and a super-heavy bottle, all inspired by Mark Pearce's time living and working in Chateauneuf. This is high quality grenache, with structure and texture ex tannins not far short of old vine shiraz, the flavours strictly red fruit grenache. Cork. 14% alc. **Rating** 97 **To** 2043 $175

ΨΨΨΨΨ **The Meister Eden Valley Shiraz 2015** From vines planted in 1906 on the Fechner Vineyard, matured in new French oak. Its deep colour is no more than expected from its parentage and very limited production; it is a newborn, and will absorb the majority of the French oak that surrounds it now, likely taking a decade or two to do so. Screwcap. 14% alc. **Rating** 96 **To** 2050 $250

The Firstborn Single Vineyard Threefold Farm Barossa Valley Shiraz 2014 From the Pearce family home vineyard, Threefold Farm. It doesn't pay to rush in and start describing the wine, for the oak and the substantial ripe tannins don't join the party until the back palate, where a wine that is Kellermeister style changes gear, with savoury black fruits, plum, licorice and tannins all arriving. Screwcap. 14% alc. **Rating** 96 **To** 2039 $45 ✪

The Pious Pioneer Dry Grown Barossa Shiraz 2014 Matured in new and used barrels. Unfurls its suite of flavours as it moves across the mouth, with a crosscut of tannins and oak intersecting with the black fruits. Medium–bodied, and perfectly balanced. Screwcap. 14.5% alc. **Rating** 95 **To** 2034 $27 ✪

Barossa Vineyards Shiraz 2014 From a patchwork of vineyards spread across the Barossa and Eden Valleys, matured in French hogsheads. Has retained exceptional colour, and has that wild black fruits/savoury character of the Kellermeister wines that I find so attractive. One of the bargains of the year. Screwcap. 14.5% alc. **Rating** 94 **To** 2034 $20 ✪

🍷🍷🍷🍷🍷 **Ralph's Ensemble Barossa Shiraz Cabernet 2013** Rating 92 To 2028 $27
The Funk Wagon GSM Barossa 2014 Rating 92 To 2029 $27
Barossa Vineyards Shiraz 2013 Rating 91 To 2028 $20 ✪

Kennedy   ★★★★☆

Maple Park, 224 Wallenjoe Road, Corop, Vic 3559 (postal) **Region** Heathcote
T (03) 5484 8293 **www.**kennedyvintners.com.au **Open** Not
Winemaker Sandro Mosele (Contract) **Est.** 2002 **Dozens** 1000 **Vyds** 29.2ha
Having been farmers in the Colbinabbin area of Heathcote for 27 years, John and Patricia Kennedy were on the spot when a prime piece of red Cambrian soil on the east-facing slope of Mt Camel Range became available for purchase. They planted 20ha of shiraz in 2002. As they gained knowledge of the intricate differences within the site, and worked with contract winemaker Sandro Mosele, further plantings of shiraz, tempranillo and mourvedre followed in '07. The Shiraz is made in small open fermenters, using indigenous yeasts and gentle pigeage before being taken to French oak (20% new) for 12 months' maturation prior to bottling.

🍷🍷🍷🍷🍷 **Cambria Heathcote Shiraz 2014** Hand-picked, destemmed, wild yeast–open fermented with a small percentage of whole bunches (less than 15%); after mlf in French barriques (15% new), the best barrels selected for this wine and matured for 18 months. A richly textured and flavoured full-bodied shiraz with multiple folds of velvety flavours tracking the bouquet's red and black fruit aromas and spices. The moderate alcohol allows the weaving of the tapestry without any sense of undue weight or heat. Diam. 13.5% alc. **Rating** 95 **To** 2044 $32 ✪

Pink Hills Heathcote Rose 2016 Mourvedre, hand-picked, a short time on skins, fermented in used French oak. Pale salmon hue; it is every bit as complex and savoury as its vinification (and variety) would suggest. Dry and very spicy, but also fruity. Bargain++. Screwcap. 13.5% alc. **Rating** 94 **To** 2020 $20 ✪

Heathcote Shiraz 2014 Differs from its Cambria sibling only by no use of whole bunches and 12 months in oak, not 18. The colour is excellent, and the wine is alive from start to finish with its mix of red and black cherry fruit, sweet tannins and lively spices. Screwcap. 13.5% alc. **Rating** 94 **To** 2030 $25 ✪

🍷🍷🍷🍷🍷 **Henrietta Heathcote Shiraz 2015** Rating 90 To 2025 $20 ✪

Kensington Wines   ★★★★

1590 Highlands Road, Whiteheads Creek, Vic 3660 **Region** Upper Goulburn
T (03) 5796 9155 **www.**kensingtonwines.com.au **Open** Sun 11–5
Winemaker Nina Stocker, Frank Bonic **Est.** 2010 **Dozens** 20 000 **Vyds** 4ha
This is the venture of husband and wife Anddy and Kandy Xu, born and raised in China, but now resident in Australia, who have built up Kensington Wines over the past six years. They have created a broad portfolio of wines by sourcing grapes and wines, mostly from regions across Vic, but also SA. While the primary market is China (and other Asian countries), the

wines have not been made with residual sugar sweetness, and are also sold in Australia. Kandy and Anddy's purchase of the Rocky Passes Vineyard (and cellar door) in the Upper Goulburn region in 2015 was a significant development in terms of their commitment to quality Australian wine, as was securing the services of winemaker Nina Stocker, daughter of Dr John Stocker, former chairman of the Grape and Wine Research and Development Corporation. Kandy has broadened her experience and wine qualifications by completing the WSET Diploma, and undertaking a vintage at Brown Brothers. She was co-founder of the Chinese Wine Association of Australia and continues as the chair. She has translated wine books into Mandarin, including my *Top 100 Wineries of Australia*.

ȲȲȲȲȲ **Benalla Single Vineyard Shiraz 2015** Fermented with a combination of cultured and wild yeast in open fermenters, before maturation over 12–16 months in used French oak. This wine sings a soprano of violet and roses. The palate is impactful and warm, with the alcohol levels pushing the envelope of excess. Satsuma plum and kirsch flavours ooze through the wine's midriff, only to be swept up by well managed, tightly meshed tannins. Well made. Screwcap. 15.5% alc. **Rating** 92 **To** 2032 $65 NG

Barossa Valley Shiraz 2015 Barossa's Christmas cake spice, black plum and cherry notes are swept across a bold palate by dusty, pliant tannins. Maturation for 12–16 months in an arsenal of new and used American oak combines with the regional voice to confer a ring of dried sage and eucalyptus to the finish. Cork. 15.5% alc. **Rating** 92 **To** 2032 $45 NG

Goulburn Valley Shiraz 2014 A wine that holds its plummy fruit and warmth well, all bound by a fine weave of slinky grape tannins and cedary oak pillars. The wine saw an elevage in French oak, 20% of which was new, for 18–20 months. Bright crimson and bursting with energy, this will develop well. Screwcap. 14.7% alc. **Rating** 92 **To** 2032 $32 NG

Heathcote Shiraz 2015 This wine has a chocolatey intensity that smacks of Heathcote. A fully extracted phalanx of dark fruit flavours and charred meat is slung across earthy, tightly furled coffee grind tannins, an echo of acidity and plenty of lavish oak. The only caveat is the alcohol. Screwcap. 15.5% alc. **Rating** 91 **To** 2025 $35 NG

Mundarlo Vineyard Gundagai Shiraz 2014 Plenty of buoyant blueberry, violet, cinnamon spice and black pepper grind flavours here, laced across finely wrought tannins and bright acidity. Maturation in 2yo French oak has imparted some textural breadth and a hint of bitter chocolate. Nicely put together. Screwcap. 14.5% alc. **Rating** 91 **To** 2026 $28 NG

Moppity Vineyard Hilltops Cabernet Sauvignon 2014 Bell pepper, blackcurrant and vivid cigar box aromas recall a classic, medium-bodied claret. An edge of brick is creeping across the crimson hue. The wine is highly savoury, with 18 months in an even split of used and new French oak providing a further drying agent to the bow of lengthening, astringent tannins. Screwcap. 13% alc. **Rating** 91 **To** 2026 $28 NG

Kerrigan + Berry ★★★★★

PO Box 221, Cowaramup, WA 6284 **Region** South West Australia
T (08) 9755 6046 **www.**kerriganandberry.com.au **Open** At Hay Shed Hill
Winemaker Michael Kerrigan, Gavin Berry **Est.** 2007 **Dozens** 1200
Owners Michael Kerrigan and Gavin Berry have been making wine in WA for a combined period of over 40 years, and say they have been most closely associated with the two varieties that in their opinion define WA: riesling and cabernet sauvignon. This is strictly a weekend and after-hours venture, separate from their respective roles as chief winemakers at Hay Shed Hill and West Cape Howe. They have focused on what is important, and explain, 'We have spent a total of zero hours on marketing research, and no consultants have been injured in the making of these wines.' Exports to the UK, the US, Denmark, Singapore and China.

ΨΨΨΨΨ **Frankland River Shiraz 2014** From a single vineyard. Fragrant black fruits, multi-spices, licorice and a subnote of tar presage a totally distinguished and focused cool palate, cool in the sense of grapes that have been cool-grown and picked at optimal ripeness, in turn reflected by the sheer intensity of the wine. Screwcap. 14% alc. **Rating** 97 **To** 2044 $35 **☉**

ΨΨΨΨΨ **Mt Barker Great Southern Riesling 2016** The grapes come from the large Langton Vineyard planted in the early '70s, and revered for the quality of its grapes. The wine is at once delicate yet intense, airy yet focused, citrussy yet minerally. These contradictions will all resolve themselves over the next 5–10+ years, richly rewarding patience. Screwcap. 12% alc. **Rating** 95 **To** 2029 $28 **☉**

Kidman Wines

13713 Riddoch Highway, Coonawarra, SA 5263 **Region** Coonawarra
T (08) 8736 5071 **www**.kidmanwines.com.au **Open** 7 days 10–5
Winemaker Sid Kidman **Est.** 1984 **Dozens** 6000 **Vyds** 17.2ha
Sid Kidman planted the first vines on the property in 1971, and has been managing the vineyard ever since. Over the years it has grown to include cabernet sauvignon, shiraz, riesling and sauvignon blanc. The cellar door is housed in the old stables on the property; they were built in 1859 and are a great link with the district's history. Susie and Sid have recently been joined by their son George, who becomes the fourth generation of the Kidman family to be involved with the property. Exports to Malaysia and China.

ΨΨΨΨ **Coonawarra Shiraz 2014** You have to scratch the surface to find the varietal character, hidden as it is beneath the menthol/gum leaf regionality, American oak, and the warm breath of 15% alcohol, but it's there, with spicy, peppery aromas (and flavours) and dark-berried fruit that runs through the palate. The finish is a touch rough and ready, but overall there's some unsophisticated appeal here. Screwcap. **Rating** 89 **To** 2021 $20 SC
Coonawarra Cabernet Sauvignon 2014 No doubting this wine's provenance from the bouquet: blackcurrant and mulberry, limestone and choc-mint are pure Coonawarra cabernet. A dash of French oak sits easily. On tasting, all those characters are present, and welcome, but the structure lacks definition. The flavours wallow around, and the tannin is a little broad. Just less than the sum of its parts. Screwcap. 14% alc. **Rating** 89 **To** 2023 $22 SC

Kilikanoon Wines

Penna Lane, Penwortham, SA 5453 **Region** Clare Valley
T (08) 8843 4206 **www**.kilikanoon.com.au **Open** 7 days 11–5
Winemaker Kevin Mitchell, Barry Kooij **Est.** 1997 **Dozens** 90000 **Vyds** 117.14ha
Kilikanoon has travelled in the fast lane since winemaker Kevin Mitchell established it in 1997 on the foundation of 6ha of vines he owns with father Mort. With the aid of investors, its 80000-dozen production comes from over 300ha of estate-owned vineyards, and access to the best grapes from a total of 2266ha across SA. Between 2013 and early '14 all links between Kilikanoon and Seppeltsfield were ended; the sale of Kilikanoon's share in Seppeltsfield, together with the sale of Kilikanoon's Crowhurst Vineyard in the Barossa Valley, led to the purchase by Kilikanoon of the winery which it had previously leased, and purchase of the Mount Surmon Vineyard. Exports to most major markets.

ΨΨΨΨΨ **Attunga 1865 Clare Valley Shiraz 2013** The 150+yo vines are among the oldest in the world; destemmed, open-fermented with cultured yeast, matured in French oak (30% new) for 18 months. Exceptionally youthful; blackberry fruit and oak spice, licorice and earth are some of the strings of this Stradivarius violin. The tannin strings are, as always, all-important in providing texture to the structure, and also in their contribution to flavour. The French oak is evident, but is totally in balance. Screwcap. 14.5% alc. **Rating** 97 **To** 2053 $250
Revelation Shiraz 2012 Revelation is the best wine of each vintage of Kilikanoon, and could come from any of the estate vineyards in the Clare or

Barossa regions. Mt Surmon is just within the Clare Valley GI boundary, and was the source of this superb wine. Destemmed, open-fermented with cultured yeast, matured for 20 months in French oak (50% new). Dense colour, still to show much change; incredibly powerful and focused. Midnight black fruits have savoury handmaidens of forest floor, licorice and some recognition of the French oak in which it spent (only) 18 months. Perfect line, length and balance. Screwcap. 14.5% alc. **Rating** 97 **To** 2052 $550

♥♥♥♥♥ **Crowhurst Reserve Barossa Valley Shiraz 2013** Destemmed, open-fermented, matured for 20 months in new French oak. This is Kilikanoon's flagship Barossa Valley wine, proudly full-bodied, and is the only wine matured in 100% new French oak. It has a very complex texture and flavour profile, and it will be at least 10 years before all the components, most obviously the oak, develop into a harmonious palate. Screwcap. 14.5% alc. **Rating** 96 **To** 2043 $120

Miracle Hill McLaren Vale Shiraz 2013 Destemmed, open-fermented with cultured yeast, matured for 20 months in French oak (50% new). Tasting Revelation, Attunga, Crowhurst Reserve, Oracle and this wine next to each other lays out the differences of flavour and structure in high relief – the sheer power of this full-bodied group might disguise some of the differences that would be apparent if tasted separately. Mind you, this wine does shriek McLaren Vale with its dark chocolate and the glossy texture of its super-abundant fruits. It's the easiest to appreciate now, and will develop most quickly, all things being relative. Screwcap. 14.5% alc. **Rating** 96 **To** 2038 $80

Oracle Clare Valley Shiraz 2013 From the estate Golden Hillside and Mt Surmon vineyards. All of Kevin Mitchell's cellaring recommendations are very short: this is the longest, with a 12-year frame. This is the most savoury, and in some ways, the most refined, of the '13 super-premium shiraz releases. It brings red, purple and black fruits into the fray, the tannins polished, the French oak balanced and integrated. Screwcap. 14.5% alc. **Rating** 96 **To** 2033 $80

Baudinet Blend Clare Valley Grenache Shiraz Mataro 2014 A 50/40/10% blend, matured in French oak (15% new) for 18 months. Deep, bright crimson-purple, exceptional for this blend. Without question the best GSM ex the Clare Valley, the three varieties welded together in a great display of red and black fruits on the medium to full-bodied palate, the supporting tannins of high quality and in perfect balance. Will live for decades. Screwcap. 14.5% alc. **Rating** 96 **To** 2039 $55 ✪

Tregea Reserve Clare Valley Cabernet Sauvignon 2013 Only produced in the best vintages is one of the most hackneyed mistruths (yes, Donald) in the game, but it's true here. Sourced from the estate property at Penwortham, production less than 300 dozen of what is Kilikanoon's finest cabernet. The colour looks as if it were bottled yesterday, and the river of cassis flowing between the headlands of tannin is equally youthful. Screwcap. 14% alc. **Rating** 96 **To** 2030 $80

Mort's Block Watervale Riesling 2016 Like all Kilikanoon's rieslings, no-frills to the vinification, just attention to detail. Incongruously, it is a blend of three vineyards. The bouquet owes as much to minerally notes as to citrus fruit, and the palate duly brings structure and length to the lemon/lime flavours and firm finish. Screwcap. 12.5% alc. **Rating** 95 **To** 2031 $25 ✪

Testament Barossa Valley Shiraz 2015 Fermented with cultured yeast, matured for 20 months, 30% in tank with staves, and 55% in French oak (15% new). There's ample, but not excessive, oak, and the wine has layer upon layer of blackberry fruit on the full-bodied but balanced palate. Screwcap. 14.5% alc. **Rating** 95 **To** 2035 $44

Parable McLaren Vale Shiraz 2014 Destemmed, open-fermented with cultured yeast, matured for 18 months in French oak (15% new). The regional signature of McLaren Vale is as immediate as it is clear, with dark chocolate wrapped around the fruit in a public demonstration of its love for shiraz. It's hard not to get in on the act; this is a very drinkable medium to full-bodied wine now. Screwcap. 14.5% alc. **Rating** 95 **To** 2030 $44

Kelly 1932 Clare Valley Grenache 2013 Machine-harvested, open-fermented, cultured yeast, matured for 15 months in used French oak. Why machine harvest a small single vineyard such as this? It is head and shoulders above all other Clare Valley grenache, with a silky smooth, but focused, palate of delicious red and maraschino cherries. It's expensive, but you can see why. Screwcap. 14.5% alc. **Rating** 95 **To** 2025 $120

Mr Hyde Bliss Clare Valley Riesling 2016 From the Trillians Hill Vineyard, wild-yeast fermented free-run juice. The intensely juicy fruit and polished acidity are perfectly balanced and have well above average length, leaving the mouth fresh. The comic strip label will appeal to some (I assume), but not everyone – I'm the old fart disliking it. Screwcap. 12.5% alc. **Rating** 94 **To** 2026 $23 **☉**

Killerman's Run Clare Valley Riesling 2016 Despite the same alcohol as Golden Hillside, is very fresh and lively in the mouth following a bouquet with flowery notes and a hint of spice; lemon sherbet flavours fit neatly into its elegant palate. Screwcap. 12.5% alc. **Rating** 94 **To** 2029 $20 **☉**

Exodus Barossa Valley Shiraz 2015 Cultured yeast, matured in French oak (30% new) for 20 months. Good colour; the fragrant red and black fruits of the bouquet and palate are neatly framed by well handled oak; the tannins are fine, and complete a wine with a long drinking span. Screwcap. 14.5% alc. **Rating** 94 **To** 2035 $40

Covenant Clare Valley Shiraz 2014 Machine-harvested, destemmed, open-fermented with cultured yeast, matured for 18 months in French oak (30% new). The bouquet is complex, with a spicy charcuterie edge, the palate also complex with a firm savoury thrust to the black fruits and licorice. That firmness is a trifle sharp on the first encounter, but goes on a 180° change as it morphs into fresh dark fruits, promising much for the future. Screwcap. 14.5% alc. **Rating** 94 **To** 2034 $44

ŢŢŢŢŢ Second Fiddle Clare Valley Grenache Rose 2016 Rating 93 To 2018 $22 **☉**
Mr Hyde Le Petit Lapin Syrah 2015 Rating 93 To 2025 $25 **☉**
Blocks Road Clare Valley Cabernet Sauvignon 2013 Rating 93 To 2028 $33
Skilly Valley Clare Valley Pinot Gris 2016 Rating 91 To 2017 $25
Golden Hillside Watervale Riesling 2016 Rating 90 To 2026 $20 **☉**
Mr Hyde High & Dry Mourvedre 2015 Rating 90 To 2023 $25

Killara Estate   ★★★★☆

773 Warburton Highway, Seville East, Vic 3139 **Region** Yarra Valley
T (03) 5961 5877 **www.**killaraestate.com.au **Open** Wed–Sun 11–5
Winemaker Travis Bush, Mac Forbes **Est.** 1997 **Dozens** 7000 **Vyds** 29.5ha
Owned by Leo and Gina Palazzo, the Sunnyside Vineyard is the new home of Killara Estate. It features the Racers and Rascals Cafe and cellar door, enjoying sweeping views of the valley and nearby mountain ranges. The vineyard is planted to pinot noir (10ha), chardonnay (6.5ha), pinot gris (3.8ha), nebbiolo (3ha), shiraz (2.3ha) and sangiovese (1.2ha). Exports to China.

ŢŢŢŢŢ Palazzo Yarra Valley Nebbiolo 2013 Estate-grown, foot-stomped, transferred to an old oak vat for fermentation, matured for 20 months in barrel (no detail given, but likely used). The colour is exceptional for nebbiolo, bright garnet; the bouquet exudes rose petals, spices and a hint of Campari. The red fruits of the palate rest on a bed of civilised tannins. Right out of left field. Cork. 13.5% alc. **Rating** 95 **To** 2028 $50

ŢŢŢŢŢ Yarra Valley Chardonnay 2015 Rating 91 To 2020 $35

Killiecrankie Wines   ★★★★

103 Soldier Road, Ravenswood, Vic 3453 **Region** Bendigo
T (03) 5435 3155 **www.**killiecrankiewines.com **Open** W'ends 11–6
Winemaker John Monteath **Est.** 2000 **Dozens** 400 **Vyds** 1ha

John Monteath moved to the Bendigo region in 1999 to pursue his interest in viticulture and winemaking, and while helping to establish the vineyard from which the grapes are sourced, gained experience at Water Wheel, Heathcote Estate, Balgownie and BlackJack. The vineyard is planted to four shiraz clones, and is the backbone of the Bendigo wine. The small crop is hand-picked, with the resultant wines made in true garagiste style. Small parcels of premium fruit are also sourced from meticulously tended vineyards in Bendigo and Heathcote.

Crankie Pearl 2016 This is a textural and highly aromatic wine of peach, apricot, marzipan and dried straw aromas. These slink along a palate of dutifully handled phenolic grip and a waft of barrel-fermented curd, vanilla and truffle notes. Mid-weighted and easygoing, with slippery length and a punchy persistence of flavour. Made up of 60% viognier, 20% marsanne and 20% roussanne as a worthy homage to the Rhône. Screwcap. 13.5% alc. **Rating** 92 $23 **To** 2019 NG ✪

Kimbarra Wines   ★★★★☆
422 Barkly Street, Ararat, Vic 3377 **Region** Grampians
T (03) 5352 2238 **www.**kimbarrawines.com.au **Open** By appt
Winemaker Peter Leeke, Ian MacKenzie **Est.** 1990 **Dozens** 200 **Vyds** 11ha
Peter Leeke has 9ha of shiraz and 2ha of riesling, varieties that have proven best suited to the Grampians region. The particularly well made, estate-grown wines deserve a wider audience.

Great Western Riesling 2016 The back label speaks of 'the full middle pallet' (sic), but I am blown away by its length and the trumpeting aftertaste, drawing saliva from the mouth. Razor sharp natural acidity drives the unsweetened lime juice flavours. Great stuff. Screwcap. 12% alc. **Rating** 95 **To** 2031 $28 ✪

Great Western Shiraz 2010 **Rating** 93 **To** 2025 $30
Eric Great Western Sparkling Shiraz 2008 **Rating** 90 **To** 2017 $32 TS

Kimbolton Wines   ★★★★☆
The Winehouse Cellar Door, 1509 Langhorne Creek Road, Langhorne Creek, SA 5255
Region Langhorne Creek
T (08) 8537 3002 **www.**kimboltonwines.com.au **Open** 7 days 10–5
Winemaker Contract **Est.** 1998 **Dozens** 1200 **Vyds** 54.8ha
The Kimbolton property originally formed part of the Potts Bleasdale estate; in 1946 it was acquired by Henry and Thelma Case, parents of current owner, Len Case. The grapes from the vineyard plantings (cabernet sauvignon, shiraz, chardonnay, carignan and montepulciano) are sold to leading wineries, with small amounts retained for the Kimbolton label. The name comes from a medieval town in Bedfordshire, UK, from which some of Len's wife Judy's ancestors emigrated.

The Rifleman Langhorne Creek Shiraz 2013 Estate-grown, destemmed and crushed, small batch open-fermented, 7–8 days on skins, hand-plunged three times daily, mlf completed in barrel, the best selected and matured for 14 months in new American oak, then 6 months in French oak, 45 dozen made. This has the edge of elegance, the X-factor, that is missing from the '14. The colour is still in full crimson-purple form, the palate with some spicy, bitter chocolate notes, and excellent tannins. A pair of most unusual wines that must have cost a fortune to produce. Screwcap. 14.5% alc. **Rating** 95 **To** 2044 $50
The Rifleman Langhorne Creek Shiraz 2014 46 dozen made. A super-opulent style built from the ground up. It doesn't go OTT, and offers hedonistic pleasure, especially with wagyu beef or similar. So much effort deserves points, even if the American oak is a constant companion. It will live off its fruit for many years to come. Screwcap. 14.3% alc. **Rating** 94 **To** 2044 $50
Special Release The L.G. Langhorne Creek Cabernet Sauvignon 2010
From the Fig Tree Block planted '88, the 100+yo fig tree on the border of the vineyard, only pressings used, matured for 32 months in new French oak. It has to be an utterly exceptional wine base to stand up to 32 months in new oak,

and it must have been an octave or similar miniature barrel, because a barrique holds 22 dozen, and only 13 dozen (plus 4 bottles) were made. So was the wine exceptional? Almost. Cork. 14.5% alc. **Rating** 94 To 2040 $100

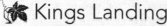 The Rifleman Cabernet Sauvignon 2012 Rating 93 To 2027 $50
The Rifleman Cabernet Sauvignon 2014 Rating 92 To 2034 $50
Cabernet Sauvignon Shiraz 2014 Rating 92 To 2029 $25 ✪
Fig Tree Cabernet Sauvignon 2014 Rating 91 To 2029 $25
Block 9 Langhorne Creek Chardonnay 2016 Rating 90 To 2022 $25
K Block Langhorne Creek Pinot Gris 2015 Rating 90 To 2017 $18 ✪
House Block Langhorne Creek Shiraz 2015 Rating 90 To 2025 $25

🍃 Kings Landing ★★★★

9 Collins Place, Denmark, WA 6333 (postal) **Region** Great Southern
T 0432 312 918 **www**.kingslandingwines.com.au **Open** Not
Winemaker Coby Ladwig, Luke Eckersley **Est.** 2015 **Dozens** 2500 **Vyds** 9ha
Winemakers Coby Ladwig and Luke Eckersley have accumulated many years making wines for others, so this is in some ways a busman's holiday. But it's also a serious business, with 9ha of vineyard plantings (3ha of chardonnay and 2ha each of shiraz, riesling and cabernet sauvignon) making this much more than a virtual winery. I have the feeling it would be a good idea to watch this space.

♟♟♟♟♟ Mount Barker Riesling 2016 A riesling with above-average weight and depth to its aromas and flavours when compared with some current vintage Clare Valley wines. Lime, with hints of pineapple, fills the mouth, acidity providing balance and length. Screwcap. 12% alc. **Rating** 92 To 2026 $32

Kirrihill Wines ★★★★

12 Main North Road, Clare, SA 5453 **Region** Clare Valley
T (08) 8842 4087 **www**.kirrihillwines.com.au **Open** 7 days 10–4
Winemaker Will Shields **Est.** 1998 **Dozens** 35 000
Kirrihill was founded in 1998 in the picturesque Clare Valley. Grapes are sourced from specially selected parcels of Kirrihill's 600ha of managed vineyards, as well as the Edwards and Stanway families' properties in the region. The Regional Range comprises blends from across the region, while the Vineyard Selection Series aims to elicit a sense of place from the chosen vineyards. The Alternative range features Fiano, Vermentino, Montepulciano, Nebbiolo, Tempranillo and Sangiovese. Exports to all major markets.

♟♟♟♟♟ E.B.'s The Squire Clare Valley Shiraz 2014 The Squire is seriously full-bodied, dispensing rich and complex forest berry and spice aromas and flavours without giving a backward glance; nor is he concerned about the alcohol or tannins that give the wine its power. Screwcap. 14.9% alc. **Rating** 94 To 2034 $45

♟♟♟♟♟ E.B.'s The Settler Clare Valley Riesling 2016 Rating 93 To 2021 $35
Regional Selection Clare Valley Riesling 2016 Rating 92 To 2031 $16 ✪
E.B.'s The Peacemaker Clare Valley Shiraz 2013 Rating 90 To 2028 $65
Regional Selection Clare Valley Cabernet Sauvignon 2015 Rating 90
To 2025 $18 ✪

KJB Wine Group ★★★☆

2 Acri Street, Prestons, NSW 2170 (postal) **Region** McLaren Vale
T 0409 570 694 **Open** Not
Winemaker Kurt Brill **Est.** 2008 **Dozens** 550
KJB Wine Group (formerly Oenotria Vintners) is the venture of Kurt Brill, who began his involvement in the wine industry in 2003, largely through the encouragement of his wife Gillian. He commenced the wine marketing course at the University of Adelaide, but ultimately switched from that to the winemaking degree at CSU. His main business is the

distribution company Grace James Fine Wines, but he also runs a virtual winery operation, purchasing cabernet and shiraz from McLaren Vale. Exports to the UK and The Netherlands.

ŶŶŶŶŶ **Land of the Vines McLaren Vale Shiraz 2015** Complexity is the first name of this wine; from a single vineyard and matured for 22 months in used French and American oak. Spicy foresty notes are woven through blackberry fruits in a carapace of dark chocolate and fine-ground tannins, the balance likewise impressive. Screwcap. 14.5% alc. **Rating** 94 **To** 2030 $25 ●

Knappstein   ★★★★★

2 Pioneer Avenue, Clare, SA 5453 **Region** Clare Valley
T (08) 8841 2100 **www.**knappstein.com.au **Open** Mon–Fri 9–5, w'ends 11–4
Winemaker Glenn Barry **Est.** 1969 **Dozens** 40 000 **Vyds** 114ha

Knappstein's full name is Knappstein Enterprise Winery & Brewery, reflecting its history before being acquired by Petaluma, then part of Lion Nathan, and now Accolade. Despite these corporate chess board moves, wine quality has remained excellent. The substantial mature estate vineyards in prime locations supply grapes both for the Knappstein brand and for wider Petaluma use. Exports to all major markets.

ŶŶŶŶŶ **Bryksy's Hill Vineyard Watervale Riesling 2016** Like the Ackland Vineyard, planted in '69. While finely structured, it has energy and intensity to its perfumed bouquet and long, lively palate. Its perfect acidity freshens the mouth now, and will sustain the long-term development of this classic Clare riesling. Screwcap. 11.5% alc. **Rating** 96 **To** 2036 $30

Slate Creek Vineyard Watervale Riesling 2016 Planted in '74. Like its siblings, crystal white at this stage. You become aware of the innate power of this wine on the finish and aftertaste – here its powerful acidity is on display, albeit with considerable citrus-driven fruit. Screwcap. 12% alc. **Rating** 95 **To** 2036 $30

Clare Valley Shiraz 2015 The harmonious bouquet promises an easy ride, and the palate duly delivers just that. Dark cherry fruit provides the core of the wine, its juicy mouthfeel very attractive; spicy tannins promote texture and structure alongside the fruit. Screwcap. 13.5% alc. **Rating** 95 **To** 2030 $22 ●

The Mayor's Vineyard Clare Valley Shiraz 2014 The fragrance of the bouquet tells you of what is to come: a vibrantly fresh, only just medium-bodied palate with red fruits and superfine tannins, oak barely worth mentioning. In the context of the Clare Valley, pure magic. Screwcap. 13.5% alc. **Rating** 95 **To** 2034 $46

Enterprise Vineyard Clare Valley Cabernet Sauvignon 2014 Has excellent crimson-purple colour, an expressive cabernet bouquet and a complex palate. The perfectly ripened fruit (and linked) tannins provide focus and power to the palate and its quality French oak, with no semblance of eye-watering alcohol. Screwcap. 13.5% alc. **Rating** 95 **To** 2035 $40

Ackland Vineyard Watervale Riesling 2016 From the estate vineyard planted in '69. A very well balanced and long palate with lime, lemon and green apple flavours intersecting with crisp, minerally acidity. Only the X-factor is missing. Screwcap. 12.5% alc. **Rating** 94 **To** 2031 $30

The Insider Limited Release Clare Valley Riesling 2016 Picked later than normal, crushed, 48 hours skin contact, wild-yeast fermented. A very complex wine, its 5.5g/l of residual sugar swallowed by the texture and semi-tropical fruits. Full of interest. Screwcap. 12.5% alc. **Rating** 94 **To** 2023 $28

ŶŶŶŶŶ **Clare Valley Cabernet Sauvignon 2015 Rating** 93 **To** 2030 $22
Clare Valley Riesling 2016 Rating 92 **To** 2023 $20 ●
The Insider Limited Release Clare Valley Shiraz Malbec 2016 Rating 90 **To** 2020 $28

Knee Deep Wines

160 Johnson Road, Wilyabrup, WA 6280 **Region** Margaret River
T (08) 0755 6776 www.kneedeepwines.com.au **Open** 7 days 10–5
Winemaker Bruce Dukes **Est.** 2000 **Dozens** 7500 **Vyds** 20ha
Perth surgeon and veteran yachtsman Phil Childs and wife Sue have planted their property in Wilyabrup to chardonnay (3.2ha), sauvignon blanc (4ha), semillon (1.48ha), chenin blanc (4ha), cabernet sauvignon (6.34ha) and shiraz (1.24ha). The name, Knee Deep Wines, was inspired by the passion and commitment needed to produce premium wine and as a tongue-in-cheek acknowledgement of jumping in 'boots and all' during a testing time in the wine industry, the grape glut building more or less in tune with the venture. Exports to Germany.

Kim's Limited Release Margaret River Chardonnay 2014 This has so much flavour and power packed in it will stop you in your tracks. And yet it manages to harness all that power with an air of lightness, the fine line of acidity driving through barrel-ferment nutty, leesy notes, savoury through and through. A classy wine. Screwcap. 13.5% alc. **Rating** 96 **To** 2024 $45 JF ✪
Kelsea's Limited Release Margaret River Cabernet Sauvignon 2013 This will last for years. It opens up now with all its varietal and regional flavours from currants, mulberries and blackberries to eucalypt and more earthy tones. Also meshed in neatly are oak spice, pepper, curry leaves and florals, with decisive tannins on its full frame. Screwcap. 14.5% alc. **Rating** 95 **To** 2036 $65 JF

Premium Margaret River Shiraz 2015 Rating 93 **To** 2025 $28 JF
Margaret River Sauvignon Blanc 2016 Rating 92 **To** 2020 $22 JF ✪
Premium Cabernet Sauvignon 2015 Rating 92 **To** 2026 $28 JF

 # Koerner Wine

935 Mintaro Road, Leasingham, SA 5452 **Region** Clare Valley
T 0408 895 341 **www.**koernerwine.com.au **Open** By appt
Winemaker Damon Koerner **Est.** 2014 **Dozens** 2000 **Vyds** 60ha
Brothers Damon and Jonathan (Jono) Koerner grew up in the Clare Valley, but flew the coop to work and study in other parts of Australia and abroad. The substantial vineyards had been owned and managed by their parents, Anthony and Christine Koerner, for 35 years, but they have passed ownership and management of the vineyards on to their sons. While the major part of the crop is sold to other wineries, in 2016, Damon made 11 wines, a major point of difference from other Clare Valley wineries being the use of synonyms for well known varieties, as well as adopting Australian name usage, turning the world upside down with left-field winemaking practices exemplified by the 2016 Watervale Riesling. The 2016 Rolle Vermentino has the nomenclature trail to follow as well as ceramic egg winemaking.

Watervale Riesling 2016 This rather austere riesling is a result of 12 hours of skin contact, ambient yeast fermentation in tank and ceramic eggs, followed by extended lees handling to build up crunch and texture. Quince, candied citrus and quinine notes are strung across riesling's high acidity and the phenolic bite of the work with the grape skins. The end impression is one of texture and savoury bitterness. Screwcap. 12% alc. **Rating** 94 **To** 2024 $27 NG ✪
Rolle Vermentino 2016 Vermentino is the name used in Sardinia, pigato in Liguria, and rolle in Provence. Thicker of texture and more stone-fruited and marzipan of aroma, this rolle is a viscous tour de force. Fermented in ceramic egg and neutral oak, with a tightening up across an oatmeal leesy thread. 12 hours of skin contact adds further bite and aromatic pungency. Screwcap. 12.3% alc. **Rating** 94 **To** 2020 $35 NG
Rose 2016 Copper apricot hue; this rose is reliant on a slaking, gently tannic thrust rather than acidity and CO_2. Dry and highly refreshing across bitter red fruit flavours, pink lady apple, orange marmalade and bitter almond. The dry, dusty pitch echoes the voices of 50% sangiovese, 35% sciaccarello and 15% vermentino. Very good. Screwcap. 11.4% alc. **Rating** 94 **To** 2018 $27 NG ✪

ŸŸŸŸŸ Pigato Vermentino 2016 Rating 92 To 2018 $30 NG
Cannanou Grenache 2016 Rating 91 To 2019 $35 NG
Cabernet Sauvignon Malbec 2016 Rating 91 To 2021 $50 NG
Nielluccio Sangiovese 2016 Rating 91 To 2019 $35 NG
Mammolo Sciaccarello 2016 Rating 91 To 2019 $40 NG
The Clare 2016 Rating 90 To 2019 $27 NG

Koonara ★★★★☆

44 Main Street, Penola, SA 5277 **Region** Coonawarra
T (08) 8737 3222 **www**.koonara.com **Open** Mon–Thurs 10–5, Fri–Sat 10–6, Sun 10–4
Winemaker Peter Douglas **Est.** 1988 **Dozens** 10 000 **Vyds** 9ha
Koonara is a sister, or, more appropriately, a brother company to Reschke Wines. The latter is
run by Burke Reschke, Koonara by his brother Dru. Both are sons of Trevor Reschke, who
planted the first vines on the Koonara property in 1988. Peter Douglas, formerly Wynns'
chief winemaker before moving overseas for some years, has returned to the district and
is consultant winemaker. Since 2013 Koonara have leased and managed the Kongorong
Partnership Vineyard in Mount Gambier, which had previously sold its grapes to Koonara.
Exports to the US, Canada, Europe, Singapore and China.

ŸŸŸŸŸ Family Reserve Ambriel's Gift Coonawarra Cabernet Sauvignon 2014
Estate-grown, matured in French oak (some obviously new) for 26 months,
custom made, strongly branded bottles. Deeply coloured, the flavours range
through cassis, choc mint and strong pencilly oak. The tannins are substantial due
to small berries and bunches. Screwcap. 14% alc. **Rating** 94 **To** 2034 $40

ŸŸŸŸŸ Sofiel's Gift Mount Gambier Riesling 2013 Rating 91 To 2028 $20
Angel's Peak Coonawarra Shiraz 2014 Rating 91 To 2027 $25

Koonowla Wines ★★★★☆

18 Koonowla Road, Auburn, SA 5451 **Region** Clare Valley
T (08) 8849 2270 **www**.koonowla.com **Open** details on website
Winemaker O'Leary Walker Wines **Est.** 1997 **Dozens** 7000 **Vyds** 48.77ha
Koonowla is a historic Clare Valley property; situated just east of Auburn, it was first planted
with vines in the 1890s, and by the early 1900s was producing 60 000 litres of wine annually.
A disastrous fire in '26 destroyed the winery and wine stocks, and the property was converted
to grain and wool production. Replanting of vines began in '85, and accelerated after Andrew
and Booie Michael purchased the property in '91; there are now almost 50ha of cabernet
sauvignon, riesling, shiraz, merlot and semillon. In an all-too-familiar story, the grapes were
sold until falling prices forced a change in strategy; now a major part of the grapes is vinified
by the infinitely experienced David O'Leary and Nick Walker. Exports to the UK, the US,
Scandinavia, Malaysia, China and NZ.

ŸŸŸŸŸ The AJM Reserve Clare Valley Shiraz 2014 Destemmed, crushed, open-
fermented, hand-plunged for 14 days, basket-pressed, matured in new French
hogsheads for 14 months. The new oak has been absorbed into the fabric of the
wine and is balanced. There is a trio of juicy black fruits, cedary oak and fine,
ripe tannins all singing from the same medium to full-bodied page. Screwcap.
14.8% alc. **Rating** 95 **To** 2034 $45

ŸŸŸŸŸ Clare Valley Riesling 2016 Rating 92 To 2025 $20 CM
Clare Valley Fortified Riesling NV Rating 90 $20 ●

Kooyong ★★★★★

PO Box 153, Red Hill South, Vic 3937 **Region** Mornington Peninsula
T (03) 5989 4444 **www**.kooyongwines.com.au **Open** At Port Phillip Estate
Winemaker Glen Hayley **Est.** 1996 **Dozens** 13 000 **Vyds** 40ha

Kooyong, owned by Giorgio and Dianne Gjergja, released its first wines in 2001. The vineyard is planted to pinot noir (20ha), chardonnay (10.4ha) and, more recently, pinot gris (3ha). In July '15, following the departure of Sandro Mosele, his assistant of six years, Glen Hayley, was appointed to take his place. The Kooyong wines are made at the state-of-the-art winery of Port Phillip Estate, also owned by the Gjergjas. Exports to the UK, the US, Canada, Sweden, Norway, Singapore, Hong Kong, Japan and China.

ΨΨΨΨΨ **Ferrous Single Vineyard Mornington Peninsula Pinot Noir 2015** Kooyong's Single Vineyard Pinots exhibit darker shades across the variety's multitude of personalities. There is an energy, a weightlessness, together with a richness. The fruit ekes its way out of the savoury maze, licked with bramble, beetroot and etched by a whole cluster spike of aniseed and cardamom. The balance of fruit intensity and structural attributes augur well for a very bright future. Screwcap. 13.5% alc. **Rating** 96 **To** 2030 $76 NG

Meres Single Vineyard Mornington Peninsula Pinot Noir 2015 Far and away the most aromatic of Kooyong's trio of Pinot Noirs, this is a high pitched soprano brimming with red fruits, all. The emphasis is on strawberry, red cherry and raspberry, given a creamy lick of vanillan cinnamon oak at the seams and a sprightly tang of candied orange rind beaming across the wine's centre. Amen! Screwcap. 13% alc. **Rating** 96 **To** 2025 $76 NG

Estate Mornington Peninsula Chardonnay 2015 From the outset the accent is on stone fruit (nectarine, white peach) and fig, with creamy nuances from oak and maybe mlf. The finish is on another path, citrus and acidity tightening and brightening the aftertaste in particular. Despite this change in flavour, the wine has good line and focus. Screwcap. 13% alc. **Rating** 95 **To** 2025 $44

Farrago Single Vineyard Mornington Peninsula Chardonnay 2015 Tangy stone fruit flavours cut a swathe across one's first impressions. The high quality oak sits in there, too, merely an adjunct to guide the unwinding flavours, rather than a shout above the wine's inherent complexity. The intensity of flavour, rapier-like initially before expanding to a broader blade, is impressive. The finish is exceptionally long. A wine to drift off to. Screwcap. 13% alc. **Rating** 95 **To** 2025 $61 NG

Faultline Single Vineyard Mornington Peninsula Chardonnay 2015 Tangy and redolent of white peach, tangerine and nectarine out of the gates. Tensile, mineral-clad and tightly furled across its aft, reined in by a framework of high quality French oak and the oatmeal, truffled curd and reductive tension of extended lees handling. This wine will billow across its structural seams with age. Screwcap. 13% alc. **Rating** 94 **To** 2023 $61 NG

Massale Mornington Peninsula Pinot Noir 2015 Bright, clear crimson hue; a complex pinot from start to finish, with spicy/woodsy notes to the bouquet and a complementary savoury edge to the plummy fruits of the palate. Already good, but its best years are in front of it. Screwcap. 13% alc. **Rating** 94 **To** 2027 $32

Haven Single Vineyard Mornington Peninsula Pinot Noir 2015 Sturdy and dark-fruited as is Kooyong's stamp, Haven is a plume of bing cherry, blueberry, black plum and cinnamon flavours, given energy by bright acidity and silken tannins following. This is pinot's domain, in a riper sense. Vanillan, cedar oak frames and creams the wine's edges, nestling in nicely to be absorbed, surely, into the generous melee in time. Screwcap. 13.5% alc. **Rating** 94 **To** 2025 $76 NG

ΨΨΨΨΨ **Beurrot Pinot Gris 2016 Rating** 93 **To** 2021 $30 NG
Estate Pinot Noir 2015 Rating 93 **To** 2023 $54 NG
Clonale Chardonnay 2016 Rating 90 **To** 2021 $32 NG

Krinklewood Biodynamic Vineyard ★★★★☆

712 Wollombi Road, Broke, NSW 2330 **Region** Hunter Valley
T (02) 6579 1322 **www.krinklewood.com Open** Fri–Sun 10–5
Winemaker Rod and Peter Windrim **Est.** 1981 **Dozens** 10 000 **Vyds** 19.9ha

Krinklewood is a family-owned certified biodynamic organic winery. Every aspect of the property is managed in a holistic and sustainable way, Rod Windrim's extensive herb crops, native grasses and farm animals all contribute to biodynamic preparations to maintain healthy soil biology. The small winery is home to a Vaslin Bucher basket press and two Nomblot French fermentation eggs, a natural approach to winemaking.

ŢŢŢŢŢ Spider Run Red 2014 Only the finest parcels of fruit in the best vintages are selected for this reserve shiraz. Leads with a heady fragrance, a little volatile acidity lift, while keeping within a savoury spectrum: earthy rhubarb, dark plums. But it's the palate that makes this rather special. Medium-bodied, and with a neat tension between the tannins and acidity. There's a palpable energy and drive to this – captivating. Screwcap. 14.5% alc. **Rating** 95 **To** 2028 $50 JF

ŢŢŢŢŢ Basket Press Shiraz 2015 Rating 93 **To** 2025 $45 JF
The Gypsy Sparkling Shiraz 2014 Rating 90 **To** 2021 $50 TS

Kurtz Family Vineyards ★★★★

731 Light Pass Road, Angaston, SA, 5353 **Region** Barossa Valley
T 0418 810 982 **www**.kurtzfamilyvineyards.com.au **Open** By appt
Winemaker Steve Kurtz **Est.** 1996 **Dozens** 2500 **Vyds** 15.04ha
The Kurtz family vineyard is at Light Pass, with 9ha of shiraz, the remainder planted to chardonnay, cabernet sauvignon, semillon, sauvignon blanc, petit verdot, grenache, mataro and malbec. Steve Kurtz has followed in the footsteps of his great-grandfather Ben Kurtz, who first grew grapes at Light Pass in the 1930s. During a career working first at Saltram, and then at Foster's until 2006, Steve gained invaluable experience from Nigel Dolan, Caroline Dunn and John Glaetzer, among others. Exports to the US, Canada and China.

ŢŢŢŢŢ Boundary Row Barossa Valley Shiraz 2014 Eperosa has a wine made from a literal boundary row, and here the wine is simply made from parcels of Barossa Valley fruit. It's a big, brawling child with black and red cherry and chocolate dribbling down its chin – time will see a tissue wiping the face clean. Screwcap. 14.5% alc. **Rating** 92 **To** 2022 $26
Seven Sleepers Barossa Valley Shiraz 2015 Elegant packaging for an $18 wine. It's medium to full-bodied with plum and blackberry fruit in abundance. There are sufficient savoury tannins to provide balance. Ready now, and the price is right. Screwcap. 14.5% alc. **Rating** 90 **To** 2020 $18 **☉**
Lunar Block Individual Vineyard Barossa Valley Shiraz 2013 Ultra-full-bodied, grown and made on the more is better, most is best axiom. It assaults the mouth, and doesn't relent. There are consumers in Aus and overseas who love the shock and awe nature of Barossa Valley wines of this style, and they shouldn't be badgered into changing their views, which they are fully entitled to hold. In that context, this is a good wine. Screwcap. 15% alc. **Rating** 90 **To** 2043 $60
Boundary Row Barossa Cabernet Sauvignon 2014 A surprise packet with its cabernet varietal expression; it is full-bodied and a bit raw-boned, but the blackcurrant/cassis fruit is there, and it hasn't been smothered by oak. Will hang around for years to come. Screwcap. 14.5% alc. **Rating** 90 **To** 2029 $26

Kyneton Ridge Estate ★★★★

90 Blackhill School Road, Kyneton, Vic 3444 **Region** Macedon Ranges
T (03) 5422 7377 **www**.kynetonridge.com.au **Open** W'ends & public hols 10.30–5.30
Winemaker John and Luke Boucher **Est.** 1997 **Dozens** 1200 **Vyds** 4ha
Established by John Boucher and partner Pauline Russell in the shadow of Black Mountain, an ideal environment for pinot noir and chardonnay vines. They maintain traditional processes but new facilities have recently been introduced to enhance the production process for the sparkling wines. The additional production capacity gives the opportunity to source additional suitable quality parcels of shiraz and cabernet sauvignon from Macedon and Heathcote. A small amount is exported to Taiwan.

ΨΨΨΨΨ **Macedon Pinot Noir Chardonnay 2012** The tension of cool Macedon fruit meets the texture and complexity of full French oak fermentation, interrupting fruit purity with savoury, charcuterie and boiled sausage notes. Lees age has built good mouthfeel and persistence. Diam. 13.2% alc. **Rating** 90 **To** 2020 $32 TS

L.A.S. Vino

★★★★☆

PO Box 361 Cowaramup, WA 6284 **Region** Margaret River
www.lasvino.com **Open** Not
Winemaker Nic Peterkin **Est.** 2013 **Dozens** 800

Nic Peterkin, owner of this newly established business, is the grandson of the late Diana Cullen (Cullen Wines) and the son of Mike Peterkin (Pierro). After graduating from Adelaide University with a Masters Degree in oenology, and travelling the world as a Flying Winemaker, he came back to roost in Margaret River with the ambition of making wines that are a little bit different, but also within the bounds of conventional oenological science. The intention is to keep the project small, and thus make only 200 dozen of each of Chardonnay, Chenin Blanc, Pinot Noir (Albino Pinot) and Touriga Nacional (Pirate Blend). Exports to the UK, Singapore and Japan.

ΨΨΨΨΨ **Margaret River Nebbiolo 2015** A beautiful package and a floral, svelte, sleek and incredibly attractive wine to boot. The wine is clearly gently extracted. Whole berries were gently plunged in open fermenters, before half of the cuve spent 400 days on skins. The result echoes a top flight cru Beaujolais with an emphasis on red cherry, strawberry, rosewater and floral perfumes, rather than structural grit. This said, some sandalwood washes across the mid-palate, while nebbiolo's genetic stamp of high-toned acidity and fibrous tannins – toned down and almost gossamer for the style at hand – imbue freshness to a growing sweetness in the glass. Cork. 14% alc. **Rating** 96 **To** 2020 $60 NG

ΨΨΨΨΨ **Barossa Valley Syrah 2015** Rating 93 To 2030 $60 NG
Portuguese Pirate Blend NV Rating 93 To 2021 $65
The Pirate Blend NV Rating 93 To 2020 $55 NG
St Mary's Jerusalem Margaret River Chardonnay 2015 Rating 90 To 2021 $65

La Bise

★★★★

PO Box 918, Williamstown, SA 5351 **Region** Adelaide Hills/Southern Flinders
T 0439 823 251 **www**.labisewines.com.au **Open** Not
Winemaker Natasha Mooney **Est.** 2006 **Dozens** 1500

This is a reasonably significant busman's holiday for Natasha Mooney, a well known and highly regarded winemaker whose 'day job' (her term) is to provide winemaking consultancy services for some of SA's larger wineries. This allows her to find small, unique parcels of grapes that might otherwise be blended into large-volume brands. She manages the arrangements so that there is no conflict of interest, making wines that are about fruit and vineyard expression. She aims for mouthfeel and drinkability without high alcohol, and for that she should be loudly applauded.

ΨΨΨΨΨ **Adelaide Hills Arneis 2016** Agreement between sources of information pinpoints the Amadio Vineyard at Kersbrook, the vines 10–12yo. A small portion is fermented in old oak, all given time on lees. A fresh and juicy citrus-accented palate reflects the care taken to prevent sunburn of the grapes (an issue for arneis). Screwcap. 13.2% alc. **Rating** 90 **To** 2018 $22
Le Petite Frais Adelaide Hills Rose 2016 A sangiovese-dominant wine, with tempranillo and a dash of pinot gris, all from Caj Amadio's Kersbrook vineyard. Spicy, savoury fresh red fruits ring true to the sangiovese/tempranillo varietal base – nice wine. Screwcap. 13.2% alc. **Rating** 90 **To** 2018 $22
Adelaide Hills Sangiovese 2015 Also from the Amadio vineyard, different vinification each year, other than only using old, large oak. The bouquet offers equal time to red fruits and a scatter of spices. Good blend and length to the

light-bodied palate which puts no roadblocks in the way of its harmonious flavours. Screwcap. 14% alc. **Rating** 90 **To** 2023 $25

ŸŸŸŸ   Adelaide Hills Pinot Gris 2016 Rating 89 To 2018 $22
Adelaide Hills Tempranillo 2015 Rating 89 To 2021 $25

La Curio   ★★★★★

Cnr Foggo Road/Kangarilla Road, McLaren Vale, SA 5171 **Region** McLaren Vale
T (08) 8323 7999 **www**.lacuriowines.com **Open** By appt
Winemaker Adam Hooper **Est.** 2003 **Dozens** 1500
At 17, winemaker and owner Adam Hooper enrolled in the Bachelor of Oenology degree course at Roseworthy College, and got off to a flying start. Working as a winemaker in McLaren Vale for 20 years, with some of the best known wineries, interspersed with Flying Winemaker trips to Italy and France. The wines have always had a certain frisson, largely as a result of extreme cold soak prior to the fermentation of uncrushed whole berries.

ŸŸŸŸŸ   **Reserve McLaren Vale Shiraz 2014** 100yo vines, small batch fermented, basket-pressed, matured for 30 months in American oak (50% new). Dark, bright, crimson-purple; an absolute powerhouse with sultry black fruits, tar, earth and bitter chocolate flavours. The tannin and oak supports are of appropriate size to match the fruit. Needs at least 10 years. Screwcap. 14.5% alc. **Rating** 95 **To** 2039 $38
Reserve Bush Vine McLaren Vale Grenache 2014 100yo dry-grown bushvines, 30% whole bunches, 30% extended skin contact 10 weeks post-fermentation, matured in French hogsheads (33% new) for 30 months. This is McLaren Vale in all its glory, with great fruit flavour, texture and structure, replaying and reflecting the complex vinification. It has fine tannins supporting its cherry and spice plum fruit. Screwcap. 14.5% alc. **Rating** 95 **To** 2029 $31 ✪
The Nubile McLaren Vale Grenache Shiraz Mataro 2015 A 65/25/10% blend, small batch fermented, basket-pressed, matured in used French hogsheads for 20 months. There is a coherence and consistency in the mouthfeel of the La Curio red wines that transcends vintage and variety. The palate has a vibrancy and freshness to the array of red, purple and black fruits, oak merely a vehicle, the fine, slightly savoury, tannins of more importance. Screwcap. 14.5% alc. **Rating** 95 **To** 2030 $25 ✪
The Dandy McLaren Vale Shiraz 2015 Average vine age 45 years, basket-pressed, matured for 20 months in 3yo French-coopered American oak. Has more elegance than many McLaren Vale shirazs, perhaps due to the light hand on the oak tiller; spicy notes are also different from the average run. It all adds up to a dandy wine. Screwcap. 14.5% alc. **Rating** 94 **To** 2028 $25✪

ŸŸŸŸŸ   The Original Zin McLaren Vale Primitivo 2015 Rating 93 To 2025 $25✪
The Selfie McLaren Vale Aglianico Rose 2016 Rating 90 To 2018 $19✪

La Linea   ★★★★☆

36 Shipsters Road, Kensington Park, SA 5068 (postal) **Region** Adelaide Hills
T (08) 8431 3556 **www**.lalinea.com.au **Open** Not
Winemaker Peter Leske **Est.** 2007 **Dozens** 3500 **Vyds** 9.5ha
La Linea is a partnership of several experienced wine industry professionals, including Peter Leske and David LeMire MW. Peter was among the first to recognise the potential of tempranillo in Australia, and his knowledge of it is reflected in the three wine styles made from the variety: Tempranillo Rose, Tempranillo blended from several Adelaide Hills vineyards, and Norteno, from a single vineyard at the northern end of the Hills. Two Rieslings are produced under the Vertigo label: TRKN (short for trocken), and the off-dry 25GR (25g/l residual sugar). Exports to the UK.

ŸŸŸŸŸ   **Cellar Release Vertigo TRKN Adelaide Hills Riesling 2011** 6 years in the bottle have barely touched this classic and elegant wine. The colour is still pale green, the first hint of toast wafts from the glass, and precisely shaped flavours of lemon/lime fruit on the palate are cradled by crisp, minerally acidity (due to its low pH of 2.88) on the fresh, dry finish. Only 50 dozen held back in the winery cellar. Screwcap. 11.5% alc. **Rating** 95 **To** 2021 $26 **✪**

Adelaide Hills Mencia Rose 2016 Mencia is a newcomer to Australia, originating from rocky hillsides in northern Spain; fermented in used barriques. The expressive bouquet offers a mix of spices and red berries, the bone-dry, textured palate following suit, adding red apple to the palette of flavours. The juicy element is downright seductive. Screwcap. 12.5% alc. **Rating** 94 **To** 2019 $25 **✪**

Adelaide Hills Tempranillo Rose 2015 No-frills winemaking, with a couple of hours of low temperature skin contact, then a cool stainless steel fermentation. The bouquet is remarkably complex, with spice and musk conducting the music of the bouquet and of the juicy, yet intense, palate. Has the rose X-factor writ large. Screwcap. 12.5% alc. **Rating** 94 **To** 2017 $22 **✪**

ΨΨΨΨΨ Adelaide Hills Tempranillo Rose 2016 **Rating** 93 **To** 2020 $22 **✪**
Adelaide Hills Tempranillo 2014 **Rating** 93 **To** 2024 $26 **✪**
Adelaide Hills Tempranillo 2015 **Rating** 92 **To** 2025 $27
Adelaide Hills Mencia 2016 **Rating** 92 **To** 2021 $29
Vertigo 25GR Adelaide Hills Riesling 2016 **Rating** 92 **To** 2029 $24 **✪**

La Pleiade ★★★★★

c/- Jasper Hill, Drummonds Lane, Heathcote, Vic 3523 **Region** Heathcote
T (03) 5433 2528 **www**.jasperhill.com.au **Open** By appt
Winemaker Ron Laughton, Michel Chapoutier **Est.** 1998 **Dozens** 1000 **Vyds** 9ha
A joint venture of Michel and Corinne Chapoutier and Ron and Elva Laughton. In spring 1998 a vineyard of Australian and imported French shiraz clones was planted. The vineyard is run biodynamically, and the winemaking is deliberately designed to place maximum emphasis on the fruit quality. Exports to the UK, the US, France, Singapore and Hong Kong.

ΨΨΨΨΨ Heathcote Shiraz 2013 Estate-grown; as usual, fermented in an open wax-lined concrete vat, matured for 12 months in new and second-use French barriques. Takes full-bodied shiraz onto a new level, so dense is the complex web of black fruits, licorice and spice, achieving this without the intrusion of alcohol or heavy tannins. To drink it now or soon would be vinocide, but some will be unable to avoid that sin. Cork. 14% alc. **Rating** 96 **To** 2053 $68

Lake Breeze Wines ★★★★★

Step Road, Langhorne Creek, SA 5255 **Region** Langhorne Creek
T (08) 8537 3017 **www**.lakebreeze.com.au **Open** 7 days 10–5
Winemaker Greg Follett **Est.** 1987 **Dozens** 20000 **Vyds** 90ha
The Folletts have been farmers at Langhorne Creek since 1880, and grapegrowers since the 1930s. Part of the grape production is sold, but the quality of the Lake Breeze wines is exemplary, with the red wines particularly appealing. Lake Breeze also owns and makes the False Cape wines from Kangaroo Island. Exports to the UK, Switzerland, Denmark, Germany, Peru, Vietnam, Singapore, Hong Kong, Japan and China.

ΨΨΨΨΨ Arthur's Reserve Langhorne Creek Cabernet Petit Verdot Malbec 2014 Lake Breeze's flagship wine showcases the class of its cabernet sauvignon by selecting the 10 best barrels then adding petit verdot (9%) and malbec (5%) for their unique elements, florals/spice and drive respectively. There's a finesse to this depth of flavour: the wine is rich but not heavy, long, pure, and really detailed. Screwcap. 14% alc. **Rating** 96 **To** 2032 $44 JF **✪**

Section 54 Langhorne Creek Shiraz 2015 Bright dark purple, with a vibrancy to match; plums, blueberries in the main, with raspberry-like acidity. Aged for 15 months in French oak (35% new) and seamlessly integrated; hits a lovely sweet spot with plenty of spice, chocolate and florals for added pleasure. Screwcap. 14.5% alc. **Rating** 95 **To** 2029 $26 JF **✪**

Old Vine Langhorne Creek Grenache 2015 It's not because the fruit comes off a mere 1 acre vineyard planted in '32 (although that helps), nor the fact that there's no new oak interfering with the heady aromas and fruit flavours (just 10 months in 2yo French barriques). It's captivating because it's so well crafted. Unadulterated, beautifully weighted, grainy, fine tannins, long and with pure sweet fruit. Screwcap. 14.8% alc. **Rating** 95 **To** 2023 $26 JF ✪

Langhorne Creek Cabernet Sauvignon 2015 Such a distinctive wine because it can come from nowhere other than Langhorne Creek, or rather Lake Breeze, as the vines hover around 50yo. The incredible tang and vibrancy of blackberry and mulberry fruit is always packed into this wine. Built for ageing, always made for drinking. Screwcap. 14% alc. **Rating** 95 **To** 2030 $26 JF ✪

False Cape The Captain Kangaroo Island Cabernet Sauvignon 2014 Aged in French oak for 20 months (70% new); seamlessly integrated. There's a firmness on the palate, a creamy vanillan character, but the fruit does hold its own. Plenty of savouriness, menthol and spice, too, with ripe, grippy yet detailed tannins. Screwcap. 14% alc. **Rating** 95 **To** 2029 $32 JF ✪

ΨΨΨΨ **Reserve Langhorne Creek Chardonnay 2015** **Rating** 93 **To** 2020 $24 SC ✪
Bernoota Shiraz Cabernet 2015 **Rating** 92 **To** 2028 $23 JF ✪
Bernoota Shiraz Cabernet 2014 **Rating** 92 **To** 2022 $22 SC ✪
Montebello Kangaroo Island Pinot Grigio 2015 **Rating** 91 **To** 2017 $18 ✪
Ship's Graveyard Kangaroo Island Shiraz 2015 **Rating** 91 **To** 2024 $20 JF ✪
The Captain Kangaroo Island Chardonnay 2015 **Rating** 90 **To** 2022 $28 JF
False Cape Unknown Sailor Kangaroo Island Cabernet Merlot 2015 **Rating** 90 **To** 2025 $20 JF ✪
Bullant Cabernet Merlot 2014 **Rating** 90 **To** 2021 $17 SC ✪

Lake Cooper Estate   ★★★★

1608 Midland Highway, Corop, Vic 3559 **Region** Heathcote
T (03) 9387 7657 **www**.lakecooper.com.au **Open** W'ends & public hols 11–5
Winemaker Donald Risstrom, Sam Brewer **Est.** 1998 **Dozens** 7800 **Vyds** 29.8ha
Lake Cooper Estate is a substantial venture in the Heathcote region, set on the side of Mt Camel Range with panoramic views of Lake Cooper, Greens Lake and the Corop township. Planting began in 1998 with 12ha of shiraz, subsequently extended to 18ha of shiraz and 9.5ha of cabernet sauvignon. Small amounts of merlot, chardonnay, sauvignon blanc and verdelho have since been planted. Exports to China.

ΨΨΨΨ **Reserve Heathcote Shiraz 2015** This has a very savoury, fine-boned and well appointed blend of judicious oak and clustery briar. A fine thread of white pepper, freshly ground, works its way across the lithe, sinewy limbs of this mid-weighted shiraz. Violet, iodine, smoked meat and blueberry, all definitive of the variety at is coolest, appear. Most impressive are the sinuous, palate-toning tannins. Cork. 14.5% alc. **Rating** 93 **To** 2030 $49 NG

Well Bin 1962 Heathcote Shiraz 2015 Red cherry, blood plum, iodine and purple fruit flavours. This wine builds across the palate nicely. The oak, too, is exceptionally well handled. Layered across a firm platform of slatey, finely tuned tannins with a crackle of briar, this is fun to drink. Cork. 14% alc. **Rating** 93 **To** 2030 $29 NG

Rhapsody Heathcote Shiraz 2015 This is lustrous and powerful but also vibrant, layered and long. There is a pulse here: blue and black fruits stride across the mouth, elevated by lilac florals and a faint whiff of mint. The oak, generous as usual, is cuddled by the glycerol; the railing of grape tannins is pliant and savoury. Cork. 14.5% alc. **Rating** 92 **To** 2035 $38 NG

Lake's Folly   ★★★★★

2416 Broke Road, Pokolbin, NSW 2320 **Region** Hunter Valley
T (02) 4998 7507 **www**.lakesfolly.com.au **Open** 7 days 10–4 while wine available
Winemaker Rodney Kempe **Est.** 1963 **Dozens** 4000 **Vyds** 12.2ha

The first of the weekend wineries to produce wines for commercial sale, long revered for its Cabernet Sauvignon and nowadays its Chardonnay. Very properly, terroir and climate produce a distinct regional influence and thus a distinctive wine style. Lake's Folly no longer has any connection with the Lake family, having been acquired some years ago by Perth businessman Peter Fogarty. Peter's family company previously established the Millbrook Winery in the Perth Hills and has since acquired Deep Woods Estate in Margaret River and Smithbrook Wines in Pemberton, so is no stranger to the joys and agonies of running a small winery. Peter has been an exemplary owner of all the brands in the group, providing support where needed, but otherwise not interfering.

ΨΨΨΨΨ **Hunter Valley Chardonnay 2016** Estate-grown, hand-picked, fermented in a mix of 1yo and 2yo French oak. This is an elegant, superbly balanced chardonnay that has perfect varietal expression in a calm and detailed fashion. It is not alone in demonstrating that the idiosyncratic nature of the Hunter Valley climate doesn't always impact adversely on chardonnay. Screwcap. 13% alc. **Rating** 95 **To** 2023 $75

ΨΨΨΨ **Hunter Valley Cabernets 2015 Rating** 89 **To** 2021 $75

Lambloch Estate

2342 Broke Road, Pokolbin, NSW 2320 **Region** Hunter Valley
T (02) 4998 6722 **www**.lambloch.com **Open** 7 days 10–5
Winemaker Scott Stephens **Est.** 2008 **Dozens** 4000 **Vyds** 8ha
Whether it be upmarket housing or mining tenements, the address is all important. Jas Khara acquired the 8ha vineyard now known as Lambloch Estate, adjoining Lake's Folly and directly opposite McWilliam's Rosehill Vineyard. All three share the red volcanic soils not often found in the Hunter Valley. With a strong marketing background in brand creation, he has invested in a new cellar door on Broke Road (itself an all-important artery) with large open areas overlooking the vines and a backdrop of the Brokenback Range in the middle distance. Currently almost all of the production is sold in Belgium, Hong Kong, Macau, Singapore, Thailand, Malaysia, Taiwan and China.

ΨΨΨΨΨ **The Loch Hunter Valley Shiraz 2014** A vibrant medium crimson, there is a complex array of red fruits, licorice and earth on the nose of this single-vineyard wine while the palate is youthful and nicely concentrated. It simply needs another 5 years or so for the 100% new oak to integrate and the wine to become even more complex. Screwcap. 13.8% alc. **Rating** 93 **To** 2030 $95 PR
The Loch Hunter Valley Shiraz 2013 More approachable now than the very good and what will be more long-lived '14, this elegant yet persistent medium-bodied Hunter shiraz is nicely perfumed, with some savoury notes to go with the mainly blackberry fruit. Beautifully balanced superfine tannins round out a wine to enjoy now and over the next 5–10 years. Screwcap. 13.5% alc. **Rating** 92 **To** 2023 $95 PR
Aged Release The Loch Hunter Valley Shiraz 2011 Deep brick red. Made from 50yo vines, there is a core of red fruit to go with the baked earth aromas and cedary wood, which is slowly integrating over time. The palate has equally good depth and tension, and there is more than enough fruit and fine tannins to suggest that this classic, medium to full-bodied Hunter shiraz will reward another 5–10 years, if not longer, in the cellar. Screwcap. 12.7% alc. **Rating** 92 **To** 2030 $125 PR
Classic Hunter Valley Merlot 2014 A light to medium cherry red in colour, this single-vineyard wine has aromas of red fruits, dried herbs and a little cedar from 12 months in French oak; the medium-bodied and fruit-driven palate is nicely framed by some gentle, grippy tannins. A wine with both good varietal character and interest. Screwcap. 12.7% alc. **Rating** 90 **To** 2024 $29 PR

ΨΨΨΨ **Classic Hunter Valley Shiraz 2014 Rating** 89 **To** 2021 $29 PR

Lambrook Wines

PO Box 3640, Norwood, SA 5067 **Region** Adelaide Hills
T 0437 672 651 **www**.lambrook.com.au **Open** By appt
Winemaker Adam Lampit **Est.** 2008 **Dozens** 5000
This is a virtual winery created by husband and wife team Adam and Brooke Lampit. With
almost two decades of industry experience between them, they began purchasing sauvignon
blanc, shiraz and pinot noir (for sparkling) in 2008. Adam's experience has come through
working with Stonehaven, Norfolk Rise and Bird in Hand.

Adelaide Hills Rose 2016 Fuchsia pink and pretty, as are the aromatics. A burst
of red berries on the palate, crunchy watermelon, raspberry-lemony acidity with
a drop of sweetness softening the finish. Screwcap. 12% alc. **Rating** 92 **To** 2018
$20 JF

Amelia Adelaide Hills Shiraz 2013 No details other than what the label
states, as in Amelia is part of the Lambrook reserve range – aged in French oak
for 18 months and 1 year in bottle. So there. Dark garnet hue; super-rich palate
densely packed with black fruit, plush tannins, tar, herbs and oak flavours. A big
wine but there's balance. Screwcap. 14.5% alc. **Rating** 92 **To** 2025 $45 JF

Emerson 2012 Adelaide Hills pinot noir declares its depth and presence in red
apple and subtle strawberry fruit, layered with the toasty, roast nut complexity
of 4 years of lees age. A noble effort for a first release, upholding the focus and
restraint of cool climate acidity, carrying the finish long and restrained, well
matched to a low dosage. A little phenolic grip on the end is characteristic of the
Adelaide Hills sparkling wines. Diam. 12% alc. **Rating** 92 **To** 2019 $50 TS

Adelaide Hills Shiraz 2015 A fabulous deep purple-red-black colour, followed
by a bouquet of black sweet plums, currants, licorice and mint, with the oak
offering up vanilla and woodsy spices. Full-bodied with plush tannins and fine
acidity to carry all those flavours, and does it well. Screwcap. 14.5% alc. **Rating** 91
To 2025 $25 JF

Family Reserve Clare Valley Riesling 2016 A soft rendition of Watervale
riesling thanks to the talc-like acidity and its estery-yeasty character, almost a
lemongrass flavour which is distinctive on the palate. Add lemon-lime drops and
juice, lavender, curry leaves and pepper to the mix and it's ready to go. Screwcap.
12.5% alc. **Rating** 90 **To** 2024 $20 JF ✪

Adelaide Hills Chardonnay 2015 A rich, more voluptuous interpretation of
chardonnay with ripe yellow stone fruit, dried mango, grilled nuts and creamed
honey to butterscotch flavours. It's not over the top as there's good acidity keeping
it buoyant. Screwcap. 13% alc. **Rating** 90 **To** 2020 $30 JF

Family Reserve Adelaide Hills Shiraz 2014 There's an easy-drinking appeal
to this with ripe sweet plums and black-berried fruits offset by savoury, oak-
derived wood spice. It's medium-bodied with supple tannins, and the wafts of
black pepper, licorice and candied blood orange peel add a dash of interest.
Screwcap. 14.5% alc. **Rating** 90 **To** 2021 $25 JF

Spark 2016 A fresh and young charmat method sparkling pinot noir of ultra pale
salmon hue, accented with tangy strawberry and elegant red apple fruit. Lively
acidity and well integrated dosage cover for a little phenolic grip on the finish,
but at this price, who's counting? It's clean, refreshing and vibrant. Cork. 12% alc.
Rating 90 **To** 2017 $25 TS

Adelaide Hills Sauvignon Blanc 2016 **Rating** 89 **To** 2018 $20 JF

Lamont's Winery

85 Bisdee Road, Millendon, WA 6056 **Region** Swan Valley
T (08) 9296 4485 **www**.lamonts.com.au **Open** Thurs–Sun 10–5
Winemaker Digby Leddin **Est.** 1978 **Dozens** 7000 **Vyds** 2ha
Corin Lamont, daughter of the late Jack Mann, oversees the making of wines in a style that
would have pleased her father. Lamont's also boasts a superb restaurant run by granddaughter
Kate Lamont. The wines are going from strength to strength, utilising both estate-grown and

contract-grown (from southern regions) grapes. Another of Lamont's restaurants in Perth is open for lunch and dinner Mon–Fri, offering food of the highest quality, and is superbly situated. The Margaret River cellar door is open 7 days 11–5 for wine tasting, sales and lunch.

ŸŸŸŸŸ **Swan Valley Muscat NV** This wine has a green edge to its tawny hue, suggesting wines of considerable age across the cuvee. Alongside the Turkish Delight, lychee, molasses and the scents of Kublai Khan, there is a welcome thread of citrus-laced acidity, keeping the wine tingly and energetic as it thrusts ever onward. 375ml. Screwcap. 19% alc. **Rating** 96 $35 NG **○**
MR Cab! Margaret River Cabernet Sauvignon 2014 From a select block of cabernet sauvignon within one of Margaret River's oldest plots, pastille, anise and mint ooze from the glass. The palate is reined in by fine-boned tannins, judicious oak handling, a mineral edge and gravelly acidity, bolstering the wine's spine and auguring well for ageing. Screwcap. **Rating** 95 To 2033 $45 NG
Great Southern Riesling 2016 Lamont's riesling attests to Great Southern's potential with the variety. Telltale notes of lime, grapefruit skin and white flower are given pulse by a mineral talc crunch. Modest in alcohol, yet palpably dry and energetic, the finish careens across notes of pez and slatey acidity that draw out the saliva and make one crave for food while reaching for another glass. Screwcap. 12% alc. **Rating** 94 To 2025 $25 NG **○**
Black Monster Donnybrook Malbec 2014 Keeping to type, blue and black fruits, smoked meat, mint and the bitter chocolate edge of lavish new oak synergise with a graphite mineral undertow. In all, a liquid package of power hewn by superb tannin management. Screwcap. 13% alc. **Rating** 94 To 2039 $55 NG

ŸŸŸŸŸ **White Monster Chardonnay 2015** Rating 93 To 2022 $45 NG
Margaret River Cabernet Sauvignon 2014 Rating 92 To 2027 $35 NG
Frankland Iced Riesling 2012 Rating 92 To 2025 $30 NG
Pemberton Pinot Gris 2016 Rating 91 To 2019 $25 NG
Frankland Shiraz 2014 Rating 91 To 2030 $35 NG
Swan Valley Pedro X 2005 Rating 91 $50 NG
Margaret River SBS 2016 Rating 90 To 2018 $25 NG

Lana ★★★★

2 King Valley Road, Whitfield, Vic 3678 **Region** King Valley
T (03) 5729 9278 **www**.lanawines.com.au **Open** 7 days 11–5
Winemaker Joel Pizzini **Est.** 2011 **Dozens** 2000
This is a new venture of siblings Carlo, Joel and Natalie Pizzini, whose grandparents migrated to Australia from Lana, a town in Italy's Trentino-Alto Adige region at the foot of the Italian Alps. The strikingly labelled wines are made by Joel from grapes purchased from King Valley producers, and are a promising start.

ŸŸŸŸŸ **King Valley Nebbiolo Barbera 2015** It's light in colour, but don't be dissuaded. This is a beautiful, flowing red wine, it's tannic heart overwhelmed by fresh cherry-berry flavours. Tobacco, fennel and earth notes make cameo appearances but the charm of fresh fruit is the real winner. Screwcap. 13.8% alc. **Rating** 93 To 2021 $28 CM

Landaire

PO Box 14, Padthaway, SA 5271 **Region** Padthaway
T 0417 408 147 **www**.landaire.com.au **Open** Not
Winemaker Pete Bissell **Est.** 2012 **Dozens** 2000 **Vyds** 200ha
David and Carolyn Brown have been major grapegrowers in Padthaway over the past 18 years, David having had a vineyard and farming background, Carolyn with a background in science. Landaire has evolved from a desire after many years of growing grapes at their Glendon Vineyard to select small quantities of the best grapes and have them vinified by Pete Bissell, chief winemaker at Balnaves. It has proved a sure-fire recipe for success. Exports to the UK.

ΨΨΨΨΨ **Single Vineyard Chardonnay 2015** Bernard clones 95 and 277, whole-bunch pressed, fermented in French oak, matured for 11 months. This has been very well made, protecting the inherent extra quality of the grapes (courtesy of their distinguished clones) and enshrining the white peach fruit in superior French oak. Screwcap. 12% alc. **Rating** 95 **To** 2024 $35 ✪

Single Vineyard Graciano 2016 Whole-bunch fermented in 2t fermenters, 8 days on skins, matured in used oak for 5 months. Graciano can be savoury to the point of bitterness, but that's not an issue here. The bouquet has a distinct hint of lavender, allied with spice; the palate is rich and succulent, totally unexpected, but delicious. Screwcap. 13.5% alc. **Rating** 94 **To** 2026 $26 ✪

ΨΨΨΨΫ **Single Vineyard Tempranillo 2016 Rating** 92 **To** 2023 $26
Single Vineyard Vermentino 2016 Rating 90 **To** 2021 $26
Single Vineyard Shiraz 2014 Rating 90 **To** 2039 $40
Single Vineyard Cabernet Graciano 2016 Rating 90 **To** 2023 $32

Landhaus Estate   ★★★★★

PO Box 2135, Bethany SA 5352 **Region** Barossa Valley
T (08) 8353 8442 **www**.landhauswines.com.au **Open** Not
Winemaker Kane Jaunutis **Est.** 2002 **Dozens** 10 000 **Vyds** 1ha
John, Barbara and son Kane Jaunutis purchased Landhaus Estate in 2002, followed by 'The Landhaus' cottage and 1ha vineyard at Bethany. Bethany is the oldest German-established town in the Barossa (1842) and the cottage was one of the first to be built. Kane has worked vintages for Mitolo and Kellermeister, as well as managing East End Cellars, one of Australia's leading fine wine retailers, while John brings decades of owner/management experience and Barbara 20 years in sales and marketing. Rehabilitation of the estate plantings and establishing a grower network have paid handsome dividends. Exports to Canada, Singapore and China.

ΨΨΨΨΨ **Rare Barossa Valley Shiraz 2013** Rare represents the best parcels of fruit from outstanding vintages, this from the Hoffman vineyard in Ebenezer producing a single new French puncheon; 3 years on lees. It is so fresh, with terrific dark garnet-purple colour, full-bodied with swathes of velvety, yet strong tannins. Densely packed fruit, layers of spice with an overall savoury outlook. Demands to be noticed, all in good time. Screwcap. 14.3% alc. **Rating** 97 **To** 2045 $140 JF ✪

ΨΨΨΨΨ **The Saint 2015** Shiraz sourced from five parishes – of low-yielding 65–75yo vineyards, aged for 15 months in older French oak. Everything about this wine is on song with beauty and power. Supple, perfectly ripe fruit flavour on the rich palate yet silky, fine tannins, fresh acidity and elegance. Screwcap. 14% alc. **Rating** 96 **To** 2030 $20 JF ✪

The Saint 2013 A smashing wine at $30, let alone $20. The colour is still deep crimson-purple, the bouquet furiously waving flags to grab attention with its seductive plum, chocolate and black cherry fruit, the palate a high-fidelity replay of the flavours promised by the bouquet. The tannins are supple and round, the balance impeccable, the mouthfeel satin and velvet. Screwcap. 14.1% alc. **Rating** 96 **To** 2028 $20 ✪

Classics Barossa Valley Shiraz Mourvedre 2015 50/50%, 20 months in French oak (50% new). While there's more grunt to the tannin structure via the integrated oak, shiraz and mourvedre unite their flavours and shapes into a harmonious whole. Vibrant red plums, cherries and blueberries sprinkled with chocolate shavings, cinnamon and crushed juniper berries. Screwcap. 14% alc. **Rating** 96 **To** 2030 $30 JF ✪

Classics Barossa Valley Mourvedre Grenache Shiraz 2015 There's exceptional quality right across the '15 Landaus range. A 44/42/14% blend from low-yielding 70–100yo vines, 16 months in French oak (20% new). Savoury-toned, earthy and spicy, deep fruit flavours, lithe tannins, excellent length and so fresh. Screwcap. 14% alc. **Rating** 96 **To** 2027 $30 JF ✪

Siren Grenache Mourvedre Rose 2015 49% grenache, 51% mourvedre. Bright salmon-pink; a highly expressive bouquet, with flowery red fruits, musk and spice, the palate taking a promising start onto another level with the intensity of the fruit flavours offset to perfection by the faintly savoury, bone-dry finish. Exceptional value. Screwcap. 13% alc. **Rating** 95 **To** 2017 $20 ✪
Classics Barossa Valley Shiraz 2015 Dark purple black; 18 months in 100% new French oak – every skerrick of rawness obliterated, and woodsy spices and rich vanillan notes added. Dark fruits abound, overlaid with cinnamon, cloves and licorice. Full-bodied, fleshy round tannins and chalky acidity; overall, has remarkable balance. Screwcap. 14.1% alc. **Rating** 95 **To** 2040 $50 JF
The Hero 2015 Kane Jaunutis says shiraz is regarded as Australia's hero grape but he nominates mourvedre for its unique characters. Hedging his bets, this is a 50/50% blend. Aged 10 months in used French oak, this starts out reductive but soon goes into overdrive with florals, pepper, salami; savoury notes on the palate too. Medium-bodied, exhilaratingly fresh with supple, detailed tannins. Screwcap. 13.8% alc. **Rating** 95 **To** 2023 $20 JF ✪
The Sinner 2015 Grenache 60%/mourvedre 30%/shiraz 10% fermented and blended in stainless steel. Well, given the depth of flavour and fruit tannin structure, this clearly didn't need any oak – it's convincing and delicious. Heady with raspberry, cherries and pips, spicy too, with a really juicy palate, lacy tannins with talc-like acidity. Screwcap. 13.8% alc. **Rating** 95 **To** 2022 $20 JF ✪
Barossa Valley Tempranillo Garnacha 2016 A bright, juicy and cheery wine aimed solely at drinkability. Tempranillo leads at 70%. This sees no oak so the vibrancy of the fruit is key but so, too, is the tannin structure, all supple and fine. Heady aromas and refreshing acidity a given. A little beauty. Screwcap. 13.7% alc. **Rating** 95 **To** 2020 $15 JF ✪
Classics Barossa Valley Shiraz Cabernet 2015 60/40% and aged in French oak (70% new) for 18 months. Deep, vibrant crimson with the roasted tomato, leafy and curranty freshness of cabernet poking out, not unduly. Lots of cedary spice notes, and again the exuberance, vitality on the palate that seems to be a theme at Landhaus. Tannins ripe, if a little raspy. Screwcap. 14% alc. **Rating** 94 **To** 2029 $40 JF
Classics Barossa Valley Grenache 2015 It's the savouriness and lightness of touch that sets this wine apart, bolstered perhaps by the fruit from 50–70yo vines, and thoughtful winemaking. The fruit is gorgeous, all wild berries, plus a spicy overlay with dried Mediterranean herbs; just medium-bodied, with bright crackling acidity and grainy tannins. Screwcap. 14% alc. **Rating** 94 **To** 2022 $27 JF ✪
Classics Barossa Valley Cabernet Sauvignon 2015 Sourced from an old low-yielding vineyard in Bethany deep in black Biscay clay; aged for 22 months in 100% new French oak. Dark purple-garnet; an array of blueberries, blackberries and currant, plus a leafy freshness, flow through on the medium–full-bodied palate. Angular grippy tannins and sparky acidity enliven to the end. Needs more time. Screwcap. 14% alc. **Rating** 94 **To** 2029 $50 JF

🍷🍷🍷🍷🍷 **Adelaide Hills Sauvignon Blanc 2016** **Rating** 93 **To** 2019 $20 JF ✪
Adelaide Hills Arneis 2015 **Rating** 92 **To** 2021 $20 ✪
The Sinner 2013 **Rating** 91 **To** 2020 $20 ✪
Adelaide Hills Gruner Veltliner 2016 **Rating** 90 **To** 2019 $22 JF
Barossa Valley Mourvedre Grenache 2015 **Rating** 90 **To** 2019 $15 JF ✪

Lane's End Vineyard ★★★★★

885 Mount William Road, Lancefield, Vic 3435 **Region** Macedon Ranges
T (03) 5429 1760 **www**.lanesend.com.au **Open** By appt
Winemaker Howard Matthews, Kilchurn Wines **Est.** 1985 **Dozens** 500 **Vyds** 2ha
Pharmacist Howard Matthews and family purchased the former Woodend Winery in 2000, with 1.8ha of chardonnay and pinot noir (and a small amount of cabernet franc) dating back to the mid-1980s. The cabernet franc has been grafted over to pinot noir, and the vineyard

is now made up of 1ha each of chardonnay and pinot noir (five clones). Howard has been making the wines for over a decade.

🍷🍷🍷🍷🍷 **Macedon Ranges Pinot Noir 2015** 70% MV6, 30% 115 and 115, 20% whole bunches, 80% destemmed, 4–5 days cold soak, wild yeast initiating a 6-day ferment, 6 days post-ferment maceration, matured in French oak (33% new). First class colour; a powerful pinot with excellent varietal expression, cherry allsorts and blood plum to the fore. Screwcap. 13.3% alc. **Rating** 96 **To** 2029 $40 ❂
Macedon Ranges Chardonnay 2015 Matured for 11 months with lees stirring and 30% mlf. 7.2g/l of acidity remained after mlf, demonstrating that mlf was needed for balance. Grapefruit, pear and white peach flavours run through the elegant palate and long finish. Screwcap. 12.8% alc. **Rating** 95 **To** 2027 $38
Cottage Macedon Ranges Chardonnay 2016 Whole-bunch pressed, fermented with cultured yeast, no mlf, battonage every 2–3 weeks, crossflow-filtered. An elegant chardonnay filled with white peach fruit and lively acidity. While battonage (lees stirring) was used, it's not obvious whether this was in barrel or in tank – seemingly the latter. Screwcap. 13% alc. **Rating** 94 **To** 2023 $25 ❂

Lange's Frankland Wines ★★★★

633 Frankland-Cranbrook Road, Frankland River, WA 6396 **Region** Frankland River
T 0438 511 828 **www.**langesfranklandwines.com.au **Open** Not
Winemaker James Kellie **Est.** 1997 **Dozens** 200 **Vyds** 13.5ha
This venture involves three generations of this branch of the Lange family, with Don and Maxine grandparents, son Kim and wife Chelsea the second generation, and their children Jack, Ella and Dylan the third generation. The first vines were planted in 1997 and the vineyard now consists of 8ha of shiraz, 3ha of sauvignon blanc and 2.5ha of semillon.

🍷🍷🍷🍷🍷 **Frankland River Shiraz 2012** 20yo estate vines, matured in French oak for 24 months. An impressive shiraz, initially with opulently rich black cherry and blackberry fruit, then moving into notes of licorice and dark chocolate, natural leaders in the final phase of fine-grained, persistent, tannins. Screwcap. 14.5% alc. **Rating** 94 **To** 2037 $35

🍷🍷🍷🍷🍷 **Frankland River Semillon Sauvignon Blanc 2016 Rating** 91 **To** 2020 $17 ❂

Langmeil Winery ★★★★★

Cnr Para Road/Langmeil Road, Tanunda, SA 5352 **Region** Barossa Valley
T (08) 8563 2595 **www.**langmeilwinery.com.au **Open** 7 days 10.30–4.30
Winemaker Paul Lindner, Tyson Bitter **Est.** 1996 **Dozens** 35 000 **Vyds** 31.4ha
Vines were first planted at Langmeil (which possesses the oldest block of shiraz in Australia) in the 1840s, and the first winery on the site, known as Paradale Wines, opened in 1932. In '96, cousins Carl and Richard Lindner with brother-in-law Chris Bitter formed a partnership to acquire and refurbish the winery and its 5ha vineyard (planted to shiraz, and including 2ha planted in 1843). Another vineyard was acquired in '98, which included cabernet sauvignon and grenache. In late 2012 the Lindner family put a succession plan into action: Richard and Shirley Lindner, and their sons Paul and James, have acquired 100% ownership of the business. In terms of management, little changes: Paul has been chief winemaker and James the sales and marketing manager since the winery began in '96. Exports to all major markets.

🍷🍷🍷🍷🍷 **The Freedom 1843 Barossa Shiraz 2014** Oddly, this feels lighter on its feet than the Orphan Bank, with a melody of red and dark fruits slung across a sumptuous palate of bitter chocolate tannins, charred meat, plus a solo of high-toned volatility and sneaky acidity, imbuing focus and poise in the context of the ancient vine hedonism of this wine. The caveat is the burn across the Adam's apple. Put it this way, though: such a wine cannot be replicated elsewhere. Screwcap. 14.5% alc. **Rating** 94 **To** 2034 $125 NG
Orphan Bank Barossa Shiraz 2014 A blend of a majority of Barossan fruit, together with a good percentage of Eden Valley material. After 24 months in French hogsheads, a solid percentage new, this wine exhibits full-throttle dried

dark-fruit aromas sewn to a toasty veneer of vanilla pod and coconut notes. Tar, bitter chocolate, anise and cardamom all wait in the wings. The overall impression is of latent power, in an inimitable and traditional Barossa mould. Screwcap. 14.5% alc. Rating 94 To 2039 $50 NG

♥♥♥♥♡ Jackaman's Barossa Cabernet Sauvignon 2014 Rating 93 To 2029 $50 NG
Resurrection Barossa Mataro 2014 Rating 93 To 2022 $20 NG
Blockbuster Barossa Shiraz 2015 Rating 92 To 2023 $25 NG ❍
The Long Mile Barossa Shiraz 2015 Rating 92 To 2023 $25 NG ❍
The Fifth Wave Barossa Grenache 2015 Rating 92 To 2020 $40 NG
Barossa Valley Viognier 2016 Rating 91 To 2018 $20 NG ❍
Blacksmith Barossa Cabernet Sauvignon 2014 Rating 91 To 2025 $30 NG
Valley Floor Barossa Shiraz 2014 Rating 90 To 2029 $30 NG

Lanz Vineyards ★★★★★

220 Scenic Road, Lyndoch, SA 5351 **Region** Barossa Valley
T 0417 858 967 **www.**lanzvineyards.com **Open** By appt
Winemaker Michael Paxton, Richard Freebairn **Est.** 1998 **Dozens** 800 **Vyds** 16ha
The major part of the grape production is sold to premium producers in the Barossa Valley. However, Marianne and Thomas Lanz take enough of the grapes to make their Shiraz and Grenache Shiraz Mourvedre. Their choice of Michael Paxton as winemaker is no accident; he is a committed biodynamic grower (as is his father, David) and the Lanzs are aiming at the 'three L' wine style: Lower alcohol, Lower intervention, and Lower carbon footprint. Exports to Switzerland, Germany and Singapore.

♥♥♥♥♥ Limited Edition The Grand Reserve Barossa Valley Shiraz 2014 The wine has excellent bloodlines through previous vintages, and this lives up to expectations. Its texture and structure are features of the medium-bodied palate, but so is the suite of spicy fruits and cedary oak. If there is a question, it relates to the level of new oak, but as time goes by it will disappear back into the fabric of the wine. Screwcap. 14% alc. Rating 95 To 2034 $39 ❍

Lark Hill ★★★★☆

521 Bungendore Road, Bungendore, NSW 2621 **Region** Canberra District
T (02) 6238 1393 **www.**larkhillwine.com.au **Open** Wed–Mon 10–5
Winemaker Dr David, Sue and Chris Carpenter **Est.** 1978 **Dozens** 4000 **Vyds** 10.5ha
The Lark Hill vineyard is situated at an altitude of 860m, offering splendid views of the Lake George escarpment. The Carpenters have made wines of real quality, style and elegance from the start, but have defied all the odds (and conventional thinking) with the quality of their Pinot Noirs in favourable vintages. Significant changes have come in the wake of son Christopher gaining three degrees, including a double in wine science and viticulture through CSU, and the biodynamic certification of the vineyard. In 2011 Lark Hill purchased one of the two Ravensworth vineyards from Bryan Martin, with plantings of sangiovese, shiraz, viognier, roussanne and marsanne; they will also be converting it (renamed Dark Horse) to biodynamic farming. Exports to the UK.

♥♥♥♥♡ Canberra District Gruner Veltliner 2016 All the appeal of the variety is right here with wafts of white pepper, chamomile, fresh herbs, baked quince and lemon. The palate is deceptive, as there's tangy acidity, but a slippery, silky texture too. Screwcap. 12.5% alc. Rating 93 To 2026 $45 JF
Canberra District Riesling 2016 A steely line of acidity straight through the middle pulls together threads of citrussy flavours, sweet-sour lemon drops, fresh herbs with some florals and a smidge of texture. Screwcap. 11.5% alc. Rating 91 To 2026 $35 JF
Canberra District Shiraz Viognier 2015 The 4% viognier is co-fermented then matured in French oak hogsheads (25% new) for 8 months. Initially this seems tough, with dusty oak, but it evolves into a savoury zone of dark chocolate, new leather and dried herbs. Screwcap. 14% alc. Rating 90 To 2024 $40 JF

Scuro Canberra District Sangiovese Shiraz 2015 The varieties are split evenly and integrated into a savoury wine with plenty going on aromatically: rosemary, cherry pips, plums, bitter chocolate and Dutch licorice. A tightish palate, sinewy with grippy, drying tannins. Screwcap. 14% alc. **Rating** 90 **To** 2021 $65 JF

Larry Cherubino Wines   ★★★★★

15 York Street, Subiaco, WA 6008 **Region** Western Australia
T (08) 9382 2379 **www.**larrycherubino.com **Open** Not
Winemaker Larry Cherubino, Andrew Siddell, Matt Bucham **Est.** 2005 **Dozens** 8000
Vyds 120ha
Larry Cherubino has had a particularly distinguished winemaking career, first at Hardys Tintara, then Houghton, and thereafter as consultant/Flying Winemaker in Australia, NZ, South Africa, the US and Italy. He has developed three ranges: at the top is Cherubino (Riesling, Sauvignon Blanc, Shiraz and Cabernet Sauvignon); next The Yard, single vineyard wines from WA; and at the bottom the Ad Hoc label, all single region wines. The range and quality of his wines is extraordinary, the prices irresistible. The runaway success of the business has seen the accumulation of 120ha of vineyards, the appointment of additional winemakers, and Larry's own appointment as Director of Winemaking for Robert Oatley Vineyards. Exports to all major markets.

🍷🍷🍷🍷🍷 **Cherubino Beautiful South White Blend 2016** 85% sauvignon blanc, 15% semillon from Porongurup; wild-yeast fermented, matured for 4 months in barrel. The wine is indeed beautiful, with its multitude of fruit flavours seamlessly bound together, only leaving room for the texture of the barrel-ferment oak, not its flavour per se. In a tropical mode throughout until the finish, when cleansing citrussy acidity surges on the aftertaste. Screwcap. 11.5% alc. **Rating** 97 **To** 2021 $35 ❂
Cherubino Pemberton Chardonnay 2016 Cool/dry conditions resulted in low crops with small bunches, gently destemmed, cool-fermented with wild yeast. The palate has a juicy, almost sherbet-like, intensity that is akin to a celestial breath freshener; it also has a startling precision and length, fruit, rather than artifact, paramount. Screwcap. 12.5% alc. **Rating** 97 **To** 2030 $49 ❂
Cherubino Frankland River Cabernet Sauvignon 2015 Hand-picked, chilled overnight and hand-sorted, 6 weeks fermentation and maceration, settled for 7 days prior to oak maturation. Deeply coloured; awesome intensity and focus, cassis oozing from every pore, aristocratic tannins in close attendance serving, not competing with, the fruit. The long maceration of great fruit is the key to this superb full-bodied cabernet. Screwcap. 14.5% alc. **Rating** 97 **To** 2045 $110 ❂

🍷🍷🍷🍷🍷 **Cherubino Porongurup Riesling 2016** Made from the best blocks of the Cherubino vineyard in Porongurup, this is a riesling all about finesse, purity and Porongurup's regional stamp. The bouquet has a haunting touch of crushed sea shell, the palate rapidly building a stream of lime zest, green apple and a savoury touch on the banks of that stream. As with all top class rieslings, acidity is the glue that binds. Screwcap. 11.2% alc. **Rating** 96 **To** 2031 $40 ❂
Cherubino Great Southern Riesling 2016 The gently floral bouquet gives no warning of the intense and pure palate that ripples through the mouth, building progressively through to the finish and aftertaste in the manner of a great pinot noir. The texture of the wine is written in the stars. Screwcap. 12% alc. **Rating** 96 **To** 2036 $35 ❂
Cherubino Margaret River Chardonnay 2016 A complex, powerful wine that captures attention from the first whiff of its funky personality, with grapefruit zest and pith leading the way into the layered palate. The elements of reduction are the product of the protective vinification, and will ensure its calm evolution of style through the coming years. Screwcap. 12.6% alc. **Rating** 96 **To** 2036 $49 ❂
Cherubino Frankland River Shiraz 2015 From the best clones on Cherubino's Riversdale vineyard. The crimson-purple colour introduces a wine that is bursting with all things bright and beautiful: black fruits, licorice, pepper, firm, ripe tannins

and quality French oak all sewn seamlessly together, and will continue thus long into the future of maturity. Screwcap. 14% alc. **Rating** 96 **To** 2040 $55 **✪**

Cherubino Margaret River Cabernet Sauvignon 2015 While this has had the same prolonged maceration pre, during and post-fermentation, the mouthfeel is rounder and fleshier than its Frankland River sibling. The tannins are there, but are also rounder, the sum total a medium to full-bodied wine offering a wide window of optimal consumption. Screwcap. 13.9% alc. **Rating** 96 **To** 2035 $75 **✪**

Cherubino River's End Cabernet Sauvignon 2014 A blend of some of the best Margaret River and Frankland River parcels in the Cherubino cellars. It has an exceptional, deep purple-crimson colour that accurately semaphores the quality of the wine, with the cassis, fleshy mid-palate fruit ex Margaret River and the great texture and structure of Frankland River. The perfect balance will ensure a long future. Screwcap. 13.2% alc. **Rating** 96 **To** 2036 $40 **✪**

Ad Hoc Wallflower Great Southern Riesling 2016 Quartz-white; the floral bouquet has a mix of blossom and talc, the palate literally alive with piercing citrus, green apple and crisp acidity. Fantastic value for a drink whenever the mood takes you. Screwcap. 12% alc. **Rating** 95 **To** 2029 $21 **✪**

The Yard Riversdale Frankland River Riesling 2016 The Riversdale Vineyard was planted in '97 on the banks of the Frankland River. Pale quartz-green, and has a particular complex bouquet and equally complex palate that fills the mouth with a wondrous array of citrus, apple and nashi pear fruit, sustained and lengthened by inbuilt acidity. Screwcap. 11.8% alc. **Rating** 95 **To** 2033 $25 **✪**

Cherubino Pemberton Sauvignon Blanc 2016 From the mature Channybearup Vineyard now owned by Larry Cherubino Wines; wild-yeast fermented and matured in French oak for 4 months. It is intense and complex, with snap pea, fresh cut grass and crunchy/citrussy acidity flavours. A mouthwatering sauvignon blanc with real attitude. Screwcap. 12.1% alc. **Rating** 95 **To** 2018 $35 **✪**

Cherubino Laissez Faire Chardonnay 2016 From the Porongurup subregion, which always has an extra degree of precision and elegance, here with emphasis. It's one of those wines that makes analytical deconstruction redundant: its length, purity, stone fruit and citrus duo are all on the money. Screwcap. 12.5% alc. **Rating** 95 **To** 2026 $39

Ad Hoc Middle of Everywhere Frankland River Shiraz 2015 This is vibrantly fresh, black pepper with spice, juicy black and purple fruits a jet stream across the middle of the palate, the hypnotically spicy/savoury tannins of the finish repeating endlessly. Screwcap. 13.7% alc. **Rating** 95 **To** 2025 $21 **✪**

The Yard Acacia Frankland River Shiraz 2015 The medium to full-bodied palate is particularly intense, with a savoury/earthy chord running through the heart of the black fruits. The firm finish demands more time in bottle. Screwcap. 13.9% alc. **Rating** 95 **To** 2035 $35 **✪**

The Yard Riversdale Frankland River Shiraz 2015 Hand-picked and sorted prior to wild yeast fermentation. As much spicy as savoury, the mouthfeel of the medium to full-bodied palate criss-crossed with cedary notes from oak and tannins providing the framework for the blackberry, licorice and sooty plum flavours. Screwcap. 14.2% alc. **Rating** 95 **To** 2035 $35 **✪**

The Yard Riversdale Frankland River Cabernet Sauvignon 2015 Full colour; a fresh, medium-bodied, skilfully sculpted cabernet with positive tannins giving the wine the length and balance for a long life. As with most of the Cherubino cabernets, oak plays a pure support role, the tannins well educated. Screwcap. 14.3% alc. **Rating** 95 **To** 2030 $35 **✪**

Cherubino River's End Cabernet Sauvignon 2015 A full-bodied cabernet that catches you gently, the answer to the seemingly impossible coming from a blend of Frankland River and Margaret River fruit, and the very long maceration, which leads to polymerisation (softening) of the tannins. Screwcap. 14% alc. **Rating** 95 **To** 2035 $40

Pedestal Vineyard Elevation 2015 55% cabernet sauvignon, 40% merlot, 5% malbec from the highest vineyard in Wilyabrup. A luscious wine, its cassis fruits balanced by persistent, fine, savoury tannins; excellent length and balance. Screwcap. 14% alc. **Rating** 95 **To** 2030 $32 ✪

Ad Hoc Avant Gardening Frankland Cabernet Sauvignon Malbec 2015 Hand picking and sorting is a costly start to making a $21 wine, as is the remainder of the vinification (maturation in 20% new French oak for 9 months). The malbec introduces plums into the mix, cabernet its formidable tannins. Good as it is now, it will lift the bar dramatically over the next 10 or so years. Screwcap. 14.2% alc. **Rating** 95 **To** 2030 $21 ✪

Ad Hoc Straw Man Margaret River Sauvignon Blanc Semillon 2016 Free-run juice, 10% fermented in 2yo oak for 2 months before blending. A relief to taste a wine of flavour, body and length in a lucklustre string of wines from eastern states. Lemon and lemongrass open proceedings, snow pea and a savoury mouthfeel ex the barrel-ferment component coming next, and tart, minerally acidity drawing out the finish of a long palate. Screwcap. 12.5% alc. **Rating** 94 **To** 2022 $21 ✪

Ad Hoc Cruel Mistress Great Southern Pinot Noir 2015 The back label (always brief) simply says, 'Hints of lipstick and leather', which leaves much for the imagination to feed on. Inch by inch, pinot quality in the Great Southern continues to grow. This offers a lot at the price, varietal expression clear on the bouquet and palate alike, with dark cherry and a savoury/foresty crosscut of finely tuned tannins on the finish, oak in its due place. Screwcap. 13.5% alc. **Rating** 94 **To** 2025 $25 ✪

The Yard Justin Frankland River Shiraz 2015 The Justin vineyard was planted in '73, the grapes were hand-picked and sorted, the wine spent 4 weeks on skins in small fermenters, then was matured in new and 1yo oak for 6 months. An elegant wine that neatly balances red, black and morello cherry with more spicy, savoury notes, the tannins like the veil on a wedding dress. Screwcap. 13.7% alc. **Rating** 94 **To** 2030 $35

Cherubino Laissez Faire Syrah 2015 From dry-grown bushvines, the grapes hand-picked and sorted before a wild yeast fermentation. While the cool climate and modest alcohol impose a stamp on the wine, the savoury and black fruit components of the palate are well balanced, the finish offering a reprise of the flavours encountered along the way. All the Cherubino Shirazs of this vineyard are deeply, but brightly, coloured. Screwcap. 13.6% alc. **Rating** 94 **To** 2035 $39

Cherubino Beautiful South Red Wine 2015 Cabernet sauvignon, malbec and merlot. Great crimson-purple; curious labelling, no region on the front label, Great Southern on the back label, but is in fact from the estate Riversdale Vineyard in Frankland River, with a collection of the best clones of the three varieties. All the components (fruit, oak and tannins) are in balance, but need a couple of years to integrate. Screwcap. 13.5% alc. **Rating** 94 **To** 2030 $40

Cherubino Beautiful South Red Wine 2014 Cabernet sauvignon, merlot and malbec from the Riversdale Vineyard in Frankland River. Deep, bright crimson-purple, it has an expressive dark berry bouquet with cedary oak to the fore; the youthful palate brings fruit, oak and tannins into play simultaneously, each seeking to dominate. When it calms down in a few years, could be a knockout. Screwcap. 13.7% alc. **Rating** 94 **To** 2034 $40

ⵟⵟⵟⵟⵟ **Pedestal Margaret River SSB 2016** Rating 93 To 2021 $22 ✪
The Yard Channybearup Sauvignon Blanc 2016 Rating 92 To 2018 $25
Ad Hoc Nitty Gritty Pinot Grigio 2016 Rating 92 To 2017 $21 ✪
Cherubino Laissez Faire Fiano 2016 Rating 92 To 2020 $29
Cherubino Laissez Faire Pinot Blanc 2016 Rating 92 To 2018 $29
Pedestal Margaret River Chardonnay 2016 Rating 91 To 2023 $25
Cherubino Laissez Faire Field Blend 2016 Rating 91 To 2018 $29
Apostrophe Possessive Reds' Great Southern Shiraz Grenache Mourvedre 2015 Rating 91 To 2022 $16 ✪

Apostrophe Possessive Reds' Great Southern Shiraz Grenache
Mourvedre 2014 Rating 91 To 2024 $16 **○**
Ad Hoc Hen & Chicken Chardonnay 2016 Rating 90 To 2020 $21 **○**
Pedestal Margaret River Pinot Gris 2016 Rating 90 To 2018 $22

Latitude 34 Wine Co

St Johns Brook, 283 Yelverton North Road, Yelverton, WA 6281 **Region** Margaret River
T (08) 9417 5633 **www.**barwickwines.com **Open** By appt
Winemaker Mark Thompson, Giulio Corbellani **Est.** 1997 **Dozens** 70 000 **Vyds** 120ha
Latitude 34 is the parent company of wine brands Optimus, St Johns Brook, The Blackwood
and Barwick Estates (www.barwickwines.com). Margaret River is the physical base of the
business, the winery being St Johns Brook. The 120ha of vineyards is made up of 37ha in
Margaret River, and 83ha in the Blackwood Valley, the Pemberton vineyards (68ha) having
been sold in 2015. Exports to the UK, the US and other major markets.

St Johns Brook Reserve Margaret River Chardonnay 2014 Hand-picked,
whole bunches, barrel-fermented with wild and cultured yeast, matured in French
oak (40% new) for 10 months. The complex bouquet has a touch of funk that
appeals; it also has a racy feel to the palate, grapefruit and white peach the main
contributors to the flavour other than neatly handled French oak. Screwcap.
12.5% alc. **Rating** 95 To 2024 $50

St Johns Brook Single Vineyard Shiraz 2014 Rating 93 To 2029 $24 **○**
Barwick Estates Cabernet Sauvignon 2014 Rating 92 To 2025 $18 SC **○**
Optimus The Terraces Blackwood Valley Shiraz 2015 Rating 91 To 2026
$100 JF
Barwick Estates Black Label Margaret River Shiraz 2014 Rating 91
To 2024 $32 SC
Barwick Estates White Label Margaret River SBS 2015 Rating 90
To 2023 $18 SC **○**
St Johns Brook Reserve Chardonnay 2016 Rating 90 To 2023 $50 JF
The Blackwood Sir Henry Blackwood Valley Shiraz 2015 Rating 90
To 2029 $50 JF
Barwick Estates White Label Margaret River Shiraz 2014 Rating 90
To 2022 $18 SC **○**
Barwick Estates White Label Margaret River Cabernet Merlot 2014
Rating 90 To 2021 $18 SC **○**

Laughing Jack ★★★★★

194 Stonewell Road, Marananga, SA 5355 **Region** Barossa Valley
T (08) 8562 3878 **www.**laughingjackwines.com.au **Open** By appt
Winemaker Shawn Kalleske **Est.** 1999 **Dozens** 3000 **Vyds** 38.88ha
The Kalleske family has many branches in the Barossa Valley. Laughing Jack is owned by
Shawn, Nathan, Ian and Carol Kalleske, and Linda Schroeter. The lion's share of the vineyard
is planted to shiraz, with lesser amounts of semillon and grenache. Vine age varies considerably,
with old dry-grown shiraz the jewel in the crown. A small part of the grape production is
taken for the Laughing Jack Shiraz. As any Australian knows, the kookaburra is also called the
laughing jackass, and there is a resident flock of kookaburras in the stands of blue and red gums
surrounding the vineyards. Exports to Malaysia, Hong Kong and China.

Moppa Block Barossa Valley Shiraz 2014 Destemmed and crushed, open-
fermented, 14 days on skins, matured for 20 months in French oak. Deep,
dense crimson-purple; here purple and black fruits are wrapped in a fur coat of
expensive French oak trimmed by tassels of ripe tannins. It's seductive enough
to drink now, but has a long widow of opportunity stretching out for decades to
come. Cork. 14.5% alc. **Rating** 96 To 2044 $85
Greenock Barossa Valley Shiraz 2014 Destemmed and crushed, post-ferment
maceration, matured for 24 months in French and American hogsheads. An

ultra-powerful full-bodied shiraz that shouts 'coming ready or not', very much in the style of earlier vintages. Very savoury, tarry black fruits are perched on a tannin bedrock. Despite its raw-boned palate, it has the marks of a true stayer. Screwcap. 14.5% alc. **Rating** 95 **To** 2044 $45

Jack's Barossa Valley Shiraz 2015 From the highly regarded districts of Greenock and Moppa, open-fermented, basket-pressed, matured for 19 months in American and French hogsheads. It's a powerful wine with drive and a savoury depth to the black fruits that fill the flavour spectrum. The tannin and oak roles have been well cast. Screwcap. 14.8% alc. **Rating** 94 **To** 2030 $23 **O**

ꪛꪛꪛꪛ   Jack's Barossa Valley GSM 2015 **Rating** 89 **To** 2020 $23

Laurel Bank   ★★★★

130 Black Snake Lane, Granton, Tas 7030 **Region** Southern Tasmania
T (03) 6263 5977 **www**.laurelbankwines.com.au **Open** By appt
Winemaker Greer Carland **Est.** 1987 **Dozens** 1500 **Vyds** 3.5ha
Laurel (hence Laurel Bank) and Kerry Carland's north-facing vineyard, overlooking the Derwent River, is planted to sauvignon blanc, riesling, pinot noir, cabernet sauvignon and merlot. They delayed the first release of their wines for some years and (by virtue of the number of entries they were able to make) won the trophy for Most Successful Exhibitor at the Hobart Wine Show '95. Things have settled down since; wine quality is reliable.

ꪛꪛꪛꪛꪛ   **Riesling 2015** Leaf-plucking the eastern side of the vines is usual in Tasmania, and carried out here, plus usual vinification and early bottling. Gleaming straw-green; laden with delicious lime/citrus fruits and balanced (not fearsome) acidity. Watch for the gold medal-winning '16 (Tasmanian Wine Show). Screwcap. 13% alc. **Rating** 93 **To** 2025 $22 **O**

Pinot Noir 2014 Multiple clones, all wild-yeast fermented and matured for 10 months in French oak (20% new). The colour is deep, not surprising for Tasmania or Central Otago, rarer elsewhere; the powerful palate is rich and layered, with plum and black cherry fruit supported by tannins of the kind found only in Tasmania. Screwcap. 13.7% alc. **Rating** 92 **To** 2024 $33

Sauvignon Blanc 2016 Low-yielding vines on stony, sandy soil. Mostly tank-fermented with a specific sauvignon blanc yeast, a very small portion barrel-fermented with some lees stirring. The aim is to build on the depth of the fruit ex the vines, and it achieves just that. It's not particularly aromatic; more in a European style. Screwcap. 13% alc. **Rating** 91 **To** 2017 $22 **O**

Leconfield   ★★★★★

Riddoch Highway, Coonawarra, SA 5263 **Region** Coonawarra
T (08) 8737 2326 **www**.leconfieldwines.com **Open** details on website
Winemaker Paul Gordon, Tim Bailey **Est.** 1974 **Dozens** 25 000 **Vyds** 43.7ha
Sydney Hamilton purchased the unplanted property that was to become Leconfield in 1974, having worked in the family wine business for over 30 years until his retirement in the mid-'50s. When he acquired the property and set about planting it he was 76, and reluctantly bowed to family pressure to sell Leconfield to nephew Richard in '81. Richard has progressively increased the vineyards to their present level, over 75% to cabernet sauvignon, for long the winery's specialty. Exports to all major markets.

ꪛꪛꪛꪛꪛ   **The Sydney Reserve Coonawarra Cabernet Sauvignon 2013** A true Reserve from the best rows planted 30 years ago, picked 20 Mar, in a single open fermenter, pressed before dryness to finish fermentation in new French hogsheads, matured for 29 months. This really is a beautiful cabernet, the barrels made by Dargaud & Jaegle imparting less oak flavour than those of other coopers. It is totally integrated with the opulent cassis fruit. Screwcap. 14% alc. **Rating** 97 **To** 2043 $80 **O**

ŶŶŶŶŶ **Old Vines Coonawarra Riesling 2016** From the dry-grown estate vineyard planted in '74, cool-fermented with cultured yeast. A wine of remarkable power and intensity, reflected in its very low pH of 2.69 and titratable acidity over 8g/l residual sugar below threshold at 3.1g/l and – of course – 42yo vines. It is tailor-made for extended cellaring, and will never lose its sublime power and energy. Screwcap. 12% alc. **Rating** 95 **To** 2031 $26 ✪

Coonawarra Merlot 2015 It's easy to see why this should have won a gold medal at the Limestone Coast Wine Show '16. Its juicy cassis fruit is augmented by the spicy fruit and tannin extract, the result of barrel fermentation of part of the wine. This is right up there in the context of traditional Aus clones available between '82 and '99. Screwcap. 14% alc. **Rating** 95 **To** 2030 $26 ✪

Coonawarra Cabernet Merlot 2015 A 76/24% blend matured in French oak (18% new) for 15 months. The deep, bright crimson purple colour signals a bouquet of exceptional fragrance, laden with cassis fruit plus a garland of oak. The splendidly upholstered palate is full of rich fruit, but still retains shape and faultless balance. Screwcap. 14.5% alc. **Rating** 95 **To** 2035 $26 ✪

Coonawarra Cabernet Sauvignon 2015 Good colour; the excellent vintage has provided winemaker Paul Gordon with a full hand of cassis and mulberry to play with, and he's played his cards well. The overall result is a medium-bodied cabernet that is already seductive, but please keep your hands off it for the first few years of what will be a long life. Screwcap. 14.5% alc. **Rating** 95 **To** 2035 $35

McLaren Vale Shiraz 2015 Night-harvested from the estate Farm Block, fermented on skins for 7 days, a portion barrel-fermented, matured in French oak (21% new) for 16 months. Good, deep colour; a very well made medium to full-bodied shiraz, its terroir first and foremost with supple black fruits, a dash of chocolate, good length and balance, the tannins ripe and round, the oak totally integrated. Screwcap. 14.5% alc. **Rating** 94 **To** 2035 $26 ✪

ŶŶŶŶŶ **Coonawarra Chardonnay 2015 Rating** 93 **To** 2021 $26 ✪
Hamilton Block Coonawarra Cabernet 2015 Rating 93 **To** 2029 $25 ✪
Coonawarra Petit Verdot 2015 Rating 90 **To** 2025 $29

Leeuwin Estate ★★★★★

Stevens Road, Margaret River, WA 6285 **Region** Margaret River
T (08) 9759 0000 **www.**leeuwinestate.com.au **Open** 7 days 10–5
Winemaker Paul Atwood, Tim Lovett, Phil Hutchison **Est.** 1974 **Dozens** 50 000
Vyds 121ha

This outstanding winery and vineyard is owned by the Horgan family, founded by Denis and Tricia, who continue their involvement, with son Justin Horgan and daughter Simone Furlong joint chief executives. The Art Series Chardonnay is, in my opinion, Australia's finest example, based on the wines of the last 30 vintages. The move to screwcap brought a large smile to the faces of those who understand just how superbly the wine ages. The large estate plantings, coupled with strategic purchases of grapes from other growers, provide the base for high quality Art Series Cabernet Sauvignon and Shiraz; the hugely successful, quick-selling Art Series Riesling and Sauvignon Blanc; and lower-priced Prelude and Siblings wines. Exports to all major markets.

ŶŶŶŶŶ **Art Series Margaret River Chardonnay 2014** Part hand, part machine-picked, part wild and part cultured yeast, matured for 11 months in new French oak. Incredibly youthful quartz-green colour; a great chardonnay, its intensity and length right up there with the best prior vintages; white peach and nectarine open the batting, pink grapefruit coming swiftly thereafter, creamy/nutty oak almost lost in the crowd. If this weren't enough, the aftertaste is a work of art, complete in itself. Screwcap. 13.5% alc. **Rating** 98 **To** 2029 $95 ✪

ŶŶŶŶŶ **Art Series Margaret River Shiraz 2014** Part hand-picked for whole bunches, part Selectiv machine–harvested for whole berries, matured in French oak (50% new) for 18 months. A wine that combines grace and power: fruit complexity with varietal expression and savoury tannins. Blackberry and plum fruits are the mainstays of the layered flavours, the darker notes worthy of the northern Rhône Valley. Screwcap. 13.5% alc. **Rating** 96 **To** 2044 $36 ○

Art Series Margaret River Cabernet Sauvignon 2013 Destemmed, crushed, matured for 12 months in French oak (40% new). The unadorned purity of this cabernet follows precisely in the footsteps of its predecessors. It is unlike most other Margaret River cabernets, a red brother to the Art Series Chardonnay, even if not quite as magical as that wine. The '13 regional vintage was highly rated at the time, a rating justified today. Screwcap. 13.5% alc. **Rating** 96 **To** 2038 $67 ○

Prelude Vineyards Margaret River Chardonnay 2015 If you didn't know about its Art Series sibling, you would be perfectly happy to accept this as a high class part of the Leeuwin Estate portfolio (which in a sense it is). A beautifully balanced wine, in terms both of its suite of stone fruit, citrus and pear flavours, and of the subtle barrel-ferment oak inputs. Its length is no less impressive. Screwcap. 14% alc. **Rating** 95 **To** 2025 $34 ○

Siblings Margaret River Sauvignon Blanc Semillon 2016 A 60/40% blend, and a case of seek and ye shall find almost any aroma or flavour that you might (or might not) expect. Snow pea and grass in the vegetal quadrant, guava and Granite Belt in the tropical quadrant, lime and lemon in the dominant citrus suite, green apple also sneaking in. Only Margaret River can achieve this alchemy. Screwcap. 13% alc. **Rating** 94 **To** 2020 $22 ○

ⵏⵏⵏⵏⵏ   **Art Series Margaret River Sauvignon Blanc 2015** Rating 93 To 2019 $30
Siblings Margaret River Shiraz 2015 Rating 92 To 2029 $22 ○
Prelude Vineyards Margaret River Cabernet Sauvignon 2013 Rating 92 To 2030 $27
Art Series Margaret River Riesling 2016 Rating 91 To 2021 $22 ○
Pinot Noir Chardonnay Brut 2013 Rating 90 To 2019 $35 TS

Lenton Brae Wines   ★★★★★

3887 Caves Road, Margaret River, WA 6285 **Region** Margaret River
T (08) 9755 6255 **www.**lentonbrae.com **Open** 7 days 10–6
Winemaker Edward Tomlinson **Est.** 1982 **Dozens** NFP **Vyds** 9ha
The late architect Bruce Tomlinson built a strikingly beautiful winery (heritage-listed by the Shire of Busselton), now in the hands of winemaker son Edward (Ed), who consistently makes elegant wines in classic Margaret River style. A midwinter (French time) trip to Pomerol in Bordeaux to research merlot is an indication of his commitment. Exports to Indonesia, Singapore and China.

ⵏⵏⵏⵏⵏ   **Wilyabrup Margaret River Chardonnay 2014** This is a compelling chardonnay with the region's signature 'peaches and cream' aroma, offset by a mid-palate core of oatmeal, nougatine, truffle and curd that massages the high beam of maritime acidity to the point where it is almost imperceivable. Such is the wine's poise; luminous flavours and length. Screwcap. 13.5% alc. **Rating** 95 **To** 2026 $70 NG

Margaret River Semillon Sauvignon Blanc 2016 Wow – this marks the 30th consecutive vintage of a distinct Margaret River style, and one Lenton Brae has helped shape. Brimming with grapefruit, ripe honeydew melon, lime oil, grassiness, ginger spice and more complex flinty notes, while the neat acidity keeps the sweetness and richness contained. Screwcap. 13% alc. **Rating** 94 **To** 2019 $22 JF ○

ⵏⵏⵏⵏⵏ   **Southside Margaret River Chardonnay 2016** Rating 93 To 2024 $26 NG ○
Margaret River No Way Rose 2016 Rating 93 To 2018 $18 NG ○
Lady Douglas Margaret River Cabernet Sauvignon 2015 Rating 93 To 2031 $30 JF
Margaret River Shiraz 2015 Rating 92 To 2027 $30 NG
Margaret River Cabernet Merlot 2015 Rating 90 To 2025 $26 JF

Leo Buring ★★★★★

Sturt Highway, Nuriootpa, SA 5355 **Region** Eden Valley/Clare Valley
T 1300 651 650 **Open** Not
Winemaker Peter Munro **Est.** 1934 **Dozens** NFP

Between 1965 and 2000, Leo Buring was Australia's foremost producer of rieslings, with a rich legacy left by former winemaker John Vickery. After veering away from its core business into other varietal wines, it has now refocused on riesling. Top of the range are the Leopold Derwent Valley and the Leonay Eden Valley Rieslings, under a changing DW bin no. (DWS for '15, DWT for '16 etc), supported by Clare Valley and Eden Valley Rieslings at significantly lower prices, and expanding its wings to Tasmania and WA.

ⓎⓎⓎⓎⓎ **Leopold Tasmania Riesling 2016** DWT20. From the White Hill Vineyard in northeast Tasmania acquired by TWE from Brown Brothers. Both its region and varietal character contribute to the mouthwatering response as the wine enters the mouth and lime juice and crunchy acidity strike simultaneously. Screwcap. 13% alc. **Rating** 96 **To** 2031 $40 ✪
Leonay Riesling 2016 DWT18 Watervale. The quality of this wine shines through immediately. While the citrus fruit flavours are generous, they have balanced acidity to provide shape and a long, clean finish. It's a traditional Australian riesling of high quality. Screwcap. 11.5% alc. **Rating** 95 **To** 2031 $40
Eden Valley Riesling Dry 2016 No finer riesling pedigree in this country than from this producer and this region. Classic citrus aromas hold sway on the bouquet, more towards lemon than lime, which is entirely appropriate. Elements of honeysuckle juxtaposed with the essence of the land's rocky outcrops. Textural but reserved on the palate, the acidity seeming elemental in nature. Needs time. Screwcap. 12% alc. **Rating** 94 **To** 2035 $20 SC ✪

ⓎⓎⓎⓎⓎ **Eden Valley Riesling Dry 2015 Rating** 91 **To** 2024 $20 ✪
Clare Valley Riesling Dry 2016 Rating 90 **To** 2023 $20 ✪

Leogate Estate Wines ★★★★★

1693 Broke Road, Pokolbin, NSW 2320 **Region** Hunter Valley
T (02) 4998 7499 **www**.leogate.com.au **Open** 7 days 10–5
Winemaker Mark Woods **Est.** 2009 **Dozens** 30000 **Vyds** 127.5ha

Since purchasing the substantial Brokenback Vineyard in 2009 (a key part of the original Rothbury Estate, with vines over 40 years old), Bill and Vicki Widin have wasted no time. Initially the Widins leased the Tempus Two winery, but prior to the '13 vintage they completed the construction of their own winery and cellar door. They have also expanded the range of varieties, supplementing the long-established 30ha of shiraz, 25ha of chardonnay and 3ha of semillon with between 0.5 and 2ha of each of verdelho, viognier, gewurztraminer, pinot gris and tempranillo. They have had a string of wine show successes for their very impressive portfolio. In 2016 Leogate purchased a 61ha certified organic vineyard at Gulgong (Mudgee) planted to shiraz, cabernet sauvignon and merlot. Exports to Malaysia, Hong Kong and China.

ⓎⓎⓎⓎⓎ **Museum Release Brokenback Hunter Valley Shiraz 2011** First tasted early '13, now for the third time. This will outlive most wine lovers because it is now, as it always has been, luscious and full of red and black fruits, supple tannins and positive oak. It is a near-perfect example of balance, and with my knowlede of great old Hunter shirazs, I stick to the '41 drink-to date. This will be singing in the rain when it's 30yo. Screwcap. 14% alc. **Rating** 96 **To** 2041 $70 ✪
Museum Release Western Slopes Reserve Hunter Valley Shiraz 2011 This wine won three trophies and five gold medals (including the National Wine Show) in its youth, and I was swept away by its richness and complexity, and tannins that now seem more obvious than before, causing me to give it a 50-year life. Screwcap. 14% alc. **Rating** 96 **To** 2061 $150
Brokenback Vineyard Hunter Valley Semillon 2014 Has taken the first steps towards the full spectrum of flavours that will emerge over the coming years, its promise underlined by the length of its finish and aftertaste. It's a weird world in

which to suggest that 11% alcohol may be pushing the upper limit, but it does mark the difference between this wine and its younger sibling. That it's done the wine no harm is evident in the points. Screwcap. 11% alc. **Rating** 95 **To** 2024 **$22** ✪

Brokenback Vineyard Hunter Valley Semillon 2015 The 45yo vines have responded in fine style to the revitalisation of the vineyard since being acquired by the Widins. The vintage certainly threw out its challenges, but semillon seems to meet them despite its thin skins and relatively large berries. This has a delicious mix of citrus of various kinds, crisp acidity providing the platform for a wine almost as good today as it will be in 5 years. Screwcap. 10.5% alc. **Rating** 94 **To** 2025 **$22** ✪

Creek Bed Reserve Hunter Valley Semillon 2013 First tasted Mar '14, and has moved slowly on from that date, maintaining its mix of lemon, grass and herb. Much more lies down the track. Screwcap. 11.5% alc. **Rating** 94 **To** 2028 **$30** ✪

Vicki's Choice Reserve Hunter Valley Chardonnay 2015 Hand-picked, fermented in French hogsheads, matured on lees with some stirring. Quite apart from the oak, this has more fruit concentration than its siblings, with whole bunches joining the citrus and stone fruits on the long palate. Screwcap. 13.5% alc. **Rating** 94 **To** 2024 **$70**

Brokenback Vineyard Hunter Valley Shiraz 2014 The vineyard was planted circa '70 by Rothbury Estate, and was ultimately sold in two parts, thereafter reunited by Leogate. The bouquet has more spicy notes than most Hunter Valley shiraz, amplified this vintage, but backed up by a full spectrum of red, purple and black fruits matured in French oak. Will be a classic, but needs a degree of patience. Screwcap. 14% alc. **Rating** 94 **To** 2034 **$40**

🍷🍷🍷🍷☐ **Museum Release Reserve Shiraz 2010** **Rating** 93 **To** 2030 **$70**
H10 Block Reserve Chardonnay 2015 **Rating** 92 **To** 2022 **$38**
Creek Bed Reserve Chardonnay 2014 **Rating** 92 **To** 2022 **$38**
Brokenback Vineyard Shiraz Viognier 2014 **Rating** 92 **To** 2029 **$40**
Brokenback Vineyard Chardonnay 2014 **Rating** 91 **To** 2020 **$26**
Creek Bed Reserve Chardonnay 2015 **Rating** 90 **To** 2021 **$38**

Lerida Estate ★★★★☆

The Vineyards, Old Federal Highway, Lake George, NSW 2581 **Region** Canberra District
T (02) 6295 6640 **www**.leridaestate.com.au **Open** 7 days 10–5
Winemaker Malcolm Burdett **Est.** 1997 **Dozens** 6000 **Vyds** 7.93ha

Lerida Estate, owned by Jim Lumbers and Anne Caine, owes a great deal to the inspiration of Dr Edgar Riek, planted as it is immediately to the south of his former Lake George vineyard, and also planted mainly to pinot noir (there are smaller plantings of pinot gris, chardonnay, shiraz, merlot, cabernet franc and viognier). The Glenn Murcutt-designed winery, barrel room, cellar door and cafe complex has spectacular views over Lake George. In May 2017 Jim and Anne decided to retire, and Lerida was purchased by Michael McRoberts. Exports to China.

🍷🍷🍷🍷🍷 **Canberra District Shiraz Viognier 2015** A 95/5% blend, co-fermented, matured for 10 months in French oak (20% new). By some distance the most complex and convincing of the Lerida Estate red wines, bordering on outright full-bodied. Purple and black fruits have a strong spice and cracked black pepper substrate, the fruit framed by ripe, but persistent, tannins and cedary oak. Screwcap. 14.2% alc. **Rating** 95 **To** 2039 **$75**

Canberra District Pinot Grigio 2016 Hand-picked, fermented in stainless steel, matured for 3 months. One of Lerida's most impressive white wines, a grigio that has abundant flavours in a broader than usual spectrum, coursing through apple, stone fruit, pear and ripe citrus on a long, intense palate. Screwcap. 13.5% alc. **Rating** 94 **To** 2020 **$24** ✪

🍷🍷🍷🍷☐ **Josephine Lake George Canberra District Pinot Noir 2014** **Rating** 92 **To** 2023 **$65**
Canberra District Pinot Noir Rose 2016 **Rating** 90 **To** 2018 **$19** ✪
Cullerin Canberra District Pinot Noir 2015 **Rating** 90 **To** 2021 **$35**

Lethbridge Wines ★★★★★

74 Burrows Road, Lethbridge, Vic 3222 **Region** Geelong
T (03) 5281 7279 **www**.lethbridgewines.com **Open** Mon-Fri 11-5, W'ends 11-5
Winemaker Ray Nadeson, Maree Collis **Est.** 1996 **Dozens** 6000 **Vyds** 10ha
Lethbridge was founded by scientists Ray Nadeson, Maree Collis and Adrian Thomas. In Ray's words, 'Our belief is that the best wines express the unique character of special places.' As well as understanding the importance of terroir, the partners have built a unique straw-bale winery, designed to recreate the controlled environment of cellars and caves in Europe. Winemaking is no less ecological: hand-picking, indigenous yeast fermentation, small open fermenters, pigeage (foot-stomping) and minimal handling of the wines throughout the maturation process are all part and parcel of the highly successful Lethbridge approach. Ray also has a distinctive approach to full-blown chardonnay and pinot noir. There is also a contract winemaking limb to the business. Exports to the UK, Denmark, Singapore and China.

♟♟♟♟♟ **Allegra Geelong Chardonnay 2013** Low-yielding 35yo vines from Rebenberg Vineyard at Mt Duneed, whole-bunch pressed to new French oak puncheons, wild yeast, mlf and left on lees for 15 months. Wow – what a wine. At once full-bodied, rich and complex, yet vibrantly fresh and tight. The palate is stunning – a gorgeous lemon ginger-infused clotted cream character, and super length. Screwcap. 13.5% alc. **Rating** 96 **To** 2025 $85 JF
Mietta Geelong Pinot Noir 2013 At once powerful yet incredibly detailed and refined. Macerated cherries, pips and spice, jamon, dried herbs, quite mouthwatering. Nothing out of place – the oak and 80% whole bunches are woven into the fabric of this full-bodied pinot. Tannins like velvet, persistent and long. Screwcap. 13% alc. **Rating** 96 **To** 2024 $85 JF
The Bartl Geelong Chardonnay 2015 The first chardonnay with fruit entirely estate-grown, and named after Stefan Bartl, who has helped with every vintage and in between to look after these vines. Richly flavoured in the Lethbridge way, with nuanced oak, creamy lees, grilled nuts, plenty of spice to the ripe stone fruit with citrus freshness. The palate is a knockout, full of power and finesse. Screwcap. 13.5% alc. **Rating** 95 **To** 2025 $45 JF
Pinot Gris 2016 What a terrific pinot gris, with its pale copper hue and crunchy fresh and poached pears flecked with powdered ginger, vanilla and cardamom. Loads of creamy texture and lemon curd, but sprightly acidity keeps it buoyant given its complexity and depth. Screwcap. 12.5% alc. **Rating** 95 **To** 2021 $30 JF ✪
Geelong Pinot Noir 2015 This has a thirst-quenching quality about it: there's acidity and an abundance of juicy, tangy cherry fruit with whole-bunch qualities, and overall freshness. It's by no means simple. The tannins are supple, the body compact, oak part of the equation but not dominating – this is special. Screwcap. 12.8% alc. **Rating** 95 **To** 2026 $45 JF
Hillside Haven Single Vineyard Geelong Pinot Noir 2015 Of all the Lethbridge Pinots, this has the most colour, the sweetest fruit and the richest flavour; fruit comes off a vineyard in Anakie. Floral, with dark cherries and raspberries, a whisper of balsam and wood spice with poised tannins and fresh acidity to close. Just lacks some oomph midway. But a lovely wine. Screwcap. 13.2% alc. **Rating** 94 **To** 2024 $45 JF
Que Syrah Syrah Pyrenees Shiraz 2016 Fruit from the Malakoff vineyard in the Pyrenees. This is concentrated and intense, with an astonishing dark-purple colour and fragrance – a very good wine. Full-bodied, supple, plentiful tannins, some sweet-sour acid drops and loads of spicy fruit. Screwcap. 14.5% alc. **Rating** 94 **To** 2025 $30 JF ✪

♟♟♟♟♡ **Hat Rock Single Vineyard Geelong Pinot Noir 2015** **Rating** 91 **To** 2022 $45 JF

Leura Park Estate ★★★★☆

1400 Portarlington Road, Curlewis, Vic 3222 **Region** Geelong
T (03) 5253 3180 **www**.leuraparkestate.com.au **Open** W'ends 10.30–5, 7 days Jan
Winemaker Darren Burke **Est.** 1995 **Dozens** 5000 **Vyds** 15.94ha
Leura Park Estate's vineyard is planted to chardonnay (50%), pinot noir, pinot gris, sauvignon blanc, riesling and shiraz. Owners David and Lyndsay Sharp are committed to minimal interference in the vineyard, and have expanded the estate-grown wine range (Sauvignon Blanc, Pinot Gris, Chardonnay, Pinot Noir and Shiraz) to include Vintage Grande Cuvee. The next step was the erection of a winery for the 2010 vintage, leading to increased production and ongoing wine show success. Exports to South Korea and Singapore.

♆♆♆♆♆ **Block 1 Reserve Geelong Chardonnay 2015** Finesse and detail here. A full-bodied and flavoursome wine with stone fruit, grapefruit pith and grilled cashews, creamy lees and lemon curd. The French oak, 35% new, impacts on flavour and shape but all positively, the end result a moreish, savoury-toned wine. Screwcap. 13% alc. **Rating** 95 **To** 2024 $45 JF

♆♆♆♆♆ **Geelong Riesling 2016 Rating** 93 **To** 2024 $25 JF ✪
Geelong Pinot Noir 2015 Rating 92 **To** 2022 $33 JF
Geelong Chardonnay 2015 Rating 90 **To** 2022 $25 JF
Geelong Shiraz 2015 Rating 90 **To** 2025 $35 JF

Lightfoot & Sons ★★★★★

Myrtle Point Vineyard, 717 Calulu Road, Bairnsdale, Vic 3875 **Region** Gippsland
T (03) 5156 9205 **www**.lightfootwines.com **Open** Not
Winemaker Alastair Butt, Tom Lightfoot **Est.** 1995 **Dozens** 10 000 **Vyds** 29.3ha
Brian and Helen Lightfoot have established pinot noir, shiraz, chardonnay, cabernet sauvignon and merlot, the lion's share to pinot noir and shiraz. The soil is very similar to that of Coonawarra, with terra rossa over limestone. Most of the grapes are sold (as originally planned) to other Vic winemakers. With the arrival of Alastair Butt (formerly of Brokenwood and Seville Estate), and supported by son Tom, production has increased, and may well rise further. Second son Rob has also come onboard, bringing 10 years' experience in sales and marketing.

♆♆♆♆♆ **Home Block Gippsland Chardonnay 2015** Hand-picked, pressed straight to French oak (30% new) for fermentation on full solids, matured for 10 months, 146 dozen made. The depth, intensity and length of the fruits are utterly exceptional, throwing down the gauntlet at the feet of top class Yarra chardonnay. The grapefruit component is mouthwatering, drawing saliva from the mouth, crunchy acidity an ally. Will be very long-lived. Screwcap. 13.2% alc. **Rating** 97 **To** 2030 $50 ✪

♆♆♆♆♆ **River Block Gippsland Shiraz 2015** Hand-picked, 100 days post-ferment maceration, matured in French oak (50% new). Technically difficult vinification has achieved all of its aims: the fruit is intense and long, yet elegant, and very expressive of cool-grown shiraz with its red and black cherry composition. The new oak has been totally integrated, the mouthfeel supple and persuasive. Screwcap. 13.8% alc. **Rating** 96 **To** 2035 $50 ✪

Myrtle Point Vineyard Gippsland Chardonnay 2016 Picked over 2 weeks, different clones/vineyard blocks, free-run juice and light pressings fermented in French oak (15% new) with yeasts. Attention to detail has paid dividends: this combines elegance and intensity, balance and length. White peach and citrussy acidity soar on the finish, imprinting themselves permanently on the very long palate and aftertaste. All class. Screwcap. 13.2% alc. **Rating** 95 **To** 2028 $28 ✪
Cliff Block Gippsland Pinot Noir 2015 Estate-grown on an exposed limestone bluff, hand-picked, 30% whole bunches, 70% destemmed; open-fermented, matured for 10 months in French puncheons (30% new). Very good depth to the colour; this has the potential to become wonderfully complex over the years

to come. In the meantime, its intense black cherry fruit with a savoury fringe commands respect. Screwcap. 13% alc. **Rating** 95 **To** 2030 $50

Myrtle Point Single Vineyard Gippsland Lakes Shiraz 2015 Estate-grown, open-fermented, matured for 11 months in new and used French oak. The bouquet is positively fragrant with red fruits and spices, the elegant light to medium-bodied palate a silk tapestry of red and purple fruits, superfine but persistent tannins and perfectly balanced and integrated French oak. A lovely shiraz for pinot noir devotees looking for the occasional dalliance. Screwcap. 13.8% alc. **Rating** 95 **To** 2027 $28 **❂**

Myrtle Point Single Vineyard Gippsland Lakes Shiraz 2014 Destemmed into open fermenters, cold-soaked for 3 days, 4 days post-fermentation maceration, pressed to French oak (15% new) for maturation. Bright, full colour; a seriously impressive cool-grown medium-bodied shiraz rippling with glistening black and red fruits, a rainbow of spice, pepper and licorice, ripe but fine tannins and a whisper of French oak. Has an unlimited drinking span. Screwcap. 14% alc. **Rating** 95 **To** 2030 $26 **❂**

Myrtle Point Vineyard Gippsland Pinot Noir 2016 Estate-grown MV6 planted in '97, eight picking days 4–25 Mar, destemmed, open-fermented with cultured yeast, 15% fermented with 30% whole bunches for carbonic maceration, matured in new and used French oak. This complex vinification has resulted in a very complex pinot, with red and purple fruits, abundant spices and savoury/earthy fine-grained tannins. This in turn leads to good length and texture. Screwcap. 13.4% alc. **Rating** 94 **To** 2023 $28 **❂**

ꟿꟿꟿꟿꟿ **Myrtle Point Vineyard Gippsland Pinot Noir 2014** Rating 92 **To** 2025 $28
Myrtle Point Single Vineyard Gippsland Lakes Rose 2016 Rating 91 **To** 2018 $22 **❂**

Lillian   ★★★★

Box 174, Pemberton, WA 6260 **Region** Pemberton
T (08) 9776 0193 **Open** Not
Winemaker John Brocksopp **Est.** 1993 **Dozens** 280 **Vyds** 3.2ha
Long-serving (and continuing consultant) viticulturist to Leeuwin Estate John Brocksopp has established 2.8ha of the Rhône trio of marsanne, roussanne and viognier, and 0.4ha of shiraz. He is also purchasing grapes from other growers in Pemberton. Exports to Japan.

ꟿꟿꟿꟿꟿ **Pemberton Marsanne Roussanne 2015** 83/17% with the fruit basket pressed, wild-yeast fermented and left on lees in old oak for 14 months. All that has created a complex, pitch-perfect wine. Pale straw and bright; a depth of flavour to this, with white peach in cream sprinkled with ginger spice – the palate glides. Superb balance. Screwcap. 14% alc. **Rating** 95 **To** 2021 $21 JF **❂**

ꟿꟿꟿꟿꟿ **Lefroy Brook Pemberton Pinot Noir 2015** Rating 93 **To** 2023 $32 JF

Lillypilly Estate   ★★★★☆

47 Lillypilly Road, Leeton, NSW 2705 **Region** Riverina
T (02) 6953 4069 **www**.lillypilly.com **Open** Mon–Sat 10–5.30, Sun by appt
Winemaker Robert Fiumara **Est.** 1982 **Dozens** 8000 **Vyds** 27.9ha
Botrytised white wines are by far the best offering from Lillypilly, with the Noble Muscat of Alexandria unique to the winery; these wines have both style and intensity of flavour and can age well. Table wine quality is always steady – a prime example of not fixing what is not broken. Exports to the UK, the US, Canada and China.

ꟿꟿꟿꟿꟿ **Noble Blend 2015** Sauvignon blanc and semillon. Lillypilly is one of a handful of makers of the blend used in Sauterne (there with an unimportant amount of muscadelle). This is rich, luscious, yet almost (but not quite) savoury. Needs a rich dessert. 375ml. Screwcap. 12% alc. **Rating** 91 **To** 2020 $34

Noble Harvest NV Sauvignon blanc, semillon gewurztraminer. The trouble with a NV without numeric identification of some kind is you can't relate a tasting note to any particular wine. This is a well balanced wine, its luscious stone fruit flavours balanced by acidity. Screwcap. 10% alc. **Rating** 90 **To** 2018 $24

Lindeman's (Coonawarra)   ★★★★★

58 Queensbridge Street, Southbank, Vic 3006 (postal) **Region** Coonawarra
T 1300 651 650 **www**.lindemans.com **Open** Not
Winemaker Brett Sharpe **Est.** 1965 **Dozens** NFP
Lindeman's Coonawarra vineyards have assumed a greater importance than ever thanks to the move towards single region wines. The Coonawarra Trio of Limestone Ridge Vineyard Shiraz Cabernet, St George Vineyard Cabernet Sauvignon and Pyrus Cabernet Sauvignon Merlot Malbec are all of exemplary quality.

🍷🍷🍷🍷🍷 **Coonawarra Trio Limestone Ridge Vineyard Shiraz Cabernet 2015**
A 75/25% blend, 'Trio' referring to the other two wines in this release. While it's strongly arguable that Lindeman's Coonawarra wines haven't been given the marketing support they deserve, the quality has been protected by the winemaking team, as this beautiful medium-bodied wine so eloquently proves. Blackberry, blackcurrant and mulberry fruit floats in silky tannins and quality oak. Screwcap. 13.5% alc. **Rating** 96 **To** 2035 $70 ✪
Coonawarra Trio St George Vineyard Cabernet Sauvignon 2015 It's a shame this wine slips through the cracks when the discussion turns to cabernet's place in Coonawarra or vice versa. This is a wine of high quality that should be put forward as a great example of the synergy between place and variety. Screwcap. 14.5% alc. **Rating** 95 **To** 2030 $70
Coonawarra Trio Pyrus Cabernet Sauvignon Merlot Malbec 2015 An 81/13/6% blend. Deep crimson-purple; by some distance the most full-bodied of the Trio, the tannins more marked, the span of fruit flavours broader, taking in plum alongside cassis. It needs – and will repay – cellaring. Screwcap. 14.5% alc. **Rating** 94 **To** 2030 $70

Lindenderry at Red Hill   ★★★★★

142 Arthurs Seat Road, Red Hill, Vic 3937 **Region** Mornington Peninsula
T (03) 5989 2933 **www**.lindenderry.com.au **Open** W'ends 11–5
Winemaker Barnaby Flanders **Est.** 1999 **Dozens** 1000 **Vyds** 3.35ha
Lindenderry at Red Hill is a sister operation to Lancemore Hill in the Macedon Ranges and Lindenwarrah at Milawa. It has a five-star country house hotel, conference facilities, a function area, day spa and restaurant on 16ha of gardens, but also has a little over 3ha of vineyards, planted equally to pinot noir and chardonnay over 15 years ago. Notwithstanding the reputation of the previous winemakers for Lindenderry, the wines now being made by Barney Flanders are the best yet. He has made the most of the estate-grown grapes, adding cream to the cake by sourcing some excellent Grampians shiraz.

🍷🍷🍷🍷🍷 **Grampians Shiraz 2015** The nuts and bolts are: hand-sorted in the vineyard then in the winery, destemmed by gravity to small open fermenters, wild yeast, 40 days on skins, aged 14 months in French hogsheads, 10% new. What a glorious wine. The palate is silky and smooth, with the finest, laciest tannins tied to a ball of perfectly ripe red-black fruit, dotted with black pepper, licorice, star anise and crushed juniper berries. Screwcap. 13.5% alc. **Rating** 96 **To** 2035 $35 JF ✪
Mornington Peninsula Chardonnay 2015 This fits and sits well. The barrel ferment adds depth and flavour to the fresh, lemony acidity plus the stone fruit and citrus fruit at the fore. Some oak spice along the way and a persistent finish; all up, quite moreish. Screwcap. 13% alc. **Rating** 95 **To** 2025 $40 JF

🍷🍷🍷🍷🍷 **Mornington Peninsula Pinot Noir 2015** **Rating** 93 **To** 2023 $45 JF
Macedon Ranges Pinot Noir 2015 **Rating** 93 **To** 2023 $40 JF
Macedon Ranges Pinot Gris 2016 **Rating** 90 **To** 2021 $35 JF

Linfield Road Wines

65 Victoria Terrace, Williamstown, SA 5351 **Region** Barossa Valley
T (08) 8524 7355 **www**.linfieldroadwines.com.au **Open** Thurs–Sun 10–5
Winemaker Daniel Wilson, Steve Wilson **Est.** 2002 **Dozens** 2500 **Vyds** 19ha
Linfield Road produces small batches of single vineyard wines from the Wilson family vineyard at Williamstown. The story began in 1860 when Edmund Major Wilson planted the first vines on the outskirts of Williamstown. Since Edmund's first plantings, the Wilsons have fostered a viticulture tradition that now spans five generations; three generations of the family currently live and work on the property, located at the very southern edge of the Barossa. It is situated high above the valley floor, with cooler nights and longer ripening periods. Exports to Canada, Malaysia, Singapore, Japan and China.

Whole Bunch Grenache 2016 From 46yo dry-grown vines, hand-picked, 100% whole bunches, basket pressed into a stainless steel tank, no oak used. From one of the highest and coolest parts of the Barossa Valley. The whole bunch fermentation has introduced a strong, savoury line of firm tannins, and the volume of red and purple fruits is above expectations. Moderate patience required. Cork. 15% alc. **Rating** 90 **To** 2026 $25

The Steam Maker Barossa Riesling 2016 **Rating** 89 **To** 2023 $20

Lino Ramble

2 Hall St, McLaren Vale, SA 5171 (postal) **Region** McLaren Vale
T 0409 553 448 **www**.linoramble.com.au **Open** Not
Winemaker Andy Coppard **Est.** 2012 **Dozens** 700
After 20 years of working for other wine companies, big and small, interstate and international, Andy Coppard and Angela Townsend say, 'We've climbed on top of the dog kennel, tied a cape around our necks, held our breaths, and jumped.' And if you are curious about the name (as I was), the story has overtones of James Joyce's stream of consciousness mental rambles.

Gomas McLaren Vale Grenache 2015 Wild yeast, 25% whole bunch, 21 days on skins, basket-pressed into old French oak. Light in colour but ever so characterful. Nuts, roasted coffee, cherries, sweetness and sourness. Leather. Spice. Behind every door, a new twist, a new turn. Bring out your best glassware; this deserves it. Screwcap. 14.4% alc. **Rating** 95 **To** 2026 $30 CM ✪

Ludo McLaren Vale Fiano 2016 **Rating** 93 **To** 2020 $30 JF
Blind Man's Bluff McLaren Vale Bastardo 2016 **Rating** 92 **To** 2020 $30 JF
Vinyl McLaren Vale Shiraz 2016 **Rating** 91 **To** 2022 $20 JF ✪
Pee Wee McLaren Vale Noro d'Avola 2016 **Rating** 91 **To** 2019 $25 JF
Tom Bowler McLaren Vale Nero d'Avola 2015 **Rating** 90 **To** 2020 $30 CM

Little Brampton Wines

PO Box 61, Clare, SA 5453 **Region** Clare Valley
T (08) 8843 4201 **www**.littlebramptonwines.com.au **Open** At the Clare Valley Tourism Centre
Winemaker Parlette Wines **Est.** 2001 **Dozens** 650
Little Brampton Wines is a boutique, family-owned business operated by Pamela Schwarz with the able assistance of the next generation, Edward and Victoria. The vineyards have been sold, but fruit for Little Brampton is still sourced from it, especially for the Flagpole Riesling. Exports to the UK.

Flagpole Clare Valley Riesling 2016 There's a good feeling of energy about this wine. You'll find all the expected and desirable aroma and flavour characters, along with the acidity that goes with the style, but it just has a bit more zip than some of its peers. The bouquet has a little extra lift, and on the palate, there's thrust and dimension to the flavours, with particularly good length. A cellaring certainty. Screwcap. 12% alc. **Rating** 94 **To** 2031 $24 SC

Little Creek Wines

15 Grantley Avenue, Victor Harbor, SA 5211 (postal) **Region** McLaren Vale
T 0415 047 719 **www**.littlecreekwines.com **Open** Not
Winemaker Duane Coates **Est.** 2014 **Dozens** 60

This is a partnership between Sam Gibson and brother-in-law Patrick Coghlan. Their real jobs are an archery wholesale business (Pats Archery) situated on the Fleurieu Peninsula. Pat is the leading compound archer in Australia and Sam is the manager of the business, importing and distributing all types of archery equipment. Sam is the one with wine in his veins; his father, Rob Gibson, owns the 5 red star Gibson Wines, and Sam's brother Abel Gibson has his own label, Ruggabellus. For many years Sam and Pat became (archery) friends with Duane Coates, which ultimately led to the creation of this micro-business, with Duane the winemaker. The grapes come from premium growers, and the partners have no intention of establishing/ purchasing vineyards or increasing the amount of wine at the present time.

ΨΨΨΨΨ Cabernet Shiraz 2015 Cabernet sauvignon 55% from Langhorne Creek and 45% Blewitt Springs shiraz aged for 18 months in French hogsheads. There's such a vibrancy of fruit leading the way, with each variety morphed into a balanced whole. Juicy red and black berries, cedary oak spice and Cherry Ripe all roll onto the supple palate with more intense fruit meeting the tannin and acid. Screwcap. 14.5% alc. **Rating** 95 **To** 2028 $30 JF **○**

Little Yarra Wines

PO Box 2311, Richmond South, Vic 3121 **Region** Yarra Valley
T 0401 228 196 **www**.littleyarra.com.au **Open** Not
Winemaker Dylan McMahon, Matt Pattison **Est.** 2013 **Dozens** 500 **Vyds** 1.2ha

Little Yarra Wines is a family partnership between Ian, Pip and Matt Pattison and Pip's sister Mary Padbury. The Pattisons previously operated a vineyard and winery in the Macedon Ranges (Metcalfe Valley Wines), but could not resist buying the Little Yarra Wines property and its plantings of 0.6ha each of pinot noir and chardonnay. The quality of the grapes also allowed them to secure Dylan McMahon as winemaker, with input from Matt Pattison.

ΨΨΨΨΨ Chardonnay 2016 A chardonnay bursting with life and energy, the bouquet half warning what is coming on the palate. Here intensity and purity drive the agenda, with white peach and grapefruit engaged in a dawn duel for primacy, oak acting as a second for both. The length of the palate and the aftertaste are stunning. Screwcap. 13.2% alc. **Rating** 97 **To** 2030

ΨΨΨΨΨ Pinot Noir 2016 Deep and clear crimson; a powerful and clear expression of pinot, with layers of plum and cherry fruit; no sense of heat, simply balanced generosity. A truly attractive and well made wine, a very good outcome for '16. Screwcap. 13.3% alc. **Rating** 95 **To** 2023

Livewire Wines

PO Box 369, Portarlington, Vic 3223 **Region** Geelong
T 0439 024 007 **www**.livewirewines.com.au **Open** Not
Winemaker Anthony Brain **Est.** 2011 **Dozens** 1000

Anthony Brain started working life as a chef, but in the late 1990s 'took a slight bend into the wine industry'. He started gathering experience in the Yarra Valley, and simultaneously started oenology studies at CSU. Margaret River followed, as did time in SA before a return to the Yarra, working at De Bortoli from 2003 to '07 (undertaking vintages in the Hunter, King and Yarra valleys). Five vintages as winemaker at Bellarine Estate followed, giving him 'a platform and understanding of the Geelong region and the opportunity to learn more about sites, viticulture and winemaking decisions'. It hasn't prevented him from foraging far and wide.

ΨΨΨΨΨ Swanno Heathcote Tempranillo 2016 The fruit for this delicious tempranillo was sourced from the Heathcote Ridge Vineyard, before gentle extraction and maturation in 80% French and 10% American oak for 10 months. Unfiltered and

gently turbid, this wine is indeed a livewire. Black cherry, raspberry, bitter cola
and anise notes jitterbug from nose to palate, with crunchy acidity towing the
flavours along. The oak, well nestled into the flowing fruit, helps to steer the ship
Dangerous! Screwcap. 14.2% alc. **Rating** 95 To 2021 $28 NG ✪

🍷🍷🍷🍷🍷 Geelong Orange Viognier 2016 **Rating** 93 To 2019 NG
Grampians Shiraz 2016 **Rating** 93 To 2022 $32 NG
Whole Bunch Love Grampians Shiraz 2016 **Rating** 93 To 2022 NG
Riverland Montepulciano 2016 **Rating** 93 To 2019 $24 NG ✪
The Blood of Hipsters 2016 **Rating** 92 To 2021 $26 NG
Bellarine Peninsula Pinot Noir 2016 **Rating** 90 To 2021 $32 NG

Lloyd Brothers

34 Warners Road, McLaren Vale, SA 5171 **Region** McLaren Vale
T (08) 8323 8792 **www.lloydbrothers.com.au Open** 7 days 11–5
Winemaker Ross Durbidge **Est.** 2002 **Dozens** 5000 **Vyds** 38ha
Lloyd Brothers Wine and Olive Company is owned and operated by David and Matthew
Lloyd, third-generation McLaren Vale vignerons. Their 25ha estate overlooks the township,
and is planted to 12ha shiraz, 0.8ha bushvine grenache and 0.4ha bushvine mataro (plus
sauvignon blanc, chardonnay, pinot gris and shiraz in the Adelaide Hills). The shiraz planting
allows the creation of a full range of styles, including Rose, Sparkling Shiraz, Fortified Shiraz
and Estate Shiraz, along with the White Chalk Shiraz, so named because of the white chalk
used to mark each barrel during the classification process. Exports to the UK.

🍷🍷🍷🍷🍷 Adelaide Hills Sauvignon Blanc 2016 No tricks to the vinification: machine-
harvested, crushed, pressed, cool-fermented in stainless steel with cultured yeast
(presumably the yeast enhancing the varietal expression). It has an unexpected
depth and intensity to the flavours, pitched midway between tropical and citrus.
Screwcap. 13.5% alc. **Rating** 90 To 2017 $20 ✪

🍷🍷🍷🍷 McLaren Vale Grenache Rose 2016 **Rating** 89 To 2018 $20

Lobethal Road Wines

2254 Onkaparinga Valley Road, Mount Torrens, SA 5244 **Region** Adelaide Hills
T (08) 8389 4595 **www.lobethalroad.com Open** W'ends & public hols 11–5
Winemaker David Neyle, Michael Sykes **Est.** 1998 **Dozens** 6500 **Vyds** 10.5ha
Dave Neyle and Inga Lidums bring diverse, but very relevant, experience to the Lobethal
Road vineyard, the lion's share planted to shiraz, with smaller amounts of chardonnay,
tempranillo, sauvignon blanc and graciano. Dave has been in vineyard development and
management in SA and Tasmania since 1990. Inga has 25+ years' experience in marketing and
graphic design in Australia and overseas, with a focus on the wine and food industries. The
property is managed with minimal chemical input. Exports to the UK.

🍷🍷🍷🍷🍷 Bacchant Adelaide Hills Chardonnay 2015 Has an attractive line of lemony
acidity anchoring the white nectarine, grapefruit and creamy leesy flavours, and
it's subtle. Supple, savoury and moreish. Screwcap. 12.6% alc. **Rating** 92 To 2020
$45 JF
Adelaide Hills Pinot Gris 2015 From a single elevated site at Lenswood,
hand-picked and whole-bunch pressed into stainless steel (80%) and used French
barriques for fermentation (20%), the latter component lees-stirred and taken
through partial mlf. This is fairly and squarely in gris territory, with layered texture
and structure to the varietal fruit in a Granny Smith apple/nashi pear group of
flavours. Screwcap. 13% alc. **Rating** 92 To 2017 $25 ✪
Adelaide Hills Roussanne 2015 Hand-picked from the estate Mt Torrens
Vineyard (475m) on 5 Apr, whole-bunch pressed into used French barriques for
fermentation and maturation. It's early days, but the wine already has complexity
and depth to its mix of citrus and Granny Smith apple flavours. The length and
depth of the fruit profile makes it an each-way proposition to cellar for more

complexity or simply drink now for freshness. Screwcap. 13.4% alc. **Rating** 92 To 2020 $31

Adelaide Hills Tempranillo Graciano 2015 First of all the colour entices – a vibrant purple-black red – then the aromas take you in with a flurry of raspberry, cherry-cola, jubes (but not confected), with plenty of spice, Dutch licorice and earthy tones. Supple palate, juicy and fresh, effortless to drink. Screwcap. 13.3% alc. **Rating** 92 **To** 2023 $25 JF ✪

Adelaide Hills Sauvignon Blanc 2016 As it should be, this is juicy and lively, with ripe nashi pears, prickly pear too, cinnamon spice and a flutter of tropical fruit with crushed herbs. A touch of sweetness yet remains refreshing. Screwcap. 12.5% alc. **Rating** 91 **To** 2018 $22 JF ✪

Bacchant Adelaide Hills Chardonnay 2014 A voluptuous and mouthfilling style, taking on yellow stone fruit, poached quince, roasted hazelnuts and creamed honey. The oak/lees characters add to the body, and good acidity keeps it afloat (just). Screwcap. 13.1% alc. **Rating** 90 **To** 2019 $45 JF

Adelaide Hills Pinot Gris 2016 There's texture and richness, the right mix of ripe pears sprinkled with spice, some sweetness kept in check by creamed honey notes. This holds interest. Screwcap. 13.1% alc. **Rating** 90 **To** 2019 $25 JF

ΨΨΨΨ   Adelaide Hills Pinot Noir 2015 Rating 89 **To** 2020 $25 JF

Logan Wines   ★★★★★

Castlereagh Highway, Apple Tree Flat, Mudgee, NSW 2850 **Region** Mudgee
T (02) 6373 1333 **www**.loganwines.com.au **Open** 7 days 10–5
Winemaker Peter Logan **Est.** 1997 **Dozens** 45 000

Logan is a family-owned and operated business with emphasis on cool climate wines from Orange and Mudgee. The business is run by husband and wife team Peter (winemaker) and Hannah (sales and marketing). Peter majored in biology and chemistry at Macquarie University, moving into the pharmaceutical world working as a process chemist. In a reversal of the usual roles, his father encouraged him to change careers, and Peter obtained a graduate diploma of oenology from the University of Adelaide in 1996. The winery and tasting room are situated on the Mudgee vineyard, but the best wines are all made from grapes grown in the Orange region. Exports to the EU, Japan and other major markets.

ΨΨΨΨΨ   **Orange Sauvignon Blanc 2016** Crushed and remained on skins for 10 hours before pressing, 20% fermented on skins, remaining on skins for 2 weeks before pressing, 15% barrel-fermented in 500l Hungarian and French barrels, undergoing partial mlf, the remainder in stainless steel. Courageous winemaking has paid off with a wine of unusual, zingy flavours that include ginger as well as a more normal span of citrus/grapefruit, tropical/guava. Screwcap. 13% alc. **Rating** 95 **To** 2017 $23 ✪

Ridge of Tears Mudgee Shiraz 2014 From a vineyard only 70km from the Orange Shiraz vineyard, and yet a completely different beast. This is beefy and substantial, with a swagger of tannin holding it all in firm place. Blackberry, woody herbs, chocolate, coffee grounds. It's dense and long and shows all the signs that it will be a long-termer. Screwcap. 14% alc. **Rating** 95 **To** 2034 $45 CM

Hannah Orange Rose 2016 35% pinot meunier, 30% shiraz, 20% cabernet franc and 15% pinot gris, the shiraz and cabernet franc fermented in a mix of stainless steel and French and Hungarian oak, the remainder in stainless steel. Pink tinged with salmon; the exceptional complexity in the winemaking process is reflected in the bouquet of red fruits, spices and red flowers/rose petals, the palate following every step of the bouquet. It is savoury and dry, but has enough fruit flavours to satisfy. Screwcap. 13% alc. **Rating** 94 **To** 2018 $23 ✪

Ridge of Tears Orange Shiraz 2014 Black cherry infused with roasted nut and black pepper notes. In flavour profile terms it's an 'oldie but a goodie', executed here with aplomb. Tannin is fine, intricate, woven into the wine. Acidity is refreshing, but also a conveyor of flavour. We have a very good wine on our hands here. Screwcap. 13% alc. **Rating** 94 **To** 2030 $45 CM

ŶŶŶŶŶ Weemala Orange Gewurztraminer 2016 Rating 92 To 2022 $20
Weemala Orange Riesling 2016 Rating 91 To 2023 $20 **✪**
Weemala Orange Pinot Gris 2016 Rating 91 To 2020 $20 **✪**
Weemala Mudgee Tempranillo 2015 Rating 91 To 2025 $20 **✪**
Orange Shiraz 2014 Rating 90 To 2029 $28
Central Ranges Shiraz Viognier 2014 Rating 90 To 2020 $20 CM **✪**
Weemala Mudgee Tempranillo 2014 Rating 90 To 2019 $20 CM **✪**

Lome   ★★★★☆

83 Franklings Road, Harcourt North, Vic 3453 **Region** Bendigo
T 0438 544 317 **Open** Not
Winemaker Tony Winspear **Est.** 2004 **Dozens** 800 **Vyds** 5ha
Tim and Diane Robertson lived and worked for 23 years in the Bendigo region, and
happened to be in the right place at the right time when, in 2008, they were able to purchase
a newly established vineyard at Harcourt North. They called their venture 'Lome', and have
since expanded the vineyard to 5ha of shiraz, marsanne, viognier and roussanne. Their interest
sprang from past times of backyard viticulture and garage-based winemaking at their home in
Burgundy, interspersed with holiday travels elsewhere in France.

ŶŶŶŶŶ **Bendigo Shiraz 2013** You can save a lot of words by using just one: elegant (or
pure, or focused, or balanced). There's simply no question about its calm quality,
nor the come-back-quickly call of the spicy black cherry/blackberry fruits.
Screwcap. 14.5% alc. **Rating** 95 **To** 2028 $45

ŶŶŶŶŶ **Bendigo Shiraz 2014** Rating 93 To 2029 $45
Bendigo Marsanne Viognier Roussanne 2015 Rating 91 To 2022 $25

Lonely Vineyard   ★★★★☆

61 Emmett Road, Crafers West, SA 5152 (postal) **Region** Eden Valley
T 0413 481 163 **www.lonelyvineyard.com.au** **Open** Not
Winemaker Michael Schreurs **Est.** 2008 **Dozens** 400 **Vyds** 1.5ha
This is the venture of winemaker Michael Schreurs and Karina Ouwens, a commercial lawyer
from Adelaide. Daughter Amalia Schreurs can 'hoover a box of sultanas in record time' while
Meesh, the family cat, 'treats Karina and Amalia well, and Michael with the contempt he
deserves. As cats do.' One or other of the partners (perhaps both) has a great sense of humour.
Michael's winemaking career began with Seppelt Great Western winery for three years,
followed by six years at Henschke, and, more recently, The Lane Vineyard in the Adelaide Hills,
backed up by stints in Burgundy, the Rhône Valley, the US and Spain. Exports to the UK.

ŶŶŶŶŶ **Eden Valley Montepulciano 2015** I like this! An inky purple to opaque hue
brims with intent, yet the elevated Horseshoe Vineyard confers a granitic energy
and pulpy savouriness to the parade of iodine and black fruits that storm the palate.
An Italianate dry, structural focus sculpts the wine, the tannins offering a welcome
respite of savour to the finish. Screwcap. 13.5% alc. **Rating** 95 **To** 2025 $36 NG
Eden Valley Riesling 2016 Hailing from the Cactus Vineyard, 73yo vines at an
altitude of 460m, this is delicate, racy and pure. A surety over the next decade and
more, this energetic wine is braced along a steely trajectory of mineral-infused
lime, grapefruit and the faintest hint of ginger. Screwcap. 12.5% alc. **Rating** 95
To 2030 $26 NG **✪**
Eden Valley Shiraz 2015 Quintessentially old vine Eden Valley, this polished
magenta-hued shiraz displays the variety's chiaroscuro of florals, blue fruits and
spice against black cherry, plum, salami and iodine. Impeccably managed, with
just the right amount of oak serving as an adjunct rather than a yell. Vinous and
pulsating to a long finish. Screwcap. 13.5% alc. **Rating** 94 **To** 2032 $36 NG

Long Rail Gully Wines

161 Long Rail Gully Road, Murrumbateman, NSW 2582 **Region** Canberra District
T 0419 257 574 **www.**longrailgully.com.au **Open** W'ends & hols 11–4
Winemaker Richard Parker **Est.** 1998 **Dozens** 12000 **Vyds** 24ha
Long Rail Gully is operated by the Parker family, established by Barbara and Garry Parker, who began the planting of the 24ha vineyard in 1998. The plantings comprise shiraz (8ha), cabernet sauvignon (4ha), merlot, riesling and pinot gris (3.5ha each) and pinot noir (1.5ha). Winemaker son Richard studied winemaking at CSU, and was responsible for selecting the natural amphitheatre site for the vineyard, designing the layout, and supervising the planting. He also operates a successful contract winemaking business for wineries situated in Orange, Hilltops, Cowra and locally. Exports to China.

Murrumbateman Riesling 2016 Yet another example of a Canberra District riesling of the highest quality. Its purity is flawless, the citrus blossom-filled bouquet flowing into its perfectly balanced palate with lime juice and bright acidity bouncing off each other. It screams out drink me, and most will not be able to resist that siren call. Value+. Screwcap. 11.9% alc. **Rating** 95 **To** 2026 $22 **✪**

Murrumbateman Shiraz 2015 Bright, full crimson-purple; the expressive bouquet tells of the spicy cherry-accented fruit of the fresh, supple medium-bodied palate. Additional complexity comes via notes of pepper joining the spice, superfine tannins and oak, the last integrated. Screwcap. 13.8% alc. **Rating** 94 **To** 2029 $25 **✪**

Four Barrels 2013 An intriguing red blend of the selection of the best four barrels of the vintage, presumably not all the same variety. It works: there are very attractive black cherry, blackberry and blackcurrant flavours, with balanced tannins. Screwcap. 14% alc. **Rating** 94 **To** 2028 $60

Murrumbateman Rose 2016 Rating 92 **To** 2018 $22 **✪**
Murrumbateman Pinot Gris 2016 Rating 91 **To** 2018 $22 **✪**

Longline Wines ★★★★

PO Box 28, Old Noarlunga, SA 5168 **Region** McLaren Vale/Adelaide Hills
T 0415 244 124 **www.**longlinewines.com.au **Open** Not
Winemaker Paul Carpenter **Est.** 2013 **Dozens** 1000
The name reflects the changing nature of the Carpenter family's activities. Over 40 years ago Bob Carpenter gave up his job as a bank manager, becoming a longline fisherman at Goolwa; this was in turn replaced by a move to McLaren Vale for farming activities. Son Paul graduated from Adelaide University and began his professional life as a cereal researcher for the university, but a vintage job at Geoff Merrill Wines at the end of his university studies led to the decision to switch to winemaking. Over the next 20 years he worked both locally and internationally, in the Rhône Valley and Beaujolais, and at Archery Summit in Oregon. Back in Australia he worked for Hardys and Wirra Wirra and is currently senior winemaker at Hardys Tintara. Together with partner Martine, he secures small parcels of outstanding grapes from four grower vineyards of grenache and shiraz (three vineyards in McLaren Vale, the fourth in the Adelaide Hills).

Blood Knot McLaren Vale Shiraz 2015 This vintage is 100% McLaren Vale from the dry-grown Demasi Vineyard at Blewitt Springs, open-fermented for 10 days, matured in a combination of used demi-muids and puncheons. Right on the bullseye of McLaren Vale shiraz style, most coming from the vineyard, with rampant black fruits, dark chocolate, licorice and earth. It is full-bodied, but happily allows you time and space to reflect on all it offers. Screwcap. 14.5% alc. **Rating** 95 **To** 2036 $26 **✪**

Albright McLaren Vale Grenache 2015 From two old vine sites at Onkaparinga and Blewitt Springs, hand-picked, 15% whole bunches; 3 weeks extended skin contact, matured for 9 months in used puncheons. Light but bright colour; a masterclass in McLaren Vale grenache with a multifaceted array of red

and black fruits, spice and fine tannins to sustain the wine over the coming years. Makes the mouth truly happy. Screwcap. 14.5% alc. **Rating** 94 **To** 2029 $26 ✪
GSM McLaren Vale Grenache Shiraz Mourvedre 2015 From 3 dry-grown vineyards, 20yo shiraz and mourvedre, 55yo grenache, open-fermented with a small amount of whole bunches, extended post-ferment maceration, matured in used puncheons. Blewitt Springs adds a touch of austerity to all wines that come from it, which adds to their quality and complexity, and this brightly coloured wine is no exception. The perfume of the grenache refuses to allow the darker fruits of the shiraz or the tannins of the mourvedre to dominate the wine. Screwcap. 14.5% alc. **Rating** 94 **To** 2025 $22 ✪

♀♀♀♀♀ **Bimini Twist McLaren Vale Rose 2016 Rating** 93 **To** 2018 $20 ✪

Longview Vineyard

Pound Road, Macclesfield, SA 5153 **Region** Adelaide Hills
T (08) 8388 9694 **www.**longviewvineyard.com.au **Open** 7 days 11–5
Winemaker Ben Glaetzer **Est.** 1995 **Dozens** 20 000 **Vyds** 63ha
With a lifelong involvement in wine and hospitality, the Saturno family are now approaching their 10th vintage at the helm of Longview. With a focus on the 63ha vineyard, recent plantings of barbera, gruner veltliner, new clones of chardonnay and pinot grigio add to significant holdings of 20-year-old shiraz, cabernet sauvignon, nebbiolo and sauvignon blanc. Winemaking is overseen by Ben Glaetzer, in close consultation with Peter and Mark Saturno. A new cellar door and kitchen was unveiled in 2017, adding to 12 accommodation suites, a popular function room and unique food and wine events on the vineyard. In 10 years, this 100% family-owned, estate-grown producer has gone from two markets to selling in more than 17 countries.

♀♀♀♀♀ **Macclesfield Chardonnay 2016** Entav clones 76, 95, 589 and I10V1 clones, hand-picked, whole-bunch pressed, wild-yeast fermented in French oak (70% new), 50% mlf, matured for 9 months (3 months lees contact). The distinguished line-up of clones has obviously contributed to the complexity of both the texture and the flavour of this impressive chardonnay; it has layers of fruit, with some creamy complexity ex the mlf matching the crunchy natural acidity, and quality French oak providing another layer. Screwcap. 12.5% alc. **Rating** 95 **To** 2026 $40
Yakka Adelaide Hills Shiraz 2015 Crushed and destemmed, fermented in open fermenters on skins for 14 days using cultured yeast, daily pumpovers, matured for 15 months in French hogsheads (20% new). The ability of the Longview vineyard to perfectly ripen shiraz was proved many years ago. The wine has good colour, the bouquet and palate constructed around red and black cherry fruit with sides of black pepper, licorice and a smidgeon of cedary French oak. Fine-grained tannins are a feature. Screwcap. 14.5% alc. **Rating** 94 **To** 2029 $29 ✪
The Piece Shiraz 2013 Hand-picked, destemmed and berry-sorted, wild yeast– open fermented in 5 separate batches, matured for 18–20 months before barrel selection. A very powerful, complex and focused wine, in contradistinction to its silk screen-printed bottle plastered with skin scraps that turn out to be a paper label of mind-snapping difficulty to make and apply. There is little of the often pretty red wines from '13 here, but the stark alternative does have its place picked out, with a European element to it. Diam. 14.5% alc. **Rating** 94 **To** 2033 $70
Adelaide Hills Nebbiolo Riserva 2014 Hand-picked, 5 days cold soak, 30 days wild yeast–open fermentation on skins, matured for (18% new) in used French hogsheads, plus 12 months bottle age before release. It certainly comes in a handsome bottle, and is equally certainly varietal. The tannins stay under control, and there are violets and rose petal aromas. It's on the edge of greatness, and would be a fine match for all foods Italian. Diam. 14% alc. **Rating** 94 **To** 2029 $45

♀♀♀♀♀ **Nebbiolo Rosato 2016 Rating** 92 **To** 2020 $25 ✪
Devil's Elbow Cabernet Sauvignon 2014 Rating 92 **To** 2029 $29

Lost Buoy Wines

c/- Evans & Ayers, PO Box 460, Adelaide, SA 5001 **Region** McLaren Vale
T 0400 505 043 **www.**lostbuoywines.com.au **Open** Not
Winemaker Phil Christiansen **Est.** 2010 **Dozens** 8000 **Vyds** 18.5ha
The Lost Buoy vineyard and estate is perched high on the cliffs at Port Willunga in McLaren Vale, overlooking the Gulf of St Vincent. The 6ha 'home block' is planted to grenache and shiraz, the region's foundation varieties. The red wines are made by experienced local contract winemaker Phil Christiansen. A rose is made from estate-grown grenache, while a series of white wines, sourced from McLaren Vale and Adelaide Hills, are made by experienced local winemakers. Exports to Canada, Singapore and Hong Kong.

ΤΤΤΤΤ **Gulf View Adelaide Hills Sauvignon Blanc 2016** A vibrant and lively wine guaranteed to wake up the taste buds, with its tropical fruit flavours veering more towards lemons and limes. Juicy with snappy acidity and loads of fun. Screwcap. 12% alc. **Rating** 91 **To** 2018 $18 JF ✪
The Edge McLaren Vale Shiraz 2016 Bright and juicy, with a focus on drinkability, so there's upfront fresh fruit and acidity, a sprinkling of spice, and savouriness with supple tannins. Screwcap. 14.5% alc. **Rating** 90 **To** 2021 $18 JF ✪

Lou Miranda Estate

1876 Barossa Valley Way, Rowland Flat, SA 5352 **Region** Barossa Valley
T (08) 8524 4537 **www.**loumirandaestate.com.au **Open** Mon–Fri 10–4.30, w'ends 11–4
Winemaker Lou Miranda, Janelle Zerk **Est.** 2005 **Dozens** 20 000 **Vyds** 23.29ha
Lou Miranda's daughters Lisa and Victoria are the driving force behind the estate, albeit with continuing hands-on involvement from Lou. The jewels in the crown of the estate plantings are 0.5ha of mourvedre planted in 1897 and 1.5ha of shiraz planted in 1907. The remaining vines have been planted gradually since '95, the varietal choice widened by cabernet sauvignon, merlot, chardonnay and pinot grigio. Exports to the UK, the US, and other major markets.

ΤΤΤΤΤ **Old Vine Barossa Valley Shiraz Grenache 2014** Hand-picked from vines over 100yo, open-fermented, matured in American oak (50% new). Vivid crimson-purple; a luscious and generous blend, shiraz providing the framework, grenache adding a layer of red fruits for the black fruits of the shiraz, the merger synergistic in producing this medium to full-bodied blend. The one comment is that it seems every bit of its 14% alcohol. Screwcap. **Rating** 95 **To** 2030 $60

ΤΤΤΤΤ **Golden Lion Barossa Valley Shiraz 2015** **Rating** 90 **To** 2025 $46

Lowe Wines

Tinja Lane, Mudgee, NSW 2850 **Region** Mudgee
T (02) 6372 0800 **www.**lowewine.com.au **Open** 7 days 10–5
Winemaker David Lowe, Liam Heslop **Est.** 1987 **Dozens** 116 000 **Vyds** 41.3ha
Lowe Wines has undergone a number of changes in recent years, the most recent the acquisition of Louee and its two vineyards. The first is at Rylstone, led by shiraz, cabernet sauvignon, petit verdot and merlot, with chardonnay, cabernet franc, verdelho and viognier making up the balance. The second is on Nullo Mountain, bordered by the Wollemi National Park, at an altitude of 1100m, high by any standards, and often the coolest location in Australia. Lowe Wines continues with its organic profile. The Tinja property has been in the Lowe family ownership for five generations.

ΤΤΤΤΤ **Nullo Mountain Mudgee Riesling 2016** This hails from a fully organic certified site, nestled circa 1100m. This is very high even by international standards (except Argentina). Lime blossom, quince and lemon zest make the introduction to this delicate wine, brimming with intent but in need of time. A chalkiness edges the palate before a stream of cool, altitudinal acidity rushes through the wine's centre, bringing a balletic tension, precision and great length. Screwcap. 11% alc. **Rating** 95 **To** 2026 $50 NG

Nullo Mountain Sauvignon Blanc 2015 Isolated from the main brigade of Mudgee vineyards, this sauvignon is sourced from an escarpment planted at 1100m, subject to both maritime and sub-alpine influences. This is a wine built around texture. Barrel fermentation with wild yeast and the subsequent build-up of tension and detail following lees handling, form its fabric. Flavours of quince, assorted stone fruits glazed with honey and a herbaceous zing at the back end, complete the package. Screwcap. 13.1% alc. **Rating** 94 **To** 2020 $30 NG ❖

🍷🍷🍷🍷🍷 **Museum Release Louee Nullo Mountain Riesling 2010** Rating 93 To 2026 $50 NG
Block 5 Mudgee Shiraz 2013 Rating 93 To 2030 $50 NG
Headstone Mudgee Rose 2016 Rating 92 $28 NG
Mudgee Zinfandel 2013 Rating 91 To 2025 $75 NG

Lyons Will Estate

60 Whalans Track, Lancefield, Vic 3435 **Region** Macedon Ranges
T 0412 681 940 **www**.lyonswillestate.com.au **Open** By appt
Winemaker Llew Knight (Contract) **Est.** 1996 **Dozens** 600 **Vyds** 4.2ha
Oliver Rapson (with a background in digital advertising) and Renata Morello (a physiotherapist with a PhD in public health) believe the Macedon Ranges has the best of both worlds: less than an hour's drive to Melbourne, ideal for pinot and chardonnay, and still sparsely settled. The property had 2ha of vines planted in 1996 (pinot noir clones D5V12, D4v2 and 115 and chardonnay), and they have extended the pinot noir to 1.2ha, increasing the 115 and introducing MV6, and planted 1ha each of riesling and gamay. A new winery was completed for the 2016 vintage, and they also have visions of planting a further 0.8ha of chardonnay. The local knowledge of Llew Knight, and of course his vast winemaking experience, will prove very useful.

🍷🍷🍷🍷🍷 **Macedon Ranges Pinot Noir 2015** Estate-grown clones D5V12, D4V2 and 115, open-fermented, 14 days on skins, matured in French oak (33% new) for 16 months. Bright, clear crimson-purple; an altogether impressive wine, all its parts in alignment; the fragrant red flower aromas presage a red cherry, damson plum and spice palate. The wine glides along and across the mouth, fruit to the fore, but cedary oak makes a quiet statement as it joins with superfine tannins on the finish and aftertaste. Diam. 13.5% alc. **Rating** 95 **To** 2025 $33 ❖

🍷🍷🍷🍷🍷 **Macedon Ranges Chardonnay 2015** Rating 91 To 2022 $35

Mac Forbes

Graceburn Wine Room, 11a Green Street, Healesville, Vic 3777 **Region** Yarra Valley
T (03) 9005 5822 **www**.macforbes.com **Open** Thurs–Sat 11–9, Sun–Tues 11–5
Winemaker Mac Forbes, Austin Black **Est.** 2004 **Dozens** 6000
Mac Forbes cut his vinous teeth at Mount Mary, where he was winemaker for several years before heading overseas in 2002. He spent two years in London working for Southcorp in a marketing liaison role, then travelled to Portugal and Austria to gain further winemaking experience. He returned to the Yarra Valley prior to the '05 vintage, purchasing grapes for the two-tier portfolio: first, the Victorian range (employing unusual varieties or unusual winemaking techniques); and second, the Yarra Valley range of multiple terroir-based offerings of Chardonnay and Pinot Noir. Exports to the UK, the US, Canada, Spain, Sweden, Norway, Hong Kong and Thailand.

🍷🍷🍷🍷🍷 **Black Label Woori Yallock Pinot Noir 2014** A barrel selection from the best section of the 1.36ha block of MV6 clone planted in '95. Good depth of hue; has significantly more power, complexity and length than the '15 standard releases, with dark cherry and plum fruit woven through with spices and fine tannins. Serious pinot with a long life ahead, retaining elegance and balance despite that power. 26 dozen made. Cork. 12.5% alc. **Rating** 97 **To** 2030 $140 ❖

ΨΨΨΨΨ Hoddles Creek Chardonnay 2015 I10V1 clone planted in '97; hand-picked, crushed, wild-yeast fermented in new and used French oak, 9 months' maturation, sterile-filtered. Exemplary tension, drive and finesse; natural minerally acidity a whip cord running through the palate. Minerally notes ex low pH (no mlf). Retasting highlights juicy grapefruit flavours. Cork. 13% alc. **Rating** 96 **To** 2027 $50 **◯**

Yarra Valley Chardonnay 2015 You can ask for little more. It offers funk, flavour and finesse in elegant form. Grapefruit and stone fruit with citrus, struck match and wheat. It all combines beautifully. It all lingers on the finish. Screwcap. 13% alc. **Rating** 95 **To** 2023 $30 CM **◯**

Coldstream Pinot Noir 2015 Serious pinot, not at all plump, with strings of herbs and spiced cherry characters sizzling along firm lines of tannin. More tension than richness; it's wine as a psychological drama. Light, long, highly strung and ultimately highly impressive. Synthetic. 12.5% alc. **Rating** 95 **To** 2025 $50 CM

Woori Yallock Pinot Noir 2015 MV6 planted in '95, standard Mac Forbes vinification/maturation, 300 dozen made. Good hue and clarity; red cherry fruit with a hint of rhubarb comes in a pure stream of light, but juicy, flavour on the long, well balanced palate. Cork. 12.5% alc. **Rating** 95 **To** 2026 $75

Wesburn Pinot Noir 2015 MV6 planted in '81, hand-picked, 10% whole bunch, part foot-stomped; 12 months in used oak. Bright crimson-purple; fragrant red and black cherry fruit on the bouquet, changing gears on the complex, savoury sour cherry palate with some echoes of stemmy whole bunch. Works very well, almost in spite of itself. Cork. 12.5% alc. **Rating** 95 **To** 2025 $75

Woori Yallock Chardonnay 2015 I10V1 clone planted in '97; hand-picked, crushed, wild-yeast fermented in new and used French oak, 10 months maturation, sterile-filtered. Elegant and poised; slides effortlessly through the length of the palate, but doesn't have quite the same intensity as the Hoddles Creek. Cork. 13% alc. **Rating** 94 **To** 2022 $50

Yarra Valley Pinot Noir 2015 It's difficult to taste this wine without looking at the price and thinking: look how far we've come. This is a complex, savoury, spice-riddled, non-sweet pinot noir of style, poise and length. It's pinot noir for grownups, at a terrific price. Screwcap. 12.5% alc. **Rating** 94 **To** 2023 $30 CM **◯**

Yarra Junction Pinot Noir 2015 Similar slightly developed hue to the other ArdeaSealed wine (Hoddles Creek), matured in new and used oak, 150 dozen made. Counterintuitively, plum replaces cherry, with a supple, light-bodied palate, the balance very good. ArdeaSeal. 12% alc. **Rating** 94 **To** 2023 $50

Hugh 2013 All manner of goings on. Honey, soy, blackcurrant, mint, redcurrant and violets. A whisper of truffles too. Pretty, firm and lively, like walking through a vineyard during a storm. Chaos as a spellbinding force. Cabernet sauvignon, merlot, cabernet franc, petit verdot and malbec from a vineyard at Gruyere in the Yarra Valley. Low alcohol is apparent but it does not taste unripe. Interest plus. Synthetic. 12.8% alc. **Rating** 94 **To** 2028 $70 CM

ΨΨΨΨΨ Hoddles Creek Pinot Noir 2015 Rating 92 To 2022 $50

Macaw Creek Wines   ★★★★

Macaw Creek Road, Riverton, SA 5412 **Region** Mount Lofty Ranges
T (08) 8847 2657 www.macawcreekwines.com.au **Open** By appt
Winemaker Rodney Hooper **Est.** 1992 **Dozens** 10000 **Vyds** 10ha
The property on which Macaw Creek Wines is established has been owned by the Hooper family since the 1850s, but development of the estate vineyards did not begin until 1995. The Macaw Creek brand was established in '92 with wines made from grapes from other regions. Rodney Hooper is a highly qualified and skilled winemaker with experience in many parts of Australia, and in Germany, France and the US.

ΨΨΨΨΨ Reserve Mt Lofty Ranges Shiraz Cabernet 2012 An estate-grown 60/40% blend mostly aged in new French puncheons and some 1yo American hogsheads for 18 months. A super-generous wine with a profusion of blackberry and blackcurrant fruit opening the batting, met mid-pitch by vanillan American oak and ripe tannins. It all works very well in a big bash way. Screwcap. 14.5% alc. **Rating** 93 **To** 2030 $28

Em's Table Premium Organic Clare Valley Riesling 2015 NASAA-certified organic from the Sevenhill district. Mainstream Clare Valley style, but of very good quality. The core is the trifecta of lemon, lime and acid, here with very good balance and length. Made with the addition of SO_2, and will develop for many years. Screwcap. 12.5% alc. **Rating** 92 **To** 2025 $19 **○**

Organic Preservative Free Mt Lofty Ranges Shiraz 2016 Deep, dense crimson-purple; a massive full-bodied shiraz overflowing with black fruits, spices, dark chocolate and savoury tannins. Organically grown and made without any additions, most notably no SO_2. The combined effect of its certified organic status, no additions, oxygen-scavenging tannins, no oak, and the screwcap make this a very long-lived 'natural' wine. 14.5% alc. **Rating** 90 **To** 2026 $17 **○**

♥♥♥♥ **Em's Table Premium Organic Preservative Free Clare Valley Shiraz 2015** **Rating** 89 **To** 2018 $21

McGlashan's Wallington Estate ★★★★★

225 Swan Bay Road, Wallington, Vic 3221 **Region** Geelong
T (03) 5250 5760 **www**.mcglashans.com.au **Open** details on website
Winemaker Robin Brockett (Contract) **Est.** 1996 **Dozens** 2000 **Vyds** 12ha
Russell and Jan McGlashan began the establishment of their vineyard in 1996. Chardonnay (6ha) and pinot noir (4ha) make up the bulk of the plantings, the remainder shiraz and pinot gris (1ha each); the wines are made by Robin Brockett, with his usual skill and attention to detail. The cellar door offers food and music, and will see an increase in direct sales.

♥♥♥♥♥ **Townsend Reserve Bellarine Peninsula Shiraz 2015** Matured for 18 months in French and American oak. This has a depth and richness of varietal fruit beyond that of its lower-priced sibling, yet the alcohol is the same; as ever, not all grapes are equal. The colour is deeper, satsuma plum and blackberry joining black cherry, licorice too, providing another dimension. The length and balance are also of the highest order. Screwcap. 14% alc. **Rating** 96 **To** 2035 $45 **○**

Bellarine Peninsula Chardonnay 2015 Matured in French oak for 12 months. Bright straw-green; an immaculately balanced wine with an established pedigree stretching back some years; savoury notes pervade the flesh of white peach and grapefruit. The disciplined approach to the winemaking pays dividends. Screwcap. 13.5% alc. **Rating** 95 **To** 2027 $32 **○**

Bellarine Peninsula Pinot Grigio 2016 Hand-picked, crushed, free-run cool-fermented in tank. Very faint pink; this has quite exceptional depth to its melody of fruit flavours: strawberry, pear, stone fruit, Granny Smith apple and citrus all register at one point or another. This is truly made in the vineyard, pure quality control in the winery. Screwcap. 12.5% alc. **Rating** 95 **To** 2019 $28 **○**

Bellarine Peninsula Shiraz 2015 Best's clone, hand-picked, matured in French and American oak for 18 months. A highly expressive cool-grown medium-bodied shiraz, its fragrant bouquet precisely replicated on the palate with its black cherry fruit in the compliant arms of warm spices and black pepper, the tannins fine and savoury. Screwcap. 14% alc. **Rating** 95 **To** 2030 $35 **○**

♥♥♥♥♡ **Single Stave Bellarine Peninsula Chardonnay 2016** **Rating** 90 **To** 2023 $25
Bellarine Peninsula Pinot Noir 2015 **Rating** 90 **To** 2029 $32

McGuigan Wines ★★★★☆

Cnr Broke Road/McDonalds Road, Pokolbin, NSW 2321 **Region** Hunter Valley
T (02) 4998 7400 **www**.mcguiganwines.com.au **Open** 7 days 9.30–5
Winemaker Peter Hall, James Evers **Est.** 1992 **Dozens** 1.5 million
McGuigan Wines is an Australian wine brand operating under parent company Australian Vintage Ltd. McGuigan represents four generations of Australian winemaking, and while its

roots are firmly planted in the Hunter Valley, its vine holdings extend across SA, from the Barossa Valley to the Adelaide Hills and the Eden and Clare valleys, into Victoria and NSW. McGuigan Wines' processing facilities operate out of three core regions: the Hunter Valley, Sunraysia and the Barossa Valley. Exports to all major markets.

🍷🍷🍷🍷🍷 **The Shortlist Hunter Valley Semillon 2013** On its way to the first stage of maturity, the citrus components starting to build significantly. Its birthmark of acidity is guiding the wine down the path to full-fledged maturity around '20. Screwcap. 10.5% alc. **Rating** 95 **To** 2028 $35 ✪
The Shortlist Adelaide Hills Chardonnay 2015 Wild-yeast fermented in French hogsheads. This over-delivers on its price. It is complex and layered, with the length one expects more from the Yarra Valley, but here is a feature reflecting the balance of the wine. The flavours are more or less evenly divided between stone fruit and citrus, with some smoky notes from the barrel ferment. Screwcap. 13.5% alc. **Rating** 94 **To** 2022 $29 ✪

🍷🍷🍷🍷🍷 **The Shortlist Eden Valley Riesling 2016 Rating** 93 **To** 2029 $29
Museum Release Bin 9000 Hunter Semillon 2007 Rating 92 **To** 2020 $50
Farms Barossa Valley Shiraz 2014 Rating 92 **To** 2034 $75
Hand Made Langhorne Creek Shiraz 2015 Rating 91 **To** 2025 $48
The Shortlist Barossa Valley Shiraz 2015 Rating 90 **To** 2035 $29

McHenry Hohnen Vintners ★★★★★

5962 Caves Road, Margaret River, WA 6285 **Region** Margaret River
T (08) 9757 7600 **www**.mchenryhohnen.com.au **Open** 7 days 10.30–4.30
Winemaker Julian Grounds **Est.** 2004 **Dozens** 10 000 **Vyds** 56ha
McHenry Hohnen is owned by the McHenry and Hohnen families, sourcing grapes from three vineyards owned by various members of the families. Vines have been established on the McHenry, Calgardup Brook and Rocky Road properties, all farmed biodynamically. The family members with direct executive responsibilities are leading Perth retailer Murray McHenry and Cape Mentelle founder and former long-term winemaker David Hohnen. Exports to the UK, Ireland, Sweden, Indonesia, Japan, Singapore, Hong Kong and NZ.

🍷🍷🍷🍷🍷 **Calgardup Brook Vineyard Margaret River Chardonnay 2015** Wild yeast ferment, evident lees handling and maturation in French oak of the utmost quality, to boot. More generous aromatically than wines made of fruit from the southern zones, the wine nevertheless boasts a nervous mineral tension underlying its swag of stone fruit flavours. Screwcap. 12.9% alc. **Rating** 96 **To** 2024 $55 NG ✪
Burnside Vineyard Margaret River Chardonnay 2015 Situated on the bend of the Margaret River in the centre of the region, Burnside is a unique site of black, micaceous soils. Presumably their capacity for heat retention serves to enhance ripening, manifest in abundant peach and apricot aromas. This is the most opulent expression of the swag. The artillery of crunchy acidity, fine oak and mealy lees, dutifully serving detail and freshness, remain. Full, long and very fine. Screwcap. 13.1% alc. **Rating** 95 **To** 2023 $55 NG
Rocky Road Margaret River Cabernet Merlot 2014 65% cabernet sauvignon, 25% merlot and 5% each of malbec and shiraz; the vinification is in the usual McHenry Hohnen template, with whole berry, partial wild yeast ferment in a stone vat, basket pressed, no additions other than minimal SO_2. Deeply coloured, it has a medium to full-bodied palate replete with blackcurrant, redcurrant, black olive and bay leaf flavours within a mesh of fine-grained tannins. Screwcap. 14.5% alc. **Rating** 95 **To** 2029 $25 ✪
Rolling Stone 2014 38% cabernet sauvignon, 38% merlot and the remainder petit verdot. This is a polished, forcefully ripe and assiduously structured blend. The wave of dark fruit aromas, the waft of cedar and reassuring bite of high quality French oak (18 months in 2 and 3yo barrels) and the stiff upper lip of acidity melded to finely woven grape tannins, are all class. This is best laid down as a test of mettle and patience. Screwcap. 13.8% alc. **Rating** 95 **To** 2035 $95 NG

Hazel's Vineyard Margaret River Chardonnay 2015 The wine boasts intensity of flavour and sneaky persistence, building nicely as it opens. Still, the overall impression is one of tension, smoky chiselled phenolics and punchy acidity steering the ship. Cool and brimming with intent. Screwcap. 13.2% alc. **Rating** 94 To 2023 $55 NG

Rocky Road Margaret River Shiraz 2014 A 90% whole berry/10% whole bunch ferment with partial wild yeast in a stone vat, hand-plunged, basket-pressed, no additions other than low level SO_2. While licorice and black fruits are regional, there is a hint of the dark chocolate found in McLaren Vale shiraz, which has contributed an X-factor to a thoroughly enjoyable, fleshy wine that has excellent structure framing that fruit. Patience strictly optional. Screwcap. 14.5% alc. **Rating** 94 To 2029 $25 ✪

Amigos Margaret River Shiraz Mataro Grenache 2014 The sole Rhône blend from the Margaret River. The colour is still vibrant, the blend utterly harmonious and satisfying thanks to the continuous interplay between red and black fruits plus savoury spices. Drink-whenever style. Screwcap. 14.5% alc. **Rating** 94 To 2022 $28 ✪

Hazel's Vineyard Margaret River Cabernet Sauvignon 2014 This is sumptuous Margaret River cabernet, displaying all the regional virtues: cassis, black plum, pastille, dried sage and a firm tea tannin spine. Yet it is the generosity of fruit that is the wine's calling card. Pillars of French oak (14 months, 20% new) keep this wine postured and proudly youthful, yet the wine's poise and extract bode very well for maturity when it all loosens up. Screwcap. 14.7% alc. **Rating** 94 To 2034 $60 NG

Tiger Country 2014 A 61/24/15% blend of tempranillo, petit verdot and graciano from three estate vineyards, separately vinified. Bright crimson; the bouquet is super-fragrant, with predominantly red cherry and some blueberry fruits, the palate upping the game with purple (plum), licorice and strongly textured tannins. Unusual wine. Screwcap. 14.8% alc. **Rating** 94 To 2029 $30 ✪

🍷🍷🍷🍷♀ **Rocky Road SSB 2016** Rating 93 To 2020 $20 NG ✪
Rocky Road Chardonnay 2015 Rating 93 To 2022 $25 ✪
Amigos Marsanne Chardonnay Roussanne 2013 Rating 93 To 2023 $28 NG
Tiger Country Tempranillo 2015 Rating 93 To 2027 $35 NG
Rocky Road Cabernet Merlot 2015 Rating 91 To 2023 $25 NG
Amigos Shiraz Grenache Mataro 2015 Rating 90 To 2023 $28 NG
Hazel's Vineyard Zinfandel 2014 Rating 90 To 2019 $40

McKellar Ridge Wines   ★★★★★

Point of View Vineyard, 2 Euroka Avenue, Murrumbateman, NSW 2582
Region Canberra District
T 0409 789 861 **www**.mckellarridgewines.com.au **Open** Sun 12–5 Sept–Jun
Winemaker Dr Brian Johnston **Est.** 2000 **Dozens** 600 **Vyds** 5.5ha
Dr Brian Johnston has completed a postgraduate diploma in science at CSU, focusing on wine science and wine production techniques. The wines come from low-yielding mature vines (shiraz, cabernet sauvignon, chardonnay, merlot and viognier), the white wines cool-fermented in stainless steel, the reds open-fermented with gentle hand plunging and basket pressing.

🍷🍷🍷🍷🍷 **Canberra District Shiraz Viognier 2015** Co-fermented with 4% viognier, matured for 9 months in French oak, mostly new. The promise of the complex, dark fruits of the bouquet is fulfilled by the elegant, yet intense, medium-bodied palate. It has superb shape, texture and balance. Small wonder Brian Johnston says it's the best so far. Screwcap. 13.8% alc. **Rating** 96 To 2035 $34 ✪
Canberra District Shiraz Viognier 2016 Bright crimson-purple; the bouquet and palate are given life and lift by 15% whole bunches and co-fermentation of 4% viognier. Plum and cherry fruit flavours are juicy and enticing, given a degree of gravitas by the oak and tannin management. Top result from a very good vintage. Screwcap. 13.6% alc. **Rating** 95 To 2026 $34

ŢŢŢŢ℃ Canberra District Pinot Noir 2015 Rating 90 To 2022 $30
Canberra District Merlot Cabernet Franc 2015 Rating 90 To 2025 $30

McLaren Vale III Associates ★★★★☆

309 Foggo Road, McLaren Vale, SA 5171 **Region** McLaren Vale
T 1800 501 513 **www**.mclarenvaleiiiassociates.com.au **Open** details on website
Winemaker Campbell Greer **Est.** 1999 **Dozens** 12 000 **Vyds** 34ha
McLaren Vale III Associates is a very successful boutique winery owned by Mary and John Greer and Reg Wymond. An impressive portfolio of estate-grown wines allows them control over quality and consistency, and thus success in Australian and international wine shows. The signature wine is Squid Ink Shiraz. Exports to the US, Canada, Indonesia, Hong Kong, Singapore, South Korea, Japan and China.

ŢŢŢŢŢ **Squid Ink Reserve Shiraz 2014** Open-fermented with cultured yeast, 8 days on skins, matured in new American oak for 18 months. Lives up to its name, with very good hue and depth; you might expect the American oak to dominate the bouquet and palate, but it doesn't, thanks to the density and power of the full-bodied array of black fruits and plentiful ripe tannins. This cries out for a decade (or more) in the cellar. Screwcap. 14.5% alc. **Rating** 95 **To** 2034 $55
Legacy McLaren Vale Shiraz 2013 French oak barrels 50% new and aged for 18 months. There could be no more concentration in this wine even if there were room – the intense plum and black-berried fruit, licorice, choc-mints and cedary wood take up every bit of space. The plush ripe tannins and big velvety texture across this full-bodied wine will excite many. Screwcap. 14.5% alc. **Rating** 94 **To** 2033 $120 JF

ŢŢŢŢ℃ **Squid Ink Reserve Shiraz 2015** Rating 93 To 2030 $55 JF
The Descendant of Squid Ink Shiraz 2016 Rating 91 To 2024 $35 JF

McLean's Farm ★★★★

Barr-Eden Vineyard, Menglers Hill Road, Tanunda, SA 5352 **Region** Eden Valley
T (08) 8564 3340 **Open** W'ends 10–5
Winemaker Bob and Wilma McLean **Est.** 2001 **Dozens** 6000 **Vyds** 5.3ha
The ever-convivial, larger-than-life Bob McLean covered a lot of wine turf until his death in April 2015. Many people, myself included, were good friends with Bob, and all of us were immensely saddened by his death. Exports to the UK.

ŢŢŢŢ℃ **Eden Valley Riesling 2016** Sitting in a nice spot, with country garden florals and wafts of powdered ginger, flavours of white pepper and raw ginger. Softish acidity with some roundness on the palate. Screwcap. 12.5% alc. **Rating** 93 **To** 2025 $20 JF ❂
Master Barossa Shiraz 2013 Excellent dark crimson with sweet fruit to match amid the lashings of oak (cedary and vanillan flavours), plus chocolate-coated coffee beans and blackberry-toffee. Ripe and full-bodied with ample tannins, yet there's vivacity too. Screwcap. 14.5% alc. **Rating** 93 **To** 2028 $52 JF
Reserve Eden Valley Riesling 2015 The bright pale-straw colour belies the toasty development on the nose and palate. Burnt lemon ricotta, lime marmalade and ripe fruit, yet racy acidity is keeping this alive. One to watch in terms of ageing; best start drinking now. Screwcap. 12% alc. **Rating** 92 **To** 2023 $24 JF ❂

McLeish Estate ★★★★★

462 De Beyers Road, Pokolbin, NSW 2320 **Region** Hunter Valley
T (02) 4998 7754 **www**.mcleishhunterwines.com.au **Open** 7 days 10–5
Winemaker Andrew Thomas (Contract) **Est.** 1985 **Dozens** 8000 **Vyds** 17.3ha
Bob and Maryanne McLeish have established a particularly successful business based on estate plantings. The wines are of consistently high quality, and more than a few have accumulated show records leading to gold medal-encrusted labels. The quality of the grapes is part of the

equation, the other the skills of winemaker Andrew Thomas. 2015 marked McLeish Estate's 30th vintage. Over the years, there have been 30 trophies, 76 gold, 66 silver, and 80 bronze medals, the majority won in the Hunter Valley Wine Show and Sydney Wine Show. Exports to the UK, the US and Asia.

ŶŶŶŶŶ **Hunter Valley Semillon 2009** Aged release. The colour is still bright, light straw-green, the palate as fresh as a daisy, with lemon sorbet and Meyer lemon juice couched comfortably in non-threatening acidity. Close to its peak, but it will hold for years to come. Screwcap. 11% alc. **Rating** 96 **To** 2024 $70 ✪
Hunter Valley Semillon 2016 Nothing reticent about this wine. Right from the outset it offers a seamless flow of lemongrass, lemon zest, Meyer lemon and a core of life-giving and sustaining acidity. Screwcap. 10.5% alc. **Rating** 95 **To** 2029 $25 ✪

ŶŶŶŶŶ **Hunter Valley Semillon 2011 Rating** 92 **To** 2023 $50 PR
Reserve Hunter Valley Chardonnay 2015 Rating 91 **To** 2022 $45
Dwyer Hunter Valley Rose 2016 Rating 91 **To** 2019 $18 ✪

McPherson Wines   ★★★★

6 Expo Court, Mount Waverley, Vic 3149 **Region** Nagambie Lakes
T (03) 9263 0200 **www**.mcphersonwines.com.au **Open** Not
Winemaker Jo Nash **Est.** 1993 **Dozens** 150 000 **Vyds** 262ha
McPherson Wines is, by any standards, a substantial business. Its wines are largely produced for the export market, with enough sales in Australia to gain some measure of recognition here. Made at various locations from the estate vineyards and contract-grown grapes, they represent very good value. McPherson Wines is a joint venture between Andrew McPherson and Alister Purbrick (Tahbilk), both of whom have had a lifetime of experience in the industry. Quality is unfailingly good. Exports to all major markets.

ŶŶŶŶŶ **Don't tell Gary. 2015** Sourced from the Grampians, matured in new and used French oak. Toasty oak accompanies the black fruits of the bouquet and medium to full-bodied palate; the fruit is vibrant and juicy, savoury tannins part fruit, part oak derived. A worthy follow on to the gold medal-winning '14 – could be a blockbuster shiraz with a few more years under its belt. (Gary is the accountant.) Screwcap. 14.5% alc. **Rating** 94 **To** 2030 $24 ✪

ŶŶŶŶŶ **MWC Pinot Noir 2015 Rating** 92 **To** 2023 $22 ✪
MWC Shiraz Mourvedre 2015 Rating 92 **To** 2025 $22 ✪
La Vue Grenache Rose 2016 Rating 91 **To** 2017 $19 ✪

McWilliam's   ★★★★★

Jack McWilliam Road, Hanwood, NSW 2680 **Region** Riverina
T (02) 6963 3400 **www**.mcwilliams.com.au **Open** Wed–Sat 10–4
Winemaker Bryan Currie, Russell Cody, Andrew Higgins **Est.** 1916 **Dozens** NFP
Vyds 455.7ha
The best wines to emanate from the Hanwood winery are in whole or part from other regions, notably the Hilltops, Coonawarra, Yarra Valley, Tumbarumba, Margaret River and Eden Valley. As McWilliam's viticultural resources have expanded, it has been able to produce regional blends from across Australia of startlingly good value. The winery rating is strongly reliant on the exceptional value for money of the Hanwood Estate and Inheritance brands. The value of Mount Pleasant (Hunter Valley), Barwang (Hilltops) and Evans & Tate (Margaret River) will become ever more apparent as the ability of these brands to deliver world-class wines at appropriate prices is leveraged by group chief winemaker Jim Chatto. A founding member of Australia's First Families of Wine, 100% owned by the McWilliam family. Exports to all major markets.

ŶŶŶŶŶ **1877 Canberra Shiraz 2015** Hand-picked, 5 days cold soak, open-fermented, up to 50% whole bunches; 14 days on skins, matured for 9 months in French puncheons (35% new). Fragrance and elegance personified. Juicy cherry fruit opens proceedings, then mouthwatering acidity and fine-grained tannins draw out the lingering finish. Amen. Screwcap. 13.5% alc. **Rating** 97 **To** 2035 $80 ○

♀♀♀♀♀ **Single Vineyard Glenburnie Tumbarumba Chardonnay 2014** This wine is all about the striking natural acidity that in turn has kept the pH low. This is why its colour, from which the pink grapefruit, Meyer lemon and white peach draw their freshness, has barely changed. It's taken almost 3 years for the wine to achieve the balance it now has. Screwcap. 13% alc. **Rating** 95 **To** 2024 $40

Single Vineyard Block 19 & 20 Hilltops Cabernet Sauvignon 2014 Destemmed, open-fermented, 14 days on skins, airbag-pressed, matured in French oak (35% new) for 16 months. Excellent crimson-purple; one of those rare full-bodied cabernets that calm the taster as it rests easily in the mouth, allowing the exploration of the blackcurrant and bay leaf fruit that is framed by ripe tannins and cedary oak. The keyword is balance. Screwcap. 13.5% alc. **Rating** 95 **To** 2044 $40

Appellation Series Orange Sauvignon Blanc 2015 Orange has long since established itself as a producer of quality sauvignon blanc, but some are a little too light and ephemeral. This wine, by contrast, is anything but. It has one pillar of passionfruit, and another of ruby grapefruit, and a connecting line of high-tensile acidity. While arguably at its best now, has enough going for it to take it through the next year. Screwcap. 13% alc. **Rating** 94 **To** 2018 $25 ○

♀♀♀♀♀ **Tightrope Walker Yarra Valley Pinot Noir 2016** Rating 93 To 2026 $25 ○
Tightrope Walker Yarra Valley Chardonnay 2015 Rating 91 To 2023 $25
High Altitude Hilltops Shiraz 2014 Rating 91 To 2029 $19 ○
Hanwood Estate 1913 Riverina Touriga 2016 Rating 91 To 2021 $25

Maddens Rise   ★★★★

Cnr Maroondah Highway/Maddens Lane, Coldstream, Vic 3770 **Region** Yarra Valley
T (03) 9739 1977 **www**.maddensrise.com **Open** Fri–Mon 11–5
Winemaker Anthony Fikkers **Est.** 1996 **Dozens** 2000 **Vyds** 22.5ha
Justin Fahey has established a vineyard planted to pinot noir (three clones), chardonnay (two clones), cabernet sauvignon, merlot, shiraz and viognier. Planting began in 1996, but the first wines were not released until 2004. The vines are grown using organic/biological farming practices that focus on soil and vine health, low yields and hand-picking to optimise the quality. Part of the grape production is sold to other Yarra Valley wineries.

♀♀♀♀♀ **Yarra Valley Viognier 2013** Estate-grown, wild-yeast fermented. This is an impressive viognier, winemaker Anthony Fikkers having successfully negotiated his way through the shoals that sink so many viognier ships. It has varietal fruit, but in conjunction with citrussy acidity on the long finish. Screwcap. 13.6% alc. **Rating** 93 **To** 2020 $30

Yarra Valley Pinot Noir 2013 From four blocks, 90% MV6, hand-picked and sorted, wild-fermented, matured in French oak for 9 months. Bright and clear colour with no sign of browning. An impressive pinot with a fragrant bouquet of red cherry and plum, the palate long, even and supple, with forest floor notes joining the dominant fruits on the finish and aftertaste. Screwcap. 13.2% alc. **Rating** 93 **To** 2023 $30

Yarra Valley Shiraz 2013 Includes 2% wild-yeast co-fermented viognier. Has retained a bright crimson-purple hue at 4yo; a juicy mix of red fruits, spice and bramble on the bouquet and palate alike. Intriguing wine. Screwcap. 13.8% alc. **Rating** 91 **To** 2023 $30

Yarra Valley Cinq Amis 2013 73% cabernet sauvignon, 22% merlot, 2% each of malbec and cabernet franc, 1% petit verdot. There's a lot going on here: the fruit more luscious and ripe than the alcohol would suggest, and creating no issue. You have to wait until the aftertaste to find the structure, but it's there (just). Screwcap. 12.9% alc. **Rating** 91 **To** 2025 $40

♀♀♀♀ **Yarra Valley Chardonnay 2013** Rating 89 To 2020 $30
Yarra Valley Nebbiolo 2013 Rating 89 To 2020 $40

Magpie Estate

PO Box 126, Tanunda, SA 5352 **Region** Barossa Valley
T (00) 0562 0300 www.magpieestate.com **Open** At Rolf Binder
Winemaker Rolf Binder, Noel Young **Est.** 1993 **Dozens** 10000 **Vyds** 16ha
This is a partnership between Rolf Binder and Cambridge (UK) wine merchant Noel Young.
Conceived in the early 1990s when grenache and mourvedre were largely forgotten varieties,
the two Rhône-philes have adopted that great larrikin of the Australian sky – the magpie – as
their mascot for the brand. Fruit is mainly sourced from a group of select growers, the recently
purchased 16ha (14ha of shiraz, 2ha of cabernet sauvignon) Smalltown vineyard in Ebenezer
providing estate-grown grapes for the 2017 vintage. Rolf and Noel say they have a lot of fun
making the wines, but are also serious about quality and delivering value for money. Exports
to the UK, Canada, Denmark, Poland, Finland and Singapore.

ΨΨΨΨΨ **The Sack Barossa Valley Shiraz 2015** A more conventional approach from
this increasingly interesting domain, with Barossan fruitcake and its assortment of
spice, dried fruits and candied orange peel all on full display. The oak, too, shifts
to an assortment of French and American (30% new), conferring a sprinkle of
coconut and bourbon-like sweetness. Familiarity breeds comfort and, for many,
contentment. Screwcap. 14% alc. **Rating** 94 **To** 2027 $30 NG ✪

ΨΨΨΨΨ **Rag & Bones Eden Valley Riesling 2016 Rating** 93 **To** 2026 $25 NG ✪
The Fixed Gear Grenache 2016 Rating 93 **To** 2021 $22 NG ✪
Natural Mourvedre Grenache 2016 Rating 93 **To** 2020 $25 NG ✪
The Call Bag Mourvedre Grenache 2013 Rating 93 **To** 2023 $25 CM ✪
Black Craft Barossa Valley Shiraz 2015 Rating 92 **To** 2025 $25 NG ✪
The Scoundrel Barossa Valley Shiraz 2015 Rating 92 **To** 2023 $20 NG ✪
The Mixed Thing 2016 Rating 92 **To** 2019 $20 NG ✪
The Scoundrel Grenache 2015 Rating 91 **To** 2020 $20 NG ✪
The Scoundrel Grenache Mataro Shiraz 2015 Rating 91 **To** 2021 $20
NG ✪
Clovella Mourvedre Grenache 2015 Rating 90 **To** 2021 $25 NG
The Tight Cluster Sparkling Shiraz 2012 Rating 90 **To** 2017 $48 TS

Main & Cherry

Main Road, Cherry Gardens, SA 5157 **Region** Adelaide Hills
T 0431 692 791 **www.**mainandcherry.com.au **Open** By appt
Winemaker Michael Sexton **Est.** 2010 **Dozens** 2500 **Vyds** 4.5ha
Michael Sexton grew up on the property, and graduated in oenology at Adelaide University
in 2003. Grapes from the existing shiraz plantings were sold to other wineries, but in '10 the
first single-vineyard Shiraz was made and the Main & Cherry brand name chosen. Since then
plantings of bushvine grenache and mataro have been made. The business continues to grow,
with the purchase of an established vineyard in Clarendon planted to 2.4ha of shiraz and 0.9ha
of grenache (the plantings at the Cherry Gardens vineyard consist of 0.8ha shiraz and
0.2ha each of mataro and grenache). Exports to Vietnam and China.

ΨΨΨΨΨ **Gruner Veltliner 2016** Ever so clear white pepper leaps from the glass on the
bouquet, followed by a riveting palate with citrus/grapefruit/pomelo flavours
running across river pebbles. Screwcap. 12.5% alc. **Rating** 95 **To** 2026 $25 ✪
Sangiovese 2015 A portion fermented in a ceramic egg-shaped amphora and
left on skins for 150 days, the balance open-fermented and basket pressed to used
French oak. Light but clear colour; fragrantly intense on both the bouquet and
palate with pure red and morello cherry fruit typical of the variety, and a carpet
of fine tannins. One is left to wonder what was the character of each of the
components, for the blend has an air of logic and inevitability about it. Screwcap.
14% alc. **Rating** 94 **To** 2030 $25 ✪

ΨΨΨΨΨ **Sauvignon Blanc 2016 Rating** 93 **To** 2021 $25 ✪
Shiraz 2015 Rating 91 **To** 2030 $25
Tempranillo 2015 Rating 90 **To** 2025 $25

Main Ridge Estate ★★★★★

80 William Road, Red Hill, Vic 3937 **Region** Mornington Peninsula
T (03) 5989 2686 www.mre.com.au **Open** Mon–Fri 12–4, w'ends 12–5
Winemaker James Sexton, Linda Hodges, Nat White (Consultant) **Est.** 1975
Dozens 1200 **Vyds** 2.8ha

Quietly spoken and charming Nat and Rosalie White founded the first commercial winery on the Mornington Peninsula, with an immaculately maintained vineyard and equally meticulously run winery. In December 2015, ownership of Main Ridge Estate passed to the Sexton family, following the retirement of Nat and Rosalie after 40 years. Tim and Libby Sexton have an extensive background in large-scale hospitality, first in the UK, then with Zinc at Federation Square, Melbourne, and the MCG. Son James Sexton completed the Bachelor of Wine Science degree at CSU in 2015. Nat will continue as a consultant to Main Ridge.

ΨΨΨΨΨ **Mornington Peninsula Chardonnay 2015** Hand-picked, crushed, 12 hours skin contact, wild-yeast fermented in new and 1yo French barriques, 100% mlf, matured for 11 months on lees. This has tremendous drive and complexity, but it's the length that takes it into the highest realm – and a long life. Screwcap. 13.5% alc. **Rating** 97 **To** 2028 $65 ❂

ΨΨΨΨΨ **Half Acre Mornington Peninsula Pinot Noir 2015** Wild yeast–open fermented, no whole bunches, 18 days on skins, matured for 17 months in new and used French barriques. Excellent colour; a complex but pure pinot with layers of red and black cherry fruit, fine tannins and perfect oak choice and handling. Will go on for many years. Screwcap. 13.5% alc. **Rating** 96 **To** 2030 $90
The Acre Mornington Peninsula Pinot Noir 2015 Identical vinification to the Half Acre. Light colour; perfectly ripened, fragrant and fresh red fruits with spices just starting to show. Suffers only in comparison to Half Acre (although it doesn't always work out this way). Screwcap. 13.5% alc. **Rating** 95 **To** 2025 $75

Majella ★★★★★

Lynn Road, Coonawarra, SA 5263 **Region** Coonawarra
T (08) 8736 3055 www.majellawines.com.au **Open** 7 days 10–4.30
Winemaker Bruce Gregory, Michael Marcus **Est.** 1969 **Dozens** 25 000 **Vyds** 55ha

The Lynn family has been in residence in Coonawarra for over four generations, starting as storekeepers, later graduating into grazing. The Majella property was originally owned by Frank Lynn, then purchased in 1960 by nephew George, who ran merinos for wool production and prime lambs. In '68 Anthony and Brian (the Prof) Lynn established the vineyards, since joined by Peter, Stephen, Nerys and Gerard. Bruce Gregory has been at the helm for every wine made at Majella. The Malleea is one of Coonawarra's classics, The Musician one of Australia's most outstanding red wines selling for less than $20 (having won many trophies and medals). The largely fully mature vineyards are principally shiraz and cabernet sauvignon, with a little riesling and merlot. Exports to the UK, Canada and Asia.

ΨΨΨΨΨ **Coonawarra Shiraz 2014** Fermentation completed (after pressing) in hogsheads, matured for 18 months in French and American oak. Just when you think the oak may have been overplayed, the fruit comes charging through on the back-palate, finish and aftertaste. It lifts the whole feel of the wine, and is the consequence of sophisticated winemaking from vines planted as far back as '69. Screwcap. 14.5% alc. **Rating** 95 **To** 2034 $37
Coonawarra Cabernet Sauvignon 2014 The hue is good, although not particularly deep; conclusion of fermentation in barrel integrates the oak better than can be achieved any other way – viz Grange. This is a lovely fruit-sweet (not sugar-sweet) and juicy cassis-laden cabernet ready for immediate drinking – or cellaring for up to 20 years. Screwcap. 14.5% alc. **Rating** 95 **To** 2034 $37
The Malleea 2013 An archetype of the Coonawarra idiom and a classic in the making, this Malleea is 55% cabernet sauvignon, 45% shiraz. The fruit is sourced from the oldest vines, abstemiously selected. The extraction is gentle and it shows, with finely tuned tannins framing and drawing up the saliva, forcing one to reach

for another glass as waves of blackcurrant, bitter chocolate and a hint of pimento waft across the finish. Cork. 14.5% alc. **Rating** 95 **To** 2035 **$**80 NG

🍷🍷🍷🍷 **Coonawarra Merlot 2015** **Rating** 93 **To** 2030 **$**30 NG
Coonawarra Sparkling Shiraz 2009 **Rating** 92 **To** 2019 **$**30 TS
The Musician Cabernet Shiraz 2015 **Rating** 90 **To** 2023 **$**18 NG ✪
Minuet NV **Rating** 90 **To** 2019 **$**30 TS

Malcolm Creek Vineyard ★★★★☆

33 Bonython Road, Kersbrook, SA 5231 **Region** Adelaide Hills
T (08) 8389 3619 **www**.malcolmcreekwines.com.au **Open** By appt
Winemaker Peter Leske, Michael Sykes **Est.** 1982 **Dozens** 800 **Vyds** 2ha
Malcolm Creek was the retirement venture of Reg Tolley, who decided to upgrade his retirement by selling the venture to Bitten and Karsten Pedersen in 2007. The wines are invariably well made and develop gracefully; they are worth seeking out, and are usually available with some extra bottle age at a very modest price. However, a series of natural disasters have decimated Malcolm Creek's production in recent years: '11 cabernet sauvignon not harvested due to continuous rain; '14 chardonnay not produced because of microscopic yield following rain and wind at flowering; and the '15 vintage truncated by bushfire and smoke taint. Exports to the UK, the US, Denmark, Malaysia and China.

🍷🍷🍷🍷🍷 **Ashwood Estate Adelaide Hills Cabernet Sauvignon 2012** Estate grown, hand-picked, matured for 20 months in French oak, then held for a further 30 months in bottle before release. The colour is still deep; it has clear-cut cassis fruit with black olive and fine, ripe tannins. It was picked at precisely the right time, the legacy being a wine with freshness that will never leave it. Cork. 13.5% alc. **Rating** 95 **To** 2037 **$**30 ✪

🍷🍷🍷🍷 **Adelaide Hills Chardonnay 2016** **Rating** 92 **To** 2020 **$**25 ✪
The Reginald Blanc de Blanc 2011 **Rating** 90 **To** 2019 **$**40 TS

Mandala ★★★★★

1568 Melba Highway, Dixons Creek, Vic 3775 **Region** Yarra Valley
T (03) 5965 2016 **www**.mandalawines.com.au **Open** Mon–Fri 10–4, w'ends 10–5
Winemaker Scott McCarthy, Andrew Santarossa, Charles Smedley **Est.** 2007
Dozens 8000 **Vyds** 29ha
Mandala is owned by Charles Smedley, who acquired the established vineyard in 2007. The vineyard has vines up to 25 years old, but the spectacular restaurant and cellar door complex is a more recent addition. The vineyards are primarily at the home base, Dixons Creek, with chardonnay (8ha), cabernet sauvignon (6ha), sauvignon blanc and pinot noir (4ha each), shiraz (2ha) and merlot (1ha). There is a separate 4ha vineyard at Yarra Junction planted entirely to pinot noir with an impressive clonal mix. Exports to China.

🍷🍷🍷🍷🍷 **The Mandala Matriarch Yarra Valley Pinot Noir 2015** From the estate's Dixon's Creek vineyard, in French oak (50% new) for 1 year. A deeply coloured wine richly flavoured and perfumed with cherries and damson plums, pepper and Middle Eastern spices, all enticing. Fuller-bodied, yet with a lovely flow to the palate and ripe, fleshy tannins. Screwcap. 13.7% alc. **Rating** 96 **To** 2025 **$**50 JF ✪
Yarra Valley Pinot Noir 2015 115, 114 and MV6 clones were hand-picked, destemmed and separately open-fermented, matured in French oak (25% new) for 12 months. A pinot with attitude and numerous nooks and crannies of different aroma and flavour contributions to its complexity. In the broad perspective it brings powerful red and black cherry fruits into a web of sour cherry and spicy tannins. A top vintage for Yarra Valley pinot, this wine a bargain. Screwcap. 12.9% alc. **Rating** 95 **To** 2025 **$**30 ✪
The Mandala Butterfly Yarra Valley Cabernet Sauvignon 2014 The colour and aromatics are convincing with well placed flavours of blackberries, juicy currants and cedary oak (which is integrated), sluiced with savouriness and

freshness. The medium-bodied palate sits neatly; so, too, the fine tannins. Screwcap. 13% alc. **Rating** 95 **To** 2026 $50 JF

Yarra Valley Chardonnay 2015 Wild-yeast fermented in French barriques (25% new), 20% undergoing mlf, matured for 9 months. Bright green-gold; grapefruit is the primary driver of the bouquet and palate, with a strong minerally streak providing focus and length. It is a prime example of the modern Yarra Valley chardonnay style, the finish and aftertaste expanding with power and intensity. Screwcap. 13.2% alc. **Rating** 94 **To** 2023 $30 ●

ⵟⵟⵟⵟⵟ **Yarra Valley Shiraz 2015 Rating** 92 **To** 2023 $30 JF
The Mandala Rock Yarra Valley Shiraz 2014 Rating 92 **To** 2026 $50 JF
Late Disgorged Blanc de Blancs 2010 Rating 91 **To** 2022 $70 TS
Yarra Valley Cabernet Sauvignon 2015 Rating 90 **To** 2025 $30 JF

Mandalay Estate ★★★☆

Mandalay Road, Glen Mervyn via Donnybrook, WA 6239 **Region** Geographe
T (08) 9732 2006 www.mandalayroad.com.au **Open** 7 days 11–5
Winemaker Peter Stanlake, John Griffiths **Est.** 1997 **Dozens** 600 **Vyds** 4.2ha
Tony and Bernice O'Connell left careers in science and education to establish plantings of shiraz, chardonnay, zinfandel and cabernet sauvignon on their property in 1997 (followed by durif). A hands-on approach and low yields have brought out the best characteristics of the grape varieties and the region. Exports to Taiwan.

ⵟⵟⵟⵟⵟ **Mandalay Road Geographe Durif 2015** The only wine from Mandalay Estate released in time for this edition of the *Wine Companion*. It has all that is typical of the variety: a deep colour, a deep well of black fruits given texture by ripe, but fine, tannins. Oak plays no significant role. Screwcap. 13.5% alc. **Rating** 90 **To** 2025 $35

Mandoon Estate ★★★★★

10 Harris Road, Caversham, WA 6055 **Region** Swan District
T (08) 6279 0500 www.mandoonestate.com.au **Open** for details see website
Winemaker Ryan Sudano **Est.** 2009 **Dozens** 10 000 **Vyds** 10ha
Mandoon Estate, headed by Allan Erceg, made a considerable impression with its wines in a very short time. In 2008 the family purchased a 13.2ha site in Caversham in the Swan Valley, on a property that had been in the hands of the Roe family since its initial settlement in the 1840s. Construction of the winery was completed in time for the first vintage, in 2010. Winemaker Ryan Sudano has metaphorically laid waste to Australian wine shows with the quality of the wines he has made. Since '11 Mandoon has collected 123 gold medals and 60 trophies.

ⵟⵟⵟⵟⵟ **Reserve Margaret River Chardonnay 2015** This is a beautifully elegant chardonnay, picked at exactly the right time, and not stage-managed at any point from vineyard to bottle. It is on a stage of its own, full of grace and charm, and has pure white peach/pink grapefruit aromas and flavours doing all the combination needed, oak used strictly as a means to an end. Screwcap. 12.5% alc. **Rating** 97 **To** 2027 $39 ●

ⵟⵟⵟⵟⵟ **Reserve Frankland River Shiraz 2013** Open-fermented for 14 days, then matured for 18 months in French oak. The vibrant, full crimson-purple colour signals a vibrantly juicy and intense array of blackberry, black cherry, licorice and spice held within a finely spun web of ripe tannins. Will outlive your patience. Screwcap. 14.5% alc. **Rating** 96 **To** 2038 $49 ●
Reserve Research Station Margaret River Cabernet Sauvignon 2013 From the Research Station set up by the Dept of Agriculture in '76. Bright crimson-purple; impeccable winemaking provides a brilliant display of cassis fruit, French oak and tannins in disciplined support. This wine really highlights the synergy between the region and variety, brilliant stuff. Screwcap. 14% alc. **Rating** 96 **To** 2038 $79

Margaret River Cabernet Merlot 2015 An 80/20% blend from the Bramley Research Station Vineyard, hand-picked, open-fermented 14 days on skins, matured in French hogsheads (40% new) for 14 months. Given its pedigree, its fruit significant gold medals, and above all else, its quality, its price is hard to follow, but no cause for complaint. It is brimful with cassis fruit, its tannins superfine, the oak integrated and the length exceptional. A standout bargain. Screwcap. 14% alc. **Rating** 96 **To** 2035 $29 ✪

Reserve Frankland River Riesling 2016 Light straw-green; complex aromas range through citrus (lime and grapefruit) and a hint of orange blossom, the palate seizing those characters in a millisecond, adding fruit spice and potent minerally acidity. A bred in the purple stayer. Screwcap. 12% alc. **Rating** 94 **To** 2036 $29 ✪

🍷🍷🍷🍷🍷 **Surveyors Red 2015 Rating** 93 **To** 2022 $24 ✪
The Pact Swan Valley Shiraz 2014 Rating 92 **To** 2044 $110
Old Vine Shiraz 2015 Rating 90 **To** 2035 $29

Marchand & Burch   ★★★★★

PO Box 180, North Fremantle, WA 5159 **Region** Great Southern
T (08) 9336 9600 **www**.burchfamilywines.com.au **Open** Not
Winemaker Janice McDonald, Pascal Marchand **Est.** 2007 **Dozens** 1100 **Vyds** 8.46ha
A joint venture between Canadian-born and Burgundian-trained Pascal Marchand and Burch Family Wines. Grapes are sourced from single vineyards, and in most cases, from single blocks within those vineyards (4.51ha of chardonnay and 3.95ha of pinot noir, in each case variously situated in Mount Barker and Porongurup). Biodynamic practices underpin the viticulture in the Australian and French vineyards, and Burgundian viticultural techniques have been adopted in the Australian vineyards (eg narrow rows and high-density plantings, Guyot pruning, vertical shoot positioning, and leaf and lateral shoot removal). Exports to the UK, the US and other major markets.

🍷🍷🍷🍷🍷 **Porongurup Mount Barker Chardonnay 2016** Hand-picked and sorted batches from each vineyard, cooled, whole-bunch pressed, wild-yeast fermented in all sizes of French oak (40% new), a portion of each batch undergoing mlf, matured for 9 months with continuous lees stirring until dry. The weight and balance of the wine have been precisely calibrated, opening with a floral bouquet leading into an assemblage of citrus (grapefruit), stone fruit (nectarine) and melon, oak providing a tattoo of grilled nuts. Screwcap. 13% alc. **Rating** 96 **To** 2029 $73

Villages Chardonnay 2016 From the Burch Family Mount Barrow vineyard at Mount Barker, predominantly Dijon clones 76, 95, 96 and 277, each separately vinified. Hand-picked and sorted, cooled, whole-bunch pressed, wild-yeast fermented in 50/50% used French oak and tank, matured for 9 months, part of each taken through mlf. The palate takes its time, minerally grapefruit juice and zest driving the considerable length. Screwcap. 13% alc. **Rating** 94 **To** 2026 $22

🍷🍷🍷🍷🍷 **Villages Rose 2016 Rating** 93 **To** 2018 $26
Mount Barrow Mount Barker Pinot Noir 2016 Rating 92 **To** 2023 $60

Marcus Hill Vineyard   ★★★★☆

560 Banks Road, Marcus Hill, Vic 3222 (postal) **Region** Geelong
T (03) 5251 3797 **www**.marcushillvineyard.com.au **Open** Not
Winemaker Darren Burke (Contract), Richard Harrison **Est.** 2000 **Dozens** 1000 **Vyds** 3ha
In 2000, Richard and Margot Harrison, together with 'gang pressed friends', planted 2ha of pinot noir overlooking Port Lonsdale, Queenscliff and Ocean Grove, a few kilometres from Bass Strait and Port Phillip Bay. Since then chardonnay, shiraz, more pinot noir, and three rows of pinot meunier have been added. The vineyard is run with minimal sprays, and the aim is to produce elegant wines that truly express the maritime site.

ΨΨΨΨΨ **Bellarine Peninsula Chardonnay 2014** Wild-yeast fermented in French barriques (40% new), lees-stirred, 50% mlf, matured for 12 months. This is a very attractive chardonnay with abundant personality and flavour, having taken full advantage of the '14 vintage (low yields are not all downside). It has grip without phenolics, the fruit with savoury elements that add complexity. The oak, too, makes a positive contribution. Screwcap. 12.5% alc. **Rating** 95 **To** 2024 $27 ○

ΨΨΨΨΨ **Bellarine Peninsula Rose 2016 Rating** 93 **To** 2018 $19 ○
Bellarine Peninsula Shiraz 2014 Rating 92 **To** 2023 $22 ○
People Madly Stomping Bellarine Peninsula Pinot Noir 2015 Rating 91 **To** 2022 $19 ○
Bellarine Peninsula Pinot Gris 2016 Rating 90 **To** 2018 $22

Margan Family   ★★★★★

1238 Milbrodale Road, Broke, NSW 2330 **Region** Hunter Valley
T (02) 6579 1317 **www**.margan.com.au **Open** 7 days 10–5
Winemaker Andrew Margan **Est.** 1997 **Dozens** 30 000 **Vyds** 98ha
Andrew Margan, following in his late father's footsteps, entered the wine industry over 20 years ago, working as a Flying Winemaker in Europe, then for Tyrrell's. The growth of the Margan Family business over the following years has been the result of unremitting hard work and a keen understanding of the opportunities Australia's most visited wine region provides. They have won innumerable awards in the tourism sector, against competition in the Hunter Valley, across NSW, and Australia-wide. The next generation will be able to cover all bases when their parents retire. Eldest son Ollie is finishing a double degree in winemaking and viticultural science at the University of Adelaide; daughter Alessa is studying communications at UTS while working in wine and food PR, and younger son James is enrolled in economics at Sydney University. Andrew has continued to push the envelope in the range of wines being made, without losing focus on the varieties that have made the Hunter famous. He began the development with barbera in 1998, and since then has progressively planted mourvedre, albarino, tempranillo and graciano. Exports to the UK, Germany, Norway, Indonesia, Malaysia, Vietnam, Hong Kong and China.

ΨΨΨΨΨ **White Label Hunter Valley Shiraz 2014** Dry-grown, 1t/acre, 20% whole bunch. Great synergy between the region and variety. Hunter terroir coming through strongly, with the red fruits and pepper of shiraz given an extra layer of complexity by the whole-bunch component. Densely flavoured but only medium-bodied; supple, but structured, founded more on acidity than tannin. A long life ahead. Screwcap. 13.5% alc. **Rating** 95 **To** 2030 $40 SC

ΨΨΨΨΨ **Hunter Valley Tempranillo Graciano Shiraz 2015 Rating** 92 **To** 2022 $40 JF
White Label Hunter Valley Semillon 2016 Rating 90 **To** 2025 $30 JF
Hunter Valley Albarino 2016 Rating 90 **To** 2018 $30 CM
Hunter Valley Shiraz 2015 Rating 90 **To** 2020 $20 ○
Breaking Ground Hunter Valley Shiraz Mourvedre 2015 Rating 90 **To** 2023 JF
Hunter Valley Merlot 2015 Rating 90 **To** 2022 $20 SC ○

Marko's Vineyard   ★★★★☆

PO Box 7518, Brisbane, Qld 4169 **Region** Adelaide Hills
T 0418 783 456 **www**.markosvineyard.com.au **Open** At Ekhidna
Winemaker Darryl Catlin, Matt Rechner **Est.** 2014 **Dozens** 21 000 **Vyds** 41.5ha
This is the reincarnation of the former Shaw + Smith M3 Vineyard, established in 1994 by Mark, Margie, Matthew and Michael Hill Smith, collectively owners of 70%, and Shaw + Smith, 30%. The split ownership wasn't generally understood, and in September 2014 Matthew Hill Smith and daughter Christobel purchased the shares hitherto owned by Margie Hill Smith, Michael Hill Smith and Shaw + Smith. In a parallel sale, Matthew Hill Smith sold his shares in Shaw + Smith and Tolpuddle Wines. The M3 Vineyard is a registered trademark

of Shaw + Smith, hence the renaming. What does not change is the planting of 27ha of sauvignon blanc, chardonnay and shiraz.

🍷🍷🍷🍷🍷 C3 Adelaide Hills Chardonnay 2016 C3 because the 3 clones are Mendoza, Bernard 95 and 76; aged in French oak 11 months. Bodes well with the pristine pale-straw hue with a shimmer of olive; stone fruit, restrained leesy characters of ginger and cream — a lovely fragrance. It's textural, but not too much, and ends softly. Screwcap. 12.9% alc. **Rating** 93 **To** 2025 $37 JF

Marq Wines   ★★★★★

860 Commonage Road, Dunsborough, WA 6281 **Region** Margaret River
T (08) 9756 6227 **www**.marqwines.com.au **Open** Fri–Sun & public hols 10–5
Winemaker Mark Warren **Est.** 2011 **Dozens** 2500 **Vyds** 1.5ha
Mark Warren has a degree in wine science from CSU and a science degree from the University of WA; to complete the circle, he is currently lecturing in wine science and wine sensory processes at Curtin University, Margaret River. He also has 27 years' experience in both the Swan Valley and Margaret River, and his current major commercial role is producing the extensive Happs range as well as wines under contract for several other Margaret River brands. When all of this is added up, he is responsible for 60 to 70 individual wines each year, now including wines under his own Marq Wines label. A quick look at the list – Vermentino, Fiano, Wild & Worked Sauvignon Blanc Semillon, Wild Ferment Chardonnay, Rose, Gamay, Tempranillo, Malbec, and Cut & Dry Shiraz (Amarone style) – points to the underlying philosophy: an exploration of the potential of alternative varieties and unusual winemaking methods by someone with an undoubted technical understanding of the processes involved.

🍷🍷🍷🍷🍷 **Serious Margaret River Rose 2016** Wild yeast–barrel fermented grenache has produced a textural, flavoursome wine. Super pale salmon-pink for starters, with watermelon and tangy red fruit, not too much, plus spice and lemony acidity. This is a serious rose, but it has a fair amount of fun about it, too. Screwcap. 12.8% alc. **Rating** 95 **To** 2019 $25 JF ✪

🍷🍷🍷🍷🍷 **Wild Ferment Margaret River Chardonnay 2015 Rating** 93 **To** 2024 $30 JF
Margaret River Vermentino 2016 Rating 93 **To** 2020 $25 JF ✪
DNA Margaret River Cabernet 2015 Rating 93 **To** 2027 $35 JF
Margaret River Gamay 2015 Rating 91 **To** 2021 $25 JF
Margaret River Fiano 2016 Rating 90 **To** 2020 $25 JF

Massena Vineyards   ★★★★★

PO Box 643, Angaston, SA 5353 **Region** Barossa Valley
T (08) 8564 3037 **www**.massena.com.au **Open** At Artisans of Barossa
Winemaker Jaysen Collins **Est.** 2000 **Dozens** 3000 **Vyds** 4ha
Massena Vineyards draws upon 1ha each of mataro, saperavi, petite syrah and tannat at Nuriootpa, also purchasing grapes from other growers. It is an export-oriented business, although the wines can also be purchased by mail order, which, given both the quality and innovative nature of the wines, seems more than ordinarily worthwhile. Exports to the US, Switzerland, Denmark, South Korea, Hong Kong and China.

🍷🍷🍷🍷🍷 **The Moonlight Run 2015** Mataro (from Moppa) and whole-bunch cinsaut co-fermented, old vine grenache (Vine Vale) and shiraz all wild-yeast fermented, bottled without fining or filtration. Its crimson colour is excellent, the bouquet full of spicy purple and black fruits, its mouthfeel simply outstanding. A tour de force of winemaking. Screwcap. 14% alc. **Rating** 97 **To** 2035 $32 ✪

🍷🍷🍷🍷🍷 **The Eleventh Hour 2015** Destemmed, open-fermented with wild yeast, basket pressed, matured in used French oak. A very rich and complex full-bodied shiraz, opening with an expressive spice and licorice bouquet, the palate with a savoury edge within the folds of its black fruits. It has an X-factor of freshness, too. Screwcap. 14.5% alc. **Rating** 95 **To** 2030 $40

The Twilight Path 2015 A 66/27/7% estate-grown blend of primitivo (aka zinfandel), mataro and graciano, wild-yeast fermented, the primitivo with 30% whole bunches, and unoaked. Bright colour; a resoundingly fresh sunburst of red and purple fruits, the mouthfeel supple and smooth. Drink asap, although it won't die anytime soon. Screwcap. 13.5% alc. **Rating** 95 **To** 2025 $28 **○**
The Howling Dog 2015 Estate-grown saperavi, no vineyard sprays, destemmed, wild-yeast fermented, neither fined or filtered. The black fruit flavours could have come from the River Styx; the bouquet is super-complex, the texture likewise – the latter creates an airy feel to the palate. Screwcap. 13.5% alc. **Rating** 94 **To** 2030 $40

♥♥♥♥♡ The Surly Muse 2016 **Rating** 92 **To** 2021 $26

Maverick Wines

981 Light Pass Road, Vine Vale, Moorooroo, SA 5352 **Region** Barossa Valley
T (08) 8563 3551 **www**.maverickwines.com.au **Open** Mon–Tues 1.30–4.30 or by appt
Winemaker Ronald Brown, Leon Deans **Est.** 2004 **Dozens** 10 000 **Vyds** 61.7ha
This is the business established by the then already highly experienced vigneron Ronald Brown. It has evolved with the transition of the seven vineyards it now owns across the Barossa and Eden Valleys into biodynamic grape production. The vines range from 40 to almost 150 years old, underpinning the consistency of the quality wines produced under the Maverick label. Exports to the UK, France, Russia, Thailand, Japan and China.

♥♥♥♥♥ Ahrens' Creek Barossa Valley Shiraz 2014 The 8ha Ahrens Creek vineyard was planted by the Lehmann family in the 1870s, yet this is the first single-vineyard release of 50 dozen bottles. Matured in used oak to throw attention onto the supple, long and perfectly balanced collage of juicy plum and blackberry fruit, the tannins pure silk. Bargain. Cork. 14.7% alc. **Rating** 97 **To** 2039 $60 **○**

♥♥♥♥♥ Trial Hill Eden Valley Shiraz 2014 From the 1.6ha Trial Hill vineyard in Pewsey Vale, 200 dozen made. An elegant medium to full-bodied wine that avoided the toughness of many parts of southeastern Australia in the wake of low yields. Its moderate – indeed perfect – alcohol is one of the reasons, its Eden Valley heritage another. The tannins are superfine, and good acidity results in a mouthwatering finish. Cork. 13.4% alc. **Rating** 96 **To** 2040 $80
Twins Barossa Cabernet Sauvignon 2015 Matured in French barriques for 18 months. The wine is medium-bodied, fresh and lively, cassis to the fore, with just the right amount of tannin and oak in support. Great value. Screwcap. 14.7% alc. **Rating** 94 **To** 2030 $27 **○**
Twins Barossa Valley Cabernet Sauvignon Merlot Petit Verdot Cabernet Franc 2016 All the varieties come from the estate Barossa Ridge Vineyard, and the wine spends 18 months in French barriques. Light to medium-bodied and fresh, juicy cassis fruits sing soprano, relegating all else to respectful support roles. Screwcap. 13.5% alc. **Rating** 94 **To** 2030 $27 **○**
Twins Barossa Valley Cabernet Sauvignon Merlot Petit Verdot Cabernet Franc 2014 In the face of the challenges of the vintage, the varieties were all picked (at different times) early, the upshot very low alcohol; matured in French barriques for 18 months. The result is a slight, but clear, minty nuance to the light to medium-bodied palate. Screwcap. 12% alc. **Rating** 94 **To** 2028 $27 **○**

♥♥♥♥♡ Trial Hill Eden Valley Shiraz 2013 **Rating** 92 **To** 2029 $80
Twins Barossa Shiraz 2016 **Rating** 90 **To** 2031 $27
Twins Barossa Shiraz 2015 **Rating** 90 **To** 2030 $27

Maxwell Wines

Olivers Road, McLaren Vale, SA 5171 **Region** McLaren Vale
T (08) 8323 8200 **www**.maxwellwines.com.au **Open** 7 days 10–5
Winemaker Andrew Jericho, Mark Maxwell **Est.** 1979 **Dozens** 30 000 **Vyds** 40ha

Maxwell Wines has carved out a reputation as a premium producer in McLaren Vale. The brand has produced some excellent red wines in recent years. The majority of the vines on the estate were planted in 1972, and include 19 rows of the highly regarded Reynella clone cabernet sauvignon. The Ellen Street shiraz block in front of the winery was planted in '53. Owned and operated by Mark Maxwell. Exports to all major markets.

ŸŸŸŸŸ **Eocene Ancient Earth McLaren Vale Shiraz 2014** This wine needs time. It's unashamedly full-bodied, with densely packed inky tannins and a ball of rich dark fruits injected with licorice and cedary, vanillan oak. There is no room to move. Yet there's an appealing voluptuousness. It's a style sure to resonate with fans of big reds. Screwcap. 14.5% alc. **Rating** 95 **To** 2034 $55 JF

ŸŸŸŸŸ **Minotaur Reserve Shiraz 2013 Rating** 93 **To** 2032 $75 JF
Lime Cave Cabernet Sauvignon 2014 Rating 92 **To** 2029 $40 JF
Four Roads Old Vine Grenache 2015 Rating 91 **To** 2021 $28 JF
Silver Hammer Shiraz 2015 Rating 90 **To** 2025 $20 JF ✪
Ellen Street Shiraz 2014 Rating 90 **To** 2024 $40 JF
Little Demon Cabernet Malbec 2015 Rating 90 **To** 2020 $18 JF ✪

Mayer ★★★★★

66 Miller Road, Healesville, Vic 3777 **Region** Yarra Valley
T (03) 5967 3779 **www.timomayer.com.au Open** By appt
Winemaker Timo Mayer **Est.** 1999 **Dozens** 1000 **Vyds** 2.4ha
Timo Mayer, also winemaker at Gembrook Hill Vineyard, teamed with partner Rhonda Ferguson to establish Mayer on the slopes of Mt Toolebewong, 8km south of Healesville. The steepness of those slopes is presumably 'celebrated' in the name given to the wines (Bloody Hill). Pinot noir has the lion's share of the high-density vineyard, with smaller amounts of shiraz and chardonnay. Mayer's winemaking credo is minimal interference and handling, and no filtration. Exports to the UK, Germany, Denmark, Singapore and Japan.

ŸŸŸŸŸ **Yarra Valley Pinot Noir 2015** The fractionally dark fruits of the bouquet are repeated on the powerful, tightly focused palate with its extra dimension of black cherry and blueberry fruit. It is supple, yet has a fine filigree of texture ex tannins. Diam. 13.5% alc. **Rating** 96 **To** 2030 $55 ✪
Granite Upper Yarra Valley Pinot Noir 2015 The wildly different label designs are a nihilist marketing approach, but there Timo goes. The bouquet has a touch of perfume and rose petal, the palate with a subtly different flavour spectrum of red and dark cherry. A slinky pinot of considerable length and charm. Diam. 13.5% alc. **Rating** 96 **To** 2029 $55 ✪
Dr Mayer Yarra Valley Pinot Noir 2015 Bright, clear crimson-purple; the fragrant bouquet is brimming with cherry and blueberry fruit entwined with attractive stemmy notes ex 100% whole bunch fermentation, a technique that may seem easy, but isn't. Timo Mayer has nailed the top vintage with this wine. Diam. 13% alc. **Rating** 95 **To** 2027 $55
Yarra Valley Syrah 2015 The colour is good, bright and full, the perfumed bouquet with its exotic spices likewise. The juicy medium-bodied palate provides yet more of the same good thing, with a display of red cherry and blueberry fruits; a lingering finish and aftertaste. Cool-grown, but without a hint of green. Diam. 13.5% alc. **Rating** 95 **To** 2030 $55
Bloody Hill Yarra Valley Pinot Noir 2015 The fragrant bouquet points to the extensive use of whole bunch fermentation, the palate simply underlining the spicy/savoury nuances of whole bunches. But there is considerable wiry strength to the interplay of red fruits. Diam. 13.5% alc. **Rating** 94 **To** 2025 $30 ✪

ŸŸŸŸŸ **Yarra Valley Cabernet 2015 Rating** 92 **To** 2029 $55

Mayford Wines

6815 Great Alpine Road, Porepunkah, Vic 3740 **Region** Alpine Valleys
T (03) 5756 2528 **www.**mayfordwines.com **Open** By appt
Winemaker Eleana Anderson **Est.** 1995 **Dozens** 800 **Vyds** 3ha
The roots of Mayford go back to 1995, when forester Brian Nicholson planted a small amount
of shiraz, since extended to 0.8ha, chardonnay (1.6ha) and tempranillo (0.6ha). In their words,
'In-house winemaking commenced shortly after he selected his seasoned winemaker bride
in 2002'. Wife and co-owner Eleana Anderson became a Flying Winemaker, working four
vintages in Germany while completing her wine science degree at CSU (having much earlier
obtained an arts degree). Vintages in Australia included one at Boynton's Feathertop (also at
Porepunkah), where she met her husband-to-be. Initially, she was unenthusiastic about the
potential of tempranillo, which Brian had planted after consultation with Mark Walpole,
Brown Brothers' viticulturist, but since making the first vintage in '06 she has been thoroughly
enamoured of the variety. Eleana practises minimalist winemaking, declining to use enzymes,
cultured yeasts, tannins and/or copper. Exports to Singapore.

TTTTT **Porepunkah Chardonnay 2015** The grapes were picked at exactly the right
time, maximising their freshness and vibrancy, and also their varietal character. It is
an outstanding achievement given its region, the actual vinification also high class.
Screwcap. 13% alc. **Rating** 95 **To** 2023 $36
Porepunkah Shiraz 2014 Handsomely packaged, and delivers a beautifully
made medium-bodied wine presenting varietal fruit without fuss, just effortless
class. Red and black cherry and juicy satsuma plum flow through the mouth,
sustained by ripe tannins. Screwcap. 13.9% alc. **Rating** 95 **To** 2030 $40
Porepunkah Tempranillo 2015 Tempranillo was the wine that gained fame for
Mayford, and this is a worthy member of the following vintages. It is bright, juicy
and fresh, with red cherry fruit to the fore, and a long, convincing finish. Screwcap.
13.9% alc. **Rating** 95 **To** 2025 $36

Maygars Hill Winery

53 Longwood-Mansfield Road, Longwood, Vic 3665 **Region** Strathbogie Ranges
T 0402 136 448 **www.**maygarshill.com.au **Open** By appt
Winemaker Contract **Est.** 1997 **Dozens** 900 **Vyds** 3.2ha
Jenny Houghton purchased this 8ha property in 1994, planting shiraz (1.9ha) and cabernet
sauvignon (1.3ha). The name comes from Lieutenant Colonel Maygar, who fought with
outstanding bravery in the Boer War in South Africa in 1901, and was awarded the Victoria
Cross. In World War I he rose to command the 8th Light Horse Regiment, winning yet
further medals for bravery. Exports to Fiji and China.

TTTTT **Reserve Shiraz 2015** Has far more things in common with its sibling than
points of difference – not surprising given the small size of the estate vineyard.
There appears to be more new oak, but it's largely submerged in the fruit. Despite
its higher alcohol, the fruit has more cadences than its sibling. All of this said, the
alcohol of both wines is a challenge. Screwcap. 15.3% alc. **Rating** 95 **To** 2030 $42
Cabernet Sauvignon 2015 This is closer to the long-term pattern of Maygars
Hill than the Shiraz is. It has fresh cassis fruit throughout the bouquet and
medium-bodied palate, given flavour complexity by a dusting of dried herbs and
some touches of French oak. Screwcap. 14.5% alc. **Rating** 95 **To** 2030 $28
Shiraz 2015 Deep colour; a very full-bodied shiraz with scads of black fruits,
licorice and dark chocolate all jostling for first foot on the ladder of flavours. Many
who taste the wine will be impressed, fewer will be delighted. Screwcap. 15% alc.
Rating 94 **To** 2028 $30

TTTTT **Reserve Cabernet Sauvignon 2015 Rating** 93 **To** 2030 $42

Mayhem & Co

49 Collingrove Avenue, Broadview, SA 5083 **Region** Adelaide Hills

T 0468 384 817 www.mayhemandcowine.com.au **Open** Not

Winemaker Andrew Hill **Est.** 2009 **Dozens** 1400

Mayhem & Co is owned by Andrew Hill. Andrew worked vintages at Wirra Wirra and Chapel Hill before taking on senior sales and marketing roles with Koonara, Tomich Hill and Reschke Wines. The wines are made from grapes purchased from various growers in the Adelaide Hills, Eden Valley and McLaren Vale. Exports to Hong Kong and China.

ŤŤŤŤŤ **Small Berries Blewitt Springs Syrah 2015** Fruit comes from a biodynamically farmed 40yo vineyard, whole berries to new French oak puncheons for 14 months. This is fabulous – the berried fruit vibrant, intense, sweet and savoury, wafts of dried herbs, florals and wood spice unfolding onto a plush palate, velvety, ripe tannins and bright acidity to close. Doesn't get any better. Screwcap. 14.3% alc. **Rating** 95 **To** 2026 $36 JF

ŤŤŤŤŸ **Hipster Eden Valley Riesling 2016** **Rating** 93 **To** 2026 $30 JF
Small Berries Blewitt Springs Syrah 2014 **Rating** 93 **To** 2029 $36

Mazza Wines

★★★★

PO Box 480, Donnybrook, WA 6239 **Region** Geographe

T (08) 9201 1114 **www**.mazza.com.au **Open** Not

Winemaker Contract **Est.** 2002 **Dozens** 1000 **Vyds** 4ha

David and Anne Mazza were inspired by the great wines of Rioja and the Douro Valley, and continue a long-standing family tradition of making wine. They have planted the key varieties of those two regions: tempranillo, graciano, bastardo, souzao, tinta cao and touriga nacional. They believe they were the first Australian vineyard to present this collection of varieties on a single site, and I am reasonably certain they are correct in this belief. Whether it is still true is a matter of conjecture – it's a fast-moving scene in Australia these days. Exports to the UK.

ŤŤŤŤŸ **Geographe Bastardo Rose 2016** This rose boasts a gorgeous copper-pink hue, all limpid and inviting. Red fruit flavours are peeled away by the wine's bright acidity, complemented by wafting notes of musk, cherry blossom, rosewater and tangy orange peel. Dry, mid-weighted and as eminently drinkable, as its energetic poise is effusive. Screwcap. 14% alc. **Rating** 93 **To** 2019 $19 NG
Cinque 2014 This mid-weighted wine, a multitudinous blend of 35% tempranillo, 35% touriga nacional, 20% souzao, 5% tinto cao and 5% graciano is quintessentially Iberian and eminently gulpable, as so many are. The tannins are dusty, ultra-savoury, the acidity bright and juicy. The fruit, dark, floral and attractively bitter, stains the mouth with flavour while ricocheting across the structural pillars with the energy and bounce of a pinball. Screwcap. 14% alc. **Rating** 93 **To** 2022 $32 NG
Geographe Tinta Cao 2014 Tinta cao is seldom made as a straight varietal, yet its overall aura of savour and clear herbal voice are attractive. Peppery briar, clove and star anise are nestled amid flavours of raspberry and mulberry. While the fruit allusions are strong, this wine does not stray into sweetness for a moment. A spindle of bright acidity and edgy grape tannins twirl across the palate. The fruit then spurts back across the palate, readying one for another glass. Screwcap. 14% alc. **Rating** 93 **To** 2022 $35 NG
Geographe Graciano 2014 Graciano, a back blender in Rioja, has an ingratiating floral lilt, sour red fruits to blood plum flavours and firm, dusty, tongue-basting and gum-licking tannins. While not fine-boned and of the utmost refinement, the structural pillars are pliant, savoury, and make for a vigorous drink. Mid-weighted and delicious, this is a highly versatile wine at the table. Screwcap. 14.5% alc. **Rating** 93 **To** 2022 $30 NG
Geographe Touriga Nacional 2014 The easiest wine to 'get' among this intriguing swag of wines, all based on indigenous Iberian varieties. It fills the month and leaves the drinker hanging out for more to chew. It is all sexy thrust,

with little parry, pull or vinous length. Nothing wrong with this, but it makes one realise that the variety is largely blended for a reason. Screwcap. 14% alc. **Rating** 92 **To** 2020 $35 NG

Geographe Tempranillo 2014 The fruit is dark and red cherry, sapid and attractively sour in an amaro sort of way. This rich bundle is smacked by oak-derived bitter chocolate tannins, all grit and chew, along with sweet mocha vanilla notes. A seam of anise-doused acidity threads it all together. A lot of yeoman grunt over finesse here, but the wine is certainly high on personality. Screwcap. 14.5% alc. **Rating** 90 **To** 2022 $25 NG

 # Meadowbank Wines ★★★★★

652 Meadowbank Road, Meadowbank, Tas 7140 **Region** Southern Tasmania
T 0439 448 151 **Open** Not
Winemaker Peter Dredge **Est.** 1976 **Vyds** 52ha
The establishment date tells you this is when Gerald and Sue Ellis picked the first grapes from their large Glenora property at the top end of the Derwent River, the vines planted in 1974. There have been four major expansions since, most recently a 10ha planting of pinot noir, chardonnay, syrah and gamay in 2016, lifting the total to 52ha, the major part fully mature vines. Meadowbank Wines opened its Meadowbank Estate cellar door and restaurant in July '00 at Cambridge in the Coal River Valley. The wines were made next door at what is now Frogmore Creek, which had a winery but not a restaurant or cellar door; in the fullness of time Frogmore purchased the restaurant and cellar door, leaving Meadowbank to further develop its vineyards. At all times Meadowbank has supplied grapes to six or so small wineries, but leases 32ha to Accolade. Peter Dredge, having been intimately associated with the vineyard for six years, formed a partnership with the Ellis family (Gerald, Sue, daughter Mardi and her husband, Alex Dean) to relaunch Meadowbank. The Meadowbank wines from '16 were made by Peter at Moorilla Estate from the 2ha of the vineyard set aside for the Meadowbank wines.

🍷🍷🍷🍷🍷 **Riesling 2016 Tasmanian** Fresh green apples and citrus drive the bouquet and palate. It is a dry and refreshing style, balancing its 8g/l residual sugar seamlessly, with a racy, natural Tasmanian acid spine that is beautifully long and fresh. Drink now or over the next few decades. Screwcap. 11.5% alc. **Rating** 95 **To** 2030 $32

Chardonnay 2016 A typically tight and reserved Tasmanian chardonnay, with fresh nectarine, lemon curd and a dusting of candied nuts. The palate is driven by nervy Tasmanian acidity, delving into citrus notes; the soft unpretentious use of oak complements the package. Has the length of a freight train with quality fruit and extract on display. Screwcap. 12.5% alc. **Rating** 95 **To** 2027 $50

Pinot Noir 2016 There is a slight lift on the bouquet from partial barrel fermentation and long lees contact. This is a fitting complement to the power of the primary fruit flavours of strawberry and fresh berry compote. There is a softness to this pinot noir; the silky or satin-like tannin structure is first rate, with just enough back-palate weight from stalk use and light French oak to hold its length. Screwcap. 13% alc. **Rating** 95 **To** 2029 $55

🍷🍷🍷🍷🍷 **Gamay 2016** Very bright colour; the vivid blueberry fruit core supports the natural gamey nuances of the variety. Possibly early picking, as it is tangy with some herb and spice notes in the background. A drink-now style, but should still drink well for some years to come. Screwcap. 12% alc. **Rating** 94 **To** 2021 $32

🍷🍷🍷🍷🍷 **Blanc de Blancs 2011 Rating** 90 **To** 2018 $45 TS
Chardonnay Pinot Noir NV Rating 90 **To** 2017 $32 TS

Medhurst ★★★★★

24–26 Medhurst Road, Gruyere, Vic 3770 **Region** Yarra Valley
T (03) 5964 9022 **www.**medhurstwines.com.au **Open** Thurs–Mon & public hols 11–5
Winemaker Simon Steele **Est.** 2000 **Dozens** 4500 **Vyds** 12.21ha
The wheel has come full circle for Ross and Robyn Wilson. In the course of a very distinguished corporate career, Ross was CEO of Southcorp when it brought the Penfolds,

Lindemans and Wynns businesses under its banner. Robyn spent her childhood in the Yarra Valley, her parents living less than a kilometre away from Medhurst. The vineyard is planted to sauvignon blanc, chardonnay, pinot noir, cabernet sauvignon and shiraz, all running on a low-yield basis. The winery focuses on small batch production, and also provides contract winemaking services. The visual impact of the winery has been minimised by recessing the building into the slope of land and locating the barrel room underground. The winery was recognised for its architectural excellence at the Victorian Architecture Awards. The arrival of Simon Steele from Brokenwood (his loss much mourned by Brokenwood) has enhanced the already considerable reputation of Medhurst.

ŸŸŸŸŸ **Estate Vineyard Yarra Valley Pinot Noir 2015** Crafted across 8 separate wild-yeast ferments, 30% of which contained whole bunches, this textural, energetic and sublimely elegant pinot noir was facilitated by minimal extraction. All tangy red fruit and baking spice, detailed tannins faintly grip the mouth and provide focus for the ethereal finish. A floating world in a glass. Screwcap. 13.5% alc. **Rating** 96 **To** 2022 $38 NG ✪

Estate Vineyard Yarra Valley Sauvignon Blanc 2016 Races out of the gates. Tight and pointed, this is spicy and tensile, challenging jaded perceptions of sauvignon blanc. Crafted with partial oak fermentation on full solids, with wild yeast. Further lees handling has served to tighten and embed texture. This is highly sophisticated fare, finishing with a spray of menthol. Screwcap. 13% alc. **Rating** 95 **To** 2020 $25 NG ✪

Estate Vineyard Yarra Valley Chardonnay 2015 Stone fruits, nashi pear and preserved lemon drip from this tensile, mineral-framed chardonnay. Flecked with a flinty bite and imbued with a creamy core of oatmeal and nougat flavours following a wild yeast ferment in an assortment of new and used French oak and 10 months on lees. Compelling intensity of flavour here. Screwcap. 13.5% alc. **Rating** 95 **To** 2022 $35 NG ✪

Estate Vineyard Rose 2016 Cabernet sauvignon and shiraz, whole-bunch pressed, which necessarily means the grapes were grown and used specifically for this wine, and the intensity of the red fruit flavours likewise attest to this expensive method – appropriately rewarded with a gold medal at the Yarra Valley Wine Show '16. Its length, balance and juicy mouthfeel are given an all-important degree of spicy/savoury complexity. Screwcap. 13% alc. **Rating** 95 **To** 2017 $25 ✪

Estate Vineyard Yarra Valley YRB 2016 A vibrant, light to mid-weighted 50/50% blend of pinot noir and shiraz that is a joy to drink and a worthy homage to Maurice O'Shea. Satsuma plum, licorice root and a floral lift set this wine racing across the mouth; it is spindly of tannin and lilting of acidity. A mellifluous flow from beginning to end, this is a unique Australian cool climate expression and the type of wine I wish people would make. Screwcap. 12.5% alc. **Rating** 94 **To** 2022 $33 NG

Estate Vineyard Yarra Valley Cabernet Sauvignon 2015 'Estate' wines represent the best parcels from the vineyard. This is from a warm site facing due north. It yields pliant, ripe cabernet. Redolent of cassis, thyme and a dusting of cedar following 18 months in a combination of new and used French barriques, it is polished. Screwcap. 14% alc. **Rating** 94 **To** 2035 $38 NG

ŸŸŸŸŸ **Estate Vineyard Yarra Valley Shiraz 2015** **Rating** 93 **To** 2023 $38 NG

Meehan Vineyard ★★★★

4536 McIvor Highway, Heathcote, Vic 3523 **Region** Heathcote
T 0407 058 432 **www**.meehanvineyard.com **Open** W'ends & public hols 10–5
Winemaker Phil Meehan **Est.** 2003 **Dozens** 1200 **Vyds** 2ha

In 1999, after their children had left the nest, Phil and Judy Meehan decided to return to the country and grow grapes for sale to wineries. In that year they took the first step, planting a small pinot noir vineyard at Bannockburn. It then took until April 2003 to find a near-perfect site, just within the Heathcote town boundary, its northeast-facing gentle slope on the famous Cambrian soil. Phil graduated with a Diploma of Winemaking and a Diploma of Viticulture in '05, saying, 'After a mere six years of study I only learned, after all that time, just how much more to winemaking there was to learn.' Exports to Malaysia and Hong Kong.

ŶŶŶŶŶ William Heathcote Shiraz 2015 Very good deep crimson colour; the price differential between this and its sibling is justified: here there is depth to the purple and black fruits, and just a whisper of lemon on the otherwise soft finish. Screwcap. 14.5% alc. **Rating** 93 **To** 2029 $55

Meerea Park ★★★★★

Pavilion B, 2144 Broke Road, Pokolbin, NSW 2320 **Region** Hunter Valley
T (02) 4998 7474 **www.meereapark.com.au Open** 7 days 10–5
Winemaker Rhys Eather **Est.** 1991 **Dozens** 11 000
This is the project of Rhys and Garth Eather, whose great-great-grandfather, Alexander Munro, established a famous vineyard in the 19th century, known as Bebeah. While the range of wines chiefly focuses on semillon and shiraz, it extends to other varieties (including chardonnay), and also into other regions. Meerea Park has moved its cellar door to the striking Tempus Two winery, now owned by the Roche family, situated on the corner of Broke Road and McDonald Road. It hardly need be said that the quality of the wines, especially with 5 years' cellaring, is outstanding. Exports to the US, Canada, Singapore and China.

ŶŶŶŶŶ Aged Release Alexander Munro Individual Vineyard Hunter Valley Shiraz 2007 From the dry-grown Ivanhoe vineyard in Pokolbin, the vines averaging 50+yo, 35% whole bunches, open-fermented, matured in French barriques (40% new) for 20 months. 10 years young, not old. There is a delicious interplay of black fruits, licorice, earth, leather, plum, blackberry and herbs. This takes place on a palate that is no more than medium-bodied at best. Screwcap. 13.5% alc. **Rating** 97 **To** 2037 $120 **✪**

ŶŶŶŶŶ Alexander Munro Individual Vineyard Hunter Valley Semillon 2012 While there was virtually no shiraz of consequence in the rain-soaked vintage, semillon defied the weather. Hand-picked and (importantly) sorted, then stainless steel–fermented – no tricks here. Toasty nuances are starting to build on the bouquet, but the power and drive of the palate comes as a shock, the finish a clap of cymbals. Screwcap. 10.5% alc. **Rating** 95 **To** 2032 $45
Old Vine Hunter Valley Shiraz 2013 Matured in French hogsheads for 18 months. This vintage stands overshadowed by the '14, but is very good by normal Hunter Valley standards. The wine is medium-bodied, the alcohol typical of the Hunter, imparting freshness to the wine, the superfine tannins holding hands with the purple and black fruits, oak playing a respectful role. Screwcap. 13.5% alc. **Rating** 95 **To** 2038 $60

ŶŶŶŶŶ Indie Individual Vineyard Hunter Valley Shiraz Marsanne 2014 **Rating** 92 **To** 2024 $40 SC
Indie Individual Vineyard Hunter Valley Marsanne Roussanne 2015 **Rating** 91 **To** 2020 $30 SC
The Aunts Individual Vineyard Hunter Valley Shiraz 2015 **Rating** 91 **To** 2025 $30
Orange Hunter Valley Sauvignon Blanc Semillon 2015 **Rating** 90 **To** 2017 $17 **✪**
Indie Hunter Valley Semillon Chardonnay 2015 **Rating** 90 **To** 2020 $30 SC

Merindoc Vintners ★★★★

Merindoc Vineyard, 2905 Lancefield-Tooborac Road, Tooborac, Vic 3522
Region Heathcote
T (03) 5433 5188 **www.merindoc.com.au Open** W'ends 10–4
Winemaker Steve Webber, Sergio Carlei, Bryan Martin **Est.** 1994 **Dozens** 2500
Vyds 60ha

Stephen Shelmerdine has been a major figure in the wine industry for over 25 years, like his family (who founded Mitchelton Winery) before him, and has been honoured for his many services to the industry. Substantial quantities of the grapes produced are sold to others, a small amount of high quality wine is contract-made. The Merindoc and Willoughby Bridge wines are produced from the two eponymous estate vineyards in Heathcote. Exports to China.

🍷🍷🍷🍷🍷 **Willoughby Bridge Heathcote Shiraz 2014** Good colour; aromas of spice and cedar join with the red and black fruits of the bouquet, the medium to full-bodied palate rumbling with savoury plum and blackberry flavours, tannins and oak both contributing to a wine that will always have much to offer. Screwcap. 14.3% alc. **Rating** 94 **To** 2034 $29 ❍

🍷🍷🍷🍷🍷 **Willoughby Bridge Heathcote Cabernet Sauvignon 2014 Rating** 92 **To** 2031 $29 NG
Merindoc Vineyard Heathcote Shiraz 2014 Rating 90 **To** 2027 $49 NG

Mermerus Vineyard   ★★★★

60 Soho Road, Drysdale, Vic 3222 **Region** Geelong
T (03) 5253 2718 **www**.mermerus.com.au **Open** Sun 11–4
Winemaker Paul Champion **Est.** 2000 **Dozens** 600 **Vyds** 2.5ha
Paul Champion has established pinot noir, chardonnay and riesling at Mermerus. The wines are made from the small but very neat winery on the property, with small batch handling and wild yeast fermentation playing a major part in the winemaking, oak taking a back seat. Paul also acts as contract winemaker for small growers in the region.

🍷🍷🍷🍷🍷 **Bellarine Peninsula Pinot Noir 2015** Hand-picked, open-fermented, matured for 12 months in French barriques. An expressive and substantial pinot with plummy fruit doing the heavy lifting on the bouquet and palate alike. Will richly repay 5+ years in the cellar. Screwcap. 13.5% alc. **Rating** 92 **To** 2026 $32
Bellarine Peninsula Chardonnay 2016 Wild yeast–barrel fermentation, partial mlf and extended lees contact have left the varietal fruit intact; nectarine, fig, creamy nuances ex mlf, and citrus acidity, fill the palate. Screwcap. 13.5% alc. **Rating** 90 **To** 2023 $26

🍷🍷🍷🍷 **Bellarine Peninsula Shiraz 2015 Rating** 89 **To** 2021 $30

Merricks Estate   ★★★★

Thompsons Lane, Merricks, Vic 3916 **Region** Mornington Peninsula
T (03) 5989 8416 **www**.merricksestate.com.au **Open** 1st w'end of month
Winemaker Paul Evans, Alex White **Est.** 1977 **Dozens** 2500 **Vyds** 4ha
Melbourne solicitor George Kefford, with wife Jacky, runs Merricks Estate as a weekend and holiday enterprise. It produces distinctive, spicy, cool climate shiraz, which has accumulated an impressive array of show trophies and gold medals. As the current tasting notes comprehensively demonstrate, the fully mature vineyard and skilled contract winemaking are producing top class wines. Exports to Hong Kong.

🍷🍷🍷🍷🍷 **Mornington Peninsula Chardonnay 2015** A bright yellow flecked with green, this wine expresses the richer equation of Mornington chardonnay. Apricot, white peach and quince mosey with a core of cashew and a highwire, mineral-clad pulse melded to juicy natural acidity. The wine is at once generous and restrained; warm and sleek. The oak is a supporting player. Screwcap. 13.5% alc. **Rating** 94 **To** 2023 $35 NG
Mornington Peninsula Cabernet Sauvignon 2009 This is very fine and pleasantly surprising given the penchant of the region for cooler climate varietal expressions. A wine that is almost Bordelais in its tightly knit tannic composure and free-flowing acidity. This is long, savoury and graceful, with the pillars of its construction finding an effortless confluence with currant, dried sage, cedar and tobacco notes. An aged beauty, with plenty of life left. Diam. 13.5% alc. **Rating** 94 **To** 2025 $35 NG

🍷🍷🍷🍷🍸 Mornington Peninsula Pinot Noir 2014 Rating 93 To 2023 $40 NG
Thompson's Lane Shiraz 2013 Rating 93 To 2025 $25 NG ✪
Thompson's Lane Rose 2016 Rating 91 To 2018 $25 NG

Merum Estate ★★★★

PO Box 840, Denmark, WA 6333 **Region** Pemberton
T (08) 9848 3443 **www**.merumestate.com.au **Open** Not
Winemaker Harewood Estate (James Kellie) **Est.** 1996 **Dozens** 4000
Merum Estate stirred from slumber after morphing from grower and winemaker to pure
grapegrowing after the 2006 vintage. Viticulturist Mike Melsom is the link with the past, for
it was he and partner Julie Roberts who were responsible for the extremely good wines made
in '05 and '06. The wines are released at three levels, headed by the Premium Reserve range.

🍷🍷🍷🍷🍷 Premium Reserve Single Vineyard Pemberton Chardonnay 2015 Bright
straw-green; significantly better than its lower-priced sibling, it has good varietal
character, texture and, in particular, length, all components working together well.
Screwcap. **Rating** 94 **To** 2023 $29 ✪

🍷🍷🍷🍷🍸 Pemberton Semillon Sauvignon Blanc 2016 Rating 93 To 2020 $20 ✪
Premium Reserve Pemberton Shiraz 2014 Rating 91 To 2029 $29

Mia Valley Estate ★★★★

203 Daniels Lane, Mia Mia, Vic 3444 **Region** Heathcote
T (03) 5425 5515 **www**.miavalleyestate.com.au **Open** 7 days 10–5
Winemaker Norbert & Pamela Baumgartner **Est.** 1999 **Dozens** 1000 **Vyds** 3.2ha
Norbert and Pamela Baumgartner both had indirect connections with wine, plus a direct
interest in drinking it. In the early 1980s, based in Melbourne, they began a search for suitable
vineyard land. However, it proved too difficult to find what they wanted, and the plans were
put on hold. It took until '98 for them to discover their property: 40ha with softly undulating
land and the Mia Mia (pronounced mya-mya) Creek running through it. They planted 1.6ha
of shiraz and in 2002 produced their first vintage. It encouraged them to plant another 1.6ha.
Along the way Norbert completed winemaking and viticulture courses, and worked with
David Anderson of Wild Duck Creek, and Peter Beckingham. They made their wines for
the '02 to '05 vintages in their air-conditioned garage in Melbourne. In '05 they converted
the vineyard shed into a mini-winery, expanding it in '06 to a winery and temporary
accommodation, commuting on weekends from Melbourne until '09. They then ran into the
'09 bushfires, the '11 rains, floods and disease, a '12 vintage more than they could handle, '14
decimated by frosts, and late '15 and '16 severe drought. Are they giving up? No sign of it so
far. Exports to the UK, the US and China.

🍷🍷🍷🍷🍸 Heathcote Cabernet Malbec 2016 An avuncular Bordeaux blend. The wine is
all red to dark berry compote, given flight by a whiff of violet, a lick of anise, mint
and a solid rub down of American oak, segueing into some coffee grind tannins.
The overall impression is one of detailed restraint, rather than buxom weight.
Cork. 14% alc. **Rating** 93 **To** 2028 $28 NG
MAP XLVII Heathcote Viognier 2016 The wine showcases peach, apricot and
a giddy floral and honeysuckle lilt across its aromatic spectrum. The palate, mid-
weighted and vibrant, finishes with a gentle mealiness. Cork. 13.3% alc. **Rating** 91
To 2020 $24 NG
Ode to Maestro Sparkling Riesling 2016 A sparkling riesling more Germanic
than Australian in style, tactically deploying the apricot, spice and ginger notes
of botrytis to build body and interest. There is depth to its baked apple fruit and
tension and cut to its citrus accents, culminating in a long finish. Crown seal.
11.5% alc. **Rating** 90 **To** 2018 $30 TS

Miceli ★★★★

60 Main Creek Road, Arthurs Seat, Vic 3936 **Region** Mornington Peninsula
T (03) 5989 2755 **www**.miceli.com.au **Open** W ends 12–5, public hols by appt
Winemaker Anthony Miceli **Est.** 1991 **Dozens** 4000 **Vyds** 5.5ha
This may be a part-time labour of love for general practitioner Dr Anthony Miceli, but that hasn't prevented him taking the venture very seriously. He acquired the property in 1989 specifically to establish a vineyard, planting 1.8ha in '91. Subsequent plantings have brought it to its present size, with pinot gris, chardonnay and pinot noir the varieties grown. Between '91 and '97 Dr Miceli completed the wine science course at CSU; he now manages both vineyard and winery. One of the top producers of sparkling wine on the Peninsula.

🍷🍷🍷🍷🍷 **Michael Brut 2007** Mornington Peninsula pinot noir (predominantly), chardonnay and pinot gris build a powerful style of bubblegum complexity that has amassed considerable toasty character over the past decade. Tense, heightened acidity rises to the challenge, keeping the finish focused and honed, if not searing. 11.5% alc. **Rating** 90 **To** 2019 $35 TS

Michael Hall Wines ★★★★★

10 George Street, Tanunda, SA 5352 (postal) **Region** Mount Lofty Ranges
T 0419 126 290 **www**.michaelhallwines.com **Open** Not
Winemaker Michael Hall **Est.** 2008 **Dozens** 1800
For reasons no longer relevant (however interesting), Michael Hall was once a jewellery valuer for Sotheby's in Switzerland. He came to Australia in 2001 to pursue winemaking, a lifelong interest, and undertook the wine science degree at CSU, graduating as dux in '05. His vintage work in Australia and France is a veritable who's who: in Australia with Cullen, Giaconda, Henschke, Shaw + Smith, Coldstream Hills and Veritas; in France with Domaine Leflaive, Meo-Camuzet, Vieux Telegraphe and Trevallon. He is now involved full-time with his eponymous brand, and does some teaching at the Nuriootpa TAFE. The wines are as impressive as his CV suggests they should be. Exports to the UK.

🍷🍷🍷🍷🍷 **Piccadilly Adelaide Hills Sauvignon Blanc 2016** Left-field winemaking has been a remarkable success. 90% pressed to French oak (33% new), 10% fermented on skins in tank then pressed to barrel, both components spending 9 months on lees in barrel. It is very complex and vinous, with texture to burn, but not at the expense of the intensity and drive of the fruit. Cleansing acidity on the finish makes the wine what it is. Screwcap. 13.3% alc. **Rating** 96 **To** 2021 $35 ✪
Triangle Block Stone Well Barossa Valley Shiraz 2015 Hand-picked, 100% destemmed, fermented in a combination of puncheons and open vats, matured in French oak (12% new) for 21 months. Has the good colour of all the Michael Hall Shirazs in this vintage, and is the richest in terms of both structure and black fruit flavours. Black cherry and blackberry do the heavy lifting in a complete and very satisfying wine. Screwcap. 14.4% alc. **Rating** 96 **To** 2035 $50 ✪
Stone Well Barossa Valley Shiraz 2014 Destemmed, part fermented in a puncheon, part open-fermented, matured for 21 months in French oak (22% new). Has had time for its components to knit on a long, well balanced, medium-bodied wine with cherry/berry fruits, delicious spices and fine tannins. Screwcap. 14.4% alc. **Rating** 96 **To** 2034 $47 ✪
Piccadilly and Lenswood Adelaide Hills Chardonnay 2015 Barrel-fermented, 75% mlf, 11 months on lees in French oak, 140 dozen made. A complex, slightly funky/struck match bouquet devolves into a fine, elegant and long palate, notable for its purity of expression and its length, citrussy acidity to the fore. Its best years are still in front of it. Screwcap. 13.4% alc. **Rating** 95 **To** 2025 $50
Mount Torrens Adelaide Hills Syrah 2015 Hand-picked, wild-yeast fermented with 15% whole bunches, pressed to barrel for 14 months in French oak. The colour shows the first signs of development, the bouquet with a hint of charcuterie and poached plum. The light to medium-bodied palate has

cool-grown red and black cherry to the fore, fine tannins and oak extending the long, well balanced finish. Screwcap. 14% alc. **Rating** 95 **To** 2025 $50

Sang de Pigeon Barossa Valley Shiraz 2015 Picked 27 Feb, crushed to a truncated oak vat and a stainless steel vat, open-fermented, matured in French oak for 20 months, blended with 15% Eden Valley shiraz. While medium to full-bodied, and with a complex texture and structure from the outset, has the touch of elegance that illuminates all of Michael Hall's wines. Screwcap. 14.4% alc. **Rating** 95 **To** 2030 $30 **❂**

Flaxman's Valley Eden Valley Syrah 2015 Rating 94 **To** 2029 $50

ΨΨΨΨΨ **Sang de Pigeon Blanc de Pigeon 2016 Rating** 93 **To** 2028 $28
Greenock Barossa Valley Roussanne 2016 Rating 90 **To** 2019 $38
Sang de Pigeon Adelaide Hills Pinot Noir 2015 Rating 90 **To** 2025 $30

Michelini Wines   ★★★☆

Great Alpine Road, Myrtleford, Vic 3737 **Region** Alpine Valleys
T (03) 5751 1990 **www**.micheliniwines.com.au **Open** 7 days 10–5
Winemaker Federico Zagami **Est.** 1982 **Dozens** 10000 **Vyds** 60ha
The Michelini family are among the best-known grapegrowers in the Buckland Valley of northeast Victoria. Having migrated from Italy in 1949, they originally grew tobacco, diversifying into vineyards in '82. The main vineyard, on terra rossa soil, is at an altitude of 300m, mostly with frontage to the Buckland River. The Devils Creek Vineyard was planted in '91 on grafted rootstocks, merlot and chardonnay taking the lion's share. A vineyard expansion program has seen the vineyards reach 60ha. Exports to China.

ΨΨΨΨΨ **Italian Selection Pinot Grigio 2016** Really crisp and savoury, with a dash of lemon salts, lime juice, some Granny Smith apple. Rather moreish. Screwcap. 12.5% alc. **Rating** 90 **To** 2018 $20 JF **❂**

Mike Press Wines   ★★★★★

PO Box 224, Lobethal, SA 5241 **Region** Adelaide Hills
T (08) 8389 5546 **www**.mikepresswines.com.au **Open** Not
Winemaker Mike Press **Est.** 1998 **Dozens** 12000 **Vyds** 22.7ha
Mike and Judy Press established their Kenton Valley Vineyards in 1998, when they purchased 34ha of land in the Adelaide Hills at an elevation of 500m. They planted mainstream cool climate varieties (merlot, shiraz, cabernet sauvignon, sauvignon blanc, chardonnay and pinot noir), intending to sell the grapes to other wine producers. Even an illustrious 43-year career in the wine industry did not prepare Mike for the downturn in grape prices that followed, and that led to the development of the Mike Press wine label. They produce high quality Sauvignon Blanc, Chardonnay, Pinot Noir, Merlot, Shiraz, Cabernet Merlot and Cabernet Sauvignon, which are sold at mouthwateringly low prices. I've decided to give this winery/maker proprietary five stars because there is no other producer offering estate-grown and made wines at prices to compete with these.

ΨΨΨΨΨ **Single Vineyard Adelaide Hills Cabernet Sauvignon 2015** I never cease to be amazed at the ease with which Mike Press strides across all the main varieties in his small vineyard, and handles each as if it was his only wine. This is a ridiculously good cabernet at the price, with bell-clear blackcurrant fruit backlit by warm herbs and black olive, the tannins positively silky. Screwcap. 14.5% alc. **Rating** 92 **To** 2025 $14 **❂**

Adelaide Hills Sauvignon Blanc 2016 The vineyard is planted around Mike Press's house, and he makes the wine, delivering unbeatable value. Sub-$20 sauvignon blancs often wobble around the mouth with vague tropical fruits neither seeking nor delivering cause for thought. This has vital cut and thrust to its array of snow pea, gooseberry and guava flavours, the package neatly tied by no-nonsense acidity. Screwcap. 13.9% alc. **Rating** 91 **To** 2017 $12 **❂**

MP One Single Vineyard Adelaide Hills Shiraz 2014 This name and label design is only used in exceptional vintages. While only light-bodied, it has immaculate balance and a super-silky mouthfeel, its spicy fruit, tannins and oak sewn together by old-time invisible mending. Moreover, it is ready now. Screwcap. 14.4% alc. **Rating** 91 **To** 2024 $20 ✪

Single Vineyard Adelaide Hills Pinot Noir Rosé 2016 Vivid crimson, way beyond the norm – the wine must have been scrupulously protected from oxygen at every stage. Red and maraschino cherry and strawberry fruit is trimmed by savoury acidity. Screwcap. 13.9% alc. **Rating** 90 **To** 2017 $12 ✪

Single Vineyard Adelaide Hills Pinot Noir 2015 Has retained its primary crimson hue to an impressive degree; red and black cherry fruit are the flavour drivers, steering provided by some earthy/foresty varietal characters on the long palate. Is there nothing Mike Press can't do? Screwcap. 13.8% alc. **Rating** 90 **To** 2017 $16 ✪

Single Vineyard Adelaide Hills Shiraz 2015 A classic light to medium-bodied cool-grown shiraz, with spicy/peppery diamonds sewn through the fabric of the predominantly black fruits. The length and intensity of the wine grow each time you retaste it: remarkable stuff. Screwcap. 14.4% alc. **Rating** 90 **To** 2022 $14 ✪

Single Vineyard Adelaide Hills Merlot 2015 It should come as no surprise that Mike Press comes closer than many in grasping the elusive core of merlot (or what it should be). This is only just medium-bodied; it is pleasingly soft and fruity, with cassis the dominatrix without a tannin whip to use. Clarity and purity are its calling cards. Screwcap. 14.5% alc. **Rating** 90 **To** 2021 $14 ✪

♀♀♀♀ Single Vineyard Adelaide Hills Chardonnay 2016 Rating 89 To 2021 $12 ✪

Miles from Nowhere   ★★★★

PO Box 197, Belmont, WA 6984 **Region** Margaret River
T (08) 9267 8555 **www**.milesfromnowhere.com.au **Open** Not
Winemaker Rory Clifton-Parks, Gary Stokes **Est.** 2007 **Dozens** 16 000 **Vyds** 46.9ha
Miles from Nowhere is one of the two wineries owned by Franklin and Heather Tate. Franklin returned to Margaret River in 2007 after working with his parents establishing Evans & Tate from 1987 until 2005. The Miles from Nowhere name comes from the journey Franklin's ancestors made over 100 years ago from Eastern Europe to Australia: upon their arrival, they felt they had travelled 'miles from nowhere'. The winery produces a series of wines, and the Best Blocks' range. The plantings include petit verdot, chardonnay, shiraz, sauvignon blanc, semillon, viognier, cabernet sauvignon and merlot, spread over two vineyards planted 20 years ago. Exports to the UK, Canada, Asia and NZ.

♀♀♀♀♀ **Best Blocks Margaret River Chardonnay 2015** This chardonnay has chutzpah in its strident, stone-fruited swagger across the palate. Intensely flavoured with a lick of truffle and nougat at its core, the wine was barrel-fermented with both cultured and wild yeast, before ageing. The oak regime consists of 80% new and 20% used oak, all French. A cedar edge from the oak needs time to nestle into the fruit. Screwcap. 12.9% alc. **Rating** 92 **To** 2020 $32 NG

Best Blocks Margaret River Semillon Sauvignon Blanc 2016 As the name implies, superior parcels of fruit were selected for this cuvee. A smidgen was barrel-fermented, imparting a welcome creamy core, while counterbalancing the racy, herbal and vegetal tones of snow pea, nettle, hedgerow and greengage that cut across aroma and palate. Screwcap. 12.3% alc. **Rating** 91 **To** 2019 $32 NG

Best Blocks Margaret River Shiraz 2015 Blue and black fruits set the tone, with an emphasis on boysenberry and mulberry. Vanillan oak provides accent, lashings of tannin and a cedar-inflected savoury focus. Given the richness of the fruit, the oak should eventually find a home. Screwcap. 14.8% alc. **Rating** 91 **To** 2025 $32 NG

Margaret River Cabernet Merlot 2015 Less ambitious perhaps than its upper tier sibling, this is nevertheless a far easier ride across a waft of red and dark fruits, pastille and some strewn herbs led by dried sage. The oak is there, guiding and conferring a tannic authority without overwhelming the interplay of elements. Screwcap. 14.5% alc. **Rating** 91 **To** 2023 $18 NG ✪

♀♀♀♀ Margaret River Sauvignon Blanc 2016 Rating 89 To 2018 $18 NG ✪

Millbrook Winery   ★★★★★

Old Chestnut Lane, Jarrahdale, WA 6124 **Region** Perth Hills
T (08) 9525 5796 **www.**millbrookwinery.com.au **Open** Wed–Mon 10–5
Winemaker Damian Hutton, Adair Davies **Est.** 1996 **Dozens** 15 000 **Vyds** 7.8ha
The strikingly situated Millbrook Winery is owned by highly successful Perth-based entrepreneur Peter Fogarty and wife Lee. They also own Lake's Folly in the Hunter Valley, Smithbrook in Pemberton and Deep Woods Estate in Margaret River. Millbrook draws on vineyards in the Perth Hills planted to sauvignon blanc, semillon, chardonnay, viognier, cabernet sauvignon, merlot, shiraz and petit verdot. The wines are of consistently high quality. Exports to Germany, Malaysia, Hong Kong, Singapore, China and Japan.

ᵀᵀᵀᵀᵀ **LR Chardonnay 2015** Whole-bunch pressed direct to French oak (75% new) for wild yeast fermentation and maturation. While green-tinged, there has been a touch more colour development than expected, the oak a little more obvious. Carping criticisms of a wine with resplendent depth to its mix of white peach, nectarine and grapefruit. Screwcap. 13.5% alc. **Rating** 95 **To** 2023 $45
Estate Shiraz Viognier 2014 4% co-fermented viognier, matured in French oak for 20 months (30% new). The oak threatens to dominate proceedings, but in the end the luscious array of red and black fruits stands firm on the medium-bodied palate, its length and finish excellent. As good as they come from the Perth Hills. Screwcap. 14.5% alc. **Rating** 95 **To** 2034 $35 ✪
Geographe Tempranillo 2015 Matured in used French puncheons for 12 months. An unqualified success. Luscious, yet light on its feet, with a peacock's tail of red fruits on a cushion of persistent but soft and juicy tannins. Ready right now. Great hedonistic value. Screwcap. 14.5% alc. **Rating** 94 **To** 2020 $22 ✪

ᵀᵀᵀᵀ **Barking Owl Shiraz 2014 Rating** 93 **To** 2029 $18 ✪
Geographe Grenache Shiraz Mourvedre 2016 Rating 93 **To** 2026 $22 ✪
Margaret River Sauvignon Blanc 2016 Rating 92 **To** 2017 $22 ✪
Margaret River Vermentino 2016 Rating 92 **To** 2020 $22 ✪
Estate Viognier 2016 Rating 91 **To** 2018 $35
Geographe Sangiovese 2015 Rating 91 **To** 2023 $22 ✪
PX Pedro Ximenes NV Rating 91 $60 CM
Barking Owl Margaret River SSB 2016 Rating 90 **To** 2018 $18 ✪
Perth Hills Viognier 2015 Rating 90 **To** 2018 $22

Milton Vineyard   ★★★★★

14635 Tasman Highway, Swansea, Tas 7190 **Region** East Coast Tasmania
T (03) 6257 8298 **www.**miltonvineyard.com.au **Open** 7 days 10–5
Winemaker Winemaking Tasmania **Est.** 1992 **Dozens** 6000 **Vyds** 19ha
Michael and Kerry Dunbabin have one of the most historic properties in Tasmania, dating back to 1826. The property is 1800ha, meaning the vineyard (9ha of pinot noir, 6ha pinot gris, 1.5ha chardonnay, 1ha each of gewurztraminer and riesling, plus 10 rows of shiraz) still has plenty of room for expansion.

ᵀᵀᵀᵀᵀ **Pinot Noir 2015** Vivid, clear crimson-purple; the bouquet and palate are in total accord; brilliant, fresh red cherry fruit is allied with a waft of new French oak and fine-grained tannins that pick up a touch of forest floor on the way through. Line, length and balance are all perfect. Screwcap. 13.4% alc. **Rating** 96 **To** 2027 $37 ✪
Dunbabin Family Reserve Pinot Noir 2012 Has the depth of colour that is only found with Tasmanian pinot, not on the mainland (if it's found there, the fruit will have no varietal character). Built for the ages, with soaked plums and black cherry fruits, fresh acidity nipping the bud of any fancied detection of over-extraction. Remarkable wine. Screwcap. 13.7% alc. **Rating** 96 **To** 2032 $65 ✪
Riesling 2016 Vividly fresh and lively, with a blend of Bickford's lime juice, crystalline acidity, and an unexpected touch of tropical fruit – which doesn't

impinge on the purity and line of a high class wine with a long future. Screwcap. 12.5% alc. **Rating** 95 **To** 2036 $27

Pinot Gris 2016 A very interesting wine with a great deal more fruit weight on the palate than normal, coupled with a range of flavours that puts stone fruit on the same table as pear and apple. Indeed, this has elements of Alsace to it. Screwcap. 13.5% alc. **Rating** 94 **To** 2021 $27 ✪

Iced Gewurztraminer 2015 In a word, delicious. Andrew Hood did much of the early work in exploring what could be achieved by stripping water out of crushed grapes, intensifying both residual sugar and titratable acidity, and therefore the flavour. Moreover, unlike botrytis or super-late picking, leaves the varietal character intact. Screwcap. 8.2% alc. **Rating** 94 **To** 2020 $32

♥♥♥♥♀ **Gewurztraminer 2016** Rating 91 **To** 2022 $27
Shiraz 2014 Rating 91 **To** 2029 $55
Freycinet Coast Pinot Noir Rose 2016 Rating 90 **To** 2017 $27

Ministry of Clouds ★★★★★

39a Wakefield Street, Kent Town, SA 5067 **Region** Various
T 0417 864 615 **www**.ministryofclouds.com.au **Open** By appt
Winemaker Julian Forwood, Bernice Ong, Tim Geddes **Est.** 2012 **Dozens** 3500 **Vyds** 9ha
Bernice Ong and Julian Forwood say, 'The name Ministry of Clouds symbolises the relinquishing of our past security and structure (ministry) for the beguiling freedom, independence and adventure (clouds) inherent in our own venture.' I doubt whether there are two partners in a young wine business with such extraordinary experience in sales and marketing of wine, stretching back well over 20 years. They bypassed owning vineyards or building wineries, instead headhunting key winemakers in the Clare Valley and Tasmania for riesling and chardonnay respectively, and the assistance of Tim Geddes at his winery in McLaren Vale, where they make the red wines. In 2016 they took the plunge and purchased part of the elevated Seaview block adjacent to Chapel Hill, Samuels Gorge, Coriole and Hardys' Yeenunga vineyard, with 7ha of shiraz and 2ha of cabernet sauvignon, and have enlisted the very experienced Richard Leaske to help manage the vineyard. Exports to the UK, Singapore and Hong Kong.

♥♥♥♥♥ **Clare Valley Riesling 2015** Light straw-green; a perfumed talc and tangerine blossom bouquet leads into an intense palate flooded with juicy lemon/lime fruit elongated by crisp, lingering acidity. A classic each-way bet, now or later. Screwcap. 12.3% alc. **Rating** 95 **To** 2028 $30 ✪

♥♥♥♥♀ **McLaren Vale Tempranillo Grenache 2015** Rating 93 **To** 2019 $30
McLaren Vale Tempranillo Grenache 2014 Rating 93 **To** 2020 $30
McLaren Vale Grenache 2014 Rating 92 **To** 2021 $38
McLaren Vale Tempranillo Grenache 2016 Rating 92 **To** 2023 $30 NG
Clare Valley Riesling 2016 Rating 91 **To** 2030 $30 NG
McLaren Vale Shiraz 2015 Rating 90 **To** 2023 $30 NG

Minko Wines ★★★☆

13 High Street, Willunga, SA 5172 **Region** Southern Fleurieu
T (08) 8556 4987 **www**.minkowines.com **Open** Wed–Fri, Sun 11–5, Sat 9.30–5
Winemaker James Hastwell **Est.** 1997 **Dozens** 1800 **Vyds** 15.8ha
Mike Boerema (veterinarian) and Margo Kellet (ceramic artist) established the Minko vineyard on their cattle property at Mt Compass. The vineyard, which uses biodynamic methods, is planted to pinot noir, merlot, cabernet sauvignon, chardonnay, pinot gris and savagnin; 60ha of the 160ha property is heritage-listed. Exports to the UK.

♥♥♥♥ **Half Tonne Reserve Pinot Noir 2014** Has largely overcome the 'dry red' flavours that are common on the Fleurieu Peninsula and the limitations of its elevage in a polyethylene flextank. However, it must be said that the price is very challenging. Screwcap. 13.4% alc. **Rating** 89 **To** 2021 $50

Reserve Cabernet Sauvignon 2014 There's good varietal fruit expression (blackcurrant and bay leaf), obvious oak and ample tannins. The issue is the lack of texture that would have been gained by the gently oxidative process of barrel maturation. Screwcap. 13.3% alc. **Rating** 89 **To** 2029 $35

Mino & Co   ★★★★

113 Hanwood Avenue, Hanwood, NSW 2680 **Region** Riverina
T (02) 6963 0200 **www.**minoandco.com.au **Open** Mon–Fri 8–5
Winemaker Greg Bennett **Est.** 1997 **Dozens** NFP
The Guglielmino family, specifically father Domenic and sons Nick and Alain, founded Mino & Co in 1997. From the outset they realised that their surname could cause problems of pronunciation, so they simply took the last four letters of their name for the business. Mino & Co has created two brands, the first Signor Vino, the second A Growers Touch. Signor Vino covers wines made from Italian varieties sourced from the Adelaide Hills, Riverina and Riverland. The A Growers Touch brand covers traditional varieties, often with local growers who have been working with the family for two decades. The wines are made at the Hanwood Winery (established on what was once a drive-in cinema). Greg Bennett has previously worked in the Mornington Peninsula, Central Victoria and Riverina, and brings a broad understanding of the markets in which the wines are to be sold, and prices that are sustainable. Exports to China are a significant part of the business.

♟♟♟♟♀ **Signor Vino Fiano 2014** Very, very interesting: the colour pick-up speaks of development, but it's the nature of that development which is so good, for it amplifies all the desirable characters fiano has in its youth. Long and – within its context – satisfying. My drink-to date may prove conservative. Screwcap. 11.5% alc. **Rating** 90 **To** 2020 $18 ✪
Signor Vino Adelaide Hills Sangiovese 2015 This throws a wicked curve ball into the ring. It's not especially complex, but has good, clear varietal colour. It is well balanced, the tannins fine, the length excellent. It's a world apart from the A Growers Touch wines (durif excepted). Screwcap. 14% alc. **Rating** 90 **To** 2020 $19

♟♟♟♟ **A Growers Touch Durif 2015 Rating** 89 **To** 2025 $15 ✪

Mistletoe Wines   ★★★★★

771 Hermitage Road, Pokolbin, NSW 2320 **Region** Hunter Valley
T (02) 4998 7770 **www.**mistletoewines.com.au **Open** 7 days 10–6
Winemaker Scott Stephens **Est.** 1989 **Dozens** 5000 **Vyds** 5.5ha
Mistletoe Wines, owned by Ken and Gwen Sloan, can trace its history back to 1909, when a vineyard was planted on what was then called Mistletoe Farm. The Mistletoe Farm brand made a brief appearance in the late '70s. The quality and consistency of these wines is irreproachable, as is their price.

♟♟♟♟♀ **Museum Release Grand Reserve Hunter Valley Shiraz 2007** First tasted Feb '10 and received a 97-point rating. The price has gone from $40 to $90, the colour shows no sign of brick, still crimson-purple, the original note follows verbatim: Great colour, deep and intense crimson-purple; an outstanding wine, combining richness with grace and elegance; layers of plum and blackberry fruit, the tannins ripe and balanced, oak subtle. From low-yielding, dry-grown 40yo vines. Will be a great Hunter shiraz in the decades to come. Screwcap. 14% alc. **Rating** 97 **To** 2040 $90 ✪

♟♟♟♟♀ **Museum Release Reserve Hunter Valley Semillon 2006** The elixir of near eternal life, still vibrant and wonderfully fresh. The original back label suggested cellaring to '14, but that can be upgraded to '24 without a shadow of doubt, its lemony acidity sheer pleasure, no pain. Great value for an 11yo wine. Screwcap. 10% alc. **Rating** 96 **To** 2024 $32 ✪
Reserve Hunter Valley Semillon 2016 An incisive and vibrant wine with Meyer lemon, lemon zest and lemongrass on a path of crystalline acidity. Has

enough flavour to justify drinking tonight, but will become a different wine with 5+ years in bottle. The choice is yours, and you can't lose. Screwcap. 10.6% alc. **Rating** 95 **To** 2029 $26 **○**

Reserve Hilltops Cabernet 2015 It has super crimson-purple colour, and quality oak has been used to cushion the luscious cassis and black olive fruit flavours. There are no issues of reduction, making this an all the way winner. Screwcap. 14.2% alc. **Rating** 95 **To** 2035 $32 **○**

ΨΨΨΨ Hilltops Shiraz Viognier 2015 Rating 93 To 2030 $25 **○**
Home Vineyard Hunter Semillon 2016 Rating 93 To 2025 $23 **○**
Hilltops Noble Viognier 2016 Rating 93 $23 **○**
Wild Hunter Valley Semillon 2016 Rating 90 To 2021 $25
Barrel Fermented Hunter Valley Rose 2016 Rating 90 To 2018 $23
Home Vineyard Hunter Valley Shiraz 2015 Rating 90 To 2025 $40

Mitchell ★★★★★

Hughes Park Road, Sevenhill via Clare, SA 5453 **Region** Clare Valley
T (08) 8843 4258 **www.**mitchellwines.com **Open** 7 days 10–4
Winemaker Andrew Mitchell **Est.** 1975 **Dozens** 30000 **Vyds** 75ha
One of the stalwarts of the Clare Valley, established by Jane and Andrew Mitchell, producing long-lived Rieslings and Cabernet Sauvignons in classic regional style. The range now includes very creditable Semillon, Grenache and Shiraz. A lovely old stone apple shed provides the cellar door and upper section of the upgraded winery. Children Angus and Edwina are now working in the business, heralding generational changes. Over the years the Mitchells have established or acquired 75ha of vineyards on four excellent sites, some vines over 50 years old; all are managed organically, with the use of biodynamic composts for over a decade. Exports to the UK, the US, Canada, Singapore, Hong Kong, China and NZ.

ΨΨΨΨΨ McNicol Clare Valley Riesling 2009 Quince marmalade, lime, ginger, cumquat and candied citrus beam from the glass, reverberating on a palate that is layered, slightly warm vintage skinsy, yet riding a riesling undercarriage of vibrant acidity. A far more spicy, complex, richer Germanic take than the Clare Valley norm, yet the Clare's lime splice notes remain unmistakable. Screwcap. 13.5% alc. **Rating** 96 **To** 2022 $35 NG **○**

Watervale Riesling 2016 Mitchell has really stepped up to the plate of contemporary taste over recent years, making poised Rieslings with less shrill acidity than in the past, yet still with the tensile line of limey flavour and febrility that has always marked the region. This is a light to mid-weighted wine, strutting across the palate with flavours of citrus rind, quince, green apple, curd and a finish dusted with pumice and driven by a pungent mineral crunch. Screwcap. 13% alc. **Rating** 94 **To** 2028 $24 NG **○**

Sevenhill Clare Valley Cabernet Sauvignon 2013 Blackcurrant, bay leaf, cherry and plum aromas are inflected with a slight smudge of Clare Valley mint and bitter chocolate, yet the wine is pointed, medium-bodied, detailed, vibrant and long. The level of extraction – 6 weeks on skins before 2 years in barriques – is perfectly tuned to the style. Screwcap. 13% alc. **Rating** 94 **To** 2028 $28 NG **○**

ΨΨΨΨ Clare Valley Semillon 2015 Rating 92 To 2021 $24 NG **○**
McNicol Clare Valley Shiraz 2009 Rating 91 To 2022 $45 NG

Mitchell Harris Wines ★★★★★

38 Doveton Street North, Ballarat, Vic 3350 **Region** Pyrenees
T 0417 566 025 **www.**mitchellharris.com.au **Open** Sun–Tues 11–6, Wed 11–9, Thurs–Sat 11–11
Winemaker John Harris **Est.** 2008 **Dozens** 1700
Mitchell Harris Wines is a partnership between Alicia and Craig Mitchell and Shannyn and John Harris, the latter winemaker for this eponymous producer. John began his career at Mount Avoca, then spent eight years as winemaker at Domaine Chandon in the Yarra Valley,

cramming in northern hemisphere vintages in California and Oregon. The Mitchells grew up in the Ballarat area, and have an affinity for the Macedon and Pyrenees districts. While the total make is not large, a lot of thought has gone into the creation of each of the wines. In 2012 a multipurpose space was created in an 1880s brick workshop and warehouse, the renovation providing a cellar door and education facility. Exports to China.

🍷🍷🍷🍷🍷 **Pyrenees Rose 2016** This is a red wine drinker's rose, serious in intent and outcome. The savoury overcoat is no surprise, but within its folds there is crisp and lively rosehip and cherry fruit. Screwcap. 12.6% alc. **Rating** 95 **To** 2018 $25 ✪
Pyrenees Shiraz 2015 Includes 2% co-fermented viognier. Bright crimson; a delicious medium-bodied shiraz with the bright red fruit flavours John Harris invests in his wine, contrary to the darker fruit of other makers in the Pyrenees. The alcohol (which I hadn't noticed earlier) is also a major factor in the style. Screwcap. 13.5% alc. **Rating** 95 **To** 2030 $35 ✪
Pyrenees Cabernet Sauvignon 2015 From the Peerick Vineyard, matured for 18 months in French hogsheads (15% new). The bright, clear crimson-purple colour signals a vibrantly fresh and cool cabernet in best Mitchell Harris style. Is varietal to its bootstraps, but the ever-so-fine tannins mean it is ready and awaiting your pleasure. Screwcap. 13.5% alc. **Rating** 95 **To** 2030 $30 ✪
Curious Winemaker Pyrenees Grenache 2016 From the DogRock Vineyard, matured for 6 months in used French hogsheads. Grenache with a savoury Rhône Valley twist to the vibrant, supple red fruits. A light year away from McLaren Vale style, true unto itself. Screwcap. **Rating** 94 **To** 2030 $27 ✪

🍷🍷🍷🍷♀ **Pyrenees Sauvignon Blanc Fume 2016 Rating** 93 **To** 2021 $27 ✪
Blanc #1 by The Maker, the Muse and the Alchemist NV Rating 92 $35
Sabre 2012 Rating 90 **To** 2018 $42 TS

Mitchelton   ★★★★☆

Mitchellstown via Nagambie, Vic 3608 **Region** Nagambie Lakes
T (03) 5736 2222 **www**.mitchelton.com.au **Open** 7 days 10–5
Winemaker Travis Clydesdale **Est.** 1969 **Dozens** 12 000 **Vyds** 148ha
Mitchelton was founded by Ross Shelmerdine, who had a vision splendid for the striking winery, restaurant, observation tower and surrounding vineyards. The expected volume of tourism did not eventuate, and the business became embroiled in a long-running dispute. In 1994 it was acquired by Petaluma, but, once again, did not deliver the expected financial return, notwithstanding the long and faithful service of chief winemaker Don Lewis, or the quality of its best wines. In Aug 2012 a new chapter opened for Mitchelton, with the completion of an acquisition agreement by Gerry Ryan OAM, and son Andrew. Gerry founded caravan company Jayco in 1975, and as a consequence of the success of that company, has a virtually unlimited budget to take Mitchelton to the next level. Winemaker Travis Clydesdale has had a long association with Mitchelton, dating back to when he was a small boy and his father was cellar manager. Exports to all major markets.

🍷🍷🍷🍷🍷 **Chardonnay 2016** Estate-grown, vinified in separate batches from different blocks, each fermented and matured in new and used French oak. There is excellent varietal expression coming through a complex palate that also retains freshness. Screwcap. 13.5% alc. **Rating** 94 **To** 2023 $22 ✪
Airstrip Marsanne Roussanne Viognier 2016 Each variety, and each batch of each variety, was separately barrel-fermented, resulting in a tapestry of flavours and textures to be mixed and matched in a complex exercise that has landed safely. While the stone fruit, apple, citrus and pear fruit inputs are a given, the key to the wine is its freshness and impressive grip to the finish. Screwcap. 13.5% alc. **Rating** 94 **To** 2022 $28 ✪

🍷🍷🍷🍷♀ **Marsanne 2015 Rating** 93 **To** 2030 $22 ✪
Airstrip Marsanne Roussanne Viognier 2015 Rating 92 **To** 2023 $28
Crescent Shiraz Mourvedre Grenache 2014 Rating 92 **To** 2021 $28
Blackwood Park Riesling 2016 Rating 91 **To** 2026 $19 ✪

Chardonnay 2015 Rating 90 To 2021 $22
Shiraz 2014 Rating 90 To 2023 $22
Cabernet Sauvignon 2014 Rating 90 To 2024 $22

Mitolo Wines

141 McMurtrie Road, McLaren Vale, SA 5171 **Region** McLaren Vale
T (1300 571 233 **www**.mitolowines.com.au **Open** 7 days 11–5
Winemaker Ben Glaetzer **Est.** 1999 **Dozens** 40 000
Mitolo had a meteoric rise once Frank Mitolo decided to turn a winemaking hobby into a business. In 2000 he took the plunge into the commercial end of the business, inviting Ben Glaetzer to make the wines. Split between the Jester range and single vineyard wines, Mitolo began life as a red wine-dominant brand, but now also produces Rose and Vermentino. Exports to all major markets.

🍷🍷🍷🍷🍷 **Marsican McLaren Vale Shiraz 2014** '14 seems an odd year in which to make a new super-cuvee flagship, but it may be the Chinese factor in play. It is by far the most intense of the Shirazs in the Mitolo toolbox, but no more full-bodied than Savitar. New oak plays a major role, but so does the brighter, more juicy fruit. Cork. 14% alc. **Rating** 96 **To** 2039 $200
Cantiniere McLaren Vale Shiraz 2014 A seductive best-barrel selection that instantaneously fills every corner of the mouth with its chocolate-coated liqueur plum flavours that counterintuitively don't cloy, nor leave a sticky aftertaste. The tannins and oak management are both precisely engineered. Screwcap. 14.5% alc. **Rating** 95 **To** 2034 $68
Savitar McLaren Vale Shiraz 2014 On the third step of the ladder in the Mitolo Shiraz hierarchy, sharing the depth of colour of all its siblings. The bouquet is strikingly different, with spicy, savoury, woody aromas leaping out of the glass. The full-bodied palate borrows heavily from the bouquet with its complex web of dark fruits and earthy notes. Screwcap. 14.5% alc. **Rating** 95 **To** 2034 $80
Jester McLaren Vale Vermentino 2016 A wine with considerable attitude and punch. While the dominant flavours are fruity, crisp and bright with some of the same attributes of good pinot gris, there is also a textural play of crushed citrus leaves. Intriguing. Screwcap. 11.5% alc. **Rating** 94 **To** 2021 $22 ○
Small Batch Series McLaren Vale Vermentino 2016 A distinctly complex bouquet with exotic spices, flowers and powder puff. Wild yeast and barrel fermentation both add to the complexity and length of the palate. Drink anywhere, anytime – simply make sure it's fully chilled. Vino-Lok. 12.5% alc. **Rating** 94 **To** 2019 $28 ○
G.A.M. McLaren Vale Shiraz 2014 This is on the second step up the ladder, and has the power and complexity of all Ben Glaetzer's red wines: deep-seated ripe fruit, soft tannins, and overall mouthfeel, dark chocolate a bonus extra. A Linus blanket. Screwcap. 14.5% alc. **Rating** 94 **To** 2034 $58

🍷🍷🍷🍷♀ **Jester McLaren Vale Shiraz 2015** Rating 92 To 2030 $25 ○
The Furies McLaren Vale Shiraz 2013 Rating 92 To 2027 $58 CM
Small Batch Series McLaren Vale Rose 2016 Rating 91 To 2018 $28
Reiver Barossa Valley Shiraz 2013 Rating 91 To 2024 $58 CM
Ourea McLaren Vale Sagrantino 2014 Rating 91 To 2024 $35
The Nessus McLaren Vale Malbec 2016 Rating 90 To 2022 $15 ○

Molly Morgan Vineyard

496 Talga Road, Rothbury, NSW 2320 **Region** Hunter Valley
T (02) 4930 7695 **www**.mollymorgan.com **Open** Not
Winemaker Rhys Eather **Est.** 1963 **Dozens** 2000 **Vyds** 7.65ha
Established by the Roberts family in 1963, later acquired by a syndicate headed by Andrew Simon of Camperdown Cellars fame, Molly Morgan focuses on estate-grown wines from vines up to 50+ years old (the semillon planted in 1963, shiraz and chardonnay following in stages through to '97). The vineyard is named after an exceptionally resourceful woman who

was twice convicted and sent to NSW, married three times (the last time when she was 60, her husband aged 31). Out of this improbable background she emerged as a significant benefactor of the sick, earning the soubriquet 'Queen of the Hunter'.

🍷🍷🍷🍷🍷 **Semillon 2016** Hand-picked, whole-bunch pressed, matured for 5 months in tank. Those who met the challenges of the '16 vintage made semillons such as this. Despite its low-end alcohol, it has considerable mouthfeel and depth to the varietal lemon/lemongrass fruit. Screwcap. 10% alc. **Rating** 92 **To** 2026 $25 ❂

Molly's Cradle ★★★☆

17/1 Jubilee Avenue, Warriewood, NSW 2102 **Region** Hunter Valley
T (02) 9979 1212 **www**.mollyscradle.com.au **Open** By appt
Winemaker Various Contract **Est.** 2002 **Dozens** 20 000 **Vyds** 9ha
Steve Skidmore and Deidre Broad created the Molly's Cradle brand concept in 1997, moving to reality with the first planting of estate vines in 2000, the first vintage following in '02. They have 2ha each of verdelho, chardonnay, merlot and shiraz, plus 1ha of petit verdot, but also look to other regions to supplement the estate-grown grapes. Exports to China.

🍷🍷🍷🍷🍷 **Cradle Vignerons Selection McLaren Vale Shiraz 2014** 2 days cold soak, 7 days on skins, matured in used French and American hogsheads for 14 months. A solidly built McLaren Vale shiraz with layers of blackberry fruit, oak and dark chocolate, tannins also very much in play. Patience will be rewarded. Screwcap. 14.6% alc. **Rating** 90 **To** 2034 $40

Mon Tout

PO Box 283, Cowaramup, WA 6284 **Region** Margaret River
T (08) 9336 9600 **www**.montout.com.au **Open** Not
Winemaker Janice McDonald, Mark Bailey **Est.** 2014 **Dozens** NFP **Vyds** 28ha
Mon Tout is the venture of second-generation vintner Richard Burch, son of Jeff and Amy Burch. Between 2003 and '12 he managed to spend two years at Curtin University studying viticulture and oenology, before deciding this wasn't his thing. He then had a gap year, travelling through Europe and Asia with friends, before homing pigeon-like returning to Perth to enrol in a three-degree wine marketing course at Edith Cowan University. Mon Tout is a small separate venture from his position as brand manager for the east coast of Australia for Burch Family Wines. The wines reflect Janice McDonald's exceptional experience and skill.

🍷🍷🍷🍷🍷 **Biodynamic Shiraz 2015** Fermented on wild yeast in stainless steel before going to a mix of old and new French oak. No whole bunches but plenty of spice and savoury stem-like flavour. Freshness is key here. Cherry-plum and peanut shells with leaf matter and garden herbs. Scent, personality, life. Rather than challenge, it brings you along with it. Screwcap. 14% alc. **Rating** 94 **To** 2027 $30 CM ❂

🍁 Monkey Business

2 Headingly Street, Hope Valley, SA 5090 (postal) **Region** Adelaide Hills/Clare Valley
T 0400 406 290 **www**.monkeybiz.net.au **Open** Not
Winemaker Jo Irvine **Est.** 2012 **Dozens** 2000
Tom Maxwell has a 30+year track record in sales and management, his initial plan to provide a conduit between growers, makers and the retail market. Monkey Business developed its own brands alongside those of its external clients, and ultimately decided to simplify its business structure, establishing Eccentric Wines and purchasing Leabrook Estate in the Adelaide Hills.

🍷🍷🍷🍷🍷 **Eccentric Wines Great Little Grooner Adelaide Hills Gruner Veltliner 2016** Hand-picked, crushed, cool-fermented in stainless steel, bottled within 6 weeks of harvest. Despite the strict detuned protocol, the wine has considerable energy, with citrus and green apple flavours running through to a long finish. Has undoubted development potential. Screwcap. 12% alc. **Rating** 92 **To** 2026
Leabrook Estate Adelaide Hills Sauvignon Blanc 2016 'Lightweight French oak influence' is an ambiguous expression on the back label, and it's far from

obvious. The wine is actually quite intense, but one is left with citrus, apple and stone fruit more than tropical, which some may praise the lord for; the length and aftertaste are also good. Screwcap. 13% alc. Rating 90 To 2017

Eccentric Wines Great Little Feeano Clare Valley Fiano 2016 Attractive juicy flavours midway between citrus and stone fruit, but without the texture that many fianos show. The concern was that by not fining, the wine might develop too quickly – a walk on the wild side might be a better way forward. Screwcap. 12.5% alc. **Rating** 90 To 2017

ƤƤƤƤ **Leabrook Estate Adelaide Hills Pinot Noir 2015** Rating 89 To 2023
Eccentric Wines Great Little Neeyo Clare Valley Tempranillo 2014
Rating 89 To 2020

Mons Rubra ★★★★☆

Cheveley Road, Woodend North, Vic 3442 **Region** Macedon Ranges
T 0457 777 202 **www**.monsrubra.com **Open** Not
Winemaker Passing Clouds (Cameron Leith) **Est.** 2004 **Dozens** 400 **Vyds** 1ha
Mons Rubra has been developed by Max and Susan Haverfield. With a broad-based interest in wine, and after some research, they purchased their property in the Macedon Ranges; it is situated in the 600–700m elevation range, with friable volcanic soils. They settled on the most widely propagated clone of pinot noir in Australia, MV6, which seems to perform well wherever it is planted. Initially the wine was made by John Ellis at Hanging Rock (2004 to '10), but it is now being made by the Leith family at their Passing Clouds winery at Musk.

ƤƤƤƤƤ **Macedon Ranges Pinot Noir 2015** Very light colour, although the hue is bright; spice and forest nuances underlie the red fruits of the bouquet, in turn faithfully replayed on the seductively silky palate and long finish. Sensitive winemaking of fruit with low level of tannins. Arguably will never be better than it is today, although, of course, it will change with age. Screwcap. 12.9% alc. **Rating** 95 To 2027 $42

Mont Rouge Estate ★★★★☆

232 Red Hill Road, Red Hill, Vic 3937 **Region** Mornington Peninsula
T (03) 5931 0234 **www**.montrougeestate.com.au **Open** Fri–Mon 11–5
Winemaker Michael Kyberd **Est.** 1989 **Dozens** 400 **Vyds** 3.23ha
Mont Rouge Estate was purchased in late 2016 by Jennifer Smith, Thea Salter and Jeffrey Smith, with Michael Kyberd (winemaker) and Geoff Clarke (vineyard manager) onboard. Both are veterans of the Mornington Peninsula, able to pick up the reins of the two vineyards (1.6ha each) in Red Hill and Main Ridge. The aim of the partners is disarmingly simple: to produce fine wine and fine food.

ƤƤƤƤƤ **Single Vineyard Red Hill Vineyard Mornington Peninsula Chardonnay 2015** Clones P58 and 96. Has slightly more breadth to the fruit on the upside, and, after much tasting of the two wines, came out marginally on top. Screwcap. 13.5% alc. **Rating** 95 To 2026 $45
Single Vineyard Main Ridge Mornington Peninsula Chardonnay 2015 Clone P58. A linear, fresh and crisp wine that has good length and balance. There isn't any profundity or X-factor in either this or its sibling, but they have been made to behave themselves. Screwcap. 13.5% alc. **Rating** 94 To 2025 $40

ƤƤƤƤƟ **Family Reserve Single Vineyard Main Ridge Mornington Peninsula Pinot Noir 2015** Rating 90 To 2023 $55

Montalto ★★★★★

33 Shoreham Road, Red Hill South, Vic 3937 **Region** Mornington Peninsula
T (03) 5989 8412 **www**.montalto.com.au **Open** 7 days 11–5
Winemaker Simon Black **Est.** 1998 **Dozens** 10 000 **Vyds** 57.7ha

John Mitchell and family established Montalto in 1998, but the core of the vineyard goes back to '86. The vineyard is planted to pinot noir, chardonnay, pinot gris, riesling, shiraz, tempranillo and sauvignon blanc. Intensive vineyard work opens up the canopy, with yields ranging between 3.7 and 6.1 tonnes per hectare. Wines are released in three ranges: the flagship Single Vineyard, Montalto and Pennon Hill. Montalto leases several vineyards that span the Peninsula, giving vastly greater diversity of pinot noir sources, and greater insurance against weather extremes. There is also a broad range of clones adding to that diversity. Montalto has hit new heights with its wines from these blocks. Exports to the Philippines and China.

ṬṬṬṬṬ **Single Vineyard Main Ridge Block Mornington Peninsula Pinot Noir 2015** Bright, light crimson; this is one extremely complex pinot noir, with all the floral spices and highways and byways of the palate, which is equally devoted, twiggy/foresty on one side, small red fruits on the other. Its magic lies with the way the red fruits flow around the foresty notes without any apparent effort, and guide the wine through to its delicious finish and aftertaste. Screwcap. 13.7% alc. **Rating** 97 **To** 2029 $70 ✪

ṬṬṬṬṬ **Estate Mornington Peninsula Chardonnay 2015** A decidedly funky complexity plays throughout the bouquet and the long palate, yet breaks free into utter purity on the finish and – in particular – the aftertaste. Grapefruit is the key in terms of fruit, giving emphasis on the back-palate and finish. Screwcap. 13.3% alc. **Rating** 96 **To** 2025 $42 ✪

Single Vineyard The Eleven Mornington Peninsula Chardonnay 2015 Has the intensity and sense of purpose lacking from a fair few Mornington chardonnays. Its bouquet is complex, thanks to a degree of engineered funk, then a vigorous and long palate leaving no questions unanswered. It will cruise through the next 5–10 years. Screwcap. 12.9% alc. **Rating** 96 **To** 2027 $60 ✪

Pennon Hill Mornington Peninsula Rose 2016 The bouquet radiates red cherry and plum fruits with a subtext of the gently spicy/savoury nuances that take form and shape on the bone-dry palate – a dryness that is absolute yet doesn't imperil the fluid, almost slippery, character of the palate. Bravo. Screwcap. 13.4% alc. **Rating** 96 **To** 2020 $25 ✪

Single Vineyard Merricks Block Mornington Peninsula Pinot Noir 2015 A hyper-fragrant bouquet sends multiple messages of fruit and forest, not letting you proceed to the palate. Breaking free, the Montalto magic cleaves a way through the forest for the river of beautifully cadenced red fruits and plums, acidity and oak drawing out the finish of a beautiful pinot. Two gold medals '16. Screwcap. 13.5% alc. **Rating** 96 **To** 2029 $70 ✪

Single Vineyard Tuerong Block Mornington Peninsula Pinot Noir 2015 This plays a tap dance between spice and fruit to set the tone for all the rest that lies behind. Again you have a pinot that flashes all the complexity of the four single vineyards. There is an overarching elegance in all these wines. Screwcap. 13.4% alc. **Rating** 96 **To** 2027 $70 ✪

Pennon Hill Mornington Peninsula Pinot Noir 2014 This has a tapestry of dark fruits, stem, spice and fine tannins, the fruit and savoury forces locked in combat with neither winning. Gold medals Melbourne Wine Show '15 and Winewise Small Vignerons Awards '15, where it was also awarded the trophy for Best Pinot Noir. Screwcap. 13.1% alc. **Rating** 96 **To** 2026 $32 ✪

Pennon Hill Mornington Peninsula Chardonnay 2015 As ever, winemaker Simon Black walks on the wild side, yet the wine's abundant complexity is coherent, with both the grapefruit and acidity weaving a grainy textural play through to the long, harmonious finish. Screwcap. 13.3% alc. **Rating** 95 **To** 2023 $28 ✪

Estate Mornington Peninsula Pinot Noir 2015 Excellent bright clear crimson hue; the complex bouquet sets the scene for what follows: spice, plum and black cherry on the bouquet, and a no-compromise palate and palette bordering on medium to full-bodied. Will repay extended cellaring. Screwcap. 13.6% alc. **Rating** 95 **To** 2030 $50

Single Vineyard Red Hill Block Mornington Peninsula Pinot Noir 2015
Simon Black clearly uses left-field techniques when he thinks they will result in
better wine, but there are wines such as this which call for a mainstream approach.
Here the plum family provides the engine that drives the bouquet and palate alike.
It results in a cool, calm and collected pinot that simply says 'Drink me'. Screwcap.
13.6% alc. **Rating** 95 **To** 2025 $70

Pennon Hill Mornington Peninsula Shiraz 2015 Conventional vinification of
grapes not up to the standard for Montalto Estate hasn't dimmed its show career;
indeed the reverse (a trophy and three gold medals). It is an emblematic statement
of cool climate shiraz, red fruits splattered with bursts of spices and cracked pepper,
the tannins fine and smooth, new oak held on a tight leash. Screwcap. 13.6% alc.
Rating 95 **To** 2030 $32 ✪

Estate Mornington Peninsula Shiraz 2015 Savoury tannins are men at work
from the outset, the fruits a profusion of red, purple and black. Gold medals at
Mornington Peninsula and the National Cool Climate Wine Show show that
judges didn't regard the challenges inherent in the wine to be too great. Screwcap.
13.7% alc. **Rating** 95 **To** 2029 $50

Pennon Hill Sauvignon Blanc 2016 Rating 94 **To** 2020 $25 ✪
Pennon Hill Pinot Noir 2015 Rating 94 **To** 2023 $32

ŶŶŶŶŶ **Pennon Hill Pinot Grigio 2016 Rating** 93 **To** 2020 $25 ✪
Pennon Hill Tempranillo 2015 Rating 92 **To** 2027 $32
Estate Mornington Peninsula Riesling 2016 Rating 90 **To** 2023 $25
Estate Mornington Peninsula Pinot Gris 2016 Rating 90 **To** 2021 $36

Montara   ★★★★★

76 Chalambar Road, Ararat, Vic 3377 **Region** Grampians
T (03) 5352 3868 **www**.montarawines.com.au **Open** Fri–Sun 11–4
Winemaker Leigh Clarnette **Est.** 1970 **Dozens** 3000 **Vyds** 19.2ha
Gained considerable attention for its Pinot Noirs during the 1980s, and continues to produce
wines of distinctive style under the ownership of no less than six siblings of the Stapleton
family. As I can attest from several visits over the years, the view from the cellar door is one
of the best in the Grampians region. Between 1984 and 2006, when he was appointed chief
winemaker at Montara, Leigh Clarnette had an exceptionally intense and varied career. He
worked at Chateau Yarrinya (now De Bortoli) and Tarrawarra Estate, and helped produce
base wine for Domaine Chandon's first venture in the Yarra Valley. He moved to Padthaway
Estate in 1990, installed the first traditional wooden champagne press in Australia, returned
to Vic to Seppelt Great Western's production of sparkling wines and top-class Shirazs, joined
McPherson Wines in '99 as chief winemaker, thence in 2003 to the Pyrenees as chief
winemaker at Taltarni. Exports to the US, Canada, Indonesia, Hong Kong and China.

ŶŶŶŶŶ **Grampians Riesling 2016** An off-dry style, this has texture galore filling out
the palate; mostly it's an ode to citrus with grapefruit pith and juiciness, homemade lemon-lime cordial and cleansing acidity. Sure, it'll age, but it's stunning now.
Screwcap. 12% alc. **Rating** 95 **To** 2025 $23 JF

Chalambar Road Grampians Shiraz 2014 Impressive and easy to like. This is
a full-bodied, richly flavoured spicy shiraz with a dark purple-black impenetrable
hue. Concentrated dark fruit, pepper, earth, bitumen and more, with grainy,
textural and sweet tannins. Just tastes good. Will age effortlessly, but looks smart
now. Cork. 14% alc. **Rating** 95 **To** 2034 $70 JF

Grampians Shiraz 2015 Wonderful dark-red hue, reductive, opens up to reveal
lots of ripeness and succulence with a whirl of dark fruit and woodsy spices,
pepper and juniper. Full-bodied with restrained gritty tannins and has all the joy of
shiraz from the Grampians. Screwcap. 14% alc. **Rating** 94 **To** 2025 $25 JF

ŶŶŶŶŶ **Grampians Cabernet Sauvignon 2015 Rating** 93 **To** 2024 $25 JF ✪
Chalambar Road Grampians Pinot Noir 2015 Rating 92 **To** 2023 $70 JF
Gold Rush Grampians Chardonnay 2015 Rating 90 **To** 2023 $23 JF
Gold Rush Pinot Noir 2015 Rating 90 **To** 2020 $25 JF

Moody's Wines

'Fontenay', Stagecoach Road, Orange, NSW 2800 **Region** Orange
T (02) 6365 9117 **www**.moodyswines.com **Open** W'ends 10–5
Winemaker Madrez Wine Services (Chris Derrez) **Est.** 2000 **Dozens** 200 **Vyds** 1ha
Tony Moody's great-grandfather started a chain of retail shops in Merseyside, England, under the banner Moody's Wines. The business ultimately sold in 1965 to a brewery seeking to minimise competition. Tony planted 1ha of shiraz 'in a promising sheep paddock' in 2000, and has subsequently added 1ha of sauvignon blanc. Moody's is in the east of the Orange region, with lighter rainfall than the west, the soils clay rather than red earth.

Orange Sauvignon Blanc 2015 A clean-cut sauvignon blanc with an aromatic bouquet and a fresh, inviting palate where tropical fruit flavours play hide and seek with acidity and raw snow pea components. Screwcap. 13% alc. **Rating** 90 To 2017 $20 **○**

Orange Paquita Rose 2016 **Rating** 89 To 2017 $20

Moombaki Wines

341 Parker Road, Kentdale via Denmark, WA 6333 **Region** Denmark
T (08) 9840 8006 **www**.moombaki.com **Open** 7 days 11–5
Winemaker Harewood Estate (James Kellie) **Est.** 1997 **Dozens** 600 **Vyds** 2.4ha
David Britten and Melissa Boughey established vines on a north-facing gravel hillside with picturesque Kent River frontage. Not content with establishing the vineyard (cabernet sauvignon, shiraz, cabernet franc, malbec and chardonnay), they put in significant mixed tree plantings to increase wildlife habitats. They chose Moombaki as their vineyard name: it is a local Aboriginal word meaning 'where the river meets the sky'.

Reserve 2013 36% cabernet sauvignon, 31% shiraz, 20% malbec, 13% cabernet franc, a best barrels selection chosen for further maturation in oak. Excellent retention of colour and of the delicious array of blackcurrant, blackberry, plum and spice fruits. Supple tannins are a feature, as is the quality oak. A lovely wine with a long future. Screwcap. 14% alc. **Rating** 96 To 2033 $55 **○**

Shiraz 2014 67% Denmark, 33% Frankland River. Bright, clear crimson; a medium to full-bodied shiraz with complexity that stems from both black fruit flavours and the coupling of tannins and oak. It's a whizz-bang wine needing time to grow into what will be a splendid maturity. Screwcap. 14% alc. **Rating** 94 To 2029 $39

Cabernet Sauvignon Cabernet Franc Malbec 2014 74% cabernet sauvignon, 14% cabernet franc, 12% malbec. Crimson-purple; a fresh, medium-bodied fragrant and juicy wine with redcurrant joining the more usual blackcurrant fruit, fine-grained and supple tannins joining with cedary French oak on the long finish. Screwcap. 14% alc. **Rating** 94 To 2034 $39

Moondarra

Browns Road, Moondarra via Erica, Vic 3825 (postal) **Region** Gippsland
T 0408 666 348 **www**.moondarra.com.au **Open** Not
Winemaker Neil Prentice **Est.** 1991 **Dozens** 3000 **Vyds** 10ha
Neil Prentice and family established their Moondarra Vineyard in Gippsland, eventually focusing on the 2ha of low-yielding pinot noir. Subsequently, they planted their Holly's Garden vineyard at Whitlands in the King Valley, where they have 8ha of pinot gris and pinot noir. It is from this vineyard that much of their wine comes. Exports to the US, Singapore, Hong Kong, the Philippines, South Korea and Japan.

Conception Gippsland Pinot Noir 2015 Spent 2 years in French oak, which is very evident on the bouquet and palate. If this doesn't worry you, there is good varietal fruit expression with that Gippsland inflection of warm plummy/strawberry flavours. Screwcap. 13% alc. **Rating** 94 To 2025 $60

Studebaker Pinot Noir 2015 **Rating** 92 To 2023 $35
Holly's Garden Pinot Gris 2015 **Rating** 90 To 2018 $28

Moores Hill Estate

3343 West Tamar Highway, Sidmouth, Tas 7270 **Region** Northern Tasmania
T (03) 6394 7649 **www**.mooreshill.com.au **Open** 7 days 10–5
Winemaker Julian Allport **Est.** 1997 **Dozens** 5000 **Vyds** 7ha
The Moores Hill Estate vineyard (jointly owned by winemaker Julian Allport with Fiona
Weller and Tim and Sheena High) consists of pinot noir, riesling, pinot gris and chardonnay,
with a very small amount of cabernet sauvignon and merlot. The vines are located on a
northeast-facing hillside, 5km from the Tamar River and 30km from Bass Strait.

Riesling 2016 So brisk, so fresh, so full of florals, plus wet stones, spearmint,
lime/lemon juice and zest, all leading onto a superfine palate. There's the necessary
smidge of sweetness to rein in the puckering natural acidity. Screwcap. 12.2% alc.
Rating 94 **To** 2027 $30 JF ✪
Pinot Noir 2015 Foresty red and black berries with plenty of spice and an
assertive churn of tannin. This is an imposing pinot noir; and by imposing read
impressive. It's juicy, fragrant, doesn't sit too dark or weighty but reeks of authority.
There's a bit of crackle and crunch to this; it's excellent. Screwcap. 13.5% alc.
Rating 94 **To** 2025 $40 CM

Chardonnay 2015 Rating 90 **To** 2022 $35 JF

Moorilla Estate

655 Main Road, Berriedale, Tas 7011 **Region** Southern Tasmania
T (03) 6277 9900 **www**.moorilla.com.au **Open** Wed–Mon 9.30–5
Winemaker Conor van der Reest **Est.** 1958 **Dozens** 10 500 **Vyds** 15.36ha
Moorilla Estate was the second winery to be established in Tasmania in the 20th century,
Jean Miguet's La Provence beating it to the punch by two years. However, through much of
the history of Moorilla Estate, it was the most important winery in the state, if not in size
but as the icon. Magnificently situated on a mini-isthmus reaching into the Derwent River,
it has always been a must-visit for wine lovers and tourists. Production is around 90 tonnes
per year, sourced entirely from the vineyards around Moorilla and its St Matthias Vineyard
(Tamar Valley). The winery is part of an overall development said by observers (not Moorilla)
to have cost upwards of $150 million. Its raison d'être is the establishment of an art gallery
(MONA) that has the highest atmospheric environment accreditation of any gallery in the
southern hemisphere, housing both the extraordinary ancient and contemporary art collection
assembled by Moorilla's owner, David Walsh, and visiting exhibitions from major art museums
around the world. Exports to the UK and Hong Kong.

Muse St Matthias Vineyard Sauvignon 2015 Demonstrates the strong affinity
between barrel fermentation and sauvignon blanc. Piercing aromas of blackcurrant,
lemon oil, anise and durian wax lyrical at the attack, while the barrel work
(1500l foudres) imbues a textural breadth and detail, without impinging on the
herbaceous cut and thrust of the varietal personality. Top gold Tas Wine Show '17.
Screwcap. 12.7% alc. **Rating** 96 **To** 2023 $30 NG ✪
Muse Riesling 2015 An exceptional riesling, transcending the usual Aussie lime,
citric, talc and battery acid ensemble, and instead delivering ripe apple, apricot,
ginger and peach: verging on complex Germanic territory. Sublime! The acidity
is juicy, mellifluous and palpably natural. Screwcap. 13.1% alc. **Rating** 95 **To** 2025
$39 NG
Praxis St Matthias Vineyard Pinot Noir 2015 Presses all the hedonic pleasure
points, with a light cherry hue alluding accurately to the crunchy red fruit to
come. Sewn immaculately to a dusting of French oak, a thread of juicy cool
climate acidity, and a lick of peppery briar and forest floor, the savoury elements
sop up any hint of sweetness. A beautifully rendered light, easygoing pinot noir
that is nevertheless admirably complex. Screwcap. 13.3% alc. **Rating** 95 **To** 2021
$32 NG ✪
Muse Cabernet Sauvignon Cabernet Franc 2014 A wine that ably proves
the merit of later ripening Bordeaux varieties in parts of Tasmania. The tiniest hint

of mint confers a lift to the red and black currant flavours interspersed with dried sage, tobacco and cocoa. Tightly furled, finely ground tannins corset the wine's sapidity, drawing it across the palate into an effortless glide. Juicy acidity keeps the pulse. Screwcap. 14.2% alc. **Rating** 95 **To** 2026 $40 NG

Cloth Series St Matthias Vineyard 2013 Tangy red, mottled blue and black fruits mingle with star anise, sarsaparilla, a lick of mint and some dried sage strewn across damp undergrowth and a fetid floor of carnal desire. Glass after glass disappears while one mulls over this highly successful blend of a majority of cabernet and shiraz, alongside dollops of pinot noir and riesling as the glue. 13.3% alc. **Rating** 95 **To** 2021 NG

St Matthias Vineyard Chardonnay 2015 A fine expression of tensile, contemporary Australian chardonnay, honed across a complex, multitudinous array of micro-ferments: some inoculated, others ambient. A citric core segues to a spray of nectarine on the febrile finish as dutifully ripe fruit is welded to flinty mineral notes and leesy hay. A glaze of sexy new oak polishes it all. A bit jangly now, but will come together with a little patience. **Rating** 94 **To** 2024 NG

ҀҀҀҀҀ Muse Pinot Noir 2014 Rating 93 To 2024 $60 NG
Moorilla Vineyard Pinot Noir 2014 Rating 93 To 2030 NG
Muse St Matthias Vineyard Chardonnay 2015 Rating 92 To 2023 $41 NG
Praxis St Matthias Vineyard Sauvignon 2016 Rating 91 To 2019 $26 NG
Muse St Matthias Vineyard Syrah 2014 Rating 91 To 2020 $65 NG
Extra Brut Rose Methode Traditionelle 2011 Rating 91 To 2031 $49 TS
Praxis Sparkling Riesling 2016 Rating 90 To 2021 $29 TS

Moorooduc Estate

501 Derril Road, Moorooduc, Vic 3936 **Region** Mornington Peninsula
T (03) 5971 8506 **www.moorooducestate.com.au** **Open** 7 days 11–5
Winemaker Dr Richard McIntyre **Est.** 1983 **Dozens** 5000 **Vyds** 6.5ha
Richard McIntyre has taken Moorooduc Estate to new heights, having completely mastered the difficult art of gaining maximum results from wild yeast fermentation. Starting with the 2010 vintage, there was a complete revamp of grape sources, and hence changes to the tiered structure of the releases. These changes were driven by the simple fact that the estate vineyards had no possibility of providing the 5000–6000 dozen bottles of wine sold each year. The entry point wines under the Devil Bend Creek label remain, as before, principally sourced from the Osborn Vineyard. The mid-priced Chardonnay and Pinot Noir are no longer single-estate vineyard wines, and are now simply labelled by vintage and variety. Next come the Robinson Vineyard Pinot Noir and Chardonnay, elevated to reserve wine status, priced a little below the ultimate 'Ducs' (The Moorooduc McIntyre). Exports to the UK, the US, Hong Kong and Singapore.

ҀҀҀҀҀ **Robinson Vineyard Pinot Noir 2015** A complex bouquet with cherry, plum and spice aromas full of promise delivered – and then some – on the long, intricately detailed palate. The varietal fruit remains centre stage, but savoury/ spicy/foresty notes provide a continuous drum beat urging you to return again and again, glorying in the wine's complexity. Screwcap. 13.5% alc. **Rating** 97 **To** 2030 $55 ✪

The Moorooduc McIntyre Pinot Noir 2015 The bouquet is pure and perfumed, the palate pure silk, with wild strawberry and red cherry fruits so intense they all but hide the complex fabric underneath. The balance and length are such that you might think the wine has arrived at its destination, but it has years before all its secondary fruits can be explored. Screwcap. 13.5% alc. **Rating** 97 **To** 2030 $65 ✪

ҀҀҀҀҀ **Robinson Vineyard Chardonnay 2015** Grapefruit shares the podium with white peach on the bouquet and the fresh, vibrant palate; these Dijon clones 95 and 96 are the white version of pinot noir clone MV6, both giving star-bright varietal fruit expression almost everywhere they are planted. I really love this wine. Screwcap. 12.5% alc. **Rating** 96 **To** 2025 $55 ✪

Shiraz 2014 The deep, bright purple-crimson hue signals a bouquet stacked with smoky bacon, spice, leather and plum aromas, the palate reinforcing the intensity of the black cherry/blackberry fruits and a pepper/spice/anise trifecta. A spectacular Mornington Peninsula shiraz. Screwcap. 14% alc. **Rating** 96 **To** 2029 $38 ○

The Moorooduc McIntyre Chardonnay 2015 The most compex and richest of the 2015 Moorooduc Chardonnays, deeper in colour, and laden with opulent fruit, cream, grilled nuts and oak – it is amazing that all this has come from a wine with only 12.5% alcohol. It will carry on serenely for years, but I doubt whether it will ever be better than it is today. Screwcap. **Rating** 95 **To** 2025 $65

Pinot Gris 2015 The colour pick-up from barrel fermentation, and time in bottle, is bright, setting the scene for a wine totally deserving the gris label, and Alsace-like in its mouthfeel and depth of ripe flavours. The Mornington Peninsula is arguably the premier region in Aus for pinot gris. Screwcap. 13.5% alc. **Rating** 95 **To** 2023 $38

Garden Vineyard Pinot Noir 2015 Bright, clear crimson-purple; the high percentage of whole bunch fruit comes through the bouquet with a slight herbal/pine needle/spice nuance, and intersects like lattice work on the red fruits and fine tannins of the palate. Vive la différence. Screwcap. 14% alc. **Rating** 95 **To** 2027 $55

Shiraz 2015 Hand-picked, 100% whole bunches, wild yeast–open fermented, 18 days maceration, matured in French oak (25% new) new for 17 months. Excellent colour; has all the structure and depth of fruit one could wish for, and also brings textural characters into play. Screwcap. 14% alc. **Rating** 95 **To** 2030 $55

Chardonnay 2015 **Rating** 94 **To** 2022 $38
Pinot Gris 2014 **Rating** 94 **To** 2018 $38
Pinot Noir 2015 **Rating** 94 **To** 2025 $38
Garden Vineyard Pinot Noir 2014 **Rating** 94 **To** 2029 $55

♟♟♟♟♟ **Chardonnay 2014** **Rating** 93 **To** 2021 $38
Pinot Noir 2014 **Rating** 92 **To** 2024 $38

Moppity Vineyards ★★★★★

Moppity Road, Young, NSW 2594 (postal) **Region** Hilltops
T (02) 6382 6222 **www**.moppity.com.au **Open** Not
Winemaker Jason Brown **Est.** 1973 **Dozens** 30 000 **Vyds** 73ha
Jason Brown and wife Alecia, with backgrounds in fine wine retail and accounting, purchased Moppity Vineyards in 2004 when it was already 31 years old. Initially they were content to sell the grapes to other makers, but that changed with the release of the '06 Shiraz, which won top gold in its class at the London International Wine & Spirit Competition. In Nov '09 the '08 Eden Road Long Road Hilltops Shiraz, made from Moppity Vineyards grapes, won the Jimmy Watson Trophy. These awards are among a cascade of golds for its Shirazs, Riesling, Tumbarumba Chardonnay and Cabernet Sauvignon. Production (and sales) have soared, and all the grapes from the estate are now used for the Moppity Vineyards brand. The Lock & Key range provides exceptional value for money. Moppity has also established Coppabella, a separate venture, in Tumbarumba. Exports to the UK and China.

♟♟♟♟♟ **Escalier Shiraz 2013** Moppity's new flagship release, from a tiny parcel of grapes from the original block planted in 1973, considered too good to blend. This is an exceptional shiraz, its greatest assets balance and extreme length. The colour is good, the plum and blackberry fruits with a juicy intensity, the tannins lined up in respectful support, the high quality oak having done its job to perfection. Screwcap. 14% alc. **Rating** 98 **To** 2043 $120 ○

Reserve Hilltops Shiraz 2015 Superb fruit and superb winemaking create the illusion that this is a medium-bodied wine when in fact it is full-bodied. This is achieved through the total fusion and perfect balance of its black fruits, lifted by some co-fermented viognier, its Rolls Royce tannins and their stealthy power, and quality oak knowing its role is no more than supporting. Screwcap. 13.9% alc. **Rating** 97 **To** 2045 $80 ○

ŢŢŢŢŢ **Estate Hilltops Cabernet Sauvignon 2015** I absolutely do not see this as
more dark and brooding than the '14s; it's flamboyant and generous, yet is true
unto its varietal self, with a flood of cassis, bay leaf and black olive flavours. The
impact of tannins ex the oak (12 months in new and used French hogsheads) and
fruit can be seen, but is no more than one facet of the wine. Screwcap. 14% alc.
Rating 96 **To** 2035 $35 **☉**

Estate Hilltops Shiraz 2015 The bouquet is very expressive, bordering on
floral, with nuances of sandalwood and fresh leather underneath; the palate has
an incisive, fresh mouthfeel to the display of cherry and plum fruits, here with
forest notes in the background. It has excellent length, yet achieves all this with a
lightness of touch. Screwcap. 14% alc. **Rating** 95 **To** 2035 $35 **☉**

Lock & Key Reserve Hilltops Cabernet Sauvignon 2015 This is old school
cabernet sauvignon with a formidable austerity to the blackcurrant fruit and
tannins, which will please those looking for cabernets pre Robert J Parker. Bring
on the lamb. Screwcap. 14% alc. **Rating** 95 **To** 2030 $30 **☉**

Lock & Key Hilltops Cabernet Sauvignon 2014 Excellent, deep crimson-
purple colour; intense blackcurrant and black olive fruit is given additional context
by its fine web of ripe, balanced tannins. Top fruit, top winemaking. Screwcap.
13.9% alc. **Rating** 95 **To** 2034 $22

Lock & Key Single Vineyard Reserve Hilltops Tempranillo 2015
Everything about this wine is as it should be: bright crimson-purple hue, a
forthright bouquet traversing berries small and large, flavours from red (cherry)
to black (blackcurrant) all with a seductive juicy character to the long, medium-
bodied palate, the farewell bringing echoes of spice and licorice into play.
Screwcap. 14% alc. **Rating** 95 **To** 2025 $30 **☉**

Estate Tumbarumba Chardonnay 2016 **Rating** 94 **To** 2024 $35
Lock & Key Tumbarumba Chardonnay 2016 **Rating** 94 **To** 2023 $25 **☉**
Lock & Key Single Vineyard Reserve Hilltops Shiraz 2015 **Rating** 94
To 2030 $30 **☉**
Cato La Promessa Hilltops Nebbiolo 2015 **Rating** 94 **To** 2029 $35

ŢŢŢŢŢ **Cato La Pendenza Hilltops Sangiovese 2016** **Rating** 93 **To** 2023 $35
Cato La Lucha Hilltops Tempranillo 2015 **Rating** 93 **To** 2029 $35

Morambro Creek Wines   ★★★★☆

PMB 98, Naracoorte, SA 5271 **Region** Padthaway
T (08) 8765 6043 **www.**morambrocreek.com.au **Open** Not
Winemaker Ben Riggs **Est.** 1994 **Dozens** 30000 **Vyds** 178.5ha
The Bryson family has been involved in agriculture for more than a century, moving to
Padthaway in 1955 as farmers and graziers. From the '90s they have progressively established
large plantings of shiraz (88.5ha), cabernet sauvignon (47.5ha), chardonnay (34.5ha) and
sauvignon blanc (8ha). The Morambro Creek and Mt Monster wines have been consistent
winners of wine show medals, but the current releases take the wines onto a level not
previously achieved. Exports to the UK, the US and other major markets.

ŢŢŢŢŢ **The Bryson Barrel Select 2014** A 60/40% blend of shiraz and cabernet
sauvignon matured in a mix of new and used French and American oak for
18 months. It is full-bodied, but has excellent balance and structure, black fruits
and oak operating hand in glove, kept honest by the fine, but persistent, tannins.
Screwcap. 14.5% alc. **Rating** 95 **To** 2034 $55

Padthaway Chardonnay 2015 Fermented in separate parcels with various use
of wild yeast, mlf and extended lees contact, matured for 12 months in French
oak. Keeps the essence of grapefruit at its core, adding nuances of pear and
Granny Smith apple. Good length and balance. Screwcap. 13.5% alc. **Rating** 94
To 2023 $35

Padthaway Cabernet Sauvignon 2014 Bright, deep crimson-purple; a purebred cabernet with powerful varietal fruit on a foundation of firm tannins that will
soften nicely over the next 5 or so years while the fruit retains all its depth. French
oak also plays a part here. Screwcap. 14.5% alc. **Rating** 94 **To** 2032 $35

ＹＹＹＹＹ Jip Jip Rocks Shiraz 2015 Rating 92 To 2030 $21
Padthaway Shiraz 2014 Rating 91 To 2030 $35
Jip Jip Rocks Cabernet Sauvignon 2014 Rating 91 To 2020 $21
Jip Jip Rocks Sauvignon Blanc 2016 Rating 90 To 2017 $21
Jip Jip Rocks Shiraz Cabernet 2015 Rating 90 To 2030 $21

Morgan Simpson   ★★★☆

PO Box 39, Kensington Park, SA 5068 **Region** McLaren Vale
T 0417 843 118 **www**.morgansimpson.com.au **Open** Not
Winemaker Richard Simpson **Est.** 1998 **Dozens** 1200 **Vyds** 17.1ha
Morgan Simpson was founded by SA businessman George Morgan (since retired) and
winemaker Richard Simpson, who is a graduate of CSU. The grapes are sourced from the
Clos Robert Vineyard, planted to shiraz (9ha), cabernet sauvignon (3.5ha), mourvedre (2.5ha)
and chardonnay (2.1ha), established by Robert Allen Simpson in 1972. Most of the grapes are
sold, the remainder used to provide the reasonably priced, drinkable wines for which Morgan
Simpson has become well known: they are available through their website.

ＹＹＹＹＹ Row 42 McLaren Vale Cabernet Sauvignon 2015 Sustains the synergy
between McLaren Vale's maritime climate and cabernet sauvignon. Blackcurrant
fruit, with a gently savoury edge, has a long finish, the tannins as fine as they come
with cabernet, the French oak present but subtle. Screwcap. 15% alc. Rating 91
To 2029 $20

ＹＹＹＹ Two Clowns McLaren Vale Chardonnay 2015 Rating 89 To 2017 $20

Morningside Vineyard   ★★★★

711 Middle Tea Tree Road, Tea Tree, Tas 7017 **Region** Southern Tasmania
T (03) 6268 1748 **Open** By appt
Winemaker Peter Bosworth **Est.** 1980 **Dozens** 600 **Vyds** 2.8ha
The name 'Morningside' was given to the old property on which the vineyard stands because
it gets the morning sun first; the property on the other side of the valley was known as
Eveningside. Consistent with the observation of the early settlers, the Morningside grapes
achieve full maturity with good colour and varietal flavour. Production will increase as the
vineyard matures; recent additions of clonally selected pinot noir (including 8104, 115 and
777) are now in bearing. The Bosworth family, headed by Peter and wife Brenda, do all the
vineyard and winery work, with conspicuous attention to detail.

ＹＹＹＹＹ Riesling 2016 An engine of juicy, cool climate acidity is melded to a chassis of
talc and pumice-like pucker. The cylinders are fuelled by lime and Meyer lemon,
candied grapefruit rind and orange blossom. Palpably dry, this is mellifluous stuff
and fine drinking now, although it will age for many years to come. Screwcap.
11.5% alc. Rating 94 To 2025 $25 NG
Pinot Noir 2014 Cherries red and black, an exotic lilt of anise and cardamom,
together with a glimpse of autumnal mulch, collude on the aromatic front. The
sweetness gains speed through the middle, careening along a carriage of vivid
acidity and nicely arranged tannins, grape and oak. A finely tuned and very well
poised pinot noir. Screwcap. 13.5% alc. Rating 94 To 2022 $37 NG

ＹＹＹＹＹ Six Long Rows Pinot Noir 2014 Rating 93 To 2024 $27 NG

Morris   ★★★★★

Mia Mia Road, Rutherglen, Vic 3685 **Region** Rutherglen
T (02) 6026 7303 **www**.morriswines.com.au **Open** Mon–Sat 9–5, Sun 10–5
Winemaker David Morris **Est.** 1859 **Dozens** 100 000 **Vyds** 96ha
One of the greatest of the fortified winemakers, ranking with Chambers Rosewood. Morris
has changed the labelling system for its sublime fortified wines, with a higher-than-average
entry point for the (Classic) Liqueur Muscat; Tokay and the ultra-premium wines are being

released under the Old Premium Liqueur (Rare) label. The art of these wines lies in the blending of very old and much younger material. These Rutherglen fortified wines have no equivalent in any other part of the world (with the honourable exception of Seppeltsfield in the Barossa Valley). In July 2016 Casella Family Brands acquired Morris after decades of uninterested ownership by Pernod-Ricard.

ΥΥΥΥΥ **Old Premium Rare Liqueur Rutherglen Topaque NV** It's possible to contemplate the meaning of life with this wine. The epitome of complexity yet it's seamless and so fresh. There's a depth of flavour, with impeccable balance of richness and sweetness to acidity. In another stratosphere. Take your time coming down. 500ml. Screwcap. 18% alc. **Rating** 99 $70 JF ✪
Old Premium Rare Liqueur Muscat NV Imagine the aromas of a cloved orange pomander, the best dark chocolate and toffee, and raisins plumped up with brandy: this Rare has that and a hundred times more. The palate ineffably complex: smooth, warming and in tiptop shape. 500ml. Screwcap. 17.5% alc. **Rating** 98 $75 JF ✪
Cellar Reserve Grand Liqueur Rutherglen Topaque NV Once topaque is in grand territory it's made it to another level, actually a few levels, of complexity. The colour of cedar wood with a light olive rim, layers of richness and flavour but nothing more heavy, more panforte than fruitcake, with cardamom and pepper. Silky, luscious and rather special. 500ml. Screwcap. 17.3% alc. **Rating** 97 $50 JF ✪

ΥΥΥΥΥ **Cellar Reserve Grand Tawny NV** Mid-brown with a red sheen through it – à la tawny; a heady mix of spiced orange cake, cloves and cedar wood, toffee, coffee and chocolate licorice bullets. Such a smooth palate, with everything in its place. Beautifully crafted. Screwcap. 19% alc. **Rating** 96 $50 JF ✪
Cellar Reserve Grand Liqueur Rutherglen Muscat NV This is what Willy Wonka's chocolate factory must smell like – a melange of orange chocolate, Pontefract licorice, brittle toffee, and yet so much more complex. A seamless, slinky palate, lemon zest freshness with the spirit subtle and beautifully balanced. 500ml. Screwcap. 17% alc. **Rating** 96 $50 JF ✪
Cellar One Classic Liqueur Rutherglen Topaque NV Mid-walnut-olive with ruby tones; perfectly composed, with the spirit integrated and balanced. Dances across the palate with its richness of lemon madeira and fruitcakes, cold black tea, plump raisins and dried rose petals. The finish is long and oh so light. 500ml. Screwcap. 17.5% alc. **Rating** 95 $35 JF ✪
Cellar One Classic Liqueur Rutherglen Muscat NV Mid-cedar with an abundance of dried fruit – seedless raisins and sultanas, chocolate-coated toffee and coffee beans. Already a complex wine with the spirit integrated and the acidity keeping it from feeling too sweet. Spot on. 500ml. Screwcap. 17.5% alc. **Rating** 95 $35 JF ✪
Classic Liqueur Rutherglen Topaque NV Rating 94 $22 JF ✪
Classic Liqueur Muscat NV Rating 94 $22 JF ✪

ΥΥΥΥΡ **Black Label Liqueur Rutherglen Muscat NV** Rating 93 $20 JF ✪
Rutherglen VP Vintage 2006 Rating 93 $25 JF ✪
Blue Imperial Bin No. 80 Cinsault 2013 Rating 90 To 2025 $25 JF
Aged Amber Rutherglen Apera NV Rating 90 $50 JF
Classic Rutherglen Tawny NV Rating 90 $22 JF

Mosquito Hill Wines   ★★★☆

18 Trinity Street, College Park, SA 5069 (postal) **Region** Southern Fleurieu
T 0411 661 149 **www.**mosquitohillwines.com.au **Open** Not
Winemaker Glyn Jamieson **Est.** 2004 **Dozens** 1700 **Vyds** 4.2ha
This is the venture of Glyn Jamieson, who happens to be the prestigious Dorothy Mortlock Professor and Chairman of the Department of Surgery of the University of Adelaide. His interest in wine dates back decades, and in 1994 he commenced the part-time (distance) degree at CSU: he says that while he never failed an exam, it did take him 11 years to

complete the course. A year in France directed him to Burgundy, rather than Bordeaux, hence the planting of chardonnay, pinot blanc and savagnin on the slopes of Mt Jagged on the Magpies Song Vineyard and pinot noir (clones 114 and MV6) on the Hawthorne Vineyard. He built a small onsite winery for the first vintage in 2011. Exports to Hong Kong.

ⓉⓉⓉⓉⓎ **Savagnin Blanc 2015** An attractive lemon colour segues to aromas of Meyer lemon, dried straw and a build-up of custard cream solids across the textural, truffled palate. A mealy texture and tension from extended lees handling are contrasted nicely against the breadth imparted by barrel fermentation. Screwcap. 13% alc. **Rating** 92 **To** 2020 $28 NG

Moss Wood
926 Metricup Road, Wilyabrup, WA 6284 **Region** Margaret River
T (08) 9755 6266 **www**.mosswood.com.au **Open** By appt
Winemaker Clare and Keith Mugford **Est.** 1969 **Dozens** 12000 **Vyds** 18.14ha
Widely regarded as one of the best wineries in the region, producing glorious Chardonnay, power-laden Semillon and elegant Cabernet Sauvignon that lives for decades. Moss Wood also owns the Ribbon Vale Estate, the wines treated as vineyard-designated within the Moss Wood umbrella. Exports to all major markets.

ⓉⓉⓉⓉⓉ **Wilyabrup Margaret River Cabernet Sauvignon 2014** Moss Wood's flagship wine is a structured beauty with nothing out of place: the gloss of the colour, the florals, blackberries and mulberries infused with black olives, dried herbs and eucalypt. The French oak and the fine-grained tannins seal the deal. Very even and will reward the patient. Screwcap. **Rating** 97 **To** 2044 $125 JF ⊙

ⓉⓉⓉⓉⓉ **Wilyabrup Margaret River Semillon 2016** Vibrant and the long, pure acid line will ensure this keeps going for quite some time. It's intensely flavoured with whirls of citrus, lemongrass, Meyer lemon and zest with dried herbs and camomile. Complex and really spunky. Screwcap. **Rating** 95 **To** 2024 $38 JF
Wilyabrup Margaret River Chardonnay 2015 A lot of flavour gets stitched into Moss Wood's chardonnay, with the new oak adding to the nose and palate as do the complex creamy leesy notes. No shortage of acidity, which is the main driver that keeps this from being just too big. It stays moreish and savoury. Screwcap. **Rating** 95 **To** 2024 $65 JF
Ribbon Vale Vineyard Wilyabrup Margaret River Merlot 2014 Don't rush this. It needs a few more years to come around. It's sturdily built for ageing although the fragrance entices now, brimming with red and black currants, black olives and rosemary. The palate is dominated by oak and significant tannins, hence leaving it for the time being. The 11% cabernet franc adds the X-factor. Screwcap. **Rating** 95 **To** 2030 $65 JF
Ribbon Vale Vineyard Wilyabrup Margaret River Sauvignon Blanc Semillon 2016 No blend percentages given, but likely 75/25%. Tropical fruit foremost, backed by tangy lemony acidity on the long, well balanced palate, no overt oak. Screwcap. 12.5% alc. **Rating** 94 **To** 2020 $32

ⓉⓉⓉⓉⓎ **Ribbon Vale Vineyard Wilyabrup Margaret River Cabernet Sauvignon 2014 Rating** 93 **To** 2034 $65 JF
Amy's 2015 Rating 92 **To** 2026 $38 JF

Mount Avoca
Moates Lane, Avoca, Vic 3467 **Region** Pyrenees
T (03) 5465 3282 **www**.mountavoca.com **Open** 7 days 10–5
Winemaker Dominic Bosch **Est.** 1970 **Dozens** 10000 **Vyds** 23.46ha
A winery that has long been one of the stalwarts of the Pyrenees region, owned by Matthew and Lisa Barry. The estate vineyards (shiraz, sauvignon blanc, cabernet sauvignon, chardonnay, merlot, cabernet franc, tempranillo, lagrein, viognier, sangiovese, nebbiolo and semillon) are organically managed. The Moates Lane, Back Block and some Limited Release wines are

partly or wholly made from contract-grown grapes, but other releases are estate-grown. Winemaker Dominic Bosch and viticulturist Luke Polson joined Mount Avoca just before vintage 2015. Both with degrees from the University of Adelaide, they have continued implementing organic practices, and have obtained full organic certification for some of the estate-grown wines; the winery was certified organic in '16. Exports to China.

ＹＹＹＹＹ **Estate Range Pyrenees Cabernet Sauvignon 2015** This is a very good release. Lovely varietal bouquet; blackcurrant, leafy, dusty and cedary. Well matched French oak is right on the money. Perfect medium-to-full cabernet weight on the palate with depth and length of flavour and elegance of form. Screwcap. 14% alc. **Rating** 95 **To** 2030 $38 SC
Old Vine Pyrenees Shiraz 2015 Multi-faceted bouquet, with ripe dark fruit, chocolate, earth, pepper and licorice framed by well judged French oak. A more medium than full-bodied palate, with quietly saturating depth of flavour. Slightly assertive astringency on the finish should soften with time. Screwcap. 14% alc. **Rating** 94 **To** 2030 $46 SC

ＹＹＹＹＹ **Estate Range Pyrenees Shiraz 2015 Rating** 93 **To** 2030 $38 SC
Malakoff Pyrenees Shiraz 2015 Rating 93 **To** 2030 $46 SC
Limited Release Pyrenees Sangiovese 2016 Rating 93 **To** 2025 $46 SC
Limited Release Tempranillo 2015 Rating 92 **To** 2025 $46 SC
Jack Barry Pyrenees Sparkling Shiraz NV Rating 92 **To** 2021 TS
Estate Range Pyrenees Viognier 2015 Rating 91 **To** 2020 $38 SC
Limited Release Tempranillo 2016 Rating 91 **To** 2025 $46 SC

Mount Beckworth   ★★★☆

46 Fraser Street, Clunes, Vic 3370 **Region** Ballarat
T (03) 5343 4207 **www**.mountbeckworthwines.com.au **Open** W'ends 11–5
Winemaker Paul Lesock **Est.** 1984 **Dozens** 800 **Vyds** 4ha
Mount Beckworth vineyard was planted between 1984 and '85, but it was not until '95 that the full range of wines under the Mount Beckworth label appeared. Until then much of the production was sold to Seppelt (Great Western) for sparkling wine use. Owned and managed by Paul Lesock, who studied viticulture at CSU, and wife Jane.

ＹＹＹＹＹ **Chardonnay 2015** A sleek, tightly woven chardonnay that plays the contemporary card of reductive lees tension embellished with a smear of creamy French oak, all nicely melded to stone-fruited generosity. Screwcap. 13% alc. **Rating** 92 **To** 2023 $18 NG **○**

Mount Cathedral Vineyards   ★★★★

125 Knafl Road, Taggerty, Vic 3714 **Region** Upper Goulburn
T 0409 354 069 **www**.mtcathedralvineyards.com **Open** By appt
Winemaker Oscar Rosa, Nick Arena **Est.** 1995 **Dozens** 950 **Vyds** 5ha
The Rosa and Arena families established Mount Cathedral Vineyards in 1995, at an elevation of 300m on the north face of Mt Cathedral. The first plantings were 1.2ha of merlot and 0.8ha of chardonnay, followed by 2.5ha of cabernet sauvignon and 0.5ha of cabernet franc in 1996. No pesticides or systemic chemicals are used in the vineyard. Oscar Rosa, chief winemaker, has a Bachelor of Wine Science from CSU, and gained practical experience working at Yering Station in the late '90s. The 2014 red wines were tasted too late for 2018 *Wine Companion* book, but do appear on www.winecompanion.com.au Exports to Singapore.

ＹＹＹＹＹ **Oh Oh Merlot Merlot 2013** The wine has very deep colour and great depth to the fruit. It is in very similar style to the standard release, and there's no doubt the vineyard produces great colour and rich fruit at low baumes. The future of the wine is measured in decades rather than years. A rare wine and a rare bargain. Screwcap. 13% alc. **Rating** 93 **To** 2033 $19 **○**
Chardonnay 2016 Hand-picked, whole-bunch pressed, matured in French oak for 9 months. Has good varietal expression and length; apple, stone fruit

and honeydew melon are tied together by citrussy acidity. Screwcap. 13% alc.
Rating 91 **To** 2022
Rose 2016 Pink, tinged with salmon: a complex, textured palate which, together
with its colour, suggests barrel fermentation (in used oak). It has a pleasingly dry
finish – this is a good meat friend. Screwcap. 13% alc. **Rating** 90 **To** 2018
Cabernet Sauvignon 2013 Like the other Mount Cathedral wines, grown on
an estate vineyard that produces wine of amazingly deep colour and full flavour.
It's a left-field wine that skirts being musclebound, and needs more time to reveal
its true personality. Screwcap. 13% alc. **Rating** 90 **To** 2028 $26

ŢŢŢŢ   **Cabernet Merlot 2014** Rating 89 To 2029

Mount Coghill Vineyard ★★★★

Cnr Pickfords Road/Coghills Creek Road, Coghills Creek, Vic 3364 **Region** Ballarat
T (03) 5343 4329 www.ballaratwineries.com/mtcoghill.htm **Open** W'ends 10–5
Winemaker Owen Latta **Est.** 1993 **Dozens** 400 **Vyds** 0.7ha
Ian and Margaret Pym began planting their tiny vineyard in 1995 with 1280 pinot noir
rootlings, adding 450 chardonnay rootlings the next year. Wine has been made and released
under the Mount Coghill Vineyard label since 2001. Ian is an award-winning photographer,
and his photographs are on display at the cellar door.

ŢŢŢŢ   **Ballarat Pinot Noir 2015** Made at nearby Eastern Peak by Owen Latta, the
light cherry-red brick colour is deceptive. Aromas of spiced cherries and a little
undergrowth lead onto the palate, which has good depth and enough fine grained
tannins to suggest that this will only improve and open up over the next 4–6 years.
Screwcap. 13% alc. **Rating** 89 $25 PR

Mount Eyre Vineyards ★★★★

173 Gillards Road, Pokolbin, NSW 2320 **Region** Hunter Valley
T 0438 683 973 www.mounteyre.com **Open** At Garden Cellars, Hunter Valley Gardens
Winemaker Andrew Spinaze, Mark Richardson **Est.** 1970 **Dozens** 1000 **Vyds** 45.5ha
This is the venture of two families whose involvement in wine extends back several centuries
in an unbroken line: the Tsironis family in the Peleponnese, Greece, and the Iannuzzi family in
Vallo della Lucania, Italy. Their largest vineyard is at Broke, with a smaller vineyard at Pokolbin.
The three principal varieties planted are chardonnay, shiraz and semillon, with small amounts
of merlot, viognier, chambourcin, verdelho, negro amaro, fiano and nero d'Avola. Exports to
Canada, Vanuatu, Hong Kong and China.

ŢŢŢŢŢ   **Three Ponds Hunter Valley Fiano 2016** Pale straw; works off a citrus theme
with its lemony-bath salts, lime zest, hint of creamed honey and crisp lemon-
sorbet acidity on the finish. Screwcap. 12.8% alc. **Rating** 90 $25 **To** 2019 JF

Mount Horrocks ★★★★★

The Old Railway Station, Curling Street, Auburn, SA 5451 **Region** Clare Valley
T (08) 8849 2243 www.mounthorrocks.com **Open** W'ends & public hols 10–5
Winemaker Stephanie Toole **Est.** 1982 **Dozens** 3500 **Vyds** 9.4ha
Owner/winemaker Stephanie Toole has never deviated from the pursuit of excellence in
the vineyard and winery. She has three vineyard sites in the Clare Valley, each managed using
natural farming and organic practices. The attention to detail and refusal to cut corners is
obvious in all her wines. The cellar door is in the old, but renovated, Auburn railway station.
Exports to the UK, the US and other major markets.

ŢŢŢŢŢ   **Clare Valley Shiraz 2015** Manages to be unashamedly full-bodied and decidedly
complex, yet retains perfect balance, with a fresh, juicy quality reflecting its modest
alcohol. There is a rainbow of fruit flavours on the long palate and lingering
aftertaste. Screwcap. 13.8% alc. **Rating** 96 **To** 2035 $43 ✪
Watervale Riesling 2016 The meticulously trained vineyards are all in their
prime, and are the springboard for the equally meticulously made Mount

Horrocks rieslings. These are old money, and the wine is never less than great, its balance and length the keys for its long-term development as citrus takes on a slight honey edge, acidity the fulcrum for the change. Screwcap. 12.7% alc. Rating 95 To 2029 $34 ✪

Clare Valley Semillon 2016 It is barrel-fermented, yet the oak is under tight control, acting as a framework for the fruit, which remains centre stage, zesty and tangy, but with lemon curd joining the lemon citrus fruit of the long, lingering finish. Screwcap. 13.5% alc. Rating 95 To 2026 $33 ✪

Clare Valley Cabernet Sauvignon 2015 The gleaming crimson-purple colour waves the flag for a pure, medium-bodied cabernet that captures the mouth with its delicious cassis fruit, a wisp of bay leaf, ultra-fine, but persistent, tannins and integrated French oak. Screwcap. 13.8% alc. Rating 95 To 2035 $45

Clare Valley Nero d'Avola 2015 Bright crimson-purple; there is a brightness to the predominantly red fruits that do the heavy lifting on the bouquet and palate alike; it bubbles with juicy life, and the tannins are only just sufficient to complete the picture. Screwcap. 13.7% alc. Rating 94 To 2025 $38

Clare Valley Nero d'Avola 2014 This wine spent 18 months in French oak, its crimson colour heralding a fragrant, spicy red fruits bouquet, the medium-bodied palate providing a zesty replay of the bouquet. Screwcap. 13.5% alc. Rating 94 To 2024 $37

♀♀♀♀♀ Cordon Cut Clare Valley Riesling 2016 Rating 92 To 2026 $40

Mount Langi Ghiran Vineyards ★★★★★

80 Vine Road, Buangor, Vic 3375 **Region** Grampians
T (03) 5354 3207 **www**.langi.com.au **Open** 7 days 10–5
Winemaker Ben Haines, Jessica Robinson **Est.** 1963 **Dozens** 60 000 **Vyds** 86ha
A maker of outstanding cool climate peppery Shiraz, crammed with flavour and vinosity, and very good Cabernet Sauvignon. The Shiraz has long pointed the way for cool climate examples of the variety. The business was acquired by the Rathbone family group in 2002, and the marketing integrated with the Yering Station and Xanadu Estate wines, a synergistic mix with no overlap. Wine quality is exemplary. Exports to all major markets.

♀♀♀♀♀ **Langi Grampians Shiraz 2015** The supremely fragrant bouquet has a platform of black fruits so tightly laced with charcuterie, licorice, spice and black pepper that you can't break free until you reach the mouthwatering, medium-bodied palate of exceptional length and balance. The mouthfeel is of silk with a velvet rim, radiating red and black cherry fruits with a drumbeat of flavours matching those of the bouquet. Screwcap. 13.8% alc. Rating 98 To 2045 $120 ✪

Mast Grampians Shiraz 2015 The bouquet is extremely expressive, with pepper and French oak joining hands with the polished, glossy black cherry fruit and black pepper. French oak is of greater importance for this wine than for either of its siblings. What a magnificent trio of wines. Screwcap. 13.7% alc. Rating 97 To 2040 $70 ✪

♀♀♀♀♀ **Spinoff Chardonnay 2015** The chardonnay, planted in '85, is usually used for the Blanc de Blancs, but in '15 a few rows were left for table wine. The raw power of the wine is exceptional. White and pink grapefruit zest, pith and juice are David Warner's now banned bat, but long live those who challenge the norms. Screwcap. 12.8% alc. Rating 96 To 2023 $40 ✪

Cliff Edge Grampians Shiraz 2015 Both bouquet and medium-bodied palate offer a tapestry of black fruits, spices and black pepper, tannins woven through the succulent, juicy black fruits, French oak there or thereabouts, and fine lingering tannins. Screwcap. 13.8% alc. Rating 96 To 2035 $30 ✪

Spinoff Barbera 2015 What a tragedy there are only 40 dozen – it is by far the best Australian barbera I've tasted, brilliantly perfumed, the palate caressed by red and blue fruits, the finale a breath of tannins. Light to medium-bodied, and could stand tall in any place or time. Where does winemaker Ben Haines go from here? Screwcap. 13% alc. Rating 96 To 2025 $45 ✪

Cliff Edge Grampians Riesling 2015 Never fails to please, a legacy of love Trevor Mast had for riesling after his time making it in Germany. It has begun inching its way to maturity, and is best left at the job without interference over the next 4 years. Screwcap. 13.2% alc. **Rating** 94 **To** 2030 $20

🍷🍷🍷🍷🍷 **Cliff Edge Grampians Pinot Gris 2015** Rating 93 To 2019 $20 ✪
Cliff Edge Grampians Cabernet Sauvignon 2015 Rating 92 To 2025 $30
Cliff Edge Grampians Riesling 2014 Rating 91 To 2026 $20 ✪
Cliff Edge Grampians Viognier 2015 Rating 91 To 2020 $20 SC ✪

Mt Lofty Ranges Vineyard ★★★★★

Harris Road, Lenswood, SA 5240 **Region** Adelaide Hills
T (08) 8389 8339 **www**.mtloftyrangesvineyard.com.au **Open** Fri–Sun 11–5
Winemaker Peter Leske, Taras Ochota **Est.** 1992 **Dozens** 3000 **Vyds** 4.6ha
Mt Lofty Ranges is owned and operated by Sharon Pearson and Garry Sweeney. Nestled high in the Lenswood subregion of the Adelaide Hills at an altitude of 500m, the very steep north-facing vineyard (pinot noir, sauvignon blanc, chardonnay and riesling) is hand-pruned and hand-picked. The soil is sandy clay loam with a rock base of white quartz and ironstone, and irrigation is kept to a minimum to allow the wines to display vintage characteristics.

🍷🍷🍷🍷🍷 **Hand Picked Lenswood Riesling 2016** It's a wistful kind of wine – offers immediate pleasure but in no hurry whatsoever. The palate is gentle, with chalky acidity, some roundness and texture – not entirely dry, which adds to the mouthfeel. It's moreish. Screwcap. 12.5% alc. **Rating** 95 **To** 2024 $29 JF ✪
S&G Lenswood Chardonnay 2015 Whole-bunch pressed, wild yeast ferment in used French oak, then does its thing for 10 months. A very tidy wine. Supple, textural, creamy, citrussy, spicy and beautifully composed. Screwcap. 12.4% alc. **Rating** 95 **To** 2023 $85 JF
S&G Adelaide Hills Shiraz 2015 Excellent purple-red hue then whoa! – an explosion of spices: pepper, five-spice, dried herbs and some meaty reduction. The palate backs up those flavours, adding juicy black plums and a savoury twist with ripe, textural tannins. Terrific wine – only 600 bottles produced. Screwcap. 13.2% alc. **Rating** 95 **To** 2025 $85 JF

🍷🍷🍷🍷🍷 **S&G Lenswood Pinot Noir 2015** Rating 93 To 2022 $85 JF
Old Cherry Block Lenswood Sauvignon Blanc 2016 Rating 92 To 2019 $22 JF ✪
Pinot Noir Chardonnay 2013 Rating 92 To 2018 $40 TS
Old Apple Block Lenswood Chardonnay 2015 Rating 91 To 2021 $30 JF
Old Pump Shed Lenswood Pinot Noir 2015 Rating 91 To 2025 $34 JF
Adelaide Hills Shiraz 2015 Rating 91 To 2024 $32 JF
Not Shy Lenswood Pinot Noir Rose 2016 Rating 90 To 2019 $22 JF

Mount Majura Vineyard ★★★★★

88 Lime Kiln Road, Majura, ACT 2609 **Region** Canberra District
T (02) 6262 3070 **www**.mountmajura.com.au **Open** Thurs–Mon 10–5
Winemaker Dr Frank van de Loo **Est.** 1988 **Dozens** 4000 **Vyds** 9.3ha
Vines were first planted in 1988 by Dinny Killen on a site on her family property that had been especially recommended by Dr Edgar Riek; its attractions were red soil of volcanic origin over limestone, with reasonably steep east and northeast slopes providing an element of frost protection. The tiny vineyard has been significantly expanded since it was purchased in '99. Blocks of pinot noir and chardonnay have been joined by pinot gris, shiraz, tempranillo, riesling, graciano, mondeuse, cabernet franc and touriga nacional. In addition, there has been an active planting program for the pinot noir, introducing Dijon clones 114, 155 and 777. All the grapes used come from these estate plantings. One of the star performers in the Canberra District.

🍷🍷🍷🍷🍷 **Canberra District Riesling 2016** Pale quartz; the perfumed citrus blossom and talc bouquet leads into an utterly beguiling palate simultaneously pure, intense and focused, with ripe lime, lemon and apple flavours, the finish stretching out for a full minute. Screwcap. 12.5% alc. **Rating** 96 **To** 2036 $29 ❍
Canberra District Shiraz 2015 This is an aristocratic shiraz that could stand shoulder to shoulder with cabernet sauvignon (although never confused with it). The medium to full-bodied palate is packed with blackberry and plum fruit swathed in fine, but persistent, tannins, oak merely an observer. The wine has flawless balance and length, its end point shrouded in the mists of the far future. Screwcap. 14% alc. **Rating** 96 **To** 2045 $34 ❍

🍷🍷🍷🍷🍷 **Canberra District Tempranillo 2016** **Rating** 93 **To** 2025 $45 JF
Canberra District Chardonnay 2016 **Rating** 92 **To** 2022 $29 JF
Canberra District Touriga 2016 **Rating** 91 **To** 2020 $29 JF
Canberra District Mondeuse 2016 **Rating** 90 **To** 2020 $29 JF

Mount Mary   ★★★★★

Coldstream West Road, Lilydale, Vic 3140 **Region** Yarra Valley
T (03) 9739 1761 **www**.mountmary.com.au **Open** Not
Winemaker Sam Middleton **Est.** 1971 **Dozens** 4000 **Vyds** 12ha
Mount Mary was one of the foremost pioneers of the rebirth of the Yarra Valley after 50 years without viticultural activity, and right from the outset produced wines of rare finesse and purity. Today its star shines brighter than that of any of the 174 wineries in the Yarra Valley. The late founder, Dr John Middleton, practised near-obsessive attention to detail long before that phrase slid into oenological vernacular. He relentlessly strove for perfection, and all four of the wines in the original Mount Mary portfolio achieved just that (within the context of each vintage). Charming grandson Sam Middleton is equally dedicated. An all-encompassing recent tasting of every vintage of these four wines left me in no doubt he is making even better wines since assuming the winemaker mantle in June 2011. Moreover, after protracted trials, two Rhône Valley–inspired wines have been released, looking to the future yet also honouring John's late wife, Marli Russell. Winery of the Year 2018.

🍷🍷🍷🍷🍷 **Yarra Valley Pinot Noir 2015** Bright, clear crimson-purple; everything about this wine exudes supreme class: the bouquet has a rose garden of perfume and spice, the palate a concerto for strings and clarinets, as predominantly red berry fruits glide around the finest quality tannins of the cello. The length and balance are awesome, and the wine will be singing soprano 20 years on from vintage. Cork. 13.5% alc. **Rating** 99 **To** 2028
Yarra Valley Chardonnay 2015 Most of the wine is closed with a screwcap, a small amount with Diam 30, the tightest form of Diam. Gleaming light green-gold, this is no pale and wan lover: its embrace is intense, white peach just in front of grapefruit. As one would expect from Mount Mary, the oak has been as important in shaping texture and mouthfeel as in imparting flavour. All up, an icon for Yarra Valley chardonnay. 13.4% alc. **Rating** 97 **To** 2025
Yarra Valley Triolet 2014 A 65/25/10% blend of sauvignon blanc, semillon and muscadelle; hand-picked, destemmed, lightly crushed, different cultured yeast strains for each parcel, 100% barrel-fermented, matured for 11 months in oak on partial solids with some stirring. Without question, the best white Bordeaux blend in Australia, combining richness with finesse and length – and above all else – dazzling complexity. Screwcap. 12.8% alc. **Rating** 97 **To** 2022 $90 ❍
Yarra Valley Quintet 2015 Just because the Mount Mary wines are famed for their purity, elegance and balance doesn't man that they eschew power and layered complexity. Quintet (the five Bordeaux varieties) is the king of the portfolio, the wine that was closest to founder Dr John Middleton's irascible heart. The rainbow of cassis, redcurrant, dried herb and bramble flavours is absolutely exemplary. Cork. 13.3% alc. **Rating** 97 **To** 2035

ΨΨΨΨΨ **Yarra Valley Triolet 2015** 65% sauvignon blanc, 21% semillon, 14% muscadelle, fermented separately in used oak, matured for 11 months. This is an uncommonly rich Triolet at this early stage, but that is all to the good, for it will mature majestically, as all the vintages that preceded it have done. Diam. 13% alc. **Rating 96 To 2025 $95**

Marli Russell Marsanne Roussanne 2015 A 60/40% blend. Initially Marli keeps her skirt tucked tight around her ankles, then just when you think you'd better come back later, the wine soars on the back-palate and aftertaste. These are typically reticent varieties – they're not aromatic, so there's everything to look forward to. Screwcap. 13% alc. **Rating 95 To 2025 $55**

Marli Russell Marsanne Roussanne 2014 A 70/30% blend. This was a top vintage for chardonnay in the Yarra Valley, and so it seems in this wine: it has a juicy quality that really catches you, sweeping from the fore-palate through to the aftertaste. Its flavours are still primary; honeyed notes are far distant, but will arrive. Screwcap. 12.5% alc. **Rating 95 To 2039 $55**

Marli Russell Grenache Mourvedre Shiraz 2015 A 65/20/15% blend. Lighter, but brighter colour than the '14; bursts into song, reflecting the great vintage and the inclusion of the mourvedre. The bouquet is fragrant, with red fruits joining the fray, the tannins superfine, the finish long, the aftertaste fresh. Screwcap. 13.2% alc. **Rating 95 To 2030 $70**

Marli Russell Grenache Shiraz 2014 Rating 94 To 2024 $70

Mt Pilot Estate ★★★☆

208 Shannons Road, Byawatha, Vic 3678 **Region** Northeast Victoria
T 0419 243 225 **www**.mtpilotestatewines.com.au **Open** By appt
Winemaker Marc Scalzo **Est.** 1996 **Dozens** 550 **Vyds** 11ha
Lachlan and Penny Campbell have planted shiraz (6ha), cabernet sauvignon (2.5ha), and viognier (2.5ha). The vineyard has been planted on deep, well drained granitic soils at an altitude of 250m near Eldorado, 20km from Wangaratta and 35km from Beechworth.

ΨΨΨΨΨ **Reserve Viognier 2016** Made in small quantities in only the best vintages, from Montpellier clone planted on 1103 Paulsen rootstocks, machine-harvested, wild-yeast fermented in French oak (50% new), matured on lees for 9 months. A remarkable result given the climate. There are as many citrus-linked flavours as there are stone fruit/apricot, and the balance is good, the absorption of the new oak quite remarkable. Well done indeed. Screwcap. 13.8% alc. **Rating 92 To 2021 $35**

Mount Pleasant ★★★★★

401 Marrowbone Road, Pokolbin, NSW 2320 **Region** Hunter Valley
T (02) 4998 7505 **www**.mountpleasantwines.com.au **Open** 7 days 10–4
Winemaker Jim Chatto, Adrian Sparks **Est.** 1921 **Dozens** NFP **Vyds** 88.2ha
McWilliam's Elizabeth and the glorious Lovedale Semillon were generally commercially available with four to five years of bottle age; they were treasures with a consistently superb show record. The individual vineyard wines, together with the Maurice O'Shea memorial wines, add to the lustre of this proud name. However, the appointment of Jim Chatto as group chief winemaker in 2013, and the '14 vintage, the best since 1965, has lifted the range and quality of the red wines back to the glory days of Maurice O'Shea in the 1930s and '40s. Henceforth it will be known as Mount Pleasant, severing the (name) connection with McWilliam's. Winery of the Year in the *Wine Companion* 2017. Exports to all major markets.

ΨΨΨΨΨ **Lovedale Hunter Valley Semillon 2011** Gleaming, almost iridescent, straw-green; the wine's trophy and eight gold medal show record (culminating in Sydney in '16) covers every relevant show. Moreover, it still has room to develop even greater richness, a faint touch of CO_2 spritz intensifying the lemon/lemongrass fruit flavours, the acidity spot on. Screwcap. 10% alc. **Rating 97 To 2031 $70** ✪

ŢŢŢŢŢ **Mountain D Full Bodied Dry Red 2014** Full-bodied in Hunter Valley terms, but medium to full-bodied at most by the standards of SA. Earthy blackberry fruit rides shotgun on the bouquet and palate alike, new French oak on its flank, firm, but ripe, tannins bringing up the rear. One of a brilliant posse of shirazs bringing Maurice O'Shea back to life. Screwcap. 14% alc. **Rating** 96 **To** 2044 $75 ✪

Mount Henry Hunter Valley Shiraz Pinot Noir 2014 The evocative front label and the informative back label subliminally reflect the yin and yang of this blend: vibrant and juicy red fruits set against regional earthy/leather nuances. It all adds up to a medium-bodied wine with an urgency and thrust to its mouthfeel. Screwcap. 13.5% alc. **Rating** 96 **To** 2039 $48 ✪

Eight Acres Hunter Valley Semillon 2016 Hand-picked early in the morning, free-run juice cool-fermented in stainless steel for 14 days, bottled early. Quartz-green; an expensive way to make semillon dictated by the later than usual vintage following the wettest Jan since 1972, but the outcome made it all worthwhile. This is semillon walking on a high-tensile wire of acidity, lemon to the fore and green apple insistently pushing the wine through to the finish and aftertaste. Will flower with 5+ years. Screwcap. 10% alc. **Rating** 95 **To** 2030 $35 ✪

High Paddock Hunter Valley Shiraz 2014 From three blocks of vines planted in '02, relatively young for Mount Pleasant, matured for 15 months in French puncheons (30% new). Clear colour; the highly expressive bouquet brings purple and black fruits into alignment with a sweet leather, earth and briar subtext, all adding up to Hunter Valley in giant neon letters. A beautiful medium-bodied shiraz from a great vintage. Screwcap. 14% alc. **Rating** 95 **To** 2039 $35 ✪

Leontine Hunter Valley Chardonnay 2015 Clone I10V5, hand-picked, whole-bunch pressed direct to French puncheons for wild fermentation and 9 months maturation. It's a very complex Hunter Valley chardonnay made with infinite attention to detail, with stone fruit, melon, fig and brioche flavours. Screwcap. 13%alc. **Rating** 94 **To** 2024 $48

ŢŢŢŢŢ **Philip Hunter Valley Shiraz 2015 Rating** 93 **To** 2030 $27 ✪
Philip Hunter Valley Shiraz 2014 Rating 92 **To** 2030 $27
Elizabeth Hunter Valley Semillon 2016 Rating 90 **To** 2028 $27 JF
Mothervine Hunter Valley Pinot Noir 2015 Rating 90 **To** 2035 $48

Mount Stapylton Wines   ★★★★☆

14 Cleeve Court, Toorak, Vic 3142 (postal) **Region** Grampians
T 0425 713 044 **www**.mts-wines.com **Open** Not
Winemaker Don McRae **Est.** 2002 **Dozens** 250 **Vyds** 1ha

Mount Stapylton's vineyard is planted on the historic Goonwinnow Homestead farming property at Laharum, on the northwest side of the Grampians in front of Mt Stapylton. In 2010 founders Howard and Samantha Staehr sold the homestead property, but leased back the vineyard. The Little Yarra Station Vineyard (1.2ha planted in '09) in the Yarra Valley provides the grapes for the Pamela Chardonnay and the Victoria Pinot Noir. The wines are listed with several iconic restaurants in Sydney and Melbourne. Exports to the UK.

ŢŢŢŢŢ **Robert Grampians Shiraz 2015** Good depth, the best yet from Mount Stapylton; the bouquet has predominantly black fruits (cherry/berry) with a generous whiff of spice and black pepper, the palate juicy and rich, freshness and vibrancy reflecting its modest alcohol. Its best years are still in front of it. Screwcap. 13.5% alc. **Rating** 95 **To** 2035 $45

Mount Terrible   ★★★★★

289 Licola Road, Jamieson, Vic 3723 **Region** Central Victoria
T (03) 5777 0703 **www**.mountterriblewines.com.au **Open** By appt
Winemaker John Eason **Est.** 2001 **Dozens** 350 **Vyds** 2ha

John Eason and wife Janene Ridley began the long, slow (and at times very painful) business of establishing their vineyard just north of Mt Terrible in 1992 – hence the choice of name. In 2001 they planted 2ha of pinot noir (MV6, 115, 114 and 777 clones) on a gently sloping, north-facing river terrace adjacent to the Jamieson River. DIY trials persuaded John to have the first commercial vintage in '06 contract-made, but he has since made the wines himself in a fireproof winery built on top of an underground wine cellar. John has a sense of humour second to none, but must wonder what he has done to provoke the weather gods, alternating in their provision of fire, storm and tempest. Subsequent vintages have provided some well earned relief. Exports to the UK.

ΨΨΨΨΨ **Jamieson Pinot Noir 2014** A bolshy pinot noir with a ton of personality, this alpine expression is hewn from low yields, maceration pre and post-ferment with a seasoning of stems and 18 months in French oak. Rich and moreish, with damson plum, mulch and cedar combining into a textural whole. The intensity of flavour is compelling, as are the layers, all auguring well for a bright future. Needs time. Screwcap. 13.5% alc. **Rating** 95 **To** 2025 $42 NG

Mount Trio Vineyard

2534 Porongurup Road, Mount Barker, WA 6324 **Region** Porongurup
T (08) 9853 1136 **www**.mounttriowines.com.au **Open** By appt
Winemaker Gavin Berry, Andrew Vesey **Est.** 1989 **Dozens** 4000 **Vyds** 8.8ha
Mount Trio was established by Gavin Berry and wife Gill Graham (plus partners) shortly after they moved to the Mount Barker area in late 1988, Gavin to take up the position of chief winemaker at Plantagenet, which he held until 2004, when he and partners acquired the now very successful and much larger West Cape Howe. They have slowly built up the business, increasing estate plantings with riesling (2.7ha), shiraz (2.4ha), sauvignon blanc (2ha) and pinot noir (1.7ha). Exports to the UK, Denmark and China.

ΨΨΨΨΨ **Home Block Porongurup Pinot Noir 2015** Porongurup has established its pre-eminent position for producing pinot noir in WA, Mount Trio doing its bit with the '14 and now this high quality follow-on. The varietal quality is faultless, the red and black cherry fruit allied with a mouthwatering, long finish. The only issue here is the mere 99 dozen. Screwcap. 13.2% alc. **Rating** 96 **To** 2025 $35 ❂
Geographe Sangiovese Rose 2016 The spicy, savoury backbone and ribcage establishes its imprint on the bouquet and palate in quick time. The palate does put some red berry flesh on the bones, giving length and balance. A lot of rose for your dollar. Screwcap. 13.5% alc. **Rating** 94 **To** 2020 $17 ❂
Porongurup Shiraz 2015 A tapestry of blackberry and black cherry, spice, savoury tannins and cedary oak is an each way special – cellar or enjoy it now. At this price you can surely have your wine and drink it too. Screwcap. 14% alc. **Rating** 94 **To** 2025 $22 ❂

ΨΨΨΨΨ **Porongurup Riesling 2016** **Rating** 92 **To** 2021 $22 ❂
Porongurup Pinot Noir 2015 **Rating** 92 **To** 2021 $22 ❂
Great Southern Chardonnay 2015 **Rating** 91 **To** 2022 $17 ❂

Mount View Estate

Mount View Road, Mount View, NSW 2325 **Region** Hunter Valley
T (02) 4990 3307 **www**.mtviewestate.com.au **Open** Mon–Sat 10–5, Sun 10–4
Winemaker Scott Stephens **Est.** 1971 **Dozens** 4000 **Vyds** 16ha
Mount View Estate's vineyard was planted by the very knowledgeable Harry Tulloch 45 years ago; he recognised the quality of the red basalt volcanic soils of the very attractive hillside vineyard. Prior owners John and Polly Burgess purchased the adjoining Limestone Creek Vineyard in 2004 (planted in 1982), which fits seamlessly into Mount View Estate's production. The quality of the wines is outstanding. The business changed hands in '16, now owned by a Chinese national, but no further details are available. Exports to China.

ΨΨΨΨΨ **Reserve Hunter Valley Chardonnay 2016** A fair amount of colour, but the nose and palate are fresh and on the lean side, with perky lemony acidity, some stone fruit and sweet-sour drops. Hardly a skerrick of oak character though it's aged in French oak hogsheads (40% new) for 9 months. Just a little out of kilter; time might help. Screwcap. 13% alc. **Rating** 93 **To** 2023 $40 JF

Flagship Liqueur Shiraz NV Wonderful vibrant purple-garnet colour for this solera with vintages dating back to 1983. Very fresh and robust, with fruitcake spices, dark fruits, grainy tannins and the spirit balanced. Screwcap. 19% alc. **Rating** 92 $55 JF

Reserve Hunter Valley Semillon 2016 Pale straw and bright, with wafts of lemon-lime blossom and lemongrass, and a citrus bent that defines the variety. The difference is the softish acidity. Approachable now. Screwcap. 11% alc. **Rating** 91 **To** 2023 $40 JF

Reserve Hilltops Shiraz Viognier 2015 Hilltops fruit to the rescue after a difficult vintage in the Hunter. Excellent dark crimson, not surprising given the 2% splash of viognier; a rich, savoury style laden with black fruit, licorice and tar. Screwcap. 14.5% alc. **Rating** 90 **To** 2025 $40 JF

Reserve Hunter Valley Merlot 2015 Bright ruby with equally bright red fruits, some Ribena and blackcurrant sweetness on the medium-bodied palate. Tannins have weight and grip, and it's a convincing example for the Hunter Valley. Screwcap. 13.5% alc. **Rating** 90 **To** 2023 $40 JF

ŶŶŶŶ V Hunter Valley Verdelho 2016 **Rating** 89 **To** 2019 $25 JF
Reserve Hunter Valley Pinot Noir 2015 **Rating** 89 **To** 2022 $40 JF
Flagship Liqueur Verdelho NV **Rating** 89 $55 JF

Mountadam ★★★★★

High Eden Road, Eden Valley, SA 5235 **Region** Eden Valley
T (08) 8564 1900 **www**.mountadam.com.au **Open** By appt
Winemaker Helen McCarthy **Est.** 1972 **Dozens** 15 000 **Vyds** 80ha
Founded by the late David Wynn for the benefit of winemaker son Adam, Mountadam was (somewhat surprisingly) purchased by Cape Mentelle (doubtless under the direction of Möet Hennessy Wine Estates) in 2000. Rather less surprising was its sale in '05 to Adelaide businessman David Brown, who has extensive interests in the Padthaway region. This acquisition was of the vineyard on the western side of the High Eden Road. In '07 David purchased a parcel of land on the opposite (eastern) side of the road, which was unplanted, and in '15 he acquired the large vineyard on the eastern side of the road from TWE, thus reassembling all of the land originally purchased by David Wynn in the late 1960s. The Brown family has decided that the original vineyard will be known as 'Mountadam West', and the newly acquired vineyard as 'Mountadam East'. Exports to the UK, France, Switzerland, Poland and Hong Kong.

ŶŶŶŶŶ **Eden Valley Riesling 2016** From low-yielding vines planted in '68. The wine has naked power that builds relentlessly across the length of the palate and searching aftertaste. The lemon and Meyer lemon flavours have a hint of lime juice, but are definitely Eden Valley. Screwcap. 13% alc. **Rating** 95 **To** 2036 $27

Eden Valley Gewurztraminer 2016 A delicious wine, although without the exuberant aromas and flavours of Alsace. It has spice, lychee and rose petal notes to a larger or lesser degree, but it's the intensity, length, grip and balance that really appeal. Screwcap. 13.5% alc. **Rating** 95 **To** 2026 $27 ✪

Eden Valley Shiraz 2015 This is a very good Eden Valley shiraz. The colour is bright, the bouquet with scents of spice and pepper as well as fruit; the texture of the medium-bodied palate, and its length and balance, are all very good. The black cherry fruit is delicious. Screwcap. 14.5% alc. **Rating** 95 **To** 2030 $27

Eden Valley Cabernet Sauvignon 2015 Another example of Helen McCarthy's skills as winemaker, sculpting a cabernet with razor-sharp varietal definition, providing textural complexity going beyond the tannins that are part and parcel of the variety. It all adds up to a cabernet that is already enjoyable, but also has a long future. Screwcap. 14.6% alc. **Rating** 95 **To** 2035 $27

Eden Valley Pinot Gris 2016 The climate endows the wine with drive and intensity, giving it stature, and forcing me to sew my lips together so I won't dismiss all pinot gris out of hand. And it is driven by pear, apple and citrus, not residual sugar. Screwcap. 13% alc. **Rating** 94 **To** 2020 $27

ŢŢŢŢŢ Pinot Chardonnay NV **Rating** 92 To 2018 $27 TS
        Marble Hill High Eden Chardonnay 2015 **Rating** 91 To 2022 $100 PR

Mr Barval Fine Wines   ★★★★☆

7087 Caves Road, Margaret River, WA 6285 **Region** Margaret River
T 0481 453 038 **www**.mrbarval.com **Open** By appt
Winemaker Robert Gherardi **Est.** 2015 **Dozens** 900
Robert Gherardi was born with wine in his blood, as a small boy going to Margaret River
to pick grapes with three generations of his extended Italian family. The grapes were taken to
his grandmother's suburban backyard to begin the fermentation, followed by a big lunch or
dinner to celebrate the arrival of the new vintage-to-be. Nonetheless, his first degree was in
marine science and biotechnology; while completing the course he worked in an independent
wine store in Perth. Having tasted his way around the world in the bottle, and aged 25, he
enrolled in the full oenology and viticulture degree. This led to employment at Moss Wood
for four years, then Brown Hill Estate as assistant winemaker, and finally to Cullen for three
years. Vanya Cullen encouraged him to travel to Barolo and work with Elio Altare for three
harvests over a five-year period. This included moving to Barolo with his wife and children to
experience the full four seasons of viticulture and winemaking. He returns to Italy each year
for his boutique travel business, with customised tours of Barolo, Valtellina and further north.
And so he arrived at the name for his winery: Margaret River, Barolo and Valtellina.

ŢŢŢŢŢ **Margaret River Cabernet Merlot 2015** The calling card of the range is
        texture: sensitive oak is an adjunct and little more. Joyous, vivid, detailed grape
        tannins draw the saliva and make one, time and time again, return to the glass. The
        acid is a natural free-flow across pastille, dark cherry, cassis and sage notes, all drawn
        across cabernet's stiff upper lip of astringency. Screwcap. 13.7% alc. **Rating** 96
        To 2033 $38 NG ✪
        Margaret River Chardonnay 2016 Ripe quince, peach, marzipan and curd
        spread their way from nose to a round palate edged by oak. The wine stains the
        cheeks, yet is not heavy. It finishes relatively long by sheer weight of extract and
        intensity of flavour. Screwcap. 12.8% alc. **Rating** 94 To 2025 $38 NG
        Mistral 2016 This is a Rhône-inspired blend of 67% viognier and 33% marsanne.
        Extensive lees handling strikes a taut mineral bow across the mid-palate, finding an
        energetic confluence with the vanilla bean oak. This serves to harness the varietal
        slipperiness into a streamlined, mineral-clad tour de force of apricot, marzipan and
        rooibos tea notes, all cushioned by the wine's inherent viscosity. This is a thrilling
        wine. Screwcap. 13.3% alc. **Rating** 94 To 2023 $27 NG ✪

ŢŢŢŢŢ Rosso 2015 **Rating** 93 To 2023 $29 NG
        Nebbia 2016 **Rating** 91 To 2021 $29 NG

Mr Mick   ★★★★

7 Dominic Street, Clare, SA 5453 **Region** Clare Valley
T (08) 8842 2555 **www**.mrmick.com.au **Open** 7 days 10–5
Winemaker Tim Adams, Brett Schutz **Est.** 2011 **Dozens** 30 000
This is the venture of Tim Adams and wife Pam Goldsack, the name chosen to honour KH
(Mick) Knappstein, a legend in the Clare Valley and the broader Australian wine community.
Tim worked at Leasingham Wines with Mick between 1975 and '86, and knew him well.
When Tim and Pam acquired the Leasingham winery in January 2011, together with its
historic buildings, it brought the wheel full circle. Various commentators (including myself)
have used Mick's great one-liner, 'There are only two types of people in the world: those who
were born in Clare, and those who wish they had been.' Exports to China and NZ.

ŢŢŢŢŢ **Clare Valley Tempranillo 2014** You certainly get your money's worth with
        this wine, the mix of cherry, raspberry and strawberry fruit cosseted by a well
        judged touch of French oak. Good now, but it'll hang around for another 5 years.
        Screwcap. 13.5% alc. **Rating** 91 To 2022 $17 ✪

Clare Valley Riesling 2016 Pale straw-green; there's a lot of easily accessible juicy riesling flavours presented in a wine with very good line, length and balance. Good now, or for short to medium-term cellaring – and the price is right. Screwcap. 11% alc. **Rating** 90 **To** 2022 $17 **✪**

ŸŸŸŸ   **Limestone Coast Pinot Grigio 2016 Rating** 89 **To** 2018 $17 **✪**
        Clare Valley Vermentino 2016 Rating 89 **To** 2020 $17 **✪**

Mr Riggs Wine Company   ★★★★★

55a Main Road, McLaren Flat, SA 5171 **Region** McLaren Vale
T (08) 8383 2055 **www.mrriggs.com.au Open** Sat–Thurs 10–5, Fri 10–late
Winemaker Ben Riggs **Est.** 2001 **Dozens** 20 000 **Vyds** 7.5ha
With over a quarter of a century of winemaking experience, Ben Riggs is well established under his own banner. Ben sources the best fruit from individual vineyards in McLaren Vale, Clare Valley, Adelaide Hills, Langhorne Creek, Coonawarra, and from his own Piebald Gully Vineyard (shiraz and viognier). Each wine expresses the essence of not only the vineyard, but also the region's terroir. The vision of the Mr Riggs brand is unpretentious and personal: 'to make the wines I love to drink'. He drinks very well. Exports to the US, Canada, Denmark, Sweden, Germany, The Netherlands, Switzerland, China, Hong Kong, Singapore, Japan and NZ.

ŸŸŸŸŸ   **McLaren Vale Shiraz 2014** A full-bodied shiraz with more of everything, and doing it well. The flavours are savoury, but not the least green or sour, the powerful tannins likewise ripe. Not for everyone, but the rest are simply glad they can find it and buy it. Diam. 14.5% alc. **Rating** 95 **To** 2039 $50
        Generation Series Sticky End McLaren Vale Viognier 2016 The grapes were dried in small perforated crates for 3 weeks in the Italian Passito style, then fermented and matured for 6 months in French barriques. Bright gold; it's a labour of love, with an array of orange marmalade and apricot jam flavours cut by crisp acidity. Screwcap. 13% alc. **Rating** 95 **To** 2020 $25 **✪**
        Watervale Riesling 2016 Classic Clare Valley Watervale style, with abundant varietal fruit covering all the various citrus bases and sustained by positive minerally/slatey acidity. Good now, greater still in 5+ years. Screwcap. 12.5% alc. **Rating** 94 **To** 2026 $24 **✪**
        Generation Series The Elder McLaren Vale Fortified Shiraz 2014 From the estate vineyard in Clarendon, crushed into an open fermenter and fortified on skins: an expensive way of halting fermentation, but it leads to greater colour and tannin extract. This is, of course, what we used to call vintage port, and is a very good example. You can drink it now, but I would leave it for at least 20 years. Screwcap. 18% alc. **Rating** 94 **To** 2034 $30 **✪**

ŸŸŸŸ♀   **Piebald Adelaide Syrah 2014 Rating** 93 **To** 2028 $27 CM **✪**
        Scarce Earth McLaren Vale Shiraz 2014 Rating 93 **To** 2029 $50
        The Magnet McLaren Vale Grenache 2015 Rating 93 **To** 2025 $30
        Outpost Coonawarra Cabernet 2015 Rating 93 **To** 2030 $25 **✪**
        Montepulciano d'Adelaide 2015 Rating 93 **To** 2025 $30
        Yacca Paddock Adelaide Hills Tempranillo 2015 Rating 92 **To** 2025 $30
        Ein Riese Adelaide Hills Riesling 2016 Rating 92 **To** 2023 $24 **✪**

Munari Wines   ★★★★☆

Ladys Creek Vineyard, 1129 Northern Highway, Heathcote, Vic 3523 **Region** Heathcote
T (03) 5433 3366 **www.munariwines.com Open** Tues–Sun 11–5
Winemaker Adrian Munari **Est.** 1993 **Dozens** 3000 **Vyds** 6.9ha
Established on one of the original Heathcote farming properties, Ladys Creek Vineyard is situated on the narrow Cambrian soil strip 11km north of the town. Adrian Munari has harnessed traditional winemaking practices to New World innovation to produce complex, fruit-driven wines that marry concentration and elegance. They are produced from estate

plantings of shiraz, cabernet sauvignon, merlot, cabernet franc and malbec. Exports to France, Denmark, Taiwan and China.

ŢŢŢŢŢ **Baby Black Barossa Heathcote Shiraz 2014** It is fair to assume that this is a 50/50% blend of a best barrel selection between Richard Sheedy of Glen Eldon and Adrian Munari. It has been matured in a mix of American and French oak for 2 years, yet the black cherry and blackberry fruit comes out on top, with ripe tannins going about their business. Screwcap. 14% alc. **Rating** 95 **To** 2034 $60 TS

🍂 Municipal Wines ★★★★

320 Moreland Road, Brunswick, Vic 3055 (postal) **Region** Strathbogie Ranges
T 0401 354 611 **www**.municipalwines.com.au **Open** Not
Winemaker Matt Froude **Est.** 2014 **Dozens** 600 **Vyds** 1.8ha
Owner and winemaker Matt Froude had the unlikely 10-year background of environmental engineer, tour guide and manager of English schools in Asia before returning to Australia in 2009 to study winemaking. Since 2010 he has managed to cram in winemaking at Yarra Yering (two vintages) and De Bortoli in the Yarra Valley, Argyle in Oregon, Craggy Range in Hawke's Bay, Pierre Gaillard in the northern Rhône Valley, Rioja in Spain and Yamanashi in Japan, finishing with Wine x Sam, where he is currently winemaker. He explains the rationale of Municipal Wines: cool climate winemaking of low-alcohol, food-friendly wines. He leases a pocket handkerchief 1.8ha vineyard of five varieties, and purchases another three. His viticulture is unique: he doesn't spray the vineyard at all (not even sulphur or copper) and only prunes the vines every second year. By contrast, the winemaking is conventional and sophisticated, the only quasi-exception that three of his wines are neither fined nor filtered. Given that all are grown and made in the Strathbogie Ranges, the name requires explanation: he plans to open a winery and cellar door in the northern suburbs of Melbourne.

ŢŢŢŢŢ **Whitegate Vineyard Double Gate Block Shiraz 2015** Good depth to the crimson-purple hue; it is true that the texture, structure and flavour are complex even though mlf was conducted in tank and there is no oak use. Radically different (riper and richer) than Home Vineyard. Diam. 14.4% alc. **Rating** 92 **To** 2027 $29

Home Vineyard Shiraz 2015 Three parcels, picked 2 Mar, 14 Mar and 12 Apr, fermented and matured separately, the first with 15% whole bunches, the second destemmed and including 4% viognier, the third 100% whole bunches. The elaborate picking diary is justified, first up by the elegant cool-grown varietal fruit expression. It's only just on the cusp of ripeness – the first pick must have been very low baume. Diam. 12.7% alc. **Rating** 91 **To** 2022 $45

Whitegate Vineyard Old Block Riesling 2016 A period of skin contact has given the wine a green tinge to its colour, the long, cool ferment offsetting any extract from the skin contact. Very high acidity (8.9g/l) and low pH (2.99) drive the palate and finish. If there is any residual sugar, it's not easy to see. Patience should be rewarded. Screwcap. 12.3% alc. **Rating** 90 **To** 2026 $29

Reserve Whitegate Vineyard Stretcher Block Tempranillo 2014 Matured for 24 months in French, American and Hungarian (50% new) oak. The high yield of 15.5t/ha comes through in the light colour, although the hue is good; the ripeness issue comes from the yield: it's on the cusp, and seems to follow Municipal Wines wherever it goes. Diam. 13.1% alc. **Rating** 90 **To** 2020 $45

ŢŢŢŢ **Home Vineyard Cabernets 2015 Rating** 89 **To** 2021 $45

Murdoch Hill

260 Mappinga Road, Woodside, SA 5244 **Region** Adelaide Hills
T (08) 8389 7081 **www**.murdochhill.com.au **Open** By appt
Winemaker Michael Downer **Est.** 1998 **Dozens** 4000 **Vyds** 20.48ha
A little over 20ha of vines have been established on the undulating, gum-studded countryside of Charlie and Julie Downer's 60-year-old Erika property, 4km east of Oakbank. In descending order of importance, the varieties planted are sauvignon blanc, shiraz, cabernet sauvignon and

chardonnay. Son Michael, with a Bachelor of Oenology degree from Adelaide University, is winemaker. Exports to the UK and China.

ㅜㅜㅜㅜㅜ **The Landau Single Vineyard Oakbank Adelaide Hills Syrah 2016** 32% whole bunches, wild-yeast fermented as are all the Murdoch Hills red wines, matured in French oak (5% new). This takes the Cronberry Block one large step further, not by increasing the flavour package, but by refining it. Here savoury, brambly tannins are present from the first sip, but are surrounded by multiple fruits on the medium-bodied palate. Diam. 13.5% alc. **Rating** 96 **To** 2041 $50 ✪
The Tilbury Adelaide Hills Chardonnay 2016 Dijon clones 76, 95, I10V1 and G9V7, wild-yeast fermented in French oak (20% new). Has high class, high tension, fruit expression; grapefruit, Granny Smith apple and white peach all play a role in a wine with an ocean of attitude. Screwcap. 13% alc. **Rating** 95 **To** 2026 $50
The Phaeton Piccadilly Valley Adelaide Hills Pinot Noir 2016 Clones 114, 115 and MV6, wild-yeast fermented, 40% whole bunches, matured in French oak (13% new). The colour is super-bright and clear, getting them off to a flying start. A spicy, slightly savoury bouquet introduces a focused, linear wine that has great integrity and a lengthy, brambly finish. Diam. 13.5% alc. **Rating** 95 **To** 2027 $50
Cronberry Block Oakbank Adelaide Hills Syrah 2016 30% whole bunches, matured in French oak (15% new). A very intense and powerful syrah with black fruits liberally doused with black pepper, spice and licorice. Despite this full-bodied assault on the senses, the wine retains shape, and has excellent balance. Top class cool climate style. Screwcap. 13.5% alc. **Rating** 95 **To** 2036 $30 ✪
Halfway Block Adelaide Hills Sauvignon Blanc 2016 Fermentation in three batches – one on skins, one in used French oak and one in stainless steel – achieves the desired texture and structure, phenolic notes part and parcel of the vinification. That said, the fruit base of the standard version is still apparent. Screwcap. 12.5% alc. **Rating** 94 **To** 2020 $30 ✪
Adelaide Hills Chardonnay 2016 Indecipherable background notes on a sticker on the bottle didn't help me, but the quality of the wine is more than able to send its own message of barrel ferment with a modest amount of new oak allowing fresh, tangy citrus/stone fruit flavours to have their head. Screwcap. 13% alc. **Rating** 94 **To** 2023 $30 ✪

ㅜㅜㅜㅜㅜ **Adelaide Hills Sauvignon Blanc 2016** Rating 93 **To** 2018 $22 ✪
The Surrey Adelaide Hills Pinot Meunier 2016 Rating 93 **To** 2024 $40
Ridley Adelaide Hills Pinot X Two 2016 Rating 92 **To** 2026 $34
Sulky Blanc 2016 Rating 90 **To** 2020 $34
Adelaide Hills Pinot Noir 2016 Rating 90 **To** 2021 $30

Murray Street Vineyards   ★★★★★

Murray Street, Greenock, SA 5360 **Region** Barossa Valley
T (08) 8562 8373 **www**.murraystreet.com.au **Open** 7 days 10–6
Winemaker Craig Viney **Est.** 2001 **Dozens** 20 000 **Vyds** 50ha
Andrew Seppelt and business partner Bill Jahnke (the latter a successful investment banker) established Murray Street Vineyards in 2001. It very quickly established itself as a producer of exceptionally good wines. In '14, with the knowledge and consent of Bill, Andrew began to establish a separate business, and in '15 Bill assumed total ownership, appointing Craig Viney (who had worked alongside Andrew for the previous eight years) as winemaker. Bill intends to upscale the production capability and distribution network. In future, the two brands of Murray Street and MSV will carry the flag. Exports to Denmark, Laos, Macau, Singapore and NZ.

ㅜㅜㅜㅜㅜ **Reserve Barossa Valley Shiraz Viognier 2014** Good colour; the expressive and fragrant bouquet leads into a medium to full-bodied palate rich in dark berry fruits, the texture softened to an extent by the viognier, ripe but gentle tannins and integrated oak all contributing to an exceptionally balanced and inviting palate. Diam. 14.5% alc. **Rating** 97 **To** 2039 $80 ✪

Reserve Barossa Valley Shiraz Mataro 2014 A medium-bodied blend with a juicy edge to the display of purple and black fruits that enliven the palate, but in no way threaten the balance, simply adding to its freshness and textural qualities. Diam. 13.5% alc. **Rating** 97 **To** 2034 $80 ○

Reserve Barossa Valley Shiraz Cabernet 2014 Stands apart from its two '14 Reserve siblings with a firmer palate introducing blackcurrant into the other black fruits. It seems lower in alcohol than 14.5% (no bad thing, of course). This blend also has the medium-bodied freshness of the Shiraz Mataro. Diam. **Rating** 97 **To** 2034 $80 ○

ŸŸŸŸŸ **The Barossa 2014** 47% grenache, 30% shiraz, 23% mataro. Strongly grenache-influenced, as you might expect, but the other varieties play their part admirably. Both sweet-fruited and savoury on the bouquet, with ripe red berry fruit, perfume and spice. The flavours wend their way from warm earthiness to dark vinosity with perfectly applied astringency. Screwcap. 13.6% alc. **Rating** 95 **To** 2024 $35 SC ○

ŸŸŸŸŸ **White Label Barossa Semillon 2016** Rating 93 To 2023 $23 SC ○
Black Label Barossa Mataro 2015 Rating 93 To 2026 $25 SC ○
Gomersal Barossa Valley Shiraz 2014 Rating 91 To 2030 $60 PR

Murrindindi Vineyards ★★★★☆

1018 Murrindindi Road, Murrindindi, Vic 3717 **Region** Upper Goulburn
T 0438 305 314 **www.**murrindindivineyards.com **Open** Not
Winemaker Hugh Cuthbertson **Est.** 1979 **Dozens** 30 000 **Vyds** 70ha
This small winery is owned and run by Hugh Cuthbertson, established by parents Alan and Jan (now retired) as a minor diversification from their cattle property. Hugh, himself with a long and high-profile wine career, has overseen the marketing of the wines, including the Family Reserve and Don't Tell Dad brands. Exports to the UK and China.

ŸŸŸŸŸ **Yarradindi Family Reserve Cabernet Sauvignon 2015** A well made, full-bodied cabernet, its Chinese back label interesting. Cassis/blackcurrant fruit is the core of the wine on the bouquet and palate, the firm cabernet tannins correct and, I suspect, exactly what sophisticated Chinese consumers would look for. Quality French oak is another plus. Screwcap. 14% alc. **Rating** 95 **To** 2030 $38

Family Reserve Yea Valley Shiraz 2015 From a small 2ha block on the home vineyard, matured in French oak (33% new) for 18 months. A full-bodied shiraz with a power of fruit backed by ripe tannins and cedary French oak. The fruit flavours range through black cherry, blackberry and licorice, and the tannins are evident, providing a savoury offset to the luscious fruit. Its best years are in front of it. Screwcap. 14% alc. **Rating** 94 **To** 2035 $38

ŸŸŸŸŸ **Mr Hugh Chardonnay 2016** Rating 91 To 2021 $48
Mr Hugh Pinot Noir 2016 Rating 91 To 2026 $48
Mr Hugh Pinot Noir 2015 Rating 90 To 2023 $55 JF

🍂 Murrora Wines NR

124 Gooromon Ponds Road, Wallaroo, NSW 2618 **Region** Canberra District
T 0414 230 677 **www.**wine.murrora.com.au **Open** Not
Winemaker Joshua Murray **Est.** 2013 **Dozens** 500 **Vyds** 1ha
Murrora is a small vineyard and winery in Wallaroo started by Joshua and Joanna Murray in 2013. The derivation of the business name needs no explanation. The vines were planted in the late 1990s by previous owners, the property purchased by the Murrays in 2009. Rehabilitation work in the vineyard to increase manageability and yield/quality began with the sale of the grapes to other wineries in the Canberra District. A change of plan in '13 saw Joshua taking on the role of winemaker and the cessation of grape sales.

Murrumbateman Winery

Cnr Barton Highway/McIntosh Circuit, Murrumbateman, NSW 2582
Region Canberra District
T (02) 6227 5584 **www**.murrumbatemanwinery.com.au **Open** Fri–Sun 10–5
Winemaker Bobbie Makin **Est.** 1972 **Dozens** 1000 **Vyds** 4ha
Draws upon 4ha of estate-grown sauvignon blanc and shiraz. It also incorporates an à la carte restaurant and function room, together with picnic and barbecue areas.

Sangiovese 2016 A pure red cherry bouquet leads into an equally pure, and totally delicious, palate, again with red cherry first and foremost. Drink it tonight, not tomorrow. Screwcap. 14% alc. **Rating** 93 **To** 2020 $25 ✪
Malbec 2015 Good colour, both hue and depth; an appealing example of a variety that can be pernickety. There is an unusual waft of freshly brewed coffee over the plum and black cherry fruit of the bouquet and medium-bodied palate. Screwcap. 13% alc. **Rating** 92 **To** 2029 $30
Riesling 2016 The label describes the wine as crisp and dry, but there is plenty of sweet lime juice fruit, making this an early-drinking proposition – and an enjoyable one. Whether there is some residual sugar is irrelevant. Screwcap. 11.5% alc. **Rating** 90 **To** 2023 $30

Mollie's Block Sauvignon Blanc 2016 Rating 89 **To** 2017 $25

Muster Wine Co

c/- 60 Sheffield Street, Malvern, SA 5061 **Region** Barossa Valley
T 0430 360 350 **www**.musterwineco.com.au **Open** By appt
Winemaker David Muster **Est.** 2007 **Dozens** 2500
Gottfried Muster arrived from Europe with his young family in 1859, settling in the Barossa Valley. Thus direct descendent David Muster was born and bred in the wine purple. This is a virtual winery business; David Muster has been buying and selling wine since 2007. He forages for small batches of wines in the Barossa and Clare valleys, and clearly has developed some very useful contacts, allowing the release of relatively small amounts under each label, sometimes offering very good value. Exports to the US.

Polish Hill River Riesling 2016 Nothing quite like a sprightly zesty and fresh young Clare Valley riesling to enliven the taste buds. Requisite white blossom and wet pebble aromas, the palate with lemon-lime juice, sweet-sour drops, crunchy acidity and a lot of verve. Screwcap. 11.5% alc. **Rating** 93 **To** 2027 $22 JF ✪
Greenock Barossa Valley Shiraz 2015 Give this time, because at first it's closed, somewhat oaky and contrived. Then it unfurls, exposing a core of densely packed dark sweet fruits and blackstrap licorice and ripe fleshy tannins on its structured palate. Screwcap. 13.7% alc. **Rating** 92 **To** 2028 $30 JF
Le Vaillant Rose 2016 Starts promisingly with its pale salmon-pink hue, then offers up a light mix of spice, red fruit and lemony acidity before it ends as it should – crisp, dry and fresh. Screwcap. 12% alc. **Rating** 91 **To** 2018 $24 JF

MyattsField Vineyards

Union Road, Carmel Valley, WA 6076 **Region** Perth Hills
T (08) 9293 5567 **www**.myattsfield.com.au **Open** Fri–Sun and public hols 11–5
Winemaker Josh and Rachael Davenport, Josh Uren **Est.** 2006 **Dozens** NA
MyattsField Vineyards is owned by Josh and Rachael Davenport, both with extensive winemaking experience. Both have oenology degrees, and both have domestic and Flying Winemaker experience, especially Rachael. In '06 they decided they would prefer to work for themselves. They left their employment, building a winery in time for the '07 vintage. Their vineyards include cabernet sauvignon, merlot, petit verdot, shiraz and chardonnay, and they also take small parcels of grapes from regions as far away as Manjimup.

ŸŸŸŸŸ **Kenneth Green Vintage Fortified 2014** A blend of touriga nacional, shiraz and durif, this is an exceptional fortified wine. Despite its heady, intoxicative powers, all the more alluring due to aromas of dried herb, tobacco and saturated dark fruits, this compact wine speaks of savour, rather than excessive sweetness. Cork. 18.2% alc. **Rating** 95 $35 NG **◐**

ŸŸŸŸ♀ **Cabernet Sauvignon Merlot Franc 2015 Rating** 92 **To** 2023 $26 NG
Joseph Myatt Reserve 2014 Rating 90 **To** 2024 $45 NG

Myrtaceae ★★★★

53 Main Creek Road, Main Ridge, Vic 3928 **Region** Mornington Peninsula
T (03) 5989 2045 **www.**myrtaceae.com.au **Open** W'ends & public hols 12–5
Winemaker Julie Trueman **Est.** 1985 **Dozens** 300 **Vyds** 1ha
John Trueman (viticulturist) and wife Julie (winemaker) purchased their Mornington Peninsula hinterland property near Arthurs Seat in 1984. Chardonnay (0.6ha) was planted in '98, and the initial plantings of cabernet were replaced with pinot noir (0.4ha) in '99. Just one Chardonnay and one Pinot Noir are made each year from the estate grapes, a Rose made from pinot is a more recent addition. Meticulous viticulture using Scott Henry trellising is used to maximise sunlight and airflow at this cool, elevated site. Extensive gardens surround the winery.

ŸŸŸŸ♀ **Selwyns Fault Mornington Peninsula Rose 2016** Made from pinot noir. Very pale pink; its strength is the way it imparts its message on the palate, delicate yet mouthfilling, gently coating the mouth with strawberry fruit before finishing dry. Screwcap. 13.5% alc. **Rating** 93 **To** 2017 $25 **◐**
Mornington Peninsula Pinot Noir 2014 Good colour; has the power and concentration of the '14 vintage, but handles it better than many from the Peninsula. Red and black cherry, plus some plummy notes, drive the palate, and the balance and length are good, giving every confidence that this will mature very well indeed. Screwcap. 13.5% alc. **Rating** 92 **To** 2029 $40

Naked Run Wines ★★★★☆

36 Parawae Road, Salisbury Plain, SA 5109 (postal) **Region** Clare Valley/Barossa Valley
T 0408 807 655 **www.**nakedrunwines.com.au **Open** Not
Winemaker Steven Baraglia **Est.** 2005 **Dozens** 1200
Naked Run is the virtual winery of Jayme Wood, Bradley Currie and Steven Baraglia, their skills ranging from viticulture through to production, and also to the all-important sales and marketing (and not to be confused with Naked Wines). The riesling is sourced from Clare Valley, grenache from the Williamstown area of the Barossa Valley, and shiraz from Greenock.

ŸŸŸŸŸ **The First Clare Valley Riesling 2016** A multi-gold medal winner following in the footsteps of the '15. Fine and precise from start to finish. Perfumed talc, lemon pith and lime leaf aromas of great purity, reprised on the palate, which rides on a slatey, minerally, acid backbone. Gorgeous drinking now, and structured to live long and well. Screwcap. 12% alc. **Rating** 95 **To** 2035 SC
Place in Time Sevenhill Clare Valley Riesling 2011 Fascinating to see a riesling with bottle age from this famously challenging cool vintage. Aromas show the classic qualities of development: honey, toast, freshly cut hay – and then some lime juice liveliness as a bonus. The flavours have life and energy, and although not possessed of great depth, it's simply a pleasure to drink. Screwcap. 12% alc. **Rating** 94 **To** 2021 SC

Nannup Ridge Estate ★★★★☆

PO Box 2, Nannup, WA 6275 **Region** Blackwood Valley
T (08) 9286 2202 **www.**nannupridge.com.au **Open** Not
Winemaker Bruce Dukes **Est.** 1998 **Dozens** 4000 **Vyds** 30ha

The business is owned by the Blizard and Fitzgerald families, who purchased the then unplanted property from the family that had farmed it since the early 1900s. Mark and Alison Blizard had in fact moved to the region in the early '90s and established a small vineyard on the banks of the beautiful Donnelly River. The partners established 12ha of mainstream varieties (and 1ha of tempranillo) backed by a (then) grape sale agreement with Constellation. They still regard themselves as grapegrowers, but have successful wines skilfully contract-made from the (now-expanded) estate production. Terrific value is par for the course. Exports to China.

ŸŸŸŸŸ **Rolling Hills Chardonnay 2015** Gleaming straw-green; has more depth and complexity than most encountered in the Blackwood Valley, perhaps due to sophisticated winemaking. The wine fills the mouth with richly textured stone fruit and fig flavours, French oak obvious yet balanced. Screwcap. 13.2% alc. **Rating** 95 **To** 2025 $28 ✪

Reserve Chardonnay 2015 This is a streamlined beauty, brimming with white peach and nectarine flavours clinging to smart oak supports and a core of creamy oatmeal. There are matchstick to mineral notes, too, but the purity of fruit and intensity of flavour gives one an overall impression of generosity. Screwcap. 13.1% alc. **Rating** 94 **To** 2025 $40 NG

ŸŸŸŸŸ **Firetower Sauvignon Blanc 2016 Rating** 93 **To** 2019 $21 NG ✪
Rolling Hills Merlot 2015 Rating 93 **To** 2025 $30 NG
Rolling Hills Shiraz 2015 Rating 91 **To** 2025 $30 NG

Narkoojee   ★★★★★
170 Francis Road, Glengarry, Vic 3854 **Region** Gippsland
T (03) 5192 4257 **www.**narkoojee.com **Open** 7 days 10.30–4.30
Winemaker Axel Friend **Est.** 1981 **Dozens** 5000 **Vyds** 10.3ha
Narkoojee (originally a dairy farm owned by the Friend family) is near the old gold-mining town of Walhalla and looks out over the Strzelecki Ranges. The wines are produced from a little over 10ha of estate vineyards, with chardonnay accounting for half the total. Former lecturer in civil engineering and extremely successful amateur winemaker Harry Friend changed horses in 1994 to take joint control, with son Axel, of the family vineyard and winery, and hasn't missed a beat since; their skills show through with all the wines, none more so than the Chardonnay. Exports to Canada, Japan and China.

ŸŸŸŸŸ **Reserve Gippsland Chardonnay 2014** It was an exceptional vintage for chardonnay, and this wine fully reflects the vintage. It is as intense as one could imagine, but doesn't go OTT, its balance and length perfect; grapefruit, white peach, creamy cashew and lingering acidity all join seamlessly. Screwcap. 13.5% alc. **Rating** 97 $48 ✪

ŸŸŸŸŸ **Lily Grace Gippsland Chardonnay 2015** Gleaming straw-green; it uncoils sinuously in the mouth, the fruit profile changing through white peach, nectarine and grapefruit in a seamless stream, the natural acidity giving it a major X-factor. This is a truly lovely chardonnay. Screwcap. 13.5% alc. **Rating** 96 $26 ✪

Valerie Gippsland Chardonnay 2015 It's not just the higher percentage of new oak that differentiates this from the '15 Reserve; it's the greater power, complexity and length of the varietal fruit expression with white peach, grapefruit and creamy/nutty nuances. Screwcap. 14% alc. **Rating** 96 $60 ✪

Four Generations Gippsland Merlot 2015 A final barrel selection only made in exceptional vintages. This has distinctly greater depth and flavour, and commensurately greater length, than The Athelstan. Screwcap. 14% alc. **Rating** 95 **To** 2030 $43

Reserve Gippsland Chardonnay 2015 I'm not going to argue about the use of 50% mlf, but it does increase complexity with the right hand, taking away natural acidity with the left. I'm not disappointed with the wine, which has excellent balance and a supple, nutty palate that is long and even. Screwcap. 14% alc. **Rating** 94 $48

Gippsland Pinot Noir 2015 Good colour; the dark cherry, plum and savoury spice notes of the bouquet are mirrored by the powerful and long palate. The only thing missing is time in bottle. Leave it until '19 and you will congratulate yourself. Screwcap. 14% alc. **Rating** 94 **To** 2023 $28 **O**

Reserve Gippsland Pinot Noir 2014 Deep, bright crimson-purple hue; a layered and rich palate with glossy black cherry fruit in the vanguard, a touch of plum to follow. An attractive, indeed seductive, wine with a broad span of drinking pleasure – now to whenever. Screwcap. 14% alc. **Rating** 94 **To** 2030 $38

Reserve Isaac Gippsland Shiraz 2013 A powerful medium to full-bodied shiraz with more black than red or purple fruits; multiple layers on the palate bring spice and bramble into play, along with notes of cedary French oak, the tannins built to size. Still very young, and sure to develop slowly and gracefully. Screwcap. 14% alc. **Rating** 94 **To** 2033 $38

The Athelstan Gippsland Merlot 2015 Has that medium-bodied mix of cassis and savoury tannins with a touch of plum and spice that differentiate it from cabernet, but doesn't go too far down the plum path. Screwcap. 13.5% alc. **Rating** 94 **To** 2025 $29 **O**

ŸŸŸŸŸ **Valerie Gippsland Pinot Noir 2015** **Rating** 93 **To** 2027 $43
Gippsland Viognier 2015 **Rating** 90 $26

Nashwauk ★★★★

PO Box 852, Nuriootpa, SA 5355 **Region** McLaren Vale
T (08) 8562 4488 **www.**nashwaukvineyards.com.au **Open** Not
Winemaker Reid Bosward, Stephen Dew **Est.** 2005 **Dozens** 5000 **Vyds** 20ha
This is an estate-based venture, with 17ha of shiraz, 2ha of cabernet sauvignon and 1ha of tempranillo, all except the tempranillo between 15 and 40+ years old. It is a stand-alone business of the Kaesler family, and the first time it has extended beyond the Barossa Valley. The striking label comes from satellite photos of the vineyard, showing the contour planting; the name Nashwauk comes from Canada's Algonquin language, meaning 'land between'. The property is situated in the (unofficial) Seaview subregion, with Kays, Chapel Hill and Coriole as its neighbours; they all benefit from sea breezes and cooler nights. Exports to the US, Singapore, Malaysia, Hong Kong and China.

ŸŸŸŸŸ **Beacon McLaren Vale Shiraz 2013** Relatively light, slightly diffuse colour, certainly not deep or black; the fruit flavours are true to McLaren Vale, and very nearly carry the alcohol; Cherry Ripe echoes, and there is some freshness. Cork. 15.5% alc. **Rating** 92 **To** 2028 $120

McLaren Vale Cabernet Sauvignon 2014 Excellent dark garnet; powerfully built, with grunt and sturdy tannins yet plenty of blackberry fruit and essence and cedary oak spice. Screwcap. 14.5% alc. **Rating** 90 **To** 2024 $25 JF

ŸŸŸŸ **Wrecked McLaren Vale Shiraz 2013** **Rating** 89 **To** 2023 $70

Nazaaray ★★★★

266 Meakins Road, Flinders, Vic 3929 **Region** Mornington Peninsula
T (03) 5989 0126 **www.**nazaaray.com.au **Open** 1st w'end of month
Winemaker Paramdeep Ghumman **Est.** 1996 **Dozens** 800 **Vyds** 2.28ha
Paramdeep Ghumman is, as far as I am aware, the only Indian-born winery proprietor in Australia. He and his wife purchased the Nazaaray vineyard property in 1991. An initial trial planting of 400 vines in '96 was gradually expanded to the present level of 1.6ha of pinot noir, 0.44ha of pinot gris and 0.12ha each of sauvignon blanc and shiraz. Notwithstanding the micro size of the estate, all the wines are made and bottled onsite.

ŸŸŸŸŸ **Single Vineyard Mornington Peninsula Sauvignon Blanc 2016** Fermented and matured in oak for 8 months. Well made, the oak imparting more texture than flavour. The flavours are more citrussy than tropical, which is a statement not a criticism – I like the wine. Screwcap. 13.5% alc. **Rating** 92 **To** 2018 $30

Single Vineyard Mornington Peninsula Pinot Rose 2015 Nazaaray Pinot Noir provided the base for the wine, the juice with 12–14 hours of skin contact, matured for 9 months. The salmon-pink hue comes from the barrel ferment, as does the spicy/savoury/bramble underplay of the red fruits. A good, dry finish to a wine worth more than a mere second glance. Screwcap. 14% alc. **Rating** 91 To 2017 $30

Single Vineyard Mornington Peninsula Pinot Gris 2016 Wild yeast–barrel fermented, nashi pear and citrus-dominant, and with good line and length. Well made. Screwcap. 14.% alc. **Rating** 90 To 2019 $30

Nepenthe   ★★★★☆

Jones Road, Balhannah, SA 5242 **Region** Adelaide Hills
T (08) 8398 8888 **www**.nepenthe.com.au **Open** 7 days 10–4
Winemaker Alex Trescowthick **Est.** 1994 **Dozens** 40 000 **Vyds** 108.68ha
Nepenthe quickly established its reputation as a producer of high quality wines, but founder Ed Tweddell died unexpectedly in 2006, and the business was purchased by Australian Vintage Limited the following year. The winery was closed in '09, and winemaking operations transferred to McGuigan Wines (Barossa Valley). The Nepenthe winery has since been purchased by Peter Leske and Mark Kozned, and provides contract winemaking services via their Revenir venture. Nepenthe has over 100ha of close-planted vines spread over four vineyards in the Adelaide Hills, with an exotic array of varieties. Exports to the UK, the US and other major markets.

ΨΨΨΨΨ Pinnacle Ithaca Adelaide Hills Chardonnay 2015 A wine with a long history, and this lives up to its pedigree. There's harmony between the white peach-led fruit and the gently nutty/creamy French oak; the balance and length are impeccable. Screwcap. 13.5% alc. **Rating** 95 To 2025 $32 ✪
Pinnacle The Good Doctor Adelaide Hills Pinot Noir 2015 The fragrant bouquet leads into a light to medium-bodied palate that has a very attractive silky, supple mouthfeel displaying a bevy of red, forest floor-accented flavours. There is a savoury/stemmy wild strawberry showcase of complex fruits. More or less ready now. Screwcap. 13% alc. **Rating** 94 To 2022 $32
Pinnacle Gate Block Adelaide Hills Shiraz 2015 Bright crimson-purple; the bouquet offers predominantly black fruits backed by spice and pepper, the palate a study in elegance, red and black cherry competing, neither dismissing the other. Screwcap. 14.5% alc. **Rating** 94 To 2030 $32

ΨΨΨΨΩ Winemaker's Selection Arneis 2016 Rating 90 To 2018 $25
Winemaker's Selection Gruner Veltliner 2016 Rating 90 To 2018 $25
Tempranillo 2015 Rating 90 To 2021 $20 ✪

New Era Vineyards   ★★★★

PO Box 391, Woodside, SA 5244 **Region** Adelaide Hills
T 0413 544 246 **www**.neweravineyards.com.au **Open** Not
Winemaker Robert and Iain Baxter **Est.** 1988 **Dozens** 500 **Vyds** 13ha
The New Era vineyard is situated over a gold reef that was mined for 60 years until all recoverable gold had been extracted (mining ceased in 1940). The vineyard was originally planted to chardonnay, shiraz, cabernet sauvignon, merlot and sauvignon, mostly contracted to Foster's. Recently 2ha of cabernet sauvignon and 1.1ha of merlot have been grafted over to sauvignon blanc. Much of the production is sold to other winemakers in the region. The small amount of wine made has been the subject of favourable reviews.

ΨΨΨΨΩ Adelaide Hills Pinot Rose 2016 Fuchsia colour with pretty aromatics dotted with raspberry, strawberry and cream; some texture, with a lick of sweetness, yet a lively fresh finish. Screwcap. 13% alc. **Rating** 91 To 2019 $20 JF ✪
Langhorne Creek Touriga Nacional 2015 Mid-purple and as tutti-frutti as touriga nacional can be, fragrant with musk, red licorice, roses, violets and

sweet juicy raspberries. Medium-bodied, bright acid, ripe tannins and ready now. Screwcap. 13.5% alc. **Rating** 90 **To** 2019 $25 JF

🍷🍷🍷🍷 Adelaide Hills Sauvignon Blanc 2016 **Rating** 89 **To** 2018 $20 JF

Newbridge Wines ★★★☆

18 Chelsea Street, Brighton, Vic 3186 (postal) **Region** Bendigo
T 0417 996 840 **www**.newbridgewines.com.au **Open** At Newbridge Hotel, Newbridge
Winemaker Mark Matthews, Andrew Simpson **Est.** 1996 **Dozens** 300 **Vyds** 1ha
The Newbridge property was purchased by Ian Simpson in 1979, partly for sentimental family history reasons and partly because of the beauty of the property, situated on the banks of the Loddon River. It was not until '96 that Ian decided to plant shiraz, and up to and including the 2002 vintage the grapes were sold to several local wineries. Ian retained the grapes and made wine in '03, and lived to see that and the following two vintages take shape before his death. The property is now run by his son Andrew, the wines contract-made by Mark Matthews, with enthusiastic support from Andrew.

🍷🍷🍷🍷🍷 Bendigo Shiraz 2013 Contains close to (but less than) 15% wine from the frost-ravaged '14 vintage. The colour is still very good, with full purple-crimson hue; an elegant wine with spicy/savoury black fruits and substantial oak (which is still in balance). It enjoys exposure to air, according to Newbridge. Screwcap. 14.5% alc. **Rating** 90 **To** 2028 $25

Newtons Ridge Estate ★★★★

1170 Cooriemungle Road, Timboon, Vic 3268 **Region** Geelong
T (03) 5598 7394 **www**.newtonsridgeestate.com.au **Open** Thurs–Mon 11–4 Oct–Easter
Winemaker David Falk **Est.** 1998 **Dozens** 850 **Vyds** 5ha
David and Carla Falk have operated a real estate and livestock agency in since 1989, the property 'just a couple of ridges away' from Newtons Ridge Estate. When they heard that founder David Newton was contemplating pulling out the vines, they purchased the vineyard, in 2012, completing a circle that began in the 1880s when Carla's family were among the first vignerons in Geelong – they produce wine in Switzerland to this day.

🍷🍷🍷🍷🍷 Port Campbell Pinot Noir 2015 Interesting colour, purple dominant; a very attractive pinot that fully reflects the great '15 vintage. The flavours of plum and cherry are succulent, yet are light on their feet. I'm inclined to say this wine will never be better than it is now, but if I'm wrong, it will be a great pinot. Screwcap. 12.8% alc. **Rating** 94 **To** 2023 $50

🍷🍷🍷🍷🍷 Sauvignon Blanc 2016 **Rating** 93 **To** 2017 $25 ✪
Shiraz 2015 **Rating** 92 **To** 2030 $35
Chardonnay 2015 **Rating** 91 **To** 2023 $30

Ngeringa ★★★★☆

119 Williams Road, Mount Barker, SA 5251 **Region** Adelaide Hills
T (08) 8398 2867 **www**.ngeringa.com **Open** Last Sun month 11–5 or by appt
Winemaker Erinn Klein **Est.** 2001 **Dozens** 2000 **Vyds** 5ha
Erinn and Janet Klein say, 'As fervent practitioners of biodynamic winegrowing, we respect biodynamics as a sensitivity to the rhythms of nature, the health of the soil and the connection between plant, animal and cosmos. It is a pragmatic solution to farming without the use of chemicals and a necessary acknowledgement that the farm unit is part of a great whole.' It is not an easy solution, and the Kleins have increased the immensity of the challenge by using ultra-close vine spacing of 1.5m × 1m, necessitating a large amount of hand-training of the vines plus the use of a tiny crawler tractor. Lest it be thought they have stumbled onto biodynamic growing without understanding wine science, they teamed up while studying at Adelaide University in 2000 (Erinn – oenology, Janet – viticulture/wine marketing), and then spent time looking at the great viticultural regions of the Old World, with a particular emphasis on biodynamics. The JE label is used for the basic wines, Ngeringa only for the very

best (NASAA Certified Biodynamic Cert No. 5184). Exports to the US, Canada, Austria, Belgium, Norway, Japan, Taiwan, Hong Kong and China.

ŸŸŸŸŸ **Single Vineyard Adelaide Hills Sangiovese 2015** Terrific varietal bouquet; sour cherry, savoury/earthy spice and the faintest hint of reduction, which adds to the Italianate feel. Balanced and poised, the fruit is juicy but not sweet, building flavour as it goes. Fine, filigreed tannins run through the palate and gather on the finish, providing the persistence and length of quality sangiovese. Screwcap. 12.5% alc. **Rating** 94 **To** 2021 $35 SC

ŸŸŸŸŸ **Adelaide Hills Rose 2015** **Rating** 93 **To** 2018 $28 SC
Single Vineyard Adelaide Hills Syrah 2013 **Rating** 93 **To** 2025 $50 SC
Adelaide Hills Chardonnay 2014 **Rating** 91 **To** 2020 $40 SC

Nicholson River   ★★★☆

57 Liddells Road, Nicholson, Vic 3882 **Region** Gippsland
T (03) 5156 8241 **www**.nicholsonriverwinery.com.au **Open** 7 days 10–5 during hols
Winemaker Ken Eckersley **Est.** 1978 **Dozens** 1000 **Vyds** 8ha
Nicholson River's fierce commitment to quality in the face of the temperamental Gippsland climate and frustratingly small production has been handsomely repaid by some massive Chardonnays and impressive red wines. Ken Eckersley refers to his Chardonnays not as white wines but as gold wines, and lists them accordingly in his newsletter.

ŸŸŸŸ **Unwooded Chardonnay 2016** A fair amount of colour for a young, unwooded white – it's mid-gold and bright; aromas of hay, stone fruit and ginger spice with some leesy nutty nuances. Quite sprightly acidity, somewhat pinched on the finish. Screwcap. 11.8% alc. **Rating** 89 **To** 2021 $24 JF

Nick Haselgrove Wines   ★★★★☆

281 Tatachilla Road, McLaren Vale, SA 5171 **Region** Adelaide
T (08) 8383 0886 **www**.nhwines.com.au **Open** By appt
Winemaker Nick Haselgrove, Marcus Hofer **Est.** 1981 **Dozens** 10 000
After various sales, amalgamations and disposals of particular brands, Nick Haselgrove now owns The Old Faithful (the flagship brand, see separate entry), Blackbilly, Clarence Hill, James Haselgrove, Tir na N'Og and Wishing Tree brands. Exports to the US and other major markets.

ŸŸŸŸŸ **James Haselgrove Futures McLaren Vale Shiraz 2014** Vines over 100yo gave this crimson-purple wine a handy start, but it has been intelligently made. It has lipsmacking elegance, content with its medium-bodied weight and fine tannins. Diam. 14.5% alc. **Rating** 95 **To** 2034 $40
Clarence Hill Reserve McLaren Vale Shiraz 2013 A powerful, full-bodied shiraz with a lot of American oak in its make-up, but also has the black fruits to better able carry that oak. That said, it does need time to settle down: 5 years should do the trick. Diam. 14.5% alc. **Rating** 94 **To** 2030 $32
Blackbilly McLaren Vale Grenache Shiraz Mourvedre 2014 A 60/32/8% blend. An attractive medium-bodied blend which carries the American oak without blinking. Juicy red fruits dance on the tongue, and – better still – leave the mouth fresh and looking for the next glass. Great value for a wine with a lot of inputs. Screwcap. 14.5% alc. **Rating** 94 **To** 2029 $23 ✪

ŸŸŸŸŸ **Blackbilly McLaren Vale Shiraz 2013** **Rating** 93 **To** 2038 $23 ✪
Blackbilly Langhorne Creek Sangiovese 2015 **Rating** 92 **To** 2023 $23 ✪
Adelaide Winemakers The Peer Shiraz 2014 **Rating** 91 **To** 2029 $24

Nick O'Leary Wines   ★★★★★

149 Brooklands Road, Wallaroo, NSW 2618 **Region** Canberra District
T (02) 6230 2745 **www**.nickolearywines.com.au **Open** By appt
Winemaker Nick O'Leary **Est.** 2007 **Dozens** 7500

At the ripe old age of 28, Nick O'Leary had been involved in the wine industry for over a decade, working variously in retail, wholesale, viticulture and winemaking. Two years earlier he had laid the foundation for Nick O'Leary Wines, purchasing shiraz from local vignerons (commencing in 2006); riesling following in '08. His wines have had extraordinarily consistent success in local wine shows and competitions since the first vintages, and are building on that early success in spectacular fashion. At the NSW Wine Awards '15, the 2014 Shiraz was awarded the NSW Wine of the Year Trophy exactly as the 2013 Shiraz was in the prior year – the first time any winery had won the award in consecutive years.

🍷🍷🍷🍷🍷 **Bolaro Shiraz 2015** This single vineyard, medium-bodied cool climate shiraz has a complex blend of red and black fruits together with some spice rack spices. The palate is compact and tightly wound, ensuring a long life ahead. Screwcap. 13.5% alc. **Rating** 92 **To** 2025 $55 PR
Shiraz 2015 Brightly coloured, this light to medium-bodied wine has aromas of red fruits, white pepper and more than enough grip to reward 3–5 years in the cellar. A touch closed at present: a quick decant is recommended and will reap rewards. Screwcap. 13.5% alc. **Rating** 90 **To** 2023 $30 PR

Night Harvest

PO Box 921, Busselton, WA 6280 **Region** Margaret River
T (08) 9755 1521 **www**.nightharvest.com.au **Open** Not
Winemaker Bruce Dukes **Est.** 2005 **Dozens** 40 000 **Vyds** 300ha
Andy and Mandy Ferreira arrived in Margaret River in 1986 as newly married young migrants. They soon became involved in the construction and establishment of new vineyards, as well as growing vegetables for the local and export markets. Their vineyard-contracting business expanded quickly when the region experienced its rapid growth in the late '90s, so the vegetable business was closed, and they put all their focus into wine. They were involved in the establishment of about 300ha of Margaret River vineyards, many of which they continue to manage today (Woodside Valley Estate and Chapman Grove are among the 16 estates that fall into this category.) As their fortunes grew, they purchased their own property and produced their first wines in 2005. Harvesting is a key part of their business, and currently they harvest fruit from over 100 sites. Hence the Night Harvest brand was born, and Butler Crest was added as a premium label. Exports to the UK, the US, Thailand, Hong Kong and China.

🍷🍷🍷🍷🍷 **John George Chardonnay 2014** True to Campbell Mattinson's prediction, has benefited greatly from 2 years in bottle since first tasted Mar '15. The grapefruit and white peach flavours have asserted themselves over the oak, and the acidity seems fresher. Still developing slowly. Screwcap. 12.5% alc. **Rating** 95 **To** 2024 $35 ❂

🍷🍷🍷🍷🍷 **John George Cabernet Sauvignon 2015 Rating** 90 **To** 2022 $40

Nillumbik Estate

195 Clintons Road, Smiths Gully, Vic 3760 **Region** Yarra Valley
T 0408 337 326 **www**.nillumbikestate.com.au **Open** Not
Winemaker John Tregambe **Est.** 2001 **Dozens** 1250 **Vyds** 2ha
In establishing Nillumbik Estate, John and Chanmali Tregambe shared the multi-generational winemaking experience of John's parents, Italian immigrants who arrived in Australia in the 1950s. The estate plantings of pinot noir are supplemented by cabernet sauvignon, chardonnay, shiraz and nebbiolo purchased from Sunbury, Heathcote and the King Valley.

🍷🍷🍷🍷🍷 **Old Earth Barrel Reserve Heathcote Shiraz 2013** This shiraz boasts all the bells and whistles: indigenous yeast fermentation, lavish mocha oak and dutifully concentrated dark and red fruit flavours oozing across a palate of prodigious density and force. This is the liquid voice of Heathcote in all its flamboyance and virulence. Screwcap. 14% alc. **Rating** 95 **To** 2028 $48 NG
Pinnacle Yarra Valley Cabernet Sauvignon 2015 Both of Nillumbik's cabernets are very good, but this is more reliant on grape tannins and natural acidity for its structural supports. The tannins are cedar-inflected and finely

wrought, corralling sumptuous currant fruit flavours and Yarra's scent of green bean. Medium-bodied and highly savoury. Despite its evident structure, this is supine now, in its youth, and long and thoroughly delicious. Screwcap. 13% alc. **Rating** 95 **To** 2025 $36 NG

Pinnacle Barrel Reserve Yarra Valley Cabernet Sauvignon 2015 Made in a fruit-forward, sinuous and eminently drinkable fashion. Varietal regalia is on full show with blackcurrant, pastille, anise and butter bean aromas. The palate is mid-weighted, with cabernet's tension eased across gently extracted fruit, partial barrel fermentation and 20 months in oak, imparting a hint of coffee mocha and vanilla pod to the finish. Suave. Screwcap. 13% alc. **Rating** 94 **To** 2025 $90 NG

 Old Earth Heathcote Shiraz 2014 Rating 91 **To** 2026 $36 NG
The Back Block King Valley Petit Verdot 2014 Rating 91 **To** 2028 $28 NG
Domenic's Paddock Pinot Noir 2015 Rating 90 **To** 2022 $36 NG

Nine Fingers ★★★☆

PO Box 212, Lobethal, SA 5241 **Region** Adelaide Hills
T (08) 8389 6049 **Open** By appt
Winemaker Michael Sykes (Contract) **Est.** 1999 **Dozens** 250 **Vyds** 1ha
Simon and Penny Cox established their sauvignon blanc vineyard after encouragement from local winemaker Robb Cootes of Leland Estate. The small vineyard has meant that they do all the viticultural work, and meticulously tend the vines. They obviously have a sense of humour, which may not be shared by their youngest daughter Olivia. In 2002, 2-year-old Olivia's efforts to point out bunches that needed to be thinned resulted in Penny's secateurs cutting off the end of Olivia's finger. A race to hospital and successful microsurgery resulted in the full restoration of the finger; strangely, Olivia has shown little interest in viticulture since. Exports to Singapore.

 Adelaide Hills Sauvignon Blanc 2016 A pure, unadorned Adelaide Hills sauvignon blanc traversing cut grass, gooseberry, passionfruit and lychee, mooching quietly along until it markedly lifts its intensity on the finish, with citrussy acidity joining the fray. Screwcap. 12.7% alc. **Rating** 90 **To** 2017 $20 **❂**

916 ★★★★★

916 Steels Creek Road, Steels Creek, Vic 3775 (postal) **Region** Yarra Valley
T (03) 5965 2124 **www**.916.com.au **Open** Not
Winemaker Ben Haines **Est.** 2008 **Dozens** 260 **Vyds** 2ha
916, established by John Brand and Erin-Marie O'Neill, is one of three wineries in the *Wine Companion* using three digits as their name, others being 919 and 201. A year after they acquired their 8ha property, bushfires destroyed their home and all their possessions, but they rebuilt their lives and home, reinvesting in wine and vineyard alike. Viticulturist John Evans, formerly at Yering Station and now at Rochford Wines, became involved with the vineyard in 1996. They chose their viticulturist well and they have a highly gifted winemaker in the form of Ben Haines. Exports to the US, China and Singapore.

 Yarra Valley Pinot Noir 2015 Estate-grown MV6, hand-picked, whole bunches and whole berries cold-soaked and open-fermented, 3 weeks post-ferment maceration for the whole-berry parcels, matured for 16 months in used French oak, not fined or filtered. Clear, bright crimson-purple; despite its lengthy elevage, it is as fresh and crisp as a spring day; its cherry/berry fruit flavours positively sing in the mouth. Natural wine at its greatest. Diam. 13% alc. **Rating** 95 **To** 2030 $90

919 Wines ★★★★☆

39 Hodges Road, Berri, SA 5343 **Region** Riverland
T 0408 855 272 **www**.919wines.com.au **Open** Wed–Sun & public hols 10–5
Winemaker Eric and Jenny Semmler **Est.** 2002 **Dozens** 2000 **Vyds** 17ha

Eric and Jenny Semmler have been involved in the wine industry since 1986, and have a special interest in fortified wines. Eric previously made fortified wines for Hardys, and worked at Brown Brothers. Jenny has worked for Swathbogie Vineyards, Pennyweight Wines and St Huberts. They have planted micro-quantities of varieties for fortified wines: palomino, durif, tempranillo, muscat à petits grains, tinta cao, shiraz, tokay and touriga nacional. They use minimal water application, deliberately reducing the crop levels, practising organic and biodynamic techniques. In 2011 they purchased the 12.3ha property at Loxton they now call Ella Semmler's Vineyard.

ΨΨΨΨΨ **Pale Dry Apera NV** This is exactly what pale dry apera should be – full of summer with its sea spray/briny character, and with preserved lemons, cut apple, grilled almonds and spirit integrated perfectly. And dry as the Sahara on the finish. Screwcap. 15.5% alc. **Rating** 95 $32 JF

ΨΨΨΨΨ **Tempranillo 2015** Rating 93 To 2024 $45 JF
Classic Muscat NV Rating 91 $42 JF
Shiraz 2016 Rating 90 To 2028 $42 JF
Touriga Nacional 2016 Rating 90 To 2025 $45 JF

Nintingbool ★★★★
56 Wongerer Lane, Smythes Creek, Vic 3351 (postal) **Region** Ballarat
T (03) 5342 4393 **www**.nintingbool.com **Open** Not
Winemaker Peter Bothe **Est.** 1998 **Dozens** 480 **Vyds** 2ha
Peter and Jill Bothe purchased the Nintingbool property in 1982 and built their home in '84, using bluestone dating back to the goldrush period. They established an extensive Australian native garden and home orchard, but in '98 diversified by planting pinot noir, a further planting the following year lifting the total to 2ha. This is one of the coolest mainland regions, and demands absolute attention to detail (and a warm growing season) for success.

ΨΨΨΨΨ **Smythes Creek Pinot Noir 2014** Estate-grown MV6, the very low yield fermented using three yeasts, matured in French oak. This is a particularly good example of ultra-cool-grown pinot, with fully ripe juicy red and dark berry fruit, the tannins superfine. Screwcap. 13% alc. **Rating** 94 To 2022 $35

ΨΨΨΨΨ **Smythes Creek Rose 2016** Rating 90 To 2018 $23

Noble Red ★★★★
18 Brennan Avenue, Upper Beaconsfield, Vic 3808 (postal) **Region** Heathcote
T 0400 594 440 **www**.nobleredwines.com **Open** Not
Winemaker Roman Sobiesiak, Osicka Wines **Est.** 2002 **Dozens** 700 **Vyds** 6ha
Roman and Margaret Sobiesiak acquired their property in 2002. There was 0.25ha of shiraz planted in the 1970s, and a progressive planting program has seen the area increase to 6ha, shiraz (3.6ha) accounting for the lion's share, the remainder equally split to tempranillo, mourvedre, merlot and cabernet sauvignon. They adopted a dry-grown approach, which meant slow development during the prolonged drought, but their commitment remains undimmed. Indeed, visiting many wine regions around the world and working within the industry locally has increased their determination. Exports to China.

ΨΨΨΨΨ **Special Release Arek Heathcote Shiraz 2014** A corpulent wine of prodigious power and concentration, this has an assemblage of muscular dark fruit with a sinew of pepper, seamlessly hewn to a firm carapace of well managed tannins, just on the better side of drying. Tactile and coating the mouth, the wine is pushed long by sheer force of will and personality. Screwcap. 14.4% alc. **Rating** 93 To 2028 $45 NG
Heathcote Cabernet Sauvignon 2015 Noble Red's penchant for dry-grown, powerful fruit is fully displayed across this cabernet. The result echoes both the voice of the ancient soils and clear varietal personality, with currant, dried sage, cedar and oak strewn across a ferruginous core and a litany of other herbal notes. Screwcap. 14.5% alc. **Rating** 93 To 2030 $30 NG

Heathcote Shiraz 2015 Opaque with a rim of garnet, this shiraz is high octane, with an edge of livewire volatility providing some necessary lift and requisite fireworks across the olfactory receptors. The finish is dense and almost impenetrable; reminiscent of tar, with black fruit compote and seize-the-day tannins. Screwcap. 14.7% alc. **Rating** 90 **To** 2023 $25 NG

Noble Road ★★★

206A Hutt Street, Adelaide, SA 5000 **Region** Clare Valley
T 0400 742 603 www.nobleroad.com.au **Open** 7 days 11–4
Winemaker Scott Curtis **Est.** 2007 **Dozens** 5000 **Vyds** 80ha
Owner and winemaker Scott Curtis has four occupations: first, to manage/advise grapegrowers over three regions, with an off-take of 9000 tonnes per year; second, to continue work with grape varieties bred by the CSIRO; third, to make and sell small amounts of Clare Valley Shiraz and Cabernet Sauvignon; and finally, to make Vermentino, Montepulciano, Fiano, Lagrein and Saperavi. Exports to Singapore, Hong Kong, Taiwan and China.

Nocton Vineyard ★★★★

373 Colebrook Road, Richmond, Tas 7025 **Region** Southern Tasmania
T (03) 6260 2688 www.noctonwine.com.au **Open** Wed–Sat 10–4
Winemaker Frogmore Creek **Est.** 1998 **Dozens** 8000 **Vyds** 34ha
Nocton Vineyard is the reincarnation of Nocton Park. After years of inactivity (other than the ongoing sale of the grapes from what is a first class vineyard) it largely disappeared from sight. Wines are released under the Nocton Vineyard and Willow (Reserve) labels. The quality across the two labels is very good. Exports to China.

🍷🍷🍷🍷🍷 Estate Pinot Noir 2015 An essay in cool climate pinot, with black cherry fruit leading the way, gamey whole-bunch aromas falling in behind, and what seems to be a touch of smoky oak rounding it off. While fleshy and juicy on the mid-palate, slightly tart cranberry-like flavours and savoury, almost edgy astringency, mark the finish. Screwcap. 13.8% alc. **Rating** 93 **To** 2023 $29 SC
Willow Pinot Noir 2015 A complex pinot in terms of texture, structure and flavour; dark berry (cherry, blueberry) fruits have a bramble/forest underlay, extending the finish and aftertaste. Silver medal Tasmanian Wine Show '17. Screwcap. 13.5% alc. **Rating** 93 **To** 2023 $40
Tasmania Sparkling NV The blend is not declared, but strawberry, red apple and red cherry fruit are the unmistakable fingerprints of pinot noir, while the acid cut and citrus expression of chardonnay tone a well honed finish. It's young and fruit-focused, with fine texture, lingering acid line and a touch of sweet dosage on the finish. Diam. 12% alc. **Rating** 93 **To** 2017 TS
Estate Chardonnay 2015 Just-ripe stone fruit and green melon aromas with a hint of creamy lees character. Plenty of flavour, but in a moderated Tasmanian way. The winemaking has added dimension, but overall this is more about attractive, easy drinking than complexity. A wine fabulous with oysters. Screwcap. 14.1% alc. **Rating** 92 **To** 2020 $27 SC

🍷🍷🍷🍷 Sauvignon Blanc 2015 **Rating** 89 **To** 2017 $27

Norton Estate ★★★★★

758 Plush Hannans Road, Lower Norton, Vic 3401 **Region** Western Victoria
T (03) 5384 8235 **Open** Fri–Sun & public hols 11–4
Winemaker Best's Wines **Est.** 1997 **Dozens** 1300 **Vyds** 4.66ha
In 1996 the Spence family purchased a rundown farm at Lower Norton and, rather than looking to the traditional wool, meat and wheat markets, trusted their instincts and planted vines on the elevated, frost-free, buckshot rises. The surprising vigour of the initial planting of shiraz prompted further plantings of shiraz, cabernet sauvignon and sauvignon blanc, plus a small planting of the American variety 'Norton'. The vineyard is halfway between the

Grampians and Mt Arapiles, 6km northwest of the Grampians region, and has to be content with the Western Victoria zone, but the wines show regional Grampians character and style.

🍷🍷🍷🍷🍷 Arapiles Run Shiraz 2015 The expressive bouquet offers black cherry, a touch of plum and a licorice/spice duo; the medium-bodied palate has an underlying freshness to its fleshy and supple mouthfeel, the French oak making a distinct, but not excessive, contribution to a complex wine. Screwcap. 13.5% alc. **Rating** 95 To 2030 $38

Wendy's Block Shiraz 2015 Made from a tiny block of 600 vines. The most intense and powerful of the '15 Norton Estate trio of shirazs, reflecting the extra degree of ripeness to the assemblage of blackberry, satsuma plum and licorice fruits on the full-bodied palate. Despite its power, the tannins are silky and refined, the oak in play, but no more. Screwcap. 14% alc. **Rating** 95 To 2035 $65

Rockface Shiraz 2015 A powerful, medium to full-bodied shiraz, its polished tannins and glossy black fruits giving a distinctive and edgy intensity on the palate, a savoury tweak appearing on the finish and aftertaste. Screwcap. 13.8% alc. **Rating** 94 To 2030 $25 ❂

🍷🍷🍷🍷🍷 Sauvignon Blanc 2016 **Rating** 92 $22 ❂
Cabernet Sauvignon 2015 **Rating** 91 To 2030 $25

Nugan Estate ★★★★☆

Kidman Way, Wilbriggie, NSW 2680 **Region** Riverina
T (02) 9362 9993 **www**.nuganestate.com.au **Open** Mon–Fri 9–5
Winemaker Daren Owers **Est.** 1999 **Dozens** 500 000 **Vyds** 491ha

Nugan Estate arrived on the scene like a whirlwind. It is an offshoot of the Nugan Group headed by Michelle Nugan (until her retirement in Feb 2013), inter alia the recipient of an Export Hero Award in '00. In the mid-1990s the company began developing vineyards, and it is now a veritable giant, with five vineyards: Cookoothama (335ha) and Manuka Grove (46ha) in the Riverina, Frasca's Lane (100ha) in the King Valley and McLaren Parish (10ha) in McLaren Vale. The wine business is now in the energetic hands of Matthew and Tiffany Nugan, Michelle's children. Exports to the UK, the US and other major markets.

🍷🍷🍷🍷🍷 Cookoothama Limited Release Darlington Point Botrytis Semillon 2012 It all seems so easy: botrytis at a high level, crushed, chilled and pressed immediately, juice settled for 18 hours, ferment initiated in stainless steel tanks, thence to French and American oak for 18 months, then back to tank before bottling in Oct '16. It's a beautifully balanced wine with luscious underlying residual sugar and fresh acidity (9.8g/l), alcohol perfectly pitched. Don't assume this will live for a long time – drink it soon. 375ml. Screwcap. 11% alc. **Rating** 95 To 2020 $21 ❂

🍷🍷🍷🍷🍷 Frasca's Lane King Valley Sauvignon Blanc 2015 **Rating** 93 To 2017 $20 ❂
Alcira Coonawarra Cabernet 2015 **Rating** 93 To 2020 $23 ❂
Yarra Valley Chardonnay 2014 **Rating** 91 To 2021 $20 ❂
Manuka Grove Riverina Durif 2012 **Rating** 91 To 2022 $23 ❂
Cookoothama King Valley SBS 2016 **Rating** 90 To 2017 $15 ❂
Frasca's Lane King Valley Pinot Grigio 2015 **Rating** 90 To 2017 $20 ❂
Alfredo Dried Grape Shiraz 2014 **Rating** 90 To 2023 $23
Alfredo Frasca's Lane Sangiovese 2014 **Rating** 90 To 2024 $23

O'Leary Walker Wines ★★★★★

Horrocks Highway, Leasingham, SA 5452 **Region** Clare Valley
T (08) 8843 0022 **www**.olearywalkerwines.com **Open** Mon–Sat 10–4, Sun 11–4
Winemaker David O'Leary, Nick Walker **Est.** 2001 **Dozens** 20 000 **Vyds** 35ha

David O'Leary and Nick Walker together had more than 30 years' experience as winemakers working for some of the biggest Australian wine groups when they took the plunge in 2001 and backed themselves to establish their own winery and brand. Initially the principal focus was on the Clare Valley, with 10ha of riesling, shiraz, cabernet sauvignon and semillon the main plantings; thereafter attention swung to the Adelaide Hills, where they now have 25ha of chardonnay, cabernet sauvignon, pinot noir, shiraz, sauvignon blanc and merlot. Exports to the UK, Ireland, the UAE and Asia.

🍷🍷🍷🍷🍷 **Claire Reserve Shiraz 2013** From Martin and Joan Smith's 123yo dry-grown vineyard in Polish Hill River, NASAA organic certified since '12, matured in French oak for 30 months. A wonderfully sumptuous and supple wine, its bouquet and palate a treasure trove of blackberry, red and black cherry, spice, cedar and chocolate; fine-grained tannins provide support, as does the French oak. Once you've got a glass in your hand, you're not likely to put it down. Screwcap. 14.5% alc. **Rating** 96 **To** 2038 $90

Polish Hill River Riesling 2016 Bright, light straw-green; a strongly floral citrus blossom bouquet with just a hint of spice leads into an intense, tightly focused palate, with lemon, lime and crisp acidity all contributing to a classic Polish Hill River style. Screwcap. 11.5% alc. **Rating** 95 **To** 2029 $25 **○**

Clare Valley Gruner Veltliner 2016 Its bouquet of pear and citrus is varietal (a good start), but it's the drive and exuberance that are as impressive as they are unexpected. There is a tactile quality conferred by the crunchy acidity that runs through the length of the palate. Bargain extraordinaire. Screwcap. 11.5% alc. **Rating** 94 **To** 2023 $18 **○**

Final Instructions Adelaide Hills Shiraz 2015 From a vineyard at Oakbank purchased by David O'Leary's grandfather in 1904, and still family-owned. There is a cornucopia of purple, red and black fruits with a sheen of spice that lifts the finish and aftertaste. The oak and tannin balance is another plus for a very good wine with a long future. Screwcap. 14% alc. **Rating** 94 **To** 2035 $35

Clare Valley Shiraz 2014 An attractive, well made shiraz speaking with equal character about its birthplace and its variety. Satsuma plum, blackberry and just the right amount of oak are seamlessly joined, fine-grained tannins underlining the bond. Screwcap. 14.5% alc. **Rating** 94 **To** 2030 $25 **○**

Wyatt Earp Vintage Shiraz 2015 How it won a gold medal and trophy (as per the back label) in '10, 5 years before it was made, is anyone's guess. This is a very good fortified shiraz with a lower baume than used to be the case, highlighting the shiraz varietal character, and also providing balance. 500ml. Screwcap. 18.5% alc. **Rating** 94 **To** 2040 $35

🍷🍷🍷🍷🍷 **Clare Valley Cabernet Sauvignon 2014** Rating 93 To 2029 $25 **○**
First Past The Post Chardonnay 2016 Rating 92 To 2020 $22 **○**
First Past The Post Chardonnay 2015 Rating 92 To 2020 $22 CM **○**
Hurtle Adelaide Hills Pinot Noir Chardonnay 2011 Rating 92 To 2020 $28
Watervale Riesling 2016 Rating 90 To 2021 $20 **○**
Clare Valley Poppy Rouge 2016 Rating 90 To 2018 $18 **○**
The Bookies' Bag Adelaide Hills Pinot Noir 2016 Rating 90 To 2026 $25
The Great Eastern Sparkling Shiraz NV Rating 90 To 2021 $28 TS

Oakdene   ★★★★★

255 Grubb Road, Wallington, Vic 3221 **Region** Geelong
T (03) 5256 3886 **www**.oakdene.com.au **Open** 7 days 10–4
Winemaker Robin Brockett, Marcus Holt **Est.** 2001 **Dozens** 7500 **Vyds** 12ha
Bernard and Elizabeth Hooley purchased Oakdene in 2001. Bernard focused on planting the vineyard (shiraz, pinot gris, sauvignon blanc, pinot noir, chardonnay, merlot, cabernet franc and cabernet sauvignon) while Elizabeth worked to restore the 1920s homestead. Much of the wine is sold through the award-winning Oakdene Restaurant and cellar door. The quality is exemplary, as is the consistency of that quality; Robin Brockett's skills are on full display.

🍷🍷🍷🍷🍷 **Jessica Single Vineyard Bellarine Peninsula Sauvignon 2016** Fermented in French oak (15% new), matured for 8 months. The bouquet is perfumed, rare for sauvignon blanc, and the palate has great precision and drive, the overall complexity compelling. The barrel fermentation has worked like a charm, making me reluctant to spit the wine out – unheard of. If entered in wine shows it should sweep the field; the length is amazing Screwcap. 13% alc. **Rating** 96 To 2020 $28 ✪

William Single Vineyard Bellarine Peninsula Shiraz 2015 Matured in French barriques (30% new) for 16 months. Excellent colour; a powerful cool-grown shiraz with black fruits (cherries and berries) on the medium to full-bodied palate. The tannins are firm but ripe and balanced, the oak precisely judged; great length and balance. Screwcap. 14.3% alc. **Rating** 96 To 2035 $43 ✪

Liz's Single Vineyard Bellarine Peninsula Chardonnay 2015 Bright, light straw-green; while the wine is complex, its cornerstone is its effortless elegance and semi-hidden power. The fruit spectrum is somewhat left field, white peach sharing the field with apple and pear before citrussy acidity joins the game. Its claims can't be ignored. Screwcap. 13.2% alc. **Rating** 95 To 2023 $35 ✪

Peta's Single Vineyard Bellarine Peninsula Pinot Noir 2015 Very good depth to the bright colour; at the fuller end of the pinot noir spectrum, with a garland of spice strung around the red and black cherry fruit of the bouquet, a theme effortlessly picked up by the intense palate. Savoury/earthy nuances add further interest Gold medals Vic Wine Show and National Wine Show '16. Screwcap. 13.6% alc. **Rating** 95 To 2025 $43

Bellarine Peninsula Shiraz 2015 10% new, matured for 11 months in French oak. Deep crimson-purple; takes you on a roller-coaster ride as its red, purple and black fruits take turns to capture your attention, likewise juicy freshness and firm tannins, the latter on the aftertaste. Screwcap. 14.5% alc. **Rating** 95 To 2030 $24 ✪

Bernard's Single Vineyard Bellarine Peninsula Cabernets 2015 47% merlot, 40% cabernet franc and 13% cabernet sauvignon. Luscious and mouthfilling, yet fresh and focused, the seeming contradiction explained by the unusual co-fermentation of the three varieties – a positive step made feasible by the normal ripening gap being compressed by the vintage, everything ripening together. Climate change – bring it on! Screwcap. 13.4% alc. **Rating** 95 To 2030 $30 ✪

Bellarine Peninsula Chardonnay 2015 Rating 94 To 2023 $24 ✪
Ly Ly Bellarine Peninsula Pinot Gris 2016 Rating 94 To $28 ✪

♙♙♙♙♙ **Bellarine Peninsula Pinot Grigio 2016** Rating 91 To 2018 $23 ✪
Bellarine Peninsula Pinot Noir 2015 Rating 90 To 2021 $24

Oakridge Wines ★★★★★

864 Maroondah Highway, Coldstream, Vic 3770 **Region** Yarra Valley
T (03) 9738 9900 **www**.oakridgewines.com.au **Open** 7 days 10–5
Winemaker David Bicknell **Est.** 1978 **Dozens** 35 000 **Vyds** 22ha
Winemaker and CEO David Bicknell has proved his worth time and again as an extremely talented winemaker. At the top of the brand tier is 864, all Yarra Valley vineyard selections, only released in the best years (Chardonnay, Pinot Noir, Shiraz, Cabernet Sauvignon, Riesling); next is the Oakridge Local Vineyard Series (the Chardonnay, Pinot Noir and Sauvignon Blanc come from the cooler Upper Yarra Valley; the Shiraz, Cabernet Sauvignon and Viognier from the Lower Yarra); and the Over the Shoulder range, drawn from all of the sources available to Oakridge (Sauvignon Blanc, Pinot Grigio, Pinot Noir, Shiraz Viognier, Cabernet Sauvignon). The estate vineyards are Oakridge Vineyard (10ha), Hazeldene Vineyard (10ha) and Henk Vineyard (12ha). Exports to the UK, the US, Canada, Sweden, The Netherlands, Norway, Fiji, Papua New Guinea, Singapore, Hong Kong and China.

♙♙♙♙♙ **864 Single Block Release Drive Block Funder & Diamond Vineyard Yarra Valley Chardonnay 2015** Made simply, with whole bunch pressing to oak, 20% new, fermentation taking place under the aegis of ambient yeasts. The result is a stunning wine of verve, with stone fruit, oatmeal and truffle splayed across a tensile spine of bright acidity and smoky mineral crunch. The oak imparts some cinnamon cream. The finish is driven long by the immaculate structural supports and intensity of fruit. Screwcap. 13.5% alc. **Rating** 97 **To** 2027 $78 NG ✪

864 Single Block Release Drive Block Funder & Diamond Vineyard Yarra Valley Chardonnay 2014 P58 clone, matured on lees in Frnch oak for 10 months. Prophetically described as a late bloomer needing more time when tasted a year ago, now quite simply superb. Upper Yarra chardonnay at its best, with another level of complexity, depth and length achieved with unmatched finesse. Screwcap. 13.5% alc. **Rating** 97 $77 ✪

Local Vineyard Series Lusatia Park Vineyard Yarra Valley Pinot Noir 2015 Matured for 10 months in French oak. Bright crimson, and typical of the Upper Yarra Lusatia Park Vineyard, with linear drive and power to its blend of red fruits and fine-grained savoury/foresty tannins. The length and depth of the palate are exceptional. Screwcap. 13.5% alc. **Rating** 97 **To** 2030 $38 ✪

864 Single Block Release A4 Block Willowlake Vineyard Yarra Valley Pinot Noir 2015 Matured in French oak for 11 months. The gently spicy, perfumed bouquet and the perfectly shaped, extremely long palate bring all the red berry fruits into play. This Upper Yarra pinot simply needs time to show the myriad of spicy foresty notes now waiting in the wings. Screwcap. 13.5% alc. **Rating** 97 **To** 2030 $78 ✪

♟♟♟♟♟ **Local Vineyard Series Willowlake Vineyard Yarra Valley Chardonnay 2015** Hand-picked, whole-bunch pressed direct to French puncheons for wild yeast fermentation and 10 months maturation. All about its extreme length and balance, less about its depth. Only a low percentage of new oak was employed, leaving the back-palate and finish to proclaim the intense, ripe grapefruit and melon flavours from centre stage. Screwcap. 13% alc. **Rating** 96 **To** 2025 $38 ✪

Local Vineyard Series Lusatia Park Vineyard Yarra Valley Chardonnay 2015 Has the Upper Yarra tightness and intensity, the bouquet with a pleasant touch of reduction, the palate taking that intro with both hands on its ultra-long, citrus-infused, minerally flavours, oak a means, not an end. Screwcap. 13% alc. **Rating** 96 **To** 2025 $38 ✪

Local Vineyard Series Willowlake Vineyard Yarra Valley Pinot Noir 2015 A perfectly constructed pinot, its fragrant, red-fruited bouquet foreshadowing a palate of immaculate balance and length. It has a particular juicy mouthfeel born of the whole-berry fermentation of perfectly ripened fruit, underlined by the aftertaste. Screwcap. 13.5% alc. **Rating** 96 **To** 2028 $38 ✪

864 Single Block Release Winery Block Oakridge Vineyard Yarra Valley Cabernet Sauvignon 2014 4-day soak pre-fermentation, 4 weeks post-fermentation maceration was followed by 15 months in French oak. Vivid, deep crimson-purple; has the perfect poise and focus of all Oakridge wines, and one of the best new-style cabernets to come from the Yarra Valley. The cassis fruit is intense and bright enough to seduce even the most rabid pinotphiles. Screwcap. 13.7% alc. **Rating** 96 **To** 2039 $78

Local Vineyard Series Yarra Valley Cabernet Sauvignon 2014 This was made in traditional Bordelais fashion, with extended fermentation on skins, followed by 17 months in barriques, a high percentage of which were new. Medium-bodied and impeccably crafted, based on the quality of the gravelly tannins alone, this is modern-day claret minus the obtrusive oak of other modern-day expressions. Currant, tobacco, Yarra's stamp of green bean and some verdant hedgerow notes are carried long and wide by juicy acidity. Savoury, classy and pointed. Screwcap. 13.7% alc. **Rating** 96 **To** 2035 $38 NG ✪

Rose of Baton Rouge 2016 Screwcap. 14% alc. **Rating** 95 $22 NG ✪

Local Vineyard Series Willowlake Vineyard Yarra Valley Pinot Noir 2016 Screwcap. 14.5% alc. **Rating** 95 **To** 2025 $38 NG

Local Vineyard Series Hazeldene Vineyard Yarra Valley Botrytis Gris 2016 Screwcap. 10% alc. **Rating** 95 **To** 2030 $40

Over the Shoulder Yarra Valley Chardonnay 2015 **Rating** 94 **To** 2021 $23 ✪

Over the Shoulder Yarra Valley Rose 2016 Rating 94 To 2019 $23 ☻
Over the Shoulder Yarra Valley Pinot Noir 2015 Rating 94 To 2025 $23 ☻
Local Vineyard Series Oakridge Vineyard Yarra Valley Shiraz 2013
Rating 94 To 2035 $38

🍷🍷🍷🍷🍷 Meunier 2016 Rating 93 To 2023 $28
Over the Shoulder Pinot Grigio 2016 Rating 92 To 2020 $23 NG ☻
Local Vineyard Series Willowlake Vineyard Yarra Valley Sauvignon 2015
Rating 91 To 2017 $33
Local Vineyard Series Murrummong Vineyard Yarra Valley Arneis 2016
Rating 91 To 2020 $28 NG
Over the Shoulder Pinot Noir 2016 Rating 91 To 2020 $23 NG ☻
Local Vineyard Series Hazeldene Vineyard Yarra Valley Pinot Gris 2016
Rating 90 To 2027 $32
Local Vineyard Series Blanc de Blancs 2012 Rating 90 To 2018 $42 TS

Occam's Razor | Lo Stesso   ★★★★

c/- Jasper Hill, Drummonds Lane, Heathcote, Vic 3523 **Region** Heathcote
T (03) 5433 2528 **www.**jasperhill.com.au **Open** By appt
Winemaker Emily McNally **Est.** 2001 **Dozens** 300 **Vyds** 2.5ha

Emily McNally (née Laughton) decided to follow in her parents' footsteps after first seeing the world and having a range of casual jobs. Having grown up at Jasper Hill, winemaking was far from strange, but she decided to find her own way, buying the grapes from a small vineyard owned by Jasper Hill employee Andrew Conforti and his wife Melissa. She then made the wine 'with guidance and inspiration from my father'. The name comes from William of Ockham (1285–1349), also spelt Occam, a theologian and philosopher responsible for many sayings, including that appearing on the back label of the wine: 'what can be done with fewer is done in vain with more'. Lo Stesso is made by Emily and friend Georgia Roberts, who purchase 2.5 tonnes of fiano from a vineyard in Heathcote, making the wine at Jasper Hill. Exports to the UK, the US, Canada and Singapore.

🍷🍷🍷🍷🍷 Lo Stesso Heathcote Fiano 2015 Bright straw-green; the distinctly fresher flavours are simply the outcome of growing season and vintage conditions. The core of the style remains unchanged – the site and vinification are the same in all four vintages. Screwcap. 13% alc. **Rating** 93 **To** 2025 $30
Lo Stesso Heathcote Fiano 2013 The colour of this is little changed from that of the '15; in the mouth the wine has excellent drive and the citrus and pear notes that give the variety its attitude. It also underlines the longevity we can expect. Cork. 13% alc. **Rating** 93 **To** 2023 $30
Lo Stesso Heathcote Fiano 2016 Pale straw-green; fiano is likely to increase its foothold in Australia, and the four vintages of Lo Stesso are full of interest. In white wine terms this is full-bodied and well balanced, with honeyed nuances to the stone fruit and pear flavours. Screwcap. 13.5% alc. **Rating** 92 **To** 2026 $30
Lo Stesso Heathcote Fiano 2014 The cork gods at work. This has more colour development than the '13, the acid more apparent due to the slight flattening of the fruit profile – often called scalping. It's still got its birthmark, but simply drink up. 12.5% alc. **Rating** 90 **To** 2018 $30
Occam's Razor Heathcote Shiraz 2015 From a single vineyard south of Heathcote on granite-derived soils. It is powerful, and exceedingly savoury, with drying tannins adding to the impression. How these characters come from such ripe shiraz I simply don't know. Cork. 15% alc. **Rating** 90 **To** 2025 $46

Oceans Estate   ★★★★

290 Courtney Road, Karridale, WA 6288 (postal) **Region** Margaret River
T 0419 916 359 **www.**tomasiwines.com.au **Open** Not
Winemaker Skigh McManus **Est.** 1999 **Dozens** 1500 **Vyds** 6.4ha

Oceans Estate was purchased by the Tomasi family (headed by Frank and Attilia) in 1995, and has 4ha of sauvignon blanc, 1ha each of pinot noir and merlot and 0.4ha of semillon. The wines are made onsite.

ŶŶŶŶŶ Tomasi Margaret River Merlot 2015 Vivid crimson-purple hue. Margaret River strikes again. For my part, merlot should be a blend of red and black currant fruits with savoury, yet warm, tannins. It shouldn't be driven by plum (which I see in the shiraz and pinot spectrums), but should be medium-bodied. Screwcap. 13.5% alc. **Rating** 94 **To** 2025 $30 ✪

Ochota Barrels   ★★★★★

Merchants Road, Basket Range, SA 5138 **Region** Adelaide Hills
T 0400 798 818 **www.**ochotabarrels.com **Open** Not
Winemaker Taras Ochota **Est.** 2008 **Dozens** 900 **Vyds** 0.5ha
Taras Ochota has had an incredibly varied career as a winemaker after completing his oenology degree at Adelaide University. He has not only made wine for top Australian producers, but has had a Flying Winemaker role in many parts of the world, most recently as consultant winemaker for one of Sweden's largest wine-importing companies, working on Italian wines from Puglia and Sicily made specifically for Oenoforos. Wife Amber has accompanied him to many places, working in a multiplicity of technical and marketing roles. Exports to the UK, the US, Canada, Denmark, Norway and Japan.

ŶŶŶŶŶ The Slint Vineyard Chardonnay 2015 An exceptionally good chardonnay, walking on the cliff edge with its alcohol, but doing so with nonchalance. It has a diamond cut to its dazzling mouthfeel, grapefruit and white peach both adding more than fruit flavours to the structure and texture; oak has been an important transport vehicle, but no more than that. Screwcap. 12.4% alc. **Rating** 97 **To** 2025 $40 ✪

ŶŶŶŶŶ The Fugazi Vineyard Grenache 2016 Unadulterated. There's a concentration of flavour, not extraction, of red tangy-tart fruit, Mediterranean herbs and a savoury overlay of cured meats. It pulsates with energy. A seamless line of fine tannins and acidity flow right through the medium-bodied palate. Cork. 12.8% alc. **Rating** 96 **To** 2026 $40 JF ✪

Weird Berries in the Woods Gewurztraminer 2016 As the beautiful variety gewurztraminer slips further into the uncool zone, it is difficult to find outstanding examples. The swooning aromatics of the variety – lychees, musk, roses, preserved ginger and Turkish Delight – are subtly composed on a palate alive with bright acidity. Just gorgeous. Screwcap. 12.2% alc. **Rating** 95 **To** 2025 $35 JF ✪

5VOV Chardonnay 2016 A classy, moreish wine dazzling with flavour yet with a tight profile. The natural acidity shoots its arrow through the middle of a frame filled with lemon curd, grilled nuts and ginger spice. Complex, heady and beguiling. Cork. 12.3% alc. **Rating** 95 **To** 2022 $60 JF

I am the Owl Syrah 2016 Wow. What a wine – it's refined, yet has a ball of energy to it. A heady fragrance of florals and fruit, and smells of an Italian deli full of smoked meats. Medium-bodied, delightfully savoury, with lacy tannins and raspberry sorbet acidity. Cork. 12.7% alc. **Rating** 95 **To** 2028 $40 JF

Surfer Rosa McLaren Vale Garnacha 2016 Sounds cool. Surfer Rosa: a person or perhaps more likely a reference to an album from alternative band The Pixies. Well this rosado/rose rocks: bone dry, textural, savoury, jamon and spice, crunchy acidity and red-fruited. 12% alc. **Rating** 95 **To** 2020 $25 JF ✪

The Fugazi Vineyard Grenache 2015 Happily, everything has worked with this wine: its colour is light but bright, red berries and satsuma plum flavours feeding off the spidery strains of tannins. Screwcap. 13.8% alc. **Rating** 95 **To** 2024 $40

The Green Room Grenache Syrah 2016 92%/8%. This is the finely tuned wine to wind down with after a hard day – or any day. It promises so much and delivers, from its heady fragrance to its supple savoury palate. Screwcap. 12.2% alc. **Rating** 95 **To** 2021 $35 JF ✪

A Forest Pinot Noir 2016 Rating 94 To 2023 $40 JF
The Price of Silence Gamay 2016 Rating 94 To 2021 $40 JF
Texture Like a Sun Caster Red 2016 Rating 94 To 2022 $55 JF

🍷🍷🍷🍷🍷 Impeccable Disorder Pinot Noir 2016 Rating 93 To 2021 $80 JF
Go with the Flow Mataro 2016 Rating 93 To 2026 $80 JF
Kids of the Black Hole Riesling 2016 Rating 92 To 2026 $35 JF
A Sense of Compression Grenache 2015 Rating 92 To 2023 $80
A Forest Pinot Noir 2015 Rating 91 To 2022 $40

Old Oval Estate ★★★★

18 Sand Road, McLaren Vale, SA 5171 **Region** McLaren Vale
T (08) 8323 9100 **www**.oldovalestate.com.au **Open** Fri–Sun 11–5
Winemaker Phil Christiansen, Matt Wenk **Est.** 1998 **Dozens** 1000 **Vyds** 6ha
Joan Rowley purchased an 8ha allotment in the heart of McLaren Vale, where she built a new family home for herself and her three children. Ben Paxton (Paxton Wines) was working at Hardys at the time, and arranged a 10-year grape supply contract if she were to plant vines on the property. When the contract came to an end in 2007, Joan recruited local winemaker Phil Christiensen to make the wines. Joan had established the gardens and grounds at the Old Oval Estate for a weddings/functions business, with sales of the wines. Daughter Patrisse Caddle (with a bed & breakfast in McLaren Vale) assists with the marketing and strategy of Old Oval. Son Cameron has purchased a vineyard in Whiting's Road to contribute to the supply of grapes, and yet another daughter, Amanda, works in the cellar door on weekends, and does the bookkeeping. Grandchildren are all already in Joan's sights to work at the cellar door while they undertake their university studies.

🍷🍷🍷🍷🍷 **Fork in the Road Adelaide Hills Sauvignon Blanc 2015** No frills apparent on the bouquet or palate, but this has served to allow the very attractive lychee and gooseberry tropical notes, cut grass and snow pea on the opposite side of the flavour wheel to flower. Screwcap. 12.5% alc. **Rating** 91 **To** 2018 $20 ✪
Fork in the Road McLaren Vale Shiraz 2014 Made in collaboration with Phil Christiansen (the '14 that appeared in the *Wine Companion* 2017 was made in conjunction with Matt Wenk). A rich, full-bodied, bold shiraz that could only have come from McLaren Vale. Screwcap. 14.6% alc. **Rating** 91 **To** 2029 $20 ✪

Old Plains ★★★☆

71 High Street, Grange, SA 5023 (postal) **Region** Adelaide Plains
T 0407 605 601 **www**.oldplains.com **Open** Not
Winemaker Domenic Torzi, Tim Freeland **Est.** 2003 **Dozens** 4000 **Vyds** 14ha
Old Plains is a partnership between Tim Freeland and Domenic Torzi, who have acquired small parcels of old vine shiraz (3ha), grenache (1ha) and cabernet sauvignon (4ha) in the Adelaide Plains region. A portion of the wines, sold under the Old Plains and Longhop labels, is exported to the US, Denmark, Hong Kong, Singapore and China.

🍷🍷🍷🍷🍷 **Power of One Old Vine Adelaide Plains Shiraz 2014** From 50yo vines, the oldest in the region, hand-picked, destemmed, whole berries open-fermented with cultured yeast, 7 days on skins, matured in French oak (25% new) for 22 months. A huge wine, even beyond the normal max of full-bodied, yet there is nothing unusual in the vinification, leaving you to wonder if the 14.5% alcohol might be significantly higher than stated (there is an allowable margin of 1.5%, so the wine could legally be 16%). A good wine for those seeking maximum flavour. Screwcap. **Rating** 91 **To** 2034 $35

🍷🍷🍷🍷 **Longhop Adelaide Hills Pinot Gris 2016** Rating 89 To 2017 $18 ✪

Olivers Taranga Vineyards ★★★★★

246 Seaview Road, McLaren Vale, SA 5171 **Region** McLaren Vale
T (08) 8323 8498 **www**.oliverstaranga.com **Open** 7 days 10–4
Winemaker Corrina Wright **Est.** 1841 **Dozens** 8000 **Vyds** 85.42ha
William and Elizabeth Oliver arrived from Scotland in 1839 to settle at McLaren Vale. Six
generations later, members of the family are still living on the Whitehill and Taranga farms. The
Taranga property has 15 varieties planted (the lion's share to shiraz and cabernet sauvignon,
with lesser quantities of chardonnay, chenin blanc, durif, fiano, grenache, mataro, merlot, petit
verdot, sagrantino, semillon, tempranillo, viognier and white frontignac). Corrina Wright (the
Oliver family's first winemaker) makes the wines and in 2011 the family celebrated 170 years
of grapegrowing. Exports to Canada, Hong Kong and China.

♀♀♀♀♀ **Corrina's McLaren Vale Shiraz Cabernet Sauvignon 2014** Unusually,
co-fermented (normally shiraz ripens before cabernet), but some adroit picking
decisions resulted in a most attractive wine that has the best of both varietal
worlds, and a sense of place to boot. The colour is superb, the melange of red,
purple and black fruits putting the wine high on the hedonic scale. Screwcap.
14% alc. **Rating** 95 **To** 2034 $32 ✪
McLaren Vale Shiraz 2014 From vines 7–70yo. Shouts McLaren Vale from the
rooftops as black fruits and black chocolate dance around the medium to full-
bodied palate, tannins and a swish of oak relegated to observer status. A unique
regional style in world terms, its best is stretching out years ahead. Screwcap.
14.5% alc. **Rating** 94 **To** 2034 $30 ✪

♀♀♀♀♀ **McLaren Vale Fiano 2016 Rating** 93 **To** 2020 $25 ✪
Corrina's Shiraz Cabernet Sauvignon 2015 Rating 93 $32 PR
McLaren Vale Shiraz 2015 Rating 92 $30 PR
McLaren Vale Grenache 2015 Rating 91 $30 PR
DJ Reserve McLaren Vale Cabernet Sauvignon 2013 Rating 91 $55 PR
Small Batch McLaren Vale Vermentino 2016 Rating 90 **To** 2017 $25
Chica McLaren Vale Mencia Rose 2016 Rating 90 **To** 2019 $25 PR

Onannon ★★★★★

PO Box 190, Flinders, Vic 3929 **Region** Mornington Peninsula
T 0409 698 111 **www**.onannon.com.au **Open** Not
Winemaker Sam Middleton, Kaspar Hermann, Will Byron **Est.** 2008 **Dozens** 1450
Vyds 3ha
Sam Middleton, Kaspar Hermann and Will Byron have donated the last two or three letters
of their surnames to come up with Onannon. They have many things in common, not the
least working vintages at Coldstream Hills, Will for six years, Sam for two (before ultimately
returning to the family's winery, Mount Mary) and Kaspar for one. Since then they have
bounced between vintages in Burgundy and Australia. Strictly speaking, I should disqualify
myself from making any comment about them or their wine, but you would have to go a
long way to find three more open-hearted and utterly committed winemakers; the world is
their oyster, their ambitions unlimited. They lease and manage a Red Hill vineyard with 3ha
of pinot noir. Exports to the UK.

♀♀♀♀♀ **Single Vineyard Mornington Peninsula Pinot Noir 2016** It's exquisitely
tuned with a core of tangy-tart cherry fruit, judicious use of whole bunches and
oak, really earthy damp autumn leaves and wood spices. Sapid with shapely, raw
silk tannins and with a denser structure than the Gippsland single vineyard wine.
Screwcap. 14% alc. **Rating** 96 **To** 2028 $75 JF ✪
Single Vineyard Gippsland Pinot Noir 2016 50 dozen made. It's a
shimmering bright garnet. A core of beautiful ripe fruit, subtle fine tannins,
refreshing acidity and a savoury overlay keeps this in the moreish spectrum.
Screwcap. 13.8% alc. **Rating** 96 **To** 2028 $75 JF ✪
Mornington Peninsula Chardonnay 2016 There's flavour, texture and
length jam-packed into this. Oak adds spice, depth and some structure, a mere

component though; the stone fruit is laced with citrussy notes and spice. Nothing else to add. Just drink it. Screwcap. 13.5% alc. **Rating** 95 **To** 2025 $41 JF
Mornington Peninsula Pinot Noir 2016 From the moment the fragrance of wild strawberries, spiced black cherries and warm earth hits, you'll swoon. This has all the plushness, ripe tannins and structure typical of the region. It is fuller bodied but far from heavy, and has beautiful composure. Screwcap. 13.8% alc. **Rating** 95 **To** 2026 $41 JF
Gippsland Pinot Noir 2016 Pale garnet with a lithe profile and restrained style; barely medium-bodied but the tannins are fine. Crisp acidity, sweet-spicy cherries and plums with a hint of eucalypt. Screwcap. 13.6% alc. **Rating** 94 **To** 2024 $41 JF

🍷🍷🍷🍷🍷 Yarra Valley Rose 2016 **Rating** 93 **To** 2020 $27 JF ✪

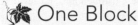

One Block ★★★★★

Nyora Road, Mt Toolebewong, Vic 3777 **Region** Yarra Valley
T 0419 186 888 **www**.oneblock.com.au **Open** By appt
Winemaker Jayden Ong **Est.** 2010 **Dozens** 1200 **Vyds** 5ha

Jayden Ong, a first-generation Eurasian-Australian, was infected by the wine virus working at the Melbourne Wine Room from 2000–06, and has moved with bewildering speed across all facets of the wine industry since then. Wedging in vintages at Curly Flat ('06), Moorooduc Estate ('07) and Allies/Garagiste ('08–'09) while completing the CSU oenology course degree and (in a throwaway line) opened Cumulus Inc, a restaurant and bar in Melbourne, with superstar chef Andrew McConnell and business partners; he continues to mentor the wine team at both venues. Apart from an annual pilgrimage to France to further his grapegrowing and winemaking experience, he went to Italy in '06 and '12, Germany in '10, Spain in '11 and '13, and California in '14. He founded One Block in '10 with the philosophy of making single vineyard wines 'from quality individual vineyard sites where the variety grown suits the site', making 100 dozen of his first love, chardonnay, in '10. In '15 he and partner Morgan Ong purchased a small property and home at Mt Toolebewong, 700m above sea level in the Yarra Valley. They immediately began biological site preparation for a close-planted vineyard with three new clones of chardonnay. He also leases the dry-grown Chestnut Hill vineyard and winery at Mt Burnett, and has begun conversion of the vineyard to organic and biological farming methods. He doesn't intend to slow down, with all sorts of projects in mind for the coming years. A star in the making. Exports to the US.

🍷🍷🍷🍷🍷 **Merricks Mornington Peninsula Pinot Gris 2015** Hand-picked and sorted, whole-bunch pressed, wild-yeast fermented in used French barriques, matured for 7 months on lees (no stirring). The funky bouquet is interesting, the layered palate even more so. It has nashi pear, apple and stone fruit held in a silvery screen of lemony acidity. Amazingly, there is no colour development at 21 months old. This is a very distinguished pinot gris. Screwcap. 13% alc. **Rating** 96 **To** 2025 $28 ✪
La Maison de Ong The Hermit Yarra Valley Syrah 2013 Hand-picked and twice-sorted, 40% whole bunches, the remainder whole berries, open-fermented with wild yeast, 31 days on skins, matured for 14 months in French puncheons (30% new), gold medal Yarra Valley Wine Show '15. Excellent depth to the black cherry, blackberry and spice fruits adorned with fine, ripe tannins. An argument for keeping it simple? Screwcap. 13% alc. **Rating** 95 **To** 2028 $48
The Quarry Yarra Valley Chardonnay 2014 This is a very good chardonnay from a very good chardonnay vintage in the Yarra Valley, fully deserving its silver medal at the Yarra Valley Wine Show '16. The nutty, complex bouquet is followed by an intense, linear palate with white peach and grapefruit sharing the flavour honours 50/50. Screwcap. 13% alc. **Rating** 94 **To** 2024 $33

🍷🍷🍷🍷🍷 Glory Yarra Valley Shiraz 2014 **Rating** 93 **To** 2025 $38
Yellingbo Yarra Valley Shiraz 2014 **Rating** 92 **To** 2024 $38
La Maison de Ong Dark Moon Syrah 2015 **Rating** 90 **To** 2035 $48

Oparina Wines ★★★★

126 Cameron Road, Padthaway, SA 5271 **Region** Padthaway
T 0448 966 553 **www**.oparinawines.com.au **Open** Not
Winemaker Phil Brown, Sue Bell **Est.** 1997 **Dozens** 500 **Vyds** 32ha
Oparina is the venture of Phil and Debbie Brown (along with father Terry and the three third-generation Brown children). Phil grew up in the Padthaway region on the family farm, moving to the Barossa Valley to first study and then teach agriculture. He returned to the family farm (with newly planted vineyards) in 1998, simultaneously enrolling in and completing an oenology degree. The majority of the grapes are sold, shiraz and cabernet sauvignon finding their way into top-tier wines such as Penfolds Bin 389, Bin 707 and St Henri. Family and community commitments limited the amount of time he could devote to winemaking, and in '14 Sue Bell of Bellwether Wines was contracted to make the wines, with input from Phil. The range has already been increased with a Rose and Methode Champenoise, and further vineyard plantings were made in '16 with small blocks of less traditional varieties.

ŸŸŸŸŸ **Padthaway Cab/Shiraz 2014** A 60/40% blend, wild-yeast fermented, basket-pressed, matured in new French oak for 18 months. Good colour; richly fruited, with blackberry, blackcurrant and a whisper of dark chocolate, the tannins soft but persistent. Screwcap. 14% alc. **Rating** 93 **To** 2029 $35
Padthaway Chardonnay 2015 Hand-picked, basket-pressed, wild-yeast fermented in French oak. Light straw-green; fresh and lively, with the fruit flavours in a grapefruit/melon spectrum, the oak subtle and well integrated; good finish and aftertaste. Screwcap. 12.8% alc. **Rating** 91 **To** 2022 $28
Padthaway Shiraz 2006 Lots of toasty vanillan oak doesn't hide the plum and blackberry fruit that is remarkably fresh for its age and, above all else, its alcohol. This didn't worry the judges at the Limestone Coast Wine Show '15, where it won a silver medal in the museum class. Screwcap. 15.9% alc. **Rating** 91 **To** 2026 $30

Orange Mountain Wines ★★★★☆

10 Radnedge Lane, Orange, NSW 2800 **Region** Orange
T (02) 6365 2626 **www**.orangemountain.com.au **Open** Wed–Fri 9–3, w'ends 9–5
Winemaker Terry Dolle **Est.** 1997 **Dozens** 2000 **Vyds** 1ha
Having established the business back in 1997, Terry Dolle made the decision to sell the Manildra vineyard in 2009. He now makes wine from small parcels of hand-picked fruit, using an old basket press and barrel maturation. These are in principle all single vineyard wines reflecting the terroir of Orange. Exports to China.

ŸŸŸŸŸ **Viognier 2015** Orange Mountain has a solid track record with this hedonistic grape variety and this wine is no exception. Optimally ripe, notes of apricot, orange blossom and vanilla pod oak are given an icing of ginger spice. The palate is appropriately viscous, with a delicate chew. The flavours sapid and long, the acidity just fresh enough. Screwcap. 14% alc. **Rating** 95 $35 **To** 2018 NG ✪

ŸŸŸŸŸ **Mountain Ice Viognier 2016 Rating** 93 **To** 2023 $25 NG ✪
1397 Shiraz Viognier 2014 Rating 92 **To** 2023 $42 NG
Sauvignon Blanc 2016 Rating 90 $22 **To** 2018 NG

Oranje Tractor ★★★★☆

198 Link Road, Albany, WA 6330 **Region** Albany
T (08) 9842 5175 **www**.oranjetractor.com **Open** Sun 11–5 or by appt
Winemaker Rob Diletti **Est.** 1998 **Dozens** 1000 **Vyds** 2.9ha
The name celebrates the 1964 vintage orange-coloured Fiat tractor acquired when Murray Gomm and Pamela Lincoln began the establishment of the vineyard. Murray was born next door, but moved to Perth to work in physical education and health promotion. Here he met nutritionist Pamela, who completed the wine science degree at CSU in 2000, before being

awarded a Churchill Fellowship to study organic grape and wine production in the US and Europe. When the partners established their vineyard, they went down the organic path.

ŸŸŸŸŸ Aged Release Albany Riesling 2005 Gleaming straw-green; first tasted Jan '07, then Dec '08, now Feb '17 – each time it has offered more. Now at its peak, with vibrant citrus and green pineapple flavours backed by crisp acidity. It will age gracefully for another decade. Screwcap. 12.5% alc. **Rating** 95 **To** 2027 $45

Orlando ★★★★☆

Barossa Valley Way, Rowland Flat, SA 5352 **Region** Barossa Valley
T (08) 8521 3111 **www**.pernod-ricard-winemakers.com **Open** Not
Winemaker Ben Bryant **Est.** 1847 **Dozens** NFP **Vyds** 1000ha
Orlando is the parent who has been divorced by its child, Jacob's Creek (see separate entry). While Orlando is 170 years old, Jacob's Creek is little more than 40 years old. For what are doubtless sound marketing reasons, Orlando aided and abetted the divorce, but the average consumer is unlikely to understand the logic, and – if truth be known – will care about it even less. The vineyard holding is for all brands (notably Jacob's Creek) and for all regions across SA, Vic and NSW; it will likely be less in coming years.

ŸŸŸŸŸ Jacaranda Ridge Coonawarra Cabernet Sauvignon 2012 It's no wallflower: its layers of flavour and concentration demand attention. Fresh blackberries and cassis essence with red currants mingle with licorice, cloves and choc-mint. Structured, mouthfilling, and with a thrust of bold tannins. Certainly a ripe style, and well packaged. Screwcap. 15.1% alc. **Rating** 95 **To** 2032 $110 JF

ŸŸŸŸŸ St Helga Eden Valley Riesling 2016 Rating 93 **To** 2027 $20 JF **⊘**
Lawson's Padthaway Shiraz 2012 Rating 93 **To** 2032 $65 JF
St Hilary Adelaide Hills Chardonnay 2016 Rating 91 **To** 2021 $22 JF **⊘**

Ottelia ★★★★

2280 V&A Lane, Coonawarra, SA 5263 **Region** Coonawarra
T 0409 836 298 **www**.ottelia.com.au **Open** Thurs–Mon 10–4
Winemaker John Innes **Est.** 2001 **Dozens** 5000 **Vyds** 9ha
John and Melissa Innes moved to Coonawarra intending, in John's words, to 'stay a little while'. The first sign of a change of heart was the purchase of a property ringed by red gums, and with a natural wetland dotted with *Ottelia ovalifolia*, a native water lily. They still live in the house they built there, John having worked as winemaker at Rymill Coonawarra while Melissa established a restaurant. After 20 years at Rymill, John left to focus on consultancy work throughout the Limestone Coast, and to establish and run Ottelia.

ŸŸŸŸŸ Wrattonbully Merlot 2014 The key aspect to this wine is the newly available Q47 clone. Notwithstanding the young vines, the wine has presence and excellent varietal expression, reflected in dark berry fruit flavours framed by perfectly pitched tannins. In coming vintages one hopes all the wine will be matured in French oak. Screwcap. 13.6% alc. **Rating** 92 **To** 2024 $27
Coonawarra Cabernet Sauvignon 2013 An elegant, light to medium-bodied Coonawarra cabernet with a fragrant and expressive bouquet with predominantly red fruits (cherry uppermost) and an unexpected waft of dark chocolate. Cherry, cassis and a sprig of dried herbs join on the palate alongside French oak and fine tannins. Screwcap. 13.6% alc. **Rating** 92 **To** 2028 $32
Mount Gambier Riesling 2016 The flinty minerality is no surprise given the rocky, lunar landscape of the Mount Gambier soil. A word of warning: the acidity of this wine is 9.7g/l, the residual sugar of 4.8g/l lost in the wash. I am acid tolerant, so don't have any issue with the wine. Screwcap. 11.7% alc. **Rating** 91 **To** 2031 $22 **⊘**

ŸŸŸŸ Limestone Coast Pinot Gris 2016 Rating 89 **To** 2018 $22
Mount Gambier Pinot Noir 2015 Rating 89 **To** 2018 $38

Out of Step   ★★★★★

6 McKenzie Avenue, Healesville, Vic 3777 (postal) **Region** Yarra Valley
T 0419 681 577 **www.**outofstepwineco.com **Open** Not
Winemaker David Chatfield, Nathan Reeves **Est.** 2012 **Dozens** 1000
Out of Step is the micro virtual winery of David Chatfield and Nathan Reeves. At the time
of printing Nathan is in Tasmania on a sabbatical from the business, while David continues
to work on the label as well as helping to look after the vineyards at Oakridge. Along the
way they have variously chalked up experience at Stella Bella (Margaret River), Lusatia Park
Vineyard, Sticks (Yarra Valley) and Vinify (California). Their initial foray with a Sauvignon
Blanc sourced from Lusatia Park was spectacular; they also now make Sauvignon Blanc from
the acclaimed Willowlake Vineyard (Yarra Valley), have a Chardonnay from Denton View Hill
Vineyard (Yarra Valley) and a Nebbiolo from the Malakoff Vineyard in the Pyrenees.

ΨΨΨΨΨ **Willowlake Vineyard Yarra Valley Sauvignon Blanc 2016** This really has
    echoes of the Loire Valley's Didier Dageneau: unashamedly opulent and complex,
    with a washing basket packed with fruits of every shape and description held
    together by bright, citrussy acidity and a savoury note poking its nose through just
    to help the complexity flag fly. Another universe away from sauvignon blanc from
    Margaret River or Marlborough. Screwcap. 13.5% alc. **Rating** 96 **To** 2018 $28 ✪
    Lusatia Park D Block Yarra Valley Sauvignon Blanc 2016 100% wild-yeast
    fermented whole bunches, 70% in used oak, 30% in tank. Significant colour
    development, but not an issue, just a fact. The bouquet is complex, gently smoky,
    but the wine comes thundering through on the intense, layered palate with cut
    grass, green capsicum, Meyer lemon and gooseberry fruit, the acidity breathing life
    into the wine from start to finish. Screwcap. 13% alc. **Rating** 95 **To** 2018 $28
    Denton View Hill Yarra Valley Chardonnay 2016 The Denton vineyard is a
    unicorn: a meagre granitic outcrop amid the Yarra's loamy soils, boasting a diversity
    of chardonnay clones. Unusually, at least among the 'less is more' vanguard, the
    wine underwent full malolactic conversion. Extensive use of the lees has allowed
    this to impart a curdy, billowy softness, rather than the oft-spoken 'butter'. This
    confers a balanced tension to the many nuances of stone jittering along the wine's
    stony, slatey carapace. Screwcap. 13.5% alc. **Rating** 95 **To** 2026 $33 NG ✪
    Lusatia Park Vineyard Margin Walker 2015 'This is not a wine about variety.
    This is a wine about a place … and a winemaking ethos.' A single barrique made.
    Has the resplendent generosity and complexity that winemaker David Chatfield so
    effortlessly produces; he is able to lift the wine onto another plane altogether yet
    not give any indication of over-oaking, over-extracting or, for that matter, over-
    anything. Screwcap. 13% alc. **Rating** 95 **To** 2018 $50

ΨΨΨΨΨ **Malakoff Estate Vineyard Pyrenees Nebbiolo 2015** Rating 91 **To** 2029 $33
    Daytime Red 2015 Rating 90 **To** 2017 $26

Palmer Wines   ★★★★★

1271 Caves Road, Dunsborough, WA 6281 **Region** Margaret River
T (08) 9756 7024 **www.**palmerwines.com.au **Open** 7 days 10–5
Winemaker Mark Warren, Bruce Jukes **Est.** 1977 **Dozens** 6000 **Vyds** 51.39ha
Steve and Helen Palmer have mature plantings of cabernet sauvignon, sauvignon blanc, shiraz,
merlot, chardonnay and semillon, with smaller amounts of malbec and cabernet franc. Recent
vintages have had major success in WA and national wine shows. Exports to Indonesia, Hong
Kong and China.

ΨΨΨΨΨ **Purebred by Clive Otto Chardonnay 2015** This refuses to be pigeon-holed,
    for it is radically richer than the '16, and it's not just a question of time in bottle.
    That said, it has magnificent length and drive stemming from a minerally, carefully
    detailed palate, the extra level of alcohol a circuit breaker. Screwcap. 13.3% alc.
    Rating 96 **To** 2025
    Purebred by Bruce Dukes Cabernet Merlot 2014 That the quality and
    complexity of the wine is flawless should surprise no one. It's on the full side of

medium-bodied, ripe tannins and French oak sewn through the rich fruit fabric, glistening with cassis and splashes of bay leaf. Screwcap. 14% alc. **Rating** 96 To 2039

Purebred by Clive Otto Sauvignon Blanc Semillon 2016 A 50/50% blend fermented in French oak (30% new), matured for 10 months. A totally delicious – and seriously good – mouthwatering wine, the varietal fruits fused together, with citrus and snow pea flavours that momentarily slide behind the barrel-ferment notes before re-emerging on the long finish. Screwcap. 13% alc. **Rating** 95 To 2021

Reserve Sauvignon Blanc Semillon 2015 A very long back label in three sections is notable for the lack of information, the only pearl 'a hint of French oak'. I suppose you can justifiably say the wine speaks for itself, for the fruit flavours are remarkably intense, with passionfruit, pink grapefruit and hints of green pea and oak in the background. Screwcap. 12.9% alc. **Rating** 95 To 2020 $25 ✪

Purebred by Clive Otto Chardonnay 2016 In the restrained and precise style of Clive Otto, in particular the careful use of new oak and modest alcohol. The result is a wine that is pure class, differing from the fully mature vines of the excellent terroir of the Palmer Vineyard; the length is akin to that expected from the Yarra Valley. Screwcap. 12.6% alc. **Rating** 95 To 2026

Purebred by Bruce Dukes Chardonnay 2015 The back label says 'outstanding', but is otherwise identical to Mark Warren's wine, both from Wilyabrup, both excellent. This has finesse, purity and length to its palate, grapefruit balanced by stone fruit, the barrel-ferment oak inputs subtle. Screwcap. 12.8% alc. **Rating** 95 To 2025 $30 ✪

Reserve Margaret River Shiraz 2015 This sings 'anything you can do, I can do better'. The colour is a shade deeper and brighter, the bouquet is more expressive, the palate is juicier and more supple, and quality oak is very much more obvious. It delivers all this from a full-bodied throne, and can be enjoyed now or much, much later. Screwcap. 14.8% alc. **Rating** 95 To 2035

Margaret River Cabernet Sauvignon 2015 Good colour; the wine is only medium-bodied, but has all the autocratic attitude of thoroughbred cabernet. There's blackcurrant (rather than cassis), dried herbs and bay leaf, black olive and a hint of earth. French oak is a pure support act, tannins thumping the big bass drum on the finish. Screwcap. 14.3% alc. **Rating** 95 To 2033

Margaret River Reserve Cabernets The Grandee 2015 Cabernet sauvignon, merlot, malbec and cabernet franc. Well named, for this Bordeaux blend has all the flags of Margaret River flexing at the top of the mast. It is full-bodied, with a luscious array of cassis fruits held within a framework of tannins and French oak. It will be very long-lived, with so much to feed on under the security of its screwcap. Screwcap. 14.6% alc. **Rating** 95 To 2040

Margaret River Cabernet Franc Merlot 2015 Even in the Margaret River (where it does best), cabernet franc is a problematic variety, and the blend with merlot makes sense. It is dusty, spicy, briary and tobacco-like, all presented in a light to medium-bodied framework. I like this wine a lot. Screwcap. 14.8% alc. **Rating** 95 To 2023

Purebred by Mark Warren Chardonnay 2015 **Rating** 94 To 2023 $30 ✪
Purebred by Bruce Dukes Shiraz 2015 **Rating** 94 To 2029 $30 ✪
Margaret River Merlot 2015 **Rating** 94 To 2035

♙♙♙♙♙ **Margaret River Malbec 2015** **Rating** 93 To 2035
Krackerjack Bin 4 2014 **Rating** 91 To 2024 $25
Purebred by Clive Otto Shiraz 2015 **Rating** 91 To 2030
Margaret River Shiraz 2015 **Rating** 91 To 2035

Panther's Patch Wines ★★★★

1827 The Escort Way, Borenore, NSW 2800 **Region** Orange
T (02) 6360 1639 **www**.pantherspatch.com.au **Open** By appt
Winemaker Chris Derrez, Lucy Maddox **Est.** 2015 **Dozens** 350 **Vyds** 2.2ha
Hakan and Virginia Holm acquired the 10ha property and its abandoned vineyard in 2009 as a country retirement retreat. Little did they know about the effort required to rehabilitate the vineyard and look after the rest of the property, they confess. 2012 saw the first vintage, and they decided to enter the wine in the Orange Wine Show, where they were awarded a silver medal, each and every successive vintage winning some award. They named the vineyard after the 5-week-old black barb kelpie puppy dropped on their doorstep shortly after they acquired the vineyard. Panther keeps the place clear of rabbits, foxes, cockatoos, etc, and most of the vineyard work is done by Hakan and Virginia (the exception is vintage, when a contractor transports the grapes to the highly experienced Madrez Wine Services).

🍷🍷🍷🍷🍷 **Panther's Vineyard Orange Sauvignon Blanc 2016** While Orange quickly established a reputation for sauvignon blanc 20 years ago, which continues to this day, the flavour and mouthfeel have remained subtly different. Sauvignon blanc often has a hard edge that serves to contrast the fruit. Orange sauvignon blanc moves more softly, the flavours tropical and clearly defined yet gentle. Screwcap. 12.5% alc. **Rating** 94 **To** 2020 $22 ✪

🍷🍷🍷🍷 **Orange Cabernet Sauvignon 2014** **Rating** 93 **To** 2029 $22 ✪

Paracombe Wines ★★★★☆

294b Paracombe Road, Paracombe, SA 5132 **Region** Adelaide Hills
T (08) 8380 5058 **www**.paracombewines.com **Open** By appt
Winemaker Paul Drogemuller, James Barry **Est.** 1983 **Dozens** 13 000 **Vyds** 22.1ha
Paul and Kathy Drogemuller established Paracombe Wines in 1983 in the wake of the devastating Ash Wednesday bushfires. The winery is located high on a plateau at Paracombe, looking out over the Mount Lofty Ranges, and the vineyard is run with minimal irrigation and hand-pruning to keep yields low. The wines are made onsite, with every part of the production process through to distribution handled from there. Exports to Canada, Denmark, Sweden, Indonesia, Singapore, Taiwan, Hong Kong, Malaysia, Japan and China.

🍷🍷🍷🍷🍷 **The Reuben 2013** A traditional Bordeaux blend. And it sure works, reminding one of Graves: ripe, warm and smelling of terracotta, blackcurrant, plum and tobacco, albeit in a riper Australian idiom. Paracombe's signature tannins are again detailed, precise and tightly wound, corseting the fruit and reining in any excess. A delicious, restrained and pointed example of the style. A steal at the price. Screwcap. 14.5% alc. **Rating** 95 **To** 2024 $23 NG ✪

Adelaide Hills Cabernet Sauvignon 2012 Images of pre-Rolland Bordeaux come to mind, when the region produced gravelly, cedary wines of stony roll-in-the-mouth tannins, like ball bearings across the gums massaging currant, cedar and tobacco leaf flavours. Elegance is written all over this. Drinking well now, but will continue to impress. And the price! Screwcap. 14.5% alc. **Rating** 94 **To** 2022 $23 NG ✪

Adelaide Hills Cabernet Franc 2012 Some years ago, hidden beneath a bushel well before Loire Valley expressions of this versatile variety became popular among the sommelier tribes, Paracombe set the standard for sappy, eminently digestible domestic cabernet franc. Varietally pure in every way, with a thread of herb tucked in behind the black and blue fruits, this struts across the mouth as a savoury, mature *bella figura*. Screwcap. 14.5% alc. **Rating** 94 **To** 2020 $27 NG ✪

🍷🍷🍷🍷 **Adelaide Hills Tempranillo 2014** **Rating** 93 **To** 2022 $22 NG ✪
Adelaide Hills Shiraz 2013 **Rating** 92 **To** 2023 $23 NG ✪
Adelaide Hills Shiraz Nebbiolo 2013 **Rating** 92 **To** 2022 $27 NG
Holland Creek Adelaide Hills Riesling 2016 **Rating** 91 **To** 2022 $20 NG ✪
Adelaide Hills Sauvignon Blanc 2016 **Rating** 90 **To** 2019 $21 NG ✪

Adelaide Hills Red Ruby 2016 Rating 90 To 2020 $21 SC ✪
Adelaide Hills Pinot Noir 2014 Rating 90 To 2020 $21 SC ✪
Adelaide Hills Shiraz 2012 Rating 90 To 2022 $23 SC

Paradigm Hill ★★★★★

26 Merricks Road, Merricks, Vic 3916 **Region** Mornington Peninsula
T (03) 5989 9000 **www**.paradigmhill.com.au **Open** W'ends 12–5
Winemaker Dr George Mihaly **Est.** 1999 **Dozens** 1200 **Vyds** 4.2ha
Dr George Mihaly (with a background in medical research, biotechnology and pharmaceutical industries) and wife Ruth (a former chef and caterer) realised a 30-year dream of establishing their own vineyard and winery, abandoning their previous careers to do so. George had all the necessary scientific qualifications, and built on those by making the 2001 Merricks Creek wines, moving to home base at Paradigm Hill in '02, all along receiving guidance and advice from Nat White of Main Ridge Estate. The vineyard, under Ruth's control with advice from Shane Strange, is planted to 2.1ha of pinot noir, 0.9ha of shiraz, 0.82ha of riesling and 0.38ha of pinot gris. Exports to the US, Germany and China.

🍷🍷🍷🍷🍷 **Les Cinq Mornington Peninsula Pinot Noir 2015** Clone 115, wild-yeast fermented, 4 days post-ferment maceration, matured in French oak (33% new) for 18 months. Clear, bright, crimson-purple; a perfumed bouquet of rose petals, spice and red fruits, the pure palate joyously fruity, the texture silky, the structure exemplary. Attention to detail is a common buzz word/phrase these days, and this has it in spades. Screwcap. 12.1% alc. **Rating** 97 **To** 2027 $85 ✪

🍷🍷🍷🍷🍷 **L'ami Sage Mornington Peninsula Pinot Noir 2015** Clones MV6 and 115, 3 days post-ferment maceration, matured in French oak (24% new) for 18 months. Vivid purple-crimson, attesting to the very low yield; a seriously good pinot, full of gorgeous red fruits and no sign of excessive extract. There are some fine oak tannins that simply underwrite the fruit and length of the palate. Screwcap. 12.8% alc. **Rating** 96 **To** 2028 $72 ✪

Mornington Peninsula Pinot Gris 2016 Paradigm Hill was the first to use substantial new French oak to make pinot gris, and hence charge more for its wine than any other Australian producer. Is it worth it? Well, the cost certainly justifies the price, and it's full of strawberry fruit. It has no residual sugar, yet there is an impression of sweetness. I would be inclined to tweak the acidity, but I'm not the maker. Screwcap. 13.7% alc. **Rating** 94 **To** 2023 $59

Transition Mornington Peninsula Rose 2016 Pale puce hue with none of the browning normally associated with barrel ferment; the bouquet is fragrant, the palate a delight. It is bone dry, but insistently fruity, underwritten by crisp acidity. Screwcap. 12.5% alc. **Rating** 94 **To** 2021 $39

Col's Block Mornington Peninsula Shiraz 2015 Full to the brim with spicy, juicy red fruits with savoury charcuterie notes on the finish of the medium-bodied palate. Classy cool climate style. Screwcap. 13.3% alc. **Rating** 94 **To** 2030 $49

🍷🍷🍷🍷🍷 **Mornington Peninsula Riesling 2016** Rating 92 To 2026 $39
Arrivé Mornington Peninsula Riesling 2016 Rating 91 To 2026 $39

Paradise IV ★★★★★

45 Dog Rocks Road, Batesford, Vic 3213 (postal) **Region** Geelong
T (03) 5276 1536 **www**.paradiseivwines.com.au **Open** Not
Winemaker Douglas Neal **Est.** 1988 **Dozens** 800 **Vyds** 3.1ha
The former Moorabool Estate has been renamed Paradise IV for the very good reason that it is the site of the original Paradise IV Vineyard, planted in 1848 by Swiss vigneron Jean-Henri Dardel. It is owned by Ruth and Graham Bonney. The winery has an underground barrel room, and the winemaking turns around wild yeast fermentation, natural mlf, gravity movement of the wine and so forth. Exports to China.

🍷🍷🍷🍷🍷 **J.H. Dardel 2015** Doug Neal has made the most of the '15 vintage, producing what he believes to be the best yet, never to be challenged in the future. It has a brilliant crimson-purple hue, and an exceptionally juicy flavour that centres on the tip of the tongue (very unusual) before moving in a more textured form on to the back-palate and finish. Cool-grown shiraz doesn't come better than this. Screwcap. 13.5% alc. **Rating** 97 **To** 2035 $70 **○**

♥♥♥♥♥ Chaumont 2015 Cabernet sauvignon, shiraz and cabernet franc. Deep colour; a fresh and vibrant bouquet leads into a juicy cassis-dominated medium-bodied palate, tannins lurking behind the fruit throughout. Just when you think you have the wine sorted out, a touch of cedar, then moments later tobacco and dark chocolate, come and go. Screwcap. 13.5% alc. **Rating** 95 **To** 2035 $60

Paringa Estate ★★★★★

44 Paringa Road, Red Hill South, Vic 3937 **Region** Mornington Peninsula
T (03) 5989 2669 **www**.paringaestate.com.au **Open** 7 days 11–5
Winemaker Lindsay McCall **Est.** 1985 **Dozens** 15 000 **Vyds** 24.7ha
Schoolteacher-turned-winemaker Lindsay McCall has shown an absolutely exceptional gift for winemaking across a range of styles, but with immensely complex Pinot Noir and Shiraz leading the way. The wines have an unmatched level of success in the wine shows and competitions Paringa Estate is able to enter, the limitation being the relatively small production of the top wines in the portfolio. His skills are no less evident in contract winemaking for others. Exports to the UK, Canada, Denmark, Ukraine, Singapore, Hong Kong, China and Japan.

♥♥♥♥♥ Estate Pinot Noir 2015 So heady you'll swoon with the blend of exotic spice, pomegranate juice and the usual dark cherries and pips and radicchio bitterness. There's exuberance of fruit on the beautifully weighted palate – medium-bodied, precise tannins and fine acidity to close. Screwcap. 14% alc. **Rating** 96 **To** 2028 $60 JF **○**

The Paringa Single Vineyard Chardonnay 2015 Always a richer style, with ripe stone fruit, creamed honey, smells of chicken stock, gingery and lemony acidity. Fuller-bodied, there's richness, length and layers of flavour, yet counterintuitively, a really tight palate. Screwcap. 13.5% alc. **Rating** 95 **To** 2025 $55 JF

Robinson Vineyard Pinot Noir 2015 For a number of years, Paringa Estate has sourced fruit from Hugh Robinson's meticulous vineyard at Tuerong, and in '14 made the first single vineyard wine. This follow-up is a humdinger. Mid-garnet and awash with dark cherries, damp earth, musk and woodsy spices, with raw silk tannins and plushness on the palate. Screwcap. 13.5% alc. **Rating** 95 **To** 2026 $60 JF

The Paringa Pinot Noir 2014 The lighter colour is deceptive, for it bursts with aromatic life: red cherries, satsuma plums, joss stick, cinnamon quills and menthol. The palate is svelte, with velvety tannins and Angostura bitters on the finish. Ultimately, quite ethereal. Screwcap. 13.5% alc. **Rating** 95 **To** 2026 $90 JF

The Paringa Shiraz 2014 Dark purple-red; not quite as peppery as the Estate. There's more fruit weight to buffer the spice rack of aromas with a touch ferrous. A mix of sweet tangy plums and stewed rhubarb. The French oak barriques, 40% new, add woodsy spices and char, neatly paired into the wine. Full-bodied with a bolt of tannin and plenty to like. Screwcap. 13.5% alc. **Rating** 95 **To** 2028 $80 JF

Peninsula Pinot Noir 2015 100% destemmed fruit fermented in open 2.5t lots, 21 days on skins, matured for 11 months on lees in French barriques. Light, bright and clear crimson-purple. The multifaceted bouquet leads into a succulently fruited cherry and plum palate surrounded by gently briary tannins, the two parts combining synergistically. Likely to be formidably good by '20. Screwcap. 13.5% alc. **Rating** 94 **To** 2025 $29 **○**

Peninsula Shiraz 2015 Contract-grown, co-fermented with 5% viognier; matured for 11 months in used French barriques. The fragrant bouquet has a clear lift from the viognier, the juicy collage of spice, pepper, black fruits and

plum seamlessly joined with fine, but firm, tannins. Screwcap. 14% alc. **Rating** 94
To 2030 $27 ○

ΥΥΥΥΥ **Estate Chardonnay 2015** Rating 93 To 2025 $40 JF
Estate Shiraz 2014 Rating 93 To 2026 $50 JF
Estate Pinot Gris 2016 Rating 92 To 2021 $22 JF ○
Peninsula Chardonnay 2016 Rating 91 To 2022 $27 JF

Parker Coonawarra Estate   ★★★★★

15688 Riddoch Highway, Penola, SA 5263 **Region** Coonawarra
T (08) 8737 3525 **www.**parkercoonawarraestate.com.au **Open** 7 days 10–4
Winemaker Phil Lehmann, Charlie Ormsby **Est.** 1985 **Dozens** 30 000 **Vyds** 20ha
Parker Coonawarra Estate is at the southern end of Coonawarra, on rich terra rossa soil over
limestone. Cabernet sauvignon is the dominant variety (17.45ha), with minor plantings of
merlot and petit verdot. It is now part of WD Wines Pty Ltd, which also owns Hesketh Wine
Company and St John's Road in the Barossa Valley. Production has risen substantially since the
change of ownership. Exports to all major markets.

ΥΥΥΥΥ **First Growth 2013** The best cabernet from the estate's Abbey vineyard and
8% merlot from its Terry block, aged 2 years in 100% new French oak barriques.
An astonishing array of complex flavours – mulberries, cassis, dark choc-mint,
iodine and ferrous earth, but the palate is king. There's depth, detailed, powerful
tannins and a secure place in the ageing stakes. Screwcap. 14% alc. **Rating** 96
To 2038 $110 JF
95 Block 2014 Planted in '95. Comprising 27 rows of cabernet sauvignon and
four of petit verdot, with the latter making up 7% in the blend. Excellent dark
crimson colour, wafts of menthol and dark chocolate sprinkled on blackberry
and plum compote, deep, earthy. Complex, very complete palate, tannins ripe and
plentiful. Screwcap. 14.5% alc. **Rating** 96 To 2034 $65 JF ○
Terra Rossa Shiraz 2015 Really slick, with a core of dark fruit bound by
licorice, eucalypt, choc-mint and inky notes; slips into overdrive to cruise along
a glossy palate with the oak seamlessly integrated. Good tannin structure and a
persistent finish. Screwcap. 14.5% alc. **Rating** 95 To 2030 $34 JF ○
Terra Rossa Cabernet Sauvignon 2015 There is more finesse with Parker
wines of late. This beauty is right up there with its atypical, pleasing aromas of
blackberry and boysenberries, a sprinkle of spice, freshly rolled tobacco, dried mint
and earth. The palate is very neatly contained, textured tannins balanced; a long
finish. Screwcap. 14.5% alc. **Rating** 95 To 2035 $34 JF ○

ΥΥΥΥΥ **Cabernet Sauvignon 2015** Rating 93 To 2027 $24 JF ○
Shiraz 2015 Rating 92 To 2023 $24 JF ○
Terra Rossa Merlot 2015 Rating 92 To 2023 $34 JF
Chardonnay 2016 Rating 90 To 2020 $24 JF

Pasadera Wines   ★★★★

3880 Frankston-Flinders Road, Shoreham, Vic 3916 **Region** Mornington Peninsula
T 0413 602 023 **www.**pasadera.com.au **Open** Not
Winemaker Michael Kyberd **Est.** 2014 **Dozens** 600 **Vyds** 5.2ha
The vineyard was planted in 1990, and for a number of years (and owners) the property
was called The Pines, hence the stylised pine cone on the label. The grapes were sold for
many years, and at various times the vineyard was leased. Then, in early 2014, owners Rusty
and Nancy French decided to cease selling the grapes and take control of the mature, low-
cropping vines, retaining the services of contract winemaker Michael Kyberd. Into the bargain,
Pasadera is also a horse stud, with a number of Arabian thoroughbreds.

ΥΥΥΥΥ **Mornington Peninsula Chardonnay 2014** Built around a core of smoky
solids, pungent and mineral-clad, this generous chardonnay boasts white peach
and hazelnut notes reverberating across a textural medium-bodied palate, plied

deftly with well appointed oak and the tangerine tang of lees. Truffles emerge as the wine billows across the palate. This is definitely more Meursault than Chablis, and there isn't anything wrong with that. Screwcap. 13.5% alc. **Rating** 95 **To** 2022 $65 NG

ŶŶŶŶŶ **Mornington Peninsula Pinot Noir 2014 Rating** 91 **To** 2022 $65 NG

Passel Estate

655 Ellen Brook Road, Cowaramup, WA 6284 **Region** Margaret River
T (08) 9717 6241 **www.**passelestate.com **Open** Fri–Sun 10.30–5 or by appt
Winemaker Bruce Dukes **Est.** 1994 **Dozens** 1500 **Vyds** 6.7ha
Wendy and Barry Stimpson were born in England and South Africa respectively, and during numerous visits to Margaret River over the years fell in love with the region's environment. They made Margaret River their home in 2005, and in '11 purchased the vineyard planted in 1994 to 2.6ha of shiraz and 1.5ha of cabernet sauvignon, 2.6ha of chardonnay established later. Viticulturist Andy Ferreira manages the vineyard year round, with sustainable practices throughout the total of 6.7ha under vine, keeping yields restricted to 6.5–7t/ha. The very talented and highly experienced contract winemaker Bruce Dukes is responsible for the wines. Exports to Singapore.

ŶŶŶŶŶ **Margaret River Shiraz 2015** Matured in French oak (one-third new) for
10 months. There's a lot of high quality French oak stamped on the bouquet and medium-bodied palate, creating both flavour and texture for the plum and savoury black cherry fruit. The finish is long and convincing, and gets it over the oak line. Screwcap. 14.5% alc. **Rating** 95 **To** 2030 $35 ✪
Margaret River Cabernet Sauvignon 2015 Includes 12.5% merlot, blended post-fermentation, matured in French oak (one-third new) for 10 months. Passel Estate has quickly established a distinct house style, with fine-grained tannins derived from both the fruit and the new oak woven through the medium-bodied palate. The bouquet is entirely at one with the palate, blackcurrant/cassis to the fore, elegance derived from the timing of the harvest. Throw in the perfect balance, and say no more. Screwcap. 14% alc. **Rating** 95 **To** 2030 $42

ŶŶŶŶŶ **Margaret River Chardonnay 2015 Rating** 92 **To** 2021 $30

Passing Clouds

30 Roddas Lane, Musk, Vic 3461 **Region** Macedon Ranges
T (03) 5348 5550 **www.**passingclouds.com.au **Open** 7 days 10–5
Winemaker Cameron Leith **Est.** 1974 **Dozens** 4600 **Vyds** 9.8ha
Graeme Leith and son Cameron undertook a monumental vine change when they moved the entire operation that started way back in 1974 in Bendigo to its new location at Musk, near Daylesford. The vines at the original vineyard had been disabled by ongoing drought and all manner of pestilence, and it was no longer feasible to continue the business there. The emphasis has moved to elegant Pinot Noir and Chardonnay, with a foot still in Bendigo courtesy of their friends, the Adams at Riola. Satisfied with his work, Graeme Leith has now left the winemaking in the hands of Cameron, and is using his formidable skills as a writer. Exports to all major markets.

ŶŶŶŶŶ **The Angel Bendigo Cabernet 2015** The cabernet spends 1 year in French oak, 25% new, then a judicious barrel selection before blending and another 4 months to mesh. And it certainly has – this is very fine. The fruit has clarity and brightness, heady spicy aromas, and there's detail on the medium-bodied palate thanks to the beautiful tannin structure. Screwcap. 14% alc. **Rating** 96 **To** 2033 $53 JF
Graeme's Shiraz Cabernet 2015 The varieties are aged separately in French oak (25% new) for 1 year; come blending time, the percentage gave shiraz the edge at 55%. It smells of Bendigo, a fragrance of damson plum, poached blackberries, earthy/eucalypt from the Aussie bush and sarsaparilla. Lots of flavour

on the fuller palate, plump tannins, yet everything in its place. Thoroughly pleasing to drink and a keeper. Screwcap. 14.7% alc. **Rating** 95 **To** 2030 $34 JF ❍

🟡🟡🟡🟡🟡 The Fools on the Hill Pinot Noir 2015 **Rating** 93 **To** 2026 $47 JF
The Fools on the Hill Chardonnay 2015 **Rating** 92 **To** 2022 $47 JF
Macedon Ranges Chardonnay 2016 **Rating** 90 **To** 2021 $29 JF
Bendigo Shiraz 2015 **Rating** 90 **To** 2025 $31 JF

Patrick of Coonawarra ★★★★★

Cnr Ravenswood Lane/Riddoch Highway, Coonawarra, SA 5263 **Region** Coonawarra
T (08) 8737 3687 **www**.patrickofcoonawarra.com.au **Open** 7 days 10–5
Winemaker Luke Tocaciu **Est.** 2004 **Dozens** 5000 **Vyds** 79.5ha
Patrick Tocaciu (who died in 2013) was a district veteran, with prior careers at Heathfield Ridge Winery and Hollick Wines. Wrattonbully plantings (41ha) cover all the major varieties, while the Coonawarra plantings (38.5ha) give rise to the Home Block Cabernet Sauvignon. Patrick of Coonawarra also carries out contract winemaking for others. Son Luke, with a degree in oenology from Adelaide University and vintage experience in Australia and the US, has taken over in the winery.

🟡🟡🟡🟡🟡 Aged Coonawarra Riesling 2012 Don't put this in the cellar, under the stairs or anywhere other than in a glass. It's ready now, and reveals a raft of gorgeous aged characters from lime marmalade on buttered toast to lemon semolina cake. Fine acidity and great length. Screwcap. 10.5% alc. **Rating** 95 **To** 2019 $39 JF
Estate Grown Mount Gambier Pinot Noir 2015 Light, but bright, colour; the savoury/stemmy background to the small red fruits works well; there is no longer any doubt that Mount Gambier, the coolest region in SA, is a force to be reckoned with when it comes to pinot noir. The length and aftertaste are excellent. Screwcap. 12.8% alc. **Rating** 95 **To** 2023 $29 ❍
Estate Wrattonbully Shiraz 2012 Aged in American and French oak (both 40% new) for 20 months. Dark purple-garnet and bursting with black and red fruit, some pepper and wood spice. Full-bodied and richly flavoured with substantial tannins abetted by the oak, but with a freshness and succulence, too. Screwcap. 14% alc. **Rating** 95 **To** 2022 $29 JF ❍
Joanna Wrattonbully Shiraz 2012 Aged in 80% American and 20% French oak, all new, for 20 months, and even with all that coffee-cream and vanillan oak, the Wrattonbully fruit shines through and leads the charge. Very good colour, a melange of dark fruit and spice. Full-bodied, long and with precise tannins. Screwcap. 14% alc. **Rating** 95 **To** 2025 $45 JF
Home Block Cabernet Sauvignon 2012 Matured in new French and American oak for 28 months. Unsurprisingly, there is some colour development; the question with the wine turns on the extravagant use of oak, à la Katnook Odyssey. There's no right or wrong, it's strictly a question of style, one much loved by many Aus consumers. My points are a compromise. Screwcap. 13.8% alc. **Rating** 95 **To** 2027 $45
Estate Grown Fume Blanc 2015 Sauvignon blanc fermented and matured in French puncheons. The bouquet has smoky barrel ferment notes (as it should), the juicy palate focusing on citrus and gooseberry fruits. A very good sauvignon blanc from a region that doesn't often do justice to the variety. Screwcap. 11.5% alc. **Rating** 94 **To** 2019 $25 ❍

🟡🟡🟡🟡🟡 Estate Riesling 2016 **Rating** 92 **To** 2020 $25 JF ❍

Patritti Wines ★★★★★

13–23 Clacton Road, Dover Gardens, SA 5048 **Region** Adelaide
T (08) 8296 8261 **www**.patritti.com.au **Open** Mon–Sat 9–5 (7 days Dec)
Winemaker James Mungall, Ben Heide **Est.** 1926 **Dozens** 190 000 **Vyds** 16ha
A family-owned business offering wines at modest prices, but with impressive vineyard holdings of 10ha of shiraz in Blewitt Springs and 6ha of grenache at Aldinga North. The

surging production points to success in export markets and also to the utilisation of contract-grown as well as estate-grown grapes. Patritti is currently releasing wines of very high quality at enticing prices, and a range of lesser quality wines at unfathomably low prices. The JPB Single Vineyard celebrates the arrival of Giovanni Patritti in Australia in 1925; he sold his wines under the 'John Patritti Brighton' label. Exports to the US and other major markets.

𝟃𝟃𝟃𝟃𝟃 **JPB Single Vineyard Shiraz 2015** From the low-yielding (1.4t/a) estate vineyard at Blewitt Springs, matured for 17 months in new puncheons, 60% American, 40% French. Immaculate cork. The seamless integration of the new oak tells you just how great the quality of the fruit is; blackberry and satsuma plum occupy centre stage, but allow regional dark chocolate to make its mark. One of the unsung heroes of SA shiraz. Cork. 14.5% alc. **Rating** 97 **To** 2055 $60 ✪

𝟃𝟃𝟃𝟃𝟃 **Lot Three Single Vineyard McLaren Vale Shiraz 2015** Hand-picked from the estate Blewitt Springs vineyard, matured for 18 months in French oak (33%). Bright crimson-purple; a full-bodied wine with the same family marks as its JPB sibling; black fruits with a savoury aspect conceivably ex some whole bunches, dark chocolate, profound tannin and oak influences in a seriously great wine. Cork. 14% alc. **Rating** 96 **To** 2050 $35 ✪

Section 181 Single Vineyard McLaren Vale Grenache 2015 From the 6ha of dry-grown grenache already planted when it was purchased by the Patritti family in '60 (Section 181, Branson Rd). McLaren Vale grenache at its imperious best, the fruit with exceptional texture and structure derived from its fine but persistent tannins, oak merely a means, not an end in itself. A 20-year grenache? Absolutely, and then some. Cork. 14.5% alc. **Rating** 96 **To** 2035 $35 ✪

Marion Vineyard Adelaide Grenache Shiraz 2015 From the 110yo vineyard owned by the city of Marion, but leased to Patritti since '06 in recognition of its long association with grapegrowing in the region. A rich, deep-seated mouthful of succulent red and purple fruits sustained by fine, yet firm, tannins. The Rhône Valley would be proud of this. Cork. 14.5% alc. **Rating** 96 **To** 2040 $30 ✪

Old Gate McLaren Vale Shire Shiraz 2015 87.5% from the estate Blewitt Springs vineyard, 12.5% from the Barossa Valley, matured for 4–18 months in 60% American and 40% French puncheons. This is ludicrously good value, a full-bodied wine that will live and prosper for decades. Had it been fined, its finish might have been easier to deal with, but the question would have been did it detract from the sumptuous palate? Cork. 14.5% alc. **Rating** 95 **To** 2045 $20 ✪

Merchant McLaren Vale Shiraz 2015 The screwcap signals a wine for domestic release only. From the estate Blewitt Springs vineyard, the grapes from this 'square block' previously sold to local wineries, mainly crushed and destemmed, some whole bunches, matured for 18 months in American puncheons (56% new). Crimson-purple; vanilla/mocha oak is an integral part of the wine, contrasting with the fresh red and black fruit flavours. Tasting after Patritti's two icon siblings did it no favours. Screwcap. 13.5°alc. **Rating** 94 **To** 2035 $30 ✪

Merchant McLaren Vale Grenache Shiraz Mourvedre 2015 Hand-picked grenache (60%) and shiraz (10%) from Patritti's McLaren Vale vineyards, 10% mataro machine-harvested from the Adelaide Hills, all parcels vinified and matured separately until blending after 15 months in French demi-muids and puncheons (20% new), 70% held in tank, the overall aim fruit intensity, structure and feel without excessive alcohol. It fulfils all of those aims, albeit with a minor question about the alcohol. Screwcap. 15°alc. **Rating** 94 **To** 2030 $30 ✪

𝟃𝟃𝟃𝟃𝟃 **Limited Release Fortified Viognier 2006 Rating** 92 $20 ✪

Paul Conti Wines   ★★★★

529 Wanneroo Road, Woodvale, WA 6026 **Region** Greater Perth
T (08) 9409 9160 **www.paulcontiwines.com.au Open** Mon–Sat 10–5, Sun by appt
Winemaker Paul and Jason Conti **Est.** 1948 **Dozens** 4000 **Vyds** 14ha

Third-generation winemaker Jason Conti has assumed control of winemaking, although father Paul (who succeeded his own father in 1968) remains involved in the business. Over the years Paul challenged and redefined industry perceptions and standards, the challenge for Jason is to achieve the same degree of success in a relentlessly and increasingly competitive market environment, and he is doing just that. Plantings at the Carabooda Vineyard have been expanded with tempranillo, petit verdot and viognier, and pinot noir and chardonnay are purchased from Pemberton. In a further extension, a property at Cowaramup in Margaret River with sauvignon blanc, shiraz, cabernet sauvignon, semillon, muscat and malbec has been aquired. The original 2ha vineyard (shiraz) of the Mariginiup Vineyard remains the cornerstone. Exports to Japan.

ΨΨΨΨΨ **Pemberton Pinot Noir 2015** MV6, hand-picked, 30% whole bunches, wild-yeast fermented, 9 days fermentation including 2 days cold soak, matured in French oak (10% new) for 10 months. Deeply coloured, and (in pinot terms) full-bodied, it is just embarking on what will be a long journey to maturity, when it will garner even more points. Screwcap. 14% alc. **Rating** 93 **To** 2028 $25 ✪

Margaret River Chardonnay 2016 Hand-picked, whole-bunch pressed, 25% fermented and matured in new French oak for 4 months. The varietal definition is not in question; the oak plays a support role for texture and flavour alike, leaving it to white peach, nectarine and melon to do the heavy lifting. Crisp, citrussy acidity freshens and lengthens the finish. An A-grade bargain. Screwcap. 13% alc. **Rating** 92 **To** 2024 $20 ✪

Tuart Block Chenin Blanc 2016 The areas around Perth make many of the best chenin blancs in Australia (some will say this is an oxymoron), and only Coriole stands tall in competition. This has remarkable intensity and fruit freshness; stone and tropical fruits have zesty citrussy acidity to enliven the finish and aftertaste. Screwcap. 12.5% alc. **Rating** 92 **To** 2021 $18 ✪

Tempranillo 2015 From the Blackwood Valley, matured for a short time in used American oak, and incorporating a small amount of malbec. Juicy black cherry and spice flavours are front and centre. A wine that comprehensively over-delivers on its price. Screwcap. 14.5% alc. **Rating** 91 **To** 2023 $18 ✪

Mariginiup Shiraz 2014 Different vinification of the dominant Swan Coastal Mariginiup portion from that of the Miamup Road Vineyard in Margaret River (both estate), resulted in a mix of 30% new American oak and 10% new French oak, the Swan wine pressed direct to the former, the Margaret River to the latter, in each case with used French oak making up the balance. Red cherry and plum fruits have a savoury backdrop, the tannins fine but persistent. Screwcap. 15% alc. **Rating** 90 **To** 2029 $28

Margaret River Cabernet Malbec 2015 A 70/30% blend, open-fermented, matured for 12 months in French oak (25% new). Bright, clear crimson-purple; rich blackcurrant and plum fruit fills the mouth on entry before the line is broken and tannins ex fruit and oak appear on the finish. The price should facilitate cellaring and a consequent smoothing of those tannins. Screwcap. 14% alc. **Rating** 90 **To** 2029 $18 ✪

Paul Morris   ★★★★☆

3 Main Street, Minlaton, SA 5575 (postal) **Region** Clare Valley
T 0427 885 321 **www.paulmorriswines.com.au Open** Not
Winemaker Paul Morris **Est.** 2014 **Dozens** 300
Paul Morris has been in the broader wine business since 2002. Vineyard roles in McLaren Vale and Lyndoch were followed by vintages in the Barossa Valley, Magill and Marlborough, NZ. These periods of hands-on winery work were interspersed with sales and marketing positions, broadening his experience. His main job at the present time is winemaking in the Clare Valley, but he plans to buy/create his own boutique winery if/when finances permit. Paul has plans to expand the range in the future.

ΨΨΨΨΨ **Single Vineyard Adelaide Hills Pinot Noir 2015** This has many good things going for it, not the least its satin mouthfeel, its vibrant red fruits part of the story, as is its fragrance of red flowers (rose petals) and strawberries. Its length is all you could ask for. This is amazing. Screwcap. 14.3% alc. **Rating** 95 **To** 2027 $24 **✪**

Paul Nelson Wines ★★★★★

14 Roberts Road, Denmark, WA 6333 (postal) **Region** Great Southern
T 0406 495 066 **www.**paulnelsonwines.com.au **Open** School hols 11–5
Winemaker Paul Nelson **Est.** 2009 **Dozens** 1500 **Vyds** 2ha
Paul Nelson started making wine with one foot in the Swan Valley, the other in the Great Southern, while completing a bachelor's degree in viticulture and oenology at Curtin University. He then worked successively at Houghton in the Swan Valley, Goundrey in Mount Barker, Santa Ynez in California, South Africa (for four vintages), hemisphere-hopping to the Rheinhessen, three vintages in Cyprus, then moving to a large Indian winemaker in Mumbai before returning to work for Houghton. He has since moved on from Houghton and (in partnership with wife Bianca) makes small quantities of table wines.

ŢŢŢŢŢ **Karriview Denmark Chardonnay 2015** Intriguing bouquet; oatmeal, dry biscuit, spicy oak and a whiff of lanolin. The varietal character is subtle, but the overall impression is unequivocally of complex, cool climate chardonnay. The palate echoes this theme, with slinky texture, perfectly integrated acidity and length of flavour the defining elements. Grapefruit and just-ripe white peach may be the best descriptors of the primary fruit input, just for the record. Top drawer. Screwcap. 13.4% alc. **Rating** 96 **To** 2027 $70 SC **✪**
Heathbank 2013 A complex 70/20/10% blend of cabernet sauvignon, cabernet franc and malbec from Frankland River, Denmark and Mount Barker. The bright crimson-purple colour might be expected from a newly bottled 18-month-old wine, setting the wine off to a flying start. It then ticks all the boxes, with perfect structure underpinning the interplay between cassis, bay leaf, cedar and fine tannins. Screwcap. 14% alc. **Rating** 96 **To** 2028 $48 **✪**
Karriview Pinot Noir 2015 Clear crimson purple; an unambiguously good pinot noir with drive and intensity to its bell-clear varietal expression coupled with fine, persuasive tannins and crisp acidity; fragrant red cherry fruit carries its line confidently through the long, perfectly balanced, palate; some expensive oak has been worth the money. Very good now, even better in 5–10 years. Screwcap. 14% alc. **Rating** 95 **To** 2026 $70
P.N. Geographe G.M.T Grenache Mourvedre Tempranillo 2014 This has morphed into a harmonious wine. It has vibrant fruit and spice stamped all over it from raspberries, red berries to musk, Middle Eastern fragrances and sopressa salami. Savoury ripe tannins, fine acidity and everything on song. Screwcap. 14% alc. **Rating** 95 **To** 2023 $42 JF
P.N. The Little Rascal Geographe Arneis 2016 Arneis hails from Piedmont, Italy and in dialect means little rascal. This is a bit special, as the lemony zesty acidity flows through onto a chalky-textural palate. Not overly aromatic, it never is, with just a whisper of florals and spice. Happy days. Screwcap. 13% alc. **Rating** 94 **To** 2019 $28 JF **✪**
Maison Madeleine Geographe Rose 2016 Pale pink cherry hue; watermelon and rind, freeze-dried strawberries, spicy with zesty acidity – really refreshing. Some texture too. This is an excellent rose. Flavoursome, dry and delicious. Screwcap. 13.2% alc. **Rating** 94 **To** 2019 $30 JF **✪**

ŢŢŢŢŢ **Heathbank 2014 Rating** 93 **To** 2028 $48 JF
Great Southern Riesling 2016 Rating 92 **To** 2028 $28 JF
Karriview Denmark Pinot Noir 2016 Rating 91 **To** 2021 $55 JF

Paul Osicka ★★★★★

Majors Creek Vineyard at Graytown, Vic 3608 **Region** Heathcote
T (03) 5794 9235 **Open** By appt
Winemaker Paul and Simon Osicka **Est.** 1955 **Dozens** NFP **Vyds** 13ha

The Osicka family arrived in Australia from Czechoslovakia in the early 1950s. Vignerons in their own country, their vineyard was the first new venture in Central and Southern Victoria for over half a century. With the return of Simon Osicka to the family business, there have been substantial changes. Simon had senior winemaking positions at Houghton, Leasingham, and as group red winemaker for Constellation Wines Australia, interleaved with vintages in Italy, Canada, Germany and France, working at the prestigious Domaine J.L. Chave in Hermitage for the '10 vintage. The fermentation of the red wines has been changed from static to open fermenters, and French oak has replaced American oak. 2015 marked the 60th anniversary of the planting of the vineyard. Exports to Denmark.

ϷϷϷϷϷ **Moormbool Reserve Heathcote Shiraz 2015** This is an inimitable expression of shiraz steeped in Heathcote's genetic footprint of ferruginous tannins, dark fruit flavours, a whiff of eucalyptus and thick, coffee bean tannins. Powerful and expressive, the persistence of flavour and poise bodes for something special in time. Screwcap. 14.5% alc. **Rating** 95 **To** 2035 $48 NG
Heathcote Cabernet Sauvignon 2015 A lead of dark fruits and graphite notes explode across the nose, reverberating over a fully packed palate. The power chord eases into cassis and a herbal backing vocal of sage and licorice. This is exemplary Heathcote cabernet harnessing power, yet displaying a textural wealth founded on impeccably hewn tannins, both grape and oak, and an overall aura of savouriness. Screwcap. 14.5% alc. **Rating** 95 **To** 2035 $35 NG ✪
Old Vines Heathcote Cabernet Sauvignon 2015 A dollop of cabernet franc (10%) gives a violet soprano and verdant lift to a baritone of currant and black fruits; a bass of dried sage, Australian scrub and anise. This boasts compelling vinosity and length, despite its arsenal of classy oak and its indomitable power. The finish is punchy and sweet, offset by bitter chocolate and coffee grind notes. Screwcap. 14.5% alc. **Rating** 94 **To** 2035 $48 NG

ϷϷϷϷϙ **Heathcote Shiraz 2015 Rating** 92 **To** 2035 $35 NG
Bull Lane Heathcote Shiraz 2015 Rating 91 **To** 2022 $28 NG
Via del Toro Pyrenees Nebbiolo 2015 Rating 91 **To** 2023 $32 NG

Paulett Wines ★★★★★

752 Jolly Way, Polish Hill River, SA 5453 **Region** Clare Valley
T (08) 8843 4328 www.paulettwines.com.au **Open** 7 days 10–5
Winemaker Neil Paulett, Kirk McDonald **Est.** 1983 **Dozens** 15 000 **Vyds** 61ha
The Paulett story is a saga of Australian perseverance, commencing with the 1982 purchase of a property with 1ha of vines and a house, promptly destroyed by the terrible Ash Wednesday bushfires the following year. Son Matthew joined Neil and Alison Paulett as a partner in the business some years ago; he is responsible for viticulture on the property holding, much expanded following the purchase of a large vineyard at Watervale. The winery and cellar door have wonderful views over the Polish Hill River region, the memories of the bushfires long gone. Exports to the UK, Singapore, Malaysia, China and NZ.

ϷϷϷϷϷ **Antonina Polish Hill River Riesling 2016** The astonishing analysis leaves only one conclusion: have soda or sparkling water at hand before tasting it. The wine has a pH of 2.83 and titratable acidity of 9.6gl, the pitiful residual sugar a non-detectable 1.5g/l. The outcome is a delicate, poised wine with citrus fruits and Granny Smith apple providing the fruit on the long palate, the finish of steely acidity, clean and fresh. Screwcap. 12.5% alc. **Rating** 96 **To** 2035 $50 ✪

ϷϷϷϷϙ **Polish Hill River Riesling 2016 Rating** 92 **To** 2030 $23 SC ✪

Paxton ★★★★★

68 Wheaton Road, McLaren Vale, SA 5171 **Region** McLaren Vale
T (08) 8323 9131 www.paxtonvineyards.com **Open** 7 days 10–5
Winemaker Richard Freebairn **Est.** 1979 **Dozens** 25 000 **Vyds** 82.7ha
David Paxton is of one Australia's most successful and respected viticulturists, with a career spanning more than 30 years. He started his successful premium grower business in 1979

and has been involved with planting and managing some of the most prestigious vineyards in McLaren Vale, Barossa Valley, Yarra Valley, Margaret River and Adelaide Hills for top global wineries. There are six vineyards in the family holdings in McLaren Vale: Thomas Block (25ha), Jones Block (22ha), Quandong Farm (18ha), Landcross Farm (2ha), Maslin (3ha) and 19th (12.5ha). All are certified organic and biodynamic, making Paxton one of the largest biodynamic producers in Australia. The vineyards have some of the region's oldest vines, including the 125-year-old EJ shiraz. His principal focus is on his own operations in McLaren Vale with Paxton Wines, established in '98 as a premium Shiraz, Grenache and Cabernet producer. Winemaker Richard Freebairn joined Paxton Wines as head winemaker in 2014, with the '15 vintage being his first. The cellar door sits on Landcross Farm, a historic 1860s sheep farm in the original village consisting of limestone houses and shearing shed. Exports to the UK, the US, Canada, Denmark, France, Germany, Sweden, The Netherlands, Russia, Finland, Japan, Malaysia, Singapore, Hong Kong, Taiwan and China.

♀♀♀♀♀ **Elizabeth Jean 100 Year McLaren Vale Shiraz 2013** Only a fierce determination to make the best possible wine could see 20% of this wine (produced from 125yo vines) drained off the open ferment to maximise concentration. This is nectar of the gods, the colour still brilliant, the medium-bodied palate held in the embrace of perfectly weighted French oak and a star dust of tannins. Glorious stuff, its freshness with a lifetime guarantee. Screwcap. 14% alc. **Rating** 98 **To** 2043 $100 **۞**

♀♀♀♀♀ **Jones Block McLaren Vale Shiraz 2014** Biodynamic-grown fruit, open-fermented, matured in French and American barriques for 18 months. A celebrated McLaren Vale single vineyard wine, effortlessly providing a deep well of black fruits and fine-grained tannins, the oak a positive contributor, not a rabble rouser. Screwcap. 14% alc. **Rating** 96 **To** 2034 $40
Cracker Barrels McLaren Vale Shiraz Cabernet 2014 The Cracker Barrel series comes at the very end of the vintage, when a special barrel (or barrels) demands to be separately bottled. It may be a single varietal, but in '14 it was this blend – with four cracker barrels the result. Paxton gets it like few others do – you can have all the flavour intensity you want at modest alcohol levels. This is delicious, bursting with juicy energy and as fresh as a spring day, but also wondrously complex. Screwcap. 13.5% alc. **Rating** 96 **To** 2034 $55
AAA McLaren Vale Shiraz Grenache 2015 A 65/35% blend, matured in French barriques. A shiraz grenache that only McLaren Vale can provide: complex, rich and layered, black and red fruits providing a mosaic of flavours on the medium+-bodied palate. The tannin and oak management can't be faulted – it's a lovely wine at a bargain basement price. Screwcap. 14% alc. **Rating** 96 **To** 2030 $25 **۞**
Quandong Farm Single Vineyard McLaren Vale Shiraz 2015 Hand-picked, 20% whole bunches, matured in French barriques. A velvety medium to full-bodied wine that is delicious now thanks to its red berries and plum fruit that open confidently on the palate and push through to the finish and aftertaste without losing shape or freshness. Screwcap. 14% alc. **Rating** 95 **To** 2030 $30 **۞**
MV Organic McLaren Vale Cabernet Sauvignon 2015 Parcels from various Paxton vineyards were separately vinified in open and closed fermenters, pumped over twice daily for 14 days, matured in new and used French puncheons for 14 months prior to final blending. A tightly focused, and appropriately firm, palate offers abundant blackcurrant and savoury tannins that are in perfect balance. A distinguished cabernet. Screwcap. 14% alc. **Rating** 94 **To** 2035 $20 **۞**

♀♀♀♀♀ **Organic McLaren Vale Tempranillo 2016 Rating** 93 **To** 2022 $25 SC **۞**
MV McLaren Vale Shiraz 2015 Rating 92 **To** 2025 $20 SC **۞**
McLaren Vale Grenache 2016 Rating 91 **To** 2022 $35 SC
Organic McLaren Vale Pinot Gris 2016 Rating 90 **To** 2017 $20 **۞**
The Vale Biodynamic Cabernet Sauvignon 2014 Rating 90 **To** 2024 $20

Payne's Rise

10 Paynes Road, Seville, Vic 3139 **Region** Yarra Valley
T (03) 5964 2504 **www.**paynesrise.com.au **Open** Thurs–Sun 11–5
Winemaker Franco D'Anna (Contract) **Est.** 1998 **Dozens** 1500 **Vyds** 5ha
Tim and Narelle Cullen have progressively established 5ha of cabernet sauvignon, shiraz, pinot noir, chardonnay and sauvignon blanc since 1998, new plantings continuing on a small scale, including several clones of chardonnay in 2014. They carry out all the vineyard work; Tim is also a viticulturist for a local agribusiness, and Narelle is responsible for sales and marketing. The contract-made wines have won both gold medals and trophies at the Yarra Valley Wine Show since '10, echoed by success at the Victorian Wines Show.

Redlands Yarra Valley Shiraz 2015 30% whole bunches in the ferment adds that extra vibrancy, that extra oomph to the fragrance, and this has plenty. All peppery and spicy with a core of juicy plums; very savoury, with detailed tannins and superfine natural acidity sealing the deal. Screwcap. 13.2% alc. **Rating** 95 To 2025 $30 JF ✪

Yarra Valley Chardonnay 2016 Rating 93 To 2025 $25 JF ✪
Mr Jed Yarra Valley Pinot Noir 2016 Rating 93 To 2026 $30 JF
Yarra Valley Cabernet Sauvignon 2015 Rating 93 To 2026 $30 JF

Peccavi Wines

1121 Wildwood Road, Yallingup Siding, WA 6282 **Region** Margaret River
T 0423 958 255 **www.**peccavi-wines.com **Open** By appt
Winemaker Brian Fletcher **Est.** 1996 **Dozens** 2500 **Vyds** 16ha
Jeremy Muller was introduced to the great wines of the world by his father when he was young, and says he spent years searching New and Old World wine regions (even looking at the sites of ancient Roman vineyards in England), but did not find what he was looking for until one holiday in Margaret River. There he found a vineyard in Yallingup that was available for sale, and he did not hesitate. He quickly put together an impressive contract winemaking team, and appointed Colin Bell as viticulturist. The wines are released under two labels: Peccavi, for 100% estate-grown fruit (all hand-picked) and No Regrets, for wines with contract-grown grapes and estate material. The quality of the wines is very good, reflecting the skills and experience of Brian Fletcher. Exports to the UAE, Singapore, Hong Kong and China.

Margaret River Shiraz 2014 The fragrant bouquet and deep colour signal a shiraz with great complexity to its array of spice, licorice and dark forest fruits. Tannin and oak both make positive contributions to a wine with a long future. Screwcap. 14% alc. **Rating** 96 To 2034 $52 ✪
Margaret River Sauvignon Blanc Semillon 2014 In very different style from its No Regrets sibling, with delicate but persistent tropical fruits to the fore on the long, refreshing palate. This is all about the vineyard and careful fruit selection. Screwcap. 13% alc. **Rating** 95 To 2018 $46
Margaret River Syrah 2013 This is a powerhouse. Full-bodied, deep and penetrating – oak adding to the shape as well as spice. The core of fruit is very good, concentrated and savoury with juniper and pepper; tannins are grainy and expansive. A little unforgiving – needs time. Screwcap. 14% alc. **Rating** 95 To 2024 $52 JF
Margaret River Sauvignon Blanc Semillon 2013 I don't know whether this bright straw-green wine was deliberately held back or if this is a re-release. Whichever, its incisive flavours show no sign of breaking up thanks to slatey acidity (from the semillon). The flavours hinge on Meyer lemon and snow pea, the length of the palate excellent. Screwcap. 12.5% alc. **Rating** 94 To 2018 $46
Margaret River Cabernet Sauvignon 2013 Good colour for age; a powerful, intense, single-minded style with blackcurrant fruit trimmed by dried bay leaf and black olive/savoury notes. There is enough fruit depth, not to mention oak, to get it over the line. Screwcap. 13.5% alc. **Rating** 94 To 2033 $68

𝗬𝗬𝗬𝗬𝗬 Margaret River Sauvignon Blanc Semillon 2015 Rating 92 To 2018 $42
Margaret River Chardonnay 2014 Rating 92 To 2020 $58 JF
No Regrets Cabernet Merlot 2014 Rating 92 To 2022 $26 JF
No Regrets Sauvignon Blanc Semillon 2015 Rating 90 To 2018 $28

Peel Estate ★★★★☆

290 Fletcher Road, Karnup, WA 6176 **Region** Peel
T (08) 9524 1221 **www**.peelwine.com.au **Open** 7 days 10–5
Winemaker Will Nairn, Mark Morton **Est.** 1974 **Dozens** 4000 **Vyds** 16ha
Peel's icon wine is the Shiraz, a wine of considerable finesse and with a remarkably consistent track record. Every year Will Nairn holds a Great Shiraz Tasting for six-year-old Australian Shirazs, and pits Peel Estate (in a blind tasting attended by 100 or so people) against Australia's best; it is never disgraced. The wood-matured Chenin Blanc is another winery specialty. Exports to the UK, Ireland, China and Japan.

𝗬𝗬𝗬𝗬𝗬 **Cabernet Sauvignon 2011** This is fully flared wine that manages to harness Peel's tendency towards largesse – generosity of fruit flavour, intensity and abundant oak – with a disciplined line of cabernet currant, dried tobacco, stiff upper-lipped tannins and bright acidity. There is something 'warm vintage Bordeaux' about this, with gravelly ball-bearing tannins growing in authority as the wine opens. This will age very well. Screwcap. 14% alc. **Rating** 95 To 2036 $34 NG ✪

𝗬𝗬𝗬𝗬𝗬 Margaret River Peel Chardonnay 2014 Rating 90 To 2022 $25 NG

Penfolds ★★★★★

30 Tanunda Road, Nuriootpa, SA 5355 **Region** Barossa Valley
T (08) 8568 8408 **www**.penfolds.com **Open** 7 days 10–5
Winemaker Peter Gago **Est.** 1844 **Dozens** NFP
Penfolds is the star in the crown of Treasury Wine Estates (TWE), but its history predates the formation of TWE by close on 170 years. Its shape has changed in terms of its vineyards, its management, its passing parade of great winemakers, and its wines. There is no other single winery brand in the New, or the Old, World with the depth and breadth of Penfolds. Retail prices range from less than $20 to $850 for Grange, which is the cornerstone, produced every year, albeit with the volume determined by the quality of the vintage, not by cash flow. There is now a range of regional wines of single varieties, and the Bin Range of wines that include both regional blends and (in some instances) varietal blends. Despite the very successful Yattarna and Reserve Bin A Chardonnays, and some impressive Rieslings, this remains a red wine producer at heart. Exports to all major markets.

𝗬𝗬𝗬𝗬𝗬 **Bin 95 Grange 2012** Bottle no. AV 697. This vintage was destined to be one of the greatest Granges. In the flesh it is majestically complex, superbly focused and intense, and wondrously balanced. It has every black fruit flavour known to man or woman, and will become more magical with each passing decade. Oh for a screwcap. Cork. 14.5% alc. **Rating** 99 To 2062 $850
Reserve Bin A Adelaide Hills Chardonnay 2015 Bin 15, bottle no. AF 308. Over the past 10 years this wine has (I suspect) won more gold medals than any other Australian chardonnay (Yattarna isn't entered in shows). Apart from maturation in French oak at 10°C or less, the magic lies in the fruit and (ultimately) barrel selection. It has a diamond-like intensity and purity to the fruit flavours, natural acidity and new French oak observers from the wings. Screwcap. 13% alc. **Rating** 97 To 2025 $100 ✪
Bin 144 Yattarna Chardonnay 2014 Bottle no. AE 904. This is the 20th vintage of the Penfolds Queen to sit alongside King Grange. Whereas the King is all about complexity, power and extreme longevity, this is all about elegance, finesse, purity and perfect balance. The move to screwcap for Yattarna allowed it to fulfil its destiny, and (in chardonnay terms) to challenge Grange in longevity. Screwcap. 13% alc. **Rating** 97 To 2022 $150 ✪

Bin 798 RWT Barossa Valley Shiraz 2014 Bottle no. BX 084. The quixotic RWT (Red Wine Trial) name used since '87 now has a bin number and a bottle number, the latter to thwart counterfeiting. It completed fermentation in French hogsheads, followed by 17 months maturation. The power and length of the wine are awesome, as is the price – but it's what the global market is prepared to pay. Screwcap. 14.5% alc. **Rating** 97 **To** 2049 $200

ΨΨΨΨΨ **Bin 707 Cabernet Sauvignon 2014** Bottle no. AT 665. Matured for 17 months in new American oak barriques of such quality that it doesn't go to war with the fruit – or is it simply that the fruit has sucked it up? It really doesn't matter any more that some will politely move to one side and let others buy (and even drink) this wine, revelling in the mega amounts of fruit, oak and tannins. Cork. 14.5% alc. **Rating** 96 **To** 2040 $500

Bin 407 Cabernet Sauvignon 2014 A multi-regional blend first made in '90, the Limestone Coast regions having an important role, the oak likewise a mix of new and used French and American. It's first and foremost Penfolds, second cabernet sauvignon, and there's no point moaning about the price, which is made to seem frugal by that of Bin 707. In the scheme of things, it will travel easily, thanks to the balance of fruit, oak and tannins. Screwcap. 14.5% alc. **Rating** 96 **To** 2039 $90

Bin 389 Cabernet Shiraz 2014 First made in '60, and for long called 'poor man's Grange', a strange name for a $90 wine. There is much conjecture about the amount of Dom Perignon made each year, and the same is true of this wine. A bottle number could cause embarrassment. It's seriously good, its palate of black fruits, licorice, oak and earth held tight by tannins as only Penfolds can make. Screwcap. 14.5% alc. **Rating** 96 **To** 2044 $90

Bin 51 Eden Valley Riesling 2016 The blossom spray of the rose petal and lime aromas leads into a juicy, expressive palate, all the citrus flavours coming out to play in the 'garden of the mouth', natural acidity providing the dew of the early morning. Screwcap. 12% alc. **Rating** 95 **To** 2026 $30 ❂

Max's Chardonnay 2015 A delicious display of pear, apple, grapefruit and white peach flavour, its sense of generosity and sizzling length both in the higher echelons. Steel and spice notes add both interest and race to the wine's overall character. Screwcap. 13% alc. **Rating** 95 **To** 2022 $35 CM ❂

Bin 311 Tumbarumba Chardonnay 2015 Intense grapefruit/white peach/ melon aromas and flavours drive through the palate in a chariot of natural acidity, making French oak an incidental extra. When Tumbarumba has a good (ie dry) vintage, everything falls into place. Screwcap. 13.5% alc. **Rating** 95 **To** 2025 $45

Bin 150 Marananga Shiraz 2014 A relatively recent arrival into the Penfolds Bin range, and has been a success from the outset. A dense and rich full-bodied shiraz, with a phalanx of purple and black fruits framed by 14 months maturation in French and American oak. Ripe tannins put the seal on the future of a long-lived wine. Screwcap. 14.5% alc. **Rating** 95 **To** 2039 $90

Bin 28 Kalimna Shiraz 2014 This is the mother of the Bin range, first made in '59 from shiraz largely ex Penfolds Kalimna Vineyard. Kalimna is now a registered trademark, the wine coming from vineyards spread across SA. It spent 12 months in American oak, but it is all about the saturated black fruits and black licorice at the steering wheel of this multilayered, full-bodied shiraz, its future still in front of it. Screwcap. 14.5% alc. **Rating** 95 **To** 2039 $45

Bin 138 Barossa Valley Shiraz Grenache Mataro 2014 From old, dry-grown vines, reflecting the low yields of the vintage. I like this wine, which has far less confection/poached fruit flavours than usual, and correspondingly more tannins. Shiraz is doing the heavy lifting, but the grenache and mataro add distinctive spicy red notes. Screwcap. 14.5% alc. **Rating** 95 **To** 2029 $45

Bin 128 Coonawarra Shiraz 2014 **Rating** 94 **To** 2034 $45

ΨΨΨΨΩ **St Henri Shiraz 2013** **Rating** 90 **To** 2028 $100
Koonunga Hill Shiraz Cabernet 2014 **Rating** 90 **To** 2025 $18 CM ❂
Bin 8 Cabernet Shiraz 2014 **Rating** 90 **To** 2029 $45

Penfolds Magill Estate ★★★★★

78 Penfold Road, Magill, SA 5072 **Region** Adelaide
T (08) 8301 5569 **www**.penfolds.com **Open** 7 days 9–6
Winemaker Peter Gago **Est.** 1844 **Dozens** NFP **Vyds** 5.2ha
This is the birthplace of Penfolds, established by Dr Christopher Rawson Penfold in 1844; his house is still part of the immaculately maintained property. It includes 5.2ha of precious shiraz used to make Magill Estate Shiraz; and the original and subsequent winery buildings, most still in operation or in museum condition. In May 2015, Penfolds unveiled the redevelopment of Magill Estate with the opening of a new cellar door (where visitors can taste Grange by the glass) and Magill Estate Kitchen, a casual dining environment with a grazing menu built on local and fresh ingredients, and meant for sharing. The much-awarded Magill Estate Restaurant, with its panoramic views of the city, remains a temple for sublime food and wine matching. Exports to al major markets.

ΨΨΨΨΨ Magill Estate Shiraz 2014 From the 5ha vineyard surrounded by suburban housing and the Magill winery where Grange was first made – in the same wax-lined square open fermenters as are used today. It is more powerful than most releases, and – in the manner of Grange – will need a decade for the fruit, oak and tannins to soften and mould together. Cork. 14.5% alc. **Rating** 96 **To** 2039 $130

Penley Estate ★★★★★

McLeans Road, Coonawarra, SA 5263 **Region** Coonawarra
T (08) 8736 3211 **www**.penley.com.au **Open** 7 days 10–4
Winemaker Kate Goodman, Matt Tilby **Est.** 1988 **Dozens** 35 000 **Vyds** 111ha
In 1988 Kym, Ang and Bec Tolley joined forces to buy a block of land in Coonawarra and Penley Estate was underway. In 2015 Ang and Bec took full ownership of the company. They have made a number of changes, including appointing general manager Michael Armstrong and, even more importantly, Kate Goodman as winemaker. Behind the scenes Ang's husband David Paxton, one of Australia's foremost viticulturists, has been working as a consultant, with improvements in vineyard performance already evident. Exports to all major markets.

ΨΨΨΨΨ Helios Coonawarra Cabernet Sauvignon 2013 A wine of formidable density, bristling with a firm carapace of ambitious grape and oak tannins, all vanilla pod and cedar-scented. The fruit oozes across the linear seams, but only just. There are blackcurrant, cherry and boysenberry, nestled into a herb and spice patch of anise, cardamom, clove and spearmint. This needs time. Cork. 14.5% alc. **Rating** 93 **To** 2033 $100 NG
Atlas Coonawarra Shiraz 2015 This mid-weighted wine boasts blue and black fruits, a skein of peppery acidity, deli smoked meats and sinewy, mid-range tannins, far less bracing than those exhibited by the Cabernets of the range. This wine plays the herbal card well, without straying into excess or hardness. Screwcap. 14.5% alc. **Rating** 92 **To** 2029 $20 NG ❂
Gryphon Cabernet Sauvignon Merlot Cabernet Franc 2014 Of all the wines at this tier, this is by far the most mellifluous. More than a sum of its parts, there is an aromatic esprit, more energetic red fruit than molten dark, and sage-soused tannins, still drying but somehow apt given the garden bed of herbs that define the finish. Screwcap. 14.6% alc. **Rating** 92 **To** 2029 $20 NG ❂
Chertsey 2013 52% cabernet sauvignon, 36% shiraz 12% merlot. Savoury, with a sappy red-fruited floral note, effortlessly combining with the red and black currant, anise and more brooding baritones. The finish is long and of a flowing fruit-driven nature, with oak guiding, rather than serving as a drying rasp. Screwcap. 14.5% alc. **Rating** 92 **To** 2030 $45 NG
Argus Coonawarra Shiraz Cabernet Sauvignon Merlot Cabernet Franc 2014 This comes across as a mid-weighted fountain of fruity softness in the context of the cabernet-driven cuvees that make up most of Penley's arsenal of releases. An avuncular meld of soy, five-spice and boot polish notes mingle

with dark and red fruit flavours, all given a heavy accent of menthol. Screwcap.
14.5% alc. **Rating** 91 **To** 2021 $20 NG ◐

Tolmer Coonawarra Cabernet Sauvignon 2014 A seductive nose of vanilla
pod, cedar, coffee bean and mocha is dictated by the 21 months the wine spent in
a combination of new and used French oak. This said, the nose is not oaky. The
palate, however, makes up for that. The aromas reverberate across a sinuous, fullish
palate, taking on some menthol, a herbal potpourri and blackcurrant, all ebbing
across and squeezing between grape and oak tannins, before skittering across the
mouth into a dry, hot finish. Screwcap. **Rating** 91 **To** 2028 $30 NG

Steyning Coonawarra Cabernet Sauvignon 2013 This sturdy, strongly
regional cabernet spent 24 months in oak, 5% new. Blackcurrant aromas verge
on Ribena in terms of their vivacity and intensity. After dinner–mint flavours
lean towards spearmint and bitter chocolate, freshening the palate with a spray of
menthol. The oak confers a mocha edge to the stern tannins, shaping the fully
loaded palate. Screwcap. 15% alc. **Rating** 90 **To** 2027 $45 NG

ŸŸŸŸ   Phoenix Cabernet Sauvignon 2015 **Rating** 89 **To** 2025 $20 NG

Penna Lane Wines

Lot 51 Penna Lane, Penwortham via Clare, SA 5453 **Region** Clare Valley
T 0403 162 431 **www**.pennalanewines.com.au **Open** Fri–Sun 11–5
Winemaker Peter Treloar, Chris Proud **Est.** 1998 **Dozens** 4500 **Vyds** 4.37ha
Penna Lane is located in the beautiful Skilly Valley, 10km south of Clare. The estate vineyard
(shiraz, cabernet sauvignon and semillon) is planted at an elevation of 450m, which allows
a long, slow ripening period, usually resulting in wines with intense varietal fruit flavours.
Exports to Hong Kong, South Korea, Fiji, Vietnam, Thailand, China and Japan.

ŸŸŸŸŸ   Skilly Valley Riesling 2016 Machine-harvested at night, cool fermentation of
        clean juice. The flowery, citrus-accented bouquet leads into a lively, fresh and juicy
        palate, lime and crisp acidity powering the long finish. Lovely wine. Screwcap.
        12% alc. **Rating** 95 **To** 2029 $25 ◐

ŸŸŸŸŸ   Watervale Riesling 2016 **Rating** 91 **To** 2031 $22 ◐

Penny's Hill

281 Main Road, McLaren Vale, SA 5171 **Region** McLaren Vale
T (08) 8557 0800 **www**.pennyshill.com.au **Open** 7 days 10–5
Winemaker Alexia Roberts **Est.** 1988 **Dozens** 85000 **Vyds** 44ha
Founded in 1988 by Tony and Susie Parkinson, Penny's Hill produces high quality Shiraz
(Footprint and The Skeleton Key) from its close-planted McLaren Vale estate, also the source
of the Edwards Road Cabernet Sauvignon and The Experiment Grenache. Malpas Road and
Goss Corner Vineyards complete the estate holdings, providing fruit for Cracking Black Shiraz
and Malpas Road Merlot. White wines (The Agreement Sauvignon Blanc and The Minimalist
Chardonnay) are sourced from 'estates of mates' in the Adelaide Hills. Also includes the Black
Chook and Thomas Goss Brands. Penny's Hill cellars are located at the historic Ingleburne
Farm, which also houses the award-winning The Kitchen Door restaurant and Red Dot
Gallery. Noted for its distinctive 'red dot' packaging. Exports to all major markets.

ŸŸŸŸŸ   Footprint McLaren Vale Shiraz 2015 Comes from 12 selected rows on the
        original Penny's Hill vineyard, aged in 50% new, 50% 1yo French barriques for
        18 months. Latent depth and power here, the seemingly formidable oak absorbed
        easily by the intense black fruit and minerality of the terroir. Demands time.
        Screwcap. 14.5% alc. **Rating** 95 **To** 2035 $65 SC

        Skeleton Key McLaren Vale Shiraz 2015 This is perhaps the most idiomatic
        of the '15 vintage Penny's Hill shiraz releases. Lashings of blackberry, plum,
        chocolate and sweet/spicy oak fill the bouquet, and then flood onto the palate,
        effortlessly rippling along with gently persuasive tannin as the guiding hand.
        Screwcap. 14.5% alc. **Rating** 94 **To** 2030 $35 SC

The Experiment Single Vineyard McLaren Vale Grenache 2015 A 1.9 acre site where old vine stocks are trellised in an 'experimental' fashion to reduce vigour and increase flavour. Cherry and raspberry aromas with a touch of sweet spice. A lovely feeling of freshness, with vibrant fruit and supple tannins. Drink now or cellar, it's win-win. Screwcap. 14.5% alc. **Rating** 94 **To** 2025 $35 SC

ΨΨΨΨΨ Cracking Black McLaren Vale Shiraz 2015 Rating 93 To 2030 $25 SC ✪
Edwards Road Cabernet Sauvignon 2015 Rating 93 To 2025 $25 SC ✪
The Veteran Very Old Fortified NV Rating 92 $35 SC
The Specialized McLaren Vale Shiraz Cabernet Merlot 2015 Rating 91 To 2025 $25 SC
The Black Chook Shiraz 2015 Rating 90 To 2030 $18 ✪
Thomas Goss McLaren Vale Shiraz 2015 Rating 90 To 2022 $15 ✪

Peos Estate ★★★★★

Graphite Road, Manjimup, WA 6258 **Region** Manjimup
T (08) 9772 1378 **www**.peosestate.com.au **Open** Not
Winemaker Coby Ladwig, Michael Ng **Est.** 1996 **Dozens** 12 000 **Vyds** 36.8ha
The Peos family has farmed the West Manjimup district for over 50 years, the third generation of four brothers commencing the development of the vineyard in 1996. There is a little over 34ha of vines, including shiraz (10ha), merlot (6.8ha), chardonnay (6.7ha), cabernet sauvignon (4ha), sauvignon blanc (3ha), and pinot noir and verdelho (2ha each). Exports to China.

ΨΨΨΨΨ Four Aces Single Vineyard Manjimup Shiraz 2014 Deep crimson-purple; this is a wine that balances intensity and elegance with its multiple layers of bramble/forest fruits, pepper, licorice and persistent fine-grained tannins. Oak, too, sends a message of approval. Screwcap. 14.5% alc. **Rating** 95 **To** 2029 $35 ✪
Four Aces Single Vineyard Manjimup Cabernet Sauvignon 2014 Strongly pushes the view that Manjimup is better suited to cabernet than to pinot noir. The deep crimson-purple colour announces a complex texture and suite of flavours, dusty tannins woven throughout the length of the palate. French oak has also made a positive contribution. Screwcap. 14.5% alc. **Rating** 95 **To** 2034 $35 ✪

ΨΨΨΨΨ Four Aces Single Vineyard Manjimup Chardonnay 2015 Rating 92 To 2023 $35

Pepper Tree Wines ★★★★★

86 Halls Road, Pokolbin, NSW 2320 **Region** Hunter Valley
T (02) 4909 7100 **www**.peppertreewines.com.au **Open** Mon–Fri 9–5, w'ends 9.30–5
Winemaker Gwyn Olsen **Est.** 1991 **Dozens** 50 000 **Vyds** 172.1ha
Pepper Tree is part of a complex that also contains The Convent guest house and Circa 1876 Restaurant. It is owned by a company controlled by Dr John Davis, who owns 50% of Briar Ridge. It sources the majority of its Hunter Valley fruit from its Tallavera Grove vineyard at Mt View, but also has premium vineyards at Orange, Coonawarra and Wrattonbully. Self-evidently, the wines are exceptional value for money. The highly credentialled Gwyn Olsen ('12 Dux, Advanced Wine Assessment course, AWRI; '14 Young Winemaker of the Year, *Gourmet Traveller WINE*; '15 Rising Star of the Year, Hunter Valley Legends Awards; and '15 Len Evans Tutorial Scholar) was appointed winemaker in '15. Exports to the UK, Denmark, Singapore and China.

ΨΨΨΨΨ Single Vineyard Reserve Tallawanta Hunter Valley Shiraz 2014 Hunter shiraz in all its medium-weight glory. Earthen but not gamey, spicy but neatly so, awash with cherry and plum fruit flavour and appropriately adorned in cedary oak. Tannin pours and churns through, firm but fair. A gorgeous wine, with a wonderful future ahead. Screwcap. 14.2% alc. **Rating** 97 **To** 2036 $145 CM ✪

ΨΨΨΨΨ Premium Reserve Single Vineyard 8R Wrattonbully Merlot 2015 The 8R clone, recently arrived from Bordeaux, is living up to expectations, especially given the youth of the vines. Good hue; its structure and texture are borrowed from cabernet, but there is no aggression, just supple dark red fruits. Watch this space. Screwcap. 14.1% alc. **Rating** 96 **To** 2035 $60 ✪

Premium Reserve Single Vineyard Block 21A Wrattonbully Cabernet Sauvignon 2015 Polished, dextrous winemaking of high quality grapes. Vivid crimson-purple; it immediately imparts its DNA of fresh, bright, intensely flavoured cassis fruits. Naturally, French oak and tannins provide context, but the focus never shifts from the fruit, picked at the zenith of its flavour. Screwcap. 13.9% alc. **Rating** 96 **To** 2035 $60 ✪

Single Vineyard Premium Reserve Alluvius Hunter Valley Semillon 2016 Pale straw-green; lime, lemon and citrus zest race across the palate at mesmerising speed, leaving the mouth as fresh as a spring day. Acidity provides the fuel for the engine and for the energy of an exceptionally good young semillon with a great future. Screwcap. 10.5% alc. **Rating** 95 **To** 2030 $35 ✪

Limited Release Wrattonbully Tempranillo 2015 Marches to the tune of the tempranillo drum we have come to expect from this variety in cooler climates. It is bracingly fresh and crisp, medium-bodied (as all good tempranillos are), with a cross-current of dark cherry fruit, spices and gently savoury tannins. The length and balance are admirable. Screwcap. 14% alc. **Rating** 95 **To** 2025 $25 ✪

Premium Reserve Single Vineyard Venus Block Orange Chardonnay 2016 Hand-picked, whole-bunch pressed, wild fermented, matured in French oak (30% new) for 12 months. An elegant style bringing an edge of funky complexity to fine stone fruit flavours; good length thanks to balanced acidity. Screwcap. 13.2% alc. **Rating** 94 **To** 2023 $35

Limited Release Orange Shiraz 2015 Destemmed ex machine harvester, matured for 18 months in French oak (25% new). A fragrant and vibrant red and black cherry medium-bodied palate, lifted by notes of spice and pepper, guided by fine tannins and carefully calibrated French oak; very good length. Screwcap. 14.2% alc. **Rating** 94 **To** 2030 $30 ✪

Premium Reserve Single Vineyard The Gravels Wrattonbully Shiraz 2015 Identical vinification to the Limited Release Orange Shiraz. Plum and blackberry fruit is punctuated with savoury/earthy notes on the bouquet and full-bodied palate alike. Needs more time, but will repay patience because it is balanced. Screwcap. 14.1% alc. **Rating** 94 **To** 2035 $42

Wrattonbully Merlot 2014 While the wine is no more than medium-bodied, it has life and lift that immediately grab attention, allied with a seductive mix of red and black currant fruit, oak spice and dried bay leaf. Even the tannins are warm and inviting, the finish leaving the mouth in a good frame of mind. A surprise packet in every way. Screwcap. 14% alc. **Rating** 94 **To** 2024 $19 ✪

♈♈♈♈♈ **Limited Release Orange Chardonnay 2015** Rating 93 To 2024 $22 ✪
Limited Release Wrattonbully Pinot Gris 2016 Rating 93 To 2019 $22 ✪
Limited Release Hunter Valley Semillon 2016 Rating 91 To 2022 $22 ✪
Hunter Valley Orange SSB 2016 Rating 91 To 2020 $19 ✪
Premium Reserve Single Vineyard Elderslee Road Wrattonbully Cabernet Sauvignon 2015 Rating 91 To 2030 $42
Limited Release Classics Wrattonbully Cabernet Sauvignon Merlot Petit Verdot 2014 Rating 91 To 2029 $25
Limited Release Wrattonbully Tempranillo 2016 Rating 91 To 2022 $25

Petaluma ★★★★★

254 Pfeiffer Road, Woodside, SA 5244 **Region** Adelaide Hills
T (08) 8339 9300 **www**.petaluma.com.au **Open** Fri–Mon 10–4
Winemaker Andrew Hardy, Mike Mudge **Est.** 1976 **Dozens** 100 000 **Vyds** 240ha
The Petaluma range has been expanded beyond the core group of Croser Sparkling, Clare Valley Riesling, Piccadilly Chardonnay and Coonawarra (cabernet sauvignon merlot). Newer arrivals of note include Adelaide Hills Viognier and Adelaide Hills Shiraz. The SA plantings in the Clare Valley, Coonawarra and Adelaide Hills provide a more than sufficient source of estate-grown grapes for the wines. A new winery and cellar door were opened in 2015 on a

greenfield site with views of Mt Lofty. In '17 it (along with all wine brands owned by Lion Nathan) was acquired by Accolade. Exports to all major markets.

ΨΨΨΨΨ **Tiers Piccadilly Valley Chardonnay 2015** From a small portion of the pioneering 30yo vineyard. The sheer intensity, power and linear drive of the wine is a direct reflection of the site, complexity and length given as it surges on the finish and aftertaste. Unpicking the contributions of the stone fruit, the oak and acidity is pointless so tightly are they bound together, the screwcap guaranteeing the future. Screwcap. 14.5% alc. **Rating** 96 **To** 2029 $115

Piccadilly Valley Chardonnay 2015 A high quality, high impact wine, its power coherent and impressive, stone fruit (white peach, nectarine) and zesty, citrussy acidity all contributing equally, having largely swallowed up the French oak. Screwcap. 14% alc. **Rating** 95 **To** 2024 $40

Coonawarra Merlot 2014 Matured for 18 months in new French barrels. Surprisingly, the oak sits comfortably with the fruit rather than dominating it, seemingly adding as much texture as flavour. Soft blackcurrant fruit has shadows of black olive adding to its complexity, the tannins superfine. Screwcap. 14% alc. **Rating** 95 **To** 2030 $50

Coonawarra Merlot 2013 Initially oaky on the bouquet, with a definite whiff of vanilla, it reveals the more expected aromas of mulberry, green leaf, Christmas cake and limestone-based earth. Relaxed and comfortable on the palate, the flavours meld seamlessly with the velvety tannin in a gently mouthfilling, effortlessly engaging style. Screwcap. 14.5% alc. **Rating** 95 **To** 2034 $50 SC

Evans Vineyard Coonawarra 2013 73% cabernet sauvignon, 19% merlot and 8% shiraz, matured in new French oak for 22 months. The hue is very good, fresh and bright; an elegant wine with vibrant cassis-accented flavours, but you have to wonder whether less new oak would have made an even better wine. Screwcap. 14.5% alc. **Rating** 95 **To** 2033 $60

Essence Botrytis 2010 55% sauvignon blanc/45% semillon from Coonawarra. Dark in the glass, looking like an old amontillado. Heady impact of concentrated apricot nectar and marmalade on the bouquet, with a typically volatile lift. Intensely luscious and rich on the palate, the flavours of dried fruit, honey and sweet baked biscuit are immersed in the deep viscosity and linger almost indefinitely. Despite the hedonistic descriptors, it has freshness. 375ml. Screwcap. 13% alc. **Rating** 95 **To** 2025 $45 SC

Hanlin Hill Clare Valley Riesling 2016 Screwcap. 12.5% alc. **Rating** 94 **To** 2031 $28 ❂

White Label Adelaide Hills Pinot Gris 2016 Screwcap. 13.5% alc. **Rating** 94 **To** 2019 $22 ❂

ΨΨΨΨΩ **White Label Coonawarra Nebbiolo Dry Rose 2016** Rating 93 To 2018 $22
Croser Pinot Noir Chardonnay 2012 Rating 93 To 2020 $38 TS
White Label Adelaide Hills Sauvignon Blanc 2016 Rating 92 To 2017 $22 ❂
B & V Vineyard Adelaide Hills Shiraz 2014 Rating 92 To 2029 $45
Project Co. Coonawarra Malbec 2014 Rating 92 To 2029 $40 SC
Croser Late Disgorged 2004 Rating 92 To 2017 $55 TS
Hanlin Hill Vineyard Cane Cut Riesling 2012 Rating 91 To 2025 $32 SC
White Label Adelaide Hills Chardonnay 2016 Rating 90 To 2019 $22
Croser NV Rating 90 To 2017 $25 TS
Croser Rose NV Rating 90 To 2017 $25 TS

Peter Lehmann   ★★★★★

Para Road, Tanunda, SA 5352 **Region** Barossa Valley
T (08) 8565 9555 **www**.peterlehmannwines.com **Open** Mon–Fri 9.30–5, w'ends & public hols 10.30–4.30
Winemaker Nigel Westblade **Est.** 1979 **Dozens** 750 000
The seemingly indestructible Peter Lehmann (the person) died in June 2013, laying the seeds for what became the last step in the sale of the minority Lehmann family ownership in the

company. The Hess Group of California had acquired control in '03 (leaving part of the capital with the Lehmann family), but a decade later it became apparent that Hess wished to quit its holding. Various suitors put their case forward, but Margaret Lehmann (Peter's widow) wanted ongoing family, not corporate, ownership. Casella thus was able to make the successful bid in November '14, followed by the acquisition of Brand's Laira in December '15. Exports to the UK, the US and Canada.

ⵟⵟⵟⵟⵟ **Wigan Eden Valley Riesling 2012** It's toasty yet fresh. It's complex yet approachable. A glorious amalgam of flavours from glace lemon and lime, juicy, with superfine acidity ensuring it's in a good spot today and for some time yet. Screwcap. 11.5% alc. **Rating** 97 **To** 2027 $35 JF ✪

Stonewell Barossa Shiraz 2012 Has retained exceptional deep crimson-purple colour, as the time perspective increases, so does the longevity stature of the '12 vintage. Here an ocean of full-bodied black fruits has tides of tannins and quality oak all playing off and enhancing each other on the prodigiously long palate. Screwcap. 14.5% alc. **Rating** 97 **To** 2042 $100 ✪

ⵟⵟⵟⵟⵟ **Portrait Eden Valley Riesling 2016** Indeed a lovely portrait of Eden Valley riesling. Pale bright quartz-green; the bouquet is floral with citrus blossom to the fore, the palate finely etched lime juice, the long finish with perfectly balanced acidity. Bargain, with even more to come over the next 5+ years. Screwcap. 11% alc. **Rating** 95 **To** 2029 $18 ✪

Margaret Barossa Semillon 2011 It hits the right flavour notes, from lemon zest and lemongrass to a hint of creamed honey and stone fruit. Just a bit of spice and the long flow of flavours and acidity across the palate make this top notch. Screwcap. 10.5% alc. **Rating** 95 **To** 2024 $26 JF ✪

VSV 1885 Barossa Valley Shiraz 2015 The Schrapel family in Ebenezer are 6th generation custodians of these 1885 shiraz vines, which again have produced a remarkable wine. Everything is in its place on the more medium-weighted palate – the dark fruit, the tannins tucked in, the savoury overlay and the satisfying presence. 320 dozen made. Screwcap. 14.5% alc. **Rating** 95 **To** 2042 $60 JF

VSV Hongell Barossa Valley Shiraz 2015 What's pleasing about this very special vineyard wine, grown by the Hongells on the western ridge of the Barossa, is the balance it achieves. It's full-bodied, deep, savoury and flavoursome, but also fresh, with an intriguing lightness despite its killer tannins. 511 dozen made. Screwcap. 14.5% alc. **Rating** 95 **To** 2035 $60 JF

Moppa Barossa Valley Shiraz 2014 The fruit is grown by the Hallion and Mulraney families. This kicks off with a savoury outpouring of black licorice, cloves, bitter chocolate and warm earth, then moves on to a full-bodied palate with ripe and plentiful tannins and the necessary dark fruit flavours to enrich it all. Screwcap. 14.5% alc. **Rating** 95 **To** 2030 $30 JF ✪

H&V Eden Valley Riesling 2015 Screwcap. 11% alc. **Rating** 94 **To** 2025 $22 ✪

ⵟⵟⵟⵟⵟ **Futures Barossa Shiraz 2014** Rating 93 To 2030 $26 JF ✪
Portrait Eden Valley Riesling 2015 Rating 92 To 2023 $19 ✪
Stonewell Barossa Shiraz 2013 Rating 92 To 2045 $100 JF
Mentor Barossa Cabernet 2013 Rating 92 To 2028 $45 JF
Portrait Barossa Shiraz 2014 Rating 91 To 2024 $18 ✪
Light Pass Barossa Valley Shiraz 2014 Rating 91 To 2030 $30 JF
8 Songs Barossa Shiraz 2013 Rating 91 To 2040 $45 JF
Futures Barossa Shiraz Cabernet 2014 Rating 91 To 2024 $26
H&V Eden Valley Pinot Gris 2015 Rating 90 To 2017 $22

Pewsey Vale   ★★★★★

Eden Valley Road, Eden Valley, SA 5353 **Region** Eden Valley
T (08) 8561 3200 **www.pewseyvale.com Open** By appt
Winemaker Louisa Rose **Est.** 1847 **Dozens** 20 000 **Vyds** 65ha

Pewsey Vale was a famous vineyard established in 1847 by Joseph Gilbert, and it was appropriate that when the Hill-Smith family began the renaissance of the Eden Valley plantings in 1961, it should do so by purchasing Pewsey Vale and establishing 50ha of riesling. The Riesling also finally benefited from being the first wine to be bottled with a Stelvin screwcap, in '77. While public reaction forced the abandonment of the initiative for almost 20 years, Pewsey Vale never lost faith in the technical advantages of the closure. A quick taste (or better, a share of a bottle) of five to seven-year-old Contours Riesling will tell you why. Exports to all major markets.

🍷🍷🍷🍷🍷 **Prima Single Vineyard Estate Eden Valley Riesling 2016** This is a lovely off-dry, kabinett style, 24g/l of residual sugar giving the wine a vivid profile in the mouth, with pure lime juice flavours and great length. Do not serve it with desserts – drink it on its own or with Chinese cuisine. Screwcap. 9.5% alc. **Rating** 96 **To** 2031 $26 ✪

The Contours Museum Reserve Single Vineyard Estate Eden Valley Riesling 2012 Still pale straw-green; this wine is not 5 years old, it is 5 years young. It's just starting to build the lime marmalade on buttered toast flavours of full maturity coming another 5, perhaps 10, years down the track. However, it will always have a delicate disposition. Screwcap. **Rating** 95 **To** 2032 $36

10 Years Cellar Aged The Contours Museum Reserve Single Vineyard Estate Eden Valley Riesling 2006 A celebration of mature riesling, still with time in front of it. The bouquet is toasty and spicy, the palate pure and long, with no sign of kerosene on its bone-dry finish. This is very much a style for Cantonese cuisine. Screwcap. 12.5% alc. **Rating** 94 **To** 2021

🍷🍷🍷🍷 **Single Vineyard Estate Eden Valley Riesling 2016** **Rating** 90 **To** 2026 $25

Pfeiffer Wines ★★★★★

167 Distillery Road, Wahgunyah, Vic 3687 **Region** Rutherglen
T (02) 6033 2805 **www**.pfeifferwines.com.au **Open** Mon–Sat 9–5, Sun 10–5
Winemaker Chris and Jen Pfeiffer **Est.** 1984 **Dozens** 20 000 **Vyds** 32ha

Family-owned and run, Pfeiffer Wines occupies one of the historic wineries (built in 1880) that abound in Northeast Victoria, and which is worth a visit on this score alone. In 2012 Chris Pfeiffer was awarded an Order of Australia Medal (OAM) for his services to the wine industry. Both hitherto and into the future, Pfeiffer's Muscats, Topaques and other fortified wines are a key part of the business. The arrival of daughter Jen, by a somewhat circuitous and initially unplanned route, has dramatically lifted the quality of the table wines, led by the reds. Chris Pfeiffer celebrated his 40th vintage in '13, having well and truly set the scene for supremely gifted daughter Jen to assume the chief winemaking role in due course. Exports to the UK, the US, Canada, Belgium, Malaysia, Singapore and China.

🍷🍷🍷🍷🍷 **Rare Rutherglen Muscat NV** Average age 25 years. Similar depth to the colour of the Grand, but more olive/mahogany; a wonderful bouquet, of raisins and spices, the palate of exceptional lusciousness (different from and more than just sweetness), the flavours running through Christmas pudding, raisins, burnt toffee, and distinct rancio cleansing the finish. 500ml. Screwcap. 17.5% alc. **Rating** 98 $123 ✪

Rare Rutherglen Topaque NV Muscadelle, average age 25 years. Deep but clear burnt amber colour, grading to olive on the rim; unbridled power and complexity. No calm moments here, its flavours intense and mouth-gripping, yet not sweet in conventional terms. Has exceptional length, with flavours of tea leaf, honey, cake and exotic spices. 500ml. Screwcap. 17.5% alc. **Rating** 97 $123 ✪

🍷🍷🍷🍷🍷 **Rare Rutherglen Tawny NV** Amazing that only 24 litres are released each year, with a total of 150 000 litres of tawny in the cellar. It's far from the normal Rare Tawny, with a degree of freshness that is seriously engaging. 500ml. Screwcap. 20.2% alc. **Rating** 96 $95

Grand Rutherglen Topaque NV Muscadelle, average age 18 years. Mid-mahogany colour; a perfumed and rich bouquet, the lift of the rancio providing extra complexity and feeding through into the palate; here burnt toffee, Christmas cake and malt provide a luscious and complex, yet not heavy, finish. Is very much in the Pfeiffer style, intensity with lightness of foot. 500ml. Screwcap. 17.8% alc. Rating 96 $85

Grand Rutherglen Muscat NV Average age 23 years. Deep colour; muscat to its back teeth, with glorious Arabian spice and raisin interplay interwoven with touches of toffee and bitter chocolate; the length and balance are perfect, as is the rancio. In the Pfeiffer style, intensity with elegance. 500ml. Screwcap. 17.5% alc. Rating 96 $83

Shiraz 2015 While having much in common with Carlyle, it has greater focus and intensity. The highly unusual treatment of the barrel-ferment parcels (post-ferment lees stirring) is a white wine practice, and the extent to which it is done here is unique. How much this has influenced the wine, and how much the quality of the fruit parcels has driven quality and mouthfeel is anyone's guess. Screwcap. 14.8% alc. Rating 95 To 2035 $25 ✪

Classic Rutherglen Topaque NV Bright gold-amber; it is radically different from, and more complex than, its lesser sibling, with sweet honey, malt and cake flavours, balanced by the rancio, which also extends the finish. 500ml. Screwcap. 17.5% alc. Rating 95 $29 ✪

Seriously Nutty NV Screwcap. 21.5% alc. Rating 94 $50

Rutherglen Topaque NV Screwcap. 18% alc. Rating 94 $20 ✪

Classic Rutherglen Muscat NV Screwcap. 17.8% alc. Rating 94 $29 ✪

ŶŶŶŶŶ **Riesling 2016** Rating 93 To 2025 $20 ✪
Carlyle Shiraz 2015 Rating 93 To 2025 $18 ✪
Seriously Fine NV Rating 93 $29
Classic Rutherglen Tawny NV Rating 93 $20 ✪
Rutherglen Muscat NV Rating 93 $20 ✪
Gamay 2016 Rating 91 To 2018 $18 ✪
Tempranillo 2015 Rating 91 To 2030 $25
Christopher's Rutherglen VP 2015 Rating 91 $30
Carlyle Cabernet Merlot 2015 Rating 90 To 2035 $18 ✪

Phaedrus Estate

220 Mornington-Tyabb Road, Moorooduc, Vic 3933 **Region** Mornington Peninsula
T (03) 5978 8134 **www**.phaedrus.com.au **Open** W'ends & public hols 11–5
Winemaker Ewan Campbell, Maitena Zantvoort **Est.** 1997 **Dozens** 3000 **Vyds** 2.5ha
Since Maitena Zantvoort and Ewan Campbell established Phaedrus Estate, they have gained a reputation for producing premium cool climate wines. Their winemaking philosophy brings art and science together to produce wines showing regional and varietal character with minimal winemaking interference. The vineyard includes 1ha of pinot noir and 0.5ha each of pinot gris, chardonnay and shiraz. Exports to Hong Kong.

ŶŶŶŶŶ **Single Vineyard Reserve Mornington Peninsula Pinot Noir 2015** It's plush and ripe and has the X-factor necessary for a reserve. Bountiful dark cherry fruit, pippy, plums too, with the sprinkle of spice, the dash of blood orange zest and velvety tannins all coming together and creating one harmonious drink. Screwcap. 13.5% alc. Rating 96 To 2025 $45 JF ✪

ŶŶŶŶŶ **Mornington Peninsula Pinot Noir 2015** Rating 93 To 2023 $26 JF ✪
Mornington Peninsula Chardonnay 2016 Rating 91 To 2022 $26 JF
Reserve Mornington Peninsula Shiraz 2014 Rating 90 To 2022 $45 JF

PHI

Lusatia Park Vineyard, Owens Road, Woori Yallock, Vic 3139 **Region** Yarra Valley/Heathcote
T (03) 5964 6070 **www**.phiwines.com **Open** By appt
Winemaker Steve Webber **Est.** 2005 **Dozens** 1700 **Vyds** 15ha
This was a joint venture between two very influential wine families: De Bortoli and Shelmerdine. The key executives are Stephen Shelmerdine and Steve Webber (and wives Kate

and Leanne). It rests upon the selection and management of specific blocks of vines, without regard to cost. The wines are made from the 7.5ha Lusatia Park Vineyard in the Yarra Valley, and the estate-owned 7.5ha vineyard in Heathcote. The vineyard was acquired by De Bortoli in November '15, effective after the '16 harvest. At the time of going to print, no further details were available. Exports to the UK and China.

♟♟♟♟♟ Lusatia Park Vineyard Yarra Valley Pinot Noir 2014 MV6, hand-picked and sorted, open-fermented, 20% whole bunches, matured in French barriques (35% new) for 8 months. The fragrant red berry sets the ball rolling in the right direction, and the elegant, savoury palate continues the story, with spicy red and purple berry fruits, fine tannins and integrated French oak already offering an open window into its future. Screwcap. 13.5% alc. **Rating** 95 **To** 2024 $55

♟♟♟♟♀ Lusatia Park Vineyard Yarra Valley Chardonnay 2014 Rating 91 To 2022 $45

Philip Shaw Wines   ★★★★★

Koomooloo Vineyard, Caldwell Lane, Orange, NSW 2800 **Region** Orange
T (02) 6365 2334 **www**.philipshaw.com.au **Open** 7 days 11–5
Winemaker Daniel Shaw **Est.** 1989 **Dozens** 25 000 **Vyds** 47ha
Philip Shaw, former chief winemaker of Rosemount Estate and then Southcorp, first became interested in the Orange region in 1985. In '88 he purchased the Koomooloo Vineyard and began extensive plantings, the varieties including shiraz, merlot, pinot noir, sauvignon blanc, cabernet franc, cabernet sauvignon and viognier. Son Daniel has joined Philip in the winery, at a time when the quality of the portfolio of wines is going from strength to strength. Exports to the UK, Norway, Mauritius, the Philippines, Indonesia, Hong Kong, China and NZ.

♟♟♟♟♟ No. 11 Orange Chardonnay 2015 From three vineyard blocks, vinified separately, matured for 10 months in French oak with regular lees stirring. Philip Shaw has been making chardonnay since Adam was a boy, and his experience blazes through this super-elegant wine. It combines juicy white peach fruit with a garnish of grapefruit, oak relegated to a purely functional role, not a decorative one. Screwcap. 12.5% alc. **Rating** 95 **To** 2025 $35 ✪
No. 89 Orange Shiraz 2015 Very good crimson-purple; an elegant and vibrantly fresh medium-bodied shiraz, replete with red and blue fruits that have made relatively light work of the new oak, and are not challenged by the fine, persistent tannins. Lovers of Burgundy/pinot noir will love the airy touch this shiraz has. Screwcap. 13.8% alc. **Rating** 95 **To** 2030 $50
The Dreamer Orange Viognier 2016 If you want to find the theoretical apricot in viognier (more often missing than not), go no further than this wine: it is loaded with it on what is a long and penetrating finish. I'm uncertain about the presence/absence of some residual sugar, which means it doesn't/shouldn't matter. Screwcap. 11.5% alc. **Rating** 94 **To** 2021 $22 ✪
No. 8 Orange Pinot Noir 2015 Fermented in batches, 15% of each parcel whole bunches, the remainder destemmed, matured in oak for 10 months. Has plenty going for it, the fragrant bouquet attractive, but not telling of the intensity and drive on the palate, where red and black cherry fruit meshes with spices and fine-grained savoury tannins, the oak subtle and integrated. Screwcap. 12.5% alc. **Rating** 94 **To** 2025 $40
No. 17 Orange Merlot Cabernet Franc 2015 Matured in oak for 16 months. It would seem there has been contact with new oak in one or other shape or form; certainly it shows more oak influence than The Conductor. The underlying black and red currant fruit has good tannin structure and presence, suggesting it will outlive the oak, not vice versa. Screwcap. 13.8% alc. **Rating** 94 **To** 2030 $28 ✪

♟♟♟♟♀ No. 5 Orange Cabernet Sauvignon 2013 Rating 93 **To** 2030 $75
The Wire Walker Orange Pinot Noir 2016 Rating 90 **To** 2023 $22
The Idiot Orange Shiraz 2013 Rating 90 **To** 2023 $22
The Conductor Orange Merlot 2015 Rating 90 **To** 2023 $22

Piano Piano ★★★★★

852 Beechworth-Wangaratta Road, Everton Upper, Vic 3670 **Region** Beechworth
T (03) 5727 0382 **www**.pianopiano.com.au **Open** By appt
Winemaker Marc Scalzo **Est.** 2001 **Dozens** 1500 **Vyds** 4.6ha
'Piano piano' means 'slowly slowly' in Italian, and this is how Marc Scalzo and wife Lisa Hernan have approached the development of their business. Marc has a degree in oenology from CSU, many years' practical experience as a winemaker with Brown Brothers and vintage experience with Giaconda, John Gehrig, and in NZ with Seresin Estate and Delegat's. In 1997 they planted 2.6ha of merlot, cabernet sauvignon, tempranillo and touriga nacional on their Brangie Vineyard in the King Valley; they followed up with 1.2ha of chardonnay ('06) and 0.8ha of shiraz ('08) on their Beechworth property.

Sophie's Block Beechworth Chardonnay 2015 There is virtually nothing fruity about this, although for those desperate for descriptives, there is some stone fruit tucked behind sleek gills of granitic crunch and mineral-clad pungency; juxtaposed beautifully against a generous build of creamy lees work as the wine opens in the glass. Reminiscent of the Maconnais. Screwcap. 13.2% alc. **Rating** 96 **To** 2027 $38 NG ✪
Sophie's Block Beechworth Chardonnay 2014 This is a bracing chardonnay, firmly planted in Beechworth's subalpine, granitic soils. Unusual in Australia – although the rites of passage for many great Burgundian producers – the fruit was gently crushed to maximise aromatic release and complexity. A small percentage of whole berry/whole cluster were retained. All of this explains why the wine is bursting with flavour and personality given that mlf was eschewed. Truffles and oatmeal flavours are splayed across this wine's tensile, chalky spine. French oak is there, but merely as a support. Screwcap. 13% alc. **Rating** 95 **To** 2025 $38 NG
Henry's Block Beechworth Shiraz 2014 This is gorgeous cool climate shiraz. Boysenberry, iodine, violet and blueberry set the tone. The wine free-flows across juicy, mouthwatering acidity; gentle tannins and pulpy fruit, blue and red. A zesty tamarind spice pushes through the finish. There is nothing drying, nothing excessive. Mellifluous. Screwcap. 14% alc. **Rating** 95 **To** 2023 $38 NG

Pierrepoint Wines ★★★★

271 Pierrepoint Road, Tarrington, Vic 3300 **Region** Henty
T (03) 5572 5553 **www**.pierrepointwines.com.au **Open** Most days 11–6
Winemaker Scott Ireland (Contract) **Est.** 1998 **Dozens** 250 **Vyds** 5ha
Pierrepoint was established by Andrew and Jennifer Lacey on the foothills of Mt Pierrepoint between Hamilton and Tarrington at an altitude of 200m. The predominantly red buckshot soils of the vineyard are derived from ancient volcanic basalt, rich in minerals and free-draining. Two hectares each of pinot noir and pinot gris, and 1ha of chardonnay are planted on an ideal north-facing slope.

Pinot Noir 2015 A little dusty, then opens up to reveal an earthy-toned pinot, its cherry fruit and pips in the background. Ferrous, radishes and new leather, quite an intriguing mix; some oak spice before moving onto a medium-bodied palate with ripe, sinewy tannins and a sweet-sour edge but clean and refreshing. Screwcap. 13% alc. **Rating** 92 **To** 2021 $39 JF

Pierro ★★★★★

Caves Road, Wilyabrup via Cowaramup, WA 6284 **Region** Margaret River
T (08) 9755 6220 **www**.pierro.com.au **Open** 7 days 10–5
Winemaker Dr Michael Peterkin **Est.** 1979 **Dozens** 10 000 **Vyds** 7.85ha
Dr Michael Peterkin is another of the legion of Margaret River medical practitioner-vignerons; for good measure, he married into the Cullen family. Pierro is renowned for its stylish white wines, which often exhibit tremendous complexity; the Chardonnay can be monumental in its weight and texture. That said, its red wines from good vintages can be every

bit as good. Exports to the UK, Denmark, Belgium, Russia, Malaysia, Indonesia, Hong Kong, Singapore and Japan.

ΨΨΨΨΨ Reserve Margaret River Cabernet Sauvignon Merlot 2013 71% cabernet sauvignon, 22% merlot and a smattering of other Bordeaux grape varieties. A sublimely graceful confluence of red and black currant fruits, punctuated by dried sage and a litany of other herbs, all waiting in the wings of time. The delicacy, detail and impeccable poise between fruit and structural adjuncts allows for enjoyment now, yet those with patience will be rewarded. Screwcap. 13.5% alc. **Rating** 97 **To** 2036 $77 NG ✪

ΨΨΨΨΨ Margaret River Cabernet Sauvignon Merlot L.T.Cf. 2014 Majestic in its elegance, this is very different from the Reserve. Redcurrant, sage, licorice and a smidgeon of cedar oak are drawn long and sapid by finely ground chalky tannins and assuaging acidity. A gentle glide across the palate with just enough pucker to keep one coming back. Screwcap. 14% alc. **Rating** 95 **To** 2034 $40 NG
L.T.C. 2016 A long-established semillon sauvignon blanc, with a little touch of chardonnay, complexity coming from the blend, not barrel fermentation. Always hits the mark, and will certainly gain complexity without losing its freshness if cellared for up to 5 years. Screwcap. 13.5% alc. **Rating** 94 **To** 2021 $33.50

Pig in the House   ★★★☆

Balcombe Road, Billimari, NSW 2804 **Region** Cowra
T 0427 443 598 **www**.piginthehouse.com.au **Open** Fri–Sun 11–5 by appt
Winemaker Antonio D'Onise **Est.** 2002 **Dozens** 1500 **Vyds** 25ha
Jason and Rebecca O'Dea established their vineyard (7ha shiraz, 6ha cabernet sauvignon, 5ha merlot, 4.5ha chardonnay and 2.5ha sauvignon blanc) on a block of land formerly used as home for 20 free-range pigs – making any explanation about the name of the business totally unnecessary. Given its prior use, one would imagine the vines would grow lustily, and it is no surprise that organic certification has been given by Biological Farmers of Australia. The O'Deas have in fact taken the process several steps further, using biodynamic preparations and significantly reducing all sprays. The wines made are good advertisements for organic/biodynamic farming. Exports to Japan and China.

ΨΨΨΨΨ Organic Shiraz 2016 A vibrant, juicy wine with a core of intense fruit, sweet, and as if this has been made via carbonic maceration. Add to that a black pepper lift, dried herbs, lithe tannins and a cheery outlook. Shame about the name. Screwcap. 14.6% alc. **Rating** 91 **To** 2021 $30 JF

Pike & Joyce   ★★★★★

730 Mawson Road, Lenswood, SA 5240 **Region** Adelaide Hills
T (08) 8389 8102 **www**.pikeandjoyce.com.au **Open** Not
Winemaker Neil Pike, Steve Baraglia **Est.** 1998 **Dozens** 5000 **Vyds** 18.5ha
This is a partnership between the Pike family (of Clare Valley fame) and the Joyce family, related to Andrew Pike's wife, Cathy. The Joyce family have been orchardists at Lenswood for over 100 years, and also have extensive operations in the Riverland. Together with Andrew they have established a vineyard planted to sauvignon blanc (5.9ha), pinot noir (5.73ha), pinot gris (3.22ha), chardonnay (3.18ha) and semillon (0.47ha). The wines are made at the Pikes' Clare Valley winery. Exports to the UK, China and other major markets.

ΨΨΨΨΨ The Kay Reserve Adelaide Hills Chardonnay 2015 The bouquet wastes no time in establishing its complexity via a low-pitched note of funk/reduction, the palate sliding in without any hesitation to support the bouquet. It is intense and long, with grapefruit covering the entrance to and exit from the palate, white peach on the fine mid-palate. French oak has been given a limited, but still important, supporting role. Screwcap. 13.5% alc. **Rating** 95 **To** 2025 $55
Separe Adelaide Hills Gruner Veltliner 2016 Cool-fermented in stainless steel. This is a truly different and interesting play of pinot gris. Pale straw-green;

Pike & Joyce's keywords introduction on the back label starts with pear and finishes with lemon, but it's what comes in between that is so unusual, with arugula and root vegetables suggested with absolute accuracy. No white pepper, but lots of other facets to explore. As I say, fascinating. Screwcap. 13% alc. **Rating** 95 **To** 2024 $26 **✪**

Beurre Bosc Adelaide Hills Pinot Gris 2016 This has more flavour and attitude than most of its peers, and has a veritable rainbow of fruit flavours ranging well into tropical fruits, pink grapefruit helping corral the fruits with its acidity. Screwcap. 13% alc. **Rating** 94 **To** 2020 $26 **✪**

W.J.J. Reserve Adelaide Hills Pinot Noir 2015 MV6, 115, 115 and 777 clones blended post ferment, matured in French oak (30–50% new) for 10–12 months. A thoroughly attractive wine with a purity to its red cherry and forest strawberry fruit heightened by its satin smooth texture and balance; the length, too, is impeccable. Screwcap. 13.5% alc. **Rating** 94 **To** 2025 $55

ŢŢŢŢŢ **Les Saignees Pinot Noir Rose 2016 Rating** 93 **To** 2020 $22 **✪**
Descente Adelaide Hills Sauvignon Blanc 2016 Rating 90 **To** 2017 $25

Pikes

Polish Hill River Road, Sevenhill, SA 5453 **Region** Clare Valley
T (08) 8843 4370 **www.pikeswines.com.au Open** 7 days 10–4
Winemaker Neil Pike, Steve Baraglia **Est.** 1984 **Dozens** 35 000 **Vyds** 73ha
Owned by the Pike brothers: Andrew was for many years the senior viticulturist with Southcorp, Neil was a winemaker at Mitchell. Pikes now has its own winery, with Neil presiding. In most vintages its white wines, led by Riesling, are the most impressive. Planting of the vineyards has been an ongoing affair, with a panoply of varietals, new and traditional. The Merle is Pikes' limited-production flagship Riesling. Exports to the UK, the US, China, and other major markets.

ŢŢŢŢŢ **The Merle Clare Valley Riesling 2016** This wine always has an extra dimension to its fruit and structure. Bright pale straw-green; Neil Pike's comment that 'it is citrussy, lean, pure and slatey' is true, but doesn't address the exceptional drive and length the wine has. It is a great riesling, lovely now, but with even more in store in the far distant future. Trophies Clare Valley Wine Show '16. Screwcap. 12% alc. **Rating** 97 **To** 2036 $45 **✪**

ŢŢŢŢŢ **Traditionale Clare Valley Riesling 2016** Traditionale? Well, it's from all the best districts of the Clare Valley, and made in a very, very good vintage. Its bouquet is flowery, the mouthwatering palate with an electric intensity to its lime and lemon fruit that draws out the finish and aftertaste. It has one foot planted here and now, another 5–10 years down the track (and more points). Screwcap. 11.5% alc. **Rating** 95 **To** 2031 $25 **✪**

The E.W.P. Clare Valley Shiraz 2014 The colour is far from deep, and the light to medium-bodied palate has spicy savoury notes underpinning its main game of black and red cherry fruits. The mark of high quality comes with its great length and finesse, which you normally see in cool climate wines. The key? 13.5% alcohol. Screwcap. **Rating** 95 **To** 2029 $70

Premio Clare Valley Sangiovese 2015 Neil Pike thinks this is the best of the 20 vintages of sangiovese from the vineyard, and – by extension – the best of the nine Premio releases. And indeed it's a very smart sangio, its vibrant red fruits neatly framed by fine, persistent, savoury tannins that will always play second fiddle to the fruit. Screwcap. 14% alc. **Rating** 95 **To** 2025 $40

The Assemblage Clare Valley Shiraz Mourvedre Grenache 2014 No blend percentages supplied, but shiraz would certainly have the whip hand if the flavours and structure are any guide, rounding up the sometimes wayward flavours of Clare Valley mourvedre and grenache. The result is an attractive mix of black fruits punctuated by splashes of red fruit, tannins and oak well handled. Screwcap. 14% alc. **Rating** 94 **To** 2024 $23 **✪**

ŶŶŶŶẎ Clare Hills Riesling 2016 Rating 93 To 2031 $15 ✪
Eastside Clare Valley Shiraz 2014 Rating 92 To 2029 $28
Impostores Clare Valley Savignan 2016 Rating 91 To 2020 $22 JF ✪

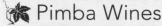 # Pimba Wines ★★★★★

495 Parkinsons Road, Gladysdale, Vic 3797 **Region** Yarra Valley
T 0401 228 196 **www**.pimbawines.com.au **Open** Not
Winemaker Dylan McMahon, Matt Pattison **Est.** 2015 **Dozens** 220
The owners are Ian, Matt and Alex Pattison, Pierre Van Der Heyde and Ben Hobson, who bring different skills and experience to the business, plus the all-important hand of Dylan McMahon, co-worker with Matt Pattison. There is as yet another unseen: the Syme on Yarra Vineyard, an extraordinary east-facing vineyard that is 30 years old, and from which Coldstream Hills has purchased pinot noir for many years. The Pimba partners believe this is one of the great syrah sites in the Yarra Valley, under the care of one of Australia's best viticulturists, Stuart Proud. Pimba is a one-variety, one-purpose business, to prove that the syrah can show as much poise, purity and character as any other expression of syrah/shiraz across the globe. 2016 wasn't a particularly good vintage in the Yarra Valley, but it's arguable that the extra warmth was to the advantage of shiraz. Time will tell how far Pimba wines can go.

ŶŶŶŶŶ Yarra Valley Syrah 2016 Brilliant crimson-purple hue; a wonderfully juicy and seductive wine with a pure silk texture to the long, pirouetting palate of red and black fruits. Not the greatest of wines, but one of the most magical. Just love it. Screwcap. 13.7% alc. **Rating** 97 **To** 2031

Pimpernel Vineyards ★★★★★

6 Hill Road, Coldstream, Vic 3770 **Region** Yarra Valley
T 0457 326 436 **www**.pimpernelvineyards.com.au **Open** Fri–Sat & public hols 11–5
Winemaker Damien Archibald, Mark Horrigan **Est.** 2001 **Dozens** 3000 **Vyds** 6ha
Lilydale-based cardiologist Mark Horrigan's love affair with wine started long before he had heard about either the Yarra Valley or his family's links, centuries ago, to Condrieu, France. He is a direct descendant of the Chapuis family, his ultimate ancestors buried in the Church of St Etienne in 1377. In a cosmopolitan twist, his father came from a Welsh mining village, but made his way to university and found many things to enjoy, not the least wine. When the family moved to Australia in 1959, wine remained part of everyday life and, as Mark grew up in the '70s, the obsession passed from father to son. In 2001 he and wife Fiona purchased a property in the Yarra Valley on which they have built a (second) house, planted a vineyard, and erected a capacious winery designed by WA architect Peter Moran. In the course of doing so they became good friends of near-neighbour the late Dr Bailey Carrodus; some of the delphic labelling of Pimpernel's wines is pure Carrodus. Exports to the UK and Singapore.

ŶŶŶŶŶ Grouch 2015 95% shiraz, 5% marsanne, 'moderate' post-ferment maceration, matured in used French oak for 15 months. The bright, deep colour suggests that co-fermentation of marsanne works as well as viognier, although the immediacy of the power and tannins on the palate takes the wine out of the normal soothing of co-fermented viognier. The answer lies in the post-ferment maceration, the oak influence a mystery. Diam. 14.8% alc. **Rating** 96 **To** 2040 $80
Yarra Valley GSM2 2015 50% grenache, 26% shiraz, 23% mourvedre, 1% muscat of Alexandria, the grenache and muscat of Alexandria co-fermented, matured for 12 months in used oak. A highly fragrant and expressive bouquet is no false dawn: this is a lovely Rhône red with tuck and pike, and a high degree of difficulty to bring it all together in the cool climate of the Yarra Valley (Serrat and Mount Mary two other skilled practitioners). It'll live, but surely can never be better than it is today. Diam. 14.5% alc. **Rating** 96 **To** 2021 $50 ✪
Yarra Valley Shiraz 2015 Matured in French oak (50% new) for 12 months. The fragrant bouquet, offering spices and dark berry aromas, flows into a supple, medium-bodied palate with a complex web of gently savoury/earthy flavours supporting the black cherry fruits of the long finish. Diam. 14.7% alc. **Rating** 95 **To** 2030 $45

Shiraz Viognier 2014 Includes 2% co-fermented viognier, matured in new (30%) and used oak. The colour is bright, although not especially deep; even though 2% viognier is tiny, it has brightened the colour and seems to have helped lift the challenge of the alcohol; the wine is charged with juicy red and black cherry fruits, the palate long, the finish neatly tying up the parcel with the aid of fine-spun tannins. Diam. 14.8% alc. **Rating** 95 **To** 2029 $50

♟♟♟♟♡ Yarra Valley Chardonnay 2015 Rating 91 To 2022 $50

Pindarie   ★★★★

946 Rosedale Road, Gomersal, SA 5352 **Region** Barossa Valley
T (08) 8524 9019 **www**.pindarie.com.au **Open** Mon–Fri 11–4, w'ends 11–5
Winemaker Peter Leske **Est.** 2005 **Dozens** 8000 **Vyds** 32.4ha
Owners Tony Brooks and Wendy Allan met at Roseworthy College in 1985. Tony was the sixth generation of farmers in SA and WA, and was studying agriculture; NZ-born Wendy was studying viticulture. On graduation Tony worked overseas managing sheep feedlots in Saudi Arabia, Turkey and Jordan, while Wendy worked for the next 12 years with Penfolds, commencing as a grower liaison officer and working her way up to become a senior viticulturist. She also found time to study viticulture in California, Israel, Italy, Germany, France, Portugal, Spain and Chile, working vintages and assessing vineyards for wine projects. In 2001 she completed a graduate diploma in wine business. The cellar door and cafe (which won a major tourism award in '12) has panoramic views. Exports to Japan and China.

♟♟♟♟♟ T.S.S. Barossa Valley Tempranillo Sangiovese Shiraz 2016 A 70/24/6% blend fermented separately, matured in used French oak. This is a particularly nice medium-bodied wine, alive with red berry/cherry fruits and perfectly weighted, savoury tannins. Screwcap. 13.5% alc. **Rating** 94 **To** 2026 $24 ✪

♟♟♟♟♡ Black Hinge Reserve Shiraz Cabernet 2015 Rating 93 To 2035 $60
The Risk Taker Tempranillo 2016 Rating 91 To 2023 $26

Pinelli Wines   ★★★★

30 Bennett Street, Caversham, WA 6055 **Region** Swan District
T (08) 9279 6818 **www**.pinelliwines.com.au **Open** Mon–Sat 9–5, Sun 10–5
Winemaker Robert and Daniel Pinelli **Est.** 1980 **Dozens** 17 000 **Vyds** 9.78ha
Domenic and Iolanda Pinelli emigrated from Italy in the mid-1950s, and it was not long before Domenic was employed by Waldeck Wines, then one of the Swan Valley's more important wineries. With the benefit of 20 years' experience gained with Waldeck, in '80 he purchased a 2.8ha vineyard that had been established many years previously. It became the site of the Pinelli family winery, cellar door and home vineyard, subsequently significantly expanded, with cabernet sauvignon, colombard, merlot and shiraz. Son Robert graduated with a degree in oenology from Roseworthy in 1987, and has been the winemaker at Pinelli for over 20 years. His brother Daniel obtained a degree in civil engineering from the University of WA in '94, but eventually the lure of the family winery became too strong, so he joined his brother in '02, and obtained his oenology degree from CSU in '07. He graduated with distinction, and was awarded the Domaine Chandon Sparkling Wine Award for best sparkling wine production student.

♟♟♟♟♟ Aged Release Family Reserve Chenin Blanc 2007 Very good colour; there's never been any question about the ability of chenin blanc to benefit from age, but this is a particularly good example, sharing with semillon and marsanne the ability to cruise along powered by natural acidity. Another 10 years won't damage its flight path, but will bring only modest improvement, so don't hang back. Screwcap. 13% alc. **Rating** 95 **To** 2027 $35 ✪

♟♟♟♟♡ Reserve Vermentino 2016 Rating 90 To 2018 $18 ✪

Pinemount

PO Box 290, Somers, Vic 3927 **Region** Various Victoria
T 0431 057 574 **www**.pinemount.com.au **Open** Not
Winemaker Imogen Dillon **Est.** 2016 **Dozens** 250

Imogen Dillon graduated from Curtin University with a degree in oenology, and went on to work two vintages with Houghton, two with Plantagenet, fitting in further vintages at Goundrey, and Tintara in McLaren Vale, while doing the Flying Winemaker trick – completing vintages in the Napa Valley and Bordeaux. In 2007 she joined West Cape Howe as winemaker before moving to Margaret River in '09 working as a winemaker with Larry Cherubino, where she had a number of specific areas of responsibility. She also completed a vintage in Washington State, US, where Larry had a consultancy job at the time. In '13 she gave birth to twins, resulting in a winemaking hiatus. Fermoy Estate was her next job through '14, but this, too, was cut short by her husband Peter being given a winemaking position with Handpicked Wines on the Mornington Peninsula. She started at Yabby Lake for the '15 harvest, and has been retained there through to the present. In between times she has kept herself busy by starting Pinemount, producing Pinot Gris and Syrah from the Yarra Valley in the inaugural '16 vintage. The aim is to expand her grower base with specific styles, extending to Chalmers fiano from Heathcote and an Upper Yarra pinot, both in the '17 vintage.

ＹＹＹＹＹ **Yarra Valley Syrah 2016** Matured for 8 months in French puncheons (40% new). Full, deep crimson-purple; the bouquet (and colour) start the ball rolling in a direction the full-bodied palate doesn't deviate from; satsuma plum, dark cherry and savoury/herbal/forest floor notes are an undercarpet for the fruit and French oak. Needs time to relax and open its fierce grip. Great label graphics. Screwcap. 14.2% alc. **Rating** 94 **To** 2030 $32

ＹＹＹＹＹ **Yarra Valley Pinot Gris 2016 Rating** 93 **To** 2020 $25 ✪

Pipers Brook Vineyard

1216 Pipers Brook Road, Pipers Brook, Tas 7254 **Region** Northern Tasmania
T (03) 6382 7527 **www**.pipersbrook.com.au **Open** 7 days 10–5
Winemaker Brian Widstrand **Est.** 1974 **Dozens** 70 000 **Vyds** 194ha

The Pipers Brook empire has almost 200ha of vineyard supporting the Pipers Brook and Ninth Island labels, with the major focus, of course, being on Pipers Brook. Fastidious viticulture and winemaking, immaculate packaging and enterprising marketing create a potent and effective blend. Pipers Brook operates two cellar door outlets, one at headquarters, the other at Strathlyn. Pipers Brook is owned by Belgian-owned sheepskin business Kreglinger, which has also established the large Norfolk Island winery and vineyard at Mount Benson in SA (see separate entry). Exports to the UK, the US and other major markets.

ＹＹＹＹＹ **Gewurztraminer 2016** This boasts a peacock's plume of flavour and impressive, punchy length that lingers on and on. Lychee, ginger spice, cumquat and rosewater notes spring from the glass. And they don't lose focus, reverberating across a chassis of fine-tuned astringency and gentle acidity, while gaining a souk of sweetness in the mouth. Screwcap. 13% alc. **Rating** 94 **To** 2020 $34 NG

Pinot Noir 2016 Pipers Brook has long made compelling, sinuously tannic and long-lived pinot noirs. It is rewarding to see that the range is on song. This is extremely delicate, yet in a way forceful, with pumice-like, powdery tannins defining a pinot of riveting, cerebral texture. It is across this spider web of chiffon that sour red cherry, strawberry, vanilla and satsuma plum have their way, ever so gradually seeping across the textural, taut mid-palate. This will age very well, belying its initial lighter complexion. Screwcap. 13% alc. **Rating** 94 **To** 2028 $45 NG

Kreglinger Brut Rose 2006 Medium to full salmon hue. There is elegance here: a gorgeous fragrance of rose petals, Turkish Delight and cherry liqueur, and a characterful presence of structure. Subtle brioche complexity and silky creaminess proclaim 9 years on lees, with the finely textural grip of tannin structure. It carries

with excellent line and length, concluding with fine-tuned acid tension. Cork.
Rating 94 **To** 2018 $65 TS

ΨΨΨΨΨ **Pinot Gris 2016 Rating** 93 **To** 2021 $34 NG
Ninth Island Rose 2016 Rating 93 **To** 2018 $24 NG **☺**
Kreglinger Vintage Brut 2007 Rating 93 **To** 2018 $55 TS
Late Disgorged Vintage Cuvee 2007 Rating 93 **To** 2017 $42.50 TS
Chardonnay 2016 Rating 92 **To** 2026 $34 NG
Pinot Gris 2015 Rating 92 **To** 2017 $34 CM
Reserve Pinot Noir 2015 Rating 92 **To** 2025 $95 NG
Kreglinger Vintage Brut de Blancs 2004 Rating 92 **To** 2017 $65 TS
Tasmania NV Rating 92 **To** 2018 TS

Pirramimma

Johnston Road, McLaren Vale, SA 5171 **Region** McLaren Vale
T (08) 8323 8205 **www.**pirramimma.com.au **Open** Mon–Fri 10–4.30, w'ends 10.30–5
Winemaker Geoff Johnston **Est.** 1892 **Dozens** 50 000 **Vyds** 91.5ha
A long-established family-owned company with outstanding vineyard resources. It is using
those resources to full effect, with a series of intense old vine varietals including Semillon,
Sauvignon Blanc, Chardonnay, Shiraz, Grenache, Cabernet Sauvignon and Petit Verdot, all
fashioned without over-embellishment. Wines are released under several ranges: Pirramimma,
Stock's Hill, Pirra, Gilden Lily, Eight Carat, Wattle Park, Vineyard Select, Katunga and Lion's
Gate. Exports to all major markets.

ΨΨΨΨΨ **Ironstone Low Trellis McLaren Vale Shiraz 2013** 40% matured for
28 months in new French oak and American oak, the remainder in older
barriques. Deep crimson-purple; this is a rich and luscious wine, but keeps a sense
of proportion and balance, with fruit and tannins simply acknowledging the oak.
Will live for many decades. Cork. 14.8% alc. **Rating** 95 **To** 2043 $50
Ironstone Old Bush Vine McLaren Vale Grenache 2014 50% matured in
new French puncheons, 50% in used French and American oak, for 18 months.
This has the structure that separates McLaren Vale grenache from all others in SA,
giving this deliciously pliant wine an almost regal air. The use of so much new
French oak was brave, but it's part of that regal DNA. Cork. 14.6% alc. **Rating** 95
To 2029 $50
McLaren Vale Shiraz 2014 Only 30% matured in new French and
American barriques, the balance in tank. This approach has worked well, with
a combination of freshness and complexity of fruit and oak, fine but persistent
tannins lengthening the finish. During the journey, black cherry, blackberry and
(guess what) dark chocolate have all added to the package. Screwcap. 14.7% alc.
Rating 94 **To** 2034 $30 **☺**
McLaren Vale Cabernet Sauvignon 2013 Shows that, when conditions are
right, McLaren Vale can produce cabernet with convincing varietal character,
needing no embellishment from lots of new French oak, bringing with it its own
structure and texture. This really is a smart wine, with a juicy cassis component to
finish it off. Screwcap. 14.6% alc. **Rating** 94 **To** 2033 $30 **☺**
McLaren Vale Petit Verdot 2014 Dense crimson-purple; Pirramimma has
some of the oldest petit verdot plantings in Aus, if not the oldest. This has relaxed
power, with layer upon layer of dark berry fruits interleaved with ripe tannins, oak
a minor player. Has time on its side, but no issue if enjoyed now rather than later.
Screwcap. 14.5% alc. **Rating** 94 **To** 2030 $30 **☺**
Ironstone McLaren Vale Malbec 2015 20% fermented in new French
barriques, 80% in a mix of used French and American oak, matured for 9 months.
This is unapologetically full-bodied, but has a power of satsuma and blood plum,
blackberry and licorice – and a slew of tannins. Cork. 14.5% alc. **Rating** 94
To 2030 $50

ΨΨΨΨ **Old Bush Vine McLaren Vale Grenache 2014 Rating** 89 **To** 2029 $30
Vineyard Select McLaren Vale GSM 2013 Rating 89 **To** 2023 $35

Pizzini ★★★★☆

175 King Valley Road, Whitfield, Vic 3768 **Region** King Valley
T (03) 5729 8278 **www**.pizzini.com.au **Open** 7 days 10–5
Winemaker Joel Pizzini **Est.** 1980 **Dozens** 40 000 **Vyds** 48.7ha
Fred and Katrina Pizzini have been grapegrowers in the King Valley for over 30 years, with a substantial vineyard. Originally much of the grape production was sold, but today 80% is retained for the Pizzini brand, and the focus is on winemaking, which has been particularly successful. Their wines rank high among the many King Valley producers. It is not surprising that their wines should span both Italian and traditional varieties, and I can personally vouch for their Italian cooking skills. Katrina's A tavola! cooking school gives lessons in antipasti, gnocchi, risotto, cakes and desserts – and, of course, pasta. Exports to the UK and Japan.

ΨΨΨΨΨ **White Fields King Valley Pinot Grigio 2016** One parcel of the grapes comes from the best estate block, the other from Whitlands, hand-picked bunches are stored at 6°C for 2 days, pressed, only free-run juice fermented, 50% in tank with cultured yeast, 50% in used French oak with wild yeast, matured for 5 months with stirring. The resulting wine is of high quality and will age with grace thanks to its texture, structure, tight pear/apple flavours and (finally) acidity. Screwcap. 13.5% alc. **Rating** 95 To 2021 $28 **O**

ΨΨΨΨΨ **King Valley Shiraz 2015 Rating** 92 To 2025 $25 **O**
King Valley Barbera 2015 Rating 92 To 2025 $35
King Valley Arneis 2016 Rating 91 To 2020 $24
King Valley Nebbiolo 2012 Rating 91 To 2022 $55 CM
King Valley Riesling 2016 Rating 90 To 2021 $18 **O**
King Valley Rosetta 2016 Rating 90 To 2017 $19 **O**
Lana King Valley Nebbiolo Barbera 2015 Rating 90 To 2021 $25
Nonna Gisella Sangiovese 2015 Rating 90 To 2019 $21.50 CM
Lana Il Nostro Gallo King Valley Sangiovese Canaiolo Colorino 2014
Rating 90 To 2020 $24 CM
La Volpe King Valley Nebbiolo 2014 Rating 90 To 2021 $28 CM

Plan B Wines ★★★★

Freshwater Drive, Margaret River, WA 6285 **Region** Great Southern/Margaret River
T 0413 759 030 **www**.planbwines.com **Open** Not
Winemaker Bill Crappsley, Vanessa Carson **Est.** 2005 **Dozens** 40 000 **Vyds** 20ha
Plan B is a joint venture between Terry Chellappah, wine consultant, Bill Crappsley, a veteran winemaker/consultant, and Andrew Blythe. The Shiraz is sourced from Bill's Calgardup Vineyard, the remaining wines from Arlewood, and all are single vineyard releases. It has been a notably successful Plan B under Terry's management, with significant increases in production. In 2014 Bill Crappsley was awarded the Jack Mann Memorial Medal for significant services to the WA Wine Industry, coinciding with his 50 years in winemaking in WA. He has also won the Di Cullen Award (in '07), and the George Mulgrue Award (in 1999), both recognising his services to the industry. Exports to all major markets.

ΨΨΨΨΨ **GT Cabernet Sauvignon Sangiovese 2015** The tangy savoury spectrum of the sangiovese adds a neat dimension to this medium-weighted blend. Ferrous, earth and tangy currants and cassis, bright acidity and sinewy tannins – a real livewire. Screwcap. 14.2% alc. **Rating** 92 To 2025 $22 JF **O**
TV Geographe Tempranillo Viognier 2015 Thankfully just 2% of viognier, so it's not OTT; instead it bolsters the terrific colour and adds a lift to the aromatics. The bright red fruits, savouriness and raspy, textual and slightly drying tannins of the tempranillo are key. Screwcap. 14.5% alc. **Rating** 92 To 2022 $30 JF
CV Margaret River Chardonnay Viognier 2016 There's 9% viognier from Geographe and it makes its presence felt positively as it plumps out the palate, adds some apricot kernel notes to the citrus-fig characters. Zesty acidity from chardonnay keeps this light on its feet. Screwcap. 13% alc. **Rating** 90 To 2020 $22 JF

ΨΨΨΨ **OD Frankland River Riesling 2016 Rating** 89 To 2025 $22 JF

Plantagenet

Albany Highway, Mount Barker, WA 6324 **Region** Mount Barker
T (08) 9851 3111 **www.**plantagenetwines.com **Open** 7 days 10–4.30
Winemaker Luke Eckerseley, Chris Murtha **Est.** 1974 **Dozens** 25 000 **Vyds** 130ha
Plantagenet was established by Tony Smith, who continues to be involved in its management over 40 years later, notwithstanding that it has been owned by Lionel Samson & Son for many years. He established five vineyards: Bouverie in 1968, Wyjup in '71, Rocky Horror 1 in '88, Rocky Horror 2 in '97 and Rosetta in '99. These vineyards are the cornerstone of the substantial production of the consistently high quality wines that have always been the mark of Plantagenet: highly aromatic Riesling, tangy citrus-tinged Chardonnay, glorious Rhône-style Shiraz and ultra-stylish Cabernet Sauvignon. Exports to the UK, the US, Canada, China and Japan.

ŸŸŸŸŸ **The House of Plantagenet 'York' Mount Barker Chardonnay 2015** A very impressive Plantagenet chardonnay, its seamless fusion of citrus, stone fruit and creamy, spicy oak laying the foundations for the long, lingering palate. The balance is such that it can be enjoyed at any time along the journey, starting now. Screwcap. 14% alc. **Rating** 95 **To** 2025 $35 ❂
The House of Plantagenet 'Lancaster' Mount Barker Shiraz 2014 Clear crimson-purple; the fragrant red fruit and spice bouquet provides a perfect launch pad for the fresh, lively medium-bodied palate that follows. It is positively silky in its texture, and equally mouthwatering, as red and black cherries are joined by savoury/spicy tannins. The length of the wine builds and strengthens each time it is retasted. Screwcap. 14% alc. **Rating** 95 **To** 2029 $35 ❂
The House of Plantagenet 'Aquitaine' Mount Barker Cabernet Sauvignon 2014 Plantagenet is in a happy place at the moment. This deliciously juicy cassis-accented wine should melt the heart of the most dedicated pinot noir drinker; the palate is the epitome of elegance, the finish sustained by superfine tannins. Screwcap. 14% alc. **Rating** 95 **To** 2034 $35 ❂

ŸŸŸŸ♀ **The House of Plantagenet 'Angevin' Riesling 2016 Rating** 92 **To** 2026 $28 NG
Three Lions Cabernet Merlot 2014 Rating 92 **To** 2024 $24 SC ❂
Three Lions Mount Barker Chardonnay 2016 Rating 91 **To** 2022 $23 NG ❂
Three Lions Great Southern Shiraz 2014 Rating 91 **To** 2024 $24 SC
The House of Plantagenet 'Angevin' Mount Barker Riesling 2015 Rating 90 **To** 2023 $30

Poacher's Ridge Vineyard

1630 Spencer Road, Narrikup, WA 6326 **Region** Mount Barker
T (08) 9857 6066 **www.**poachersridge.com.au **Open** Fri–Sun 10–4
Winemaker Robert Diletti (Contract) **Est.** 2000 **Dozens** 900 **Vyds** 6.9ha
Alex and Janet Taylor purchased the Poacher's Ridge property in 1999. It had previously been used for cattle grazing. The vineyard includes shiraz, cabernet sauvignon, merlot, riesling, marsanne and viognier. Winning the Tri Nations 2007 merlot class against the might of Australia, NZ and South Africa with its '05 Louis' Block Great Southern Merlot was a dream come true. Nor was it a one-time success: Poacher's Ridge Merlot is always at, or near, the top of the tree.

ŸŸŸŸŸ **Great Southern Cabernet Sauvignon 2015** Picked at 14° baume to avoid dead fruit, and has produced a classy, full-bodied cabernet following 17 months maturation in French oak (35% new). Blackcurrant, bay leaf and dried herbs out-muscle the firm cabernet tannins, thus creating the balance that will underwrite the long future of the wine. Screwcap. 13.5% alc. **Rating** 95 **To** 2040 $30 ❂
Great Southern Merlot 2015 Deep crimson-purple; Great Southern merlot meets the challenge of Margaret River merlot head on: blue and red berry fruits, fine tannins and French oak are all focused on the same page of what is a very

good medium-bodied wine with excellent balance and length, the oak integrated. Screwcap. 13.5% alc. **Rating** 94 **To** 2030 $30 ✪

🍷🍷🍷🍷 Great Southern Riesling 2016 **Rating** 89 **To** 2021 $26

Pokolbin Estate ★★★★★

McDonalds Road, Pokolbin, NSW 2321 **Region** Hunter Valley
T (02) 4998 7524 **www**.pokolbinestate.com.au **Open** 7 days 9–5
Winemaker Andrew Thomas (Contract) **Est.** 1980 **Dozens** 4000 **Vyds** 15.7ha
Pokolbin Estate has a very unusual, but very good, multi-varietal, multi-vintage array of wines always available for sale. The Riesling is true riesling, not misnamed Semillon, the latter being one of their best wines, and wines under screwcap going back six or seven vintages, and single vineyard offerings to boot, are available.

🍷🍷🍷🍷🍷 Phoenix Hunter Valley Shiraz Tempranillo 2014 A 50/50% blend, matured in French oak for 15 months. Light, but bright, hue; the blend works well, even though tempranillo theoretically demands a cool climate; there is a display of juicy red berry fruits that leads to the idea of a second glass pronto (tannins not in play). Screwcap. 13.5% alc. **Rating** 92 **To** 2021 $28

Polperro | Even Keel ★★★★☆

150 Red Hill Road, Red Hill, Vic 3937 **Region** Mornington Peninsula
T 0405 155 882 **www**.polperrowines.com.au **Open** Thurs–Mon 11–2
Winemaker Samuel Coverdale **Est.** 2006 **Dozens** 3000 **Vyds** 13ha
Sam Coverdale lives on the Mornington Peninsula, makes wine there full-time and surfs part-time. Before taking up residence on the Peninsula, he obtained his degree in oenology from CSU, and accumulated 10 years of winemaking experience in Australia, France, Spain and Italy. Polperro is his single vineyard Mornington Peninsula range, and includes Pinot Noir, Chardonnay and Pinot Gris. Second label Even Keel uses grape varieties that best represent their region. Exports to Hong Kong.

🍷🍷🍷🍷🍷 Even Keel Canberra District Syrah 2015 Clear, full crimson-purple; a very well made cool climate shiraz with all the vibrancy of the best examples; juicy, bright red berry fruits are set in a wreath of spice and black pepper, with superfine tannins and quality oak in respectful support on the long palate. Screwcap. 13.5% alc. **Rating** 95 **To** 2030 $35 ✪

Even Keel Tumbarumba Chardonnay 2016 A really moreish style. There's an evenness on the palate, with tangy juicy citrus notes and stone fruit plus more complex leesy and oak influenced characters – neatly balanced. Screwcap. 12.8% alc. **Rating** 94 **To** 2023 $35 JF

🍷🍷🍷🍷🍷 Polperro Mill Hill Chardonnay 2015 **Rating** 93 **To** 2022 $60 JF
Even Keel Mornington Peninsula Pinot Gris 2016 **Rating** 92 **To** 2020 $29 JF
Polperro Mornington Peninsula Pinot Noir 2015 **Rating** 92 **To** 2020 $55
Polperro Landaviddy Lane Mornington Peninsula Pinot Noir 2015 **Rating** 92 **To** 2022 $65 JF
Polperro Mill Hill Pinot Noir 2015 **Rating** 91 **To** 2021 $65 JF
Polperro Talland Hill Pinot Noir 2015 **Rating** 91 **To** 2021 $65 JF

Pondalowie Vineyards ★★★★★

55 Bambra School Road, Bambra, Vic 3241 **Region** Bendigo
T 0439 373 366 **www**.pondalowie.com.au **Open** W'ends by appt
Winemaker Dominic Morris, Krystina Morris **Est.** 1997 **Dozens** 3000 **Vyds** 10ha
Dominic and Krystina Morris both have strong winemaking backgrounds gained in Australia, France and Portugal, where Dominic worked alternate vintages from 1995 to 2012. They have established 5.5ha of shiraz, 2ha each of tempranillo and cabernet sauvignon, and a little malbec at Bridgewater on Loddon in Central Victoria. They are also establishing a cool climate

vineyard at Bambra in the Otways, south-west of Melbourne. Incidentally, the illustration on the Pondalowie label is not a piece of barbed wire, but a very abstract representation of the winery kelpie dog. Exports to Hong Kong and Japan.

🍷🍷🍷🍷🍷 **Reserve Heathcote Shiraz 2015** Deeply coloured; the power and intensity of the black fruits is exceptional, yet there is a generosity that means it's possible to enjoy it now, even though it will take a decade to approach its best. Screwcap. 14% alc. **Rating** 96 **To** 2035 $50 ✪

Old Clones Shiraz 2015 Dense, deep crimson-purple colour is the first sign; spiced berry/plum aromas the second; the plush, powerful palate, replete with poached plum and blackberry fruits, the third; licorice and ripe tannins fourth; the cuttings from century-old vines around Bendigo the final note. A story in a glass. Screwcap. 14% alc. **Rating** 95 **To** 2035 $40

Pooley Wines   ★★★★★

Butcher's Hill Vineyard, 1431 Richmond Road, Richmond, Tas 7025
Region Southern Tasmania
T (03) 6260 2895 **www**.pooleywines.com.au **Open** 7 days 10–5
Winemaker Anna Pooley **Est.** 1985 **Dozens** 5000 **Vyds** 16ha

Three generations of the Pooley family have been involved in the development of Pooley Wines, although the winery was previously known as Cooinda Vale. Plantings have now reached over 12ha in a region that is warmer and drier than most people realise. In 2003 the family planted pinot noir and pinot grigio (with more recent plantings of pinot noir and chardonnay) at Belmont Vineyard, a heritage property with an 1830s Georgian home and a (second) cellar door in the old sandstone barn and stables.

🍷🍷🍷🍷🍷 **Cooinda Vale Single Vineyard Chardonnay 2015** The wine hits the mouth with the crack of a whip, taking me out of my comfort zone. Its length and intensity are awesome – small wonder that from '05–'14 the fruit was purchased by Penfolds for Yattarna. A triumphant homecoming: unsweetened citrus/grapefruit, white peach and cleansing acidity ends up with the finish balanced. Screwcap. 13% alc. **Rating** 98 **To** 2030 $58 ✪

Riesling 2016 You can't make wine by numbers, nor rate them. This won the trophy for Best Riesling at the Melbourne Wine Awards '16 off the back of 9.5g/l titratable acidity, pH 2.9 and residual sugar 3.5g/l. This should by rights be fearsome, but it's not – it's just awesomely delicious, with a bouquet full of white flowers, the palate with pink grapefruit and Granny Smith apple. It's virtually immune from ageing. Screwcap. 12.3% alc. **Rating** 97 **To** 2041 $36 ✪

🍷🍷🍷🍷🍷 **Butcher's Hill Single Vineyard Pinot Noir 2015** Clones 114, 115, MV6 and 777, 15% whole bunches, the remainder destemmed whole berries, open-fermented, matured in French barriques (35% new) for 13 months. Vibrant and lively, with a super-fragrant red berry bouquet and palate; the most instantly enjoyable of the four Pooley pinots, with a long and airy finish. Screwcap. 13.5% alc. **Rating** 96 **To** 2030 $58 ✪

Family Reserve Single Vineyard Pinot Noir 2015 From the original Cooinda Vale vineyard planted in 1983 by grandparents Dennis and Margaret Pooley. Has significantly greater power, fruit intensity and forest floor than its siblings, and achieves all this while as light on its feet as a ballet dancer. Screwcap. 13.1% alc. **Rating** 96 **To** 2031 $85

Pinot Noir 2015 A blend of declassified barrels from Cooinda Vale and Butchers Hill, but predominantly from the Clarence House Vineyard in the Coal River Valley (clones 777 and 2051). A fragrant and juicy bouquet and palate with a savoury/foresty subtext in small print, but running alongside the red and dark berry fruits. Screwcap. 13.5% alc. **Rating** 95 **To** 2028 $46

Cooinda Vale Single Vineyard Pinot Noir 2015 Clones 114 and 115, with an average age of 15 years, 10% whole bunches, matured in French barriques (35% new) for 13 months. Touches of herb and mint lurk behind the red fruit façade on both bouquet and palate, but don't dominate the fruit on the finish. Screwcap. 13.3% alc. **Rating** 95 **To** 2029 $58

Gewurztraminer 2016 Rating 94 $36

Poonawatta

1227 Eden Valley Road, Flaxman Valley, SA 5235 **Region** Eden Valley
T (08) 8565 3248 **www.**poonawatta.com **Open** By appt
Winemaker Reid Bosward, Andrew Holt **Est.** 1880 **Dozens** 1800 **Vyds** 3.6ha
The Poonawatta story is complex, stemming from 0.8ha of shiraz planted in 1880. When Andrew Holt's parents purchased the Poonawatta property, the vineyard had suffered decades of neglect, and the slow process of restoration began. While that was underway, the strongest canes available from the winter pruning of the 1880 block were slowly and progressively dug into the stony soil of the site. It took seven years to establish the 0.8ha Cuttings Block, and the yield is even lower than that of the 1880 Block. Second label, Monties Block, sits underneath The Cuttings (from the 'new' vines) and at the top is The 1880. The Riesling is produced from a single vineyard of 2ha hand-planted by the Holt family in the 1970s. Exports to Canada, France, Denmark, Taiwan, Hong Kong and China.

The Eden Riesling 2016 45yo low-yielding vines, sustainably farmed, free-run juice fermented slowly (18–22 days). A marvellous riesling, majestically perfumed, intensely lime juice-flavoured and exceptionally long. I couldn't resist the temptation to swallow half of the first sip. Just under 400 dozen made. Screwcap. 12% alc. **Rating** 97 **To** 2036 $26 **○**

Valley of Eden Off Dry Riesling 2016 The balance between residual sugar and titratable acidity is nigh-on perfect, and leaves the lime juice and Meyer lemon flavours complete freedom in semaphoring their message. It's dangerously drinkable now, but give it 5 years and it'll be nectar of the gods. Screwcap. 10.8% alc. **Rating** 94 **To** 2030 $26 **○**

The 1880 Eden Valley Shiraz 2014 Rating 90 **To** 2029 $90

Port Phillip Estate

263 Red Hill Road, Red Hill, Vic 3937 **Region** Mornington Peninsula
T (03) 5989 4444 **www.**portphillipestate.com.au **Open** 7 days 11–5
Winemaker Glen Hayley **Est.** 1987 **Dozens** 7000 **Vyds** 9.3ha
Port Phillip Estate has been owned by Giorgio and Dianne Gjergja since 2000. The ability of the site to produce outstanding Syrah, Pinot Noir and Chardonnay, and very good Sauvignon Blanc, is something special. In July '15, following the departure of Sandro Mosele, his assistant of six years, Glen Hayley, was appointed to take his place. Quite possibly the estate may have answers for decades to come. The futuristic, multimillion-dollar restaurant, cellar door and winery complex, designed by award-winning Wood/Marsh Architecture, overlooks the vineyards and Westernport Bay. Exports to the UK, Canada, Singapore and China.

Mornington Peninsula Sauvignon 2016 A relatively unusual but welcome, and indeed refreshing, take on this variety in Australia. More reminiscent of Loire Valley expressions, with lanolin, quince, candied grapefruit and stone fruit notes; verdant fennel pungency lingers in the background. There is nothing exuberantly tropical or sherbet-lime about this wine and it is all the more restrained, savoury and drinkable because of it. Screwcap. 13.8% alc. **Rating** 95 **To** 2019 $27 NG **○**

Single Site Red Hill Chardonnay 2015 The bouquet has a touch of à la mode funk, and the palate has more depth and power than Kooyong's '15 Chardonnay. If there's a criticism, it's that its richness and punch don't leave much airspace for finesse, but that's no crime in a chardonnay world so fixated on elegance. Screwcap. 13% alc. **Rating** 95 **To** 2024 $35 **○**

Serenne Mornington Peninsula Shiraz 2015 This is cool climate shiraz all the way. Green olive, black and red cherries, deli cold cuts, fennel and cardamom all slink along a skein of white peppery acidity and fibrous tannins. Violet lifts the attack and the finish. An understated wine of real pedigree. Screwcap. 13% alc. **Rating** 95 **To** 2023 $51 NG

Salasso Mornington Peninsula Rose 2016 A blend of 69% pinot noir and 31% shiraz, this provides thrills with a chill! Sweet and sour red fruits pop across the mouth, all strung across a bow of crunchy acidity, mineral timbre and tangy orange zest lifting the finish. Screwcap. 13% alc. **Rating** 94 **To** 2018 $26 NG ✪
Red Hill Mornington Peninsula Pinot Noir 2015 Red and black cherry, rhubarb, orange zest and a mulch of wet leaves and clove make the introduction. This sappy, mid-weighted pinot expands across a spider web of savoury whole cluster spike, sandy yet firm tannins and well appointed French oak. Screwcap. 13.5% alc. **Rating** 94 **To** 2025 $39 NG

♥♥♥♥♡ **Balnarring Pinot Noir 2015 Rating** 93 **To** 2023 $39 NG

Portsea Estate

7 Pembroke Place, Portsea, Vic 3944 **Region** Mornington Peninsula
T (03) 5984 3774 **www**.portseaestate.com **Open** By appt
Winemaker Tim Elphick **Est.** 2000 **Dozens** 3000 **Vyds** 3.5ha

♥♥♥♥♥ **Estate Chardonnay 2015** A full-flavoured, generously proportioned wine that carries its shape at the upper end of alcohol for an à la mode Australian chardonnay. It starts with ripe white stone fruit before doing a U-turn to grapefruit on the finish, achieving this without faltering or losing its line. Screwcap. 13.9% alc. **Rating** 95 **To** 2028 $36
Stonecutters Block Single Vineyard Chardonnay 2015 Here there is no U-turn; it starts with lots of opulent stone fruit, creme bulee and omnipresent oak, which is precisely where it finishes. Heston Blumenthal's lobster would meet it eye to eye. Screwcap. 13.8% alc. **Rating** 95 **To** 2025 $55
Estate Pinot Gris 2016 Half gris, half grigio, simply because of its intensity and focus. There's also a delectably juicy, faintly citrussy, line of flavour running alongside pear and citrus. Screwcap. 13.2% alc. **Rating** 95 **To** 2019 $27 ✪
Estate Pinot Gris 2015 Here gris is the style leader, although whether this is simply a year's extra bottle age or a vintage effect isn't easy to say. Those who study cool-grown pinot gris suggest it responds to 5+ years in bottle. Screwcap. 13.8% alc. **Rating** 95 **To** 2018 $27 ✪
Birthday Hill Single Vineyard Pinot Noir 2015 Deeply coloured; this shows serious intent right from the outset, whole-bunch inclusion providing a forest floor carpet for multi-cherry and plum fruit, new oak providing both flavour and structure, closely aligned with tannins. The only thing the wine needs is years to come, during which time it will switch on the lights. Screwcap. 13.4% alc. **Rating** 95 **To** 2030 $55
Estate Pinot Noir 2015 The great colour tells you this is a Siamese twin to Birthday Hill; the power, intensity and depth of the wine are exceptional, but result in a wine that is even more in need of bottle development, the rewards of patience likewise. Screwcap. 13.2% alc. **Rating** 94 **To** 2030 $42

♥♥♥♥♡ **Estate Pinot Noir Rose 2016 Rating** 93 **To** 2018 $27 ✪

Possums Vineyard

88 Adams Road, Blewitt Springs, SA 5171 **Region** McLaren Vale
T (08) 8272 3406 **www**.possumswines.com.au **Open** By appt
Winemaker Pieter Breugem **Est.** 2000 **Dozens** 8000 **Vyds** 44.8ha
Possums Vineyard is owned by Dr John Possingham and Carol Summers. They have two vineyards in McLaren Vale – one at Blewitt Springs, the other at Willunga – covering shiraz (20a), cabernet sauvignon (16ha) and chardonnay (14ha), with lesser plantings of pinot gris, viognier and malbec. Winemaker Pieter Breugem has come from South Africa via the US and Constellation Wines. At the end of 2016 the property was for sale on a walk-in, walk-out basis, complete with staff. Unless a sale materialises before going to print, the intention is to sell the '17 crop. In all of these circumstances, the rating has been maintained. Exports to the UK, Denmark, Germany, Hong Kong and China.

 Possingham & Summers McLaren Vale Malbec 2015 Deep colour; the complex bouquet is full of perfumed spices, even violets, the full-bodied palate living up to the promise of the bouquet and belies the overall misperception of the inability to make malbec as a straight varietal rather than part of a multi-varietal blend. It is redolent of saturated plum fruits, dark chocolate and dark cherry, the tannins fine but persistent. An absolute steal at the price. Screwcap. 14.5% alc. **Rating** 92 **To** 2025 $18 **☉**

Prancing Horse Estate   ★★★★☆

39 Paringa Road, Red Hill South, Vic 3937 **Region** Mornington Peninsula
T (03) 5989 2602 **www.**prancinghorseestate.com **Open** W'ends 12–5
Winemaker Sergio Carlei, Pascal Marchand, Patrick Piuze **Est.** 1990 **Dozens** 2000
Vyds 6.5ha

Anthony and Catherine Hancy acquired the Lavender Bay Vineyard in early 2002, renaming it Prancing Horse Estate and embarking on increasing the estate vineyards, with 2ha each of chardonnay and pinot noir, and 0.5ha of pinot gris. The vineyard moved to organic farming in '03, progressing to biodynamic in '07. They appointed Sergio Carlei as winemaker, and the following year became joint owners with Sergio in Carlei Wines. An additional property 150m west of the existing vineyard was purchased, and 2ha of vines planted. Prancing Horse has become one of a small group of Australian wineries having wines made for them in Burgundy. Pascal Marchand makes an annual release of Morey-St-Denis Clos des Ormes Premier Cru and Meursault Premier Cru Blagny, while Patrick Piuze makes four Chablis appellation wines. Exports to the UK, the US and France.

 Reserve Mornington Peninsula Pinot Noir 2015 Deep colour; not just a prancing horse, but a prancing stallion. It has both power and breed, its dark cherry and plum fruit with balance and length. Dijon clone 777 performs very well in the cool Mornington Peninsula climate, and this wine will run the length of the Melbourne Cup. Screwcap. 12.5% alc. **Rating** 95 **To** 2030

 Reserve Mornington Peninsula Chardonnay 2015 **Rating** 92
Mornington Peninsula Pinot Noir 2015 **Rating** 92 **To** 2025 SC
Mornington Peninsula Pinot Gris 2016 **Rating** 91 $44 SC
The Pony Mornington Peninsula Chardonnay 2016 **Rating** 90 $35 SC

Precipice Wines   ★★★★

25 Maddens Lane, Gruyere, Vic 3770 (postal) **Region** Yarra Valley
T 0403 665 980 **Open** Not
Winemaker Marty Singh **Est.** 2011 **Dozens** 500

Marty Singh says that after 20 years of selling, tasting, drinking and making wine the temptation to start his own brand was just too strong, although the production means that it is still very much a part-time job. His practical skills were learned over a decade of working alongside winemakers such as David Bicknell and Adrian Rodda. The first vintage, in 2012, was of a Shiraz grown on the Hyde Park Vineyard in the Coldstream area; it was backed up by the '13 production of the same wine, coupled with Chardonnay from the Willow Lake Vineyard in the Upper Yarra Valley.

 Willow Lake Vineyard Yarra Valley Chardonnay 2016 Plenty of good wine folk source fruit from Willow Lake Vineyard in Gladysdale and it's fascinating to taste the differences: Precipice takes a soft approach, creating a subtle wine with fine acidity, some leesy nuances and a mix of figs and stone fruit. It finishes with great satisfaction. Screwcap. 13.5% alc. **Rating** 93 **To** 2024 $38 JF
Hyde Park Vineyard Yarra Valley Syrah 2014 Reductive, dense and richly flavoured with layers of woodsy spice, plums, currants. A touch sweet-sour, with grainy tannins, full-bodied and citrussy acidity to close. This smells of warm earth/compost – I like it. Screwcap. 13% alc. **Rating** 91 **To** 2024 $38 JF
Stewart's Vineyard Yarra Valley Pinot Noir 2016 Pale garnet with pretty aromatics of raspberries, spiced cherries and Mediterranean herbs; fruity on the

palate, with fine, easy tannins and refreshing acidity. A lighter style to enjoy now.
Screwcap. 13.5% alc. **Rating** 90 **To** 2020 $38 JF

Pressing Matters

665 Middle Tea Tree Road, Tea Tree, Tas 7017 **Region** Southern Tasmania
T (03) 6268 1947 **www**.pressingmatters.com.au **Open** By appt 0408 126 668
Winemaker Winemaking Tasmania, Paul Smart **Est.** 2002 **Dozens** 2300 **Vyds** 7.2ha
Greg Melick simultaneously wears more hats than most people manage in a lifetime. He is
a top-level barrister (Senior Counsel), a Major General (the highest rank in the Australian
Army Reserve) and has presided over a number of headline special commissions and enquiries
into subjects as diverse as cricket match-fixing allegations and the Beaconsfield mine collapse.
More recently he has become Deputy President of the Administrative Appeals Tribunal and
Chief Commissioner of the Tasmanian Integrity Commission. Yet, if asked, he would probably
nominate wine as his major focus in life. Having built up an exceptional cellar of the great
wines of Europe, he has turned his attention to grapegrowing and winemaking, planting 2.9ha
of riesling at his vineyard in the Coal River Valley. It is a perfect north-facing slope, and the
Mosel-style Rieslings are sweeping all before them. His multi-clone 4.2ha pinot noir block is
also striking gold. Exports to the US and Singapore.

R69 Riesling 2016 Exotic and alluring, this is light-bodied and chiselled; a
tightrope walker deftly tiptoeing across a beam of high voltage acidity while
pondering the allure of exotica across candied quince, orange marmalade, ginger
and honeysuckle flavours on the long finish. Screwcap. 11.5% alc. **Rating** 96
To 2030 $36 NG ✪

Coal River Valley Pinot Noir 2013 There's quite a bit of sulphur-stink,
especially on opening, but the wine's long lines of acidity and tannin have no
trouble pulling cherry-plum flavours through to a long finish. Foresty notes add
another dimension. This has a future ahead of it. Screwcap. 13.7% alc. **Rating** 94
To 2026 $56 CM

R139 Riesling 2016 While virtually every other grape variety would be
challenged by 139g/l of residual sugar, riesling is a crusader of impeccable balance
due to its whirlwind of high acidity, sweeping across the dainty palate and
whisking the sweetness into an ether of dryness. Pear Eau de Vie, ginger, quince
and citrus chutney stream across the mouth before being corralled into the long,
precise, delicate finish. Screwcap. 9.4% alc. **Rating** 94 **To** 2030 $33 NG

R9 Riesling 2016 Rating 92 **To** 2028 $36 NG
Coal River Valley Pinot Noir 2014 Rating 91 **To** 2022 $56 NG

Preveli Wines

Prevelly Liquor Store, 99 Mitchell Drive, Prevelly, WA 6285 **Region** Margaret River
T (08) 9757 2374 **www**.preveliwines.com.au **Open** Mon–Fri 8.30–7, w'ends 10–7
Winemaker Fraser Gallop Estate **Est.** 1995 **Dozens** 4500 **Vyds** 5.5ha
While Preveli Wines is a relative newcomer, its owners, the Home family, have lived on the
property for three generations. Vince and Greg Home also operate the Prevelly Park Beach
Resort and Prevelly Liquor Store, where the wines are available for tasting. Fruit from the
vineyard at Rosa Brook (semillon, sauvignon blanc, cabernet sauvignon, pinot noir and
merlot) is supplemented by contracts with local growers.

Wild Thing Margaret River Pinot Rose 2016 99% pinot noir, 1% chardonnay.
Pale pink; the aromatic bouquet is full of wild strawberries, as is the palate, albeit
in a strictly dry mode; excellent length and balance. Well deserved gold medal
Margaret River Wine Show '16. Screwcap. 13.5% alc. **Rating** 95 **To** 2018 $24 ✪
Wild Thing Margaret River Sauvignon Blanc 2016 Bright straw-green;
complex vinification can obscure varietal expression, but here it rides high, wide
and handsome with a display of tropical fruit, passionfruit leading the charge,
coupled with lemon curd and citrussy acidity. Screwcap. 13% alc. **Rating** 94
To 2019 $24 ✪

ΨΨΨΨΩ Wallcliffe Cabernet Sauvignon 2013 Rating 93 To 2028 $35
Margaret River Cabernet Sauvignon 2014 Rating 92 To 2029 $35
Margaret River Semillon Sauvignon Blanc 2016 Rating 90 To 2019 $20 ✪
Margaret River Cabernet Merlot 2014 Rating 90 To 2021 $26
Bombora Red 2014 Rating 90 To 2019 $19 ✪
Blanc de Noir Methode Traditionelle 2010 Rating 90 To 2018 $35 TS

Primo Estate   ★★★★★

McMurtrie Road, McLaren Vale, SA 5171 **Region** McLaren Vale
T (08) 8323 6800 **www**.primoestate.com.au **Open** 7 days 11–4
Winemaker Joseph Grilli, Daniel Zuzolo **Est.** 1979 **Dozens** 30 000 **Vyds** 34ha
Joe Grilli has always produced innovative and excellent wines. The biennial release of the
Joseph Sparkling Red (in its tall Italian glass bottle) is eagerly awaited, the wine immediately
selling out. Also highly regarded are the vintage-dated extra-virgin olive oils. However, the
core lies with the La Biondina, the Il Briccone Shiraz Sangiovese and the Joseph Moda
Cabernet Merlot. The business has expanded to take in both McLaren Vale and Clarendon,
with plantings of colombard, shiraz, cabernet sauvignon, riesling, merlot, sauvignon blanc,
chardonnay, pinot gris, sangiovese, nebbiolo and merlot. Exports to all major markets.

ΨΨΨΨΨ Joseph Sparkling Red NV A deep purple hue heralds a universe of expansive
complexity, spanning primary black plum and black cherry fruit, secondary roast
nuts, dark chocolate and coffee and the tertiary allure of black olives. Another great
in the grand lineage of Joseph. Cork. 13.5% alc. **Rating** 96 To 2020 $90 TS
Joseph Angel Gully Clarendon Shiraz 2014 Hand-picked, a portion air-
dried in Amarone style. Imposing bouquet, with layered aromas of blueberry,
pepper, spicy oak and the Amarone component having an influence. Deep in
flavour but fresh and elegant, its complexity makes it worth drinking now, but
there's no hurry. Screwcap. 14.5% alc. **Rating** 95 To 2026 $90 SC
Joseph Moda McLaren Vale Cabernet Sauvignon Merlot 2014 An
80/20% blend made in the Italian 'Moda' fashion (with partially dried grapes),
which adds a great deal to its texture and structure. Here blackcurrant, plum and
dark chocolate coalesce in a coherent fashion; there's no equivalent outcome
elsewhere in McLaren Vale. Screwcap. 14.5% alc. **Rating** 95 To 2034 $90
Joseph The Fronti NV Fruitcake and dried muscatel aromas, intense but not
overwhelming. Certainly luscious on the palate, but it does retain a certain restraint
and elegance that sets it apart from the real heavyweights in this category. A wine
to be enjoyed at the table rather than revered in isolation. Screwcap. 19.5% alc.
Rating 95 $50 SC
Joseph d'Elena Clarendon Pinot Grigio 2016 Its relatively cool origins, and
the considerable accumulated knowledge of one of the pioneers of the variety, are
all reflected in this wine, its grainy/lemony acidity a backdrop for the first-up nashi
pear and Granny Smith apple. Screwcap. 12% alc. **Rating** 94 To 2020 $30 ✪
Primo & Co The Tuscan Shiraz Sangiovese Toscana 2015 An 85/15%
blend matured in barriques for 7 months, made in collaboration with Italian
oenologist Gianpaolo Chiettini. A whirling dervish of cherry, spice, bramble and
fresh earth, fine but firm tannins another plus. Great value and interest. Screwcap.
14% alc. **Rating** 94 To 2029 $28 ✪
Il Briccone McLaren Vale Shiraz Sangiovese 2015 Dark plum, bitter
chocolate and molten raspberry liqueur aromas are welded to a spike of coffee-
grind oak and sangiovese's frisky tannins, sculpting a medium body. In all, a
successful confluence with plenty of verve and crunchy sass. Screwcap. 14.5% alc.
Rating 94 To 2023 $25 NG ✪

ΨΨΨΨΩ Shale Stone McLaren Vale Shiraz 2015 Rating 93 To 2028 $35 JF
Joseph La Magia Botrytis 2016 Rating 91 To 2023 $35 JF
La Biondina Colombard 2016 Rating 90 To 2017 $17 JF ✪
Zamberlan Cabernet Sangiovese 2015 Rating 90 To 2030 $40 JF

Principia ★★★★☆

139 Main Creek Road, Red Hill, Vic 3937 (postal) **Region** Mornington Peninsula
T (03) 5931 0010 **www**.principiawines.com.au **Open** By appt
Winemaker Darrin Gaffy **Est.** 1995 **Dozens** 600 **Vyds** 3.5ha

Darrin Gaffy's guiding philosophy for Principia is minimal interference, thus the vines (2.7ha of pinot noir and 0.8ha of chardonnay) are not irrigated, yields are restricted to 3.75 tonnes per hectare or less, and all wine movements are by gravity or by gas pressure, which in turn means there is no filtration, and both primary and secondary fermentation are by wild yeast. 'Principia' comes from the word 'beginnings' in Latin.

Mornington Peninsula Chardonnay 2015 Hand-picked, whole-bunch pressed, wild-yeast fermented and matured in French oak (25% new) for 18 months. Has excellent intensity, with pink grapefruit to the fore, and a lingering, fresh finish and aftertaste. Screwcap. 13.3% alc. **Rating** 95 **To** 2023 $40

Altior Mornington Peninsula Pinot Noir 2015 **Rating** 93 **To** 2022 $50
Mornington Peninsula Pinot Noir 2015 **Rating** 91 **To** 2020 $40

Printhie Wines ★★★★☆

489 Yuranigh Road, Molong, NSW 2866 **Region** Orange
T (02) 6366 8422 **www**.printhiewines.com.au **Open** Mon–Sat 10–4
Winemaker Drew Tuckwell **Est.** 1996 **Dozens** 20 000 **Vyds** 30ha

Owned by the Swift family, and the next generation Edward and David have taken over (from Ed Swift) the reins to guide the business into its next era. In 2016 Printhie 'clocked up' 10 years of commercial wine production, and the vineyards are now reaching a good level of maturity at 20 years. The 30ha of estate vineyards are planted at lower elevations and supply all the red varieties and the pinot gris; other varieties are purchased from other growers in the region. Winemaker Drew Tuckwell has been at Printhie for nearly a decade, and has over 20 years of winemaking experience in Australia and Europe. Exports to Canada and China.

Super Duper Orange Chardonnay 2014 From a single vineyard in Nashdale at 1050m, hand-picked, cloudy juice wild-yeast fermented and matured in two new hogsheads, limited mlf and some battonage, only 65 dozen made. This succeeds where the Super Duper Shiraz failed; it has a feline grace, a willowy suppleness, and precision. It is in a citrus/citrus zest orbit, but that's almost a sine qua non. Screwcap. 12.4% alc. **Rating** 96 **To** 2024 $85

Swift Blancs Brut No. 1 2010 **Rating** 93 **To** 2020 $85 TS
Swift Rose Brut 2011 No. 1 NV **Rating** 93 **To** 2018 $40 TS
MCC Orange Riesling 2016 **Rating** 92 **To** 2026 $25 ✪
Swift Cuvee Brut NV **Rating** 92 **To** 2020 $40 TS
MCC Orange Chardonnay 2015 **Rating** 91 **To** 2022 $35
Swift Vintage Brut 2011 **Rating** 91 **To** 2021 $50 TS
Super Duper Orange Syrah 2014 **Rating** 90 **To** 2020 $85
Super Duper Orange Cabernet Sauvignon 2015 **Rating** 90 **To** 2025 $85

Project Wine ★★★★

83 Pioneer Road, Angas Plains, SA 5255 **Region** South Australia
T (08) 73424 3031 **www**.projectwine.com.au **Open** Not
Winemaker Peter Pollard **Est.** 2001 **Dozens** 150 000

Originally designed as a contract winemaking facility, Project Wine has developed a sales and distribution arm that has rapidly developed markets, both domestically and overseas. Located in Langhorne Creek, it sources fruit from most key SA wine regions, including McLaren Vale, Barossa Valley and Adelaide Hills. The diversity of grape sourcing allows the winery to produce a wide range of products under the Tail Spin, Pioneer Road, Parson's Paddock, Bird's Eye View and Angas & Bremer labels. Exports to the UK, Canada, Japan and China.

ŶŶŶŶ♀ **Pioneer Road Langhorne Creek Cabernet Sauvignon 2015** The best of
the '15 red wines from Project Wines. It has good varietal character in the typical
style of Langhorne Creek, relaxed and juicy. The tannins are fine, the only faint
query the quality of the used oak. Screwcap. 14.5% alc. **Rating** 90 **To** 2025 $18
Pioneer Road Langhorne Creek Sangiovese 2015 Matured for 12 months
in used French hogsheads. The inclusion of 10% shiraz has worked very well
indeed, with red and purple fruits to the fore on a medium-bodied, well balanced
palate. Great value. Screwcap. 14.5% alc. **Rating** 90 **To** 2022 $18 ✪

ŶŶŶŶ **Angas & Bremer Shiraz Cabernet 2015** **Rating** 89 **To** 2025 $15 ✪

Provenance Wines   ★★★★★

100 Lower Paper Mills Road, Fyansford, Vic 3221 **Region** Geelong
T (03) 5222 3422 **www**.provenancewines.com.au **Open** By appt
Winemaker Scott Ireland, Sam Vogel **Est.** 1997 **Dozens** 2500 **Vyds** 5ha
Scott Ireland and partner Jen Lilburn established Provenance Wines in 1997 as a natural
extension of Scott's years of winemaking experience, both here and abroad. Located in the
Moorabool Valley, the winery team focuses on the classics in a cool climate sense – Pinot
Gris, Chardonnay and Pinot Noir in particular, as well as Shiraz. Fruit is sourced from both
within the Geelong region and further afield (when the fruit warrants selection). The future
of Provenance will be influenced by its 2012 acquisition of 30ha a property with red volcanic
soil and a spring-fed dam; 1.5ha or pinot noir was planted in '12. They are also major players
in contract making for the Geelong region.

ŶŶŶŶŶ **Geelong Shiraz 2015** 20% whole bunches, wild-yeast fermented, 20 days on
skins, 75% transferred to used French oak, 25% to concrete eggs, matured for
12 months. The adventurous winemaking has worked a treat, investing this deeply
coloured, multilayered, medium to full-bodied shiraz with both flavoured and
textured complexity. It has a well of red and black cherry fruit, spice and pepper
dancing around its rim. Screwcap. 13.8% alc. **Rating** 96 **To** 2040 $32 ✪
Golden Plains Chardonnay 2015 45% from Ballarat, 40% Geelong,
15% Henty. A classic cool climate chardonnay with grapefruit and mineral
providing the drive, barrel fermentation and mlf the complexity on the long, fresh
palate. Will be long-lived. Value+. Gold medal Ballarat Wine Show '16. Screwcap.
13.5% alc. **Rating** 95 **To** 2025 $29 ✪
Golden Plains Pinot Noir 2015 76% from Geelong, 24% from Ballarat. A
powerful wine with at least 5 years of development in front of it as the tannins
soften, and scented, spicy secondary notes join the dark cherry fruit that presently
rides high. Screwcap. 13.2% alc. **Rating** 94 **To** 2020 $30 ✪

ŶŶŶŶ♀ **Tarrington Pinot Gris 2015** **Rating** 91 **To** 2017 $26

Punch   ★★★★★

2130 Kinglake Road, St Andrews, Vic 3761 **Region** Yarra Valley
T (03) 9710 1155 **www**.punched.com.au **Open** Most Sundays 12–5
Winemaker James Lance **Est.** 2004 **Dozens** 1800 **Vyds** 3.45ha
In the wake of Graeme Rathbone taking over the brand (but not the real estate) of Diamond
Valley, the Lances' son James and his wife Claire leased the vineyard and winery from David
and Catherine Lance, including the 0.25ha block of close-planted pinot noir. In all, Punch has
2.25ha of pinot noir (including the close-planted), 0.8ha of chardonnay and 0.4ha of cabernet
sauvignon. When the 2009 Black Saturday bushfires destroyed the crop, various grapegrowers
wrote offering assistance, which led to the purchase of the grapes used for that dire year, and
the beginning of the 'Friends of Punch' wines.

ŶŶŶŶŶ **Lance's Vineyard Yarra Valley Pinot Noir 2015** 5% whole bunches, wild-
yeast fermented, matured in French oak (40% new) for 10 months. Bright, full
colour; a very complex, spicy wine, the bouquet and palate singing the same
song. It gives the impression of more than 5% whole bunches, but regardless, it

has utterly exceptional length and drive. Screwcap. 13.5% alc. **Rating** 97 **To** 2030 $55 ✪

𝟬𝟬𝟬𝟬𝟬 **Lance's Vineyard Yarra Valley Chardonnay 2015** Gleaming, pale straw-green; it is the complexity, integrity and length of Yarra Valley chardonnays as good as this that show the limitations of warmer regions' wines. Here white peach/nectarine flavours lead the way, albeit with complex texture and structure built on the back-palate by citrussy acidity and the positive influence of seriously good Burgundian oak. Screwcap. 13.5% alc. **Rating** 96 **To** 2025 $45 ✪
Lance's Vineyard Close Planted Yarra Valley Pinot Noir 2015 Deep, clear colour; a pocket rocket, built to travel far and live long. Black cherry, plum and spice all come through strongly after the lengthy elevage. Its tiny production (69 dozen, sold in 6-packs) is a shame, but it enabled James Lance to calculate an average 91g bunch weight! Its best is years away. Screwcap. 13.5% alc. **Rating** 96 **To** 2035 $90
Lance's Vineyard Yarra Valley Cabernet Sauvignon 2015 Matured in French oak for 18 months, 65 dozen made. Making in micro-quantities like this isn't easy – it's just that James Lance makes it look easy. Cassis and bay leaf run the flavour line perfectly, with the usual balance of quality oak and fine tannins. Screwcap. 13.5% alc. **Rating** 95 **To** 2035 $45

Punt Road ★★★★★

10 St Huberts Road, Coldstream, Vic 3770 **Region** Yarra Valley
T (03) 9739 0666 **www**.puntroadwines.com.au **Open** 7 days 10–5
Winemaker Tim Shand **Est.** 2000 **Dozens** 20000 **Vyds** 65.61ha
Punt Road is owned by the Napoleone family. All the wines are produced from vineyards owned by the family; this has resulted in the introduction of the Airlie Bank range, a mostly sub-$20 Yarra Valley range made in a fruit-driven, lightly oaked style to complement the successful Punt Road range at the premium end of their offerings. There is also more focus on small-production single vineyard wines under the Punt Road label. Exports to the US, Canada, Singapore, Hong Kong, Japan, China and other major markets.

𝟬𝟬𝟬𝟬𝟬 **Napoleone Vineyard Yarra Valley Shiraz 2015** Trophies for Best Shiraz and Best Single Vineyard Wine at Melbourne Wine Awards '16 and trophy for Best Single Vineyard at the Yarra Valley Wine Show '16. It's not a giant killer: its place is in the bedroom, not on the battlefield. For yes, it is seductively crafted, the emphasis on red and black cherries, plus a flourish of blackberry, the tannins calculated with extreme sensitivity. One of the best value wines in the 31-year history of the Companion. Screwcap. 13.5% alc. **Rating** 97 **To** 2035 $27 ✪

𝟬𝟬𝟬𝟬𝟬 **Napoleone Vineyard Yarra Valley Chardonnay 2016** A complex wine, the bouquet opening the batting with a (deliberate) touch of struck match funk, the palate taking another direction as it justifies the mlf without losing freshness or length. Screwcap. 12.5% alc. **Rating** 94 **To** 2023 $23 ✪
Napoleone Vineyard Yarra Valley Pinot Gris 2016 Bright straw-green; no hint of pink despite 5 hours skin contact. The vinification has worked a treat, resulting in a vibrant wine with drive and length, pear and citrus contesting primacy; excellent balance. Screwcap. 12% alc. **Rating** 94 **To** 2020 $23 ✪

𝟬𝟬𝟬𝟬𝟬 **Napoleone Vineyard Block 12 Yarra Valley Gamay 2016 Rating** 92 $23 ✪
Airlie Bank Yarra Valley Pinot Noir 2015 Rating 91 **To** 2023 $22 ✪
Airlie Bank Gris Fermented on Skins 2016 Rating 90 **To** 2017 $22
Airlie Bank Franc 2016 Rating 90 **To** 2021 $22
Airlie Bank Chardonnay Pinot Noir NV Rating 90 **To** 2017 $22 TS

Purple Hands Wines ★★★★★

32 Brandreth Street, Tusmore, SA 5065 (postal) **Region** Barossa Valley
T 0401 988 185 **www**.purplehandswines.com.au **Open** Not
Winemaker Craig Stansborough **Est.** 2006 **Dozens** 2500 **Vyds** 14ha

This is a partnership between Craig Stansborough, who provides the winemaking know-how and an 8ha vineyard of shiraz, northwest of Williamstown in a cooler corner of the southern Barossa, and Mark Slade, who provides the passion. Don't ask me how this works – I don't know, but I do know they are producing outstanding single vineyard wines (the grenache is contract-grown) of quite remarkable elegance. The wines are made at Grant Burge, where Craig is chief winemaker. Exports to the Philippines and Singapore.

ΨΨΨΨΨ **Barossa Valley Mataro Grenache Shiraz 2016** 52/26/22% forms the blend and the result is harmony in a glass. Vivid crimson, bright red fruit, Middle Eastern spices, earthy and with a silkiness to the full palate, even if there's grip to the tannin. Effortless really. Screwcap. 14% alc. **Rating** 95 **To** 2025 $30 JF ✪
Old Vine Barossa Valley Grenache 2016 Old bush vines (50+ years), 30% whole bunches in the fermentation and ageing in used puncheons for 9 months has resulted in an ethereal, elegant wine. It's heady with red fruit, licorice, potpourri and cinnamon, and has a palate so smooth the silky tannins glide across to a long finish. Screwcap. 13.8% alc. **Rating** 95 **To** 2021 $30 JF ✪
Barossa Valley Montepulciano 2015 Pretty simple winemaking, they say – wild yeast fermentation, 10 days on skins, basket-pressed to older oak for 18 months and ta da! A captivating drink. There's a succulence here, fineness too, with its flourish of red fruits, maraschino cherry, ferrous and with silky Italianate tannins. Well played. Screwcap. 13.5% alc. **Rating** 95 **To** 2021 $30 JF ✪

ΨΨΨΨΨ **Barossa Valley Shiraz 2015 Rating** 93 **To** 2028 $30 JF
Barossa Valley Mataro 2015 Rating 92 **To** 2022 $30 JF
Barossa Valley Aglianico 2015 Rating 92 **To** 2023 $30 JF

Pyren Vineyard   ★★★★

Glenlofty-Warrenmang Road, Warrenmang, Vic 3478 **Region** Pyrenees
T (03) 5467 2352 **www.**pyrenvineyard.com **Open** By appt
Winemaker Leighton Joy **Est.** 1999 **Dozens** 5000 **Vyds** 29ha
Brian and Leighton Joy have 23ha of shiraz, 5ha of cabernet sauvignon and 1ha malbec, cabernet franc and petit verdot on the slopes of the Warrenmang Valley near Moonambel. Yield is restricted to between 3.7 and 6.1 tonnes per hectare. Exports to the US.

ΨΨΨΨΨ **Block E Pyrenees Shiraz 2015** A soaringly aromatic wine of violet, iodine, blueberry and licorice tones. The tannins are seamless, a beam of stems and fibre, with nothing green about them. The finish is taut, yet lively, a ricochet of all described above. The finish is long. Screwcap. **Rating** 94 **To** 2025 $55 NG

ΨΨΨΨΨ **Little Ra Ra Pyrenees Rose 2015 Rating** 92 **To** 2017 $28
Yardbird Pyrenees Shiraz 2015 Rating 92 **To** 2020 $35 NG
Yardbird Union 2015 Rating 91 **To** 2023 $35 NG
Little Ra Ra Franc Pyrenees Cabernet Franc 2015 Rating 90 **To** 2017 $28

Quarisa Wines   ★★★★

743 Slopes Road, Tharbogang, NSW 2680 (postal) **Region** South Australia
T (02) 6963 6222 **www.**quarisa.com.au **Open** Not
Winemaker John Quarisa **Est.** 2005 **Dozens** NFP
John Quarisa has had a distinguished career as a winemaker spanning over 20 years, working for some of Australia's largest wineries, including McWilliam's, Casella and Nugan Estate. He was also chiefly responsible in 2004 for winning the Jimmy Watson Trophy (Melbourne) and the Stodart Trophy (Adelaide). John and Josephine Quarisa have set up a very successful family business using grapes from various parts of NSW and SA, made in leased space. Production has risen in leaps and bounds, doubtless sustained by the exceptional value for money provided by the wines. Exports include the UK, Canada, Denmark, Sweden, Malaysia, Indonesia, Hong Kong, Japan and NZ.

ΨΨΨΨΨ **Johnny Q Adelaide Hills Sauvignon Blanc 2015** The intensity of the varietal fruit aromas of citrus, fresh-cut grass and gooseberry makes this a quite exceptional bargain. It would still offer value at twice the price. Screwcap. 13% alc. **Rating** 92 To 2017 $12 ❂

Treasures McLaren Vale Shiraz 2014 Good colour; a medium to full-bodied shiraz that has depth to all its flavour and structural components, oak and tannins tending to encircle the fruit. It's not ready, and in a weird way, offers too much at this price unless accompanied by rich flame-grilled/barbecued beef. Difficult to point, but whichever way you look at it, it's exceptional value. Screwcap. 14.5% alc. **Rating** 90 To 2024 $15 ❂

ΥΥΥΥ Enchanted Tree Cabernet Sauvignon 2014 Rating 89 To 2019 $14 ❂

Quarry Hill Wines ★★★★

8 Maxwell Street, Yarralumla, ACT 2600 (postal) **Region** Canberra District
T (02) 6223 7112 **www**.quarryhill.com.au **Open** Not
Winemaker Collector Wines (Alex McKay) **Est.** 1999 **Dozens** 600 **Vyds** 4.5ha
Owner Dean Terrell is the ex-Vice Chancellor of the Australian National University and a Professor of Economics. The acquisition of the property, originally used as a quarry for the construction of the Barton Highway and thereafter as a grazing property, was the brainchild of his family, who wanted to keep him active in retirement. The vineyard was established in 1999, with further plantings in 2001 and '06; there are 2ha of shiraz, 1ha of sauvignon blanc, and 0.25ha each of savagnin, sangiovese, tempranillo, grenache, pinot noir and sagrantino. Only part of the production is released under the Quarry Hill label, as grapes are sold to wineries, including Clonakilla and Collector Wines.

ΥΥΥΥΥ Canberra District Shiraz 2015 Deep crimson-purple hue; a compellingly rich, intense and focused shiraz with black cherry and anise aromas and flavours that relegate oak and tannins into second-tier importance. Screwcap. 13.2% alc. Rating 94 To 2035 $25 ❂

ΥΥΥΥΥ Two Places Pinot Gris 2016 Rating 90 To 2018 $24
Canberra District Shiraz 2013 Rating 90 To 2020 $22

Quattro Mano ★★★☆

PO Box 189, Hahndorf, SA 5245 **Region** Barossa Valley
T 0430 647 470 **www**.quattromano.com.au **Open** By appt
Winemaker Anthony Carapetis, Christopher Taylor, Philippe Morin **Est.** 2006
Dozens 2500 **Vyds** 3.8ha
Anthony Carapetis, Philippe Morin and Chris Taylor have collective experience of over 50 years working in various facets of the wine industry, Philippe as a leading sommelier for over 25 years, and presently as Director of French Oak Cooperage, Anthony and Chris as winemakers. The dream of Quattro Mano began in the mid-1990s, becoming a reality in 2006 (I'm still not sure how three equals four). They produce an eclectic range of wines, Tempranillo the cornerstone. It's an impressive, albeit small, business. Exports to the US and Japan.

ΥΥΥΥ Duende Pinta 2015 Tempranillo, mourvedre and grenache. A light-bodied, savoury, spicy wine for immediate drinking. Screwcap. 13.5% alc. **Rating** 89 To 2018 $19 ❂

Quealy Winemakers ★★★★

62 Bittern-Dromana Road, Balnarring, Vic 3926 **Region** Mornington Peninsula
T (03) 5983 2483 **www**.quealy.com.au **Open** 7 days 11–5
Winemaker Kathleen Quealy, Kevin McCarthy **Est.** 1982 **Dozens** 8000 **Vyds** 8ha
Kathleen Quealy and Kevin McCarthy were among the early waves of winemakers on the Mornington Peninsula. They challenged the status quo – most publicly by introducing Mornington Peninsula pinot gris/grigio (with great success). Behind this was improvement and diversification in site selection, plus viticulture and winemaking techniques that allowed their business to grow significantly. The estate plantings are 2ha each of pinot noir, pinot gris

and friulano as well as smaller plots of riesling, chardonnay and moscato giallo. Their leased vineyards are established on what Kathleen and Kevin consider to be premium sites for pinot gris and pinot noir, and are now single vineyard wines: Musk Creek and the newer Tussie Mussie Vineyard. Kathleen and Kevin are assisted by winemaker Dan Calvert, who has worked with Quealy for 7 years. Their son Tom has joined the business, with a particular focus on natural wine, Turbul Friulano his first such wine. Exports to the UK and France.

ꟼꟼꟼꟼꟼ **Campbell & Christine Pinot Noir 2015** Firm, dry and slightly reductive, with stewy red berries and an itch of woody spice. Looks to have plenty of development up its sleeve. Will be interesting to follow. Screwcap. 13.5% alc. **Rating** 90 **To** 2021 $45 CM

R. Paulazzo
852 Oakes Road, Yoogali, NSW 2680 **Region** Riverina
T 0412 969 002 **www**.rpaulazzo.com.au **Open** By appt
Winemaker Rob Paulazzo **Est.** 2013 **Dozens** NFP **Vyds** 12ha
Rob Paulazzo began winemaking in 1997, and covered a lot of ground before establishing his eponymous Riverina business. In Australia he worked for McWilliam's and Orlando, in NZ for Giesen, also completing four vintages in Burgundy, plus vintages in Tuscany, the Napa Valley and Niagara Peninsula (Canada). In addition to the family's vineyard, established over 80 years ago, Rob is also sourcing fruit from Hilltops, Tumbarumba, Orange and Canberra District. Unfortunately the top-tier wines were not tasted in time for this edition.

ꟼꟼꟼꟼꟼ **Nero d'Avola 2015** From the Riverina (86%), Hilltops (10%) and Heathcote (4%). The colour is light and clear; the spiced red fruits also with a lively, fresh mouthfeel to a range of red cherries of all kinds, from maraschino to sour. Interesting wine. Screwcap. 13.5% alc. **Rating** 90 **To** 2018 $17 ❂

Raidis Estate
147 Church Street, Penola, SA 5277 **Region** Coonawarra
T (08) 8737 2966 **www**.raidis.com.au **Open** Thurs–Sun 12–6
Winemaker Steven Raidis **Est.** 2006 **Dozens** 5000 **Vyds** 24.29ha
The Raidis family has lived and worked in Coonawarra for over 40 years. Chris Raidis was only three years old when he arrived in Australia with his parents, who were market gardeners in Greece before coming here. In 1994 he planted just under 5ha of cabernet sauvignon; son Steven significantly expanded the vineyard in 2003 with sauvignon blanc, riesling, pinot gris, merlot and shiraz. The cellar door was opened by then Deputy Prime Minister Julia Gillard in Nov '09, an impressive example of pulling power. Exports to the UK and the US.

ꟼꟼꟼꟼꟼ **PG Project Oak Coonawarra Pinot Gris 2015** The difference between this and PG Project Skins? This spends less time on skins (4 days), before it's matured in a new French oak puncheon for 1 year. A pale amber hue, the core of fruit has depth of flavour, the texture of pear skins and peach fuzz, and is spicy and gingery, with its phenolics nicely handled. Screwcap. 14% alc. **Rating** 94 **To** 2021 $35 JF

ꟼꟼꟼꟼꟼ **Cheeky Goat Coonawarra Pinot Gris 2016 Rating** 93 **To** 2020 $24 JF ❂
The Kid Coonawarra Riesling 2016 Rating 91 **To** 2023 $20 JF ❂
PG Project Skins Coonawarra Pinot Gris 2015 Rating 91 **To** 2021 $35 JF
Wild Goat Coonawarra Shiraz 2014 Rating 91 **To** 2022 $28 JF
The Trip 2013 Rating 90 **To** 2026 $80 JF

Rambouillet
403 Stirling Road, Pemberton, WA 6260 **Region** Pemberton
T (08) 9776 0114 **www**.rambouillet.com.au **Open** 7 days 11–5
Winemaker Mike Garland **Est.** 2005 **Dozens** NFP **Vyds** 4.5ha
Alan and Leanne Rowe acquired their 40ha property in 2003, planting the first vines in '05. Their lack of capital, a common scenario, meant that Alan decided he would do all the work

in establishing the vineyard, complete with trellis and drip irrigation. Although 4.5ha may not seem much, it was a major undertaking for one person, even though Leanne was always on hand to help where she could. They chose sauvignon blanc, chardonnay and shiraz, offering the Chardonnay in three versions: unwooded, lightly oaked and barrel-fermented, all under the aegis of contract winemaker Mike Garland. Even though the vineyard is remote, they live and work full-time on the property, with a de facto cellar door open 'most days'.

ŸŸŸŸŸ **Aever Series Pemberton Shiraz Excellence 2014** The hue is good, although not deep; the bouquet is spicy and inviting, and the palate grows on you, initially seeming too oaky, but gaining fruit strength as it was retasted. Screwcap. 14.5% alc. **Rating** 91 **To** 2024 $28

Ravens Croft Wines ★★★★

274 Spring Creek Road, Stanthorpe, Qld 4380 **Region** Granite Belt
T (07) 4683 3252 **www**.ravenscroftwines.com.au **Open** Fri–Sun 10.30–4.30
Winemaker Mark Ravenscroft **Est.** 2002 **Dozens** 800 **Vyds** 1.2ha
Mark Ravenscroft was born in South Africa and studied oenology there. He moved to Australia in the early 1990s, and in '94 became an Australian citizen. His wines come from estate plantings of verdelho and pinotage, supplemented by contract-grown grapes from other vineyards in the region. The wines are made onsite.

ŸŸŸŸŸ **Granite Belt Pinotage 2015** It is not often that we see pinotage in Australia. And for good reason. This cross of cinsault and pinot noir is often medicinal and thoroughly unattractive. This is svelte, sexy and bouncing with tangy red berry fruit as an expression of pinot's best side, while also exhibiting strewn herb and a whiff of pepper for lift. Screwcap. 13.5% alc. **Rating** 94 **To** 2022 $40 NG

ŸŸŸŸŸ **Granite Belt Petit Verdot 2015 Rating** 93 **To** 2028 $35 NG
Granite Belt Tempranillo 2016 Rating 90 **To** 2022 $28 NG

Ravensworth ★★★★★

312 Patemans Lane, Murrumbateman, ACT 2582 **Region** Canberra District
T (02) 6226 8368 **www**.ravensworthwines.com.au **Open** Not
Winemaker Bryan Martin **Est.** 2000 **Dozens** 2000
Winemaker, vineyard manager and partner Bryan Martin (with dual wine science and winegrowing degrees from CSU) has a background in wine retail, and food and beverage work in the hospitality industry, and teaches part-time. He is also assistant winemaker to Tim Kirk at Clonakilla, after seven years at Jeir Creek. Judging at wine shows is another string to his bow. Ravensworth has two vineyards: Rosehill (cabernet sauvignon, merlot and sauvignon blanc) and Martin Block (shiraz, viognier, marsanne and sangiovese).

ŸŸŸŸŸ **Riesling 2016** There's no beating around the bush: this is a first rate riesling, its floral bouquet an instant come-on, followed by a riveting palate of lemon, lime and green apple fruit within the embrace of flinty/minerally acidity. Moreover, it is a wine bred to stay the distance. Screwcap. 12% alc. **Rating** 95 **To** 2026 $25 ✪
Pinot Gris 2016 From Canberra and Tumbarumba, fermented in ceramic eggs. Full-on pink; a bright, almost jaunty, pinot gris with an intangible Siren-like pull. Deserves 110 points as a full-on natural wine. Screwcap. 12.5% alc. **Rating** 95 **To** 2023 $28 ✪
Sangiovese 2016 Light red colour and light red fruits, with a fine skein of tannins in balanced support. This is pure unadorned sangiovese à la Australia. No need for extended cellaring. Screwcap. 13% alc. **Rating** 95 **To** 2021 $25 ✪
The Grainery 2016 Estate-grown marsanne, roussanne, viognier, chardonnay and 5% contract-grown gewurztraminer, whole-bunch pressed directly to oak, matured in large-format oak and ceramic eggs. Full yellow-gold; given the whole bunch pressing and maturation, there's an extraordinary amount of flavour and texture in the wine. Screwcap. 13% alc. **Rating** 94 **To** 2026 $36

Charlie-Foxtrot Gamay Noir 2016 Good depth to the colour; suffers in comparison to the beautiful '15, but not (in comparison) to other Australian gamays. The satusma plum and raspberry fruit on the bouquet and palate shouldn't be sneezed at, the tingle on the tip of the tongue reinforcing its undoubted presence and length. Screwcap. 13% alc. **Rating** 94 **To** 2023 $36

The Tinderry 2016 Estate-grown cabernet franc and sauvignon blanc, matured for 5 months in used barriques. It's an attractive redcurrant and spice combination, the medium-bodied palate supple and friendly. I'd drink it sooner rather than later, enjoying its audacious freshness with eyes averted from its gruesome label. Screwcap. 13.5% alc. **Rating** 94 **To** 2021 $36

Barbera 2016 One of the best barberas I have come across in Australia. It often looks one-dimensional, but certainly doesn't do so here. There is a profusion of fresh red and black juicy fruits making you want to quaff this, not just sip it. And it has texture in its light to medium-bodied mode. Screwcap. 14% alc. **Rating** 94 **To** 2022 $30 ✪

🍷🍷🍷🍷🍷 **Seven Months 2016** **Rating** 91 **To** 2020 $36

Red Art | Rojomoma ★★★★

16 Sturt Road, Nuriootpa, SA 5355 **Region** Barossa Valley
T 0421 272 336 **www**.rojomoma.com.au **Open** By appt
Winemaker Bernadette Kaeding, Sam Kurtz **Est.** 2004 **Dozens** 400 **Vyds** 5.4ha

2015 was a momentous year for the Red Art | Rojomoma business, when winemaker and life partner of Bernadette Kaeding, Sam Kurtz, left his position as chief winemaker within the Orlando group, where he had worked for over 20 years. He had in fact helped Bernadette with the care of Red Art since 1996, when Bernadette purchased the nucleus of the vineyard. It had 1.49ha of 80-year-old dry-grown grenache; the remaining 3.95ha were planted over several years to shiraz, cabernet sauvignon, petit verdot and tempranillo. Until 2004 the grapes from the old and new plantings were sold to Rockford, Chateau Tanunda, Spinifex and David Franz. In that year she decided to make a small batch of wine (with advice from Sam) and continued to accumulate wine until '11, when she began selling wines under the Red Art label. With Sam coming onboard full-time it seems likely that all the grapes will be henceforth used in making the Red Art wines.

🍷🍷🍷🍷🍷 **Red Art Barossa Cabernet Sauvignon 2015** Plenty of varietal personality across cassis, dark plum, crushed herb and an underlying carriage of mint. The tannins are tactile, yet plush, oak serving its purpose to harness it all into a greater whole. Holds its alcohol with aplomb. Screwcap. 14.6% alc. **Rating** 93 **To** 2030 $30 NG

Red Art Chiaro Barossa Tempranillo Grenache 2016 A successful and highly intriguing blend of 86% tempranillo and the remainder grenache, with 20% whole bunches in the ferment. The tempranillo was dried on racks for 2 weeks to concentrate the sugars and to build up the solids to liquid ratio. The result is a deep vermilion, all pulpy dark fruits, violet and rose petal florals slung across sassy tannins. Screwcap. 12.8% alc. **Rating** 93 **To** 2019 $25 NG ✪

Red Art Barossa Shiraz 2013 Dark fruits, grilled meats, soy and star anise emerge from the brooding inky hue. This estate's signature pulpy, coffee-grind tannins, seasoned with a lash of oak, tame and massage the forceful flavours, squelching them into a moreish, pliant whole. Screwcap. 14.5% alc. **Rating** 92 **To** 2025 $30 NG

🍷🍷🍷🍷 **Red Art Barossa Grenache 2015** **Rating** 89 **To** 2025 $30

Red Edge ★★★★☆

Golden Gully Road, Heathcote, Vic 3523 **Region** Heathcote
T 0407 422 067 **www**.rededgewine.com.au **Open** By appt
Winemaker Peter Dredge **Est.** 1971 **Dozens** 1500 **Vyds** 14ha

Red Edge's vineyard dates back to 1971 and the renaissance of the Victorian wine industry. In the early '80s it produced the wonderful wines of Flynn & Williams and was rehabilitated by Peter and Judy Dredge, producing two quite lovely wines in their inaugural vintage and continuing that form in succeeding years. Exports to the US, Canada and China.

ŦŦŦŦŦ **71 Block Heathcote Shiraz 2014** The wine is a manifest of their struggle, striking as much for its sheer density as for the baritone of cardamom, anise and turmeric. French oak, and plenty of it, is a necessary corset to the wine's force. Sweet berry fruit explodes across its midriff, with Red Edge's detailed, coffee grind to bitter chocolate tannins conferring pliancy, authority and age-worthiness. Screwcap. 14.5% alc. **Rating** 95 **To** 2028 $60 NG

ŦŦŦŦŦ **Degree Heathcote Shiraz 2014** **Rating** 93 **To** 2022 $20 NG
Heathcote Cabernet Sauvignon 2014 **Rating** 93 **To** 2022 $30 NG
Heathcote Shiraz 2014 **Rating** 91 **To** 2025 $40 NG

Red Hill Estate

53 Shoreham Road, Red Hill South, Vic 3937 **Region** Mornington Peninsula
T (03) 5989 2838 **www.**redhillestate.com.au **Open** 7 days 11–5
Winemaker Donna Stephens **Est.** 1989 **Dozens** 25 000 **Vyds** 9.7ha
Red Hill Estate was established in 1989 by the Derham family. It is now owned and run by the Fabrizio family. Fruit is sourced from two estate vineyards, the main property and the Merricks Grove Vineyard. The cellar door and Max's Restaurant have spectacular views across the Red Hill vineyard and Western Port Bay.

ŦŦŦŦŦ **Single Vineyard Mornington Peninsula Pinot Noir 2015** Full crimson-purple; this is in stark contrast to the curiously named Cool Climate Pinot Noir, bordering on full-bodied, with lashings of savoury, foresty dark plum and black cherry fruit. It needs, and will handle, 10+ years in the cellar. Screwcap. 14% alc. **Rating** 95 **To** 2027 $70
Single Vineyard Mornington Peninsula Chardonnay 2014 Bright straw-green; this is a wine that Red Hill Estate can be proud of: it has concentration, complexity and balance between its stone fruit, mlf creaminess and gently nutty oak. It deserved better than its bronze medal at the National Cool Climate Wine Show. Screwcap. 13.5% alc. **Rating** 94 **To** 2024 $60
Cordon Cut Pinot Grigio 2016 An unusually sweet cordon-cut wine, the bouquet with a clear jasmine scent, the palate with crystallised pear and peach fruit, its acidity exactly balanced with the fruit, cleansing the finish. Screwcap. 11% alc. **Rating** 94 **To** 2022 $30 ●

ŦŦŦŦŦ **Cellar Door Release Chardonnay 2015** **Rating** 93 **To** 2021 $28
Single Vineyard Shiraz 2014 **Rating** 93 **To** 2030 $70
Cellar Door Release Pinot Noir 2015 **Rating** 91 **To** 2022 $28
Merricks Grove Pinot Noir 2014 **Rating** 90 **To** 2023 $37

Redbank

Whitfield Road, King Valley, Vic 3678 **Region** King Valley
T 0411 404 296 **www.**redbankwines.com **Open** Not
Winemaker Nick Dry **Est.** 2005 **Dozens** 33 000 **Vyds** 15ha
The Redbank brand was for decades the umbrella for Neill and Sally Robb's Sally's Paddock. In 2005 Hill-Smith Family Vineyards acquired the Redbank brand from the Robbs, leaving them with the winery, surrounding vineyard and the Sally's Paddock label. Redbank purchases grapes from the King Valley, Whitlands, Beechworth and the Ovens Valley (among other vineyard sources). Exports to all major markets.

ŦŦŦŦ **King Valley Fiano 2015** Fiano is a variety that deserves recognition for its ability to invest a wine with texture, even when from young vines with generous crops. It has it all together here. Screwcap. 13.5% alc. **Rating** 89 **To** 2018 $22

Redesdale Estate Wines ★★★★★

c/o Post Office, Redesdale, Vic 3444 **Region** Heathcote
T 0408 407 108 **www**.redesdale.com **Open** By appt
Winemaker Alan Cooper **Est.** 1982 **Dozens** 800 **Vyds** 4ha

Planting of the Redesdale Estate vines began in 1982 on the northeast slopes of a 25ha grazing property fronting the Campaspe River on one side. The rocky quartz and granite soil meant the vines had to struggle, and the annual yield is little more than 1.2t/acre. The vineyard property has since been sold, allowing Peter and Suzanne Williams more time to market their wines.

♀♀♀♀♀ Heathcote Shiraz 2014 This has come together rather well with its plush, bright red fruits, hint of blueberries, bay and curry leaves leading onto a fine palate, grippy ripe tannins – full-bodied but reined in. Slurpy and eerily light. Screwcap. 14.2% alc. **Rating** 95 **To** 2025 $37 JF
Heathcote Cabernet Sauvignon Cabernet Franc 2013 What a pleasant surprise: this is spine-tinglingly gorgeous and supple. No hard edges, just lacy tannins, spice, zesty tangy red-black fruits, black olives, Mediterranean herbs and a medium-bodied palate. Screwcap. 13.1% alc. **Rating** 95 **To** 2022 $37 JF

Redgate ★★★★★

659 Boodjidup Road, Margaret River, WA 6285 **Region** Margaret River
T (08) 9757 6488 **www**.redgatewines.com.au **Open** 7 days 10–4.30
Winemaker Joel Page **Est.** 1977 **Dozens** 6000 **Vyds** 18ha

Founder and owner of Redgate, the late Bill Ullinger, chose the name not simply because of the nearby eponymous beach, but also because – so it is said – a local farmer (with a prominent red gate at his property) had run an illegal spirit-still 100 or so years ago, and its patrons would come to the property and ask whether there was any 'red gate' available. True or not, Redgate was one of the early movers in the Margaret River, now with close to 20ha of mature estate plantings (the majority to sauvignon blanc, semillon, cabernet sauvignon, cabernet franc, shiraz and chardonnay, with smaller plantings of chenin blanc and merlot). Exports to Denmark, Switzerland, Singapore, Japan and China.

♀♀♀♀♀ Margaret River Cabernet Sauvignon 2015 This is a more detailed, precise and eminently drinkable wine out of the gates than the headier Reserve. Both wines have the same extraction period of 8–10 days on skins, so presumably this is largely down to the lower percentage of new oak. Pastille, bay leaf, mint and black and red currant flavours are all in full regalia. Screwcap. 14.2% alc. **Rating** 95 **To** 2035 $38 NG
Reserve Margaret River Chardonnay 2015 This is tighter and more energetic than previous Reserves. That said, it is a richly flavoured chardonnay leading off with an aromatic plume of vanilla pod, peaches and cream. A nectarine tang cuts through the midriff, pulling the flavours along. A hint of oak adds a punctuation mark. Screwcap. 13.1% alc. **Rating** 94 **To** 2025 $60 NG
Reserve Margaret River Cabernet Sauvignon 2015 Blackcurrant, bitter chocolate, spearmint, cedar and tobacco leaf aromas ply a florid solo, pushing the envelope of expression across a taut bow of grainy, espresso-laced tannins, crunchy acidity and some cardamom oak. Dripping, too, with Margaret River's telltale pastille notes. Screwcap. 14.3% alc. **Rating** 94 **To** 2035 $65 NG

♀♀♀♀♀ Reserve Margaret River Sauvignon Blanc 2016 Rating 92 **To** 2017 $29
Reserve Margaret River Sauvignon Blanc 2015 Rating 92 **To** 2021 $29 NG
Margaret River Shiraz 2015 Rating 92 **To** 2035 $33
Margaret River Cabernet Franc 2015 Rating 92 **To** 2035 $40

RedHeads Studios ★★★★

733b Light Pass Road, Angaston, SA 5353 **Region** South Australia
T 0457 073 347 **www**.redheadswine.com **Open** By appt
Winemaker Dan Graham **Est.** 2003 **Dozens** 10000

Redheads was established by Tony Laithwaite in McLaren Vale, and has since moved to the Barossa Valley. The aim was to allow winemakers working under corporate banners to produce small batch whites. The team liberates premium parcels of grapes from large companies 'a few rows at a time, to give them the special treatment they deserve and to form wines of true individuality and character. It's all about creating wines with personality, that are made to be enjoyed.'

ΥΥΥΥΥ Vin'Atus Tempranillo Graciano Garnacha 2015 The link is obvious on paper and even more obvious in the glass. It's elegant, very fresh and (less probably) complex, with cooking spices and superfine tannins. Screwcap. 14% alc. **Rating** 92 To 2029 $28

Dogs of the Barossa Shiraz 2014 The label may appeal to some, and seem pointless to others, and so may the wine. It has good colour, good fruit, and an embarrassment of riches of oak. Less would have been so much more. Cork. 14.5% alc. **Rating** 90 To 2029 $60

ΥΥΥΥ The Corroboree Barossa Shiraz 2015 Rating 89 To 2022 $30

Redman

Main Road, Coonawarra, SA 5263 Region Coonawarra
T (08) 8736 3331 **Open** Mon-Fri 9–5, w'ends 10–4
Winemakers Bruce, Malcolm and Daniel Redman **Est.** 1966 **Dozens** 18000 **Vyds** 34ha
In March 2008 the Redman family celebrated 100 years of winemaking in Coonawarra. The '08 vintage also marked the arrival of Daniel, fourth-generation Redman winemaker. Daniel gained winemaking experience in Central Victoria, the Barossa Valley and the US before taking up his new position. It was felicitous timing, for the '04 Cabernet Sauvignon and '04 Cabernet Merlot were each awarded a gold medal from the national wine show circuit in '07, the first such accolades for a considerable time. A major vineyard rejuvenation program is underway, but there will be no change to the portfolio of wines. The quality has stabilised at a level in keeping with the long-term history of the winery and its mature vines.

ΥΥΥΥΥ Coonawarra Shiraz 2012 From an exceptionally good vintage, and the wine reflects this. Matured for 12 months in American and French hogsheads. Bright colour, then a bouquet filled with black cherry/blackberry fruit, oak also in the picture. A rich and long palate with great balance across the fruit, oak and tannins. Exceptional bargain. Cork. 14.1% alc. **Rating** 95 To 2037 $19

The Last Row Limited Release Coonawarra Shiraz 2014 From a single block of 80yo vines planted by Arthur Hoffman in the '30s, wild yeast–open fermented, 13 days on skins, 18 months in French oak (66% new). Has the old vine structure and depth of blackberry/black cherry/plum fruit to last for decades, underwritten by fine tannins. Screwcap. 14% alc. **Rating** 95 To 2039 $30

Coonawarra Cabernet Sauvignon Merlot 2013 A 52/48% blend, machine-harvested and field-crushed, matured for 24 months in French oak (35% new). Attractive crimson-purple hue; the juicy red and black currant palate leads to balanced but firm tannins, extending the finish. Cork. 13.6% alc. **Rating** 94 To 2033

Coonawarra Cabernet Sauvignon 2014 A pure, slightly austere, cabernet, with one foot in the past, one in the future, and a third in the present, reflected by the consequences of poor flowering. The result is an intense wine made from small berries and elevated tannins which, if nothing else, means a long life. Cork. 13.4% alc. **Rating** 94 To 2034 $28

Reillys Wines

Cnr Leasingham Road/Hill Street, Mintaro, SA 5415 **Region** Clare Valley
T (08) 8843 9013 **www**.reillyswines.com.au **Open** 7 days 10–4
Winemaker Justin Ardill **Est.** 1994 **Dozens** 25 000 **Vyds** 115ha
This has been a very successful venture for Adelaide cardiologist Justin Ardill and wife Julie, beginning as a hobby in 1994, but growing significantly over the intervening years. They now

have vineyards at Watervale, Leasingham and Mintaro, growing riesling, cabernet sauvignon, shiraz, grenache, tempranillo and merlot. The cellar door and restaurant were built between 1856 and 1866 by Irish immigrant Hugh Reilly; 140 years later they were restored by the Ardills, distant relatives of Reilly who have been making wines in the Clare Valley for a mere 20 years or so. Exports to the US, Canada, Ireland, Malaysia, China and Singapore.

ŸŸŸŸŸ **Dry Land Clare Valley Cabernet Sauvignon 2014** This is a very useful Clare Valley cabernet, reliant on its sheer power and its pure blackcurrant fruit, which make as good an opening as you could expect. The brush of eucalypt doesn't clash with cabernet, and the tannins are precisely in specification. Good to run for years yet. Screwcap. 15% alc. **Rating** 95 To 2029 $38

ŸŸŸŸŸ **Aged Release Watervale Riesling 2010** Rating 93 To 2022 $38
Watervale Riesling 2016 Rating 92 To 2029 $25 ●
Clare Valley Shiraz 2014 Rating 91 To 2029 $25
Barking Mad Watervale Riesling 2016 Rating 90 To 2026 $20 ●

Relbia Estate
★★★☆

1 Bridge Road, Launceston, Tas 7250 **Region** Northern Tasmania
T (03) 6332 1000 **www.relbiaestate.com.au** **Open** Mon–Thurs 10–5, Fri–Sat 10–11
Winemaker Ockie Myburgh **Est.** 2011 **Dozens** 2350
Dean Cocker is the grandson of Josef Chromy, and managing director of Josef Chromy Wines, and has worn two hats: one as a commercial lawyer in Melbourne and Sydney, the other with personal involvement in the Tasmanian wine industry since 1994. He has retained Ockie Myburgh as winemaker, stating the obvious in revealing Ockie's South African heritage and first winemaking degree, complemented by a Bachelor in Winemaking from the University of Western Sydney in 2005. Ockie has made wine in many parts of Australia, the most important and most recent as assistant winemaker at Bay of Fires in Tasmania. Exports to the UK.

ŸŸŸŸŸ **Methode Traditionelle NV** A fruity and tangy cuvee in which pinot noir takes a confident lead, via a faint blush hue and lively strawberry, red cherry and pink grapefruit characters. Cool northern Tasmanian acidity makes for a tense finish that would appreciate longer lees age to soften, integrate and build complexity. 12.3% alc. **Rating** 92 To 2019 $29 TS

Renards Folly
★★★☆

PO Box 499, McLaren Vale, SA 5171 **Region** McLaren Vale
T (08) 8556 2404 **www.renardsfolly.com** **Open** Not
Winemaker Tony Walker **Est.** 2005 **Dozens** 3000
The dancing foxes on the label, one with a red tail, give a subliminal hint that this is a virtual winery, owned by Linda Kemp. Aided by friend and winemaker Tony Walker, they source grapes from McLaren Vale, and allow the Vale to express itself without too much elaboration, the alcohol nicely controlled. Exports to the UK and Germany.

ŸŸŸŸŸ **Fighting Fox McLaren Vale Shiraz 2015** A buxom red with ample dark fruits hewn to a whack of vanillan oak tannins. Pulls no punches, and does so with considerable aplomb. Packed and fully loaded! Screwcap. 14.5% alc. **Rating** 90 To 2022 $28 NG

Renzaglia Wines
★★★★

38 Bosworth Falls Road, O'Connell, NSW 2795 **Region** Central Ranges
T (02) 6337 5756 **www.renzagliawines.com.au** **Open** By appt
Winemaker Mark Renzaglia **Est.** 2011 **Dozens** 2000 **Vyds** 5ha
Mark Renzaglia is a second-generation vigneron, his father growing vines in southern Illinois, US. Mark and wife Sandy planted their first vineyard in 1997 (1ha of chardonnay, cabernet sauvignon and merlot), Mark making wine in small quantities while working as a grapegrower/winemaker at Winburndale Wines for 11 years. In 2011 he left Winburndale

and he and Sandy started their own business. He also manages a vineyard in the middle of the famous Mount Panorama race circuit, and has access to the grapes from the 4ha Mount Panorama Estate (another vineyard, from which Brokenwood purchased chardonnay for some years). This gives him access to shiraz, semillon, cabernet sauvignon and chardonnay. He also purchases grapes from other local growers. Exports to the US.

ΨΨΨΨΨ **Mount Panorama Estate Chardonnay 2016** Partial wild yeast fermentation in barrel, 6 months on lees. Considerable colour pickup, and some phenolics on the finish, point to earlier rather than later consumption, its white peach, nectarine and melon providing the flavour. Screwcap. 13% alc. **Rating** 93 **To** 2024 $30
Mount Panorama Estate Shiraz 2015 Matured in a range of barrels of different origins and ages, which has worked the proverbial treat. Red (cherry), purple (plum) and black (berry) fruits tightly clasp each other's hands on this expansive, medium-bodied palate. Screwcap. 14% alc. **Rating** 93 **To** 2029 $30
Cabernet Sauvignon 2015 From the estate Mount Panorama Vineyard at Bathurst. This is in fact a delicious, easy-access light to medium-bodied cabernet, with cassis driving the juicy palate, and no green tannin or other unripe flavours whatsoever. Screwcap. 14.1% alc. **Rating** 91 **To** 2020 $22 ❂

ΨΨΨΨ **Shiraz 2015 Rating** 89 **To** 2021 $22

Reschke Wines

Level 1, 183 Melbourne Street, North Adelaide, SA 5006 (postal) **Region** Coonawarra
T (08) 8239 0500 www.reschke.com.au **Open** Not
Winemaker Peter Douglas (Contract) **Est.** 1998 **Dozens** 25000 **Vyds** 155ha
The Reschke family has been a landowner in Coonawarra for 100 years, with a large holding that is part terra rossa, part woodland. Cabernet sauvignon (with 120ha) takes the lion's share of the plantings, with merlot, shiraz and petit verdot making up the balance. Exports to the UK, Canada, Germany, Malaysia, Japan, Hong Kong and China.

ΨΨΨΨΨ **Vitulus Coonawarra Cabernet Sauvignon 2011** The decision not to produce Empyrean or Bos Cabernet Sauvignon in this vintage was repaid; this isn't a great Coonawarra cabernet, but is nonetheless among the best of the vintage, its cassis fruit plain for all to see and enjoy. Cork. 14% alc. **Rating** 90 **To** 2021 $28
Rufus The Bull Coonawarra Cabernet Sauvignon 2010 Distinctively Coonawarra cabernet from start to finish. Varietal aromas of green leafiness with a touch of blackcurrant; just medium-bodied, with the flavour running evenly through the palate. The fruit is ripe, but imbued with a herbal, minty feel. A solid citizen. Screwcap. 13.8% alc. **Rating** 90 **To** 2025 $22 SC

Reynella

Reynell Road, Reynella, SA 5161 **Region** McLaren Vale/Fleurieu Peninsula
T 1800 088 711 www.reynellawines.ocm.au **Open** Fri 11–4
Winemaker Paul Carpenter **Est.** 1838 **Dozens** NFP
John Reynell laid the foundations for Chateau Reynella in 1838; over the next 100 years the stone buildings, winery and underground cellars, with attractive gardens, were constructed. Thomas Hardy's first job in SA was with Reynella; he noted in his diary that he would be able to better himself soon. He did just that, becoming by far the largest producer in SA by the end of the 19th century; 150 or so years after Chateau Reynella's foundation, CWA (now Accolade Wines) completed the circle by making it its corporate headquarters, while preserving the integrity of the Reynella brand in no uncertain fashion. Exports to all major markets.

ΨΨΨΨΨ **Basket Pressed McLaren Vale Shiraz 2015** Deep but brilliant crimson-purple; takes complexity onto another level with black fruits, dark earthy notes, bitter 70% cacao chocolate, black pepper and cedary oak all held in a wickerwork of ripe, insistent tannins. This will never chuck the towel in. Screwcap. 14.5% alc. **Rating** 97 **To** 2045 $70 ❂

🍷🍷🍷🍷🍷 **Basket Pressed McLaren Vale Cabernet Sauvignon 2015** The colour is full and deep, the bouquet alive with black fruits, spice and distinct sandalwood aromas, the palate adding some earthy notes to the parade of blackcurrant, plum and mulberry fruits, savoury tannins providing the necessary structure for a very long life. Screwcap. 14.5% alc. **Rating** 96 **To** 2040 $70 ✪

Rhythm Stick Wines ★★★★★

89 Campbell Road, Penwortham, SA 5453 **Region** Clare Valley
T (08) 8843 4325 **www**.rhythmstickwines.com.au **Open** By appt
Winemaker Tim Adams **Est.** 2007 **Dozens** 1060 **Vyds** 1.62ha
Rhythm Stick has come a long way in a short time, and with a small vineyard. It is owned by Ron and Jeanette Ely, who in 1997 purchased a 3.2ha property at Penwortham. The couple had already decided that in the future they would plant a vineyard, and simply to obtain experience they planted 135 cabernet sauvignon cuttings from Waninga Vineyards in four short rows. They produced a few dozen bottles of Cabernet a year, sharing it with friends. In 2002 they planted riesling, and the first harvest followed in '06, the grapes from this and the ensuing two vintages sold to Clare Valley winemakers. Prior to the '09 harvest they were advised that due to the GFC no grapes would be required, which advanced Ron's planned retirement after 40 years in electrical engineering consulting and management.

🍷🍷🍷🍷🍷 **Aged Release Red Robin Reserve Clare Valley Riesling 2010** Bright straw-green, looking more like a 2yo than a 7yo wine, and the palate every bit as fresh as the colour suggests. Crisp citrus and Granny Smith apple drive the long palate, owing nothing to residual sugar, everything to the conjunction of a pH of 2.91, and titratable acidity of 7.18g/l. Another 10 years won't tire it. Screwcap. 11.4% alc. **Rating** 95 **To** 2027 $25 ✪
Red Robin Reserve Single Vineyard Clare Valley Riesling 2009 Has fulfilled the exceptional potential it had when given 94 points in Jan '11. Its floral bouquet, perfectly poised lime fruit on the palate and finely drawn acidity tick all the boxes. Screwcap. 11% alc. **Rating** 95 **To** 2024 $25

🍷🍷🍷🍷🍷 **Red Robin Clare Valley Riesling 2015 Rating** 93 **To** 2031 $19
Red Robin Clare Valley Riesling 2016 Rating 90 **To** 2023 $19 ✪

Richard Hamilton ★★★★★

Cnr Main Road/Johnston Road, McLaren Vale, SA 5171 **Region** McLaren Vale
T (08) 8323 8830 **www**.leconfieldwines.com **Open** Mon–Fri 10–5, w'ends 11–5
Winemaker Paul Gordon, Tim Bailey **Est.** 1972 **Dozens** 25 000 **Vyds** 71.6ha
Richard Hamilton has outstanding estate vineyards, some of great age, all fully mature. An experienced and skilled winemaking team has allowed the full potential of those vineyards to be realised. The quality, style and consistency of both red and white wines has reached a new level; being able to keep only the best parcels for the Richard Hamilton brand is an enormous advantage. For reasons outside the *Wine Companion*'s control, not all the current releases were available for tasting for the 2018 edition. Exports to the UK, the US, Canada, Denmark, Sweden, Germany, Belgium, Malaysia, Vietnam, Hong Kong, Singapore, Japan, China and NZ.

🍷🍷🍷🍷🍷 **Centurion McLaren Vale Shiraz 2015** Grapes from 123yo vines have been given Rolls Royce treatment from the hand-picked start through to bottling. The high quality of the wine is beyond doubt, its long-term future guaranteed thanks to the inherent balance between the lush dark fruits, silky tannins and French oak. A word of warning: the oak is very obvious now, but will sink back into the flavour profile (think Grange) with 5–10 years in bottle. Screwcap. 14.5% alc. **Rating** 97 **To** 2043 $80 ✪

🍷🍷🍷🍷🍷 **Centurion McLaren Vale Shiraz 2014** Vines planted in 1892, dry-grown and hand-tended. Remarkable. A wine clearly made with due reverence for this amazing fruit resource. Completely unforced from start to finish, the deep blue and black fruit character is sympathetically dressed in high quality oak, and the regional milk chocolate adds a touch of sweet complexity. Deep and long in flavour, the tannin is superfine, framing the palate without ever becoming obtrusive. A winemaking work of art. Screwcap. 14.5% alc. **Rating** 95 **To** 2040 $80 SC

Burton's Vineyard Old Bush Vine McLaren Vale Grenache 2015 This is at the full-bodied end of the spectrum for high quality McLaren Vale grenache, but keeps its shape well. Juicy red fruits of all kinds fill the mouth in a hedonistic display of generosity. Its breeding and quality mean it will live long, but I'd be drinking it right now. Screwcap. 14.5% alc. **Rating** 95 **To** 2025 $30

Burton's Vineyard Old Bush Vine McLaren Vale Grenache 2014 From 67yo dry-grown estate vines, matured in used French oak for 18 months. It's fuller-bodied than many McLaren Vale grenaches, and needs food. In that context, it will shine, its varietal cherry-accented fruit coming to the fore, alcohol pushed back. Screwcap. 15% alc. **Rating** 94 **To** 2029 $30 ○

ΨΨΨΨΨ **Watervale Riesling 2016** Rating 93 To 2025 $20 SC ○
The Smuggler McLaren Vale Shiraz 2015 Rating 93 To 2025 $21 ○
Hut Block Cabernet Sauvignon 2014 Rating 92 To 2024 $20 CM ○
Hut Block Cabernet Sauvignon 2015 Rating 90 To 2024 $21 SC ○

Ridgemill Estate   ★★★★☆

218 Donges Road, Severnlea, Qld 4352 **Region** Granite Belt
T (07) 4683 5211 **www**.ridgemillestate.com **Open** Fri–Mon 10–5, Sun 10–3
Winemaker Martin Cooper, Peter McGlashan **Est.** 1998 **Dozens** 900 **Vyds** 2.1ha
Martin Cooper and Dianne Maddison acquired what was then known as Emerald Hill Winery in 2004. In '05 they reshaped the vineyards, which now have plantings of chardonnay, tempranillo, shiraz, merlot, cabernet sauvignon, saperavi, verdelho and viognier, setting a course down the alternative variety road. There is a quite spectacular winery and cellar door facility, and self-contained cabins in the vineyard.

ΨΨΨΨΨ **Granite Belt Chardonnay 2014** Half fermented in stainless steel, half in French oak, no mlf, matured in new French oak. You can see why this wine should have won three trophies at the Australian Small Winemakers Show '15 – but not what the trophies were for; this show has for years used stickers that immediately become illegible as the black print wears off. The fermentation has worked well here, with gentle stone fruit trimmed by grapefruit zest. Screwcap. 12.8% alc. **Rating** 95 **To** 2019 $40

ΨΨΨΨΨ **Granite Belt Mourvedre 2014** Rating 91 To 2029 $45
WYP Granite Belt Chardonnay 2015 Rating 90 To 2019 $35 SC

RidgeView Wines   ★★★★

273 Sweetwater Road, Pokolbin, NSW 2320 **Region** Hunter Valley
T (02) 6574 7332 **www**.ridgeview.com.au **Open** Wed–Sun 10–5
Winemaker Darren Scott, Gary MacLean **Est.** 2500 **Dozens** 5000 **Vyds** 9ha
Darren and Tracey Scott have transformed a 40ha timbered farm into a vineyard, together with self-contained accommodation and a cellar door. The lion's share of the plantings are 4.5ha of shiraz, with cabernet sauvignon, chambourcin, merlot, pinot gris, viognier and traminer making up a somewhat eclectic selection of other varieties.

ΨΨΨΨΨ **Aged Release Generations Reserve Hunter Valley Semillon 2009** As expected, this has taken on some toasty buttered brioche notes, as well as lemon oil and candied peel with crushed coriander and white pepper. While there's plenty of lively acidity, it's in a good place and best drunk soon. Screwcap. 10.8% alc. **Rating** 93 **To** 2020 $40 JF
Generations Single Vineyard Reserve Hunter Valley Semillon 2016 Mid-straw and bright; a delicate mix of citrus blossom, Meyer lemon juice and lemongrass. A lovely freshness and softish acidity, so best enjoyed now. Screwcap. 11% alc. **Rating** 91 **To** 2020 $25 JF

Impressions Single Vineyard Hunter Valley Shiraz 2014 Tangy briary and plum fruits with lots of acidity locking in wood spices, supple tannins and ease on the palate. Mid-ruby and bright, even if the fresher flavours seem to be dissipating into some tertiary notes. 13.5% alc. **Rating** 91 **To** 2023 $35 JF

Rieslingfreak ★★★★★

8 Roenfeldt Drive, Tanunda, SA 5352 **Region** Clare Valley
T (08) 8563 3963 **www**.rieslingfreak.com **Open** By appt
Winemaker John Hughes **Est.** 2009 **Dozens** 5000 **Vyds** 35ha
The name of John Hughes' winery leaves no doubt about his long-term ambition: to explore every avenue of riesling, whether bone-dry or sweet, coming from regions across the wine world, albeit with a strong focus on Australia. The wines made from his Clare Valley vineyard offer dry (No. 2, No. 3 and No. 4) and off-dry (No. 5 and No. 8) styles. Exports to Canada, Norway, Hong Kong and NZ.

No. 4 Riesling 2016 Elegance is the first name of this wine, quickly pursued by purity and silky acidity, then lemon and green apple fruit flavours. A lovely wine to drink now or much later. Fully deserved its gold medals at the Adelaide and Melbourne wine shows '16. Screwcap. 11% alc. **Rating** 96 **To** 2031 $24 ❂
No. 3 Riesling 2016 A generous riesling, opening up immediately on the lime-filled palate before life-giving minerally acidity takes control on the palate and aftertaste. Gold medal Adelaide Wine Show '16, silver medal Clare Valley Wine Show '16. Screwcap. 11.5% alc. **Rating** 95 **To** 2026 $24 ❂

No. 5 Riesling 2016 Rating 93 **To** 2031 $24 ❂
No. 8 Riesling 2016 Rating 91 **To** 2036 $35

Rileys of Eden Valley ★★★★

PO Box 71, Eden Valley, SA 5235 **Region** Eden Valley
T (08) 8564 1029 **www**.rileysofedenvalley.com.au **Open** Not
Winemaker Peter Riley, Jo Irvine (Consultant) **Est.** 2006 **Dozens** 2000 **Vyds** 11.24ha
Rileys of Eden Valley is owned by Terry and Jan Riley with son Peter, who, way back in 1982, purchased 32ha of a grazing property that they believed had potential for quality grape production. The first vines were planted in that year and now extend to over 12ha. In '98 Terry retired from his position (Professor of Mechanical Engineering) at the University of SA, allowing him to concentrate on the vineyard, and, more recently, winemaking activities, but the whole family (including granddaughter Maddy) have been involved in the development of the property. It had always been intended that the grapes would be sold, but when not all the grapes were contracted in '06, the Rileys decided to produce some wine (even though they ended up with buyers for all the production that year).

Jump Ship Shiraz 2014 A medium to full-bodied, generously flavoured shiraz with well above average texture and structure. The flavours are right in the mainstream of Eden Valley shiraz, supple and darker than those of the Barossa Valley. Screwcap. 14.5% alc. **Rating** 94 **To** 2029 $25 ❂
Cabernet Sauvignon 2015 The saints (and Jo Irvine) be praised, for the wine is as fresh and vibrant as young cabernet should be. It is full of varietal cassis fruit, while the tannins are soft (again an Irvine mark of some barrel ferment). Screwcap. 13.5% alc. **Rating** 94 **To** 2030 $25 ❂

Aged Release The Family Riesling 2009 Rating 90 **To** 2020 $35
The Engineer Merlot 2014 Rating 90 **To** 2024 $28

 # Rill House Vineyard ★★★★☆

O'Leary's Lane, Spring Hill, Vic 3444 **Region** Macedon Ranges
T 0408 388 156 **www**.rillhouse.com.au **Open** Not
Winemaker Matt Harrop **Est.** 1986 **Dozens** 100 **Vyds** 1.8ha

The vineyard was planted 30 years ago to 1.2ha of chardonnay and 0.6ha of sauvignon blanc; the grapes were sold to other makers in the region until the vineyard was purchased by Caroline Achersold and Richard Price in 2013. They decided to sell part of the production and vinify the remainder. The one wine so far released under the Rill House label, made by Matt Harrop, should absolutely guarantee that it won't be the last.

ΤΤΤΤΤ My Deer Bride Chardonnay 2015 From the 30yo estate Quartz Block, matured for 12 months in new and used French hogsheads. Given the age of the vines and the region, the sheer power and concentration of this wine should not surprise. The oak flavours have been easily swallowed by the fruit, which is equal parts white peach, grapefruit and crunchy acidity. It is clearly destined for a long life, but I'm resisting the temptation to make comparisons with Montrachet. Screwcap. 12.5% alc. **Rating** 96 **To** 2025 $48 ✪

Riposte   ★★★★★

PO Box 256, Lobethal, SA 5241 **Region** Adelaide Hills
T (08) 8389 8149 **www**.timknappstein.com.au **Open** Not
Winemaker Tim Knappstein **Est.** 2006 **Dozens** 11 000
It's never too late to teach an old dog new tricks when the old dog in question is Tim Knappstein. With 50+ years of winemaking and more than 500 wine show awards under his belt, Tim started yet another new wine life in 2006 with Riposte, a subtle response to the various vicissitudes he has suffered over the years. While having no continuing financial interest in Lenswood Vineyards, established many years ago, Tim is able to source grapes from it and also from other prime sites in surrounding areas. The prices for almost all the wines are astonishingly low. Exports to the UK, US, Canada, Indonesia and China.

ΤΤΤΤΤ The Sabre Adelaide Hills Pinot Noir 2015 A sabre, it seems, can cleave a pinot that is alive with a fragrant red flower (roses) perfumed bouquet and a juicy/spicy palate that welcomes all who draw near. Relaxed, silky tannins and a quick kiss on the cheek by the oak complete a wine that is ready now (but with more to come). Screwcap. 13.5% alc. **Rating** 95 **To** 2027 $35 ✪
The Cutlass Adelaide Hills Shiraz 2015 Tim Knappstein has had a lifetime of practice, and his wines continue to reflect both his technical skills across a range of varieties and his abiding belief in reflecting terroir. This wine starts with dark cherry before moving into spiced dark plum fruit with an oompapah beat of ripe tannins. Screwcap. 14% alc. **Rating** 95 **To** 2030 $28 ✪
The Scimitar Clare Valley Riesling 2016 Lime and apple blossom aromas lead into a dazzling pure and crisp palate, finely etched acidity driving the long finish and cleansing aftertaste. A 10-year outlook may be way short of the mark, but either way, it's an automatic choice for any BYO Asian restaurant. Screwcap. 11.5% alc. **Rating** 94 **To** 2026 $20 ✪
The Katana Adelaide Hills Chardonnay 2015 Gleaming straw-green; there's a lot of wine for the price, as fruit, oak and acidity (not softened by partial mlf) play off against each other in synergistic fashion. The flavour spectrum reflects the climate, comfortably spanning stone fruit and citrus. Has time to go. Screwcap. 13.2% alc. **Rating** 94 **To** 2021 $25 ✪
The Dagger Adelaide Hills Pinot Noir 2016 Light, but bright crimson hue; a surprise packet, until the memory of prior vintages clicks in. This has an indecent amount of complex varietal fruits; cherry and plum fruit engage in a duel to establish primacy, the referee coming in with spicy/savoury tannins to give context to the duel – which ultimately remains unresolved. Screwcap. 13.5% alc. **Rating** 94 **To** 2025 $20 ✪

ΤΤΤΤΤ The Foil Adelaide Hills Sauvignon Blanc 2016 Rating 93 **To** 2018 $20 ✪
The Stiletto Adelaide Hills Pinot Gris 2015 Rating 93 **To** 2017 $20 ✪
The Cutlass Adelaide Hills Shiraz 2014 Rating 91 **To** 2021 $27
Aged Release The Rapier 'Traminer 2010 Rating 90 **To** 2020 $28

Rise Vineyards   ★★★★☆

PO Box 7336, Adelaide, SA 5000 **Region** Clare Valley
T 0419 844 238 **www.**risevineyards.com.au **Open** Not
Winemaker Matthew McCulloch **Est.** 2009 **Dozens** 1200
Rise is very much a busman's holiday for Grant Norman and Matthew McCulloch. The two are a close-knit team, Grant looking after the business and Matt the wine. Matt spent more than a decade in the UK wine trade. In 2006 Matt and wife Gina moved to the Clare Valley, where he was responsible for sales and marketing at Kirrihill Wines, of which Grant, an Australian wine industry veteran, was general manager. The move to Clare enabled Matt and Gina to realise a long-held dream of owning their own vineyard, growing the grapes and making the wine, with the help of Grant and his wife Alice. Having spent 11 years on the road working with more than 70 winemakers in 13 countries, Matt was convinced the focus of Rise should be on making small-scale, terroir-driven Riesling, Cabernet Sauvignon, Grenache and Shiraz, reflecting the unique vineyard sites from which they come. Exports to China.

ϱϱϱϱϙ **Watervale Riesling 2016** No doubting the region this hails from: it practically shouts Watervale. All lemon blossom, lemon-lime juice freshness and zest with a slight yeasty-leesy character – not unpleasant, just noticeable. Still, it's steely and crisp on the finish. Screwcap. 11.5% alc. **Rating** 93 **To** 2025 $23 JF **O**

ϱϱϱϱ **Clare Valley Mourvedre 2015 Rating** 89 **To** 2022 $22 JF

Risky Business Wines   ★★★★

PO Box 6015, East Perth, WA 6892 **Region** Various
T 0457 482 957 **www.**riskybusinesswines.com.au **Open** Not
Winemaker Michael Kerrigan, Andrew Vesey, Gavin Berry **Est.** 2013 **Dozens** 3500
The name Risky Business is decidedly tongue-in-cheek, for the partnership headed by Rob Quenby has neatly side-stepped any semblance of risk. First up, the grapes come from vineyards in Great Southern and Margaret River that are managed by Quenby Viticultural Services. Since the batches of wine are very small (150–800 dozen), the partnership is able to select grapes specifically suited to the wine style and price. So there is no capital tied up in vineyards, nor in a winery – the wines are contract-made. Exports to Japan and China.

ϱϱϱϱϙ **White Knuckle Chardonnay 2015** The combined effect of fruit and oak makes this a pleasure to drink. White peach, creamy/toasty/cedary oak, a whisper of chalk and a burst of citrus. It works, handsomely. Screwcap. 13% alc. **Rating** 93 **To** 2020 $25 CM **O**

Malbec 2015 5 days on skins reflects the rapid accumulation of colour and tannins with malbec in Margaret River; matured in new and used French oak for 14 months. Deeply coloured, and with tannins on parade from the outset, dark plummy fruit holding the mid-palate. Screwcap. 14.5% alc. **Rating** 90 **To** 2023 $25

ϱϱϱϱ **King Valley Pinot Grigio 2016 Rating** 89 **To** 2017 $25 CM

Riversdale Estate   ★★★★★

222 Denholms Road, Cambridge, Tas 7170 **Region** Southern Tasmania
T (03) 6248 5555 **www.**riversdaleestate.com.au **Open** 7 days 10–5
Winemaker Nick Badrice **Est.** 1991 **Dozens** 9000 **Vyds** 37ha
Ian Roberts purchased the Riversdale property in 1980 while a university student, and says he paid a record price for the district. The unique feature of the property is its frontage to the Pittwater waterfront, which acts as a buffer against frost, and also moderates the climate during the ripening phase. It is a large property, with 37ha of vines and one of the largest olive groves in Tasmania, producing 50 olive-based products. Five families live permanently on the estate, providing all the labour for the various operations, which also include four 5-star French Provincial cottages overlooking the vines. A new cellar door and French bistro opened in Jan '16. Wine quality is consistently good, and can be outstanding.

ŸŸŸŸŸ **Crater Chardonnay 2015** A beautifully crafted chardonnay, ticking each and
every box, and a vast relief after a string of chardonnays in its tasting with all
manner of problems. Here white peach and grapefruit zest are held in a finely
structured basket of high quality oak. Screwcap. 13.5% alc. **Rating** 96 **To** 2027
$50 **○**
Botrytis Riesling 2014 Botrytis at its best, introducing complexity yet without
in any way obscuring the delicious juicy Bickford's lime juice flavours, in turn
balanced by cleansing acidity. Tasmania does this so well. 375ml. Screwcap.
6.1% alc. **Rating** 95 **To** 2021 $26 **○**
Pinot Gris 2016 The quality of the fruit is the springboard for the flavour and
texture of a very good gris. Nashi pear is a confident leader of the flavour pack,
spice and stone fruit brining up the rear. Screwcap. 12.5% alc. **Rating** 94 **To** 2021
$26 **○**
Pinot Noir 2015 This is old money pinot, self-assured and with nothing to prove.
Wild forest fruits, cadenced spices, silky tannins and French oak are all at ease with
each other. A pinot to drink. Screwcap. 14.5% alc. **Rating** 94 **To** 2025 $26 **○**

ŸŸŸŸŸ **Pinot Noir 2014 Rating** 93 **To** 2029 $36
Musca Syrah 2014 Rating 92 **To** 2022 $57 SC
Crux NV Rating 92 **To** 2017 $38 TS
Sauvignon Blanc 2015 Rating 90 **To** 2017 $23

Rob Dolan Wines ★★★★☆

21–23 Delaneys Road, South Warrandyte, Vic 3134 **Region** Yarra Valley
T (03) 9876 5885 **www**.robdolanwines.com.au **Open** 7 days 10–5
Winemaker Rob Dolan, Mark Nikolich **Est.** 2010 **Dozens** 20 000 **Vyds** 20ha
Rob Dolan has been making wine in the Yarra Valley for over 20 years, and knows every
nook and cranny there. In 2011 he was able to purchase the Hardys Yarra Burn winery at an
enticing price. It is singularly well equipped, and as well as making the excellent Rob Dolan
wines there, he carries on an extensive contract winemaking business. Business is booming,
production having doubled, with exports driving much of the increase. Exports to the UK,
the US, Canada, Malaysia, Singapore, Hong Kong and China.

ŸŸŸŸŸ **White Label Yarra Valley Pinot Gris 2016** It is refreshing to see a gris that
has not had the colour and stuffing knocked out of it by carbon fining. This wine
is of a bright copper hue, segueing to crunchy red apple, nashi pear, a melody of
citrus and ginger notes. The palate is suitably rich and viscous; the wine's modus
operandi, texture. Gentle acidity and a phenolic pucker keep things on the straight
and narrow. A good drink. Screwcap. 14.2% alc. **Rating** 93 **To** 2019 $30 NG
White Label Yarra Valley Chardonnay 2016 Stone fruits spring from the
glass, framed by cedar and vanilla. The palate unfurls across more spicy oak,
presumably helping to mitigate the lower acidity and ripe fruit from such a warm
year. Peach, citrus and toasted nuts careen along oaky rails. The finish is long and
penetrative, if not slightly hot. Screwcap. 14% alc. **Rating** 92 **To** 2022 $30 NG
True Colours Yarra Valley Chardonnay 2015 This is a sophisticated, mineral-
clad chardonnay etched with the attributes of a far more expensive offering. There
is a hint of stone fruit, oatmeal and nougat from lees handling, and a brushstroke
of vanilla across the finish, suggesting a modicum of oak in support. Mid-weighted,
energetic and highly drinkable. Screwcap. 13.5% alc. **Rating** 92 **To** 2020 $24
NG **○**
White Label Bon Blanc Yarra Valley Savagnin 2016 Autumnal fruits,
camomile and curry powder make for an intriguing aroma. The palate, mid-
weighted and intensely flavoured, is furled around a core of mineral crunch, bright
acidity and the textural drift of gentle grape skin tannins. The finish is long and
moreish. Screwcap. 13.5% alc. **Rating** 91 **To** 2021 $30 NG
White Label Yarra Valley Pinot Noir 2016 Pallid is the visage of this ethereal
variety and this wine no different. Yet in stark contrast, punchy red fruit flavours
kick off a stream of prickly briar, a whiff of musk and a growing cascade of

sweetness as the wine grows across the mouth. Screwcap. 14% alc. **Rating** 91 **To** 2022 $35 NG

White Label Yarra Valley Cabernet Sauvignon 2015 Firm and bracing, this cabernet hails from an extremely dry year and the thick-skinned grape tannins are the wine's signature. These tannins, monumental and chocolatey, harness the flow of currant, mocha and sage. Some vanilla-pod oak adds further support. Screwcap. 14.5% alc. **Rating** 91 **To** 2029 $35 NG

True Colours Dry Rose 2016 Rating 90 **To** 2018 $24 NG

True Colours Pinot Noir 2015 Rating 90 **To** 2023 $24 NG

True Colours Cabernet Shiraz Merlot 2015 Rating 90 $24 NG

ΨΨΨΨ **True Colours Sauvignon Blanc 2016 Rating** 89 **To** 2018 $24 NG

Robert Channon Wines ★★★★

32 Bradley Lane, Amiens, Qld 4352 **Region** Granite Belt
T (07) 4683 3260 **www**.robertchannonwines.com **Open** Mon, Tues & Fri 11–4, w'ends 10–5
Winemaker Paola Cabezas **Est.** 1998 **Dozens** 2500 **Vyds** 8ha

Peggy and Robert Channon have established verdelho, chardonnay, pinot gris, shiraz, cabernet sauvignon and pinot noir under permanent bird protection netting. The initial cost of installing permanent netting is high, but in the long term it is well worth it: it excludes birds and protects the grapes against hail damage. Also, there is no pressure to pick the grapes before they are fully ripe. Exports to NZ.

ΨΨΨΨΨ **Granite Belt Shiraz 2016** Extended maceration has resulted in a deeply coloured, full-bodied shiraz with spicy notes to the black fruits (cherry, berry) of the palate. Needs a year or two to settle down, the extract a touch tough at the moment. Screwcap. 14% alc. **Rating** 94 **To** 2030 $25 ✪

Granite Belt Cabernet Sauvignon 2016 Estate-grown, hand-picked, open-fermented, 10 days on skins, but no mention of oak. Medium to full-bodied, with good varietal expression, juicy cassis and black olive waving the semaphore flags. Impressive. Screwcap. 14% alc. **Rating** 94 **To** 2031 $25 ✪

ΨΨΨΨΫ **Granite Belt Cabernet Shiraz 2015 Rating** 90 **To** 2023 $25

Robert Johnson Vineyards ★★★★★

Old Woollen Mill, Lobethal, SA 5241 **Region** Eden Valley
T (08) 8359 2600 **www**.robertjohnsonvineyards.com.au **Open** W'ends 11–5
Winemaker Robert Johnson **Est.** 1997 **Dozens** 3000 **Vyds** 3.86ha

The home base for Robert Johnson is a 12ha vineyard and olive grove purchased in 1996, with 0.4ha of merlot and 5ha of olive trees. The olive grove has been rehabilitated, and 2.1ha of shiraz, 1.2ha of merlot and a small patch of viognier have been established. Wines made from estate-grown grapes are released under the Robert Johnson label; these are supplemented by Alan & Veitch wines, made from grapes purchased from the Sam Virgara vineyard in the Adelaide Hills, and named after Robert Johnson's parents. Exports to the US and Poland.

ΨΨΨΨΨ **Eden Valley Viognier 2015** A similar winemaking approach to the previous vintage, with wild yeast ferment on solids in 1yo and seasoned French oak. Whether the oak is too dominant is something that could be argued, but there's no disputing that this wine has a bold personality. The apricot-like varietal character is full-on in the bouquet, and the palate is rich in texture and multilayered flavour. Screwcap. 13.5% alc. **Rating** 94 **To** 2019 $32 SC

ΨΨΨΨΫ **Adelaide Hills Pinot Noir 2016 Rating** 93 **To** 2025 $30 SC

Alan & Veitch Adelaide Hills Sauvignon Blanc 2016 Rating 91 **To** 2019 $20 SC ✪

Eden Valley Merlot 2015 Rating 91 **To** 2021 $48 SC

Alan & Veitch Adelaide Hills Merlot 2014 Rating 90 **To** 2020 $26 SC

Robert Oatley Vineyards

Craigmoor Road, Mudgee, NSW 2850 **Region** Mudgee
T (02) 6372 2208 **www**.robertoatley.com.au **Open** 7 days 10–4
Winemaker Larry Cherubino, Rob Merrick **Est.** 2006 **Dozens** NFP **Vyds** 440ha
Robert Oatley Vineyards is the venture of the Oatley family, previously best known as the
owners of Rosemount Estate until it was sold to Southcorp. Sandy Oatley is chairman
following the death of father Bob in 2016. Wild Oats, as anyone with the remotest interest in
yachting and the Sydney–Hobart Yacht Race will know, has been the name of Bob's racing
yachts. The family has long owned vineyards in Mudgee, but the new business was rapidly
expanded by the acquisition of the Montrose winery and the Craigmoor cellar door and
restaurant. The recruitment of Larry Cherubino as a winemaker has been a major factor in
the radical reshaping of the overall business, with most the best wines now coming coming
from WA. While there is a plethora of wines, the portfolio is easy to understand: at the bottom,
Pocketwatch; next Wild Oats; Robert Oatley Signature Series; Robert Oatley Finisterre; and
at the top, Robert Oatley The Pennant. The Cornucopia wines are a joint project with Larry
Cherubino. Exports to the UK, the US and other major markets (including China).

ΨΨΨΨΨ **Robert Oatley Great Southern Riesling 2015** The highly floral rose petal
and citrus blossom bouquet is the foreplay for the will-o'-the-wisp acidity of the
palate as it dances in time with the lime/lemon fruit duo. This is a beautifully
cadenced riesling that will reveal all its secrets in 10 years, and live for another
10 years beyond that. Screwcap. 12.5% alc. **Rating** 97 **To** 2035 $23 ✪
Robert Oatley The Pennant Margaret River Chardonnay 2012 Gleaming
straw-green; a high quality chardonnay that is ageing with grace, still fresh as
a daisy with years to go before reaching its zenith. The bouquet is decidedly
complex, the palate with grapefruit zest and precise acidity drawing out its length
and aftertaste. Screwcap. **Rating** 97 **To** 2021 $70 ✪

ΨΨΨΨΨ **Robert Oatley Margaret River Sauvignon Blanc 2016** It's as racy as one
of (the late) Robert Oatley's yachts. Laser precision with its acidity and flavours –
more in the citrus spectrum, with crunchy star fruit, fresh basil and cut grass – and
offers a lot of pleasure. Gold medal and subsequent trophy Sydney Royal Wine
Show '16 and fair enough, too. Screwcap. **Rating** 95 **To** 2021 $23 JF ✪
Robert Oatley Margaret River Chardonnay 2015 Plots its course quietly but
expertly, the colour still undeveloped (a good thing), white peach and nectarine
fruit setting the course for now or later, because there will be no fundamental
change with bottle age, just a slow increase in weight from mid to full. Screwcap.
12.5% alc. **Rating** 95 **To** 2025 $23 ✪
Robert Oatley Finisterre Great Southern Syrah 2014 Everything from the
colour, flavour profile to the shape of this wine sings. A flourish of bright, dark
cherries and plums, star anise and cinnamon. The palate flows evenly with supple
yet decisive tannins, the cedary oak integrated and part of the wine's detailed
structure. Screwcap. **Rating** 95 **To** 2030 $40 JF
Robert Oatley Finisterre Mudgee Chardonnay 2015 The explosion in
the number of high quality chardonnays from the Hunter Valley suggest Mudgee
should be on the same page, and this marks a step along the way with its pink
grapefruit and melon flavours augmented by cashew oak. Screwcap. 12.5% alc.
Rating 94 **To** 2025 $33

ΨΨΨΨΩ **Robert Oatley Finisterre Margaret River Chardonnay 2016** Rating 93
To 2023 $37 JF
Robert Oatley Heathcote Shiraz 2015 Rating 93 To 2024 $23 JF ✪
Wild Oats Mudgee Pinot Grigio 2016 Rating 92 To 2019 $18 JF ✪
Robert Oatley McLaren Vale GSM 2016 Rating 92 To 2024 $23 JF ✪
Robert Oatley Margaret River Cabernet Sauvignon 2015 Rating 92
To 2026 $23 JF ✪
Robert Oatley The Pennant Mudgee Chardonnay 2015 Rating 91
To 2022 $70 JF

Robert Oatley Finisterre Margaret River Cabernet Sauvignon 2014
Rating 91 To 2024 $40 JF
Wild Oats Sauvignon Blanc 2016 Rating 90 To 2019 $18 JF ✪
Montrose Stony Creek Mudgee Chardonnay 2015 Rating 90 To 2021
$23 JF
Wild Oats Mudgee Rose 2016 Rating 90 To 2017 $18
Robert Oatley Yarra Valley Pinot Noir 2015 Rating 90 To 2025 $23
Robert Oatley The Pennant Margaret River Cabernet Sauvignon 2013
Rating 90 To 2030 $80 JF

Robert Stein Vineyard   ★★★★★

Pipeclay Lane, Mudgee, NSW 2850 **Region** Mudgee
T (02) 6373 3991 **www.robertstein.com.au Open** 7 days 10–4.30
Winemaker Jacob Stein **Est.** 1976 **Dozens** 20 000 **Vyds** 18.67ha
While three generations of the family have been involved since Robert (Bob) Stein began
the establishment of the vineyard, the chain stretches even further back, going to Bob's great-
great-grandfather, Johann Stein, who was brought to Australia in 1838 by the Macarthur
family to supervise the planting of the Camden Park Vineyard. Bob's son Drew and grandson
Jacob have now taken over winemaking responsibilities. Jacob worked vintages in Italy,
Canada, Margaret River and Avoca, and, more particularly, in the Rheingau and Rheinhessen
regions of Germany. Since his return one success has followed another. Exports to Germany,
Hong Kong, Singapore and China.

🍷🍷🍷🍷🍷 **Mudgee Riesling 2016** The acidity is true to form and rapier-like, yet stone
fruit, quince and an assortment of citrus flavours flow across a cool stream of
wet rocks, effortlessly and forcefully, before an exclamation of white pepper and
a phenolic bite. This is highly Germanic and far from the Madding Australian
Crowd. Screwcap. 12% alc. **Rating** 96 **To** 2030 $30 NG ✪
Reserve Mudgee Riesling 2016 Less opulent than the '15, the wine is a taut
bow of citrus and pungent mineral. Smoky. There is quince, too. Tensile acidity
streams from fore to aft, with a whiff of white pepper on the finish bringing to
mind fine Austrian and German examples. Austere and in a nascent stage, this
needs time. Screwcap. 11.5% alc. **Rating** 96 **To** 2032 $50 NG ✪
Reserve Mudgee Riesling 2015 More concentrated and less tightly knit
than the '16, this is a tour de force of stone fruits, ginger and quince flavours that
stain the gums, as a trickle of lime cordial runs through it all. The dry extract is
monumental, and smothers riesling's telltale acidity at this embryonic stage; still
energetic behind the scenes, tactile and jittery with time in the glass. Screwcap.
13% alc. **Rating** 95 **To** 2031 $50 NG
Half Dry Mudgee Riesling 2016 RS10. As the label implies, this riesling is
equipped with 10g/l residual sugar. In effect the variety's high acidity negates
sweetness and any sense of cloying. The combination of skin contact, wild yeast
fermentation and partial oak handling tightens this up even further, as lime
and candied citrus rind unravel across a beam of energy. Finishes dry. Screwcap.
11.5% alc. **Rating** 95 **To** 2032 $40 NG
Museum Release Mudgee Riesling 2009 Developed notes of exotic spice
from ginger, honey blossom and saffron stream along a tangy rail of lime cordial,
quince marmalade and juicy acidity. A bead of spritz resolves itself in the glass,
but keeps things perky until the crescendo of building flavours and pumice-like
texture. Screwcap. 11% alc. **Rating** 94 **To** 2023 $80 NG
Third Generation Mudgee Chardonnay 2016 Part fermented in used French
puncheons, part with with wild, part with cultured yeast and part taken through
mlf, the remainder fermented and matured in stainless steel with full solids. It is
nigh-on impossible to do more without impinging on the varietal character of
the fruit, or filling the palate with phenolics, neither of which has occurred here.
Screwcap. 12.5% alc. **Rating** 94 **To** 2026 $25 ✪
The Kinnear Mudgee Shiraz Cabernet 2014 This is a wine far lighter on
its feet than regional expectations would suggest. Red and black currant, satsuma

plum, five-spice, licorice and cinnamon are all present. The palate is full, but at this stage tightly bound to a phalanx of well massaged, vanilla-soaked tannins All augurs well for a long future. Screwcap. 14% alc. Rating 94 To 2034 $80 NG

🍷🍷🍷🍷🍷 Mudgee Rose 2016 Rating 93 To 2018 $25 ☻
Reserve Mudgee Shiraz 2014 Rating 92 To 2031 $50 NG
Mudgee Gewurztraminer 2016 Rating 91 $20 ☻
Gewurztraminer 2016 Rating 91 To 2019 $20 NG ☻
Reserve Mudgee Chardonnay 2015 Rating 91 To 2021 $40 NG
Mudgee Shiraz 2014 Rating 90 To 2022 $25
Reserve Mudgee Merlot 2014 Rating 90 To 2032 $40 NG

Robertson of Clare   ★★★☆

PO Box 149, Killara, NSW 2071 **Region** Clare Valley
T (02) 9499 6002 **www.rocwines.com.au Open** Not
Winemaker Leigh Eldredge, Biagio Famularo **Est.** 2004 **Dozens** NFP
This is the highly unusual venture of Bryan Robertson, initially producing a single wine: MAX V. The Bordeaux varieties that go to produce MAX V are all grown in the Clare Valley, and individual varietal parcels are matured in 19 variations of 100% new French oak barrels. Primary fermentation takes place in barrel using what is called 'vinification integrale'. MAX V has been joined by the Block 6 Shiraz. Exports to Singapore, Hong Kong and China.

🍷🍷🍷🍷 MAX V 2014 80% cabernet sauvignon, 9% each malbec and merlot, 1% each cabernet franc and petit verdot. You absolutely have to love oak to enjoy this wine, which is in many ways bigger than Ben Hur – oak, oak, oak in 19 variations. 100% Clare Valley from various established growers. Cork. 14.7% alc. Rating 89 To 2034 $75

🌺 Robin Brockett Wines   ★★★★★

43 Woodville St, Drysdale, Vic 3222 (postal) **Region** Geelong
T 0418 112 223 **Open** Not
Winemaker Robin Brockett **Est.** 2013 **Dozens** 400
Robin Brockett is chief winemaker at Scotchmans Hill, a position he has held for over 30 years, making consistently very good wines through the ebbs and flows of climate. In 2013 he took the first steps towards the realisation of a 35-year dream of making and selling wines under his own label. He put in place an agreement to buy grapes from the Fenwick (2ha) and Swinburne (1ha) vineyards, and in '13 made the first wine, venturing into the unknown with the Amphora Syrah. In '16 he made Pinots from each of the two vineyards, and a Fenwick Shiraz, but left it until January '16 to come out, as it were, announcing the business and the wines available for sale.

🍷🍷🍷🍷🍷 Swinburne Vineyard Bellarine Peninsula Pinot Noir 2014 Robin Brockett has made pinot from this vineyard since '92, but this is the first single vineyard wine to come from it. The vinification is identical to that of the Fenwick Vineyard, but the fruit is richer, deeper and more complex, black cherry and spice rather than red. Screwcap. 13.5% alc. Rating 95 To 2026 $35 ☻
Fenwick Vineyard Bellarine Peninsula Shiraz 2014 This is a compelling example of cool-grown shiraz with all manner of savoury/earthy/meaty flavours alongside the more common black fruits and licorice. The tannins stand and salute at the end of the palate. Screwcap. 14.5% alc. Rating 95 To 2029 $35 ☻

🍷🍷🍷🍷🍷 Fenwick Vineyard Pinot Noir 2014 Rating 93 To 2024 $35

Rochford Wines   ★★★★★

878–880 Maroondah Highway, Coldstream, Vic 3770 **Region** Yarra Valley
T (03) 5957 3333 **www.rochfordwines.com.au Open** 7 days 9–5
Winemaker Marc Lunt **Est.** 1988 **Dozens** 16 000 **Vyds** 23.2ha

This Yarra Valley property was purchased by Helmut Konecsny in 2002; he had already established a reputation for Pinot Noir and Chardonnay from the family-owned Romsey Park vineyard in the Macedon Ranges. Since '10, Helmut has focused on his Yarra Valley winery and vineyards. Winemaker Marc Lunt had a stellar career as a Flying Winemaker over a six-year period in Bordeaux and Burgundy; in the latter region he worked at Armand Rousseau and Domaine de la Romanée-Conti. The property also has a large restaurant and cafe, cellar door, retail shop, expansive natural amphitheatre and observation tower. It is a showpiece in the region, hosting a series of popular summer concerts. Exports to China.

ΨΨΨΨΨ **Dans les Bois Chardonnay 2015** This is a beautiful wine. It is cool of fruit, finesse and aura. Myriad white peach, yellow plum and lime curd flavours curl their way around vivid acidity and a mineral drive. Nothing is hard or exaggerated. Mellifluous. From a stunning site in the upper reaches of Gembrook, this is fine Premier or Grand Cru pedigree. Is crushing, as at the best estates in Burgundy, the secret? Screwcap. 13.8% alc. **Rating** 98 **To** 2026 $49 NG ✪

ΨΨΨΨΨ **Isabella's Vineyard Yarra Valley Chardonnay 2015** Slinky phenolics, light to medium toasted French oak and a mineral sleight of hand give tone and clarity to a soprano voice of crunchy yellow plum, apricot, dried straw, toasted walnut and a leesy truffle scent. This is sprightly, jittery and bouncing with energy, but intense and packed. Screwcap. 13.2% alc. **Rating** 96 **To** 2025 $54 NG ✪
Premier Pinot Noir 2016 Moroccan exotica leads the wine out of the glass with cardamom, turmeric and saffron. Sapid cherry flavours, black and molten, fill out the palate. Strident, ebbing and flowing amid the souk of spice. The wine was aged for 10 months in French oak, a mere 15% new. It is barely detectable, so intensely flavoured and fresh is the wine's appeal. This will age very well. Screwcap. 13.5% alc. **Rating** 96 **To** 2028 $105 NG
Isabella's Vineyard Yarra Valley Cabernet Sauvignon 2015 The ripeness of the wine is impeccable. The gauntlet of tannins, finely hewn and containing a burst of pulpy black to blue fruits, serve as an assuaging balancing board between intensity and force of flavour; sinew, structure and savour. The oak is a mere adjunct, buffering the tannins as the bridge across the wine's rich fruit. Screwcap. 14.5% alc. **Rating** 96 **To** 2035 $54 NG ✪
Valle del Re King Valley Nebbiolo 2015 Teeming red and dark berries with a whiff of wood smoke, sandalwood and briar; the carapace of marked acidity and spindly tannins, firm and chalky with a frisky edge. The tannins draw out the saliva. This is among the very best Australian expressions of the variety. It demands food. Screwcap. 14.8% alc. **Rating** 96 **To** 2028 $36 NG ✪
Dans les Bois Pinot Noir 2016 Delicate, balletic and full of tangy red fruit and tiptoed poise, this is a pinot noir of grace and buoyant energy. High-toned acidity runs along a beam of 50% whole bunch spice and whispering tannins, echoing along its length. An ethereal wine with a sprinkling of 15% new French oak. Screwcap. 13% alc. **Rating** 95 **To** 2025 $54 NG
Yarra Valley Syrah 2015 A sumptuous syrah displaying the cooler climatic idiom of violet florals, iodine and purple and blue fruits of all types, carried long and finessed by a skein of peppery acidity and filmy tannins. Smoked meat and Indian spice, cardamom and clove, are evident too, delivered across sensitive oak treatment. Screwcap. 13.9% alc. **Rating** 95 **To** 2025 $33 NG ✪
L'Enfant Unique Pinot Noir 2016 **Rating** 94 **To** 2025 $68 NG
la Gauche Cabernet Sauvignon 2015 **Rating** 94 **To** 2030 $30 NG ✪

ΨΨΨΨΨ **Yarra Valley Chardonnay 2016** **Rating** 93 **To** 2022 $36 NG
Yarra Valley Savagnin 2016 **Rating** 93 **To** 2021 $30 NG
Yarra Valley Pinot Noir 2016 **Rating** 93 **To** 2024 $38 NG
Terre Pinot Noir 2016 **Rating** 93 **To** 2028 $68 NG
la Droite Merlot 2015 **Rating** 93 **To** 2023 $30 NG
Latitude Cabernet Merlot 2015 **Rating** 92 **To** 2022 $20 NG ✪
King Valley Riesling 2016 **Rating** 91 **To** 2023 $30 NG
Dans les Bois Chardonnay 2016 **Rating** 91 **To** 2022 $49 NG

Terre Chardonnay 2016 Rating 91 **To** 2023 $54 NG
Premier Chardonnay 2016 Rating 91 **To** 2023 $68 NG
Yarra Valley Pinot Gris 2016 Rating 91 **To** 2020 $30 NG

RockBare ★★★★☆

62 Brooks Road, Clarendon, SA 5157 **Region** South Australia
T (08) 8388 7155 **www**.rockbare.com.au **Open** 7 days 11–5
Winemaker Shelley Torresan **Est.** 2000 **Dozens** 10 000 **Vyds** 29ha
RockBare focuses on the distinctive expressions of the wine regions across SA and the varieties that make them famous. Under the direction of recently appointed winemaker Shelley Torresan, RockBare draws grapes from many long-term growers, supported by well established relationships. Exports to most major markets.

🍷🍷🍷🍷🍷 **McLaren Vale Shiraz 2015** A compelling wine in terms of both price and quality. Excellent colour and a super-fragrant bouquet lead into a supple medium-bodied palate that has a rare grace in the context of McLaren Vale. There is a passing note of dark chocolate, but it's really the plum and black cherry/berry fruits, allied with soft tannins, that make this hedonistic wine sing so joyfully. Screwcap. 14.5% alc. **Rating** 95 **To** 2030 $26 ✪
The Clare Valley Riesling 2016 A most attractive riesling coming into its own on the back-palate, finish and aftertaste where ripe citrus fruits and delicious grippy acidity join forces to fill all the senses with its message. Screwcap. 12.5% alc. **Rating** 94 **To** 2029 $21 ✪
Barossa Babe Shiraz 2014 It's a well constructed wine, showing depth and richness without being too obvious. Ripe, sweetish blackberry fruit and new oak are evident, but there's a concentrated, composed, balanced feel to it. Should age very well. Screwcap. 14.5% alc. **Rating** 94 **To** 2034 $46 SC
Coonawarra Cutie Cabernet Sauvignon 2014 This is the Full Monty of Coonawarra cabernet courtesy of blackcurrant, mulberry and mint flavours that have held their heads up throughout 24 months in new French oak. I think this may have only just started a journey that will either reveal an inner beauty or crash in flames. Screwcap. 14% alc. **Rating** 94 **To** 2030 $46

🍷🍷🍷🍷 **McLaren Vale Tempranillo 2014 Rating** 93 **To** 2026 $25 SC ✪
Coonawarra Cabernet Sauvignon 2015 Rating 92 **To** 2025 $26
McLaren Vale Chardonnay 2016 Rating 91 **To** 2020 $21 ✪
Wild Vine McLaren Vale Grenache Rose 2016 Rating 91 **To** 2017 $25
Tideway McLaren Vale Grenache 2016 Rating 91 **To** 2021 $35

Rockcliffe ★★★★★

18 Hamilton Road, Denmark, WA 6333 **Region** Denmark
T (08) 9848 2622 **www**.rockcliffe.com.au **Open** 7 days 11–5
Winemaker Michael Ng **Est.** 1990 **Dozens** 10 000 **Vyds** 10ha
The Rockcliffe winery and vineyard business, formerly known as Matilda's Estate, is owned by citizen of the world Steve Hall. The wine ranges echo local surf place names, headed by Rockcliffe itself, but extending to Third Reef, Forty Foot Drop and Quarram Rocks. Over the years, Rockcliffe has won more than its fair share of trophies, gold and silver medals in wine shows. Exports to Canada, Malaysia, Singapore and China.

🍷🍷🍷🍷🍷 **Single Site Mount Barker Riesling 2016** This uncoils its multi levels of lime blossom, lime zest and sweet lime fruit without any effort whatsoever. It has so much flavour that there is no need for patience, especially if you like spoonfuls of juicy primary fruits. Yet it will grow splendidly with more time in bottle. Screwcap. 12.5% alc. **Rating** 96 **To** 2029 $35 ✪
Single Site Mount Barker Shiraz 2015 The bouquet and palate are in perfect harmony; gently warm spices are sewn through fragrant aromas and the intense, yet only medium-bodied, palate. There are no challenges here, thanks to the

immaculate balance and mouthfeel of its panoply of foresty fruits. Just sit back and enjoy the ride. Screwcap. 14% alc. **Rating** 96 To 2035 $45 **○**

Single Site Mount Barker Cabernet Sauvignon 2015 Young cabernet sauvignon can be prickly and hard to handle, but that is only one face of the variety; this wine has a thoroughly inviting bouquet that is no false dawn. The palate is supple and rich, with a mix of blackcurrant and blueberry fruit, bay leaf and spice, and earthy tannins that simply reaffirm its varietal expression. Screwcap. 14% alc. **Rating** 95 To 2040 $45

Single Site Mount Barker Cabernet Sauvignon 2014 A thoroughly attractive cabernet from start to finish, sustained throughout by perfectly ripened cassis fruit, the bouquet aromatic, the palate medium-bodied, the finish balanced. This is an emphatic drink-now style, although its balance will secure its long-term future. Screwcap. 14.5% alc. **Rating** 95 To 2029 $45

Single Site Denmark Chardonnay 2016 The bouquet is slightly reduced, but will heal quickly, and is in any event redeemed by the power, precision and purity of the long palate and aftertaste. Those who wait will be rewarded. Screwcap. 13.5% alc. **Rating** 94 To 2029 $45

Third Reef Great Southern Shiraz 2015 A spicy/savoury pulsating theme runs deep below the fruits on the surface of this medium-bodied shiraz, with all the birthmarks of its cool-grown origin. Red and black cherry join blackberry to provide the melody of a more than usually complex wine. Screwcap. 14% alc. **Rating** 94 To 2030 $30 **○**

Single Site Frankland Shiraz 2014 Deep crimson-purple; an elegant, medium-bodied cool-grown shiraz with spicy/bramble/savoury fruit on the bouquet and palate alike. The tannins are fine and well integrated, as is the oak. Will repay further cellaring. Screwcap. 14.5% alc. **Rating** 94 To 2029 $45

♟♟♟♟♟ **Third Reef Riesling 2016** Rating 93 To 2026 $28
Third Reef Cabernet Sauvignon 2015 Rating 93 To 2029 $30

Rockford   ★★★★★

131 Krondorf Road, Tanunda, SA 5352 **Region** Barossa Valley
T (08) 8563 2720 **www**.rockfordwines.com.au **Open** 7 days 11–5
Winemaker Robert O'Callaghan, Ben Radford **Est.** 1984 **Dozens** NFP
Rockford can only be described as an icon, no matter how overused that word may be. It has a devoted band of customers who buy most of the wine through the cellar door or mail order (Rocky O'Callaghan's entrancing annual newsletter is like no other). Some wine is sold through restaurants, and there are two retailers in Sydney, and one each in Melbourne, Brisbane and Perth. Whether they will have the Basket Press Shiraz available is another matter; it is as scarce as Henschke Hill of Grace (but less expensive). Ben Radford, whom I first met in South Africa some years ago, has been entrenched as Rocky's right-hand man, and is destined to take over responsibility for winemaking when the time comes for Rocky to step back from an active role. Exports to the UK, Canada, Switzerland, Russia, Vietnam, Singapore, Japan, Hong Kong, Fiji and NZ.

♟♟♟♟♟ **Basket Press Shiraz 2013** The beautiful label, traditional brown bottle and the wine within all have an allure. There's the richness and depth of the tannin structure (velvety and ripe), the suppleness on the palate, the savoury thread with coffee grounds, pepper, bitumen and yes, oak (but everything in its place), plus a heady perfume with florals and red plums. Cork. 14.1% alc. **Rating** 95 To 2036 $63 JF

Black Shiraz NV The iconic Rockford Black Shiraz is as multifaceted as its vast depth of maturity predicts, with all the personality of old vine fruit ricocheting in black plum, black cherry, licorice, even a hint of sarsaparilla, and the ever-present, long-lingering delight of high cocoa dark chocolate. Age has brought notes of cedar, leather, mixed spice and orange liqueur. It's magnificently finished, with perfectly integrated dosage and firm, fine yet somehow creamy tannins that will sustain it for a good while yet. 13.5% alc. **Rating** 94 To 2026 $64 TS

▼▼▼▼♀ Rifle Range Cabernet Sauvignon 2014 Rating 92 To 2028 $45 JF
White Frontignac 2016 Rating 91 To 2018 $19 IF
Frugal Farmer 2015 Rating 90 To 2019 $22 JF

Rolf Binder ★★★★☆

Cnr Seppeltsfield Road/Stelzer Road, Tanunda, SA 5352 **Region** Barossa Valley
T (08) 8562 3300 **www**.rolfbinder.com **Open** Mon–Sat 10–4.30, Sun on long weekends
Winemaker Rolf Binder, Christa Deans **Est.** 1955 **Dozens** 28 000 **Vyds** 90ha
Rolf Binder and sister Christa Deans are following their father's winemaking philosophy, using
primarily estate-grown fruit from various districts of the Barossa and Eden Valleys, the most
recent vineyard acquisition in Vine Vale with vines planted in the 1890s, the parent vines to
the Chri-Ro Vineyard planted in the early 1970s by Rolf and his father Rolf Heinrich Binder.
They make classic Barossa wines that reflect their many years of experience. The JJ Hahn
brand was created in '97 as a joint venture between sixth-generation Barossans James and
Jacqui Hahn and Rolf Binder, Rolf continuing the brand since the Hahns' retirement in 2010.
Exports to all major markets.

▼▼▼▼▼ Eden Valley Riesling 2016 A delicate riesling of lime juice and spring water,
honey blossom and quince. The wine is of a slate-like texture, dry and balletic;
drawn long and taut by juicy, ever-flowing acidity showcasing fine intensity of
flavour. Screwcap. 12.5% alc. **Rating** 95 To 2031 $25 NG ✪
JJ Hahn 1890s Vineyard Barossa Valley Shiraz 2015 Binder's malt
chocolate tannins melt across this powerful wine's attack of dark fruit flavours
and spice: plum, dark cherry, mace and five-spice spring to the nostrils. There is
nothing whatsoever jammy about this, with the fruit held tightly to the plush
breast of American oak and impeccably drawn-out grape tannins. Screwcap.
14.5% alc. **Rating** 94 To 2032 $65 NG
Bull's Blood Barossa Valley Shiraz Mataro Pressings 2014 Smoked meat,
char and a ferruginous roar of grapey tannin across tobacco leaf and dried sage
flavours tie this full-bodied wine neatly together. The connotations of name and
method belie the savoury, textural and moreish end result. Screwcap. 14% alc.
Rating 94 To 2034 $50 NG

▼▼▼▼♀ JJ Hahn Homestead Cabernet 2015 Rating 93 To 2028 $25 NG ✪
Barossa Valley Malbec 2015 Rating 93 To 2032 $30 NG
Silvern Barossa Valley Shiraz 2015 Rating 92 To 2023 $20 NG ✪
Hales Barossa Valley Shiraz 2015 Rating 92 To 2023 $25 NG ✪
JJ Hahn Western Ridge 1975 Planting Barossa Valley Shiraz 2014
Rating 92 To 2023 $35 NG
Halliwell Shiraz Grenache 2014 Rating 92 To 2024 $25 NG ✪
JJ Hahn Stockwell Barossa Valley Cabernet Sauvignon Shiraz 2015
Rating 92 To 2032 $35 NG
Barossa Valley Shiraz Malbec 2014 Rating 91 To 2038 $30 NG
JJ Hahn Reginald Shiraz Cabernet 2014 Rating 91 To 2020 $25 NG
JJ Hahn Stelzer Road Merlot 2015 Rating 91 To 2023 $25 NG
Barossa Valley Shiraz 2015 Rating 90 To 2024 $25 NG
Eden Valley Shiraz 2014 Rating 90 To 2028 $30 NG

Romney Park Wines ★★★★★

116 Johnsons Road, Balhannah, SA 5242 **Region** Adelaide Hills
T (08) 8398 0698 **www**.romneyparkwines.com.au **Open** By appt
Winemaker Rod and Rachel Short **Est.** 1997 **Dozens** 500 **Vyds** 2.8ha
Rod and Rachel Short planted chardonnay, shiraz and pinot noir in 1997. Yields are limited to
3.7–5 tonnes per hectare for the red wines, and 2–3 tonnes for the chardonnay. The vineyard
is managed organically, with guinea fowl cleaning up the insects, all vines hand-picked and
hand-pruned. In every way (including the wines) has the beauty of a hand-painted miniature.
Exports to China.

🍷🍷🍷🍷🍷 **Gloria Adelaide Hills Chardonnay 2015** Elegance and balance are the keywords; white peach, nectarine and a hint of cashew are sustained and lengthened by citrussy acidity. When you come across a wine as perfectly balanced as this, there's not much more to say. Diam. 13.5% alc. **Rating** 95 **To** 2025 $50
Adelaide Hills Shiraz 2013 A savoury/spicy character underpins the vibrant, juicy red and black fruits of the bouquet and medium-bodied palate. Structure and length are provided by fine-grained, ripe tannins. A very attractive cool-grown shiraz. Diam. 14% alc. **Rating** 95 **To** 2033 $45
Adelaide Hills Blanc de Blancs 2012 Over 4 years on lees has led to biscuity complexity behind tangy grapefruit flavours; the length is very good, as is the relatively low dosage. Very interesting wine, with no sign of the full mlf blunting the edge of the fruit. Crown seal. 12.5% alc. **Rating** 94 **To** 2020 $45

Ros Ritchie Wines ★★★★

1974 Long Lane, Barwite, Vic 3722 **Region** Upper Goulburn
T 0448 900 541 **www**.rosritchiewines.com **Open** By appt
Winemaker Ros Ritchie **Est.** 2008 **Dozens** 2000 **Vyds** 5ha
Ros Ritchie was winemaker at the Ritchie family's Delatite winery from 1981 to 2006, but moved on to establish her own winery with husband John in '08. They lease a vineyard (merlot and cabernet sauvignon) close to Mansfield and source their white wines from growers who work in tandem with them to provide high quality grapes. Foremost are Gumbleton, Retief and Baxendale Vineyards, the last planted by the very experienced viticulturist Jim Baxendale (and wife Ruth) high above the King River Valley. All the vineyards are managed with minimal spray regimes. Exports to Hong Kong and China.

🍷🍷🍷🍷🍷 **Dead Man's Hill Vineyard Gewurztraminer 2016** Life is always better with a splash of fine gewurztraminer, because it evokes happiness. Really. It's the terpenes, those adorable aromatic and flavour compounds coating this wine in musk, ginger spice, rose petals, coriander, lychees and slivers of bitter orange. The palate is sleek, yet has a power and richness, plus a sensation of slippery glycerol. Screwcap. 14% alc. **Rating** 94 **To** 2024 $25 JF ✪

🍷🍷🍷🍷🍷 **Barwite Vineyard Riesling 2016 Rating** 93 **To** 2025 $25 JF ✪
Baxendale's Vineyard Cabernet 2015 Rating 92 **To** 2021 $28 JF
Aromatyk 2016 Rating 91 **To** 2019 $25 JF

Rosabrook Margaret River Wine ★★★★☆

1390 Rosa Brook Road, Rosabrook, WA 6285 **Region** Margaret River
T (08) 9368 4555 **www**.rosabrook.com.au **Open** Not
Winemaker Brian Fletcher **Est.** 1980 **Dozens** 12 000 **Vyds** 25ha
The original Rosabrook estate vineyards were established between 1984 and '96. In 2007 Rosabrook relocated its vineyard to the northwestern end of the Margaret River wine region, overlooking Geographe Bay and the Indian Ocean. Warm days and cool nights, influenced by the ocean, result in slow, mild-ripening conditions. Exports to the UK, Sweden, Dubai, Hong Kong and China.

🍷🍷🍷🍷🍷 **Single Vineyard Estate Cabernet Sauvignon 2014** A sturdy cabernet, this has Margaret River's signature pastille, currant and mint aromas hurtling across the aromatic spectrum, before reverberating on the long, detailed finish. The oak, while generous, feels like a mere adjunct to the wine's noble richness, intensity of flavour and penetrative vinosity. Screwcap. 14.5% alc. **Rating** 96 **To** 2032 $45 NG ✪
Single Vineyard Estate Chardonnay 2015 Subscribing to the tensile fabric of the contemporary chardonnay style, this adds Margaret River's peachy tones, some honey blossom and plenty of high quality French oak to the package. The oak harnesses the fruit, tempering the runaway, mineral-edged flavours and bringing them to a sudden conclusion. Screwcap. 12.4% alc. **Rating** 94 **To** 2026 $45 NG

🍷🍷🍷🍷🍷 **Cabernet Merlot 2015 Rating** 93 **To** 2025 $17 NG ✪
Single Vineyard Estate Tempranillo 2013 Rating 91 **To** 2030 $65 NG

Rosby ★★★★

122 Strikoo Lane, Mudgee, NSW 2050 **Region** Mudgee
T (02) 6373 3856 **www**.rosby.com.au **Open** By appt
Winemaker Tim Stevens **Est.** 1996 **Dozens** 2000 **Vyds** 9ha
Gerald and Kay Norton-Knight have 4ha of shiraz and 2ha of cabernet sauvignon established on what is truly a unique site in Mudgee. Many vignerons like to think that their vineyard has special qualities, but in this instance the belief is well based. It is situated in a small valley, with unusual red basalt over a quartz gravel structure, encouraging deep root growth, making the use of water far less critical than normal. Tim Stevens of Huntington Estate has purchased some of the ample production, and makes the Rosby wines.

🍷🍷🍷🍷🍷 **Mudgee Shiraz 2014** Full red-purple; a rich, verging on voluptuous, wine with plum, blackberry and black cherry fruits, tannins and oak adding to the package without threatening to overpower the fruit. Top outcome for a vintage not as easy as that of the Hunter Valley. Screwcap. 13.3% alc. **Rating** 91 **To** 2034 $25
Mudgee Cabernet Sauvignon 2014 Hand-picked, crushed and destemmed, open-fermented, 8 days on skins, matured for 18 months in French oak (30% new). If you are in, or thinking of a trip to, Mudgee, you will have to work hard to find a better value wine than this. In its quiet way, it ticks all the boxes. Screwcap. 13.5% alc. **Rating** 90 **To** 2029 $20 ✪

Rosemount Estate ★★★★★

The Atrium, 58 Queensbridge Street, Southbank, Vic 3006 **Region** McLaren Vale
T 1300 651 650 **www**.rosemountestate.com **Open** Not
Winemaker Randall Cummins **Est.** 1888 **Dozens** NFP
Rosemount Estate has vineyards in McLaren Vale, Fleurieu, Coonawarra and Robe that are the anchor for its top-of-the-range wines. It also has access to other TWE estate-grown grapes, but the major part of its intake for the Diamond Label wines is supplied by contract growers across SA, NSW, Vic and WA. The quality and range of the wines has greatly improved over the past few years as Rosemount Estate endeavours to undo the damage done to the brand around the new millennium. Ironically, the large McLaren Vale winery was closed in November 2014, winemaking transferred to other major wineries owned by TWE. Exports to all major markets.

🍷🍷🍷🍷🍷 **G.S.M. McLaren Vale Grenache Syrah Mourvedre 2015** Quite aromatic on the bouquet, the grenache very much on the front foot with raspberry and Turkish Delight characters most prominent. Just medium-bodied, with a savoury feel to the flavours and the tannins. A little sweet fruit on the finish adds to the easy drinkability. Screwcap. 14% alc. **Rating** 90 **To** 2022 SC

🍷🍷🍷🍷 **Little Berry Adelaide Hills Sauvignon Blanc 2015** **Rating** 89 **To** 2017 $20

Rosenthal Wines ★★★★

24 Rockford Street, Denmark, WA 6333 **Region** Great Southern
T 0417 940 851 **www**.rosenthalwines.com.au **Open** Not
Winemaker Luke Eckersley, Coby Ladwig **Est.** 2001 **Dozens** 5000 **Vyds** 17ha
Rosenthal Wines is a small part of the much larger 180ha Springfield Park cattle stud situated between Bridgetown and Manjimup. Dr John Rosenthal acquired the property from Gerald and Marjorie Richings, who in 1997 had planted a small vineyard as a minor diversification. The Rosenthals extended the vineyard, the main varieties shiraz and cabernet sauvignon. The wines have had significant show success, chiefly in WA-based shows. Rosenthal Wines is now owned by Luke Eckersley (winemaker at Willoughby Park) and Coby Ladwig. Exports to China.

🍷🍷🍷🍷🍷 **Garten Series Great Southern Chardonnay 2015** Kicks more goals than its price would suggest; an elegant fusion of white peach, nectarine, grilled cashew and grapefruit acidity; leaves the mouth fresh. Screwcap. 13% alc. **Rating** 94 **To** 2023 $25 ✪

The Marker Pemberton Pinot Noir 2016 An impressive wine with good depth, structure and varietal expression. Spicy dark cherry and plum flavours run through the long, well balanced palate, inviting you back for more. Screwcap. 14.5% alc. **Rating** 94 **To** 2023 $32

Garten Series Shiraz 2014 Good colour; a plummy/spicy/brambly bouquet adds blackberry and licorice to a very well balanced and structured palate, the finely drawn tannins typical of Great Southern in a vintage as good as this. Excellent value for what will be a very long-lived wine. Screwcap. 14.5% alc. **Rating** 94 **To** 2034 $25 ❂

Richings Great Southern Shiraz 2014 Deep crimson-purple hue; a potent wine with a velvety mouthfeel, pliant tannins adding to the equation. The rich purple and black fruits don't lose their way, and patience will be rewarded. Screwcap. 14.5% alc. **Rating** 94 **To** 2039 $42

The Marker Blackwood Valley Shiraz Cabernet 2015 Full-bodied in every respect: black fruits, new oak, dark chocolate, licorice, plum, blackberry, cedar and ripe tannins. Savoury nuances appear briefly, but are then swallowed up in the swarm of rich flavours. Screwcap. 14.5% alc. **Rating** 94 **To** 2035 $32

Garten Series Cabernet Sauvignon 2015 Bright crimson-purple; an instantaneously attractive marriage of cassis fruit and fine, savoury tannins, oak the best man. Consummation and consumption tonight a sure-fire way to go. Screwcap. 14% alc. **Rating** 94 **To** 2023 $25 ❂

ႃႃႃႃႃ **Richings Great Southern Chardonnay 2016** Rating 93 To 2025 $42
The Marker Great Southern Riesling 2016 Rating 92 To 2026 $32
The Marker Great Southern Chardonnay 2016 Rating 92 To 2024 $32
The Marker Southern Forest Shiraz 2015 Rating 92 To 2035 $32
Garten Series Great Southern Chardonnay 2016 Rating 90 To 2022 $25
Garten Series Shiraz 2015 Rating 90 To 2029 $25

Rosily Vineyard   ★★★★☆

871 Yelverton Road, Wilyabrup, WA 6284 **Region** Margaret River
T (08) 9755 6336 **www**.rosily.com.au **Open** 7 days Dec–Jan 11–5
Winemaker Mick Scott **Est.** 1994 **Dozens** 5500 **Vyds** 12.28ha
Ken Allan and Mick Scott acquired the Rosily Vineyard site in 1994, and the vineyard was planted over three years to sauvignon blanc, semillon, chardonnay, cabernet sauvignon, merlot, shiraz, grenache and cabernet franc. The first crops were sold to other makers in the region, but by '99 Rosily had built an 120-tonne capacity winery. It has gone from strength to strength, all of its estate-grown grapes being vinified under the Rosily Vineyard label, substantially over-delivering for their prices.

ႃႃႃႃႃ **Margaret River Cabernet Sauvignon 2015** A flurry of regional flavours of blackberries, boysenberries, some choc-mint, warm soil and bay leaf, with cedary oak in check. There's detail on the medium-bodied palate and the raw silk tannins add another layer of complexity. Neatly composed and drinking brilliantly now, better with extra bottle age. Screwcap. 14% alc. **Rating** 95 **To** 2030 $27 JF ❂

Margaret River Merlot 2014 How much is due to terroir and how much to the clone isn't easy to identify, but the end result is a wine that has excellent varietal expression, with cassis and plum fruit complexed by nuances of snow pea, fine-grained tannins and neatly balanced oak. Exceptional bargain. Screwcap. 14% alc. **Rating** 94 **To** 2024 $20 ❂

ႃႃႃႃႃ **Margaret River Sauvignon Blanc 2016** Rating 91 To 2019 $20 JF ❂
Cellar Release Margaret River SSB 2011 Rating 90 To 2018 $23 JF
Margaret River Shiraz 2011 Rating 90 To 2021 $23

Ross Hill Wines   ★★★★★

134 Wallace Lane, Orange, NSW 2800 **Region** Orange
T (02) 6365 3223 **www**.rosshillwines.com.au **Open** 7 days 10.30–5
Winemaker Phil Kerney **Est.** 1994 **Dozens** 25 000 **Vyds** 18.2ha

Peter and Terri Robson planted chardonnay, merlot, sauvignon blanc, cabernet franc, shiraz and pinot noir on north-facing slopes of the Griffin Road vineyard in 1994. In 2007, their son James and his wife Chrissy joined the business, and the Wallace Lane vineyard (pinot noir, sauvignon blanc and pinot gris) was planted next to the fruit-packing shed, which is now the winery. No insecticides are used, the grapes are hand-picked and the vines are hand-pruned. Exports to Germany, Singapore, Bali, Hong Kong and China.

ΨΨΨΨΨ **The Griffin 2013** Cabernet sauvignon, merlot and cabernet franc. Smoky oak and eucalyptus characters are both front and centre in the profile of the wine, but for sheer presence, fruit power and length this wine is outstanding. This can be cellared with absolute confidence. Bold ribs of tannin complete a substantial but well honed picture. Screwcap. 14.5% alc. **Rating** 96 **To** 2033 $95 CM
Pinnacle Series Griffin Road Vineyard Orange Cabernet Sauvignon 2015 Matured for 22 months in French oak (30% new). Good hue and depth; a very good cabernet, with cassis, black olive and bay leaf flavours, stately tannins and oak a precise framework for the fruit. Lives up to its reputation and then some. Screwcap. 14.9% alc. **Rating** 95 **To** 2030 $45
Pinnacle Series Griffin Road Vineyard Orange Cabernet Franc 2015 Good colour; an impressive wine, the juicy red fruit flavours are given texture and structure by the combination of the tannins and the French oak. Screwcap. 14.5% alc. **Rating** 95 **To** 2030 $45
Pinnacle Series Orange Chardonnay 2015 The flavours strike bold and pure. Grapefruit, white peach and quartz-like mineral characters give this wine both edge and oomph, and the finish doesn't let the side down either. Screwcap. 12.5% alc. **Rating** 94 **To** 2022 $35 CM
Jack's Lot Orange Shiraz 2015 There's a lot going on here, from the bouquet to the palate, to the finish and aftertaste. The richness of the varietal fruit may be partly due to its elevated alcohol, but it's not overripe, allowing blackberry, black cherry, pepper and spice to all have their say. French oak and plush tannins also make a positive contribution. Screwcap. 14.8% alc. **Rating** 94 **To** 2029 $25 ❂

ΨΨΨΨΨ **Jack's Lot Orange Shiraz 2014** Rating 93 To 2025 $25 CM ❂
Pinnacle Series Wallace Lane Pinot Gris 2016 Rating 92 To 2018 $30
Isabelle Orange Cabernet Franc Merlot 2015 Rating 92 To 2025 $25 ❂
Pinnacle Series Griffin Road Sauvignon Blanc 2016 Rating 91 To 2018 $30
Pinnacle Series Griffin Road Shiraz 2015 Rating 91 To 2029 $45
Tom & Harry Orange Cabernet Sauvignon 2015 Rating 90 To 2023 $25
Blanc de Blancs 2013 Rating 90 To 2017 $35 TS
Blanc de Blancs 2011 Rating 90 To 2026 $30 TS

Rouleur ★★★★★

150 Bank Street, South Melbourne, Vic 3205 (postal) **Region** Yarra Valley/McLaren Vale
T 0419 100 929 **www.**rouleurwine.com **Open** Not
Winemaker Rob Hall, Matthew East **Est.** 2015 **Dozens** 700
Owner Matt East's interest in wine began at an early age, growing up in the Yarra Valley and watching his father plant a vineyard in Coldstream. Between February 1999 and December 2015 his day job was in sales marketing, culminating in his appointment in '11 as National Sales Manager for Wirra Wirra (which he had joined in '08). Following his retirement from that position, he formed Mr East Wine Industry Consulting, and also set in motion the wheels of Rouleur. He lives in Melbourne, with the Yarra in easy striking distance, and together he and Rob Hall source fruit and make the wines. His time with Wirra Wirra in McLaren Vale was the final trigger for Rouleur, and he also makes wine there, using the facilities at Dennis Winery, drawing on the expertise/assistance of personal winemaking friends when needed. Back in Melbourne he is transforming a dilapidated milk bar in North Melbourne into the inner-city cellar door for Rouleur.

ΨΨΨΨΨ **Yarra Valley Chardonnay 2016** 34yo I10V1 clone, 70% whole-bunch pressed with full solids straight to barrel, 30% destemmed and gently crushed to open pots, 10% soaked on skins for 24 hours, 20% fermented on skins for 5 days, wild yeast, no mlf, matured in French oak (15% new) for 10 months. Every bit as ballsy as the vinification suggests it might be, but it's fully entitled to be so. This combines a courtesan's come-hither look with straight-backed minerally acidity and length in best Yarra Valley style, grapefruit and nectarine to the fore. Screwcap. 12.8% alc. **Rating** 95 **To** 2024 $29

McLaren Vale Grenache 2016 52yo bushvines, gently crushed and destemmed with 20% whole bunches on top, 3 days cold soak, open-fermented with cultured yeast, two ferments, one with 7 days post-ferment maceration, the other 10 days conventional, matured in used hogsheads for 11 months. Grenache à la McLaren Vale, with its unique expression, particularly if the alcohol is kept at or below 14.5%. The vinification was complex, but totally successful, with red and purple fruits supported by gently savoury tannins. Fills the mouth, but doesn't cloy. Screwcap. 14.4% alc. **Rating** 95 **To** 2026 $29

 Yarra Valley Pinot Noir 2016 **Rating** 91 **To** 2023 $29

Route du Van ★★★☆

PO Box 1465, Warrnambool, Vic 3280 **Region** Various Vic
T (03) 5561 7422 **www**.routeduvan.com **Open** Not
Winemaker Tod Dexter **Est.** 2010 **Dozens** 8000
The Dexter (Todd and Debbie) and Bird (Ian and Ruth, David and Marie) families have been making or selling wine for over 30 years. They were holidaying in the picturesque vineyards and ancient Bastide villages of southwest France when they decided to do something new that was all about fun: fun for them, and fun for the consumers who bought their wines, which would have a distinctive southern French feel to them. The prices are also friendly, bistros one of the target markets. The business is obviously enjoying great success, production up from 3500 dozen to its present level off the back of expanded export markets. Exports to the UK, the US, Norway, Sweden and Poland.

 Yarra Valley Pinot Noir 2016 Deeply coloured; it has good texture and structure, with layers of dark cherry and plum fruit. A good outcome for a challenging vintage, and will repay cellaring. Screwcap. 13% alc. **Rating** 92 **To** 2026

♀♀♀♀ **Yarra Valley Chardonnay 2016** **Rating** 89 **To** 2019

Rowlee ★★★★☆

19 Lake Canobolas Road, Orange, NSW 2800 **Region** Orange
T (02) 6365 3047 **www**.rowleewines.com.au **Open** 7 days 11–5
Winemaker PJ Charteris (Consultant) **Est.** 2000 **Dozens** 3000 **Vyds** 7.71ha
Rowlee first evolved as a grazing property of 2000 acres in the 1850s. It is now 80 acres, but still with the original homestead built circa 1880. The property has retired from its grazing days and is now home to 20 acres of vineyards, first planted in 2000 by the Samodol family. Varieties include pinot noir, pinot gris, nebbiolo, arneis, chardonnay, riesling and sauvignon blanc. The Rowlee vineyard is situated on the sloping northerly face of an extinct volcano, Mt Canobolas, and at 920m is rich in basalt soils. Wine production commenced in 2013, in partnership with viticulturist Tim Esson and family.

♀♀♀♀♀ **Orange Chardonnay 2015** Cool climate white peach varietal aromas are fully matched by the French oak influence, but so well meshed that it seems natural and unforced. Beautifully textured palate, the acidity and barrel-derived complexity enhancing rather than competing with the pure, crystal-clear fruit character. Screwcap. 13.5% alc. **Rating** 95 **To** 2022 $35 SC ✪

Orange Pinot Noir 2014 Sappy raspberry and sour cherry varietal aromas are skilfully enhanced with toasty, top shelf oak on the bouquet; fresh and complex. Similar themes on the palate; bright, juicy, and lively, with the underlying depth and length of flavour, accompanied by fine acidity, that are the hallmarks of high quality. Screwcap. 13% alc. **Rating** 94 **To** 2027 $35 SC

ＹＹＹＹＹ Orange Riesling 2016 Rating 93 To 2023 $28 JF
R-Series Orange Pinot Noir 2016 Rating 93 To 2025 $45 JF
Orange Pinot Noir 2015 Rating 93 To 2024 $30 JF
Orange Chardonnay 2016 Rating 92 To 2021 $28 JF
Friends Blend 2016 Rating 92 To 2020 $25 JF ○
Orange Pinot Noir 2016 Rating 91 To 2022 $30 JF
Orange Pinot Gris 2015 Rating 90 To 2017 $25
Orange Arneis 2016 Rating 90 To 2020 $25 JF
Single Vineyard Orange Nebbiolo 2015 Rating 90 To 2023 $38 JF

Ruckus Estate

PO Box 167, Penola, SA 5277 **Region** Wrattonbully
T 0437 190 244 **www.**ruckusestate.com **Open** Not
Winemaker Mike Kloak **Est.** 2000 **Dozens** 1000 **Vyds** 40ha
Ruckus Estate was established in 2000 after a protracted search for high quality viticultural land, with a particular focus on the production of merlot utilising recently released clones that hold the promise of producing wine of a quality not previously seen. However, it's not a case of all eggs in the same basket, for malbec, cabernet sauvignon and shiraz have also been planted. It was not until '13 that the first small amount of wine was made (most of the grapes were, and will continue to be, sold to other winemakers). Given the quality of the Merite Merlot, the plan to increase production to 2000 dozen should be achieved with ease, with Shiraz Malbec released in May '16, and Cabernet Sauvignon in the pipeline.

ＹＹＹＹＹ **Merite Single Vineyard Wrattonbully Merlot 2015** The vineyard's planting of five merlot clones (including 8R and Q45) is capable of producing very high quality wine. If you want to go nitpicking, the French oak (40% new) is a touch too obvious, but it will almost certainly diminish with age. It raises the question whether 30% new oak might have done an even better job. That said, the '14 had 50%. The mouthfeel, weight and flavours of cassis, plum and herb have a base of exquisite tannins. Screwcap. 14% alc. **Rating** 96 To 2035 $60 ○
Merite Single Vineyard Wrattonbully Cabernet 2015 A powerful, rich and ripe (not too ripe) wine with luscious fruit and oak in an arm wrestle for dominance. Even now they are evenly matched, so with another 5 or so years the fruit will be foremost. Tannins – both fruit and oak-derived – play a significant role, and will continue to do so. A classy wine in every way. Cork. 14.2% alc. **Rating** 96 To 2035 $60 ○
The Q Merlot 2015 This has remarkable focus and purity, gossamer tannins threaded through the predominantly red fruits of the mid palate, thence to the gently earthy/savoury flavours and mouthfeel on the finish. It's medium-bodied, but has great balance and precise use of new oak. As the vines mature, even greater things lie in store. Screwcap. 14% alc. **Rating** 95 To 2030 $32 ○

Rudderless

Victory Hotel, Main South Road, Sellicks Beach, SA 5174 **Region** McLaren Vale
T (08) 8556 3083 **www.**victoryhotel.com.au **Open** 7 days
Winemaker Pete Fraser (Contract) **Est.** 2004 **Dozens** 450 **Vyds** 2ha
It's a long story how Doug Govan, owner of the Victory Hotel (circa 1858), came to choose the name Rudderless for his vineyard. The vineyard, planted to shiraz, graciano, grenache, malbec, mataro and viognier, surrounds the hotel, which is situated in the foothills of the Southern Willunga Escarpment as it falls into the sea. The wines are mostly sold through the Victory Hotel, where the laid-back Doug Govan keeps a low profile.

ＹＹＹＹＹ **Sellicks Hill McLaren Vale Grenache 2014** It has that extra something. Cherry, plum, cola and anise flavours flood the palate before earth and spice notes explode through the finish. A rip of tannin comes pulsed with flavour. A beauty. Screwcap. 14.5% alc. **Rating** 95 To 2027 $35 CM ○

Sellicks Hill McLaren Vale Grenache Mataro Graciano 2014 1500 vines of shiraz, 864 graciano, 538 grenache, 487 malbec and 294 mataro. Glory be to McLaren Vale and to this eclectic blend that pulls the bouquet and the palate every which way. There are luscious plummy fruits, slashes of red cherry, pots of spices and a gloriously fresh mouthfeel that lifts the finish onto another plane. Screwcap. 14% alc. **Rating** 95 **To** 2034 $35 ✪

Sellicks Hill McLaren Vale Malbec 2014 Punchy with dark, inky fruit. It's not a hulking wine, but it has a presence. It's all violet and rose, tar and plum, with a ribbon of smoky oak helping to tie it all together. Tannin asserts itself impressively through the back half of the wine. Only 95 dozen made; it'll pay to get in quickly on this. Screwcap. 14% alc. **Rating** 95 **To** 2030 $35 CM ✪

ꞏꞏꞏꞏ **Sellicks Hill McLaren Vale Shiraz 2014 Rating** 92 **To** 2028 $35 CM
Sellicks Hill McLaren Vale GSM 2014 Rating 92 **To** 2024 $35 CM

Rusty Mutt   ★★★★

26 Columbia Avenue, Clapham, SA 5062 (postal) **Region** McLaren Vale
T 0402 050 820 **www**.rustymutt.com.au **Open** Not
Winemaker Scott Heidrich **Est.** 2009 **Dozens** 1000
Scott Heidrich has lived under the shadow of Geoff Merrill for 20 years, but has partially emerged into the sunlight with his virtual micro-winery. Back in 2006 close friends and family (Nicole and Alan Francis, Stuart Evans, David Lipman and Phil Cole) persuaded Scott to take advantage of the wonderful quality of the grapes that year and make a small batch of Shiraz. The wines are made at a friend's micro-winery in McLaren Flat. The name Rusty Mutt comes from Scott's interest in Chinese astrology, and feng shui; Scott was born in the year of the dog, with the dominant element being metal, hence Rusty Mutt. What the ownership group doesn't drink is sold through fine wine retailers and selected restaurants, with a small amount exported to the UK and China.

ꞏꞏꞏꞏ **Vermilion Bird McLaren Vale Shiraz 2013** Dense and rich, with cedary/coconut oak, vanilla cream and tar enclosing the dark ripe fruit, a slight sweet-sour note and gritty powerful tannins, drying on the finish. Glossy full-bodied palate – stylistically, archetypal McLaren Vale shiraz and a lot to ponder. It gets better in the glass. Cork. 14.5% alc. **Rating** 92 **To** 2023 $75 JF
Original McLaren Vale Shiraz 2014 Bright crimson-garnet and awash with spice, chocolate and ripe plum fruit, with the oak in check. It's full-bodied but not heavy, with the tannins ripe and powerful, and all in balance. Screwcap. 14.5% alc. **Rating** 91 **To** 2023 $27 JF

Rutherglen Estates   ★★★★☆

Tuileries, 13 Drummond Street, Rutherglen, Vic 3685 **Region** Rutherglen
T (02) 6032 7999 **www**.rutherglenestates.com.au **Open** 7 days 10–5.30
Winemaker Marc Scalzo **Est.** 1997 **Dozens** 70 000 **Vyds** 184ha
Rutherglen Estates is one of the larger growers in the region. The focus of the business has changed: it has reduced its own fruit intake while maintaining its contract processing. Production has turned to table wine made from parcels of fruit hand-selected from five Rutherglen vineyard sites. Rhône and Mediterranean varieties such as durif, viognier, shiraz and sangiovese are a move away from traditional varieties, as are alternative varieties including zinfandel, fiano and savagnin. Exports to Singapore, Thailand and China.

ꞏꞏꞏꞏ **Renaissance Zinfandel 2014** Reminiscent of high-end gear from Sonoma (at a fraction of the price), this is a mouthfilling expression of sapid blue and red fruit flavours sewn to zin's dusty tannins, a complex oak regime and acidity from the uneven nature of zin's ripening pattern. Screwcap. 14.5% alc. **Rating** 95 **To** 2022 $35 NG ✪

ꞏꞏꞏꞏ **Classic Muscat NV Rating** 93 $28 NG
Renaissance Viognier Roussanne Marsanne 2015 Rating 92 **To** 2020 $32 NG

Arneis 2016 Rating 91 To 2019 $24 NG
Tempranillo 2015 Rating 91 To 2023 $24 NG
Muscat NV Rating 91 $20 NG ✪
Shelley's Block Marsanne Viognier Roussanne 2015 Rating 90 To 2020
$19 NG ✪
Durif 2014 Rating 90 To 2038 $24 NG
Renaissance Durif 2014 Rating 90 To 2040 $50 NG

Rymill Coonawarra

Riddoch Highway, Coonawarra, SA 5263 **Region** Coonawarra
T (08) 8736 5001 **www**.rymill.com.au **Open** 7 days 10–5
Winemaker Sandrine Gimon, Federico Zaina, Joshua Clementson **Est.** 1974
Dozens 40 000 **Vyds** 137ha
The Rymills are descendants of John Riddoch and long owned some of the finest Coonawarra soil, upon which they grew grapes since 1970. Champagne-trained Sandrine Gimon is a European version of a Flying Winemaker, having managed a winery in Bordeaux, and made wine in Champagne, Languedoc, Romania and WA; she became an Australian citizen in 2011. In '16 the Rymill family sold the winery, vineyards and brand to a Chinese investor. The management, vineyard and winery teams have remained in place and new capital has financed moves to improve the vineyards and winery. Specifically, Sandrine, who has been with Rymill for the past 9 vintages, has been joined by Australian-born Josh Clementson (winemaker and vineyard manager) and Argentinean-born Frederico Zaina. The winery building also houses the cellar door and art exhibitions, which, together with viewing platforms over the winery, make it a must-see destination for tourists. Exports to all major markets.

ɿɿɿɿɿ **Sandstone Single Vineyard Cabernet Sauvignon 2015** This is a pure-bred stallion, its muscles rippling, its coat glossy, its gaze imperious. Its moderate alcohol is another seriously good attribute, anchored without any loss or perversion of flavour. Top marks for Coonawarra. Diam. 13.5% alc. **Rating** 96 To 2040 $60 ✪

ɿɿɿɿɿ **June Traminer Botrytis Gewurztraminer 2016** Rating 92 To 2020 $20 ✪
The Dark Horse Cabernet Sauvignon 2015 Rating 91 To 2030 $23 ✪
The Yearling Cabernet Sauvignon 2015 Rating 90 To 2025 $15 ✪

Saddler's Creek

Marrowbone Road, Pokolbin, NSW 2320 **Region** Hunter Valley
T (02) 4991 1770 **www**.saddlerscreek.com **Open** 7 days 10–5
Winemaker Brett Woodward **Est.** 1989 **Dozens** 6000 **Vyds** 10ha
Saddler's Creek is a boutique winery that is little known outside the Hunter Valley but has built a loyal following of dedicated supporters. It came onto the scene over 25 years ago with some rich, bold wines, and maintains this style today. Fruit is sourced from the Hunter Valley and Langhorne Creek, with occasional forays into other premium regions.

ɿɿɿɿɿ **Ryan's Reserve Hunter Valley Semillon 2016** Given the precarious vintage, this is super sharp and exacting. Linear and long with driving acidity but plenty of flavour from lemongrass, cider apple juice, grapefruit with wafts of blossom, curry leaves and wet stones. Screwcap. 11% alc. **Rating** 94 To 2027 $36 JF

ɿɿɿɿɿ **Hunter Valley Semillon 2016** Rating 92 To 2025 $26 JF
Ryan's Reserve Tumbarumba Chardonnay 2016 Rating 90 To 2022 $36 JF

Sailor Seeks Horse

102 Armstrongs Road, Cradoc, Tas 7109 **Region** Southern Tasmania
T 0418 471120 **www**.sailorseekshorse.com.au **Open** Not
Winemaker Paul and Gilli Lipscombe **Est.** 2010 **Dozens** 400 **Vyds** 6.5ha
While I was given comprehensive information about the seriously interesting careers of Paul and Gilli Lipscombe, and about their vineyard, I am none the wiser about the highly unusual and very catchy name. The story began in 2005 when they resigned from their (unspecified)

jobs in London, did a vintage in Languedoc, and then headed to Margaret River to study oenology and viticulture. While combining study and work, their goal was to learn as much as possible about pinot noir. They worked in large, small, biodynamic, conventional, minimum and maximum intervention vineyards and wineries – Woodlands, Xanadu, Beaux Freres, Chehalem and Mt Difficulty, all household names. By '10 they were in Tasmania working for Julian Alcorso's Winemaking Tasmania and found a derelict vineyard that had never cropped, having been abandoned not long after being planted in '05. It was in the Huon Valley, precisely where they had aimed to begin, the coolest district in Tasmania. They are working as winemakers for celebrated Home Hill wines and manage Jim Chatto's vineyard in Glaziers Bay. Exports to Singapore.

ΨΨΨΨΨ **Pinot Noir 2015** Sumptuous red and blue fruit flavours are seasoned with a sprinkle of 5% whole cluster, adding a dimension of five-spice and clove to the flow. The oak is impeccably integrated, imbuing a creamy edge as the fruit skirts effortlessly across it. This never slips into excessive sweetness. All class. Screwcap. 12.7% alc. **Rating** 97 **To** 2026 $50 NG ✪

ΨΨΨΨΨ **Tasmania Chardonnay 2015 Rating** 93 **To** 2026 $45 NG

St Hallett ★★★★★

St Hallett Road, Tanunda, SA 5352 **Region** Barossa
T (08) 8563 7000 **www**.sthallett.com.au **Open** 7 days 10–5
Winemaker Toby Barlow, Shelley Cox, Darin Kinzie **Est.** 1944 **Dozens** 210 000
St Hallett sources all grapes from within the Barossa GI, and is synonymous with the region's icon variety, shiraz. Old Block is the ultra-premium leader of the band (using old vine grapes from Lyndoch and Eden Valley), supported by Blackwell (Greenock, Ebenezer and Seppeltsfield). The winemaking team headed by Toby Barlow continues to explore the geographical, geological and climatic diversity of the Barossa, manifested through individual processing of all vineyards and single vineyard releases. In 2017 it was acquired by Accolade. Exports to all major markets.

ΨΨΨΨΨ **Old Block Barossa Shiraz 2014** Average vine age 88 years, hand-picked, a combination of open and tank fermentation, some whole bunches included, matured in French oak. A masterpiece created from ancient vines and the skilled winemaking team at St Hallett. This is elegance of the highest degree, with medium-bodied, supple red and black fruits flowing along the prodigiously long palate and aftertaste, the use of French oak the key. Screwcap. 14.5% alc. **Rating** 97 **To** 2039 $110 ✪

ΨΨΨΨΨ **Single Vineyard Release Dawkins Eden Valley Shiraz 2016** Bright, deep crimson-purple; a quick sniff and taste and you'll know that this full-bodied shiraz comes from the Eden Valley. It has a vibrancy and insouciant power and lift to its blue and black fruits that puts it in a pigeonhole all of its own. A lovely wine. Screwcap. 14.5% alc. **Rating** 96 **To** 2041 $55 ✪
Single Vineyard Release Scholz Estate Barossa Valley Shiraz 2016 A monster of a wine, forged without compromise. It is still at the very start of its life, raw with power, like a top of the range BMW or Mercedes. Blood plum, blackberry, black cherry, earth and licorice are just some of its calling cards; many are held in reserve. Needless to say, the tannins are made to match. Screwcap. 14.5% alc. **Rating** 96 **To** 2046 $55 ✪
Single Vineyard Release Mattschoss Eden Valley Shiraz 2015 Avant-garde winemaking in 3-tonne fermenters using partial whole-bunch carbonic maceration in various ways. It is as expressive as it is elegant, with a pinot-ish display of red fruits and spices on its long and silky palate, freshness and balance its watch words. New French oak (less than 20%) sits perfectly with its modest alcohol. Screwcap. 13.5% alc. **Rating** 96 **To** 2030 $50 ✪
Single Vineyard Release Mattschoss Eden Valley Shiraz 2016 This is a shiraz with lots to say about itself, and is very different from its siblings. It is medium to full-bodied, fruit, oak and tannins in symbiotic union, with a printed

fabric that has spice and oak in rhythmic, repeating patterns. Needs time, but will repay it. Screwcap. 14.5% alc. Rating 95 To 2041 $55

Single Vineyard Release Materne Barossa Valley Shiraz 2016 The bouquet is embryonic, but the medium to full-bodied palate is surprisingly open, the balance excellent, with a precocious display of red and black fruits. The tannins are plentiful, but supple, and no money has been wastefully spent on oak that the wine doesn't need. Screwcap. 14% alc. **Rating** 95 **To** 2036 $55

Single Vineyard Release Scholz Estate Barossa Valley Shiraz 2015 Blackberry, dark chocolate and a hint of eucalypt on the bouquet swell on the opulent and very long palate. Calculated to have great appeal to a broad church of consumers. Screwcap. 14.5% alc. **Rating** 95 **To** 2040 $50

Single Vineyard Release Materne Barossa Valley Shiraz 2015 It is highly fragrant, with an echo of the ironstone that is in the soil. It has a very firm structure, but the balance is such that it will age with assured grace. Screwcap. 14.5% alc. **Rating** 95 **To** 2040 $50

Blackwell Barossa Shiraz 2015 I assume Stuart Blackwell kept a close watch on the grape selection and vinification of this wine, and claims responsibility for its quality. Black fruits in profusion embrace the scaffold of ripe tannins and American oak to display their wares. Screwcap. 14.5% alc. **Rating** 95 **To** 2035 $40

Garden of Eden Barossa Shiraz 2016 Rating 94 To 2030 $25 **◎**
The Reward Barossa Cabernet Sauvignon 2015 Rating 94 To 2030 $30 **◎**

ΨΨΨΨΨ **Butcher's Cart Barossa Shiraz 2015** Rating 93 To 2035 $30
Barossa Touriga Nacional 2015 Rating 93 $30
Eden Valley Riesling 2016 Rating 92 To 2028 $19 **◎**
Black Clay Barossa Valley Shiraz 2016 Rating 90 To 2036 $18 **◎**
Faith Barossa Shiraz 2016 Rating 90 To 2026 $20 **◎**
Old Vine Barossa Grenache 2016 Rating 90 To 2021 $30

St Huberts ★★★★★

Cnr Maroondah Highway/St Huberts Road, Coldstream, Vic 3770 **Region** Yarra Valley
T (03) 5960 7096 **www**.sthuberts.com.au **Open** 7 days 10–5
Winemaker Greg Jarratt **Est.** 1966 **Dozens** NFP **Vyds** 20.49ha
The St Huberts of today has a rich 19th century history, not least in its success at the 1881 Melbourne International Exhibition, which featured every type of agricultural and industrial product. The wine section alone attracted 711 entries. The Emperor of Germany offered a Grand Prize, a silver gilt epergne, for the most meritorious exhibit in the show. A St Huberts wine won the wine section, then competed against objects as diverse as felt hats and steam engines to wine the Emperor's Prize, featured on its label for decades thereafter. Like other Yarra Valley wineries, it dropped from sight at the start of the 20th century, was reborn in 1966, and after several changes of ownership, became part of what today is TWE. The wines are made at Coldstream Hills, but have their own, very different, focus. St Huberts is dominated by Cabernet and the single vineyard Roussanne. Its grapes come from warmer sites, particularly the valley floor, that are part owned and part under contract.

ΨΨΨΨΨ **Yarra Valley Chardonnay 2015** Bright straw-green; a gold-plated bargain if ever there was one; it has a touch of funky complexity that immeasurably adds to its appeal, but is still (Yarra Valley) chardonnay to its core, and will flourish with more years in bottle. Screwcap. 13% alc. **Rating** 95 $27 **◎**
Yarra Valley Cabernet Merlot 2015 There's a fineness yet depth to cabernet sauvignon and friends from the valley – the distinct shape of the supple, fine tannins, the restraint in the fruit profile, the whisper of cassis, plums and tamarillos, the palate that's elegant and long. Both subtle and persuasive. Screwcap. 13.5% alc. **Rating** 95 **To** 2033 $27 JF **◎**
Yarra Valley Cabernet Sauvignon 2015 This is refined and elegant. No more than medium-bodied, with supple, detailed and beautiful tannins matched to the subtle oak influence. Defined by its savouriness but plenty of cassis, chocolate and spice dust. Lots to enjoy here. Screwcap. 13.5% alc. **Rating** 95 **To** 2030 JF

Yarra Valley Pinot Noir 2015 A powerful pinot, with black cherry, plum and spice leading the fruit on the bouquet and palate, along with some cedary oak and, of course, tannins bringing up the rear. Needs a year or two, but should develop very well indeed, and merit higher points. Screwcap. 13.5% alc. **Rating** 94 To 2027 $33

Yarra Valley Roussanne 2016 Rating 93 $30
The Stag Yarra Valley Pinot Noir 2016 Rating 91 To 2021 $24 JF
Yarra Valley Late Harvested Viognier 2016 Rating 91 To 2019 $30 JF
The Stag Cool Climate Chardonnay 2016 Rating 90 $20 ○
The Stag Cool Climate Shiraz 2015 Rating 90 To 2020 $20 ○

St Hugo ★★★★☆

2141 Barossa Valley Way, Rowland Flat, SA 5352 **Region** Barossa Valley
T (08) 8115 9200 **www**.sthugo.com **Open** 7 days 10.30–4.30
Winemaker Daniel Swincer **Est.** 1983 **Dozens** NFP
This a standalone business within the giant bosom of Pernod-Ricard, focused on the premium and ultra-premium end of the market, thus differentiating it from Jacob's Creek. It is presumably a substantial enterprise, even though no information about its size or modus operandi is forthcoming.

Barossa Grenache Shiraz Mataro 2015 A 54/29/17% blend, old vine grenache parcels with 20–50% whole bunches, shiraz and mataro destemmed, mainly open-fermented, matured in French oak. A very well made GSM, faithfully reflecting the quality of the grapes used, and maximising the flavour contribution of the grenache. The choice of used oak was 100% correct. Screwcap. 14.3% alc. **Rating** 95 To 2030 $58
Barossa Shiraz 2014 A rich, complex and layered shiraz with blood plum and blackberry varietal fruit, the one fairly obvious question whether less new oak would have made a better wine – and yes, it would have. Screwcap. 14.7% alc. **Rating** 94 To 2034 $58
Coonawarra Cabernet Sauvignon 2014 Matured for 19 months in 60% new French and Hungarian hogsheads, and 10% new American, the balance used. The oak is more obvious than I would like, but it could easily slip back into the fruit over coming years. At the risk of harping on, I can't for the life of me see the reason for 10% new American oak, but there you go. Screwcap. 14.1% alc. **Rating** 94 To 2039 $58
Private Collection Barossa Valley Coonawarra Shiraz Cabernet 2012 Beginning to show some mature characters, as you would expect. The youthful mint and leaf of the Coonawarra cabernet component has evolved and meshed comfortably with the berried fruit and spice of the Barossa shiraz, and there's both a richness and an elegance to the wine which reflects its classy pedigree. Should continue to develop gracefully. Screwcap. 14.8% alc. **Rating** 94 To 2024 $65 SC
Coonawarra Cabernet Sauvignon 2013 Matured for 22 months in 55% new French oak and 7% new American oak, the balance used French and American. While the oak is still in the front row of the flavour theatre, it leaves room for the cabernet to join in, and they then try, largely successfully, to repulse the overtures of the tannins. It's too early to be sure, but this could surprise with age. Screwcap. 14.3% alc. **Rating** 94 To 2033 $58

Vetus Purum Barossa Shiraz 2013 Rating 93 To 2053 $240
Coonawarra Cabernet Sauvignon 2012 Rating 93 To 2032 $75 JF
Coonawarra Barossa Cabernet Shiraz 2014 Rating 90 To 2039 $58

St Ignatius Vineyard ★★★☆

5434 Sunraysia Highway, Lamplough, Vic 3352 **Region** Pyrenees
T (03) 5465 3542 **www**.stignatiusvineyard.com.au **Open** 7 days 10–5
Winemaker Enrique Diaz **Est.** 1992 **Dozens** 2000 **Vyds** 9ha

Silvia Diaz and husband Enrique began establishing their vineyard (shiraz, cabernet sauvignon, malbec and chardonnay), winery and restaurant complex in 199? The vineyard has received three primary production awards. Wines are released under the Hangmans Gully label. Exports to the UK.

ŸŸŸŸ **Contemplation Pyrenees Chardonnay 2016** Unoaked, deep straw-gold with ripe yellow peaches, mango and charry pineapple slices. Simple, sweetish, a hint of creaminess with fresh acidity to close. Screwcap. 13% alc. **Rating** 89 **To** 2019 $25 JF

Contemplation Reserve Pyrenees Malbec 2014 Good dark ruby hue; there are Arnold Schwarzenegger muscles latching on to this full-bodied frame with lashings of oak and bulky tannins. Flavours of chocolate, macerated cherries, Cherry Ripe and rolled tobacco, hot on the finish. Cork. 15.5% alc. **Rating** 89 **To** 2023 $28 JF

St John's Road ★★★★★

1468 Research Road, St Kitts, SA 5356 **Region** Barossa Valley
T (08) 8362 8622 **www.**stjohnsroad.com **Open** Not
Winemaker Phil Lehmann, Charlie Ormsby **Est.** 2002 **Dozens** 20000 **Vyds** 20ha
St John's Road is now part of WD Wines Pty Ltd, which also owns Hesketh Wine Company and Parker Coonawarra Estate. It brings together a group of winemakers with an intimate knowledge of the Barossa Valley, and a fierce pride in what they do. Curiously, each obtained their first degree in other disciplines, Phil Lehmann as an electrical engineer, Charlie Ormsby as a librarian with a Bachelor of Arts degree and James Lienert with a Bachelor of Science (organic and inorganic chemistry) from the University of Adelaide. Others in the ownership group have extensive sales and marketing expertise. Exports to all major markets.

ŸŸŸŸŸ **Block 8 Maywald Clone Resurrection Vineyard Barossa Valley Shiraz 2015** Full crimson-purple; if only more Barossa Valley shiraz could taste and feel like this. Purity and intensity, its characters border on minerality – great life, vitality and length. The reason? Its alcohol, compared to a weighted Barossa Valley average of over 14.5%. Screwcap. 13.4% alc. **Rating** 96 **To** 2035 $38 ❂

The Evangelist Barossa Valley Shiraz 2014 Strong colour; exceptional mouthfeel ex tannins; much more savoury, but not at the expense of dark black fruits, anise; distinguished wine from three old vine vineyards in Eden and Barossa Valleys; very good tannins. Screwcap. 14.5% alc. **Rating** 96 **To** 2039 $50 ❂

Block 3 Old Vine 1935 Plantings Resurrection Vineyard Barossa Valley Shiraz 2015 Fabulous shiraz. Meaty, peppery, earthen and yet flush with ripe blackberry, even tipping into blackcurrant. Presents a fresh face and backs it with substance. Smoky oak never intrudes, only adds. No doubt it will cellar, but it's thoroughly irresistible now. Screwcap. 14.5% alc. **Rating** 95 **To** 2030 $35 CM ❂

Prayer Garden Selection Resurrection Vineyard Barossa Valley Grenache 2015 Aromatic lively red fruits, with some red jube nuances. This is grenache as it should be: no mawkish confection, and doesn't go soft on repeated tastes; as much dark as red fruit, its length and balance as pleasurable today as it will be in 5+ years. Screwcap. 14.5% alc. **Rating** 94 **To** 2023 $28 ❂

ŸŸŸŸŸ **Peace of Eden Riesling 2016 Rating** 92 **To** 2022 $22 CM ❂
PL Eden Valley Chardonnay 2015 Rating 92 **To** 2022 $30 SC
LSD Barossa Lagrein Shiraz Durif 2015 Rating 91 **To** 2029 $26

St Leonards Vineyard ★★★★☆

St Leonards Road, Wahgunyah, Vic 3687 **Region** Rutherglen
T 1800 021 621 **www.**stleonardswine.com.au **Open** Thurs–Sun 10–5
Winemaker Nick Brown, Chloe Earl **Est.** 1860 **Dozens** 5000 **Vyds** 12ha
An old favourite, relaunched in late 1997 with a range of premium wines cleverly marketed through an attractive cellar door and bistro at the historic winery on the banks of the Murray. It is run by Eliza Brown (CEO), sister Angela (online communications manager) and brother

Nick (vineyard and winery manager). They are perhaps better known as the trio who fulfil the same roles at All Saints Estate. Exports to the UK and the US.

ΨΨΨΨΨ **Wahgunyah Shiraz 2015** A very attractive medium-bodied shiraz that has greatly benefited from the use of French barriques. I tasted the wine (with the benefit of vinification details), but didn't notice the price. It all hangs together, and shows exactly the quality that can be coaxed out of Rutherglen shiraz. Screwcap. 14% alc. **Rating** 95 **To** 2030 $62

Shiraz 2015 Exceeds expectations, probably due to its flying start in picking before the alcohol started to fire up. It's positively elegant, with a chess board of red and black fruits, then fine tannins to complete the flavour story, oak merely a means to an end. Screwcap. 14.4% alc. **Rating** 94 **To** 2030 $30 ✪

ΨΨΨΨ **Durif 2015 Rating** 92 **To** 2030 $30 SC
Classic Rutherglen Muscat NV Rating 90 $35 CM

St Michael's Vineyard   ★★★★

503 Pook Road, Toolleen, Vic 3521 **Region** Heathcote
T 0427 558 786 **Open** By appt
Winemaker Mick Cann **Est.** 1994 **Dozens** 300 **Vyds** 4.5ha
Owner/winemaker Mick Cann has established vines on the famous deep-red Cambrian clay loam on the east face of the Mt Camel Range. Planting began in 1994–95, with a further extension in 2000. Shiraz (3ha), merlot (1ha) and petit verdot (0.3ha) and cabernet sauvignon (0.2ha) are grown. Part of the grape production is sold to David Anderson of Wild Duck Creek Estate, the remainder made by Mick, using open fermentation, hand-plunging of skins and a basket press, a low-tech but highly effective way of making high quality red wine. The period poster-style labels do the wines scant justice.

ΨΨΨΨΨ **Personal Reserve Heathcote Petit Verdot 2015** 48 hours cold soak, wild yeast until near the end of fermentation then cultured yeast added to ensure completion, matured in new French oak. Plum, blackcurrant and redcurrant fruit establish themselves before the full tannins counterattack, but they don't unseat the fruit. Screwcap. 13.5% alc. **Rating** 90 **To** 2025

Personal Reserve Heathcote Durif 2015 Matured for 13 months in new American oak. The inky colour stains the glass when swirled, unusual for table wine – it is a sign of the total extract of the wine, and of the long, long period needed for the wine to become enjoyable, the alcohol a coup de grace. Screwcap. 15.2% alc. **Rating** 90 **To** 2040

Saint Regis   ★★★★

35 Waurn Ponds Drive, Waurn Ponds, Vic 3216 **Region** Geelong
T 0432 085 404 **www.**saintregis.com.au **Open** Thurs–Sun 11–5
Winemaker Peter Nicol **Est.** 1997 **Dozens** 500 **Vyds** 1ha
Saint Regis is a family-run boutique winery focusing on estate-grown shiraz, and locally sourced chardonnay and pinot noir. Each year the harvest is hand-picked by members of the family and friends, with Peter Nicol (assisted by wife Viv) the executive onsite winemaker. Peter, with a technical background in horticulture, is a self-taught winemaker, and has taught himself well, also making wines for others. His son Jack became the owner of the business in 2015 and took on the management of the newly constructed restaurant and wine bar. Peter continues to be the winemaker.

ΨΨΨΨ **The Reg Geelong Shiraz 2015** Matured for 12 months in French oak (30% new). Black cherry and blackberry, splashes of spice and licorice, and gently savoury tannins all work well. This is typical of the depth and flavour Geelong can provide. Screwcap. 15% alc. **Rating** 91 **To** 2025 $30

Geelong Pinot Noir 2015 Matured for 12 months in French oak (25% new). Deeply coloured; a powerful pinot with baker's spices on the bouquet and luscious plum on the palate. Screwcap. 13.3% alc. **Rating** 90 **To** 2025 $30

Salomon Estate

17 High Street, Willunga, SA 5171 **Region** Southern Fleurieu
T 0412 412 228 **www.**salomonwines.com **Open** Not
Winemaker Bert Salomon, Mike Farmilo **Est.** 1997 **Dozens** 6500 **Vyds** 12.1ha
Bert Salomon is an Austrian winemaker with a long-established family winery in the Kremstal region, not far from Vienna. He became acquainted with Australia during his time with import company Schlumberger in Vienna; he was the first to import Australian wines (Penfolds) into Austria, in the mid-1980s, and later became head of the Austrian Wine Bureau. He was so taken by Adelaide that he moved his family there for the first few months each year, sending his young children to school and setting in place an Australian red winemaking venture. He retired from the Bureau and is now a full-time travelling winemaker, running the family winery in the northern hemisphere vintage, and overseeing the making of the Salomon Estate wines at Chapel Hill. Salomon Estate now shares a cellar door with Hither & Yon, just a few steps away from the Saturday farmers' market in Willunga. Exports to all major markets.

ττττ **Finniss River Braeside Vineyard Cabernet Sauvignon 2014** A wine that broods over a core of molten dark fruits – plum, cherry and cassis – all pinned to varietal herb and mint. The chassis of firm grape tannins finds confluence with well applied French oak. The maceration was extensive, serving to leach the tannins, pliant and tactile, as a platform for the performance of intense flavours. Cork. 14.5% alc. **Rating** 95 **To** 2045 $37 NG
Finniss River Sea Eagle Vineyard Southern Fleurieu Shiraz 2014 This is a statuesque wine defined by a stream of juicy, blue and black fruits. The tannins are beautifully defined, allowing the fruit to gush either side. There is a skein of peppery acidity, conferring a verve and je ne sais quoi energy to lingering notes of mocha. Cork. 14.5% alc. **Rating** 94 **To** 2040 $42 NG

ττττ **Alttus Southern Fleurieu Shiraz 2012** **Rating** 93 **To** 2025 $110 NG
Norwood Shiraz Cabernet 2015 **Rating** 93 **To** 2025 $25 NG ✪
Finniss River Cabernet Sauvignon 2009 **Rating** 92 **To** 2022 $48 NG

Saltram

Murray Street, Angaston, SA 5353 **Region** Barossa Valley
T (08) 8561 0200 **www.**saltramwines.com.au **Open** 7 days 10–5
Winemaker Shavaughn Wells, Richard Mattner **Est.** 1859 **Dozens** 150 000
There is no doubt that Saltram has taken strides towards regaining the reputation it held 30 or so years ago. Grape sourcing has come back to the Barossa Valley for the flagship wines. The red wines, in particular, have enjoyed great show success over the past decade, with No. 1 Shiraz and Mamre Brook leading the charge. Exports to all major markets.

ττττ **Single Vineyard Moculta Rd Vineyard Barossa Shiraz 2010** First tasted 4 years ago, and all I can do is briefly remark on the still brilliant crimson colour, the freshness and the elegance of the wine, and retain the original tasting note and points, the drink to date unchanged. 'Deep crimson-purple; the wine spent 24 months in used vats (large upright format), which has served to place all the emphasis on the excellent black fruits, spice and licorice flavours, the fine, but persistent and savoury, tannins adding to the overall appeal of a remarkable wine.' Screwcap. 14.5% alc. **Rating** 96 **To** 2035 $95
Mr Pickwick's Limited Release Particular Tawny NV Crushing intensity and length. Sour and nutty with slick, sweet, fresh toffee, dried fruits, rancio and coffee notes. Dances out through the finish. Cork. 19.5% alc. **Rating** 95 $60 CM
Single Vineyard Basedow Road Barossa Shiraz 2014 A deep, dark and densely packed celebration of Barossa Valley shiraz, conjured from the '14 vintage, turning the limitations of the year to the advantage of the wine. It is long, with spices and savoury nuances, the finish harmonious in every way, tannins and oak supporting the black fruits. Screwcap. **Rating** 95 **To** 2034 $95
No. 1 Barossa Shiraz 2014 Rich, black fruit aromas jump from the glass, with spicy oak playing a supporting role. Deep layers of flavour vie for attention with

the vice-like grip of the tannin, and it's probably about a draw. Really a little impenetrable now, but it's unequivocally built for the future. Screwcap. 14.5% alc. **Rating** 95 **To** 2034 $100 SC

No. 1 Barossa Shiraz 2013 The colour is deep, and the varietal flavours of blackberry and plum finish with gentle savoury tannins. Yet it is only medium-bodied, and the freshness of the mouthfeel suggests an alcohol level closer to 13.5% than the actual 14.5% (frequently alcohol seems higher than that on the label). Screwcap. **Rating** 95 **To** 2033 $100

Pepperjack Cabernet Sauvignon 2014 Rating 94 **To** 2034 $30 ❂

ＹＹＹＹＹ **Mamre Brook Eden Valley Riesling 2016 Rating** 92 **To** 2026 $23 ❂
Pepperjack Barossa Shiraz 2015 Rating 92 **To** 2025 $30
Metala Shiraz Cabernet 2014 Rating 92 **To** 2024 $20 SC ❂
Winemaker's Selection Grenache 2014 Rating 92 **To** 2025 $50 SC
1859 Eden Valley Chardonnay 2015 Rating 91 **To** 2020 $21 SC ❂
Winemaker's Selection Fiano 2015 Rating 90 **To** 2020 $25 SC
Pepperjack Scotch Fillet Graded Shiraz 2014 Rating 90 **To** 2034 $50
Pepperjack Sparkling Shiraz NV Rating 90 **To** 2019 $39 TS

Sam Miranda of King Valley ★★★★☆

1019 Snow Road, Oxley, Vic 3678 **Region** King Valley
T (03) 5727 3888 **www**.sammiranda.com.au **Open** 7 days 10–5
Winemaker Sam Miranda **Est.** 2004 **Dozens** 25 000 **Vyds** 55ha
Sam Miranda, grandson of Francesco Miranda, joined the family business in 1991, striking out on his own in 2004 after Miranda Wines was purchased by McGuigan Simeon. The Myrrhee Estate vineyard is at 450m in the upper reaches of the King Valley. This is where the varieties for Sam Miranda's Signature Range of wines are sourced, each with the name of the nearest town or named district. In 2016 Sam Miranda purchased the Oxley Estate vineyard on Snow Road with 40ha of vines to be reworked over coming years. Exports to the UK, Fiji and China.

ＹＹＹＹＹ **Estate Sangiovese 2015** A chameleon – at first all upfront spiced cherries and plums, then a savoury spectrum with roasted coffee beans, warm earth and wood spices. Fleshy, just shy of full-bodied, with sangiovese's acidity and tannins neatly meshed with the oak. Screwcap. 13.5% alc. **Rating** 95 **To** 2027 $50 JF

ＹＹＹＹＹ **Super King Sangiovese Cabernet 2015 Rating** 93 **To** 2021 $25 JF ❂
Durif 2015 Rating 93 **To** 2026 $30 JF
Dry Bianco 2016 Rating 91 **To** 2018 $20 JF ❂
Estate Nebbiolo 2014 Rating 91 **To** 2025 $75 JF
Chardonnay 2016 Rating 90 **To** 2021 $30 JF
Rosato 2016 Rating 90 **To** 2018 $20 JF ❂
Super King Sangiovese Cabernet 2014 Rating 90 **To** 2021 $25 JF

Sandalford ★★★★★

3210 West Swan Road, Caversham, WA 6055 **Region** Margaret River
T (08) 9374 9374 **www**.sandalford.com **Open** 7 days 9–5
Winemaker Hope Metcalf **Est.** 1840 **Dozens** 60 000 **Vyds** 105ha
Sandalford is one of Australia's oldest and largest privately owned wineries. In 1970 it moved beyond its original Swan Valley base, purchasing a substantial property in Margaret River that is now the main source of its premium grapes. Wines are released under the Element, Winemakers, Margaret River and Estate Reserve ranges, with Prendiville Reserve at the top. Exports to all major markets.

ＹＹＹＹＹ **Prendiville Reserve Margaret River Chardonnay 2016** It hardly need be said the wine is delicate, if not ephemeral, yet it has presence and length, the 5% mlf portion giving rise to some creamy mouthfeel. It's not possible to be didactic, but a gaudy butterfly might emerge from the chrysalis in 5 or 50 years. Screwcap. 12% alc. **Rating** 96 **To** 2026 $75 ❂

Prendiville Reserve Margaret River Shiraz 2015 Matured for 13 months in top class French barriques (70% new), then a final barrel selection. It is full bodied, rollicking with blue and black fruits in a cedary oak shroud, tannin the clasp. Desperately needs time. Screwcap. 14.5% alc. **Rating** 95 **To** 2040 $120

Prendiville Reserve Margaret River Cabernet Sauvignon 2015 Matured for 12 months, the best six barrels selected for this wine. Every aspect is scaled up from the Estate Reserve, although not dramatically so. This is very well bred, but is determined not to frighten the horses. Screwcap. 13.5% alc. **Rating** 95 **To** 2035 $120

Estate Reserve Margaret River Sauvignon Blanc Semillon 2016 Far more intense than its entry-point sibling, the difference lying in the vineyard, not the winery. Tropical and stone fruits dance a pas de deux to the rhythm of tangy acidity. Screwcap. 12% alc. **Rating** 94 **To** 2019 $25 ◐

Estate Reserve Margaret River Chardonnay 2016 Grapefruit and other citrus get a clear run up the straight. I am tolerant of high acidity, but this tests me. What it must do to others I have no idea. Screwcap. 12% alc. **Rating** 94 **To** 2026 $35

Estate Reserve Margaret River Shiraz 2014 Elegance is the keyword of a supple, fluid and fresh wine, red and black cherry to the fore, the oak totally integrated, the tannins fine. Screwcap. 14.5% alc. **Rating** 94 **To** 2025 $35

Estate Reserve Margaret River Cabernet Sauvignon 2015 Light, but bright hue; a pretty Margaret River cabernet, oxymoronic though that may be, its varietal fruit fresh and vibrant. Screwcap. 14% alc. **Rating** 94 **To** 2030 $45

🍷🍷🍷🍷 Margaret River Shiraz 2016 Rating 90 To 2026 $20 ◐
Margaret River Cabernet Merlot 2015 Rating 90 To 2025 $20 ◐

Sandhurst Ridge ★★★★☆

156 Forest Drive, Marong, Vic 3515 **Region** Bendigo
T (03) 5435 2534 **www**.sandhurstridge.com.au **Open** 7 days 11–5
Winemaker Paul Greblo **Est.** 1990 **Dozens** 3000 **Vyds** 7.3ha
The Greblo brothers (Paul is the winemaker, George the viticulturist), with combined experience in business, agriculture, science and construction and development, began the establishment of Sandhurst Ridge in 1990, planting the first 2ha of shiraz and cabernet sauvignon. Plantings have increased to over 7ha, principally cabernet and shiraz, but also a little merlot, nebbiolo and sauvignon blanc. As the business has grown, the Greblos have supplemented their crush with grapes grown in the region. Exports to Norway, Malaysia, Taiwan, Hong Kong, Japan and China.

🍷🍷🍷🍷🍷 Reserve Bendigo Shiraz 2014 This is so explosive that it takes little time to coax the avalanche of red, mottled blue and black fruits from the glass. The oak is embedded, following 19 months in French barriques, merely adding a patina of vanilla to boysenberry, dark plum and a core of molten kirsch. The acidity edges the fruit, beaming towards a long finale. Cork. 15% alc. **Rating** 95 **To** 2035 $45 NG

🍷🍷🍷🍷 Fringe Bendigo Cabernet Sauvignon 2015 Rating 92 To 2025 $22 NG ◐
Bendigo Cabernet Sauvignon 2015 Rating 90 To 2027 $30 NG

Sanguine Estate ★★★★★

77 Shurans Lane, Heathcote, Vic 3523 **Region** Heathcote
T (03) 5433 3111 **www**.sanguinewines.com.au **Open** W'ends & public hols 10–5
Winemaker Mark Hunter **Est.** 1997 **Dozens** 10 000 **Vyds** 21.57ha
The Hunter family – parents Linda and Tony at the head, and their children Mark and Jodi, with their respective partners Melissa and Brett – have 20ha of shiraz, with a 'fruit salad block' of chardonnay, viognier, merlot, tempranillo, petit verdot, cabernet sauvignon and cabernet franc. Low-yielding vines and the magic of the Heathcote region have produced Shiraz of exceptional intensity, which has received rave reviews in the US, and led to the 'sold out' sign

being posted almost immediately upon release. With the ever-expanding vineyard, Mark has become full-time vigneron and winemaker, and Jodi has taken over from her father as CEO and general manager. Exports to Singapore and China.

ŸŸŸŸŸ Robo's Mob Heathcote Shiraz 2015 This has an attractive and compelling savoury quality in the midst of its luscious black fruits, suggesting a high level of whole bunches in the ferment, and providing an interplay between the dark/black fruits and ripe tannins. Screwcap. 14.8% alc. **Rating** 95 **To** 2035 $30 **✪**
Inception Heathcote Shiraz 2015 The focus and intensity of the wine lifts it above the rest of Sanguine's '15 wines. Black fruits, spice and licorice do most of the work, keeping the wine well within the boundaries of the style. The fact that it has by far the highest alcohol is surprising, for there is no heat or dead fruit. Screwcap. 15.5% alc. **Rating** 95 **To** 2035 $40
Wine Club Heathcote Shiraz 2015 Blended by wine club members from four batches of shiraz. While black fruits are the core of the wine, there are touches of red and purple (plum) fruits also contributing to the total. This lengthens the palate, and freshens the finish. Screwcap. 14.8% alc. **Rating** 94 **To** 2030 $30 **✪**

ŸŸŸŸŸ Progeny Heathcote Shiraz 2015 Rating 93 **To** 2030 $25 **✪**
Heathcote Cabernet Sauvignon Petit Verdot Cabernet Franc Merlot 2013 Rating 92 **To** 2033 $25 **✪**
Music Festival Heathcote Shiraz 2015 Rating 91 **To** 2025 $30
Heathcote Cabernets 2015 Rating 90 **To** 2025 $25

Santa & D'Sas ★★★★

2 Pincott Street, Newtown, Vic 3220 **Region** Various
T 0417 384272 **www.**santandsas.com.au **Open** Not
Winemaker Andrew Santarossa, Matthew Di Sciascio **Est.** 2014 **Dozens** 5000
Santa & D'Sas is a collaboration between the Santarossa and Di Sciascio families. Andrew Santarossa and Matthew Di Sciascio met while studying for a Bachelor of Applied Science (Wine Science). Wines are released under the label Valentino (Fiano, Sangiovese and Shiraz), dedicated to Matthew's father; the remaining labels simply identify the region and variety.

ŸŸŸŸŸ Henty Pinot Gris 2016 When the fruit is sourced from an established cool climate site, about 22yo, made using wild yeast fermentation in older French oak puncheons plus barriques, and left on lees for 5 months, the end result should have some pizzazz, and it does. Racy with lemon juice and lemon meringue pie flavours, new season pears, a smidge of creaminess and an ultra-fine acid line ensuring a long, pure end. Screwcap. 13.5% alc. **Rating** 94 **To** 2022 $33 JF

ŸŸŸŸŸ Henty Riesling 2016 Rating 93 **To** 2025 $33 JF
Valentino King Valley Fiano 2016 Rating 93 **To** 2020 $40 JF
Valentino Heathcote Shiraz 2015 Rating 93 **To** 2025 $40 JF
Valentino Heathcote Sangiovese 2015 Rating 93 **To** 2023 $40 JF
King Valley Pinot Grigio 2016 Rating 92 **To** 2020 $24 JF **✪**
King Valley Rosato 2016 Rating 92 **To** 2019 $24 JF **✪**
Yarra Valley Pinot Noir 2015 Rating 92 **To** 2021 $33 JF
Heathcote Shiraz 2015 Rating 90 **To** 2024 $33 JF
D'Sas King Valley Prosecco 2016 Rating 90 **To** 2017 $32 TS

Santarossa Vineyards ★★★★

2 The Crescent, Yea, Vic 3717 (postal) **Region** Yarra Valley/Heathcote
T 0419 117 858 **www.**betterhalfwines.com.au **Open** Not
Winemaker Andrew Santarossa **Est.** 2007 **Dozens** NFP **Vyds** 16ha
Santarossa Vineyards, formerly known as Fratelli, started out as a virtual winery business, owned and run by three brothers of Italian heritage. It is now solely owned by winemaker Andrew and wife Megan Santarossa. The Yarra Valley and Heathcote are the focus of the business.

ΨΨΨΨΨ **Better Half Chardonnay 2016** Popcorn, vanillan oak and a reductive mineral smokiness dominate this wine. A tale of two halves, with plenty of ????? ?????? warmth tucked in beneath the structural attributes. Opens to a tangy citric twist and the tang of nectarine on the finish. Screwcap. 13% alc. **Rating** 92 **To** 2021 $35 NG

ΨΨΨΨ **Better Half Pinot Noir 2016 Rating** 89 **To** 2019 $35 NG

Santolin Wines   ★★★★★

c/- 21–23 Delaneys Road, South Warrandyte, Vic 3136 **Region** Yarra Valley
T 0402 278 464 **www**.santolinwines.com.au **Open** Not
Winemaker Adrian Santolin **Est.** 2012 **Dozens** 500
Adrian Santolin grew up in Griffith, NSW, and has worked in the wine industry since he was 15. He moved to the Yarra Valley in '07 with wife Rebecca, who has worked in marketing roles at various wineries. Adrian's love of pinot noir led him to work at wineries such as Wedgetail Estate, Rochford, De Bortoli, Sticks and Rob Dolan Wines. In '12 his dream came true when he was able to buy 2 tonnes of pinot noir from the Syme-on-Yarra Vineyard, increasing production in '13 to 4 tonnes, split between chardonnay and pinot noir. The Boy Meets Girl wines are sold through www.nakedwines.com.au Exports to the UK and the US.

ΨΨΨΨΨ **Willowlake Vineyard Yarra Valley Pinot Noir 2015** The difference between the vinification of this wine and that of Syme is 50% lower whole-bunch inclusion and the use of cold soak. The bouquet is very fragrant, almost scented, with a spray of red fruits, sous bois and spice. This lovely pinot glides along and across the palate, thence into the aftertaste. Screwcap. 13% alc. **Rating** 96 **To** 2030 $45 ✪
Syme on Yarra Vineyard Yarra Valley Pinot Noir 2015 30% whole bunches, matured in French oak (30% new) for 10 months. An instantaneously expressive bouquet of red cherry and plum, bracken and spice, leads with total assurance into the complex, but not the least heavy or aggressive, palate, freshened and extended by fresh acidity on the finish. '15 was a great pinot vintage in southern Vic. Screwcap. 13% alc. **Rating** 95 **To** 2026 $45

Saracen Estates   ★★★★

Level 10, 225 St Georges Terrace, Perth, WA 6000 **Region** Margaret River
T (08) 9486 9410 **www**.saracenestates.com.au **Open** Mon–Fri 9–5
Winemaker Paul Dixon, Bob Cartwright (Consultant) **Est.** 1998 **Dozens** 5000
The sale of the Saracen Estate property has left a cloud of uncertainty over how the business intends to operate into the future. Maree Saraceni and her brother Dennis Parker are running a virtual winery operation through their Perth office, employing contract winemaker Bob Cartwright, who is buying Margaret River harvest and making wine at Thompson's Estate.

ΨΨΨΨΨ **Margaret River Chardonnay 2016** Contract-grown, made by Clive Otto, whose predilection for restrained use of new oak comes through clearly in this fresh, elegant wine. Natural acidity also plays a role in the white peach and tangy citrus palate. As fresh as a daisy. Screwcap. 13% alc. **Rating** 94 **To** 2023 $35

ΨΨΨΨΨ **Cabernet Merlot 2015 Rating** 93 **To** 2025 $26 ✪
Reserve Cabernet Sauvignon 2012 Rating 93 **To** 2027 $56
Sauvignon Blanc Semillon 2016 Rating 92 **To** 2019 $22 ✪

Sassafras Wines   ★★★☆

20 Grylls Crescent, Cook, ACT 2614 (postal) **Region** Canberra District
T 0476 413 974 **www**.sassafraswines.com.au **Open** Not
Winemaker Paul Starr, Hamish Young **Est.** 2015 **Dozens** 300
Paul Starr and Tammy Braybrook brought unusual academic knowledge with them when they established Sassafras Wines. Tammy has a science degree, has worked as an economist, and is now an IT professional and part-time florist. Paul has a PhD in cultural studies and intended to be an academic in humanities before a detour into environment work in government.

Tammy knew Mark Terrell, of Quarry Hill, and the pair ended up working in the Terrell Vineyard with pruning and vintage work, leading to local college courses in winemaking. Paul worked at Eden Road cellar door on weekends for four years. History is an interest for both, and when thinking of heading in an altogether new wine direction, they read of what they describe as the ancestral method of making sparkling wine using the original yeast and fermentable sugar to create the mousse, bypassing disgorgement altogether.

🍷🍷🍷🍷 **Salita Sagrantino Nebbiolo 2015** Canberra sagrantino jumps into bed with some Gundagai nebbiolo (8%) and it's a lovely surprise: heady aromatics of licorice, tobacco, maraschino cherries and amaro. Of course it's tannic and mouth-puckering, but there's suppleness too. Screwcap. 14% alc. **Rating** 90 **To** 2022 $25 JF

🍷🍷🍷🍷 **Riverland Fiano 2016 Rating** 89 **To** 2018 $25 JF

Savaterre   ★★★★☆

PO Box 337, Beechworth, Vic 3747 **Region** Beechworth
T (03) 5727 0551 **www**.savaterre.com **Open** Not
Winemaker Keppell Smith **Est.** 1996 **Dozens** 1500
Keppell Smith embarked on a career in wine in 1996, studying winemaking at CSU and (at a practical level) with Phillip Jones at Bass Phillip. He purchased the 40ha property on which Savaterre has been established, and has close-planted (7500 vines per hectare) 1ha each of chardonnay and pinot noir at an elevation of 440m. Organic principles govern the viticulture, and the winemaking techniques look to the Old World rather than the New. Smith's stated aim is to produce outstanding individualistic wines far removed from the mainstream.

🍷🍷🍷🍷🍷 **Chardonnay 2015** Yet another producer of chardonnay able to exploit the synergy between the Beechworth climate and chardonnay. Its flavours are rich and complex, with white stone fruit in abundance, then tucked into bed with lively acidity. Screwcap. 13.4% alc. **Rating** 96 **To** 2025 $70 ✪

SC Pannell   ★★★★★

60 Olivers Road, McLaren Vale, SA 5171 **Region** McLaren Vale
T (08) 8323 8000 **www**.scpannell.com.au **Open** 7 days 11–5
Winemaker Stephen Pannell **Est.** 2004 **Dozens** 20 000 **Vyds** 22ha
The only surprising piece of background is that it took (an admittedly still reasonably youthful) Stephen (Steve) Pannell (and wife Fiona) so long to cut the painter from Constellation/Hardys and establish their own winemaking and consulting business. Steve radiates intensity, and extended experience has resulted in wines of the highest quality right from the first vintage. The Pannells have two vineyards in McLaren Vale, the first planted in 1891 with a precious 3.6ha of shiraz. A second property was purchased in 2014, lifting the estate vineyards to a total of 22ha. The future for the Pannells is limitless, the icon status of the label already established. Exports to the UK.

🍷🍷🍷🍷🍷 **McLaren Vale Grenache 2015** Red fruits of every description lead the wine out of the glass. Plenty of black cherry too. The wine is mid-weighted, with growing sweetness as bright acidity and fine, sandy tannins propel the wine across the gums and down the throat. The core of this seductive elixir is kirsch, pomegranate and a tang of whole cluster spice. Screwcap. 14.5% alc. **Rating** 96 **To** 2038 $55 NG ✪

McLaren Vale Touriga Cabernet Mataro 2015 An allusion, perhaps, to a Mediterranean vine-scape that is less water hungry and more sustainable; in synergy with later-ripening, more tannic varieties capable of mitigating fruit sweetness and imbuing texture and an aura of savouriness. This wine achieves all of this, with touriga's aromatic soprano of violet soaring amid cabernet's bass and mataro's ferruginous, meaty baritone, scraping the fruit together. Screwcap. 13.9% alc. **Rating** 96 **To** 2032 $40 NG ✪

Aromatico 2016 Largely gewurztztraminer, with 29% riesling and 4% pinot gris, this is a potpourri of rosehip, lychee and Turkish Delight doused in a floral perfume. The phenolics are perfectly controlled – delicate and detailed – serving to steer this exotic ship to Asian locations on the palate. A thoroughly delicious wine. Screwcap. 13.5% alc. **Rating** 95 **To** 2021 $25 NG **○**

Adelaide Hills Pinot Noir 2015 Red fruits, briar, and piercing bing cherry notes soar from the glass without the inflection of excessive sweetness. The wine's tension from fore to aft is testimony to the optimal fruit ripeness and tannin management from judicious use of stems, extraction and diplomatic choice of oak. Screwcap. 13% alc. **Rating** 95 **To** 2024 $35 NG **○**

Adelaide Hills Syrah 2015 This wine sheds its initial shaft of reduction with a twirl of the wrist, delivering tapenade, blue and black fruit flavours and a skein of peppery tannin melded to a rasp of briar, indicating the 20% of stems in the ferment. The oak is absorbed by the fruit; the finish is taut, persistent and highly refreshing. Screwcap. 13.5% alc. **Rating** 95 **To** 2035 $35 NG **○**

The Vale McLaren Vale Shiraz Grenache 2015 Indelibly of place, the wine's aroma sings strongly of a maritime salinity, embedded in which are iron, blue and black fruits, raw meat and a hint of mace. The palate, while concentrated, plays a savoury chord of spiky whole cluster notes, licorice-soaked tannins and a veil of lively acidity. Screwcap. 14.5% alc. **Rating** 95 **To** 2035 $40 NG

Adelaide Hills Sauvignon Blanc 2016 **Rating** 94 **To** 2018 $25 NG **○**
McLaren Vale Grenache Shiraz Touriga 2015 **Rating** 94 **To** 2025 $30 NG **○**
McLaren Vale Barossa Valley Tempranillo Touriga 2015 **Rating** 94 **To** 2030 $30 NG **○**

ŸŸŸŸŸ **Adelaide Hills Nebbiolo Rose 2016** **Rating** 93 **To** 2018 $35 NG
Adelaide Hills Pinot Grigio 2016 **Rating** 92 **To** 2018 $25 NG **○**
Field Street McLaren Vale Shiraz 2015 **Rating** 92 **To** 2030 $30 NG
Langhorne Creek Montepulciano 2015 **Rating** 92 **To** 2028 $30 NG
Dead End McLaren Vale Tempranillo 2015 **Rating** 91 **To** 2022 $30 NG

Scarborough Wine Co   ★★★★☆

179 Gillards Road, Pokolbin, NSW 2320 **Region** Hunter Valley
T (02) 4998 7563 **www.**scarboroughwine.com.au **Open** 7 days 9–5
Winemaker Ian and Jerome Scarborough **Est.** 1985 **Dozens** 25 000 **Vyds** 14ha
Ian Scarborough honed his white winemaking skills during his years as a consultant, and has brought all those skills to his own label. He makes three different styles of Chardonnay: the Blue Label is a light, elegant, Chablis style for the export market; a richer barrel-fermented wine (Yellow Label) is primarily directed to the Australian market; the third is the White Label, a cellar door-only wine made in the best vintages. The Scarborough family also acquired a portion of the old Lindemans Sunshine Vineyard (after it lay fallow for 30 years) and planted it with semillon and (quixotically) pinot noir. Exports to the UK and the US.

ŸŸŸŸŸ **The Obsessive Vanessa Vale Vineyard Hunter Valley Shiraz 2014** Perfect fruit, alcohol, tannin and oak balance are the hallmarks of a superlative vintage, all carefully guarded by the Scarborough family. This wine will coast through the next 40 years. Screwcap. 13.7% alc. **Rating** 97 **To** 2054 $60 **○**

ŸŸŸŸŸ **The Obsessive Gillards Road Vineyard Chardonnay 2015** **Rating** 93 **To** 2022 $40
Yellow Label Chardonnay 2014 **Rating** 90 **To** 2021 $28

Scarpantoni Estate   ★★★★

Scarpantoni Drive, McLaren Flat, SA 5171 **Region** McLaren Vale
T (08) 8383 0186 **www.**scarpantoniwines.com **Open** Mon–Fri 9–5, w'ends 11.30–4.30
Winemaker Michael and Filippo Scarpantoni **Est.** 1979 **Dozens** 37 000 **Vyds** 40ha
Scarpantoni has come a long way since Domenico Scarpantoni purchased his first vineyard in 1958. He worked for Thomas Hardy at its Tintara winery, then as vineyard manager for

Seaview Wines, and soon became one of the largest private grapegrowers in the region. The winery was built in '79 with help from sons Michael and Filippo, who continue to manage the company. Michael and Filippo grew up on part of Oxenberry Farm, originally settled in 1840, and in 1998 were able to purchase part of the property. The Oxenberry wines are made in a different style from that of Scarpantoni, and are available only from its cellar door, at 24–26 Kangarilla Road, McLaren Flat. Exports to the UK and other major markets.

ΨΨΨΨΩ **Block 3 McLaren Vale Shiraz 2014** From the estate's oldest, this is quintessential McLaren Vale in its brooding guise: black cherry, menthol and anise notes are whiplashed into gear by high-toned American oak handling. The sort of avuncular expression of a region that we all seek at times for comfort and solace. Screwcap. **Rating** 91 **To** 2030 $30 NG
Brothers' Block McLaren Vale Cabernet Sauvignon 2014 Cabernet sauvignon's mint, tobacco and cedar rims are fully flared against the glossy engine room of saturated dark fruits with further lashings of pastille flavours and generous oak. A full-bodied wine of force, yet there is as much substance as style in these bones. Screwcap. **Rating** 91 **To** 2026 NG

ΨΨΨΨ **Gamay 2015 Rating** 89 **To** 2023 $25 NG

Schild Estate Wines   ★★★★☆

Cnr Barossa Valley Way/Lyndoch Valley Road, Lyndoch, SA 5351 **Region** Barossa Valley
T (08) 8524 5560 **www.**schildestate.com.au **Open** 7 days 10–5
Winemaker Scott Hazeldine **Est.** 1998 **Dozens** 40 000 **Vyds** 163ha
Ed Schild is a Barossa Valley grapegrower who first planted a small vineyard at Rowland Flat in 1952, steadily increasing his vineyard holdings over the next 50 years to their present level. The flagship wine is made from 170-year-old shiraz vines on the Moorooroo Vineyard. The cellar door is in the old ANZ Bank at Lyndoch, and provides the sort of ambience that can only be found in the Barossa Valley. Exports to all major markets.

ΨΨΨΨΨ **Moorooroo Barossa Valley Shiraz 2013** Made from four rows of 165yo vines, this was fermented in open-top fermenters before being matured in new French barriques. The result is a wine that smells of dark fruits, chocolate and leather, while the palate has an old vine creaminess together with very ripe tannins, ensuring that this classic, old-school Barossa shiraz will still be looking good 20 years from now. Cork. 14.5% alc. **Rating** 95 **To** 2035 $100 PR
Edgar Schild Reserve Barossa Valley Grenache 2014 French oak influence isn't heavy but it's clearly present, the run of raspberry and earth flavours only just managing to keep pace. It's in need of some time to show its best. The way tannin curls through the finish, and indeed the general blossoming of fruit as the wine breathes, are distinctly positive signs. Screwcap. 14.9% alc. **Rating** 94 **To** 2027 $40 CM

ΨΨΨΨΩ **Barossa Valley GSM 2014 Rating** 93 **To** 2022 $18 CM ✪
Prämie Barossa Valley Shiraz 2014 Rating 92 $70 PR
Ben Schild Reserve Barossa Valley Shiraz 2013 Rating 91 $40 PR
Museum Release Moorooroo Shiraz 2008 Rating 90 $165 PR

Schubert Estate   ★★★★★

26 Kensington Road, Rose Park, SA 5067 **Region** Barossa Valley
T (08) 8562 3375 **www.**schubertestate.com **Open** Mon–Fri 11–5
Winemaker Steve Schubert **Est.** 2000 **Dozens** 4200 **Vyds** 14ha
Steve and Cecilia Schubert are primarily grapegrowers, with 12.8ha of shiraz and 1.2ha of viognier. They purchased the 25ha property in 1986, when it was in such a derelict state that there was no point trying to save the old vines. Both were working in other areas, so it was some years before they began replanting, at a little under 2ha per year. Almost all the production is sold to Torbreck. In 2000 they decided to keep enough grapes to make a barrique of wine for their own (and friends') consumption. They were sufficiently encouraged

by the outcome to venture into the dizzy heights of two hogsheads a year (since increased to four or so). The wine is made with wild yeast–open fermentation, basket pressing and bottling without filtration. In 2016 Schubert Estate opened a cellar door in Adelaide in a renovated stone villa. Exports to Germany, Malaysia, Hong Kong and China.

TTTTT The Gander Reserve Shiraz 2013 To date only four vintages of The Gander Reserve ('04, '07, '08 and '13). Deep, dense crimson-purple; the quality of the fruit has made light work of the additional year in barrel (and of its 15% alcohol). It is as good an example of uninhibited Barossa Valley shiraz as you are likely to find. Cork. **Rating** 97 **To** 2053 $90 ✪

TTTTT Goose-yard Block Barossa Valley Shiraz 2014 Full crimson-purple; while the vineyard is relatively young (20yo), the quality of the fruit is exceptional, the wine itself very well made, flooded with dark cherry and plum fruit, pliable tannins and integrated French oak. Cork. 14.5% alc. **Rating** 96 **To** 2044 $69 ✪
The Gosling Single Vineyard Barossa Valley Shiraz 2015 This full-bodied shiraz has all the traditional richness of Barossa Valley shiraz gift-wrapped in contemporary French oak and neatly dialled tannins that add length and complexity. Cork. 14.5% alc. **Rating** 95 **To** 2035 $28 ✪
The Lone Goose Barossa Valley Shiraz 2015 Includes 5% co-fermented viognier. This has greater intensity and drive than The Gosling, the alcohol and viognier adding to the tension created on the full-bodied palate. There are notes of licorice, dark chocolate and briar underlying the black fruits. Pepsodent-wise, you'll wonder where the viognier went. Diam. 15% alc. **Rating** 95 **To** 2045 $42

TTTTT Le Jars Blanc Dry Viognier 2016 Rating 92 **To** 2020 $36
The Golden Goose Sweet Viognier 2016 Rating 90 **To** 2020 $26

Schulz Vignerons   ★★★★★

PO Box 121, Nuriootpa, SA 5355 **Region** Barossa Valley
T (08) 8565 6257 **www.**schulzwines.com.au **Open** By appt
Winemaker Marcus Schulz, Neville Falkenberg **Est.** 2003 **Dozens** 500 **Vyds** 58.5ha
Marcus and Roslyn Schulz are the fifth generation of one of the best-known (extended) wine families in the Barossa Valley. Four generations of grapegrowing and winemaking precede them, but in 2002 they went down a new path by initiating 'biological farming' of the 50+yo wines. They have moved away from irrigation and extensive spraying and now the vines are virtually dry-grown, producing generous yields of high quality grapes, using natural nitrogen created by the active soil biology, and minimal chemical input. The vineyard is planted to 12 varieties, shiraz, mourvedre, grenache and cabernet sauvignon leading the band. As might be imagined, the lion's share of the grapes is sold to other makers in the Barossa.

TTTTT Grandies Barossa Valley Shiraz 2014 Blue fruits charge. Dark plum and cherries swathed in cardamom, vanilla, anise, liqueur and Indian curry powder clean out the trenches between nose and palate. This is smooth as silk, but amplified in its vinosity and carpet ride of textures. A polished solo of fruit, tannic supports and pulpy, bouncy energy beneath. An exemplary wine for the idiom. Screwcap. 14% alc. **Rating** 96 **To** 2034 $50 NG ✪
Benjamin Barossa Valley Shiraz 2014 Following the impact of brazen dark fruits, molten coffee-grind tannins and barbecue-charred oak, the mind may be abuzz, but the palate is whetted and ready for more. Texturally, this wine is lavishly handled. There is plenty of plush, impeccably tannin-managed cushion to leave the palate primed. Screwcap. 14% alc. **Rating** 95 **To** 2033 $30 NG ✪

TTTTT Marcus Old Vine Barossa Valley Shiraz 2013 Rating 93 **To** 2030 $60 NG
Maria Barossa Valley Mataro 2015 Rating 93 **To** 2023 $25 NG ✪
Clara Reserve Barossa Valley Semillon 2016 Rating 90 **To** 2023 $25 NG

Schwarz Wine Company ★★★★★

PO Box 779, Tanunda, SA 5352 **Region** Barossa Valley
T 0417 881 923 **www.**schwarzwineco.com.au **Open** At Artisans of Barossa
Winemaker Jason Schwarz **Est.** 2001 **Dozens** 4500

The economical name is appropriate for a business that started with 1 tonne of grapes making two hogsheads of wine in 2001. Shiraz was purchased from Jason Schwarz's parents' vineyard in Bethany, the vines planted in 1968; the following year half a tonne of grenache was added, once again purchased from the parents. In '05, grape sale agreements with another (larger) winery were terminated, freeing up 1.8ha of shiraz and 0.8ha of grenache. From this point on things moved more quickly: in '06 Jason formed a partnership (Biscay Road Vintners) with Peter Schell of Spinifex, giving them total control over production. Exports to the US, France, Singapore and China.

ŶŶŶŶŶ The Schiller Single Vineyard Barossa Valley Shiraz 2014 The 400-vine vineyard planted in 1881 is still owned by the sixth generation of the Schiller family. Bright colour, French oak integrated into the fabric of the wine through barrel fermentation. Spicy, savoury flavours abound in this lively, medium-bodied shiraz, freshness its keyword. Screwcap. 14.5% alc. **Rating** 96 **To** 2040 $70 ✪
Meta Barossa Shiraz 2015 An attractive medium to full-bodied shiraz with black cherry, plum and oak showing the way, the juicy mouthfeel created by the whole-bunch inclusion and modest alcohol. Screwcap. 14% alc. **Rating** 95 **To** 2035 $35 ✪
Nitschke Block Single Vineyard Barossa Valley Shiraz 2015 Picked in two portions, 20–25% whole bunches, wild yeast–open fermented, 20–25 days on skins, matured in French oak (25% new). Sophisticated winemaking, the only question the amount of French oak apparent now, but it will regress with more time in bottle. Screwcap. 14.2% alc. **Rating** 95 **To** 2035 $40
Nitschke Block Single Vineyard Barossa Valley Shiraz 2014 Full-bodied, and filled with black fruits and a dab of dark chocolate supported by fine but firm tannins; built to last decades. Despite all this, it has no dead/overripe fruit flavours, just seductive complexity. Screwcap. 14.5% alc. **Rating** 95 **To** 2034 $40
Meta Barossa Valley Mataro 2016 The fragrant and complex bouquet has unexpected exotic spice nuances that come through on the lively medium-bodied palate that is also (delightfully) unusual. Raspberry and cinnamon are all in the flavour mix, the tannins fine. Screwcap. 14.1% alc. **Rating** 95 **To** 2023 $35 ✪

ŶŶŶŶŶ Thiele Road Barossa Valley Grenache 2015 **Rating** 92 **To** 2020 $38
Barossa Valley GSM 2015 **Rating** 92 **To** 2023 $28
Barossa Valley Shiraz 2015 **Rating** 91 **To** 2025 $30
Barossa Valley Rose 2016 **Rating** 90 **To** 2018 $22 CM
Meta Barossa Valley Grenache 2016 **Rating** 90 **To** 2020 $35

Scion Vineyard & Winery ★★★★

74 Slaughterhouse Road, Rutherglen, Vic 3685 **Region** Rutherglen
T (02) 6032 8844 **www.**scionvineyard.com **Open** 7 days 10–5
Winemaker Rowly Milhinch **Est.** 2002 **Dozens** 1650 **Vyds** 3.2ha

Scion Vineyard was established by retired audiologist Jan Milhinch, who is a great-great-granddaughter of GF Morris, founder of the most famous Rutherglen wine family. Jan has now handed the baton to son Rowland (Rowly), who continues to manage the vineyard, planted on a quartz-laden red clay slope to durif, viognier, brown muscat and orange muscat, and make the wines.

ŶŶŶŶŶ Rutherglen Durif Viognier 2014 With 3% co-fermented viognier, 15% whole-bunch durif and 20% new French oak, Rowly Milhinch has made the traditional image of durif stand on its head. It is vibrant, fresh and juicy, interposing red nuances in the foundation of dark berry fruit flavours. Its balance is such that it can be enjoyed tonight or in 10 years. Screwcap. 13.2% alc. **Rating** 94 **To** 2026 $42

Scorpo Wines ★★★★★

23 Old Bittern Dromana Road, Merricks North, Vic 3926 **Region** Mornington Peninsula
T (03) 5989 7697 **www**.scorpowines.com.au **Open** By appt
Winemaker Paul Scorpo **Est.** 1997 **Dozens** 3500 **Vyds** 9.64ha
Paul Scorpo has a background as a horticulturist/landscape architect, working on major projects ranging from private gardens to golf courses in Australia, Europe and Asia. His family has a love of food, wine and gardens, all of which led to their buying a derelict apple and cherry orchard on gentle rolling hills between Port Phillip and Western Port bays. They have established pinot gris (4.8ha), pinot noir (2.8ha), chardonnay (1ha) and shiraz (1ha). Exports to Singapore and Hong Kong.

ŸŸŸŸŸ **Eocene Single Vineyard Chardonnay 2013** From a 0.3ha block of mainly Dijon clone 95 and a small amount of P58, only made in exceptional vintages. By shunning both mlf and lees stirring (battonage), Paul Scorpo goes along a different path from almost all of his confreres on the Mornington Peninsula. It could be mistaken for a 1yo chardonnay; its structure, texture and flavour of exceptional delicacy. Screwcap. 13.5% alc. **Rating** 96 **To** 2028 $62 ✪
Mornington Peninsula Chardonnay 2014 When 3yo looked like a yearling, pale in colour, intense and precisely fixed on a path stretching out to the horizon. The acidity is a (positive) feature, with no mlf to moderate its intensity. White peach and green apple drive through the palate with unstoppable power, the mlf suppressed at birth. Screwcap. 13% alc. **Rating** 95 **To** 2025 $49
Mornington Peninsula Pinot Noir 2015 The palate is outstanding in depth, line and length, the fragrance growing each time it was tasted. Slightly left field for '15 (some darker cherry notes) but has great structure, reflecting the low yield. Screwcap. 13.5% alc. **Rating** 95 **To** 2030 $55
Aubaine Mornington Peninsula Chardonnay 2016 Mornington Peninsula may not have the depth of Margaret River chardonnays, nor the length of those of the Yarra Valley, but it produces wines with very good elegance and balance, exemplified by this wine. It has white peach, Granny Smith apple and pear within a fine clasp of French oak. Screwcap. 13.5% alc. **Rating** 94 **To** 2023 $31

ŸŸŸŸŸ **Mornington Peninsula Pinot Gris 2016 Rating** 92 **To** 2020 $35
Noirien Mornington Peninsula Pinot Noir 2016 Rating 91 **To** 2031 $31

Scotchmans Hill ★★★★★

190 Scotchmans Road, Drysdale, Vic 3222 **Region** Geelong
T (03) 5251 3176 **www**.scotchmans.com.au **Open** 7 days 10.30–4.30
Winemaker Robin Brockett, Marcus Holt **Est.** 1982 **Dozens** 50 000 **Vyds** 40ha
Established in 1982, Scotchmans Hill has been a consistent producer of well made wines under the stewardship of long-term winemaker Robin Brocket and assistant Marcus Holt. The wines are released under the Scotchmans Hill, Cornelius, Jack & Jill and Swan Bay labels. A change of ownership in 2014 has resulted in significant vineyard investment.

ŸŸŸŸŸ **Cornelius Single Vineyard Bellarine Peninsula Pinot Noir 2013** A particularly fresh and bright crimson colour for a 3+yo pinot; plum is in the foreground, red and black cherry in the mix of the background; fills the mouth with luscious, yet not the least jammy, fruit supported by high quality French oak and excellent tannins. Will be long-lived, and is well priced for a cellaring special. Screwcap. 13% alc. **Rating** 96 **To** 2028 $55 ✪
Bellarine Peninsula Chardonnay 2014 Bright straw-green; over-delivers in emphatic fashion, celebrating the vintage; the complex bouquet is first class, the palate likewise, its fruit span in the classic stone fruit/grapefruit spectrum, acidity precisely managed, oak likewise. Screwcap. 13% alc. **Rating** 95 **To** 2022 $28 ✪
Cornelius Sutton Vineyard Bellarine Peninsula Chardonnay 2014
A fascinating and compelling wine which, despite boasting lower alcohol than the other single sites, feels palpably riper. Vividly ripe apricot, white peach and nectarine flavours are catapulted across a ribcage of tensile acidity, a nutty kernel

and a saline mineral punch; the finish is very long. Screwcap. 12.5% alc. **Rating** 95 To 2024 $50 NG

Cornelius Single Vineyard Bellarine Peninsula Chardonnay 2013 A high quality chardonnay with a complex bouquet of sea shells and grapefruit pith, expanding in every dimension on the palate, with layered white peach, nectarine and grapefruit, oak flavour subtle, but with all-important structure. Screwcap. 13% alc. **Rating** 95 To 2023 $55

Cornelius Bellarine Peninsula Pinot Gris 2014 No winemaking information available, but having regard to the bouquet and palate one assumes this wine was fermented and matured in high quality French oak. The fruit flavours are a mix of citrus, pear and apple, and stand firm against the oak on the long palate. Screwcap. 13.5% alc. **Rating** 95 To 2019 $46

Jack & Jill Bellarine Peninsula Pinot Noir 2015 Good hue, depth and clarity; a complex, layered and powerful pinot with plum and black cherry fruit. Good now, but will be even better in 5 years, and through another 5 thereafter. Very much in the Scotchmans style developed by long-serving winemaker Robin Brockett. Screwcap. 13.5% alc. **Rating** 95 To 2027 $40

Cornelius Armitage Vineyard Bellarine Peninsula Pinot Noir 2014 A free-flowing, transparent wine of bing cherry, damson plum, red currant and very ripe strawberry notes, interlaced with autumnal mulch, briar and gentle whole cluster spike. The effect is soothing and engaging, the oak well bosomed and the finish long and effortless, verging on ethereal. **Rating** 95 To 2023 $50 NG

Jack & Jill Bellarine Peninsula Shiraz 2014 Destemmed, 5 days cold soak, wild yeast–open ferment, matured in a mix of new and used French oak for 10 months. 'This is how pinot noir makers make shiraz', says the background info. The fragrant, spicy bouquet leads sinuously into the medium-bodied palate with a complex interplay between red, purple and black fruits on the one hand, and savoury tannins on the other. Screwcap. 14.5% alc. **Rating** 95 To 2039 $40

Geelong Cabernet Sauvignon 2013 The yield was 1t/acre; open-fermented, 5 days cold soak, 6-day wild yeast ferment, 7 days post-ferment maceration, matured in new and used French oak for 16 months. A classy wine, with juicy blackcurrant fruit, fine-grained tannins and a long finish. Very good value. Screwcap. 13.5% alc. **Rating** 95 To 2028 $30 ✪

Bellarine Peninsula Sauvignon Blanc 2015 Rating 94 To 2017 $21 ✪
Jack & Jill Sauvignon Blanc 2015 Rating 94 To 2018 $40
Jack & Jill Chardonnay 2015 Rating 94 To 2023 $40
Cornelius Chardonnay 2014 Rating 94 To 2024 $50 NG

♥♥♥♥♡ **Bellarine Peninsula Chardonnay 2015** Rating 93 To 2023 $30 NG
Cornelius Armitage Vineyard Chardonnay 2014 Rating 93 To 2024 $50 NG
Cornelius Single Vineyard Pinot Gris 2015 Rating 93 To 2021 $40 NG
Bellarine Peninsula Pinot Noir 2015 Rating 93 To 2023 $33 NG
Cornelius Pinot Noir 2014 Rating 93 To 2023 $50 NG
Jack & Jill Bellarine Peninsula Shiraz 2015 Rating 93 To 2022 NG
Cornelius Single Vineyard Syrah 2014 Rating 93 To 2022 $60 NG
Bellarine Peninsula Riesling 2016 Rating 92 To 2026 $27 NG
Jack & Jill Pinot Gris 2016 Rating 92 To 2019 $40
Cornelius Norfolk Vineyard Bellarine Peninsula Pinot Noir 2014 Rating 92 To 2022 $50 NG
Swan Bay Shiraz 2014 Rating 92 To 2021 $20 NG ✪
Swan Bay Pinot Noir 2015 Rating 91 To 2021 $20 NG ✪
Ferryman Mornington Peninsula Pinot Noir 2013 Rating 91 To 2023 $26
Late Harvest Riesling 2016 Rating 91 To 2025 $22 NG ✪
Late Harvest Riesling 2015 Rating 91 To 2025 $21 ✪
Sauvignon Blanc 2016 Rating 90 To 2019 $22 NG
Cornelius Sauvignon 2015 Rating 90 To 2023 $40 NG
Swan Bay Chardonnay 2015 Rating 90 To 2021 $20 NG ✪
Ferryman Mornington Peninsula Chardonnay 2013 Rating 90 To 2019 $26

Swan Bay Bellarine Peninsula Shiraz 2013 Rating 90 To 2021 $18 SC ✪
Hill Adelaide Cabernet Shiraz 2013 Rating 90 To 2021 $15 NO ✪

Scott ★★★★★

102 Main Street, Hahndorf, SA 5245 **Region** Adelaide Hills
T (08) 8388 7330 **www**.scottwines.com.au **Open** 1st w'end of the month 11–5
Winemaker Sam Scott **Est.** 2009 **Dozens** 4000
Sam Scott's great-grandfather worked in the cellar for Max Schubert, and passed his knowledge on to Sam's grandfather. It was he who gave Scott his early education. Sam enrolled in business at university, continuing the casual retailing with Booze Brothers he had started while at school, picking up the trail with Baily & Baily. Next came wine wholesale experience with David Ridge, selling iconic Australian and Italian wines to the trade. This led to a job with Michael Fragos at Tatachilla in 2000, and since then he has been the 'I've been everywhere man', working all over Australia and in California. He moved to Bird in Hand winery at the end of '06, where Andrew Nugent indicated that it was about time he took the plunge on his own account, and this he has done. Scott is a star in the making. Exports to the UK and Singapore.

🍷🍷🍷🍷🍷 **Piccadilly Valley Chardonnay 2014** The ultra-minimalist label gives no clue to what is a complex, well made chardonnay. It has layers of fruit, the accent on citrus zest and grapefruit, the acidity fine-boned and precise, the oak simply a member of the orchestra. Screwcap. 13% alc. **Rating** 95 **To** 2024 $40
Hope Forest Adelaide Hills Syrah 2015 Light, bright crimson-purple; this combines fragrance, finesse and elegance on the one hand, and fine-grained, savoury tannins on the other. Unfined and unfiltered, the only addition SO_2, leaving the red fruits intact. This is a world apart from Barossa Valley shiraz – only some will like both. Screwcap. 13.8% alc. **Rating** 95 **To** 2035 $40
The Denizen Adelaide Hills Chardonnay 2015 Grown on a south-facing slope, the wine is more luscious than its region and site would suggest, but retains brightness and shape thanks to citrus/grapefruit acidity. The bouquet, too, has a nice touch of reductive funk. All up, a very attractive wine at the price. Screwcap. 13% alc. **Rating** 94 **To** 2025 $26 ✪
La Prova Adelaide Hills Fiano 2016 From the Amadio vineyard at Kersbrook, super-tiny berries were crushed (usually whole-bunch pressed), fermented in barrel and tank. A floral bouquet and a decidedly complex palate in terms of both structure and fruit flavour, the latter from the tiny berries, the former from the barrel-ferment component. No wonder Scott is excited about the potential of the variety ex this vineyard. Screwcap. 13.5% alc. **Rating** 94 **To** 2021 $26 ✪

🍷🍷🍷🍷🍷 **La Prova Adelaide Hills Pinot Grigio 2016** Rating 93 To 2019 $25 ✪
La Prova Adelaide Hills Aglianico Rosato 2016 Rating 92 To 2018 $25 ✪
La Prova Rosso 2015 Rating 92 To 2020 $20 ✪
La Prova Bianco 2016 Rating 90 To 2017 $20 ✪

Seabrook Wines ★★★★

1122 Light Pass Road, Tanunda, SA 5352 **Region** Barossa Valley
T 0427 224 353 **www**.seabrookwines.com.au **Open** By appt
Winemaker Hamish Seabrook **Est.** 2004 **Dozens** 1200 **Vyds** 10ha
Hamish Seabrook is the youngest generation of a proud Melbourne wine family once involved in wholesale and retail distribution, and as leading show judges of their respective generations. Hamish, too, is a wine show judge, but was the first to venture into winemaking, working with Best's and Brown Brothers in Vic before moving to SA with wife Joanne. In 2008 Hamish set up his own winery, on the family property in Vine Vale, having previously made the wines at Dorrien Estate and elsewhere. Here they have shiraz (4.4ha), cabernet sauvignon (3.9ha), and mataro (1.8ha), and also continue to source small amounts of shiraz from the Barossa, Langhorne Creek and Pyrenees. Exports to Hong Kong and China.

ΨΨΨΨΨ **The Judge Eden Valley Riesling 2015** Pale straw-green; while the bouquet is relatively muted, the exotic palate has Meyer lemon and pink grapefruit flavours, and an emphatic finish. Slightly left field, but out to please. Screwcap. 12.5% alc. **Rating** 93 To 2027 $23 ✪

Lineage Langhorne Creek Shiraz 2014 An impressive wine by any standards, doubly so at its price. Good colour, the bouquet enticing and the palate overflowing with soused plum, blackberry and mocha oak, the tannins pillowy. Terrific value for current drinking. Screwcap. 14.5% alc. **Rating** 93 To 2018 $20 ✪

The Chairman Great Western Shiraz 2013 Includes 5% '14 Barossa Valley Shiraz. Speaks clearly of its place, the fruit flavours spinning blackberry, spice, cedar and licorice and earth into a coherent, medium-bodied whole, the line, length and balance all exemplary. Screwcap. 14.5% alc. **Rating** 93 To 2028 $33

See Saw Wines   ★★★★

Annangrove Park, 4 Nanami Lane, Cargo, NSW 2800 **Region** Orange
T (02) 6364 3118 **www**.seesawwine.com **Open** By appt
Winemaker Contract **Est.** 1995 **Dozens** 4000 **Vyds** 170ha
Justin and Pip Jarrett have established one of the largest vineyards in the Orange region. Varieties include chardonnay (51ha), sauvignon blanc (28ha), shiraz and merlot (22ha each), pinot gris (15ha), cabernet sauvignon (14ha), pinot noir (11ha), gewurztraminer and prosecco (3ha each), and marsanne (2ha). They also provide management and development services to growers of another 120ha in the region. A substantial part of the annual production is sold to others. One of the purchasers of Jarretts' grapes was See Saw, a venture owned by Hamish MacGowan (of Angus the Bull) and Andrew Margan. In 2014 Hamish and Andrew decided to concentrate on other wine activities, and the Jarretts were the logical purchasers. Exports to the UK.

ΨΨΨΨΨ **Orange Sauvignon Blanc 2015** See Saw has vineyards at 700, 800 and 900m, the grapes harvested between 12 Feb and 2 Mar; 5 hours' skin contact, cool-fermented in stainless steel. The result is a particularly intense and long palate awash with citrus and tropical fruit. The best from See Saw to date, and the wine has time to go. Screwcap. 12.6% alc. **Rating** 94 To 2018 $20 ✪

ΨΨΨΨΨ **Orange Sauvignon Blanc 2016 Rating** 90 To 2018 $25
Orange Pinot Gris 2016 Rating 90 To 2018 $25

Sentio Wines   ★★★★★

23 Priory Lane, Beechworth, Vic 3437 (postal) **Region** Various Vic
T 0433 773 229 **www**.sentiowines.com.au **Open** Not
Winemaker Chris Catlow **Est.** 2013 **Dozens** 800
This is a winery to watch. Owner/winemaker Chris Catlow was born (1982) and raised in Beechworth, and says, 'A passion for wine was inevitable.' He drew particular inspiration from Barry Morey of Sorrenberg, working there in his late teens. He completed a double-major in viticulture science and wine science at La Trobe University, working with Paringa Estate, Kooyong and Portsea Estate from 2006–13. Here Sandro Mosele led him to his fascination with the interaction between place and chardonnay, and he in turn worked with Benjamin Leroux in Burgundy during vintage '13, '14 and '16.

ΨΨΨΨΨ **Yarra Valley Chardonnay 2015** A captivating wine for its detail and precision: a mineral thread and lemon sorbet acidity drive this. Flinty, wet stones with a sprinkling of white pepper, a hint of lees just adding a layer to the otherwise tight palate. The fruit comes from the Lusatia Park vineyard, now owned by De Bortoli. Screwcap. 12.6% alc. **Rating** 95 To 2026 $43 JF

Beechworth Blanc 2015 A blend of 90% savagnin with 10% arneis. While subtly aromatic – white blossom, ginger powder and citrus – its claim to fame is texture. Well handled phenolics add shape and mingle with flavours of lemon barley water and lemon drops. Some creaminess and zesty acidity enhance complexity. Screwcap. 12.8% alc. **Rating** 95 To 2020 $30 JF ✪

Beechworth Shiraz 2015 Chris Catlow's father grows the fruit – a mere 450 vines on a cool, rocky site to produce just two barrels. It's long on. Perfectly ripe fruit, spice, oak seamlessly integrated, full-bodied, with the silkiest tannins and long on the finish. Screwcap. 13.5% alc. **Rating** 95 **To** 2027 $43 JF

Macedon Chardonnay 2015 This works off a linear theme – long and pure with the fruit in the citrus spectrum, grapefruit and pith, flinty, moreish, and yet it's restrained, gentle even: it's not ready to reveal all. It will flesh out in time but wow, what a drink now. Screwcap. 12.5% alc. **Rating** 94 **To** 2025 $43 JF

Beechworth Pinot Noir 2015 Ethereal aromatics and detailed tannin structure have been teased out of the fruit. It's full-bodied and there's a core of intensely sweet cherries and spiced rhubarb with cedary oak spice. The wine glides across the palate. Screwcap. 13% alc. **Rating** 94 **To** 2024 $38 JF

♟♟♟♟♟ **Beechworth Chardonnay 2015 Rating** 93 **To** 2023 $43 JF

Seppelt

36 Cemetery Road, Great Western, Vic 3377 **Region** Grampians
T (03) 5361 2239 **www.**seppelt.com.au **Open** 7 days 10–5
Winemaker Adam Carnaby **Est.** 1851 **Dozens** NFP **Vyds** 500ha

Seppelt once had dual, very different, claims to fame. The first was as Australia's foremost producer of both white and red sparkling wine, the former led by Salinger, the latter by Show Sparkling and Original Sparkling Shiraz. The second claim, even more relevant to the Seppelt of today, was based on the small-volume superb red wines made by Colin Preece from the 1930s through to the early '60s. These were ostensibly Great Western-sourced, but – as the laws of the time allowed – were often region, variety and vintage blends. Two of his labels (also of high quality) were Moyston and Chalambar, the latter recently revived. Preece would have been a child in a lolly shop if he'd had today's viticultural resources to draw on, and would be quick to recognise the commitment of the winemakers and viticulturists to the supreme quality of today's portfolio. Ararat businessman Danile Ahchow has leased the cellar door and surrounds, including the underground drives. Exports to the UK, Europe and NZ.

♟♟♟♟♟ **Drumborg Vineyard Riesling 2016** This has it all, bringing finesse and luxuriant varietal character onto the table at the first moment of the bouquet and of the palate. It is literally loaded with power in the fashion of a fine, dry Rheingau riesling. It is utterly irresistible now, and will become even more so with extended cellaring. Screwcap. 11% alc. **Rating** 97 **To** 2036 $40 ✪

Show Sparkling Limited Release Shiraz 2007 Grand longevity is the key to this style, and even on release at a decade of age (8 years of which were spent on lees) the fruit of the Seppelt Great Western vineyard itself demands a long time yet to fully blossom. Enticingly poised, effortless, medium-bodied black cherry liqueur, black plum and blackberry fruit are here aplenty, framed in high cocoa dark chocolate, but the real distinction of this cuvee lies in its impeccably mineral, powder-fine tannins. Crown seal. 13% alc. **Rating** 97 **To** 2047 $100 TS ✪

♟♟♟♟♟ **Drumborg Vineyard Henty Pinot Noir 2015** Brilliant, vibrant crimson-purple, and an equally vibrant and fragrant bouquet; the palate is long, verging on luscious, with red fruits and spices rampant. Ticks all the boxes, as they say, and does so with gusto. While its balance is so good, there is every reason for having a bottle tonight, as long as you keep a bottle for 10 years hence. Screwcap. 12.5% alc. **Rating** 96 **To** 2027 $45 ✪

Great Western Riesling 2016 From the estate vineyard planted in '76, early-picked to retain natural balance/acidity – and succeeding. I'm mystified about the price compared to $40 for the premium Leo Buring Rieslings. Bright and juicy, it has great life, and history shows just how well this will age. Screwcap. 10.5% alc. **Rating** 95 **To** 2031 $27 ✪

Jaluka Henty Chardonnay 2016 Even though tasted in unavoidably warm conditions, came through with flying colours. It has a vibrancy and intensity that brings you up with a jolt, but you settle down quickly, enjoying the typical white peach/pink grapefruit flavour spectrum. Screwcap. 12.5% alc. **Rating** 95 **To** 2031 $27

Drumborg Vineyard Henty Chardonnay 2015 Fermented in large French oak vessels which have left minimal impact on the wine, which is a panegyric to its unsweetened lemony acidity and the consequent mouthwatering lipsmacking flavours and mouthfeel. Those who like tight, flinty chardonnay will love this potentially long-lived example. Screwcap. 12.5% alc. **Rating** 95 **To** 2039 $40

Mount Ida Heathcote Shiraz 2015 Matured in French barriques, some old, some new, the latter obvious. A strong tannin structure achieved by extended maceration on skins takes the hands of the oak and blackberry fruits in a wine with a pure-bred bloodline. Screwcap. 14.5% alc. **Rating** 95 **To** 2040 $55

Chalambar Grampians Heathcote Shiraz 2015 Spicy, peppery aromas upfront which is likely the cooler Grampians component in play. The fruit is ripe, with the impression of dark berries and plums, but overall there's a savoury, restrained feel. Beautifully textured, supple and fine, but built on a firm base. The cellar awaits. Screwcap. 14% alc. **Rating** 95 **To** 2035 $27 SC ○

Drumborg Vineyard Pinot Meunier 2015 Rating 94 **To** 2025 $36

Salinger Henty Methode Traditionelle Vintage Cuvee 2013 Rating 94 **To** 2018 $30 TS ○

🍷🍷🍷🍷🍷 **Original Sparkling Shiraz 2014 Rating** 92 **To** 2022 $27 TS

The Victorians Heathcote Shiraz 2014 Rating 91 **To** 2029 $15 ○

NV Salinger Premium Cuvee Rating 91 **To** 2017 $25 TS

Seppeltsfield   ★★★★★

Seppeltsfield Road, Seppeltsfield via Nuriootpa, SA 5355 **Region** Barossa Valley
T (08) 8568 6200 **www.**seppeltsfield.com.au **Open** 7 days 10.30–5
Winemaker Fiona Donald **Est.** 1851 **Dozens** 10000 **Vyds** 100ha

This historic Seppelt property and its treasure trove of fortified wines dating back to 1878 was purchased by Janet Holmes à Court, Greg Paramor and Kilikanoon Wines in 2007, from Foster's Wine Estates (now Treasury Wine Estates). Foster's kept the Seppelt brand for table and sparkling wines, mostly produced at Great Western, Vic (see separate entry). In '09 Warren Randall (ex sparkling winemaker for Seppelt at Great Western in the 1980s) acquired 50% of Seppeltsfield and became Managing Director. In February '13, Randall increased his shareholding in Seppeltsfield to over 90%. The change also marks a further commitment to the making of table wine as well as more focused marketing of the fortified wines. On 31 March '17 Seppeltsfield acquired the Ryecroft winery (with a production capacity of around 30000 tonnes) from TWE, together with 40ha of adjoining vineyard and water licences. Winetitles Daily Wine News reported that the acquisition would increase Seppeltsfield's collective ownership of SA vineyards to a little over 2300ha. Exports to Hong Kong and China.

🍷🍷🍷🍷🍷 **100 Year Old Para Liqueur 1917** The consistency is not far short of treacle, pouring reluctantly from the bottle to the glass, and even more reluctantly from the glass into the mouth, which is already quivering like a bird dog after swirling the glass to savour the toweringly rich and complex bouquet. The aromas are a distillation of every spice you have ever encountered, whether on its own, mixed with others, or in a fruit compote, or a Christmas cake or pudding. An electric current trickles into the mouth along with the wine when you can't bear waiting any longer before taking your first sip, and your senses spin. 100ml. Cork. 21.4% alc. **Rating** 100 $700

Vintage Tawny Para Liqueur 1987 This gives a good picture of the way the 100 Year Old Para looked when it was 30yo. Its colour is full-on tawny-brick, the rim grading towards olive, the intensity and complexity of the bouquet catching you unawares, if you've not previously experienced a barrel-aged wine of this stature. Warm spices and melted toffee one starting point, but expanding rapidly into an Aladdin's Cave of textures, flavours and yet more spices than you have ever previously enountered. Cork. 20% alc. **Rating** 97 $120 ○

🍷🍷🍷🍷🍷 **Barossa Grenache 2016** This has exceptional richness and succulence to its dark, brooding fruits and savoury tannins. The estate vineyard is exceptional, the wine made in honour of the late wine writer Mark Shield. Just as he was a rare

and wonderful character, so was the wine then, and so (albeit by a different team)
is this wine. Screwcap. 14.0% alc. Rating 96 To 2031 $50 ●

Para Tawny 1996 Well into tawny colour, with only a faint twitch of red,
powerful and intense, said on the back label to be a reflection of the growing
conditions during the season, and a reflection of a year long gone. It's already
a complete wine, rancio hard at work introducing an edge that cuts across the
intense, layered sweetness of the palate. These Seppeltsfield tawnies are all rare
beasts. Screwcap. 19.7% alc. **Rating** 96 $88

Barossa Shiraz 2015 This was made in the winery built in 1888, 120 years
ahead of its time, built into the slope of a long hill obviating the need of pumps
in most of the vinification. A high quality wine, matured in French oak, with the
thumbprint of the Barossa Valley deeply imprinted on it. Screwcap. 14.8% alc.
Rating 95 To 2035 $38

♟♟♟♟♟ **Barossa Vermentino 2016 Rating** 91 To 2020 $22 ●

Serafino Wines   ★★★★★

Kangarilla Road, McLaren Vale, SA 5171 **Region** McLaren Vale
T (08) 8323 0157 **www.**serafinowines.com.au **Open** Mon–Fri 10–4.30, w'ends 10–4.30
Winemaker Charles Whish **Est.** 2000 **Dozens** 30 000 **Vyds** 100ha
After the sale of Maglieri Wines to Beringer Blass in 1998, Maglieri founder Serafino (Steve)
Maglieri acquired the McLarens on the Lake complex originally established by Andrew Garrett.
The operation draws upon 40ha each of shiraz and cabernet sauvignon, 7ha of chardonnay, 2ha
each of merlot, semillon, barbera, nebbiolo and sangiovese, and 1ha of grenache. Part of the
grape production is sold. Serafino Wines has won a number of major trophies in Australia and
the UK. Exports to the UK, the US, Canada, Hong Kong, Malaysia and NZ.

♟♟♟♟♟ **Terremoto Single Vineyard McLaren Vale Syrah 2014** Night-harvested,
destemmed, 3 days cold soak, open-fermented with cultured yeast, pumped over
twice daily, matured for 8 months in used French oak. Fascinating – when you
read the vinification of this and Sharktooth, you'd expect the latter to wear the
big price tag. The moment you taste this wine it all makes sense, for it lances the
mouth with the vibrancy and intensity of the fruit, shoot-thinning providing
part of the answer. As well as intensity, it has purity and vibrancy, all far removed
from normal expectations of McLaren Vale (and the vintage). Screwcap. 14.5% alc.
Rating 97 To 2039 $120 ●

♟♟♟♟♟ **McLaren Vale Shiraz 2015** Deep, bright purple; the bouquet and medium to
full-bodied palate sing loud and clear from the same page, with blackberry and
plum fruit skilfully enshrined in fine, ripe tannins, plus a nudge of oak. There is
a harmony, a completeness, to the wine that means it is totally open-ended, its
drinking window without borders. Screwcap. 14% alc. **Rating** 96 To 2040 $28 ●

Malpas Vineyard McLaren Vale Shiraz 2015 Deep crimson-purple; all of the
focus is on the fruit and its birthplace, precisely fulfilling its place in the region's
Scarce Earth program designed to pinpoint the characteristics of the multitude
of micro-terroirs found in the region. This is an elegant, spicy wine with marked
freshness to the fruit, the relative absence of dark chocolate a positive. Screwcap.
14.5% alc. **Rating** 95 To 2035 $45

Malpas Vineyard McLaren Vale Shiraz 2014 Deep crimson-purple;
archetypal medium to full-bodied McLaren Vale shiraz, bitter chocolate advertising
its presence from the first whiff through to the luxuriant black fruits of the finish
and aftertaste, the intervening dots all neatly joined. Impossible to fault. Screwcap.
14.5% alc. **Rating** 95 To 2034 $45

Sharktooth McLaren Vale Shiraz 2014 Machine-harvested, wild-yeast
fermented in open and closed fermenters, 7 days on skins, 30% given 14 days post-
ferment maceration, the fermentation completed in barrel and tank, matured for
24 months in new (50% French and 10% American) and used oak. While it's very
much of its variety and place, the wine has real elegance and length; black cherry
and plum lead the fruit brigade, spice and dark chocolate following, finishing with

cedary French oak. A wine made for drinking, not sipping. Screwcap. 14.5% alc.
Rating 95 **To** 2034 $70

Reserve McLaren Vale Grenache 2015 Light colour even in the context of
grenache; the riposte comes when you smell and taste the wine. It has the red
fruits to nail its variety to the mast, but it's more than that: it has purity and refined
balance, its freshness carefully retained during relatively brief maturation. Screwcap.
14.5% alc. **Rating** 95 **To** 2029 $40

🍷🍷🍷🍷🍷 **Sharktooth Wild Ferment McLaren Vale Chardonnay 2015** Rating 93
To 2022 $40

Sorrento McLaren Vale Shiraz 2015 Rating 91 To 2021 $20 ❂
Magnitude McLaren Vale Shiraz 2013 Rating 91 To 2029 $40
**BDX McLaren Vale Cabernet Sauvignon Cabernet Franc Carmenere
Merlot 2015** Rating 91 To 2025 $28
Bellissimo Pinot Grigio 2016 Rating 90 To 2017 $20 ❂
Bellissimo Fiano 2016 Rating 90 To 2020 $20 ❂
GSM McLaren Vale Grenache Shiraz Mataro 2015 Rating 90 To 2023 $28

Seraph's Crossing   ★★★★

PO Box 5753, Clare, SA 5453 **Region** Clare Valley
T 0412 132 549 **Open** Not
Winemaker Harry Dickinson **Est.** 2006 **Dozens** 450 **Vyds** 5ha
In a moment of enlightened madness, Harry Dickinson gave up his career as a lawyer in
a major London law firm to work in the wine industry. He helped run the International
Wine Challenge for three years, followed by stints with various wine retailers, and some PR
work for the German Wine Information Service. He worked his first vintage in Australia at
Hardys Tintara winery in 1997 with Stephen Pannell and Larry Cherubino; their work with
open fermenters, basket presses, and their winemaking philosophy, made a huge impression.
Following a period as a wine retailer in North Adelaide, he returned to winery work in 1999,
in various wineries in the Clare Valley, where he and wife Chan bought a 75ha property. They
restored the 1880s house on the property, and the vineyards have been extended from the
original 1ha to now comprise shiraz (2ha), grenache, mourvedre and zinfandel (1ha each).
Exports to the UK, the US and Ireland.

🍷🍷🍷🍷 **Seraph's Clare Valley Shiraz 2012** A real concentration about the bouquet,
reminiscent of pressed dried fruit packs and nougat, but remarkably, some freshness
as well. Elixir-like on the palate, the fruit grappling with the tannin, and no clear
winner. Screwcap. 16.4% alc. **Rating** 93 **To** 2025 $40 SC

Venus and Mars Clare Valley Shiraz 2012 Made unconventionally, and
difficult to judge within conventional parameters. 40% new oak and aged on lees
for 52 months. No racking, no fining, no filtration. There are elements here which
would normally be called winemaking faults, but to see the bigger picture, it has
imposing character, and a sense of highly individual identity. The score is arbitrary.
Screwcap. 15.7% alc. **Rating** 90 **To** 2022 $34 SC

Serrat   ★★★★★

PO Box 478, Yarra Glen, Vic 3775 **Region** Yarra Valley
T (03) 9730 1439 **www.serrat.com.au** **Open** Not
Winemaker Tom Carson **Est.** 2001 **Dozens** 1000 **Vyds** 2.95ha
Serrat is the family business of Tom Carson (after a 12-year reign at Yering Station, now
running Yabby Lake and Heathcote Estate for the Kirby family) and wife Nadege Suné. They
have close-planted (at 8800 vines per hectare) 0.8ha each of pinot noir and chardonnay, 0.4ha
of shiraz, and a sprinkling of viognier. Most recent has been the establishment of an esoteric
mix of 0.1ha each of malbec, nebbiolo, barbera and grenache. As well as being a consummate
winemaker, Tom has one of the best palates in Australia, and a deep understanding of the
fine wines of the world, which he and Nadege drink at every opportunity (when they aren't
drinking Serrat). Viticulture and winemaking hit new heights with the 2014 Yarra Valley

Shiraz Viognier named *Wine Companion* 2016 Wine of the Year (from a field of 8863 wines). Exports to Singapore and Hong Kong.

🍷🍷🍷🍷🍷 **Yarra Valley Shiraz Viognier 2016** Brightly coloured and extremely expressive on the bouquet, and no less so on the palate; red berries and spices are inextricably bonded by fine, supple tannins. Has exemplary line, length and balance, and has made light of the challenges of the vintage. As ever, will sell in a trice at this price. Screwcap. 13.5% alc. **Rating** 97 **To** 2031 $42 ✪

🍷🍷🍷🍷🍷 **Yarra Valley Chardonnay 2016** Precision winemaking; classic Yarra Valley chardonnay flavours, very long, and led by white peach with a kiss of oak, 20% new exactly balanced by the fruit; grapefruit haunts the backdrop and aftertaste. Screwcap. 12.5% alc. **Rating** 96 **To** 2028 $42 ✪
Yarra Valley Pinot Noir 2016 Deep colour; the '16 Yarra Valley pinots don't lack power and depth: the fruits are purple and black rather than red, and reluctantly reveal their secrets. But enough escapes to establish its balance and length, thus ensuring that it will open up with time in bottle (3+ years) and go on from there. Screwcap. 13.5% alc. **Rating** 95 **To** 2029 $42
Yarra Valley Grenache Noir 2016 Brilliantly clear crimson, and equally clear rose petal, spice and red berry aromas, the positively crisp palate with a reprise of the bouquet. Begs to be consumed tonight. Screwcap. 13.5% alc. **Rating** 95 **To** 2021 $42

Sevenhill Cellars ★★★★★

111c College Road, Sevenhill, SA 5453 **Region** Clare Valley
T (08) 8843 5900 **www**.sevenhill.com.au **Open** 7 days 10–5
Winemaker Liz Heidenreich, Brother John May **Est.** 1851 **Dozens** 25 000 **Vyds** 95.8ha
One of the historical treasures of Australia; the oft-photographed stone wine cellars are the oldest in the Clare Valley, and winemaking remains an enterprise within the Jesuit Province of Australia. All the wines reflect the estate-grown grapes from old vines. Notwithstanding the difficult economic times, Sevenhill Cellars has increased its vineyard holdings from 74ha to 95ha, and, naturally, production has risen. Exports to the UK, Switzerland, Indonesia, Malaysia, Vietnam, Japan, Hong Kong and Taiwan.

🍷🍷🍷🍷🍷 **Inigo Clare Valley Riesling 2016** Has picked up some colour, but is bright, with no cause for concern; there is a lot of high quality wine here at the price, the floral citrus bouquet starting the show. It's bone dry, but there is a wealth of lime juice, pith and zest backed by crunchy acidity. Outstanding value. Screwcap. 10.5% alc. **Rating** 95 **To** 2030 $22 ✪
St Francis Xavier Single Vineyard Riesling 2016 More refined and elegant than its Inigo sibling, and richly deserves time in bottle to build on the picture-perfect base it already has. Demure lime and Granny Smith apple is swathed in fine shards of acidity that prolong the finish and aftertaste – where the quality of the wine shines. Screwcap. 11% alc. **Rating** 95 **To** 2031 $35 ✪
St Ignatius 2014 52% cabernet sauvignon, 25% merlot, 14% malbec and 9% cabernet franc. Has more elegance than most of Sevenhill Cellars' normally robust full-bodied reds, but nonetheless has a full boat of purple and black fruits, slightly sandy tannins and cedary oak. Its undoubted balance will serve it well in the years to come. Screwcap. 14.5% alc. **Rating** 94 **To** 2029 $45
Inigo Clare Valley Barbera 2014 All the levers were pulled at the right time with this wine, its faintly spicy black cherry fruit sitting comfortably in a settee of compatible tannins and fresh acidity. Elegance and grace are the markers of a very good barbera. Screwcap. 14% alc. **Rating** 94 **To** 2034 $28 ✪

🍷🍷🍷🍷🍷 **Inigo Clare Valley Cabernet Sauvignon 2014 Rating** 90 **To** 2029 $28

Seville Estate ★★★★★

65 Linwood Road, Seville, Vic 3139 **Region** Yarra Valley
T (03) 5964 2622 **www.sevilleestate.com.au Open** 7 days 10–5
Winemaker Dylan McMahon **Est.** 1972 **Dozens** 700 **Vyds** 8.08ha

Brokenwood acquired Seville Estate in 1997 from the founding ownership of Dr Peter and Margaret McMahon. In 2005 ownership passed to Graeme and Margaret Van Der Meulen, who retained the services of Dylan McMahon as winemaker. Graeme and Margaret's divorce led to yet another sale, this time to a wealthy Chinese investor (with a chain of wine shops in China) who bought the business outright in '16. Despite these changes in ownership, the quality of the wines has never been higher. Dylan McMahon's knowledge and skills provides continuity, which is helped by Graeme Van Der Meulen remaining as General Manager.

⟡⟡⟡⟡⟡ Dr McMahon Yarra Valley Shiraz 2014 It's not about throwing everything at this wine; it's about the inherent quality. This is in mighty good form. Full-bodied, powerful tannin structure with a depth of flavour from the dark fruit, spice, pepper and more. Looks fabulous now, with those patient better rewarded. Screwcap. 13% alc. **Rating** 97 **To** 2034 $125 JF ✪

⟡⟡⟡⟡⟡ Yarra Valley Chardonnay 2016 A wine of precision, with everything perfectly placed, from the citrus and white stone-fruit profile to the oak integration with ginger and wood spices. Finally the leesy flavours add a dash of creaminess to the palate. Plus there's exceptional length. Screwcap. 13% alc. **Rating** 96 **To** 2028 $36 JF ✪

Reserve Yarra Valley Chardonnay 2016 There is definitely an added layer of complexity and flavour here. A touch more stone fruit and spice to the fore, more length and finesse, flinty with superfine acidity. Stonkingly good. Screwcap. 13.5% alc. **Rating** 96 **To** 2028 $70 JF ✪

Old Vine Reserve Yarra Valley Shiraz 2015 The first part of the seduction is the dark purple colour, then the aromas of black cherries, plums, licorice, black pepper and roasted hazelnuts unfurl on the palate. Vibrant acidity, beautifully shaped ripe tannins and a finish that will leave you breathless. Screwcap. 13% alc. **Rating** 96 **To** 2030 $70 JF ✪

Old Vine Reserve Yarra Valley Cabernet Sauvignon 2015 A beautiful purple-red hue, heady aromas of violets, roses, blackberries and currants, all given an edge with oak spice. But it is the medium-bodied palate that'll cause the heart to miss a beat – velvety, glossy with silky tannins and with a certain power woven in. Bright acidity keeps this lively and it promises a long future. What a wine. Screwcap. 13% alc. **Rating** 96 **To** 2040 $70 JF ✪

Yarra Valley Riesling 2016 Wild yeast ferment in used French oak puncheons for Yarra Valley riesling – you don't see that every day. Dylan McMahon has nailed it. Textural, vibrant, loaded with spiced lemon and ginger, plus fine acidity and a lemon barley water freshness. Screwcap. 13% alc. **Rating** 95 **To** 2026 $36 JF

Old Vine Reserve Yarra Valley Pinot Noir 2016 Elegance comes through this vintage, while old vines offer beautiful fragrance and restrained flavours of red cherries and light, woody spices. Builds on the palate; finely tuned, svelte tannins and a long, persistent finish. Screwcap. 13.5% alc. **Rating** 95 **To** 2028 $70 JF

Yarra Valley Shiraz 2015 It has all the appeal and vibrancy of youth with its dark red fruit, the lifted fragrance from 20% whole bunches in the ferment, the pepper, the gum leaves and the savoury tone. It's medium-bodied, with ripe, finely shaped tannins and raspberry-fresh acidity. Youth will give way to a more complex wine in a few years. That's life. Screwcap. 13% alc. **Rating** 95 **To** 2026 $36 JF

Yarra Valley Pinot Noir 2016 This floats along, ethereal, all subtle spice with cherries, wild strawberries in its light frame plus fine, lacy tannins and fresh acidity. Its elegance is a drawcard. Screwcap. 13% alc. **Rating** 94 **To** 2025 $36 JF

⟡⟡⟡⟡⟡ The Barber Yarra Valley Chardonnay 2016 Rating 92 **To** 2021 $24 JF ✪
The Barber Yarra Valley Shiraz 2015 Rating 91 **To** 2021 $24 JF
The Barber Yarra Valley Rose 2016 Rating 90 **To** 2019 $24 JF
The Barber Yarra Valley Pinot Noir 2016 Rating 90 **To** 2020 $24 JF

Seville Hill

8 Paynes Road, Seville, Vic 3139 **Region** Yarra Valley
T (03) 5964 3284 **www**.sevillehill.com.au **Open** 7 days 10–5
Winemaker Dominic Bucci, John D'Aloisio **Est.** 1991 **Dozens** 4000 **Vyds** 6ha
John and Josie D'Aloisio have had a long-term involvement in the agricultural industry, which
ultimately led to the establishment of Seville Hill in 1991. Plantings of cabernet sauvignon
replaced the old apple and cherry orchard on the site. A small winery was established, with
long-term friend Dominic Bucci and John D'Aloisio making the wines. In 2011 1ha of the
original 6ha was grafted over to nebbiolo, barbera, sangiovese and tempranillo. John and Josie's
sons (Christopher, Jason and Charles) are also involved in all aspects of the business.

Yarra Valley Cabernet Sauvignon 2012 Yarra's stamp of green bean plies its
verdant note, along with dried sage, mulch and tobacco – all herbal pummel. The
tannins are just on the better side of drying; the oak arches over all. I wouldn't
hold on to this indefinitely. Cork. 14% alc. **Rating** 91 **To** 2020 $30 NG

Reserve Yarra Valley Chardonnay 2015 Rating 89 **To** 2021 $30 NG

Sew & Sew Wines

PO Box 1924, McLaren Flat, SA 5171 **Region** Adelaide Hills
T 0419 804 345 **www**.sewandsewwines.com.au **Open** Not
Winemaker Jodie Armstrong **Est.** 2004 **Dozens** 630
Co-owner and winemaker Jodie Armstrong works as a viticulturist by day, consulting to
vineyards in the Adelaide Hills and McLaren Vale, at night making small amounts of wine.
Grapes are chosen from the vineyards that Jodie manages, and she makes the wines in garagiste
facilities in the Adelaide Hills and McLaren Vale, with the support of local oenological talent
and her Sydney-based partner Andrew Mason. Exports to Denmark.

Contour Series Adelaide Hills Syrah 2015 Lovely aromatics on the bouquet,
with spicy cool climate characters of black fruit, licorice and white pepper, along
with a dusting of mocha oak. Supple and seamless, with depth and length of
flavour perfectly integrated, and tannin just so. Screwcap. 13.7% alc. **Rating** 94
To 2027 $39 SC

Contour Series Adelaide Hills Chardonnay 2016 Rating 93 **To** 2022
$35 SC
Sashiko Series Adelaide Hills Fiano 2016 Rating 92 **To** 2019 $25 SC ✪
Sashiko Series McLaren Vale Shiraz 2015 Rating 92 **To** 2025 $25 SC ✪
Contour Series Adelaide Hills Pinot Noir 2015 Rating 91 **To** 2023 $35 SC

Shadowfax

K Road, Werribee, Vic 3030 **Region** Geelong
T (03) 9731 4420 **www**.shadowfax.com.au **Open** 7 days 11–5
Winemaker Matt Harrop **Est.** 2000 **Dozens** 15 000
Shadowfax is part of an awesome development at Werribee Park, a mere 20 minutes from
Melbourne. The truly striking winery, designed by Wood Marsh Architects and built in 2000,
is adjacent to the extraordinary private home built in the 1880s by the Chirnside family and
known as The Mansion. It was then the centrepiece of a 40 000ha pastoral empire, and the
appropriately magnificent gardens were part of the reason for the property being acquired by
Parks Victoria in the early 1970s. The Mansion is now The Mansion Hotel, with 92 rooms
and suites. Exports to the UK, Japan, NZ and Singapore.

Glenfern Chardonnay 2015 Matured for 10 months on lees. A super-intense
wine shaped first and foremost by the climate in which the grapes are grown.
There is a broad spectrum of stone fruit and citrus expanding past the usual
suspects of white peach and grapefruit; the length and balance are faultless.
Screwcap. 13% alc. **Rating** 96 **To** 2030 $50 ✪

Geelong Chardonnay 2016 Matured on lees in French hogsheads (30% new) for 8 months. Combines elegance, balance and intensity with very good complexity, oak barely intrudes in the flavour frame, but has provided the all-important texture. Screwcap. 13% alc. **Rating** 95 **To** 2026 $32 ✪

Macedon Ranges Chardonnay 2015 Matured on lees in new and used hogsheads for 12 months. Gleaming straw-green; this is a wine built around a framework of crisp, minerally acidity that underpins the white peach, Granny Smith apple and grapefruit flavours; such new oak as was used now absorbed into the fabric of the wine. Screwcap. 13% alc. **Rating** 95 **To** 2027 $35 ✪

Little Hampton Pinot Noir 2015 A high quality estate-grown pinot, with great intensity and drive to its varietal expression. Satsuma plum is given depth and complexity by the inclusion of 50% whole bunches in the open ferment and 27 days on skins. Screwcap. 13% alc. **Rating** 95 **To** 2028 $60

Macedon Ranges Pinot Gris 2015 Wild yeast fermentation and maturation in used French hogsheads has created a great deal out of nothing; aromas of spice, pear and baked apple introduce a layered palate full of flavour and character. There's no compelling need to cellar it, but it could gain even greater richness and interest than it has now. Screwcap. 13% alc. **Rating** 94 **To** 2022 $24 ✪

Port Phillip Heathcote Shiraz 2015 Spices are woven through plum and blackberry fruit on the medium-bodied palate; stretches out impressively on the finish and aftertaste on the back of savoury tannins. Screwcap. 13.5% alc. **Rating** 94 **To** 2029 $25 ✪

ŢŢŢŢ♀ **Macedon Ranges Pinot Gris 2016 Rating** 93 **To** 2020 $30
Macedon Ranges Pinot Noir 2015 Rating 93 **To** 2025 $35
Minnow Rose 2016 Rating 92 **To** 2018 $25 ✪
Geelong Pinot Noir 2016 Rating 90 **To** 2023 $32

Sharmans   ★★★★☆

175 Glenwood Road, Relbia, Tas 7258 **Region** Northern Tasmania
T (03) 6343 0773 **www.**sharmanswines.com.au **Open** W'ends 11–5 Mar–May & Sept
Winemaker Jeremy Dineen, Ockie Myburgh **Est.** 1986 **Dozens** 2200 **Vyds** 7ha
When Mike Sharman planted the first vines at Relbia in 1986, he was the pioneer of the region, and he did so in the face of a widespread belief that it was too far inland, and frost-prone. He proved the doomsayers wrong, helped by the slope of the vineyard draining cold air away from the vines. In 2012 the property was acquired by Dr Ian and Melissa Murrell and Matt and Miranda Creak. Both Mike and his viticulturist, Bill Rayner, continue to help with the management of the vineyard, with direction from Matt. An additional 3.5ha of vines were planted, the larger plantings being 2.3ha of pinot noir and 1ha each of chardonnay and pinot gris; the balance is made up of smaller plantings of riesling, sauvignon blanc, cabernet sauvignon, merlot, shiraz, muscat, saperavi and dornfelder – a mixed grill if ever there was one.

ŢŢŢŢŢ **Pinot Noir 2014** Excellent hue and depth; the voluminous cherry/plum bouquet is replicated on the voluptuous palate, full to the brim with pinot fruit, persistent fine tannins and quality French oak. A thunderous answer to Central Otago's biggest and best. Screwcap. 14% alc. **Rating** 95 **To** 2030 $35 ✪

ŢŢŢŢ♀ **Chardonnay 2014 Rating** 93 **To** 2021 $35
Merlot 2014 Rating 92 **To** 2029 $35

Shaw + Smith   ★★★★★

136 Jones Road, Balhannah, SA 5242 **Region** Adelaide Hills
T (08) 8398 0500 **www.**shawandsmith.com **Open** 7 days 11–5
Winemaker Martin Shaw, Adam Wadewitz **Est.** 1989 **Dozens** NFP **Vyds** 80.9ha
Cousins Martin Shaw and Michael Hill Smith MW already had unbeatable experience when they founded Shaw + Smith as a virtual winery in 1989. In '99 Martin and Michael purchased the 36ha Balhannah property, building the superbly designed winery in 2000 and planting more sauvignon blanc, shiraz, pinot noir and riesling. It is here that visitors can taste the wines in appropriately beautiful surroundings. Exports to all major markets.

ŸŸŸŸŸ Lenswood Adelaide Hills Chardonnay 2015 Whole-bunch pressed to new and used French puncheons for fermentation and 10 months' maturation. The bright quartz-green colour signals a wine of exceptional intensity and purity, pink grapefruit embracing white peach, oak watching on from the sideline. A truly great chardonnay. Screwcap. 13% alc. **Rating** 98 **To** 2028 $85 ○

M3 Adelaide Hills Chardonnay 2015 M3 now comes from selected sites over the Adelaide Hills, not from the vineyard previously called M3. Pale straw-green; it may be autosuggestion, but this has great freshness, vibrancy and finesse, the flavours pitched halfway between white peach/stone fruit on the one hand, grapefruit/citrus on the other. Obviously fermented in French oak, but is not obviously oaky. Screwcap. 13% alc. **Rating** 97 **To** 2023 $46 ○

Adelaide Hills Shiraz 2015 The colour is bright, the bouquet full of red fruits, darker fruit notes and delicious pepper and spice nuances. These characters flow through to the medium-bodied palate of Shaw + Smith's most consistently outstanding wine, the '15 vintage making it seem so easy. Screwcap. 14.5% alc. **Rating** 97 **To** 2030 $46 ○

Balhannah Vineyard Adelaide Hills Shiraz 2015 Matured in French puncheons for 14 months, with a further 14 months in bottle before release. This is an exercise in power, bay leaf staring down any attempt to add red fruits, the tannins of the same ilk, ditto oak. Despite the power, the balance and synergy of the components is undeniable. Screwcap. 14% alc. **Rating** 97 **To** 2035 $85 ○

Balhannah Vineyard Adelaide Hills Shiraz 2014 A joyously lively cool-grown shiraz. The bouquet is particularly fragrant and fruit-driven, the medium-bodied palate laden with black cherry, spice, licorice and pepper. Its aftertaste is exceptional, underlining the length and quality of the wine. Screwcap. 14.5% alc. **Rating** 97 **To** 2039 $85 ○

ŸŸŸŸŸ Adelaide Hills Sauvignon Blanc 2016 Long accepted as the benchmark for Adelaide Hills sauvignon blanc, and you don't have to go past the bouquet to figure out why: just about every tropical fruit you can imagine is on display, from custard apple at one extreme, kiwi fruit and green pineapple at the other. It all adds up to a complete wine made to be enjoyed until the queue forms for the next release. Screwcap. 12% alc. **Rating** 95 **To** 2017 $26 ○

Adelaide Hills Pinot Noir 2015 Light crimson; the bouquet is fragrant and floral with red fruit, spice and forest notes, the palate building on the scaffold of the bouquet. Here the accent is on excellent texture and length replaying the cherry fruit held in a savoury clasp. Screwcap. 12.5% alc. **Rating** 95 **To** 2020 $46

Adelaide Hills Riesling 2016 Screwcap. 12% alc. **Rating** 94 **To** 2030 $30 ○

Shaw Family Vintners ★★★★★

Myrtle Grove Road, Currency Creek, SA 5214 **Region** Currency Creek/McLaren Vale
T (08) 8555 4215 **www**.shawfamilyvintners.com **Open** 7 days 10–5
Winemaker John Loxton **Est.** 2001 **Dozens** 100 000 **Vyds** 461ha
Richard and Marie Shaw ventured into the wine industry by planting shiraz in the early 1970s at McLaren Flat. They still have the original vineyards, and during the Vine Pull Scheme of the '80s saved several neighbours' valuable old shiraz and grenache. Their three sons are also involved in the family business. Extensive vineyards are now held in Currency Creek (350ha) and McLaren Vale (64ha), with a modern winery in Currency Creek. RMS is the flagship release, named in honour of founder Richard Morton Shaw. In April '17 the winery, vineyards, stock and brands were purchased by Casella Family Brands. Exports to the UK, the US, Canada, Fiji, NZ and China.

ŸŸŸŸŸ RMS Limited Release McLaren Vale Cabernet Sauvignon 2013 The bright colour announces an exceedingly well made cabernet with wonderfully fresh fruit coming from 65yo vines, cassis to the fore, supple tannins and precisely calibrated French oak all making positive contributions without tripping over each other. Cork. 14.5% alc. **Rating** 95 **To** 2033 $60

Ballast Stone RMS McLaren Vale Cabernet Sauvignon 2004 Has retained very good depth of colour, and has equally well dismissed the last 12+ years. Black fruits, cedar and dark chocolate fill the palate, the velvety tannins perfectly weighted. Won a string of silver medals in '08, but not shown since. Cork. 14.5% alc. **Rating** 95 **To** 2029 $60

The Figurehead Shiraz 2012 Yes, the wine is ultra-full-bodied, but yes, it's balanced by its fruit, its tannins and its oak, all firing at once, with maximum power. Some will prostrate themselves at the foot of the wine, lost in admiration, others may end up in the same position in fear of their lives (or palates). Cork. 15.5% alc. **Rating** 94 **To** 2042 $100

Ballast Stone Emetior McLaren Vale Shiraz 2009 Doesn't show its age, the colour still deep, with no transition to brick; it has all manner of full-bodied, earthy, briary, savoury and spicy/peppery notes – and no alcohol-induced heat. It's only on the finish that McLaren Vale chocolate appears. Cork. 15% alc. **Rating** 94 **To** 2029 $60

ᵞᵞᵞᵞ   **Moonraker McLaren Vale Merlot 2016** Rating 89 To 2023 $29
Monster Pitch Cabernet Sauvignon 2016 Rating 89 To 2026 $29
The Back-up Plan Petit Verdot 2014 Rating 89 To 2029 $50

Shaw Vineyard Estate   ★★★★

34 Isabel Drive, Murrumbateman, NSW 2582 **Region** Canberra District
T (02) 6227 5827 **www.**shawvineyards.com.au **Open** Wed–Sun & public hols 10–5
Winemaker Graeme Shaw, Tony Steffania **Est.** 1999 **Dozens** 12000 **Vyds** 33ha
Graeme and Ann Shaw established their vineyard (cabernet sauvignon, merlot, shiraz, semillon and riesling) in 1998 on a 280ha fine wool-producing property established in the mid-1800s and known as Olleyville. It is one of the largest privately owned vineyard holdings in the Canberra area. Their children are fully employed in the family business, Michael as viticulturist and Tanya as cellar door manager. Shaw Vineyard Estate operates a 'wine shop' cellar door in conjunction with Suntay Wines in Hainan Island, China, with plans for further cellar doors in Shi Jia Zuang and Changzhi. Exports to The Netherlands, Vietnam, Singapore, Thailand, the Philippines, South Korea, Hong Kong and China.

ᵞᵞᵞᵞ̣   **Estate Riesling 2016** Sitting pretty and young with its lime juice, red apple tang and slate, quite juicy and moreish. Very precise talc-like acidity, the backbone to this, ensures it will unfurl and gain more complexity in time. Screwcap. 12.5% alc. **Rating** 93 **To** 2027 $30 JF

Reserve Merriman Cabernet Sauvignon 2015 A whirl of dark concentrated blackberries and currants, cedary oak, licorice and dark chocolate mints and coffee grounds lead the charge. It's not shy – has layers of complexity and needs more time in bottle. Screwcap. 14.5% alc. **Rating** 93 **To** 2030 $65 JF

Estate Cabernet Sauvignon 2015 Dark black-garnet; no shortage of flavour or depth. Plenty of juicy blackberries, Black Forest cake, mint and cedary oak make their mark, yet there's a vivacity too. Needs more time Screwcap. 14.5% alc. **Rating** 92 **To** 2027 $30 JF

Winemakers Selection Riesling 2016 All pure citrus, from kaffir lime leaf fragrance, juice and zest, with a focus on lemons. Sprightly acidity drives this. Crisply refreshing. Screwcap. 12.5% alc. **Rating** 90 **To** 2026 $18 JF ✪

Winemakers Selection Semillon Sauvignon Blanc 2016 Mid-straw-gold. The sprightly acidity of the semillon acts as a driving force, with lemon and hay aromas and the merest hint of tropical fruits. Simple, bright and breezy. Screwcap. 13% alc. **Rating** 90 **To** 2019 $18 JF ✪

Estate Canberra Merlot 2014 Makes its presence known, starting with the excellent purple-red hue, bright jubey raspberry fruit and boot polish. Tannins have plenty of oomph – partly oak-derived. On the lighter side of medium-bodied. Screwcap. 14% alc. **Rating** 90 **To** 2023 $26 JF

Winemakers Selection Cabernet Sauvignon 2015 Vibrant violets, cassis and boysenberries. Medium-bodied, supple tannins, some grip, pepper and spice.

Uncomplicated, keenly priced and in the zone. Screwcap. 14.5% alc. **Rating** 90
To 2021 $18 JF ✪

🍷🍷🍷🍷 Reserve Merriman Shiraz 2014 Rating 89 To 2027 $65 JF
Estate Shiraz 2014 Rating 89 To 2024 $34 JF
Winemakers Selection Shiraz 2014 Rating 89 To 2029 $18 JF ✪

She-Oak Hill Vineyard ★★★★

82 Hope Street, South Yarra, Vic 3141 (postal) **Region** Heathcote
T (03) 9866 7890 **www**.sheoakhill.com.au **Open** Not
Winemaker Sanguine Estate (Mark Hunter) **Est.** 1995 **Dozens** 400 **Vyds** 5ha
This is the venture of Judith Firkin and Gordon and Julian Leckie, who (in 1975 and '95)
planted shiraz (4.5ha) and chardonnay (0.5ha). The vineyard is located on the southern and
eastern slopes of She Oak Hill, 6km north of Heathcote. It lies between Jasper Hill's Emily's
Paddock and Mt Ida vineyards, and thus has the same type of porous, deep red Cambrian soil.
The decision to opt for dry-grown vines has meant low yields.

🍷🍷🍷🍷🍷 Estate Heathcote Shiraz 2014 At the bigger, denser end of the Heathcote
shiraz spectrum, this large-framed and darkly fruited wine has aromas of blackberry,
black plums, licorice and dark chocolate; the palate remains balanced despite the
relatively high alcohol. Firm tannins round out a wine that can be cellared for at
least the next 6–10 years. Screwcap. 14.8% alc. **Rating** 92 $25 PR ✪

Shingleback ★★★★★

3 Stump Hill Road, McLaren Vale, SA 5171 **Region** McLaren Vale
T (08) 8323 7388 **www**.shingleback.com.au **Open** 7 days 10–5
Winemaker John Davey, Dan Hills **Est.** 1995 **Dozens** 160 000 **Vyds** 120ha
Brothers Kym and John Davey planted and nurture their family-owned and sustainably
managed vineyard on land purchased by their grandfather in the 1950s. Shingleback has
been a success story since its establishment. Its 110ha of estate vineyards are one of the keys
to that success, which includes winning the Jimmy Watson Trophy 2006 for the '05 D Block
Cabernet Sauvignon. The well made wines are rich and full-flavoured, but not overripe (and,
hence, not excessively alcoholic). Exports to the UK, the US, Canada, Cambodia, Vietnam,
China and NZ.

🍷🍷🍷🍷🍷 Unedited McLaren Vale Shiraz 2015 Sit back, relax and be mesmerised by
this black beauty. Nothing is out of place. It has depth of flavour and power yet
superb balance. The palate teases: it's full-bodied, yet perfect fruit and fine-grained
tannins ensure that it's velvety and seamless right through to the persistent finish.
Due for release Mar '18. Screwcap. 14.5% alc. **Rating** 96 To 2040 $80 JF
The Gate McLaren Vale Shiraz 2015 The Gate is a barrel selection made
from estate-grown fruit with the aim being to highlight McLaren Vale shiraz at its
best. It succeeds. Excellent inky-red colour, a flush of dark fruit, a tease of licorice,
sarsaparilla, mint chocolate and cedary oak spices. Full-bodied with perfectly
placed tannins. A complete wine. Screwcap. 14.5% alc. **Rating** 95 To 2035 $35
JF ✪
Red Knot Classified McLaren Vale Shiraz 2015 You'd be hard-pressed to
find a better example at this price point. Dark fruits whip up a glossy texture onto
the fuller body with plump tannins and lively acidity – the end result is succulent,
savoury and satisfying. Screwcap. 14% alc. **Rating** 94 To 2023 $19 JF ✪

🍷🍷🍷🍷🍷 Davey Estate Reserve Shiraz 2015 Rating 93 To 2030 $25 JF ✪
Davey Brothers Shiraz 2015 Rating 93 To 2023 $18 JF ✪
Local Heroes Shiraz Grenache 2015 Rating 93 To 2021 $25 JF ✪
Davey Estate Reserve Cabernet 2015 Rating 93 To 2029 $25 JF ✪
Kitchen Garden Mataro 2016 Rating 93 To 2023 $25 JF ✪
Red Knot Classified Shiraz 2014 Rating 92 To 2022 $20 CM ✪
Haycutters Shiraz 2015 Rating 91 To 2022 $17 JF ✪
Black Bubbles NV Rating 91 To 2019 $23.50 TS

Vin Vale Shiraz 2015 Rating 90 To 2021 $15 JF ✪
Aficionado Red Blend 2015 Rating 90 To 2020 $18 JF ✪
Aficionado Cabernet Sauvignon 2015 Rating 90 To 2022 JF
Los Trios Bravos Tempranillo Monastrell Grenache 2016 Rating 90
To 2021 $25 JF
El Capitan Tempranillo 2016 Rating 90 To 2021 $25 JF

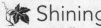 Shining Rock Vineyard ★★★★★

165 Jeffrey Street, Nairne, SA 5252 **Region** Adelaide Hills
T 0448 186 707 **www**.shiningrock.com.au **Open** By appt
Winemaker Con Moshos, Darren Arney **Est.** 2000 **Dozens** 1200 **Vyds** 14.4ha
Agronomist Darren Arney and psychologist wife Natalie Worth had the opportunity to
purchase the Shining Rock Vineyard from Lion Nathan in 2012. It had been established
by Petaluma in '00, and until '15 the grapes were sold to various premium wineries in the
Adelaide Hills. Darren graduated from Roseworthy Agricultural College in the late 1980s,
and saw the vineyard as the opportunity of a lifetime to produce top quality grapes from a
very special vineyard. They hit the ground running with the inaugural vintage of '15 made by
Peter Leske (Revenir), but since '16 Con Moshos has taken over the task in conjunction with
Darren. It hardly need be said that the wines reflect the expertise of those involved, with the
éminence grise of Brian Croser in the background.

🍷🍷🍷🍷🍷 **Adelaide Hills Shiraz 2015** Co-fermented with 6% viognier, 20% whole
bunches, matured in French oak (25% new). Is every bit as complex as the
vinification would suggest. The spicy bouquet is particularly fragrant, and the
medium-bodied palate is quite special in the way it dances in the mouth, luscious
dark fruits and licorice giving way to flashes of elegant freshness, and finally
high quality tannins. This is a winery to watch. Screwcap. 14.5% alc. **Rating** 96
To 2035 $35
Adelaide Hills Sangiovese 2015 Hand-picked, matured in French oak
(10% new), bottled Jan '16. A totally delicious wine, full of red cherry fruits with
typically fine yet firm sangio tannins adding complexity to a high quality palate.
Screwcap. 14% alc. **Rating** 95 To 2023 $30

🍷🍷🍷🍷🍷 **Adelaide Hills Viognier 2016** Rating 93 To 2020 $28
Monsoon Adelaide Hills Viognier 2015 Rating 91 To 2018 $28

Shirvington ★★★★☆

PO Box 220, McLaren Vale, SA 5171 **Region** McLaren Vale
T (08) 8323 7649 **www**.shirvington.com **Open** Not
Winemaker Kim Jackson **Est.** 1996 **Dozens** 950 **Vyds** 23.8ha
The Shirvington family began the development of their McLaren Vale vineyards in 1996
under the direction of viticulturist Peter Bolte, and now have almost 24ha under vine, the
majority to shiraz and cabernet sauvignon, with small additional plantings of mataro and
grenache. A substantial part of the production is sold as grapes, the best reserved for the
Shirvington wines. Exports to the UK and the US.

🍷🍷🍷🍷🍷 **The Redwind McLaren Vale Shiraz 2014** Deeply coloured, this impressive
single vineyard McLaren Vale shiraz has a combination of red and black fruits,
dark chocolate and a little vanillan from the oak, which is already well integrated,
while the full-bodied but not full-throttled palate is equally complex and balanced.
Screwcap. 14% alc. **Rating** 92 To 2029 $65 PR

🍷🍷🍷🍷 **McLaren Vale Shiraz 2014** Rating 89 $37 PR

Shottesbrooke ★★★★

Bagshaws Road, McLaren Flat, SA 5171 **Region** McLaren Vale
T (08) 8383 0002 **www**.shottesbrooke.com.au **Open** Mon–Fri 10–4.30, w'ends 11–5
Winemaker Hamish Maguire **Est.** 1984 **Dozens** 12 000 **Vyds** 30.64ha

Founded by Nick Holmes, who has since passed the winemaking baton on to Flying Winemaker stepson Hamish Maguire, who completed two vintages in France, and one in Spain before settling permanently at Shottesbrooke. The capacity of the winery has been increased to 1200 tonnes annually, and it has a storage capacity for almost 1 million litres. This is far in excess of the amount made under the Shottesbrooke label: the remainder is for contract winemaking for a number of other independent brands. Hamish also travels both nationally and internationally promoting the Shottesbrooke brand. Exports to all major markets.

ŸŸŸŸŸ **Eliza Reserve McLaren Vale Shiraz 2013** Unashamedly in the old-school 'reserve shiraz' style; rich and ripe with a hearty dollop of meaty oak. In that context it's well executed. The wood is nicely integrated with the fruit, its smoky, mocha character matched by a wave of smooth and seamless shiraz flavour. Screwcap. 14.5% alc. **Rating** 94 **To** 2030 $60 SC
Bush Vine McLaren Vale Grenache 2015 Sweetly perfumed, with top-end aromas ranging from ripe cherry to musky spice and a back-note of gentle, warm earthiness. Excellent concentration of flavour typical of old, low-yielding vines, the fruit rich and generous but maintaining a line and firmness of structure. Lovely wine. Screwcap. 14.5% alc. **Rating** 94 **To** 2025 $30 SC ❂

ŸŸŸŸŸ **Tom's Block McLaren Vale Shiraz 2014** Rating 93 To 2044 $50
Limited Release Icon Series McLaren Vale Shiraz Cabernet Sauvignon 2010 Rating 93 To 2035 $85
McLaren Vale Shiraz 2014 Rating 91 To 2022 $20 SC ❂
Estate Series McLaren Vale GSM 2015 Rating 91 To 2025 $20 ❂
McLaren Vale Merlot 2014 Rating 90 To 2021 $20 SC ❂

Shut the Gate Wines ★★★★

2 Main North Road, Watervale, SA 5452 **Region** Clare Valley
T 0488 243 200 **Open** 7 days 10–4.30
Winemaker Contract **Est.** 2013 **Dozens** 6000
Shut the Gate is the venture of Richard Woods and Rasa Fabian, which took shape after five years' involvement in the rebranding of Crabtree Watervale Wines, followed by 18 months of juggling consultancy roles. During this time Richard and Rasa set the foundations for Shut the Gate, with striking and imaginative labels (and parables) catching the eye. The engine room of the business is the Clare Valley, where the wines are contract-made and the grapes for many of the two ranges of wines are sourced. They have chosen their grape sources and contract winemakers with considerable care.

ŸŸŸŸŸ **For Love Watervale Riesling 2016** A filigreed expression of riesling from this hallowed subregion, this is dainty and balletic, tiptoeing across a myriad of citrus, quince and jasmine scents. What makes this wine stand out, however, is its glaze of crystalline acidity and texture of talc and pumice: stony, mineral-clad and the architecture of the wine. Screwcap. 11% alc. **Rating** 94 **To** 2031 $25 NG ❂

ŸŸŸŸŸ **For Freedom Polish Hill River Riesling 2016** Rating 92 To 2031 $25 NG ❂
Fur Elise Clare Valley Grenache Rose 2016 Rating 92 $20 NG ❂
Rosie's Patch Watervale Riesling 2016 Rating 91 To 2028 $25 NG
The Rose Thief Hilltops Shiraz 2015 Rating 90 To 2022 $22 NG
Blossom 26G RS Riesling 2016 Rating 90 To 2022 $20 NG ❂

Side Gate Wines ★★★☆

57 Rokeby Street, Collingwood, Vic 3066 **Region** South Eastern Australia
T (03) 9417 5757 **www.**sidegate.com.au **Open** Mon–Fri 8–5
Winemaker Josef Orbach **Est.** 2001 **Dozens** 50 000
Side Gate is a Melbourne-based multi-regional producer, specialising in cool climate reds and whites. Founder Josef Orbach lived and worked in the Clare Valley from 1994 to '98 at Leasingham, and completed a winemaking degree at the University of Melbourne in 2010. His is a classic negociant business, buying grapes and/or wines from various regions; the

wines may be either purchased in bulk, then blended and bottled by Orbach, or purchased as cleanskins. Exports to Canada, Thailand, Singapore and China.

ŸŸŸŸŸ Organic Clare Valley Riesling 2016 You get a lot of classic Clare Valley riesling for a small price. No-frills winemaking of organically grown fruit throws the focus on ripe lime and Meyer lemon with good acid balance. There's every reason to drink this now rather than in 5 years' time, but by all means cellar some if you so wish. Screwcap. **Rating** 90 **To** 2023 $15 ●

Sidewood Estate

Maximillian's Restaurant, 15 Onkaparinga Road, Oakbank, SA 5245 **Region** Adelaide Hills
T (08) 8389 9234 **www**.sidewood.com.au **Open** Wed–Sun 11–5
Winemaker Darryl Catlin **Est.** 2004 **Dozens** NFP **Vyds** 93ha
Sidewood Estate is part-vineyard and part-horse stables and racehorse training. Owned by Owen and Cassandra Inglis since 2004, both aspects of the business are flourishing. Sidewood Estate lies in the Onkaparinga Valley, with the vines weathering the coolest climate in the Adelaide Hills. Significant expenditure on regeneration of and increase in the size of the vineyards was already well underway when Sidewood obtained a SA State Regional Government Fund grant of $856 000, being part of a $3.5 million expansion of the winery capacity from 500 to 2000 tonnes each vintage. The expenditure includes new bottling and canning facilities capable of handing 400 000 bottles of wine and cider annually. Wines are released under the Sidewood Estate, Stable Hill and Mappinga labels, the last the Reserve range. Exports to the UK, the US and other major markets.

ŸŸŸŸŸ Adelaide Hills Pinot Noir 2015 The spicy bouquet shows unmistakable, complex, whole-bunch aromas, the palate with a finely pitched savoury edge. Screwcap. 12.5% alc. **Rating** 96 **To** 2025 $35 ●
Adelaide Hills Sauvignon Blanc 2016 Free-run juice chilled, wild yeast, cool-fermented in tank, and kept on lees for 4 months to successfully build mid-palate texture without compromising drive and length. The only gold in the sauvignon blanc class at the National Wine Show '16. Screwcap. 12.5% alc. **Rating** 95 **To** 2017 $20 ●
777 Adelaide Hills Pinot Noir 2015 Estate-grown utilising one of the newer clones from Burgundy. Light, clear colour; the highly fragrant red cherry/wild strawberry bouquet shapes the elegant palate. Gold medal Adelaide Hills Wine Show '16. Screwcap. 12.5% alc. **Rating** 95 **To** 2023 $35 ●

ŸŸŸŸŸ Adelaide Hills Chardonnay 2015 Rating 92 **To** 2023 $20 ●
Late Disgorged Isabella Rose 2011 Rating 92 **To** 2017 $60 TS
Stable Hill Adelaide Hills Palomino Pinot Grigio 2016 Rating 90 **To** 2018 $15 ●
Chloe Methode Traditionelle Cuvee 2013 Rating 90 **To** 2017 $28 TS

Sieber Road Wines

Sieber Road, Tanunda, SA 5352 **Region** Barossa Valley
T (08) 8562 8038 **www**.sieberwines.com **Open** 7 days 11–4
Winemaker Tony Carapetis **Est.** 1999 **Dozens** 4500 **Vyds** 18ha
Richard and Val Sieber are the third generation to run Redlands, the family property, traditionally a cropping/grazing farm. They have diversified into viticulture with shiraz (14ha) the lion's share, the remainder viognier, grenache and mourvedre. Son Ben Sieber is the viticulturist. Exports to Canada and China.

ŸŸŸŸŸ Reserve Barossa Valley Shiraz 2014 Hand-picked from a low-yielding 3ha rock-strewn estate block, crushed into a small open fermenter, matured in 60% new French puncheons, the remainder in used French and American hogsheads. This is a monolithic wine, built for giants to consume, not mere mortals. Impossible to give normal points, mine a compromise. Cork. 15.5% alc. **Rating** 94 **To** 2054 $100

🍷🍷🍷🍷🍷 **Barossa Valley Viognier 2015** **Rating** 90 **To** 2019 $18 ✪
Barossa Valley GSM 2014 **Rating** 90 **To** 2024 $20 ✪

Signature Wines ★★★★

31 King Street, Norwood, SA 5067 **Region** Adelaide Hills/Barossa Valley
T (08) 8568 1757 **www**.signaturewines.com.au **Open** Mon–Fri 9–5, w'ends by appt
Winemaker Warwick Billings (Contract) **Est.** 2011 **Dozens** 15 000 **Vyds** 16ha

Signature Wines, owned by Daniel Khouzam and family, has formed a special relationship with core growers in the Adelaide Hills and the greater Barossa. Daniel has been in the industry for over 20 years, and during that time has slowly developed its export markets. It operates out of the one-time Penfolds winery in the Eden Valley. Exports to the UK, Malaysia, Singapore, Hong Kong, China and NZ.

🍷🍷🍷🍷🍷 **Reserve Barossa Valley Shiraz 2014** Dark crimson and bright; an assortment of red and black plums, lots of spice, with charry/cedary/vanillan oak fragrance and flavours somewhat dominating on the palate. Tannins a tad raw but bright acidity enlivens. Screwcap. 14.5% alc. **Rating** 90 **To** 2025 $35 JF

The Summons McLaren Vale Shiraz 2013 Big. That's what this wine is in every way, from the saturating vanillan cedary oak, dense tannins and ripe fruit to its structure. Flavours of satsuma plums doused in dark chocolate are an added bonus. Screwcap. 15% alc. **Rating** 90 **To** 2026 $68 JF

🍷🍷🍷🍷 **Reserve Adelaide Hills Sauvignon Blanc 2016** **Rating** 89 **To** 2019 $27 JF

Silent Way ★★★★

PO Box 630, Lancefield, Vic 3435 **Region** Macedon Ranges
T 0409 159 577 **www**.silentway.com.au **Open** Not
Winemaker Matt Harrop **Est.** 2009 **Dozens** 1000 **Vyds** 1.2ha

This is a busman's holiday for partners Matt Harrop and Tamara Grischy, who purchased their small property in 2007, 10 years after they were married. They have planted 1.2ha of chardonnay, and buy semillon and pinot noir from the Quarry Ridge Vineyard at Kilmore. The name comes from a Miles Davis record made in February 1969, regarded as a masterpiece and one of the most inventive recordings of all time. The labels feature artwork originally created by friend Daniel Wallace for their wedding, turned into labels by friend Mel Nightingale. Earthworms, birds, snakes, friendship and love are the symbols for Silent Way.

🍷🍷🍷🍷🍷 **Macedon Ranges Chardonnay 2015** A minimally messed-with wine from one of Australia's coolest GI, this is reminiscent of a good, swigging chardonnay from France's Maconnais. Peaches, apple and oyster shell notes mingle with perfectly nestled oak, a guiding hand for the stream of juicy fruit. Mellifluous, delicious and highly versatile, confident in its generosity and easygoing nature while being faithful to place. This is surely the point. Screwcap. 13% alc. **Rating** 93 **To** 2023 $35 NG

Pinot Noir 2016 This is a generously flavoured, lithe pinot noir brimming with dark and red cherry scents, rhubarb and root spice. The oak (12% new, all French) confers a waft of cinnamon spice, and together with a gentle rasp from a smidgen of whole bunch, creates a framework within which the sassy, sapid fruit flavours flow. Screwcap. 13.5% alc. **Rating** 93 **To** 2024 $25 NG ✪

🍷🍷🍷🍷 **Serpens Semillon Viognier 2015** **Rating** 89 **To** 2020 $22 NG

Silkman Wines ★★★★★

c/- The Small Winemakers Centre, McDonalds Road, Pokolbin, NSW 2320
Region Hunter Valley
T 0414 800 256 **www**.silkmanwines.com.au **Open** 7 days 10–5
Winemaker Shaun and Liz Silkman **Est.** 2013 **Dozens** 3500

Winemaking couple Shaun and Liz Silkman (one-time dux of the Len Evans Tutorial) were both born and raised in the Hunter Valley, and worked many vintages (both in Australia and abroad) before joining forces at First Creek Wines, where Liz is senior winemaker. This gives them the opportunity to make small quantities of the three classic varieties of the Hunter Valley: Semillon, Chardonnay and Shiraz. Unsurprisingly, the wines so far released have been of outstanding quality. Exports to the US.

ŢŢŢŢŢ **Reserve Hunter Valley Semillon 2016** Bright straw-green; brimful of crushed lemon, lemon juice, lime juice and lemongrass aromas, the flavours rushing along the same path. A celebration of exuberant modern semillon, presumably using carefully selected yeast. Screwcap. **Rating** 97 **To** 2030 $35 ✪

ŢŢŢŢŢ **Hunter Valley Semillon 2015** Made from an extremely small parcel of semillon grown in the heart of Pokolbin. It takes a millisecond into the first sip to understand why the Silkman duo were so focused on the fruit: a citrus rainbow of flavours shower the palate, acidity underlining the intensity of those flavours. Great now or in 10+ years. Screwcap. 10.5% alc. **Rating** 96 **To** 2030 $25 ✪
Hunter Valley Semillon 2013 A very good white (semillon) vintage has resulted in a wine of explosive power and intensity, aflame with a fusillade of lemongrass, citrus pith, skin and juice. Hunter Valley acidity provides the framework for a wine still on an upwards trajectory. Screwcap. 10.5% alc. **Rating** 96 **To** 2025 $25 ✪
Hunter Valley Semillon 2016 Bright straw-green; purity, precision and gun barrel-straight acidity all point to the same bullseye — '30 — but sightings can be taken any time from '20 on. Screwcap. **Rating** 95 **To** 2029 $25 ✪

ŢŢŢŢŢ **Reserve Shiraz Pinot Noir 2016** **Rating** 93 **To** 2030 $40
Reserve Shiraz Pinot Noir 2014 **Rating** 92 **To** 2024 $40

Silkwood Estate   ★★★★

5204/9649 Channybearup Road, Pemberton, WA 6260 **Region** Pemberton
T (08) 9776 1584 **www**.silkwoodwines.com.au **Open** Fri–Mon & public hols 10–4
Winemaker Coby Ladwig, Tim Redlich **Est.** 1998 **Dozens** 10 000 **Vyds** 23.5ha
Silkwood Wines has been owned by the Bowman family since 2004. The vineyard is patrolled by a large flock of guinea fowl, eliminating most insect pests and reducing the use of chemicals. In '05 the adjoining vineyard was purchased, lifting the estate plantings to 23.5ha; plantings include shiraz, cabernet sauvignon, merlot, sauvignon blanc, chardonnay, pinot noir, riesling and zinfandel. The cellar door, restaurant and four luxury chalets overlook the large lake on the property. Exports to Malaysia, Singapore and China.

ŢŢŢŢŢ **The Walcott Pemberton Sauvignon Blanc 2016** You catch the touch of French oak on the first whiff of the bouquet, but thereafter tropical fruits do all the talking and walking. Guava, passionfruit and cut grass combine with very good acidity to give the palate serious length. Screwcap. 13% alc. **Rating** 92 **To** 2018 $28
Pemberton Malbec 2014 Classic varietal aromas with red fruit of all sorts. Fragrant oak plays its part as well. Nicely supple on the palate, the flavours showing a little more earthiness and a touch of stewed plum. Just misses on real complexity, often the case with straight malbec, but very good drinking. Screwcap. 13.2% alc. **Rating** 92 **To** 2022 $30 SC
The Walcott Pemberton Riesling 2016 An attractive riesling with a faint passionfruit edge to the lemon/lime core of fruit that throws out a couple of false trails before its acidity takes over to tie the flavours up into a neat parcel. Screwcap. 12.5% alc. **Rating** 91 **To** 2031 $28
The Walcott Pemberton Shiraz 2014 20yo vines, machine-harvested, whole berries open-fermented, 4 days cold soak, matured for 15 months in French oak (35% new). Red and black cherry fruit drives the bouquet and medium-bodied palate alike, spice and pepper providing the seasoning, French oak the polish. Sparks with life. Screwcap. 14% alc. **Rating** 91 **To** 2029 $30

The Walcott Pemberton Malbec 2015 Malbec is most reliable when grown in temperate regions, providing structure and texture to carry its dark berry and satsuma plum fruit. The influence of the new French oak is another plus for the wine, which is medium-bodied and welcoming, with a light savoury twist on the farewell. Screwcap. 14% alc. **Rating** 91 **To** 2024 $30

Silverstream Wines

2365 Scotsdale Road, Denmark, WA 6333 **Region** Denmark
T (08) 9840 9119 **www.**silverstreamwines.com **Open** By appt
Winemaker James Kellie, Michael Garland **Est.** 1997 **Dozens** 2500 **Vyds** 9ha
Tony and Felicity Ruse have 9ha of chardonnay, merlot, cabernet franc, pinot noir, riesling and viognier in their vineyard 23km from Denmark. The wines are contract-made, and after some hesitation, the Ruses decided their very pretty garden and orchard more than justified opening a cellar door, a decision supported by the quality of the wines on offer at very reasonable prices.

ƮƮƮƮƮ **Single Vineyard Denmark Riesling 2012** When first tasted almost 4 years ago its restraint, acidity and freshness were noted, with a drink-to date of '17. It still has all those characters (and a light colour), and one is left to wonder how long it will continue to coast. Gold medal Mount Barker Wine Show '16 and a gold medal and two trophies WA Wine Awards '16. Screwcap. 12.2% alc. **Rating** 96 **To** 2032 $30
Denmark Chardonnay 2010 Gleaming straw-green; has grown a leg, if not two, since first tasted over 5 years ago, with a drink-to date of '15. Its melon and nectarine fruit are still the drivers, partial barrel fermentation being as valid now as it was back then. Screwcap. 13.5% alc. **Rating** 94 **To** 2020 $22

ƮƮƮƮ♀ **Single Vineyard Denmark Pinot Noir 2012 Rating** 90 **To** 2021 $29

Simon Whitlam & Co

PO Box 1108, Woollahra, NSW 1350 **Region** Hunter Valley
T (02) 9007 5331 **Open** Not
Winemaker Edgar Vales (Contract) **Est.** 1979 **Dozens** 2000
My association with the owners of Simon Whitlam – Andrew and Hady Simon, Nicholas and Judy Whitlam, and Grant Breen – dates back to the late 1970s, at which time I was a consultant to the Simons' leading wine retail shop in Sydney, Camperdown Cellars. The association continued for a time after I moved to Melbourne in '83, but ceased altogether in '87 when Camperdown Cellars was sold; it was later merged with Arrowfield Wines. The Simon Whitlam label was part of the deal, and it passed through a number of corporate owners until 20 years later, when the original partners regained control of the business.

ƮƮƮƮ♀ **Hunter Valley Semillon Sauvignon Blanc 2012** A blend of 94% semillon and 6% sauvignon blanc which sits discreetly in the background, this very brightly coloured wine has some lemon butter on toast, citrus and gently tropical aromas while the palate is racy and long. Approachable now, this will still be looking good 3–5 years from now. Screwcap. 11.3% alc. **Rating** 93 **To** 2020 $24 PR ●
Hunter Valley Traminer 2014 Brightly coloured and youthful looking, this textbook example is super varietal with lashings of rosewater, Turkish Delight and quince aromas, while the palate manages to remain balanced and long despite the obvious sweetness. Screwcap. 12.7% alc. **Rating** 92 **To** 2018 $24 PR ●
Hunter Valley Verdelho 2011 A still vibrant and youthful looking green-gold. This wine has continued to improve since it was last tasted for the *Wine Companion*, in '14. Now fully ready, there is some toast to go with the lemony fruit and custard apple aromas, while the palate is creamy, gently sweet and balanced. Screwcap. 13.9% alc. **Rating** 90 **To** 2020 $24 PR

Sinapius Vineyard ★★★★★

4232 Bridport Road, Pipers Brook, Tas 7254 **Region** Northern Tasmania
T 0417 341 764 **www.**sinapius.com.au **Open** Thur–Mon 12–5 Aug–Jun
Winemaker Vaughn Dell **Est.** 2005 **Dozens** 1200 **Vyds** 4.07ha
Vaughn Dell and Linda Morice purchased the former Golders Vineyard in 2005 (planted in 1994). More recent vineyard plantings include 13 clones of pinot noir and eight clones of chardonnay, as well as a small amount of gruner veltliner. The vineyard is close-planted, ranging from 5100 vines per hectare for the gruner veltliner to 10 250 vines per hectare for the pinot noir and chardonnay. The wines are made with a minimalist approach: natural ferments, basket pressing, extended lees ageing and minimal fining and filtration.

♈♈♈♈♈ **Home Vineyard Chardonnay 2015** This wine's modus operandi is surely its extremely long finish, due to what feels like an effortless confluence of grape variety, site and a sensitive winemaking hand. Surely a great deal of effort was needed. The wine is crammed full of creamy cashew, truffle, peach, apricot and a whiplash of nectarine tang. Screwcap. 13.5% alc. **Rating** 97 **To** 2023 $50 NG ✪
The Enclave Pinot Noir 2015 A compact, tightly wound wine, drawing upon a core of damson plum, sour cherry, bonbon and forest floor notes. The plume of flavour is given crunchy energy by sinuous tannins, livewire acidity and a mineral tang. Well handled oak and some whole cluster briar round out the package. Screwcap. 13.5% alc. **Rating** 97 **To** 2024 $80 NG ✪

♈♈♈♈♈ **Home Vineyard Pinot Noir 2015** A transparent, ever so elegant melody of crushed strawberries, white pepper, whole cluster twig and herb laces the mouth. Silky and spicy at once, this is a sublimely elegant wine with sap, vigour and plenty of glide. Screwcap. 13.5% alc. **Rating** 94 **To** 2022 $55 NG

♈♈♈♈♈ **Clem Blanc 2016 Rating** 93 **To** 2021 $38 NG

Sinclair of Scotsburn ★★★★

256 Wiggins Road, Scotsburn, Vic 3352 **Region** Ballarat
T (03) 5341 3936 **www.**sinclairofscotsburn.com.au **Open** W'ends by appt
Winemaker Scott Ireland **Est.** 1997 **Dozens** 135 **Vyds** 2ha
David and (the late) Barbara Sinclair purchased their property in 2001. At that time 1.2ha of chardonnay and 0.8ha of pinot noir had been planted, but had struggled, the pinot noir yielding less than 0.25 tonnes in '02. With the aid of limited drip irrigation, cane pruning, low crop levels and bird netting, limited quantities of high quality chardonnay and pinot have since been produced. Two-thirds of the annual production is sold to Tomboy Hill and Provenance Wines, the remaining third made for the Sinclair of Scotsburn label.

♈♈♈♈♈ **Wallijak Chardonnay 2015** Well made, with a complex web of grapefruit, Granny Smith apple and pear flavours, sparkling citrus and minerally acidity cleansing the long finish. Screwcap. 13% alc. **Rating** 91 **To** 2025
Manor House Pinot Noir 2015 This is a very cool, highly continental climate with cold nights that slow ripening. The bouquet is fragrant, with attractive fruits, the palate moving into a more savoury/spicy mode, but is definitively pinot, and has good length. Screwcap. 13% alc. **Rating** 90 **To** 2021

Sinclair's Gully ★★★★

288 Colonial Drive, Norton Summit, SA 5136 **Region** Adelaide Hills
T (08) 8390 1995 **www.**sinclairsgully.com **Open** Sun & public hols 12–4 (Aug–June)
Winemaker Contract **Est.** 1998 **Dozens** 900 **Vyds** 1ha
Sue and Sean Delaney purchased their property at Norton Summit in 1997. The property had a significant stand of remnant native vegetation, with a State Conservation Rating, and much energy has been spent on restoring 8ha of pristine bushland, home to 130 species of native plants and 66 species of native birds, some recorded as threatened or rare. The adoption of biodynamic viticulture has coincided with numerous awards for the protection of the natural

environment and, more recently, eco-tourism; they operate the only eco-certified cellar door in the Adelaide Hills, and have won innumerable ecological and general tourism awards. Sparkling wine disgorgement demonstrations are a particular attraction.

🍷🍷🍷🍷♀ **Susanne Joy 2014** This soft and creamy Adelaide Hills blanc de noirs has a distinct copper tint to its medium salmon hue. New French oak maturation has built creamy texture without oak flavour. Gentle red apple fruits and savoury spice mark out a well balanced finish of fruit sweetness, albeit without the primary fruit lift and perfume that would be expected at this young age. 12.5% alc. **Rating** 90 To 2017 $40 TS

Sparkling Grenache 2014 True to the mood of grenache, there is a lightness to the body of this sparkling red, with gentle red berry fruits accented by savoury tomato notes. Tannins are firm, dry and astringent on the finish, a little too much for the restraint of its fruit. Cork. 13% alc. **Rating** 90 To 2017 $40 TS

Singlefile Wines

90 Walter Road, Denmark, WA 6333 **Region** Great Southern
T (08) 9840 9749 www.singlefilewines.com **Open** 7 days 11–5
Winemaker Mike Garland, Coby Ladwig **Est.** 2007 **Dozens** 6000 **Vyds** 3.75ha
In 1968 geologist Phil Snowden and wife Viv moved from South Africa to Perth, where they developed their successful multinational mining and resource services company, Snowden Resources. Following the sale of the company in 2004, they turned their attention to their long held desire to make and enjoy fine wine. In '07 they bought an established vineyard (planted in '89) in the beautiful Denmark subregion. They pulled out the old shiraz and merlot vines, kept and planted more chardonnay, and retained Larry Cherubino to set up partnerships with established vineyards in Frankland River, Porongurup, Denmark, Pemberton and Margaret River. The cellar door, tasting room and restaurant are strongly recommended. The consistency of the quality of the Singlefile wines is outstanding, as is their value for money. Exports to the US, Japan and China.

🍷🍷🍷🍷🍷 **The Vivienne Denmark Chardonnay 2014** Whole-bunch pressed to a French barrique, wild fermentation on full solids, matured for 6 months. Singlefile says the wine exceeded its expectations, and it's not hard to see why: the wine is immensely complex and equally rich, yet has the lightness of foot one would expect from 12.6% alcohol. Every box is ticked three times. Screwcap. **Rating** 98 To 2026 $80 ✪

Single Vineyard Mount Barker Riesling 2015 Bright, pale straw-green; the wine's pH of 2.95 and 7.47g/l of acidity have no relevant residual sugar (1 47g/l) to provide the inherent balance the wine has, this coming from the vines and vineyard. The result is a flavour intensity that is distinctly Germanic, rich citrus in a pas de deux with crunchy, minerally acidity. A wine of the highest calibre. Screwcap. 11.2% alc. **Rating** 97 To 2030 $30 ✪

Single Vineyard Family Reserve Denmark Chardonnay 2015 A very, very different wine from its Great Southern sibling, with intense grapefruit leading white peach through the bouquet and into a complex palate. One of those all-too-rare wines that manage to combine elegance with intensity and complexity, notes of cashew and cream swirling around in the background. Screwcap. 13.6% alc. **Rating** 97 To 2030 $50 ✪

The Philip Adrian Frankland River Cabernet Sauvignon 2015 Good crimson-purple; an unambiguously full-bodied cabernet, laden to the gills with all things cabernet – blackcurrant, black olive, earth, tar and tannins genuflecting to no one, new French oak (60%) and 18 months in barrel. All these provide the answers to the secrets of this majestic wine. Screwcap. 14.5% alc. **Rating** 97 To 2049 $80 ✪

Single Vineyard Frankland River Cabernet Sauvignon 2014 Taut, powerful, lengthy and exquisitely well polished. This doesn't put a foot wrong, and (given appropriate storage) won't do for many a decade to come. You can bank on this wine. It tastes of bay leaves, blackcurrant, cocoa and (subtle) tobacco, and feels strong and secure at every turn. It's the kind of anvil cellar collections can be built on. Screwcap. 13.8% alc. **Rating** 97 **To** 2040 $37 CM ✪

The Philip Adrian Frankland River Cabernet Sauvignon 2014 Cold-soaked for 6 weeks before undergoing an extended maceration, thereafter spending 18 months in French barriques (65% new) and bottle-aged for 12 months before release. This is a luxuriantly full-bodied cabernet with exemplary varietal character, and shows no sign of over-extraction. It will be exceptionally long-lived. Screwcap. 13.6% alc. **Rating** 97 **To** 2044 $80 ✪

ΨΨΨΨΨ **Single Vineyard Mount Barker Riesling 2016** The perfumed citrus and apple blossom bouquet introduces an elegant, fresh, well balanced palate nimbly following the footsteps of the bouquet; citrus fruit is the lead player until the finish, when acidity takes command through to the aftertaste. All up, a little finer and more elegant than its Great Southern sibling. Screwcap. 11.9% alc. **Rating** 96 **To** 2029 $30 ✪

Clement V 2015 66% shiraz, 27% grenache and 7% mataro. The spicy array of black fruits from shiraz, and red fruits from grenache and mataro, combine synergistically. It is supple and finely structured, and its perfect balance makes it an each-way proposition for drinking now or in 10 years. Screwcap. 14.2% alc. **Rating** 96 **To** 2027 $30 ✪

Single Vineyard Frankland River Cabernet Sauvignon 2015 A precision-plus wine. There's a gossamer thread of acidity holding it securely in place. Fuller-bodied, with filigreed tannins, savoury tones of graphite, menthol and woodsy spices mingling with the blackberries and dark plums. Very polished, and everything in its place. Screwcap. 14.3% alc. **Rating** 96 **To** 2033 $37 JF ✪

Great Southern Riesling 2016 Rating 95 **To** 2030 $25 ✪
Single Vineyard Family Reserve Denmark Chardonnay 2016 Rating 95 **To** 2025 $50 JF
Single Vineyard Frankland River Shiraz 2015 Rating 95 **To** 2030 $37
Great Southern Cabernet Merlot 2015 Rating 95 **To** 2028 $25 JF ✪
Frankland River Cabernet Merlot 2014 Rating 95 **To** 2034 $25 ✪
Single Vineyard Pemberton Fume Blanc 2016 Rating 94 **To** 2021 $30 JF ✪
Great Southern Chardonnay 2015 Rating 94 **To** 2028 $30 ✪
Pemberton Pinot Gris 2015 Rating 94 **To** 2019 $30 ✪

ΨΨΨΨΨ **Great Southern Chardonnay 2016 Rating** 93 **To** 2024 $30 JF
Great Southern Semillon Sauvignon Blanc 2016 Rating 92 **To** 2019 $25 JF ✪
Run Free Great Southern Chardonnay 2016 Rating 91 **To** 2023 $25 JF
Single Vineyard Denmark Pinot Noir 2015 Rating 91 **To** 2020 $33
Run Free Great Southern Shiraz 2015 Rating 91 **To** 2022 $25 JF

Sirromet Wines   ★★★★☆

850–938 Mount Cotton Road, Mount Cotton, Qld 4165 **Region** Granite Belt
T (07) 3206 2999 **www**.sirromet.com **Open** 7 days 9–4.30
Winemaker Adam Chapman, Jessica Ferguson **Est.** 1998 **Dozens** 40 000 **Vyds** 98.7ha
This ambitious venture has succeeded in its aim of creating Qld's premier winery. The founding Morris family retained a leading architect to design the striking state-of-the-art winery; the state's foremost viticultural consultant to plant three major vineyards (in the Granite Belt); and the most skilled winemaker practising in Qld, Adam Chapman, to make the wine. It has a 200-seat restaurant, a wine club, and is firmly aimed at the tourist market, taking advantage of its situation, halfway between Brisbane and the Gold Coast. Exports to Sweden, South Korea, Papua New Guinea, Hong Kong, China and Japan.

ΨΨΨΨΨ **Private Collection LM Assemblage Reserve 2014** 47% cabernet sauvignon, 34% merlot, 19% petit verdot. The major components were matured for 16 months in used French barriques, but counterintuitively, the 10% new oak used for the cabernet component was American, not French. No matter, this is an extremely well balanced wine, the palate long, the finish fresh, but with

the necessary tannins. I fancy one of the keys is the 13.8% alcohol. Screwcap.
Rating 96 To 2031 $120

🍷🍷🍷🍷♀ **Severn River Granite Belt Shiraz Viognier 2014** Rating 93 To 2029 $45
Signature Collection Terry Morris Granite Belt Chardonnay 2014
Rating 92 To 2021 $35
Wild Granite Belt Syrah Viognier 2014 Rating 92 To 2034 $65
Vineyard Selection Granite Belt Pinot Gris 2016 Rating 91 To 2018 $21
Vineyard Selection Granite Belt Verdelho 2016 Rating 91 To 2018 $21 ✪
**Club Member Release Bald Rock Creek Granite Belt Merlot Cabernet
2014** Rating 91 To 2020 $35
Signature Collection Terry Morris Granite Belt Merlot 2014 Rating 90
To 2022 $35

Sister's Run   ★★★★

PO Box 382, Tanunda, SA 5352 **Region** Barossa
T (08) 8563 1400 **www**.sistersrun.com.au **Open** Not
Winemaker Elena Brooks **Est.** 2001 **Dozens** NFP
Sister's Run is owned by noted Barossa Valley vignerons Carl and Peggy Lindner (owners of
Langmeil), directly employing the skills of Elena Brooks as winemaker, and, indirectly, the
marketing know-how of husband Zar Brooks. The Stiletto and Boot are those of Elena, and
the motto 'The truth is in the vineyard, but the proof is in the glass' is, I would guess, the work
of Zar Brooks. Exports to all major markets.

🍷🍷🍷🍷♀ **Epiphany McLaren Vale Shiraz 2015** Full colour, both depth and hue; a
medium to full-bodied wine that takes McLaren Vale shiraz from a good vintage,
the winemaking simply taking best advantage of the fruit quality. Blackberry, plum,
bitter chocolate and briar all contribute to a savoury palate and finish. Screwcap.
14.5% alc. **Rating** 91 **To** 2025 $22 ✪
Calvary Hill Lyndoch Shiraz 2015 There's no artifice about this wine: it is an
unrestrained exercise in the heartland of Barossa Valley shiraz style, full of purple
and black fruits, ripe tannins and a quick salute from compatible oak. Screwcap.
14.5% alc. **Rating** 90 **To** 2025 $22

🍷🍷🍷🍷 **St Petri's Eden Valley Riesling 2016** Rating 89 To 2021 $18 ✪
Sunday Slippers Lyndoch Barossa Chardonnay 2016 Rating 89 To 2018
$18 ✪

Sittella Wines   ★★★★★

100 Barrett Street, Herne Hill, WA 6056 **Region** Swan Valley
T (08) 9296 2600 **www**.sittella.com.au **Open** Tues–Sun & public hols 11–5
Winemaker Colby Quirk, Yuri Berns **Est.** 1998 **Dozens** 8000 **Vyds** 10ha
Simon and Maaike Berns acquired a 7ha block (with 5ha of vines) at Herne Hill, making
the first wine in 1998 and opening a most attractive cellar door facility. They also own the
Wildberry Estate vineyard in Margaret River. Consistent and significant wine show success
has brought well deserved recognition for the wines. Exports to the US, Japan and China.

🍷🍷🍷🍷🍷 **Reserve Wilyabrup Margaret River Chardonnay 2016** Estate-grown Dijon
clones 95 and 96, hand-picked, whole-bunch pressed, wild-yeast fermented in
French oak (20% new), matured for 10 months, no mlf. Precision engineering
from vineyard to glass (and impossible to resist the second glass), so perfect is the
mouthfeel and balance. A wine with a rich history strewn with success. Screwcap.
13% alc. **Rating** 95 **To** 2024 $32 ✪
Coffee Rock Swan Valley Shiraz 2015 Hand-picked from 66yo vines,
100% whole berry, complex fermentation, part in French hogsheads (30% new)
for 18 months. It's all paid dividends: this is a full-bodied wine measured in terms
of intensity rather than extract, the cherry and plum fruit fresh, the finish clean
and lively. Screwcap. 14.5% alc. **Rating** 95 **To** 2030 $55

The Wild One Margaret River Sauvignon Blanc 2016 Hand-picked, chilled overnight, 75% wild-yeast fermented in tank, 25% in French oak on lees for 14 weeks. The funky bouquet and vibrant, edgy fruits are exactly as intended. This is all herb, grass, citrus and mineral-infused, bypassing the tropical notes waiting on the kerbside. Screwcap. 12.5% alc. **Rating** 94 **To** 2021 $21 ✪

Tinta Rouge Swan Valley Shiraz Grenache Tempranillo 2016 Bright, clear crimson; there's a lot going on here, all good. Colour, juicy plum fruit, savoury tannins ex whole bunches, good length. Exceptional value. Screwcap. 14.5% alc. **Rating** 94 **To** 2021 $19 ✪

Swan Valley Grenache Tempranillo 2016 Light, clear crimson-purple; a compote of raspberry, cherry and plum with a sprinkling of spice; supple lightweight tannins, fresh, juicy finish. Delicious immediate drinking proposition. Clever winemaking. Screwcap. 14% alc. **Rating** 94 **To** 2020 $30 ✪

Berns Reserve 2015 94% cabernet sauvignon, 4% malbec and 1.5% petit verdot. The wine is only medium-bodied despite the lengthy maceration. Blackcurrant fruit has an ephemeral discordant note on the bouquet, swept away by the wiry strength of the palate and tannin structure. Screwcap. 14% alc. **Rating** 94 **To** 2030 $55

Avant-Garde Series Margaret River Malbec 2015 Matured in French hogsheads and barriques (35% new) for 16 months, a micro barrel selection. Deep, dense crimson-purple; there is layer upon layer of luscious purple and black fruits with French oak still in action, and soft tannins to close. Screwcap. 14% alc. **Rating** 94 **To** 2025 $38

ᵀᵀᵀᵀᵞ **Single Vineyard Cabernet Malbec 2015** Rating 93 To 2030 $27 ✪
Marie Christien Lugten Grand Vintage Methode Traditionelle 2012 Rating 93 To 2019 $35 TS
Late Disgorged Methode Traditionelle Pinot Noir Chardonnay 2008 Rating 92 To 2017 $40 TS
The Calling Swan Valley Verdelho 2016 Rating 91 To 2022 $19 ✪
Berns and Walsh Pemberton Pinot Noir 2014 Rating 91 To 2020 $31
Swan Valley Shiraz 2015 Rating 91 To 2025 $26
Swan Valley Petit Verdot 2014 Rating 91 To 2024 $27
Methode Traditionnelle Chenin Blanc NV Rating 91 To 2017 $22 TS ✪
Avant-Garde Series Swan Valley Tempranillo 2016 Rating 90 To 2020 $38
Blanc de Blancs NV Rating 90 To 2018 $32 TS

Six Acres   ★★★★☆

20 Ferndale Road, Silvan, Vic 3795 **Region** Yarra Valley
T 0408 991 741 **www**.sixacres.com.au **Open** W'ends 10–4
Winemaker Aaron and Ralph Zuccaro **Est.** 1999 **Dozens** 470 **Vyds** 1.64ha
Ralph and Lesley Zuccaro, who have a successful optical dispensing business, decided to plant a vineyard in 1999 to pinot noir (0.82ha), cabernet sauvignon (0.62ha) and merlot (0.2ha). Son Aaron, a biochemist, grew restless in the confines of a laboratory, and started his winemaking career in 2007, graduating in '12 from CSU. During his time at CSU he worked at Chandon Australia. The small size of the property means that all the work is carried out by the family.

ᵀᵀᵀᵀᵞ **Black Label Yarra Valley Pinot Noir 2015** Part estate-grown at Silvan, part from vineyards at Gruyere and St Andrews on opposite sides of the Yarra Valley. Relatively light-bodied, with a mix of sweet berry, earth and forest notes each tugging at the other. The war games need a truce to resolve the differences presently on display. Very different from the '14 Pinot. Screwcap. 13.5% alc. **Rating** 90 **To** 2021 $32

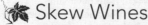 # Skew Wines   ★★★★

17a Edward Street, Norwood, SA 5067 **Region** Various
T 0407 972 064 **www**.skew.com.au **Open** By appt
Winemaker Andrew Ewart **Est.** 2014 **Dozens** 300

Andrew Ewart's involvement in wine dates back 40 years, covering South Africa, the US and NZ, but always making Australia home. A multi-decade career in research/academia has covered scientific advances in both the winery and the vineyard, over-qualifying him for his role as head of a still small family wine business which started even smaller – wine for family consumption. Son Simon describes himself as a trainee winemaker, his wife Kylie (a lawyer) describes herself as breadwinner and taster. The portfolio is currently an Eden Valley riesling, a Bordeaux blend from a single vineyard in the Fleurieu Peninsula and a McLaren Vale grenache.

�♥♥♥♥ Eden Valley Riesling 2015 Plain KISS winemaking. Springs into life on the palate with mouthwatering Meyer lemon and lime fruit coating every tastebud in the mouth. There is ample acidity to underwrite the medium to long-term future of the wine, yet it doesn't put up a barrier to those wanting to crack a bottle tonight. Screwcap. 11.3% alc. **Rating** 94 **To** 2029 $24 ✪

♥♥♥♥♡ Fleurieu BDX 2015 Rating 90 **To** 2025 $24

Skillogalee   ★★★★☆

Trevarrick Road, Sevenhill via Clare, SA 5453 **Region** Clare Valley
T (08) 8843 4311 **www.**skillogalee.com.au **Open** 7 days 7.30–5
Winemaker Dave Palmer, Emma Walker **Est.** 1970 **Dozens** 15 000 **Vyds** 50.3ha
David and Diana Palmer have fully capitalised on the exceptional fruit quality of the Skillogalee vineyards. All the wines are generous and full-flavoured, particularly the reds. In 2002 the Palmers purchased next-door neighbour Waninga Vineyards, with 30ha of 30-year-old vines, allowing an increase in production without any change in quality or style. Exports to the UK, Denmark, Switzerland, Malaysia, Thailand and Singapore.

♥♥♥♥♡ Clare Valley Riesling 2016 This brightly coloured wine is redolent with white flowers and kaffir lime, while the juicy, textured and flavoursome palate is balanced and long. Delicious now, this will reward at least another 5–10 years in the cellar. Screwcap. 12.5% alc. **Rating** 92 **To** 2025 $25 PR ✪
Clare Valley Chardonnay 2016 A high quality wine from a region that one doesn't normally associate with this variety. Attractive stone fruit and gently nutty aromas lead onto the palate which is restrained, balanced and long. Screwcap. 13% alc. **Rating** 91 **To** 2020 $27 PR

 # Slain Giant Wines   ★★★★

PO Box 551, Tanunda, SA 5352 **Region** Barossa Valley
T 0427 524 161 **www.**slaingiant.com **Open** Not
Winemaker Tyson Bitter **Est.** 2016 **Dozens** 3500
Founder and winemaker Tyson Bitter has had nearly two decades of experience in the wine industry, from vineyards to the cellar, to assistant winemaker and cellar manager, and now – after finishing a wine science degree at CSU – has decided to start his own business. Slain Giant Wines takes its name from the story of the Kaurna people who named SA's Mount Lofty Ranges Yurrebilla after a dreamtime giant ancestral figure who travelled from the mountains to the east to attack the tribes through the plains. Yurrebilla was slain, and back in real time, Tyson is slaying all the current ideas about winemaking. Thus his wines are a blend of vintages, varieties and/or regions. Just to complicate the picture, the Medium Bodied Dry White does have a vintage.

♥♥♥♥♡ Full Bodied Dry Red NV Cabernet sauvignon, petit verdot and tannat from Clare Valley, Langhorne Creek and Barossa Valley from the '15 and '16 vintages. It is indeed rich and full-bodied, with ripe flavours and tannins. What is not obvious is the rationale/need for the two-vintage blend (and the percentage contribution of each vintage and variety). Screwcap. 14.5% alc. **Rating** 91 **To** 2026 $28
Medium Bodied Dry Red NV Shiraz, barbera and malbec from the Barossa Valley, McLaren Vale and Adelaide Hills from the '15 and '16 vintages. It is indeed medium-bodied, and is fresh and juicy, the complexity there or thereabouts. Screwcap. 14.5% alc. **Rating** 91 **To** 2022 $28

Small Island Wines ★★★★★

Drink Co, Shop 10, 33 Salamanca Place, Hobart 7004 **Region** Southern Tasmania
T 0414 896 930 **www.**smallislandwines.com **Open** Mon–Sat 10–8
Winemaker James Broinowski **Est.** 2015 **Dozens** 3500 **Vyds** 3ha

Tasmanian-born James Broinowski completed his Bachelor of Viticulture and Oenology degree at the University of Adelaide in 2013. He was faced with the same problem as many other young graduates wanting to strike out on their own: cash. While others in his predicament may have found the same solution, his is the first wine venture to successfully seek crowd funding. His payback will be an e-real-life access into sharing the journey of the winemaking at Small Island, and some wine at the end. The first year ('15) allowed him to purchase pinot noir from Glengarry in the north of the island, making 2100 bottles of Pinot Noir which won a gold medal at the Royal International Hobart Wine Show '16, and 200 bottles of Rose that sold out in four days at the Taste of Tasmania Festival. In '16 he was able to buy pinot from the highly rated Gala Estate on the east coast, and backup the '15 purchase from Glengarry vineyard with '16. It looks very much like a potential acorn to oak story, for the quality of the wines is seriously good.

🍷🍷🍷🍷🍷 **Pinot Noir 2015** Wow. Small island, but a big pinot noir, Tasmania's answer to Central Otago. The colour is deep, and both the texture and tannin structure are powerful. But amid this feast of plenty, there is purity and restraint to the cherry fruit that emerges to claim the finish and aftertaste. Gold medal Hobart Wine Show '16 richly deserved. Screwcap. 13.5% alc. **Rating** 96 **To** 2029 $45
Patsie's Blush Rose 2016 Pale salmon-pink; spicy savoury notes on the bouquet lead into a richly flavoured and textured palate with a core of small red and forest berries; exceptional mouthfeel and length. A very attractive, serious pinot noir rose, a rare beast indeed. Screwcap. 13.5% alc. **Rating** 95 $30

Smallfry Wines ★★★★☆

13 Murray Street, Angaston, SA 5353 **Region** Barossa Valley
T (08) 8564 2182 **www.**smallfrywines.com.au **Open** By appt tel 0412 153 243
Winemaker Wayne Ahrens **Est.** 2005 **Dozens** 1500 **Vyds** 27ha

The engagingly named Smallfry Wines is the venture of Wayne Ahrens and partner Suzi Hilder. Wayne is from a fifth-generation Barossa family; Suzi is the daughter of well known Upper Hunter viticulturist Richard Hilder and wife Del, former partners in Pyramid Hill Wines. Both have degrees from CSU, and both have extensive experience – Suzi was a consultant viticulturist, and Wayne's track record includes seven vintages as a cellar hand at Orlando Wyndham and other smaller Barossa wineries. Their vineyards in the Eden Valley (led by cabernet sauvignon and riesling) and the Vine Vale area of the Barossa Valley (shiraz, grenache, semillon, mourvedre, cabernet sauvignon and riesling) are certified biodynamic/ organic. Exports to the UK, the US, the Philippines, Singapore, Hong Kong, Japan and China.

🍷🍷🍷🍷🍷 **Barossa Riesling 2016** Well made; rieslings with residual sugar can fall between two stools, often with insufficient sugar. This has nailed it, with pristine lime juice balancing sweetness and acidity. It will flower further over the next 5 years, and go on thereafter. Screwcap. 11% alc. **Rating** 95 **To** 2031 $25 ❂
Eden Valley Riesling 2016 Real life can be cruel when it comes to grape growing, but also uplifting if you can make a wine with the quality of this one. It has 6g/l residual sugar (deliberate) largely hidden by crisp, crunchy acidity and a generous burst of lime juice. Screwcap. 11.8% alc. **Rating** 94 **To** 2026 $25 ❂

🍷🍷🍷🍷🍷 **Stella Luna Barossa Cinsault Shiraz 2016** Rating 93 **To** 2018 $28
Barossa Joven 2016 Rating 92 **To** 2019 $28
Barossa Rose 2016 Rating 90 **To** 2017 $28

Smidge Wines

62 Austral Terrace, Malvern, SA 5061 (postal) **Region** South Eastern Australia
T (08) 8272 0369 **www**.smidgewines.com **Open** Not
Winemaker Matt Wenk **Est.** 2004 **Dozens** 1000
The business is owned by Matt Wenk and wife Trish Callaghan, and was for many years
an out-of-hours occupation for Matt; his day job was as winemaker for Two Hands Wines
(and Sandow's End). In 2013 he retired from Two Hands, and plans to increase production
of Smidge to 8000 dozen over the next few years. His retirement meant the Smidge wines
could no longer be made at Two Hands, and the winemaking operations have been moved
to McLaren Vale, where Smidge is currently leasing a small winery. Smidge owns the vineyard
in Willunga which provides the grapes for all the Cabernet Sauvignon releases and some of
the McLaren Vale Shiraz. The vision is to build a modern customised facility on the Willunga
property in the not-too-distant future. Exports to the UK and the US.

Magic Dirt Mengler's Hill Eden Valley Shiraz 2014 Red and black fruits,
spice and pepper course through the expressive bouquet and animated medium
to full-bodied palate, with a juicy, spicy red licorice farewell, the tannins perfectly
weighted. It's the perfect compromise between power and pure expression of place.
Screwcap. 14.2% alc. **Rating** 97 **To** 2039 $100 ○

S Barossa Valley Shiraz 2014 The slightly less full-bodied weight of this wine
allows more light and shade, more complex fruit expression. It's very much a
matter of personal taste, and I can't differentiate (in terms of points) between the
wines, other than the Mengler's Hill. Screwcap. 14.6% alc. **Rating** 96 **To** 2039
$65 ○

Magic Dirt Stonewell Barossa Valley Shiraz 2014 Like all its siblings,
extremely complex, extremely powerful; here some bitter chocolate insinuates its
way into the long, dark-toned palate coming, as they all do, from low-yielding
vineyards (typically less than 0.5t/acre). These wines are all (with the exception of
Mengler's Hill) full-bodied. Screwcap. 14.6% alc. **Rating** 96 **To** 2039 $100

Magic Dirt Greenock Barossa Valley Shiraz 2014 There is only one
barrique (22 dozen) made of each of these regional wines, and only used oak
employed. Like all, needed a degree of patience (and swirling in the glass) before
opening up. The dark berry bouquet then became ascendant with the least twitch
of the glass, spicy black fruits studded with fine tannins on the full-bodied palate
closing the deal. Screwcap. 14.8% alc. **Rating** 96 **To** 2039 $100

Magic Dirt Moppa Barossa Valley Shiraz 2014 Dark, brooding fruits on
the bouquet lead the way into a firm, full-bodied palate, with savoury characters
dominant, part fruit, part tannin-derived. Screwcap. 14.6% alc. **Rating** 96
To 2039 $100

The GruVe Adelaide Hills Gruner Veltliner 2016 Rating 93 **To** 2023 $30
The Ging McLaren Vale Shiraz 2014 Rating 90 **To** 2026 $30 JF

Smithbrook ★★★☆

Smithbrook Road, Pemberton, WA 6260 **Region** Pemberton
T (08) 9750 2150 **www**.smithbrookwines.com.au **Open** By appt
Winemaker Ben Rector **Est.** 1988 **Dozens** 10 000 **Vyds** 57ha
The picturesque Smithbrook property is owned by Perth businessman Peter Fogarty and
family, who also own Lake's Folly in the Hunter Valley, Deep Woods Estate in Margaret River
and Millbrook in the Perth Hills. Originally planted in the 1980s and one of the first in the
Pemberton region, the Smithbrook vineyard covers over 57ha of the 110ha property and
focuses on sauvignon blanc, chardonnay and merlot.

Pemberton Chardonnay 2016 The cool climate gives the wine intensity and
shape, with white peach and citrus blossom aromas intertwined with grapefruit
and stone fruit on the palate. Its length is good, and you don't stop to try to
unpick the subtle, integrated oak. Screwcap. 13.5% alc. **Rating** 90 **To** 2019 $17 ○

Snake + Herring

PO Box 918, Dunsborough, WA 6281 **Region** South West Australia
T 0419 487 427 **www**.snakeandherring.com.au **Open** Not
Winemaker Tony Davis **Est.** 2010 **Dozens** 7000

Tony (Snake) Davis and Redmond (Herring) Sweeny both started university degrees before finding that they were utterly unsuited to their respective courses. Having stumbled across Margaret River, Tony's life changed forever; he enrolled at Adelaide University, thereafter doing vintages in the Eden Valley, Oregon, Beaujolais and Tasmania, before three years at Plantagenet, next Brown Brothers, then a senior winemaking role at Yalumba, a six-year stint designing Millbrook Winery in the Perth Hills, and four years with Howard Park in Margaret River. Redmond's circuitous course included a chartered accountancy degree and employment with an international accounting firm in Busselton, and the subsequent establishment of Forester Estate in 2001, in partnership with Kevin McKay. Back on home turf he is the marketing and financial controller of Snake + Herring. Exports to China.

🍷🍷🍷🍷🍷 **Corduroy Karridale Margaret River Chardonnay 2014** Karridale is the coolest and southernmost part of Margaret River, and the wine proclaims that origin loud and clear with its tangy, zesty fruit driving it at high speed across the palate and into the long aftertaste. Its purity is quite exceptional. Screwcap. 13.5% alc. **Rating** 96 **To** 2024 $38 ○

Cannonball Margaret River Cabernet Sauvignon Merlot Petit Verdot 2013 64% cabernet sauvignon, 21% merlot, 12% petit verdot and 4% malbec separately open-fermented, matured in French barriques and puncheons (50% new). The efforts in the winery have paid big dividends. This is an Aladdin's Cave of aromas and flavours, each having its say, ultimately uniting in the joyously juicy red fruits of the medium-bodied palate, framed by a complex chord of savoury, herbal tannins. Screwcap. 13.5% alc. **Rating** 96 **To** 2033 $38 ○

Perfect Day Margaret River Sauvignon Blanc Semillon 2016 There's more to this than meets the eye, both the bouquet and palate suggesting flavour augmentation by all or some of oak, skin contact and lees contact. The clever aspect is the uncertainty about which has been responsible: what is certain is the extra length and depth of the mouthfeel – or, in a word, its complexity. Screwcap. 13% alc. **Rating** 95 **To** 2018 $24 ○

Dirty Boots Margaret River Cabernet Sauvignon 2014 Scores with its elegance rather than its power, its purity rather than its complexity. It's a cassis-driven cabernet that has no excess tannin to soften, and the oak is not intrusive. Made for drinking tonight. Screwcap. 14% alc. **Rating** 94 **To** 2024 $24 ○

🍷🍷🍷🍷🍸 **Redemption Great Southern Shiraz 2013 Rating** 90 **To** 2023 $24

Snobs Creek Wines ★★★★

486 Goulburn Valley Highway, via Alexandra, Vic 3714 **Region** Upper Goulburn
T (03) 9596 3043 **www**.snobscreekvineyard.com.au **Open** W'ends 11–5
Winemaker Marcus Gillon **Est.** 1996 **Dozens** 1500 **Vyds** 5ha

In the 1860s, well respected West Indian shoemaker 'Black' Brookes occupied a cottage at the bridge over Cataract Creek. After he passed away in the late 1880s the creek was renamed Snobs Creek, 'snob' being an old English term for cobbler (shoe repairer), and the last that shapes the toe end of the shoe. The vineyard is situated where Snobs Creek joins the Goulburn River, 5km below the Lake Eildon wall. The varieties grown are shiraz (2.5ha), sauvignon blanc (1.5ha) and chardonnay (1ha); all manage to produce no more than 7.4 tonnes per hectare. Is described as a 'cool climate vineyard in a landscaped environment'.

🍷🍷🍷🍷🍷 **Brookes Shiraz Cabernet Merlot 2015** 65% shiraz, 28% cabernet sauvignon, 7% merlot, hand-picked, cultured yeast, matured in American oak. Lateral thinking and skilful handling in the winery have paid significant dividends; this is a prime example of varietal blending chosen for positive reasons, not by default. Blackberry, plum, spice and licorice are supported by balanced oak and ripe tannins. Screwcap. 14.3% alc. **Rating** 94 **To** 2029 $25

🍷🍷🍷🍷🍷 The Artisan Heathcote Shiraz 2015 Rating 93 To 2028 $23 SC
VSP Shiraz 2015 Rating 91 To 2030 $23

Sons & Brothers Vineyard ★★★★

Spring Terrace Road, Millthorpe, NSW 2798 **Region** Orange
T (02) 6366 5117 **www**.sonsandbrothers.com.au **Open** Not
Winemaker Dr Chris Bourke **Est.** 1978 **Dozens** 300 **Vyds** 2ha
Chris and Kathryn Bourke do not pull their punches when they say, 'Our vineyard has had a chequered history, because in 1978 we were trying to establish ourselves in a non-existent wine region with no local knowledge and limited personal knowledge of grapegrowing and winemaking. It took us about 15 years of hit and miss before we started producing regular supplies of appropriate grape varieties at appropriate ripeness levels for sales to other NSW wineries.' Chris has published two fascinating papers on the origins of savagnin in Europe; he has also traced its movements in Australia after it was one of the varieties collected by James Busby – and moved just in time to save the last plantings in NSW of Busby's importation.

🍷🍷🍷🍷🍷 **Cabernet of Millthorpe 2015** The light but bright colour reflects the co-fermentation of 5% savagnin, the vineyard at 935m in Orange. Chris Bourke says the bouquet has a touch of musk ex the savagnin, and I agree. The bright cassis fruit of the cabernet shows no unripe characters whatsoever, and the tannins are in no way assertive. As enjoyable as it is unusual. Crown seal. 13.5% alc. **Rating** 94 **To** 2029 $30 **❂**

Sons of Eden ★★★★★

Penrice Road, Angaston, SA 5353 **Region** Barossa
T (08) 8564 2363 **www**.sonsofeden.com **Open** 7 days 11–6
Winemaker Corey Ryan, Simon Cowham **Est.** 2000 **Dozens** 9000 **Vyds** 60ha
Corey Ryan and Simon Cowham both learnt and refined their skills in the vineyards and cellars of Eden Valley. Corey is a trained oenologist with over 20 vintages under his belt, having cut his teeth as a winemaker at Henschke. Thereafter he worked for Rouge Homme and Penfolds in Coonawarra, backed up by winemaking stints in the Rhône Valley, and in 2002 he took the opportunity to work in NZ for Villa Maria Estates. In '07 he won the Institute of Masters of Wine scholarship. Simon has had a similarly international career, covering such diverse organisations as Oddbins, UK and the Winemakers' Federation of Australia. Switching from the business side to grapegrowing when he qualified as a viticulturist, he worked for Yalumba as technical manager of the Heggies and Pewsey Vale vineyards. With this background, it comes as no surprise to find that the estate-grown wines are of outstanding quality, nor that in '13 they were awarded the title of Barossa Winemaker of the Year by the Barons of Barossa. Exports to the UK, the US, Germany, Switzerland, Hong Kong, the Philippines, Taiwan and China.

🍷🍷🍷🍷🍷 **Cirrus Single Vineyard High Eden Valley Riesling 2016** The difference between this magnificent riesling and Freya is startling. It rides on a magic carpet of lime, lemon sherbet and thrilling acidity. Only riesling can produce such intensity with such delicacy, with a fresh, airy spring day mouthfeel. It's worth every penny, and is a privilege to taste. Screwcap. 12% alc. **Rating** 98 **To** 2036 $42 **❂**
Zephyrus Barossa Shiraz 2015 A seriously complex and intense wine, combining raw power and finesse on the prodigiously long palate, piano keys from all parts of the keyboard being played from the opening stanza to the aftertaste, sour cherries and dried herbs, licorice and black pepper soprano to the bass of blackberry, in a coruscating display of daring to be different shiraz. Screwcap. 14.5% alc. **Rating** 97 **To** 2040 $48 **❂**
Remus Old Vine Eden Valley Shiraz 2014 The bouquet's harmony of red and black fruits and oak aromas flows into the medium-bodied palate, perfectly ripened shiraz standing proudly centre stage. Secondary, savoury notes get air time, but the core is this beautifully detailed and supple palate of red and black cherry fruit, elegance the last thought. Screwcap. 14.5% alc. **Rating** 97 **To** 2040 $75 **❂**

🍷🍷🍷🍷🍷 **Freya Eden Valley Riesling 2016** Meyer lemon fruit overshadows (in a good way) the lime-accented fruit on the generous palate. No more could have been done to maximise the high quality fruit. It is full of charm – and flavour. Screwcap. 12.5% alc. **Rating** 95 **To** 2031 $27 ◎

Marschall Barossa Shiraz 2015 The bouquet and medium to full-bodied palate waste no time in communicating the intensely complex tower of dark fruits, spice, dried herbs and tannins derived in part from the fruit, part from the oak. Very impressive. Screwcap. 14.5% alc. **Rating** 95 **To** 2035 $31 ◎

Romulus Old Vine Barossa Valley Shiraz 2014 Matured in new and used French and American hogsheads for 20 months. Unapologetically full-bodied, but not brazenly so. The predominantly black fruits are joined by ripe tannins and mocha notes ex the American oak. The wine needs a decade to show its best, but will live and prosper for many years thereafter. Screwcap. 14.5% alc. **Rating** 95 **To** 2030 $75

Kennedy Barossa Valley Grenache Shiraz Mourvedre 2015 A 40/34/26% blend, matured in used French oak for 16 months before blending. Avoids confection/sweet fruit flavours, and does so with panache, ringing red, purple and black fruits into the very complex medium to full-bodied palate, cherry/plum and blackberry flavours welded together with a savoury, spicy subtext. Screwcap. 14.5% alc. **Rating** 95 **To** 2025 $31 ◎

Selene Barossa Valley Tempranillo 2014 **Rating** 94 **To** 2034 $48

🍷🍷🍷🍷🍺 **Pumpa Eden Valley Cabernet Shiraz 2014** **Rating** 92 **To** 2034 $31

Soul Growers ★★★★★

218–230 Murray Street, Tanunda, SA 5352 **Region** Barossa Valley
T 0410 505 590 **www**.soulgrowers.com **Open** Thurs–Sat 11–4 or by appt
Winemaker Paul Heinicke, Stuart Bourne **Est.** 1998 **Dozens** 5000 **Vyds** 4.85ha
In January 2014 Paul Heinicke (one of the four founders of the business) purchased the shares previously held by David Cruickshank and James and Paul Lindner. The vineyards are mainly on hillside country in the Seppeltsfield area, with shiraz, cabernet sauvignon, grenache and chardonnay the most important varieties, and lesser plantings of mataro and black muscat; there are then pocket-handkerchief blocks of shiraz at Tanunda, mataro at Nuriootpa and a 1.2ha planting of grenache at Krondorf. Exports to the US, Canada, Singapore, Hong Kong and China.

🍷🍷🍷🍷🍷 **106 Vines Barossa Valley Mourvedre 2015** This is made across 106 individual vines, all over 130yo, that have survived the encroaching sprawl of Nuriootpa, enough to make a single hogshead. Each bottle was then filled by hand. The wine's bright, natural acidity is palate whetting, giving the impression of a mid-weight boxer's prowess, with a heavyweight puncher's heft. Across this, smoked meat, blood plum, iodine, dried tobacco, pepper, sage and peat are strewn. This is compelling upon entry, cool and building, layer upon layer, into a savoury tour de force. Not once does it strike a pose of jam. Not once did I spit it. Diam. 14.3% alc. **Rating** 97 **To** 2035 $110 NG ◎

🍷🍷🍷🍷🍷 **Single Vineyard Hampel Barossa Valley Shiraz 2015** This buxom and beautifully polished wine hails from an ancient parcel, the finest contribution from the Hampel family's vineyards. Blueberry, boysenberry and mulberry are slung across a statuesque, billowing palate that feels like a satin cushion in the mouth so well are the tannins polished and massaged. Some anise and a gentle drift of pepper, too. Diam. 14.5% alc. **Rating** 95 **To** 2035 $150 NG

Slow Grown Barossa Shiraz 2015 This is an impeccably polished wine of buoyant blue and black fruits, lilac floats, a thread of anise and spice and well embedded oak. A blend of Barossan and Eden Valley fruit, this is exceptionally poised between innate richness, a corset of finely tuned structural pillars in the oak, and well managed tannins. Diam. 14.5% alc. **Rating** 94 **To** 2035 $55 NG

Single Vineyard Kroehn Eden Valley Shiraz 2015 An elegant, pulpy and highly aromatic shiraz when viewed from within the prism of Barossa, this has soaring purple florals, slinky tannins, a prickle of aniseed and a densely packed mid-palate of blue and dark fruits. Eden Valley embellishes the natural potency of the region's wines with a cooler shade, without necessarily relinquishing shiraz's innate power. Diam. 14.5% alc. **Rating** 94 **To** 2035 $150 NG

Defiant Barossa Valley Mataro 2013 Rich and full-bodied, yet retains a surprising degree of elegance, reflecting the balance between fruit and tannin. There are elements of spice to go with the plum and mulberry of the mid-palate, oak kept to a minimal role. Diam. 15% alc. **Rating** 94 **To** 2028 $50

ŦŦŦŦŦ Cellar Dweller Cabernet Sauvignon 2015 Rating 93 To 2035 $55 NG
Defiant Barossa Valley Mataro 2015 Rating 93 To 2027 $55 NG
Slow Grown Barossa Shiraz 2014 Rating 92 To 2026 $55 NG
Cellar Dweller Cabernet Sauvignon 2014 Rating 92 To 2029 $55 NG
El Mejor Barossa Valley Cabernet Shiraz Mourvedre 2015 Rating 91 To 2030 $110 NG
Wild Iris Eden Valley Chardonnay 2014 Rating 90 To 2019 $25 SC
Provident Barossa Valley Shiraz 2015 Rating 90 To 2023 $28 NG

Soumah ★★★★★

18 Hexham Road, Gruyere, Vic 3770 **Region** Yarra Valley
T (03) 5962 4716 **www**.soumah.com.au **Open** 7 days 10–5
Winemaker Scott McCarthy **Est.** 1997 **Dozens** 15000 **Vyds** 19.57ha
Unravelling the story behind the exotically named Soumah, and its strikingly labelled Savarro (reminiscent of 19th-century baroque design), was a voyage of discovery. Soumah is in fact an abbreviation of South of Maroondah (Highway), and Savarro is an alternative name for savagnin. This is the venture of Brett Butcher, who has international experience in the hospitality industry as CEO of the Langham Group, and a long involvement in retailing wines to restaurants in many countries. Tim Brown is viticultural director. The many varieties planted have been clonally selected and grafted onto rootstock with the long-term future in mind, although some of the sauvignon blanc is already being grafted over to bracchetto. Exports to the UK, Canada, Denmark, South Korea, Singapore, Hong Kong, Japan and China.

ŦŦŦŦŦ Hexham Single Vineyard Yarra Valley Chardonnay 2015 Estate-grown, hand-picked, wild yeast–barrel fermented, matured in a mix of new and used French oak for 8 months, mlf allowed in the new oak. The complex vinification has worked well, the mlf component introducing touches of fig and cream to offset the white peach and grapefruit of the major part of the wine. The overall length and balance can't be faulted. Screwcap. 13% alc. **Rating** 95 **To** 2023 $39

Equilibrio Single Vineyard Yarra Valley Pinot Noir 2015 Clones D4V2, 777 and MV6, a best barrels selection, effectively Soumah's reserve pinot. A worthy example of a great Yarra Valley vintage with an extra level of intensity to its sour and red cherry fruit flavours, which easily carry French oak, ditto the savoury/spicy tannins on the finish. Screwcap. 13% alc. **Rating** 95 **To** 2024 $68

Hexham Single Vineyard Yarra Valley Viognier 2016 The difficulty in picking the right time to harvest viognier is legendary, but Soumah pretty well nailed it here. There is apricot and yellow peach fruit in abundance, but it sidesteps the issue of an excessively phenolic finish – instead there is a jab of citrussy acidity. Screwcap. 13% alc. **Rating** 94 **To** 2021 $35

Hexham Single Vineyard Yarra Valley Syrah 2015 Good hue and depth; the scented bouquet has spice, pepper, balance and cedary oak all on show, the medium-bodied palate providing an instant replay. Screwcap. 13.8% alc. **Rating** 94 **To** 2035 $35

ŦŦŦŦŦ Hexham Yarra Valley Savarro 2016 Rating 92 To 2021 $28
U. Nygumby Yarra Valley Pinot Noir 2016 Rating 92 To 2023 $35
Equilibrio Yarra Valley Syrah 2014 Rating 91 To 2029 $68

Hexham Yarra Valley Chardonnay 2016 Rating 90 To 2023 $39
Hexham Yarra Valley Pinot Noir 2016 Rating 90 To 2025 $35
Hexham Yarra Valley Nebbiolo 2015 Rating 90 To 2030 $49

Spence ★★★★★

760 Burnside Road, Murgheboluc, Vic 3221 **Region** Geelong
T (03) 5265 1181 **www.spencewines.com.au Open** 1st Sun each month
Winemaker Peter Spence, Scott Ireland **Est.** 1997 **Dozens** 1300 **Vyds** 3.2ha
Peter and Anne Spence were sufficiently inspired by an extended European holiday, which
included living on a family vineyard in Provence, to purchase a small property and establish a
vineyard and winery. They have planted 3.2ha on a north-facing slope in a valley 7km south of
Bannockburn, the lion's share to three clones of shiraz (1.83ha), the remainder to chardonnay,
pinot noir and fast-diminishing cabernet sauvignon (it is being grafted over to viognier for
use in the Shiraz). The vineyard attained full organic status in 2008, since then using only
biodynamic practices.

♀♀♀♀♀ **Geelong Shiraz 2015** Includes 3% viognier. 60% whole bunches; wild-yeast
co-fermented in open vats, matured for 12 months in barriques (20% new), gold
medal Geelong Wine Show '16. Brilliant crimson-purple; a tautly strung, intensely
flavoured and powerfully structured shiraz with its whole life in front of it. A wine
of true distinction. Screwcap. 13.7% alc. **Rating** 96 **To** 2035 $30 ✪
Geelong Chardonnay 2015 Gold medal Geelong Wine Show '16. An incisive
chardonnay, brilliantly cut in the fashion of a diamond, with zesty grapefruit (skin,
pith and juice) driving the palate through to the finish without so much as a side
glance. Polarising at gold medal level. Needs time. Screwcap. 12.6% alc. **Rating** 95
To 2023 $30 ✪
Geelong Pinot Noir 2015 Bright, clear colour; a light-bodied, elegant style,
red cherry/berry fruits given complexity by oak and fruit tannins. Gold medal
Geelong Wine Show '16. Screwcap. 13.6% alc. **Rating** 94 **To** 2025 $30 ✪

Spinifex ★★★★★

PO Box 511, Nuriootpa, SA 5355 **Region** Barossa Valley
T (08) 8564 2059 **www.spinifexwines.com.au Open** At Artisans of Barossa
Winemaker Peter Schell **Est.** 2001 **Dozens** 6000
Peter Schell and Magali Gely are a husband and wife team from NZ who came to Australia in
the early 1990s to study oenology and marketing at Roseworthy College. They have spent four
vintages making wine in France, mainly in the south, where Magali's family were vignerons
for generations near Montpellier. The focus at Spinifex is the red varieties that dominate in the
south of France: mataro (more correctly mourvedre), grenache, shiraz and cinsaut. The wine
is made in open fermenters, basket-pressed, with partial wild (indigenous) fermentation and
relatively long post-ferment maceration. This is a very old approach, but nowadays à la mode.
Exports to the UK, Canada, Belgium, Singapore, Hong Kong, China and NZ.

♀♀♀♀♀ **La Maline Barossa Shiraz 2015** This is nothing short of electrifying. It's as
if a ball of energy has been created with a core of tiptop dark fruit laced with
pepper, menthol, star anise and patchouli. There are high tones to the floral notes,
creaminess on the full-bodied palate, velvety tannins and integrated cedary oak. It
has power, design and structure yet purity, too, and extraordinary length. It takes
complexity to a new level. Screwcap. 14.5% alc. **Rating** 97 **To** 2045 $70 JF ✪
Moppa Shiraz 2015 The inaugural release of this single vineyard wine. It exudes
a certain power yet dances to an elegant tune. Exemplary purple-dark crimson
hue; meaty and reductive at first, but soon enough revealing dark fresh fruit with
umami flavours of soy, and warm earth in a savoury spectrum. Full-bodied with
supple powerful tannins. Screwcap. 14.5% alc. **Rating** 97 **To** 2045 $60 JF ✪

♀♀♀♀♀ **Single Vineyard Old Vine Barossa Valley Shiraz 2012** The utterly
remarkable crimson-purple colour of a 4yo shiraz, and the sheer intensity of the
flavour, do speak of great vine age. I also suspect this wine spent much time in

oak, with a significant percentage new, France its likely provenance. Screwcap. 14.5% alc, Rating 96 To 2042 $70 🔞

Single Vineyard Old Vine Barossa Valley Mataro 2012 The identity of the vineyard is not disclosed, but it's very good on the incontrovertible evidence of this remarkable mataro, a variety that is notoriously difficult to manage on its own in the winery. The colour is excellent, as is the depth of the complex fruits that range across red and purple and then into a savoury/earthy eventide of flavours and dusty tannins. Screwcap. 14.5% alc. **Rating** 96 **To** 2032 $50 ✪

Barossa Syrah 2016 It's easy to be enchanted by this wine. It'll garner complexity in time, but it's sheer bliss to drink now thanks to its excellent fruit and perfectly poised tannins. A cascade of red fruits picks up a spice trail of star anise and cinnamon, some menthol too, en route to a full-bodied, very detailed, palate. Screwcap. 13.5% alc. **Rating** 95 **To** 2027 $28 JF ✪

Barossa Syrah 2015 There's only one word to describe a wine such as this: delicious – perhaps with a swear word or two to add emphasis. Its flowery, fragrant bouquet leads into a juicy red berry melange with rivulets of flavour skipping across the palate and into the fresh finish. You can cellar the wine for a decade if you wish, but I can't imagine it will ever be better than it is now. Screwcap. 13% alc. **Rating** 95 **To** 2025 $30 ✪

Bête Noir 2014 Shiraz is mentioned in small handwriting on the back label, the use of the phrase left to the imagination, but surely nothing to do with this wine, with its spicy, savoury, essency, juicy dark fruit flavours that ask you back again and again as you taste it. Screwcap. 14.5% alc. **Rating** 95 **To** 2034 $40

Miette 2015 58% grenache, 32% mataro, 10% cinsaut is the final blend and wow, what a beautiful wine. Not the most complex, but for sheer drinking pleasure, it's right up there, as lofty as the aromatics of red licorice, musk, menthol and spice. A silky sensation to the tannins, a bit of grunt too, and a lively acid kick to finish. Screwcap. 14.5% alc. **Rating** 95 **To** 2022 $23 JF ✪

Miette Barossa Valley Shiraz 2015 Rating 94 To 2030 $24 ✪

🍷🍷🍷🍷🍷 **Barossa Valley Rose 2016** Rating 93 To 2019 $28 JF
Esprit 2014 Rating 93 To 2029 $35
Adelaide Hills Aglianico 2015 Rating 93 To 2020 $30
Miette 2013 Rating 92 To 2020 $22.50 ✪
Miette Barossa Valley Shiraz 2014 Rating 91 To 2024 $22 ✪
Miette Barossa Valley Vermentino 2015 Rating 90 To 2018 $19 ✪
Single Vineyard Barossa Valley Clairette 2015 Rating 90 To 2019 $26
Louis Sparkling Shiraz NV Rating 90 To 2017 $60 TS

Spring Vale Vineyards ★★★★

130 Spring Vale Road, Cranbrook, Tas 7190 **Region** East Coast Tasmania
T (03) 6257 8208 **www**.springvalewines.com **Open** 7 days 11–4
Winemaker Matt Wood **Est.** 1986 **Dozens** 8000 **Vyds** 17.6ha
Rodney Lyne has progressively established pinot noir (6.5ha), chardonnay (2ha), gewurztraminer (1.6ha), pinot gris and sauvignon blanc (1ha each). Spring Vale also owns the Melrose vineyard, which is planted to pinot noir (3ha), sauvignon blanc and riesling (1ha each) and chardonnay (0.5ha). Exports to Singapore and Hong Kong.

🍷🍷🍷🍷🍷 **Pinot Noir 2015** With its floral, perfumed nose, dark plum and cherry fruit and a hint of vanilla from 9 months in French oak (25% new), there's plenty going on aromatically here. The damson plums continue onto the sweetly fruited palate and the tannins are supple, meaning that this can be enjoyed now and over the next 5–7 years. Screwcap. 13.7% alc. **Rating** 92 **To** 2023 $45 PR

Family Selection Repose Extra Brut 2009 The strawberry fruits of pinot meet the tense citrus of chardonnay, layered with bubblegum notes of fermentation and the candied almond complexity of 5 years of lees age. Acidity remains tense and firm, with contrasting sweet dosage on a long finish. Diam. 12% alc. **Rating** 91 **To** 2019 TS

Springington Hills Wines   ★★★★☆

41 Burnbank Grove, Athelstone, SA 5076 (postal) **Region** Eden Valley
T (08) 8337 7905 **www**.springtonhillswines.com.au **Open** Not
Winemaker John Ciccocioppo **Est.** 2001 **Dozens** 2000 **Vyds** 12ha
The Ciccocioppo family migrated from central Italy in the 1950s; as is so often the case, wine
was in their veins. In 2001, second-generation John and wife Connie purchased a grazing
property at Springton, and began the planting of shiraz and riesling. Each year they increased
the shiraz and riesling blocks, but also added smaller amounts of cabernet sauvignon, grenache
and a smaller amount still of montepulciano. The wines are available for tasting at Taste Eden
Valley in Angaston. Good label design and packaging.

🍷🍷🍷🍷🍷 **Eliza's Eden Valley Riesling 2016** A high quality Eden Valley riesling, already
showing its birthplace courtesy of outstanding mouthfeel to its interplay of
lemon/lime flavours and soft, but persistent, acidity. One of those wines happy
to be opened today, but with a bare minimum of a decade to show all its wares.
Screwcap. 11.5% alc. **Rating** 95 **To** 2029 $22

🍷🍷🍷🍷🍷 **Harvey's Eden Valley Cabernet Grenache Montepulciano Blend 2012**
Rating 90 **To** 2027 $30

Squitchy Lane Vineyard   ★★★★★

Medhurst Road, Coldstream, Vic 3770 **Region** Yarra Valley
T (03) 5964 9114 **www**.squitchylane.com.au **Open** W'ends 11–5
Winemaker Robert Paul **Est.** 1982 **Dozens** 2000 **Vyds** 5.75ha
Mike Fitzpatrick acquired a taste for fine wine while a Rhodes scholar at Oxford University
in the 1970s. Returning to Australia he guided Carlton Football Club to two premierships
as captain, then established Melbourne-based finance company Squitchy Lane Holdings.
The wines of Mount Mary inspired him to look for his own vineyard, and in '96 he found
a vineyard of sauvignon blanc, chardonnay, pinot noir, merlot, cabernet franc and cabernet
sauvignon, planted in '82, just around the corner from Coldstream Hills and Yarra Yering.

🍷🍷🍷🍷🍷 **The Key Single Vineyard Yarra Valley Chardonnay 2016** A little over
100 dozen bottles made of this intense, powerful chardonnay that ticks every box
with emphatic precision. The fruit is the key to the high quality of the wine, but
winemaking has protected, indeed embellished, it. White peach, nectarine and
grapefruit all contribute. Screwcap. 13% alc. **Rating** 96 **To** 2025 $40 ❂
Yarra Valley Cabernet Sauvignon 2015 30+yo estate vines, matured in
French oak for 15 months. The colour is bright crimson–purple, and the medium-
bodied palate is fresh and vibrant, the picking decision nailing the quality that is
now in the glass. Typical Yarra Valley fine-grained tannins are the icing on the cake.
Screwcap. 13.5% alc. **Rating** 95 **To** 2035 $45
Yarra Valley Pinot Noir 2015 MV6 and 114 clones, matured in French oak
for 11 months. A fragrant red berry and spice bouquet is followed by a long and
intense palate with good balance and length. Needs yet more time to fully open
up, but the basics are there – this is from the great '15 vintage, after all. Screwcap.
14% alc. **Rating** 94 **To** 2029 $35

🍷🍷🍷🍷🍷 **Yarra Valley Rose 2016 Rating** 90 **To** 2020 $25

Stage Door Wine Co   ★★★★★

22 Whibley Street, Henley Beach, SA 5022 **Region** Eden Valley
T 0400 991 968 **www**.stagedoorwineco.com.au **Open** Not
Winemaker Graeme Thredgold **Est.** 2013 **Dozens** 2500
It took a long time for Graeme Thredgold to establish this still-embryonic wine business.
Having been a successful professional musician for 15 years during the 1980s and '90s, he
developed vocal nodules in the early '90s, putting an end to his musical career. Having spent
so much time working in hotels and night clubs, a new occupation stared him in the face:

the liquor industry. In '92 he began working for Lion Nathan as a sales representative, then spent five years with SA Brewing, and in '08 ventured into the world of wine as national sales manager for Andrew Garrett. In around 2000 he moved on to the more fertile pasture of Tucker Seabrook as state sales manager for SA. Further roles with Barossa Valley Estate and as general manager of Chain of Ponds Wines added to an impressive career in sales and marketing, before he made his final move – to general manager of Eden Hall Wines, which just happens to be owned by his sister and brother-in-law, David and Mardi Hall. Exports to Canada.

ΨΨΨΨΨ **The Green Room Eden Valley Riesling 2016** Eden Valley riesling often has an element of Meyer lemon that emerges with lime in a different fashion from that of the Clare Valley. It always appeals to me as a point of difference, not necessarily quality. It certainly drives this wine, which has a fresh and lively finish and aftertaste. Good grapes and good wine. Screwcap. 12% alc. **Rating** 95 **To** 2029 $25 ✪

Eden Valley Shiraz 2015 The wine has very good texture, and the integration and balance of cedary French oak is as good as it gets. It looks to me as if the alcohol might even be a little bit less, rather than more, than the stated figure. By all means cellar it, but that's purely optional. Screwcap. 14.5% alc. **Rating** 95 **To** 2030 $50

Eden Valley Cabernet Sauvignon 2015 Has the same felicitous oak handling as its Shiraz sibling, even staring down the challenge of cabernet sauvignon. Mind you, it is a powerful cabernet, with a depth and range of cassis/blackcurrant/mulberry flavours tied to its bedrock of tannin, and does need patience. Screwcap. 14.5% alc. **Rating** 95 **To** 2035 $50

Front and Centre Barossa Shiraz 2015 87% Eden Valley, 13% Barossa Valley. A pretty good wine, the fruit more luscious and overt than its Eden Valley sibling. Luscious plum and blackberry fruit has ripe tannins to balance, and it's still in medium-bodied territory. Screwcap. 14.5% alc. **Rating** 94 **To** 2030 $25 ✪

ΨΨΨΨΨ **Full House Barossa Cabernet Sauvignon 2015** **Rating** 93 **To** 2029 $25 ✪

Staindl Wines   ★★★☆

63 Shoreham Road, Red Hill South, Vic 3937 (postal) **Region** Mornington Peninsula
T 0419 553 299 **www**.staindlwines.com.au **Open** By appt
Winemaker Rollo Crittenden (Contract) **Est.** 1982 **Dozens** 400 **Vyds** 3.1ha
As often happens, the establishment date for a wine producer can mean many things. In this instance it harks back to the planting of the vineyard by the Ayton family, and the establishment of what was thereafter called St Neots. Juliet and Paul Staindl acquired the property in 2002, and have extended the plantings to 2.6ha of pinot noir, 0.4ha of chardonnay and 0.1ha of riesling, the vineyard run biodynamically. Ironically, all the 30-year-old chardonnay vines have been removed (and replanted) due to eutypa, a die-back disease that decimates the crop – it is an increasing problem in many parts of Victoria and SA.

ΨΨΨΨΨ **Mornington Peninsula Riesling 2016** Bright straw-green; has very good acidity, giving the wine texture, structure and the freshness often absent from riesling grown in maritime climates. The flavours are green apple and citrus. Nice wine. Don't pay attention to the Burgundy bottle. Screwcap. 12.5% alc. **Rating** 93 **To** 2024 $25 ✪

ΨΨΨΨ **Mornington Peninsula Pinot Noir 2015** **Rating** 89 **To** 2020 $55

Staniford Wine Co   ★★★★★

20 Jackson Street, Mount Barker, WA 6324 **Region** Great Southern
T 0405 157 687 **www**.stanifordwineco.com.au **Open** By appt
Winemaker Michael Staniford **Est.** 2010 **Dozens** 500
Michael Staniford has been making wine in the Great Southern since 1995, principally as senior winemaker for Alkoomi at Frankland River, with additional experience as a contract

maker for other wineries. The business is built around single vineyard wines; a Chardonnay from a 20+-year-old vineyard in Albany and a Cabernet Sauvignon from a 15+-year-old vineyard in Mount Barker. The quality of these two wines is every bit as one would expect. Michael plans to introduce a Riesling and a Shiraz with a similar individual vineyard origin, quality being the first requirement.

🍷🍷🍷🍷🍷 **Great Southern Reserve Chardonnay 2015** Gloriously rich and flavoursome, yet neatly zipped together thanks to its fine acidity. White stone fruit, dried figs, grapefruit and woodsy spice are to the fore. The fuller-bodied palate causes quite a sensation with its flavours of grilled nuts, creamed honey and creamy lees. Top stuff. Screwcap. 13.5% alc. **Rating** 95 **To** 2023 $38 JF

🍷🍷🍷🍷🍷 **Great Southern Reserve Cabernet Franc 2015** **Rating** 93 **To** 2021 $31 JF

Stanton & Killeen Wines ★★★★★

440 Jacks Road, Murray Valley Highway, Rutherglen, Vic 3685 **Region** Rutherglen
T (02) 6032 9457 **www**.stantonandkilleen.com.au **Open** Mon–Sat 9–5, Sun 10–5
Winemaker Andrew Drumm, Joe Warren **Est.** 1875 **Dozens** 12 000 **Vyds** 34ha
In 2015 Stanton & Killeen celebrated its 140th anniversary, with a number of changes throughout the business. Andrew Drumm, formerly the CSU winemaker, was in place for his first vintage at Stanton & Killeen. He joined Ruston Prescott, who had been appointed vineyard manager in December '13. The business is owned by Wendy Killeen and her two children, Simon and Natasha. Wendy had embraced the role of CEO in July '11, using skills learnt working in the business community in northeast Victoria. Natasha manages the website, newsletter production and all consumer-focused communications. Simon has chosen to broaden his winemaking knowledge and skills by working outside the company. Exports to the UK, Switzerland, Hong Kong and China.

🍷🍷🍷🍷🍷 **The Prince Reserva 2015** This is a compelling Iberian blend and a homage to port given Chris Killeen's passion for the style. This is a sturdy, dry table wine. The varieties were largely co-fermented, resulting in a tarry lick to dark plum, liqueured cherry and a melody of spice and herbal notes. The tannins are pulpy and easygoing. Screwcap. 13.8% alc. **Rating** 94 **To** 2023 $45 NG
Classic Rutherglen Muscat NV Lusciously sweet but with real intensity and finish. It takes all the required components and slots them into the correct places. Leather, toffee, rancio, spice. Cleansing acidity sits at one with the overall wine. In a word, seamless. 500ml. Screwcap. 18% alc. **Rating** 94 $35 CM

🍷🍷🍷🍷🍷 **Reserve Rutherglen Durif 2015** **Rating** 91 **To** 2030 $35 NG
Rutherglen Shiraz Durif 2015 **Rating** 90 **To** 2025 $22 NG

Stargazer Wine ★★★★★

37 Rosewood Lane, Tea Tree, Tas 7017 **Region** Tasmania
T 0408 173 335 **www**.stargazerwine.com.au **Open** By appt
Winemaker Samantha Connew **Est.** 2012 **Dozens** 1200 **Vyds** 1ha
Samantha (Sam) Connew has racked up a series of exceptional achievements, commencing with Bachelor of Law and Bachelor of Arts degrees, majoring in political science and English literature, from the University of Canterbury, Christchurch, NZ, but showing her future direction by obtaining a postgraduate diploma of oenology and viticulture from Lincoln University, Canterbury, NZ. Sam moved to Australia, undertaking the advanced wine assessment course at the Australian Wine Research Institute in 2000, being chosen as a scholar at the '02 Len Evans Tutorial, winning the George Mackey Award for the best wine exported from Australia in '04; and in '07 was made International Red Winemaker of the Year at the International Wine Challenge, London. After a highly successful and lengthy position as chief winemaker at Wirra Wirra, Sam moved to Tasmania (via the Hunter Valley) to make the first wines for her own business, something she said she would never do. The emotive name (and label) is in part a tribute to Abel Tasman, the first European to sight Tasmania before proceeding to the South Island of NZ, navigating by the stars. Exports to the UK and the US.

ŶŶŶŶŶ **Coal River Valley Riesling 2016** Whole-bunch pressed, fermented in stainless steel, old oak and a ceramic egg, 2 months on lees with stirring. The complex vinification has worked perfectly: it has intense lime juice and lime zest flavours, but even more striking is the opulent juiciness of the mouthfeel before acidity on the finish cleanses the mouth. Screwcap. 12% alc. **Rating** 97 **To** 2031 $35 **○**

ŶŶŶŶŶ **Coal River Valley Chardonnay 2015** Bright, light straw-green, just as it should be, as is everything else. Grapefruit is the driving force on a very long, super-intense palate and aftertaste, the new oak totally absorbed by the fruit. Screwcap. 12.5% alc. **Rating** 96 **To** 2023 $45 **○**

ŶŶŶŶŶ **Tupelo 2016 Rating** 91 **To** 2018 $30

Steels Creek Estate

1 Sewell Road, Steels Creek, Vic 3775 **Region** Yarra Valley
T (03) 5965 2448 **www**.steelsckestate.com.au **Open** W'ends & public hols 10–6
Winemaker Simon Peirce **Est.** 1981 **Dozens** 400 **Vyds** 1.7ha
The Steels Creek vineyard (chardonnay, shiraz, cabernet sauvignon, cabernet franc and colombard), family-operated since 1981, is located in the picturesque Steels Creek Valley, with views towards the Kinglake National Park. All the wines are made onsite by winemaker and owner Simon Peirce, following renovations to the winery.

ŶŶŶŶŶ **Single Vineyard Yarra Valley Cabernet Sauvignon 2015** A well structured cabernet with firm granular tannins, well applied cedary oak and a flow of acidity all serving to give currency to the blackcurrant, bitter cola, mint and plum flavours. Finishes gently astringent with a dusting of vanilla and eucalyptus. Diam. 13.5% alc. **Rating** 93 **To** 2030 $35 NG
Single Vineyard Yarra Valley Shiraz 2015 A wine of bouncy purple and blue fruits as a result of what feels to be a gentle extraction regime. Some oak and pepper-infused acidity frame the pulpy fruit, almost like biting into a ripe bunch of grapes, and makes this mid-weighted wine fun to drink. Diam. 14% alc. **Rating** 91 **To** 2030 $35 NG
Single Vineyard Yarra Valley Colombard 2015 Punchy, tangy and very well made, this would make a sophisticated substitute for a whole slew of sauvignons. Tangerine, cumquat, dried mango and some herb leap from the glass. The exuberant aromas are bound to a zesty, light, crunchy palate, reverberating across a slate-like texture and vibrant acid crunch. Screwcap. 13% alc. **Rating** 90 **To** 2018 $22 NG

Steels Gate

227 Greenwoods Lane, Steels Creek, Vic 3775 **Region** Yarra Valley
T 0419 628 393 **www**.steelsgate.com.au **Open** Not
Winemaker Aaron Zuccaro **Est.** 2010 **Dozens** 500 **Vyds** 2ha
Brad Atkins and Matthew Davis acquired a 2ha vineyard of 25 to 30-year-old dry-grown chardonnay and pinot noir in 2009. For reasons unexplained, the owners have a particular love of gates, and as the property is at the end of Steels Creek, the choice of Steels Gate was obvious. The next step was to engage French designer Cecile Darcy to create what is known today as the Steels Gate logo.

ŶŶŶŶŶ **Yarra Valley Chardonnay 2012** Has developed as expected (first tasted Oct '13): great value at $25 for a Yarra Valley chardonnay now ready to drink. Screwcap. 12% alc. **Rating** 92 **To** 2019 $25 **○**

Stefani Estate

122 Long Gully Road, Healesville, Vic 3777 **Region** Yarra Valley/Heathcote
T (03) 9570 8750 **www**.stefaniestatewines.com.au **Open** By appt
Winemaker Peter Mackey **Est.** 1998 **Dozens** 6800 **Vyds** 30ha

Stefano Stefani came to Australia in 1985. Business success has allowed Stefano and wife Rina to follow in the footsteps of Stefano's grandfather, who had a vineyard and was an avid wine collector. The first property they acquired was at Long Gully Road in the Yarra Valley, planted to pinot grigio, cabernet sauvignon, chardonnay and pinot noir. The next was in Heathcote, where they acquired a property adjoining that of Mario Marson (ex Mount Mary), built a winery and established 14.4ha of shiraz, cabernet sauvignon, merlot, cabernet franc, malbec and petit verdot. In 2003 a second Yarra Valley property, named The View, reflecting its high altitude, was acquired and Dijon clones of chardonnay and pinot noir were planted. In addition, 1.6ha of sangiovese have been established, using scion material from the original Stefani vineyard in Tuscany. Exports to China.

🍷🍷🍷🍷🍷 **Barrel Selection Heathcote Vineyard Shiraz 2015** Matured in new and used French oak for 12 months, this a best barrels selection. It is a very complex wine with a core of luscious black fruits given context and flavour balance by an amalgam of spice, pepper and licorice on the finish and aftertaste. Diam. 14.5% alc. **Rating** 95 **To** 2040 $65

Boccallupo Mauro Nostrum Yarra Valley Sangiovese 2015 Matured for 12 months in French oak. Bright colour; this has the brightness and red-berried elegance that the '16 lacks, but is still very complex, and has excellent colour. Sour cherry, red cherry and savoury spices all contribute. Diam. 14% alc. **Rating** 95 **To** 2029 $65

🍷🍷🍷🍷 **The Gate Yarra Valley Cabernet Sauvignon 2014 Rating** 93 **To** 2028 $65
The View Yarra Valley Vineyard Pinot Gris 2016 Rating 91 **To** 2019 $30
The View Yarra Valley Vineyard Pinot Noir 2015 Rating 91 **To** 2025 $65
Heathcote Vineyard Shiraz 2015 Rating 91 **To** 2030 $40
Vigna Stefani Heathcote Malbec 2016 Rating 90 **To** 2021 $30

Stefano de Pieri ★★★★

27 Deakin Avenue, Mildura, Vic 3502 **Region** Murray Darling
T (03) 5021 3627 **www**.stefano.com.au **Open** Mon–Fri 8–6; w'ends 8–2
Winemaker Sally Blackwell, Stefano de Pieri **Est.** 2005 **Dozens** 25 000

Stefano de Pieri decided to have his own range of wines, wines that reflect his Italian spirit and the region he lives in. Mostly hand-picked, the fruit comes from a variety of Mildura vineyards, including the highly respected Chalmers Nursery vineyard. They are intended to be fresh and zesty, deliberately aiming at lower alcohol, to retain as much natural acidity as possible, designed to go with food, and inexpensive and easy to enjoy, reflecting Stefano's philosophy of generosity and warmth. The emphasis is on the Italian varieties, from arneis to aglianico, including a frizzante pinot grigio and the innovative blend of moscato gialla, garganega and greco, while retaining some of the local workhorses such as cabernet and chardonnay.

🍷🍷🍷🍷 **Pinot Grigio 2016** Matches Stefano's personality: bright and forthcoming. Nashi pear and green apple flavours are in complete accord, lemony acidity on the finish precisely weighted. Great value. Screwcap. 12% alc. **Rating** 90 **To** 2018 $17 ✪

L'Unico 2013 This blend of cabernet and sangiovese was born to be married to food, and in particular that of Stefano de Pieri. It is light to medium-bodied, savoury, and has the persistence needed in this context. Screwcap. 13.5% alc. **Rating** 90 **To** 2019 $24

Stefano Lubiana ★★★★★

60 Rowbottoms Road, Granton, Tas 7030 **Region** Southern Tasmania
T (03) 6263 7457 **www**.slw.com.au **Open** Thurs–Mon 11–4 (closed Jul)
Winemaker Steve Lubiana **Est.** 1990 **Dozens** NFP **Vyds** 25ha

Monique and Steve Lubiana moved from the hot inland of a brown Australia to the beautiful banks of the Derwent River in 1990 to pursue Steve's dream of making high quality sparkling wine. The sloping site allowed them to build a gravity-fed winery, and his whole winemaking approach since that time has been based on attention to detail within a biodynamic environment. The first sparkling wines were made in 1993 from the first plantings of chardonnay and pinot noir. Over the years they have added riesling, sauvignon blanc, pinot gris and merlot. The Italian-inspired Osteria restaurant is based on their own biodynamically produced vegetables and herbs, the meats (all free-range) are from local farmers, and the seafood is wild-caught. In 2016 the Lubianas purchased the Panorama Vineyard, first planted in 1974, in the Huon Valley. Exports to the UK, Singapore, Indonesia, Japan, Hong Kong and China.

ŸŸŸŸŸ **Sasso Pinot Noir 2013** The colour gleams deep and bright; the aromas soar and the palate holds you captivated with its complexity and depth of flavour. It ebbs and flows: first the fruit appears intensely sweet and spicy, then the fine natural acidity comes through with spice, warm earth and leaves to the fore. And the velvety, yet strong, tannins are the deal maker. Cork. 13.5% alc. **Rating** 96 **To** 2025 $125 JF
Riesling 2016 A wine with depth and texture, instructing the acidity to back down and flow right through the palate. Complex florals and spice, Meyer lemon curd and tangerine unfold like pure silk velvet. Quite a profound wine. Screwcap. 13.5% alc. **Rating** 95 **To** 2030 $35 JF ✪
Sauvignon Blanc 2016 Complex, textural and a livewire of racy acidity. The flavours aren't overt: there's some guava, pine needle freshness, lemon balm, grapefruit and pith with creaminess, too, all dancing across the palate. Screwcap. 13.5% alc. **Rating** 95 **To** 2020 $35 JF ✪
Primavera Chardonnay 2015 It's best to open Primavera and let it breathe – as the seemingly fuller fruit and oak come out at once. Then they fall back into the wine, letting lemon blossom emerge, plus ginger spice on the finely tuned palate. The leesy, creamy texture and acidity are spot on. Screwcap. 13% alc. **Rating** 95 **To** 2020 $35 JF ✪
Estate Pinot Noir 2015 Complex, with macerated cherries sprinkled with five-spice and Satsuma plums, rhubarb, damp earth; stemmy, yet remains sapid. Builds on the velvety palate – a bit tangier, a bit juicier and savoury – with a TheraBand of tannin wrapping itself around this ball of flavour and keeping everything perfectly in place. Screwcap. 13% alc. **Rating** 95 **To** 2025 $53 JF
Grande Vintage 2008 '08 is one of my favourite seasons in Tasmania, possessed of a grace, elegance and endurance rarely encountered outside Champagne itself. Steve Lubiana has captured the essence of the season in this bright and pale-coloured blend. A creamy texture marries seamlessly with bright, cool Tasmanian acidity and intricately integrated dosage on a very long and seamless finish. Cork. 12.5% alc. **Rating** 95 **To** 2020 $60 TS

ŸŸŸŸŸ **Pinot Gris 2015 Rating** 91 **To** 2020 $35 JF
Brut Rose 2011 Rating 90 **To** 2017 $45 TS

Stella Bella Wines ★★★★★
205 Rosabrook Road, Margaret River, WA 6285 **Region** Margaret River
T (08) 9758 8611 **www**.stellabella.com.au **Open** 7 days 10–5
Winemaker Luke Jolliffe, Michael Kane **Est.** 1997 **Dozens** 50 000 **Vyds** 87.9ha
This enormously successful winemaking business produces wines of true regional expression, with fruit sourced from the central and southern parts of Margaret River. The company owns and operates six vineyards, and also purchases fruit from small contract growers. Substantial quantities of wine covering all styles and price points make this an important producer for Margaret River. Exports Stella Bella, Suckfizzle and Skuttlebutt labels to all major markets.

ŸŸŸŸŸ **Serie Luminosa Margaret River Cabernet Sauvignon 2014** Bright, clear crimson-purple – quite striking; a wine made without any compromise in the fruit selection or in the vinification, with a long pedigree of prior vintages of high quality. The bouquet is perfumed, the medium-bodied palate with a full array of cassis, redcurrant and blueberry fruits and bay leaf, and superfine but persistent tannins. Oh, and yes, French oak does make a contribution. Screwcap. 14.3% alc. **Rating** 97 **To** 2034 $75 ✪

ŦŦŦŦŦ **Margaret River Sauvignon Blanc 2016** In distinctive Stella Bella fashion, the wine is loaded with tropical fruits fit for an Arabian feast, starting with passionfruit and gooseberry, continuing with green pineapple, finishing with punchy citrussy acidity that intensifies and prolongs the impact. Screwcap. 13.2% alc. **Rating** 96 To 2018 $24 ✪

Suckfizzle Margaret River Sauvignon Blanc Semillon 2014 If you are absolutely confident about the quality of the grapes, and the synergy between the varieties, you can afford the luxury of barrel fermentation and extended maceration in French oak. This is one of a handful of Margaret River sauvignon blancs that move into another universe of complexity and longevity. No one should dismiss this wine without tasting it and learning of its majesty. Screwcap. 13% alc. **Rating** 96 To 2024 $45 ✪

Margaret River Chardonnay 2016 Brimming with life and energy, the fragrant bouquet of citrus and white flowers, the palate intense and very long; the flavours are spun around beacons of white peach and grapefruit, the barrel-ferment inputs simply adding complexity. Screwcap. 12.5% alc. **Rating** 95 To 2026 $35 ✪

Margaret River Chardonnay 2015 Matured in French oak for 12 months. Stella Bella cruises effortlessly these days, this wine a prime example. Nothing is overplayed, allowing the peach and nectarine flavours free expression, yet also providing texture and gentle complexity. Screwcap. 13% alc. **Rating** 95 To 2023 $32 ✪

Suckfizzle Margaret River Cabernet Sauvignon 2014 The richest and most forthright of the '14 Cabernets, firm tannin guy ropes running through the blackcurrant fruits from start to finish. As ever, the balance and varietal integrity are unquestioned, time the only missing ingredient at this point. Screwcap. 13.8% alc. **Rating** 95 To 2039 $55

Skuttlebutt Sauvignon Blanc Semillon 2016 Rating 94 To 2017 $18 ✪
Margaret River Cabernet Merlot 2015 Rating 94 To 2028 $24 ✪

ŦŦŦŦ♀ **Skuttlebutt Margaret River Rose 2016 Rating** 93 To 2019 $18 ✪
Margaret River Shiraz 2015 Rating 93 To 2030 $30
Margaret River Cabernet Sauvignon 2014 Rating 93 To 2029 $35
Margaret River Semillon Sauvignon Blanc 2016 Rating 92 To 2022 $24 ✪
Margaret River Sangiovese Cabernet 2015 Rating 91 To 2023 $30

Steve Wiblin's Erin Eyes ★★★★★

58 Old Road, Leasingham, SA 5452 **Region** Clare Valley
T (08) 8843 0023 **www**.erineyes.com.au **Open** Not
Winemaker Steve Wiblin **Est.** 2009 **Dozens** 2500

Steve Wiblin became a winemaker accidentally, when he was encouraged by his mentor at Tooheys Brewery who had a love of fine art and fine wine. This was 38 years ago, and because Tooheys owned Wynns and Seaview, the change in career from beer to wine was easy. He watched the acquisition of Wynns and Seaview by Penfolds and then Seppelt, before moving to Orlando. He moved from the world of big wineries to small when he co-founded Neagles Rock in 1997. In 2009 he left Neagles Rock and established Erin Eyes, explaining, 'in 1842 my English convict forebear John Wiblin gazed into a pair of Erin eyes. That gaze changed our family make-up and history forever. In the Irish-influenced Clare Valley, what else would I call my wines but Erin Eyes?'

ŦŦŦŦŦ **Pride of Erin Single Vineyard Reserve Clare Valley Riesling 2016** The single vineyard in question is in Penwortham. This adds another level of flavour to its Emerald Isle sibling, although the actual characters are similar. A delicious riesling to be sure, to be sure, but it's a question of swings and roundabouts. Screwcap. 12% alc. **Rating** 95 To 2026 $35 ✪

Emerald Isle Watervale Riesling 2016 Bright straw-green; gloriously fresh and pure, lime and lemon joined by a touch of Granny Smith apple and, more importantly, crisp acidity on the long, perfectly balanced, breezy finish. Screwcap. 11.5% alc. **Rating** 95 To 2031 $25 ✪

Clare Valley Sangiovese 2014 Bright, clear crimson-garnet; a delicious cherry-filled wine with a floral bouquet and a supple, lively and long palate. The handling of sangiovese's tannins is perfect. Scores for its hedonistic qualities. Screwcap. 13.5% alc. **Rating** 95 To 2020 $30 ○

Celtic Heritage Cabernet Shiraz 2015 Rating 92 To 2025 $30 NG
Ballycapple Cabernet Sauvignon 2015 Rating 91 $30 NG
Gallic Connection Cabernet Malbec Merlot 2014 Rating 90 To 2024 $30
Gallic Connection Cabernet Malbec 2015 Rating 90 To 2028 $30 NG

Sticks Yarra Valley ★★★★☆

206 Yarraview Road, Yarra Glen, Vic 3775 **Region** Yarra Valley
T (03) 9925 1911 **www**.sticks.com.au **Open** Not
Winemaker Travis Bush, Tom Belford **Est.** 2000 **Dozens** 25 000
Sticks acquired the former Yarra Ridge 3000-tonne capacity winery in 2005, and 24ha of estate vineyards, mainly planted in 1983. The estate production is significantly supplemented by contract-grown grapes sourced elsewhere in the Yarra Valley and surrounding regions. Sticks also provides substantial contract-making facilities for wineries throughout the Yarra Valley. Exports to the UK, the US, Hong Kong and China.

Cabernet Sauvignon 2014 Bright colour; the fragrant bouquet of cassis and dried herbs is replayed on the medium-bodied palate, cassis riding high, wide and handsome, given an edge of intensity by green capsicum. The tannins are particularly well behaved, insisting that the wine's elegance be recognised and rewarded. Screwcap. 12.5% alc. **Rating** 95 To 2029

Sauvignon Blanc 2015 Rating 90 To 2017 $19 ○
Pinot Grigio 2016 Rating 90 To 2017

Stockman's Ridge Wines ★★★★

21 Boree Lane, Lidster, NSW 2800 **Region** Orange
T (02) 6365 6512 **www**.stockmansridge.com.au **Open** Thurs–Mon 1105
Winemaker Jonathan Hambrook **Est.** 2002 **Dozens** 1500 **Vyds** 3ha
Stockman's Ridge Wines, founded and owned by Jonathan Hambrook, started its wine life in Bathurst, before relocating to its present vineyard on the northwest slopes of Mt Canobolas, at an elevation of 800m. Jonathan has planted 1.2ha of pinot noir and 1ha of gruner veltliner. His next door neighbour is the Booree Lane Vineyard, owned by Bob Clark, who has 21.6ha of shiraz, merlot, cabernet franc, chardonnay and gewurztraminer – a significant part of the grapes go next door to Stockman's Ridge. Exports to the US and China.

Handcrafted Central Ranges Savagnin 2014 Hand-picked, whole-bunch pressed. Has that faintly savoury character that savagnin can display, plus pear, green apple and citrussy acidity. A very good example. Screwcap. 11.5% alc. **Rating** 94 To 2020 $30

Handcrafted Orange Zinfandel 2015 Rating 91 To 2023 $30
Rider Orange Merlot Cabernet Franc 2015 Rating 90 To 2029 $25

Stomp Wine ★★★★

1273 Milbrodale Road, Broke, NSW 2330 **Region** Hunter Valley
T 0409 774 280 **www**.stompwine.com.au **Open** Fri–Sun 10.30–4.30
Winemaker Michael McManus **Est.** 2004 **Dozens** 1000
After a lifetime in the food and beverage industry, Michael and Meredith McManus moved to full-time winemaking. They have set up Stomp Winemaking, a contract winemaker designed to keep small and larger parcels of grapes separate through the fermentation and maturation process, thus meeting the needs of boutique wine producers in the Hunter Valley. The addition of their own Stomp label is a small but important part of their business.

🍷🍷🍷🍷🍷 **Limited Release Fiano 2016** Not sure why this is a limited release or what that exactly means, but it's a perky wine with fine texture, lemon pith, a hint of honeysuckle and ginger. Screwcap. 12.5% alc. **Rating** 90 **To** 2020 $28 JF

Stonefish   ★★★★☆

24 Kangarilla Road, McLaren Vale, SA 5171 **Region** Various
T (02) 9668 9930 **www**.stonefishwines.com.au **Open** Not
Winemaker Contract, Peter Papanikitas **Est.** 2000 **Dozens** 10 000
Peter Papanikitas has been involved in various facets of the wine industry for the past 30+ years. Initially his contact was with companies that included Penfolds, Lindemans and Leo Buring, then he spent five years working for Cinzano, gaining experience in worldwide sales and marketing. In 2000 he established Stonefish, a virtual winery operation, in partnership with various grapegrowers and winemakers, principally in the Barossa Valley and Margaret River, who provide the wines. The value for money has never been in doubt, but Stonefish has moved to another level with its Icon and Reserve Barossa wines. Exports to China, Thailand, Vietnam, Hong Kong, Indonesia, the Philippines, the Maldives, Singapore and Fiji.

🍷🍷🍷🍷🍷 **Nero Margaret River Cabernet Sauvignon 2014** This sways with energy, concentrated cassis, currants and boysenberries doused in Middle Eastern spices and cedary oak. Full-bodied and structured with substantial tannins, yet maintains a vibrancy and freshness throughout. Screwcap. 14% alc. **Rating** 95 **To** 2029 $40 JF

🍷🍷🍷🍷🍷 **Reserve Barossa Valley Shiraz 2015 Rating** 92 **To** 2028 $36 JF
Reserve Margaret River Cabernet 2015 Rating 92 **To** 2027 $36 JF
Nero Barossa Valley Shiraz 2013 Rating 91 **To** 2024 $60 JF

Stonehurst Cedar Creek   ★★★★

1840 Wollombi Road, Cedar Creek, NSW 2325 **Region** Hunter Valley
T (02) 4998 1576 **www**.stonehurst.com.au **Open** 7 days 10–5
Winemaker Tamburlaine **Est.** 1995 **Dozens** 4000 **Vyds** 6.5ha
Stonehurst Cedar Creek has been established by Daryl and Phillipa Heslop on a historic 220ha property in the Wollombi Valley, underneath the Pokolbin Range. The vineyards (chambourcin, semillon, chardonnay and shiraz) are organically grown. A substantial part of the business, however, is the six self-contained cottages on the property. Exports to all major markets.

🍷🍷🍷🍷🍷 **Hunter Valley Semillon 2014** While this Hunter semillon is already showing attractive toast and lemon butter aromas and flavours, there is more than enough stuffing and structure to suggest that this will continue to improve for the next 5 years, if not longer. Screwcap. 10.5% alc. **Rating** 91 **To** 2025 $25 PR
Methode Champenoise 2010 The creamy, biscuity, toasty complexity of lees age lends compelling complexity and texture to the bright, crunchy lemon, apple, pear and cut grass of chardonnay and semillon fruit with a wisp of struck flint reduction. There's some skill in the execution here, with texture, acidity and dosage uniting in a harmonious finish. 11.5% alc. **Rating** 90 **To** 2020 $35 TS

Stoney Rise   ★★★★★

96 Hendersons Lane, Gravelly Beach, Tas 7276 **Region** Northern Tasmania
T (03) 6394 3678 **www**.stoneyrise.com **Open** Thurs–Mon 11–5
Winemaker Joe Holyman **Est.** 2000 **Dozens** 2000 **Vyds** 7.2ha
The Holyman family had been involved in vineyards in Tasmania for 20 years, but Joe Holyman's career in the wine industry, first as a sales rep, then as a wine buyer, and more recently working in wineries in NZ, Portugal, France, Mount Benson and Coonawarra, gave him an exceptionally broad-based understanding of wine. In 2004 Joe and wife Lou purchased the former Rotherhythe Vineyard, which had been established in 1986, and set about restoring it to its former glory. There are two ranges: the Stoney Rise wines, focusing on fruit and

early drinkability, and the Holyman wines, with more structure, more new oak and the best grapes, here the focus on length and potential longevity. Exports to the UK, The Netherlands, Singapore and Japan.

🍷🍷🍷🍷🍷 **Holyman Pinot Noir 2015** Clear, vivid crimson-purple, it leaps from the glass with its perfumed red and blue fruits, then captures the palate in a split second with its array of those fruits on the one side, spicy, savoury tannins ex the whole bunches on the other. Yet another beautiful Tasmanian pinot attesting to the great vintage. Screwcap. 13% alc. **Rating** 96 **To** 2027 $50 ☉

Holyman Project X Pinot Noir 2014 Excellent Tasmanian crimson-purple hue; this packs power into its 12% alcohol frame, the whole-bunch bouquet and palate exuding red cherry, blueberry and plum fruit and easily absorbing 100% new oak. The only question is whether the finish is a little acidic; the accompanying low pH should, however, underwrite its future. Screwcap. **Rating** 95 **To** 2030 $90

Holyman Chardonnay 2015 Pale quartz-green; the wine is still in the first phase of its life, the bouquet reticent, the reduced palate tight but very long and well balanced, its future assured. Pink grapefruit and green apple have a chorus line of Tasmanian acidity, the oak likewise subdued. Will flourish with more time in bottle. Screwcap. 13.5% alc. **Rating** 94 **To** 2024 $50

🍷🍷🍷🍷🍷 Gruner Veltliner 2016 **Rating** 92 **To** 2026 $32
No Clothes No SO$_2$ Pinot Noir 2016 **Rating** 90 **To** 2017 $32

Stonier Wines   ★★★★★

Cnr Thompson's Lane/Frankston-Flinders Road, Merricks, Vic 3916
Region Mornington Peninsula
T (03) 5989 8300 **www**.stonier.com.au **Open** 7 days 11–5
Winemaker Michael Symons, Will Byron, Luke Burkley **Est.** 1978 **Dozens** 35 000
Vyds 17.6ha

This may be one of the most senior wineries on the Mornington Peninsula, but that does not stop it moving with the times. It has embarked on a serious sustainability program that touches on all aspects of its operations. It is one of the few wineries in Australia to measure its carbon footprint in detail, using the officially recognised system of WFA; it is steadily reducing its consumption of electricity; it uses rainwater, collected from the winery roof, for rinsing and washing in the winery, as well as for supplying the winery in general; it has created a balanced ecosystem in the vineyard by strategic planting of cover crops and reduction of sprays; and has reduced its need to irrigate. All the Stonier wines are estate-grown and made with a mix of wild yeast (from initiation of fermentation) and cultured yeast (added towards the end of fermentation to ensure that no residual sugar remains), and almost all are destemmed to open fermenters; all have a two-stage maturation, always French oak and variable use of barriques and puncheons for the first stage. Exports to all major markets.

🍷🍷🍷🍷🍷 **W-WB Mornington Peninsula Pinot Noir 2015** The wine is suitably statuesque, silken of texture, forceful of fruit and impressive of punchy length. Unlike the lesser cuvees, the wine never becomes too sweet or palpably alcoholic, due to well applied structural attributes and the stem component's edgy spike. This is very good. Screwcap. 14.5% alc. **Rating** 96 **To** 2027 $85 NG

KBS Vineyard Mornington Peninsula Chardonnay 2015 This is cool and inviting; not giving too many of its components and their application techniques away. Oak, plus wafting vanilla and cedar, admittedly drifts across the nostrils, yet is to be expected at this nascent stage. Curd, truffle, the straw from a freshly laid tatami mat and a faint whiff of stone fruit are mere teases. Rich, yet tensile; febrile, yet round, warm and mouth-coating. This is a stunning wine of intriguing dichotomies. Screwcap. 13.5% alc. **Rating** 95 **To** 2027 $50 NG

Mornington Peninsula Chardonnay 2015 In typical precisely crafted Stonier style, not a hair out of place. It would be fatuous to question whether that is the style best suited, or whether it would be better with a wind-blown hair or two. Screwcap. 13.5% alc. **Rating** 94 **To** 2027 $25 ☉

Jimjoca Vineyard Mornington Peninsula Chardonnay 2015 The steeliest chardonnay of the gaggle, with a resolute urgency thrumming down its tensile spine of bracing acidity. However, the wine is far from ungenerous. Truffled lees and oak (15% new French; 10 months on lees following barrel fermentation) are effortlessly nestled into allusions to stone fruit, particularly nectarine and apricot, hints of dried straw and green apple. This fine chardonnay will age very well. Screwcap. 14% alc. **Rating** 94 **To** 2025 $38 NG

Gainsborough Park Vineyard Mornington Peninsula Chardonnay 2015 Riper than the Jimjoca and reminiscent of yellow plum, apricot and white peach, this boasts plenty of grunt, propelling the fruit across its angular ridges of oak, lees and punchy acidity. The finish is long and persistent, yet this is still elemental and very much a number of parts striving to mesh, with the dusty vanillan oak carving an etching across the roof of the mouth. Needs time. Screwcap. 14% alc. **Rating** 94 **To** 2025 $45 NG

KBS Vineyard Mornington Peninsula Pinot Noir 2015 The KBS Vineyard is in Merrick's, facing due east. The fruit reflects this, with a bright, lipsmacking red cherry sass and orange-rind amaro hitting the nostrils. The palate, fleshy and sweet, is wound around some fine-boned grape tannins, vanillan-edged creamy oak and crunchy acidity, serving it well in the name of energetic poise and drinkability. Screwcap. 14.5% alc. **Rating** 94 **To** 2023 $75 NG

Merron's Vineyard Mornington Peninsula Pinot Noir 2015 There is more of a baritone of black cherry, satsuma plum and Chinotto about this wine. Its sinew of tannin, too, is thicker, chewier, more resinous and of deeper soils. It serves the wine well by taming the sweetness. Bountiful of flavour and rich of texture, there is a warm bouillon enveloping the fruit, with plenty of acidity. Among the most savoury of the range with, again, the alcohol as the caveat. Screwcap. 14.5% alc. **Rating** 94 **To** 2025 $60 NG

Stonier Family Vineyard Mornington Peninsula Pinot Noir 2015 The price leaps with the familial label and one immediately understands why upon nosing the wine. Black and red fruits merge into a tight ball of more ambitious extraction – grape tannin, colour and oak. Orange rind and five-spice flicker at the edges. The oak manifests as vanilla and mocha characters, managing to tuck the powerful, fleshy nature of the fruit into cedar seams. Screwcap. 14.2% alc. **Rating** 94 **To** 2027 $85 NG

ŸŸŸŸŸ Reserve Chardonnay 2015 **Rating** 93 **To** 2027 $48 NG
Reserve Pinot Noir 2015 **Rating** 93 **To** 2023 $60 NG
Lyncroft Pinot Noir 2015 **Rating** 93 **To** 2023 $35 NG
Mornington Peninsula Pinot Noir 2015 **Rating** 92 **To** 2024 $28
Windmill Pinot Noir 2015 **Rating** 92 **To** 2023 $65 NG
Jimjoca Pinot Noir 2015 **Rating** 91 **To** 2023 $45 NG
Chardonnay Pinot Noir 2015 **Rating** 90 **To** 2017 $30 TS
Chardonnay Pinot Noir 2014 **Rating** 90 **To** 2020 $30 TS

Studley Park Vineyard   ★★★★

5 Garden Terrace, Kew, Vic 3101 (postal) **Region** Port Phillip
T (03) 9254 2777 **Open** Not
Winemaker Llew Knight (Contract) **Est.** 1994 **Dozens** 500 **Vyds** 0.5ha
Geoff Pryor's Studley Park Vineyard is one of Melbourne's best-kept secrets. It is on a bend of the Yarra River barely 4km from the Melbourne CBD, on a 0.5ha block once planted to vines, but for a century used for market gardening, then replanted with cabernet sauvignon. A spectacular aerial photograph shows that immediately across the river, and looking directly to the CBD, is the epicentre of Melbourne's light industrial development, while on the northern and eastern boundaries are suburban residential blocks.

ŸŸŸŸŸ Cabernet Sauvignon 2012 Mid-garnet tinged with brick, this highly savoury, light to mid-weighted wine is gracefully glimpsing senescence, but with another 5 years or so left in its bones. Reminiscent of a Cru Bourgeois, a stream of red and black currant flavours mingle with Darjeeling tea, dried sage, bay leaf and pimento. The tannins are finely tuned; the acid gently lilting and carrying the wine to a lingering finish. Far from a blockbuster, but this is a pleasant drink. Screwcap. 13% alc. **Rating** 90 **To** 2022 $25 NG

Stumpy Gully ★★★☆

1247 Stumpy Gully Road, Moorooduc, Vic 3933 **Region** Mornington Peninsula
T 1800 STUMPY (788679) **www**.stumpygully.com.au **Open** Thurs–Sun 10–5
Winemaker Wendy, Frank and Michael Zantvoort **Est.** 1988 **Dozens** 12 000 **Vyds** 40ha
Frank and Wendy Zantvoort began planting their first vineyard in 1988; Wendy, having enrolled in the oenology course at CSU, subsequently graduated with a B.App.Sc. (Oenology). In addition to the original vineyard, they have deliberately gone against prevailing thinking with their Moorooduc vineyard, planting it solely to red varieties, predominantly cabernet sauvignon, merlot and shiraz. They believe they have one of the warmest sites on the Peninsula, and that ripening should present no problems to late-ripening varieties such as shiraz and sangiovese. Exports to all major markets.

♥♥♥♥♡ **Crooked Post Zantvoort Reserve Shiraz 2014** Certainly proclaims its cool climate origins, with black pepper, licorice and savoury tannins all underpinning the unusual combination of black fruits and sour cherries. A headline-grabber, and doesn't let go. Screwcap. 14.2% alc. **Rating** 91 **To** 2025 $48

♥♥♥♥ **Riesling 2015 Rating** 89 **To** 2021 $25
Chardonnay 2015 Rating 89 **To** 2020 $28
Pinot Noir 2015 Rating 89 **To** 2023 $28
Magic Black Pinot Noir 2015 Rating 89 $48 PR

Summerfield ★★★★★

5967 Stawell-Avoca Road, Moonambel, Vic 3478 **Region** Pyrenees
T (03) 5467 2264 **www**.summerfieldwines.com **Open** Mon–Sat 10–5, Sun 10–3
Winemaker Mark Summerfield **Est.** 1979 **Dozens** 7500 **Vyds** 40.5ha
Founder Ian Summerfield handed over the winemaker reins to son Mark several years ago. Mark has significantly refined the style of the wines with the introduction of French oak, and by reducing the alcohol without compromising the intensity and concentration of the wines. If anything, the longevity of the wines produced by Mark will be even greater than that of the American-oaked wines of bygone years. Exports are now directed solely to China.

♥♥♥♥♥ **Saieh Shiraz 2015** This is a single vineyard, single block wine, showcasing Summerfield's salubrious fruit massaged by the estate's indelible stamp of impeccably hewn tannins. A floral nose of lilac and musk leads one astray into a richly endowed nether world of dark cherries and plum, basted with five-spice, anise and cinnamon. The American oak is buried beneath the avalanche of fruit. A wine of immense force, yet paradoxically, a wine that is light on its feet. Screwcap. 14% alc. **Rating** 96 **To** 2030 $55 NG
Sahsah Shiraz 2015 From an original 46yo plot, this is all molten black fruits on one hand; a savoury melody of clove, worn leather, anise, cardamom, bitter chocolate and bay leaf on the other. Fragrant and of multitudinous layers, each revealing itself with time in the glass. Poised. The tannins are substantial on the back end: this augurs very well for a long time in the cellar. Screwcap. 14% alc. **Rating** 95 **To** 2030 $55 NG
Reserve Shiraz 2015 This preens the regular Shiraz's mane with added flair, giving greater gusto to the intensity of the fruit and the oak applied. Sourced from the original '70s plantings, there is an additional element of spice, too: clove and cardamom. Betel leaf and anise ply their intrigue across a kaleidoscope of dark fruit flavours, blue and black all. The finish is penetrating and long, driving across the mouth and down the throat. Cola and barbecue notes linger. Nothing is out of place. Screwcap. 14% alc. **Rating** 95 **To** 2035 $55 NG

R2 Shiraz 2014 The most vibrant, varietally floral and poised R2 of the bunch, this full-weighted wine wears a satin robe of black fruit woven across a wheel of bitter chocolate, pulpy tannins and vanillan oak. Strong threads of anise, clove and olive provide an assortment of colours. The Pyrenees' whiff of eucalyptus provides a reference to provenance, rather than an exclamation. The tannins are a tour de force, grapey and tactile, portending well for a long future. Screwcap. 14.6% alc. **Rating** 95 **To** 2045 $50 NG

Taiyo Cabernet Sauvignon 2015 This has the Pyrenees' coffee-grind riff planted in its firm tannins, segueing to spearmint, sage, assorted dried herbs and briar. Unusually for cabernet, this was made intuitively, with some whole cluster fruit, adding a savoury tone to the sculpture of tightly furled tannins, lavish oak and concentrated fruit. There is nothing excessive about it despite its unbridled richness. Screwcap. 14% alc. **Rating** 95 **To** 2035 $63 NG

Shiraz 2015 Rating 94 **To** 2034 $35 NG
Reserve Cabernet Sauvignon 2015 Rating 94 **To** 2035 $55 NG

ŸŸŸŸŸ **R2 Shiraz 2015 Rating** 93 **To** 2040 $50 NG
Cabernet Sauvignon 2015 Rating 92 **To** 2030 $35 NG
Tradition 2015 Rating 92 **To** 2030 $35 NG

Sunshine Creek ★★★★☆

350 Yarraview Road, Yarra Glen, Vic 3775 **Region** Yarra Valley
T (03) 9818 5142 **www.**sunshinecreek.com.au **Open** Not
Winemaker Mario Marson, Chris Lawrence **Est.** 2009 **Dozens** 7000 **Vyds** 20ha
Packaging magnate James Zhou has a wine business in China, and, over the years, has worked with an A–Z of distinguished Australian winemakers, including Grant Burge, Philip Shaw, Phillip Jones, Pat Carmody, Geoff Hardy and Mario Marson, in bringing their wines to China. It was a logical extension to produce Australian wine of similar quality, and he commissioned Mario Marson to find an appropriate existing vineyard. They discovered Martha's Vineyard, which was planted in the 1980s by Olga Szymiczek. The site was a particularly good one, which compensated for the need to change the existing spur-pruned vineyard (for mechanisation) to vertical shoot position (VSP) for increased quality and hand picking. At the same time, an extensive program of grafting was undertaken and new clones planted. In 2011 Andrew Smith (formerly of Lusatia Park Vineyard) was appointed vineyard manager to change the focus of management to sustainability and minimal interference. In '13 winemaker Chris Lawrence joined the team, and an onsite winery (capable of handing 275 tonnes) was completed prior to the '16 vintage. Exports to Hong Kong and China.

ŸŸŸŸŸ **Heathcote Shiraz 2013** Matured in French oak for 15 months. Licorice, clove spice and dried dark fruit aromas and flavours give the wine remarkable depth and concentration on its medium to full-bodied palate. Diam. 14.5% alc. **Rating** 95 **To** 2038 $45

ŸŸŸŸŸ **Yarra Valley Pinot Noir 2013 Rating** 93 **To** 2028 $45

Surveyor's Hill Vineyards ★★★★

215 Brooklands Road, Wallaroo, NSW 2618 **Region** Canberra District
T (02) 6230 2046 **www.**survhill.com.au **Open** W'ends & public hols
Winemaker Brindabella Hills (Dr Roger Harris), Greg Gallagher (sparkling) **Est.** 1986
Dozens 1000 **Vyds** 10ha
Surveyor's Hill vineyard is on the slopes of the eponymous hill, at 550–680m above sea level. It is an ancient volcano, producing granite-derived, coarse-structured (and hence well drained) sandy soils of low fertility. This has to be the ultimate patchwork-quilt vineyard, with 1ha each of chardonnay, shiraz and viognier; 0.5ha each of roussanne, marsanne, aglianico, nero d'Avola, mourvedre, grenache, muscadelle, moscato giallo, cabernet franc, riesling, semillon, sauvignon blanc, touriga nacional and cabernet sauvignon.

ΨΨΨΨ? **Hills of Hall Shiraz 2015** The seal of the screwcap was mysteriously broken, but that didn't seem to adversely impact on the wine. The colour is bright, the spicy bouquet leading into a medium-bodied palate with some of the characters found in Hunter Valley shiraz. The use of a mix of French and American oak is a plus, not (as often happens) a negative. Screwcap. 14% alc. **Rating** 92 **To** 2025 $25 **○**

Hills of Hall Riesling 2016 Has very good varietal expression courtesy of a trio of lime, lemon and apple fruit playing throughout the bouquet and long, dry and crisp palate. Has the balance to handsomely repay patience. Screwcap. 11.5% alc. **Rating** 91 **To** 2026 $22 **○**

Hills of Hall Viognier Roussanne 2015 Viognier has a higher fruit presence (on its own) than roussanne (ditto), and here has a higher share of the volume – the inevitable result is that the viognier drives the flavour with its apricot trademark. Screwcap. 12% alc. **Rating** 90 **To** 2018 $18 **○**

Hills of Hall Tinto 2015 The blend of tempranillo and graciano, two of the most frequently encountered varieties in the Rioja region of Spain, works well here, with an energetic synergy between the red fruits. The tempranillo contributes a rainbow of cherry-based flavours, the graciano high-toned savoury notes. Screwcap. 13.5% alc. **Rating** 90 **To** 2027 $22

ΨΨΨΨ **Hills of Hall Sauvignon Blanc 2016 Rating** 89 **To** 2018 $18 **○**

Sussex Squire ★★★★

PO Box 1361, Clare, SA 5453 **Region** Clare Valley
T 0458 141 169 **www.**sussexsquire.com.au **Open** 7 days 10–5
Winemaker Daniel Wilson, Mark Bollen **Est.** 2014 **Dozens** 500 **Vyds** 6ha
There's a long family history attached to this embryonic wine business. The history began with Walter Hackett (1827–1914), a Sussex farmer; next came Joseph Hackett (1880–1958), followed by Joseph Robert Hackett (1911–98), and now fourth-generation Mark and Skye Bollen. Over the generations, the family worked in a successful major grain and seed business, then established the Nyora grazing property near Mintaro and Wyndham Park near Sevenhill, which is still farmed today with herds of black and red Angus cattle. Mark and Skye returned to the Clare Valley after spending 25 years working in other pursuits, Mark in wine sales and marketing, Skye in 5-star hotels for a decade before embarking on a successful career in recruitment. In 1998 Mark and Skye planted 6ha of dry-grown, organically managed, shiraz, and in lieu of Angus cattle, have a flock of Black Suffolk sheep that roam the vineyard during winter to provide natural weed control and fertilise the soil.

ΨΨΨΨΨ **The Raging Bull Single Vineyard Limited Release Clare Valley Malbec 2015** From a vineyard in Watervale, matured in French oak for 12 months. It has very good deep scarlet colour, and has the confit plum fruit I often see in malbec. It has been very well made, with an almost velvety mid-palate before tannins tidy up the finish. Screwcap. 14.5% alc. **Rating** 94 **To** 2029 $30 **○**

ΨΨΨΨ? **The Prancing Pony Riesling 2016 Rating** 91 **To** 2026 $24
Thomas Block Shiraz 2015 Rating 91 **To** 2030 $28
The Partnership Shiraz Mataro 2015 Rating 91 **To** 2035 $35
The Darting Hare Sangiovese 2015 Rating 91 **To** 2025 $25
JRS The Sussex Squire Shiraz 2015 Rating 90 **To** 2030 $65

Sutherland Estate ★★★★★

2010 Melba Highway, Dixons Creek, Vic 3775 **Region** Yarra Valley
T 0402 052 287 **www.**sutherlandestate.com.au **Open** W'ends & public hols 10–5
Winemaker Cathy Phelan, Angus Ridley, Rob Hall **Est.** 2000 **Dozens** 1500 **Vyds** 4ha
The Phelan family established Sutherland Estate in 2000 when they purchased a mature 2ha vineyard at Dixons Creek. Further plantings followed: the plantings now consist of 1ha each of chardonnay and pinot noir, and 0.5ha each of gewurztraminer, cabernet sauvignon, tempranillo and shiraz. Ron Phelan designed and built the cellar door, which enjoys stunning views over the Yarra Valley, while daughter Cathy studied Wine Science at CSU. The sparkling

wines are made by Phil Kelly, the reds by Cathy and partner Angus Ridley (who has been at Coldstream Hills for the last decade), and the Chardonnay by Rob Hall.

🍷🍷🍷🍷🍷 **Daniel's Hill Vineyard Yarra Valley Cabernet Sauvignon 2016** Angus Ridley aspires to make this medium-bodied in Mount Mary style, but I think the quality of the varietal character in the fruit is always going to express itself more vocally, unless there is much gentler handling in the winery – and I wouldn't suggest this for even a split second. Screwcap. 14% alc. **Rating** 96 **To** 2036 $30 ✪
Daniel's Hill Vineyard Yarra Valley Chardonnay 2016 Fermented in French puncheons and barriques (33% new). The bouquet is expressive, the palate building complexity and depth as it is retasted, and will replicate this as it matures in bottle: give it 3–5 years. Screwcap. 13.4% alc. **Rating** 95 **To** 2024 $30 ✪
Daniel's Hill Vineyard Yarra Valley Shiraz 2016 Good, deep crimson-purple hue; a very well made, complex medium-bodied shiraz that ticks all the boxes, with plum, blackberry, multi-spice, fine tannins and integrated French oak; the finish is fresh, and the palate long. Screwcap. 13.9% alc. **Rating** 95 **To** 2031 $30 ✪
Daniel's Hill Vineyard Yarra Valley Tempranillo 2016 Very different from most Australian tempranillos, this with more texture and structure to its darker fruits on the medium to full-bodied palate. Tempranillo should be grown only in cool regions, not indiscriminately – even the Hunter Valley and Swan Valley and Riverland-grown vines are forced to play host. Screwcap. 14.1% alc. **Rating** 94 **To** 2031 $30

🍷🍷🍷🍷🍷 **Daniel's Hill Vineyard Gewurztraminer 2015** Rating 91 To 2023 $24
Daniel's Hill Vineyard Gewurztraminer 2016 Rating 90 To 2021 $24
Daniel's Hill Vineyard Pinot Noir 2016 Rating 90 To 2024 $30

Sutton Grange Winery   ★★★★☆

Carnochans Road, Sutton Grange, Vic 3448 **Region** Bendigo
T (03) 8672 1478 **www.suttongrange.com.au Open** Sun 11–5
Winemaker Melanie Chester **Est.** 1998 **Dozens** 5000 **Vyds** 12ha
The 400ha Sutton Grange property is a horse training facility acquired in 1996 by Peter Sidwell, a Melbourne businessman with horse racing and breeding interests. A lunch visit to the property by long-term friends Alec Epis and Stuart Anderson led to the decision to plant shiraz, merlot, cabernet sauvignon, viognier and sangiovese. The winery is built from WA limestone. Exports to the UK, the US, Canada, Switzerland and China.

🍷🍷🍷🍷🍷 **Fairbank Rose 2016** This is very fine rose indeed. On the pallid side of salmon, with a touch of partridge, this licks the nostrils with a salty, herbal tang. Sweet and sour red berries pop across the mouth, never straying into sweetness. The finish has a mineral crunch, with a sapid stream of saline, herbal goodness towed long by bright acidity. Screwcap. 13% alc. **Rating** 95 **To** 2018 $22 NG ✪
Estate Fiano 2015 Assorted stone fruit notes are given plenty of pungent, herbal thrust by fiano's verdant personality. Barrel-fermented with wild yeast, there is a leesy, mineralic vibrato to lift it all, before the wine finishes with a gentle oaky bite. Screwcap. 14% alc. **Rating** 94 **To** 2022 $60 NG

🍷🍷🍷🍷🍷 **Fairbank Sangiovese 2016** Rating 93 To 2022 $25 NG ✪
Fairbank Syrah 2016 Rating 92 To 2028 $25 NG ✪
Fairbank Viognier 2015 Rating 90 To 2018 $25 NG

Sweetwater Wines   ★★★★★

PO Box 256, Cessnock, NSW 2325 **Region** Hunter Valley
T (02) 4998 7666 **www.sweetwaterwines.com.au Open** Not
Winemaker Bryan Currie **Est.** 1998 **Dozens** NFP **Vyds** 13.5ha
Sweetwater Wines is in the same ownership as Hungerford Hill, and wouldn't normally have a separate winery entry in the *Companion*. But it's a single vineyard winery making only two wines, Shiraz and Cabernet Sauvignon, the wines made by Andrew Thomas from 2003 to '16

and all stored in a temperature-controlled underground wine cellar that is part of the very large ornate house and separate guest accommodation built on the property. The reason for the seemingly unusual focus on cabernet sauvignon (true, second to shiraz) is the famed red volcanic soil over limestone.

Shiraz 2014 Bright crimson; has nailed the '14 vintage with its vibrant medium-bodied array of red and black fruits, a balanced infusion of earth, spice and leather, and a long, graceful palate. The aftertaste embodies all of the above in its farewell. Screwcap. 14% alc. **Rating** 96 **To** 2044 $90

Shiraz 2007 Exceptional retention of colour and hue, not possible under cork. This hot year produced shiraz with masses of plum and blackberry fruit that will slowly become even more regional as leather and earth notes grow. Screwcap. 14.5% alc. **Rating** 95 **To** 2037 $90

Hunter Valley Shiraz 2005 Earthy/leathery regional flavours have now taken hold of the palate, but not to its detriment, for there is no break-up or loss of overall flavour. Its future rests to a degree with the cork gods, but on the evidence of this bottle, go for it. 13.4% alc. **Rating** 95 **To** 2030 $90

Cabernet Sauvignon 2014 Hunter Valley cabernet is an oxymoron, but earnest efforts have been made with this wine, and have succeeded in teasing out cassis fruit while keeping tannins under control. Back vintages are variable, some as good as this wine, others not. Screwcap. 13.5% alc. **Rating** 94 **To** 2029 $90

Hunter Valley Cabernet Sauvignon 2006 Rating 93 To 2021 $90
Hunter Valley Cabernet Sauvignon 2013 Rating 91 To 2025 $90

Swinging Bridge ★★★★

33 Gaskill Street, Canowindra, NSW 2804 **Region** Central Ranges
T 0409 246 609 **www**.swingingbridge.com.au **Open** Fri–Sun 11–6
Winemaker Tom Ward **Est.** 1995 **Dozens** 4000 **Vyds** 45ha
Swinging Bridge was founded by Mark Ward, who immigrated to Australia in 1965 from the UK with an honours degree in agricultural science from Cambridge University. Its original purpose was to grow grapes for others, with a small winemaking business alongside. Since then, under the direction of Mark's son, Tom, and daughter-in-law, Georgie, it has moved to effectively become an Orange winery. The 45ha of vines are all planted in Orange. In addition, Tom Ward has been involved with Justin Jarrett in the Balmoral Vineyard at Orange since 2012.

Single Vineyard Series Mrs Payten Orange Chardonnay 2014 Fermented and matured in French oak for 10 months. It has a complex touch of funk (or reduction) on its bouquet that doesn't disturb me one iota – it adds an edge (good) to the grapefruit and white peach fruit on the palate, and doesn't bite on the finish and aftertaste. Screwcap. 12.9% alc. **Rating** 95 **To** 2024 $32 ✪

Orange Sauvignon Blanc 2015 Rating 89 To 2017 $20

Swings & Roundabouts ★★★★☆

2807 Caves Road, Yallingup, WA 6232 **Region** Margaret River
T (08) 9756 6640 **www**.swings.com.au **Open** 7 days 10–5
Winemaker Brian Fletcher **Est.** 2004 **Dozens** 20 000 **Vyds** 5ha
The Swings & Roundabouts name comes from the expression used to encapsulate the eternal balancing act between the various aspects of grape and wine production. Swings aims to balance the serious side with a touch of fun. There are four ranges: Kiss Chasey, Life of Riley, Swings & Roundabouts and Backyard Stories. Exports to the US, China, Canada and Japan.

Backyard Stories Margaret River Cabernet Sauvignon 2015 A best barrels selection given further maturation. A classy medium-bodied cabernet, silky and suave on entry to the mouth, then firm, savoury cabernet tannins shepherd the wine along the palate and into the finish. Its fruit/oak/tannin balance is faultless, and the wine will age majestically. Screwcap. 14% alc. **Rating** 96 **To** 2040 $45 ✪

🍷🍷🍷🍷 Margaret River Sauvignon Blanc Semillon 2016 Rating 92 To 2019 $24
Margaret River Chardonnay 2015 Rating 90 To 2019 $24

Swinney Vineyards ★★★★☆

325 Franland-Kojimup Road, Frankland River, WA 6396 **Region** Frankland River
T (08) 9200 4483 **www**.swinneyvineyards.com.au **Open** Not
Winemaker Cherubino Consulting **Est.** 1998 **Dozens** 1500 **Vyds** 160ha
The Swinney family (parents Graham and Kaye, and son and daughter Matt and Janelle) has been resident on their 2500ha property since it was settled by George Swinney in 1922. In the '90s they decided to diversify, and now have 160ha of vines across four vineyards, including the Powderbark Ridge vineyard in Frankland River (planted in '98, purchased in partnership with former Hardys winemaker Peter Dawson). The lion's share goes to shiraz (67ha) and cabernet sauvignon (48ha), followed by riesling, semillon, pinot gris, gewurztraminer, viognier, vermentino and malbec. They also pushed the envelope by establishing grenache, tempranillo and mourvedre as bushvines, a rarity in this part of the world. Exports to the UK.

🍷🍷🍷🍷 Tirra Lirra Great Southern Shiraz 2015 A natural yeast fermentation and the judicious use of whole bunches have resulted in a wine that is bright crimson ruby in colour and has aromas of dark fruits and a little chocolate. The palate is ripe, generous and balanced and fine tannins round out a wine that will still be looking good in 5–7 years. Screwcap. 14% alc. **Rating** 90 To 2022 $35 PR

Symphonia Wines ★★★★

1699 Boggy Creek Road, Myrrhee, Vic 3732 **Region** King Valley
T (03) 4952 5117 **www**.symphoniafinewines.com.au **Open** By appt
Winemaker Lilian Carter **Est.** 1998 **Dozens** 1500 **Vyds** 28ha
Peter Read and his family are veterans of the King Valley, commencing the development of their vineyard in 1981. After extensive trips to both Western and Eastern Europe, Peter embarked on an ambitious project to trial a series of grape varieties little known in this country. Current owners Peter and Suzanne Evans are committed to continuing Peter Read's pioneering legacy, making Arneis, Petit Manseng, Pinot Grigio, Savagnin, Tannat, Tempranillo and Saperavi.

🍷🍷🍷🍷 Quintus King Valley Saperavi Tannat Shiraz Cabernet Sauvignon Tempranillo 2015 This is an intriguing hodgepodge of varieties. Each imbues an element of fruit and structure to varying degrees. The end result is one of grapey, pulpy richness with clear attention to tannin detail and resolution evident in the glass. The oak is well handled, the wine with darker fruits and an Italianate dryness. Screwcap. 14.5% alc. **Rating** 92 To 2027 $35 NG
Prosecco 2016 Enticingly understated, beautifully poised and refreshingly dry, this is a prosecco of accurate fruit expression of lemon, nashi pear and Granny Smith apple, with low dosage giving freedom to cool King Valley acidity of great persistence and perfectly harmonious integration. A beautifully composed and delicately poised aperitif. Crown seal. 11.2% alc. **Rating** 91 To 2017 $25 TS

Symphony Hill Wines ★★★★☆

2017 Eukey Road, Ballandean, Qld 4382 **Region** Granite Belt
T (07) 4684 1388 **www**.symphonyhill.com.au **Open** 7 days 10–4
Winemaker Mike Hayes **Est.** 1999 **Dozens** 6000 **Vyds** 3.5ha
Ewen Macpherson purchased an old table grape and orchard property in 1996. A partnership with his parents, Bob and Jill Macpherson, led to development of the vineyard, while Ewen completed his Bachelor of Applied Science in viticulture (2003). The vineyard (now much expanded) was established using state-of-the-art technology; vineyard manager/winemaker Mike Hayes is a third-generation viticulturist in the Granite Belt region, and became an equal co-owner of Symphony Hill in '14. He also has impressive academic achievements, with a degree in viticulture, followed by a Masters in Professional Studies – Viticulture, and was awarded a Churchill Fellowship (in '12) to study alternative wine grape varieties in Europe.

Symphony Hill has firmly established its reputation as one of the Granite Belt's foremost wineries. Exports to China.

🍷🍷🍷🍷🍷 **The Rock Reserve Shiraz 2015** A medium crimson-red, this wine is showing a little new oak at present. However, there is admirable depth of fruit on the medium-bodied, structured and balanced palate and once the wood integrates, this should be a lovely drink. Screwcap. 14.6% alc. **Rating** 90 **To** 2022 $65 PR

Syrahmi ★★★★

2370 Lancefield–Tooborac Road, Tooborac, Vic 3523 **Region** Heathcote
T 0407 057 471 **www.**syrahmi.com.au **Open** Not
Winemaker Adam Foster **Est.** 2004 **Dozens** 2000
Adam Foster worked as a chef in Vic and London before moving to the front of house and becoming increasingly interested in wine. He then worked as a cellar hand with a who's who in Australia and France, including Torbreck, Chapoutier, Mitchelton, Domaine Ogier, Heathcote Winery, Jasper Hill and Domaine Pierre Gaillard. He became convinced that the Cambrian soils of Heathcote could produce the best possible shiraz, and since 2004 has purchased grapes from the region, using the full bag of winemaking techniques. Exports to the US, Japan and Hong Kong.

🍷🍷🍷🍷🍷 **Demi Heathcote Shiraz 2015** An extremely complex shiraz with a jumble sale of aromas and flavours from wild-grown raspberry through to smoked meats, thence licorice and black pepper, black cherry adding its voice the second time around. Screwcap. 14% alc. **Rating** 93 **To** 2028 $25 ❂

Garden of Earthly Delights Riesling 2016 Chilled for 24 hours before being pressed, wild-yeast fermented, one-third fermented on skins in a 675l ceramic egg with no temperature control. Throw conceptions of quality riesling out the window when approaching this wine. Don't be put off by the unusual bouquet (wet sand shoe), and proceed to the deep flavours of the palate – earthy and minerally, with all sorts of citrus and rock notes just for starters. This isn't a yellow wine (it is quartz-white) but it should hold natural wine devotees in its thrall. Points for wines such as this are like overcoats on a nudist beach. Screwcap. 12.6% alc. **Rating** 92 **To** 2020

Garden of Earthly Delights Riesling 2015 Funky elements on the bouquet and palate add to the complexity rather than the varietal expression of the wine. There is a break in the line as it dips on the back-palate that should be filled with bottle age. Full of interest for those looking for something very different. Screwcap. 12.3% alc. **Rating** 92 **To** 2023 $32

Last Dance Heathcote Shiraz 2014 100% whole bunches, wild yeast–open fermented, 52 days on skins, matured in used French oak for 15 months. How you can achieve part carbonic, part alcoholic (ie with yeast) fermentation for 52 days in an open vessel with no plunging is extraordinary – all sorts of bacterial and volatile acidity issues would be normal. One saving grace is the near perfect alcohol that has bequeathed sweet red berry fruits at a relatively low pH. Screwcap. 13.8% alc. **Rating** 92

T'Gallant ★★★★

1385 Mornington–Flinders Road, Main Ridge, Vic 3928 **Region** Mornington Peninsula
T (03) 5931 1300 **www.**tgallant.com.au **Open** 7 days 9–5
Winemaker Adam Carnaby **Est.** 1990 **Dozens** NFP **Vyds** 8ha
Husband and wife winemakers Kevin McCarthy and Kathleen Quealy carved out such an important niche market for the T'Gallant label that in 2003, after protracted negotiations, it was acquired by Beringer Blass (now part of TWE). The acquisition of a 15ha property and the planting of 8ha of pinot gris gave the business a firm geographic base, as well as providing increased resources for its signature wine.

🍷🍷🍷🍷🍷 **Cape Schanck Pinot Grigio 2016** Pale blush-pink ex skin contact; a well made wine with crisp acidity underpinning and lengthening the palate and its nashi pear flavour. Screwcap. 12.5% alc. **Rating** 91 **To** 2017 $20 ❂

Imogen Pinot Gris 2015 In the unique T'Gallant high alcohol style, which has its upside (enhanced flavour) and downside (a peppery warmth to the finish). Not easy to judge by conventional standards, but loyal customers should pay no attention. Screwcap. 15% alc. **Rating** 90 **To** 2018 $25

ΥΥΥΥ **Imogen Pinot Gris 2016 Rating** 89 **To** 2019 $25 SC
Cape Schanck Heathcote Rose 2016 Rating 89 **To** 2017 $20

Tahbilk ★★★★★

254 O'Neils Road, Tabilk, Vic 3608 **Region** Nagambie Lakes
T (03) 5794 2555 **www**.tahbilk.com.au **Open** Mon–Sat 9–5, Sun 11–5
Winemaker Alister Purbrick, Neil Larson, Alan George **Est.** 1860 **Dozens** 120 000
Vyds 221.5ha
A winery steeped in tradition (with National Trust classification), which should be visited at least once by every wine-conscious Australian, and which makes wines – particularly red wines – utterly in keeping with that tradition. The essence of that heritage comes in the form of the tiny quantities of Shiraz made from vines planted in 1860. The quality of the 2012 and '13 wines continued to underwrite the reputation of Tahbilk. A founding member of Australia's First Families of Wine. *Wine Companion* 2016 Winery of the Year. Exports to all major markets.

ΥΥΥΥΥ **1927 Vines Marsanne 2011** As always, this has an extra degree of concentration and complexity, partly due to vine age, partly to the extra years in bottle, and – in this year at least, the cool climate. This is wonderfully fresh and delicate, citrus, apple and honeysuckle all on the same page. Sometimes the acidity can be too obvious for some, but not here. A glorious wine, its future stretching out for decades. Screwcap. 11% alc. **Rating** 97 **To** 2031 $46 ❂
1860 Vines Shiraz 2013 Lighter colour than usual, but has an excellent clear crimson hue; the winemaking team has resisted the temptation to extract more fruit and tannins, letting the purity of the fruit light up the room, red cherry to the fore. The silky tannins and overall weight are akin to a high quality pinot noir, so it's no surprise I should love it even if others may not. Screwcap. 13.5% alc. **Rating** 97 **To** 2038 $320

ΥΥΥΥΥ **1927 Vines Marsanne 2010** Gleaming straw-green; superb balance and length are the usual hallmarks, the trademark honeysuckle and a touch of honey smartly followed by precisely balanced acidity. This is one of the best vintages of this unique wine, made from the only block of 90yo marsanne vines in Australia. Screwcap. 11.5% alc. **Rating** 96 **To** 2030 $45 ❂
1860 Vines Shiraz 2012 It is only medium-bodied, but has a quiet insistence that brooks no argument, opening proceedings with the fragrant spicy/earthy/ red fruits triptych of the bouquet (oak doesn't seek to dominate at any stage). The medium-bodied palate is supple, perfectly balanced and has great length. In many ways, this could be argued to be the ultimate distillation of Australian red wines made over the past 155 years. Screwcap. 12.5% alc. **Rating** 96 **To** 2042 $298
Eric Stevens Purbrick Cabernet Sauvignon 2012 The bouquet replays the aromas of a warm day in the Australian bush, the aromas of earth, dried grass and eucalypt coupled with a powerful blast of blackcurrant and dried herbs on the long, full-bodied palate. The management of oak and tannins has been exemplary. Screwcap. 14% alc. **Rating** 96 **To** 2042 $70 ❂
Museum Release Marsanne 2011 The bright green-golden colour is marvellous; the bouquet and palate operate in perfect harmony with lime, lemon, lemon curd, honeysuckle and toast all on eloquent parade. A unique Australian classic with no contender in sight. Screwcap. 11.5% alc. **Rating** 95 **To** 2025 $24 ❂
Eric Stevens Purbrick Shiraz 2013 The colour is deep, the wine medium to full-bodied, with fruit ranging through red to purple to black; the tannins are ripe and supple, oak contributing a little more than usual, but not egregiously so. Screwcap. 14.2% alc. **Rating** 95 **To** 2038 $72

Eric Stevens Purbrick Shiraz 2012 Shares many things with the 1860 Vines, but in a more generous framework, making instant gratification easier to come by. The earthy/spicy notes are common to the bouquet and the tannins, and there are fleshy elements filling in the mid-palate, albeit without undue fuss. A gentleman's shiraz. Screwcap. 13.5% alc. **Rating** 95 **To** 2031 $70

Eric Stevens Purbrick Cabernet Sauvignon 2013 A rock of ages full-bodied cabernet, dark in colour and full-bodied in the mouth. It's savoury blackcurrant more than cassis, with a sprig of herbs, a dash of black olive, sober-sided tannins, and French oak that won't be (entirely) intimidated. Screwcap. 13% alc. **Rating** 95 **To** 2038 $72

Old Vines Cabernet Shiraz 2013 First made – and labelled as Cabernet Shiraz – in '57 and '58, believed to be the first such wine so labelled in Aus; after intermittent releases, returns to a permanent position in the Tahbilk premium range with this 60/40% blend. Black fruits, firm tannins and integrated oak are talismans for the long-term development of this wine. Screwcap. 14% alc. **Rating** 95 **To** 2038 $46

Cabernet Sauvignon 2014 Rating 94 **To** 2034 $26 ✪
Old Vines Cabernet Shiraz 2014 Rating 94 **To** 2030 $45

 Grenache Shiraz Mourvedre 2015 Rating 92 **To** 2030 $26
Cane Cut Marsanne 2013 Rating 92 **To** 2021 $25 ✪
Riesling 2016 Rating 90 **To** 2023 $19 JF ✪
Marsanne 2016 Rating 90 **To** 2023 $18 ✪
Cellar Door Exclusive Roussanne 2016 Rating 90 **To** 2021 $18 ✪
Shiraz 2014 Rating 90 **To** 2034 $26
Cane Cut Marsanne 2012 Rating 90 **To** 2024 $25 JF

Talbots Block Wines   ★★★★☆

62 Possingham Pit Road, Sevenhill, SA 5453 **Region** Clare Valley
T 0402 649 979 **www.**talbotsblock.com.au **Open** By appt
Winemaker Contract **Est.** 2011 **Dozens** 1000 **Vyds** 5ha

Thanks to careers in government and the oil industry, Alex and Bill Talbot started their journey to wine in 1997 while working and living at Woomera in the SA desert. They purchased land in the Sevenhill area of the Clare Valley, having fallen in love with the place, and dreamed of some day making wine for their friends. They then moved to various places in Asia, including Kuala Lumpur, Jakarta and Singapore, their minds always returning to their Sevenhill vineyard. They now live in the house they built high on the block, giving views across the vineyard, and have the opportunity to tend the vines whenever they please. Initially the grapes were sold, but since 2012 they have kept enough of the production to have 1000 dozen made across their two distinctly different Shiraz styles. The labels are striking and evocative.

♟♟♟♟♟ **The Sultan Clare Valley Shiraz 2014** The long, cool '14 vintage allowed the grapes to reach full ripeness at a lower baume than in '15, but didn't scrimp on the velvety texture and mouthfeel this wine has. The flavours, too, are neatly balanced between red and black, bringing out the best of each. Screwcap. 14.3% alc. **Rating** 95 **To** 2030 $36

The Prince Clare Valley Shiraz 2015 A brilliant full crimson-purple, the bouquet with licorice, spice, olive tapenade and black fruits, the palate a swelling wave of black fruits; angular but not rough tannins, the alcohol curiously (but happily) submerged in all the good attributes of the wine. Screwcap. 14.9% alc. **Rating** 94 **To** 2035 $25

Talijancich   ★★★★

26 Hyem Road, Herne Hill, WA 6056 **Region** Swan Valley
T (08) 9296 4289 **www.**taliwine.com.au **Open** Wed–Mon 10.30–4.30
Winemaker James Talijancich **Est.** 1932 **Dozens** 10000 **Vyds** 6ha

A former fortified wine specialist (with old Liqueur Tokay) now making a select range of table wines, with particular emphasis on Verdelho – each year there is a tasting of fine three-year-old

Verdelho from both Australia and overseas. James Talijancich is an energetic and effective ambassador for the Swan Valley as a whole. Exports to the UK.

ŢŢŢŢŢ **Reserve Swan Valley Verdelho 2008** Has transformed itself from duckling to swan (pun intended) with a honey on buttered toast flavour-set, allied with a hint of crystallised lemon. Fully developed. Screwcap. 14% alc. **Rating** 94 **To** 2020 $35

Talisman Wines   ★★★★★

PO Box 354, Cottesloe, WA 6911 **Region** Geographe
T 0401 559 266 **www.**talismanwines.com.au **Open** Not .
Winemaker Peter Stanlake **Est.** 2009 **Dozens** 2700 **Vyds** 9ha
Kim Robinson (and wife Jenny) began the development of their vineyard in 2000, and now have cabernet, shiraz, malbec, zinfandel, chardonnay, riesling and sauvignon blanc. Kim says that 'after eight frustrating years of selling grapes to Evans & Tate and Wolf Blass, we decided to optimise the vineyard and attempt to make quality wines'. The measure of their success has been consistent gold medal performance at (and some trophies) the Geographe Wine Show. They say this could not have been achieved without the assistance of vineyard manager Victor Bertola and winemaker Peter Stanlake. Exports to the UK.

ŢŢŢŢŢ **Gabrielle Ferguson Valley Chardonnay 2015** Complex, detailed, textural and alluring. It sums up great chardonnay. It sums up Gabrielle. The fruit is top notch and the winemaking a smart fit: wild yeast fermentation and new and older French barriques create flavours of creamed honey, lemon curd, baked quinces, and complex sulphides – the moreish mouthwatering kind – and textural fine lees. Screwcap. 13.9% alc. **Rating** 96 **To** 2021 $35 JF ✪
Ferguson Valley Riesling 2016 More texture than usual, perhaps due to the warmer vintage, yet showing all the vibrancy of lime-lemon zest with a fine acid line running the length of the palate. It's backed up with a whisper of citrus blossom. Ready now. Screwcap. 11.8% alc. **Rating** 95 **To** 2023 $22 JF ✪
Ferguson Valley Merlot 2014 This is good. Really good merlot. It's just started to hit its straps, revealing a core of perfectly ripe plum fruit and squishy currants, florals and woodsy spices, leather and the attractive varietal top note of crushed herbs – not weedy, but savoury. Finely tuned, oak integrated, and tannins superb. Screwcap. 14.5% alc. **Rating** 95 **To** 2021 $35 JF ✪

ŢŢŢŢŢ **Ferguson Valley Cabernet Malbec 2013** **Rating** 93 **To** 2023 $25 JF ✪
Barrique Ferguson Valley Sauvignon Blanc Fume 2015 **Rating** 92
To 2021 $27 JF
Ferguson Valley Zinfandel 2013 **Rating** 92 **To** 2021 $42 JF
Ferguson Valley Zinfandel 2010 **Rating** 90 **To** 2019 $42 JF

Tallavera Grove | Carillion   ★★★★★

749 Mount View Road, Mount View, NSW 2325 **Region** Hunter Valley
T (02) 4990 7535 **www.**tallaveragrove.com.au **Open** Thurs–Mon 10–5
Winemaker Gwyn Olsen **Est.** 2000 **Dozens** 15 000 **Vyds** 188ha
Tallavera Grove is one of the many wine interests of Dr John Davis and family. The family is a 50% owner of Briar Ridge, and also owns a 12ha vineyard in Coonawarra, the 100ha Stonefields Vineyard at Wrattonbully and a 36ha vineyard at Orange (the Carillion wines are sourced from this vineyard). The 40ha Hunter Valley vineyards are planted to chardonnay, shiraz, semillon, verdelho, cabernet sauvignon and viognier.

ŢŢŢŢŢ **Carillion The Crystals Orange Chardonnay 2014** An elegant, understated wine that grows each time you go back to it, and which has years to go before it reaches its prime. In between, its stone fruit and apple flavours will grow, sustained by crunchy acidity and understated oak on the finish. Screwcap. 13% alc. **Rating** 95 **To** 2029 $35 ✪
Carillion The Volcanics Orange Cabernet Sauvignon 2015 Wears its origins on its sleeve, with cool climate cabernet's tomato bush, bay leaf and herbal characters all in evidence, and a cedary overlay which is probably partly French

oak, partly varietal. Silky and elegant on the palate, the ripe red berry and cassis flavours mesh seamlessly with the fine tannin. Screwcap. 14% alc. **Rating** 95 To 2030 $45 SC

Stonefields Block 22 Wrattonbully Cabernet Sauvignon 2014
Wrattonbully is often forgotten in discussions about the best Aus regions, Coonawarra heading the Limestone Coast board of honour. Wines such as this, with its juicy cassis fruit tempered by bay leaf and black olive, are right up there in the sub-$50 bracket, tannin and oak contributions well measured. Screwcap. 13.8% alc. **Rating** 95 To 2034 $45

Carillion Orange Riesling 2015 Has a certain delicacy to its bouquet and palate, but no shortage of varietal expression as it moves through its blossom and spice bouquet to its elegant lime and apple-infused palate. Bright acidity will be a friend forever. Screwcap. 12.5% alc. **Rating** 94 To 2025 $25 ⚫

Stonefields Arbitrage Wrattonbully Cabernet Merlot Shiraz 2014
A blend which is perfectly suited to this region, with each variety in its element here, and all equally capable of a worthwhile contribution. It's actually the regional quality which stands out on the bouquet, with aromatic mint and limestone much in evidence. Cassis, red fruit and spice flow through the palate with supple richness and an impeccable balance. Screwcap. 13.8% alc. **Rating** 94 To 2028 $38 SC

🍷🍷🍷🍷🍷 **Tallavura Grove Hunter Valley Semillon 2016** Rating 93 To 2030 $25 SC ⚫
Carillion The Crystals Orange Chardonnay 2015 Rating 93 To 2023 $35 SC
Carillion Orange Sauvignon Blanc 2015 Rating 92 To 2017 $20 ⚫
Carillion The Crystals Chardonnay 2016 Rating 91 To 2021 $35 SC
Davis Premium Vineyards Lovable Rogue Funky Ferment Orange Verduzzo 2016 Rating 91 To 2020 $30
Carillion Orange Pinot Noir 2015 Rating 91 To 2023 $25
Carillion Orange Riesling 2016 Rating 90 To 2023 $25
Davis Premium Vineyards Rogue Series Field Blend Wild in the Wood 2016 Rating 90 To 2024 $30
Carillion Cabernet Merlot Petit Verdot 2014 Rating 90 To 2022 $25 SC

Taltarni ★★★★★
339 Taltarni Road, Moonambel, Vic 3478 **Region** Pyrenees
T (03) 5459 7900 **www.**taltarni.com.au **Open** 7 days 11–5
Winemaker Robert Heywood, Peter Warr **Est.** 1969 **Dozens** 80 000 **Vyds** 78.5ha
The American owner and founder of Clos du Val (Napa Valley), Taltarni and Clover Hill (see separate entry) has brought the management of these three businesses and Domaine de Nizas (Languedoc) under the one roof, the group known as Goelet Wine Estates. Taltarni is the largest of the Australian ventures, its estate vineyards of great value and underpinning the substantial annual production. Insectariums are established in permanent vegetation corridors, each containing around 2000 native plants that provide a pollen and nectar source for the beneficial insects, reducing the need for chemicals and other controls of the vineyards. In recent years Taltarni has updated its winemaking techniques, and in 2017 celebrated 40 years of winemaking. Exports to all major markets.

🍷🍷🍷🍷🍷 **Fume Blanc 2016** A blend of Pyrenees and Coal River (Tasmania) grapes, fermented in used French barriques and aged on lees in barrel. Skilled winemaking has taken full advantage of the inherent complexity of the process, yet kept the tropical fruit flavours fresh and vibrant, the finish long and clean. Screwcap. 13% alc. **Rating** 95 To 2019 $26 ⚫

Old Block Pyrenees Shiraz 2015 Complex, rich, perfumed wine. Take some dark fruit, add pepper, crushed juniper and choc-mint, with Mediterranean dried herbs, and cedary oak for good measure, and a profile forms. Grainy tannins, a touch drying but the palate doesn't waver. Screwcap. 14.5% alc. **Rating** 95 To 2035 $45 JF

Reserve Pyrenees Shiraz Cabernet 2013 Layer upon layer of aromas and flavours of black cherry, plum, licorice, cassis, dark chocolate, oak and mint are evident in this luscious, full-bodied wine. It has only just embarked on what will be a long life, with the best yet to come. Cork. 14.5% alc. **Rating** 94 **To** 2030 $65

🍷🍷🍷🍷🍷 Estate Pyrenees Shiraz 2015 Rating 93 To 2026 $40 JF
Reserve Pyrenees Shiraz Cabernet 2014 Rating 93 To 2036 $65 JF
Estate Pyrenees Cabernet Sauvignon 2014 Rating 93 To 2035 $40 JF
Old Block Pyrenees Cabernet Sauvignon 2014 Rating 93 To 2029 $45 JF
Cuvee Rose 2012 Rating 92 To 2017 $26 TS
Tache 2012 Rating 92 To 2017 $26 TS
Barossa Heathcote Pyrenees GSM 2016 Rating 90 To 2022 $26 JF
Sparkling Shiraz 2015 Rating 90 To 2020 TS

Tamar Ridge | Pirie   ★★★★★

1a Waldhorn Drive, Rosevears, Tas 7277 **Region** Northern Tasmania
T (03) 6330 0300 **www.**tamarridge.com.au **Open** 7 days 10–5
Winemaker Tom Wallace **Est.** 1994 **Dozens** 14 000 **Vyds** 120ha
In August 2010 Brown Brothers purchased Tamar Ridge from Gunns Limited for $32.5 million. While Dr Andrew Pirie has retired from his former position of CEO and chief winemaker, he points out that the end of his five-year tenure happened to coincide with the acquisition. Tasmania is the one region of Australia with demand for grapes and wine exceeding supply. Tamar Ridge was well managed during the seven years it was owned by Gunns, avoiding the financial meltdown of Gunns. Exports to all major markets.

🍷🍷🍷🍷🍷 **Tamar Ridge Single Block Pinot Noir 2015** MV6 clone from the Kayena vineyard, 5 days cold soak, wild yeast–open fermented, matured for 12 months in French barriques (30% new). Light crimson; there is no mention of whole bunch use, but the powerful savoury tannins that permeate the long palate seem to have at least some whole bunch origin. Red fruits stand up to the tannins. Screwcap. 14.1% alc. **Rating** 95 **To** 2030 $100

🍷🍷🍷🍷🍷 Tamar Ridge Reserve Pinot Noir 2014 Rating 92 To 2025 $65 JF
Traditional Method Non Vintage NV Rating 92 To 2019 $32 TS

Tambo Estate   ★★★★★

96 Pages Road, Tambo Upper, Vic 3885 **Region** Gippsland
T (03) 5156 4921 **www.**tambowine.com.au **Open** Thurs–Sun 11–5, 7 days Dec–Jan
Winemaker Alastair Butt **Est.** 1994 **Dozens** 1380 **Vyds** 5.11ha
Bill and Pam Williams returned to Australia in the early 1990s after seven years overseas, and began the search for a property which met the specific requirements for high quality table wines established by Dr John Gladstones in his masterwork *Viticulture and Environment*. They chose a property in the foothills of the Victorian Alps on the inland side of the Gippsland Lakes, with predominantly sheltered, north-facing slopes. They planted a little over 5ha of chardonnay (the lion's share of the plantings, with 3.4ha), sauvignon blanc, pinot noir, cabernet sauvignon and a splash of merlot. They are mightily pleased to have secured the services of Alastair Butt (one-time winemaker at Seville Estate).

🍷🍷🍷🍷🍷 **Reserve Gippsland Lakes Chardonnay 2015** A striking wine of very high quality: white peach with a twist of limey acidity, the oak extract exactly positioned in support. It's the attention to detail that makes it special, the palate so long. Screwcap. 13.3% alc. **Rating** 97 **To** 2028 $48 ✪

🍷🍷🍷🍷🍷 **Gippsland Lakes Sauvignon Blanc 2016** Marches convincingly to the tune of its own drum. The texture is outstanding, with slinky acidity contrasting with the faintly nutty/smoky notes created by barrel ferment. This could so easily be mistaken for a Loire Valley sauvignon blanc in the Dageneau style. And it will live. Screwcap. 12.7% alc. **Rating** 95 **To** 2021 $26 ✪
Gippsland Lakes Unwooded Chardonnay 2016 Shows just how good unoaked chardonnay can be. It has precise varietal definition in that midpoint

between grapefruit and white peach. A few years in bottle will add complexity to the equation. Screwcap. 12.7% alc. Rating 94 To 2021 $22 ☺

♈♈♈♈♈ Reserve Cabernet Sauvignon 2015 Rating 90 To 2030 $38
Field Blend 2015 Rating 90 To 2029 $28

Tamburlaine   ★★★★☆

358 McDonalds Road, Pokolbin, NSW 2321 **Region** Hunter Valley
T (02) 4998 4200 **www**.mywinery.com **Open** 7 days 9.30–5
Winemaker Mark Davidson, Ashley Horner **Est.** 1966 **Dozens** 60 000 **Vyds** 125ha
A thriving business that (until exports started to grow significantly) sold over 90% of its wine through the cellar door and by mailing list (with an active tasting club members' cellar program). The maturing of the estate-owned Orange vineyard led to the introduction of reserve varietals across the range. The Hunter Valley and Orange vineyards are all now certified organic. Exports to Malaysia, South Korea, Nepal, Japan and China.

♈♈♈♈♈ Reserve Hunter Valley Semillon 2013 On a dark night, or with the bottle out of sight, many would be tossing up in answer to the question 'is this wine semillon or riesling?' I'm not going to jump ship from the tasting note or drink-to date given when tasted in Jan '14. 'Pale quartz green; the fragrant lemon/citrus bouquet leads into a palate that opens with imperious lemon/lemongrass flavours, but – improbably given this start – becomes even more intense and probing on the long finish and aftertaste.' Screwcap. 10% alc. Rating 96 To 2025 $50 ☺
Museum Release Reserve Orange Riesling 2004 A riesling with depth and power to its citrus rind fruit, and at no risk of fading away. Indeed, I think it will continue to grow in bottle for up to 5 years. Screwcap. 12.1% alc. Rating 94 To 2024 $49

♈♈♈♈♈ Reserve Orange Riesling 2016 Rating 93 To 2021 $33
Reserve Hunter Valley Semillon 2016 Rating 93 To 2021 $33
Reserve Orange Syrah 2015 Rating 92 To 2040 $44
Reserve Orange Merlot 2015 Rating 91 To 2025 $44
Reserve Orange Cabernet Sauvignon 2015 Rating 90 To 2030 $44
Reserve Orange Malbec 2015 Rating 90 To 2023 $44

Tapanappa   ★★★★★

15 Spring Gully Road, Piccadilly, SA 5151 **Region** Adelaide Hills
T (08) 7324 5301 **www**.tapanappawines.com.au **Open** Thurs–Mon 11–4
Winemaker Brian Croser **Est.** 2002 **Dozens** 2500 **Vyds** 16.7ha
Tapanappa came home in many ways in 2015. It has the original Petaluma winery back, and a cellar door at the picturesque Tiers vineyard. Equally importantly, it is now wholly owned by Brian and Ann Croser, albeit with the involvement of daughter and son-in-law Lucy and Xavier Bizot. The business as usual components are the Whalebone Vineyard at Wrattonbully (planted to cabernet sauvignon, shiraz and merlot over 30 years ago), the Tiers Vineyard at Piccadilly in the Adelaide Hills (chardonnay), and the Foggy Hill Vineyard on the southern tip of the Fleurieu Peninsula (pinot noir). Exports to the UK, France, Sweden, Singapore, the UAE, Hong Kong and China.

♈♈♈♈♈ Single Vineyard Eden Valley Riesling 2016 From the 50yo Bartholomeus Vineyard, hand-picked, chilled, destemmed and crushed, pressed at 2°C, the free-run and first-press juice fermented over a 3-month period, which is astonishingly long. Quartz-white; it is almost painfully intense and long, and will mature superbly. The return of some of the stalks to the press may be the cause of the X-factor. Screwcap. 12.5% alc. Rating 96 To 2030 $29 ☺
Piccadilly Valley Chardonnay 2015 A very well made and stylish chardonnay that elegantly picks its way between citrus and stone fruit, and in so doing adds a savoury component. A tight rein on the percentage of new oak has impacted on texture, not flavour. Screwcap. 13.5% alc. Rating 95 To 2023 $39

Tiers Vineyard 1.5m Piccadilly Valley Chardonnay 2015 Offers citrus blossom and white peach aromas with a touch of mealy, nutty oak in the background. Ripe but restrained flavours, and a lovely line of fine acidity through the palate to a fresh finish. Screwcap. 13.7% alc. **Rating** 95 **To** 2023 $55 SC
Tiers Vineyard Piccadilly Valley Chardonnay 2015 Spicy oak is upfront in the bouquet, the aromas of lemon and white nectarine needing encouragement to emerge. The palate is lean and taut; very much the coiled spring. The flavours are strongly citrus-accented, the minerally texture and slatey acidity leading to a long, grapefruit pith-like finish. Be patient. Screwcap. 13.6% alc. **Rating** 94 **To** 2025 $79 SC

ȲȲȲȲȲ Single Vineyard Eden Valley Riesling 2015 Rating 93 To 2025 $29

Tar & Roses ★★★★

61 Vickers Lane, Nagambie, Vic 3608 **Region** Heathcote
T (03) 5794 1811 **www.tarandroses.com.au Open** 1st w'end each month 10–4
Winemaker Don Lewis, Narelle King **Est.** 2006 **Dozens** 18 000
Literally days before this edition was about to go to press, the news came through that Don Lewis had died. It's impossible to know what the owners of the business (John Valmorbida and David Jemmeson) may decide. It may be perfectly able to continue, giving support to Narelle King, part of the winemaking team of Tar & Roses since its inception. Exports to the UK, the US, Canada, Switzerland, Singapore, Japan, China and NZ.

ȲȲȲȲȲ **Heathcote Sangiovese 2015** It's quite a hefty style, in a varietal context, but with the heft comes seduction. Sweet spice, ripe plum, a run of red cherry and a lacing of cedar wood. It smells enticing and engages you on the palate. It's hard to go wrong here. Screwcap. 14.5% alc. **Rating** 93 **To** 2021 $24 CM ✪
Heathcote Tempranillo 2016 A bright purple robe verging on opaque sets the tone. The bounce of violet florals, the pulp of red and black cherry, the decadence of booze-soused cherry bonbons and hints of anise and root spice, all edge along a scale of well managed oak tannins. Screwcap. 14.6% alc. **Rating** 92 **To** 2025 $24 NG ✪
Lewis Riesling 2016 A luminescent straw flecked with yellow, this is attractive from the first whiff. Quince, Granny Smith apple and citrus zest form the cavalcade. While dry, the acidity is not forced. The path is brightly laid. The finish is bracing and long. Screwcap. 13.8% alc. **Rating** 91 **To** 2024 $20 NG ✪
Heathcote Nebbiolo 2015 Mid-garnet; tomato bush, sarsaparilla and creamy strawberry notes make the wine's entrance. Some sandalwood and orange zest spring up on the back end. The tannins are twiggy and firm, delivering a savoury rasp. The acidity is all soprano, sweeping the wine along. Screwcap. 13.5% alc. **Rating** 91 **To** 2024 $45 NG
Heathcote Shiraz 2015 This is a full-bodied, powerful shiraz without any sign of jammy fruit. Brooding and reticent at this early stage; there is a whiff of tapenade, coffee bean, camphor, salami and dark fruits strung across a densely packed mid-palate defined by a reductive tension and oak supports. Screwcap. 14.8% alc. **Rating** 90 **To** 2030 $22 NG
Heathcote Tempranillo 2015 10% new oak but mostly older French. Firm and solid. The fruit seems slightly cooked but there's ample weight and indeed impact. Tar, black cherry and mocha-like notes, lifted by dried spice. Muscular. Screwcap. 14.5% alc. **Rating** 90 **To** 2021 $24 CM

ȲȲȲȲ Central Victoria Pinot Grigio 2016 Rating 89 To 2019 $18 NG ✪

Tarrahill. ★★★★★

340 Old Healesville Road, Yarra Glen, Vic 3775 **Region** Yarra Valley
T (03) 9730 1152 **www.tarrahill.com Open** By appt
Winemaker Jonathan Hamer, Geof Fethers **Est.** 1992 **Dozens** 700 **Vyds** 6.5ha

Owned by former Mallesons Lawyers partner Jonathan Hamer and wife Andrea, a former doctor and daughter of Ian Hanson, who made wine for many years under the Hanson-Tarrahill label. Ian had a 0.8ha vineyard at Lower Plenty, but needed 2ha to obtain a vigneron's licence. In 1990 the Hamers purchased a property in the Yarra Valley and planted the requisite vines (pinot noir – ultimately destroyed by the 2009 bushfires). Jonathon and company director friend Geof Fethers worked weekends in the vineyard, and in '04 decided that they would undertake a wine science degree (at CSU); they graduated in '11. In '12 Jonathan retired from law and planted more vineyards (cabernet sauvignon, cabernet franc, merlot, malbec and petit verdot) and Ian (aged 86) retired from winemaking. Andrea has also contributed, with a second degree (horticulture); she is a biodynamics advocate.

ŶŶŶŶ **Le Batard 2015** An interesting blend of 65% pinot and 35% shiraz, this spicy, red and black-fruited wine has good depth on the youthful, straightforward and delicious palate with some gently grippy tannins giving the wine structure and backbone. Nice wine. Screwcap. 14.5% alc. **Rating** 89 **To** 2020 $25 PR

TarraWarra Estate ★★★★★

311 Healesville-Yarra Glen Road, Yarra Glen, Vic 3775 **Region** Yarra Valley
T (03) 5962 3311 **www.**tarrawarra.com.au **Open** Tues–Sun 11–5
Winemaker Clare Halloran **Est.** 1983 **Dozens** 15 000 **Vyds** 28.98ha
TarraWarra is, and always has been, one of the top-tier wineries in the Yarra Valley. Founded by Marc Besen AO and wife Eva, it has operated on the basis that quality is paramount, cost a secondary concern. The creation of the TarraWarra Museum of Art (twma.com.au) in a purpose-built building provides another reason to visit; indeed, many visitors come specifically to look at the ever-changing displays in the Museum. Changes in the vineyard include the planting of shiraz and merlot, and in the winery, the creation of a four-tier range: a deluxe MDB label made in tiny quantities and only when the vintage permits; the single vineyard range; a Reserve range; and the 100% estate-grown varietal range. Exports to France, the Maldives, Vietnam, Singapore, Hong Kong and China.

ŶŶŶŶŶ **MDB Yarra Valley Chardonnay 2015** This wine is very good. Seldom made, it is a reflection of select, high-performing plots preening in top vintages such as this. Stone fruit comes a distant second to the wine's structural pedigree. There is plenty of oak slung across its frame, too. However, it nestles effortlessly into the wine's weight and precision, channelling it towards a long life. Screwcap. 12.8% alc. **Rating** 96 **To** 2027 $110 NG

Reserve Yarra Valley Pinot Noir 2014 Clear crimson hue; a truly delicious wine built around a heart of fresh red cherries and red berries, with gossamer silk tannins and perfectly judged French oak. This will change as it ages, with more foresty nuances, but will never be better than it is now. Screwcap. 13% alc. **Rating** 96 **To** 2029 $70 ❂

Reserve Yarra Valley Chardonnay 2015 This is a rich, flavourful chardonnay despite its modest alcohol. Built solidly around a mid-palate of creamy, lees-driven nougat notes and vanilla pod oak supports, the aromas are all truffled corn, popcorn and funk. A stone fruit-inflected mineral tang reveals itself, bosomed beneath the billowy creaminess. A generous wine packed with flavour, but far from fat. Screwcap. 13.2% alc. **Rating** 95 **To** 2025 $50 NG

K Block Yarra Valley Merlot 2014 Clever work in the vineyard and a sensitive approach in the winery have produced a merlot with clear-cut varietal character, something missing from most Australian merlots. It has a silken web of red fruits, green olive, fine-spun tannins on the light to medium-bodied palate, all in harmony. Screwcap. 13.5% alc. **Rating** 95 **To** 2024 $35 ❂

Yarra Valley Pinot Noir Rose 2016 From a single block grown exclusively for this wine. The palest of pink colour; strawberry/spicy aromas; the palate is savoury, coupled with intriguing lemony acidity to provide length. Screwcap. 12.3% alc. **Rating** 94 **To** 2018 $25 ❂

K Block Yarra Valley Merlot 2015 This is exactly what one should expect from merlot: similar aromatic traits to cabernet, albeit with the piercing blackcurrant

notes of the latter replaced by a plummy tone. In this case, blood plum, but also red cherry, anise and cola. The undercarriage of leaf and dried herbs bears similarities too. In all, a savoury wine of stature and complexity, buffered by salubrious, well handled oak. Screwcap. 14.5% alc. **Rating** 94 **To** 2025 $35 NG
Yarra Valley Barbera 2015 Excellent colour; most assuredly a barbera with attitude, and fully entitled to that. It has more depth, more precision and more mouthfeel to its supple purple fruit flavours. Screwcap. 14.2% alc. **Rating** 94 **To** 2023 $28 ⊙

ŸŸŸŸŸ **Yarra Valley Roussanne Marsanne Viognier 2015** Rating 93 To 2025 $30
Late Disgorged Vintage Reserve Yarra Valley Blanc de Blanc 2010 Rating 93 To 2020 $60
Reserve Yarra Valley Pinot Noir 2015 Rating 92 To 2024 $70 NG
South Block Yarra Valley Chardonnay 2015 Rating 91 To 2023 $35 NG
Reserve Yarra Valley Chardonnay 2014 Rating 91 To 2024 $50 CM
Q Block Yarra Valley Pinot Noir 2015 Rating 91 To 2023 $35 NG
Yarra Valley Chardonnay 2015 Rating 90 To 2023 $28 NG
Yarra Valley Pinot Noir 2015 Rating 90 To 2024 $28 NG
Yarra Valley Nebbiolo 2014 Rating 90 To 2024 $35

Taylor Ferguson ★★★★

Level 1, 62 Albert Street, Preston, Vic 3072 (postal) **Region** South Eastern Australia
T (03) 9487 2599 **www**.alepat.com.au **Open** Not
Winemaker Norman Lever **Est.** 1996 **Dozens** 40 000

Taylor Ferguson is the much-altered descendant of a business of that name established in Melbourne in 1898. A connecting web joins it with Alexander & Paterson (1892) and the much more recent distribution business of Alepat Taylor, formed in 1996. The development of the Taylor Ferguson wines has been directed by winemaker Norman Lever, using grapes sourced from various regions, mainly Coonawarra, Langhorne Creek and the Riverina. Exports to Germany, Iraq, Singapore, Malaysia, Vietnam, Taiwan and China.

ŸŸŸŸŸ **Special Release Fernando The First Barossa Shiraz 2013** The most ambitious wine of the stable, with old vine Barossan fruit aged for 18 months in assorted oak. Still a monster of a wine, the coal face of cooked black plum, cinnamon oak spice, vanilla bean, soy, dried fruits and boozy liqueur met, gallantly, by assuaging oak. Charred and assertive, the oak somehow manacles the fruit into a compact whole. Cork. 14.8% alc. **Rating** 91 **To** 2028 $75 NG
Fernando The First Barossa Valley Cabernet Sauvignon 2013 Suave, saturated and full, this is far from the oaky idiom displayed across this producer's other cuvees, suggesting that the handling of oak is becoming more sensitive over time. That said, the wine is still fleshy, very ripe and a morass of dark fruit flavours, hoisin and an attractive juicy stream of kirsch and bitter chocolate through its core. Cork. 14% alc. **Rating** 91 **To** 2023 $25 NG

Taylors ★★★★★

Taylors Road, Auburn, SA 5451 **Region** Clare Valley
T (08) 8849 1111 **www**.taylorswines.com.au **Open** Mon–Fri 9–5, w'ends 10–4
Winemaker Adam Eggins, Phillip Reschke, Chad Bowman **Est.** 1969 **Dozens** 250 000
Vyds 400ha

The family-founded and owned Taylors continues to flourish and expand – its vineyards are now by far the largest holding in the Clare Valley. There have also been changes in terms of the winemaking team and the wine style and quality, particularly through the outstanding St Andrews range. With each passing vintage, Taylors is managing to do for the Clare Valley what Peter Lehmann did for the Barossa Valley. Recent entries in international wine shows have resulted in a rich haul of trophies and gold medals for wines at all price points. A founding member of Australia's First Families of Wine. Exports (under the Wakefield brand due to trademark reasons) to all major markets.

ΨΨΨΨΨ **St Andrews Single Vineyard Release Clare Valley Riesling 2015** Has won three gold medals at even more questionable US competitions than those won by its Clare Valley sibling, including the 'World Wine Championship Awards '15'. A very elegant wine with diamond-cut varietal delineation, pure riesling fruit the centrepiece. Lovely now, better in a decade. Screwcap. 12.5% alc. **Rating** 96 **To** 2029 $40 ✪

TWP Taylors Winemaker's Project Clare Valley Riesling 2015 A cellar door release quixotically sold in a claret bottle, which can distract until you taste the wine, which is exceptionally good, with razor-sharp varietal definition (lime, lemon, apple) and very good acidity. The wine still has to develop colour, and will outlast many of its peers. Screwcap. 12.5% alc. **Rating** 96 **To** 2030 $25 ✪

The Visionary Exceptional Parcel Release Clare Valley Cabernet Sauvignon 2013 This is slightly more restrained and elegant than the '14 St Andrews Cabernet Sauvignon. It is still very concentrated and very long in the mouth, and is fruit (rather than oak or tannin) driven. Screwcap. 14.5% alc. **Rating** 96 **To** 2043 $200

St Andrews Single Vineyard Release Clare Valley Riesling 2016 A very good wine with purity and intensity underpinning the vibrantly fresh palate and long finish. Citrus/orange blossom aromas and flavours are just as they should be. Screwcap. 12.5% alc. **Rating** 95 **To** 2031 $40

TWP Taylors Winemaker's Project Clare Valley Chardonnay 2015 The claret bottle and the maddening unreadable blurb on the bottle itself to one side, this is an amazing achievement. Obviously, a patch of the very best chardonnay was identified, picked early with natural acidity; barrel fermentation and maturation in French oak are the keys to the best Clare Valley chardonnay I have tasted to date. Screwcap. 13.5% alc. **Rating** 95 **To** 2025 $25 ✪

Jaraman Clare Valley McLaren Vale Shiraz 2015 This is as complex as it is full-bodied, with an inky black fruit bouquet, the palate filled to overflowing, with black fruits, spice, licorice and dark chocolate all contributing. Has the X-factor, especially if it is given 10+ years in the bottle. Great value too. Screwcap. 14.5% alc. **Rating** 95 **To** 2040 $29 ✪

St Andrews Clare Valley Shiraz 2014 Machine-harvested, destemmed not crushed, 4 days cold soak, 10–14 days fermentation, 8–12 weeks post-ferment maceration, matured for 22 months in American oak (50% new). This is extreme winemaking, full of traps, but you have to say it worked. The wine manages to absorb the American oak without castrating the fruit, and has excellent length. Screwcap. 14.5% alc. **Rating** 95 **To** 2034 $70

The Pioneer Exceptional Parcel Release Clare Valley Shiraz 2013 Machine-harvested, destemmed not crushed, 4 days cold soak, 10–14 days fermentation, 8–12 weeks post-ferment maceration, matured for 28 months in American oak (50% new). I'm not convinced the extra 6 months in oak, and presumably even better fruit selection, has produced a wine three times as great as the St Andrews. Screwcap. 14.5% alc. **Rating** 95 **To** 2034 $200

St Andrews Single Vineyard Release Clare Valley Cabernet Sauvignon 2014 It is massively full-bodied, and really needs decades to reach its best à la Wynns' John Riddoch, but it does have balance, and the varietal character is not lost. Screwcap. 14.5% alc. **Rating** 95 **To** 2038 $70

TWP Taylors Winemaker's Project Clare Valley Fiano 2016 Rating 94 To 2020 $25 ✪

Clare Valley Shiraz 2014 Rating 94 To 2025 $20 ✪

Reserve Parcel Clare Valley Shiraz 2014 Rating 94 To 2034 $22 ✪

St Andrews Clare Valley Shiraz 2013 Rating 94 To 2028 $70

ΨΨΨΨΨ **Clare Valley Adelaide Hills Pinot Gris 2016** Rating 93 To 2020 $19 ✪

Jaraman Clare Valley McLaren Vale Shiraz 2014 Rating 93 To 2029 $30

Jaraman Clare Valley Coonawarra Cabernet Sauvignon 2014 Rating 93 To 2029 $30

Clare Valley Riesling 2015 Rating 92 To 2025 $20 ✪

Clare Valley Cabernet Sauvignon 2015 Rating 92 To 2025 $19 ✪
Taylor Made American Oak Clare Valley Malbec 2015 Rating 92
To 2025 $28
TWP Taylors Winemaker's Project McLaren Vale Nero d'Avola 2015
Rating 92 To 2021 $25 ✪
Clare Valley Riesling 2016 Rating 90 To 2023 $19 ✪
St Andrews Single Vineyard Release Clare Valley Chardonnay 2014
Rating 90 To 2020 $40
Taylor Made Adelaide Hills Pinot Noir Rose 2016 Rating 90 To 2018 $28
Adelaide Hills Pinot Noir 2015 Rating 90 To 2021 $20 ✪
Reserve Parcel Clare Valley Cabernet Sauvignon 2014 Rating 90
To 2025 $22

Telera   ★★★★

PO Box 3114, Prahran East, Vic 3181 **Region** Mornington Peninsula
T 0407 041 719 **www**.telera.com.au **Open** Not
Winemaker Michael Telera **Est.** 2007 **Dozens** 190 **Vyds** 0.4ha
Telera was established by Michael and Susanne (Lew) Wynne-Hughes, who planted the
vines in 2000, naming the venture MLF Wines. In '11 Michael Telera leased the vineyard,
and, following the death of Michael Wynne-Hughes in that year, the name was changed to
Telera. He has learnt the trade through six vintages as a cellar hand/assistant winemaker at Dr
George Mihaly's Paradigm Hill winery, and produces shiraz sourced from other growers on
the Peninsula. He plans to plant 12 rows of pinot noir on the leased property, making the total
20 rows of pinot noir and nine rows of sauvignon blanc. Production is increased with small
amounts of contract-grown sauvignon blanc.

♀♀♀♀♀ **Pernella Fume Sauvignon Blanc 2016** Crisper and brighter than its sibling
Itana. Pernella takes off on a citrus route with crunchy, lemony acidity, lemon peel
and pith and some grassy, daikon radish undertones. Plenty of joy here. Screwcap.
13.1% alc. **Rating** 92 **To** 2021 $29 JF
Itana Fume Sauvignon Blanc 2016 Wild yeast fermentation in French oak,
lees stirring and in barrel for 6 months: Itana gets the full Fume Monty. As
expected, there's some creamy texture, with white stone fruit, fresh horseradish,
lemony notes, too; refreshing acidity. Screwcap. 13.1% alc. **Rating** 92 **To** 2022
$39 JF
Del Su Pinot Noir 2015 Made from the aromatic 777 Dijon clone, estate-
grown, hand-picked, 15% whole bunches in the fermentation then aged in French
oak for 14 months. A pretty wine with pleasing upfront sweet cherry fruit and
Campari-esque flavours and fine tannins; a lighter style. 22 dozen made. Screwcap.
13.5% alc. **Rating** 90 **To** 2023 $55 JF

Tellurian   ★★★★☆

408 Tranter Road, Toolleen, Vic 3551 **Region** Heathcote
T 0431 004 766 **www**.tellurianwines.com.au **Open** By appt
Winemaker Tobias Ansted **Est.** 2002 **Dozens** 3000 **Vyds** 21.87ha
The vineyard is situated on the western side of Mt Camel at Toolleen, on the red Cambrian
soil that has made Heathcote one of the foremost regions in Australia for the production of
shiraz (Tellurian means 'of the earth'). Viticultural consultant Tim Brown not only supervises
the Tellurian estate plantings, but also works closely with the growers of grapes purchased
under contract for Tellurian. Further Rhône red and white varieties were planted on the
Tellurian property in 2011. Exports to the UK and China.

♀♀♀♀♀ **Heathcote Viognier 2016** Shows great promise, with a brushing of vanillan
oak and leesy detail laying the foundation for the exuberant regalia of stone
fruit aromas, a lick of honeysuckle and a pucker of talc and mineral. The oak
is beautifully handled, reining viognier's tendency towards hedonism into a
nourishing, compact whole. Viognier as it should be. Screwcap. 14.5% alc.
Rating 95 **To** 2022 $27 NG ✪

Heathcote Marsanne 2015 This is unctuous and rather glorious, with a firm nod to the Rhône. White peach, apricot and quince flavours, all ripe and slippery of texture, billow through the wine's middle. A yeasty riff of oatmeal funk comes into play, while some well handled phenolics and the warm breath of barrel fermentation imbue grip and focus. Screwcap. 14% alc. **Rating** 94 **To** 2030 $27 NG✪

Heathcote Grenache Shiraz Mourvedre 2015 A sensible blend, with grenache leading the charge rather than shiraz. This gives an intoxicating aroma of kirsch and violet, while allowing shiraz to perform best as a mid-palate filler; mourvedre as the shepherd, doling out tannins and harnessing the fruit to a meaty, ferrous clang of savouriness. The youthfulness of the vines augurs well for a bright future. Screwcap. 14.5% alc. **Rating** 94 **To** 2022 $27 NG✪

🍷🍷🍷🍷🍷 **Heathcote Grenache 2016** **Rating** 93 **To** 2021 $24 NG✪
Heathcote Fiano 2016 **Rating** 92 **To** 2020 $27 NG
Heathcote Mourvedre 2015 **Rating** 92 **To** 2022 $24 NG✪
Heathcote Riesling 2016 **Rating** 91 **To** 2028 $22 NG✪
Redline Heathcote Shiraz 2015 **Rating** 90 **To** 2021 $22 NG

Temple Bruer ★★★★

689 Milang Road, Angas Plains, SA 5255 **Region** Langhorne Creek
T (08) 8537 0203 **www**.templebruer.com.au **Open** Mon–Fri 9.30–4.30
Winemaker David Bruer, Vanessa Altmann, Verity Stanistreet **Est.** 1980 **Dozens** 18 000
Vyds 56ha

Temple Bruer was in the vanguard of the organic movement in Australia and was the focal point for the formation of Organic Vignerons Australia. Part of the production from its estate vineyards is used for its own label, part sold. Winemaker-owner David Bruer also has a vine propagation nursery, likewise run on an organic basis. Exports to the UK, the US, Canada, Sweden, Japan and China.

🍷🍷🍷🍷🍷 **Eden Valley Riesling 2012** At its optimal window of drinking, this fully certified organic producer's riesling is an archetype: quince marmalade, gasoline, ginger and ripe stone fruit flavours flaring across a shimmering, dry finish blessed with some bottle aged complexity. Screwcap. 13% alc. **Rating** 92 **To** 2022 $20 NG

Tempus Two Wines ★★★★★

Broke Road, Pokolbin, NSW 2321 **Region** Hunter Valley
T (02) 4993 3999 **www**.tempustwo.com.au **Open** 7 days 10–5
Winemaker Andrew Duff **Est.** 1997 **Dozens** 55 000

Tempus Two is a mix of Latin (Tempus means time) and English. It has been a major success story, production growing from 6000 dozen in 1997 to 55 000 dozen today. Its cellar door, restaurant complex (including the Oishii Japanese restaurant) and small convention facilities are situated in a striking building. The design polarises opinion; I like it. Exports to all major markets.

🍷🍷🍷🍷🍷 **Uno Hunter Valley Semillon 2016** What? $100! You have to be dreaming. The grapes were grown on the sandy loam soils of the '23 planting on Bainton vineyard at Broke. It's a particularly good semillon with intensity of flavour and great texture and structure. Citrus fruit and minerally acidity are in a balletic epic duel as they pirouette across the palate and into the far distance. Screwcap. 11% alc. **Rating** 97 **To** 2036 $100 ✪

🍷🍷🍷🍷🍷 **Pewter Hunter Valley Chardonnay 2016** Early picking has paid off, giving the wine freshness and intensity without losing varietal fruit and descending into the abyss of sauvignon blanc. You couldn't ask for more length, and the oak doesn't seriously challenge the fruit. The Hunter does it again. Screwcap. 12.5% alc. **Rating** 95 **To** 2024 $60

Pewter Hunter Valley Semillon 2016 Bright straw-green; a cheeky price for a current vintage semillon, but it is a quality wine, with razor-sharp varietal definition and length; lemongrass, lemon zest, lemon pith and minerally acidity are all in tune with each other. Screwcap. 10.5% alc. **Rating** 94 **To** 2026 $42

 Pewter Tumbarumba Chardonnay 2016 Rating 90 **To** 2021 $60
Copper Series Shiraz Rose 2016 Rating 90 **To** 2018 $30
Copper Shiraz 2016 Rating 90 **To** 2028 $30 SC
Pewter Pinot Noir Chardonnay Brut Cuvee 2012 Rating 90 **To** 2017 $35 TS

Ten Miles East ★★★★

8 Debneys Road, Norton Summit, SA 5136 **Region** Adelaide Hills
T (08) 8390 1723 **www**.tenmileseast.com **Open** Not
Winemaker Taiita and James Champniss **Est.** 2003 **Dozens** 400 **Vyds** 1.71ha
Ten Miles East takes its name from the fact that it is that distance and direction from the Adelaide GPO. Established by industry veteran John Greenshields (many years ago, John founded Koppamurra, the vineyard now owned by Tapanappa), and Robin and Judith Smallacombe and is, to put it mildly, an interesting one. Its vineyard in the Adelaide Hills is planted principally to shiraz, sauvignon blanc and saperavi, with smaller plantings of pinot noir (eight clones), arneis, riesling and carmenere. The winery and cellar door are in what was once the Auldwood Cider Factory, built in 1962. In January 2014, John's daughter Taiita and her husband, James Champniss, assumed ownership.

★★★★★ **Adelaide Hills Syrah 2015** Once it was called shiraz, now syrah. It's just so cool. Still, this is a very good wine – fabulous colour, awash with dark plums, blueberries, bay leaves and curry leaves. The palate is long, with silky tannins; fuller-bodied and showing a lot of restraint. Screwcap. 14% alc. **Rating** 94 **To** 2025 $55 JF

 Adelaide Hills Pinot Noir 2015 Rating 93 **To** 2024 $45 JF
Adelaide Hills Saperavi 2015 Rating 93 **To** 2025 $45 JF
Adelaide Hills Sauvignon Blanc 2016 Rating 91 **To** 2020 $28 JF
Adelaide Hills Arneis 2016 Rating 90 **To** 2019 $28 JF

Ten Minutes by Tractor ★★★★★

1333 Mornington-Flinders Road, Main Ridge, Vic 3928 **Region** Mornington Peninsula
T (03) 5989 6455 **www**.tenminutesbytractor.com.au **Open** 7 days 11–5
Winemaker Richard McIntyre, Martin Spedding, Jeremy Magyar **Est.** 1999
Dozens 12 000 **Vyds** 34.4ha
The energy, drive and vision of Martin Spedding have transformed Ten Minutes by Tractor since he acquired the business in early 2004. In mid-'06 Ten Minutes By Tractor purchased the McCutcheon vineyard; it also has long-term leases on the other two original home vineyards (Judd and Wallis), thus having complete control over grape production. Three new vineyards have been added in recent years: the one at the cellar door and restaurant site is organically certified and is used to trial organic viticultural practices that are progressively being employed across all the vineyards; the others are in the north of the peninsula. There are now three ranges: Single Vineyard, from the home Judd, McCutcheon and Wallis vineyards; Estate, the best blend of pinot and of chardonnay from the home vineyards; and finally 10X, from the other estate-owned Mornington Peninsula vineyards. The restaurant has one of the best wine lists to be found at any winery. Exports to the UK, Canada, Sweden and Switzerland.

★★★★★ **Judd Vineyard Chardonnay 2015** Judd is on the southerly side of Main Ridge, facing due west. The end result is pliant warmth, more loosely knit and bumptious than the tensile Wallis and, dare I say, reminiscent of top-grade Meursault with its arsenal of truffle, roasted hazelnut and curdy, peachy warmth. The oak has simply sunk into the wine's warm gaze. The acid drive is there, hidden behind the puppy fat. Delicious now, but will certainly go the distance. Screwcap. 13.8% alc. **Rating** 97 **To** 2026 $68 NG ✪

Wallis Mornington Peninsula Chardonnay 2015 From the oldest and lowest block among those on Main Ridge, Wallis is on the southern side, facing north to northeast. This is a flinty, pointed, saline chardonnay. Elbows and oyster-shelled knees right now, with cylinders of mineral and fine-grained oak firing far and wide across the mouth. This is more about incisive energy and compelling texture than any fruit descriptors, and rightly so. For those in need, the fruit will come in time. Screwcap. 13.8% alc. **Rating** 97 **To** 2028 $68 NG ○

McCutcheon Mornington Peninsula Pinot Noir 2015 This bridles the inherent structure of the MV6 with the cool aromatic finesse of the highest site among the estate's Main Ridge holdings. The fruit is lifted and floral, pinned to a tapestry of savoury forest floor notes, and a gauze of cobweb tannins and succulent acidity. Screwcap. 13.8% alc. **Rating** 97 **To** 2027 $78 NG ○

♟♟♟♟♟ **Judd Mornington Peninsula Pinot Noir 2015** All 115 clone, this ethereal wine boasts strawberry scents, the slightest prickle of briar. The wine spent 19 days on skins before 17 months in new and used oak. One wouldn't know, so integrated and gossamer are the tannins. Screwcap. 13.6% alc. **Rating** 96 **To** 2025 $78 NG

Estate Mornington Peninsula Chardonnay 2015 A chardonnay plying the tricks of the contemporary, cool climate Australian trade, with virtuosic effect: an artful picking window, followed by whole bunch pressing to an indigenous fermentation across an assortment of new and used French oak, all prior to 10 months of elevage. The result is an intensity of stone fruit flavours interwound with mineral-bound truffle, nougat and high quality oak. Screwcap. 13.8% alc. **Rating** 95 **To** 2022 $44 NG

McCutcheon Mornington Peninsula Chardonnay 2015 This house's triumvirate of single-site chardonnay expressions is fascinating; each has a different story to tell despite almost identical winemaking. In this case there is a hazelnut veneer, and a more incisive thrust and parry of minerality and acidity as its chassis, the oak clinging on for effect. Not as mellifluous as the other cuvees, but time may beg to differ. Screwcap. 13.8% alc. **Rating** 95 **To** 2026 $68 NG

Wallis Mornington Peninsula Pinot Noir 2015 Its MV6 genetic lineage is manifest as satsuma plum, bing cherry and a hint of undergrowth and truffle. The fruit flavours are forceful, yet this is a sexier expression than the Coolart Road, also MV6, sashaying across the mouth while bouncing off the gums, with filmy tannins, crunchy acidity, and a hinge of oak its trampoline. Screwcap. 13.8% alc. **Rating** 95 **To** 2023 $78 NG

10X Mornington Peninsula Chardonnay 2015 **Rating** 94 **To** 2022 $30 NG ○

Coolart Road Pinot Noir 2015 **Rating** 94 **To** 2025 $78 NG

♟♟♟♟♟ **10X Mornington Peninsula Pinot Noir 2015** **Rating** 93 **To** 2020 $34 NG
Estate Mornington Peninsula Pinot Noir 2015 **Rating** 93 **To** 2023 $48 NG
10X Sauvignon Blanc 2015 **Rating** 91 **To** 2019 $28 NG
10X Pinot Gris 2015 **Rating** 91 **To** 2020 $28 NG
10X Rose 2016 **Rating** 90 **To** 2022 $28 NG
Blanc de Blancs 2011 **Rating** 90 **To** 2021 $68 TS

Tenafeate Creek Wines ★★★★

1071 Gawler-One Tree Hill Road, One Tree Hill, SA 5114 **Region** Adelaide
T (08) 8280 7715 **www.tcw.com.au Open** Fri–Sun & public hols 11–5
Winemaker Larry and Michael Costa **Est.** 2002 **Dozens** 3000 **Vyds** 1ha
Larry Costa, a former hairdresser, embarked on winemaking as a hobby in 2002. The property, with its 1ha of shiraz, cabernet sauvignon and merlot, is situated on the rolling countryside of One Tree Hill in the Mount Lofty Ranges. The business grew rapidly, with grenache, nebbiolo, sangiovese, petit verdot, chardonnay, semillon and sauvignon blanc purchased to supplement the estate-grown grapes. Michael Costa, Larry's son, has now joined his father as co-owner of the business, and has 16 vintages under his belt, mainly in the Barossa Valley, with Flying

Winemaker stints in southern Italy and Provence. The red wines have won many medals over the years.

ƳƳƳƳ Adelaide Hills Sauvignon Blanc 2016 Standard cool fermentation in stainless steel. No colour pick-up, still white; a fresh, breezy, crisp wine with citrus nuances lifted by lively acidity. Best now. Screwcap. 11.5% alc. **Rating** 89 **To** 2017 $20

Terra Felix   ★★★★

52 Paringa Road, Red Hill South, Vic 3937 (postal) **Region** Central Victoria
T 0419 539 108 **www**.terrafelix.com.au **Open** Not
Winemaker Ben Haines **Est.** 2001 **Dozens** 12 000 **Vyds** 7ha
Long-term industry stalwarts Peter Simon and John Nicholson, with an involvement going back well over 30 years, have built on the estate plantings of pinot noir (5ha) and chardonnay (2ha) through purchases from Coonawarra, McLaren Vale, Barossa Valley, Langhorne Creek, Yarra Valley and Strathbogie Ranges. Terra Felix exports 70% of its production to China.

ƳƳƳƳƳ Langhorne Creek Shiraz 2015 Matured for 12 months in French and American oak, it has excellent mouthfeel, flavours of red and black fruits, and a wonderfully fresh finish, reflecting its modest alcohol. A medium-bodied wine that is a pleasure to taste. Diam. 13.5% alc. **Rating** 94 **To** 2030 $27 ✪

ƳƳƳƳƳ Harcourt Valley Bendigo Pinot Gris 2016 Rating 90 **To** 2017 $22

Terre à Terre   ★★★★★

PO Box 3128, Unley, SA 5061 **Region** Wrattonbully/Adelaide Hills
T 0400 700 447 **www**.terreaterre.com.au **Open** At Tapanappa
Winemaker Xavier Bizot **Est.** 2008 **Dozens** 5000 **Vyds** 16ha
It would be hard to imagine two better-credentialled owners than Xavier Bizot (son of the late Christian Bizot of Bollinger fame) and wife Lucy Croser (daughter of Brian and Ann Croser). 'Terre à terre' is a French expression meaning down to earth. The close-planted vineyard is on a limestone ridge, adjacent to Tapanappa's Whalebone Vineyard. The vineyard area has increased (3ha each of cabernet sauvignon and sauvignon blanc and 1ha each of cabernet franc and shiraz), leading to increased production. In 2015, Terre à Terre secured the fruit from one of the oldest vineyards in the Adelaide Hills, the Summertown Vineyard, which will see greater quantities of Daosa, and a Piccadilly Valley pinot noir. Wines are released under the Terre à Terre, Down to Earth, Sacrebleu and Daosa labels. Exports to the UK, Singapore, Taiwan and Hong Kong.

ƳƳƳƳƳ Piccadilly Valley Pinot Noir Chardonnay Rose 2016 A copper-toned rose that glimpses the herbal quench of top-drawer Provençale gear, while showcasing its Australian pedigree with a quilt of ever so subtle red fruit flavours easing across the palate. A very sophisticated rose and a benchmark for the style. Screwcap. 13.5% alc. **Rating** 95 **To** 2018 $32 NG ✪
Crayeres Vineyard Reserve Wrattonbully Cabernet Sauvignon Cabernet Franc 2014 Currants red and black, dried sage, bouquet garni, licorice and the lift of mint are all there, before a thrust of finely wrought tannins and punchy acidity take over. A parry of fruit reverberates on the compact finish, still gristle and extract. Needs time. Plenty. Cork. 14.1% alc. **Rating** 95 **To** 2035 $60 NG
Down to Earth Wrattonbully Sauvignon Blanc 2016 This is reminiscent of solid, quaffing sauvignon from the Graves, with a textural dimension seldom seen in Australia. Quince, apricot, a resinous slate component and a gloss of lemon oil are carried by a confluence of acidity and phenolic pick-up. Very good. Screwcap. 13.5% alc. **Rating** 94 **To** 2019 $26 NG✪

ƳƳƳƳƳ Summertown Reserve Pinot Noir 2016 Rating 93 **To** 2025 $60 NG
Daosa Blanc de Blancs 2011 Rating 92 **To** 2026 $55 TS

Tertini Wines

Kells Creek Road, Mittagong, NSW 2575 **Region** Southern Highlands
T (02) 4878 5213 **www.tertiniwines.com.au Open** 7 days 10–5
Winemaker Jonathan Holgate **Est.** 2000 **Dozens** 3000 **Vyds** 7.9ha
When Julian Tertini began the development of Tertini Wines in 2000, he followed in the
footsteps of Joseph Vogt 145 years earlier. History does not relate the degree of success that
Joseph had, but the site he chose then was, as it is now, a good one. Tertini has pinot noir and
riesling (1.8ha each), cabernet sauvignon and chardonnay (1ha each), arneis (0.9ha), pinot gris
(0.8ha), merlot (0.4ha) and lagrein (0.2ha). Winemaker Jonathan Holgate, who is responsible
for the outstanding results achieved at Tertini, presides over High Range Vintners, a contract
winemaking business also owned by Julian Tertini. Exports to Asia.

Private Cellar Collection Southern Highlands Chardonnay 2015 It
has been skilfully made, white peach fruit, acidity and subtle oak all playing
a coordinated role. While in one sense exactly as one might expect, it has a
different metier from almost all other Aus cool climate chardonnays. Gold
medal International Cool Climate Show '16. Screwcap. 12.6% alc. **Rating** 95
To 2023 $48
Private Cellar Collection Southern Highlands Riesling 2015 It is elegant
and delicate, bringing lime, lemon and green apple woven through with minerally
acidity. Developing at a leisurely pace, with years to go. Screwcap. 11.1% alc.
Rating 94 **To** 2025 $50
Hilltops Cabernet Sauvignon 2015 Good colour; an attractive medium-
bodied cabernet with juicy cassis fruit to spare, and balanced tannins that are
fully resolved; the touch of new French oak seals the deal. Screwcap. 13.4% alc.
Rating 94 **To** 2030 $28 **❂**

Hilltops Nebbiolo 2015 Rating 93 **To** 2023 $28
Southern Highlands Riesling 2015 Rating 92 **To** 2025 $30

Teusner

95 Samuel Road, Nuriootpa, SA 5355 **Region** Barossa Valley
T (08) 8562 4147 **www.teusner.com.au Open** By appt
Winemaker Kym Teusner, Matt Reynolds **Est.** 2001 **Dozens** 25 000
Teusner is a partnership between former Torbreck winemaker Kym Teusner and brother-in-
law Michael Page, and is typical of the new wave of winemakers determined to protect very
old, low-yielding, dry-grown Barossa vines. The winery approach is based on lees ageing, little
racking, no fining or filtration, and no new American oak. As each year passes, the consistency,
quality (and range) of the wines increases; there must be an end point, but it's not easy to guess
when, or even if, it will be reached. Exports to the UK, the US, Canada, The Netherlands,
Malaysia, Singapore, Japan, Hong Kong and China.

Albert 2014 70+yo vines, destemmed, open-fermented with cultured yeast,
6 days on skins, matured in French hogsheads (3% new) for 18 months. The highly
charged bouquet set my antennae waving furiously, and the palate instantaneously
cried wondrous quality. Black and blue fruits intersect with spices of all kinds,
augmented by quality French oak. The wine has exceptional intensity to the
bouquet and palate alike, but does so with a fresh, light touch. To know it is to
love it at first sight. Screwcap. 14.5% alc. **Rating** 98 **To** 2044 $65 **❂**
Avatar 2014 50% grenache, 26% shiraz, 24% mataro, the grenache and mataro
vines almost 100yo, matured in used puncheons and hogsheads for 16 months.
Retains both crimson hue and depth; the shiraz, despite being only a quarter
of the blend, has a significant impact, both in terms of dark/black fruit flavour
and firmer structure, but at the end of the day, it's the heady perfume and juicy
red fruits of the grenache and mataro that make this glorious wine what it is.
Screwcap. 14.5% alc. **Rating** 98 **To** 2039 $40 **❂**
Joshua 2016 60% grenache, 30% mataro, 10% shiraz, the grenache and mataro
warm-fermented, the shiraz fermented cooler. Brilliant clear purple-crimson,

exceptional for these varieties – only Teusner can achieve this depth and purity of the red and blue fruits of this blend in the Barossa Valley. It has first class texture and structure, and is so glorious now it's hard to resist wolfing it down, even though it has a great future. All this from only 6 days on skins. Screwcap. 14.5% alc. Rating 97 To 2031 $35 ✪

ΨΨΨΨΨ The Dog Strangler 2015 Very good colour; vibrant and fresh, far distant from the mataros of bygone decades, the limited skin contact and controlled alcohol two of the keys. A fragrant bouquet with a mix of spicy and savoury scents leads into a medium-bodied palate with strikingly juicy mouthfeel and a fresh aftertaste. Screwcap. 14.5% alc. Rating 96 To 2030 $35 ✪

Empress Eden Valley Riesling 2016 The naked lady on the front label with a snake's head disconcertingly placed in front of her left nipple doubtless portrays the 'strongly sensual, desirable' summary of the back label, which in turn accurately describes this lovely lime-accented wine from a tip-top vintage – Eden Valley to the core. Screwcap. 11.5% alc. Rating 95 To 2026 $24 ✪

Salsa Barossa Valley Rose 2016 Deep, bright crimson-salmon hue; the bouquet is highly aromatic, with a phalanx of red fruits, the palate even more expressive, with cherries, plums and raspberries carried along at high speed by acidity. Super rose. Screwcap. 13% alc. Rating 95 To 2020 $23 ✪

The Wark Family Shiraz 2015 You get your money's worth with this wine. It has a distinctive cool feel to it, spice and pepper whispering in the background of the medium-bodied palate, superfine tannins drawing out the length of the finish and aftertaste. Elegant and moreish, red and black fruits playing tag with each other. Screwcap. 14.5% alc. Rating 95 To 2030 $24 ✪

The Bilmore Barossa Valley Shiraz 2015 Rating 94 To 2028 $24 ✪
The Riebke Barossa Valley Shiraz 2015 Rating 94 To 2035 $24 ✪
The Independent Shiraz Mataro 2015 Rating 94 To 2029 $27 ✪
MC Barossa Valley Sparkling Shiraz 2010 Rating 94 To 2024 $65 TS

ΨΨΨΨΫ The Gentleman Barossa Cabernet Sauvignon 2015 Rating 91 To 2028 $24

The Grapes of Ross   ★★★☆

PO Box 14, Lyndoch, SA 5351 **Region** Barossa Valley
T (08) 8524 4214 **www**.grapesofross.com.au **Open** Not
Winemaker Ross Virgara **Est.** 2006 **Dozens** 1500 **Vyds** 27.1ha
Ross Virgara spent much of his life in the broader food and wine industry, taking the plunge into commercial winemaking in 2006. The grapes come from a fourth-generation family property in the Lyndoch Valley, and the aim is to make fruit-driven styles of quality wine. The estate plantings include chardonnay, shiraz, cabernet sauvignon and old vine semillon. His fondness for frontignac led to the first release of Moscato, followed in due course by Rose, Shiraz, Sparkling Shiraz, Grenache Shiraz and The Charmer Sangiovese Merlot Cabernet Sauvignon. Exports to China.

ΨΨΨΨΨ Black Sapphire Shiraz 2014 Matured for 24 months in two-thirds French and one-third American oak (33% new). Brimful of dark/black fruits on the supple, medium-bodied palate. There is no impact from the alcohol, and the oak is well integrated, the tannins ripe and balanced. Cork. 14.5% alc. Rating 94 To 2034 $45

ΨΨΨΨ Old Bush Vine Barossa Valley Grenache 2015 Rating 89 To 2023 $25

The Hairy Arm   ★★★★

18 Plant Street, Northcote, Vic 3070 (postal) **Region** Sunbury/Heathcote
T 0409 110 462 **www**.hairyarm.com **Open** Not
Winemaker Steven Worley **Est.** 2004 **Dozens** 800 **Vyds** 2.1ha
Steven Worley graduated as an exploration geologist, then added a Master of Geology degree, followed by a postgraduate Diploma in Oenology and Viticulture. Until December 2009 he was general manager of Galli Estate Winery, The Hairy Arm having started as a university

project in '04. It has grown from a labour of love to a commercial undertaking; he has an informal lease of 1.5ha of shiraz at Galli's Sunbury vineyard, which he manages, and procures 0.5ha of nebbiolo from the Galli vineyard in Heathcote. The hairy arm, incidentally, is Steven's. Exports to Canada.

🍷🍷🍷🍷 **Sunbury Shiraz 2015** A very savoury black-fruited palate with clinging tannins full of character, but needing time to open up and relax the grip of the Hairy Arm. Screwcap. 14.5% alc. **Rating** 93 **To** 2030 $35

The Islander Estate Vineyards ★★★★★

PO Box 868, Kingscote, SA 5223 **Region** Kangaroo Island
T (08) 8553 9008 **www**.iev.com.au **Open** Wed–Sun 12–5 Dec–Feb or by appt
Winemaker Jacques Lurton **Est.** 2000 **Dozens** 7000 **Vyds** 10ha
Established by one of the most famous Flying Winemakers in the world, Bordeaux-born and trained and part-time Australian resident Jacques Lurton. He has established a close-planted vineyard; the principal varieties are cabernet franc, shiraz and sangiovese, with lesser amounts of grenache, malbec, semillon and viognier. The wines are made and bottled at the onsite winery in true estate style. After several vintages experimenting with a blend of sangiovese and cabernet franc, Jacques has settled on cabernet franc as the varietal base of the signature wine, The Investigator. Exports to the UK, the US, Canada, France, Germany, Malta, Hong Kong, Taiwan and China.

🍷🍷🍷🍷🍷 **Bark Hut Road 2014** Has retained exceptional colour. The Islander has superb cabernet franc, unlike most of the eastern states, and it combines synergistically with shiraz. Purple, blue and black fruits are embraced by sultry tannins that provide both texture and structure for a high quality wine. Screwcap. 14% alc. **Rating** 96 **To** 2034 $25
The Wally White Semillon 2015 No one else in Australia makes semillon like this, neither the vinification (large French oak for extended maturation) nor the flavour, the body or the overall mouthfeel and length. It has the lemony accent of semillon, but might be missed in a blind tasting as an alternative white blend. Don't get me wrong, this is a delicious all-purpose wine of considerable length. Screwcap. 13.5% alc. **Rating** 95 **To** 2025 $35
Majestic Plough Malbec 2014 This breathes youthful character from every one of its pores, exulting in the cool maritime climate akin to Bordeaux, where it was so important prior to the arrival of phylloxera. It is deliciously, piquantly savoury, with a long, even finish. Screwcap. 14% alc. **Rating** 95 **To** 2029 $35
The Rose 2016 Almost colourless; a faint salmon yellow hue is most unusual. An exotic band of spices and savoury notes power the bouquet; the palate has excellent texture and balance, the flavours building on the bouquet. Possible amphora fermentation, with or without whole bunches in the ferment. Whatever, it works, but might well frighten the horses. Screwcap. 12.5% alc. **Rating** 94 **To** 2020 $20

🍷🍷🍷🍷 **The Wally White Semillon 2014** Rating 91 **To** 2020 $35
The Red 2015 Rating 91 **To** 2025 $20
SoFar SoGood Chardonnay 2016 Rating 90 **To** 2018 $25 SC
SoFar SoGood Shiraz 2016 Rating 90 **To** 2019 $25 SC

The Lake House Denmark ★★★★★

106 Turner Road, Denmark, WA 6333 **Region** Denmark
T (08) 9848 2444 **www**.lakehousedenmark.com.au **Open** 7 days 10–5
Winemaker Harewood Estate (James Kellie) **Est.** 1995 **Dozens** 8000 **Vyds** 5.2ha
Garry Capelli and Leanne Rogers purchased the property in 2005 and have restructured the vineyard to grow varieties suited to the climate – chardonnay, pinot noir, semillon and sauvignon blanc – incorporating biodynamic principles. They also manage a couple of small family-owned vineyards in Frankland River and Mount Barker, with a similar ethos. Wines are released in three tiers: the flagship Premium Reserve range, the Premium Block range, and

the quirky He Said, She Said easy-drinking wines. The combined cellar door, restaurant and gourmet food emporium is a popular destination.

🍷🍷🍷🍷🍷 **Premium Reserve Great Southern Chardonnay 2015** Ripe nectarine and white peach aromas intermingle with a touch of vanilla from well handled and high quality French oak. This richer style chardonnay, with its creamy mid-palate fruit, remains balanced and I would suggest drinking this now and over the next 2–3 years. Screwcap. 13% alc. **Rating** 91 **To** 2019 $40 PR

The Lane Vineyard ★★★★★

Ravenswood Lane, Hahndorf, SA 5245 **Region** Adelaide Hills
T (08) 8388 1250 **www**.thelane.com.au **Open** 7 days 10–4.30
Winemaker Michael Schreurs, Martyn Edwards **Est.** 1993 **Dozens** 25 000 **Vyds** 75ha
After 15 years at The Lane Vineyard, Helen and John Edwards, and sons Marty and Ben, took an important step towards realising their long-held dream – to grow, make and sell estate-based wines that have a true sense of place. In 2005, at the end of the (now discontinued) Starvedog Lane joint venture with Hardys, they commissioned a state-of-the-art 500-tonne winery, bistro and cellar door overlooking their vineyards on picturesque Ravenswood Lane. Having previously invested in Delatite, and much earlier established Coombe Farm in the Yarra Valley, the Vestey Group (UK), headed by Lord Samuel Vestey and the Right Honourable Mark Vestey, have acquired a significant shareholding in The Lane Vineyard. The remaining shares are owned by Martyn Edwards and Ben Tolstoshev. Exports to the UK, the US, Canada, The Netherlands, Belgium, the UAE, Hong Kong and China.

🍷🍷🍷🍷🍷 **Beginning Adelaide Hills Chardonnay 2015** This is classy and so subtle, yet unfurls with complex leesy characters, creamed honey, grilled nuts, ginger fluff cake and other moreish complex sulphides. The palate is long, pure and ultra-refined. Screwcap. 13% alc. **Rating** 95 **To** 2023 $39 JF
Block 14 Single Vineyard Basket Press Adelaide Hills Shiraz 2015 Good depth to the colour; black fruits lead the way, cherry and berry in equal parts. Controlled alcohol pays dividends on the long, medium to full-bodied palate. Tannins and oak have been skilfully handled, subtly adding to the complexity. Screwcap. 13.5% alc. **Rating** 95 **To** 2035 $39
Reunion Single Vineyard Adelaide Hills Shiraz 2014 An exercise in elegance from start to finish. There is an airy lightness to the way the wine reaches into every corner of the mouth in the same fashion as the fragrance of the bouquet. Screwcap. 13.5% alc. **Rating** 95 **To** 2030 $65
Gathering Adelaide Hills Sauvignon Blanc Semillon 2015 It's smoky, beguiling, moreish and savoury, with fresh herbs, basil, lemongrass and kaffir lime leaves. There's texture, with chalky acidity adding another layer of complexity to the palate. Screwcap. 13% alc. **Rating** 94 **To** 2021 $35 JF
Block 1 Adelaide Hills Cabernet Merlot 2015 A convincing blend, starting with good colour, then an expressive cassis-laden bouquet, the supple medium-bodied palate all about fruit, less so tannins. One of those each-way wines ready soon or in a decade+. Screwcap. 13.5% alc. **Rating** 94 **To** 2029 $39

🍷🍷🍷🍷🍷 **Single Vineyard Adelaide Hills Pinot Noir 2016 Rating** 93 **To** 2025 $39 JF
Block 5 Adelaide Hills Shiraz 2015 Rating 93 **To** 2025 $25 ❂
Block 10 Sauvignon Blanc 2016 Rating 92 **To** 2019 $25 JF ❂
Cuvée Helen Blanc de Blancs 2009 Rating 92 **To** 2017 $55 TS
Lois Brut Rose NV Rating 91 **To** 2017 $25 TS
Block 1A Chardonnay 2016 Rating 90 **To** 2020 $20 JF ❂
Block 3 Chardonnay 2016 Rating 90 **To** 2019 $25 JF
Lois Adelaide Hills Blanc de Blancs NV Rating 90 **To** 2017 $23 TS

The Old Faithful Estate

281 Tatachilla Road, McLaren Vale, SA 5171 **Region** McLaren Vale
T 0419 383 907 **www.**nhwines.com.au **Open** By appt
Winemaker Nick Haselgrove, Warren Randall **Est.** 2005 **Dozens** 2000 **Vyds** 5ha
This is a joint venture of American John Larchet, Nick Haselgrove (see separate entry) and Warren Randall. John has long had a leading role as a specialist importer of Australian wines into the US, and guarantees the business whatever sales it needs there. Its shiraz, grenache and mourvedre come from old, single site blocks in McLaren Vale. Exports to the US, Canada, Switzerland, Russia, Hong Kong and China.

ϓϓϓϓϓ **Northern Exposure McLaren Vale Grenache 2013** 95% 80+yo grenache, 5% 103yo shiraz, matured in used French oak for 40 months. Retains exceptional hue and depth given it is grenache, not shiraz. Very classy wine reminiscent of the greatest examples of the Rhône Valley. Its red and black cherry and raspberry fruit is perfectly balanced by fine tannins, and won't reach a plateau of perfection until '23. Diam. 14.5% alc. **Rating** 97 **To** 2033 $60 **◑**

ϓϓϓϓϓ **Cafe Block McLaren Vale Shiraz 2013** Vines planted in '52, matured for 6 months in new French oak, followed by 34 months in demi-muids. A powerful, uncompromising full-bodied shiraz, but retains freshness and balance, the fruit outpacing the oak and the tannins. A long and healthy future is assured. Diam. 14.5% alc. **Rating** 95 **To** 2038 $60

The Other Wine Co

136 Jones Road, Balhannah, SA 5242 **Region** South Australia
T (08) 8398 0500 **www.**theotherwineco.com **Open** At Shaw + Smith
Winemaker Martin Shaw, Adam Wadewitz **Est.** 2015 **Dozens** 1000
This is the venture of Michael Hill Smith and Martin Shaw, established in the shadow of Shaw + Smith, but with an entirely different focus and separate marketing. The name reflects the two wines, a McLaren Vale Grenache and an Adelaide Hills Pinot Gris, both intended for casual consumption, the whole focus being freshness combined with seductive mouthfeel. The concept of matching variety and place is one without any particular limits, and there may well be other wines made by The Other Wine Co in years to come. Exports to the UK, Canada and Germany.

ϓϓϓϓϓ **McLaren Vale Grenache 2016** Light, clear crimson; a vibrant wine that may or may not have been in oak. Regardless, its red cherry and raspberry fruits and crisp acidity all argue the case for immediate, joyful consumption. Screwcap. 13% alc. **Rating** 94 **To** 2019 $26 **◑**

ϓϓϓϓϓ **Adelaide Hills Pinot Gris 2016 Rating** 90 **To** 2018 $26

The Pawn Wine Co.

10 Banksia Road, Macclesfield, SA 5153 **Region** Adelaide Hills
T 0438 373 247 **www.**thepawn.com.au **Open** Not
Winemaker Tom Keelan **Est.** 2002 **Dozens** 5000 **Vyds** 54.92ha
This is a partnership between Tom and Rebecca Keelan and David and Vanessa Blows. Tom was for some time manager of Longview Vineyards at Macclesfield in the Adelaide Hills, and consulted to the neighbouring vineyard, owned by David and Vanessa. In 2004 Tom and David decided to make some small batches of Petit Verdot and Tempranillo at the Bremerton winery, where Tom is now vineyard manager. The wines are sourced from grapes grown on their Macclesfield vineyards; the remainder of the grapes supply brands such as Shaw + Smith, Penfolds, Orlando and Scott Winemaking.

ϓϓϓϓϓ **Jeu de Fin Adelaide Hills Shiraz 2015** This is (only) medium-bodied, but has the intensity and attack of a full-bodied shiraz; it sparkles with energy as it goes on the attack with pawns, knights and bishops summoning cracked black pepper, spice, licorice and an array of red and purple fruits plus tannins and French oak. Screwcap. 14.5% alc. **Rating** 95 **To** 2030 $32 **◑**

Jeu de Fin Clonal #76 Adelaide Hills Chardonnay 2016 Dijon clone 76, hand-picked, wild fermented in barrel, matured on lees for 12 months. The flavours range through stone fruit to citrus and green apple, but no one flavour comes back to contest the end game. Screwcap. 13.5% alc. **Rating** 94 **To** 2024 $32

The Austrian Attack Adelaide Hills Gruner Veltliner 2016 Has admirable power, drive and grip; the bouquet ranges through green apple, pear and white pepper, the palate ratcheting up the power and intensity of the attack. Gruner veltliner shares with riesling the capacity to expand in all directions with age. Screwcap. 12.5% alc. **Rating** 94 **To** 2026 $24 ✪

 🍷🍷🍷🍷 **Jeu de Fin Clonal #76 Chardonnay 2015 Rating** 93 **To** 2022 $36 SC
En Passant Tempranillo 2015 Rating 93 **To** 2022 $24 ✪
The Gambit Sangiovese 2015 Rating 91 **To** 2022 $24 SC
El Desperado Pinot Grigio 2016 Rating 90 **To** 2018 $19 SC ✪
El Desperado Pinot Noir 2016 Rating 90 **To** 2021 $19 SC ✪

The Story Wines   ★★★★★

170 Riverend Road, Hangholme, Vic 3175 **Region** Grampians
T 0411 697 912 **www**.thestory.com.au **Open** Not
Winemaker Rory Lane **Est.** 2004 **Dozens** 2500
Over the years I have come across winemakers with degrees in atomic science, doctors with specialties spanning every human condition, town planners, sculptors and painters, and Rory Lane adds yet another to the list: a degree in ancient Greek literature. He says that after completing his degree, and 'desperately wanting to delay an entry into the real world, I stumbled across and enrolled in a postgraduate wine technology and marketing course at Monash University, where I soon became hooked on ... the wondrous connection between land, human and liquid'. Vintages in Australia and Oregon germinated the seed, and he zeroed in on the Grampians, where he purchases small parcels of high quality grapes. He makes the wines in a small factory where he has assembled a basket press, a few open fermenters, a mono pump and some decent French oak. Exports to the UK.

🍷🍷🍷🍷 **R. Lane Vintners Westgate Vineyard Grampians Syrah 2015** From the '60 plantings of the Westgate Vineyard, the R. Lane label reserved for exceptional wines in exceptional vintages. A very complex and compelling syrah, with all the many components welded together so that no person should seek to set them asunder. It is savoury and brambly, drenched in wild blackberry and black cherry flavours, licorice a fellow traveller, as are tannins. Diam. 14% alc. **Rating** 96 **To** 2040 $75 ✪

R. Lane Vintners Westgate Vineyard Grampians Syrah 2014 Uses the multiplicity of fermentation techniques loved by Rory Lane. Unsurprisingly, a complex wine, with generous supple black fruits driving the medium to full-bodied palate from the outset, and taking attention away from the vinification. Will be very long-lived. Diam. 14% alc. **Rating** 96 **To** 2044 $75 ✪

Grampians Shiraz 2014 From three vineyards, with a variety of ferments for each, in all 46% whole bunches, very little new French oak. Opinions vary about whole bunches in fermenting shiraz, but I am on the support side. The colour hasn't suffered, and the spicy, savoury spine has no shortage of lingering red and black fruits draped around that spine. All up, medium-bodied and lively. Screwcap. 13.5% alc. **Rating** 95 **To** 2029 $30 ✪

Port Campbell Pinot Noir 2016 The colour is bright, but spectacularly deep, and the pure-fruited wine needs several years to escape from its reductive bonds, when it might soar like an eagle. Screwcap. 13% alc. **Rating** 94 **To** 2031 $29 ✪

Grampians Shiraz 2015 The savoury notes that underpin the palate are detectable on the bouquet, but aren't dominant, with spicy dark fruits also on parade. The medium-bodied palate shows the impact of the high percentage of whole bunches, but leaves room for the black fruits to express themselves. It's an open question which will prevail. Screwcap. 14% alc. **Rating** 94 **To** 2030 $29 ✪

🍷🍷🍷🍷 **Westgate Vineyard Marsanne Roussanne Viognier 2015 Rating** 91 **To** 2018 $30

The Trades

13/30 Peel Road, O'Connor, WA 6163 (postal) **Region** Margaret River
T (08) 9331 2188 **www.terrawines.com.au Open** Not
Winemaker Bruce Dukes (Contract) **Est.** 2006 **Dozens** 770
Thierry Ruault and Rachel Taylor have run a wholesale wine business in Perth since 1993, representing a group of top end Australian and foreign producers. By definition, the wines they offered to their clientele were well above $20 per bottle, and they have decided to fill the gap with a contract-made Shiraz and Sauvignon Blanc from Margaret River.

Grasscutters Margaret River Sauvignon Blanc 2016 I love the back label description of 'succulent acidity', which is the tactile quality I describe as 'squeaky', referring to the way the tongue and the roof of the mouth interact with each other, 'slippery' another description. The tropical varietal fruit stands up for its rights too. Good stuff. Screwcap. 13% alc. **Rating** 92 **To** 2018 $18 **❂**
Butchers Margaret River Shiraz 2015 I don't know of any other Margaret River producer offering shiraz at this price and quality. Contract winemaker Bruce Dukes has given the fresh red fruits a generous pinch of oak, adding complexity and value for money. Screwcap. 14% alc. **Rating** 91 **To** 2025 $18 **❂**

The Vintner's Daughter

5 Crisps Lane, Murrumbateman, NSW 2582 **Region** Canberra District
T (02) 6227 5592 **www.thevintnersdaughter.com.au Open** W'ends 10–4
Winemaker Stephanie Helm **Est.** 2014 **Dozens** 1000 **Vyds** 3ha
The Vintner's Daughter is Stephanie Helm, daughter of Ken Helm, who made her first wine when she was nine, and won her first trophy when she was 14. On finishing school she enrolled in an arts/law degree at the Australian National University, thereafter pursuing a career outside the wine industry until 2011, when she began the wine science degree at CSU. Along the way, while she was at ANU, she met a young bloke from Lightning Ridge at a pub, and introduced him to the world of wine. It wasn't too long before he was vineyard manager (with his background as a qualified horticulturist and landscaper) for Ken Helm. In late '14 all the wheels came full circle when a vineyard, originally planted in 1978 with traminer, crouchen and riesling, extended to 3ha in '99, came on the market. It was in an immaculate position between Clonakilla and Eden Road, and they purchased it in a flash and set about some urgently need rejuvenation. Stephanie (and Ben) waltzed into the trophy arena at the Canberra International Riesling Challenge '15, winning the trophy for Best Canberra District Riesling, and for good measure, winning the trophy for Best Riesling at the Winewise Small Vignerons Awards '15. Gewurztraminer is also part of the estate-based portfolio. And yes, they are life partners.

Canberra District Riesling 2016 Winemaker Stephanie Helm describes this as a challenging vintage, with Oct thunderstorms, a Dec dry spell, the wettest Jan for a decade and heatwaves at harvest. Despite all that, she has produced a very good riesling. Even with its moderate alcohol and crisp acidity, the wine has a generous feel, the bouquet and palate replete with classy cool climate varietal character. Screwcap. 11% alc. **Rating** 93 **To** 2028 $30 SC
Canberra District Gewurztraminer 2016 The spicy aromatics of the variety have been dialled down – merely a whisper of rose petal, musk and lychees – but the wine is still utterly convincing and delicious. A delicacy on the finely tuned palate, with lemon balm and cream, then softish acidity and a fresh finish. Screwcap. 11% alc. **Rating** 93 **To** 2022 $26 JF **❂**

The Wanderer

2850 Launching Place Road, Gembrook, Vic 3783 **Region** Yarra Valley
T 0415 529 639 **www.wandererwines.com Open** By appt
Winemaker Andrew Marks **Est.** 2005 **Dozens** 500
Andrew Marks is the son of Ian and June Marks, owners of Gembrook Hill, and after graduating from Adelaide University with a degree in oenology he joined Southcorp, working

for six years at Penfolds (Barossa Valley) and Seppelt (Great Western), as well as undertaking vintages in Coonawarra and France. He has since worked in the Hunter Valley, Great Southern, Sonoma County in the US and Costa Brava in Spain – hence the name of his business.

🍷🍷🍷🍷🍷 **Upper Yarra Valley Chardonnay 2015** Establishes its birthright and its quality from the first sip. High quality grapes have been barrel-fermented with skill in the choice of French oak, keeping its impact under tight control; the flavour plays the tension between white peach and grapefruit, typical of the Yarra Valley, Upper or Lower. Diam. 13.5% alc. **Rating** 95 **To** 2025 $35 ◐

Upper Yarra Valley Pinot Noir 2014 A light and bright hue; a prime example of why you should not judge a pinot by the depth of its colour: this has a beautifully shaped palate, intense and long, with red berry fruits couched within a skein of supple acidity, the finish and aftertaste reinforcing the message. Diam. 13% alc. **Rating** 95 **To** 2023 $55

Yarra Valley Shiraz 2015 A brightly coloured, thoroughly elegant yet intense wine, picked at precisely the right time. It is supple and medium-bodied, a perfect portrayal of cool-grown shiraz. Spices and pepper are threaded through red and black cherry fruit, French oak and superfine tannins bringing up the rear. Diam. 13.5% alc. **Rating** 95 **To** 2030 $38

Upper Yarra Valley Chardonnay 2016 An immaculately tailored wine, all the vinification (and viticultural) steps made to measure. The bouquet and palate both have a hint of funky/struck match character adding to the length of the palate before it backs off a trifle on the finish. Diam. 13.5% alc. **Rating** 94 **To** 2025 $38

Upper Yarra Valley Pinot Noir 2015 Light, clear crimson; this is all about the Upper Yarra's propensity to produce delicately scented, light-bodied pinots that can easily be overlooked if you don't stop to register the length of the palate and its aftertaste. It has been handled with kid gloves in the winery, and presented without any apology. Diam. 13.5% alc. **Rating** 94 **To** 2030 $55

🍷🍷🍷🍷🍷 **Yarra Valley Syrah 2015 Rating** 90 **To** 2023 $55

The Willows Vineyard ★★★★

310 Light Pass Road, Light Pass, Barossa Valley, SA 5355 **Region** Barossa Valley
T (08) 8562 1080 **www**.thewillowsvineyard.com.au **Open** Wed–Mon 10.30–4.30
Winemaker Peter and Michael Scholz **Est.** 1989 **Dozens** 6000 **Vyds** 42.74ha
The Scholz family have been grapegrowers for generations and have over 40ha of vineyards, selling part of the crop. Current-generation winemakers Peter and Michael Scholz make rich, ripe, velvety wines under their own label, some marketed with some bottle age. Exports to the UK, Canada, Switzerland, China and NZ.

🍷🍷🍷🍷🍷 **Bonesetter Barossa Shiraz 2014** This comes from the 'more is more' winemaking school of thought. No holds barred on the bouquet, with a display of luxurious oak, Christmas pudding, and minty, mentholated fruit. Rich and sweet in flavour, heavy in texture, and armed with imposing tannins, it's going to polarise opinion. You have to acknowledge its sheer intensity though, hence the score. Cork. 14.9% alc. **Rating** 94 **To** 2030 $60 SC

🍷🍷🍷🍷🍷 **Single Vineyard Semillon 2016 Rating** 91 **To** 2026 $17 SC ◐
Barossa Valley Shiraz 2014 Rating 90 **To** 2029 $28 SC

Thick as Thieves Wines ★★★★★

355 Healesville-Kooweerup Road, Badger Creek, Vic 3777 **Region** Yarra Valley
T 0417 184 690 **www**.tatwines.com.au **Open** By appt
Winemaker Syd Bradford **Est.** 2009 **Dozens** 1100 **Vyds** 1ha
Syd Bradford is living proof that small can be beautiful, and, equally, that an old dog can learn new tricks. A growing interest in good food and wine might have come to nothing had it not been for Pfeiffer Wines giving him a vintage job in 2003. In that year he enrolled in the wine science course at CSU; he moved to the Yarra Valley in '05. He gained experience at

Coldstream Hills (vintage cellar hand), Rochford (assistant winemaker), Domaine Chandon (cellar hand) and Giant Steps/Innocent Bystander (assistant winemaker). In '06 Syd achieved the Dean's Award of Academic Excellence at CSU and in '07 was the sole recipient of the A&G Engineering Scholarship. Aged 35, he was desperate to have a go at crafting his own 'babies', and in '09 came across a small parcel of arneis from the Hoddles Creek area, and Thick as Thieves was born. The techniques used to make his babies could only come from someone who has spent a long time observing and thinking about what he might do if he were calling the shots. Exports to Japan and Singapore.

🍷🍷🍷🍷🍷 **Driftwood Yarra King Valley Pinot Gamay 2016** The lipsmacking crunch of creamy strawberries, pomegranate and a spread of whole-bunch spice from ginger, sarsaparilla and cardamom, make for an absolutely delicious drink. Syd Bradford's use of whole clusters has become more deft over time, imparting a savoury edge to the flowing fruit rather than overwhelming it. A lick of amaro on the finish teases out more textural wealth. Mellifluous. Screwcap. 13.9% alc. **Rating** 95 To 2020 $30 NG ✪

The Aloof Alpaca Yarra Valley Arneis 2016 A gush of pear gelato rushes down the throat, pricked with a cool flow of acidity, hints of white fig and peach and an ever-so gentle, assuaging phenolic pucker. This is a delicious wine brimming with a dangerous drinkability factor. All here, right now. Screwcap. 13.5% alc. **Rating** 94 To 2019 $25 NG ✪

Levings Yarra Valley Pinot Noir 2016 A Jekyll and Hyde experience, this opens to fennel, pickle and a piquant pepper aroma from the 35% component of whole cluster, bridled to low alcohol and a jitter of ascetically sour red berry fruit. After an aggressive decant – read 5 years in the cellar – this begins a strut of strawberry, clove, autumnal forest floor and anise trailing across chiffon tannins and bright acidity to a long finish. Screwcap. 12.6% alc. **Rating** 94 To 2026 $60 NG

🍷🍷🍷🍷🍷 **Another Bloody Yarra Valley Chardonnay 2016** Rating 93 To 2023 $35 NG
La Vie Rustique Pinot Noir Rose 2016 Rating 93 To 2019 $25 NG ✪
Plump Yarra Valley Pinot Noir 2016 Rating 93 To 2020 $35 NG
The Love Letter Sylvaner Gewurztraminer 2016 Rating 91 To 2020 $25 NG
Purple Prose King Valley Gamay 2016 Rating 91 To 2021 $35 NG
The Gamekeeper King Valley Nebbiolo 2014 Rating 91 To 2021 $40 NG

Thistledown Wines   ★★★★

c/- Revenir, Peacock Road North, Lenswood, SA 5240 **Region** South Australia
T +44 7778 003 959 **www.**thistledownwines.com **Open** Not
Winemaker Peter Leske, Giles Cooke MW, Fergal Tynan MW **Est.** 2010 **Dozens** 3000
Giles Cooke MW and Fergal Tynan MW are based in Scotland, and have a collective 40+ years' experience in buying and selling Australian wines. They have been friends since 1998, when they met over a pint of beer on the evening before the first Master of Wine course they were about to embark on. In 2006 they established Alliance Wine Australia, which purchases Australian wines for distribution in the UK; they took the process one step further when Alliance began the Thistledown Wines venture. This focuses on Barossa Valley shiraz, McLaren Vale grenache, and smaller amounts of chardonnay from the Adelaide Hills. The wines are made under Peter Leske's direction at his Revenir small batch winery in the Adelaide Hills. Giles says he has particular affection for grenache, and is precisely right (in my view) when he says, 'McLaren Vale grenache is world class, and it best expresses itself when made in the mould of pinot noir.' Exports to the UK, the US, Canada, The Netherlands, South Korea, Singapore and NZ.

🍷🍷🍷🍷🍷 **Cunning Plan Langhorne Creek Shiraz 2016** The youthful colour has the depth to promise abundant black fruits. It has the succulence of Langhorne Creek, but with a raft of flowery/spicy notes not so common in the region. Mocha oak adds another dimension, cuddling up to the plump tannins. Hedonistic? You bet. Screwcap. 14% alc. **Rating** 94 To 2030 $25 ✪

Bachelor Block Ebenezer Shiraz 2015 A natural yeast fermentation that included 40% whole bunches then 20 months in 300l French barrels was the recipe for this very well put together Barossa shiraz. Red and black fruits, some olive tapenade and with the whole-bunch element nicely integrated, this concentrated, medium to full-bodied wine is light on its feet. Cork. 14.5% alc. **Rating** 94 **To** 2030 $70 PR

Vagabond Old Vine Blewitt Springs McLaren Vale Grenache 2016 This has more power, depth and drive than its Barossa Valley counterpart, which momentarily suggests higher alcohol. It's not, but it certainly needs more time, and will repay the patient in spades. Screwcap. 14.5% alc. **Rating** 94 **To** 2031 $50

Thorny Devil Barossa Valley Grenache 2016 Light, bright crimson; the inclusion of 9% grenache from McLaren Vale has worked very well, for there's a touch more structure and spine than many Barossa Valley grenaches at this price. The red fruits that are the heart and soul of this wine are delicious. Screwcap. 14.5% alc. **Rating** 94 **To** 2026 $30 ✪

Thomas Vineyard Estate   ★★★☆

PO Box 490, McLaren Vale, SA 5171 **Region** McLaren Vale
T 0419 825 086 **www**.thomasvineyard.com.au **Open** Not
Winemaker Mike Farmilo **Est.** 1998 **Dozens** 500 **Vyds** 5.26ha

Merv and Dawne Thomas thought long and hard before purchasing the property on which they have established their vineyard. It is 3km from the coast of the Gulf of St Vincent on the Fleurieu Peninsula, with a clay over limestone soil known locally as 'Bay of Biscay'. They had a dream start to the business when the 2004 Shiraz won the trophy for Best Single Vineyard Wine (red or white) at the McLaren Vale Wine Show '05, the Reserve Shiraz also winning a gold medal.

♟♟♟♟♟ **Merv's Signature Reserve McLaren Vale Shiraz 2015** This wine pulls even fewer punches than its sibling, with an emphasis on revved-up levels of extract and lavish oak. Yet despite the generous intent of blueberry, camphor and vanillan oak notes that loft genie-like over the glass, the tannins lash and dry the finish rather than invigorating it. The wine will yield, soften and become complex with time. **Rating** 90 **To** 2022 NG

Thomas Wines   ★★★★★

Cnr Hermitage Road/Mistletoe Lane, Pokolbin, NSW 2320 **Region** Hunter Valley
T (02) 4998 7134 **www**.thomaswines.com.au **Open** 7 days 10–5
Winemaker Andrew Thomas, Scott Comyns **Est.** 1997 **Dozens** 8000 **Vyds** 3ha

Andrew Thomas came to the Hunter Valley from McLaren Vale to join the winemaking team at Tyrrell's. After 13 years, he left to undertake contract work and to continue the development of his own label. He makes individual-vineyard wines, underlining the subtle differences between the various subregions of the Hunter. Plans for the construction of an estate winery have been abandoned for the time being, and for the foreseeable future he will continue to lease the James Estate winery on Hermitage Road. The major part of the production comes from long-term arrangements with growers of semillon (15ha) and shiraz (25ha); an additional 3ha of shiraz is leased. The quality of the wines and the reputation of Andrew Thomas have never been higher; the appointment of Scott Comyns as winemaker is also a significant step. Exports to the US and Japan.

♟♟♟♟♟ **Braemore Individual Vineyard Hunter Valley Semillon 2016** Andrew (Tommo) Thomas is acknowledged as one of the best practitioners of the fine art of coaxing young semillon to grab attention without compromising a 15+ year life, adding yet more to the flavour span. Here lime, lemon zest, grass and lemongrass all join hands, balance and length the outcome (or, if you prefer, the cause) of its extreme quality, acidity exactly where it should be. Screwcap. 13.8% alc. **Rating** 96 **To** 2031 $30 ✪

Cellar Reserve Braemore Individual Vineyard Hunter Valley Semillon 2011 Bright, gleaming straw-green; the magical transformation is now well and truly underway with a kaleidoscopic spray of lemon drop, zest and pith fruits propelled by tightly coiled acidity – and it's only halfway down the track to full maturity. Screwcap. 11.5% alc. **Rating** 96 **To** 2026 $55 ✪
Kiss Limited Release Hunter Valley Shiraz 2015 This brightly hued flagship shiraz is on the border of full-bodied status, tannins prominent from the outset, as are the mouthwatering black fruits of a wine that can stand shoulder to shoulder with some of the shirazs from the great '14 vintage. Will repay those who wait 10 years. Screwcap. 13.8% alc. **Rating** 96 **To** 2035 $75 ✪
Murphy's Individual Vineyard Hunter Valley Semillon 2016 A tightly focused, but utterly delicious palate is as long as it is fresh. Lemongrass, a sunburst of Meyer lemon and mineral fruits propel the wine at high speed through to the finish. Screwcap. 11.4% alc. **Rating** 95 **To** 2030 $26 ✪
Two of a Kind Semillon Sauvignon Blanc 2016 56% Hunter Valley semillon, 44% Adelaide Hills sauvignon blanc. A masterclass in the synergy of this blend, vibrant and fresh, lime, lemon, lemongrass and green pineapple all come and go, the nature and length of the acidity the key to the wine. Where will it be in '21? Great value, so you can afford to hold on to a bottle or two to find out. Screwcap. 11.5% alc. **Rating** 94 **To** 2021 $20 ✪
Elenay Barrel Selection Hunter Valley Shiraz 2015 Andrew Thomas wove more magic in this challenging vintage than the majority of his peers. This has excellent colour and clarity, plummy fruit, a swish of sweet oak, and gentle tannins all within a regional earthy cocoon. Screwcap. 13.8% alc. **Rating** 94 **To** 2030 $50
The Dam Block Individual Vineyard Hunter Valley Shiraz 2015 From a tiny 0.8ha vineyard across the dam from the Kiss vineyard site, and shares much of the structure of Kiss, with an edgy freshness and length. Plucked from the jaws of defeat (for some) of the vintage. Equal highest score in the '15 shiraz class at the Hunter Valley Wine Show '16. Screwcap. 13.5% alc. **Rating** 94 **To** 2035 $35

🍷🍷🍷🍷 **Broke-Fordwich Semillon 2016 Rating** 93 **To** 2021 $24 ✪
Two of a Kind Shiraz 2015 Rating 93 **To** 2035 $25 ✪
Synergy Vineyard Selection Shiraz 2015 Rating 92 **To** 2025 $25 ✪
Two of a Kind Shiraz 2014 Rating 92 **To** 2024 $25 ✪
Sweetwater Hunter Valley Shiraz 2015 Rating 91 **To** 2030 $35
Synergy Vineyard Selection Semillon 2016 Rating 90 **To** 2020 $20 ✪

Thompson Estate ★★★★★

299 Tom Cullity Drive, Wilyabrup, WA 6284 **Region** Margaret River
T (08) 9755 6406 **www**.thompsonestate.com **Open** 7 days 11–5
Winemaker Bob Cartwright, Paul Dixon **Est.** 1994 **Dozens** 10 000 **Vyds** 28.63ha
Cardiologist Peter Thompson planted the first vines at Thompson Estate in 1997, inspired by his and his family's shareholdings in the Pierro and Fire Gully vineyards, and by visits to many of the world's premium wine regions. The vineyard is planted to cabernet sauvignon, cabernet franc, merlot, chardonnay, sauvignon blanc, semillon, pinot noir and malbec. Thompson Estate wines are made by Bob Cartwright (former Leeuwin Estate winemaker) at its state-of-the-art winery. Exports to Canada, Singapore, Hong Kong and China.

🍷🍷🍷🍷🍷 **Andrea Reserve 2014** 76% cabernet sauvignon, 15% merlot, 9% 'other' varieties, matured for 16 months in new and used French oak. One of many great examples of Bordeaux-type blends which Margaret River produces with far greater regularity than any other Australian region. It is medium-bodied, and it is elegant, with perfect fruit, oak and tannin balance. I pay particular attention to the aftertaste of wines such as this, and it reaffirms the message. Screwcap. **Rating** 96 **To** 2039 $50 ✪
Margaret River Cabernet Sauvignon 2014 Includes 10% merlot, matured for 16 months in new and used French oak. Fragrance and freshness of a high order, seemingly the mark of the vintage in Thompson Estate's hands. Pure cassis and bay

leaf aromas and flavours on the bouquet and long, pure palate; tannins and oak are camouflaged and largely unseen supports. Screwcap. **Rating** 96 **To** 2039 $50 ✪

The Specialist Cabernet Sauvignon 2013 85% cabernet sauvignon, 9% merlot, 9% 'other' varieties, all matured for 18 months in French oak. A powerful, concentrated and complex wine proudly flying its colours from the main mast, and staring down anyone seeking to question its authority, but even here there is a deftness of touch with the balance between the black fruits, the firm tannins and the cedary oak. Screwcap. 14% alc. **Rating** 96 **To** 2043 $80

Margaret River Chardonnay 2016 A particularly well balanced and focused chardonnay, fruit foremost with a classic array of nectarine, white peach and grapefruit zest and juice; acidity and oak slot precisely into the fruit jigsaw, the picture complete in every respect. Screwcap. 13.5% alc. **Rating** 95 **To** 2026 $50

The Specialist Chardonnay 2013 Controlled alcohol injects a feeling of freshness and lightness in the mouth that is not expected given the age of the wine and the 100% new oak. It's altogether elegant, with Bob Cartwright's fingerprints all over it. Screwcap. 13.5% alc. **Rating** 95 **To** 2023 $70

Margaret River SSB 2016 **Rating** 94 **To** 2021 $35

Margaret River Cabernet Merlot 2014 **Rating** 94 **To** 2034 $35

🍷🍷🍷🍷🍷 **Four Chambers SBS 2016** **Rating** 90 **To** 2018 SC

Four Chambers Pinot Noir Rose 2016 **Rating** 90 **To** 2018 SC

Thorn-Clarke Wines ★★★★★

Milton Park, 266 Gawler Park Road, Angaston, SA 5353 **Region** Barossa Valley
T (08) 8564 3036 **www**.thornclarkewines.com.au **Open** Mon–Fri 9–5, w'ends 11–4
Winemaker Peter Kelly **Est.** 1987 **Dozens** 90 000 **Vyds** 268ha

Established by David and Cheryl Clarke (née Thorn), and son Sam, Thorn-Clarke is one of the largest family-owned estate-based businesses in the Barossa. Their winery is close to the border between the Barossa and Eden valleys, and three of their four vineyards are in the Eden Valley: the Mt Crawford vineyard is at the southern end of the Eden Valley, while the Milton Park and Sandpiper vineyards are further north in the Eden Valley. The fourth vineyard is at St Kitts, at the northern end of the Barossa Ranges. In all four vineyards careful soil mapping has resulted in matching of variety and site, with all the major varieties represented. The quality of grapes retained for the Thorn-Clarke label has resulted in a succession of trophy and gold medal-winning wines at very competitive prices. Exports to all major markets.

🍷🍷🍷🍷🍷 **Eden Trail Riesling 2016** Quartz-white; a wine born to rise to the very top, its finesse, purity and balance the foundations for its slow, long-term development. The balance is the outcome of the citrus/apple fruit and its finely etched acidity. Screwcap. 11% alc. **Rating** 95 **To** 2031 $24 ✪

William Randell Barossa Shiraz 2014 A wantonly luscious and complex medium to full-bodied wine with plum, fruitcake, dark chocolate and vanillan oak all having their say, yet allowing high quality tannins to infiltrate the palate and aftertaste. Hard to fault in the context of its style. Screwcap. 14.5% alc. **Rating** 95 **To** 2034 $60

Ron Thorn Single Vineyard Barossa Shiraz 2014 Best take care when lifting the dreadnought bottle, appropriately heavy – seriously heavy – given the ultra-full-bodied shiraz it contains. It oozes blackberry, blackcurrant, licorice and quality oak, tannins doing their best to provide balance. Its prime lies decades away. Cork. 14.5% alc. **Rating** 95 **To** 2044 $95

William Randell Eden Valley Cabernet Sauvignon 2014 A wholly convincing Eden Valley cabernet, purity and intensity the two pillars around which the wine is built. Cabernet is seldom as supple and immediately enjoyable as this, cassis flowing evenly across and along the palate, fine tannins and cedary French oak providing the final touches. Screwcap. 14.5% alc. **Rating** 95 **To** 2034 $60

🍷🍷🍷🍷🍷 **Barossa Malbec 2015** **Rating** 93 **To** 2025 $30 JF

Sandpiper Eden Valley Riesling 2016 **Rating** 91 **To** 2024 $19 ✪

Eden Trail Shiraz 2015 Rating 91 To 2025 $28 JF
Shotfire Barossa Quartage 2014 Rating 91 To 2029 $25
Sandpiper Barossa Shiraz 2015 Rating 90 To 2030 $19 **○**

Three Dark Horses ★★★★☆

49 Fraser Avenue, Happy Valley, SA 5159 **Region** McLaren Vale
T 0405 294 500 **www**.3dh.com.au **Open** Not
Winemaker Matt Broomhead **Est.** 2009 **Dozens** 1000
Three Dark Horses is the new project for former Coriole winemaker Matt Broomhead. After
vintages in southern Italy and the Rhône Valley he returned to McLaren Vale in 2009 and,
with his father Alan, buys quality grapes, thanks to the long experience they both have in the
region. The third dark horse is Matt's 93-year-old grandfather, a vintage regular. Exports to
NZ and China.

� **McLaren Vale Shiraz 2015** Hand-picked from vines up to 70yo, 10% whole
bunches, wild yeast fermented, matured in 40% new oak. The whole bunches lift
the fragrance of the bouquet, but McLaren Vale comes thundering through on the
palate, with dark chocolate swirling through on the savoury black fruits of this full-
bodied, but not fat, wine. Screwcap. 14.5% alc. **Rating** 95 **To** 2040 $25 **○**
GT McLaren Vale Grenache Touriga 2016 A 75/25% blend, 50% whole
bunches, co-fermented with wild yeast, no oak, no fining, no filtration. The
generosity and mouthfeel of the fruit is such that you would quite possibly not
identify the absence of oak. It is bold, voluptuous and luscious, with poached
plums and cherries dipped in dark chocolate. Bring it on. Screwcap. 14% alc.
Rating 94 **To** 2026 $25 **○**

3 Drops ★★★★★

PO Box 1828, Applecross, WA 6953 **Region** Mount Barker
T (08) 9315 4721 **www**.3drops.com **Open** Not
Winemaker Robert Diletti (Contract) **Est.** 1998 **Dozens** 5000 **Vyds** 21.5ha
3 Drops is the name given to the Bradbury family vineyard at Mount Barker. The name
reflects three elements: wine, olive oil and water, all of which come from the substantial
property. The vineyard is planted to riesling, sauvignon blanc, semillon, chardonnay, cabernet
sauvignon, merlot, shiraz and cabernet franc, and irrigated by a large wetland on the property.
3 Drops also owns the 14.7ha Patterson's vineyard, planted in 1982 to pinot noir, chardonnay
and shiraz. Exports to Canada, Singapore, South Korea, Hong Kong and China.

♥♥♥♥♥ **Great Southern Riesling 2016** In the heart of Great Southern/Mount
Barker riesling. The mouthwatering purity and intensity are exceptional, and the
attention to detail (cold-settled, free-run juice, etc) and early picking make this a
powerhouse, bred to stay for decades. Screwcap. 11.5% alc. **Rating** 95 **To** 2031
$26 **○**
Great Southern Shiraz 2014 Full crimson-purple; the expressive bouquet
spans black fruits, spicy florals and a backdrop of bitter chocolate, the palate with
a bottomless well of potent black fruits and licorice. Despite this opulent array, it
remains medium-bodied and light on its feet thanks to careful tannin extract and
controlled French oak. Screwcap. 13.5% alc. **Rating** 95 **To** 2034 $26 **○**
Great Southern Pinot Noir 2015 Excellent bright colour; it is unmistakably
pinot noir, and unquestionably good, with clear-cut cherry-accented fruit and a
supple mouthfeel to the long, light to medium-bodied palate. Screwcap. 13.5% alc.
Rating 94 **To** 2023 $28 **○**
Great Southern Cabernets 2015 A cabernet sauvignon/cabernet franc blend
matured in French oak. The colour is bright enough, but not intense, so gives
no clue about the richness and depth of the cassis and bay leaf fruit that fills the
mouth from the word go. Despite this depth, the tannins are soft and pliable.
Screwcap. 14% alc. **Rating** 94 **To** 2030 $26 **○**

🍷🍷🍷🍷� Great Southern Sauvignon Blanc 2016 Rating 90 To 2022 $24
Great Southern Chardonnay 2015 Rating 90 To 2020 $26
Great Southern Rose 2016 Rating 90 To 2018 $24 JF

Three Lads   ★★★★☆

46 Rylstone Crescent, Grace, ACT 2911 **Region** Canberra District
T 0408 233 481 **www**.threelads.com.au **Open** Not
Winemaker Bill Crowe, Aaron Harper, Luke McGaghey **Est.** 2013 **Dozens** 1000
The three lads are Luke McGaghey, Aaron Harper and Bill Crowe, who fortuitously met at a
local food and wine event in 2012, and decided that they should have some fun. Their business
plan was simplicity itself: buy small amounts of grapes from vineyards in the Canberra District
and turn them into wine. Bill Crowe had spent 10 years working at Scott Harvey Wines in
Napa Valley and came to Australia to join his wife Jaime Crowe at Four Winds Vineyard, where
he (Bill) is winemaker (his real job).

🍷🍷🍷🍷🍷 Shiraz 2015 Firstly and most importantly, this is a damn good drink. It's refined
yet full of juicy, tangy fruit, teased with pepper, crushed juniper berries with lithe
tannins. The back label says drink up to 10 years or at your next barbecue. Sums it
up perfectly. Screwcap. 13.5% alc. **Rating** 95 **To** 2025 $27 JF ✪

🍷🍷🍷🍷♈ Riesling 2016 Rating 90 To 2023 $24 JF
Gundagai Rose 2016 Rating 90 To 2019 $20 JF ✪
Gundagai Sangiovese 2015 Rating 90 To 2019 $24 JF

Tidswell Wines   ★★★☆

14 Sydenham Road, Norwood, SA 5067 **Region** Limestone Coast
T (08) 8363 5800 **www**.tidswellwines.com.au **Open** By appt
Winemaker Ben Tidswell, Wine Wise **Est.** 1994 **Dozens** 4000 **Vyds** 136.4ha
The Tidswell family (now in the shape of Andrea and Ben Tidswell) has two large vineyards in
the Limestone Coast zone near Bool Lagoon; the lion's share is planted to cabernet sauvignon
and shiraz, with smaller plantings of merlot, sauvignon blanc, petit verdot, vermentino and
pinot gris. Tidswell is a fully certified member of WFA's environmental sustainability program.
Wines are released under the Jennifer, Heathfield Ridge and The Publicans labels. Exports to
Singapore, Japan and China.

🍷🍷🍷🍷♈ Publicans Series Wild Violet Limestone Coast Sauvignon Blanc 2016
A fresh combo of all things herbaceous – wild nettles, star fruit, crunchy green
apples – then the lively lemon-lime juice kicks in. Tight acidity keeping this all in
place. Screwcap. 12% alc. **Rating** 90 **To** 2018 $18 JF ✪

Tim Adams   ★★★★

Warenda Road, Clare, SA 5453 **Region** Clare Valley
T (08) 8842 2429 **www**.timadamswines.com.au **Open** Mon–Fri 10.30–5, w'ends 11–5
Winemaker Tim Adams, Brett Schutz **Est.** 1986 **Dozens** 60000 **Vyds** 145ha
Tim Adams and partner Pam Goldsack preside over a highly successful business. Having
expanded the range of estate plantings with tempranillo, pinot gris and viognier, in 2009
the business took a giant step forward with the acquisition of the 80ha Leasingham Rogers
Vineyard from CWA, followed in '11 by the purchase of the Leasingham winery and
winemaking equipment (for less than replacement cost). The winery is now a major contract
winemaking facility for the region. Exports to the UK, The Netherlands, Sweden, Hong
Kong, China and NZ.

🍷🍷🍷🍷🍷 Clare Valley Botrytis Riesling 2016 Lovely, bright and well balanced residual
sugar/titratable acidity/alcohol guaranteeing a long life. The modest level of
botrytis means the varietal character of riesling is preserved, and the potential
elegance is fully realised. Will grow old slowly and with grace. Screwcap. 11% alc.
Rating 94 **To** 2031 $25 ✪

𝄞𝄞𝄞𝄞𝄞 Clare Valley Pinot Gris 2016 Rating 93 To 2022 $22 SC ✪
Aberfeldy Clare Valley Shiraz 2013 Rating 93 To 2030 $60 JF
Clare Valley Riesling 2016 Rating 92 To 2036 $22 SC ✪
Clare Valley Semillon 2014 Rating 92 To 2023 $24 JF ✪
Clare Valley Shiraz 2013 Rating 92 To 2026 $25 JF ✪
Reserve Clare Valley Tempranillo 2009 Rating 92 To 2021 $29 JF
Clare Valley Semillon 2013 Rating 91 To 2020 $22 ✪
Fergus 2014 Rating 91 To 2022 $24 JF

Tim Gramp ★★★★

Mintaro/Leasingham Road, Watervale, SA 5452 **Region** Clare Valley
T (08) 8344 4079 **www.timgrampwines.com.au Open** W'ends 12–4
Winemaker Tim Gramp **Est.** 1990 **Dozens** 6000 **Vyds** 16ha
Tim Gramp has quietly built up a very successful business, and by keeping overheads to a minimum provides good wines at modest prices. Over the years the estate vineyards (shiraz, riesling, cabernet sauvignon and grenache) have been expanded significantly. Exports to Malaysia, Taiwan and China.

𝄞𝄞𝄞𝄞𝄞 **Watervale Riesling 2016** A roll call of the attributes for youthful Clare riesling: perfumed bath salts, lime cordial, citrus flowers and slate, among others. Shows good intensity of flavour through the palate, and the acidity marshals the fruit all the way to the finish. Really good drinking now and will age very well. Screwcap. 11.5% alc. **Rating** 93 To 2028 $21 SC ✪
Basket Pressed Watervale Shiraz 2013 Traditional Clare Valley shiraz at its best. The foundation is a full-bodied wealth of blood plum and blackberry fruit; the oak is integrated and balanced, the supple tannins exceptionally good. Could become something special in 10+ years. Screwcap. 14.5% alc. **Rating** 93 To 2033 $35

Tim McNeil Wines ★★★★

71 Springvale Road, Watervale, SA 5452 **Region** Clare Valley
T (08) 8843 0040 **www.timmcneilwines.com.au Open** Fri–Sun & public hols 11–5
Winemaker Tim McNeil **Est.** 2004 **Dozens** 1500 **Vyds** 2ha
When Tim and Cass McNeil established Tim McNeil Wines, Tim had long since given up his teaching career, graduating with a degree in oenology from Adelaide University in 1999. He then spent 11 years honing his craft at important wineries in the Barossa and Clare valleys. In Aug 2010 Tim McNeil Wines became his full-time job. The McNeils' 16ha property at Watervale includes mature dry-grown riesling. The cellar door overlooks the riesling vineyard, with panoramic views of Watervale and beyond. Exports to Canada.

𝄞𝄞𝄞𝄞𝄞 **Watervale Riesling 2016** A finely textured and structured riesling, vital and crisp; citrus and tight-strung acidity all add up to a wine of typicity and quality. Screwcap. 12.5% alc. **Rating** 94 To 2026 $24 ✪

𝄞𝄞𝄞𝄞 **On the Wing Clare Valley Shiraz 2014** Rating 89 To 2024 $23

Tim Smith Wines ★★★★★

PO Box 446, Tanunda, SA 5352 **Region** Barossa Valley
T 0416 396 730 **www.timsmithwines.com.au Open** Not
Winemaker Tim Smith **Est.** 2002 **Dozens** 5000 **Vyds** 1ha
With a talent for sourcing exceptional old vine fruit from the Barossa floor, Tim Smith has created a small but credible portfolio of wines, currently including Mataro, Grenache, Shiraz, Viognier, and more recently Eden Valley Riesling and Viognier. Tim left his full-time winemaking role with a large Barossa company in 2011, allowing him to concentrate 100% of his energy on his own brand. In '12 Tim joined forces with the team from First Drop (see separate entry), and has moved winemaking operations to a brand-new winery fondly named

'Home of the Brave', in Nuriootpa. Exports to the UK, the US, Canada, Denmark, Taiwan and Singapore.

🍷🍷🍷🍷🍷 **Reserve Barossa Shiraz 2014** Grown on two Eden Valley vineyards, one boasting 115yo vines, the other nearing 100. It's floral, meaty, truffly, brimful of black cherry and blackcurrant, shot with plum. Mint notes add lift and life. Tannin wakes slowly in the wine before finally spreading its arms out wide through the back palate. A long life of gorgeous drinking is guaranteed. Screwcap. 14% alc. **Rating** 96 **To** 2034 $85 CM
Reserve Barossa Mataro 2015 Inaugural release. It's intense of fruit and intense of tannin, with liberal dosings of earth/rust/meat/savouriness. All this at 13.5%. It has flow, flavour and class, and more than a little exotica. Screwcap. **Rating** 96 **To** 2027 $85 CM
Barossa Mataro 2015 Cool mints and blueberries, meaty spice and jubey blackberry. It's inviting, it offers an array of flavours, it's satiny and it's all well sustained through the finish. In short, it's a beautiful red wine. Screwcap. 14% alc. **Rating** 94 **To** 2025 $38 CM

🍷🍷🍷🍷♀ **Bugalugs Barossa Valley Shiraz 2015** **Rating** 93 **To** 2025 $25 CM ○

Tinklers Vineyard   ★★★★★

Pokolbin Mountains Road, Pokolbin, NSW 2320 **Region** Hunter Valley
T (02) 4998 7435 **www**.tinklers.com.au **Open** 7 days 10–5
Winemaker Usher Tinkler **Est.** 1946 **Dozens** 5000 **Vyds** 41ha
Three generations of the Tinkler family have been involved with the property since 1942. Originally a beef and dairy farm, vines have been both pulled out and replanted at various stages, and part of the adjoining 80-year-old Ben Ean vineyard has been acquired. Plantings include semillon (14ha), shiraz (11.5ha), chardonnay (6.5ha) and smaller areas of merlot, muscat and viognier. The majority of the grape production continues to be sold to McWilliam's and Tyrrell's. Usher has resigned his roles as chief winemaker at Poole's Rock and Cockfighter's Ghost to take on full-time responsibility at Tinklers, and production has been increased to meet demand. Exports to Sweden, Singapore and China.

🍷🍷🍷🍷🍷 **Reserve Hunter Valley Semillon 2015** One of those young Hunter semillons that is already complete in its youth, its future path written in stone. Citrus, lemongrass and apple flavours are wreathed by acidity, investing the wine with excellent length and balance. Screwcap. 10.9% alc. **Rating** 95 **To** 2035 $35 ○
School Block Hunter Valley Semillon 2015 Very good drive and length, the flavours of lemongrass and citrus zest, lively acidity the king of the castle. Onwards and upwards from here. Screwcap. 10.8% alc. **Rating** 94 **To** 2035 $25 ○

🍷🍷🍷🍷♀ **School Block Hunter Valley Semillon 2013** **Rating** 93 $25 SC ○
U and I Hunter Valley Shiraz 2015 **Rating** 93 **To** 2028 $45 SC
Old Vines Hunter Valley Shiraz 2015 **Rating** 92 **To** 2030 $35 SC
Poppys Hunter Valley Chardonnay 2016 **Rating** 91 **To** 2021 $35 SC
Chardonnay 2015 **Rating** 90 **To** 2020 $25 SC
Hunter Valley Viognier 2016 **Rating** 90 **To** 2018 $25 SC
Steep Hill Shiraz 2015 **Rating** 90 **To** 2024 $25 SC

Tintilla Wines   ★★★★☆

725 Hermitage Road, Pokolbin, NSW 2320 **Region** Hunter Valley
T (02) 6574 7093 **www**.tintilla.com.au **Open** 7 days 10.30–6
Winemaker James and Robert Lusby **Est.** 1993 **Dozens** 3500 **Vyds** 6.52ha
The Lusby family has established shiraz (2.2ha), sangiovese (1.6ha), merlot (1.3ha), semillon (1.2ha) and cabernet sauvignon (0.2ha) on a northeast-facing slope with red clay and limestone soil. Tintilla was the first winery to plant sangiovese in the Hunter Valley (in 1995). The family has also planted an olive grove producing four different types of olives, which are cured and sold from the estate.

🍷🍷🍷🍷🍷 Patriarch Syrah 2011 '11 was a fine vintage in the Hunter. The aroma is
reticent, with a ferrous tone to dark plum, iodine, violet, cherry and licorice notes.
Still tightly wound across a kernel of firm tannins with oak pitching in generously,
this needs plenty of time to unravel. Screwcap. 14% alc. **Rating** 95 **To** 2025 $60
NG

Pebbles Brief Chardonnay 2015 The chassis is spicy cedar oak while the
carburettor is peaches, apricot and cream, punching long, lively and streamlined,
with a thirst-slaking citrus twist. Screwcap. 13.4% alc. **Rating** 94 **To** 2022 $30
NG

🍷🍷🍷🍷🍷 Museum Release Angus Semillon 2010 Rating 93 To 2020 $40 NG
Reserve Shiraz 2014 Rating 91 To 2025 $40 NG
Angus Semillon 2015 Rating 90 To 2025 $30 NG

Tobin Wines   ★★★☆

34 Ricca Road, Ballandean, Qld 4382 **Region** Granite Belt
T (07) 4684 1235 **www.tobinwines.com.au Open** 7 days 10–5
Winemaker Adrian Tobin **Est.** 1964 **Dozens** 1500 **Vyds** 5.9ha
In the early 1960s the Rica family planted table grapes, followed by shiraz and semillon in
'64–66: these are said to be the oldest vinifera vines in the Granite Belt region. The Tobin
family (headed by Adrian and Frances) purchased the vineyard in 2000 and has increased
the plantings, which now consist of shiraz, cabernet sauvignon, merlot, tempranillo, semillon,
verdelho, chardonnay, muscat and sauvignon blanc.

🍷🍷🍷🍷🍷 Charlotte Barrel Ferment Granite Belt Sauvignon Blanc 2016 This is
white Bordeaux-inspired, with judicious oak lending a sense of textural intrigue
and an aromatic fireworks to the pungent, herbaceous undertone of sauvignon.
Lemon oil, ripe apricot and the exotic pitch of durian all lend themselves to a
successful rendition. 12.4% alc. **Rating** 93 **To** 2023 NG

🍷🍷🍷🍷 Lily Barrel Fermented Granite Belt Chardonnay 2014 Rating 89 To 2019

Tokar Estate   ★★★★★

6 Maddens Lane, Coldstream, Vic 3770 **Region** Yarra Valley
T (03) 5964 9585 **www.tokarestate.com.au Open** 7 days 10.30–5
Winemaker Martin Siebert **Est.** 1996 **Dozens** 4000 **Vyds** 12ha
Leon Tokar established 12ha of now mature chardonnay, pinot noir, shiraz, cabernet sauvignon
and tempranillo at Tokar Estate, one of many vineyards on Maddens Lane. All the wines have
performed well in regional shows, with early success (and continued) for the Tempranillo, and
very distinguished Cabernet Sauvignon.

🍷🍷🍷🍷🍷 Yarra Valley Pinot Noir 2015 Fermented in seven small batches with varying
amounts of whole bunches, crushed berries and cap management etc, wild-yeast
ferments, maceration on skins, matured for 9 months in French oak (30% new).
The complexity of the vinification has paid dividends; plum and cherry fruits have
no problems with the foresty/savoury notes that will change to spicy with more
bottle age. Attractive wine. Screwcap. 13.5% alc. **Rating** 95 **To** 2025 $40
Yarra Valley Cabernet Sauvignon 2015 Crushed and destemmed, wild-
yeast fermented, matured for 15 months in French hogsheads (45% new), then a
barrel selection. A powerful medium to full-bodied cabernet with a clear contrast
between ripe cassis fruit on the one hand, and savoury earthy dried herb notes on
the other. Screwcap. 14.5% alc. **Rating** 95 **To** 2035 $40

🍷🍷🍷🍷🍷 Yarra Valley Chardonnay 2015 Rating 92 To 2023 $35
Carafe & Tumbler Yarra Valley Cabernet Sauvignon 2015 Rating 92
To 2025 $25
Yarra Valley Tempranillo 2015 Rating 91 To 2025 $35
Yarra Valley Shiraz 2015 Rating 90 $35

Tolpuddle Vineyard

37 Back Tea Tree Road, Richmond, Tas 7025 **Region** Southern Tasmania
T (08) 8155 6003 **www.**tolpuddlevineyard.com **Open** At Shaw + Smith
Winemaker Martin Shaw, Adam Wadewitz **Est.** 1988 **Dozens** 1800 **Vyds** 20ha

If ever a winery was born with blue blood in its veins, Tolpuddle would have to be it. The vineyard was established in 1988 on a continuous downhill slope facing northeast, and in '06 won the inaugural Tasmanian Vineyard of the Year Award. Michael Hill Smith MW and Martin Shaw are joint managing directors. David LeMire looks after sales and marketing; Adam Wadewitz, one of Australia's brightest winemaking talents, is senior winemaker. Vineyard manager Carlos Souris loses nothing in comparison, with over 30 years of grapegrowing in Tasmania under his belt, and an absolutely fearless approach to making a great vineyard even greater. Exports to the US, the UK, Canada, Denmark, China, Japan and Singapore.

ΨΨΨΨΨ **Pinot Noir 2015** Bright, clear crimson; this is right up there with the best of the best from a great Tasmanian vintage, sharing the alluring, perfumed fruits and the integrity of high quality tannins providing the structure for a long future. There is a purity to the red and black cherry/berry fruits that shines through the portals of the savoury/spicy tannins. A luminous future will richly repay those who are patient. Screwcap. 13.5% alc. **Rating** 97 **To** 2028 $78 ✪

ΨΨΨΨΨ **Chardonnay 2015** An elegant wine, quietly confident about its present and future. All the boxes have been ticked, leaving the stone fruit, pear and apple fruit to pick up citrussy/minerally acidity on the finish and aftertaste. Screwcap. 12.5% alc. **Rating** 95 **To** 2025 $67

Tomboy Hill

204 Sim Street, Ballarat, Vic 3350 (postal) **Region** Ballarat
T (03) 5331 3785 **Open** Not
Winemaker Scott Ireland (Contract) **Est.** 1984 **Dozens** 600 **Vyds** 3.6ha

Former schoolteacher Ian Watson seems to be following the same path as Lindsay McCall of Paringa Estate (also a former schoolteacher) in extracting greater quality and style than any other winemaker in his region. Since 1984 Ian has patiently built up a patchwork quilt of small plantings of chardonnay and pinot noir. In the better years, single vineyard Chardonnay and/or Pinot Noir are released; Rebellion Chardonnay and Pinot Noir are multi-vineyard blends, but all 100% Ballarat. After difficult vintages in 2011 and '12, Tomboy Hill returned in top form with the '13 and '14 wines, quietly ecstatic about the '15s.

ΨΨΨΨΨ **Rebellion Ballarat Chardonnay 2015** A mix of stone fruit, lemon peel and pith and moreish creamed honey leesy notes. Plenty of body to this, yet neat acidity ensures that it remains fairly taut, precise and alive. Screwcap. 13% alc. **Rating** 95 **To** 2024 $35 JF ✪
Clementine's Picking Ballarat Chardonnay 2015 This wine is akin to concentric circles – the centre ripe stone fruit, dried figs, then leesy flavours of grilled nuts and creamed honey, and the outer circle a layer of fine acidity drawing everything in. A richer style, luscious and well done. Only 75 dozen. Screwcap. 13.2% alc. **Rating** 95 **To** 2023 $50 JF
Rebellion Ballarat Pinot Noir 2015 From vineyards across Ballarat, aged in new and used French oak barriques. Alluring aromatics of dark cherries and spice. There's some weight, but velvety tannins keep this gliding along seamlessly. Ready now. Screwcap. 13% alc. **Rating** 95 **To** 2024 $35 JF ✪
Evie's Picking Ballarat Pinot Noir 2015 Compelling for its breadth and depth of flavour, from black cherries to olives and woodsy spices; really sturdy, though, with fine-sandpaper-like tannins. There's a slight herbal edge: not green or unripe, more rosemary, cardamom and pine needles. Screwcap. 13% alc. **Rating** 95 **To** 2026 $75 JF

Tomich Wines

87 King William Road, Unley, SA 5061 **Region** Adelaide Hills
T (08) 8299 7500 **www.**tomichhill.com.au **Open** Wed–Sat 12–5
Winemaker Randall Tomich **Est.** 2002 **Dozens** 60000 **Vyds** 180ha
Patriarch John Tomich was born on a vineyard near Mildura, where he learnt firsthand the skills and knowledge required for premium grapegrowing. He went on to become a well known Adelaide ear, nose and throat specialist. Taking the wheel full circle, he completed postgraduate studies in winemaking at the University of Adelaide in 2002, and embarked on the Master of Wine revision course from the Institute of Masters of Wine. His son Randal is a cutting from the old vine (metaphorically speaking), having invented new equipment and techniques for tending the family's vineyard in the Adelaide Hills, resulting in a 60% saving in time and fuel costs. Exports to the US, Singapore and China.

🍷🍷🍷🍷🍷 **Woodside Vineyard Adelaide Hills Shiraz 2015** You might be forgiven for swapping the regions of this and its McLaren Vale sibling in a blind tasting, for this is medium to full-bodied. It is very complex in flavour, texture and structure, dark cherry and spice lifting the back-palate, finish and aftertaste to a level all of its own. Screwcap. 14% alc. **Rating** 96 **To** 2035 $30
Tomich Hill McLaren Vale Shiraz 2015 This is a rare wine in the context of McLaren Vale, for while it is extremely intense, it is only medium-bodied. Its texture is exceptional, weaving fresh juicy fruit, pepper, fine tannins and oak into a mesmerising silken carpet. Screwcap. 14% alc. **Rating** 96 **To** 2030 $28
Woodside Vineyard Q96 Adelaide Hills Chardonnay 2015 White-fleshed stone fruit, pithy grapefruit and obviously expensive slinky oak take centre stage in the bouquet. The wine glides easily through the mouth with rippling flavour and perfectly integrated acidity, the finish long and textural. Very stylish. Cork. 12.5% alc. **Rating** 95 **To** 2022 $60 SC
Single Vineyard Adelaide Hills Gruner Veltliner 2016. A particularly successful gruner veltliner; it has considerable intensity to its unsweetened lemon, pear and white pepper aromas and flavours, bright acidity drawing out the long finish. Should develop very well. Screwcap. 12.5% alc. **Rating** 95 **To** 2020 $25
Woodside Park McLaren Vale Shiraz 2015 Deep colour; while full-bodied, this has lots of charm, its spicy, peppery nuances insinuating themselves into the velvety heart of the wine. The tannins, too, are fine. Exceptional value, and while big in body, good to go now. Screwcap. 14% alc. **Rating** 94 **To** 2025
Woodside Vineyard Adelaide Hills Shiraz 2014 Beautiful cool climate shiraz aromas as you put your nose in the glass; ultra-dark berry fruit, sweet and woody spice, and just a touch of mocha-like oak. Supple and seamless on the palate, it glides effortlessly along at just medium weight, the flavours ripe, savoury and long. Velvety tannins complete the picture. Cork. 14% alc. **Rating** 94 **To** 2027 $60 SC

🍷🍷🍷🍷🍷 **Single Vineyard Sauvignon Blanc 2016** Rating 92 To 2018 $25 ●
Woodside Vineyard Pinot Noir 2015 Rating 92 To 2025 $30 SC
Grace & Glory McLaren Vale Shiraz 2015 Rating 92 To 2025 $18 ●
Tomich Hill Winemaker's Reserve Chardonnay 2016 Rating 91 To 2020 $39
Woodside Vineyard Chardonnay 2015 Rating 91 To 2021 $25 SC
Single Vineyard Pinot Grigio 2016 Rating 91 To 2018 $25
Woodside Vineyard Gruner Veltliner 2015 Rating 91 To 2022 $25
Tomich Hill Sauvignon Blanc 2016 Rating 90 To 2018 $22 SC
Rhyme & Reason Pinot Grigio 2016 Rating 90 To 2018 $18 ●
Tomich Hill Hilltop Pinot Noir 2015 Rating 90 To 2022 $28 SC
Woodside Vineyard 1777 Pinot Noir 2015 Rating 90 To 2023 $60 SC
Adelaide Hills Chardonnay Pinot NV Rating 90 To 2017 TS
Adelaide Hills Blanc de Blanc NV Rating 90 To 2017 $25 TS

Toolangi Vineyards

PO Box 9431, South Yarra, Vic 3141 **Region** Yarra Valley
T (03) 9827 9977 **www**.toolangi.com **Open** Not
Winemaker Various contract **Est.** 1995 **Dozens** 7000 **Vyds** 12.2ha
Garry and Julie Hounsell acquired their property in the Dixons Creek area of the Yarra Valley, adjoining the Toolangi State Forest, in 1995. The primary accent is on pinot noir and chardonnay, accounting for all but 2.7ha, which is predominantly shiraz and a little viognier. Winemaking is by Yering Station (Willy Lunn), Giaconda (Rick Kinzbrunner), Hoddles Creek Estate (Franco D'Anna), Andrew Fleming (Coldstream Hills) and Oakridge (David Bicknell), as impressive a quintet of winemakers as one could wish for. Exports to the UK, Hong Kong, Singapore, Japan and China.

ꝗꝗꝗꝗꝗ **Block E Yarra Valley Pinot Noir 2015** This takes a millisecond to imprint the bouquet and palate with its sheer intensity, complexity and length. Its siblings are very, very good (and very different), but this is in a league of its own. Spices and savoury, foresty notes are all important, but don't imperil the fruit. A glorious salute to the vintage, and the very best grapes from the estate. Screwcap. 13.8% alc. **Rating** 98 **To** 2035 $100 ✪

Estate Yarra Valley Shiraz 2015 A high quality shiraz that reflects (and benefits from) the attention to detail, bunch sorting via dedicated equipment in the winery leading to whole berry sorting on the way to the fermenters. It is medium to full-bodied, its life span measured in decades, not years. Blackberry, black cherry, licorice, ripe tannins and an airbrush of French oak all contribute to a majestic palate. Screwcap. 13.8% alc. **Rating** 97 **To** 2045 $40 ✪

ꝗꝗꝗꝗꝗ **Block F Yarra Valley Chardonnay 2014** Gleaming straw-green; an extremely complex, rich and long chardonnay with high quality fruit and equally good oak. It definitely aspires to the richness of Montrachet or related Grand Crus, and does a good job. I just wonder whether 3 months (or more) less time in oak might have kept a little more freshness. Screwcap. 13.8% alc. **Rating** 96 **To** 2027 $125

Estate Yarra Valley Pinot Noir 2015 A beautiful pinot, absolutely stacked to the gills with varietal flavour, yet doesn't attack any of the senses, secure in its own beauty. Dark, spicy cherry fruit is foremost, but is as far away from simplicity as earth is from Mars. Great fragrance, great length, great balance – and every other box gets an emphatic tick. Screwcap. 13.8% alc. **Rating** 96 **To** 2030 $45 ✪

Yarra Valley Pinot Noir 2015 Bright, clear, full crimson-purple colour is a welcoming sign. 100% destemming allows the fruit total freedom of expression, and with the wind in its sails, it responds loudly and clearly. Red cherry fruit leads the way, black cherry and spice following with a touch of the forelock. This will richly repay 5 years in the cellar. Screwcap. 14% alc. **Rating** 94 **To** 2030 $28 ✪

Yarra Valley Shiraz 2015 Bright crimson-purple; ticks each and every box you can think of. The red fruits (predominantly cherry) of the bouquet effortlessly glide across and along the medium-bodied palate, the texture supple, indeed silky, the balance impeccable. Screwcap. 14.2% alc. **Rating** 94 **To** 2029 $26 ✪

ꝗꝗꝗꝗꝗ **Yarra Valley Rose 2016 Rating** 92 **To** 2019 $28

Top Note   ★★★★

546 Peters Creek Road, Kuitpo, SA 5172 **Region** Adelaide Hills
T 0406 291 136 **www**.topnote.com.au **Open** W'ends 11–4 (closed Jun–Jul)
Winemaker Nick Foskett **Est.** 2011 **Dozens** 600 **Vyds** 17ha
Computer chip designer Nick and opera singer Cate Foskett were looking for a lifestyle property in the Adelaide Hills after full-on careers in their very different occupations. By chance they came across a 24ha property planted to five varieties, all mainstream except for 0.5ha of a rare mutation of semillon turning the skin red. They say, 'Despite the small hurdles of our not knowing much about anything and none of the grapes being under contract, we sold our city house, enrolled in postgraduate viticulture and winemaking at the Waite Campus, University of Adelaide, and became grapegrowers.' Two years on, Cate became possibly the

only qualified operatic viticulturist in the world, and still works as a singer between harvests, managing the vineyard and cellar.

🍷🍷🍷🍷🍷 **Block 4 Adelaide Hills Shiraz 2015** The modest alcohol is a reflection of the elegant, red-berried, medium-bodied palate, spice and tannins adding complexity to the finish and aftertaste. Screwcap. 13.7% alc. **Rating** 94 **To** 2035 $40
Block 4 Adelaide Hills Shiraz 2014 Peppermint-cream and black pepper fragrances introduce this pretty Adelaide Hills shiraz. It certainly boasts heightened aromatics. The palate is then all cherry-plum, violet and creamy oak. It's a quality crowd-pleaser. Screwcap. 13.5% alc. **Rating** 94 **To** 2025 $40 CM

🍷🍷🍷🍷🍷 **Adelaide Hills Noble Rose 2015** Rating 93 To 2019 $24 CM ❂
Adelaide Hills Cabernet Sauvignon 2015 Rating 92 To 2030 $35
Adelaide Hills Pinot Noir 2015 Rating 91 To 2025 $35

Torbreck Vintners

Roennfeldt Road, Marananga, SA 5352 **Region** Barossa Valley
T (08) 8562 4155 **www.torbreck.com Open** 7 days 10–6
Winemaker Craig Isbel, Scott McDonald **Est.** 1994 **Dozens** 70 000 **Vyds** 86ha
Torbreck Vintners was already one of Australia's best-known high quality red wine makers when, in Sept 2013, wealthy Californian entrepreneur and vintner Peter Kight (of Quivira Vineyards) acquired 100% ownership of the Torbreck business. The winemaking team, headed by Craig Isbel, supported by Scott McDonald and Russell Burns, all in place for some years, continue to make the wines. The brand structure remains as before: the top quartet led by The Laird (single vineyard Shiraz), RunRig (Shiraz/Viognier), The Factor (Shiraz) and Descendant (Shiraz/Viognier); next The Struie (Shiraz) and The Steading (Grenache/Mataro/Shiraz). Exports to all major markets.

🍷🍷🍷🍷🍷 **RunRig 2013** All the hurly burly of immense fruit flavour and yet there are pretty elements to this wine. Inky depths of asphalt, licorice and saturated plum are met by volleys of five-spice, cloves, toast and chocolate. Tannin rumbles from the mid-palate onwards. The flavours are super-ripe but alcohol doesn't overly intrude on the palate. It's long and intense. Cork. 15.5% alc. **Rating** 96 **To** 2030 $250 CM

Torzi Matthews Vintners

Cnr Eden Valley Road/Sugarloaf Hill Road, Mt McKenzie, SA 5353 **Region** Eden Valley
T 0412 323 486 **www.torzimatthews.com.au Open** By appt
Winemaker Domenic Torzi **Est.** 1996 **Dozens** 3000 **Vyds** 10ha
Domenic Torzi and Tracy Matthews, former Adelaide Plains residents, searched for a number of years before finding a block at Mt McKenzie in the Eden Valley. The block they chose is in a hollow; the soil is meagre, but they were in no way deterred by the knowledge that it would be frost-prone. The result is predictably low yields, concentrated further by drying the grapes on racks, thus reducing the weight by around 30% (the Appassimento method is used in Italy to produce Amarone-style wines). Newer plantings of sangiovese and negro amaro, and an extension of the original plantings of shiraz and riesling, have seen the wine range increase. Exports to the UK and Denmark.

🍷🍷🍷🍷🍷 **1903 Single Vineyard of Domenico Martino Old Vines Shiraz 2015** A wonderful wine from a very old vineyard made with sensitivity, keeping the focus on the fruit, not the oak or the tannins. The decision to use 40% whole bunches was inspired, injecting a perfume to the bouquet and freshness to a palate that is no more than medium-bodied. Screwcap. 14.2% alc. **Rating** 97 **To** 2045 $50 ❂

🍷🍷🍷🍷🍷 **Frost Dodger Eden Valley Riesling 2016** Whole-bunch pressed, only the free-run juice used, wild-yeast fermented at cool temperatures for 6 weeks, aged on lees for 8 weeks. Has all the weight and texture its background suggests, with the full range of citrus fruits plus a hint of white peach; the long palate finishes with good acidity. Screwcap. 12.5% alc. **Rating** 94 **To** 2029 $25 ❂

Schist Rock Single Vineyard Barossa Shiraz 2015 This is an awesomely full-bodied, power-laden wine, deeply coloured and awash with black fruits and tannins, licorice and charry meat contributing part of the complexity. The one thing I don't get is that this vineyard is in the Eden Valley – why use the Barossa catch-all GI, especially given the wine has a powerful sense of place? Screwcap. 14.5% alc. **Rating** 94 **To** 2040 $22 ✪

🍷🍷🍷🍷🍷 **Frost Dodger Eden Valley Shiraz 2013** **Rating** 90 **To** 2028 $40

Trapeze ★★★★★

2130 Kinglake Road, St Andrews, Vic 3761 (postal) **Region** Yarra Valley
T (03) 9710 1155 **Open** Not
Winemaker James Lance, Brian Conway **Est.** 2011 **Dozens** 1600

This is the venture of friends James Lance (Punch) and Brian Conway (Izway Wines). While James is firmly attached to the Yarra Valley, Brian divides his time between the Barossa Valley and Melbourne, having made wine from the Rhône varietals for many years. He wanted to tackle the Burgundy varieties but realised this was not going to happen just because he felt the need; thus the partnership came about.

🍷🍷🍷🍷🍷 **Yarra Valley Chardonnay 2015** Slightly deeper and brighter green-gold than the Punch Lance's Vineyard Chardonnay, the palate more complex and powerful but less intense and focused. The attention to detail is extraordinary in each wine, and which you prefer is a purely personal decision. Screwcap. 13.5% alc. **Rating** 95 **To** 2024 $32 ✪

Yarra Valley Pinot Noir 2015 You realise this is upper class the second you swirl and taste it, and reflect on the great vintage. It is an exercise in silk and velvet, with length that extends further each time you return to it. Spice is a constant companion (no Le Carré) as you learn more and more about the offer. Screwcap. 13.5% alc. **Rating** 95 **To** 2027 $32 ✪

Travertine Wines ★★★☆

78 Old North Road, Pokolbin, NSW 2320 **Region** Hunter Valley
T (02) 6574 7329 **www**.travertinewines.com.au **Open** Wed–Sun 10–4
Winemaker Liz Silkman **Est.** 1988 **Dozens** 3000 **Vyds** 10.73ha

This is the reincarnation of Pendarves Estate, originally planted by medico-cum-wine historian-cum-wine health activist Dr Phillip Norrie. It was purchased by Graham Burns in January 2008, and vineyard manager Chris Dibley, who had previously worked in the vineyard, was brought back to 'get the place back up to scratch'. There is a Joseph's coat of plantings including pinot noir (2.35ha), verdelho (2.25ha), chardonnay (1.25ha) and chambourcin (1.7ha), and lesser plantings of tannat, semillon, shiraz and merlot.

🍷🍷🍷🍷🍷 **The Column Vineyard Reserve 2014** This is a shiraz-dominant blend that includes merlot and petit verdot. If ever the blend were to really work, '14 was the vintage. Fresh, light to medium-bodied, with the handling of both the oak and tannins reflecting the extreme skills of contract winemaker Liz Silkman. Screwcap. 13.6% alc. **Rating** 93 **To** 2024 $30

Trellis ★★★★

Valley Farm Road, Healesville, Vic 3777 **Region** Yarra Valley
T 0417 540 942 **www**.trelliswines.com.au **Open** By appt
Winemaker Luke Houlihan **Est.** 2007 **Dozens** 800 **Vyds** 3.2ha

This is the venture of winemaker Luke Houlihan and viticulturist Greg Dunnett. Luke was formerly winemaker at Yarra Ridge and Long Gully Estate, and Greg owns Valley Farm Vineyard. The pinot noir has had several distinguished purchasers over the years, and there has never been any doubt about the quality of the fruit, which is from the dry-grown vines.

🍷🍷🍷🍷🍷 **Yarra Valley Pinot Noir 2015** A sappy, crunchy, floral and eminently drinkable pinot noir, redolent of creamy strawberry and assorted red fruits. Despite the lowish alcohol, there is not the faintest sense of greenness, with impeccably handled vanillan oak supports, bright acidity, a whisper of whole cluster briar and a broad brushstroke of soothing, gauze-like grape tannins serving as a point of focus. Pretty and engaging, rather than cerebral. And there is nothing at all wrong with that. Screwcap. 12.9% alc. **Rating** 93 **To** 2023 $35 NG

Heathcote Syrah 2015 This is an aspirational mid-weighted syrah, as the choice of moniker suggests. It largely works well, with blueberry, black cherry, olive tapenade, a smudge of briar and smoked meat all clenched in the grip of camphor-like reduction. This blows off, boding well for ageing. Screwcap. 12.8% alc. **Rating** 92 **To** 2028 $30 NG

Trentham Estate

6531 Sturt Highway, Trentham Cliffs, NSW 2738 **Region** Murray Darling
T (03) 5024 8888 **www.**trenthamestate.com.au **Open** 7 days 10–5
Winemaker Anthony Murphy, Shane Kerr **Est.** 1988 **Dozens** 70 000 **Vyds** 49.9ha
Remarkably consistent tasting notes across all wine styles from all vintages attest to the expertise of ex-Mildara winemaker Tony Murphy, a well known and highly regarded producer. Estate vineyards are on the Murray Darling. With an eye to the future, but also to broadening the range of the wines in offer, Trentham Estate is selectively buying grapes from other regions with a track record for the chosen varieties. The value for money is unfailingly excellent. Exports to the UK, China and other major markets.

🍷🍷🍷🍷🍷 **Family Reserve Tasmania Pinot Noir 2013** Has developed very well since first tasted in Aug '14. The hue is still bright and clear, the red fruits still in control, although spicy/savoury/foresty notes are absolutely part of the mix. May be getting close to its peak, but the original drink-to year of '23 stands, as do the original points. Screwcap. 13.5% alc. **Rating** 95 **To** 2023 $26 **○**

🍷🍷🍷🍷🍷 **Family Reserve Heathcote Shiraz 2014** **Rating** 92 **To** 2029 $26
Estate Shiraz 2015 **Rating** 90 **To** 2023 $16 **○**

Trevelen Farm

506 Weir Road, Cranbrook, WA 6321 **Region** Great Southern
T (08) 9826 1052 **www.**trevelenfarm.com.au **Open** By appt
Winemaker Harewood Estate (James Kellie) **Est.** 1993 **Dozens** 3500 **Vyds** 6.5ha
In 2008 John and Katie Sprigg decided to pass ownership of their 1300ha wool, meat and grain-producing farm to son Ben and wife Louise. However, they have kept control of the 6.5ha of sauvignon blanc, riesling, chardonnay, cabernet sauvignon and merlot planted in 1993. When demand requires, they increase production by purchasing grapes from growers in the Frankland River subregion. Riesling remains the centrepiece of the range. Exports to the US, Japan and China.

🍷🍷🍷🍷🍷 **Estate Riesling 2016** Fragrant citrus blossom lifts gently on the bouquet, the palate overflowing with sweet lime juice, lemon and green apple, finishing with firm acidity providing length and balance, and scotching any thought of residual sugar that the sweet fruit might suggest. The '07 Aged Release gives you a guide to its longevity. Screwcap. 12.5% alc. **Rating** 95 **To** 2029 $25 **○**

Aged Release Riesling 2007 The bright green-straw colour sets the antennae waving furiously: this looks like a young riesling, 2–3yo at most. The bouquet is gently toasty, and the long palate has toast, herb and lime juice flavours that push forward on the finish and aftertaste, acidity helping the freshness of the wine. Screwcap. 13% alc. **Rating** 95 **To** 2020 $50

The Tunney Cabernet Sauvignon 2014 A powerful, focused and intense full-bodied cabernet with blackcurrant, bay leaf and savoury tannins all interwoven, each holding its ground, oak a bystander watching the action. Screwcap. 14.5% alc. **Rating** 95 **To** 2029 $25 **○**

Frankland Reserve Shiraz 2014 Good colour; has a strictness of flavour and structure normally reserved for young cabernet sauvignon, but the Frankland

River terroir and climate invests all red wines with a secret cache of black fruits and savoury tannins unlike those of any other region. Screwcap. 14.5% alc. **Rating** 94 To 2034 $30 **○**

🍷🍷🍷🍷♀ **Sauvignon Blanc Semillon 2016 Rating** 92 To 2021 $18 **○**

tripe.Iscariot ★★★★★

74 Tingle Avenue, Margaret River, WA 6285 **Region** Margaret River
T 0414 817 808 **www.tripeiscariot.com Open** Not
Winemaker Remi Guise **Est.** 2013 **Dozens** 250
This has to be the most way out winery name of the century. It prompted me to email South African-born and trained winemaker/owner Remi Guise asking to explain its derivation and/or meaning, and he courteously responded with a reference to Judas as 'the greatest black sheep of all time', and a non-specific explanation of tripe as 'challenging in style'. He added 'I hope this sheds some light, or dark, on the brand.' The wines provide a better answer, managing to successfully harness highly unusual techniques at various points of their elevage. His day job as winemaker at Naturaliste Vintners, the large Margaret River contract winemaking venture of Bruce Dukes, provides the technical grounding, allowing him to throw the 'how to' manual out of the window when the urge arises. His final words on his Marrow Syrah Malbec are, 'So, suck the marrow from the bone, fry the fat, and savour the warm, wobbly bits.'

🍷🍷🍷🍷🍷 **Absolution Karridale Margaret River Chenin Blanc 2015** Mid-gold and bright; distinctly varietal bouquet, with honeydew melon, preserved lemon, baked quinces with cinnamon and acacia flowers. Once on the palate, it has plenty of grip and tannins, creamy and textural, offset by uplifting, bright acidity and a dry finish. Screwcap. 13% alc. **Rating** 95 To 2024 $30 JF **○**
Absolution Wilyabrup Margaret River Chenin Blanc 2015 Straw-gold and bright; aromas of baked quince, pears and licorice root. Tasting grippy, chewy and phenolic, but in a good way, as these characters add to the texture. A tight palate and really dry on the finish. Screwcap. 12.8% alc. **Rating** 95 To 2023 $30 JF **○**
Aspic Margaret River Grenache Rose 2014 Love the gentle aromatics – a hint of Campari and soda, raspberries with clotted cream and spices, but it's the palate that makes this rose exceptional. It has texture and depth, yet its citrus-zesty and refreshing acidity keeps it delightfully buoyant, and it's super dry on the finish. Screwcap. 13% alc. **Rating** 95 To 2018 $30 JF **○**
Marrow Margaret River Syrah Malbec 2014 Crimson-purple and bright; plums, mulberries, allspice and stalks make for a seductive entree. Medium-bodied, it jumps from soy sauce, wood shavings and wheatmeal to new leather before meeting abundant ripe and plump tannins alongside crunchy acidity. Balanced and complete, but another year or so in bottle will round out the exuberance of youth. Screwcap. 13% alc. **Rating** 94 To 2024 $40 JF
Absolution Karridale Margaret River Grenache Noir Syrah Viognier Malbec 2014 It's delicious, vibrant, juicy and lithe with heady aromas of raspberries, red plums and Fuji apples, a sprinkling of white pepper, Redskin lollies and florals. Medium-bodied, supple tannins, and bursting with freshness to the very end. Screwcap. 13.8% alc. **Rating** 94 To 2020 $30 JF **○**

🍷🍷🍷🍷♀ **Brawn Margaret River Chardonnay 2014 Rating** 91 To 2020 $40 JF

Trofeo Estate ★★★★

85 Harrisons Road, Dromana, Vic 3936 **Region** Mornington Peninsula
T (03) 5981 8688 **www.trofeoestate.com Open** Thurs–Sun 10–5
Winemaker Richard Darby **Est.** 2012 **Dozens** 5000 **Vyds** 18.7ha
This property has had a chequered history. In the 1930s Passiflora Plantations Company was set up to become Australia's leading exporter of passionfruit and associated products. By '37, 120ha was covered with 70 000 passionfruit vines, and a processing factory was in operation. The following year a disease devastated the passionfruit and the company went into receivership, never to be seen again. In '48 a member of the Seppelt family planted a vineyard

on the exact site of Trofeo Estate, and it was thereafter acquired by leading Melbourne wine retailer and wine judge the late Doug Seabrook, who maintained the vineyard and made the wine until the vines were destroyed in a bushfire in '67. In '98 it was replanted, but passed through several hands and fell into and out of neglect until new owner, Jim Manolios, developed the property as a cafe restaurant, vineyard and winery, with pinot noir (6.7ha), chardonnay (4.9ha), pinot gris (2.6ha), shiraz (2.3ha), cabernet sauvignon (1.2ha) and muscat (1ha). Trofeo Estate is the exclusive Australian distributor of terracotta amphorae made in Italy, hence the involvement of amphorae in the making of a number of the wines.

🍷🍷🍷🍷🍷 **Pinot Noir 2015** Has the greatest mouthfeel of the Trofeo Pinots, oak a participant in the process; fresh and juicy red fruits reflect the vintage; very good length, with silky tannins. Cork. 13.8% alc. **Rating** 94 **To** 2025 $50

Pinot Noir 2014 Matured in a combination of terracotta amphorae and French barriques. Has good colour, and the winemaking has worked very well in a Mornington Peninsula vintage that overall was tougher and less expressive than '15. Plum and dark cherry fruits run through the long, well balanced palate and aftertaste. Screwcap. 13.9% alc. **Rating** 94 **To** 2027 $55

🍷🍷🍷🍷🍷 **Shiraz 2015 Rating** 93 **To** 2029 $50

Aged in Terracotta Single Old Block Pinot Noir 2015 Rating 90 **To** 2023 $69

Truffle & Wine Co ★★★★

Seven Day Road, Manjimup, WA 6248 **Region** Pemberton
T (08) 9777 2474 **www**.truffleandwine.com.au **Open** 7 days 10–4
Winemaker Mark Aitken, Ben Haines **Est.** 1997 **Dozens** 4000 **Vyds** 9ha
Owned by a group of investors from various parts of Australia who have successfully achieved their vision of producing fine wines and black truffles. The winemaking side is under the care of Mark Aitken, who, having graduated as dux of his class in applied science at Curtin University in 2000, joined Chestnut Grove as winemaker in '02. The truffle side of the business is run under the direction of Harry Eslick, with 13000 truffle-inoculated hazelnut and oak trees on the property. Truffle Hill is now the premium label for a range of wines that is sold domestically; the Truffle & Wine Co label is the ultra-premium label, the best from the Yarra Valley, with 50% of this range exported to international restaurant clients through the exclusive distributors of the truffles. Exports to Hong Kong and Singapore.

🍷🍷🍷🍷🍷 **Truffle Hill Manjimup Shiraz 2014** Immediately appealing and slurpable; a mix of boysenberries and red cherries, plus wood spices. There's a softness on the palate, with the cedary sweet oak integrated and the tannins plump, with some grip on the finish. Screwcap. 14.5% alc. **Rating** 91 **To** 2023 $35 JF

Truffle Hill Pemberton Cabernet Rose 2015 Attractive pale salmon hue; sweet strawberries and cream, then cranberry juice tartness with the acidity, which keeps the palate fresh and bright. Screwcap. 13.5% alc. **Rating** 90 **To** 2017 $30 JF

Trust Wines ★★★☆

PO Box 8015, Seymour, Vic 3660 **Region** Central Victoria
T (03) 5794 1811 **www**.trustwines.com.au **Open** Not
Winemaker Don Lewis, Narelle King **Est.** 2004 **Dozens** 500 **Vyds** 5ha
Partners Don Lewis and Narelle King had been making wine together for many years at Mitchelton, and Priorat, Spain. Don came from a grapegrowing family in Red Cliffs, near Mildura, and in his youth was press-ganged into working in the vineyard. When he left home he swore never to be involved in vineyards again, but in 1973 found himself accepting the position of assistant winemaker to Colin Preece at Mitchelton, where he remained until his retirement 32 years later. Narelle, having qualified as a chartered accountant, set off to travel, and while in South America met a young Australian winemaker who had just completed a vintage in Argentina, and who lived in France. The lifestyle appealed greatly, so on her return to Australia she obtained her winemaking degree from CSU and was offered work by Mitchelton as a bookkeeper and cellar hand. The estate-based wines are a reflection of

Central Victorian style. They also make the Tar & Roses wines. As this book was going to print, news of Don's death came through, causing much sadness for his innumerable friends. Understandably, no decisions have been published about the future of Trust Wines. Exports to Canada, Singapore and China.

ŸŸŸŸŸ **The Don Shiraz 2014** Made from low-cropping bushvines, which means intense manual work and often more concentrated flavours. Proof is here: a densely packed, full-bodied palate full of dark sweet and sour plums, blueberries, sage, saltbush and oak, and powdery if powerful tannins. Not shy: it's warming, soothing and pleasing. Screwcap. 14.5% alc. **Rating** 92 **To** 2026 $60 JF

ŸŸŸŸ **Crystal Hill White 2016 Rating** 89 **To** 2020 $20 JF

Tuck's Ridge   ★★★★★

37 Shoreham Road, Red Hill South, Vic 3937 **Region** Mornington Peninsula
T (03) 5989 8660 **www**.tucksridge.com.au **Open** 7 days 11–5
Winemaker Michael Kyberd **Est.** 1985 **Dozens** 6000 **Vyds** 3.4ha
Tuck's Ridge has changed focus significantly since selling its large Red Hill vineyard. It retained the Buckle Vineyards of chardonnay and pinot noir that consistently provide outstanding grapes (and wine). The major part of the production is purchased from the Turramurra Vineyard. Exports to the US and Hong Kong.

ŸŸŸŸŸ **Buckle Chardonnay 2015** A beautifully weighted and balanced wine that calmly rolls out its nectarine, white peach and citrus fruits with a background hint of creamy cashew. The balance of fruit, oak and acidity can't be faulted. Screwcap. 13.6% alc. **Rating** 96 **To** 2024 $55 ✪
Buckle Pinot Noir 2015 Has an architecture all of its own, with very intense dark cherry fruit held in a cradle of fine but persistent tannins and even finer cedary oak. Given time, all manner of flowery violets and spices will appear. Expensive? Not if you compare it with a $100 Burgundy. But be aware that it is reductive, and demands patience. Screwcap. 13.9% alc. **Rating** 96 **To** 2030 $100
Turramurra Chardonnay 2015 A wine playing out its career through the opposite headlands of grapefruit and apple, citrussy/minerally acidity flowing between those headlands. Razor-sharp definition in a different style from the vast majority of Mornington Peninsula chardonnays. Screwcap. 13.8% alc. **Rating** 95 **To** 2023 $50
Mornington Peninsula Savagnin 2016 Wow. This is a savagnin champing at the bit, with layers of fruit, zest, skin and pip taking it well into savoury territory, lengthened by handsome acidity . Screwcap. 13.8% alc. **Rating** 95 **To** 2026 $45
Mornington Peninsula Pinot Noir 2015 If you can't afford the Buckle Pinot, this is a handy pinot that is open for business and ticks all the boxes, as any good pinot from '15 should. Bright and juicy red fruits are framed by spicy flavours ex French oak and superfine tannins . Will come into full flower by '25 and charm the socks off you. Screwcap. 14.2% alc. **Rating** 95 **To** 2028 $45
Mornington Peninsula Shiraz 2015 Vivid crimson-purple; elegant, but intense and very long, with juicy red fruits dancing on the palate, and showing no sign whatsoever of becoming tired or bored. It drags you back repeatedly as you find it's not a one-trick pony, savoury/spicy tannins adding to the overall complexity of the wine. Screwcap. 14.9% alc. **Rating** 95 **To** 2030 $38
Mornington Peninsula Chardonnay 2015 Rating 94 **To** 2022 $35
Mornington Peninsula Pinot Gris 2016 Rating 94 **To** 2021 $32
Mornington Peninsula Rose 2016 Rating 94 **To** 2019 $29 ✪

ŸŸŸŸ **Mornington Peninsula Sauvignon Blanc 2016 Rating** 93 **To** 2019 $26 ✪
Mornington Peninsula Tempranillo 2015 Rating 92 **To** 2025 $45

Tulloch ★★★★★

Glen Elgin, 638 De Beyers Road, Pokolbin, NSW 2321 **Region** Hunter Valley
T (02) 4998 7580 **www.**tullochwines.com **Open** 7 days 10–5
Winemaker Jay Tulloch, First Creek **Est.** 1895 **Dozens** 45 000 **Vyds** 80ha
The Tulloch brand continues to build success on success. Its primary grape source is estate
vines owned by part-shareholder Inglewood Vineyard in the Upper Hunter Valley. It also owns
the JYT Vineyard established by Jay Tulloch in the mid-1980s at the foot of the Brokenback
Range in the heart of Pokolbin. The third source is contract-grown fruit from other growers
in the Hunter Valley and further afield. Skilled winemaking by First Creek Winemaking
Services has put the icing on the winemaking cake, and Christina Tulloch is a livewire
marketer. Exports to Belgium, the Philippines, Singapore, Hong Kong, Malaysia, Thailand
and Japan.

🍷🍷🍷🍷🍷 **Limited Release Hector of Glen Elgin Hunter Valley Shiraz 2013** Tulloch's
flagship, with its regal name befitting this wine. Dark ruby with red and black
plums and cherries encased in cedary oak and spice. Concentrated palate yet very
lively, with ripe powerful tannins – packed for the long haul. Screwcap. 12.5% alc.
Rating 96 **To** 2040 $80 JF
Cellar Door Release Limited Edition Hilltops Cabernet Sauvignon 2015
Dark crimson, savoury-toned with earth, mocha, cedary oak and upfront cassis
and black plums. A slight sweet-sour edge to the finely chiselled tannins; there's
an elegance and restraint on the palate yet it's tightly coiled, not ready to open up.
This needs more time in bottle and will reward the patient. Screwcap. 14.9% alc.
Rating 95 **To** 2030 $50 JF

🍷🍷🍷🍷🍷 **Julia Hunter Valley Semillon 2016 Rating** 92 **To** 2024 $30 JF
Cellar Door Release Hilltops Sangiovese 2015 Rating 92 **To** 2019 $25 ✪
EM Hunter Valley Chardonnay 2016 Rating 90 **To** 2022 $34 JF
Cellar Door Release Viognier 2016 Rating 90 **To** 2019 $20 JF ✪
Private Bin Pokolbin Dry Red Hunter Valley Shiraz 2015 Rating 90
To 2024 $55 JF

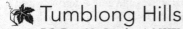 Tumblong Hills ★★★★

PO Box 38, Gundagai, NSW 2722 **Region** Gundagai
T 0427 078 636 **www.**tumblonghills.com **Open** Not
Winemaker Paul Bailey **Est.** 2009 **Dozens** 10 000 **Vyds** 202ha
This large winery was established by Southcorp Wines in the 1990s, as part of 'Project Max',
an initiative to honour Max Schubert of Penfolds Grange fame. In 2009 it was acquired by
business partners Danny Gilbert, Peter Leonard and Peter Waters. They were able to secure
the services of viticulturist and general manager Simon Robertson, who knew the vineyard
like the back of his hand, although his experience stretches far wider, over most of NSW. In
'11 close friends of Danny Gilbert, investors Wang Junfeng and Handel Lee, came onboard
to strengthen Tumblong Hills' presence in Australia and foster a strong relationship with the
Chinese premium wine market, where most of the wine goes. Winemaker Paul Bailey is
also a key figure; as a graduate from Roseworthy College he initially worked in the Barossa
Valley, and in '04 was awarded Best Red Wine at the London International Wine and Spirit
Competition's Great Australian Shiraz Challenge. He has also worked in Bordeaux for one
of the highest profile winemakers in that region, Michel Rolland. While shiraz and cabernet
sauvignon remain the two most important varieties in the vineyard, plantings now include
nebbiolo, barbera, sangiovese and pinot noir. Exports to China.

🍷🍷🍷🍷🍷 **Gundagai Premiere Cuvee Syrah 2013** Estate-grown, part machine, part
hand-picked, translating into whole bunch, whole berry and crushed/destemmed
ferments, matured for 18 months in used American (60%) and French (40%) oak.
There has also presumably been some fruit selection in the first place, as this is
fresher than J-Block. Cork. 14% alc. **Rating** 92 **To** 2028 $40

Gundagai J-Block Cuvee Syrah 2013 Made in identical fashion to the Premiere Cuvee, except 14 months maturation. A medium to full-bodied wine, honest and true to the Gundagai climate, but no X-factor. Cork. 14% alc. **Rating** 90 **To** 2023 $30

Turkey Flat   ★★★★★

Bethany Road, Tanunda, SA 5352 **Region** Barossa Valley
T (08) 8563 2851 **www.turkeyflat.com.au Open** 7 days 11–5
Winemaker Mark Bulman **Est.** 1990 **Dozens** 20 000 **Vyds** 47.83ha
The establishment date of Turkey Flat is given as 1990 but it might equally have been 1870 (or thereabouts), when the Schulz family purchased the Turkey Flat vineyard, or 1847, when the vineyard was first planted – to the very old shiraz that still grows there today and the 8ha of equally old grenache. Plantings have since expanded significantly, now comprising shiraz (24ha), grenache (10.5ha), cabernet sauvignon (5.9ha), mourvedre (3.7ha), and smaller plantings of marsanne, viognier and dolcetto. The business is run by sole proprietor Christie Schulz. Exports to the UK, the US and other major markets.

ϒϒϒϒϒ **Barossa Valley Grenache 2015** One of a handful of Barossa Valley grenaches with the same weight and power as top-flight McLaren Vale grenache. It has abundant red cherry, raspberry, blueberry and plum fruits allied with firm tannins, and no confection/Turkish Delight nuances. Moreover, it will react positively to maturation. Screwcap. 15% alc. **Rating** 96 **To** 2030 $30 ✪
Barossa Valley Rose 2016 Made with 95% grenache, but with input from cabernet sauvignon, shiraz and mataro. It's not far short of perfect; the drinkability factor here is immensely high. Rose petals, cherries and strawberries, ripe but not overtly sweet, with spice and herb notes and – the coup de grace to any attempt at resistance – texture like velvet. Screwcap. 13% alc. **Rating** 95 **To** 2017 $20 CM ✪
Barossa Valley Shiraz 2015 Deep crimson purple, this smells super with its aromas of briary dark fruits together with a little cedar/vanillan from the beautifully handled oak (the wine was matured in new and seasoned French oak hogsheads). There is an old vine creaminess to the palate, which manages to be rich and concentrated but supremely balanced at the same time. A terrific wine from go to whoa. Screwcap. 14.5% alc. **Rating** 95 **To** 2030 $47 PR
Butchers Block Red 2015 51% shiraz, 38% grenache, 11% mataro from 15–170yo vines. Given the provenance, is freakish value, its quality simply underlining that fact. It has purple and black fruits sewn together by firm tannins that add to the length of the wine (and its structure). I wouldn't hesitate to cellar the wine for 15+ years). Screwcap. 14.8% alc. **Rating** 94 **To** 2030 $20 ✪

ϒϒϒϒϒ **Barossa Valley Sparkling Shiraz NV Rating** 90 **To** 2020 $42 TS

Turner's Crossing Vineyard   ★★★★★

747 Old Bridgewater-Serpentine Road, Serpentine, Vic 3517 **Region** Bendigo
T 0427 843 528 **www.turnerscrossingwine.com Open** By appt
Winemaker Sergio Carlei **Est.** 1998 **Dozens** 4000 **Vyds** 42ha
The name of this outstanding vineyard comes from local farmers crossing the Loddon River in the mid to late 1800s on their way to the nearest town. The vineyard was planted in 1999 by former corporate executive and lecturer in the business school at La Trobe University, Paul Jenkins. However, Paul's experience as a self-taught viticulturist dates back to '85, when he established his first vineyard, at Prospect Hill, planting all the vines himself. The grapes from both vineyards have gone to a who's who of winemakers in Central Victoria, but an increasing amount is being made into wines of exceptional quality for Turner's Crossing. Phil Bennett and winemaker Sergio Carlei have joined Paul as co-owners of the vineyard, with Sergio putting his money where his winemaking mouth is. Exports to the UK, the US, Canada, Taiwan, Singapore and China.

ϒϒϒϒϒ **The Cut Shiraz 2007** Absolutely remarkable retention of hue; also still has the tannin structure noted when previously tasted in Mar '10, black fruits and spices likewise. Retains the same points and drink-to date, the only change the price, down from $90. Diam. 15% alc. **Rating** 96 To 2022 $65 ✪

Bendigo Shiraz 2013 A single wraparound label has '13 on the front portion, '12 on the side. The wine is co-fermented with some viognier (no percentage stated). This is a very smart, elegant, medium-bodied shiraz with red and black fruits on both the bouquet and the supple, fresh palate. Oak plays a positive role, and the tannins are silky. Screwcap. 14.5% alc. **Rating** 95 To 2038 $26 ✪

Bendigo Cabernet Sauvignon 2012 The colour is spectacular, the bright crimson-purple hue that of a 2yo, not a 5yo wine, possibly due to higher acidity and lower pH than that normally associated with a wine of this alcohol (and origin, for that matter). Cassis is the dominant player on the bouquet and palate, the savoury tannins finely constructed and embedded. A fine cabernet. Screwcap. 14.5% alc. **Rating** 94 To 2032 $26 ✪

ⵟⵟⵟⵟ Bendigo Viognier 2016 Rating 92 To 2020 $28
Bendigo Picolit 2016 Rating 90 To 2019 $55

Twinwoods Estate

Brockman Road, Cowaramup, WA 6284 **Region** Margaret River
T 0419 833 122 **www**.twinwoodsestate.com **Open** Not
Winemaker Deep Woods Estate (Julian Langworthy), Aldo Bratovic **Est.** 2005
Dozens 2500
This is a winery that was bound to succeed. It is owned by the Jebsen family, for many years a major player in the importation and distribution of fine wine in Hong Kong, more recently expanded into China. Fifteen years ago Jebsen invested in a NZ winery, following that with the acquisition of this vineyard in Margaret River in 2005. It brings together senior Jebsen managing director, Gavin Jones, and peripatetic winemaker Aldo Bratovic, who began his career decades ago under the tutelage of Brian Croser. Its widespread distribution is interesting, not all the eggs being put in the Hong Kong/China markets. The quality of the wines I have tasted fully lives up to what one would expect. (I tasted the wines without any knowledge of the background of Twinwoods.) It commenced selling wine in Australia in 2014, with Terroir Selections its Australian partner, another intersection with Brian Croser. Exports to Denmark, Germany, Singapore, Taiwan, Hong Kong, China and NZ.

Twisted Gum Wines

2253 Eukey Road, Ballandean, Qld 4382 **Region** Granite Belt
T (07) 4684 1282 **www**.twistedgum.com.au **Open** W'ends 10–4
Winemaker Andy Williams (Contract) **Est.** 2007 **Dozens** 700 **Vyds** 2.8ha
Tim and Michelle Coelli bring diverse and interesting backgrounds to this venture. During his university days in the early 1980s Tim began reading weekly wine columns of a certain journalist and bought recommended red wines from Wynns and Peter Lehmann, liked the wines, and with wife Michelle 'bought dozens and dozens ...' Tim became a research economist, and during periods of living and working in Europe, he and Michelle became well acquainted with the wines of France, Spain and Italy. Michelle has a degree in agricultural science which, she says, 'has not been well utilised because four children came along'. When they found a beautiful 40ha bush property on a ridge near Ballandean (at an altitude of 900m) with dry-grown vines already planted, they did not hesitate.

ⵟⵟⵟⵟ Single Vineyard Granite Belt Verdelho Semillon 2015 Clean, crisp and well made. Inevitably, it has no clear varietal fruit flavours, but will be refreshing on the hottest of summer days. Particularly impressive given that only 75 dozen bottles were made, and will cellar well if you can keep your hands off it. Screwcap. 13.5% alc. **Rating** 90 To 2020 $25

Two Hands Wines

273 Neldner Road, Marananga, SA 5355 **Region** Barossa Valley
T (08) 8562 4566 **www.**twohandswines.com **Open** 7 days 10–5
Winemaker Ben Perkins **Est.** 2000 **Dozens** 50000 **Vyds** 15ha

The 'hands' in question are those of SA businessmen Michael Twelftree and Richard Mintz, Michael in particular having extensive experience in marketing Australian wine in the US (for other producers). On the principle that if big is good, bigger is better, the style of the wines has been aimed squarely at the palate of Robert Parker Jr and *Wine Spectator*'s Harvey Steiman. Grapes are sourced from the Barossa Valley (where the business has 15ha of shiraz), McLaren Vale, Clare Valley, Langhorne Creek and Padthaway. The emphasis is on sweet fruit and soft tannin structure, all signifying the precise marketing strategy of what is a very successful business. Exports to the US and other major markets.

🍷🍷🍷🍷🍷 **Yacca Block Single Vineyard Mengler Hill Road Eden Valley Shiraz 2015** Another very different wine: it's savoury, intense and mouthwatering, the tannins with feet all of their own. It steps lightly, with red and black fruits, and has that Eden Valley ability to transcend the here and now and look into the future without conscious thought. Diam. 14.2% alc. **Rating** 97 **To** 2040 $100 ✪
Wazza's Block Seppeltsfield Road Shiraz 2015 Speaks with clarity about the Seppeltsfield terroir: an immensely attractive, savoury/spicy character permeates the black fruits, rolling on and on like peals of thunder. An outstanding wine with a great future. Diam. 14.8% alc. **Rating** 97 **To** 2045 $100 ✪
Dave's Block Blythmans Road Blewitt Springs Shiraz 2015 Deep crimson-purple; Blewitt Springs is the sacred place in McLaren Vale, imparting elegant and effortless dark berry fruits on a supple medium-bodied palate, alcohol not worth mentioning. Great fruit and great winemaking. Diam. 15.2% alc. **Rating** 97 **To** 2040 $100 ✪
Aphrodite Barossa Valley Cabernet Sauvignon 2014 Bright crimson-purple; the exemplary varietal expression is immediate in its impact, with flowing cassis supported by fine quality French oak and fine tannins. Each time you return to the wine it seems even better than it was before. A wonderful outcome for the vintage. Diam. 14% alc. **Rating** 97 **To** 2049 $165

🍷🍷🍷🍷🍷 **Windmill Block Single Vineyard Stonewell Road Barossa Valley Shiraz 2015** Great colour; the wine has a striking juicy quality that runs like a stream between the black fruits, ripe tannins, and integrated and balanced oak. The flavours continue in the mouth and aftertaste long after the wine has been swallowed or spat out. Diam. 14.2% alc. **Rating** 96 **To** 2040 $100
Secret Block Single Vineyard Wildlife Road Moppa Hills Shiraz 2015 The oak trembles on the brink of going OTT, but the depth and richness of the purple and black fruits gives every assurance that it (the oak) will be cut down to size within a few more years. The tannins are already balanced and integrated, a staff of life for the future. Diam. 14% alc. **Rating** 96 **To** 2045 $100
Ares Barossa Valley Shiraz 2014 How can you create a luscious, deep-seated array of black fruits and full-on tannins rippling through the palate from start to finish with fruit at 14%? It's an outstanding achievement from any vintage, especially '14. Diam. **Rating** 96 **To** 2044 $165
Harriet's Garden Adelaide Hills Shiraz 2015 Fresh and vibrant with a skip in its heartbeat; astute winemaking has let the cool region speak truly, with red berries, spices and a touch of oak setting the agenda on the bouquet, the medium-bodied palate an exact replay of the bouquet. Delicious now or later. Diam. 13% alc. **Rating** 95 **To** 2030 $60
Lily's Garden McLaren Vale Shiraz 2015 Rating 94 **To** 2035 $60
Twelftree Schuller Blewitt Springs Grenache 2014 Rating 94 **To** 2020 $55

🍷🍷🍷🍷🍷 **Twelftree Strout McLaren Flat Grenache 2014** Rating 93 **To** 2020 $45
Twelftree Vinegrove Greenock Grenache 2014 Rating 93 **To** 2021 $55
Tenacity Old Vine Shiraz 2015 Rating 90 **To** 2024 $18 JF ✪
Charlie's Garden Eden Valley Shiraz 2015 Rating 90 **To** 2035 $60

2 Mates

160 Main Road, McLaren Vale, SA 5171 **Region** McLaren Vale
T 0411 111 198 **www**.2mates.com.au **Open** 7 days 11–5
Winemaker Matt Rechner, Mark Venable, **Est.** 2003 **Dozens** 500 **Vyds** 20ha
The two mates are Mark Venable and David Minear, who say, 'Over a big drink in a small bar
in Italy a few years back, we talked about making "our perfect Australian Shiraz". When we
got back, we decided to have a go.' The wine ('05) was duly made, and won a silver medal at
the Decanter World Wine Awards in London, in some exalted company.

ŸŸŸŸŸ **McLaren Vale Shiraz 2014** Cold-soaked, open-fermented, 23 days on skins,
matured for 28 months in new and used French oak. Bright, full crimson-purple
hue; in heroic full-bodied style, but it brings everything to the table in impeccable
balance, the sombre black fruits with an unexpected juicy mouthfeel. Ideal for
lovers of big Aus shiraz style. Screwcap. 14.9% alc. **Rating** 95 **To** 2044 $35 **✪**

ŸŸŸŸŸ **McLaren Vale Sparkling Shiraz NV** Rating 90 To 2017 $28 TS

Two Rivers ★★★★★

2 Yarrawa Road, Denman, NSW 2328 **Region** Hunter Valley
T (02) 6547 2556 **www**.tworiverswines.com.au **Open** 7 days 11–4
Winemaker Liz Silkman **Est.** 1988 **Dozens** 10 000 **Vyds** 67.5ha
A significant part of the viticultural scene in the Upper Hunter Valley, with 67.5ha of
vineyards, involving an investment of several million dollars. Part of the fruit is sold under
long-term contracts, and part is kept for Two Rivers' winemaking and marketing operations.
The emphasis is on chardonnay and semillon, most rated 95 or 96 points. Two Rivers is also
a partner in the Tulloch business, together with the Tulloch and Angove families, and supplies
grapes for the Tulloch label. A contemporary cellar door adds significantly to the appeal of the
Upper Hunter Valley as a wine-tourist destination. The appointment of immensely talented
winemaker Liz Silkman has had an immediate impact.

ŸŸŸŸŸ **Aged Release Stones Throw Hunter Valley Semillon 2009** Full green-gold;
there's lightly browned toast with a smear of butter, honey and lemon zest, but the
acidity constantly refreshes the mouth as you taste it. At heart, this is still a young
wine. Screwcap. 10.8% alc. **Rating** 96 **To** 2024 $55 **✪**
Stones Throw Hunter Valley Semillon 2014 First tasted Mar '15. It is still
quartz-white, like the day it was born, but the palate is another thing altogether.
Its crushed lemon leaf and spice bouquet quickly leads onto the mouthwatering
flavours of the intense Meyer lemon/lemon zest/lemon juice finish. The price
when first tasted was $16. Screwcap. 10.6% alc. **Rating** 95 **To** 2029 $45
Vigneron's Reserve Hunter Valley Chardonnay 2016 Winemaker Liz
Silkman nee Jackson used 100% new oak for barrel fermentation. Elegant, fresh
and lively, it is one of those gravity-free chardonnays that could be made anywhere,
just floating around the world. Screwcap. 12.5% alc. **Rating** 94 **To** 2023 $26 **✪**

ŸŸŸŸ **Hidden Hive Hunter Valley Verdelho 2016** Rating 89 To 2020 $16 **✪**
Thunderbolt Hunter Valley Shiraz 2015 Rating 89 To 2022 $20

Twofold

142 Beulah Road, Norwood, SA 5067 (postal) **Region** Various
T (02) 9572 7285 **Open** Not
Winemaker Tim Stock, Nick Stock, Neil Pike (Contract) **Est.** 2002 **Dozens** 400
This is the venture of brothers Nick and Tim Stock, both of whom have had varied
backgrounds in the wine industry (primarily at the marketing end, whether as sommeliers
or in wholesale) and both of whom have excellent palates. Their contacts have allowed them
to source single vineyard Rieslings from Sevenhill in the Clare and Eden valleys and a single
vineyard Shiraz from Heathcote.

ΨΨΨΨΨ **Aged Release Clare Valley Riesling 2010** Bright, gleaming green-straw, it is as fresh as a daisy, beautifully balanced and very long. The lime juice of young riesling is still to change shape, giving the wine a 10-year window of opportunity. Screwcap. 12% alc. **Rating** 97 **To** 2026 $40 ◎

ΨΨΨΨΨ **Clare Valley Riesling 2016** From a single dry-grown site in Sevenhill. Quartz-white, but with an immediate burst of lime and apple on both the bouquet and very long palate, finishing with crisp acidity, leaving no doubt that this will develop in similar fashion to its '10 sibling. Screwcap. 11.5% alc. **Rating** 95 **To** 2027 $25 ◎

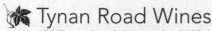 # Tynan Road Wines

185 Tynan Road, Kuitpo, SA 5172 (postal) **Region** Adelaide Hills
T 0413 004 829 **www**.tynanroadwines.com.au **Open** Not
Winemaker Duane Coates **Est.** 2015 **Dozens** 150 **Vyds** 10.25ha
This is the venture of Heidi, a lawyer who wanted a pretty outlook and tolerates the folly of her gastroenterologist husband, Sandy Craig. Living in Kuitpo made the folly eminently reasonable, and they have gone the whole way with building an onsite winery, and securing the services of the experienced and very good winemaker Duane Coates.

ΨΨΨΨΨ **Kuitpo Adelaide Hills Shiraz 2015** A brilliant purple in the glass, this svelte, mid-weighted Syrah offloads lilac, blueberry, iodine and smoked meat aromas. The wine spent close to 40 days on skins, which is considerably longer than the Australian norm, facilitating a gradual build-up of long-chained tannins that are tactile, sinuous and almost chiffon-like as they wash over the mouth. 14% alc. **Rating** 95 **To** 2025 $30 NG ◎

Tyrrell's Wines

1838 Broke Road, Pokolbin, NSW 2321 **Region** Hunter Valley
T (02) 4993 7000 **www**.tyrrells.com.au **Open** Mon–Sat 9–5, Sun 10–4
Winemaker Andrew Spinaze **Est.** 1858 **Dozens** 220 000 **Vyds** 158.22ha
One of the most successful family wineries, a humble operation for the first 110 years of its life that has grown out of all recognition over the past 40. Vat 1 Semillon is one of the most dominant wines in the Australian show system, and Vat 47 Chardonnay is one of the pacesetters for this variety. It has an awesome portfolio of single vineyard Semillons released when 5–6 years old. Its estate plantings are over 116ha in the Hunter Valley, 15ha in the Limestone Coast and 26ha in Heathcote. A founding member of Australia's First Families of Wine. Exports to all major markets.

ΨΨΨΨΨ **Museum Release Vat 1 Hunter Semillon 2005** This is where you marvel at the beauty of perfectly aged Hunter Valley semillon. In pristine condition, hallelujah screwcap, elegant, with toasty brioche and unsalted butter and lemon curd. Superfine palate, long and persistent. What a joy. 11.4% alc. **Rating** 97 **To** 2027 $150 JF ◎

ΨΨΨΨΨ **Single Vineyard Belford Hunter Semillon 2012** The vines were planted in 1933, and produce such distinctive semillon – the smell of petrichor (of rain after a warm spell), the merest hint of toasty complexity. It has the more atypical flavours of lemongrass, lime zest and creamed honey, plus superfine acidity. Stunning semillon. Screwcap. 11.8% alc. **Rating** 96 **To** 2030 $35 JF ◎
Museum Release Vat 1 Hunter Semillon 2012 The extra few years in bottle add another complex layer, a richness that still has the precise, lemony zesty acidity in tow. There's a herbal edge, fresh pine needles and lime curd tart. In a good place but plenty of life ahead of it. Screwcap. 10.5% alc. **Rating** 95 **To** 2025 $80 JF
Single Vineyard HVD Hunter Semillon 2012 There's a wonderful approach into this – nothing is out of place. Sit back and enjoy the evenness of its palate, the acidity almost softish, the lemongrass and slivers of glace lime, the texture: just the yumminess of it. Great drinking. Screwcap. 10.5% alc. **Rating** 95 **To** 2032 $35 JF ◎

Single Vineyard Stevens Hunter Semillon 2012 Heady with white blossom and all manner of citrus notes, especially lime zest and juice flavoured with lemon barley water. So lively and not even hinting at a journey towards aged complexity – it's taking its time. Screwcap. 10.5% alc. **Rating** 95 **To** 2032 $35 JF ✪

Single Vineyard Belford Hunter Chardonnay 2015 Coming off a difficult vintage, this is showing well. Complex, layered with poached quince and ginger and sun-bleached hay, yet tight. Zesty and bright with a lightning rod of acidity, so this needs more time. Screwcap. 13.2% alc. **Rating** 95 **To** 2026 $45 JF

Vat 47 Hunter Chardonnay 2012 Gleaming, full straw-green; shows the mastery Tyrrell's has with chardonnay, appropriate given its pioneer role with the Vat 47 '71. It is complex, textured and balanced, with stone fruit, fig and melon flavours to the fore, acidity tightening up and lengthening the finish. Has three trophies and six golds to its credit. Screwcap. 12.5% alc. **Rating** 95 **To** 2022 $70

🍷🍷🍷🍷🍷 **Single Vineyard SFOV Chardonnay 2013** Rating 92 To 2023 $70
HVD & The Hill Hunter Valley Pinot Noir 2014 Rating 91 To 2025 $30
Lunatiq Heathcote Shiraz 2014 Rating 91 To 2024 $40 JF

🍂 Ubertas Wines   NR

790 Research Road, Light Pass, SA 5355 **Region** Barossa Valley
T (08) 8562 4489 **www.**ubertaswines.com.au **Open** By appt
Winemaker Wine Wise **Est.** 2013 **Dozens** 3500 **Vyds** 12ha
Brothers Phil and Kevin Liu followed their father from Taiwan to mainland China, working for their father's car component factory. In 2006 they made a life-changing decision to migrate to Australia, and saw an opportunity to start a wine export business to China, their business called Rytor. It succeeded, and over the following years they both obtained masters degrees, Phil in oenology from the University of Adelaide, Kevin in marketing from the University of SA. By 2014 they had taken another major step, building and managing their own winery at Light Pass in the Barossa Valley, and are now ('17) in the process of creating a cellar door. Exports to Germany, Japan, Taiwan and China.

Ulithorne   ★★★★★

The Mill at Middleton, 29 Mill Terrace, Middleton, SA 5213 **Region** McLaren Vale
T 0419 040 670 **www.**ulithorne.com.au **Open** W'ends & public hols 10–4
Winemaker Rose Kentish, Brian Light **Est.** 1971 **Dozens** 2500 **Vyds** 7.2ha
Ulithorne produces small quantities of red wines from selected parcels of grapes from a vineyard in McLaren Vale planted by Rose Kentish's father-in-law, Frank Harrison, over 40 years ago. Rose's dream of making small batch, high quality wines from exceptional grapegrowing regions around the world has taken her to France, where she has made a Vermentinu on the island of Corsica and a Rose in Provence under the Ulithorne label. In 2013 Sam Harrison and Rose purchased an old vineyard in the heart of McLaren Vale, with 4ha of shiraz and 3.2ha of grenache dating back to 1945. Exports to the UK, Canada, The Netherlands, Malaysia and China.

🍷🍷🍷🍷🍷 **Unicus McLaren Vale Shiraz 2014** Deep crimson-purple; a striking full-bodied shiraz that keeps its varietal shape and its sense of place; black fruits blot out other fruit flavours, but not the regional dark chocolate. The tannins are plentiful, but round and balanced, and oak also makes a positive contribution. Screwcap. 14.5% alc. **Rating** 96 **To** 2034 $75

Familia McLaren Vale Shiraz 2015 A complex suite of aromas swirl out of the glass in a spicy, savoury dark berry spectrum. New oak makes its presence felt in the focused, medium-bodied palate, but doesn't hide those intriguing savoury nuances in a wine that keeps drawing you back again and again. Screwcap. 14% alc. **Rating** 95 **To** 2035 $40

Dona McLaren Vale Shiraz 2015 Influenced by the time winemaker Rose Kentish spent in the Rhône Valley. It packs a punch, but in the best possible way, distilling the essence of McLaren Vale shiraz into a wine that cannot be denied, its river of black fruits, earth, licorice and high quality tannins unstoppable. Screwcap. 14% alc. **Rating** 95 **To** 2035 $27

Frux Frugis McLaren Vale Shiraz 2014 From estate vines planted in '69. The colour is still a deep, dense crimson-purple, heralding an ultra-powerful and dense wine, its black fruits with an earthy, savoury undertow, licorice, spice and bitter chocolate all present to a lesser or greater degree. Needs time to welcome visitors. Cork. 14.5% alc. **Rating** 94 **To** 2044 $85

ΨΨΨΨΨ **Chi McLaren Vale Shiraz Grenache 2015** Rating 93 To 2021 $40
Specialis McLaren Vale Tempranillo Grenache Graciano 2015 Rating 92 To 2025 $30 SC
Dona Blanc 2016 Rating 91 To 2020 $27
Paternus McLaren Vale Cabernet Sauvignon 2014 Rating 91 To 2034

Umamu Estate ★★★★★

PO Box 1269, Margaret River, WA 6285 **Region** Margaret River
T (08) 9757 5058 **www.**umamuestate.com **Open** Not
Winemaker Bruce Dukes (Contract) **Est.** 2005 **Dozens** 1800 **Vyds** 16.8ha
Chief executive Charmaine Saw explains, 'My life has been a journey towards Umamu. An upbringing in both eastern and western cultures, graduating in natural science, training as a chef, combined with a passion for the arts and experience as a management consultant have all contributed to my building the business creatively yet professionally.' The palindrome Umamu, says Charmaine, is inspired by balance and contentment. In practical terms this means an organic approach to viticulture and a deep respect for the terroir. The plantings, dating back to 1978, include cabernet sauvignon, chardonnay, shiraz, semillon, sauvignon blanc, merlot and cabernet franc. Exports to Hong Kong, Malaysia, Indonesia and the Philippines.

ΨΨΨΨΨ **Margaret River Chardonnay 2014** A deceptive wine – the first reaction is that it is simply immaculately balanced and poised, but then the power and the zesty citrus pith and aftertaste arrive. The white peach of the mid-palate remains untarnished, as does the overall integrity of the wine. Screwcap. 13.8% alc. **Rating** 96 **To** 2024 $51

Margaret River Cabernet Sauvignon 2014 This is the king of grapes speaking, a full-bodied cabernet with blackcurrant, dried bay leaf, black olive and earth all in perfect agreement, tannins as they should be, giving savoury nuances to the finish, French oak likewise. Screwcap. 13.8% alc. **Rating** 96 **To** 2034 $64

Margaret River Cabernet Franc 2015 Good hue, although not especially deep; you can see why this cabernet franc wasn't blended, its elegant redcurrant and raspberry fruit enhanced by subtle French oak and savoury herbal and black olive. Screwcap. 13.4% alc. **Rating** 94 **To** 2028 $38

ΨΨΨΨΨ **Margaret River Sauvignon Blanc Semillon 2016** Rating 91 To 2019 $24

Underground Winemakers ★★★★

1282 Nepean Highway, Mt Eliza, Vic 3931 **Region** Mornington Peninsula
T (03) 9775 4185 **www.**ugwine.com.au **Open** 7 days 10–5
Winemaker Peter Stebbing **Est.** 2004 **Dozens** 10 000 **Vyds** 12ha
Owned by Adrian Hennessy, Jonathon Stevens and Peter Stebbing. Each has made wine in Alsace, Burgundy, Northern Italy and Swan Hill and each has extensive experience in the vineyards and wineries of the Mornington Peninsula. Their first step, in 2004, was to lease a small winery at Mt Eliza that had closed years earlier, but still had a vineyard with some of the oldest plantings of pinot noir, pinot gris and chardonnay on the peninsula. Their portfolio is nothing if not eclectic: Pinot Gris, Pinot Noir and Chardonnay from the Mornington Peninsula, and Durif, Moscato, Cabernet Merlot and Shiraz from Northern and Central Victoria. The San Pietro wines are made according to the philosophy of traditional Italian winegrower San Pietro, who has vineyards in the hills south of Benalla and the Mornington Peninsula (more information at www.sanpietrowine.com).

🍷🍷🍷🍷🍷 **San Pietro Pinot Noir 2016** This pinot noir's aromas are all class, from crunchy red fruits, bing cherry, anise and a litter of herb. The palate, while generous and bouncing with flavour, is tightly bound to ripe, impeccably detailed tannins and bright acidity. Not a hugely complex wine, but one of fruity candour and dangerous drinkability. Screwcap. 13% alc. **Rating** 93 **To** 2022 $30 NG

Black and White Mornington Peninsula Pinot Grigio 2015 Punchy, lightweight and lively, this is made with canny expertise, managing to straddle the nashi pear and marzipan licks of the variety, and with a solo of gentle phenolics and a zesty riff of bright acid crunch and unresolved CO_2. Nothing is excessive. All is in balance. Screwcap. 13% alc. **Rating** 92 **To** 2018 $18 NG ✪

Rose 2016 Comprised of Central Victorian fruit that was bled off skins following 24 hours of maceration, this went through barrel fermentation in older wood and, interestingly, partial mlf. This has conferred a creamy complexity to the wine's bright red fruit complexion, reminiscent of the seldom seen clairette styles of Bordeaux. Very well done. Screwcap. 13% alc. **Rating** 92 **To** 2023 $18 NG ✪

Black and White Mornington Peninsula Pinot Noir 2016 A bright, cool climate pinot of an attractive cherry cola crunch, violet lilt and an auspiciously confident nature. Savoury grape tannins, a dusting of oak and juicy acidity confer mid-palate tension and texture, ravelling it all up into an easygoing nugget of flavour. Screwcap. 13.5% alc. **Rating** 92 **To** 2023 $20 NG ✪

San Pietro Pinot Grigio 2016 Broader across the girth than the Underground-labelled expression, this is not afraid of amplifying its baked apple pie aromas across some phenolic detail and sudsy, warm mouthfeel. The colour is fully flared and copper-tinged, as unadulterated grigio should be. Plenty of flavour in these bones. Screwcap. 12.5% alc. **Rating** 91 **To** 2020 $20 NG ✪

Upper Reach

77 Memorial Avenue, Baskerville, WA 6056 **Region** Swan Valley
T (08) 9296 0078 **www.**upperreach.com.au **Open** 7 days 11–5
Winemaker Derek Pearse **Est.** 1996 **Dozens** 4000 **Vyds** 8.45ha
This 10ha property on the banks of the upper reaches of the Swan River was purchased by Laura Rowe and Derek Pearse in 1996. The original 4ha vineyard was expanded, and plantings now include chardonnay, shiraz, cabernet sauvignon, verdelho, semillon, merlot, petit verdot and muscat. All wines are estate-grown. Several years ago they leased the restaurant area to Anthony and Annalis Broad, who now run Broads Restaurant at Upper Reach, encased by full-length glass doors and surrounded by a deck overlooking the vineyard. They have integrated the cellar door with the restaurant, the glass walls bringing vineyard views into the cellar door, where wines are tasted in Riedel glasses. Next they constructed a deck where visitors can relax and enjoy a glass or two, resulting in *Gourmet Traveller WINE* choosing Upper Reach as the Star Cellar Door in the Swan Valley.

🍷🍷🍷🍷🍷 **Reserve Margaret River Cabernet Sauvignon 2014** From Wilyabrup, matured in new and 1yo French hogsheads. Full crimson-purple; a complex, rich and powerful cabernet awash with cassis doing (successful) battle with its attendant tannins. Add in the logistics of bringing the grapes to the Swan Valley, and the wine becomes even more impressive. Screwcap. 14% alc. **Rating** 95 **To** 2039 $38

Reserve Swan Valley Shiraz 2014 Matured for 12 months in French hogsheads (50% new). This is a very good wine, the fermentation regime allowing shiraz to show its many facets, but there is a question about the amount of oak influence. Mercurey French barrels are of very high quality, and used by many top-flight producers in Australia, so it's easy to vacillate about the answer – the rating is a compromise. Screwcap. 14.5% alc. **Rating** 94 **To** 2034 $38

🍷🍷🍷🍷🍷 **Tempranillo 2014 Rating** 91 **To** 2024 $30

Vasarelli Wines ★★★★

164 Main Road, McLaren Vale, SA 5171 **Region** McLaren Vale
T (08) 8323 7980 **Open** 7 days 8–5
Winemaker Nigel Dolan (Contract) **Est.** 1995 **Dozens** 18 000 **Vyds** 33ha

Pasquale (Pat) and Vittoria (Vicky) Vasarelli moved with their parents from Melbourne to McLaren Vale in 1976. They began the establishment of their vineyard, and over the succeeding years increased the area under vine to its present size, planted to semillon, sauvignon blanc, chardonnay, pinot gris, vermentino, shiraz, cabernet sauvignon and merlot. Until '95 the grapes were sold to other producers, but in that year they joined Cellarmaster Wines and the Vasarelli label was born. In a reverse play of the usual pattern, they opened a cellar door in 2009 on a small property they had purchased in '92.

Pasquale's Selection Single Vineyard McLaren Vale Shiraz Cabernet 2014 A 55/45% blend. The aromas and flavours have a very broad spectrum, ranging through purple and black fruits, spice, licorice and bitter chocolate, the mouthfeel picking up texture from the oak and tannins. Conquers its alcohol. Screwcap. 15% alc. **Rating** 94 **To** 2029 **$45**

Estate Grown Cabernet Sauvignon 2014 **Rating** 90 **To** 2034 **$28**

Vasse Felix ★★★★★

Cnr Tom Cullity Drive/Caves Road, Cowaramup, WA 6284 **Region** Margaret River
T (08) 9756 5000 **www**.vassefelix.com.au **Open** 7 days 10–5
Winemaker Virginia Willcock **Est.** 1967 **Dozens** 150 000 **Vyds** 232ha

Vasse Felix was the first winery to be built in the Margaret River. Owned and operated by the Holmes à Court family since 1987, Vasse Felix has undergone extensive changes and expansion. Chief winemaker Virginia Willcock has energised the winemaking and viticultural team with her no-nonsense approach and fierce commitment to quality. The estate vineyards contribute all but a small part of the annual production, and are scrupulously managed, quality the sole driver. Wines include top of the range Heytesbury (a cabernet blend) and Heytesbury Chardonnay; the premier range of mainly varietal wines; Filius Chardonnay and Cabernet Merlot; and Classic Dry White and Dry Red. Limited quantities of specialty wines include Cane Cut Semillon, Viognier and Tempranillo. Exports to all major markets.

Tom Cullity Margaret River Cabernet Sauvignon Malbec 2013 Don't pay any attention to the slightly light colour, but certainly dwell on the gloriously fragrant bouquet and the intensity of the cassis-accented palate. This is a truly sophisticated blend of 76% cabernet sauvignon, 20% malbec and 4% petit verdot, with exceptional texture, length and aftertaste. Screwcap. 14.5% alc. **Rating** 98 **To** 2033 **$200** ✪

Heytesbury Margaret River Chardonnay 2015 One of the icons of Margaret River, a chardonnay that has had spectacular success in shows over the past 5+ years, this vintage typical. The mouthfeel and balance are flawless, supple yet focused, all the ingredients – fruit, oak, acidity – in perfect harmony and balance. Screwcap. 13% alc. **Rating** 97 **To** 2028 **$75** ✪

Margaret River Chardonnay 2015 The bouquet is still developing, but the palate guarantees the medium to long-term future of a chardonnay with exceptional length and intensity, pear, white peach and grapefruit combining to make light work of the oak. Restrained like a lion on a leash. Screwcap. 13% alc. **Rating** 96 **To** 2025 **$37** ✪

Margaret River Cabernet Sauvignon 2014 It would be hard to find a more elegant, yet razor-sharp expression of Margaret River cabernet. It has cassis nailed to its mast, the sails of bay leaf, perfectly integrated oak and fine-grained, but insistent, tannins. Lovely wine. Screwcap. 14.5% alc. **Rating** 96 **To** 2034 **$45** ✪

Filius Margaret River Cabernet Merlot 2015 51% cabernet sauvignon, 43% merlot, 5% malbec and 1% petit verdot. It has all the hallmarks of the warmer part of Margaret River, flavour building relatively early and sustained throughout the length of the palate. Juicy cassis is the cornerstone, but there are notes of dried herbs, black olive and oak adding complexity and length. Screwcap. 14% alc. Rating 94 To 2029 $28 ○

🍷🍷🍷🍷♀ Margaret River Shiraz 2014 Rating 92 To 2029 $37
Filius Margaret River Cabernet Sauvignon 2015 Rating 91 To 2022 $28
Filius Margaret River Chardonnay 2015 Rating 90 To 2022 $28

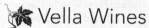 # Vella Wines

PO Box 39, Balhannah, SA 5242 **Region** Adelaide Hills
T 0499 998 484 **www**.vellawines.com.au **Open** Not
Winemaker Mark Vella **Est.** 2013 **Dozens** 750
Mark Vella was blooded at Bloodwood Estate in 1995 (an appalling but inevitable pun). Over the following 22 years Mark has plied his trade as viticulturist in Orange, the Hunter Valley and now (and permanently) the Adelaide Hills. He manages to avoid conflicts of interest in running his vineyard management company, Vitiworks, and pinpointing outstanding parcels of fruit for the Vella brand. A broader conflict (which is in fact no conflict at all) comes from his 12 years of vineyard management, supplying contract-grown fruit for more than 40 of the leading wine producers in SA. He uses Andre Bondar to make his Chardonnay, Franco D'Anna his Pinot Noir, and Daryl Catlin his Pinot Blanc blend.

🍷🍷🍷🍷🍷 Dirt Boy Pinot Noir 2015 A mix of clones MV6 and 777, matured in French oak for 10 months. The bouquet is exceptionally complex, the palate a Siamese twin with the bouquet; a seriously good pinot noir with great length and style. Screwcap. 12.5% alc. **Rating** 96 To 2025 $32 ○
Harvest Widow Chardonnay 2014 Some colour development, but no issue with this; a rich and full palate offers a creamy mix of cashew and stone fruit, balanced and lengthened by citrussy acidity. Screwcap. 12.5% alc. **Rating** 94 To 2022 $32

🍷🍷🍷🍷♀ Troublemaker Pinot Blanc Pinot Gris Gewurztraminer 2016 Rating 93 To 2021 $32

Vickery Wines

28 The Parade, Norwood, SA 5067 **Region** Clare Valley/Eden Valley
T (08) 8362 8622 **www**.vickerywines.com.au **Open** Not
Winemaker John Vickery, Phil Lehmann **Est.** 2014 **Dozens** 4000 **Vyds** 12ha
It must be a strange feeling for John Vickery to begin at the beginning again, 60 years after his first vintage, in 1951. His interest in, love of, and exceptional skills with riesling began with Leo Buring in '55 at Chateau Leonay. Over the intervening years he became the uncrowned but absolute monarch of riesling makers in Australia until, in his semi-retirement, he passed the mantle on to Jeffrey Grosset. Along the way he had (unsurprisingly) won the Wolf Blass Riesling Award at the Canberra International Riesling Challenge 2007, and had been judged by his peers as Australia's Greatest Living Winemaker in a survey conducted by The Age Epicure in '03. His new venture has been undertaken in conjunction with Phil Lehmann, with 12ha of Clare and Eden Valley riesling involved, and wine marketer Jonathon Hesketh moving largely invisibly in the background. The Da Vinci code letters and numerals are easy when it comes to EVR (Eden Valley Riesling) and WVR (Watervale Riesling), but thereafter the code strikes. The numerics are the dates of harvest, thus '103' is 10 March, '172' is 17 February. The two initials that follow are even more delphic, standing for the name of the vineyard or those of the multiple owners. Exports to the UK, the EU and Canada.

🍷🍷🍷🍷🍷 Eden Valley Riesling 2016 EVR 153 ZMR. Gleaming straw-green; classic young Eden Valley riesling, its citrus aromas and flavours on the midpoint between lime and lemon, the acidity flowing calmly on in the wake of the fruit, purity the watchword. Screwcap. 12.5% alc. **Rating** 96 To 2031 $23 ○
Watervale Riesling 2016 WVR 252 CK. Light, bright straw-green; manages to fill the senses with its Catherine wheel of citrus fruits, already with great balance and varietal expression. A prime each-way bet, now or later Screwcap. 12.5% alc. **Rating** 95 To 2029 $23 ○

Victory Point Wines   ★★★★★

4 Holben Road, Cowaramup, WA 6284 **Region** Margaret River
T 0417 954 655 **www**.victorypointwines.com **Open** By appt
Winemaker Mark Messenger (Contract) **Est.** 1997 **Dozens** 2000 **Vyds** 13ha
Judith and Gary Berson have set their sights high. They established their vineyard without
irrigation, emulating those of the Margaret River pioneers (including Moss Wood). The fully
mature plantings comprise 4.2ha chardonnay and 0.5ha of pinot noir, the remainder Bordeaux
varieties, with cabernet sauvignon (6.2ha), cabernet franc (0.5ha), malbec (0.8ha) and petit
verdot (0.7ha).

ᵀᵀᵀᵀᵀ **Margaret River Chardonnay 2013** A distinguished mix of the Dijon clones
(59%) and Mendoza (41%). This is a very good chardonnay, even by Margaret
River standards, tightly wound and focused, the fruit/oak balance perfect, likewise
that of the citrus and stone fruits. Screwcap. 13.5% alc. **Rating** 96 **To** 2023 $45 ✪
Margaret River Rose 2016 Cabernet franc, pinot noir and malbec. Pale pink; a
vibrant, pure and delicious rose, so much so I was tempted to have a mouthful at
7am on a long day of tasting. The articulation of the red fruits, the silky mouthfeel,
the length and the fruit-acid balance are all perfect. Screwcap. 13.5% alc. **Rating**
96 **To** 2017 $23 ✪
Margaret River Cabernet Sauvignon 2013 Includes 9% petit verdot and
2% malbec, matured in French oak (20% new) for 15 months before extensive
blending trials. Deep crimson-purple; while full-bodied, the fruit-tannin-oak
balance of the wine makes it seem light on its feet, and confers length (plus
longevity). Screwcap. 14% alc. **Rating** 95 **To** 2038 $45
**The Mallee Root Margaret River Malbec Cabernet Sauvignon Petit
Verdot 2015** A 62/33/5% blend vinified and matured separately. Bright colour; a
wine full of nervosity (a French word, but needed here) thanks to its bright acidity
linked with fine tannins. Screwcap. 14% alc. **Rating** 94 **To** 2029 $28 ✪

View Road Wines   ★★★★

Peacocks Road, Lenswood, SA 5240 **Region** Adelaide Hills
T 0402 180 383 **www**.viewroadwines.com.au **Open** Not
Winemaker Josh Tuckfield **Est.** 2011 **Dozens** 1000
View Road Wines sources prosecco, arneis, chardonnay, sangiovese, merlot, sagrantino and
syrah from Adelaide Hills vineyards; shiraz, aglianico and sagrantino from McLaren Vale
vineyards; and nero d'Avola and fiano from the Riverland. All of the wines are wild-yeast
fermented, and matured in used oak.

ᵀᵀᵀᵀᵀ **Picked by my Wife Lenswood Chardonnay 2015** From an undisclosed
'mystery block' that also supplies Penfolds Yattarna. High quality chardonnay; it
retains life-sustaining crunchy citrussy acidity throughout the finely strung palate
and finish, oak used as (an all-important) vehicle. If all the hullabaloo about
Penfolds is true, the price is far too low. Screwcap. 13.3% alc. **Rating** 94 **To** 2025
$25 ✪

🌿 Vigena Wines   ★★★★

210 Main Road, Willunga, SA 5172 **Region** McLaren Vale
T 0433 966 011 **Open** Not
Winemaker Ben Heide **Est.** 2010 **Dozens** 30 000 **Vyds** 15.8ha
The principal business of Vigena Wines is exports to Singapore, Hong Kong and China. In
recent years the vineyard has been revitalised, with one significant change: chardonnay being
grafted to shiraz, giving the business a 100% red wine focus.

ᵀᵀᵀᵀᵀ **Gran Reserve McLaren Vale Shiraz 2014** 87% from Blewitt Springs,
13% Moppa, matured for 18 months in American (80%) and French (20%) oak,
70% new. A very full-bodied wine with max black fruits, max tannins, although

soft, and max oak needing time to lower its lance – which it will do. More points with age. High quality cork. 14.5% alc. **Rating** 94 **To** 2044 $35

McLaren Vale Shiraz Cabernet 2014 Peculiar: the front label says 'South Australia' (normally for multi-region blends), while the back label says McLaren Vale (95%) and Barossa Valley (5%) The wine is full-bodied, but much less extractive than the '12. Oak, of course, is a major contributor, but there is plenty of supple regional blackcurrant and blackberry fruit flavour, the tannins fine. Intriguing wine. High quality cork. 14% alc. **Rating** 94 **To** 2034 $32

🍷🍷🍷🍷 **McLaren Vale Shiraz 2012 Rating** 90 **To** 2042 $28

Vigna Bottin ★★★★

Lot 2 Plains Road, Sellicks Hill, McLaren Vale, SA 5171 **Region** McLaren Vale
T 0414 562 956 **www**.vignabottin.com.au **Open** Not
Winemaker Paolo Bottin **Est.** 2006 **Dozens** 1800 **Vyds** 16.45ha

The Bottin family migrated to Australia in 1954 from Treviso in northern Italy, where they were grapegrowers. The family began growing grapes in McLaren Vale in '70, focusing on mainstream varieties for sale to wineries in the region. When son Paolo and wife Maria made a trip back to Italy in '98, they were inspired to do more, and, says Paolo, 'My love for barbera and sangiovese was sealed during a vintage in Pavia. I came straight home to plant both varieties in our family plot. My father was finally happy!' They now trade under the catchy phrase 'Italian Vines, Australian Wines'.

🍷🍷🍷🍷 **McLaren Vale Vermentino 2016** It's not surprising that vermentino is finding a happy home in the Mediterranean climes of McLaren Vale, and here's another to prove it: savoury, with lemon bath salts and citrussy saline. So crisp you can hear the crunch. Screwcap. 12.8% alc. **Rating** 92 **To** 2018 $24 JF ✪

McLaren Vale Sangiovese Rosato 2016 Pale fuchsia; this is spicy, smoky, with zesty crunchy acidity ensuring it's super lively, but there's texture too and it finishes neat and dry. Screwcap. 12.7% alc. **Rating** 92 **To** 2019 $24 JF ✪

McLaren Vale Fiano 2016 Wafts of lavender and lemon blossom, with the palate still quite reserved, offering up some pear juice, sweet-sour drops and bright acidity, all attractive elements. Screwcap. 12.7% alc. **Rating** 91 **To** 2019 $24 JF

Vignerons Schmolzer & Brown ★★★★☆

39 Thorley Road, Stanley, Vic 3747 **Region** Beechworth
T 0411 053 487 **www**.vsandb.com.au **Open** By appt
Winemaker Tessa Brown **Est.** 2014 **Dozens** 500 **Vyds** 2ha

Winemaker/viticulturist Tessa Brown graduated from CSU with a degree in viticulture in the late 1990s, and undertook postgraduate winemaking studies at Adelaide University in the mid-2000s. Her self-description of being 'reasonably peripatetic' covers her winemaking in Orange in '99, and Canberra, SA, Strathbogie Ranges, Rioja and Central Otago, before joining Kooyong and Port Phillip Estate in '08. In '09 Mark Walpole showed Tess and architect partner Jeremy Schmolzer a property that he described as 'the jewel in the crown of Beechworth'. When it came onto the market unexpectedly in '12, they were in a position to jump. The property (named Thorley) was 20ha, and cleared; they have planted chardonnay, shiraz, riesling and nebbiolo. By sheer chance, just across the road from Thorley was a tiny vineyard, a bit over 0.4ha, with dry-grown pinot and chardonnay around 20 years old. When they realised it was not being managed for production, they struck up a working relationship with the owners, getting the vineyard into shape, and made their first (very good) wines in '14.

🍷🍷🍷🍷🍷 **Brunnen Beechworth Chardonnay 2015** One of those unusual wines that becomes more elegant and refined the more you come back to it. While it has the Beechworth stamp of generosity at its heart, the oak is subtle, and the acidity is lively despite partial mlf. It is rich in stone fruit, but with a grapefruity cut linked to the acidity. Screwcap. 13% alc. **Rating** 95 **To** 2022 $41

Pret-a-Rose 2016 60/40% blend of sangiovese and pinot noir. It is a powerful, fruit-laden, yet dry, style with a background of multi-spice to its savoury red fruits. No limits to its adaptability at the table. Screwcap. 13% alc. **Rating** 94 **To** 2020 $28 ○

🍷🍷🍷🍷♀ **Brunnen Beechworth Pinot Noir 2015 Rating** 91 **To** 2022 $41

Vinaceous Wines   ★★★★★

49 Bennett Street, East Perth, WA 6004 (postal) **Region** Various
T (08) 9221 4666 **www**.vinaceous.com.au **Open** Not
Winemaker Gavin Berry, Michael Kerrigan **Est.** 2007 **Dozens** 25 000
This is the somewhat quirky venture of wine marketer Nick Stacy, Michael Kerrigan (winemaker/partner Hay Shed Hill) and Gavin Berry (winemaker/partner West Cape Howe). The fast-moving and fast-growing brand was originally directed at the US market, but has changed direction due to the domestic demand engendered (one might guess) by the decidedly exotic/erotic labels and, more importantly, by the fact that the wines are of seriously good quality and equally good value. Margaret River provides over half of the production, the remainder from McLaren Vale and the Adelaide Hills. Yet more labels, ranges and wines are in the pipeline; the website is the best method of keeping up to date. Exports to the UK, the US, Canada, South America, Denmark, Finland, Indonesia, the Philippines, Thailand, Singapore and Hong Kong.

🍷🍷🍷🍷🍷 **Right Reverend V Syrah 2014** Matured for 15 months in new and used French barriques; the texture and structure are major pluses, neatly framing the spicy/savoury/peppery mix of dark cherry and plum fruit of a thoroughly enjoyable wine. Great value. Screwcap. 14.5% alc. **Rating** 95 **To** 2024 $24 ○
Clandestine Vineyards #1 McLaren Vale Grenache 2015 A joyous celebration of grenache grown above Clarendon, super elegant and silky, made with sensitivity, throwing the focus on the purity of the fruit. Screwcap. 14.5% alc. **Rating** 95 **To** 2025 $40

🍷🍷🍷🍷♀ **Right Reverend V Riesling 2016 Rating** 93 **To** 2025 $24 JF ○
Red Right Hand Margaret River Shiraz Grenache Tempranillo 2015 **Rating** 93 **To** 2024 $25 JF ○
Right Reverend V Chardonnay 2015 Rating 92 **To** 2021 $24 ○
Impavido Mount Barker Vermentino 2016 Rating 91 **To** 2019 $22 ○
Right Reverend V Rose 2016 Rating 91 **To** 2019 $24
Salome Tempranillo Rose 2016 Rating 91 **To** 2019 $22 ○
Snake Charmer McLaren Vale Shiraz 2015 Rating 90 **To** 2023 $25 JF
Voodoo Moon Margaret River Malbec 2015 Rating 90 **To** 2023 $25

Vinden Estate   ★★★★★

138 Gillards Road, Pokolbin, NSW 2320 **Region** Hunter Valley
T (02) 4998 7410 **www**.vindenestate.com.au **Open** Wed–Sun 10–5
Winemaker Angus Vinden, Daniel Binet **Est.** 1998 **Dozens** 4000 **Vyds** 6.5ha
Sandra and Guy Vinden have a beautiful home and cellar door, landscaped gardens and a vineyard that includes shiraz (2.5ha), merlot and alicante bouschet (2ha each), with the Brokenback mountain range in the distance. The wines are made onsite, using estate-grown red grapes; semillon and chardonnay are purchased from other growers. The reds are open-fermented, hand-plunged and basket-pressed.

🍷🍷🍷🍷🍷 **The Vinden Headcase Hunter Valley Semillon 2016** Talc, oyster shell, lemon zest and a whiff of salt air in the mind's eye are its pillars. This is all tangy acid pulse and gentle phenolic pull. Far from the Madding Crowd for the region, but a winning expression of old vine Hunter semillon treated with due respect. Screwcap. 10% alc. **Rating** 95 **To** 2030 $30 NG ○

Basket Press Hunter Valley Shiraz 2014 Exemplary Hunter shiraz from a fine vintage, this is all bing cherry, black plum and warm terracotta notes wafting across a medium body. The sumptuous fruit is drawn across an energetic mineral undercurrent and Hunter's savoury, anise-macerated tannins. It would be a shame to lock this away for too long given its plenitude of exuberance. Screwcap. 14% alc. **Rating** 95 **To** 2022 $38 NG

ŸŸŸŸŸ **Hunter Valley Semillon 2016** Rating 93 To 2026 $28 NG
Hunter Valley Semillon 2014 Rating 93 To 2028 $35 NG
Reserve Hunter Valley Semillon 2015 Rating 92 To 2025 $35 NG
Back Block Hunter Valley Shiraz 2010 Rating 92 To 2025 $60 NG
The Vinden Headcase Rose 2016 Rating 91 To 2018 $30 NG

Vinea Marson ★★★★★

411 Heathcote-Rochester Road, Heathcote, Vic 3523 **Region** Heathcote
T 0417 035 673 **www**.vineamarson.com **Open** By appt
Winemaker Mario Marson **Est.** 2000 **Dozens** 2500 **Vyds** 7.12ha
Owner-winemaker Mario Marson spent many years as the winemaker/viticulturist with the late Dr John Middleton at the celebrated Mount Mary. Mario has over 35 years of experience in Australia and overseas, having undertaken vintages at Isole e Olena in Tuscany and Piedmont, and Domaine de la Pousse d'Or in Burgundy, where he was inspired to emulate the multi-clonal wines favoured by these producers, pioneered in Australia by John Middleton. In 1999 he and his wife, Helen, purchased the Vinea Marson property on the eastern slopes of the Mt Camel Range, and have planted shiraz and viognier, plus Italian varieties sangiovese, nebbiolo, barbera and refosco dal peduncolo. Marson also sources north-eastern Italian varietals from Porepunkah in the Alpine Valleys.

ŸŸŸŸŸ **Viognier 2014** Mario Marson has handled this prickly variety with panache, making it seem all too easy. It has complex flavour, texture and structure, yet avoids phenolics. The bright straw-green colour is a good guide for a wine with stone fruits, including, of course, apricot, and fresh citrus-tinged acidity, oak in its due place quietly contributing. Diam. 14% alc. **Rating** 95 **To** 2024 $30
Syrah 2013 Has impressive textural and flavour complexity to its bouquet and medium-bodied palate; the 30% new French oak has been absorbed into the fabric of the wine, as have the tannins. Mario Marson at his best. Diam. 14% alc. **Rating** 95 **To** 2033 $40
Sangiovese 2013 The bouquet is full of an Arabian bazaar of exotic warm spices over a compote of cherry and plum; the savoury side of sangiovese takes control of the palate – a tale of two cities, but a compelling one. Diam. 14% alc. **Rating** 95 **To** 2023 $40
Nebbiolo 2012 Clear red, grading to onion skin on the rim; truly interesting, with silky, spicy preserved red fruits, fresh acidity, and tannins polished to a high lustre. Diam. 14% alc. **Rating** 94 **To** 2022 $45

ŸŸŸŸŸ **Rose 2014** Rating 91 To 2019 $28

Vinifera Wines ★★★★☆

194 Henry Lawson Drive, Mudgee, NSW 2850 **Region** Mudgee
T (02) 6372 2461 **www**.viniferawines.com.au **Open** Mon–Sat 10–5, Sun 10–4
Winemaker Jacob Stein **Est.** 1997 **Dozens** 1200 **Vyds** 12ha
Having lived in Mudgee for 15 years, Tony McKendry (a regional medical superintendent) and wife Debbie succumbed to the lure; they planted their small (1.5ha) vineyard in 1995. In Debbie's words, 'Tony, in his spare two minutes per day, also decided to start Wine Science at CSU in 1992.' She continues, 'His trying to live 27 hours per day (plus our four kids!) fell to pieces when he was involved in a severe car smash in 1997. Two months in hospital stopped full-time medical work, and the winery dreams became inevitable.' Financial compensation finally came through and the small winery was built. The now-expanded vineyard includes chardonnay, cabernet sauvignon (3ha each), semillon, tempranillo, grenache (1.5ha each) and smaller plantings of graciano and monastrell.

ŶŶŶŶ **Organic Mudgee Tempranillo 2015** The colour isn't deep, and in fruit terms
the spicy red cherry fruit isn't strong – until the fine, savoury tannins swing
into play. It is disjointed right now, but should settle down given a year or two.
Screwcap. 14.5% alc. **Rating** 89 **To** 2022

Vinrock   ★★★★

1/25 George Street, Thebarton, SA 5031 (postal) **Region** McLaren Vale
T (08) 8408 8900 **www**.vinrock.com **Open** Not
Winemaker Michael Fragos **Est.** 1998 **Dozens** 13 000 **Vyds** 30ha
Owners Don Luca, Marco Iannetti and Anthony De Pizzol all have backgrounds in the wine
industry, none more than Don, a former board member of Tatachilla. He also planted the Luca
Vineyard in 1998 (21ha of shiraz, 5ha grenache and 4ha cabernet sauvignon). The majority of
the grapes are sold, but steadily increasing quantities of wine have been made from the best
blocks in the vineyard, many at tempting prices.

ŶŶŶŶŶ **McLaren Vale Grenache Shiraz Mourvedre 2015** It gets the balance right.
The sweet fruit, the leathery notes, the spice, the silky tannin. And while the fruit
almost enters ultra-ripe territory, it remains fresh/vibrant. Screwcap. 14.5% alc.
Rating 92 **To** 2021 $25 CM ✪
McLaren Vale Cabernet Sauvignon 2015 This cabernet is clearly a warm
climate expression, with oodles of blackcurrant fruit mingling with finely wrought
grape tannins and lashes of oak, all finding an uncanny confluence on the long
finish. Screwcap. 14.5% alc. **Rating** 92 **To** 2025 $25 NG ✪
Terra Mia McLaren Vale Shiraz Mataro 2015 Dark purple-garnet; pleasing
aromatics of spice, florals and fruit; fleshy tannins, fuller-bodied, with a savoury
appeal of prosciutto and warm earth and kept fresh by snappy acidity. Screwcap.
14.5% alc. **Rating** 90 **To** 2021 $18 JF ✪
McLaren Vale Grenache 2015 Grenache that's immeasurable slurpy and
gluggable now, brimming with ripe raspberries, musk and woodsy spices, which
lead onto the medium-bodied palate. It's restrained, if uncomplicated, with the
snappy acidity tempering sandy tannins. Screwcap. 14.5% alc. **Rating** 90 **To** 2020
$25 JF

ŶŶŶŶ **McLaren Vale Shiraz 2015 Rating** 89 **To** 2026 $25 JF

Vintners Ridge Estate   ★★★☆

Lot 18 Veraison Place, Yallingup, Margaret River, WA 6285 **Region** Margaret River
T 0417 956 943 **www**.vintnersridge.com.au **Open** By appt
Winemaker Flying Fish Cove (Simon Ding) **Est.** 2001 **Dozens** 500 **Vyds** 2.1ha
When Maree and Robin Adair purchased the Vintners Ridge vineyard in 2006 (cabernet
sauvignon), it had already produced three crops, having been planted in Nov '01. The vineyard
overlooks the picturesque Geographe Bay.

ŶŶŶŶŶ **Margaret River Cabernet Sauvignon 2015** Give this some time to open
up so it can fully reveal its mix of boysenberries, blackberries and mulberries.
While it holds very ripe fruit, it's largely fresh and vibrant. Full-bodied, richly
flavoured with some earthy tones and eucalypt, supple tannins and a smooth finish.
Screwcap. 15% alc. **Rating** 90 **To** 2024 $25 JF

Virago Vineyard   ★★★★☆

40 Boundary Road, Everton Upper, Vic 3678 **Region** Beechworth
T 0411 718 369 **www**.viragobeechworth.com.au **Open** By appt
Winemaker Karen Coats, Rick Kinzbrunner **Est.** 2007 **Dozens** 175 **Vyds** 1ha
Karen Coats was a tax accountant in her previous life, but has now completed a Bachelor of
Wine Science degree at CSU. It was her love of nebbiolo and the Beechworth region that
made Virago Vineyard her new office of choice. Prue Keith is an orthopaedic surgeon by day,
night and weekend, devoting her free time (whatever is not occupied by mountain biking,
skiing and trekking to the peaks of mountains) to Virago Vineyard. She clearly has the same

star sign as I do. The vines had been removed from the property long before they purchased it, but the existing terracing, old posts and broken wires laid down a challenge that was easily accepted, although the planting of nebbiolo was not so easy. The one and only Rick Kinzbrunner has a more than passing interest in nebbiolo, so it was inevitable that he would be the contract winemaker.

ꢰꢰꢰꢰꢰ **La Mistura Nebbiolo 2013** Bing cherry and the archetypal notes of sandalwood and dried flowers drift from the glass, drawing one in. Hints of root beer, mint and mulch ensue. The tannins and acidity combine to mesh the fruit into a layered whole, thrusting the flavours long and broad. The overall impression is one of juiciness, energy and delicacy; reminiscent of a fine-boned pinot noir. Rating 95 To 2025 $27 NG

Virgara Wines ★★★★
143 Heaslip Road, Angle Vale, SA 5117 **Region** Adelaide Plains
T (08) 8284 7688 **www**.virgarawines.com.au **Open** Mon–Fri 9–5, w'ends 11–4
Winemaker Tony Carapetis **Est.** 2001 **Dozens** 55 000 **Vyds** 118ha
In 1962 the Virgara family – father Michael, mother Maria and 10 children – migrated to Australia from southern Italy. Through the hard work so typical of many such families, in due course they became market gardeners on land purchased at Angle Vale ('67), and in the early '90s acquired an existing vineyard in Angle Vale. The plantings have since expanded to almost 120ha of shiraz, cabernet sauvignon, grenache, malbec, merlot, riesling, sangiovese, sauvignon blanc, pinot grigio and alicante bouschet. In 2001 the Virgara brothers purchased the former Barossa Valley Estates winery, but used it only for storage and maturation. The death of Domenic Virgara in a road accident led to the employment of former Palandri (and, before that, Tahbilk) winemaker Tony Carapetis, and the full re-commissioning of the winery. Exports to the US, Canada, China, Thailand, Malaysia and Japan.

ꢰꢰꢰꢰꢰ **Five Brothers Adelaide Shiraz 2013** 12% cabernet in the blend and maturation in French oak have transformed the wine; it would go too far to describe it as elegant, but it is balanced, and its dark berry fruits show no sign of heat. Diam. 14.8% alc. Rating 93 To 2018 $99
Adelaide Cabernet Sauvignon 2014 Matured for 15 months in new and 2yo French oak, 3% malbec a garnish. It is surprisingly tight, bay leaf and dried herbs all in play alongside blackcurrant fruit and savoury oak. A considerable achievement for such a hot region. Diam. 14.5% alc. Rating 90 To 2025 $18 ✪

Vogel ★★★★
324 Massey Road, Watchem West, Vic 3482 (postal) **Region** Grampians
T (03) 5281 2230 **Open** Not
Winemaker Sam Vogel **Est.** 1998 **Dozens** 150
Sam Vogel is a graduate in wine science from CSU, and worked in Margaret River and the Rhône Valley before joining Scott Ireland at Provenance Wines in Geelong. The eponymous winemaking venture focuses on cool climate shiraz using both Old and New World practices; he generally includes 20% whole bunches, believing this provides greater complexity, in terms of both structure and aromas.

ꢰꢰꢰꢰꢰ **Geelong Pinot Noir 2015** Good hue and depth; the '14 was whole bunches, and this could well be the same; it has attractive plum and cherry fruit with good length and overall balance. Screwcap. Rating 94 To 2024 $35

ꢰꢰꢰꢰꢰ **Otways Sauvignon Blanc 2015** Rating 90 To 2018 $35

Voyager Estate ★★★★★
Lot 1 Stevens Road, Margaret River, WA 6285 **Region** Margaret River
T (08) 9757 6354 **www**.voyagerestate.com.au **Open** 7 days 10–5
Winemaker Steve James, Travis Lemm **Est.** 1978 **Dozens** 40 000 **Vyds** 110ha

The late mining magnate Michael Wright pursued several avenues of business and agriculture before setting his sights on owning a vineyard and winery. It was thus an easy decision when he was able to buy what was then called Freycinet Estate from founder and leading viticulturist Peter Gherardi in 1991. Peter had established the vineyard in '78, and it was significantly expanded by Michael over the ensuing years. Apart from the Cape Dutch-style tasting room and vast rose garden, the signpost for the estate is the massive Australian flag pole – after Parliament House in Canberra, the largest flag pole in Australia. Michael's daughter, Alexandra Burt, has been at the helm of Voyager Estate for many years, supported by general manager Chris Furtado and a long-serving and committed staff. Michael is remembered as a larger-than life character, more at home in his favourite work pants and boots than a suit, and never happier than when trundling around the estate on a four-wheeler or fixing a piece of machinery. Exports to the UK, the US, Canada, Germany, Indonesia, Singapore, Japan, Hong Kong and China.

🍷🍷🍷🍷🍷 **Margaret River Cabernet Sauvignon Merlot 2014** Margaret River sets the standard for this and similar blends for the rest of Aus. It is delicious despite its youth and medium to full-bodied weight. It bursts with cassis fruit, earthy black olive notes merely serving to highlight the fruit, the tannins exactly as they should be, the high quality oak balanced. Screwcap. 14% alc. **Rating** 96 **To** 2044
Margaret River Chardonnay 2013 Typical Voyager style, complex and layered. While the vineyard plays a significant role (as it should), vinification and blending of barrels are also important. Stone fruit, melon and fig go hand in glove with citrussy acidity to refresh the finish and aftertaste. Screwcap. 13.5% alc. **Rating** 95 **To** 2023 $45
North Block U12 Margaret River Cabernet Sauvignon 2013 This seriously good wine is deep crimson-purple in colour with aromas of dark cherry/blackcurrant fruit and some savoury nuances. There is a core of pure and focused cabernet fruit on the palate, excellent depth, and the tannins are supremely ripe and fine. Screwcap. 14% alc. **Rating** 95 **To** 2030 $90 PR
Old Block V9 Margaret River Cabernet Sauvignon 2013 This superb expression of cabernet is sourced from the original '78 plantings, and spent 18 months in French oak. The result is a wine that is discreet yet powerful, with blackcurrant and cedar notes. Concentrated and tightly wound, the best is yet to come. Screwcap. 14% alc. **Rating** 94 **To** 2030 $90 PR

🍷🍷🍷🍷🍷 **Girt by Sea Margaret River Chardonnay 2016** Rating 92 To 2020 $28 PR
Margaret River Cabernet Sauvignon Merlot 2013 Rating 92 $70 PR
Margaret River Chenin ++ 2016 Rating 91 To 2020 $20 PR ✪
Margaret River Shiraz 2015 Rating 91 $38 PR

Walter Clappis Wine Co   ★★★★

Rifle Range Road, McLaren Vale, SA 5171 **Region** McLaren Vale
T (08) 8323 8818 **www**.hedonistwines.com.au **Open** Not
Winemaker Walter and Kimberley Clappis, James Cooter **Est.** 1982 **Dozens** 18 000
Vyds 35ha
Walter Clappis has been making wine in McLaren Vale for well over 30 years, and over that time has won innumerable trophies and gold medals, including the prestigious George Mackey Memorial Trophy with his 2009 The Hedonist Shiraz, chosen as the best wine exported from Australia for the year in question. He now has daughter Kimberley and son-in-law James Cooter, both with impressive CVs, supporting him on the winery floor. The estate plantings of shiraz (14ha), cabernet sauvignon (10ha), merlot (9ha) and tempranillo (2ha) are the cornerstone of his business, which provides the home for the Amicus and The Hedonist wines. Exports include the UK, the US, Canada and China.

🍷🍷🍷🍷🍷 **The Hedonist McLaren Vale Tempranillo 2015** Although the vines are young (7yo), this suggests the site has great potential. There is truly lovely cherry fruit on the fresh light to medium-bodied palate, thanks in part to the controlled alcohol;

the finish has gently savoury tannins that tie the parcel up ever so neatly. Screwcap.
13.5% alc. Rating 94 To 2025 $25

🍷🍷🍷🍷 The Hedonist Sangiovese Rose 2016 Rating 91 To 2021 $22
The Hedonist McLaren Vale Shiraz 2015 Rating 91 To 2030 $25
The Hedonist McLaren Vale Sangiovese 2015 Rating 91 To 2021 $25
Down the Rabbit Hole Friends & Lovers McLaren Vale Rose 2016
Rating 90 To 2020 $26
Down The Rabbit Hole McLaren Vale Shiraz 2015 Rating 90 To 2028 $26
Down the Rabbit Hole McLaren Vale Sangiovese Cabernet 2015
Rating 90 To 2023 $26

Wanted Man ★★★★

School House Lane, Heathcote, Vic 3523 **Region** Heathcote
T (03) 9654 4664 **www**.wantedman.com.au **Open** Not
Winemaker Matt Harrop, Simon Osicka **Est.** 1996 **Dozens** 2000 **Vyds** 9.3ha
The Wanted Man vineyard was planted in 1996, and has been managed by Andrew Clarke
since 2000, producing Jinks Creek's Heathcote Shiraz. That wine was sufficiently impressive
to lead Andrew and partner Peter Bartholomew (a Melbourne restaurateur) to purchase the
vineyard in 2006, and give it its own identity. The vineyard is planted to shiraz (4ha), marsanne,
viognier, grenache, roussanne and mourvedre. The quirky Ned Kelly label is the work of
Mark Knight, cartoonist for the *Herald Sun*. Exports to the UK, Canada, Denmark, France
and Hong Kong.

🍷🍷🍷🍷 White Label Heathcote Shiraz 2014 Matured in mainly older, large format
French barrels, this delicious and uncomplicated Heathcote shiraz has mainly
dark fruits, together with a little spice, which follows onto the medium-bodied,
balanced and refreshing palate. Screwcap. 13.5% alc. **Rating** 91 To 2024 $30 PR

Wantirna Estate ★★★★★

10 Bushy Park Lane, Wantirna South, Vic 3152 **Region** Yarra Valley
T (03) 9801 2367 **www**.wantirnaestate.com.au **Open** Not
Winemaker Maryann and Reg Egan **Est.** 1963 **Dozens** 830 **Vyds** 4.2ha
Reg and Tina Egan were among the early movers in the rebirth of the Yarra Valley. The
vineyard surrounds the house they live in, which also incorporates the winery. These days
Reg describes himself as the interfering winemaker, but in the early years he did everything,
dashing from his legal practice to the winery to check on the ferments. Today much of the
winemaking responsibility has been transferred to daughter Maryann, who has a degree in
wine science from CSU. Both have honed their practical skills among the small domaines
and chateaux of Burgundy and Bordeaux, inspired by single vineyard, terroir-driven wines.
Maryann was also winemaker for many years in Domaine Chandon's infancy. Exports to
Hong Kong, Singapore and Japan.

🍷🍷🍷🍷🍷 Amelia Yarra Valley Cabernet Sauvignon Merlot 2014 A very elegant cool-
grown blend with a fragrant bouquet of violets and rosehip, the supple medium-
bodied palate with savoury foresty nuances, mint notes also in play. French oak has
been carefully managed so as not to upstage the fruit and the superfine tannins.
Screwcap. 12.5% alc. **Rating** 95 To 2024 $70
Isabella Yarra Valley Chardonnay 2015 Takes no prisoners as it wends its way
across and along the palate. The texture is such that it almost brings a savoury note;
certainly fig and some grilled cashew notes build layered complexity. Screwcap.
13.5% alc. **Rating** 94 To 2025 $70

🍷🍷🍷🍷 Lily Yarra Valley Pinot Noir 2015 Rating 91 To 2022 $70

Warner Glen Estate

PO Box 218, Melville, WA 6956 **Region** Margaret River
T 0457 482 957 **Open** Not
Winemaker Various **Est.** 1993 **Dozens** 6000 **Vyds** 34.6ha
The primary fruit source for Warner Glen Estate is its Jindawarra Vineyard, located south of Karridale. With north-facing slopes and soils of gravelly loams it is the ideal site for high quality grapes. Planted in 2000, the vines are mature, balanced, and of moderate vigour. The vineyard is only 6km from the Southern Ocean and 4km from the Indian Ocean, and avoids extreme temperatures as a result of the cooling sea breezes. Plantings are of shiraz, chardonnay, sauvignon blanc, pinot noir, viognier and pinot gris. Cabernet sauvignon is sourced from the Warner Glen-managed vineyard at Wilyabrup.

ŸŸŸŸŸ **Margaret River Cabernet Sauvignon 2014** It's not often a red wine at this price has so much attitude: there's blackcurrant, bay leaf, black olive fruit, and cabernet tannins to provide back up. It has all the requisites to motor serenely into the distance. Screwcap. 14.5% alc. **Rating** 94 **To** 2029 $19 ❍

ŸŸŸŸŸ **Margaret River Chardonnay 2016 Rating** 93 **To** 2025 $20 ❍
Frog Belly Margaret River SSB 2016 Rating 90 **To** 2018 $13 ❍

Warramate

27 Maddens Lane, Gruyere, Vic 3770 **Region** Yarra Valley
T (03) 5964 9219 **www.warramatewines.com.au** **Open** Not
Winemaker Sarah Crowe **Est.** 1970 **Dozens** 3000 **Vyds** 6.6ha
A long-established and perfectly situated winery reaping the full benefits of its 47-year-old vines; recent plantings have increased production. All the wines are well made, the Shiraz providing further proof (if such be needed) of the suitability of the variety to the region. In 2011 Warramate was purchased by the partnership that owns the adjoining Yarra Yering; the Warramate brand is kept as a separate operation, using the existing vineyards. Exports to the UK, the US, Singapore, Hong Kong and China.

ŸŸŸŸŸ **Yarra Valley Chardonnay 2015** Bright light straw-green; the bouquet is decidedly complex, and the palate follows suit, but its cardinal virtues are its freshness, length and balance. Will flourish through this decade and beyond. Screwcap. 13% alc. **Rating** 95 **To** 2023 $28 ❍
Yarra Valley Pinot Noir 2015 Bright, full crimson-purple; the perfumed bouquet lays the path for the red and purple fruits, spices and whole bunch/stalk tannins of the palate. Rip-snorter value. Screwcap. 13.5% alc. **Rating** 95 **To** 2028 $28 ❍
Black Label Yarra Valley Cabernet Sauvignon 2015 Chardonnay and pinot noir might steal the limelight in the valley, but ignore cabernet sauvignon at your peril. Unique flavours of rosemary-infused blackberries, pine needles and bracken work on a finely tuned, medium-bodied palate. Screwcap. 13% alc. **Rating** 95 **To** 2027 $28 JF ❍
Black Label Yarra Valley Shiraz 2015 Good depth to the colour; an archetypal cool climate shiraz with a spice and pepper background to the front and centre juicy dark berry fruits, fine tannins and oak playing an important support role. Screwcap. 13% alc. **Rating** 94 **To** 2035 $28 ❍

ŸŸŸŸŸ **Yarra Valley Riesling 2016 Rating** 93 **To** 2024 $28 JF
Yarra Valley Pinot Noir 2016 Rating 91 **To** 2021 $28 JF

Warramunda Estate

860 Maroondah Highway, Coldstream, Vic 3770 **Region** Yarra Valley
T 0412 694 394 **www.warramundaestate.com.au** **Open** Fri–Sun 10–6
Winemaker Ben Haines **Est.** 1998 **Dozens** 2000 **Vyds** 19.2ha

Ted Vogt purchased the original Warramunda property, on which a cattle and sheep stud known as 'Warramunda Station' was run, in 1975, then extended the property by 320 acres in '80. A large dam was built in '81, and the property now supports three vineyards and some grazing land. The Magdziarz family acquired Warramunda from the Vogt family in 2007. The Magdziarz family have built on the existing solid foundations with a deep respect for the surrounding landscape, and a vision for terroir-driven wines. Exports to the UK, the US, Canada and Asia.

ŸŸŸŸŸ **Yarra Valley Marsanne 2015** This has responded very well to the oak regime, into which the fruit has slipped like a velvet glove. It is a complex wine, but you still see the chalky/juicy double faces of the grape, chalky ultimately going the whole way to honeyed. Fascinating. Screwcap. 12.8% alc. **Rating** 95 **To** 2030 $35
Yarra Valley Pinot Noir 2015 The bright, clear crimson-purple colour is a great start, and the wine doesn't blink at any stage. The fruits are in the red spectrum, balanced and complexed by some hints of herbs, fine tannins and an airbrush of French oak. Diam. 12.9% alc. **Rating** 95 **To** 2027 $40
Yarra Valley Syrah 2015 Gets off to a flying start with its super-fragrant red and purple fruit bouquet and entry into the mouth. Is the spicy/savoury/stemmy finish a plus, a negative or neither? The barrel-ferment treatment has certainly helped. Snazzy wax-dipped bottle neck. Diam. 14.2% alc. **Rating** 94 **To** 2029 $35

Warrenmang Vineyard & Resort ★★★★

188 Mountain Creek Road, Moonambel, Vic 3478 **Region** Pyrenees
T (03) 5467 2233 **www**.warrenmang.com.au **Open** 7 days 10–5
Winemaker Greg Foster **Est.** 1974 **Dozens** 10 000 **Vyds** 32.1ha
Luigi and Athalie Bazzani continue to watch over Warrenmang; a new, partially underground barrel room with earthen walls has been completed, wine quality remains high, and the accommodation for over 80 guests, plus a restaurant, underpin the business. Over the 40 years that Luigi and Athalie have been at Warrenmang, a very loyal clientele has been built up. The business is quietly on the market, Luigi and Athalie having long since earned their retirement. However, they have taken one step to reduce their workload: employing the highly experienced Elizabeth Byrne to manage the resort. Exports to Denmark, The Netherlands, Poland, Taiwan, Singapore, Malaysia and China.

ŸŸŸŸŸ **Grand Pyrenees 2012** Cabernet sauvignon, cabernet franc, merlot and shiraz, fermented separately and matured in French and American oak for upwards of 2 years. It is a distinguished wine with a track record going back decades, always having the minty notes of Central Victoria. It is medium to full-bodied, but fully complete, and now embarking on a long journey thanks to its screwcap, no tannins needing to soften. 15% alc. **Rating** 94 **To** 2032 $35

ŸŸŸŸŸ **Estate Pyrenees Shiraz 2008 Rating** 92 **To** 2028 $75
Pyrenees Sauvignon Blanc 2014 Rating 90 **To** 2020 $25
Estate Pyrenees Shiraz 2010 Rating 90 **To** 2025

Warwick Billings ★★★★

c/- Post Office, Lenswood, SA 5240 (postal) **Region** Adelaide Hills
T 0405 437 864 **www**.wowique.com.au **Open** Not
Winemaker Warwick Billings **Est.** 2009 **Dozens** 300
This is the venture of Warwick Billings and partner Rose Kemp. Warwick was a cider maker in the UK who came to study at Roseworthy, and got diverted into the wine world. He completed postgraduate oenology at Adelaide University in 1995, and worked for Miranda Wine, Orlando and Angove Family Winemakers from 2002 to '08, along the way moonlighting in France and Spain for 12 vintages. Warwick's approach to his eponymous label is self-deprecating, beginning with the name Wowique, and saying, 'Occasionally a vineyard sings to the winemaker. [We] have taken one of these songs and put it into a bottle.' The vineyard in question is planted to an unusual clone of chardonnay and nurtured on a

sloping hilltop site in Mt Torrens. Warwick's final word on all of this is, 'The winemaking is unashamedly inspired by Burgundy, but care is taken to acknowledge that the soil is different, the clones are often different, the climate is definitely different, and the end consumer is usually different.'

ỶỶỶỶỶ **Wowique Single Vineyard Lenswood Sauvignon Blanc 2016** Fermented
with cultured yeast on high solids in used French oak. A complex sauvignon, in terms of both its structure and flavour, the power of the fruit able to absorb the fermentation and oak inputs. A sauvignon blanc with purpose in life, and a tropical reprise on the aftertaste. Screwcap. 13.3% alc. **Rating** 94 **To** 2018 $26

ỶỶỶỶỸ **Wowique Lenswood Pinot Noir 2015 Rating** 91 **To** 2021 $38 JF

Watershed Premium Wines   ★★★★★

Cnr Bussell Highway/Darch Road, Margaret River, WA 6285 **Region** Margaret River
T (08) 9758 8633 **www**.watershedwines.com.au **Open** 7 days 10–5
Winemaker Severine Logan, Conrad Tritt **Est.** 2002 **Dozens** 100 000 **Vyds** 137ha
Watershed Wines has been set up by a syndicate of investors, with no expense spared in establishing the substantial vineyard and striking cellar door, with a 200-seat cafe and restaurant. Situated towards the southern end of the Margaret River region, its neighbours include Voyager Estate and Leeuwin Estate. The vineyard development occurred in three stages (2001, '04 and '06), the last in Jindong, well to the north of stages one and two. The first stage of the winery was completed prior to the '03 vintage, with a capacity of 400 tonnes, increased the following year to 900 tonnes, then another expansion in '05 to 1200 tonnes. March '08 saw the crush capacity reach 1600 tonnes; wine storage facilities have increased in lockstep with crush capacity, lifted by a further 170 000 kilolitres. Exports to Germany, Indonesia, Fiji, Thailand, Papua New Guinea, Singapore, Hong Kong and China.

ỶỶỶỶỶ **Awakening Margaret River Cabernet Sauvignon 2010** The price has come
down from the original $100 despite six trophies at the Perth Wine Show '12, one at the National Wine Show (plus all the attendant gold medals). The colour is still a superb crimson-purple, fulfilling, indeed exceeding, the promise it held when first tasted in Jan '13. It is not a powerhouse; rather it is elegant, medium-bodied and very long, its cassis fruit delicately framed by tannins woven through high quality French oak. Screwcap. 14% alc. **Rating** 98 **To** 2035 $70 ✪

ỶỶỶỶỶ **Senses Margaret River Chardonnay 2016** The combination of high quality
cool-grown grapes and sensitive winemaking has produced this lovely chardonnay, the first release of a chardonnay in the Senses range. Delicacy teams with intensity, grapefruit, white peach and nectarine the drivers, not the oak. Screwcap. 13% alc. **Rating** 96 **To** 2029 $30 ✪
Senses Margaret River Sauvignon Blanc 2016 Picked at different ripeness levels, 48% fermented in new (20%) and 1yo French oak, the balance in stainless steel, matured on lees for 5 months. The varied fruit ripeness is a contributor, alongside the complex vinification; taken together, the power of the wine is almost painful, with citrus and cut grass at one end of the spectrum, guava and passionfruit at the other end. Screwcap. 13% alc. **Rating** 95 **To** 2018 $30 ✪
Awakening Single Block A1 Margaret River Chardonnay 2015 A wine with exceptional drive, purity and an immaculately shaped varietal profile. It is lean yet intense, taking white peach, apple and wafts of grilled cashews on the long, stylish palate. It will peak in 6–7 years, and cruise on for years thereafter. Screwcap. 13.5% alc. **Rating** 95 **To** 2025 $47
Senses Margaret River Shiraz 2014 Deep colour; a very complex shiraz in terms of flavour and structure. Oak plays a significant role in the mocha/dark chocolate/spice components, but the purple and black fruits are more than a match, assisted by tannins to create the stimulating texture on the back-palate and finish. Screwcap. 14.5% alc. **Rating** 95 **To** 2039 $30 ✪
Senses Margaret River Cabernet Merlot 2014 A wine of considerable complexity and intensity, with a continuing interplay between fruit and oak.

The fruit component is a mouthwatering mix of cassis, bay leaf and black olive, the oak instilling cedary flavours and persistent, fine-grained tannins. Screwcap. 14.5% alc. **Rating** 95 **To** 2034 $30 ○

Shades Margaret River Sauvignon Blanc Semillon 2016 Rating 94 To 2018 $20 ○

Shades Margaret River Merlot 2015 Rating 94 To 2034 $20 ○

ꓬꓬꓬꓬꓕ **Margaret River Blanc de Blanc 2012** Rating 90 To 2018 $25 TS

WayWood Wines ★★★★★

67 Kays Road, McLaren Vale, SA 5171 **Region** McLaren Vale
T (08) 8323 8468 **www**.waywoodwines.com **Open** Fri–Mon 11–5
Winemaker Andrew Wood **Est.** 2005 **Dozens** 1500
This is the culmination of Andrew Wood and Lisa Robertson's wayward odyssey. Andrew left his career as a sommelier in London and retrained as a winemaker, working in Portugal, the UK, Italy and the Granite Belt (an eclectic selection), and settling in McLaren Vale in early 2004. Working with Kangarilla Road winery for the next six years, while making small quantities of shiraz, cabernets and tempranillo from purchased grapes, led them to nebbiolo, montepulciano and shiraz. Lisa's business, Luscious Red, offers food at the cellar door.

ꓬꓬꓬꓬꓕ **McLaren Vale Shiraz 2015** Archetypal McLaren Vale shiraz, with its concentration of flavour and power. Ripe plums coated in cocoa, warm bitumen, a hint of florals, coconut husk and other woodsy spices. Full-bodied and with firm, savoury tannins. Screwcap. 14.2% alc. **Rating** 92 **To** 2030 $25 JF ○
McLaren Vale Grenache 2015 Aged in older American and French hogsheads, allowing the aromatics to soar. Lavender, lots of spice (especially crushed coriander seeds) and menthol with a dab of raspberry flavour. Supple, savoury and slightly gritty tannins. Screwcap. 14.2% alc. **Rating** 91 **To** 2021 $28 JF

ꓬꓬꓬꓬ **Years 96 McLaren Vale Cabernet 2012** Rating 89 To 2028 $50 JF
McLaren Vale Montepulciano 2015 Rating 89 To 2024 $35 JF

Welshmans Reef Vineyard ★★★☆

Maldon-Newstead Road, Welshmans Reef, Vic 3462 **Region** Bendigo
T (03) 5476 2733 **www**.welshmansreef.com **Open** W'ends & public hols 10–5
Winemaker Ronald Snep **Est.** 1986 **Dozens** 6000 **Vyds** 15ha
The Snep family (Ronald, Jackson and Alexandra) began developing Welshmans Reef Vineyard in 1986, planting cabernet sauvignon, shiraz and semillon. Chardonnay and merlot were added in the early '90s, sauvignon blanc and tempranillo later. The vineyard is certified organic. For some years the grapes were sold to other wineries, but in the early '90s the Sneps decided to share winemaking facilities established in the Old Newstead Co-operative Butter Factory with several other small vineyards. When the Butter Factory facility closed down, the Sneps built a winery and mudbrick tasting room onsite. Exports to China.

ꓬꓬꓬꓬꓕ **Merlot 2013** An attractive medium-bodied merlot with nigh-on perfect varietal expression beginning with the violets and berries of the bouquet, seamlessly continuing with a juicy, gently spicy red and purple berry palate. A wine to drink anytime, anywhere. Screwcap. 14.8% alc. **Rating** 92 **To** 2028 $22 ○

ꓬꓬꓬꓬ **Black Knight Cabernet Sauvignon 2015** Rating 89 To 2023 $18 JF ○

Wendouree ★★★★★

Wendouree Road, Clare, SA 5453 **Region** Clare Valley
T (08) 8842 2896 **Open** Not
Winemaker Tony Brady **Est.** 1895 **Dozens** 2000 **Vyds** 12ha
An iron fist in a velvet glove best describes these extraordinary wines. They are fashioned with commitment from the very old vineyard (shiraz, cabernet sauvignon, malbec, mataro and muscat of alexandria), with its unique terroir, by Tony and Lita Brady, who rightly see

themselves as custodians of a priceless treasure. The 100+-year-old stone winery is virtually unchanged from the day it was built; this is in every sense a treasure beyond price. Wendouree has never made any comment about its wines, but the subtle shift from the lighter end of full-bodied to the fuller end of medium-bodied seems to be a permanent one (always subject to the dictates of the vintage). The best news of all is that I will drink some of the Wendourees I have bought over the past 10 years before I die, and not have to rely on my few remaining bottles from the 1970s (and rather more from the '80s and '90s).

♟♟♟♟♟ **Shiraz 2014** The wine takes a lot of air via glass swirling to express itself, but ultimately does so emphatically. Plum, black cherry and spices paint the flavour picture, and expand prodigiously on the back-palate and finish. As the late Len Evans would have said, it has flawless line, length and balance. Screwcap. 13.7% alc. **Rating** 97 **To** 2049
Shiraz Mataro 2014 The colour is fractionally lighter than the Shiraz, and it has the lightest body (strictly in comparison to its two siblings). It's no surprise that the bouquet is very expressive, with red berries ascendant, the palate juicy and silky until the very end, when finely assembled tannins (and oak) provide compelling structure. Screwcap. 13.3% alc. **Rating** 97 **To** 2044
Cabernet Sauvignon 2014 The moment the wine is poured into the glass, the bright, deep colour tells you this wine will assert its authority in no uncertain fashion. Yet it does so by stealth, first revealing the cassis fruit and (in the best sense) mint. There is no bombardment by often autocratic cabernet tannins; just as was the case with the '13 vintage, it is elegant, dispensing tannins slyly. Three very different wines, and I love them all, so the points are the same. Screwcap. 13.7% alc. **Rating** 97 **To** 2047

West Cape Howe Wines   ★★★★★

Lot 14923 Muir Highway, Mount Barker, WA 6324 **Region** Mount Barker
T (08) 9892 1444 **www**.westcapehowewines.com.au **Open** 7 days (various hours)
Winemaker Gavin Berry, Andrew Vasey **Est.** 1997 **Dozens** 60 000 **Vyds** 310ha
West Cape Howe is owned by a partnership of four West Australian families, including winemaker/managing partner Gavin Berry and viticulturist/partner Rob Quenby. Grapes are sourced from estate vineyards in Mount Barker and Frankland River. The Langton vineyard (Mount Barker) has 100ha planted to cabernet sauvignon, shiraz, riesling, sauvignon blanc, chardonnay and semillon, and the Russell Road vineyard (Frankland River) has 210ha planted. West Cape Howe also sources select parcels of fruit from valued contract growers. Best Value Winery *Wine Companion* 2016. Exports to the UK, the US, Denmark, Switzerland, South Korea, Singapore, Japan, Hong Kong and China.

♟♟♟♟♟ **King Billy Mount Barker Cabernet Sauvignon 2011** An exercise in the best of the best: top parcels from the Langton and Windy Hill vineyards were selected for the Book Ends Cabernet Sauvignon, the best four barriques (100% new French oak) chosen for this wine, bottled after 16 months and then matured for three and a half years prior to release. The colour is still vivid purple-crimson, the fruit and oak totally integrated and balanced, cassis riding high on the long palate, the aftertaste lingering on and on. Screwcap. 14.5% alc. **Rating** 98 **To** 2051 $50 ✪

♟♟♟♟♟ **Hannah's Hill Frankland River Cabernet Merlot 2014** This has the bearing of a $40+ wine, not a $20+ wine. Whether you look to Bordeaux or Margaret River for style references, this comes up trumps, the blackcurrant fruit held in a perfect basket of French oak and firm tannins. Exceptional bargain. Screwcap. 14% alc. **Rating** 96 **To** 2039 $22 ✪
Styx Gully Mount Barker Chardonnay 2015 No mlf; moderately high titratable acidity has given the wine a sea breeze of freshness with its grapefruit-accented fruit profile, white peach and pear also contributing, French oak providing the cream on the cake. Screwcap. 12.7% alc. **Rating** 95 **To** 2023 $28 ✪

♟♟♟♟♟ **Mount Barker Sauvignon Blanc 2016 Rating** 92 **To** 2017 $20 ✪
Tempranillo Rose 2016 Rating 92 **To** 2017 $17 ✪

Shiraz 2015 Rating 92 To 2025 $17 **O**
Frankland River Malbec 2014 Rating 92 To 2020 $22 **O**
Mount Barker Riesling 2016 Rating 91 To 2026 $20 **O**
Semillon Sauvignon Blanc 2016 Rating 91 To 2017 $17 **O**
Pinot Grigio 2016 Rating 91 To 2017 $17 **O**
Frankland River Malbec 2015 Rating 91 To 2023 $22 PR **O**
Old School Chardonnay 2016 Rating 90 To 2020 $20 **O**

Westlake Vineyards   ★★★★★

Diagonal Road, Koonunga, SA 5355 **Region** Barossa Valley
T 0428 656 208 **www**.westlakevineyards.com.au **Open** By appt
Winemaker Darren Westlake **Est.** 1999 **Dozens** 500 **Vyds** 36.2ha
Darren and Suzanne Westlake tend 22ha of shiraz, 6.5ha of cabernet sauvignon, 2ha of
viognier, and smaller plantings of petit verdot, durif, mataro, grenache and graciano planted
on two properties in the Koonunga area of the Barossa Valley. They do all the vineyard work
personally, and have a long list of high-profile winemakers queued up to buy the grapes,
leaving only a small amount for production under the Westlake label. Suzanne is a sixth-
generation descendant of Johann George Kalleske, who came to SA from Prussia in 1838;
the 717 Convicts label draws on the history of Darren's ancestor Edward Westlake, who was
transported to Australia in 1788.

ŸŸŸŸŸ **717 Convicts The Warden Barossa Valley Shiraz 2015** Like The Felon,
the palate is smooth, velvety and long. Rich flavours of blackstrap licorice and
chocolate move into a savoury realm of curry leaves and roast beef bones. Will
appeal to those who dig big reds. 14.8% alc. **Rating** 93 **To** 2030 $35 JF
717 Convicts The Felon Barossa Valley Shiraz 2015 A flurry of black sweet
fruit, wood spice, lots of coconut-oak flavours and most definitely full-bodied.
Elegant it is not, but it all comes together well, with the substantial tannins sitting
neatly into the smooth, voluptuous palate. 15% alc. **Rating** 90 **To** 2020 $25 JF

Westmere Wines   NR

916 Bool Lagoon Road, Bool Lagoon, SA 5271 **Region** Limestone Coast
T 0427 647 429 **Open** Not
Winemaker Phil Lehmann **Est.** 1998 **Dozens** 300 **Vyds** 12ha
The Bool Lagoon property has been owned by the Kay family since 1891, farming prime
lambs, cattle and cropping, but Jack Kay had long cherished the idea of a small diversification
into growing cabernet sauvignon. Phil Lehmann just happens to be a family friend, and has
duly made the wine, which is sold direct to restaurants and hotels in SA and Vic.

Whicher Ridge   ★★★★★

200 Chapman Hill East Road, Busselton, WA 6280 **Region** Geographe
T (08) 9753 1394 **www**.whicherridge.com.au **Open** Thurs–Mon 10–5
Winemaker Cathy Howard **Est.** 2004 **Dozens** 1500 **Vyds** 5ha
It is hard to imagine a founding husband-and-wife team with such an ideal blend of viticultural
and winemaking experience accumulated over a combined 40+ years. Cathy Howard (née
Spratt) was a winemaker for 16 years at Orlando and St Hallett in the Barossa Valley, and at
Watershed Wines in Margaret River. She now has her own winemaking consulting business
covering the southwest regions of WA, as well as making the Whicher Ridge wines. Neil
Howard's career as a viticulturist began in the Pyrenees region with Taltarni vineyards and
Blue Pyrenees Estate; then he moved to Mount Avoca as vineyard manager for 12 years. When
he moved to the west, he managed the Sandalford vineyard in Margaret River for several years,
then developed and managed a number of smaller vineyards throughout the region. Whicher
Ridge's Odyssey Creek vineyard at Chapman Hill has sauvignon blanc, cabernet sauvignon
and viognier. The Howards have chosen the Frankland River subregion of the Great Southern
to supply shiraz and riesling, and also buy grapes from Margaret River.

🍷🍷🍷🍷🍷 **Elevation Geographe Cabernet Sauvignon 2013** Deep crimson-purple; a distinguished cabernet in every respect. The bouquet is a complex amalgam of blackcurrant fruit, quality French oak and the earthy tannins so typical of cabernet grown in the right climate, and vinified very well. Screwcap. 13.5% alc. **Rating** 96 To 2038 $39 ☉
Geographe Sauvignon Blanc 2015 A striking sauvignon blanc, its complexity on the bouquet matched by the raw power and drive of the palate. The wine is built around a scaffold of minerally/chalky acidity. In European tradition, the composition of the fruit flavours is of lesser importance than the structure and texture of the wine. Screwcap. 12.8% alc. **Rating** 95 To 2020 $26 ☉
Frankland River Shiraz 2013 The wine is medium-bodied (not full-bodied) and has deceptive power and length – and fragrance. It is distinctly savoury, but intense blue and black fruits emerge on the finish and aftertaste. This wine and the Cabernet Sauvignon are made using complex techniques, the most unusual draining a portion of the actively fermenting must into new oak barrels, the remainder into tank, the next day returning the juice from the tank and barrels to the fermenter. Screwcap. 13.5% alc. **Rating** 95 To 2035 $34 ☉
Margaret River Chardonnay 2015 The Clairault/Striecker Vineyard is a source of high quality grapes full of varietal fruit flavours (primarily white peach, nectarine and citrus). A very good chardonnay, but there is a slight break in the line on the back-palate. Screwcap. 12.8% alc. **Rating** 94 To 2023 $34

🍷🍷🍷🍷 **Nuts & Bolts Geographe Sauvignon Blanc 2016** Rating 89 To 2020 $18 ☉

🍇 Whimwood Estate Wines ★★★★☆

PO Box 250, Nannup, WA 6275 **Region** Blackwood Valley
T 0417 003 235 **www**.whimwoodestatewines.com.au **Open** Not
Winemaker Bernie Stanlake **Est.** 2011 **Dozens** 700 **Vyds** 1.2ha
Maree Tinker and Steve Johnstone say they fell in love with the property at first sight in 2011, without even knowing that it had a vineyard. The name draws on the region's past timber milling history, where horse-drawn whims were used for hauling logs. The vineyard had been planted in 2004 to chardonnay with an agreement in place for the purchase of the grapes by a local winemaker. The grape shortage of '04 turned into a grape surplus, and it was left to Maree and Steve to remove 6000 of the 8000 chardonnay vines, and increase the handful of shiraz vines originally planted by grafting onto chardonnay rootstock. They now have 0.7ha of chardonnay and 0.5ha of shiraz. Exports to the UK and Sweden.

🍷🍷🍷🍷🍷 **Blackwood Valley Chardonnay 2016** Pressed straight to oak (30% new) and wild-yeast fermented. This is good stuff: the wine has considerable power, the impact of the pink grapefruit flavour immediate, and not backing off as the wine reaches the end of the palate. Screwcap. 12.5% alc. **Rating** 95 To 2027 $20
Blackwood Valley Chardonnay 2015 Considerable success in '16, ranging from the trophy for Best White at the Blackwood Valley and WA Boutique wine shows. It has considerable finesse, with light-fingered choice of oak to support the fresh grapefruit and Granny Smith apple flavours of the fruit. Screwcap. 13% alc. Rating 94 To 2023 $25 ☉

🍷🍷🍷🍷🍷 **Blackwood Valley Shiraz 2015** Rating 92 To 2025 $22 ☉
Blackwood Valley Shiraz 2016 Rating 91 To 2029 $19

Whispering Brook ★★★★★

Hill Street, Broke, NSW 2330 **Region** Hunter Valley
T (02) 9818 4126 **www**.whispering-brook.com **Open** W'ends 11–5, Fri by appt
Winemaker Susan Frazier, Adam Bell **Est.** 2000 **Dozens** 2000 **Vyds** 3ha
It took some time for partners Susan Frazier and Adam Bell to find the property on which they established their vineyard 15 years ago. It has a combination of terra rossa loam soils on which the reds are planted, and sandy flats for the white grapes. The partners have also

established an olive grove and accommodation for 10–18 guests in the large house set in the vineyard. Exports to Canada and Japan.

ΨΨΨΨΨ **Single Vineyard Hunter Valley Semillon 2016** Proof you shouldn't judge a wine by its label – sorry Whispering Brook, yours is nondescript, but the semillon is pitch-perfect. A gossamer thread of acidity weaves through the lemon-lime notes, the wet pebbles and dried herbs. It's complex, lively and destined to last for quite some time. Screwcap. 11.7% alc. **Rating** 95 **To** 2028 $28 JF ✪

Single Vineyard Hunter Valley Shiraz 2014 Nothing out of place, nothing overt: this is a detailed and composed wine with beautifully balanced fruit, spice, precise tannins, good acidity and drive. It's polished, highly gluggable and will appease those with cellars. Screwcap. 14.4% alc. **Rating** 95 **To** 2034 $40 JF

Basket Pressed Hunter Valley Merlot 2014 What a meritorious merlot: perfectly ripe, fresh and leafy with wafts of cassis, juniper and a smidge of florals. The palate is really good – chalky tannins, has depth and body, yet not a big wine; quite refined. A nice surprise. Cork. 13.5% alc. **Rating** 95 **To** 2024 $35 JF ✪

Whistling Kite Wines ★★★☆

73 Freundt Road, New Residence via Loxton, SA 5333 **Region** Riverland
T (08) 8584 9014 **www**.whistlingkitewines.com.au **Open** By appt
Winemaker 919 Wines (Eric and Jenny Semmler) **Est.** 2010 **Dozens** 360 **Vyds** 16ha
Owners Pam and Tony Barich have established their vineyard and house on the banks of the Murray River, a haven for wildlife. They believe custodians of the land have a duty to maintain its health and vitality – their vineyard has had organic certification for over a decade, and biodynamic certification since 2008.

ΨΨΨΨΨ **Viognier 2016** This works: it has positive fruit flavours, good texture and grip, and no oily phenolics. Screwcap. 14.5% alc. **Rating** 90 **To** 2020 $25

ΨΨΨΨ **Petit Verdot 2015 Rating** 89 **To** 2019 $38

Wicks Estate Wines ★★★★★

21 Franklin Street, Adelaide, SA 5000 (postal) **Region** Adelaide Hills
T (08) 8212 0004 **www**.wicksestate.com.au **Open** Not
Winemaker Leigh Ratzmer **Est.** 2000 **Dozens** 20000 **Vyds** 38.1ha
Tim and Simon Wicks had a long-term involvement with orchard and nursery operations at Highbury in the Adelaide Hills prior to purchasing their 54ha property at Woodside in 1999. They planted fractionally less than 40ha of chardonnay, riesling, sauvignon blanc, shiraz, merlot and cabernet sauvignon, following this with the construction of a winery in 2004. Wicks Estate has won more than its fair share of wine show medals over the years, the wines priced well below their full worth. Exports to Singapore, Hong Kong and China.

ΨΨΨΨΨ **CJ Wicks Adelaide Hills Shiraz 2014** Clones (BVRC-12/16-54), 20 days on skins, and 60% new French oak, otherwise identical vinification to the '15 Shiraz. Slightly deeper colour and more overall power and complexity, especially the new oak, but also tannins on the finish. It is not devoid of freshness, but its message is altogether more serious. Screwcap. 14.5% alc. **Rating** 96 **To** 2034 $45 ✪

Adelaide Hills Cabernet Sauvignon 2015 Selectiv machine–harvested, multiple clone and block ferments, 80% crushed and destemmed, 20% whole berries, open fermenters of various sizes, matured for 12 months in French oak (25% new). This has resulted in a seriously good cabernet, flush with blackcurrant fruit perfectly balanced by tannins and cedary oak. A price of $50 would be justified. Screwcap. 14.5% alc. **Rating** 96 **To** 2035 $25 ✪

C.J. Wicks Adelaide Hills Chardonnay 2015 Identical vinification to the '16, except for 10 months' maturation in 75% new French oak. An elegant wine without a hair out of place, varietal fruit expression, acidity and oak all lined up with military precision. Screwcap. 13.5% alc. **Rating** 95 **To** 2025 $45

Adelaide Hills Chardonnay 2016 Dijon clones 76 and 96, Selectiv machine–harvested, crushed and destemmed, wild-yeast fermented in French (25% new), matured for 8 months. Fine, elegant and long, a prime example of modern chardonnay at an affordable price. Screwcap. 12.5% alc. **Rating** 94 **To** 2025 $25 ◎

Adelaide Hills Pinot Noir 2016 Three clones, Selectiv machine–harvested (de facto sorting), open-fermented, cold soak, differing cultured yeasts, 12 days on skins, matured for 6 months in French oak (20% new). Up to Wicks' usual high standard, red and purple fruits with a spicy savoury twist complexing both texture and flavour. Time to go. Screwcap. 14% alc. **Rating** 94 **To** 2025 $25 ◎

Adelaide Hills Shiraz 2015 Individual vineyard block and clone selections (BVRC-12/16-54/712), Selectiv machine–harvested, open fermentation of various configurations, 15 different fermentations, matured for 12 months in French oak (20% new). Good hue and depth; an intense palate that has a striking texture as it enters the mouth, and equally striking freshness. Screwcap. 14.5% alc. **Rating** 94 **To** 2030 $25 ◎

Adelaide Hills Shiraz 2014 Revels in its cool climate region, bringing black cherry to the table wreathed in a bevy of spices, licorice and cedary oak, the overall mouthfeel of freshness. Utterly ridiculous value. Screwcap. 14.5% alc. **Rating** 94 **To** 2029 $20 ◎

�♥♥♥♀ **Adelaide Hills Pinot Rose 2016** Rating 91 To 2017 $18 JF ◎
Adelaide Hills Riesling 2016 Rating 90 To 2026 $20 ◎

Wignalls Wines ★★★★☆

448 Chester Pass Road (Highway 1), Albany, WA 6330 **Region** Albany
T (08) 9841 2848 **www**.wignallswines.com.au **Open** 7 days 11–4
Winemaker Rob Wignall, Michael Perkins **Est.** 1982 **Dozens** 7000 **Vyds** 18.5ha
While the estate vineyards have a diverse range of sauvignon blanc, semillon, chardonnay, pinot noir, merlot, shiraz, cabernet franc and cabernet sauvignon, founder Bill Wignall was one of the early movers with pinot noir, producing wines that, by the standards of their time, were well in front of anything else coming out of WA (and up with the then limited amounts being made in Vic and Tas). The establishment of an onsite winery, and the assumption of the winemaking role by son Rob, with significant input from Michael Perkins, saw the quality and range of wines increase. Exports to Denmark, Japan, Singapore and China.

♥♥♥♥♥ **Great Southern Shiraz 2015** Certainly has had its fair share of wine show success and other critical acclaim to date. Peppery spice leaps out of the glass, deep black fruit aromas tucked in behind. Sweet-fruited and densely flavoured on the palate, it's both rich and savoury; easy to see how it has its admirers. Screwcap. 13.8% alc. **Rating** 95 **To** 2030 $29 SC ◎

♥♥♥♥♀ **Premium Single Vineyard Albany Chardonnay 2015** Rating 93 To 2022 $30
Single Vineyard Albany Pinot Noir 2015 Rating 91 To 2025 $32 SC

Willem Kurt Wines ★★★★

Croom Lane, Beechworth, Vic 3747 **Region** Beechworth
T 0428 400 522 **www**.willemkurtwines.com.au **Open** Not
Winemaker Daniel Balzer **Est.** 2014 **Dozens** 300
This is the venture of Daniel Balzer and Marije van Epenhuijsen, he with a German background, she Dutch. The name of the winery is drawn from the middle names of their two children: Willem (Dutch) and Kurt (German), in each instance reflecting long usage in the two families. Daniel moved into the wine industry in 1998, having already obtained a science degree, working first at Yarra Ridge (including a vintage in Germany) before moving to Gapsted Wines in 2003, then completing his Bachelor of Wine Science at CSU the following year. Seven years were given over to contract winemaking for smaller producers, and it was inevitable that sooner or later they would start making wine for their own brand. They currently lease a vineyard in Beechworth, and buy select parcels of fruit. Beechworth is the

region they know and love best, the plan being to buy land and establish their own vineyard and winery. The quality of the wines made to date suggests it should succeed.

🍷🍷🍷🍷 **Beechworth Chardonnay 2015** Seriously good. Effortless but powerful. Juicy peach and nectarine, cedary oak, milk biscuits, herbs and grapefruit. As seductive as it is impressive. Screwcap. 13% alc. **Rating** 94 **To** 2023 $34 CM

Willespie ★★★★

555 Harmans Mill Road, Wilyabrup via Cowaramup, WA 6284 **Region** Margaret River
T (08) 9755 6248 **www**.willespie.com.au **Open** 7 days 10.30–5
Winemaker Loren Brown **Est.** 1976 **Dozens** 3000 **Vyds** 17.53ha
One of the pioneer wineries in Margaret River, established by local school headmaster Kevin Squance and wife Marian in 1976. They built their house from local timber and stone, set among the natural forest; it now (inter alia) houses the cellar door. Kevin and Marian have retired, and their four children, who are based in Perth and the southwest, have an active involvement in the business, developing and activating the domestic and export markets in the short to medium term. Exports to the Japan and Singapore.

🍷🍷🍷🍷 **Margaret River Shiraz 2010** A medium to full-bodied wine still in apple pie condition; blackberry and blackcurrant fruit has a savoury inflection that provides the first layer of complexity, the second layer coming from firm, but not threatening, tannins. Seven years young. Diam. **Rating** 93 **To** 2030 $30
Old School Barrel Fermented Margaret River Semillon 2010 Glowing yellow. Kaffir lime and honeysuckle, nettle and ripe tropical fruit. Full-bodied. Over-the-top in many ways yet it sizzles through the finish. Still going strong as a 7yo. Screwcap. 13.5% alc. **Rating** 91 **To** 2018 $30 CM
Old School Margaret River Cabernet Sauvignon 2008 A brooding, earthy/brambly black-fruited cabernet, still uncompromisingly full-bodied, still watching on as its fruits and tannins engage in an Indian arm-wrestle, neither yielding. Anyone wishing to retrospectively celebrate the birth of a child in '08 might well invest in this. Diam. **Rating** 90 **To** 2033 $65

Willoughby Park ★★★★★

678 South Coast Highway, Denmark, WA 6333 **Region** Great Southern
T (08) 9848 1555 **www**.willoughbypark.com.au **Open** 7 days 10–5
Winemaker Michael Ng **Est.** 2010 **Dozens** 13000 **Vyds** 19ha
Bob Fowler, who comes from a rural background and had always hankered for a farming life, stumbled across the opportunity to achieve this in early 2010. Together with wife Marilyn, he purchased the former West Cape Howe winery and surrounding vineyard that became available when West Cape Howe moved into the far larger Goundrey winery. In '11 Willoughby Park purchased the Kalgan River vineyard and business name, and winemaking operations have been transferred to Willoughby Park. There are now three labels: Kalgan River single vineyard range (Kalgan River Ironrock from single sites within the Kalgan River vineyard); Willoughby Park, the Great Southern brand for estate and purchased grapes; and Jamie & Charli, a sub-$20 Great Southern range of wines. Exports to China.

🍷🍷🍷🍷 **Ironrock Kalgan River Albany Riesling 2016** Citrus blossom fills the bouquet and leads directly into the palate, which has an unusual, but enjoyable, tactile quality. The flavours are a blend of Meyer lemon, lime and green apple. Screwcap. 12% alc. **Rating** 96 **To** 2031 $35 ✪
Ironrock Kalgan River Albany Chardonnay 2016 Matured in French oak (50% new) for 10 months with lees stirring. An intense, tightly structured chardonnay with white peach and grapefruit flavours braced by punchy acidity. A wine of restrained power. Screwcap. 13% alc. **Rating** 96 **To** 2026 $40 ✪
Kalgan River Great Southern Pinot Noir 2016 The colour is light, but bright, giving little notice of the power of the punch this pinot packs. Wild strawberry, red cherry and fine, but persistent, tannins on the long palate gain further complexity from the French oak. Screwcap. 14.5% alc. **Rating** 95 **To** 2026 $30 ✪

Ironrock Albany Shiraz 2014 Full crimson-purple; a full-on cool climate shiraz with black fruit (cherry and berry) in supple abundance, closely attended by licorice and cracked black pepper. The tannins add another dimension, part juicy (yes I know, that's an oxymoron), part savoury. Screwcap. 14.5% alc. **Rating** 95 To 2030 $55

Ironrock Kalgan River Albany Cabernet Sauvignon 2014 A powerful, full-bodied cabernet with blackcurrant fruit, earthy/savoury tannins and French oak woven together on the bouquet and palate alike. This needs the most time of the '14 Willoughby Park Cabernets, and will emerge on top down the track. Screwcap. 14.5% alc. **Rating** 95 To 2039 $55

Kalgan River Albany Riesling 2016 **Rating** 94 To 2031 $25 ✪

Kalgan River Albany Chardonnay 2016 **Rating** 94 To 2023 $30 ✪

Kalgan River Albany Chardonnay 2015 **Rating** 94 To 2025 $30 ✪

Ironrock Kalgan River Albany Chardonnay 2015 **Rating** 94 To 2030 $40

Kalgan River Albany Shiraz 2014 **Rating** 94 To 2034 $30 ✪

ⵌⵌⵌⵌⵌ Kalgan River Albany Cabernet Sauvignon 2014 **Rating** 93 To 2034 $30

Great Southern Shiraz 2014 **Rating** 92 To 2024 $22 ✪

Willow Bridge Estate ★★★★★

178 Gardin Court Drive, Dardanup, WA 6236 **Region** Geographe
T (08) 9728 0055 **www**.willowbridge.com.au **Open** 7 days 11–5
Winemaker Kim Horton **Est.** 1997 **Dozens** 20000 **Vyds** 59ha
Jeff and Vicky Dewar have followed a fast track in developing Willow Bridge Estate since acquiring the spectacular 180ha hillside property in the Ferguson Valley: chardonnay, semillon, sauvignon blanc, shiraz and cabernet sauvignon were planted, with merlot, tempranillo, chenin blanc and viognier following. Many of its wines offer exceptional value for money. On 22 March 2015, Willow Bridge's 44-year-old senior winemaker, Simon Burnell, died in a windsurfing accident off the coast of Margaret River. It revived memories of the death of Craggy Range winemaker Doug Wiser in Hawke's Bay in '04 while kite-surfing. Kim Horton, with extensive experience in WA, most recently as Senior Winemaker at Ferngrove, was appointed to take Simon's place. Exports to the UK, China and other major markets.

ⵌⵌⵌⵌⵌ Gravel Pit Geographe Shiraz 2015 This is the Willow Bridge flagship wine, matured in French oak (30% new). It has the flavours of Dragonfly, but doubles the depth and intensity of the black cherry and plum fruits, along with that of the ripe tannins. Because of this, the French oak, albeit with a greater percentage of new oak, is less obvious. Screwcap. 14.1% alc. **Rating** 96 To 2035 $30

Bookends Fume Geographe Sauvignon Blanc Semillon 2016 A complex and strongly herbal/green capsicum/asparagus bouquet changes focus on the palate, adding volumes of fruit flavours ranging from citrus to stone fruit and tropical fruits. A wine of character and quality. Screwcap. 13.9% alc. **Rating** 95 To 2021 $25 ✪

G1-10 Geographe Chardonnay 2016 Bright straw-green; a particularly elegant and refined chardonnay that will progressively gain weight and texture as it slowly matures over the next 10 years. Flavours of pink grapefruit and nectarine will yield to creamy cashew and peach with time. Screwcap. 13.4% alc. **Rating** 95 To 2027 $30 ✪

Coat of Arms Geographe Cabernet Sauvignon 2015 The section of the estate from which these grapes come is home to kangaroos and emus that (uninvited) thin the bunch numbers. This is an intense, medium to full-bodied cabernet with blackcurrant fruit, dried herbs/bay leaf and a healthy serve of tannins, part from fruit, part from oak. Screwcap. 14.7% alc. **Rating** 95 To 2035 $30

Dragonfly Sauvignon Blanc Semillon 2016 This has exceptional flavour and texture, the latter adding an edge to the fruit expression. The bouquet is complex and edgy, pointing to fragrant herbs, capsicum and an overarching mix of citrus and tropical fruits. Screwcap. 13.4% alc. **Rating** 94 To 2020 $20 ✪

Rosa de Solana Geographe Tempranillo Rose 2015 The cherry fruit (red and black) of tempranillo comes through the bouquet and palate in an unbroken

stream of aroma and flavour. The insistence of the varietal expression might be expected from a red wine tempranillo, but not in the much lighter impact of a rose. Great stuff. Screwcap. 13.4% alc. **Rating** 94 **To** 2017 $25 ✪
Dragonfly Geographe Shiraz 2015 Matured in new and used French oak. The crimson-purple colour is very, very good and points to a lively light to medium-bodied wine with red and black cherry and plum fruit supported by silky tannins and obvious French oak. Screwcap. 14% alc. **Rating** 94 **To** 2025 $20

🍷🍷🍷🍷 **Dragonfly Cabernet Sauvignon Merlot 2015 Rating** 93 **To** 2029 $20
Dragonfly Geographe Chardonnay 2016 Rating 92 **To** 2023 $20
Rosa de Solana Geographe Tempranillo Rose 2016 Rating 91 **To** 2018 $25

Willow Creek Vineyard ★★★★★

166 Balnarring Road, Merricks North, Vic 3926 **Region** Mornington Peninsula
T (03) 5931 2502 **www**.willow-creek.com.au **Open** 7 days 11–5
Winemaker Geraldine McFaul **Est.** 1989 **Dozens** 4000 **Vyds** 18ha
Significant changes have transformed Willow Creek over the past nine years. In 2008, winemaker Geraldine McFaul, with many years of winemaking in the Mornington Peninsula under her belt, was appointed, and worked with viticulturist Robbie O'Leary to focus on minimal intervention in the winery; in other words, to produce grapes in perfect condition. In '13 the Li family arrived from China and expanded its portfolio of hotel and resort properties in Australia by purchasing Willow Creek, with plans to develop a luxury 39-room boutique hotel on the site. This will be the seventh in the Li hotel group. The Rare Hare wine bar, restaurant and tasting room opened in March '17.

🍷🍷🍷🍷🍷 **Mornington Peninsula Chardonnay 2015** Vibrant white peach fruit has a lance of citrussy acidity giving it great length, but in no way diminishing the balance of the fruit. New oak (20%) has been well judged, giving a flick of nutty complexity. Screwcap. 13.5% alc. **Rating** 95 **To** 2024 $45
O'Leary Block Mornington Peninsula Pinot Noir 2015 Similar colour to its cheaper sibling, and similar weight; however, an extra 6 months in oak has given a more savoury make-up to its palate. Screwcap. 13.5% alc. **Rating** 95 **To** 2021 $75
Mornington Peninsula Pinot Noir 2015 Light-bodied, the bouquet fragrant and flowery, the juicy red fruits with a savoury/wild herb underplay. You are left to search for greater depth to the fruit from a vintage that provided so much to so many pinots. Screwcap. 13.5% alc. **Rating** 94 **To** 2019 $40

🍷🍷🍷🍷 **Malakoff Pyrenees Shiraz 2015 Rating** 93 **To** 2029 $30
Mornington Peninsula Pinot Gris 2016 Rating 91 **To** 2018 $35

Wills Domain ★★★★★

Cnr Brash Road/Abbey Farm Road, Yallingup, WA 6281 **Region** Margaret River
T (08) 9755 2327 **www**.willsdomain.com.au **Open** 7 days 10–5
Winemaker Naturaliste Vintners (Bruce Dukes) **Est.** 1985 **Dozens** 12 500 **Vyds** 20.8ha
When the Haunold family purchased the original Wills Domain vineyard in 2000, they were adding another chapter to a family history of winemaking stretching back to 1383 in what is now Austria. Remarkable though that may be, more remarkable is that Darren, who lost the use of his legs in an accident in 1989, runs the estate (including part of the pruning) from his wheelchair. The vineyard is planted to shiraz, semillon, cabernet sauvignon, sauvignon blanc, chardonnay, merlot, petit verdot, malbec, cabernet franc and viognier. Exports to Canada, Indonesia, Hong Kong and China.

🍷🍷🍷🍷🍷 **Cuvee d'Elevage Margaret River Chardonnay 2015** This covers a rich spectrum of flavours from stone fruit and Meyer lemon to vanillan-ginger oak notes. It tastes good. It's commanding. The full-bodied palate offers the gamut of lemon curd, leesy nuttiness and piercingly fresh acidity. Screwcap. 13.5% alc. **Rating** 95 **To** 2024 $60 JF
Cuvee d'Elevage Margaret River Shiraz 2015 A far more polished wine than Block 5, but as the flagship, so it should be. A glug of malbec and viognier

make their presence felt with apricot kernel and satsuma plums. The glossy palate is richly flavoured with oak, pepper, star anise and dried herbs. Screwcap. 14% alc. **Rating** 95 To 2030 $75 JF

Cuvee d'Elevage Margaret River Cabernet Sauvignon 2014 Everything has fallen into place: oak, the core of spicy blackberries, mulberries and sweet plums, and the fine tannins with a savoury lift. This has power and depth. Screwcap. 14.5% alc. **Rating** 95 To 2030 $75 JF

Cuvee d'Elevage Margaret River Matrix 2014 60% cabernet sauvignon, 20% cabernet franc with 10% each of malbec and petit verdot. Terrific wine, packed with sweet mulberries and blackberries, the right amount of spice, and nutty, cedary oak an integrated component. Amazingly supple, with the tannins holding sway over the medium-bodied palate. Screwcap. 14.5% alc. **Rating** 95 To 2030 $100 JF

ŸŸŸŸŸ   Block 8 Margaret River Chardonnay 2015 Rating 93 To 2022 $36 JF
Margaret River Rose 2016 Rating 93 To 2017 $17 ○
Block 5 Margaret River Shiraz 2015 Rating 93 To 2030 $36 JF
Margaret River Shiraz 2015 Rating 92 To 2023 $17 ○
Margaret River Cabernet Merlot 2015 Rating 92 To 2025 $25 JF ○
Block 3 Cabernet Sauvignon 2015 Rating 92 To 2030 $36 JF
Margaret River Semillon Sauvignon Blanc 2016 Rating 91 To 2022 $17 ○
Block 9 Margaret River Scheurebe 2016 Rating 91 To 2020 $29 JF

Willunga 100 Wines   ★★★★☆
PO Box 2427, McLaren Vale, SA 5171 **Region** McLaren Vale
T 0414 419 957 **www**.willunga100.com **Open** Not
Winemaker Tim James, Mike Farmilo **Est.** 2005 **Dozens** 9500
Willunga 100 is solely owned by Liberty Wines UK, sourcing its grapes from McLaren Vale and from Adelaide Hills (pinot gris and a portion of its viognier). The winemaking team these days is decidedly high-powered, with the hugely experienced Tim James and Mike Farmilo the conductors of the band. The focus is on the diverse districts within McLaren Vale and dry-grown bushvine grenache. Exports to the UK, Canada, Singapore, Hong Kong and NZ.

ŸŸŸŸŸ   The Hundred Blewitt Springs Grenache 2015 A light to mid-weighted free-flow of pomegranate, rosewater, orange rind and a litany of red fruits led by fresh strawberry, all given focus and punchy length by sandy tannins and bright, tangy acidity. There's initially a pinotesque ethereal nature to this, but the sweetness and impact grow in the glass. Screwcap. 14.5% alc. **Rating** 93 To 2023 $30 NG

The Hundred Clarendon Grenache 2015 Slightly more concentrated, brooding and of darker fruit tones, this mid-weighted wine exhibits bing cherry, bitter chocolate and raspberry bonbon, cascading down a fountain of energetic acidity and delicate tannins, etched with a dusting of sand. The finish is effortless across a gradual build-up of flavour. Screwcap. 14.5% alc. **Rating** 93 $30 NG

McLaren Vale Grenache 2015 This grenache is a fine achievement at the price, boasting the varietal genetics of kirsch and tangy red fruits, all slung across a beam of crunchy, pumice-tuned tannins and assuaging pomegranate acidity. A bit thin and green, perhaps. A gentle rasp ... and snap, crackle, pop! Screwcap. 14% alc. **Rating** 93 To 2023 $22 NG ○

McLaren Vale Cabernet Sauvignon Shiraz 2015 Blackcurrant, dark cherry, plum and bay leaf-infused bouillon: offers little room for mistaking the baritone of the choir. Indeed, cabernet makes up 65% of the blend and its aromatic harmonies soar over the blue fruits and warmth of syrah, a soprano backing vocal. Screwcap. 14% alc. **Rating** 93 To 2027 $22 NG ○

McLaren Vale Shiraz Viognier 2015 This full-bodied, juicy expression boasts a deep crimson flare, segueing righteously into a morass of blueberry, black cherry and mulberry fruits, flecked with uplifting violet florals and anise bound to an

undercarriage of peppery acidity and sinewy tannins. A scoop of vanilla pod oak provides a winning creaminess. Screwcap. 14% alc. Rating 92 To 2023 $22 NG ⊙
McLaren Vale Grenache Rose 2016 Rating 91 To 2018 $18 NG ⊙

ΨΨΨΨ McLaren Vale Tempranillo 2015 Rating 89 To 2021 $22 NG

Wilson Vineyard

Polish Hill River, Sevenhill via Clare, SA 5453 **Region** Clare Valley
T (08) 8843 4310 **Open** W'ends 10–4
Winemaker Daniel Wilson **Est.** 1974 **Dozens** 3000 **Vyds** 11.9ha
In 2009 the winery and general operations were passed on to son Daniel Wilson, the second generation. Daniel, a graduate of CSU, spent three years in the Barossa with some of Australia's largest winemakers before returning to Clare in '03. Parents John and Pat Wilson still contribute in a limited way, content to watch developments in the business they created. Daniel continues to follow John's beliefs about keeping quality high, often at the expense of volume, and rather than talk about it, believes the proof is in the bottle.

ΨΨΨΨΨ **DJW Clare Valley Riesling 2016** From a small single block (3500 vines) in the Polish Hill River vineyard, planted in '77, that immediately stood apart from the remainder. The mid-palate is generous, morphing to power on the finish and aftertaste. Screwcap. 12.5% alc. Rating 96 To 2036 $24 ⊙
Polish Hill River Riesling 2016 The wine is beautifully poised and focused, the insistent Bickford's lime juice and Meyer lemon flavours held within a crystal gauze of acidity on the very long palate. A great example of Polish Hill River riesling. Screwcap. 12.5% alc. Rating 95 To 2031 $29 ⊙

ΨΨΨΨΩ **Watervale Riesling 2016** Rating 93 To 2021 $19 ⊙

Windance Wines

2764 Caves Road, Yallingup, WA 6282 **Region** Margaret River
T (08) 9755 2293 **www**.windance.com.au **Open** 7 days 10–5
Winemaker Tyke Wheatley **Est.** 1998 **Dozens** 3500 **Vyds** 7.25ha
Drew and Rosemary Brent-White founded this family business, situated 5km south of Yallingup. Cabernet sauvignon, shiraz, sauvignon blanc, semillon and merlot have been established, incorporating sustainable land management and organic farming practices where possible. The wines are exclusively estate-grown. Daughter Billie and husband Tyke Wheatley now own the business: Billie, a qualified accountant, was raised at Windance, and manages the business and the cellar door, and Tyke (with winemaking experience at Picardy, Happs and Burgundy) has taken over the winemaking and manages the vineyard.

ΨΨΨΨΨ **Margaret River Shiraz 2015** An explosion of cassis, currants and black cherries plus loads of spice and cedary oak, all of which flow onto the full-bodied palate. There's a boldness to this, with ripe tannins, and pleasure in the silky smoothness and overall balance. Screwcap. 13.8% alc. Rating 95 To 2028 $24 JF ⊙

ΨΨΨΨΩ **Margaret River Cabernet Sauvignon 2014** Rating 93 To 2034 $32 JF
Margaret River Cabernet Shiraz 2015 Rating 92 To 2022 $28 JF
Margaret River Sauvignon Blanc Semillon 2016 Rating 91 To 2020 $20 JF ⊙

Windowrie Estate

Windowrie Road, Canowindra, NSW 2804 **Region** Cowra
T (02) 6344 3234 **www**.windowrie.com.au **Open** At The Mill, Cowra
Winemaker Antonio D'Onise **Est.** 1988 **Dozens** 30 000 **Vyds** 240ha
Windowrie Estate was established by the O'Dea family in 1988 on a substantial grazing property at Canowindra, 30km north of Cowra. A portion of the grapes is sold to other makers, but increasing quantities are being made for the Windowrie Estate and The Mill labels.

The cellar door is in a flour mill – built in 1861 from local granite – that ceased operations in 1905 and lay unoccupied for 91 years until restored by the O'Dea family. Exports to Canada, China, Japan and Singapore

ŸŸŸŸŸ Family Reserve Single Vineyard Cowra Chardonnay 2016 Hints of stone fruit with some lemon peel lead onto a subtle, almost gentle, palate, with some texture. In a word, reliable. Screwcap. 13% alc. **Rating** 90 **To** 2019 $28 JF
Family Reserve Shiraz 2015 Meaty, spicy and peppery aromas to the fore, with perhaps some whole-bunch influence coming into play. The fruit character running through the bouquet and palate is in the dark cherry, red vine-fruit vein; ripe, but not overly so. A brisk cut of acidity and lightly astringent tannin sit comfortably in the mix. Screwcap. 14.5% alc. **Rating** 90 **To** 2022 $25 SC

Windows Estate ★★★★★

4 Quininup Road, Yallingup, WA 6282 **Region** Margaret River
T (08) 9756 6655 **www.**windowsestate.com **Open** 7 days 10–5
Winemaker Chris Davies **Est.** 1996 **Dozens** 3500 **Vyds** 6.3ha
Chris Davies planted the Windows Estate vineyard (cabernet sauvignon, shiraz, chenin blanc, chardonnay, semillon, sauvignon blanc and merlot) in 1996, at the age of 19, and has tended the vines ever since. Initially selling the grapes, Chris moved into winemaking in 2006 and has had considerable show success for the consistently outstanding wines. Exports to Germany, Singapore and Taiwan.

ŸŸŸŸŸ Petit Lot Chardonnay 2014 Margaret River may do chardonnay well 90% of the time, but only 10% is as impressive as this. It is very complex and very intense, yet doesn't challenge so much as seduce the taster with its rainbow of white peach, nectarine and grapefruit flavours; the acidity and oak are judged to perfection. Screwcap. 13% alc. **Rating** 97 **To** 2024 $60 ✪
Basket Pressed Margaret River Cabernet Sauvignon 2014 Margaret River to its back teeth, with that particular profound mouthfilling expression of varietal blackcurrant fruit that doesn't need to belabour the point. It is, quite simply, of world class. Screwcap. 14% alc. **Rating** 97 **To** 2039 $39 ✪

ŸŸŸŸŸ Estate Grown Margaret River Semillon Sauvignon Blanc 2016 Early picking of the semillon has given the wine a spine of acidity and urgency to the drive, yet allowed the fruit (especially from the 50% barrel-ferment component) to effortlessly express itself on the long, elegant palate. Screwcap. 11.5% alc. **Rating** 95 **To** 2023 $26 ✪
Margaret River Chardonnay 2015 This is at the elegant end of Margaret River chardonnay style, but absolutely none the worse for that. White peach and a light garnish of gently spicy French oak run through the length of the palate and the fine, clear and clean finish. Screwcap. 13.5% alc. **Rating** 95 **To** 2025 $44
Petit Lot Fume Blanc 2015 This Margaret River wine pays homage to the Didier Dagenau (Loire Valley) style. Full straw-green; the bouquet has funky/smoky complexity (not reduction), the palate with deliberate phenolics ex skin contact during fermentation. Demands food of similar weight and complexity. Screwcap. 12% alc. **Rating** 94 **To** 2019 $32
Basket Pressed Margaret River Cabernet Merlot 2014 Matured in French barriques for 18 months. The bouquet has fresh fruit aromas, the palate more savoury than the bouquet would suggest, with spicy/earthy notes backing the blackcurrant, plum and bay leaf fruit line. Screwcap. 13.8% alc. **Rating** 94 **To** 2029 $32
Small Batch Margaret River Petit Verdot 2012 Petit verdot is grown in a multiplicity of climates in Australia, and is unfairly treated as a workhorse in the hot, unirrigated regions. Here it has a natural home, allowing its full-bodied, unmistakable earthy black fruits free play, dragging in balanced tannins and responding well to French oak. Screwcap. 14% alc. **Rating** 94 **To** 2025 $45

ŸŸŸŸŸ Estate Grown Margaret River Sauvignon Blanc 2016 Rating 93 **To** 2018 $23 ✪

Wine Unplugged ★★★★☆

PO Box 2208, Sunbury, Vic 3429 **Region** Various Vic
T 0432 021 668 **www**.wineunplugged.com.au **Open** Not
Winemaker Callie Jemmeson, Nina Stocker **Est.** 2010 **Dozens** 5000 **Vyds** 14ha
Nina Stocker and Callie Jemmeson believe that winemaking doesn't have to have barriers: what it does need is quality, focus and a destination. With a strong emphasis on vineyard selection and a gentle approach to their small batch winemaking, the wines are a true reflection of site. The wines are mainly released under the pacha mama, La Vie en Rose and Cloak & Dagger labels.

♈♈♈♈♈ **pacha mama Yarra Valley Chardonnay 2015** White peach, pink grapefruit and the barest hint of grilled nuts, likely oak-derived, provide all the flavour needed without compromising the finesse of a lovely chardonnay. Screwcap. 13.4% alc. **Rating** 95 **To** 2023 $27 ❍
pacha mama Heathcote Shiraz 2015 This is an admirable Heathcote shiraz, elegance and balance its life's mission, not ripeness and depth. It is driven by the freshness of its red (predominant) and black cherry fruits, oak and tannins little more than lift music. Screwcap. 14% alc. **Rating** 94 **To** 2029 $28 ❍

♈♈♈♈♈ **pacha mama Pinot Gris 2016** Rating 92 To 2019 $26
pacha mama Yarra Valley Pinot Noir 2015 Rating 92 To 2025 $31

Wine x Sam ★★★★☆

69–71 Anzac Avenue, Seymour, Vic 3660 **Region** Strathbogie Ranges
T 0403 059 423 **www**.winebysam.com.au **Open** 7 days 9–4
Winemaker Sam Plunkett, Matt Froude **Est.** 2013 **Dozens** 60 000 **Vyds** 10.2ha
Since 1991 Sam Plunkett and partner Bron Dunwoodie have changed shells as often as a lively hermit crab. 1991: first estate vineyard established and mud brick winery built. 2001: created a new winery at Avenel. 2004: purchased the large Dominion Wines in partnership with the Fowles family. 2011: Fowles purchased the Plunkett family's shareholding, except 7ha of shiraz and 3.2ha of chardonnay. Winemaking moved to the Taresch family's Elgo Estate winery. Within two years the Plunkett interests had leased the entire Elgo winery, now making the Elgo wines as well as their own brands. A large contract make for Naked Wines saw production increase to 20 000 dozen, and in a few blinks of the eye later production is 60 000. Exports to the UK, the US and China.

♈♈♈♈♈ **The Victorian Strathbogie Ranges Shiraz 2015** Gold medal Great Shiraz Challenge '16, trophy National Cool Climate Wine Show '16. This is an elegant shiraz from start to finish. The fragrant bouquet has red and blue fruits with a background of French oak; this follows through the medium-bodied, fresh palate. Tannins are present, but not obvious, as the wine flows evenly across and along the mouth. Screwcap. 14.5% alc. **Rating** 96 **To** 2030 $28 ❍
Tait Hamilton Vineyard Heathcote Shiraz 2015 An impressive Heathcote shiraz with black cherry, blackberry and a touch of licorice on the medium-bodied palate; the texture is especially good, with a juicy quality throughout. Carries its alcohol well. Screwcap. 14.7% alc. **Rating** 94 **To** 2030 $35

♈♈♈♈♈ **Stardust & Muscle Strathbogie Ranges Shiraz 2015** Rating 91 To 2029
Major Plains Vineyard Shiraz 2014 Rating 90 To 2024 $35

Wines by Geoff Hardy ★★★★★

327 Hunt Road, McLaren Vale, SA 5171 **Region** South Australia
T (08) 8383 2700 **www**.winesbygeoffhardy.com.au **Open** 7 days 11–5
Winemaker Geoff Hardy, Shane Harris **Est.** 1980 **Dozens** 90 000 **Vyds** 43ha
Geoff Hardy's great-great-grandfather, the original Thomas Hardy, first planted grapes in SA in the 1850s and was one of the founding fathers of the Australian wine industry. In 1980, Geoff left the then family company, Thomas Hardy & Sons, to make his own way in all sectors of the Australian wine business, together with wife Fiona. Wines by Geoff Hardy is made up

of three ventures/brands founded by Geoff: Pertaringa in McLaren Vale, K1 by Geoff Hardy in the Adelaide Hills (Tynan Rd, Kuitpo) and Hand Crafted by Geoff Hardy, sourced from a variety of premium regions across SA. Exports to Canada, the UK, Germany, Sweden, Finland, India, Malaysia, South Korea, Indonesia, Japan, Singapore, Taiwan, Hong Kong and China.

ΨΨΨΨΨ **Pertaringa The Yeoman 2014** The vines were planted by Geoff Hardy's great-great-grandfather 100 years ago. The colour is good, and the shiraz proclaims its McLaren Vale origin with its blend of blackberry fruits and dark chocolate, the supple and velvety palate of the highest quality. Diam. 14.7% alc. **Rating** 97 **To** 2039 $250

ΨΨΨΨΨ **K1 by Geoff Hardy Adelaide Hills Chardonnay 2015** A generous, well made wine, its foundation the depth of its stone fruit flavours augmented by some toasty oak and grilled nuts. The length is good, as is its price. A prime each-way bet for present or future consumption. Screwcap. 13.7% alc. **Rating** 95 **To** 2023 $35 ✪
Pertaringa Over The Top McLaren Vale Shiraz 2015 Thankfully this isn't over the top, though it is rich, ripe and commanding, certainly. There's an overlying savouriness to this, a whisper of black pepper, cinnamon quills, crushed juniper and dark chocolate. The oak is well integrated with powerful and composed tannins: everything is in balance. Diam. 15% alc. **Rating** 95 **To** 2030 $40 JF
Pertaringa The Yeoman 2015 While this shiraz demands attention, the hefty 2kg bottle really is absurd. Definitely in the full-bodied, richer and riper spectrum, with dark fruit, wood spice, black licorice, with powerful yet supple tannins. Somehow it manages to rein that in and morph into a sophisticated drink. Diam. 15% alc. **Rating** 95 **To** 2035 $250 JF
Hand Crafted by Geoff Hardy Fiano 2016 Its bouquet and fore-palate have greater flowery perfume and precision than most, but it falls into the fiano line with the power and length of its finish and aftertaste, savoury acidity a varietal hallmark. Screwcap. 13% alc. **Rating** 94 **To** 2020 $25 ✪
Pertaringa Undercover McLaren Vale Shiraz 2015 Quite apart from semaphoring its region on the fragrant bouquet, its price is mouthwatering, as are the multi-flavours in the mouth. Cherry, plum and blackberry all have their say, but there's not much point in arguing the cause of one or the other: just relax and enjoy. Screwcap. 14.5% alc. **Rating** 94 **To** 2025 $22 ✪
Hand Crafted by Geoff Hardy Shiraz 2015 A compelling example of McLaren Vale with its medium to full-bodied earthy/chocolatey black fruits reaching every corner of the mouth in a flash. Better still is the balance, which will sustain the wine as it slowly matures, its oak and tannins already an integral part of the wine. Screwcap. 14.5% alc. **Rating** 94 **To** 2035 $30 ✪
K1 by Geoff Hardy Adelaide Hills Autumn Harvest 2016 Yellow-gold; an extremely luscious and complex riesling. Autumn Harvest is a totally ambiguous name, normally reserved for barely off-dry rieslings. This is a horse of a very different colour. 375ml. Screwcap. 9.5% alc. **Rating** 94 **To** 2023 $20 ✪

ΨΨΨΨΨ **Hand Crafted Arneis 2016 Rating** 93 **To** 2021 $25 ✪
K1 Adelaide Hills Gruner Veltliner 2016 Rating 92 **To** 2023 $25 ✪
K1 Middle Hill Shiraz 2015 Rating 92 **To** 2030 $25 ✪
Pertaringa Two Gentlemen's GSM 2015 Rating 92 **To** 2020 $22 ✪
Hand Crafted Cabernet Franc 2015 Rating 92 **To** 2023 $30 JF
Hand Crafted Durif 2015 Rating 92 **To** 2020 $30 JF
Hand Crafted Lagrein 2015 Rating 92 **To** 2023 $30 JF
Hand Crafted Gruner Veltliner 2016 Rating 91 **To** 2020 $25
K1 Adelaide Hills Pinot Noir 2015 Rating 91 **To** 2023 $40
Pertaringa Stage Left Merlot 2015 Rating 91 **To** 2024 $22 ✪
Pertaringa Scarecrow Sauvignon Blanc 2016 Rating 90 **To** 2017 $20 ✪
K1 Adelaide Hills Rose 2016 Rating 90 **To** 2017 $25
K1 Adelaide Hills Shiraz 2015 Rating 90 **To** 2022 $45 JF
K1 Adelaide Hills Cabernet Sauvignon 2015 Rating 90 **To** 2027 $45 JF

K1 Sparkling NV **Rating** 90 **To** 2017 $35 TS
Pertaringa Rampart Vintage Fortified 2015 **Rating** 90 To 2028 $40 JF

Wines for Joanie ★★★★

163 Glendale Road, Sidmouth, Tas 7270 **Region** Northern Tasmania
T (03) 6394 7005 **www**.winesforjoanie.com.au **Open** 7 days 10–5
Winemaker Contract **Est.** 2013 **Dozens** 800 **Vyds** 6.5ha
Andrew (Rew) and Prue O'Shanesy lived on a small cattle and cropping farm in Qld, but
they realised it wasn't a viable stand-alone business. They sold it, and had no idea what to
do next. Northern Territory? A coffee plantation at Byron Bay? Someone mentioned that a
vineyard was for sale in northern Tasmania. Look no further: Rew is a viticulturist and both
love drinking wine. In the blink of an eye they were heading across Bass Strait 'with the ute,
two cattle dogs, a horse and a prissy cat'. They started working on a budget for a vineyard,
trying to make the budget tell them what they wanted to hear. They eventually tore up the
budget, took the plunge and bought Glendale, the little farm they now call home. They now
have three dogs, two horses, the prissy cat, a couple of chooks, some sheep, a few cows and two
small children. Joanie was Rew's mother, an inspiring, vivacious, creative and strong woman.

♀♀♀♀♀ **Pinot Gris 2016** Wham bam thank you ma'am – this is fierce in its immediate
intensity and high tension acidity, barrel fermentation and maturation having done
nothing to stop it in its tracks. Screwcap. 13% alc. **Rating** 91 **To** 2019 $35
Portrait Chardonnay 2016 The acidity in this wine is spot on. The flavours
build within a framework of grapefruit, Granny Smith apple, white peach and pear
the main contributors, oak merely an observer. Screwcap. 13.5% alc. **Rating** 90
To 2024 $30

♀♀♀♀ **Portrait Pinot Noir 2015 Rating** 89 **To** 2018 $30

Wirra Wirra ★★★★★

463 McMurtrie Road, McLaren Vale, SA 5171 **Region** McLaren Vale
T (08) 8323 8414 **www**.wirrawirra.com **Open** Mon–Sat 10–5, Sun & public hols 11–5
Winemaker Paul Smith, Tom Ravech **Est.** 1894 **Dozens** 150 000 **Vyds** 51.31ha
Long respected for the consistency of its white wines, Wirra Wirra has now established an
equally formidable reputation for its reds. The wines are of exemplary character, quality and
style, The Angelus Cabernet Sauvignon and RWS Shiraz battling each other for supremacy,
with The Absconder Grenache one to watch. Long may the battle continue under the
direction of managing director Andrew Kay and the winemaking team of Paul Smith and Tom
Ravech, who forge along the path of excellence first trod by the late (and much loved) Greg
Trott, the pioneering founder of modern-day Wirra Wirra. Its acquisition of Ashton Hills in
2015 added a major string to its top quality bow. Exports to all major markets.

♀♀♀♀♀ **Patritti McLaren Vale Shiraz 2015** A bright, booming vermilion, this is all
latent power. Boysenberry scents envelop; violet, too. Yet it is the strident, skinsy
parry of tightly meshed grape tannins, juicy and cheek-pummelling, that define
this wine. The oak, surely lavish, is buried beneath the sumptuous extract. The
finish is long and taut, the fruit barely flowing across its broad shoulders yet. This
needs plenty of time. Screwcap. 14.5% alc. **Rating** 97 **To** 2034 $130 NG ✪
Whaite Old Block Single Vineyard Shiraz 2014 40yo vines, matured in
used French puncheon for 18 months. A seriously beautiful wine celebrating the
Blewitt Springs district; it's hard to imagine how the rippling rivulet of red and
purple fruits could be bested. It's perfection, and well worth the money. Screwcap.
14.5% alc. **Rating** 97 **To** 2034 $130 ✪

♀♀♀♀♀ **Woodhenge McLaren Vale Shiraz 2015** This is very good. A plush pasture of
black fruits of every description, plus licorice, bonbon and bitter chocolate, is deftly
pruned by firm framing tannins, each impeccably detailed. The oak is beautifully
integrated, tucked in behind the veneer of polish. Screwcap. 14.5% alc. **Rating** 96
To 2029 $35 NG ✪

RSW McLaren Vale Shiraz 2015 The top-end wines of Wirra Wirra all boast an exemplary meld of tightly knit, grapey tannins, considered oak and easy flowing acidity, making them a pleasure to drink. Despite the muscle of blue to dark fruit tones and the driving vinosity of this shiraz, it is far from an assault. Violet wafts across an altogether savoury melody. Long and fine. Screwcap. 14.5% alc. **Rating** 96 **To** 2039 $70 NG ⊙

The Absconder McLaren Vale Grenache 2015 High quality old vine grenache was open-fermented and matured in French oak for 10 months. It is an exercise in purity and place, showing once again the synergy between McLaren Vale and grenache on the near-endless palate. I think the wine may prove to be exceptionally long-lived. Screwcap. 14.5% alc. **Rating** 96 **To** 2030 $70 ⊙

Catapult McLaren Vale Shiraz 2015 This is from the big boys' school, armed to the teeth with black fruits, bitter chocolate and tannins lined up with military precision. It is medium to full-bodied, and a red for prolonged cellaring, balance both now and into the far future ensuring that it hits the target dead centre. Screwcap. 14% alc. **Rating** 95 **To** 2035 $25 ⊙

Whaite Old Block Single Vineyard Shiraz 2014 Predominantly earthy, spicy and savoury on the bouquet, the fruit character expressed as a subtle red berry contribution. Flows effortlessly and elegantly on the palate, the latent depth of flavour somewhat masked (for now) by the fine but persistent tannins and fresh, lingering acidity. Screwcap. 14.5% alc. **Rating** 95 **To** 2030 $130 SC

Chook Block Shiraz 2014 Dark fruit aromas of blood plum and blueberry are the first impression on the bouquet, with chocolate, licorice and tarry notes emerging. Solidly built palate, but avoids seeming overly big or heavy, the rich fruit, oak and tannin striking an admirable balance. Screwcap. 14.5% alc. **Rating** 95 **To** 2030 $130 SC

Hiding Champion Sauvignon Blanc 2016 Rating 94 **To** 2018 $24 ⊙
The Angelus Cabernet Sauvignon 2015 Rating 94 **To** 2033 $70 NG

ŸŸŸŸŸ **The 12th Man Adelaide Hills Chardonnay 2016** Rating 93 **To** 2026 $35 NG
Amator McLaren Vale Shiraz 2015 Rating 93 **To** 2023 $30 NG
Amator McLaren Vale Shiraz 2014 Rating 93 **To** 2022 $30 SC
Mrs Wigley Grenache Rose 2016 Rating 92 **To** 2017 $20 SC ⊙
Original Blend Grenache Shiraz 2015 Rating 92 **To** 2022 $25 SC ⊙
Amator McLaren Vale Cabernet Sauvignon 2015 Rating 91 **To** 2024 $30 NG
Church Block McLaren Vale Cabernet Sauvignon Shiraz Merlot 2015 Rating 91 **To** 2024 $22 NG ⊙
The Lost Watch Adelaide Hills Riesling 2016 Rating 90 **To** 2026 $24
Amator McLaren Vale Cabernet Sauvignon 2014 Rating 90 **To** 2024 $30 SC

Wise Wine   ★★★★★

237 Eagle Bay Road, Eagle Bay, WA 6281 **Region** Margaret River
T (08) 9750 3100 **www**.wisewine.com.au **Open** 7 days 11–5
Winemaker Andrew Siddell, Matt Buchan, Larry Cherubino (Consultant) **Est.** 1986
Dozens 10000 **Vyds** 2.5ha

Wise Wine, headed by Perth entrepreneur Ron Wise, has been a remarkably consistent producer of high quality wine. The vineyard adjacent to the winery (2ha of cabernet sauvignon and shiraz, and 0.5ha of zinfandel) in the Margaret River is supplemented by contract-grown grapes from Pemberton, Manjimup and Frankland River. The value for money of many of the wines is extraordinarily good. Exports to the UK, Switzerland, the Philippines and Singapore.

ŸŸŸŸŸ **Lot 80 Margaret River Cabernet Sauvignon 2015** The region's genetic stamp of cigar box, dried sage, pastille and black cherry flavours flow-long and broad across a generous palate defined by wagyu-like grape tannins, massaged and toned; a spray of saline acidity and new oak, palpable, but nestled firmly into the ̶w̶i̶n̶e̶'̶s̶ ̶a̶r̶o̶m̶y̶ ̶core Gewürztraminer. 11% alc. Rating 95 To 2010 $15 NG

🍷🍷🍷🍷🍷 Eagle Bay Margaret River Chardonnay 2016 Rating 93 To 2024 $65 NG
Eagle Bay Margaret River Shiraz 2015 Rating 92 To 2030 $65 NG
Leaf Frankland River Riesling 2016 Rating 91 To 2024 $28 JF
Leaf Margaret River Pinot Grigio 2016 Rating 91 To 2019 $28 NG
Sea Urchin Frankland River Shiraz 2014 Rating 91 To 2022 $19 NG ✪

Witches Falls Winery ★★★★★

79 Main Western Road, Tamborine Mountain, Qld 4272 **Region** Queensland
T (07) 5545 2609 **www**.witchesfalls.com.au **Open** Mon–Fri 10–4, w'ends 10–5
Winemaker Jon Heslop, Arantza Milicua Celador **Est.** 2004 **Dozens** 12 000 **Vyds** 0.4ha
Witches Falls is the venture of Jon and Kim Heslop. Jon has a deep interest in experimenting with progressive vinification methods in order to achieve exceptional and interesting results. He has a degree in applied science (oenology) from CSU, and experience working in the Barossa and Hunter valleys as well as at Domaine Chantel Lescure, Burgundy, and with a Napa-based winegrower. Witches Falls' grapes are sourced from the Granite Belt (other than its 0.4ha of estate durif), and it is one of the consistently good performers in that context. Exports to the US, South Korea, Taiwan and China.

🍷🍷🍷🍷🍷 Wild Ferment Granite Belt Viognier 2015 This really is a success, starting with a variety that needs the skills of a horse whisperer. The apricot-tinged varietal expression is excellent, and the barrel ferment inputs, while important, have been neatly controlled. Screwcap. 13% alc. **Rating** 95 To 2019 $32 ✪
Prophecy Granite Belt Cabernet Sauvignon 2014 A complex, medium-bodied wine reflecting the time and money invested in it. The more I tasted it, the more blackcurrant/cassis I unearthed at its core, oak and tannins handmaidens. Screwcap. 13.4% alc. **Rating** 95 To 2034 $51
Wild Ferment Granite Belt Fiano 2015 The lemon zest and pith of fiano aren't particularly obvious, but are present, along with notes of stone fruit, on the long, well balanced palate, particularly commendable given the young vines. The freshness of the finish is a feature. Screwcap. 13.8% alc. **Rating** 94 To 2019 $32

🍷🍷🍷🍷🍷 Wild Ferment Granite Belt Verdelho 2015 Rating 93 To 2018 $32
Wild Ferment Granite Belt Chardonnay 2016 Rating 92 To 2010 $32 SC
Wild Ferment Granite Belt Monastrell 2015 Rating 92 To 2024 $32
Wild Ferment Sauvignon Blanc 2015 Rating 91 To 2017 $32
Granite Belt Cabernet Sauvignon 2015 Rating 91 To 2023 $28 SC
Wild Ferment Granite Belt Chardonnay 2015 Rating 90 To 2020 $32
Granite Belt Verdelho 2016 Rating 90 To 2018 $24 SC
Prophecy Granite Belt Syrah 2014 Rating 90 To 2024 $51
Granite Belt Merlot 2013 Rating 90 To 2033 $28

Witchmount Estate ★★★★☆

557 Leakes Road, Plumpton, Vic 3335 **Region** Sunbury
T (03) 9747 1055 **www**.witchmountestatewinery.com.au **Open** Wed–Sun 11–5
Winemaker Steve Goodwin **Est.** 1991 **Dozens** 8000 **Vyds** 25.5ha
Witchmount Estate, with its restaurant and function centre, is only 30 minutes from Melbourne, in the Sunbury region. The vineyard is planted to shiraz (12ha), cabernet sauvignon (6ha) and chardonnay (2ha), with lesser amounts of sauvignon blanc, pinot gris, merlot, tempranillo and barbera. The quality of the wines has been consistent, the prices very modest. Exports to China.

🍷🍷🍷🍷🍷 Reserve Shiraz 2010 Remains defiantly youthful: first tasted in '13, then in late '15, and now for the third time. The colour is still bright crimson, the palate with a mix of red and black fruits, fine, gently savoury tannins, and positive, albeit integrated, oak. The one change is in overall weight, now medium-bodied rather than full-bodied. Screwcap. 13.8% alc. **Rating** 95 To 2030 $60

Olivia's Paddock Chardonnay 2015 The wine has excellent freshness and acidity; its apple and fine-grained flavours are long and intense, and have absorbed the new oak without a word of complaint. Will develop very nicely. Screwcap. 13% alc. **Rating** 94 **To** 2025 $32

♀♀♀♀♀ **Cabernet Franc 2016 Rating** 93 **To** 2029 $32
Lowen Park Shiraz 2015 Rating 91 **To** 2030 $18 **○**
Lowen Park Sangiovese Rose 2016 Rating 90 **To** 2017 $18 **○**

Wolf Blass ★★★★★

97 Sturt Highway, Nuriootpa, SA 5355 **Region** Barossa Valley
T (08) 8568 7311 **www.**wolfblasswines.com **Open** 7 days 10–4.30
Winemaker Chris Hatcher **Est.** 1966 **Dozens** NFP
Although merged with Mildara and now under the giant umbrella of TWE, the brands (as expected) have been left largely intact. The Wolf Blass wines are made at all price points, ranging through Red, Yellow, Gold, Brown, Grey, Sapphire, Black, White and Platinum labels, at one price point or another covering every one of the main varietals. In 2016 a new range of wines labelled BLASS was introduced. The style and range of the wines continue to subtly evolve under the leadership of chief winemaker Chris Hatcher. Exports to all major markets.

♀♀♀♀♀ **Platinum Label Barossa Shiraz 2013** The nose is reticent, brooding with an uncanny latency implying graphite, basalt, cedar, anise, cardamom and an array of Indian spices. The billowing black fruits lie beneath, stretching ... edging across the palate, but kept bound, for now at least, to a carapace of pulpy grape tannin and lavish oak. Lock this away for some time. Screwcap. 14.7% alc. **Rating** 95 **To** 2035 $200 NG
Black Label Barossa Cabernet Shiraz Malbec 2014 An expression of carnal, warm climate, hedonistic and explosive fruit on one hand, and a pillow of creamy texture, built upon the foundation of superlative winemaking cum authoritative tannin management, on the other. Like most very good wine, this is as delicious now as it will be in 30 years. Only the shades of dark to light will change. Screwcap. 14.8% alc. **Rating** 95 **To** 2044 $130 NG

♀♀♀♀♀ **Blass Noir Barossa Valley Shiraz 2014 Rating** 93 **To** 2024 $35 SC
Grey Label Shiraz Cabernet 2015 Rating 93 **To** 2028 $45 NG
Grey Label McLaren Vale Shiraz 2014 Rating 92 **To** 2026 $45 SC
Gold Label Adelaide Hills Syrah 2013 Rating 92 **To** 2022 $28 SC
BLASS Black Cassis Cabernet 2015 Rating 92 **To** 2024 $22 JF **○**
Gold Label Barossa Shiraz 2015 Rating 91 **To** 2025 $28 NG
Gold Label Cabernet Sauvignon 2015 Rating 91 **To** 2026 $28 JF
Gold Label Adelaide Hills Chardonnay 2015 Rating 90 **To** 2020 $28
Blass Noir Barossa Valley Shiraz 2015 Rating 90 **To** 2025 $35 JF
Yellow Label Cabernet Sauvignon 2015 Rating 90 **To** 2021 $16 JF **○**
Gold Label Cabernet Sauvignon 2014 Rating 90 **To** 2024 $28 SC
BLASS Black Cassis Cabernet 2014 Rating 90 **To** 2021 $35 SC

Wood Park ★★★★★

263 Kneebones Gap Road, Markwood, Vic 3678 **Region** King Valley
T (03) 5727 3778 **www.**woodparkwines.com.au **Open** At Milawa Cheese Factory
Winemaker John Stokes **Est.** 1989 **Dozens** 7000 **Vyds** 16ha
John Stokes planted the first vines at Wood Park in 1989 as part of a diversification program for his property at Bobinawarrah, in the hills of the Lower King Valley, east of Milawa. The vineyard is managed with minimal chemical use, winemaking a mix of modern and traditional techniques (what wine isn't?). The reach of Wood Park has been expanded with Beechworth Pinot Noir and Chardonnay and a mix of mainstream and alternative varieties, all well made. It also has a cellar door in Ford St, Beechworth. Exports to Taiwan, Singapore and China.

�♱♱♱♱ **Beechworth Chardonnay 2015** Gleaming straw-green; a prime example of the synergy between Beechworth and chardonnay, swelling on the end of the palate, but not distorting it. A special feature is the way it folds citrussy acidity within its white and yellow peach fruit. Screwcap. 13.8% alc. **Rating** 95 **To** 2025 $30 **○**
The Tuscan 2015 Cabernet sauvignon, sangiovese, petit verdot, colorino and shiraz matured in French oak for 18 months. A gloriously juicy wine with vibrant spicy red berry fruits, fine-grained tannins and a long, well balanced palate. Screwcap. 13.5% alc. **Rating** 95 **To** 2030 $25 **○**
Home Block King Valley Viognier 2015 Bright straw-green; packs a remarkable punch given its modest alcohol and has clear-cut varietal character, apricot and a touch of fresh ginger doing the honours. Screwcap. 13.5% alc. **Rating** 94 **To** 2030 $28 **○**

♱♱♱♱♱ **Monument Lane King Valley Roussanne 2015** Rating 92 To 2027 $28
Wild's Gully King Valley Tempranillo 2015 Rating 92 To 2025 $18 **○**
Reserve King Valley Cabernet Sauvignon 2015 Rating 91 To 2025 $40
Beechworth Pinot Noir 2015 Rating 90 To 2022 $30
Monument Lane Cabernet Shiraz 2015 Rating 90 To 2030 $26

Woodgate Wines ★★★★

43 Hind Road, Manjimup, WA 6258 **Region** Manjimup
T (08) 9772 4288 **www**.woodgatewines.com.au **Open** Thurs–Sat 10–4.30
Winemaker Mark Aitken **Est.** 2006 **Dozens** 2000 **Vyds** 7.9ha
Woodgate is the family business of Mark and wife Tracey Aitken, Tracey's mother Jeannette Smith, and her brother Robert and his wife Linda Hatton. Mark became a mature- age student at Curtin University, obtaining his oenology degree in 2001 as Dux, earning a trip to Bordeaux to undertake vintage, returning to work at Manjimup's Chestnut Grove winery from '02. In '05 he and Tracey began their own contract winemaking business, as well as making wine for their Woodgate brand. Most of the grapes come from the estate plantings of cabernet sauvignon, chardonnay, sauvignon blanc, pinot noir and merlot, supplemented by grapes from a leased vineyard. The name of the sparkling wine, Bojangles, reflects the family's musical heritage, which stretches back three generations and includes vocalists, guitarists, pianists, a trumpeter, a saxophonist, two drummers and a double bass player.

♱♱♱♱♱ **Pemberton Cabernet Franc 2014** Crafted with 15% merlot in the blend, this is a sappy, savoury and agreeable confluence of violet, red and black currant, spearmint and cherry flavours, strung across a beam of gently astringent grape tannins, vital acidity and well applied oak. Highly varietal, savoury and versatile at the table. Screwcap. 14.5% alc. **Rating** 93 **To** 2022 $28 NG

Woodhaven Vineyard ★★★★

87 Main Creek Road, Red Hill, Vic 3937 **Region** Mornington Peninsula
T 0421 612 178 **www**.woodhavenvineyard.com.au **Open** By appt
Winemaker Lee and Neil Ward **Est.** 2003 **Dozens** 275 **Vyds** 1.6ha
Woodhaven is the venture of Lee and Neil Ward, both qualified accountants for 30 years in Melbourne, albeit working in different fields. They spent two years looking for a suitable site on the Mornington Peninsula, ultimately finding one high on Red Hill. Bringing the venture to the point of production has been a slow and, at times, frustrating business. They decided from the outset to be personally responsible for all aspects of growing the grapes and making the wines, relying on the advice readily given to them by George and Ruth Mihaly of Paradigm, David and (the late) Wendy Lloyd of Eldridge, John and Julie Trueman of Myrtaceae and Nat and Rose White, formerly of Main Ridge. They also decided to grow the vines organically and biodynamically, and it took eight years to produce their first two barrels of wine, in 2010. In '13 the 0.8ha each of pinot noir and chardonnay finally produced more than one barrel of each wine.

♱♱♱♱♱ **Chardonnay 2015** Fermented in new French barriques, mlf, matured in used French oak for 15 months. The oak regime is decidedly unusual, although in his prime Robert Parker Jr persuaded vignerons in France to double-oak their wines, first for fermentation, then for maturation, but Woodhaven stops short of that. If you focus on the fruit, and on the aftertaste, you can be persuaded that this wine does have balance. Screwcap. 12.8% alc. **Rating** 94 **To** 2025 $40

Woodlands ★★★★★

3948 Caves Road, Wilyabrup, WA 6284 **Region** Margaret River
T (08) 9755 6226 **www**.woodlandswines.com **Open** 7 days 10–5
Winemaker Stuart and Andrew Watson **Est.** 1973 **Dozens** 17 000 **Vyds** 26.58ha
Founder David Watson had spectacular success with the Cabernets he made in 1979 and the early '80s. Commuting from Perth on weekends and holidays, as well as raising a family, became all too much, and for some years the grapes from Woodlands were sold to other Margaret River producers. With the advent of sons Stuart and Andrew (Stuart primarily responsible for winemaking), the estate has bounced back to pre-eminence. The wines come in four price bands, the bulk of the production under the Chardonnay and Cabernet Merlot varietals, then a series of Reserve and Special Reserves, then Reserve de la Cave, and finally Cabernet Sauvignon. The top-end wines primarily come from the original Woodlands vineyard, where the vines are over 40 years old. Exports to the UK, the US, Sweden, The Netherlands, Indonesia, Malaysia, the Philippines, Singapore, Japan and China.

♥♥♥♥♥ **Reserve de la Cave Margaret River Cabernet Franc 2015** Only 300 bottles were produced of what is, unquestionably, one of the world's great cabernet francs. A gorgeous deep ruby red, this fragrant red has a core of dark cherry/mulberry fruit while 100% new oak sits very discreetly in the background. With its superb depth of fruit, silky palate and ripe, fine and very persistent tannins, there is little doubt that this will provide enormous pleasure now and over the next 10–20 years. Screwcap. 13.5% alc. **Rating** 97 **To** 2030 $90 PR **❂**

♥♥♥♥♥ **Matthew Margaret River Cabernet Sauvignon 2014** 94% cabernet, 4% malbec and 2% cabernet franc. Pure blackcurrant fruit aromas intermingle with some gentle olive tapenade and cedar notes while the medium-bodied a palate is supported by very persistent and fine-grained tannins. Screwcap. 13.5% alc. **Rating** 95 **To** 2030 $150 PR
Emily 2015 47% cabernet franc, 41% merlot, 9% malbec 2% cabernet and 1% petit verdot. Red and black fruits intermingle with bell pepper and violet aromas and the palate is textured and long. The tannins are superfine and there is a great each-way proposition here: enjoy this now or in 5–10 years. Screwcap. 13.5% alc. **Rating** 95 **To** 2025 $39 PR

♥♥♥♥♡ **Wilabrup Valley Cabernet Merlot 2015 Rating** 92 $28 PR
Margaret 2015 Rating 90 $58 PR

Woods Crampton ★★★★★

PO Box 417, Hamilton, NSW 2303 **Region** Barossa Valley
T 0417 670 655 **www**.woods-crampton.com.au **Open** Not
Winemaker Nicholas Crampton, Aaron Woods **Est.** 2010 **Dozens** 30 000
This is one of the most impressive ventures of Nicholas Crampton (his association with McWilliam's is on a consultancy basis) and winemaking friend Aaron Woods. The two make the wines at the Sons of Eden winery with input advice from Igor Kucic. The quality of the wines, and the enticing prices, has seen production soar from 1500 to 30 000 dozen, with every expectation of continued success. Exports to the UK, Canada, Denmark, Hong Kong and China.

♥♥♥♥♥ **Frances & Nicole Old Vine Single Vineyard Eden Valley Shiraz 2015** Utterly convincing colour to a wine that effortlessly captures the imagination of those who seek to understand and describe it. It achieves this through a medium-bodied palate overflowing with black fruits and an occasional lightning flash of red berries, focused yet supple tannins, oak like Le Carré's *The Constant Gardener*. Screwcap. 14% alc. **Rating** 97 **To** 2045 $60 ⚫

Old Vine Barossa Valley Mataro 2015 Excellent colour, and from this point on you know you're onto something special. It is strikingly elegant for a wine with intense purple and black fruits, tannins barely raising a ripple to disturb the surface. Screwcap. 14% alc. **Rating** 97 **To** 2035 $30 ⚫

ȲȲȲȲȲ **High Eden Riesling 2016** The bouquet is markedly more complex than that of its sibling, the palate with another drum roll of intensity and power, the lemon/lime fruit backed by minerally acidity. The exceptional length is a sine qua non. Screwcap. 12.5% alc. **Rating** 96 **To** 2036 $30 ⚫

Old Vine Eden Valley Shiraz 2015 Has that textured, plush mouthfeel that is the Woods Crampton birthmark. Perfumed black fruits and spices drive the bouquet, the palate adding blackberry, black cherry and licorice. Power and body assembled without high octane fruit. Screwcap. 14% alc. **Rating** 96 **To** 2040 $30 ⚫

Frances & Nicole Old Vine Eden Valley Shiraz 2014 A riot of spice on the bouquet: clove, cumin, anise, allspice and more. Dark, almost liqueur-like fruit and sweet/savoury oak aromas manage to find a way through. Rich and intense on the palate but blessed with a supple, velvety texture, it's mouthfilling yet not overwhelming. Screwcap. 14% alc. **Rating** 96 **To** 2034 $65 SC ⚫

Old Vine Eden Valley Shiraz 2014 A remarkably complex bouquet for a young wine. Dark fruit, licorice, Asian spice, herbs de Provence, whole bunch aromas and pepper. Supple and seamless on the palate, the dark fruit in control with the savoury, spicy elements adding their own touches; well integrated tannin is in perfect harmony. Delicious. Screwcap. 14% alc. **Rating** 95 **To** 2034 $30 SC ⚫

Three Barrels Barossa Valley Graciano 2015 Graciano can be a miserable handful, and I wondered how the 50% whole-bunch stem characters would play with it, but it has worked, with spicy, savoury stemmy notes dancing on the tongue, red fruits in the lead. Screwcap. 14% alc. **Rating** 95 **To** 2030 $30 ⚫

Third Wheel Barossa Valley Rose 2016 **Rating** 94 **To** 2018 $24 ⚫

Old Vine Barossa Shiraz 2015 **Rating** 94 **To** 2035 $22 ⚫

The Big Show Shiraz Mataro 2015 **Rating** 94 **To** 2030 $25 ⚫

ȲȲȲȲȲ **Old John Barossa Shiraz Bonvedro 2015** **Rating** 93 **To** 2020 $25 ⚫

Off the Books Heathcote Shiraz 2015 **Rating** 92 **To** 2025 $22 ⚫

Old Vine Barossa Valley Cabernet Sauvignon 2015 **Rating** 92 **To** 2035 $30

Take it to the Grave Shiraz 2016 **Rating** 91 **To** 2029 $18 ⚫

Take it to the Grave Shiraz 2015 **Rating** 91 **To** 2023 $18 ⚫

Eden Valley Dry Riesling 2016 **Rating** 90 **To** 2026 $22

The Primrose Path McLaren Vale Shiraz 2015 **Rating** 90 **To** 2025 $18 ⚫

Woodstock ★★★★☆

215 Douglas Gully Road, McLaren Flat, SA 5171 **Region** McLaren Vale
T (08) 8383 0156 **www.**woodstockwine.com.au **Open** 7 days 10–5
Winemaker Ben Glaetzer **Est.** 1905 **Dozens** 22 000 **Vyds** 18.44ha

The Collett family is among the best known in McLaren Vale, the late Doug Collett AM for his World War II exploits flying Spitfires and Hurricanes with the RAF and RAAF, returning to study oenology at Roseworthy Agricultural College, and rapidly promoted to take charge of SA's largest winery, Berri Co-operative. In 1973 he purchased the Woodstock estate, built a winery, and in '74 he crushed its first vintage. Son Scott Collett, once noted for his fearless exploits in cars and on motorcycles, became winemaker in '82, and has won numerous accolades; equally importantly, he purchased an adjoining shiraz vineyard planted circa 1900 (now the source of The Stocks Shiraz) and a bushvine grenache vineyard planted in '30. In '99, he joined forces with Ben Glaetzer, passing responsibility for winemaking to Ben, but retaining responsibility for the estate vineyards. Exports to most major markets.

🍷🍷🍷🍷🍷 **The Stocks Single Vineyard McLaren Vale Shiraz 2014** This full-bodied wine represents the best barrels of the vintage. There is substantial oak showing now, but it's good quality, and I don't have the slightest doubt that when the wine approaches maturity in '24, all the juicy black fruits, licorice and chocolate will simply acknowledge that oak is part of a complex shiraz of the utmost quality. Screwcap. 15.4% alc. **Rating** 97 **To** 2044 $80 ○

🍷🍷🍷🍷🍷 **McLaren Vale Very Old Fortified NV Rating** 92 $48
Naughty Monte Montepulciano 2015 Rating 90 **To** 2020 $30

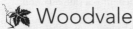 # Woodvale   ★★★★★

PO Box 54, Watervale, SA 5453 **Region** Clare Valley
T 0417 829 204 **Open** Not
Winemaker Kevin Mitchell **Est.** 2014 **Dozens** 3000 **Vyds** 7ha
This is the personal venture of Kevin Mitchell and wife Kathleen Bourne, not an offshoot of Kilikanoon (see separate entry). The main targets are what Kevin describes as 'modest, sustainable growth, working with the varieties that Clare does so well: riesling, shiraz, cabernet sauvignon, mataro, semillon, pinot gris, and of course, grenache'. Given he is a third-generation Clare Valley grapegrower, procuring grapes from mates to supplement the estate shiraz, pinot gris and riesling should not be a problem.

🍷🍷🍷🍷🍷 **Woodberry Clare Valley Shiraz 2014** Deep colour, although not as dense as Spring Gardens; a high quality shiraz that is, relatively speaking, light on its feet. It has a fresh, gently savoury, edge to black fruits and fine-grained tannins. It has also taken the oak into the folds of its fruits in convincing fashion. Screwcap. 14.5% alc. **Rating** 96 **To** 2040 $50
The Khileyre Clare Valley Riesling 2015 From two Watervale vineyards and made in precisely the same way as its Watervale sibling, but there is more tension and drive to the fruit, more cohesion to the pure stream of lime and lemon fruit; the acidity, too, is a touch more detailed. Screwcap. 12.5% alc. **Rating** 95 **To** 2030 $38
Skilly Clare Valley Riesling 2014 From a single 15yo vineyard in the Skillogalee Valley at 430m. A vibrantly fresh and crisp wine with minerally acidity woven in strands through the citrus and apple fruit. If you love 10yo Clare rieslings, this should do the trick. Screwcap. 12.5% alc. **Rating** 95 **To** 2032 $28 ○
Spring Gardens Clare Valley Shiraz 2014 Dense, deep crimson-purple; as the colour suggests, a full-bodied shiraz that manages to remain supple and rich without excessive extract. It rolls around the mouth with blackberry, plum and a neat veneer of French oak. Screwcap. 14.5% alc. **Rating** 95 **To** 2044 $35
Hootenanny Clare Valley GSM 2014 A 50/40/10% blend. Shiraz carries this wine on its back, and does so impressively, injecting both freshness and shape to the medium to full-bodied blend of red and black fruits; the tannins are fine. As good as they come from the Clare Valley. Screwcap. 14.5% alc. **Rating** 94 **To** 2029 $35
Orchard Road Clare Valley Cabernet Sauvignon 2014 High quality fruit from a region not famous for the variety, and expansive use of high quality oak, will win many friends. The tannins are present, but not intrusive, the only question the amount of oak – which will delight some, be forgiven by others. Screwcap. 14% alc. **Rating** 94 **To** 2039 $35

🍷🍷🍷🍷🍷 **The Khileyre Clare Valley Riesling 2016 Rating** 93 **To** 2026 $35
Watervale Riesling 2015 Rating 93 **To** 2022 $28
Watervale Riesling 2016 Rating 92 **To** 2026 $30
M.C.D. Clare Valley Grenache 2014 Rating 90 **To** 2023 $35

...'s Wines

kolbin, NSW 2320 **Region** Hunter Valley
woodwardswines.com.au **Open** Not
ward **Est.** 1972 **Dozens** 200 **Vyds** 7.5ha

is fascinating, and seems unreal until you learn that winemaker
as winemaker at Saddlers Creek. The business is owned by his
ng from the corporate world of Sydney to the Hunter Valley to
neyard in 1973. When water became available through a major
d the first computerised irrigation system in the Hunter Valley.
er to the likes of Mount Pleasant and Capercaillie, and, when
ed at Hungerford Hill, Rothbury Estate, Bimbadgen Estate
s. His younger son Brett, who first of all did the hard yards
and Brokenwood, obtained a Masters of Oenology from
marketing has been desultory is putting it mildly, given
non is (apparently) still available after winning trophies
ers Show in '08, '09 and '14 for Best Cabernet, and

***

rve Cabernet 2007 Made for Woodward's by
illie shortly before his death. It is only now on the
multiple layers of cassis, earth and briar, the tannins
p. 14% alc. **Rating** 92 **To** 2027 $75
Rose 2016 A dark cherry hue; lots of flavour and
spice, tangy cranberries, watermelon and rind;
cap. 12% alc. **Rating** 90 **To** 2019 $20 JF ❂

Shearer own two
ere first planted in
abernet sauvignon

nas are rich and
touch. Ripe
e tannin firm
dium-rare steak
2023 $26 SC

★★★★★

30 **Region** Margaret River
m.au **Open** 7 days 10–4.30
kerton **Est.** 1982 **Dozens** 7500 **Vyds** 14.23ha
of majestic marri and jarrah forest, doesn't have the
aret River, but has had major success in wine shows
nd Jane Bailey in 2000, and major renovations have
ery tasting room for larger groups and an alfresco
ast is Neil Gallagher's continuing role as winemaker,
il is the son of founders Jeff and Wynn Gallagher).
uda, Hong Kong and China.

et River Cabernet Sauvignon 2015 A potent,
. Something like a young, expensive Bordeaux as
cter and oak engaged in a battle for supremacy.
int of sweet fruit just a teaser. Demands bottle age.
030 $65 SC

Merlot 2015 **Rating** 93 **To** 2027 $35 SC
iver Graciano 2014 **Rating** 93 **To** 2024 $26 ❂
2015 **Rating** 92 **To** 2020 $35 SC
ver SSB 2016 **Rating** 90 **To** 2018 $23
ver Shiraz 2014 **Rating** 90 **To** 2025 $35 SC
iver Merlot 2014 **Rating** 90 **To** 2024 $26

★★★★★

E) from producing
ment Riesling and
d Michael Shiraz.
noney. Investments
enkins, and skilled
and elegance than

and the epitome
oral note
ulated palate,
such depth and
lc. **Rating** 97

e wines were
on site in
vineyard wine,
. The excellent
s. But the palate
like raw silk.

overlooked
ied palate, silky
; ultra-refreshing
0 $60 JF ❂
keen price and
lagship Michael,
oning of spice and

S

gion Orange
es.com.au **Open** 7 days 10.30–5
st. 1999 **Dozens** 750 **Vyds** 2.5ha
igure in Word of Mouth, his involvement dating
e Wines with an early planting of pinot gris. Word

of Mouth was formed when Pinnacle amalgamated with neighbouring Don
In 2013 the Donnington parcel was sold, and has since become Colmar Est
his original block, and continues under the Word of Mouth label.

ΨΨΨΨΨ **Orange Riesling 2012** The airy elegance of the wine is anchor
residual sugar, veiled by the acidity and freshness of its penetrating
the lemon sorbet on the finish. It's not 5 years old, it's 5 years you
11.1% alc. **Rating** 94 **To** 2022 $25

ΨΨΨΨΨ **Orange Petit Manseng 2015 Rating** 90 **To** 2025 $30

Wykari Wines

PO Box 905, Clare, SA 5453 **Region** Clare Valley
T (08) 8842 1841 **www**.wykariwines.com.au **Open** Not
Winemaker Neil Paulett **Est.** 2006 **Dozens** 1200 **Vyds** 20ha
Local Clare families Rob and Mandy Knight and Peter and Robyn-
vineyards, one to the north, the other to the south of Clare. The vineyards w
1974, and are dry-grown and hand-pruned. In all there are shiraz, riesling, c
and chardonnay.

ΨΨΨΨΨ **Naughty Girl Clare Valley Shiraz 2014** Juicy blackberry aro
varietal, mint and ironstone characters adding a distinctly regiona
fruit rolls along the palate with a measure of sweet oak in tow, th
enough to provide the framework and the finish. Made for a me
from a wood-fired barbecue. Screwcap. 14.6% alc. **Rating** 90 **To**

Wynns Coonawarra Estate

Memorial Drive, Coonawarra, SA 5263 **Region** Coonawarra
T (08) 8736 2225 **www**.wynns.com.au **Open** 7 days 10–5
Winemaker Sue Hodder, Sarah Pidgeon **Est.** 1897 **Dozens** NFP
Large-scale production has not prevented Wynns (an important part of TW
excellent wines covering the full price spectrum, from the bargain-base
Shiraz through to the deluxe John Riddoch Cabernet Sauvignon an
Even with steady price increases, Wynns offers extraordinary value for
in rejuvenating and replanting key blocks, under the direction of Allen
winemaking by Sue Hodder, have resulted in wines of far greater finesse
many of their predecessors. Exports to the UK, the US, Canada and Asia.

ΨΨΨΨΨ **Michael Shiraz 2014** What a wine. It's spine-tingling, thrilling
of elegance. Vivid purple with red plums and black cherries, a f
wafting in with powdered ginger and star anise. An evenly mod
extraordinarily powdery tannins and an ultra-long finish. There'
complexity here, and it just appears effortless. Screwcap. 13.5%
To 2034 $150 JF ○
Johnsons Single Vineyard Cabernet Sauvignon 2014 Th
planted in '54, making this the oldest surviving cabernet sauvig
Coonawarra. A mere 60 years later, it makes its debut as a singl
bringing forth its unique elements, which centre on savouriness
colour is a given; so, too, the fragrance of fruit, florals and flowe
is key: all poise, with vitality and quite distinct tannins, textured
Screwcap. 13.5% alc. **Rating** 97 **To** 2036 $80 JF ○

ΨΨΨΨΨ **V&A Lane Shiraz 2015** A subtle, beautiful shiraz that can be
precisely for those attributes. This glides across the medium-bo
tannins in tow, savoury and spicy elements in the succulent frui
on the long, long finish. Screwcap. 12.5% alc. **Rating** 96 **To** 20
Shiraz 2015 A youthful, vibrant shiraz with depth of flavour,
ready now. No pretensions of reaching the lofty heights of the
but this can stand proud with its core of juicy fruit, perfect seas

oak, and ultra-fine tannins on its smooth, supple, medium-bodied palate. It just tastes good. Screwcap. 13.5% alc. **Rating** 95 **To** 2024 $25 JF ✪
The Siding Cabernet Sauvignon 2014 Bright, full crimson-purple; blackcurrant, cherry and spice flavours are woven through a latticework of French oak and quite persistent tannins that add to the stature of the wine. Totally impressive. Screwcap. 13.5% alc. **Rating** 95 **To** 2029 $25 ✪
V&A Lane Cabernet Shiraz 2015 A balanced interplay between bramble berries and plums, blood orange rind and juice, and fennel and freshly rolled tobacco. The palate is textured, bolstered by plush tannins with finely cut acidity, and long on the finish. Screwcap. 13.5% alc. **Rating** 95 **To** 2030 $60 JF
Shiraz 2014 **Rating** 94 **To** 2030 $25 ✪

🍷🍷🍷🍷 **The Siding Cabernet Sauvignon 2015** **Rating** 92 **To** 2024 $25 JF ✪
Chardonnay 2016 **Rating** 91 **To** 2022 $25 JF
Cabernet Shiraz Merlot 2015 **Rating** 91 **To** 2025 $25 JF
Cabernet Shiraz Merlot 2014 **Rating** 90 **To** 2029 $25

Wynwood Estate ★★★★

310 Oakey Creek Road, Pokolbin, NSW 2320 **Region** Hunter Valley
T (02) 4998 7885 **www**.wynwoodestate.com.au **Open** 7 days 10–5
Winemaker Peter Lane **Est.** 2011 **Dozens** 7000 **Vyds** 28ha

Wynwood Estate is owned by Winston Wine Pty Ltd, the Australian arm of what is described as one of the largest and fastest-growing wine distributors in China, with 100 wine stores established across the country. Wynwood has almost 30ha of low-yielding vineyards, including shiraz (8ha), merlot (5ha), chardonnay (4ha), verdelho (3ha) and muscat (1ha). It has some dry-grown 95-year-old shiraz vines that only produce an average of 0.75 tonnes of fruit each vintage. Plantings were extended in 2014 with durif (3ha), malbec and roussanne (1ha each). Wynwood also sources cabernet franc, grenache and merlot from company-owned vineyards in the Barossa Valley. Winemaker Peter Lane has had a long career in the Hunter Valley (Mount Pleasant, Tulloch and Tyrrell's).

🍷🍷🍷🍷🍷 **Grey Gum Hunter Valley Durif 2014** The deep crimson-purple colour is a rarity in the Hunter Valley, a tribute to the great vintage and to a variety that performs well wherever grown; there is a wealth of dark berry fruits, the used French oak in which it was matured barely visible, but nonetheless important. Screwcap. 13.9% alc. **Rating** 94 **To** 2025 $40

🍷🍷🍷🍷 **Reserve Hunter Valley Chardonnay 2013** **Rating** 92 **To** 2020 $40 NG

Xabregas ★★★★★

Spencer Road, Mount Barker, WA 6324 **Region** Mount Barker
T (08) 6389 1382 **www**.xabregas.com.au **Open** Not
Winemaker Mike Garland, Andrew Hoadley **Est.** 1996 **Dozens** 10 000 **Vyds** 80ha

The Hogan family have five generations of WA history and family interests in sheep grazing and forestry in the Great Southern, dating back to the 1860s. Terry Hogan, founding Xabregas chairman, felt the Mount Barker region was 'far too good dirt to waste on blue gums', and vines were planted in 1996. The Hogan family concentrates on the region's strengths – shiraz and riesling. Exports to the US, Singapore, Japan, China and NZ.

🍷🍷🍷🍷🍷 **Mount Barker Riesling 2015** Mount Barker makes riesling so consistently good it all seems too easy. This has great length, and a wealth of aromas, blossom and otherwise, the palate responding with a stream of delicious, ever-changing flavours. Irresistible. Screwcap. 12.7% alc. **Rating** 95 **To** 2030 $25 ✪
X by Xabregas Spencer Syrah 2012 The lighter colour is relative – it's just the depth of the colour of its siblings that triggers the lighter comparison, but it's a relative indicator of a medium-bodied cool climate shiraz that is instantly appealing. It tiptoes through red, purple and black fruits, a garden of spices and fine-spun, but persistent, tannins. Screwcap. 14.4% alc. **Rating** 95 **To** 2037 $55

X by Xabregas Figtree Syrah 2012 Takes minimalist labelling to the far extreme – black on black, the wine, happily, anything but. The bouquet is very expressive, with a whirl of black fruits, licorice, pepper and spice feeding into tannins, and quality oak on the finish. Screwcap. 14.8% alc. **Rating** 94 **To** 2032 $55

ŸŸŸŸŸ **Mount Barker Sauvignon Blanc 2016 Rating** 90 **To** 2018 $25
Mount Barker Shiraz 2014 Rating 90 **To** 2027 $25

Xanadu Wines   ★★★★★

Boodjidup Road, Margaret River, WA 6285 **Region** Margaret River
T (08) 9758 9500 **www**.xanaduwines.com **Open** 7 days 10–5
Winemaker Glenn Goodall **Est.** 1977 **Dozens** 70000 **Vyds** 109.5ha
Xanadu Wines was established in 1977 by Dr John Lagan. In 2005 it was purchased by the Rathbone family, and together with Glenn Goodall's winemaking team they have significantly improved the quality of the wines. The vineyard has been revamped via soil profiling, precision viticulture, improved drainage and reduced yields, with production bolstered through the acquisition of the Stevens Road vineyard in '08. In '15 the new entry point Exmoor range replaced the Next of Kin range, made from both estate and contract-grown grapes. Exports to most major markets.

ŸŸŸŸŸ **DJL Margaret River Sauvignon Blanc Semillon 2016** Wild-yeast fermented in French oak (10% new) and lees-stirred for several months. The bouquet immediately tells you complex vinification has worked brilliantly, with struck match aromas, the layered palate of utterly exceptional intensity, with fruit, oak and acidity welded together so tightly it's impossible (and irrelevant) to unpick them. Screwcap. 13% alc. **Rating** 97 **To** 2021 $24 ❂

ŸŸŸŸŸ **Stevens Road Margaret River Chardonnay 2015** Matured for 9 months in French oak (25% new) before a best barrels selection blended in Nov '14. Has considerable drive and complexity; grapefruit and white peach utterly dominate the building up of the flavours on the long palate. Fruit, oak and acidity all act synergistically. Screwcap. 13% alc. **Rating** 96 **To** 2025 $70 ❂
Margaret River Cabernet Sauvignon 2014 91% cabernet sauvignon, 5% malbec, 4% petit verdot, matured for 14 months in French oak (40% new). Great colour is no surprise, nor is the majesty of the cassis-filled bouquet and palate. While there is an element of barrel selection (and trickle down of lesser barrels, and possible promotion) each wine does have its own personality, part shaped by the vineyard, part in the winery. Here the extended maceration has refined the tannins without stripping the fruit. Screwcap. 14% alc. **Rating** 96 **To** 2040 $37 ❂
Reserve Margaret River Cabernet Sauvignon 2014 Includes 5% each of malbec and petit verdot, matured for 14 months in French barriques before the blend assembled from a best barrels selection and then returned to oak for a further 2 months. An exceedingly clever bonding of fresh and complex fruit, fresh cassis at the core, wrapped in ripe tannins, herbs and cedary French oak; the length is impeccable, as is the balance. Easy when you're in Margaret River. Screwcap. 14% alc. **Rating** 96 **To** 2039 **To** 2023 $85
Reserve Margaret River Chardonnay 2015 Matured in French oak (30% new) for 9 months. Elegant, supple and spring-day fresh stone fruit, white peach, nectarine and a little Granny Smith apple, the oak subtle, the finish very long and clean. Screwcap. 13% alc. **Rating** 95 **To** 2023 $85
DJL Margaret River Cabernet Sauvignon 2014 86% cabernet sauvignon, 10% malbec, 4% petit verdot. The great crimson-purple colour telegraphs a steel hand in a velvet glove. The wine has great structure and texture, yet is so refined it is only medium-bodied, with all the expected cassis, blackcurrant and mulberry fruit. Bargain, of course. Screwcap. 14% alc. **Rating** 95 **To** 2039 $24 ❂
Exmoor Sauvignon Blanc Semillon 2016 Rating 94 **To** 2020 $18 ❂
DJL Chardonnay 2016 Rating 94 **To** 2026 $24 ❂
Stevens Road Cabernet Sauvignon 2014 Rating 94 **To** 2030 $70

Ɏ Ɏ Ɏ Ɏ Ɏ Exmoor Chardonnay 2016 Rating 91 To 2020 $18 ○
Exmoor Cabernet Sauvignon 2014 Rating 90 To 2022 $18 ○

Yabby Lake Vineyard ★★★★★

86–112 Tuerong Road, Tuerong, Vic 3937 **Region** Mornington Peninsula
T (03) 5974 3729 **www**.yabbylake.com **Open** 7 days 10–5
Winemaker Tom Carson, Chris Forge **Est.** 1998 **Dozens** 3350 **Vyds** 50.8ha
This high-profile wine business was established by Robert and Mem Kirby (of Village
Roadshow), who had been landowners in the Mornington Peninsula for decades. In 1998
they established Yabby Lake Vineyard, under the direction of vineyard manager Keith Harris;
the vineyard is on a north-facing slope, capturing maximum sunshine while also receiving sea
breezes. The main focus is the 25ha of pinot noir, 14ha of chardonnay and 8ha of pinot gris;
3h of shiraz, merlot and sauvignon blanc take a back seat. The arrival of the hugely talented
Tom Carson as Group Winemaker has added lustre to the winery and its wines, making the
first Jimmy Watson Trophy-winning Pinot Noir in 2014, and continuing to blitz the Australian
wine show circuit with Single Block Pinots. Exports to the UK, Canada, Sweden, Singapore,
Hong Kong and China.

Ɏ Ɏ Ɏ Ɏ Ɏ Single Vineyard Mornington Peninsula Syrah 2016 The vintage was
somewhat challenging for pinot, but not for shiraz. Both the bouquet and medium
to full-bodied palate have a smoky/savoury/spicy undertow easily dealt with by
the black fruits and generous tannins. Screwcap. 14.5% alc. **Rating** 96 **To** 2036
$33 ○
Single Vineyard Mornington Peninsula Syrah 2015 The fragrant, spicy
fruit-driven bouquet opens the door to the immaculately crafted medium-bodied
palate, where spicy red and black cherry fruit is draped on a scaffold of fine-
grained tannins and integrated French oak. As usual, a lovely wine. Screwcap.
14% alc. **Rating** 96 **To** 2030 $33 ○
Single Vineyard Mornington Peninsula Chardonnay 2016 Wild-yeast
fermented (no mlf) in French oak (20% new), matured for 11 months. Terrific
drive, focus and length, mouthwatering in its intensity. Pink grapefruit and white-
fleshed stone fruit are the centre of attention. Screwcap. 12.5% alc. **Rating** 95
To 2024 $45
Single Vineyard Mornington Peninsula Pinot Noir 2016 Matured in French
puncheons (25% new) for 11 months. Light, though bright, colour; the expressive,
flowery red fruit aromas set the scene for a palate with fine, silky tannins and a
lingering finish. Screwcap. 13% alc. **Rating** 95 **To** 2028 $60

Ɏ Ɏ Ɏ Ɏ Ɏ Red Claw Chardonnay 2016 Rating 93 To 2020 $28 PR
Red Claw Pinot Noir 2016 Rating 92 To 2024 $28 PR

Yal Yal Estate ★★★★☆

15 Wynnstay Road, Prahran, Vic 3181 (postal) **Region** Mornington Peninsula
T 0416 112 703 **www**.yalyal.com.au **Open** Not
Winemaker Sandro Mosele **Est.** 1997 **Dozens** 2500 **Vyds** 2.63ha
In 2008 Liz and Simon Gillies acquired a vineyard planted in 1997 to 1.6ha of chardonnay
and a little over 1ha of pinot noir.

Ɏ Ɏ Ɏ Ɏ Ɏ Yal Yal Rd Mornington Peninsula Chardonnay 2015 The decidedly
complex, funky bouquet melds into a rich, fruit-driven palate with nectarine,
peach and a hint of honey providing depth and length. Barrel-ferment oak is also
in play throughout, albeit in a secondary role. A wine that grew and grew each
time I went back to it. Screwcap. 13.5% alc. **Rating** 95 **To** 2023 $30 ○

Ɏ Ɏ Ɏ Ɏ Ɏ Yal Yal Rd Mornington Peninsula Pinot Gris 2015 Rating 91 To 2017 $30

Yalumba

40 Eden Valley Road, Angaston, SA 5353 **Region** Eden Valley
T (08) 8561 3200 **www**.yalumba.com **Open** 7 days 10–5
Winemaker Louisa Rose (chief) **Est.** 1849 **Dozens** 930 000 **Vyds** 180ha
Family-owned and run by Robert Hill-Smith, Yalumba has a long commitment to quality and great vision in its selection of vineyard sites, new varieties and brands. It has always been a serious player at the top end of full-bodied (and full-blooded) Australian reds, and was a pioneer in the use of screwcaps. While its estate vineyards are largely planted to mainstream varieties, it has taken marketing ownership of viognier. However, these days its own brands revolve around the Y Series and a number of stand-alone brands across the length and breadth of SA. A founding member of Australia's First Families of Wine. Exports to all major markets.

The Caley Coonawarra Barossa Cabernet Shiraz 2012 52% Coonawarra cabernet, 27% Barossa cabernet and 21% Barossa shiraz. Bright, deep crimson-purple; the bouquet instantly semaphores a glorious profusion of cassis, blackberry and black cherry fruits, flavours which are precisely mirrored by the palate. But it's the way this beautiful wine caresses the mouth that is so special, the tannins polished, the oak judged to perfection. Cork. 14% alc. **Rating** 98 **To** 2042 $349

The Octavius Old Vine Barossa Shiraz 2013 By design, and from the ground up, this is a trenchantly full-bodied shiraz, but notwithstanding this, is so well balanced it fills the mouth with black fruit flavours, then backs off so gracefully the finish and aftertaste are of pure fruit, oak and tannins dismissed with a magic wand. Cork. **Rating** 96 **To** 2043 $112

The Signature Barossa Cabernet Sauvignon Shiraz 2014 This ticks all the boxes, a rock of ages in the storm of Yalumba reds coming onto the market, led by The Caley, but numerous others seeking your company. The blackcurrant and blackberry fruit are in total harmony, and the overall texture is of a high order thanks to the management of the oak, as well as that of the tannins. A standout from a vintage that had its challenges. Cork. 13.5% alc. **Rating** 96 **To** 2040 $60 ❂

The Virgilius Eden Valley Viognier 2015 It brings you up with a jolt when you find Yalumba has had 35 years experience with this variety, and it does show in this vintage. Yalumba has perfected the approach to coax positive varietal fruit – orange zest and apricot – yet keep the finish clear of phenolic oiliness. Bravo. Screwcap. 13.5% alc. **Rating** 95 **To** 2019 $48

Samuel's Garden Collection Eden Valley Roussanne 2015 Full-bodied and textural, but not mawkish, thanks to lively acidity keeping it neatly pitched. Honeysuckle, dried herbs, white pepper and woodsy spices mingle with stone fruit, honeydew melon and creamed honey. A roussanne still definitely in the savoury spectrum. Screwcap. 12.5% alc. **Rating** 95 **To** 2021 $24 JF ❂

Paradox Northern Barossa Shiraz 2015 From the Kalimna/Ebenezer district, known for the power of its shiraz, here conferring a generous black fruit bouquet; the palate has obvious texture and structure, yet there is a special vibrancy on the back-palate and finish. Cork. 14% alc. **Rating** 95 **To** 2030 $43

Paradox Northern Barossa Shiraz 2014 While savoury black fruits (blackberry foremost) provide the drum beat for the exploration of the wine. It has a juicy elegance and intensity, elbowing tannins and oak out of the way. A really enjoyable shiraz. Cork. 13.5% alc. **Rating** 95 **To** 2034 $43

Vine Vale Barossa Valley Grenache 2016 I like this wine: it has bright, fresh red fruits and a firmness in the mouth that comes as much from the fruit as from the tannins. There is a continuity in the flow and development of flavour which puts beyond doubt the proposition that it shouldn't be an article of faith that grenache can't be picked below 14.5° baume. Cork. 13.5% alc. **Rating** 95 **To** 2026 $35 ❂

Vine Vale Barossa Valley Grenache 2015 It is as fresh as a daisy on the way in, and likewise on the finish and aftertaste. These Yalumba Grenaches are only light-bodied, but with an intensity that belies their translucency. Cork. 13.5% alc. **Rating** 95 **To** 2025 $35 ❂

Carriage Block Grenache 2015 Rating 94 To 2024 $45
Samuel's Garden Grenache 2015 Rating 94 To 2024 $20 ◐

ΨΨΨΨΨ Samuel's Garden Collection Eden Valley Viognier 2015 Rating 93
To 2021 $24 JF ○
Rogers & Rufus Rose 2016 Rating 93 To 2019 $23 JF ○
The Menzies Cabernet Sauvignon 2014 Rating 93 To 2029 $52
Ringbolt Cabernet Sauvignon 2014 Rating 92 To 2029 $28
Running With Bulls Barossa Tempranillo 2016 Rating 92 To 2020 $23 JF ○
Y Series Barossa Riesling 2016 Rating 90 To 2022 $15 ○
Samuel's Garden Collection Triangle Block Eden Valley Shiraz 2013
Rating 90 To 2023 $24
Carriage Block Grenache 2016 Rating 90 To 2021 $45

Yangarra Estate Vineyard ★★★★★

809 McLaren Flat Road, Kangarilla SA 5171 **Region** McLaren Vale
T (08) 8383 7459 **www**.yangarra.com.au **Open** 7 days 10–5
Winemaker Peter Fraser, Shelley Torresan **Est.** 2000 **Dozens** 15 000 **Vyds** 89.3ha
This is the Australian operation of Jackson Family Wines, one of the leading premium
wine producers in California, which in 2000 acquired the 172ha Eringa Park vineyard
from Normans Wines (the oldest vines dated back to 1923). The renamed Yangarra Estate
Vineyard is the estate base for the operation, and is moving to certified organic status with its
vineyards. Peter Fraser has taken Yangarra Estate to another level altogether with his innovative
winemaking and desire to explore all the possibilities of the Rhône Valley red and white styles.
Thus you will find grenache, shiraz, mourvedre, cinsaut, carignan, tempranillo and graciano
planted, and picpoul noir, terret noir, muscardin and vaccarese around the corner. The white
varieties are roussanne and viognier, with grenache blanc, bourboulenc and picpoul blanc
planned. Then you see ceramic eggs being used in parallel with conventional fermenters. In
2015 Peter was named Winemaker of the Year at the launch of the *Wine Companion* 2016.
Exports to the UK, the US and other major markets.

ΨΨΨΨΨ **Ironheart McLaren Vale Shiraz 2014** The flagship shiraz. It effortlessly reaches
a depth of flavour and presence while retaining its verve. Smells of a spice shop
next door to a baker, with the dark fruit in line with sprightly acidity and shapely
if firm tannins. Stunning now, with an even brighter future. Screwcap. 14.5% alc.
Rating 97 **To** 2038 $105 JF ○
High Sands McLaren Vale Grenache 2014 50% whole berries, wild yeast and
on lees in used French oak for 1 year. No need for winemaking accoutrements.
Perfectly modulated, the tannins enmeshed with the fruit whence they came.
Excellent fruit, yet the most savoury and earthy-toned and deepest of the three
Grenaches. Screwcap. 14.5% alc. **Rating** 97 **To** 2034 $130 JF ○

ΨΨΨΨΨ **Roux Beaute McLaren Vale Roussanne 2015** Using two ceramic egg vessels,
half the fruit is fermented on skins for 160 days in one, the other half with juice
only. The final outcome a 60/40% blend respectively. What a wine. Complex yet
refined, notes of preserved ginger, herbal tea, honeycomb and clotted cream, with
neat phenolics and gossamer-like acidity. Screwcap. 13.5% alc. **Rating** 96 **To** 2023
$72 JF ○
Ovitelli McLaren Vale Grenache 2015 A name change: goodbye Small Pot
Ceramic Egg, hello Ovitelli, sounds classier. Still made in (two) ceramic egg vessels.
The heady aromatics greet and promise more good things to come. Superfine
acidity, the pure line of fruit tannin, the energy and joy in this wine, quite
profound. Screwcap. 14.5% alc. **Rating** 96 **To** 2032 $72 JF ○
McLaren Vale Viognier 2016 It's viognier, but not as you know it. It's not big,
fat, nor riddled with apricots. Instead it's savoury and really textural, with grilled
nuts, jasmine rice, a creamed-honey leesy character and saline-like acidity. As good
as it gets and stylishly so. Screwcap. 13.5% alc. **Rating** 95 **To** 2021 $32 JF ○

McLaren Vale Roussanne 2016 While there's a whisper of nashi pears, daikon, camomile, fennel and white pepper, this runs on a savoury track, with fine acidity keeping it from ever becoming too big. Lovely drink. Screwcap. 13.5% alc. **Rating** 95 **To** 2022 $35 JF ✪

McLaren Vale Shiraz 2015 Excellent dark-purple hue; succulent and velvety texture with some power to the chiselled tannins, savoury yet pristine fruit the key. Screwcap. 14.5% alc. **Rating** 95 **To** 2032 $30 JF ✪

Old Vine McLaren Vale Grenache 2015 So fragrant it's breathtaking. To start, a whirl of perfectly ripe raspberries and redcurrants, patchouli and subtle Middle Eastern spices. The palate is tightly wound, with raspberry-like acidity, and more pronounced tannins in the background. Screwcap. 14.5% alc. **Rating** 95 **To** 2029 $35 JF ✪

GSM 2015 One of the noticeable traits of Yangarra's wines, GSM in particular, is that there's nothing harsh or worked: there's a purity of fruit that comes through, and a balance of tannins to acidity (this not shy with the latter). The right amount of spice and flavour: a really, delicious drink. Screwcap. 14.5% alc. **Rating** 95 **To** 2024 $32 JF ✪

McLaren Vale Mourvedre 2015 It has more perfume and lift than most, with currants, Treviso radicchio, crushed gravel and cinnamon quills. Ripe tannins and sprightly acidity are in sync, with the latter in the driver's seat. Come along for the ride. Screwcap. 14.5% alc. **Rating** 95 **To** 2025 $35 JF ✪

🍷🍷🍷🍷︎ PF McLaren Vale Shiraz 2016 **Rating** 93 **To** 2019 $25 JF ✪

Yarra Burn   ★★★★☆

4/19 Geddes Street, Mulgrave, Vic 3170 **Region** Yarra Valley
T 1800 088 711 **www.**yarraburn.com.au **Open** Not
Winemaker Ed Carr **Est.** 1975 **Dozens** NFP
At least in terms of name, this is the focal point of Accolade's Yarra Valley operations. However, the winery was sold, and the wines are now made elsewhere. The Upper Yarra vineyard largely remains. The lack of interest in the brand and its quality is as sad as it is obvious.

🍷🍷🍷🍷🍷 Bastard Hill Single Vineyard Yarra Valley Chardonnay 2013 Gleaming straw-green; it is a very powerful and concentrated wine that some may find too confronting, but not me; grapefruit and white peach are benchmark flavours, acidity perfectly judged. Screwcap. 13.5% alc. **Rating** 96 **To** 2025 $60 ✪

Pinot Noir Chardonnay Rose 2007 The price has risen from $20 since its initial release, but the gain in complexity justifies it. Salmon-hued, it has a spicy, floral gingerbread bouquet and a rich, creamy palate, its red fruits and spices reflecting its 66+% pinot noir base. Its length and freshness can't be faulted. Cork. 12.5% alc. **Rating** 94 **To** 2018 $25 ✪

🍷🍷🍷🍷︎ Premium Cuvee Brut NV **Rating** 90 **To** 2017 $20 TS ✪

Yarra Yering   ★★★★★

Briarty Road, Coldstream, Vic 3770 **Region** Yarra Valley
T (03) 5964 9267 **www.**yarrayering.com **Open** 7 days 10–5
Winemaker Sarah Crowe **Est.** 1969 **Dozens** 5000 **Vyds** 26.37ha
In September 2008, founder Bailey Carrodus died, and in April '09 Yarra Yering was on the market. It was Bailey Carrodus's clear wish and expectation that any purchaser would continue to manage the vineyard and winery, and hence the wine style, in much the same way as he had done for the previous 40 years. Its acquisition in June '09 by a small group of investment bankers has fulfilled that wish. The low-yielding, unirrigated vineyards have always produced wines of extraordinary depth and intensity. Dry Red No. 1 is a cabernet blend; Dry Red No. 2 is a shiraz blend; Dry Red No. 3 is a blend of touriga nacional, tinta cao, tinta roriz, tinta amarela, alvarelhao and souzao; Pinot Noir and Chardonnay are not hidden behind delphic numbers; Underhill Shiraz (planted in 1973) is from an adjacent vineyard purchased by Yarra

Yering over a decade ago. Sarah Crowe, who had carved out a remarkable reputation as a winemaker in the Hunter Valley in a relatively short time, was appointed winemaker in the wake of Paul Bridgeman's departure to Levantine Hill after the '13 vintage. She has made red wines of the highest imaginable quality from her first vintage, and to the delight of many, myself included, has offered all the wines with screwcaps. For good measure, she introduced the '14 Light Dry Red Pinot Shiraz as a foretaste of that vintage, and an affirmation of the exceptional talent recognised by her being named Winemaker of the Year in the *Wine Companion* 2017. Exports to the UK, the US, Singapore, Hong Kong and China.

ȚȚȚȚȚ **Dry Red No. 1 2015** This is a superlative, tightly furled Bordeaux blend of pedigree, age-worthiness and a sapid quiver of blackcurrant to herbal notes: crushed, dried and strewn about the palate, all tightly guarded by gravelly tannins and juicy natural acidity. The oak handling, too, smacks of expertise: a fine-grained and well trained hedge, embellishing the savoury air of the style rather than overwhelming it. A blend of 67% cabernet sauvignon, 16% merlot, 13% malbec and a mere seasoning of petit verdot synergise to make an imperious, beautiful wine with a long, long life ahead. Screwcap. 14% alc. **Rating** 99 **To** 2040 $100 NG ✪

Carrodus Shiraz 2015 High-toned violet aromas and pumice-stone tannins, all inflected with a cool stream of natural acidity lighting up blueberry, damson plum and salami notes. These are sluiced with a ferruginous tang of iodine and an impeccable spread of woven tannin, each strand impeccably bound to the glorious fruit spread across the palate. This will age beautifully, as with most of the range. Screwcap. 13% alc. **Rating** 98 **To** 2034 $250 NG

Agincourt Cabernet Malbec 2015 Violet and boysenberry set the senses alight. A lick of bay leaf brings a more savoury tone. The factor that marks the entire range more than any other is the impeccable tannin management, tactile and palpably juicy across the wine, and the oak, nestled as a classy echoing support amid the cacophonous fruit and herbal follow-through. Screwcap. 14% alc. **Rating** 98 **To** 2032 $86 NG ✪

Pinot Noir 2015 This is in classic Yarra Yering style: rich, powerful and complex, but doesn't go over the top, its varietal expression plain for all to see, its length exceptional, its longevity likewise. Screwcap. 13.5% alc. **Rating** 97 **To** 2030 $100 ✪

Carrodus Cabernet Sauvignon 2015 There are no blending agents to buffer, or mitigate, the strong thrust of cabernet's fine-boned astringency, cool climate acidity and supportive oak pillars, plinths on which the fruit stands, rigid and cool in its youth. Blackcurrant, red cherry, violet, tobacco, anise, dried sage and garden herbs swirl about the mouth, kinetic and vibrant, yet firmly bound to the wine's impeccably sculpted carapace. Screwcap. 14% alc. **Rating** 97 **To** 2040 $250 NG

ȚȚȚȚȚ **Carrodus Viognier 2015** A sublime expression of headily aromatic viognier, exhibiting varietal slipperiness underlain by a refreshing mineral clench and a textural phenolic bite. The maker understands well that the variety ripens optimally circa 14% and beyond, showcasing apricot, peach and honeysuckle against an inherent viscosity in the process. Screwcap. 14% alc. **Rating** 96 **To** 2022 $160 NG

Light Dry Red Pinot Shiraz 2016 This is a classic Australian blend of 50/50% pinot noir and shiraz originated by the Hunter's Maurice O'Shea. It is lip-smackingly delicious, with the gamut of red fruit flavours moseying with briar, cardamom and anise. The acidity trickles from forefront to aft, the tannins palpable, but little more. Screwcap. 14% alc. **Rating** 96 **To** 2028 $86 NG

Dry Red No. 2 2015 A bright vermilion robe invites one into a kaleidoscope of violet, baking spice, black cherry, and blue fruits of every description. Anise, iodine and vanillan oak sashay effortlessly with diaphanous grape tannins and a flow of natural acidity. Screwcap. 13.5% alc. **Rating** 96 **To** 2038 $100 NG

Dry Red No. 3 2015 A blend of estate-grown touriga nacional, tinta cao, tinto roriz, alvarelhao and sousao. A tour de force of winemaking, it has a highly fragrant bouquet signalling the vibrant array of warm spices, sour cherries and poached

plums on the palate. French oak has been absorbed, and the tannins are gossamer fine, the finish fresh and vibrant. Screwcap. 14% alc. **Rating** 96 **To** 2035 $100
Dry White No. 1 2015 Rating 95 **To** 2030 $50 NG
Underhill 2015 Rating 95 **To** 2030 $100 NG
Chardonnay 2015 Rating 94 **To** 2020 $100
Carrodus Pinot Noir 2015 Rating 94 **To** 2028 $250 NG

Yarrabank   ★★★★

38 Melba Highway, Yarra Glen, Vic 3775 **Region** Yarra Valley
T (03) 9730 0100 **www**.yering.com **Open** 7 days 10–5
Winemaker Michel Parisot, Willy Lunn **Est.** 1993 **Dozens** 5000 **Vyds** 4ha
Yarrabank is a highly successful joint venture between the French Champagne house Devaux and Yering Station, established in 1993. Until '97 the Yarrabank Cuvee Brut was made under Claude Thibaut's direction at Domaine Chandon, but thereafter the entire operation has been conducted at Yarrabank. There are 4ha of dedicated vineyards at Yering Station (planted to pinot noir and chardonnay); the balance of the intake comes from growers in the Yarra Valley and southern Victoria. Exports to all major markets.

ϙϙϙϙϙ **Late Disgorged 2005** A magnificent contrast between all the wonder of long lees age and the tension of malic acidity, this is a cuvee bursting with grand complexity of dried nectarine, nutmeg, ginger nut biscuits, honey, roast almonds, even tertiary hints of pipe smoke, then pulling dramatically and refreshingly into a taut finish of glittering malic acid that lingers long and bright. Dosage is intricately integrated. Diam. 13% alc. **Rating** 94 **To** 2020 $55 TS

ϙϙϙϙϙ **Creme de Cuvee NV Rating** 90 **To** 2017 $30 TS

YarraLoch   ★★★★☆

11 Range Road, Gruyere Vic 3770 **Region** Yarra Valley
T 0407 376 587 **www**.yarraloch.com.au **Open** By appt
Winemaker Contract **Est.** 1998 **Dozens** 2000 **Vyds** 6ha
This is the ambitious project of successful investment banker Stephen Wood. He has taken the best possible advice, and has not hesitated to provide appropriate financial resources to a venture that has no exact parallel in the Yarra Valley or anywhere else in Australia. Six hectares of vineyards may not seem so unusual, but in fact he has assembled three entirely different sites, 70km apart, each matched to the needs of the variety/varieties planted on that site. Pinot noir is planted on the Steep Hill vineyard, with a northeast orientation, and a shaley rock and ironstone soil. Cabernet sauvignon has been planted at Kangaroo Ground, with a dry, steep northwest-facing site and abundant sun exposure in the warmest part of the day, ensuring full ripeness. Merlot, shiraz, chardonnay and viognier are planted at the Upper Plenty vineyard, 50km from Kangaroo Ground. This has an average temperature 2°C cooler and a ripening period 2–3 weeks later than the warmest parts of the Yarra Valley.

ϙϙϙϙϙ **Single Vineyard Pinot Noir 2015** This and La Cosette have virtually identical vinification, the only difference an extra 3 days on skins and 7% new oak and this is 100% MV6 clone. Whether there was some difference in row selection or picking dates we don't know, but there is identical alcohol. Whatever, this is markedly more complex, with greater fruit depth and more savoury spice notes on the very long palate. Screwcap. 13% alc. **Rating** 95 **To** 2027 $30
Single Vineyard Chardonnay 2015 A perfect model of Yarra Valley chardonnay, making it all seem so easy, the result more to do with hands off, rather than hands on, vinification. It has the purity and length of the better Yarra chardonnays. Indeed, by the time the shouting is over, you decide it's a little too straight-laced. Perhaps more time will prove the wine had it right all along. Screwcap. 13% alc. **Rating** 94 **To** 2023 $35
Stephanie's Dream Single Vineyard Pinot Noir 2014 100% whole bunch MV6, wild yeast fermentation in stainless steel tanks, 27 days on skins, maturation in French oak (33% new), and of course, vintage, are the points of difference.

When the '15 vintage is released, it should be a knockout. Screwcap. 13% alc.
Rating 91 To 2021 050

TTTTT La Cosette Pinot Noir 2015 Rating 93 To 2025 $25

Yarran Wines ★★★★
178 Myall Park Road, Yenda, NSW 2681 **Region** Riverina
T (02) 6968 1125 **www**.yarranwines.com.au **Open** Mon–Sat 10–5
Winemaker Sam Brewer **Est.** 2000 **Dozens** 8000 **Vyds** 30ha
Lorraine Brewer (and late husband John) were grapegrowers for over 30 years, and when
son Sam completed a degree in wine science at CSU, they celebrated his graduation by
crushing 1t of shiraz, fermenting the grapes in a milk vat. The majority of the grapes from
the estate plantings are sold, but each year a little more has been made under the Yarran
banner; along the way a winery with a crush capacity of 150 tonnes has been built. Sam
worked for Southcorp and De Bortoli in Australia, and overseas (in the US and China), but
in 2009 decided to take the plunge and concentrate on the family winery with his parents.
The majority of the grapes come from the family vineyard, but some parcels are sourced
from growers, including Lake Cooper Estate in the Heathcote region. It is intended that the
portfolio of regions will be gradually increased, and Sam has demonstrated his ability to make
silk purses out of sow's ears, and sell them for the price of the latter. Exports to Singapore
and China.

TTTTT **B Series Heathcote Shiraz 2015** Has an abundance of ripe fleshy plums,
squishy tangy-tart raspberries, lots of fruit concentration yet is juicy and vibrant at
the same time. Medium-bodied, with ripe tannins. A slight singed note to the oak,
but bright acidity levels it out. Screwcap. 14.5% alc. **Rating** 92 **To** 2025 $28 JF
Leopardwood Limited Release Heathcote Shiraz 2015 Very good mid-
crimson colour, the bouquet awash with dark, juicy red plums, licorice and cloves,
charry oak just sitting slightly on the edge. The palate is medium-bodied, buoyant
with crackling acidity. Screwcap. 14.5% alc. **Rating** 91 **To** 2022 $20 JF

Yarrh Wines ★★★★
440 Greenwood Road, Murrumbateman, NSW 2582 **Region** Canberra District
T (02) 6227 1474 **www**.yarrhwines.com.au **Open** Fri–Sun 11–5
Winemaker Fiona Wholohan **Est.** 1997 **Dozens** 2000 **Vyds** 6ha
Fiona Wholohan and Neil McGregor are IT refugees, and both now work full-time running
the Yarrh Wines vineyard and making the wines. Fiona undertook the oenology and
viticulture course at CSU, and has also spent time as an associate judge at wine shows. They
say they spent five years moving to a hybrid organic vineyard, with composting, mulching,
biological controls and careful vineyard floor management. The vineyard includes cabernet
sauvignon, shiraz, sauvignon blanc, riesling, pinot noir and sangiovese. They have recently
tripled their sangiovese plantings with two new clones, and are planning to plant nero d'Avola,
montepulciano and aglianico. Yarrh was the original Aboriginal name for the Yass district.

TTTTT **Shiraz 2015** There is a lot to like about this bright, medium-bodied cool climate
shiraz, from the well handled whole berry, spicy aromas to the fine, delicately
constructed palate which has some alpine berry fruit, a touch of white pepper and
fine-grained tannins. Screwcap. 13.5% alc. **Rating** 90 **To** 2025 $28 PR

Yeates Wines ★★★★
138 Craigmoor Road, Mudgee, NSW 2850 **Region** Mudgee
T 0427 791 264 **www**.yeateswines.com.au **Open** By appt
Winemaker Jacob Stein **Est.** 2010 **Dozens** 500 **Vyds** 16ha
In 2010 the Yeates family purchased the 16ha Mountain Blue vineyard in Mudgee from Fosters,
planted in 1968 by the late Robert (Bob) Oatley. The vines have since been reinvigorated
and cane-pruned, with the grapes now being hand-picked. In '13 the use of chemicals and
inorganic fertiliser were eliminated and organic management practices introduced, in an effort

to achieve a more sustainable ecological footprint. The vines and wines have flourished under this new management regimen.

❦❦❦❦❦ The Gatekeeper Reserve 2015 96% shiraz, 4% cabernet sauvignon. The Yeates family must be delighted with the outcome of the remedial surgery and canopy work in the vineyard. Great colour; this is full-bodied in terms of its luscious cherry, plum and blackberry fruits, yet has great balance that keeps it fresh; good length, too. Screwcap. 14% alc. **Rating** 94 **To** 2035 $25 ✪

Yelland & Papps

Lot 501 Nuraip Road, Nuriootpa, SA 5355 **Region** Barossa Valley
T (08) 8562 3510 **www.**yellandandpapps.com **Open** Mon–Sat 10–4
Winemaker Michael Papps **Est.** 2005 **Dozens** 4000 **Vyds** 1ha
Michael and Susan Papps (née Yelland) set up this venture after their marriage in 2005. It is easy for them to regard the Barossa Valley as their home, for Michael has lived and worked in the wine industry in the Barossa Valley for more than 20 years. He has a rare touch, with his wines consistently excellent, but also pushing the envelope; as well as using a sustainable approach to winemaking with minimal inputs, he has not hesitated to challenge orthodox approaches to a number of aspects of conventional fermentation methods.

❦❦❦❦❦ Second Take Barossa Valley Shiraz 2016 Yelland & Papps have this marvellous ability to combine low alcohol with all the fully ripe fruit flavour you could wish for. Here black cherry and satsuma plum have just the right amount of support from classy French oak and fine tannins. Screwcap. 13.7% alc. **Rating** 95 **To** 2030 $40

Devote Greenock Barossa Valley Shiraz 2015 Elegant, juicy and full of cherry and blackberry fruit on a long, perfectly balanced palate. Much shiraz is picked in a 15–15.5% range – what a waste. Have a glass of this and don't feel ashamed. Screwcap. 13.7% alc. **Rating** 95 **To** 2029 $40

318 Days on Skins Shiraz 2014 100% whole bunches fed directly into French puncheons through purpose-built enlarged bung holes, left for 318 days, pressed at the start of '15 and left for a further year, hand-bottled during the '16 vintage (682 bottles, 10 magnums and 10 Jeroboams). You'd never guess how the wine was made and matured if served blind. Points for bravery, time and effort, and its moderate alcohol. Cork. 13.6% alc. **Rating** 95 **To** 2030 $150

Second Take Barossa Valley Grenache 2016 The colour is a clear, full crimson, the bouquet of plums and cherries, and the palate is fresh, not hot. Screwcap. 14.3% alc. **Rating** 95 **To** 2028 $40

317 Days on Skins Grenache 2014 One less day on skins than the shiraz. Good colour – this alone is amazing, but so is the wine in the mouth. Points are arbitrary – 95 or nothing. Cork. 13.8% alc. **Rating** 95 **To** 2020 $150

Barossa Valley Vermentino 2016 From the Kalleske and Mader vineyards, wild-yeast fermented in tank and 20% in used French oak, matured for 5 months on lees. This is V8-powered, with a level of flavour that takes it onto another level: stone fruit surrounded by pink grapefruit and Meyer lemon within a silken wrap of texture. Really attractive wine. Screwcap. 12% alc. **Rating** 94 **To** 2025 $25 ✪

Barossa Valley Shiraz 2015 From several vineyards, the parcels destemmed and fermented separately, average 14 days on skins, blended and matured in used French oak for 15 months. In Yelland & Papps fashion, the wine is intensely flavoured, blackberry foremost, plum and fruitcake pushing on behind. Screwcap. 13.2% alc. **Rating** 94 **To** 2030 $25 ✪

Second Take Barossa Valley Mataro 2016 Hand-picked, 73% whole bunches, 17 days on skins, matured for 9 months in French oak (23% new), and like all the Yelland & Papps red wines, not filtered or fined. Light, faintly turbid red; the savoury/earthy nature of mataro is resistant to change, but it gains a narrow margin here. Screwcap. 13.8% alc. **Rating** 94 **To** 2029 $40

ΨΨΨΨ℧ Devote Barossa Valley Roussanne 2016 Rating 93 To 2024 $40
Second Take Barossa Valley Vermentino 2016 Rating 90 To 2010 $10
Divine Barossa Valley Shiraz 2013 Rating 90 To 2023 $90
Sete di Vino 2015 Rating 90 To 2021 $25

Yellowglen ★★★☆

The Atrium, 58 Queensbridge Street, Southbank, Vic 3006 **Region** South Eastern Australia
T 1300 651 650 **www**.yellowglen.com **Open** Not
Winemaker Nigel Nesci **Est.** 1971 **Dozens** NFP
Yellowglen is not only the leading producer of sparkling wine in the TWE group, but the largest producer of sparkling wine in Australia. In 2012 it announced a major restructuring of its product range, adding single vineyard traditional-method wines under the Exceptional Vintage XV label. Exports to the UK, Canada and Japan.

ΨΨΨΨ℧ Vintage Perle 2012 This is a toasty, spicy and honeyed style that upholds the crunchy apple and bright lemon character of a strong season in the Adelaide Hills. It finishes long and accurate, with a low, well integrated dosage of 8g/l. 11.5% alc. **Rating** 90 To 2018 $25 TS

Yering Station ★★★★★

38 Melba Highway, Yarra Glen, Vic 3775 **Region** Yarra Valley
T (03) 9730 0100 **www**.ycring.com **Open** 7 days 10–5
Winemaker Willy Lunn, Darren Rathbone **Est.** 1988 **Dozens** 60 000 **Vyds** 112ha
The historic Yering Station (or at least the portion of the property on which the cellar door sales and vineyard are established) was purchased by the Rathbone family in 1996 and is also the site of the Yarrabank joint venture with French Champagne house Devaux (see separate entry). A spectacular and very large winery was built, handling the Yarrabank sparkling and the Yering Station table wines, immediately becoming one of the focal points of the Yarra Valley, particularly as the historic Chateau Yering, where luxury accommodation and fine dining are available, is next door. Willy Lunn, a graduate of Adelaide University, has more than 25 years' cool-climate winemaking experience around the world, including at Petaluma, Shaw + Smith and Argyle Winery (Oregon). Exports to all major markets.

ΨΨΨΨΨ Scarlett Pinot Noir 2015 It's a deceptive wine because it's quite ethereal, with wafts of wild strawberries and sweet cherries, pippy and spicy, all delicately constructed over the medium-weighted palate. And yet laser-precise tannins ensure that this has depth and power but never loses its class. A special wine honouring Nathan Scarlett, Rathbone's technical viticulturist, who died in '13. Screwcap. 13% alc. **Rating** 97 To 2028 $250 JF
Reserve Yarra Valley Shiraz Viognier 2015 It's stonkingly good. From the dark purple hue, the excellent fruit – an array of plum flavours, perfectly seasoned with pepper, cinnamon and oak spice – to the killer tannins encompassing restrained power. Seriously good wine. Screwcap. 13.8% alc. **Rating** 97 To 2030 $120 JF ◐

ΨΨΨΨΨ Reserve Yarra Valley Chardonnay 2015 This is both impressive and refined. It's not always easy to strike such a balance. A chardonnay that drives long and pure, yet has substance. Complex sulphides and leesy characters, flinty, balanced oak, so detailed and moreish it demands you come back for another taste. And you do. It's seamless. Screwcap. 13% alc. **Rating** 96 To 2024 $120 JF
Reserve Yarra Valley Pinot Noir 2015 This is a beautifully subtle and detailed wine. Finesse and elegance are its drivers, with silky fine tannins neatly threaded through the barely medium-bodied palate, plus refreshing acidity and a delicate mix of spiced cherries. Screwcap. 13.5% alc. **Rating** 96 To 2025 $120 JF
Reserve Yarra Valley Cabernet Sauvignon 2015 Compelling and convincing, with florals, currants and blackberries, not too sweet; it has a savoury edge, with the oak seamlessly integrated. Perfectly ripe tannins with poise and

presence ensure that this is lovely now, but will be more so in years to come. Screwcap. 14.6% alc. **Rating** 96 **To** 2040 $120 JF

Yarra Valley Chardonnay 2015 A carefully shaped wine, the emphasis on elegance and balance, length a Yarra Valley given. It is so pristine that it needs time to show its ultimate potential, but can't be gainsayed now. Screwcap. 13% alc. **Rating** 95 **To** 2025 $40

Reserve Yarra Valley Pinot Noir 2014 The colour shows expected development, the bouquet and palate likewise. It is a very complex pinot, with dark spices, cedar and forest notes intertwined with its cherry and plum fruit. A nice dab of tannin completes an impressive wine. Screwcap. 13% alc. **Rating** 95 **To** 2032 $120

Yarra Valley Pinot Noir 2015 Estate-grown, matured in French puncheons for 11 months. The highly fragrant bouquet already has bewitching spicy notes, part fruit, part oak-derived. Spicy notes continue to flow through the long palate; with time, the oak will diminish and fruit spice will increase. The '15 vintage was high in quality, as this wine demonstrates. Screwcap. 13.5% alc. **Rating** 94 **To** 2028 $40

ŸŸŸŸŸ Village Yarra Valley Pinot Noir 2015 Rating 93 To 2022 $24 SC ❍
Village Yarra Valley Shiraz Viognier 2014 Rating 92 To 2025 $24 CM ❍
Village Yarra Valley Chardonnay 2016 Rating 91 To 2020 $24 JF
Little Yering Yarra Valley Chardonnay 2015 Rating 90 To 2020 $18 JF ❍
Little Yering Yarra Valley Shiraz 2015 Rating 90 To 2022 $18 JF ❍
Yarra Valley Cabernet Sauvignon 2014 Rating 90 To 2024 $40

Yeringberg   ★★★★★

Maroondah Highway, Coldstream, Vic 3770 **Region** Yarra Valley
T (03) 9739 0240 **www**.yeringberg.com **Open** By appt
Winemaker Guill and Sandra de Pury **Est.** 1863 **Dozens** 1500 **Vyds** 3.66ha

Guill de Pury and daughter Sandra, with Guill's wife Katherine in the background, make wines for the new millennium from the low-yielding vines re-established in the heart of what was one of the most famous (and infinitely larger) vineyards of the 19th century. In the riper years, the red wines have a velvety generosity of flavour rarely encountered, while never losing varietal character; the long-lived Marsanne Roussanne takes students of history back to Yeringberg's fame in the 19th century. Exports to the US, Switzerland, Hong Kong and China.

ŸŸŸŸŸ **Yarra Valley Shiraz 2014** A superbly crafted wine with infinite attention to detail. Red and black cherry, with a faint touch of raspberry, balanced by a hint of bramble, make the task of deconstructing the palate nigh on impossible, simply because there will be so many different readings of its message – but with one common point: its undeniable quality. Screwcap. 13.5% alc. **Rating** 96 **To** 2044 $86

Yeringberg 2014 66% cabernet sauvignon, 11% cabernet franc, 10% merlot, 9% petit verdot and 4% malbec. Right in the mainstream of the Yeringberg style, refined but not apologetic. Blackcurrant/cassis, cedar, olive and earth notes all combine, the tannins pitched to perfection. A long life ahead. Gold medal Yarra Valley Wine Show '16. Screwcap. 13.5% alc. **Rating** 96 **To** 2034 $98

Yarra Valley Marsanne Roussanne 2015 A 59/41% blend, due for release Oct '17. Slightly brassy colour; a powerful, full-bodied and complex wine. Its track record of development in bottle – and the vintage – underwrites its future. Screwcap. 13.5% alc. **Rating** 95 **To** 2025 $65

Yarra Valley Chardonnay 2015 A fleshy, full-bodied chardonnay with stone fruit and cashew to the fore. To a degree, countercultural. 168 dozen, due for release Oct '17. Screwcap. 13% alc. **Rating** 94 **To** 2022 $65

Yarra Valley Pinot Noir 2014 Deeply coloured, it is full-bodied in pinot terms, the fruits purple and black, not red. Prolonged cellaring is on offer for those with the patience needed. Screwcap. 13.5% alc. **Rating** 94 **To** 2029 $95

ŸŸŸŸŸ Yarra Valley Viognier 2015 Rating 91 To 2021 $35

Yes said the Seal

1251–1269 Bellarine Highway, Wallington, Vic 3221 **Region** Geelong
T (03) 5250 6577 **www.**yessaidtheseal.com.au **Open** 7 days 10–5
Winemaker Darren Burke **Est.** 2014 **Dozens** 1000 **Vyds** 2ha
This is a new venture for David and Lyndsay Sharp, long-term vintners on Geelong's Bellarine
Peninsula. It is situated onsite at the Flying Brick Cider Co's Cider House in Wallington.
The 2ha of estate vineyard were planted to shiraz in 2010; other varieties are purchased from
growers on the Bellarine Peninsula.

ỸỸỸỸỸ **The Bellarine Chardonnay 2015** Yet another lovely wine from this vineyard,
shepherded through to bottle with a flowing, irresistible energy. White peach, pear,
apple and grapefruit are all showing their wares on the long, stylish palate and
aftertaste. Screwcap. 13.5% alc. **Rating** 95 **To** 2024 $35 ✪
The Bellarine Pinot Noir 2015 Bright purple-crimson hue; the expressive
bouquet has scents of red flowers, spices and red berries, the elegant palate with
convincing length despite its airy delicacy. A pinot for pinot devotees. Screwcap.
12.5% alc. **Rating** 95 **To** 2024 $35 ✪
The Bellarine Shiraz 2015 The colour is very good, the bouquet is fragrant,
the predominantly red fruits of the medium-bodied, long palate with intense red
cherry/berry fruit, tannin and oak contributions positive but not threatening the
fruit. Screwcap. 13.5% alc. **Rating** 95 **To** 2029 $35 ✪
The Bellarine Sauvignon Blanc 2016 Gleaming straw–green; complex, its
power lingering in the mouth long after it is tasted. It is in Loire Valley/Dageneau
style, with great vinosity, the actual fruit composition of secondary importance.
Screwcap. 12.8% alc. **Rating** 94 **To** 2020 $25 ✪

ỸỸỸỸỵ **The Bellarine Rose 2016** **Rating** 90 **To** 2018 $25

Z Wine

Shop 3, 109–111 Murray Street, Tanunda, SA 5352 **Region** Barossa Valley
T 0422 802 220 **www.**zwine.com.au **Open** Thurs–Tues 10–5
Winemaker Janelle Zerk **Est.** 1999 **Dozens** 5500 **Vyds** 1ha
Z Wine is the partnership of sisters Janelle and Kristen Zerk, whose heritage dates back five
generations at the Zerk vineyard in Lyndoch. Vineyard resources include growers that supply
old vine shiraz, old bushvine grenache and High Eden Valley riesling. Both women have
completed degrees at Adelaide University (Janelle winemaking and Kristen wine marketing).
Janelle also has vintage experience in Puligny Montrachet, Tuscany and Sonoma Valley. Wines
are released under the Z Wine, Rustica and Section 3146 labels. In 2017 Z Wine opened a
cellar door in the main street of Tanunda. Exports to Vietnam, Singapore and China.

ỸỸỸỸỸ **Saul Eden Valley Riesling 2016** This is a beautifully proportioned and
structured riesling that cries in a loud voice, 'Drink me if you must, but cellar
as many bottles as possible for drinking '23–'30'. Its acidity seems to have been
wrung from the lean and rocky Eden Valley soils. Screwcap. 12% alc. **Rating** 96
To 2030 $25 ✪
Joachim Barossa Valley Shiraz 2013 From the original Zerk property at
Lyndoch, not only a single vineyard, but a single barrel selection. It is a bold,
powerful style with black fruits, ripe tannins and oak forming a Barossa Valley
band, all the players being heard with clarity. Cork. 14.5% alc. **Rating** 96
To 2043 $180
Museum Release Barossa Valley Shiraz 2008 An unprecedented heatwave in
the first two weeks of Mar '08 meant the success or failure of the vintage turned
on whether you picked before or after. No information is given on this subject,
but I'll bet it was indeed before. The wine is full-bodied, very complex, with
bramble, blackberry and black cherry on a palate that soars on the finish. Screwcap.
14% alc. **Rating** 95 **To** 2028 $75
Roman Barossa Valley Grenache Shiraz Mataro 2014 A 45/40/15% blend.
Like the Z Wine 100% grenache releases, thrives on the freshness ex controlled

alcohol, avoiding the confection characters of overripe grenache. Screwcap. 14.5% alc. **Rating** 94 To 2024 $30 **◐**

♟♟♟♟♟ Section 3146 Barossa Valley Shiraz 2014 **Rating** 91 To 2029 $35
August Old Vine Barossa Valley Grenache 2015 **Rating** 90 To 2023 $25

Zarephath Wines   ★★★★☆

424 Moorialup Road, East Porongurup, WA 6324 **Region** Porongurup
T (08) 9853 1152 **www**.zarephathwines.com.au **Open** Mon–Sat 10–5, Sun 10–4
Winemaker Robert Diletti **Est.** 1994 **Dozens** 1500 **Vyds** 8.9ha
The Zarephath vineyard was owned and operated by Brothers and Sisters of The Christ Circle, a Benedictine community. In 2014 they sold the property to Rosie Singer and her partner Ian Barrett-Lennard, who live on the spot full-time and undertake all the vineyard work, supplemented by the local Afghani community during vintage and pruning. They have diverse backgrounds, Ian's roots in the Swan Valley, while Rosie has worked in various aspects of fine arts, first in administration and thereafter as a practising visual artist with galleries in north Queensland and regional WA.

♟♟♟♟♟ Riesling 2016 Crystal white; the expressive, flowery and talc bouquet is followed by an immaculately balanced and structured wine with a 20-year future. Lime juice flavours float across the tongue, caressing the mouth as they do so. All class. Screwcap. 11.6% alc. **Rating** 96 To 2036 $35 **◐**
Late Harvest Riesling 2016 Crisp, lively and delicious, circa 35–45g/l of residual sugar is balanced by natural acidity, and the wine will never lose its charm, the sweetness gradually receding as the wine becomes more complex with age – if that is what you want. Screwcap. 10% alc. **Rating** 94 To 2026 $30 **◐**

♟♟♟♟♟ Pinot Noir 2015 **Rating** 91 To 2027 $35
Petit Chardonnay 2016 **Rating** 90 To 2019 $30 SC

Zema Estate   ★★★★★

14944 Riddoch Highway, Coonawarra, SA 5263 **Region** Coonawarra
T (08) 8736 3219 **www**.zema.com.au **Open** Mon–Fri 9–5, w'ends & public hols 10–4
Winemaker Greg Clayfield **Est.** 1982 **Dozens** 20 000 **Vyds** 61ha
Zema is one of the last outposts of hand-pruning in Coonawarra, with members of the Zema family tending the vineyard set in the heart of Coonawarra's terra rossa soil. Winemaking practices are straightforward; if ever there was an example of great wines being made in the vineyard, this is it. Exports to the UK, Vietnam, Hong Kong, Japan, Singapore and China.

♟♟♟♟♟ Family Selection Coonawarra Cabernet Sauvignon 2013 A lovely medium-bodied Coonawarra cabernet with ultra-typical cassis, mulberry and faintly minty fruit on the long, supple palate. The oak has entirely integrated, as have the tannins. Will cruise along for many years to come. Screwcap. 14% alc. **Rating** 96 To 2030 $46 **◐**
Coonawarra Shiraz 2014 This medium to full-bodied wine paints a picture of Coonawarra in rude good health, not a deceptive note anywhere in its body. Blackberry and blood plum are built on foundations of polished tannins and an echo of oak. Demands respect for its traditional estate winemaking. Screwcap. 14% alc. **Rating** 95 To 2034 $26 **◐**
Family Selection Coonawarra Shiraz 2013 The palate has another dimension of depth and length, along with a touch of dark choc-mint borrowed, as it were, from McLaren Vale. The overall fruit impression is luscious, the tannins soft, although sufficient to do the job. The wine will calmly move through decades to come giving pleasure whenever it is tasted. Screwcap. 14.5% alc. **Rating** 95 To 2038 $46
Cluny Coonawarra Cabernet Merlot 2014 65% cabernet sauvignon, 25% merlot, 5% each cabernet franc and malbec, matured for 14 months in French and American oak (10% new). One of relatively few cabernet merlot blends in

Coonawarra, and makes you wonder why there aren't more. Supple, sweet cassis, redcurrant and dried herb flavours are supported by fine, ripe tannins and French oak. Screwcap. 13.5% alc. **Rating** 95 **To** 2034 $26 ○

🍷🍷🍷🍷🍷 **Coonawarra Cabernet Sauvignon 2014** Rating 91 To 2024 $30

Zerella Wines ★★★★★

182 Olivers Rd, McLaren Vale, SA 5171 **Region** McLaren Vale
T (08) 8323 8288/0488 929 202 **www**.zerellawines.com.au **Open** Thurs–Mon 11–4
Winemaker Jim Zerella **Est.** 2006 **Dozens** 2500 **Vyds** 58ha
In 1950 Ercole Zerella left his native Campania in southern Italy to seek a better life in SA. With a lifetime of farming and grapegrowing, the transition was seamless. Ercole's son Vic followed in his father's footsteps, becoming an icon of the SA farming and wine industries. He founded Tatachilla, where his son Jim began as a cellar hand, eventually controlling all grape purchases. While working there, Jim purchased land in McLaren Vale and, with help from family and friends, established what is now the flagship vineyard of Zerella Wines. He also established a vineyard management business catering to the needs of absentee owners. When Tatachilla was purchased by Lion Nathan in 2000 he declined the opportunity of continuing his role there, and by '06 had purchased two more vineyards, and become a shareholder in a third. These all now come under the umbrella of Zerella Wines, with its 58ha of vines. The winemaking techniques used are thoroughly à la mode, and definitely not traditional Italian.

🍷🍷🍷🍷🍷 **La Gita Fiano 2016** Has a higher aromatic profile than most of its varietal peers, elderflower an aroma rattling around in my mind as I tasted a mini-group of seven fianos from '16. There is also more juicy flavour to be had from the palate, the savoury crunchy acidity of the variety leaving it to the last minute to appear. Screwcap. 13% alc. **Rating** 95 **To** 2020 $30 ○

🍷🍷🍷🍷🍷 **Dom's Block Grenache 2015** Rating 93 To 2024 $60
Home Block Shiraz 2014 Rating 92 To 2034 $60

Zig Zag Road ★★★★

201 Zig Zag Road, Drummond, Vic 3446 **Region** Macedon Ranges
T (03) 5423 9390 **www**.zigzagwines.com.au **Open** Thurs–Mon 10–5
Winemaker Eric Bellchambers, Llew Knight **Est.** 1972 **Dozens** 700 **Vyds** 4.5ha
In 2002 Eric and Anne Bellchambers became the third owners of this vineyard, planted by Roger Aldridge in '72. The Bellchambers have extended the plantings with riesling and merlot, supplementing the older dry-grown plantings of shiraz, cabernet sauvignon and pinot noir.

🍷🍷🍷🍷🍷 **Macedon Ranges Cabernet Sauvignon 2013** A good mid-crimson, dark purple hue; a rather refreshing style, more savoury than fruit, yet some cassis and currants on the palate with black licorice, fennel and crushed juniper spice; supple, with tannins neatly wound in. Screwcap. 14% alc. **Rating** 91 **To** 2021 $23 JF ○
Macedon Ranges Riesling 2015 Mid-straw and bright; super zesty with crunchy if piercing acidity, lemon flavours, yet a bone-dry, steely austere style. Screwcap. 12.5% alc. **Rating** 90 **To** 2022 $23 JF
Macedon Ranges Shiraz 2013 Mid-garnet and bright; a lighter frame, with spiced plums, pepper and woodsy spices. Tannins are grainy and ripe. Screwcap. 13.5% alc. **Rating** 90 **To** 2021 $23 JF

Zilzie Wines ★★★☆

544 Kulkyne Way, Karadoc, Vic 3496 **Region** Murray Darling
T (03) 5025 8100 **www**.zilziewines.com **Open** Not
Winemaker Hayden Donohue **Est.** 1999 **Dozens** NFP **Vyds** 572ha
The Forbes family has been farming since the early 1990s; Zilzie is currently run by Ian and Ros Forbes, with sons Steven and Andrew, and the diverse range of farming activities includes

grapegrowing from substantial vineyards. Having established a dominant position as a supplier of grapes to Southcorp, Zilzie formed a wine company in '99 and built a winery in 2000, expanding it in '06 to its current capacity of 45 000 tonnes. The wines consistently far exceed expectations, given their enticing prices, that consistency driving the production volume to 200 000 dozen (the last known publicised amount) – this in an extremely competitive market. The business includes contract processing, winemaking and storage. Exports to the UK, Canada, Hong Kong and China.

ŸŸŸŸ   **Regional Collection Barossa Shiraz 2015** Good hue and depth; a attractive wine designed for early consumption, with minimal tannins, but sweet fruit and some spicy oak. Screwcap. 14.5% alc. **Rating** 89 **To** 2020 $18 ○
Regional Collection Coonawarra Cabernet Sauvignon 2015 A curious feature of the background info is the Coonawarra and Wrattonbully regions – presumably Wrattonbully is less than 15%. It is light-bodied, but does have pretty cassis fruit and no tannins to distract. Twin top. 13.5% alc. **Rating** 89 **To** 2018 $18 ○

Zitta Wines

3 Union Street, Dulwich, SA 5065 (postal) **Region** Barossa Valley
T 0419 819 414 **www.zitta.com.au Open** Not
Winemaker Angelo De Fazio **Est.** 2004 **Dozens** 3000 **Vyds** 26.3ha
Owner Angelo De Fazio says that all he knows about viticulture and winemaking came from his father (and generations before him). It is partly this influence that has shaped the label and brand name: Zitta is Italian for 'quiet', and the seeming reflection of the letters of the name Zitta on the bottle is in fact nothing of the kind; turn the bottle upside down, and you will see it is the word 'Quiet'. The Zitta vineyard dates back to 1864, with a few vines remaining from that time, and a block planted with cuttings taken from those vines. Shiraz dominates the plantings (22ha), the balance made up of chardonnay, grenache and a few mourvedre vines; only a small amount of the production is retained for the Zitta label. The property has two branches of Greenock Creek running through it, and the soils reflect the ancient geological history of the site, in part with a subsoil of river pebbles, reflecting the course of a long-gone river. Exports to Denmark and China.

ŸŸŸŸŸ   **Single Vineyard Greenock Barossa Valley Shiraz 2014** Matured for 24 months in French oak. The bouquet initially, and the full-bodied palate thereafter, suggests that not only is the overall make-up of the wine on another level, but that there has to be a significant percentage of new oak. Whatever be the case, this has out-performed many of its vintage peers with its fruit and the nonchalant way it deals with its Screwcap. 14.8% alc. **Rating** 95 **To** 2034 $58
Single Vineyard Bernardo Greenock Barossa Valley Shiraz 2014 Estate-grown, matured for 24 months in French and American oak, named after Frank Zitta's grandfather. It has very good focus, length and balance between black berry fruits, tannins and oak. The consequence is a full-bodied shiraz that carries its body and alcohol with grace. Screwcap. 14.7% alc. **Rating** 94 **To** 2030 $45
Single Vineyard 1864 Greenock Barossa Valley GSM 2014 Exceptionally deep and bright colour for a Barossa Valley GSM. It is a barrel selection of the best of vintage; the palate has loads of fruit and, most pleasingly, firm tannins. Screwcap. 14.5% alc. **Rating** 94 **To** 2034 $42

ŸŸŸŸ   **Union Street No 168 Barossa Valley Shiraz 2015 Rating** 89 **To** 2027 $28
Union Street No 789 Coonawarra Barossa Valley Cabernet Shiraz 2015 Rating 89 **To** 2030 $28

Zonte's Footstep

The General Wine Bar, 55a Main Road, McLaren Flat, SA 5171 **Region** McLaren Vale
T (08) 8383 2083 **www.zontesfootstep.com.au Open** 7 days 10–5
Winemaker Ben Riggs **Est.** 2003 **Dozens** 20 000 **Vyds** 214.72ha

Zonte's Footstep has been very successful since a group of long-standing friends, collectively with deep knowledge of every aspect of the wine business, decided it was time to do something together. Along the way there has been some shuffling of the deck chairs, all achieved without any ill feeling from those who moved sideways or backwards. The major change has been a broadening of the regions (Langhorne Creek, McLaren Vale, the Barossa and Clare valleys and elsewhere) from which the grapes are sourced. Even here, however, most of the vineyards supplying grapes are owned by members of the Zonte's Footstep partnership. Exports to the UK, the US, Canada, Finland, Sweden, Denmark, Thailand and Singapore.

🍷🍷🍷🍷🍷 **Z-Force 2014** 90% shiraz and 10% durif (aka petite syrah), open-fermented, matured in new and used French and American oak. McLaren Vale on steroids? That's cruel, but this is as full-bodied and intense as a wine can be before becoming a caricature. Moreover, it's the black ironstone fruit that's so intense, not the tannins or the oak. The consequent balance means this wine can outlive most who lay it down now. Screwcap. 14.5% alc. **Rating** 96 **To** 2054 $55 ✪
Avalon Tree Single Site Fleurieu Peninsula Cabernet 2015 Includes 5% tempranillo; matured for 12 months in used hogsheads. The colour is deep and bright, appropriate for the deep, medium to full-bodied varietal fruit on the bouquet and palate. The firm, but fine, tannins are pure cabernet in taste and texture, and make the wine. Screwcap. 14.5% alc. **Rating** 95 **To** 2030 $25 ✪
Violet Beauregard Langhorne Creek Malbec 2015 A juicy, bright fruit profile with damson plum the focus, black cherry in support. Good line, length and balance. Screwcap. 14% alc. **Rating** 94 **To** 2025 $25 ✪

🍷🍷🍷🍷🍷 **Lake Doctor Langhorne Creek Shiraz 2015** **Rating** 93 **To** 2030 $25 ✪
Chocolate Factory McLaren Vale Shiraz 2015 **Rating** 92 **To** 2039 $25 ✪
Canto di Lago Fleurieu Peninsula Sangiovese Barbera Lagrein 2015 **Rating** 91 **To** 2025 $25
Duck til Dawn Adelaide Hills Chardonnay 2016 **Rating** 90 **To** 2020 $30
Doctoressa Di Lago Pinot Grigio 2016 **Rating** 90 **To** 2018 $18 SC ✪
Scarlet Ladybird Rose 2016 **Rating** 90 **To** 2018 $18 SC ✪
Hills Are Alive Adelaide Hills Shiraz 2015 **Rating** 90 **To** 2035 $35

 # Zonzo Estate ★★★★

957 Healesville-Yarra Glen Road, Yarra Glen, Vic 3775 **Region** Yarra Valley
T (03) 9730 2500 **www.zonzo.com.au** **Open** Wed–Sun 12–4
Winemaker Kate Goodman, Caroline Mooney **Est.** 1998 **Dozens** 2075 **Vyds** 18.21ha
This is the new iteration of Train Trak, best known by Yarra Valley locals for the quality of its wood-fired oven pizzas. The vineyard was planted in 1995, the first wines made from the 1998 vintage. The business was acquired by Rod Micallef in 2016. It's open for lunch from Wed–Sun, dinner Fri–Sun.

🍷🍷🍷🍷🍷 **Yarra Valley Shiraz 2015** Dense crimson-purple; with the caveat that this really needs to hibernate in a cool, dark place for a minimum of 5 years, preferably 10, this full-bodied shiraz, with its sombre black fruits, licorice, spice and pepper has considerable upside potential. Cork. 14.5% alc. **Rating** 93 **To** 2035 $75
Yarra Valley Chardonnay 2015 The colour is good, and the combination of oak, ripe stone fruit, fig and melon works well to produce a full-flavoured, but not heavy, wine. The choice of cork is bewildering, so drink up asap. 13% alc. **Rating** 91 **To** 2017 $75
Yarra Valley Pinot Noir 2015 A rough-hewn pinot in keeping with its unusual heavyweight proprietary bottle. Chewy tannins and a spear of alcohol (notwithstanding the 13% measurement) make you keep your distance, for the time being at least. Cork. **Rating** 90 **To** 2024 $75

🍷🍷🍷🍷 **Yarra Valley Sauvignon Blanc 2015** **Rating** 89 **To** 2016 $30
Yarra Valley Cabernet Sauvignon 2015 **Rating** 89 **To** 2030 $75

Index

♀	Cellar door sales
⬚	Food: lunch platters to à la carte restaurants
⊨	Accommodation: B&B cottages to luxury vineyard apartments
⬚	Music events: monthly jazz in the vineyard to spectacular yearly concerts

Adelaide Hills (SA)

Alta Vineyards ⬚ ⬚ 73

Anvers 81

Artwine ♀ ⬚ ⊨ ⬚ 85

Ashton Hills ♀ ⬚ 86

Barratt ♀ ⬚ 99

Barristers Block ♀ ⬚ ⊨ ⬚ 100

Between the Vines ♀ 115

Bird in Hand ♀ ⬚ ⬚ 117

BK Wines ♀ 120

Black Bishop Wines 121

Casa Freschi ♀ 159

Chain of Ponds 166

Charlotte Dalton Wines 174

Clackers Wine Co. 178

Cloudbreak Wines 183

Coates Wines ♀ 186

Corduroy 196

Coulter Wines 198

CRFT Wines 202

Dead Man Walking 217

Deviation Road ♀ ⬚ ⬚ 222

Elderslie 247

Esto Wines 255

Geoff Weaver 288

Hahndorf Hill Winery ♀ ⬚ 307

Adelaide Hills (SA) continued

Hersey Vineyard 338

Howard Vineyard ♀ ⬚ ⬚ 352

Jericho Wines 367

Kakaba Wines 376

Karrawatta ♀ 378

La Bise 395

La Linea 396

Lambrook Wines ♀ 400

Lobethal Road Wines ♀ ⬚ ⬚ 421

Longview Vineyard ♀ ⬚ ⊨ ⬚ 425

Main & Cherry ♀ 435

Malcolm Creek Vineyard ♀ ⬚ 437

Marko's Vineyard ♀ ⬚ 440

Mayhem & Co 445

Mike Press Wines 452

Monkey Business 460

Mt Lofty Ranges Vineyard ♀ ⬚ ⬚ 475

Murdoch Hill ♀ 483

Nepenthe ♀ ⬚ ⬚ 490

New Era Vineyards 490

Ngeringa ♀ ⬚ ⬚ 491

Nine Fingers ♀ 494

Ochota Barrels 502

Paracombe Wines ♀ ⬚ ⬚ 510

Petaluma ♀ ⬚ ⬚ 527

Pike & Joyce 534

Riposte 565

Romney Park Wines ♀ 575

Scott ♀ 601

Sew & Sew Wines 609

Shaw + Smith ♀ 610

Shining Rock Vineyard ♀ 614

Sidewood Estate ♀ ⬚ 616

Signature Wines ♀ ⬚ ⬚ 617

Sinclair's Gully ♀ ⬚ ⬚ 620

Tapanappa ♀ 657

Adelaide Hills (SA) continued
Ten Miles East 664
The Lane Vineyard ♀ ⅋ 670
The Pawn Wine Co. 671
Tomich Wines ♀ ⅋ 685
Top Note ♀ 686
Tynan Road Wines 698
Vella Wines 703
View Road Wines 704
Warwick Billings 713
Wicks Estate Wines 719

Adelaide Plains (SA)

Ceravolo Estate 164
Old Plains 503
Virgara Wines ♀ ⅋ 709

Adelaide (SA)

Cantina Abbatiello 153
Heirloom Vineyards ♀ 325
Hewitson ♀ 339
Nick Haselgrove Wines ♀ 492
Patritti Wines ♀ ⅋ 515
Penfolds Magill Estate ♀ ⅋ 524
Tenafeate Creek Wines ♀ ⅋ 665

Albany (WA)

Oranje Tractor ♀ 506
Wignalls Wines ♀ ⅋ 720

Alpine Valleys (Vic)

Billy Button Wines ♀ ⅋ 116
Bush Track Wines ♀ 147
Feathertop Wines ♀ ⅋ ⊨ ⅋ 259

Alpine Valleys (Vic) continued
Gapsted ♀ ⅋ 284
Mayford Wines ♀ 444
Michelini Wines ♀ ⅋ 452

Ballarat (Vic)

Mount Beckworth ♀ ⅋ 472
Mount Coghill Vineyard ♀ ⅋ 473
Nintingbool 495
Sinclair of Scotsburn ♀ ⊨ ⅋ 620
Tomboy Hill 684

Barossa Valley (SA)

Atze's Corner Wines ♀ ⅋ 88
Auswan Creek ♀ 90
Ballycroft Vineyard & Cellars ♀ 95
Basedow Wines ♀ ⅋ ⅋ 102
Ben Murray Wines 110
Bethany Wines ♀ ⅋ ⅋ 114
Brothers at War 139
Burge Family Winemakers ♀ 146
Caillard Wine 149
Chaffey Bros Wine Co 165
Charles Cimicky ♀ ⅋ 172
Charles Melton ♀ ⅋ ⊨ 173
Chateau Tanunda ♀ ⅋ ⅋ 175
Cooper Burns ♀ 194
Curator Wine Company ♀ 205
Dell'uva Wines ♀ 221
Deonte Wines ♀ 222
Dolan Family Wines 229
Domain Barossa ♀ ⅋ ⅋ 230
Dorrien Estate 235
Dutschke Wines ♀ 241
1847 | Yaldara Wines ♀ 245
Elderton ♀ ⅋ ⊨ ⅋ 248

Barossa Valley (SA) continued
Eperosa ♀ 252
Epsilon ♀ 253
Final Cut Wines 263
First Drop Wines ♀ ⚊ 265
Fox Gordon 276
Gibson ♀ ⚑ 292
Glaetzer Wines 294
Glen Eldon Wines ♀ 295
Gomersal Wines ♀ ⚊ ⚑ 299
Grant Burge ♀ ⚊ 302
Groom 304
Haan Wines 307
Harbord Wines 313
Hare's Chase 316
Hart of the Barossa ♀ ⚑ 318
Hayes Family Wines ♀ 320
Head Wines ♀ 321
Hemera Estate ♀ ⚊ ⚑ 328
Hentley Farm Wines ♀ ⚊ 332
Hobbs of Barossa Ranges ♀ 345
Jacob's Creek ♀ ⚊ 364
jb Wines ♀ 367
John Duval Wines ♀ ⚊ 370
Kaesler Wines ♀ ⚊ ⊨ ⚑ 375
Kalleske ♀ ⚊ ⚑ 376
Kellermeister ♀ ⚊ ⚑ 382
Kurtz Family Vineyards ♀ 394
Landhaus Estate 402
Langmeil Winery ♀ 404
Lanz Vineyards ♀ 405
Laughing Jack ♀ 409
Linfield Road Wines ♀ ⚊ ⊨ ⚑ 419
Lou Miranda Estate ♀ ⚊ 426
Magpie Estate ♀ 435
Massena Vineyards ♀ ⚊ 441
Maverick Wines ♀ 442

Barossa Valley (SA) continued
Murray Street Vineyards ♀ ⚊ 484
Muster Wine Co ♀ 486
Orlando 507
Penfolds ♀ 522
Peter Lehmann ♀ ⚊ ⚑ 528
Pindarie ♀ ⚊ ⚑ 537
Purple Hands Wines 551
Quattro Mano ♀ 553
Red Art | Rojomoma ♀ 556
Rockford ♀ 574
Rolf Binder ♀ ⚊ ⊨ ⚑ 575
St Hallett ♀ ⚊ 584
St Hugo ♀ ⚊ 586
St John's Road 587
Saltram ♀ ⚊ ⚑ 589
Schild Estate Wines ♀ ⚊ 596
Schubert Estate ♀ 596
Schulz Vignerons ♀ 597
Schwarz Wine Company ♀ ⚊ 598
Seabrook Wines ♀ 601
Seppeltsfield ♀ ⚊ ⚑ 604
Sieber Road Wines ♀ 616
Sister's Run 623
Slain Giant Wines 625
Smallfry Wines ♀ ⚊ 626
Sons of Eden ♀ ⚊ 629
Soul Growers ♀ 630
Spinifex ♀ 632
Teusner ♀ 667
The Grapes of Ross 668
The Willows Vineyard ♀ 674
Thorn-Clarke Wines ♀ ⚊ ⚑ 678
Tim Smith Wines 681
Torbreck Vintners ♀ ⊨ 687
Turkey Flat ♀ ⚊ 694
Two Hands Wines ♀ 696

Barossa Valley (SA) continued

Ubertas Wines ♀ 699

Westlake Vineyards ♀ 717

Wolf Blass ♀ 732

Woods Crampton 734

Yelland & Papps ♀ 748

Z Wine ♀ 751

Zitta Wines 754

Beechworth (Vic)

A. Rodda Wines 66

Fighting Gully Road ♀ 262

Giaconda ♀ 290

Golden Ball ♀ 297

Haldon Estate Wines ♀ 308

Indigo Vineyard ♀ ⊨ ◊ 358

James & Co Wines 364

Piano Piano ♀ 533

Savaterre 594

Vignerons Schmolzer & Brown ♀ 705

Virago Vineyard ♀ 708

Willem Kurt Wines 720

Bendigo (Vic)

Balgownie Estate ♀ ⅠⅠ ⊨ ◊ 94

Belvoir Park Estate ♀ ◊ 109

BlackJack Vineyards ♀ 122

Bress ♀ ⅠⅠ ◊ 133

Glenwillow Wines ♀ 297

Harcourt Valley Vineyards ♀ ⅠⅠ ◊ 314

Killiecrankie Wines ♀ 387

Lome ⊨ 423

Newbridge Wines ♀ 491

Pondalowie Vineyards ♀ 542

Sandhurst Ridge ♀ ⊨ 591

Sutton Grange Winery ♀ ⅠⅠ ◊ 648

Bendigo (Vic) continued

Turner's Crossing Vineyard ♀ 694

Welshmans Reef Vineyard ♀ ⅠⅠ ◊ 715

Blackwood Valley (WA)

Dickinson Estate 226

Nannup Ridge Estate 487

Whimwood Estate Wines 718

Canberra District (NSW)

Barton Estate ♀ 101

Brindabella Hills ♀ ⅠⅠ ◊ 135

Capital Wines ♀ ⅠⅠ ◊ 157

Clonakilla ♀ 182

Collector Wines 190

Eden Road Wines ♀ 244

Four Winds Vineyard ♀ ⅠⅠ ◊ 274

Helm ♀ 327

Lark Hill ♀ ⅠⅠ 405

Lerida Estate ♀ ⅠⅠ ◊ 414

Long Rail Gully Wines ♀ ◊ 424

McKellar Ridge Wines ♀ 431

Mount Majura Vineyard ♀ ⅠⅠ ◊ 475

Murrora Wines 485

Murrumbateman Winery ♀ ⅠⅠ ◊ 486

Nick O'Leary Wines ♀ 492

Quarry Hill Wines 553

Ravensworth 555

Sassafras Wines 593

Shaw Vineyard Estate ♀ ⅠⅠ ◊ 612

Surveyor's Hill Vineyards ♀ ⅠⅠ ⊨ ◊ 646

The Vintner's Daughter ♀ 673

Three Lads 680

Yarrh Wines ♀ ⅠⅠ 747

Central Ranges (NSW)

Renzaglia Wines ♀ 560

Swinging Bridge ♀ 649

Central Victoria

Angus the Bull 80

Brave Goose Vineyard ♀ ⚭ 132

Four Sisters 274

Mount Terrible ♀ 478

Terra Felix 666

Trust Wines 691

Clare Valley (SA)

Adelina Wines 68

Annie's Lane ♀ ⚭ 80

Artis Wines 84

Atlas Wines 87

Bourke & Travers 129

Clare Wine Co 180

Claymore Wines ♀ ❙❙ ⚭ 181

Crabtree Watervale Wines ♀ 199

Eldredge ♀ ❙❙ 249

Fireblock 264

Gaelic Cemetery Wines 281

Georges Wines 289

Grosset ♀ 304

Jeanneret Wines ♀ 367

Jim Barry Wines ♀ 368

Kilikanoon Wines ♀ 385

Kirrihill Wines ♀ 389

Knappstein ♀ 390

Koerner Wine ♀ 391

Koonowla Wines ♀ 392

Little Brampton Wines ♀ 419

Mitchell ♀ 457

Clare Valley (SA) continued

Mount Horrocks ♀ 473

Mr Mick ♀ ❙❙ 481

Naked Run Wines 487

Noble Road ♀ 496

O'Leary Walker Wines ♀ ❙❙ ⚭ 497

Paul Morris 517

Paulett Wines ♀ ❙❙ ⚭ 519

Penna Lane Wines ♀ 525

Pikes ♀ ❙❙ 535

Reillys Wines ♀ ❙❙ ⊨ 559

Rhythm Stick Wines ♀ 562

Rieslingfreak ♀ 564

Rise Vineyards 566

Robertson of Clare 571

Seraph's Crossing 606

Sevenhill Cellars ♀ ❙❙ ⚭ 607

Shut the Gate Wines ♀ ❙❙ ⚭ 615

Skillogalee ♀ ❙❙ ⊨ ⚭ 625

Steve Wiblin's Erin Eyes 640

Sussex Squire ♀ 647

Talbots Block Wines ♀ 653

Taylors ♀ ⚭ 660

Tim Adams ♀ 680

Tim Gramp ♀ 681

Tim McNeil Wines ♀ 681

Vickery Wines 703

Wendouree 715

Wilson Vineyard ♀ 725

Woodvale 737

Wykari Wines 738

Coonawarra (SA)

Bailey Wine Co 93

Balnaves of Coonawarra ♀ 96

Bowen Estate ♀ 129

Coonawarra (SA) continued

Brand's Laira Coonawarra ♀ 130

Bundalong Coonawarra 145

DiGiorgio Family Wines ♀ ⁙ 226

Grey-Smith Wines 303

Hoggies Estate Wines ♀ 347

Hollick ♀ ⁙ ♦ 347

Jack Estate ♀ 363

Jim Brand Wines 369

Katnook Coonawarra ♀ ⁙ 380

Kidman Wines ♀ 385

Koonara ♀ ♦ 392

Leconfield ♀ ♦ 410

Lindeman's (Coonawarra) 418

Majella ♀ 436

Ottelia ♀ ⁙ 507

Parker Coonawarra Estate ♀ 513

Patrick of Coonawarra ♀ ♦ 515

Penley Estate ♀ ⁙ ♦ 524

Raidis Estate ♀ ♦ 554

Redman ♀ 559

Reschke Wines 561

Rymill Coonawarra ♀ ⁙ ♦ 583

Wynns Coonawarra Estate ♀ ♦ 738

Zema Estate ♀ 752

Cowra (NSW)

Pig in the House ♀ 534

Windowrie Estate ♀ ⁙ ♦ 725

Currency Creek (SA)

Finniss River Wines ♀ 263

Shaw Family Vintners ♀ ⁙ 611

Denmark (WA)

Apricus Hill ♀ 82

Estate 807 ♀ ⁙ 255

Harewood Estate ♀ 316

Moombaki Wines ♀ 464

Rockcliffe ♀ ⁙ ♦ 573

Silverstream Wines ♀ 619

The Lake House Denmark ♀ ⁙ ♦ 669

Eden Valley (SA)

Blue Rock Wines 125

Brockenchack ♀ ⊨ 135

Eden Hall ♀ 244

Edenmae Estate Wines ♀ ⁙ ⊨ 245

Fernfield Wines ♀ ⁙ 260

Flaxman Wines ♀ ⁙ 269

Forbes & Forbes ♀ 271

Gatt Wines 286

Heathvale ♀ 324

Heggies Vineyard ♀ 325

Henschke ♀ 329

Hill-Smith Estate ♀ 343

Irvine ♀ 361

Leo Buring 413

Lonely Vineyard 423

McLean's Farm ♀ 432

Mountadam ♀ 480

Pewsey Vale ♀ 529

Poonawatta ♀ 544

Rileys of Eden Valley 564

Robert Johnson Vineyards ♀ ♦ 568

Springton Hills Wines 634

Stage Door Wine Co 634

Torzi Matthews Vintners ♀ ⁙ 687

Yalumba ♀ ♦ 742

Frankland River (WA)

Alkoomi ♀ ⊨ 70

Ferngrove ♀ ⊨ 261

Frankland Estate ♀ 277

Lange's Frankland Wines 404

Swinney Vineyards 650

Geelong (Vic)

Attwoods Wines 87

Austins & Co. ♀ 89

Baie Wines ♀ 92

Banks Road ♀ ⁊⁊ 98

Bannockburn Vineyards ♀ 98

Barrgowan Vineyard ♀ 100

Barwon Ridge Wines ♀ 102

Bellarine Estate ♀ ⁊⁊ ⚲ 108

Bellbrae Estate ♀ ⁊⁊ 109

Bromley Wines 138

Brown Magpie Wines ♀ 142

Ceres Bridge Estate ♀ 165

Clyde Park Vineyard ♀ ⁊⁊ ⚲ 185

Curlewis Winery ♀ 206

Dinny Goonan ♀ ⁊⁊ 227

Farr | Farr Rising 258

"Heroes" Vineyard 338

Jack Rabbit Vineyard ♀ ⁊⁊ ⚲ 363

Lethbridge Wines ♀ ⁊⁊ 415

Leura Park Estate ♀ ⁊⁊ ⚲ 416

Livewire Wines 420

McGlashan's Wallington Estate ♀ ⁊⁊ ⚲ 429

Marcus Hill Vineyard 439

Mermerus Vineyard ♀ ⚲ 449

Newtons Ridge Estate ♀ 491

Oakdene ♀ ⁊⁊ ⊨ 498

Paradise IV 511

Provenance Wines ♀ 550

Geelong (Vic) continued

Robin Brockett Wines 571

Saint Regis ♀ ⁊⁊ 588

Scotchmans Hill ♀ 599

Shadowfax ♀ ⁊⁊ ⊨ 609

Spence ♀ 632

Yes said the Seal ♀ 751

Geographe (WA)

Angelicus ⁊⁊ ⊨ 78

Aylesbury Estate 91

Barton Jones Wines ♀ ⁊⁊ ⚲ 101

Bonking Frog ♀ ⊨ 128

Capel Vale ♀ ⁊⁊ 157

Green Door Wines ♀ ⁊⁊ 302

Iron Cloud Wines 361

Mandalay Estate ♀ 438

Mazza Wines 445

Talisman Wines 654

Whicher Ridge ♀ ⚲ 717

Willow Bridge Estate ♀ 722

Gippsland (Vic)

Bass Phillip ♀ 103

Bass River Winery ♀ 104

Bellvale Wine ♀ 109

Caledonia Australis | Mount Macleod 150

Cannibal Creek Vineyard ♀ ⁊⁊ ⚲ 152

Dirty Three Wines ♀ 227

Jinks Creek Winery ♀ ⁊⁊ ⊨ 369

Lightfoot & Sons 416

Moondarra 464

Narkoojee ♀ ⁊⁊ ⚲ 488

Nicholson River ♀ ⁊⁊ ⚲ 492

Tambo Estate ♀ 656

Glenrowan (Vic)

Baileys of Glenrowan ♀ ‖ ⚬ 93

Grampians (Vic)

Best's Wines ♀ 112
Clarnette & Ludvigsen Wines ♀ 181
Grampians Estate ♀ ‖ 301
Halls Gap Estate ♀ 309
Kimbarra Wines ♀ 388
Montara ♀ ‖ ⚬ 463
Mount Langi Ghiran Vineyards ♀ 474
Mount Stapylton Wines 478
Seppelt ♀ ‖ ⊨ ⚬ 603
The Story Wines 672
Vogel 709

Granite Belt (Qld)

Ballandean Estate Wines ♀ ‖ ⊨ ⚬ 95
Boireann ♀ 126
Golden Grove Estate ♀ 298
Heritage Estate ♀ ‖ ⊨ ⚬ 337
Just Red Wines ♀ 375
Ravens Croft Wines ♀ ‖ ⚬ 555
Ridgemill Estate ♀ ⊨ 563
Robert Channon Wines ♀ ‖ ⚬ 568
Sirromet Wines ♀ ‖ ⊨ ⚬ 622
Symphony Hill Wines ♀ 650
Tobin Wines ♀ 683
Twisted Gum Wines ♀ ⊨ 695

Great Southern (WA)

Across the Lake ♀ 68
Byron & Harold 148
Castelli Estate ♀ ‖ ⊨ ⚬ 161
Forest Hill Vineyard ♀ ‖ ⚬ 272

Great Southern (WA) continued
Kings Landing 389
Marchand & Burch ⚬ 439
Paul Nelson Wines ♀ 518
Plan B Wines 540
Rosenthal Wines 577
Singlefile Wines ♀ ‖ ⚬ 621
Staniford Wine Co ♀ 635
Trevelen Farm ♀ 689
Willoughby Park ♀ ‖ ⚬ 721

Great Western (Vic)

A.T. Richardson Wines 67

Greater Perth (WA)

Paul Conti Wines ♀ ‖ 516

Gundagai (NSW)

Tumblong Hills 693

Hastings River (NSW)

Cassegrain Wines ♀ ‖ ⚬ 161

Heathcote (Vic)

Barfold Estate ♀ 99
Buckshot Vineyard 143
Bull Lane Wine Company 144
Burke & Wills Winery ♀ ⚬ 147
Chalmers 169
Coliban Valley Wines ♀ 189
Condie Estate ♀ 191
Devil's Cave Vineyard ♀ 223
Domaine Asmara ♀ ⊨ 230

Heathcote (Vic) continued
Domaines Tatiarra 233
Ellis Wines 251
Farmer and The Scientist 257
Flynns Wines ♀ ⁑ ⊨ ♦ 271
Foster e Rocco 273
Heathcote Estate ♀ ⁑ 323
Heathcote II ♀ ⊨ 323
Heathcote Winery ♀ ⁑ 324
Idavue Estate ♀ ⁑ ♦ 357
Jasper Hill ♀ 366
Kennedy 383
La Pleiade ♀ 397
Lake Cooper Estate ♀ ♦ 398
Meehan Vineyard ♀ 447
Merindoc Vintners ♀ ⁑ ⊨ 448
Mia Valley Estate ♀ 450
Munari Wines ♀ 482
Noble Red 495
Occam's Razor | Lo Stesso ♀ 501
Paul Osicka ♀ 518
Red Edge ♀ 556
Redesdale Estate Wines ♀ ⊨ 558
St Michael's Vineyard ♀ 588
Sanguine Estate ♀ ♦ 591
She-Oak Hill Vineyard 613
Syrahmi 651
Tar & Roses ♀ 658
Tellurian ♀ 662
Vinea Marson ♀ 707
Wanted Man 711

Henty (Vic)

Basalt Wines ♀ ⁑ 102
Crawford River Wines ♀ 201
Henty Estate 335
Hentyfarm Wines 336

Henty (Vic) continued
Jackson Brooke 363
Pierrepoint Wines ♀ ⁑ ⊨ ♦ 533

Hilltops (NSW)

Barwang 101
Chalkers Crossing ♀ 168
Freeman Vineyards ♀ 279
Grove Estate Wines ♀ 305
Moppity Vineyards 467

Hunter Valley (NSW)

Audrey Wilkinson ♀ ⊨ 88
Belford Block Eight 107
Bimbadgen ♀ ⁑ ⊨ ♦ 116
Briar Ridge Vineyard ♀ ⊨ 134
Brokenwood ♀ 136
Capercaillie Wines ♀ ⊨ ♦ 157
Chateau Francois ♀ 174
Chateau Pâto ♀ 175
Cockfighter's Ghost ♀ ⊨ 187
Colvin Wines 191
David Hook Wines ♀ ⁑ 212
De Iuliis ♀ ⁑ 216
DEGEN ♀ ⊨ 218
Drayton's Family Wines ♀ ⁑ ⊨ 238
Eagles Rest Wines ♀ ⁑ ⊨ 242
Eclectic Wines ♀ ⁑ ⊨ 243
Elbourne Wines ♀ 247
Ernest Hill Wines ♀ 253
First Creek Wines ♀ 264
Gartelmann Wines ♀ ⁑ ♦ 286
George Wyndham ⁑ ♦ 289
Glenguin Estate ♀ 295
Goldman Wines 298
Greenway Wines ♀ 303

Hunter Valley (NSW) continued
Gundog Estate ♀ ⅋ ⊨ 306
Hanging Tree Wines ♀ ⊨ 312
Hart & Hunter ♀ 317
Hollydene Estate ♀ ⅋ 348
Horner Wines 349
Hungerford Hill ♀ ⅋ ⌕ 355
Inner City Winemakers ♀ 359
Keith Tulloch Wine ♀ ⅋ ⊨ ⌕ 381
Krinklewood Biodynamic Vineyard ♀ ⅋ 393
Lake's Folly ♀ 398
Lambloch Estate ♀ 399
Leogate Estate Wines ♀ ⅋ 413
McGuigan Wines ♀ ⅋ 429
McLeish Estate ♀ 432
Margan Family ♀ ⅋ 440
Meerea Park ♀ 448
Mistletoe Wines ♀ ⅋ 456
Molly Morgan Vineyard ⊨ 459
Molly's Cradle ♀ 460
Mount Eyre Vineyards ♀ ⊨ 473
Mount Pleasant ♀ ⅋ 477
Mount View Estate ♀ ⊨ 479
Pepper Tree Wines ♀ ⅋ ⊨ 526
Pokolbin Estate ♀ ⅋ 542
RidgeView Wines ♀ ⅋ ⊨ 563
Saddler's Creek ♀ 583
Scarborough Wine Co ♀ 595
Silkman Wines ♀ 617
Simon Whitlam & Co 619
Stomp Wine ♀ ⊨ 641
Stonehurst Cedar Creek ♀ ⊨ ⌕ 642
Sweetwater Wines 648
Tallavera Grove | Carillion ♀ ⅋ ⊨ 654
Tamburlaine ♀ ⌕ 657
Tempus Two Wines ♀ ⅋ ⌕ 663
Thomas Wines ♀ ⅋ 676

Hunter Valley (NSW) continued
Tinklers Vineyard ♀ 682
Tintilla Wines ♀ ⅋ 682
Travertine Wines ♀ 688
Tulloch ♀ ⅋ 693
Two Rivers ♀ ⅋ ⊨ ⌕ 697
Tyrrell's Wines ♀ ⌕ 698
Vinden Estate ♀ ⅋ ⊨ 706
Whispering Brook ♀ ⅋ ⊨ ⌕ 718
Woodward's Wines 737
Wynwood Estate ♀ 739

Kangaroo Island (SA)

Dudley Wines ♀ ⅋ ⌕ 240
The Islander Estate Vineyards ♀ ⅋ 669

King Valley (Vic)

Brown Brothers ♀ ⅋ ⊨ ⌕ 141
Chrismont ♀ ⅋ ⊨ ⌕ 176
Ciavarella Oxley Estate ♀ 177
Dal Zotto Wines ♀ ⅋ ⊨ ⌕ 209
Eddie McDougall Wines 243
John Gehrig Wines ♀ ⌕ 370
Lana ♀ ⅋ ⊨ ⌕ 401
Pizzini ♀ ⅋ ⊨ ⌕ 540
Redbank 557
Sam Miranda of King Valley ♀ ⅋ ⌕ 590
Symphonia Wines ♀ ⌕ 650
Wood Park ♀ ⅋ ⌕ 732

Langhorne Creek (SA)

Angas Plains Estate ♀ ⅋ ⊨ ⌕ 77
Beach Road ♀ ⅋ 106
Bleasdale Vineyards ♀ 122
Bremerton Wines ♀ ⅋ ⌕ 132

Langhorne Creek (SA) continued
Brothers in Arms ♀ 140
Gipsie Jack Wine Co ♀ 🍴 294
Heartland Wines ♀ 🍴 322
John's Blend ♀ 🍴 🍷 371
Kimbolton Wines ♀ 388
Lake Breeze Wines ♀ 🍴 🛏 🍷 397
Temple Bruer ♀ 663

Limestone Coast (SA)

Carpe Vinum 159
Tidswell Wines ♀ 680
Westmere Wines 717

Macedon Ranges (Vic)

Bindi Wine Growers 117
Birthday Villa Vineyard ♀ 119
Curly Flat ♀ 206
Gisborne Peak ♀ 🍴 🛏 294
Granite Hills ♀ 🍷 301
Hanging Rock Winery ♀ 311
Hunter-Gatherer Vintners ♀ 🍴 355
Kyneton Ridge Estate ♀ 🍴 🛏 🍷 394
Lane's End Vineyard ♀ 🍷 403
Lyons Will Estate ♀ 427
Mons Rubra 461
Passing Clouds ♀ 🍴 🍷 514
Rill House Vineyard 564
Silent Way 617
Zig Zag Road ♀ 🍴 753

McLaren Vale (SA)

Aphelion Wine 81
Arakoon ♀ 82
Aramis Vineyards ♀ 82

McLaren Vale (SA) continued
Battle of Bosworth ♀ 104
Bekkers ♀ 107
Bent Creek ♀ 111
Beresford Wines ♀ 111
Bondar Wines ♀ 127
Brash Higgins ♀ 131
Brick Kiln ♀ 134
Brini Estate Wines ♀ 135
Cape Barren Wines ♀ 153
Chalk Hill 167
Chapel Hill ♀ 🍴 🛏 🍷 171
Clarendon Hills ♀ 180
Conte Estate Wines ♀ 192
Cooter & Cooter 194
Coriole ♀ 🍴 196
cradle of hills ♀ 🍴 199
Cragg Cru Wines 200
Curtis Family Vineyards 206
d'Arenberg ♀ 🍴 207
Dandelion Vineyards 211
Doc Adams ♀ 227
Dodgy Brothers 228
DogRidge Wine Company ♀ 228
DOWIE DOOLE ♀ 🍴 🍷 236
Ekhidna ♀ 🍴 246
Five Geese 267
Fox Creek Wines ♀ 🍴 🍷 275
Gemtree Wines ♀ 🍴 🍷 287
Geoff Merrill Wines ♀ 288
Hancock & Hancock 310
Hardys ♀ 🍴 314
Haselgrove Wines ♀ 318
Hastwell & Lightfoot ♀ 319
Hickinbotham Clarendon Vineyard ♀ 341
Hither & Yon ♀ 🍴 🍷 344
Hugh Hamilton Wines ♀ 353

McLaren Vale (SA) continued

Hugo ♀ ⑪ ⚲ 354

Inkwell ♀ 359

J&J Wines ♀ 362

Kangarilla Road Vineyard ♀ 377

Kay Brothers Amery Vineyards ♀ ⚲ 380

KJB Wine Group 389

La Curio ♀ 396

Lino Ramble 419

Little Creek Wines 420

Lloyd Brothers ♀ ⑪ 421

Longline Wines 424

Lost Buoy Wines 426

McLaren Vale III Associates ♀ 432

Maxwell Wines ♀ ⑪ ⚲ 442

Mitolo Wines ♀ 459

Morgan Simpson 469

Mr Riggs Wine Company ♀ ⑪ ⚲ 482

Nashwauk 489

Old Oval Estate ♀ 503

Olivers Taranga Vineyards ♀ 504

Paxton ♀ ⚲ 519

Penny's Hill ♀ ⑪ ⚲ 525

Pirramimma ♀ ⚲ 539

Possums Vineyard ♀ 545

Primo Estate ♀ ⑪ 548

Renards Folly 560

Reynella ♀ 561

Richard Hamilton ♀ ⑪ ⚲ 562

Rosemount Estate ⑪ ⚲ 577

Rudderless ♀ ⑪ ⊨ ⚲ 581

Rusty Mutt 582

SC Pannell ♀ ⑪ 594

Scarpantoni Estate ♀ ⑪ ⊨ 595

Serafino Wines ♀ ⑪ ⊨ ⚲ 605

Shingleback ♀ ⑪ 613

Shirvington 614

McLaren Vale (SA) continued

Shottesbrooke ♀ ⑪ ⚲ 614

The Old Faithful Estate ♀ 671

Thomas Vineyard Estate 676

Three Dark Horses 679

2 Mates ♀ 697

Ulithorne ♀ ⑪ 699

Vasarelli Wines ♀ ⑪ 702

Vigena Wines 704

Vigna Bottin ♀ 705

Vinrock 708

Walter Clappis Wine Co 710

Way Wood Wines ♀ ⑪ 715

Willunga 100 Wines 724

Wirra Wirra ♀ ⑪ ⚲ 729

Woodstock ♀ ⑪ ⊨ ⚲ 735

Yangarra Estate Vineyard ♀ 743

Zerella Wines ♀ 753

Zonte's Footstep ♀ ⑪ 754

Manjimup (WA)

Peos Estate 526

Woodgate Wines ♀ 733

Margaret River (WA)

After Hours Wine ♀ 69

Amato Vino 74

Amelia Park Wines ♀ ⑪ 75

Aravina Estate ♀ ⑪ ⚲ 83

Arlewood Estate ♀ 84

Ashbrook Estate ♀ 86

Barnyard1978 ♀ 99

Brash Vineyard ⊨ 131

Brookland Valley ♀ ⑪ ⚲ 139

Brown Hill Estate ♀ 142

Brygon Reserve ♀ ⊨ 143

768   Index

Margaret River (WA) continued
Burch Family Wines ♀ ⚲ 145
Calneggia Family Vineyards Estate
     Wines 151
Cape Grace Wines ♀ 154
Cape Mentelle ♀ ⚲ 155
Cape Naturaliste Vineyard ♀ 156
Chalice Bridge Estate ♀ 166
Chapman Grove Wines 172
Churchview Estate ♀ ⅱ 177
Clairault | Streicker Wines ♀ ⅱ ⚲ 179
Cloudburst 184
Cowaramup Wines ♀ 198
Coward & Black Vineyards ♀ 199
Credaro Family Estate ♀ 201
Cullen Wines ♀ ⅱ ⊨ 203
Deep Woods Estate ♀ 217
Della Fay Wines ♀ 221
Devil's Lair 224
Domaine Naturaliste 232
Driftwood Estate ♀ ⅱ 239
Evans & Tate ♀ ⅱ 255
Evoi Wines ♀ 256
Fermoy Estate ♀ ⊨ ⚲ 260
Fire Gully ♀ 263
Firetail ♀ 264
Flametree ♀ ⚲ 268
Flowstone Wines ♀ 269
Flying Fish Cove ♀ 270
Forester Estate ♀ 273
Franklin Tate Estates 278
Fraser Gallop Estate ♀ 279
Gallows Wine Co ♀ 283
Grace Farm ♀ 300
Hamelin Bay ♀ ⅱ 310
Happs ♀ ⅱ ⚲ 313
Hay Shed Hill Wines ♀ ⅱ 319
Heydon Estate ♀ 341

Margaret River (WA) continued
Higher Plane ♀ 342
House of Cards ♀ ⚲ 351
Ibizan Wines ♀ ⊨ 357
Ipso Facto Wines 360
Juniper Estate ♀ 374
KarriBindi 379
Knee Deep Wines ♀ ⅱ ⚲ 391
L.A.S.Vino 395
Latitude 34 Wine Co ♀ 409
Leeuwin Estate ♀ ⅱ ⚲ 411
Lenton Brae Wines ♀ 412
McHenry Hohnen Vintners ♀ 430
Marq Wines ♀ 441
Miles from Nowhere 453
Mon Tout 460
Moss Wood ♀ ⊨ 471
Mr Barval Fine Wines ♀ 481
Night Harvest 493
Oceans Estate 501
Palmer Wines ♀ ⅱ ⚲ 508
Passel Estate ♀ 514
Peccavi Wines ♀ 521
Pierro ♀ 533
Preveli Wines ♀ 547
Redgate ♀ ⚲ 558
Rosabrook Margaret River Wine 576
Rosily Vineyard ♀ 578
Sandalford ♀ ⅱ ⚲ 590
Saracen Estates ♀ ⅱ 593
Stella Bella Wines ♀ 639
Swings & Roundabouts ♀ ⅱ ⚲ 649
The Trades 673
Thompson Estate ♀ 677
tripe.Iscariot 690
Twinwoods Estate 695
Umamu Estate 700

Margaret River (WA) continued

Vasse Felix ♀ ❙❙ ⚬ 702

Victory Point Wines ♀ 704

Vintners Ridge Estate ♀ 708

Voyager Estate ♀ ❙❙ 709

Warner Glen Estate 712

Watershed Premium Wines ♀ ❙❙ 714

Willespie ♀ 721

Wills Domain ♀ ❙❙ ⚬ 723

Windance Wines ♀ 725

Windows Estate ♀ ❙❙ 726

Wise Wine ♀ ❙❙ ⊨ ⚬ 730

Woodlands ♀ 734

Woody Nook ♀ ❙❙ 737

Xanadu Wines ♀ ❙❙ ⚬ 740

Mornington Peninsula (Vic)

Allies Wines 73

Avani ♀ 90

Baillieu Vineyard ♀ ❙❙ 94

Bittern Estate ♀ 119

Circe Wines 178

Crittenden Estate ♀ ❙❙ ⊨ 203

Dexter Wines 225

Dromana Estate ♀ ❙❙ 239

Eldridge Estate of Red Hill ♀ 250

Elgee Park ♀ ❙❙ 251

Foxeys Hangout ♀ ❙❙ 277

Garagiste 284

Hurley Vineyard ♀ 356

Kooyong ♀ 392

Lindenderry at Red Hill ♀ ❙❙ ⊨ ⚬ 418

Main Ridge Estate ♀ ❙❙ ⚬ 436

Merricks Estate ♀ 449

Miceli ♀ 451

Mont Rouge Estate ♀ ❙❙ 461

Montalto ♀ ❙❙ ⚬ 461

Mornington Peninsula (Vic) continued

Moorooduc Estate ♀ ❙❙ ⚬ 466

Myrtaceae ♀ 487

Nazaaray ♀ ❙❙ ⊨ ⚬ 489

Onannon 504

Paradigm Hill ♀ 511

Paringa Estate ♀ ❙❙ 512

Pasadera Wines 513

Phaedrus Estate ♀ 531

Polperro | Even Keel ♀ ❙❙ ⊨ 542

Port Phillip Estate ♀ ❙❙ ⊨ 544

Portsea Estate ♀ 545

Prancing Horse Estate ♀ 546

Principia ♀ 549

Quealy Winemakers ♀ ❙❙ 553

Red Hill Estate ♀ ❙❙ ⊨ 557

Scorpo Wines ♀ 599

Staindl Wines ♀ 635

Stonier Wines ♀ ❙❙ 643

Stumpy Gully ♀ ❙❙ 645

T'Gallant ♀ ❙❙ ⚬ 651

Telera 662

Ten Minutes by Tractor ♀ ❙❙ 664

Trofeo Estate ♀ ❙❙ ⊨ 690

Tuck's Ridge ♀ ❙❙ 692

Underground Winemakers ♀ 700

Willow Creek Vineyard ♀ ❙❙ ⊨ 723

Woodhaven Vineyard ♀ 733

Yabby Lake Vineyard ♀ ❙❙ 741

Yal Yal Estate 741

Mount Barker (WA)

Galafrey ♀ 282

Gilberts ♀ ❙❙ ⊨ ⚬ 293

Plantagenet ♀ ❙❙ ⚬ 541

Poacher's Ridge Vineyard ♀ ❙❙ ⊨ 541

3 Drops 679

Mount Barker (WA) continued

West Cape Howe Wines 🍷 🍴 716

Xabregas 739

Mount Benson (SA)

Cape Jaffa Wines 🍷 🍴 🍇 155

Mount Gambier (SA)

Herbert Vineyard 🍷 336

Mount Lofty Ranges (SA)

Macaw Creek Wines 🍷 428

Michael Hall Wines 451

Mudgee (NSW)

Botobolar 🍷 🍇 129

De Beaurepaire Wines 🍷 214

Ernest Schuetz Estate Wines 🍷 🍴 🛏 253

First Ridge 🍷 267

Gooree Park Wines 🍷 300

Heslop Wines 339

Huntington Estate 🍷 🍇 356

Jamieson Estate 365

Logan Wines 🍷 🍴 422

Lowe Wines 🍷 🍴 🍇 426

Robert Oatley Vineyards 🍷 🍴 🍇 569

Robert Stein Vineyard 🍷 🍴 570

Rosby 🍷 🛏 577

Vinifera Wines 🍷 🍴 707

Yeates Wines 🍷 747

Murray Darling (Vic and NSW)

Deakin Estate 217

Stefano de Pieri 🍷 🍴 🍇 638

Trentham Estate 🍷 🍴 🍇 689

Zilzie Wines 753

Nagambie Lakes (Vic)

Box Grove Vineyard 🍷 🍴 130

Dalfarras 🍷 🍴 210

McPherson Wines 433

Mitchelton 🍷 🍴 🛏 458

Tahbilk 🍷 🍴 652

Northeast Victoria

Eldorado Road 🍷 249

Mt Pilot Estate 🍷 477

Orange (NSW)

Angullong Wines 🍷 🍴 🛏 🍇 80

Bloodwood 🍷 124

Brangayne of Orange 🍷 130

Cargo Road Wines 🍷 🍴 158

Colmar Estate 🍷 190

Cooks Lot 🍷 🛏 192

De Salis Wines 🍷 216

Gilbert Family Wines 293

Highland Heritage Estate 🍷 🍴 343

Moody's Wines 🍷 464

Orange Mountain Wines 🍷 🍇 506

Panther's Patch Wines 🍷 510

Philip Shaw Wines 🍷 🍴 🍇 532

Printhie Wines 🍷 549

Ross Hill Wines 🍷 578

Rowlee 🍷 🍴 🛏 580

See Saw Wines 🍷 602

Orange (NSW) continued
Sons & Brothers Vineyard 629
Stockman's Ridge Wines ♀ 641
Word of Mouth Wines ♀ ₫ 737

Padthaway (SA)

Farmer's Leap Wines ‖ 257
Henry's Drive Vignerons ♀ ‖ 329
Landaire 401
Morambro Creek Wines 468
Oparina Wines 506

Peel (WA)

Peel Estate ♀ ₫ 522

Pemberton (WA)

Bellarmine Wines ♀ 108
Hillbrook Wines ♀ 344
Lillian 417
Merum Estate 450
Rambouillet ♀ 554
Silkwood Estate ♀ ‖ ⊨ 618
Smithbrook ♀ 627
Truffle & Wine Co ♀ ‖ 691

Perth Hills (WA)

Millbrook Winery ♀ ‖ 454
MyattsField Vineyards ♀ 486

Porongurup (WA)

Abbey Creek Vineyard ♀ 68
Castle Rock Estate ♀ ‖ 162
Duke's Vineyard ♀ ₫ 240

Porongurup (WA) continued
Ironwood Estate ♀ ‖ ₫ 361
Mount Trio Vineyard ♀ 479
Zarephath Wines ♀ ‖ 752

Port Phillip (Vic)

Studley Park Vineyard 644

Pyrenees (Vic)

Amherst Winery ♀ ‖ 76
Blue Pyrenees Estate ♀ ‖ ₫ 124
Camfield Family Wines 151
Dalwhinnie ♀ ‖ ⊨ 211
DogRock Winery ♀ 229
Glenlofty Wines 296
Mitchell Harris Wines ♀ ‖ 457
Mount Avoca ♀ ‖ ⊨ 471
Pyren Vineyard ♀ 552
St Ignatius Vineyard ♀ ‖ ₫ 586
Summerfield ♀ ‖ ⊨ ₫ 645
Taltarni ♀ ‖ ⊨ 655
Warrenmang Vineyard & Resort ♀ ‖ ⊨ ₫ 713

Queensland

Witches Falls Winery ♀ ₫ 731

Riverina (NSW)

Beelgara | Cumulus ₫ 106
Berton Vineyard ♀ 112
Calabria Family Wines ♀ ₫ 150
Casella Family Brands 160
De Bortoli ♀ ₫ 214
Lillypilly Estate ♀ 417

Riverina (NSW) continued
McWilliam's ♀ 433
Mino & Co ♀ 456
Nugan Estate ♀ 497
R. Paulazzo ♀ 554
Yarran Wines ♀ 747

Riverland (NSW and SA)

Cirami Estate ♀ 178
Delinquente Wine Co 220
919 Wines ♀ 494
Whistling Kite Wines ♀ 719

Robe (SA)

Karatta Wines ♀ 378

Rutherglen (Vic)

All Saints Estate ♀ ⅋ ۵ 71
Anderson ♀ 76
Buller Wines ♀ ۵ 144
Campbells ♀ ⅋ 151
Chambers Rosewood ♀ 169
Cofield Wines ♀ ⅋ ⊨ ۵ 188
Jones Winery & Vineyard ♀ ⅋ 372
Morris ♀ 469
Pfeiffer Wines ♀ ⅋ ۵ 530
Rutherglen Estates ♀ ⅋ ⊨ ۵ 582
St Leonards Vineyard ♀ ⅋ ۵ 587
Scion Vineyard & Winery ♀ 598
Stanton & Killeen Wines ♀ 636

Shoalhaven Coast (NSW)

Coolangatta Estate ♀ ⅋ ⊨ ۵ 193
Cupitt's Winery ♀ ⅋ ⊨ ۵ 204

South Australia

Angove Family Winemakers ♀ ⅋ 78
Byrne Vineyards 148
Gotham Wines 300
Ius Wines 362
Project Wine 549
Quarisa Wines 552
RedHeads Studios ♀ 558
RockBare ♀ ⅋ ۵ 573
The Other Wine Co ♀ 671
Thistledown Wines 675
Wines by Geoff Hardy ♀ 727

South Eastern Australia

Allegiance Wines 72
BackVintage Wines ♀ 91
Ben Haines Wine 110
Black Stump Wines ♀ 121
Echelon 242
Espier Estate ♀ 254
Handpicked Wines ♀ 311
Hesketh Wine Company 339
Journeys End Vineyards 374
Ministry of Clouds ♀ 455
Risky Business Wines 566
Santa & D'Sas 592
Side Gate Wines ♀ 615
Skew Wines ♀ 624
Smidge Wines 627
Stonefish 642
Taylor Ferguson 660

South Eastern Australia continued
Twofold 697
Vinaceous Wines 706
Yellowglen 749

South West Australia

Amberley 74
Kerrigan + Berry ♀ ❙❙ 384
Snake + Herring 628

Southern Fleurieu (SA)

Minko Wines ♀ ❙❙ ⊨ ⌕ 455
Mosquito Hill Wines 470
Salomon Estate 589

Southern Highlands (NSW)

Centennial Vineyards ♀ ❙❙ ⌕ 163
Cherry Tree Hill ♀ 176
Tertini Wines ♀ 667

Southern New South Wales

A. Retief 66
Hatherleigh Vineyard 319

Strathbogie Ranges (Vic)

Costanzo & Sons ♀ 197
Fowles Wine ♀ ❙❙ ⌕ 275
Garners Heritage Wines ♀ ❙❙ 285
Maygars Hill Winery ♀ ⊨ ⌕ 444
Municipal Wines 483
Wine x Sam ♀ 727

Sunbury (Vic)

Arundel Farm Estate ♀ ❙❙ ⌕ 85
Craiglee ♀ 200
Galli Estate ♀ ❙❙ 283
The Hairy Arm 668
Witchmount Estate ♀ ❙❙ 731

Swan District (WA)

Mandoon Estate ♀ ❙❙ ⊨ ⌕ 438
Pinelli Wines ♀ ❙❙ 537

Swan Hill (Vic)

Andrew Peace Wines ♀ ❙❙ 77

Swan Valley (WA)

Clockwork Wines 182
Corymbia Wine 197
Faber Vineyard ♀ ❙❙ 256
Heafod Glen Winery ♀ ❙❙ ⌕ 322
Houghton ♀ ❙❙ ⌕ 350
Jane Brook Estate Wines ♀ ❙❙ 365
John Kosovich Wines ♀ 371
Lamont's Winery ♀ ❙❙ ⌕ 400
Sittella Wines ♀ ❙❙ 623
Talijancich ♀ 653
Upper Reach ♀ ❙❙ ⊨ ⌕ 701

Tasmania

Ampel 76
Bangor Estate ♀ ❙❙ ⌕ 97
Barringwood ♀ ❙❙ ⌕ 100
Bay of Fires ♀ ❙❙ 105
Bream Creek ♀ ❙❙ 132
Cape Bernier Vineyard ♀ ⌕ 154

774 Index

Tasmania continued
Clover Hill ♀ 184
Coal Valley Vineyard ♀ ⫲ ⚲ 186
Craigow ♀ 201
Dalrymple 210
Dawson & James 213
Delamere Vineyard ♀ ⫲ ⚲ 219
Devil's Corner ♀ ⫲ ⚲ 223
Domaine A ♀ 230
Domaine Dawnelle 231
Dr Edge 237
Freycinet ♀ 280
Frogmore Creek ♀ ⫲ ⚲ 281
Gala Estate ♀ 282
Ghost Rock Vineyard ♀ ⫲ ⚲ 289
Goaty Hill Wines ♀ ⫲ ⚲ 297
Grey Sands ♀ 303
Heemskerk 325
Holm Oak ♀ 348
Home Hill ♀ ⫲ ⚲ 349
House of Arras ♀ ⫲ 350
Jansz Tasmania ♀ ⫲ 365
Josef Chromy Wines ♀ ⫲ ⚲ 372
Kate Hill Wines 379
Laurel Bank ♀ 410
Meadowbank Wines 446
Milton Vineyard ♀ ⫲ ⚲ 454
Moores Hill Estate ♀ ⫲ 465
Moorilla Estate ♀ ⫲ ⊨ ⚲ 465
Morningside Vineyard ♀ 469
Nocton Vineyard ♀ 496
Pipers Brook Vineyard ♀ ⫲ ⚲ 538
Pooley Wines ♀ ⫲ ⚲ 543
Pressing Matters ♀ 547
Relbia Estate ♀ 560
Riversdale Estate ♀ ⫲ ⊨ 566
Sailor Seeks Horse 583

Tasmania continued
Sharmans ♀ ⫲ 610
Sinapius Vineyard ♀ 620
Small Island Wines ♀ 626
Spring Vale Vineyards ♀ 633
Stargazer Wine ♀ 636
Stefano Lubiana ♀ ⫲ 638
Stoney Rise ♀ 642
Tamar Ridge | Pirie ♀ ⫲ 656
Tolpuddle Vineyard ♀ 684
Wines for Joanie ♀ ⊨ 729

Tumbarumba (NSW)

Coppabella of Tumbarumba 195

Upper Goulburn (Vic)

Black Range Estate 121
Delatite ♀ ⫲ ⚲ 220
Gioiello Estate 293
Kensington Wines ♀ ⫲ ⚲ 383
Mount Cathedral Vineyards ♀ 472
Murrindindi Vineyards 485
Ros Ritchie Wines ♀ 576
Snobs Creek Wines ♀ 628

Victoria

AAA Aaron Aardvark 68
Born & Raised 128
Di Sciascio Family Wines 225
Domaine Carlei G2 ♀ 231
Pinemount 538
Route du Van 580
Sentio Wines 602
Wine Unplugged 727

Western Australia

Domaines & Vineyards 233
Larry Cherubino Wines 406

Western Victoria

Norton Estate ♀ 496

Wrattonbully (SA)

Eight at the Gate 245
Ruckus Estate 581
Terre à Terre ♀ 666

Yarra Valley (Vic)

Alkimi Wines 70
Badger's Brook ♀ 92
Bicknell fc 115
Bird on a Wire Wines ♀ 118
Boat O'Craigo ♀ ♒ 126
Buttermans Track 147
Carlei Estate | Carlei Green Vineyards ♀ ♒ ♦ 158
Chandon Australia ♀ ♒ 170
Coldstream Hills ♀ 188
Coombe Farm ♀ ♒ ♦ 194
Dappled Wine ♀ 212
DCB Wine 213
De Bortoli (Victoria) ♀ ♒ 214
Denton Viewhill Vineyard ♀ 222
Dominique Portet ♀ ♒ 234
Drake 238
Elmswood Estate ♀ ♒ ♦ 251
Fergusson ♀ ♒ ⊨ 259
Fetherston Vintners 261
Fikkers Wine 262
First Foot Forward ♀ 266

Yarra Valley (Vic) continued

Five Oaks Vineyard ♀ 268
Gembrook Hill ♀ 287
Giant Steps ♀ ♒ ♦ 291
Goodman Wines 299
Hanrahan Estate ♀ 312
Helen & Joey Estate ♀ ♒ ♦ 326
Helen's Hill Estate ♀ ♒ ♦ 327
Hillcrest Vineyard ♀ 344
Hoddles Creek Estate ♀ 346
In Dreams 358
Innocent Bystander ♀ ♒ ♦ 360
Journey Wines 373
Killara Estate ♀ ♒ 387
Little Yarra Wines 420
Mac Forbes ♀ 427
Maddens Rise ♀ 434
Mandala ♀ ♒ 437
Mayer ♀ 443
Medhurst ♀ ♒ 446
Mount Mary 476
Nillumbik Estate ♒ ♦ 493
916 494
Oakridge Wines ♀ ♒ 499
One Block ♀ 505
Out of Step 508
Payne's Rise ♀ ♒ ♦ 521
PHI ♀ 531
Pimba Wines 536
Pimpernel Vineyards ♀ 536
Precipice Wines 546
Punch ♀ 550
Punt Road ♀ ♒ ♦ 551
Rob Dolan Wines ♀ ♒ ♦ 567
Rochford Wines ♀ ♒ ♦ 571
Rouleur 579
St Huberts ♀ ♦ 585

Yarra Valley (Vic) continued

Santarossa Vineyards 592

Santolin Wines 593

Serrat 606

Seville Estate ♀ ⁙ 608

Seville Hill ♀ ⁙ ⊨ ⚬ 609

Six Acres ♀ 624

Soumah ♀ ⁙ 631

Squitchy Lane Vineyard ♀ 634

Steels Creek Estate ♀ 637

Steels Gate 637

Stefani Estate ♀ 637

Sticks Yarra Valley 641

Sunshine Creek 646

Sutherland Estate ♀ ⁙ ⊨ ⚬ 647

Tarrahill. ♀ 658

TarraWarra Estate ♀ ⁙ 659

The Wanderer ♀ 673

Thick as Thieves Wines ♀ 674

Tokar Estate ♀ ⁙ 683

Toolangi Vineyards 686

Trapeze 688

Trellis ♀ ⊨ 688

Wantirna Estate 711

Warramate 712

Warramunda Estate ♀ ⁙ 712

Yarra Burn 744

Yarra Yering ♀ 744

Yarrabank ♀ ⁙ ⚬ 746

YarraLoch ♀ 746

Yering Station ♀ ⁙ ⚬ 749

Yeringberg ♀ 750

Zonzo Estate ♀ 755